Naturalized birds of the world

Previous works by the author

Naturalized mammals of the world
(Longman, 1985)

Chapter in Mason, I. L. (ed.) *Evolution of domesticated animals* (Longman, 1984)

The naturalized animals of the British Isles
(Hutchinson, 1977; Paladin Granada, 1979)

Naturalized birds of the world

Christopher Lever

Foreword by
Sir Peter Scott

Illustrations by
Robert Gillmor

Longman
Scientific &
Technical

Copublished in the United States with
John Wiley & Sons, Inc., New York

Longman Scientific & Technical,
Longman Group UK Limited,
Longman House, Burnt Mill, Harlow,
Essex CM20 2JE, England
and Associated Companies throughout the world.

Copublished in the United States with
John Wiley & Sons, Inc., 605 Third Avenue, New York,
NY 10158

First published 1987

British Library Cataloguing in Publication Data
Lever, Christopher
    Naturalized birds of the world.
    1. Birds   2. Animal introduction
    I. Title
    598   QL673
    ISBN 0-582-46055-7

Library of Congress Cataloging-in-Publication Data
Lever, Christopher, 1932–
    Naturalized birds of the world.

    Bibliography: p.
    Includes index.
    1. Bird populations. 2. Birds. 3. Animal
introduction. I. Gillmor, Robert. II. Title.
QL677.4.L49 1987   598.2'5   86-28727
ISBN 0-470-20789-2 (USA only)

Set in Linotron 202 10/11 pt Bembo

Printed and bound in Great Britain
at the Bath Press, Avon

Contents

CONTENTS

CONTENTS

List of tables

Foreword

Since writing *The Naturalized Animals of the British Isles*, to which I also contributed a Foreword, in 1977, Christopher Lever has produced two follow-up works on the same general theme – *Naturalized Mammals of the World* (1985) and this present volume, which is designed as a companion work. His two earlier books are each now regarded as the definitive work on their subject, and I am sure that *Naturalized Birds of the World* will come to be looked on in the same light.

Before Christopher Lever's 1977 publication, the study of naturalized exotic species had been almost entirely neglected by serious zoologists, most of whom appear to have considered them as of little ecological significance, and thus unworthy of their attention. It is surely no coincidence that since Christopher Lever's two previous works, a great many scientific papers have been published on naturalized alien animals, and that the zoological establishment has become ever more concerned about the ecological and sociobiological consequences of introducing such animals outside their natural range.

Clearly we should not do it, and indeed since 1981 it is not allowed by law in Britain. Before it became illegal, however, I was responsible for letting the North American Ruddy Duck establish itself as part of the British avifauna. It came about accidentally. Several pinioned pairs of *Oxyura jamaicensis* – a common North American breeding bird – had lived happily for some years on what is now called Swan Lake at Slimbridge. One summer in the early 1960s, a female Ruddy hid her nest very well, close beside the water's edge, and when the young ones hatched they jumped into the water before we could catch and pinion them. They flew out of our enclosure and began to breed on local gravel pits. After a few years they had spread to many local reservoirs. By the late 1970s there were apparently some 4,000 feral Ruddy Ducks in Britain. There is some evidence that the population is somewhat smaller at the present time. At first, I felt rather shamefaced about what had happened, but, when the species was adopted by the West Midland Bird Club as their emblem, I felt much better. I seriously doubt whether the Ruddy Duck will ever become a pest species, and meanwhile a delightful and decorative little duck can brighten the day for many a bird-watcher in many parts of our country.

There are, nevertheless, some examples of introduced birds, which have competed with native species to a disastrous extent, leading even to their extinction in a few cases. The early settlers in New Zealand, for instance, formed Acclimatization Societies in order to establish birds which reminded them of home. These introductions could, and sometimes did lead to the extinction of the native species, and in some parts of the world the process is still going on.

If introduction techniques are to be used at all, they should be directed towards reinforcing the populations of native birds that are in danger of extinction.

Naturalized Birds of the World is essential reading for all serious ornithologists and for those concerned with the stability of our ecosystems, and should find a place on every ornithological bookshelf.

Sir Peter Scott
Slimbridge, Gloucestershire

Preface

The object of this book is to describe when, where, why, how and by whom the various alien birds now living in a wild state throughout the world were introduced, how they subsequently became naturalized, and what effects – for good or ill – they have had on the native biota, and vice versa. The criteria for inclusion of a species are that it should have been imported from its natural range to a new country or region either deliberately or accidentally by human agency, and that it should currently be established in the wild in self-maintaining and self-perpetuating populations unsupported by, and independent of, man.

Each species account is a monograph on an individual bird: at the end of some of them are brief details of the artificial distribution of allied, related or associated species. In general, only species that have become successfully naturalized are discussed. The inclusion of those that failed to become established would have been of little value unless the precise reasons (usually a combination of various factors) for each such failure were known, and would inevitably have resulted in numerous omissions. Exceptions have been made in the case of species that have failed to become established in some regions but have succeeded elsewhere, and when initial failures have been followed by subsequent successes. Natural immigrants from one country to another have normally been included only if they have been augmented by deliberate or accidental introductions by man, or in the case of an established alien self-colonizing a new country – for example, the House Sparrow (*Passer domesticus*) in South and Central America. Translocations and/or transplantations of a species from one part of a country or its natural range to another, and from the mainland to offshore islands or vice versa, natural extensions of range and colonization of offshore islands, and acclimatized species have in general only been included if such a species has been successfully naturalized elsewhere.

Terminology

The definitions (with sources) of various terms used in the text are as follows:

Naturalization: 'The introduction (of animals and plants) to places where they are not indigenous, but in which they may flourish under the same conditions as those which are native.'[1] More particularly, 'The establishment of self-regenerating populations [unsupported by and independent of man] of an introduced species or race in a free-living state in the wild.'[2]

Acclimatization: 'Grown or become habituated to a new climate.'[3] Used to describe an exotic species living in the wild in an alien environment or climate with the support of and dependent (e.g. for food) on man.

Feral: 'Animals or plants that have lapsed into a wild from a domesticated condition.'[4] It is thus, strictly speaking, incorrect to refer to a *wild* (as opposed to a *domestic*) animal that has escaped from captivity and has become naturalized as 'feral'. The term is not, as suggested by De Vos & Petrides,[5] synonymous with 'wild'.

Introduction: 'The deliberate or accidental release of animals or plants of a species or race into an area in which it has not occurred in historical times.'[6] 'The movement by man of live organisms to a new location outside their recent natural geographic range.'[7]

Reintroduction: 'The deliberate or accidental release of a species or race into an area in which it was indigenous in historical times.'[8] 'The act of returning a species to an area within its original geographic range from which it has disappeared.'[9]

Transplantation/Translocation/Stocking: The deliberate or accidental movement by man of a species or race from one area where it is established (as either native or alien) to another area within the same range.

Restocking: 'The deliberate or accidental release of a species or race into an area in which it is already present.'[10]

Established: 'Set up on a secure or permanent basis.'[11] A successfully introduced species or race. Synonymous with 'naturalized'.

Exotic/Alien: 'A species native to an area located outside of, or foreign to, the area under review.'[12] 'An introduced species.'[13]

Adventive: An introduced species or race that is as yet unestablished.

Native/Indigene: 'An individual or population which is a member of the natural biotic community.'[14]

Classification and sequence

The classification and sequence followed is that of Peters and successors (1931–72). Also consulted were Mayr (1965a), Morony, Bock & Farrand (1975), Gruson (1976) and, for subspecies, Howard & Moore (1980).

Nomenclature

The nominate subspecies is the one occurring in the area where the holotype (the individual from which the whole species was described and scientifically named) was discovered, and which thus bears the same subspecific name as the species. The term 'subspecies' is sometimes replaced by the less-technical 'race' or 'form'.

Distribution of species

Zoogeographically, the world was divided in 1858 by P. L. Sclater into six great faunal regions: the **Palaearctic** (Europe, northern Africa south to the mid-Sahara, and northern Asia); the **Ethiopian** (Africa south of the Palaearctic and southern Arabia); the **Oriental** (tropical Asia and western Indonesia); the **Nearctic** (North America south to central Mexico); the **Neotropical** (central and South America, southern Mexico and the Antilles); and the **Australasian** (Australia, Tasmania, Papua New Guinea and some Pacific and eastern Indonesian islands). The division between the Australasian and Oriental regions is a deep trough in the ocean bed between Papua New Guinea and Borneo; this division is defined by (Alfred Russel) Wallace's Line, which extends south of the Philippines between Borneo and Celebes (now Sulawesi) and between the islands of Bali and Lombok. The Palaearctic and Nearctic regions together form the **Holarctic** region. The tropical region (not one of the faunal regions) lies between the tropics of Cancer and Capricorn (i.e. between 23 ° N and S of the equator).

Geographically, the world is divided into six continents which are politically subdivided into countries or nations: the continent of **Europe** includes Turkey-in-Europe and European USSR; **Asia** includes the remainder of Turkey, Israel, the Soviet Far East and Arabia; **Africa** includes Madagascar (the Malagasy Republic), the Seychelles, the Mascarenes (Réunion, Mauritius, Rodrigues), Cape Verde Islands, Ascension and St Helena; **North America** includes Mexico, Central America, the Caribbean territories, the West Indies, the Hawaiian Islands and Bermuda; **South America** comprises all land south of Central America; **Australasia** (and **Oceania**) include the Antarctic territories, the Malay archipelago, the East Indies, Indonesia, Borneo, Melanesia, Papua New Guinea, Polynesia, Micronesia, New Caledonia, the New Hebrides (now Vanuatu), the Solomon Islands, Fiji, the Philippines, the Celebes, the Moluccas, Tahiti, Tonga and other oceanic island groups.[15]

The system adopted here is based on these geographical and political boundaries rather than on the less-precise division into faunal regions, with the following exceptions: Australasia and Oceania have been separated – the former comprising principally Australia, Tasmania, New Zealand and New Guinea (together with their associated territories and offlying islands), and to the latter have been assigned most of the distant offshore island groups, including the Hawaiian Islands.

Old, new and alternative geographic names

Where these apply the old or principal name is normally used with the new or secondary name in parentheses.

British county names

In 1974 the names and boundaries of several counties in England and Wales, and in 1975 of some in Scotland, were changed. As many of the events described herein antedate these changes, and because it would be confusing to use both old and new names, the old names and boundaries have been adhered to throughout.

Notes

Only primary or principal references are given in the endnotes; secondary and supplementary ones will be found in the bibliography.

Nomenclature and distribution of feral domesticated species

The use of formal binominal names for domesticated animals has for long been a subject of contention among taxonomists. As those species discussed here are living in a feral state, it has been considered justifiable to treat them on the same footing as their wild congeners.

Through human agency, some domesticated birds, such as fowl, pigeons and geese, have become widely distributed in the wild. In these cases, only the ecologically, historically or morphologically more interesting and important populations are discussed in the text. Introductions of domesticated species from one country to another are only mentioned if feral populations have resulted.

Vernacular names

The English names of species are those most frequently used in Britain.

Distribution maps

These are intended to give a general indication only of the natural and naturalized distribution (both of which are in some cases discontinuous) of each species. In the case of the former, the extent of migration is indicated by arrows. In both, a dot may represent an island or group of islands.

Naturalized British birds

More detailed information on these will be found in *The Naturalized Animals of the British Isles* (Lever 1977a), which also discusses mammals, fish, reptiles and amphibians naturalized in Britain.

Errors and omissions

The author would welcome information regarding any errors and omissions in the text.

NOTES

1 *Oxford English Dictionary*.
2 Linn 1979, derived from Boitani 1976.
3 See note 1.
4 Ibid.
5 1967: 114.
6 See note 2.
7 See note 5.
8 See note 2.
9 See note 5.
10 See note 2.
11 See note 1.
12 See note 5.
13 See note 2.
14 See note 5.
15 Based on the *Universal Decimal Classification*, 4th international edn (Publication no. 179, British Standards Institution: London, 1972), Gr. 9.

Acknowledgements

Without the generous cooperation of a host of correspondents throughout the world this book could never have been written. For their assistance and patience in answering my requests for information I am greatly indebted to the following:

Mr R. Albignac (Laboratoire de Zoologie, Madagascar); Dr S. Ali (Bombay Natural History Society, India); Miss J. Allan (Australian High Commission, London); Dr H. Alvarez-Lopez (Universidad del Valle, Colombia); Dr R. Anderegg (Swiss Wildlife Information Service); Dr. R. H. Ansell (late Chief Veterinary Officer, southern Sudan); Dr J. S. Ash (United Nations Environment Programme); Dr I. A. E. Atkinson (Department of Scientific & Industrial Research, New Zealand).

Mr B. Barnett (University of California, USA); Mr J. Bensusan (Gibraltar Museum); Dr A. J. Berger (University of Hawaii, USA); Dr M. L. Birch (Edward Grey Institute of Field Ornithology, UK); Mrs M. Blakers (Royal Australasian Ornithologists' Union); Dr W. R. P. Bourne (University of Aberdeen, Scotland); Miss C. A. Bowman (Biosciences Information Service, USA); Miss P. Bradley (International Wildfowl Research Bureau/International Council for Bird Preservation Neotropical Wetlands Project, Cayman Islands); Mr and Mrs A. Braguine (Kenya); Dr M. A. Brazil (Japan); Dr N. Brickell (Avicultural Research Unit, South Africa); Sir Theodore Brinckman, Bt (Barbados); Mr R. Buckingham (International Council for Bird Preservation, Australia); Dr G. Bump (late US Department of the Interior); Mr J. A. Burton (Fauna & Flora Preservation Society, UK); Dr D. Butler (Ireland).

Dr R. W. Campbell (British Columbia Provincial Museum, Canada); Señor J. Cardona (Puerto Rico); Mr W. L. Chaplin (Lincolnshire Pheasantries, UK); Professor Cheng Tso-Hsin (Academia Sinica, Beijing, China); Dr P. A. Clancey (Durban Museum & Art Gallery, South Africa); Mr F. Clunie (Fiji Museum); Dr S. Cobb (International Union for Conservation of Nature Research Project, Mali); Professor Y. Coineau (Muséum National d'Histoire Naturelle, Paris, France); Mr D. C. Collingwood (Royal Forest & Bird Protection Society of New Zealand); Mr G. C. H. Cooper (International Council for Bird Preservation, Hong Kong); Mr J. Cooper (Percy

FitzPatrick Institute of African Ornithology, South Africa); Mrs D. Coster (Ministry of Agriculture, Fisheries & Food, England); Mrs M. Cox (Smithsonian Institution, USA); Professor K. L. Crowell (St Lawrence University, USA); Mr J. C. Cubby (Forestry Commission, UK); Mr R. A. Cuneo (USA); Dr K. Curry-Lindahl (UNESCO, Sweden).

Mr A. K. Davies (UK); Dr J. Delacour (France); Señor C. F. P. Del Prado (Ministerio de Agricultura, Peru); Professor F. S. Delgado (International Council for Bird Preservation, Panama); Mr M. Deorsola (Ente Parco Nazionale Gran Paradiso, Italy); Mr S. B. El Din (International Council for Bird Preservation, Egypt); Mr P. K. Dennis (UK); Mrs A. S. de Dod (International Council for Bird Preservation, Dominican Republic); Dr P. Dollinger (Federal Veterinary Office, Switzerland); Mr H. E. M. Dott (UK); Mr M. Doyle (Canada); Dr P. Drouilly (Seccion Chilena del CIPA, Chile); Captain H. Drummond (UK); Mr K. Duffy (Royal Zoological Society of Scotland).

Mr J. A. Fa (Gibraltar); Dr C. J. Feare (Ministry of Agriculture, Fisheries & Food, England); Mrs E. A. Feesey (the Netherlands); Miss J. Fenton (International Council for Bird Preservation, UK); Professor A. C. de Ferenzi (Instituto Nacional para la Preservacion del Medio Ambiente, Uruguay); Mr C. Ferriera (Department of Nature Conservation, South Africa); Dr L. W. Filewood (University of New South Wales, Australia); Dr O. C. Filho (Instituto Oswaldo Cruz, Brazil); Mr R. S. R. Fitter (Fauna & Flora Preservation Society, UK); Mr B. Fofana (Direction Nationale des Eaux et Forêts, Mali); Mr J. M. Forshaw (Australian National Parks and Wildlife Service); Dr R. M. Fraga (International Council for Bird Preservation, Argentina); Mr M. Framarin (Gran Paradiso National Park, Italy); Dr H. Frey (Institut für Parasitologie und Allgem. Zoologie, Austria); Dr H. J. Frith (Commonwealth Scientific & Industrial Research Organization, Australia); Professor S. Frugis (International Council for Bird Preservation, Italy).

Señor J. M. Gallardo (Museo Argentino de Ciencias Naturales, Argentina); Dr E. F. J. Garcia (Edward Grey Institute of Field Ornithology, UK); Dr P. Geroudet (Société Romande pour l'Étude et la Protection des Oiseaux, Switzerland); Mr P. D. Goriup (International Council for Bird Preservation, UK); Major I. Grahame (World Pheasant Association, UK); Dr J. C. Greig (Department of Nature & Environmental Conservation, South Africa).

Dr C. J. Hails (Ministry of National Development, Singapore); Captain J. Hamilton (Republic of Ireland); Mr N. Hammond (Royal Society for the Protection of Birds, UK); Mr F. Hannecart (Association pour la Sauvegarde de la Nature Neo-Caledonienne, New Caledonia); Mr B. Hawkes (UK); Miss M. Held (International Wildfowl Research Bureau/International Council for Bird Preservation Neotropical Wetlands Project, Suriname); Mr M. Heyman (Edward James Foundation, UK); Dr M. W. Holdgate (Department of the Environment, UK); Mr M. D. Holland (Department of Agriculture and Forestry, New Zealand); Miss S. Holowesko (Bahamas National Trust); Mr and Mrs H. Horswell (Avicultural Society, UK); Mr K. C. R. Howman (World Pheasant Association, UK); Dr P. Hudson (Game Conservancy, UK); Mr R. W. Hudson (British Trust for Ornithology); Sir Rex Hunt (Falkland Islands).

Dr J. A. Ibarra (Museo Nacional de Historia Natural, Guatemala); Dr C. Imboden (International Council for Bird Preservation, UK); Dr T. Ito (Tohoku University, Japan).

Miss Y. Kakabadse (Fundacion Nature, Ecuador); Dr H. W. Kale (Florida Audubon Society, USA); Mr J. Karpowicz (Director, Agricultural Programme of Arab Republic of Yemen); Dr J. Kear (Wildfowl Trust, UK); Dr R. E. Kenward (Institute of Terrestrial Ecology, UK); Mr W. B. King (International Council for Bird Preservation, USA); Mr R..J. Knowles (British Museum (Natural History), London).

Dr G. Le Grand (Universidade dos Açores, Azores); Dr B. Lekagul (Association for the Conservation of Wildlife, Thailand); Dr H. W. Levi (Harvard University, USA, who generously presented me with his collected bibliography of introduced and transplanted species); Dr R. Liversidge (McGregor Museum, Kimberley, South Africa); Mr J. L. Long (Agriculture Protection Board of Western Australia); Señor N. E. Lopez (Ministerio de Agricultura y Ganaderia Servicio Forestal Nacional, Paraguay); Mr J. A. Love (Nature Conservancy Council, UK); Dr T. W. I. Lovel (World Pheasant Association, UK); Mr Lu Tai-Chun (Academia Sinica, Beijing, China).

Dr L. F. G. McIntyre (Sugar Industry Research Institute, Mauritius); Dr C. McKelvie (Game Conservancy, UK); Dr M. McNicholl (Canadian Nature Federation, Ottawa); Mr I. L. Mason (Food & Agriculture Organization of the United Nations, Rome, Italy); Dr M. Marquiss (Institute of Terrestrial Ecology, UK); Mr F. Marseu (Ministry of Agriculture, Fisheries & Forests, Fiji); Señor A. O. Martinez (Dirección Forestal, Parques y Fauna, Uruguay); Dr G. E. Maul (late Museum Municipal da Funchal, Madeira); Dr A. Moreno (National Zoological Park, Academia de Ciencias, Cuba); Mr W. T. Munro (Ministry of Environment, British Columbia, Canada).

Mrs J. Nishida (Hawaiian Audubon Socciety, USA).

Mr T. B. Oatley (University of Cape Town, South Africa); Mr H. M. K. Oesman (International Council for Bird Preservation, Indonesia); Mr A. W. Owadally (Forestry Service, Mauritius); Professor O. T. Owre (University of Miami, USA).

Miss S. Palmer (World Wildlife Fund, UK); Mr J. Parslow (Royal Society for the Protection of Birds, UK); Dr J. Paton (Australia); Mr P. E. Paryski (Institut de Sauvegarde du Patrimoine Nature, Haiti); Mr and Mrs J. Pearson (British Columbia, Canada); Major A. D. Peirse-Duncombe (Scottish Ornithologists' Club); Mr J. C. Pernetta (University of Papua New Guinea); Dr C. M. Perrins (Edward Grey Institute of Field Ornithology, UK); Mrs B. Perry (UK); Drs F. and J.-J. Petter (Muséum National d'Histoire Naturelle, Paris, France); Señor W. H. Phelps (International Council for Bird Preservation, Venezuela); Mr G. Phipps (Sydney University, Australia); Mr C. Pilcher (Kuwait University); Mr M. A. Plenge (International Council for Bird Preservation, Peru); Dr G. R. Potts (Game Conservancy, UK).

Dr M. A. Ramos (International Council for Bird Preservation, Mexico); Señor J. R. Rau (Instituto de Zoologia, Valdivia, Chile); Mr P. Read (Editor, *Cage & Aviary Birds*, UK); Mrs D. J. Reynolds (Charles Darwin Research Station, Galápagos Islands); Professor S. Dillon Ripley (USA); Mr C. R. Rogers (UK); Mr M. Rogers (UK).

Dr D. G. Salmon (Wildfowl Trust, UK); Dr D. E. Samuel (West Virginia University, USA); Dr J. E. Sanchez (Ministerio de Agricultura y Ganaderia, Costa Rica); Mr C. D. W. Savage (International Trust for Nature Conservation/World Pheasant Association, UK); Sir Peter Scott (Wildfowl Trust, UK/World Wildlife Fund); Dr J. T. R. Sharrock (British Trust for Ornithology); Miss A. E. Shapiro (Florida Game & Fresh Water Fish Commission, USA); Dr C. Shroads (University of Miami, USA); Mr L. L. Shurtleff (USA); Professor H. Sick (Academia Brasileira de Ciencias, Rio de Janeiro, Brazil); Professor W. R. Siegfried (University of Cape Town, South Africa); Mr T. Silva (USA); Mr J. Skead (South Africa); Dr M. F. Stevenson (Royal Zoological Society of Scotland); Mr N. Stronach (Balamuck Station, Papua New Guinea); Mr R. Sutton (Jamaica).

Dr M. M. Terrasse (Fonds d'Intervention pour les Rapaces, France); Professor J. C. Thibault (Parc Naturel Regional de Corse, France); Major B. Thompson (Northern Ireland); Mr M. C. Thompson (Bedford Estates, UK); Miss J. Tucker (International Union for Conservation of Nature & Natural Resources).

Mr C. A. Valle (Charles Darwin Research Station, Galápagos Islands); Mr B. Vaohita (International Council for Bird Preservation, Malagasy Republic); Dr R. E. Vaughan (Mauritius); Dr J. Vincent (Natal Parks, Game & Fish Preservation Board, South Africa); Dr T. de Vries (Universidad Catolica, Ecuador).

Dr D. Watling (Fiji); Dr D. R. Wells (University of Malaya); Dr R. S. Whitley (late Grasslands Trials Unit, Falkland Islands); Professor G. R. Williams (Lincoln College, New Zealand); Dr J. G. Williams (late Coryndon Museum, Nairobi, Kenya); Mr L. E. Williams (Florida Game & Fresh Water Fish Commission, USA); Mr L. L. Williamson (Wildlife Management Institute, Washington, DC, USA); Dr D. B. Wingate (Conservation Officer, Bermuda); Professor J. M. Winterbottom (University of Cape Town, South Africa); Dr S. Wolff (Transvaal Provincial Administration, South Africa); Mr R. Woods (Falkland Islands); Dr E. Wyndham (University of New England, Australia).

Dr Y. Yamashina (Yamashina Institute for Ornithology, Japan); Mr H. G. Young (Jersey Wildlife Preservation Trust, Channel Islands).

Mr P. A. Zino (International Council for Bird Preservation, Madeira).

For their patience and diligence in tracing innumerable references for me I am grateful to the staff of the various libraries in which I conducted my researches. In particular my thanks are due to the following members of the British Museum (Natural History): Mr M.·J. Rowlands, Mr A. P. Harvey, Miss S. A. Angel, Mr P. R. Colston, Mrs C. Comben, Miss P. Cook, Mrs A. Datta, Miss N. French, Miss P. Gilbert, Miss S. Goodman, Mr M. R. Halliday, Miss D. M. Hills, Miss A. Jackson, Miss J. Jeffrey, Miss P. D. Jenkins, Miss A. Lum, Mrs K. Martin (who also researched on my behalf), Miss A. Pope, Miss M. Seely, Mr N. Thomson, Mrs D. A. Vale, Mrs D. Vines and Mrs E. Warr. The staff of the following British libraries were also of great assistance: Alexander Library of the Edward Grey Institute of Field Ornithology; British Library (Lending Division); British Museum; Commonwealth Institute of Entomology; Game Conservancy; Linnean Society of London; Ministry of Agriculture, Fisheries & Food; Nature Conservancy Council; Royal College of Veterinary Surgeons; Royal Geographical Society; Science Reference; and Zoological Society of London. I have also to thank Dr M. Boyd of the Science Reference Library for helping me carry out a computer-search of *Biological Abstracts*, and Mr R. K. Brooke of the Percy FitzPatrick Institute of African Ornithology, University of Cape Town, for providing me with a computer-printout bibliography of alien birds in southern and south-central Africa.

I am most grateful to Dr C. J. Feare (Ministry of Agriculture, Fisheries & Food); Mr D. Goodwin, Dr C. J. O. Harrison and Dr D. W. Snow (all of the British Museum (Natural History)); Mr B. Hawkes; Mr J. A. Love (Nature Conservancy Council); Dr M. A. Ogilvie (Wildfowl Trust); Mr T. Silva (USA); and Mr J. D. Summers-Smith, who kindly read and annotated the typescript for me. For drawing my attention to various errors of omission and commission and for their comments in general I am greatly indebted to them all. The responsibility for any errors that remain, however, is solely mine.

I should also like to thank the staff at Longman for their help and advice throughout: Miss S. Bunney for her patience and diligence in bringing order to my typescript and for compiling the indexes; Mr R. Gillmor for providing the illustrations; and last, but by no means least, Mrs R. Rugman for her patience in again deciphering and typing my well-nigh illegible manuscript.

To Sir Peter Scott I extend my grateful thanks for kindly contributing the Foreword to this book.

Christopher Lever

Windsor, Berkshire
November 1986

Introduction

Birds, more than any other animals, have always held a peculiar fascination for mankind. They have been admired for the beauty of their plumage, marvelled at for the variety and delicacy of their songs and, perhaps most of all, envied for their power of flight. What, then, more natural than that, in our colonization of the world, we should have endeavoured to enrich the birdlife of those areas in which we have settled?

Birds have been introduced to new regions by human agency with a variety of motives: for sport; for sentimental or nostalgic reasons; as an aesthetic amenity; as a potential source of food; as a form of biological control of insect and other pests; as scavengers; and, in pre-Columbian Central America, for their plumage, which was used for ritualistic purposes and ornamentation. Some have been released simply out of curiosity to see what would become of them in a new environment, and at least one has been introduced ostensibly as a means of conservation. Many have escaped from captivity or domesticity, and several have used man as unwitting means of sea-borne transportation.

Birds (as well as mammals and fish) have been released for sporting purposes, as Bates (1956: 798–9) points out, 'to compensate for alleged deficiencies in the local fauna; but the deficiency may be apparent [rather than real] because man is hankering after some particular kind of sport remembered from 'back home', and is unwilling to adapt his habits to the sporting possibilities of the new fauna'. Thus in the United States, a country already liberally stocked with game birds, Phillips (1928) describes attempts, which met with mixed success, to naturalize or translocate a wide variety of different species. As early as 1733, the Governor of New York, Colonel John Montgomerie, unsuccessfully released 'about half a dozen couple of English pheasants' on Nutten Island in Upper New York Bay. Further attempts by George Washington in 1786 and by Benjamin Franklin's son-in-law, Richard Bache, 4 years later, similarly failed, and almost a century was to pass before Pheasants were first successfully released in North America.

Until quite recently the importation of foreign game (and other) birds into the United States was conducted on a somewhat haphazard basis, with, as Gottschalk (1967) points out, no consideration being given to the alien's ecological requirements, to the possibility of environmental and/or economic damage, or to the importance of maintaining written records. The Foreign Game Introduction Program (a cooperative venture initiated in 1948 and involving the US Department of the Interior through the Bureau of Sport Fisheries and Wildlife and the various state fish and game departments, as well as foreign governments and such private organizations as the Wildlife Management Institute of Washington, DC) energetically sought to rectify these deficiencies. Its declared objectives were, first, 'to discourage unwise game bird introductions by making careful biological evaluations in advance of any importations', and, second, 'to meet a real recreational need by filling vacant niches with attractive, adaptable game species' (Gottschalk 1967: 137). Although the release of game birds under this scheme formally ceased in 1970, stocks of various species held at that time continued to be freed in some states until at least 1978.

In New Zealand, on the other hand, where there were few game birds, their introduction filled a genuine want. Thomson (1922: 21–2) records that the early settlers, thinking of home, 'recalled the sport which was forbidden to all but a favoured few, but which they had often longed to share in . . . the grouse on the heather-clad hills, the pheasants in the copses and plantations, the hares and partridges in the stubble and turnip fields'. To satisfy this craving, Thomson describes the introduction by early colonists of many different species with varying degrees of success. Such introductions were not only encouraged but subsidized; thus in 1864 the Auckland provincial government offered the following prices per pair to immigrants importing alien birds: Song Thrushes (*Turdus philomelos*), £3; Blackbirds (*T. merula*), Robins (*Erithacus rubecula*), Wrens (*Troglodytes troglodytes*), Wheatears (*Oenanthe oenanthe*), House Sparrows (*Passer domesticus*) and Hedge Sparrows (Dunnocks) (*Prunella modularis*), £1.10.0. In the decade after 1874 the Wellington Acclimatization Society, which included among its objectives 'the perfection, propagation, and hybridization of species newly introduced and already domesticated', imported and released no fewer than 2,112 birds, including 'Australian bell birds, cirl buntings, diamond sparrows, jager birds [skuas], Java

doves, ortolans, Wonga pigeons, Australian shrikes, and plovers'.

Similarly, in Australia, the relative paucity of native game birds compared to the numbers they were used to at home, led to efforts by early settlers – again with mixed results – to establish in their adopted homeland various alien species.

Introductions for sentimental or nostalgic reasons have almost invariably involved songbirds. In Australia, where of more than a dozen European species introduced over half became established, they were imported by homesick colonists trying to provide themselves with mementoes of their native land. In 1861, Edward Wilson founded the Acclimatization Society of Victoria, whose declared aims were 'the introduction, acclimatization and domestication of all innoxious animals, birds, fishes, reptiles, insects and vegetables whether useful or ornamental . . . the spread of indigenous animals etc. from parts of the colonies where they are already known to other localities where they are not known'. (These objectives almost precisely mirrored those of The Society for the Acclimatization of Animals, Birds, Fishes, Insects and Vegetables within the United Kingdom, which had been founded in the previous year by Francis Trevelyan Buckland. The formation of the various acclimatization societies, of which the first was the Société Impériale d'Acclimatation founded in Paris by Geoffroy Saint-Hilaire in 1854, arose from the increasing interest by naturalists in exotic species, and resulted in more intensive efforts at naturalization (Lever 1977a).) Other acclimatization societies were later founded in most Australian colonies and in New Zealand, but none seems to have been as vigorous and long-lasting as that in Victoria.

The feelings of the early Australian settlers were typified by Professor F. McCoy who, in his anniversary address to the Victoria Acclimatization Society on 24 November 1862 (quoted by Frith 1979: 138), reported that 'those delightful reminders of our English homes would even now have spread . . . over a great part of the colony, and the plains, the bush and the forest would have had their present savage silence, or worse, enlivened by those varied touching joyous strains of Heaven taught melody'. That the native fauna and flora were in no danger from these introductions was confidently believed even by such eminent naturalists as C. S. Ryan (1906) who, in his presidential address to the Australasian Ornithologists' Union (quoted by Frith), claimed that 'our native birds . . . have only seen houses for a comparatively few years, hence they retire to the bush as buildings increase. But not so most of the imported ones; these find a retreat among suburban gardens'. That this theory was not invariably correct was soon to become obvious to all.

Likewise, in New Zealand, Thomson (1922) records the importation of some two dozen or more European songbirds (of which only about half became successfully established), which were brought in by settlers whose 'thoughts went back . . . to the song birds which charmed their youthful ears'.

In the United States, the Natural History Society of America imported songbirds from Europe and these were released near Brooklyn, New York, in 1846. Others (including the House Sparrow) were brought in by the Brooklyn Institute between 1850 and 1853, and the Trustees of the Greenwood Cemetery on Long Island introduced several species late in 1852.

One of the first private individuals to import songbirds from Europe into the United States was a German immigrant, Andrew Erkenbrecher, founder of the Cincinnati Zoological Garden. These birds, Erkenbrecher (quoted by Laycock 1970: 65) claimed, would prevent the 'encroachment of insects . . . as well as enliven our parks, woods and meadows, which in comparison with European countries are so bare of feathered songsters'. Erkenbrecher announced that $5,000 – a not inconsiderable sum – would be expended in shipping European songbirds to Cincinnati, where 'it may be expected that the ennobling influence of the song of birds will be felt by the inhabitants'. Later, he informed the Cincinnati Society of Natural History that a new organization, the Cincinnati Acclimatization Society, had, between 1872 and 1874, spent $9,000 in the purchase and importation of some 4,000 European songbirds, including, according to Laycock (1970: 65), 'robin redbreast, wagtail, skylark, starling, dunnock, song thrush, blackbird, nightingale, goldfinch, siskin, great tit, dutch tit [?], dipper, Hungarian thrush [?], missel thrush, corn crake and crossbill . . . and house sparrows'. This motley collection appears to have been released en masse, since a contemporary account (quoted by Laycock, p. 65) states that 'a cloud of beautiful plumage burst through the open window, and a moment later Burnet Woods [a suburb of Cincinnati] was resonate with a melody of thanksgiving never heard before and probably never heard since'. Few of these birds were ever seen again.

In its annual report for 1884, the Cincinnati Society of Natural History, referring to Erkenbrecher's importation, said that while it could not 'but admire the sentiment which promoted the introduction of these birds, we may properly at the same time express the opinion that the general principle is, zoologically speaking, a wrong one'.

The formation of the Cincinnati Acclimatization Society encouraged the founding of others in various states. Palmer (1899) reported that 'during the last fifty years a number of acclimatization societies have been organized for the purpose of introducing animals and plants from foreign countries. Private individuals, too, have devoted both time and money to importing birds or mammals which they consider necessary or desirable additions to the native fauna. Four or five societies exist in New Zealand and several have been formed in the United States.' In New York, Eugene Scheiffelin, an eccentric pharmaceutical chemist who conceived the novel idea of introducing to the United States all the birds mentioned by Shakespeare, and John Avery, were instrumental in founding the American Acclimatization Society; in Oregon, C. F. Pfluger helped to form the Portland Song Bird Club.

Birds deliberately introduced as an aesthetic amenity – that is, for the beauty of their plumage – have mostly been wildfowl and the so-called 'ornamental' pheasants. These include the Mute Swan (*Cygnus olor*) in the United States, South Africa, Australia and New Zealand; the Black Swan (*C. atratus*) in New Zealand; the Canada Goose (*Branta canadensis*), Egyptian Goose (*Alopochen aegyptiacus*), Mandarin Duck (*Aix galericulata*), Golden Pheasant (*Chrysolophus pictus*) and Lady Amherst's Pheasant (*C. amherstiae*) in the British Isles; the Peafowl (*Pavo cristatus*) in the United States (including the Hawaiian Islands) and New Zealand; Reeves's Pheasant (*Syrmaticus reevesii*) in the British Isles and Hawaii; and the Kalij Pheasant (*Lophura leucomelana*) in Hawaii.

Birds introduced solely as a source of food

3

have usually been domestic species, such as the Red Jungle Fowl (*Gallus gallus*) – the ancestor of the Domestic Fowl – and the Feral Pigeon (*Columba livia*). The former is now widely feral, especially in Indonesia, while the latter is virtually cosmopolitan. In the nineteenth century, Wekas (*Gallirallus australis scotti*) were imported from Stewart Island, New Zealand, to sub-antarctic Macquarie Island, as a source of food for visiting whalers and sealers. The provision of an additional food supply is, of course, a concomitant feature of the naturalization of game-bird species.

Many birds have been introduced throughout the world as a form of biological control of insects and other pests. The House Sparrow, for example, was introduced to the United States in the nineteenth century partly to control the larvae of the Snow-white Linden Moth (*Ennomos subsignarius*), which was defoliating trees; to Argentina in 1872 or 1873 to kill a psychid moth *Oiketicus kirbyi*; and to Brazil in 1905 or 1906 to destroy mosquitoes, and caterpillars that were damaging ornamental shrubs, in Rio de Janeiro. Similarly, in northern Queensland, Australia, Common or Indian Mynahs (*Acridotheres tristis*) were released in the nineteenth century to combat locusts and cane-beetles that were ravaging the sugar-cane plantations. More recently, in 1959, Cattle Egrets (*Bubulcus ibis*) were imported to the Hawaiian Islands to control flies that were damaging hides and causing cattle to gain less weight, and in the following year some were freed on Frigate and Praslin in the Seychelles, also to kill flies. The introduction of the Great Kiskadee (*Pitangus sulphuratus*) to Bermuda to control lizards, *Anolis grahami*, is a classic example of the folly of releasing one animal to control another without having first considered the possible side-effects.[1] All these species, with the exception so far of the Cattle Egret in Hawaii, and many others introduced around the world for the same purpose, have eventually themselves become pests. Although some exotic species are still being used as a form of biological control, this reason for releasing alien species is now generally accepted as totally invalid.

Two birds, the Chimango Caracara (*Milvago chimango*) on Easter Island and the Turkey Vulture (*Cathartes aura*) on Puerto Rico and Hispaniola, were released to act as scavengers. The former also preys on colonies of nesting sea

birds, and has been accused of injuring cattle and damaging their hides.

If Haemig (1978 and 1979) is correct, several species of exotic birds may have been imported to pre-Columbian Central America (where they subsequently became naturalized) to satisfy the requirements of the flourishing feather trade. Of these, two, the Great-tailed Grackle (*Quiscalus mexicanus*) and the Tufted or Painted Jay (*Cyanocorax dickeyi*), were almost certainly so introduced.

Several birds have been released simply out of curiosity, to see what would become of them in an alien environment – a peculiarly irresponsible reason, but one that is probably a factor in many introductions.

At least one bird, the magnificent Greater Bird of Paradise (*Paradisaea apoda*), was in 1909 introduced as a means of conservation from the Aru Islands off New Guinea (where it was being plundered to satisfy the demands of the millinery trade) to the island of Little Tobago some 170 km off the coast of Venezuela. In an attempt to conserve dwindling populations, the endemic New Zealand Saddleback or Tieke (*Creadion carunculatus*) has been translocated to several offshore islands within its natural range, while endemic Hawaiian Geese or Nénés (*Branta sandvicensis*), bred in captivity in Hawaii and by the Wildfowl Trust in England, have been reintroduced to the islands of Hawaii and Maui. The stocks of both species had been previously devastated by introduced mammalian predators (Lever 1985).

Many birds have become naturalized in alien countries as a result of escaping from captivity or domesticity. Among the families most commonly represented in the former category are the Psittacidae (parrots), Estrildidae (waxbills) and Ploceidae (weavers and sparrows), while species in the latter include the Red Jungle Fowl and Feral Pigeon. This contradicts Liversidge's claim (1979) that 'most people's fears about exotics escaping and establishing themselves is highly exaggerated. There is in my opinion little chance of most birds establishing themselves unless they are aided and abbetted [*sic*] by man. . . . Isn't it fun to have a home sparrow on the kitchen doorstep?'

Several birds have used humans as unwitting means of transportation by stowing-away on ships; thus, House Crows (*Corvus splendens*) have been carried to the Arabian Gulf, South Africa and Australia, and House Sparrows from Montevideo in Uruguay to the Falkland Islands.

Various unfortunate consequences may attend the naturalization of animals in a new environment: of these, the most important are the transmission of parasites and diseases; damage to human food and economic resources and to buildings; disturbance of the ecosystem; interspecific competition with indigenous species; predation; and morphological and/or genetic changes in native populations.

As De Vos & Petrides (1967: 116–17) point out, most diseases are likely to have more serious effects on hosts that have not been previously exposed to them than on their original hosts, because the former have not had the opportunity to develop any in-built immunity; such diseases may prove difficult, or in some cases even impossible, to eradicate. Although in time natural selection tends to result in an accommodation between a pathogen and its host, a new host may become endangered or even exterminated before that occurs. When an alien and an indigene compete for the same ecological niche, the host that originally introduced the disease may partially or completely displace the native species.

Epizootic diseases most seriously affecting humans and transmitted through the introduction of birds include psittacosis or ornithosis (sometimes known as 'parrot-fever'), cryptococcal meningitis (caused by the fungus *Cryptococcus neoformans*), histoplasmosis, toxoplasmosis, encephalitis and encephalomyelitis. In Brazil, the House Sparrow has been implicated in the spread of Chagas's disease (a form of sleeping-sickness transmitted by blood-sucking hemipteran insects), which can prove fatal to man. Among disorders that primarily attack other birds are Newcastle disease (a respiratory ailment of domestic poultry), blackhead (which has affected Common Turkeys (*Meleagris gallopavo*) in North America via imported domestic fowl), bird pox (following the introduction to the Hawaiian Islands of the night mosquito, *Culex pipiens fatigans*), avian influenza and avian malaria introduced into the Hawaiian Islands with birds from Asia. Pathogens carried by naturalized birds may have contributed to the serious decline (and in two cases probable extinction) of endemic Hawaiian honeycreepers of the genus *Hemignathus*; to the near-eradication of another honeycreeper, the Akepa (*Loxops coccinea*), and to that of the Hawaiian Goose or Néné. In New Zealand, Oliver (1930 and 1955) has suggested that infections brought in by imported Pheasants (*Phasianus colchicus*) may have contributed to the extinction in about 1875 of the endemic New Zealand Quail (*Coturnix pectoralis novaezealandiae*), while Falla, Sibson & Turbott (1979) believed that diseases introduced by naturalized birds and domestic fowls may have been partially responsible for the fall in numbers of the New Zealand Auckland Island Teal (*Anas aucklandica*), the Weka and the Red-crowned Parakeet (*Cyanoramphus novaezelandiae*).

Ectoparasites introduced by alien birds include ticks carried by the Common Quail (*Coturnix coturnix*), which can transmit to humans such diseases as typhus and relapsing fever, and chicken mites borne by Feral Pigeons which, having killed their avian hosts, turn their attentions to man. In Western Australia, both Laughing and Spotted Doves (*Streptopelia senegalensis* and *S. chinensis*) have been accused of helping to spread stickfast fleas. On the island of Hawaii, alien game birds are known to be the hosts of intestinal endoparasite worms, and throughout the archipelago a leucocytozoan infestation has been identified in exotic pigeons and doves. Starlings (*Sturnus vulgaris*) and House Sparrows are responsible for spreading the cestodes and nematodes of domestic poultry.

Examples of naturalized birds depleting human food resources are legion. It would be tedious and unnecessary to list them here, since details of the various species' depredations are fully discussed in the text. Perhaps the most notorious are the Starling and the House Sparrow, which have become pests wherever they are naturalized. Both, together with the Feral Pigeon, have also damaged buildings by depositing excrement, by pecking at mortar, and through their nesting activities. Several species that are regarded as either harmless or, at worst, insignificant and local pests in their natural range, have become serious nuisances in their naturalized one.

Naturalized birds frequently compete – principally for food and nesting sites – with indigenous species (especially closely related ones). Here we are confronted with the concept of the 'ecological niche'. In nature, every species occupies a position or niche in the biosphere to which it is better adapted than any other creature. Thus in any given ecosystem, provided that the diffusion of species has been complete, every available niche will already be occupied. An alien animal introduced into such an environment will survive only if it can out-compete native species, or if it can find a previously unoccupied or 'empty' niche. Of these two options, the former is the more common. Thus, for example, in North America the Starling has contributed to the decline of several native hole-nesting birds, such as the Eastern Bluebird (*Sialia sialis*); wherever it has been introduced, the Common Mynah has ousted native birds by usurping their nests, and by its aggressive behaviour towards more timid species has competed successfully with them for food; in Australia, the naturalized Nutmeg Mannikin (*Lonchura punctulata*), which is adapted to a wider variety of habitats and foods than its native congeners, whom it can also outbreed, appears to be evicting the Chestnut-breasted Mannikin (*Lonchura castaneothorax*), and the Spotted Dove has taken over much of the habitat of the Bar-shouldered Dove (*Geopelia humeralis*), which it seems to be replacing.

Alien species sometimes succeed because man has created an 'artificial' niche to which they (but not indigenes) are well-adapted. Thus, the House Sparrow in Australia has colonized newly created urban environments that were unsuitable for any native species, which have therefore not been adversely affected. Similarly, in Australia, Goldfinches (*Carduelis carduelis*) thrive on disturbed wasteground overgrown with alien weeds and shrubs, where they seldom come into contact with potential competitors. On Puerto Rico, ironically, the various species of naturalized parrots are thriving in the drier urban districts, while the endemic Puerto Rican Amazon (*Amazona vittata*), which in *The ICBP Bird Red Data Book* (King 1981) is classified as critically endangered, has since 1930 been confined to the virgin and extremely humid Luquillo Experimental Forest in the north-east of the island. It would be interesting to see how *vittata* would fare if released in residential areas.

Where an alien species has food, habitat and breeding requirements that are very similar to those of native species, Gause's Principle applies. This states that two species with identical ecological requirements cannot co-exist in the same area unless there is a superabundance of their various needs.[2] Either the alien will prove stronger and more effective than the native in

utilizing the available resources, in which case the former will ultimately replace the latter, or it will prove weaker and less efficient, in which case the interloper will itself disappear.

Introduced species can also be responsible for genetic and/or morphological changes in indigenous populations. Although natural selection usually favours native genotypes, continuous infiltration or introgression of an alien's genes into an indigenous population can eventually have an effect, which may be beneficial but, especially in the case of birds, is more likely to be detrimental. The hybrid offspring of naturalized Mallards (*Anas platyrhynchos*) and native New Zealand Grey Duck (*A. s. superciliosa*), of Mallards and Australian Black Duck (*A. s. rogersi*), and of naturalized Scarlet Ibises (*Eudocimus ruber*) and native White Ibises (*E. albus*) in Florida, USA, are aesthetically and genetically inferior to both their respective parents. This negates Liversidge's statement (1979) that 'nor do I accept the fear expressed that ducks might hybridise'.

At least three naturalized raptors have been implicated in the decline or extinction of various small native birds. On Easter Island in the southeast Pacific, the Chimango Caracara preys on the young of Red-tailed Tropicbirds (*Phaethon rubricauda*) and Kermadec Petrels (*Pterodroma neglecta*). On Tahiti in the Society Islands, Marsh Harriers (*Circus aeruginosus*) kill domestic fowl; have been accused of causing a severe decline in the local populations of seven species;[3] and on circumstantial evidence may have been responsible for the extinction of local insular populations of the Tahitian Lory (*Vini peruviana*). In the Seychelles, Barn Owls (*Tyto alba*) are said to have caused a reduction or the extinction of a dozen or so endemic species.[4] On Macquarie Island, an introduced rail, the Weka, preys on ground-nesting sea birds and (with introduced rats and cats) is said to have contributed to the decline of nine species of burrow-nesting petrels (Procellariidae and Pelecanoididae).[5]

Extensions of a species' distribution sometimes result in considerable genetic variation, such as has occurred in the House Sparrow in North America and the Hawaiian Islands. Aliens all too often cause damage that is either of minor importance or unknown in their native range: thus, the Yellow-fronted Canary (*Serinus mozambicus*) in the Mascarenes and the Village Weaver

(*Ploceus cucullatus*) on Hispaniola are far more serious pests than in their African homeland, while the Grey Francolin (*Francolinus pondicerianus*), which in India is quite harmless, is regarded on the island of Rodrigues as a menace to sprouting maize. Finally, many birds – even those that in their native range are not migratory – are likely to disperse widely from the countries where they were originally introduced; a prime example is provided by the House Sparrow in South and Central America.

The benefits derived from the presence of naturalized birds include the provision of (new) game species; further sources of food; added aesthetic amenity; additional opportunities for human employment; and an economically valuable extension of a country's natural resources. Although it is possible to argue for the conservation of at least some naturalized animals because of their undoubted economic importance, it is more difficult to justify their conservation on purely scientific grounds, unless the animal concerned is a relic population of an endangered species that has been introduced for the express purpose of conservation, as in the case of the Greater Bird of Paradise on Little Tobago, or it provides an interesting example for the study of microevolution. There is, indeed, an ideological contradiction between on the one hand attempting to conserve natural ecosystems and native species, and on the other advocating the conservation of aliens that are, in general, ecologically undesirable.

The introduction or reintroduction of an endangered species can be a valuable tool in the hands of the conservationist. As the Working Group on Introductions of the UK Committee for International Nature Conservation states in its report *Wildlife Introductions to Great Britain* (Linn 1979: 10–11):

By it ecosystems can be enriched in species and this restoration of the full ecosystem complement might have an important influence on ecosystem functioning. . . . Moreover, by dispersing the populations of a species introductions or reintroductions can also lessen the risk of extinction by catastrophic changes in the original range. . . . Finally, increased diversity is generated by introductions and reintroductions and high diversity is commonly regarded as a conservation objective on both amenity and scientific grounds.[6]

The reintroduction to the wild of endangered species bred in captivity is increasingly becoming accepted as the only justification for keeping wild animals in confinement. A classic case among birds, referred to above, is that of the Hawaiian Goose or Néné. Others include the reintroduction to its native range of the Aleutian Island subspecies of the Canada Goose (*Branta canadensis leucopareia*); of the White-headed Duck (*Oxyura leucocephala*) to Hungary; of the Cheer Pheasant (*Catreus wallichii*) to Pakistan; of Swinhoe's Pheasant (*Lophura swinhoei*) to Taiwan; and the proposed reintroduction of White-winged Wood Ducks (*Cairina scutulata*) to Assam. The umbrella pretexts of 'education' and 'scientific research' are no longer – if, indeed, they ever were – valid.

As Bates (1956: 799) points out, 'It is not always easy to get a vertebrate species established in a new region, even though the new environment may seem quite suitable.' De Vos & Petrides (1967: 113), quoting Dorst (1964), explain the successful introduction of animals in the following three ways although, as they point out, many other complex factors are frequently involved.

1. In case of a vacant and suitable ecological niche, the introduced species will occupy it to become well established. It may even proliferate to pest proportions.
2. Where a closely related autochthonous species is present in an ecological niche, an introduced species may be more aggressive and successful in competition so that the native species is gradually reduced in numbers and may be eliminated.
3. Also the introduction of predatory species may threaten a predator–prey balance, and modify this to the detriment of native species.

Factors that increase the likelihood of success of an introduced species include a congenial climate; a suitable habitat; an abundant supply of acceptable food; freedom from predators; an absence of competition from more aggressive native species; the ability to reproduce rapidly; the absence of, or abandonment of, the instinct to migrate; a large-enough initial stock; and a degree of adaptability. It is seldom that all these factors occur in the case of any one species, although as De Vos & Petrides (1967: 114) point out, 'In general, the more generalized the characteristics of a vertebrate species, particularly in its food habits, the better are its chances of establishment'. The only element in species introduction that can be forecast with certainty is that of unpredictability.

As E. H. Graham (quoted by Westerskov 1953b: 1) said, 'When a species is introduced into an area where it has not lived before, it is almost impossible to foretell the consequences, although it is quite possible that it will either succeed gloriously or eventually fail entirely.'[7] When enough of the above factors do occur, a species' establishment frequently follows a typical sigmoid curve, as described by Elton (1927: 111–12) in his classic *Animal Ecology*:

When an animal spreads rapidly upon being introduced into a new country, there is usually a definite sequence of events, which is rather characteristic. At first it may be almost unnoticed for some time, or else is highly prized as forming a link with the home country. Thus the starling was introduced into New Zealand by acclimatization societies bent upon brightening the country with British birds. The next stage is that the animal may suddenly appear in the dimensions of a plague, often accompanied by a migration. . . . The starling was instrumental in spreading the seeds of the common English blackberry in New Zealand and has been undoubtedly one of the biggest factors in the production of the blackberry plague there. This has resulted in the formation of thickets of blackberry covering the country for miles, making agriculture impossible, and in some places forming a danger to lambs, since the latter get caught inextricably on the thorns of the blackberry plants. Finally, after a good many years there is often a natural dying down of the plague. This is in most cases not due to the direct efforts of mankind in killing off the pests, but appears rather to be due to the animal striking a sort of balance with its new surroundings, and acquiring a set of checks which act fairly efficiently.

The sequence of events following the successful introduction of an exotic species into an alien environment may thus be summarized as follows.

1. *Release*, followed by a marked reduction in stock due to predation or death from natural causes.
2. *Breeding*, followed – as a result of the appearance of adaptive changes in the behaviour and ecology of survivors – by a rapid increase in the population (described by Elton as an 'ecological explosion') to the maximum numbers that the colonized area will support.
3. *Establishment*, followed by a contraction in numbers and distribution until a level is reached at which both become stabilized.

It is axiomatic that alien species have their greatest impact on insular biota. As the report by the UK Working Group on Introductions (Linn 1979: 8–9) states:

Species evolved in isolation from one another to fill similar niches are potentially direct competitors should they be brought together, and one will usually (perhaps always) prove the stronger. Island species are particularly vulnerable for they are rarely equipped to contend with either direct competitors evolved in the more populous and harder school of continental evolution, or with predators or parasites absent from their own impoverished floras and faunas.

Introduced species released from competition, predation or other limiting factors of their native range can also spread rapidly. The realised range, or niche width, of a species in its indigenous ecosystems may be, because of these factors, much narrower than its potential range in their absence.

In his classic *The Naturalisation of Animals and Plants in New Zealand*, Thomson (1922: 73) wrote:

In regard to any natural enemy it is, of course, absolutely certain that it cannot exterminate, but can only keep in check, the animal it is intended to cope with. If it does more, then its own means of livelihood are imperilled, or it has to find other victims.

In other words, a predator is controlled by the amount of prey available to it, and not vice versa. Although this is certainly true in the case of continental land masses, it does not necessarily apply when an alien predator is introduced to an offshore island. With particular reference to rats and the Small Indian Mongoose (*Herpestes auropunctatus*) in Jamaica (where the former were exterminated after the introduction of the latter), but in words which are applicable also to avian predators, C. B. Lewis wrote:

The introduction of any animal into a new habitat involves certain important and highly complicated biological principles and interrelationships. In any long established and undisturbed area the native plants and animals exist in fairly constant proportions – a natural balanced condition. The balance of populations fluctuates slightly from year to year and may, over a period of years, gradually change; but if a . . . predatory animal is introduced into a community, which will provide no natural enemies, it is obvious that the natural balance of the community will be greatly upset.[8]

Research on the extinction of indigenous birds on small island groups and their replacement by exotics suggests that quite often native birds are not lost as a direct result of interspecific competition with adventives, but rather that the latter take over only after the former have been largely eradicated by introduced predators, disease or despoliation of their habitat by man or introduced wild or domestic herbivores. Thus, in the virgin forest of the Harauki Gulf islands of New Zealand there are few of the European and Australian exotic birds that live in the disturbed forests of North and South Islands. Although the exotics could easily have dispersed to these islands they have not done so, apparently because of their inability to out-compete native species for food, nesting sites, and other requirements.[9]

C. J. O. Harrison (personal communication, 1986) has noted increasing evidence that some places that have proved especially vulnerable to adventives, such as the Hawaiian Islands[10] and New Zealand, are now known to be areas in which the present endemic avifauna is only a surviving relic[11] following habitat devastation by native settlements in periods before recorded history. The island of Madagascar has suffered from such despoliation in the past, and may thus be particularly vulnerable to future introductions.

Over 30 years ago, Westerskov (1953b) suggested various questions for consideration when contemplating the introduction of an animal into a new environment. These may be summarized as follows:

1. Whether the new species would be of value for sport, food, as a form of biological control of an existing pest species [a reason for introduction of extremely dubious validity], or on amenity or aesthetic grounds.
2. Whether the new species would itself be likely to become a pest in any way, for example by causing agricultural, horticultural, silvicultural, piscicultural or other economic loss, or by competing with and/or destroying native fauna and flora.
3. Whether a vacant ecological niche exists for the new species to fill.
4. Whether the climate and habitat (including cover and roosting and nesting sites) are suitable.
5. Whether there is an abundant supply of suitable foods and sufficient water.
6. Whether, if migratory in its natural range, the species would be likely to remain where intended.
7. Whether an adequate supply of suitable stock is available.

Since Westerskov's paper three major policy manifestos for introducing animals (and plants) have been published. In chronological order these are: 'Problems in species' introductions' (Anon. 1968); *Reintroductions: Techniques and Ethics* (Boitani 1976); and *Wildlife Introductions to Great Britain* (Linn 1979). A summary of their recommendations is as follows:

1. The risk of accidental introductions should be minimized and, when these occur, the reasons should be determined.
2. Reintroductions are in general more acceptable than new introductions, provided that:
   (a) they are undertaken with individuals of a taxon as close as possible to that of the original stock; and that
   (b) their removal does not endanger the survival of the donor population;
   (c) the causes of extinction are known and no longer exist, and that the reason was not that the species was a pest or dangerous;
   (d) suitable food and habitat are available; and
   (e) the species is unlikely to become a pest in the existing demographic conditions.
3. The introduction of a new species should be permitted only when:
   (a) the factors governing its home distribution and population are properly understood;
   (b) no stock of a desirable and comparable native species already exists;
   (c) it seems likely to be an economic, sporting, and/or aesthetic asset, and ecologically and economically innoxious;
   (d) the stock to be used is free from diseases and parasites;
   (e) it would not compete with native species, other than pests;
   (f) it could, should the need arise, be eradicated or at least controlled;
   (g) its biology (especially its rate of spread and ecological – and socioeconomic – impact) is carefully studied both before and after introduction;
   (h) a suitable and, if possible, vacant ecological niche exists;
   (i) the climate and habitat are suitable; and
   (j) there is an abundant supply of acceptable food.
4. If suitable enclosed experimental areas are available, where a new species can be controlled and monitored prior to release, these should be utilized.

5. The agreement of the local human population should, if possible, be obtained, and adequate funds should be available as compensation for any economic loss incurred.

6. Where necessary, relevant legislation (e.g. for the protection of the introduced species) should be enacted before the release.

7. The control of the exportation of native species for introduction elsewhere (as exists in the United States) should become universal.

The overall policy guideline for introductions of alien species around the world – both animals and plants – is encapsulated by the declaration in Article 6.8 of *Wildlife Introductions to Great Britain* (Linn 1979: 17) (retaining the original italics):

Because of their dubious benefits to wildlife interests and our inability to predict the effects of introduced species on our native flora and fauna and ecosystems, *we accept the provision in Article 11.2b of the Draft Convention on the Conservation of European Wildlife and Habitats, 'to strictly control the introduction of non-native species'*, and *suggest that the basic premise from a conservation viewpoint should be that deliberate introductions of alien species with the intent to naturalise them in native ecosystems are for the most part undesirable.*

NOTES

Based on a paper by the author, 'Introductions: reasons, results and criteria', delivered at the British Herpetological Society, Fauna and Flora Preservation Society, and Mammal Society Joint Symposium on Introduced Species, held at the Zoological Society of London on 27 November 1982.

1 See p. 301.
2 This principle was restated in 1934 by the Russian ecologist Gause, after whom it is now named. As, however, he was not its originator it has been suggested that it should be renamed the Principle of Competitive Exclusion.
3 See p. 68.
4 See p. 288.
5 See p. 202.
6 See also A. D. Bradshaw, *Proceedings of the Royal Society* 197: 77 (1977).
7 *Natural Principles of Land Use* (1944).
8 'Rats and the mongoose in Jamaica', *Oryx* 2: 170–2 (1953).
9 Diamond & Veitch 1981; King 1984:116–17.
10 S. L. Olson & H. F. James, *Science* 217: 633–5 (1982); S. L. Olson & H. F. James, *Smithsonian Contributions to Zoology* no. 365 (1982); S. L. Olson & H. F. James, 'The role of Polynesians in the extinction of the avifauna of the Hawaiian Islands', in P. S. Martin (ed.) *Late Quaternary Extinctions* (University of Arizona Press: Tucson, 1983), 768–84.
11 See, for example, D. W. Steadman, *Bulletin of the British Ornithologists' Club* 105: 58–66 (1985).

Ostrich
(Struthio camelus)

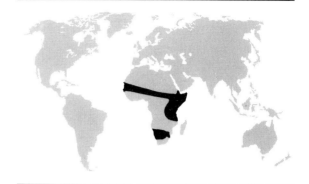

NATURAL DISTRIBUTION
Much of north and west Africa south of the Atlas Mountains to Nigeria; eastern Africa from the Sudan and northeastern Ethiopia south to Tanzania, and South Africa. Formerly also Arabia, Jordan and Syria.

NATURALIZED DISTRIBUTION
Australasia: Australia.

AUSTRALASIA

Australia[1]

The first pair of Ostriches despatched to Australia (Victoria) from Paris in 1862 as the intended founder-stock of an aigrette[2] or osprey farm died on the voyage. A second consignment of four that followed in 1869 was more successful; the birds were safely landed at Melbourne, from where they were transferred by their importer, Mr (later Sir) Samuel Wilson, a noted Australian pastoralist, to his estate at Longerenong in the

Wimmera district. Here, in the following year, one of the hens laid and hatched 12 or 13 eggs, 11 of the chicks being reared successfully.

The next season, however, was exceptionally wet, and only seven young were hatched, all of which soon died. The hens showed no discretion over their choice of nesting sites, often laying on the bare soil which flooded easily after heavy rain, causing the eggs to become addled and the brooding bird to develop rheumatism. Before long one of the cocks became extremely ill-tempered; one man had his trousers torn from the waist to the shin by a single kick, and although he was unhurt others were less fortunate. Wilson claimed to have seen a wooden fence-rail snapped in two by the kick of an angry Ostrich.

These vicissitudes, combined with a climate that was clearly too wet and predation of the young by native marsupial cats (*Dasyurus* spp.), forced Wilson in 1874 to send his surviving stock inland to a station owned by C.M. and S.H. Officer at Murray Downs near Swan Hill on the north bank of the Murray River in New South Wales. The journey was made during some of the heaviest rainstorms recorded in Victoria, causing the ox-carts to become bogged in the mud, as a result of which several of the birds died.

Soon after the arrival of the survivors at Murray Downs one of the Officers' stockmen carelessly left a yard gate open, through which a hen escaped and broke her neck by running into a wire fence. One of the two remaining hens laid a single egg and then died, leaving the Officers with a total stock of three cocks and a hen. This nucleus they attempted to augment by ordering further birds from the Cape of Good Hope, but these failed to materialize. Instead, they acquired from the Cape an incubator (for which they paid the then not inconsiderable sum of £100), in which two clutches of eggs laid by the surviving hen were successfully hatched; initially the chicks did well, but later contracted South African disease, the first symptoms of which are similar to those of 'staggers' in domestic farm stock, followed by an inability to remain standing unless in constant movement; as a result, the unfortunate birds soon succumbed to exhaustion and starvation.

The next three clutches were more successful, the four healthy offspring from the first being ready to breed in 1878. To prevent attacks by the cocks and predation by Wedge-tailed Eagles (*Aquila audax*), a keeper was appointed to guard the young birds; however, Lord Casey,[3] who in 1877 had been appointed Governor-General of Australia, recorded that many Ostrich eggs at Murray Downs were broken by stones dropped on them by Black-breasted Buzzards (*Hamirostra melanosternon*) – a mode of attack that the buzzards also practised on the eggs of Emus (*Dromaius novaehollandiae*).

The Officers' Ostriches, in addition to grazing the lush Murray Downs pastures, were fed on chopped lucerne, sorghum, maize, bonemeal and gravel. Their plumes, marketed in London, were said to be superior in quality to those produced in South Africa.

When Suetonius Officer died in 1882 the population had increased to over a hundred; in the following year, C.M. Officer sold the Murray Downs station and transferred part of the stock to a smaller property a few kilometres south at Kerang in Victoria, and part to another of his estates, the Kallara Station, on the Darling River. The stock at Kerang eventually increased to 120, but although at Kallara the older birds flourished their young were all poisoned by the mineral salts in the station's artesian wells.

In the early 1880s, Ostriches were also introduced successfully with the support of the South Australian Government to some of the drier parts of that state, such as the Younghusband Peninsula of the upper Coorong south of Adelaide, and at Port Augusta where, by 1888, the South Australia Ostrich Company had a flock of 510, some of which may have been liberated before the outbreak of the First World War. Before 1933, farm-reared birds were released at Point Sturt on Lake Alexandrina and on Mundoo Island at the mouth of the Murray River, where they increased to such an extent that they eventually became a pest.

After the First World War (not 'towards the end of the last century' as stated by Roots 1976) the trade in ospreys dramatically collapsed; this was due partly to a change in fashion, partly through the difficulties sometimes experienced in catching the birds for plucking (an adult Ostrich can easily outrun a mounted horseman), and partly when it became apparent that sheep were more profitable than plumes. Even well-established South African farmers were ruined when the price of a breeding pair of Ostriches fell from a peak of £250 in 1882 and between £140 and £200 in 1911, to only £14 in 1920. When farms closed down most of the birds escaped or were deliberately released, and feral flocks became established at Murgah, New South Wales, at Redcliffe Station north-west of Morgan near Maryan, and in the sandhills of the Coorong (where they remained until the late 1950s), Narrung and Port Augusta districts of South Australia.

Today, despite predation and shooting by Aborigines and local farmers, small feral populations survive north of Port Augusta and at Redcliffe, and hundreds or even thousands around the Flinders Range north-east of Port Augusta. The Ostriches in South Australia, many of which have been shipped to North American zoos, are believed to be mainly the southern race (*australis*) from south of the Zambesi, possibly intermixed with some *S. c. camelus* from North Africa.

Before 1912, the Acclimatization Committee of Western Australia released some Ostriches at Gingin and Mount Morgan east of Leonora in the goldfields, but none were ever established for long in the wild.

In 1882, a Dr Protheroe imported some Ostriches from Cape Town to the United States; the birds were landed at New York, from where 22 were overlanded to an osprey farm started at Anaheim in California by the California Ostrich Company. During the next 4 years three other importations of Ostriches were made to farms in California (at south Pasadena) and Arizona, all of which flourished until the collapse of the plume market. So far as is known Ostriches never became feral in the United States.

In 1985 attempts were made to reintroduce the Syrian Ostrich (*S. c. syriacus*) to Jordan, where it died out following severe floods in 1964.

A flock of some 30–40 rheas (introduced for their plumes, and believed to have been the **Lesser Rhea** (*Pterocnemia pennata*) from southern Peru, Bolivia, northwestern Argentina and Chile, but possibly the **Greater Rhea** (*Rhea americana*) from eastern and central Brazil, Paraguay, Uruguay, Bolivian Chaco and northern and central Argentina), was established in the wild near Askaniya Nova in the southern Ukraine, USSR,[4] before

the outbreak of the Second World War. Although only about half-a-dozen are known to have survived the hostilities, by 1951 the flock had recovered to its pre-war level. By the late 1950s, however, it was said to be again declining.

Some time before 1936 a number of Lesser Rheas were introduced to the western (Chilean) half of Tierra del Fuego,[5] where in 1970 a flock of about 50 was established in the wild in the northern, tree-less part of the island.

In the 1930s, an *emigré* Scottish shepherd, Mr John Hamilton, imported some rheas (probably Lesser Rheas) from Argentina to an island in the Weddell/Beaver group off West Falkland where, after persisting for a number of years, they eventually disappeared.

In 1885, the **Chilean Tinamou** of the nominate form *Northoprocta perdicaria perdicaria*, a native of northern and central Chile between the Tropic of Capricorn and about 42° S, was released on Easter Island,[6] in the South Pacific; although the birds remain established a century later, they have not succeeded in spreading far, possibly due to predation by the Chimango Caracara (*Milvago chimango*) (q.v.), which was introduced in 1928.

Between 1966 and 1978 large numbers of South American tinamous of various species were released, apparently without success, in the United States.[7] In the former year, 69 Chilean Tinamous – *Northoprocta p. perdicaria* and *N. p. sanborni* – were introduced as potential game birds to Big Island and to Kauai, respectively, in the Hawaiian group, and, between 1971 and 1977, 12,004 *sanborni* were planted in 17 counties in Washington State. From 1969 to 1974, 473 **Ornate Tinamous** (*Northoprocta ornata*) were placed in the Willamette Valley of Oregon, and in 1970–1, 110 **Red-winged Tinamous** (*Rhynchotus rufescens*) were released in two counties of Alabama. In 1966 and 1971, 128 **Spotted Nothuras** (*Nothura maculosa annectens*) were released in Florida; in 1968 and 1972, 47 were freed in Alabama, and 136 were acquired by the King Ranch of Texas in 1968. In 1969–70, 164 **Darwin's Nothuras** (*Nothura darwinii salvadorii*) were introduced in Colorado and, in 1970, 1,000 were freed in Oklahoma. Nebraska liberated 256 **Elegant Crested Tinamous** (*Eudromia elegans*) in 1971, and in 1968 and 1970, 217 *E. e. albida* were released in California.

NOTES

1 Blakers, Davies & Reilly 1984; Condon 1968, 1975; Frith 1979; Long 1972, 1981; Pizzey 1980; Rolls 1969.
2 Ostrich or egret plumes.
3 Richard G. Casey, *Australian Father and Son* (Collins: London, 1966).
4 Long 1981; Salganskii & Salganskaya 1959.
5 Humphrey, Bridge et al. 1970; Johnson 1965; Long 1981; Philippi 1954.
6 Harrisson 1971; Hellmayr 1932; Holyoak & Thibault 1984; Johnson, Millie & Moffett 1970; Long 1981; Peters 1931.
7 Banks 1981; Bohl & Bump 1970; Long 1981; Walker 1967.

Cattle Egret
(*Bubulcus ibis*)

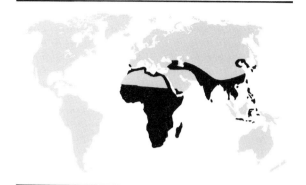

NATURAL DISTRIBUTION

Originally only locally in the southwestern Palaearctic, Ethiopian and Oriental regions, including parts of northern and tropical Africa, southern Spain and Portugal, and southwestern Arabia sporadically eastwards to southern China and Japan, Taiwan and the east Malaysian archipelago.

Cattle Egrets (also known as Buff-backed Herons) have dramatically extended their range[1] naturally to include North America – the eastern United States (since 1941) and southern California (1964), and southern and eastern Canada (1956 or 1957) and British Columbia (1973); Bermuda (1953); Central America – Panama and Costa Rica (since 1954) and Guatemala and southern Mexico (since 1958); northern and parts of western South America – Guyana (1937), Venezuela (1943), Aruba (1944), Surinam (1946), Colombia (1951), Bolivia (1953), Peru (1956), Ecuador (1958) and northern Chile (by 1970); the West Indies – especially Puerto Rico (since 1948), Trinidad (1952), St Croix (1955), Barbados, Jamaica and Haiti (all since 1956), Cuba (1957) and Antigua; the Galápagos Islands (1964); parts of Papua New Guinea (*c.* 1960); Australia, away from the interior (1948), and parts of North and South islands, New Zealand (since 1963).

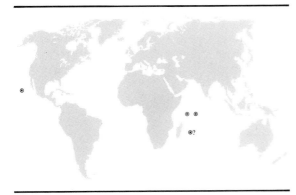

NATURALIZED DISTRIBUTION
Africa: Seychelles, ?Rodrigues; Oceania: Hawaiian Islands, Chagos Archipelago.

Seychelles[2]

On circumstantial evidence Cattle Egrets may have been first introduced to the Seychelles in the late nineteenth or early twentieth century. In 1960, some were released on Frigate and Praslin to control flies and other pests, and they are now well established on both these islands. The present stock is somewhat different to the nominate form and may be a hybrid between an earlier endemic race and the introduced birds, as early specimens of *B. i. seychellarum* show evidence of an Asiatic rather than an African origin. Cattle Egrets are now widespread throughout the Seychelles, where on Frigate Island they prey on the eggs and chicks of White Terns (*Gygis alba*) and could be effecting the relic population of the gravely endangered endemic Seychelles Magpie Robin (*Copsychus sechellarum*), known locally as the *pie chanteuse*; other species – for example, Sooty Terns (*Sterna fuscata*) – have been attacked on Bird Island, where Feare (1979) estimated the egret population to number 'probably over 40 birds'. Cattle Egrets that have spread to the Amirantes prey on nesting seabird colonies on Noeufs Island.

Rodrigues and Mauritius[3]

Cattle Egrets may have been successfully introduced to the island of Rodrigues in the Indian Ocean. From time to time, small numbers have been introduced to Mauritius, where, however, they have never become established.

OCEANIA

Hawaiian Islands[4]

According to Breese (1959), Cattle Egrets were introduced to the Hawaiian archipelago from Miami, Florida to help 'in the battle to control house flies, horn flies, and other flies that damage hides and cause lower weight gains in cattle'. Between 17 July and 24 August 1959, the Hawaiian Board of Agriculture and Forestry, the Honolulu Zoo and the Honolulu Hui Manu ('Bird Society'), funded by local cattle-ranchers, released 105 birds at single sites on Kauai, Molokai and Maui, and at two places on Oahu and Hawaii. The first nests were built near Kahuku on Oahu in 1960 in 4–5-m high thickets of mixed haole koa, lantana, Christmas berry and vines, some 24 km from the birds' point of release. In July 1961, a further 22 (followed later by 26 more from the Honolulu Zoo) were liberated on Oahu, where a year later the population exceeded 150.

As well as eating insect pests on Oahu, Cattle Egrets also feed on Louisiana red crawfish (*Procambarus clarkii*), which cause flooding by undermining with their burrows the embankments and irrigation ditches surrounding taro and watercress paddies. The birds are now common on Oahu and Kauai, and smaller numbers are established on the other main islands. On Kauai, where the population had increased from 25 to at least 6,800 by 1980, it was feared that before long they might displace nesting Red-footed Boobies (*Sula sula*) at Kilanea Crater. In recent years, Cattle Egrets have been reported from Laysan Island and Tern Island in the French Frigate Shoals.

Chagos Archipelago[5]

In 1955, a Captain Georges Lanier imported a dozen Cattle Egrets from the Seychelles to the Chagos Archipelago in an apparently successful attempt to control insect and other pests (it is possible that nine had previously been released in

1953), and by 1960 a colony of 27 nests was established at Point Est on Diego Garcia; as Bourne (1971) and Hutson (1975) point out, birds of the Asiatic subspecies *B. i. coromanda* occasionally reach Diego Garcia as natural vagrants, so the colony may consist of hybrids between this and the introduced form. Fear has been expressed that Cattle Egrets may spread to some of the other islands in the group, where they could become a serious pest to colonies of nesting sea birds.

In 1933, 20 Cattle Egrets were imported from India to Western Australia,[6] where 18 were released along the Lennard River at Kimberley Downs Station near Derby. The birds soon disappeared, having probably fallen prey to hawks, and there is no evidence that the present Australian population of Cattle Egrets are their descendants.

The Handbook of British Birds (Vol. 3, 1939) by Witherby et al. contains the following note (p. 144):

A considerable number of A[rdeola] [replaced by *Bubulcus*] *i. coromanda*, usually called the Indian Cattle-Egret, have been released by the Zoological Society [of London] each year since 1931 at Whipsnade, and a few were also released in 1930 by Mr A. Ezra at Cobham, Surrey. These birds have wandered in all directions and have been reported from time to time in many parts of the country as far apart as Devon, Somerset, Monmouth, Wiltshire, Leicester, Nottinghamshire, Merioneth, Kent, Essex, Cambridge, Norfolk, Lincolnshire, Perth, and even Iceland. . . . Some have also been released (1929 and 1938) at the Dublin Zoo.

So far as is known, none of these birds ever bred in the wild.

On 5 July 1961, two dozen eggs of the **Scarlet Ibis** (*Eudocimus ruber*), shipped from northeastern South America to Carter Bundy in North Miami Beach, Florida, USA,[7] arrived at Greynolds Park, where they were placed in the nests of native White Ibis (*E. albus*), and a fortnight later 17 hatched successfully. The two species interbred freely, but before long the scarlet-plumaged birds – vastly outnumbered by their white congeners – had all but disappeared. Apparently, the two species do not hybridize in South American rookeries where they nest sympatrically.

In the 1930s, Mr John Hamilton, an *emigré* Scottish shepherd, unsuccessfully introduced an unknown species of South American ibis (possibly the **Black-faced Ibis** (*Theristicus melanopis*) of southern Chile and Argentina) to a small island off West Falkland.

A free-flying but semi-domesticated colony of the **Greater Flamingo** (*Phoenicopterus ruber ruber*), a native of the Atlantic coast of tropical Central and South America and the West Indies, is established at Hialeah, in Florida, USA.[8] In 1929, H. D. Sloggett introduced three Greater Flamingos from Cuba to Kauai in the Hawaiian Islands,[9] where they only survived for about a year.

NOTES

1 For example, Crosby 1972.
2 Feare 1979; Long 1981; Penny 1974.
3 Rountree, Guérin et al. 1952.
4 Berger 1981; Bird, Zeillemaker & Telfer 1980; Breese 1959; Hawaiian Audubon Society 1975; Long 1981; Thistle 1962; Walker 1983.
5 Bourne 1971; Hutson 1975; Long 1981; Loustau-Lalanne 1962.
6 Hewitt 1960; Jenkins 1959; Long 1972, 1981; Serventy & Whittell 1951; Tarr 1950.
7 American Ornithologists' Union 1983; Blake 1977; King 1968; Long 1981, O'Keefe 1973; Reilly 1968.
8 Blake 1977; Long 1981.
9 Berger 1981; Long 1981; Munro 1960; Walker 1983.

Black-crowned Night Heron
(*Nycticorax nycticorax*)

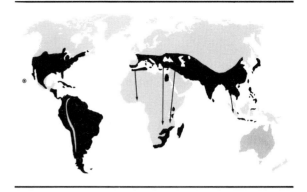

NATURAL DISTRIBUTION

Holarctic, Ethiopian, Oriental and Neotropical regions, including much of western Europe, sporadically eastwards to the Philippines and Indonesia, and parts of northern, tropical and southern Africa. In the New World, the race *N. n. obscurus* inhabits southern South America, and *N. n. hoactli* (which is the one established in Scotland) ranges from North America south to central South America and Hawaii.

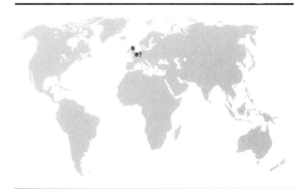

NATURALIZED DISTRIBUTION

Europe: British Isles, ?the Netherlands.

EUROPE

British Isles[1]

The European race *N. n. nycticorax* – usually known simply as the Night Heron – occurs in the British Isles naturally as an uncommon vagrant from western Europe. Only one attempt has ever been recorded to establish it as a resident species, when Lord Lilford unsuccessfully released a pair in Northamptonshire in 1887.

In December 1950, some Night Herons of the North American race *N. n. hoactli* escaped through a hole in the roof of their aviary in the grounds of the Royal Zoological Society of Scotland in Edinburgh, where they had been established since 1936. Five months later the entire roof was removed and the remaining birds escaped to join their companions in the zoo gardens. Unfortunately, and surprisingly, no census has ever been made since the birds escaped. Dorward (1957) estimated the population in 1955 at 24; by 1957, it had risen to around 30, and totals for succeeding years were about 50 (in 1960), 40 (1963), 60 (1968), 10 (1979) – following the exceptionally hard winter of 1978–9 – and 30 (since 1980). Young & Duffy (1984) consider that a population of between 25 and 40 is a realistic estimate. From time to time, some birds have been recaptured for sale to, or exchange with, other zoos, and since this has been done on a haphazard basis it may have led to an imbalance in sex and age within the colony.

Since their escape and release Night Herons have nested in a variety of deciduous and coniferous trees within the zoo grounds, including Larch (*Larix decidua*), Scots Pine (*Pinus sylvestris*), Austrian Pine (*P. laricio*), Yew (*Taxus baccata*), Holm Oak (*Quercus ilex*), Lime (*Tilia vulgaris*), Sycamore (*Acer pseudoplatanus*), Hawthorn (*Crataegus monogyna*) and Horse Chestnut (*Aesculus hippocastanum*). Nesting has been recorded in every month except August and September when the adults moult (though mainly between April and July), and as Young & Duffy state it is not unusual for chicks to be heard calling from snow-covered trees. Although some young may be killed by Carrion Crows (*Corvus corone*), Brown Rats (*Rattus norvegicus*), Domestic Cats (*Felis catus*) and Foxes (*Vulpes vulpes*), and others have been drowned in ponds and illegally removed by members of the public, Young & Duffy consider that insufficient food may be the cause of the high rate (perhaps 50 per cent or more) of fledgling mortality. Despite suggestions to the contrary, there is no evidence that nesting has yet occurred outside the zoo grounds.

The Night Herons' main source of food seems to be dead fish, day-old chicks and laboratory mice put out during the day for Sarus Cranes (*Grus antigone*), White Storks (*Ciconia ciconia*), American White Pelicans (*Pelecanus erythrorhynchos*) and Californian Sealions (*Zalophus californianus*) – though in the wild Night Herons are almost entirely crepuscular in their feeding habits. The young of various water birds may sometimes be taken, as also may be Common Toads (*Bufo bufo*), House Mice (*Mus musculus*) and shrews (Soricidae). The disappearance from the zoo grounds of the Common Frog (*Rana temporaria*) has been attributed to predation by Night Herons. After dusk, a number of birds usually leave the zoo to feed up to 15–20 km away – mainly on intertidal areas of the Firth of Forth and on the River Almond between Cramond Bridge and the coast – normally returning before dawn. Their prey on these nocturnal excursions is unknown, but probably comprises small rodents, amphibians, insects and other invertebrates. Although Young & Duffy consider that the continued provision of food by the zoo authorities is probably essential for the Night Herons' winter survival, this may not necessarily be so. Night Herons seldom nest north of 53° N, and are migratory in the north of their range. Edinburgh is situated at around 56° N, and it seems probable that the birds have abandoned their migratory instinct because of supplementary feeding by man. Were this ever to be abandoned, the birds would probably migrate south to winter in southern England, which is on much the same latitude as the Netherlands, Belgium and northern France (see below), where they would find ample food in the form of freshwater crustaceans and freshwater fish, which are respectively absent and in short supply in the Edinburgh area.

Before the Edinburgh birds' escape and subsequent release in 1950–1, Night Herons were only rarely reported in Scotland – according to Witherby et al. (Vol. 3, 1939: 150), 'six in south, one Aberdeen, two or three Argyll, one O[uter] Hebrides'. In the last 30 years, Night Herons have been regularly observed in and around the city of Edinburgh, and birds believed to be from this source have been reported from as far north as Kirkaldy, Fife (on the northern coast of the Firth of Forth), south to Westmorland in England. Other British records during the past three decades come in Scotland from as far north as Orkney, in England from Northumberland south to the Isles of Scilly, and also from Wales and Ireland. Birds observed in northeastern and southeastern England and in northern Scotland are believed to originate in the Netherlands (see below), and those in the west from southern Europe. Though as yet unconfirmed, it is not impossible that North American birds (which are virtually indistinguishable in the field from the European form) have made the transatlantic crossing as storm-carried vagrants. Although any natural colonization of Britain that may occur will presumably come from continental Europe, where after an earlier decline the species is expanding its range and population largely due to its tolerance of increasing urbanization, the North American birds at Edinburgh (which, since they cause no known damage, are tolerated and even welcomed as a local curiosity) may well become involved.

The Netherlands

In 1908–9, an attempt was made to reintroduce Night Herons to the Netherlands. Although this failed, in 1946 a small breeding population became established in the south, where the last native birds had died out by 1876. It has never been conclusively determined whether this colony resulted in the spread northwards of natural immigrants from southern Europe or from birds that escaped from a private collection formed before the Second World War in the neighbouring province of Zeeland.[2] The birds have now spread into northern France and Belgium, where they first nested in 1979.

Young (1984) refers to an introduced free-flying colony of Black-crowned Night Herons within the species' natural range. In Israel, the Tel Aviv University Zoo recently released birds of the nominate subspecies into its grounds; some remained to breed, and the increasing colony began to prey on the young of Black and White Storks (*Ciconia nigra* and *C. ciconia*), which seemed unable to cope with a nocturnal avian predator.

NOTES

1 Cramp & Simmons 1977; Dorward 1957; Fitter 1959; Hancock & Elliot 1978; Lever 1977a; Witherby et al. Vol. 3, 1939; Young 1984; Young & Duffy 1984 (and personal communications 1983–5).
2 Cramp & Simmons 1977; Lever 1977a: Voous 1960.

Yellow-crowned Night Heron
(Nycticorax violaceus)

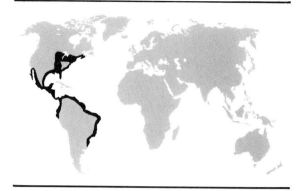

NATURAL DISTRIBUTION
The east-central USA, Central America, Baja California and Socorro (in the Ilas Revilla Gigedo) in Mexico, the West Indies, and from coastal Colombia and Peru through Venezuela to southern Brazil.

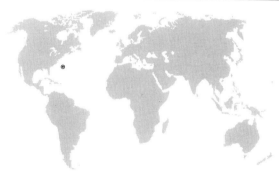

NATURALIZED DISTRIBUTION
North America: Bermuda.

NORTH AMERICA

Bermuda[1]

From subfossil bones discovered as recently as 1981 it is known that Yellow-crowned Night Herons – similar in conformation to the Socorro Island form *N. v. gravirostris* – were resident in Bermuda in precolonial times, that is before 1612. When the species died out as a breeding bird is uncertain, but being tree-nesters they were apparently able to survive the introduction of pigs in the sixteenth century by the Spanish, which so seriously affected the endemic Cahow or Bermuda Petrel (*Pterodroma cahow*). The Bermuda naturalist J. T. Bartram collected adult specimens in breeding plumage at Castle Harbour and Walsingham Bay in June 1861 and 1862, respectively, and in 1941, Hilary Moore (quoted by Wingate 1982) said that Yellow-crowned Night Herons were:

present throughout the year round Longbird Island and from the way that pairs of adults are seen with young birds in autumn I would think that it is quite likely that they breed there. One such party of two adults and a young bird was seen repeatedly in October, 1940. They are usually present in small numbers but I once saw six together and once eleven.

The destruction of the extensive mangrove swamps in which the herons nested on Longbird Island, when an airport was constructed between 1941 and 1943, may well mark the time when Yellow-crowned Night Herons ceased to breed in Bermuda. Since, however, the species is a regular visitor throughout the year, and adults in breeding plumage have been observed in every month, it is, as Wingate (1982) – from whom much of the following account is derived – points out, quite possible that the birds have nested undetected in more recent years.

The project of trying to re-establish a heronry through the reintroduction to Bermuda of a non-migratory population was a natural concomitant of the living museum programme on the 6-ha Nonsuch Island Nature Reserve in Castle Harbour, in which an attempt is being made to restore a viable sample of Bermuda's terrestrial ecosystem to its precolonial state. The project was made feasible by the Protection of Birds Acts of 1949 and 1975, which cover all but a few pest species; by a total ban on privately owned fire-arms, which has existed since 1973; by the estab-lishment since the early 1950s of a series of bird sanctuaries and wetland nature reserves; and by an almost total absence of mammalian and avian predators. Feral Cats (*Felis catus*), Black and Brown Rats (*Rattus rattus* and *R. norvegicus*), Common or American Crows (*Corvus brachy-rhynchos*) and Barn Owls (*Tyto alba*) are the only potential, but so far fortunately unrealized, threats.

The Yellow-crowned Night Heron was selected for the experiment both because it had in all probability been present before human settlement began, and because the principal prey of visiting birds between July and October, the Land Crab (*Gecarcinus lateralis*), was extremely common on Nonsuch Island – as it is on coastal hillsides along the whole of Bermuda's south shore, where its burrowing activities cause such damage to crops, lawns and gardens that it is everywhere looked on as a pest. Indeed, it was hoped that the successful reintroduction of the Yellow-crowned Night Heron as a breeding species might even result in a degree of biological control of the crabs.

In 1976, 1977 and 1978, 10, 17 and 19 nestling Yellow-crowned Night Herons, respectively (of the race *N. v. violaceus*), ranging in age from approximately 14 to 30 days, were collected in sibling groups from nests in the Alafia Banks heronry in Tampa Bay on the west coast of Florida, USA, and airfreighted via Atlanta and New York to Bermuda, where they arrived 24 hours later.

The nestlings were placed in a roofless enclosure on Nonsuch Island from which they were allowed to fly when fully fledged; they became independent of hand-feeding (almost exclusively with Land Crabs) within about 4 to 9 weeks of their arrival. It was soon apparent that the transplanted fledglings acted as decoys for their migratory brethren, which, in turn, tended to encourage the dispersal of the transplants away from Nonsuch. Thus, individuals from the first (1976) shipment were observed on Trunk Island in Harrington Sound on 2 September 1976 and in Riddell's Bay, Warwick Parish, on 7 April of the following year. Birds from the second (1977) shipment were harassed on Nonsuch by a Marsh Hawk (*Circus cyaneus*) and a Peregrine (*Falco peregrinus*) between 15 and 23 October of that year, which probably hastened their dispersal. Two were seen in Pilchard Bay, Sandy's Parish, near the western end of Bermuda, on 26 October 1977, and two more were found wintering in a mangrove swamp at Hungry Bay, Paget Parish, on Bermuda's south coast, in the following December.

Although some of the introduced birds may have left Bermuda with their migratory con-geners, at least two of the 1976 shipment remained permanently associated with Nonsuch Island, commuting daily to offlying rocky islets and mangrove swamps in and around Castle

Harbour. Some of the 1977 fledglings eventually joined these birds and adopted their routine, and by the second winter the Nonsuch Island population numbered at least four, rising by the third year (1978) to a minimum of six; by the winters of 1980–1 and 1981–2 the Nonsuch population had increased to a total of 14 birds of various ages.

After hand-feeding ceased, Land Crabs continued to comprise over 90 per cent of the birds' diet in the wild; the remainder consisted of other crabs – the Mangrove Crab (*Goniopsis cruentata*), the Blue Crab (*Callinectes ornatus*), the Ghost Crab (*Ocypode quadrata*) and a small *Pachygrapsis* sp. – and insects, including cockroaches (*Periplaneta* spp.), grasshoppers (*Neoconocephalus* and *Orphalella* spp.) and the cricket *Gryllus bermudensis*.

The first indication of possible breeding by the introduced birds was in July 1978, when two from the 1976 shipment, in definitive (adult breeding) plumage, began commuting daily to the Walsingham Bay area on the opposite side of Castle Harbour. Walsingham is a thickly wooded district with a dense understorey of vines and bushes covering some 16 ha, with an additional 1.2 ha of mangrove swamp around the bay; 9 ha form part of the Walsingham Trust Nature Reserve – the most extensive secluded area remaining on urbanized Bermuda.

Although Wingate deliberately refrained from searching for nests in 1978 for fear of disturbing the birds, he considers that successful breeding may have taken place in that year and again in 1979. On 23 June, 26 July and 30 August 1980, Wingate located three nests in the Walsingham area, which had increased to 14 by July 1982 and to around 16 by 1983 – all in living or dead Bermuda Cedars (*Juniperus bermudiana*).

By the late summer of 1982, when the fledgling crop amounted to over 30 birds, the resident population of Yellow-crowned Night Herons consisted of a minimum of 14 adult pairs plus at least 12 young, and it seemed that the population was self-perpetuating. Wingate considered that the most likely limiting factor would be a shortage of sufficiently secluded nesting sites in the densely populated islands. Although the birds are now regularly observed on all the islets in Castle Harbour and on the nearby Tucker's Town peninsula and Cooper's Point, and roost on cliffs and in mangroves at Ireland Island Lagoon, Pilchard, Riddell's and Hungry bays, Fairylands Creek in Pembroke Parish, Spittal Pond in Smith's Parish, Trunk Island and Ferry Reach, Wingate has to date found no evidence of nesting outside the Walsingham Reserve. Since even this secluded area is becoming subject to disturbance by illegal marijuana growers and timber thieves, who fell and remove the commercially valuable dead cedar trees that were devastated by an epidemic of scale insects (*Carulaspis minima*) between 1947 and 1951, Wingate considers it is unlikely that the herons will ever multiply to a point where shortage of food becomes a limiting factor. As even in the short time they have been established the herons already appear to be exerting a noticeable controlling effect on the Land Crabs, their reintroduction to Bermuda can, as Wingate points out, be considered both a biological and ecological success.

NOTE

1 For much of the history of the reintroduction of Yellow-crowned Night Herons to Bermuda I am indebted to D. B. Wingate 1982 (and personal communication, 1983). See also: Horton 1980; Lever 1984c, 1985c; Wingate 1973.

Mute Swan
(*Cygnus olor*)

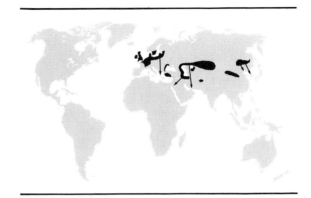

NATURAL DISTRIBUTION
Breeds from the British Isles, southern Scandinavia, Denmark, Russia, Asia Minor and Iran, discontinuously eastwards through Turkestan to Mongolia. Winters within breeding range and south to southeastern Europe and southern Asia.

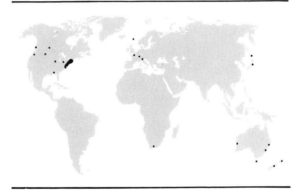

NATURALIZED DISTRIBUTION
Europe: parts of western Europe apart from the Iberian Peninsula and Italy; Asia: Japan; Africa: South Africa; North America: USA, Canada; Australasia: Australia, New Zealand.

EUROPE

British Isles[1]

Evidence that the Mute Swan was introduced to the British Isles in early times has long since been disproved. The species was a native of parts of East Anglia (Norfolk, Suffolk, Cambridgeshire, Huntingdonshire and Lincolnshire) and southern

England (the Thames Valley). It was semi-domesticated before AD 1186, but began to revert to the wild during the seventeenth or eighteenth century, and may thus now be fairly described as naturalized. Mute Swans are now widespread throughout the British Isles, where they cause a limited amount of damage by grazing water-meadows and trampling and grazing new-sown leys and winter wheat.

Mute Swans have for long been naturalized in parts of western Europe.[2] They were, for example, established on a number of rivers around Paris as early as the late seventeenth century, but during the succeeding 200 years many populations disappeared until few survived. In this century, however, the species has extended its range considerably as the result of introductions in Switzerland (*c.* 1850), Finland (the Åland Islands, *c.* 1934), Denmark (Tórshavn and Vágur on Suduroy in the Faeroes, *c.* 1940), and northern Italy and Greece (*c.* 1967), accompanied by natural spread (following increased protection) on the Danish mainland and in Bulgaria, Czechoslovakia, the Netherlands, Norway, Poland, Sweden, the Soviet Union and Yugoslavia.

ASIA

Japan[3]

In Japan, Mute Swans are currently established in the wild on several ornamental waters (e.g. at Yamanaka-ko near Mount Fuji, south-west of Tokyo) on the island of Honshu, and also in the south of the northern island of Hokkaido.

Although it has been asserted that Mute Swans have on at least two occasions arrived in Japan naturally (on Hachijo-jima, 280 km south of Tokyo, in 1933, and 50 years later in Yamanashi Prefecture on southern Honshu) – presumably from Mongolia or Ussuri on the Asian mainland, Mark Brazil is sceptical of these claims. He asserts that in their natural range Mute Swans are basically sedentary, and that the likelihood of them crossing the Sea of Japan from the mainland of Asia must be very remote. M. A. Ogilvie, on the other hand, (personal communication, 1985), points out that especially in the Far East (e.g. in the eastern USSR), Mute Swan populations are

almost certainly wholly migratory. He is thus much less sceptical than Brazil of the authenticity of these claims for natural arrival.

The Mute Swans at present established in the shallow waters of the Utonai-ko sanctuary on the southern tip of Hokkaido are descended from a group of seven that escaped from Onuma park north of Hakodate. This population is steadily increasing, and, in April 1984, eight pairs nested, of which, however, only five reared young successfully. The numbers at Utonai do not remain constant throughout the year, and appear to increase in late summer when more birds arrive to moult, and decrease again in autumn when neck-collaring has shown that some move 600 km south via Miyagi Prefecture in northern Honshu to winter on lakes in Ibaragi-ken north-west of Tokyo.

An unusually high proportion of adult Mute Swans at Utonai have pinkish or greyish instead of black legs, and some of the cygnets are ivory or white instead of the more usual dirty brownish-grey. Although first recorded in Britain as long ago as 1686, this colour variation was not scientifically described until several were collected in the hard winter of 1838. Five years later it was named '*Cygnus immutabilis*' in *A History of British Birds* by William Yarrell, who believed that a new species had been discovered. The birds came to be known as 'Polish Swans', since large numbers were imported from that country by London poulterers. It is now known, however, that this colour form, which is rare in Britain, increasing in Europe, and most common in the naturalized populations of North America, is a type of albinism that is rare in the birds' natural range, but relatively common in domesticated or naturalized populations.

Bacon (1980) has advanced an elegant hypothesis that the possible advantage of the 'Polish' morph is to the heterogametic female, enabling her to breed early in low-density populations. As a recessive condition in males its presence may prevent its extinction in high-density populations. The hypothesis predicts that 'Polish' genes should occur more frequently in low-density and expanding populations, as does in fact appear to be the case.

Mute Swans in Japan have been accused of overgrazing the vegetation on which other species feed in winter, and of directly competing for food with native Whooper Swans (*Cygnus c.*

cygnus) and Eastern Bewick's or Jankowski's Swans (*C. columbianus* (*bewickii*) *jankowskii*). So far, however, there seems little hard evidence to support this claim, and where they occur the birds are a popular local attraction.

AFRICA

South Africa[4]

Exactly when and how Mute Swans first came to South Africa is uncertain, but it is known that one breeding pair arrived in the Eastern Cape before 1920. It is believed that the birds either escaped from a passing ship or that they were deliberately introduced by a local landowner. By 1962, a herd of around 40 was established near Humansdorp at the mouth of the Krom River, and 4 years later one or two neighbouring estuaries and some lakes in the Wilderness area had been colonized. From the Krom, a number have been successfully translocated 150 km west to Green Lake near Knysna by the South African Department of Nature Conservation. In 1970, the total population in the Cape Province was about 120.

NORTH AMERICA

USA[5]

The earliest release of Mute Swans in the United States, by private landowners in New York State, took place before 1900. In 1910 and 1912, 216 and 328 birds, respectively, were imported from Europe, probably as semi-domesticated stock. On the Lower Hudson River between Stattsburg and Rhinebeck in Dutchess County, New York, and on Long Island, New York, a number escaped before 1920 when a herd of 26 is known to have been established. Before 1941, some Mute Swans were released by the Southside Club at Oakdale on Long Island, where by 1967 the population numbered about 700.

A herd on Silver Lake near Akron, Ohio, was wing-clipped annually from 1911 to 1934, when the birds were allowed to fly free. By 1940, a number of Mute Swans had escaped from estates near Ashbury Park, New Jersey, and several full-winged populations were established along the northern New Jersey coast south to Seaside Park on Barnegat Bay, where herds of up to 35 were reported; nesting occurred in the following decade, and the population had increased to 118 by 1957. Free-flying Mute Swans on private estates near Newport, Rhode Island, are believed to have been the origin of a population that multiplied and spread rapidly after the 1940s.

From New York, Ohio, New Jersey and Rhode Island, Mute Swans have wandered to eastern Massachusetts, Michigan, Pennsylvania, West Virginia, Kentucky and Alabama. Elsewhere, there have been further deliberate or accidental introductions that have assisted in the species' establishment from New Jersey northwards to Massachusetts; in Chesapeake Bay between Maryland and Virginia (where one or two pairs which escaped or were released from captivity in 1962 have multiplied to 500 individuals, which may be competing for food with other water birds); at Traverse City on Lake Michigan (where they have increased from one pair in 1948 to 500 birds); locally, according to a report by the US Fish and Wildlife Service in 1976, along the east, west (in Oregon) and gulf (in Alabama) coasts; and in the Great Lakes region. The American Ornithologists' Union (1983: 64) says that breeding has been 'recorded locally from southern Saskatchewan [Canada], northern Wisconsin, central Michigan, southern Ontario [Canada], southern New York and Connecticut south to central Missouri, northern Illinois, northwestern Indiana and, in the Atlantic region, Virginia. . . . Recorded after the breeding season from the breeding range, Minnesota, the Great Lakes and Maine south to the Ohio Valley and Virginia.'

Canada[6]

In 1966, Mute Swans were reported to be nesting and wintering in Regina, Saskatchewan, having presumably dispersed from northwestern Michigan. A population fluctuating between 10 and 50 pairs lives and breeds on southern Vancouver Island, British Columbia, where it competes with wintering native Trumpeter Swans (*Cygnus buccinator*) and Tundra Swans (*C. columbianus*).

AUSTRALASIA

Australia[7]

The earliest recorded introduction of Mute Swans to Australia took place in 1853 when the *Medway* landed four from England at Melbourne, Victoria, where they were presented to the Botanical gardens. In 1864 or 1866, two of their offspring were released on Phillip Island.

In 1886, Mr T. H. Dardel of Paradise Vineyards, Batesford, imported a pair of Mute Swans from Paris on the steamship *Kaikoura*. In 1897, three pairs, presented by the Worshipful Company of Vintners in London, were landed from the SS *Devon* at Perth, Western Australia; in 1901–2 (and/or possibly in 1912) their progeny were 'turned out for acclimatization', and the present small breeding population (amounting to only 31 in 1978) at Northam on the Avon River, 80 km east of Perth, is believed to be derived from this source. Semi-wild populations have occurred since before 1912 on such ornamental waters as those in Queen's Gardens and Hyde Park, and at Lake Coolbellup, Fremantle. Breeding pairs liberated on some rivers in the extreme south-west of Western Australia (e.g. on the Blackwood at Bridgetown, 240 km south of Perth) have resulted in further small populations, but the birds are only tenuously established and show no signs of increasing or spreading.

In Western Australia, the Mute Swan is apparently competing with the native Black Swan (*Cygnus atratus*), to the latter's disadvantage, wherever the two species live sympatrically, and steps are being taken to control the former by preventing the formation of new colonies, by killing or sending wild birds to zoos and by pinioning those on ornamental waters.[8]

Elsewhere on the Australian mainland, wild Mute Swans are established west and south of Brisbane in southeastern Queensland, and on waters near Sydney on the coast of New South Wales. At least one bird has been reported as far inland as Booligal on the Lachlan River in the latter state.

In about 1920, six Mute Swans were introduced by the city council to Launceston Park, Tasmania, from where a few years later their progeny were transferred to Lake Leake on the Eastern Tiers; according to Jenkins (1977), 'stragglers occasionally leave the lake and have been sighted on the Derwent River in the south and the Meander River in the north'.

New Zealand[9]

The first Mute Swans in New Zealand were a pair imported from England by the Canterbury Acclimatization Society in 1866 and some landed at Christchurch (both in South Island) in the same year. These were followed by introductions to Auckland (North Island) in 1867; to Dunedin in 1868; to Otago in 1868 (three) and 1869 (one); to Auckland again in 1869 (two from Sir George Grey[10]) and 1871 (a dozen presented by Captain F. W. Hutton), and others imported by dealers and private collectors.

Although Thomson (1922) found Mute Swans nowhere abundant in New Zealand in the early 1920s, Oliver, writing 30 years later, reported small populations at Pupuke Lake, Foxton, Ashley Mouth, Kaituna, Akaroa, Tomahawk, Lake Waihala and some other waters. Falla, Sibson & Turbott (1979) found a 'well-established breeding population of 50–70 on Lake Ellesmere [said to be descended from a single pair], Canterbury, and 12–20 on Lake Poukawa, Wanstead Lagoon and other lakes in central and southern Hawke's Bay'. Most Mute Swan populations in New Zealand occur south of 40° S.

In about 1920, W. H. Wise released a number of Mute Swans near Hilo on the island of Hawaii[11] where, although for a time they apparently became established, they eventually disappeared.

NOTES

1 Delacour 1954; Fitter 1959; Scott & Boyd 1957; Sharrock 1976; Witherby et al. Vol. 2, 1938.
2 American Ornithologists' Union 1983; Cramp & Simmons 1977; Delacour 1954; Long 1981; Mayaud (in Palmer 1976); Scott 1972; Williamson 1970.
3 For information on Mute Swans in Japan I am indebted to M. Brazil (1984, 1985, in press, and personal communication, 1985), and to M. A. Ogilvie (personal communication, 1985).
4 Siegfried 1962, 1970; Liversidge n.d.; Long 1981; Winterbottom 1966, 1978 (and personal communication, 1981).
5 American Ornithologists' Union 1957, 1983; Bump 1941; Cooke & Knappen 1941; Delacour

1954; Long 1981; Palmer 1976; Phillips 1928; Reese 1975; Scott 1972; Willey 1968a, b.

6 Godfrey 1966; Long 1981; Munro & Peter 1981; and W. T. Munro, personal communication, 1985.

7 Balmford 1978; Blakers, Davies & Reilly 1984; Condon 1975; Jenkins 1959, 1977; Le Souef 1912; Long 1972, 1981; Pizzey 1980; Serventy & Whittell 1962; Tarr 1950.

8 *Oryx* 15: 239 (1980).

9 Falla, Sibson & Turbott 1979; Kinsky 1970; Long 1981; Oliver 1955; Thomson 1922; Williams 1969; Wodzicki 1965.

10 1812–98; Governor of New Zealand 1845–53 and 1861–7; Prime Minister 1877–9.

11 Long 1981; Munro 1960.

Black Swan
(*Cygnus atratus*)

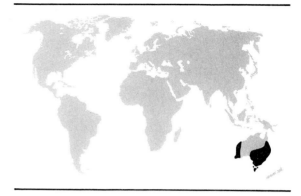

NATURAL DISTRIBUTION
Australia (except parts of the northern, central and southern regions), Tasmania and some islands in Bass Strait.

NATURALIZED DISTRIBUTION
Australasia: New Zealand.

AUSTRALASIA

New Zealand[1]

Writing about the Black Swan in 1922 Thomson said: 'This is one of the pronounced successes of naturalisation in New Zealand.'

Shortly before 1864 seven Black Swans were imported from Australia by the Nelson Acclimatization Society. In that year Sir George Grey[2] presented four to the Canterbury Acclimatization Society which, in the same year, acquired a further pair from a Mr Wilkin and in 1866 one from a Mr Mueller and four more from Grey.

According to R. C. Lamb, in *Early Christchurch* (1963), the council of that city imported 13 pairs in 1865. Twenty of these birds were released by the society and the Christchurch City Council on the Avon River, partly in an attempt, which was more or less successful, to clear the beds of Watercress (*Nasturtium officinale*), which had been introduced around 1850 and had flourished to such an extent that it was clogging up the river. Within a short time the population of swans had increased dramatically, and in 1867 many left the Avon and dispersed to Lake Ellesmere, Marlborough, Otago and the wilder country of the west coast. By 1880, up to 500 Black Swans were established on the rivers Avon, Halswell and Heathcote, and 15 years later several thousand had colonized the estuary of the Opawa River in Marlborough.

In 1866, the Otago Acclimatization Society released one bird, followed by 42 in 1867, 4 in 1868, 6 in 1869 and 8 in 1870, and in 1869 6 were freed by the Southland Acclimatization Society. These liberations proved as successful as that in Canterbury – the birds all quickly becoming established and, following a spectacular population explosion, spread to all parts of South Island from Stewart Island and the west coast sounds north to Cook Strait.

According to Buller (1872), Black Swans were first introduced into the North Island in 1864. The earliest introduction to that island traced by Thomson, however, was in 1867, when the Auckland Acclimatization Society released four; by about 1912 their progeny were said to be 'plentiful' on the Kaipara River and Kaipara Flats north of Auckland.

By 1906, Drummond claimed that Black Swans were 'now found in thousands on lakes, estuaries, and lagoons in many parts of the colony, from the extreme North to the far South. In some places, they wage a deadly war on the native ducks [the Grey Duck (*Anas superciliosa superciliosa*) – a view first propounded by Buller (1872)], taking their food supplies from them and persecuting them relentlessly'. Oliver (1930 and 1955), who concurs with Buller and Drummond, adds that Black Swans also harry the native *pukeko* or Purple Swamphen (*Porphyrio melanotus*).

Thomson reported that Black Swans were 'abundant' on the Chatham Islands before 1920, and by the following decade they were wide-spread, especially on coastal lakes and lagoons, on both main islands.

M. Williams (1979) attributes the phenomenal success of the Black Swan in New Zealand at least in part to the fact that it found an empty ecological niche left vacant by the extinction several hundred years previously of the native New Zealand swan, *Cygnus sumnerensis*.

The largest and most important breeding site for Black Swans in New Zealand is Lake Ellesmere[3] – an extensive coastal water south-west of Christchurch – from where many birds have dispersed to other areas of South Island and to some southern parts of North Island. From the early 1950s to the mid-1960s, between 40,000 and 80,000 (in 1959) Black Swans lived on Lake Ellesmere, and many birds had to be culled to reduce damage to crops. In 1959, the water level of the lake became abnormally high, and the swans were unable to reach the submerged vegetation on which they feed. As a result, many died of aspergillosis (caused by a microscopic fungus) and starvation, and, according to Cutten (1966), only 5,000 pairs nested in the 1963–4 season. In April 1968, a severe cyclonic storm (named the Wahine after an interisland ferry which it caused to sink) killed a further 5,000 Black Swans and destroyed many hectares of aquatic macrophytes (*Ruppia megacarpa* (*spiralis*) and *Potamogeton pectinatus*), which were the birds' staple food and provided the principal rearing grounds for cygnets.

The 1968–9 breeding season produced only some 50 per cent of the nests of previous years, and by January of the latter year the total population had fallen to 22,400. In 1969–70, there were only about 10 Black Swans' nests on Lake Ellesmere, but by 1970–1 (when the total adult population was around 6,200) the number of nests had recovered to around 2,500 – only some 2,000 of which, however, produced cygnets, of which barely 300 survived to the following January and February. In November 1972, some 3,100 nests were built, from which only about 4,500 cygnets (from a potential of around 12,000) survived to the end of the year – a mortality rate of around 60 per cent.

In January 1978 the population of Black Swans on Ellesmere was estimated to number about 9,500 (a fall of some 75 per cent from the average 1950s/60s figure) of which only a third were under 10 years old. M. Williams predicted that by 1981 the breeding component of the population would decline by some 50 per cent. The extensive breeding failure and poor survival of the cygnets and the increase in adult mortality and the permanent dispersal to other waters of many of the survivors, are attributed by Williams to the diminished food supply and lack of shelter for the cygnets – caused by the slow recovery rate of the aquatic macrophytes – coupled with excessive shooting and egg-collecting. Nevertheless, Druett (1983) claimed that the number of Black Swans on Lake Ellesmere was in excess of 70,000.

The population of Black Swans on Lake Ellesmere is a commercially important natural resource for New Zealand, providing both food and sport, and is managed more intensively than any other avian population in the country, many birds being shot annually and their eggs collected under licence. Elsewhere, Black Swans are resident on many of the larger lakes, lagoons and estuaries on both main islands, especially on Washdyke and Wainono lagoons, Canterbury; on Vernon Lagoon, Marlborough; on lakes Waihola, Wairarapa, Whangape and some lower Waikato waters; on Lake Alexandrina (where 23 were released by the South Canterbury Acclimatization Society as recently as 1959); at Farewell Spit; and on the central lagoon of the main island in the Chatham group. Although the number of breeding sites is relatively few, on some waters Black Swans are the most abundant species of waterfowl. Scott (1972) estimated the population at some 200,000 birds.

———————————————

Black Swans have been acclimatized and have bred successfully outside captivity in several European countries – in England[4] (where they were first imported from Australia in about 1791) at Carshalton in Surrey as early as 1851 and at Bicton in Devon in the following decade. Since 1902 they have nested intermittently on the Thames – mostly in the vicinity of London and under the nominal tutelage of the Worshipful Company of Vintners, who acquired them from Western Australia in exchange for Mute Swans (*Cygnus olor*) (q.v.). Black Swans presumably from this source have been recorded from all over the Home Counties – especially Hertfordshire, Essex, Surrey and Berkshire – and occasionally from even further afield, but have nowhere become properly established.

In the United States, Canada (eastern Quebec),[5] Hawaii and Japan[6] (in parks in Kyoto, Osaka and Tokyo) Black Swans have also nested in the wild but, as in Europe, have never become successfully naturalized.

In about 1938, some Black Swans were introduced to Tahiti[7] where they likewise failed to establish themselves.

NOTES
1 Cutten 1966; Falla, Sibson & Turbott 1979; Kinsky 1970; Long 1981; Oliver 1930, 1955; Scott 1972; Stidolph 1933; Thomson 1922; Williams 1969, 1979; Wodzicki 1965.
2 1812–98; Governor of New Zealand 1845–53 and 1861–7; Prime Minister, 1877–9.
3 M. Williams 1979.
4 Fitter 1959.
5 Blake 1975; Long 1981.
6 Kikkawa & Yamashina 1966; Long 1981.
7 Guild 1938; Long 1981.

Canada Goose
(*Branta canadensis*)

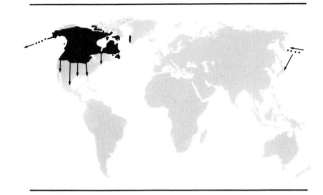

NATURAL DISTRIBUTION
A migratory Nearctic species (with some 11 subspecies), breeding in Alaska, Canada and northern USA. It is the world's most numerous goose.

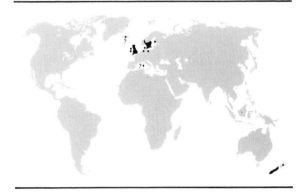

NATURALIZED DISTRIBUTION
Europe: British Isles, Sweden, Norway, Finland, Denmark, Germany, the Netherlands, Belgium, France, ?Iceland, ?Sardinia; Australasia: New Zealand.

EUROPE[1]

British Isles[2]

The earliest mention of Canada Geese in Britain, by the diarist John Evelyn on 9 February 1665, apparently refers to birds in the collection of Charles II in St James's Park in London. Francis Willughby and John Ray, in their *Ornithologia* (1676–8), say that they saw Canada Geese in the royal collection before 1672: 'the name shows the

place whence it comes. We saw and described this . . . among the King's wildfowl in St James's Park.'

The earliest record of an escaped Canada Goose in Britain appears to be one that was shot on the Thames at Brentford in Middlesex in 1731. In 1785, in *A General History of Birds*, John Latham wrote: 'In England they are thought a great ornament to the pieces of water in many gentlemen's seats, where they are very familiar and breed freely.'

In the nineteenth century, several private estates, mostly in England, are known to have contained Canada Geese among their collections of wildfowl; these include Walton Hall and Harewood House, Yorkshire; Windsor Park, Berkshire; Holkham Hall, Norfolk; Lilford Hall, Northamptonshire; Gosford House, East Lothian; the Dukeries of Nottinghamshire; and Bicton House, Devon. In 1844, a pair nested in the wild at Groby Pool, Leicestershire, and, in *A History of British Birds* (1843), William Yarrell refers to free-flying Canada Geese that were 'obtained in Cambridgeshire, Cornwall, Derbyshire, Devonshire, Hampshire, Oxfordshire and Yorkshire. . . . They have also been taken to Scotland'. In 1885, a pair nested in Edgbaston Park, Birmingham, and a second pair bred at Garendon Pond, Leicestershire, where Alexander Montague Browne, in *The Vertebrate Animals of Leicestershire* (1889), described them as 'an introduced species, often found at large, especially in winter, and roaming so far afield as to give rise to the doubt if it may not soon become feral'.

During this century several introductions of Canada Geese have been made in Britain; for example, at Leighton Park, Montgomeryshire (*c.* 1908), at Radipole Lake, Dorset (before 1932) and at West Wycombe Park, Buckinghamshire (in 1933–4). It was not, however, until 1938, after the birds had ceased to live predominantly on private and protected estates, that the Canada Goose was accorded British citizenship by their inclusion by Witherby et al. in *The Handbook of British Birds* (Vol. 3, 1939).

During the 1950s and 1960s, Canada Geese began increasingly to come into conflict with agricultural interests, as a result of which various methods of control were tried, including egg destruction, winter shooting, and translocations by the Wildfowl Trust and the Wildfowlers' Association of Great Britain and Ireland to many

new areas. This redistribution almost invariably resulted in the founding of new subpopulations, and the culled colonies soon resumed their former numbers. The policy of translocation was largely responsible for the general increase of the population and its distribution during the next two decades, and Canada Geese are now widely distributed throughout Britain, being especially numerous in northern, central, eastern and south-eastern England. In Ireland, they have been established for some years on private waters in counties Cork, Down (on Strangford Lough) and Fermanagh, from where since 1982 the National Association of Regional Game Councils has translocated small numbers to counties Tipperary, Carlow, Donegal, Westmeath, Limerick and Galway.

Between 1953 and 1969, the number of Canada Geese in Britain rose from between 2,200 and 4,000 to 10,500, of which the majority were in England; by 1976, the total had nearly doubled to 19,400 (an annual growth rate since the hard winter of 1962–3 of 8 per cent), and if the present rate of increase continues is expected to have risen to over 50,000 by 1990. Such increases cannot, as Owen, Atkinson-Willes & Salmon (1986) point out, go on indefinitely, but there seems little reason to suppose that shortage of suitable habitats will be a limiting factor. There remain large tracts of apparently ideal but so far uncolonized country, especially in Scotland, and new breeding habitats – in the form of gravel-pits (often with suitable island nesting sites) excavated during building and road-construction projects – are continually being created, particularly in the valleys of the Thames, Trent, Ouse and their tributaries. Even in areas where the geese have been long established, such as the West Midlands, the rate of increase is the same as in the rest of the country. Continued population growth, which will only be contained by rigorous control, would undoubtedly effect agricultural interests, although there are so far only a few areas where numbers are high enough to cause significant economic problems.

Canada Geese now occur, according to Owen et al., on well over 1,000 different sites in Britain, although flocks are usually small (70 per cent averaging 25 or less), and only five locations support colonies of as many as 500. Smaller subpopulations (19 in 1953, 32 in 1968 and 43 in 1976) are established on the periphery of major concentrations, particularly in the Thames Valley, the West Midlands and Yorkshire.

The principal reasons for the successful naturalization of the Canada Goose in Britain are the existence of a near-empty ecological niche for a large aquatic bird that breeds on waters in open woodland and parks (where its only competitor is the Mute Swan (*Cygnus olor*), q.v.), the continuing provision of new breeding habitats, and the species' successful abandonment of the instinct to migrate – although not all introduced birds are migratory in their natural range. Since 1947, however, a moult migration to the Beauly Firth in Inverness-shire, Scotland – similar to those that take place in North America – has evolved among non-breeding birds of central Yorkshire, involving a flight of some 500 km. This moulting flock increased from 50 or less in the 1950s to 300 in 1969 and, according to Owen et al., to around 1,000 by the early 1980s.

It has for long been known that Canada Geese from the eastern Arctic occur in the British Isles as rare but regular transatlantic winter vagrants. Most of these records are from Ireland (especially County Wexford) and Scotland (especially the Isle of Islay). These birds usually travel by way of Greenland, and normally arrive in the British Isles with flocks of White-fronted Geese (*Anser albifrons*) and Barnacle Geese (*Branta leucopsis*).

Sweden[3]

The first Canada Geese in Sweden were imported from North America via Holland by Bengt Berg, who succeeded in rearing a brood of goslings in captivity at Värnanäs in the Kalmar region in 1930. Others were imported to Hudiksvall and Eriksberg. Three years later Berg released some birds at Kalmarsund in Blekinge, where they first nested in the wild, and before long (with the help of translocations) they had colonized much of southern and central-southern Sweden, migrating in winter – presumably because of the severe weather in this northern latitude – to Denmark, East and West Germany, France, the Netherlands and Belgium. The Swedish population increased dramatically from 150 breeding pairs in 1960 to around 2,000 in 1970, with a total population of nearly 10,000 birds – about the same as in Britain at that time – making it the most abundant goose in Sweden. Although Canada Geese live sympatrically with Greylag Geese (*Anser anser*), there seems to be no competition for nesting sites and only a limited amount for food. The Canada Goose's success in Sweden is due to the existence of a vacant ecological niche and to a favourable ecosystem, because the climate and boreal forests of the Laurentian and Fennoscandian shields are very similar, and reflect the ability of the birds to colonize habitats that most wildfowl find unsuitable. The total Swedish population is estimated by Fabricius (1983a, b), as the result of a much faster growth rate than in Britain, at about 50,000, with 5,000 breeding pairs, distributed from northeastern Skåne to the River Torne.

Norway[4]

The first Canada Geese in Norway were imported from North America, and possibly also from Sweden, in 1936 by T. Røer, who released 11 at Nesodden, Oslo. No further liberations are recorded until 1958–60, when nine birds were freed in Orkdal, South Trøndelag: these were followed by 27 at Meraker in North Trøndelag (1963–6); 6 at inner Bjugn, off Ørlandet, Trondheimsfjorden, and 4 at Østensjøv, Oslo (1965–6); 25 at Steinkjer, North Trøndelag (1970); and 8 at Storelval, 10 at Bømlo, 8 at Frognerdam and 15 at Ekeberg in 1972 – a total of 112 birds.

As a result of these introductions, Canada Geese are now established around Trondheim and Oslo and in some intervening areas; Tangen (1974) suggests that if suitable habitats are colonized, and if the birds are not persecuted by man, a significant population should build up during the next 15 to 20 years.

Finland[5]

In the summer of 1964, eight Canada Geese goslings were imported from Sweden to Viksberg Manor, 50 km east of Helsinki. The birds flourished and formed three pairs, one of which was transferred to near Pori on the west coast, where it apparently disappeared. The other two pairs first nested on Lake Viksberg in 1966, and between that year and 1970 laid 49 eggs from which 29 goslings hatched successfully. The first juveniles migrated southwards in the autumn of

1967, and in most succeeding springs some have returned to the Porvoo district east of Helsinki, where the birds appear to be becoming established.

Denmark; Germany; the Netherlands; Belgium[6]

As mentioned above, Canada Geese from Sweden (and more recently from Norway and Finland) regularly winter in Belgium, East and West Germany, the Netherlands, and especially in Denmark, where increasing numbers shelter for lengthy periods both inland and along the North Sea coast. In the mid-1930s, unsuccessful attempts were made to establish Canada Geese as free-flying residents in Denmark, but the species remains in that country only as a winter visitor or as a semi-captive park bird. It has also been recorded on the Danish Faeroe Islands.

France[7]

The Canada Goose has been known in domestication in France for over 300 years. Georges Louis Leclerc, Comte de Buffon, in his *Histoire Naturelle, Générale et Particulière* (1749–1804), says that it was breeding in considerable numbers in the park at Versailles during the reign (1643–1715) of Louis XIV. Today it remains only in semi-captivity or as an occasional vagrant from Scandinavia.

AUSTRALASIA

New Zealand[8]

In 1876 and 1879, the Wellington Acclimatization Society imported and released 3 and 15 Canada Geese, respectively; according to Thomson (1922) some were surprisingly reported to have been killed by New Zealand Shelduck or Paradise Duck (*Tadorna variegata*), and before long all had apparently disappeared.

In 1905, the New Zealand Government imported 'a considerable number' of Canada Geese (believed to have been about 50 of the *maxima* form – see notes 1 and 8) from the eastern

United States as potential game birds, which they distributed among several of the acclimatization societies: 11 were sent to Southland, 10 to Otago, 'an unspecified number' (possibly 8) to Canterbury and 6 to Wellington.

The Southland Society turned their birds out on Lake Manapouri, and added a further three in 1909; others were released on Lake Te Anau, where in 1918 they were reported to be thriving. Two of the Otago Society's birds were lost in the first few years, but some of the survivors were sent to a poultry farm at Milton, where several goslings were reared successfully. In 1912, a number were liberated 'on Mr Telford's lagoon at Waiwera', and 3 years later a dozen were turned out at the head of Lake Hawea, where they apparently flourished. Six of the Canterbury Society's birds were released on a lagoon at Glenmark near Waikari in 1907–8, and a pair was kept in the gardens of Hagley Park, Christchurch, from where in succeeding years their progeny were successfully turned out on Lake Sumner and at Mount White (1912), and in the Cold Lakes region of Otago.

Although by 1915 Canada Geese were reported to be 'doing well in several parts of the dominion', in 1920 the Canterbury Society imported a further 10 birds (probably *taverneri* – see notes 1 and 8) from Dr A. R. Baker, Chairman of the Game Conservation Board in Vancouver. Ten years later Canada Geese had apparently disappeared from North Island, but were well established in several places in Otago and Canterbury in South Island, where in 1925 a limited shooting season was declared; 6 years later all protection was removed, and shooting became legal throughout the year.

In 1950, some Atlantic Canada Geese were released in north Canterbury, where the population of *maxima* and *taverneri* (and possibly *moffitti*) was already common and the birds in this (and doubtless other) areas are probably hybrids of these races – see notes 1 and 8.

Canada Geese in New Zealand today are most abundant in Canterbury and northern Otago, where they breed mainly in the grass-covered montane valleys and around high-altitude lakes. Whereas in Otago the birds tend to remain in the vicinity of their breeding grounds in winter, in Canterbury they disperse to lowland waters (especially the coastal Lake Ellesmere) between February and May; most return to the high country in early September to breed, but some 10 to 15 pairs usually remain behind to nest on Ellesmere and between 150 and 200 pairs on nearby Lake Forsyth. Non-breeding Canterbury birds leave the high country in December to moult on Ellesmere (cf. the Yorkshire to Inverness-shire moult-migration in Britain). Small numbers breed in other parts of South Island east of the divide, and a few in North Island, but wanderers have occurred in most areas. In recent years some birds have been turned out in the Wairoa district near Hawke's Bay in North Island. The successful naturalization of Canada Geese in New Zealand can be largely attributed (as in the British Isles) to their partial abandonment of the instinct to migrate.

In New Zealand, Canada Geese became a problem because they feed almost exclusively on privately owned farmland, which domestic stock are then reluctant to graze. As a result of complaints from pastoralists legal protection was removed in 1931, and large numbers were killed (e.g. 3,000 in 1950–1 and 1,700 in the north Canterbury district in 1951–2 by the New Zealand Wildlife Service). Despite this severe culling, the birds managed to increase their numbers, and complaints continued to be made until at least 1963. The present population may be in the region of about 20,000.

Canada Geese were imported as potential game birds to the south-west of Western Australia[9] between 1912 and 1920 and again at a later date, but although they were subsequently reported to be breeding freely they never became properly established.

Canada Geese were unsuccessfully introduced to the Hawaiian Islands,[10] allegedly to control insect pests.

According to the American Ornithologists' Union (1983), Canada Geese have been introduced to, and are established in, Iceland and the island of Sardinia.

In North America,[11] at least four races of Canada Geese (*canadensis, interior, maxima* and *moffitti* – see note 1) have been translocated to new areas. Of these the most successful was the reintroduction between 1951 and 1957 of 70 captive-bred birds of the *maxima* form (which at the time was

believed to be extinct in the wild) to Marsh Point, Manitoba. The birds were kept in captivity until they had nested – thus avoiding the attention of sportsmen and predators – and were initially fed even after release. Between 1957 and 1969–70, the population rose from 100 to some 10,000 birds.

One of the largest but most unsuccessful transplantation programmes (which resulted in the establishment of only one new migratory population) took place between 1953 and 1965 when no fewer than 20,734 Canada Geese were released in the southeastern United States. In October 1960 and February 1961, 27 and 34 birds, respectively, from Wisconsin were introduced to the Rockefeller Wildlife Refuge in southwestern Louisiana. One pair nested in 1961 and five pairs in 1962, and the project appears to have met with modest success.

In 1974, the Aleutian Islands subspecies (*B. c. leucopareia*) had become endangered, largely as a result of the introduction of Arctic Foxes (*Alopex lagopus*) for the fur trade (Lever 1985b). After the removal of foxes from three islands, a number of breeding birds were reintroduced, and by 1984 the population had increased to some 4,000 (Anon. 1984c). In October 1985, half-a-dozen captive-bred birds were released on one of the subspecies' former wintering waters, Lake Izunuma, in Japan.

The **Greylag Goose**[12] (*Anser anser*), which ranges over much of the Palaearctic region, is Britain's[13] only native breeding goose. Before the land reclamation and drainage schemes of the early nineteenth century it nested as far south as the fens of Cambridgeshire and Lincolnshire, but by the beginning of this century was confined largely to Wester Ross, Sutherland, Caithness (where it has been augmented by the release of captive-bred birds) and the Outer Hebrides. Since then it has been frequently reintroduced and, as Sharrock (1976) remarks, is now more widely distributed than ever before. In 1982, there were around 1,750 in the Outer Hebrides, and a similar number scattered across parks of the mainland in Ross & Cromarty and Sutherland.

In about 1930, Lord William Percy brought eggs and later goslings from South Uist to Lochinch near Stranraer in Wigtownshire, and between 1933 and 1942 Mr Gavin Maxwell released some young at Monreith in the same county from where, assisted by further plantings on Barfad and Logan House lochs in about 1960 and on Earlstoun Loch, Kirkcudbrightshire, in 1967, they have colonized much of Wigtownshire and Dumfriesshire.

In Ireland, a colony at Castlecoole in County Fermanagh is said to date from the early eighteenth century, while in England a substantial population in east Norfolk is largely descended from a pair of pricked birds brought down from Scotland before the Second World War.

Other reintroductions have been made by private individuals in Galloway and Perthshire in Scotland and in Essex and Huntingdonshire in England, and between 1961 and 1970 the Wildfowlers' Association turned down no fewer than 938 birds at 33 sites in 13 English and Welsh counties. In 1973, 39 Greylags of the eastern and southeastern European and Asian race *A. a. rubrirostris* were imported from Belgium (where, as in the Netherlands and Sweden[14] there is an expanding introduced population) to Kent in southeastern England.

Introduced Greylag populations are now widely scattered throughout Britain, with notable concentrations in County Down, Kent, Norfolk, Cumberland, Westmorland and, especially, in southwestern Scotland. Full-winged Greylags are kept in a number of waterfowl collections from which they disperse to breed, returning to their home waters in winter. There are currently believed to be some 3,000 introduced birds in Britain and Northern Ireland.

In the Falkland Islands, feral **Domestic Geese** (whose ancestors are wild Greylags) are established and breeding on West Point, Carcass, and Weddell Islands; there are a few also at Dunbar, Roy Cove, Hill Cove, and Chartres settlements on West Falkland.

The birds on West Point are descended from a pair of 'Sebastopol' (curly-feathered) east European geese, imported from Montevideo, Uruguay, by Mrs Gladys Napier in 1944. Some five or so goslings were hatched in October of that year, and within a short time the population had increased to between 50 and 60 – a figure that remained constant until around 1955. After that date, numbers gradually increased to some 150–200 by early 1982. In October of the

following year, R. W. Woods found the birds living in loose flocks along most of the lower eastern side of West Point, where he counted 132. Four varieties of plumage have been developed, probably as a result of cross-breeding with 'normal' Domestic Geese and/or reversion: about half the birds are smooth-feathered brown and white; rather less than half are smooth and all white; and a small number are partly 'Sebastopol' curly-feathered white or brown and white. All the smooth-feathered birds are strong on the wing, and are much more wary and unapproachable than the endemic Upland or Magellan Goose (*Chloëphaga picta leucoptera*).

In about 1950 or 1960 a few Domestic Geese arrived on Carcass Island – probably from West Point some 9.6 km to the south-west – where Woods counted at least 25 in October 1983. The birds at the settlement were less wary than those on West Point, whereas others a few kilometres north-west of the settlement were relatively shy. The geese at Dunbar, Roy Cove, Hill Cove and Chartres probably originate from the population on West Point either through natural colonization or by deliberate introduction.[15] In 1984 and 1985, respectively, feral Domestic Geese were sighted on the shore of Berkeley Sound and behind Gipsy Cove on East Falkland.[16]

The **Greenland White-fronted Goose** (*Anser albifrons flavirostris*) breeds in western and southwestern Greenland, and winters in Ireland, western Scotland, Wales (in small numbers), and occasionally in England and eastern North America.

In 1985, six goslings, the offspring of a pair imported with five others from Scotland by Mr Jack Whitmore, were hatched at Gorey, County Wexford, in the Republic of Ireland. Once a sufficient nucleus has been built up, they will be released into the wild. It will be interesting to see whether these birds will abandon their natural instinct to migrate.

Since 1981, attempts have been made to reintroduce the **Lesser White-fronted Goose** (*Anser erythropus*) to the mountains of southern Swedish Lapland. The species used to breed from Norwegian Lapland at least as far eastwards as the Kolyma River in the Soviet Union, but is now very rare in Sweden and in recent years has declined throughout Fennoscandia.[17]

The **Swan-Goose** (*Anser cygnoides*) of eastern Asia is the ancestor of the domesticated 'Chinese' Goose, which frequently breeds successfully in the wild in Britain, though no viable populations have ever been established.

The **Cereopsis** or **Cape Barren Goose** (*Cereopsis novaehollandiae*) is confined to islands off the south coast of Western and South Australia. Thomson (1922) records that prior to 1869 two were released by the Auckland Acclimatization Society of New Zealand at Riverhead, and that in 1871 a further two were acquired by the Canterbury Society. A pair received by the Otago Society in 1912 was despatched to the government poultry farm at Milton, from where 4 of their offspring were freed at the head of Lake Hawera in 1915, and others were sent to the society's hatchery at Clinton. According to G. R. Williams (1968), five young were reared at Lake Hawera in 1916, and more in the following year, when a pair bred at Clinton was released at Minarets Station on Lake Wanaka. Although Thomson (1922: 106) reported that 'they appear to be doing well', Williams quotes the Otago Society's annual report for 1923 as saying that only a small number survived on Hawera and Wanaka, where 27 were counted in 1927. Two were seen on Lake Thomson in 1934, a few on lakes Hawera and Thomson in 1936, and two on Lake Maree and two on Lake Hankinson in 1947. Despite Wodzicki's claim (1965: 432) that the species was 'local, South Island', it seems improbable that Cereopsis Geese were then, or currently are, established in New Zealand. Those birds seen there since the late 1940s are likely to have been storm-borne waifs from across the Tasman Sea.

Cereopsis Geese occasionally reach King Island in Bass Strait as natural vagrants from southern Australia. According to McGarvie & Templeton (1974), 38 goslings were translocated to the island in December 1972, where they subsequently became established.

NOTES

1 The Atlantic Canada Goose (*B. c. canadensis*) of eastern Canada is the principal race believed to have been introduced to the British Isles and mainland Europe: a few, however, may have been the Central or Todd's Canada Goose (*B. c. interior*) of central and eastern Canada and/or the Giant Canada Goose (*B. c. maxima*) of the Great Plains region of the central United States. Palmer (1976), on the other hand, suggests that those in the British Isles are Great Basin or Moffitt's Canada Geese (*B. c. moffitti*) of southwestern Canada and the northwestern United States, and in Norway and Sweden are either *moffitti* or *interior*.

2 Atkinson-Willes 1963; Blurton-Jones 1956; Dennis 1964; Fitter 1959; Lever 1977; Merne 1970; Ogilvie 1969, 1977; Owen 1983; Scott & Boyd 1957; Sharrock 1976; Witherby et al. Vol. 3, 1939.

3 See note 1 and Fabricius 1970, 1983a,b; Long 1981; Tangen 1974.

4 See note 1 and Long 1981; Lund 1963; Tangen 1974.

5 Korhonen 1972; Long 1981.

6 Long 1981; Peterson, Mountford & Hollom 1963.

7 Delacour 1954; Lever 1977.

8 Delacour 1954; Falla, Sibson & Turbott 1979; Imber 1971; Imber & Williams 1968; Kinsky 1970; Long 1981; Oliver 1930, 1955; Palmer 1976; Thomson 1922; Williams 1969; Wodzicki 1965; Yocum 1970. The birds in New Zealand are thought to be Taverner's (*B. c. taverneri*) of northern Canada, or Atlantic, Great Basin or Giant Canada Geese, or hybrids (see Falla et al., Imber, Palmer, Yocum, and note 1).

9 Long 1972, 1981.

10 Scheffer 1967.

11 Chalbreck, Dupuie & Belsom 1975; Hankla, 1968.

12 A possible derivation of the name is the 'grey' goose that 'lagged' behind after other species had migrated north in spring.

13 Ellwood 1971; Fitter 1959; Lever 1977; Owen 1983; Sharrock 1976; Young 1972a,b.

14 Cramp & Simmons 1977.

15 R. S. Whitley (personal communication, 1985); and R. W. Woods (personal communication, 1985, and per R. B. Napier, personal communication, 1983).

16 Falkland Islands Trust, *Trust News* No. 1 (per R. S. R. Fitter, 1986).

17 Von Essen 1982.

Egyptian Goose
(Alopochen aegyptiacus)

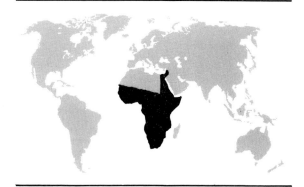

NATURAL DISTRIBUTION
Africa south of the Sahara; also the Nile Valley in Egypt and southern Palestine, where it is now scarce.

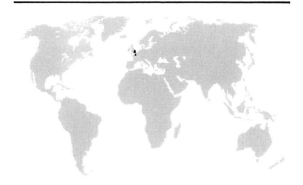

NATURALIZED DISTRIBUTION
Europe: British Isles, the Netherlands.

39

EUROPE

British Isles[1]

In their *Ornithologia* (1676–8), Francis Willughby and John Ray describe correctly 'The Gambo-Goose or Spur Wing'd Goose' (*Plectropterus gambensis*), which they saw in Charles II's collection of waterfowl in St James's Park, London. Their illustration, however, clearly shows an Egyptian Goose, and the inference must be that the latter species was known in England as early as the late seventeenth century.

In his *A General History of Birds* (1785), John Latham described the Egyptian Goose as 'common at the Cape of Good Hope, from whence numbers have been brought to England: and are now not uncommon in gentlemen's ponds in many parts of this Kingdom'.

In January 1795, an Egyptian Goose was shot at Thatcham in Berkshire, and in 1803 or 1804, a further six were killed near Buscot in the same county. In 1823, a noted wildfowler, Colonel Peter Walker, 'killed 2 [Egyptian Geese] in Norfolk and 3 at Longparish in Hampshire, and the next year again during some tremendous gales from the west, a flock of about 80 appeared near the same place'. Other references to Egyptian Geese during the first half of the nineteenth century include birds on the 'Fern' (Farne) Islands, Northumberland in 1830 (until 1880 small numbers regularly wintered on the nearby Fenham Flats, where they were known as 'Spanish geese'); Campsie, north of Glasgow (1832); Dorset (1836); the Isle of Man (1838); the River Tweed (1839); the River Severn, near Bridgwater in Somerset (1840); Leicester (1843); Romney Marsh in Kent (1846); Oxfordshire (1847); Sussex and Ormsby Broad, Norfolk (1848); Derwent Water, Cumberland (1849); and occasionally small parties in Ireland.

By the mid-nineteenth century, a considerable number of private estates, mostly in southern and eastern England, held flocks of full-winged Egyptian Geese: the largest were those at Blickling Hall, Gunton Park, Holkham Hall and Kimberley Park in Norfolk; at Bicton and Crediton, Devon; at Woburn Abbey, Bedfordshire; and at Gosford House, East Lothian, in Scotland. From these and other estates Egyptian Geese frequently strayed to different parts of the country, which led M. A. Mathew and W. S. M.

D'Urban to write in their *Birds of Devon* (1895) that 'the Egyptian Goose . . ., being so frequently kept on ponds in a semi-domesticated state, breeding freely and wandering at will over the country, [is] on the same footing as the Mute Swan and Pheasant'.

In this century Egyptian Geese have been recorded on the Thames near London, in the Royal Botanic Gardens at Kew, and in some dozen or so English counties. In spite of the species' known ability to disperse widely, it is only between Holkham and Beeston in north-western Norfolk, and to a lesser extent in the Bure Valley and the Broadland area of north-eastern Norfolk, that free-flying colonies are well established, and even there some artificial redistribution by man has taken place. In recent years, Egyptian Geese have increasingly been recorded in the Breckland region of Suffolk; these birds could be either natural immigrants from Norfolk or escapes from local wildfowl collections.

The failure of the Egyptian Goose to spread and multiply in Britain to the same extent as the Canada Goose (*Branta canadensis*) (q.v.), the Mandarin Duck (*Aix galericulata*) (q.v.) and the Ruddy Duck (*Oxyura jamaicensis*) (q.v.), suggests that ecological conditions for it are verging on marginal. What its limiting factors are have yet to be determined, but it may be significant that warmer and drier conditions prevail in its African homeland. Many goslings, which normally hatch in early spring when the weather is often cold and wet, fall prey to Carrion Crows (*Corvus corone*). Atkinson-Willes (1963) estimated the population at between 300 and 400 birds, and a census in Norfolk in 1984 revealed a total of around 450.

Although in parts of Africa Egyptian Geese are reported to have caused considerable agricultural damage, in England the population is as yet too small and too scattered for any such depredations to have occurred. Egyptian Geese can, however, be extremely aggressive to other species.

The Netherlands[2]

The free-flying population of Egyptian Geese[3] in the Netherlands dates from about 1967, when half-a-dozen birds escaped from a park at Rijswijk south-east of Den Haag in Zuid Holland. At around the same time, a pair escaped from Wassenaar Zoo north-west of Den Haag, and it seems probable that these eight birds were the origin of the population that became established in the surrounding countryside between Den Haag and Leiden, where 1 pair bred in 1971, 4 pairs in 1973, 6 pairs in 1974 and 16 pairs in 1975. In Meijendel, breeding started in about 1969, and in 1973 five pairs of goslings were recorded. It seems likely that other birds may subsequently have escaped elsewhere in Zuid Holland, where in the mid-1970s the population around Den Haag and Wassenaar increased, and by 1977 Egyptian Geese had been recorded from as far south as Rotterdam, and westwards to near Gouda and Woerden.

Egyptian Geese in Gelderland (where they first occurred on the River Ijssel north-east of Arnhem), Noord Holland (south of Amsterdam, on the coast south of the Noordzeekanaal, and on Amstelmeer), and Friesland (around Leeuwarden), are almost certainly also descended from escaped park birds. Breeding in these areas outside Zuid Holland began only in 1977.

In the Netherlands, where eggs are usually laid between February and June, Egyptian Geese are often double-brooded, and it is recorded that a pair near Wassenaar once successfully reared 19 goslings in one season. In 1977, there were estimated to be between 30 and 50 free-flying pairs in the Netherlands, and during the winter months mixed adult and juvenile flocks numbering up to 200 were not exceptional. Whether Egyptian Geese in the Netherlands compete for nesting sites, food or other requirements with native species, has not so far been recorded.

Despite assertions to the contrary, there are currently no established free-flying populations of Egyptian Geese in France.

Until at least 1928 the species was a favourite of aviculturists in the United States[4] where, although it frequently escaped, it never became established in the wild. King (1968), however, says that it was successfully introduced into Florida, where it has since apparently died out.

Egyptian Geese introduced at an unknown date on Rottnest Island off the coast of Western Australia[5] had disappeared before 1956.

In 1860, Sir George Grey imported 8 or 10 birds from Cape Province, South Africa, to Kawau Island, New Zealand[6] where they bred freely; many flew to the nearby mainland and dispersed from the Kaipara to Hawke's Bay, but all were subsequently killed. In 1869, the Auckland Acclimatization Society added some Egyptian Geese to its collection, but so far as is known none were ever released and the species never became naturalized in New Zealand.

The **Black-bellied Tree Duck** (*Dendrocygna autumnalis*) is a native of extreme southern Texas and Mexico, south through Central America and Panama to South America east of the Andes as far south as northern Argentina.

In about 1968, some escaped from Crandon Park Zoo in Miami, Florida, and in the following year and in 1972 12 and 4 ducklings, respectively, were reported on neighbouring Virginia Key. The species has been introduced unsuccessfully from Panama to Kingston, Jamaica and in 1931 from Central America to the Zapata Swamp and Pinar del Rio Province in Cuba.[7] Between January 1967 and September 1975, 243 young birds of the southern form *D. a. discolor* were released by the Pointe-à-Pierre Wildfowl Trust on Trinidad and 11 at Speyside on Tobago, where overshooting had severely reduced the population.[8]

The **West Indian Tree Duck** (*Dendrocygna arborea*), a native of the Bahamas, the Greater Antilles and the northern Lesser Antilles, also escaped from Crandon Park Zoo in the late 1960s, and was continually seen on and around Virginia Key until at least the late 1970s.

Tree or whistling ducks nest in holes in trees that are in short supply in suburban and rural areas of southern Florida; were they ever to become established in large numbers they could well come into conflict with indigenous hole-nesting species.

The wild **Muscovy Duck** (*Cairina moschata*), which occurs naturally from Mexico southwards to Colombia, Ecuador, Peru and northern Argentina, is the ancestor of the domestic variety that frequently becomes feral in many parts of the world.

Wild Muscovy Ducks (4 from Paraguay and 97 from Venezuela) were at one time released in various parts of Florida, USA,[9] where most, if not all, are believed to have succumbed to

Raccoons (*Procyon lotor*). Others (either wild or escaped feral birds) occur in San Patricio and Live Oak counties of Texas, and possibly in other Gulf Coast areas.

Thomson (1922) records that in 1865 a Captain Norman turned out six (presumably domestic) Muscovy Ducks on Adam's Island in the Auckland group, New Zealand,[10] where they failed to become established.

In parts of their natural range, feral Muscovy Ducks have probably bred with wild stock: they also interbreed freely with other wildfowl, especially Mallards (*Anas platyrhynchos*), the progeny being invariably infertile.

NOTES

1 Atkinson-Willes 1963; Fitter 1959; Lever 1977a; Owen 1983; Owen, Atkinson-Willes & Salmon 1986; Scott & Boyd 1957; Sharrock 1972.
2 Cramp & Simmons 1977; Eikhoudt 1973; Lichtenbelt 1972; Ringleben 1975; Teixeira 1979; and M. A. Ogilvie, personal communication, 1985.
3 The species is known in Dutch as *nijlgans* (= Nile Goose).
4 Long 1981; Phillips 1928.
5 King 1968; Long 1972, 1981.
6 Long 1981; Thomson 1922.
7 Bond 1979; Delacour 1954; Long 1981.
8 Ffrench 1976; Long 1981.
9 Bolen 1971; Long 1981; Palmer 1976.
10 Long 1981; Thomson 1922.

Mallard
(Anas platyrhynchos)

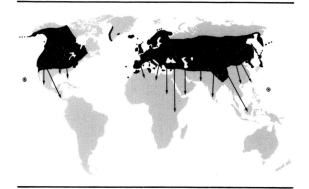

NATURAL DISTRIBUTION

A Holarctic species, breeding in: Eurasia from the Arctic Circle south to the Mediterranean, Iran, Tibet, central China, Korea and northern Japan; Iceland; southern Greenland; the Azores; and much of North America except parts of the extreme north. Winters from the southern half of its breeding range to North Africa, the Nile Valley, India, Burma, Turkistan, and southern China and Japan, and from southern Mexico and Florida to Panama.

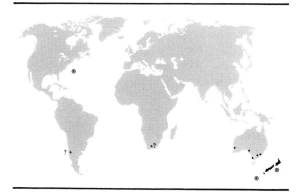

NATURALIZED DISTRIBUTION

Africa: ?South Africa; North America: Bermuda; South America: ?Chile; Australasia: Australia, New Zealand.

AFRICA

South Africa[1]

According to Siegfried (1970), 'No definite information exists concerning the status of the Mallard in Southern Africa. It is known, however, that an increasing number of waterfowl fanciers are keeping exotic waterfowl on open waters and that at present live Mallards are being freely offered for sale by dealers. It may well be that the species has already succeeded in obtaining a foothold in the wild.' This belief seems to be confirmed by Vincent who writes: 'This is a species which is starting to be of some concern in a few isolated localities. It has for long been kept as a decorative duck by many people, but where it has escaped, it has cross-bred with the indigenous African Yellowbill (*Anas undulata*), which is very widespread in its distribution, and quite common. The offspring are fertile.'

NORTH AMERICA

Bermuda[2]

Free-flying Mallard in Bermuda are descended from domestic breeding stock imported by a farm supply store in the 1950s or 1960s from Ronson Farms, Ohio, USA. Locally bred captive birds escaped or were released and gradually colonized such waters as Spittal and Warwick Ponds, and considerable numbers are now breeding in the wild. Mallard from eastern North America have sometimes occurred as accidental visitors in Bermuda.

SOUTH AMERICA

Chile

Mallard have on several occasions been introduced to high-altitude lakes in the Chilean Andes, on some of which they are said to be established.

AUSTRALASIA

Australia[3]

The first Mallard in Australia were half-a-dozen released on Phillip Island, Victoria, in 1866; what became of them is unknown. In 1871 and 1872,

40 and 80 Mallard, respectively, were placed on a lake in the Melbourne Botanical Gardens, where they promptly hybridized with the Australian Black Duck (*Anas superciliosa rogersi*), before all but disappearing by the early 1900s. In 1950, however, they were still to be found on some lakes around Melbourne.

Before 1912, Mallard were reported to be breeding on and spreading from a number of ornamental waters around Perth in Western Australia, and 8 years later they were established in several parks in the Metropolitan area (e.g. John Forrest in the north, Hackett Gully and The Dell in the east, Forrestdale in the south and Coast in the west), where they remain but show little signs of spreading or increasing. They are, however, occasionally found in the wild in the south-west of the state.

Semi-domesticated Mallard now occur on waters in many city parks and gardens (especially in Sydney, New South Wales), and on some farm dams and swamps, particularly in southeastern Australia and Tasmania. In the wild they are found in small numbers in southeastern South Australia, in the Riverina region of New South Wales, and in the south-west of Western Australia. Mallard ringed in New Zealand are occasionally recovered in Australia.

Wild Mallard and native Black Duck hybridize freely, the dominant genes of the former ensuring that in successive generations the characteristics of the latter are obliterated. Free-flying Mallard in Australia have abandoned their migratory instinct, and hybrids may not survive the changeable Australian climate as well as does the indigenous species that disperses in times of drought. Hybridization also occurs when semi-domesticated birds carrying various percentages of Mallard blood are deliberately introduced to farm dams and swamps, where they are allowed to mate with the native species to produce more alluring call-birds, whose use, incidentally, is illegal. The adulteration of the blood of a native species by that of a genetically superior alien is always to be deplored.

New Zealand[4]

In 1867, the Otago Acclimatization Society acquired a pair of Mallard from their *confrères* in Melbourne, followed by five in 1869, four in

1870, three in 1876 and nine in 1881 – all from London: some were sent north to Kakanui and others south to Riverton, but apparently all soon disappeared. In 1896, a consignment of a further 21 birds arrived from London, of which 10 were forwarded to the Southland Society while the remainder were kept at Clinton for captive breeding. In the following year, more birds were imported from England and were placed for breeding in the hands of a Mr Telford of Clinton. So many Mallard were reared and released in the early 1900s – the Southland Society alone turned down nearly 1,350 between 1910 and 1918 – that by 1915 shooting on a limited scale was permitted.

In 1870, the Auckland Society imported a pair of Mallard followed by four more in 1886; these were kept in the Domain for breeding, but appear to have met with little success.

The Canterbury Society is known to have maintained a dozen Mallard in its gardens for breeding purposes in 1873, but, as in Auckland, apparently unsuccessfully. In 1897, Canterbury joined with a number of other societies in importing Mallard from London, but what became of them is unknown. According to the society's annual report for 1908–9, the first release took place at Glenmark in the former year.

In 1893, the Wellington Society imported 19 Mallard, which they kept for breeding at Masterton, where introduced Stoats (*Mustela erminea*) and Weasels (*M. nivalis*) almost exterminated the entire stock. Some of the survivors were sent to a reserve on a Mr Martin's run in the Wairarapa where they rapidly increased, and eggs from Masterton were distributed among some of the other societies. In 1904, the New Zealand Government imported and presented four pairs of Mallard to the Wellington Society, which between 1896 and 1916 reared and subsequently released several hundred birds at Manawatu, Rangitikei and in the Wairarapa. Thomson (1922) considered that by 1920 Mallard were established in the last district, but that without careful protection they were unlikely to increase.

In 1898, the Taranaki Society acquired some Mallard from one of the other societies, but within 4 years all had disappeared. Some time after 1906 a Mr McBean turned down a quantity on Lake Okareka, where before long a flock of around 200 was established.

Although Thomson was of the opinion that by 1920 Mallard were established in the southern part of South Island, within a decade most had apparently disappeared.

At Wellington in North Island interest in re-establishing the Mallard was revived in 1939, when the society was presented with 500 eggs from the United States, and for several years thereafter an average of 300 birds were released each year – mainly in the Manawatu and Rangitikei districts. Between 1931 and 1947–9, the annual take of Mallard by New Zealand sportsmen, as a result of further large-scale liberations (which, indeed, continue today), rose from 5 per cent of the total harvest to 52 per cent.

In 1917, some ducks were shot in South Canterbury that appeared to be Mallard × New Zealand Grey Duck (*Anas s. superciliosa*) hybrids. Mallard and Grey Ducks interbreed freely, as the former does with Black Ducks in Australia, and, as in Australia, Mallard appear to be biologically superior to the native species. With an average clutch of 10–12 eggs compared with 8–9 they have a greater breeding potential and need to rear fewer young (which have a lower mortality rate) to replace their lower adult population losses. Mallard are also less easy to decoy and, being more adaptable to different habitats, have suffered to a lesser extent than Grey Ducks – with whom they compete for food – from the reclamation of wetlands for agricultural purposes, and in some areas appear to be replacing the native species.

Although most, if not all, of the early importations of Mallard to New Zealand were made with European stock, between about 1920 and 1940 many North American birds – probably the sedentary Florida Duck (*Anas platyrhynchos fulvigula*) and/or the Mexican Duck (*A. p. diazi*) – were introduced. New Zealand Mallard are thus of mixed migratory/sedentary origin, and although the latter predominate the birds do, on occasion, disperse considerable distances.

By the mid-1960s, Mallard were widespread and common on both main islands and on Stewart Island, and occurred in small numbers on the Chatham Islands; they are also occasional vagrants on the Antipodes, Auckland and Campbell islands, and may now be breeding on Macquarie Island where they were first seen in 1949. In most closely settled districts and on all lowland farms Mallard are the dominant New

Zealand duck: only in the undeveloped back country, where no Mallard were ever released, is the native Grey Duck more abundant.

————————————

In the 1930s, an *emigré* Scottish shepherd, Mr John Hamilton, released some Mallard on East Falkland,[5] where a few remained until the 1960s but have apparently since died out.

In January 1959, four pairs of Mallard were released on Kerguelen,[6] where within five years they had all disappeared. More were introduced at a later date, again apparently without success.

In 1938, Eastham Guild liberated some Mallard on Tahiti,[7] where, although they were said to be breeding shortly afterwards, they eventually died out.

————————————

The present stock of Mallard in the eastern United States[8] is derived principally from large-scale releases of captive-reared birds (around 50,000 a year over the past 30 years) augmented by a natural expansion of range eastwards during the past 50 years, and by the reversion to the wild of domestic stock and translocations of wild birds from within the species' natural range.

————————————

The endangered **Hawaiian Duck** or **Koala** (*Anas platyrhynchos wyvilliana*),[9] a subspecies of the Mallard, is resident mainly on the islands of Kauai and Oahu; it has been transplanted to Hawaii (and reinforced on Oahu) in an attempt to re-establish it in its former range. There is no evidence to support Roots's (1976) claim that the nominate form has ever been introduced to Hawaii.

————————————

In about 1850, **Meller's Duck** (*Anas melleri*),[10] a native of eastern Madagascar, was probably introduced to Mauritius, where the present population of about 50 birds – which is strictly protected – is confined to Pinton du Milieu and Valetta Lakes. Meller's Duck may also have been introduced, unsuccessfully, to the neighbouring island of Réunion.

————————————

The **Kerguelen** or **Eaton's Pintail** (*Anas acuta eatoni*),[11] a subspecies of the common or

Northern Pintail, was in 1955 successfully introduced from Îles Kerguelen to Île Amsterdam in the southern Indian Ocean, from where by 1970 it had spread naturally 80 km south to Île St Paul.

————————————

The **Gadwall** (*Anas strepera*) breeds from Iceland through central Europe and Asia to Kamchatka, and in North America from British Columbia and the Prairie Provinces of Canada south to California and Colorado.

Gadwalls did not breed in the British Isles[12] until about 1850 when a pair of migrants, caught in a decoy at Dersingham in Norfolk, were wing-clipped and turned down by the Revd John Fountaine of Southacre, on Narford Lake in the Breckland district of southwestern Norfolk. From this pair a substantial population, probably reinforced by breeding migrants from Europe, had built up by 1875, and by 1897 Gadwalls had crossed into Suffolk where, a decade later, they were breeding in the valley of the River Lark and in marshland at the source of the River Waveney. Later expansion in East Anglia, however, was slow, and east Suffolk was not colonized until the 1930s and the Norfolk Broads, Ouse Washes and east Essex not before the 1950s. Today, eastern England remains the species' principal British stronghold, where it is probably augmented from time to time by continental migrants – attracted by the introduced birds – that stay on to breed.

In London, 61 full-winged Gadwalls flew away from St James's Park in the early 1930s, and birds presumably from this source bred on Barn Elms Reservoir in Surrey in 1935. Other English colonies derived from introductions occur in Greater London; west Kent (probably from birds released by the Wildfowlers' Association after 1965); the Isles of Scilly (where birds were released in the 1930s); Somerset (mainly on Chew Valley Reservoir, which holds 20–5 pairs), resulting from escapes from the Wildfowl Trust at Slimbridge in Gloucestershire; Cumberland; Westmorland; and north Lancashire, where more birds were released by the Wildfowlers' Association.

In Scotland, Gadwalls have nested on Loch Leven in Kinross-shire (still their main breeding site with 25–30 pairs) since 1909, from where they have spread into Perthshire and Fife. Breeding was first confirmed in Ireland in 1933, since when the species has nested in half-a-dozen counties, but only regularly (1–3 pairs) in Wexford. The Scottish and Irish populations probably result from a natural extension of range from the birds' main breeding grounds in eastern Europe, southern Scandinavia and Iceland; it may be significant that the recent increase in the Scottish and Irish colonies has coincided with a marked expansion of the species in Iceland, from where large numbers migrate south to winter in Ireland and doubtless also in western Scotland, where a small breeding colony is established on North Uist in the Outer Hebrides. Owen, Atkinson-Willes & Salmon (1986) estimate the British breeding population to be at least 500 pairs.

Gadwalls breeding in parts of western Europe such as the Netherlands may have been introduced or result from a natural extension of range westward, or a combination of both.

In North America,[13] the Gadwall has recently expanded its range naturally both northwards from Canada and south from the United States, where it has also been successfully transplanted (to Massachusetts and possibly to Florida) outside its natural range.

The **Red-crested Pochard** (*Netta ruffina*) breeds in Eurasia from southern France through the lower Danube and southern USSR eastwards across the Kirghiz Steppes to western Siberia; it winters in the Mediterranean region, Asia Minor, India and Burma.

Red-crested Pochards are normally only autumn and winter vagrants in Britain,[14] where they have for long been reared by aviculturists. A pair that bred on the coast of northeastern Lincolnshire in 1937 may have wandered from the Duke of Bedford's collection at Woburn Abbey in Bedfordshire or have been migrants from Europe, where the species was then spreading northwestwards and was already breeding regularly in northern Germany and possibly the Netherlands. In 1958, a pair nested at St Osyth in Essex, and since the mid-1960s birds – probably escapes from the Wildfowl Trust at Slimbridge in Gloucestershire – have bred almost annually at Frampton-on-Severn in the same county where, however, production of young is very low. In 1971, the offspring of a pair that nested at Apethorpe in Northampton-

shire later dispersed, and probable breeding was reported in the same year at Rickmansworth in Hertfordshire. A pair that nested in 1972 in the Royal Botanic Gardens, Kew, Surrey, was probably descended from birds allowed to fly free from several Inner London parks. In 1975, two pairs (only one of which reared young successfully) nested at the Cotswold Water Park on the Gloucestershire/Wiltshire border, where although one or more pairs have bred almost annually ever since, success is clearly low, as numbers in winter hardly change. There have also been occasional breeding records from gravel-pits near Bourton-on-the Water, Gloucestershire.[15]

In the 1950s, the Red-crested Pochard was a regular autumn and winter migrant to south-eastern England, but since 1962 has reverted to its earlier vagrant status. Red-crested Pochards breeding spasmodically in Britain today are thus much more likely to have escaped or been released from waterfowl collections than to be natural immigrants from continental Europe.

NOTES

1 Liversidge n.d.; Long 1981; Siegfried 1962, 1970; and P. A. Clancey and J. Vincent, personal communications, 1981.
2 Witherby et al, Vo. 3, 1939; D. B. Wingate 1973 (and personal communication, 1981).
3 Balmford 1978; Blakers, Davies & Reilly 1984; Frith 1973; Hardy 1928; Long 1972, 1981; Pizzey 1980; Ryan 1906; Serventy & Whittell 1967; Tarr 1950.
4 Balham 1952; Balham & Miers 1959; Falla, Sibson & Turbott 1979; Gwynn 1953; Kinsky 1970; Long 1981; Oliver 1930, 1955; Sage 1958; Thomson 1922; Watson 1975; Williams 1969; Wodzicki 1965.
5 Cawkell & Hamilton 1961; Long 1981; Wood 1975.
6 Long 1981; Prévost & Mougin 1970.
7 Guild 1938; Long 1981.
8 Boyer 1966 & Foley et al. 1961 (both in Palmer 1976); Bump 1941; Delacour 1954; Long 1981.
9 Hawaiian Audubon Society 1975; Long 1981; Peterson 1961; Swedberg 1969.
10 Benedict 1957; Delacour 1954; Long 1981; Meinertzhagen 1912; Peters 1931; Scott 1965; Staub 1976. (But see also: Carié 1916 and Rountree, Guérin et al. 1952.)
11 Delacour 1954; Scott 1965; Segonzac 1972; Watson 1975; Weller 1980.
12 Delacour 1954; Fitter 1959; Lever 1977a; Sharrock 1976; Thomson 1964.
13 Palmer 1976.
14 Fitter 1959; Lever 1977a; Pyman 1959; Sharrock 1976.
15 M. A. Ogilvie, personal communication, 1985.

Wood Duck
(*Aix sponsa*)

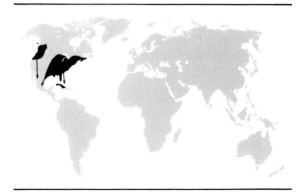

NATURAL DISTRIBUTION

North America, in two entirely separate populations: in the west from southwestern British Columbia south to the San Joaquin Valley in California, wintering in southern California; in the east from Nova Scotia and Lake Winnipeg south to southeastern Texas, Florida and Cuba, westwards to the Dakotas, eastern Nebraska, Kansas and Oklahoma, wintering in central Mexico, the northwestern Bahamas and occasionally Jamaica.

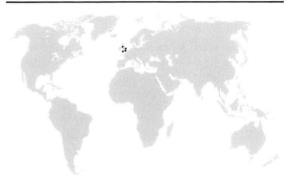

NATURALIZED DISTRIBUTION

Europe: British Isles.

EUROPE

British Isles[1]

Attempts to naturalize the Wood Duck (usually known to aviculturists as the Carolina Duck) in England date from the 1870s, when

M. A. Mathew and W. S. M. D'Urban in *The Birds of Devon* (1895) describe the 'Summer Duck' (another synonym for the Wood Duck) as 'breeding freely and wandering at will over the country'. Bicton House near Exeter possessed at the time one of the most comprehensive collections of wildfowl in England, and the full-winged Wood Ducks referred to by Mathew and D'Urban, which almost certainly came from that source, ranged as far afield as Plymouth and Slapton Ley – respectively, 65 and 50 km from Bicton.

Before the Second World War, free-flying colonies were maintained by the Duke of Bedford at Woburn Abbey in Bedfordshire, by Viscount Grey of Fallodon in Northumberland, and by Mr Alfred Ezra at Foxwarren Park in Surrey. Since the war, full-winged Wood Duck have been kept in several private collections, from which they have from time to time escaped, and in the late 1960s and early 1970s a number periodically reared young in various widely scattered localities: these include near Guildford in Surrey; on Virginia Water in Windsor Great Park on the Berkshire/Surrey border; on the River Frome near Rode in Somerset; on the River Duddon near Broughton in Cumberland; near East Dereham in Norfolk; at Cranbury Park near Winchester in Hampshire; and near Eccleshall in Staffordshire. In the late 1970s, an attempt was made to introduce Wood Duck to Grizedale Forest in north Lancashire.

Why the Wood Duck has failed to become more fully established in Britain remains something of a mystery, since it is a hardy species: it has a longer fledgling period than its close relation, the Mandarin, and Savage (1952) suggested that its ducklings would thus be vulnerable for a longer period to predators. Sharrock (1976) points out that most Wood Duck breeding records have occurred in Surrey and east Berkshire, where the birds may come into competition for food and nesting sites with the well-entrenched Mandarin (*Aix galericulata*): supplies of old decaying trees with suitable nesting holes have diminished in recent years due to 'improved' forestry methods, and shortage of nesting sites (together with an increasing population) have forced Mandarins considerably to expand their range in search of new breeding grounds.

Between 1867 and 1906, the Auckland, Canterbury, Wellington and Otago acclimatization societies introduced at least 10 Wood Duck to New Zealand,[2] of which only four were released – by the Wellington Society in 1899 – and these were said to have bred and to be thriving in Christchurch in 1908. Two years earlier some Wood Duck were turned down on Lake Okareka between Rotorua and the Tarawera Lakes, where they survived for a number of years but apparently did not breed.

Guild (1938) states that in about 1938 C. B. Nordhoff unsuccessfully introduced some Wood Duck to Tahiti.

According to Niethammer (1963), Wood Duck have also failed to become established after plantings in Germany.

In the late nineteenth and early twentieth centuries drainage schemes and widespread logging operations removed many lakeland habitats and trees with potential nesting holes for Wood Duck in North America[3] and this, coupled with overshooting, very nearly caused the species' extinction by the end of the First World War. Since then, the birds' willingness to make use of nesting boxes (of which large numbers have been provided) together with protective legislation and captive breeding programmes, have revitalized their flagging population, and the Wood Duck has been noticeably extending its range, especially in a northerly direction. Phillips (1928) traced some of the releases of captive-reared stock that are presumed to have contributed to this expansion. As early as 1884–5, some were introduced to the wild in New Jersey, and since 1913 others have been liberated in Connecticut, Indiana, Massachusetts, New York, North Dakota, Nova Scotia, Wisconsin, California, and elsewhere.

The **White-winged Wood Duck** (*Cairina scutulata*),[4] which is classified in King (1981) as 'vulnerable', formerly occurred in northern and eastern Assam, India and Bangladesh, south through Burma, western Thailand and western peninsular Malaysia to Sumatra and Java. It has seriously declined due to massive decreases in suitable habitats, isolation of local populations, increased disturbance, shooting and water pollution. In Thailand, where it has not been reported in the wild since before 1960, it is probably extinct. Now, however, an attempt is being made to reintroduce it to that country. Two pairs, bred by the Wildfowl Trust in England, have been sent to a captive-breeding centre in Thailand, from where their offspring will be released into the Huai Kha Khaeng Forest Sanctuary. In February 1986, the Wildfowl Trust sent a further eight to India, where their progeny will be freed in rainforest areas of Assam and Himachal Pradesh. There are currently believed to be less than 200 pairs of White-winged Wood Duck surviving in the wild in Southeast Asia.

NOTES

1 Fitter 1959; Lever 1957, 1977a; Savage 1952; Sharrock 1976; Wheatley 1970.
2 Thomson 1922.
3 Bump 1941; Long 1981; Palmer 1976; Phillips 1928.
4 Ali & Ripley 1968; Delacour 1959; King 1981. See also: M. J. S. Mackenzie & J. Kear, 'The White-winged Wood Duck' (unpublished report for the Wildfowl Trust, Slimbridge, England, 1976); *Birds* (*Magazine of the Royal Society for the Protection of Birds*) 10:3 (1984); *Wildfowl World* (*Magazine of the Wildfowl Trust*) 91:5, 22–3; 93:5 (1985) and *Oryx* 19:41 (1985).

Mandarin Duck
(*Aix galericulata*)[1]

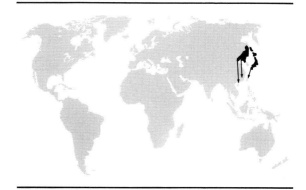

NATURAL DISTRIBUTION
Breeds in eastern Asia from the Uda (55° N), Amur and Ussuri rivers in China and the USSR south through Korea, eastern China and Japan to around 40° N on the mainland and 36° N on the Japanese island of Honshu. Winters in eastern Asia from about 38° N south to Kwangtung (Guangdong) and Taiwan (23° N), especially in Kiangsi (Jiangxi) north of Shanghai.

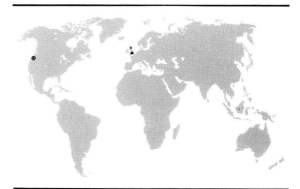

NATURALIZED DISTRIBUTION
Europe: British Isles; North America: USA.

EUROPE

The earliest mention of the Mandarin Duck in Europe appears in 1599 in the writings of the Italian naturalist Ulissi Aldrovandi, where he describes a bird called *Querquedula indica*,[2] which was portrayed in a painting brought to Rome by envoys from Japan. In his *History of Japan* (1727), the German traveller Engelbrecht Kaempfer, who was one of the earliest Europeans to visit that country, has this to say about the Mandarin:

Of ducks there are several different kinds, and as tame as the geese. One kind particularly I cannot forbear mentioning, because of the surprising beauty of its male, call'd 'Kinmodsui', which is so great, that being showed its picture in colours, I could hardly believe my own eyes.

British Isles[3]

The Mandarin Duck was first imported to England shortly before 1745, when a drawing of *La Sarcelle*[4] *de la Chine* in the gardens of Sir Matthew Decker, Bt[5] at Richmond Green in Surrey was made by George Edwards for his *History of Birds* (1743–64).

In 1830, two pairs of Mandarin were purchased for the not inconsiderable sum of £70 by the Zoological Society of London, in whose gardens they bred for the first time in England 4 years later. The first recorded specimen of a wild-living Mandarin in Britain was shot near the Thames at Cookham in Berkshire in May 1866.

Free-flying Mandarin Ducks in Britain today, however, are all descended from birds that have escaped or have been deliberately set free in this century.

In the early 1900s the Duke of Bedford introduced some Mandarin to his waterfowl collection at Woburn Abbey in Bedfordshire. By the outbreak of the First World War the population numbered over 300, but because of the difficulty of war-time feeding the total fell by half between 1914 and 1918, as it also did between 1939 and 1945.

In the years immediately preceding the First War, Sir Richard Graham, Bt introduced some Mandarin to his estate at Netherby in Cumberland on the Border Esk, where by about 1920 they had died out.

In 1918, Viscount Grey of Fallodon added some Mandarin to his extensive bird sanctuary and wildfowl collection in Northumberland; after initially doing well the population eventually became extinct when, after Lord Grey's death in 1933, the sanctuary and collection were abandoned.

Between 1910 and 1935, a free-flying colony of Mandarin was maintained by Lieutenant-Colonel E. G. B. Meade-Waldo at Stonewall Park near Edenbridge in Kent where, possibly

because of the unsuitability of the surrounding countryside, the birds failed to become established in the wild.

In 1928, M. Jean Delacour presented half-a-dozen pairs of Mandarin to Mr Alfred Ezra, who turned them out in the grounds of his home, Foxwarren Park near Cobham in Surrey. The birds bred successfully in the following year and soon spread outside the park, eventually dispersing south-west as far as Haslemere, northwards into south Buckinghamshire and south-western Middlesex, and east and west as far as Staines and Reading, respectively. In 1930, Ezra, with the help of J. Spedan Lewis and W. H. St Quintin, was involved in an unsuccessful attempt to establish full-winged Mandarin in the grounds of Buckingham and Hampton Court palaces and in Regent's and Greenwich parks in London.

The largest and most important free-flying colony of Mandarin in Britain today is centred on Virginia Water on the Berkshire/Surrey border; the birds are believed to be descended from some of Ezra's stock, perhaps supplemented by others that dispersed from the attempted plantings at Hampton Court and in inner London. By 1932 they were well established on Virginia Water and were spreading to other lakes and ponds in Windsor Great Park[6] and the adjacent forest. Their success at Windsor is due to an ideal habitat, an abundant supply of food throughout the year, a profusion of nesting sites, and, thanks to the park gamekeepers, relative freedom from predators. Since their establishment in Windsor Park, Mandarin have slowly but steadily extended their range, and by the mid-1970s occurred as far west as Swallowfield in Berkshire, east to Esher and Leatherhead in Surrey, north to Maidenhead and Wraysbury in Buckinghamshire, and south to the Surrey/Sussex border; this expansion of range continues today.

In 1935, Ronald and Noel Stevens added some Mandarin to their waterfowl collection at Walcot Hall, Shropshire, where by the outbreak of the Second World War the population numbered about 100. During the war the birds dispersed as far as north Wales and Lancashire, but after the conclusion of hostilities some returned to form a small but apparently stable colony.

Since the war, populations of free-flying Mandarin, all of which originate from escapes from nearby waterfowl collections, have been established at, among other places, Tillingbourne

Manor, Surrey; Leckford, Hampshire; Bassmead, Huntingdonshire; Eaton Hall, Cheshire; Apethorpe Lake and Milton Park in the Soke of Peterborough; Leeds Castle, Kent; Monken Hadley, Hertfordshire; Salhouse, Norfolk; Leonardslee, Sussex; the Zoological Gardens in Regent's Park, London; and on the River Tay near Perth in Scotland, where the 1984 post-breeding population numbered about 100. Isolated individuals or pairs have also been reported from the Isle of Wight in the south northwards to Loch Lomond between Dunbartonshire and Stirlingshire in Scotland.

The future of the Mandarin Duck in the Far East, following the deforestation for agricultural development after the Second World War of its two main breeding grounds, the Tung Ling and Kirin forests, must be in some doubt. In 1972, the British population was estimated to number over 250 pairs; by 1976 Sharrock judged that it had risen to between 300 and 400 pairs, and the current total may be as high as 1,000 pairs. The population in Britain may thus exceed that in the whole of the species' natural range in the Far East (outside Japan, where the total, based on counts from 1970 to 1984, is believed to be between 8,000 and 9,000), where it is probably declining. The Mandarin was admitted to the official British and Irish List in 1971.

NORTH AMERICA

USA[7]

Since about 1977, a free-flying population of Mandarin has been established on the ranches of Mr Richard A. Cuneo and Mr Lawton L. Shurtleff at Vineburg and Walnut Creek in Sonoma, in the wine-producing country of northern California to the north of San Francisco. Here the birds live in an area of rough, rolling hills, heavily wooded with various oaks, Madrone (*Arbutus menziesii* – an evergreen tree or shrub), alders (*Alnus* spp.), willows (*Salix* spp.), Bay Laurel and other species, some 50 km inland from the Pacific coast. The temperatures of this habitat, which covers some 50 km west to east and 80–160 km north to south, range between 0 °C and 37 °C, with an average of around 18 °C, and the November to April rainfall amounts to some 76 cm. This habitat and climate seem as

suitable for the Mandarin as they are for the native Wood Ducks (*Aix sponsa*), which have been released on the two properties since about 1972.

The two species share 30 or more nesting boxes on one large lake, and a further 30 on outlying ponds, although the Mandarin, which nest earlier, invariably select the optimum sites. At first, both species shared the same waters, which they now tend to occupy separately. Since the Mandarin are fed throughout the year on the main lake, and in the breeding season also on the smaller ponds, they cannot be regarded as living entirely naturally, as such artificial management alters their normal behaviour pattern, and creates an unnatural population density. In 1987, the total was estimated at about 550, and both Mr Cuneo and Mr Shurtleff consider it unlikely that the birds would flourish in the wild without supplementary feeding. Mandarin have been sighted up to 50 km away from their point of release, and nesting boxes have been erected in some of these localities in an attempt to persuade them to extend their present distribution. Their principal predators are Largemouth Bass (*Micropterus salmoides* – an imported game fish), Bobcats (*Felis rufus*), Raccoons (*Procyon lotor*), owls (Strigidae) and hawks (Accipitridae).

Full-winged Mandarin were established in the grounds of the zoo at Clères north of Rouen, France until 1940, but were subsequently destroyed by the occupying German forces. Despite several reports to the contrary there are believed to be no wild Mandarin in mainland Europe today.

In Australia,[8] a pair of Mandarin released on Macedon Reservoir, Victoria, in the 1860s apparently soon disappeared.

C. B. Nordhoff liberated a number of Mandarin on Tahiti[9] in about 1938, again apparently without success.

Between 1868 and 1907, considerable numbers of Mandarin were imported to New Zealand,[10] but there is no record of any having been released.

NOTES

1 In 1952, the Japanese ornithologist Dr Yoshimaro Yamashina proposed that, because of the number

of its chromosomes, the Mandarin Duck be placed by itself in a 'supergenus' *Dendronessa*, but most authors still place it in the genus *Aix*.

In Mandarin females only the left ovary is functional; if it becomes damaged in any way the rudimentary right ovary sometimes increases in size and acts, not as an ovary, but as a testis, resulting in a change of sex.

2 *Querquedula* = teal (Lat.).

3 Cheng 1963, 1976, 1978–9; A. K. Davies 1985a, b (and personal communication, 1985); Delacour 1954; Fitter 1959; Hughes & Codd 1980; Lever 1957, 1977a; Ogilvie 1975; Owen 1983; Parr 1972; Savage 1952; Scott & Boyd 1957; Sharrock 1976; Tomlinson 1976; and D. G. Salmon; personal communication, 1985.

4 *Sarcelle* = teal (Fr.)

5 Sir Matthew Decker was a Director of the East India Company, and imported to England many species of exotic fauna and flora from the Far East.

6 Despite this, Witherby et al. (1939) only say in a footnote (Vol. 3: 282) that 'wanderers from captivity or semi-captivity of . . . the Mandarin Duck . . . are frequently reported'.

7 R. A. Cuneo & L. L. Shurtleff, personal communications, 1985. See also M. D. F. Udvardy, *The Audubon Society Field Guide to North American Birds – Western Region* (Alfred A. Knopf: New York, 1985), 473.

8 McCance 1962.

9 Guild 1938.

10 Thomson 1922.

Ruddy Duck
(*Oxyura jamaicensis*)

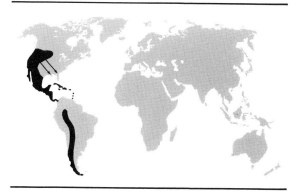

NATURAL DISTRIBUTION

Nearctic and Neotropical regions from south-western Canada through Central America and the Andean Highlands of western South America (Colombia, Ecuador, Peru and Chile) to Tierra del Fuego. The nominate North American subspecies, *O. j. jamaicensis*, which is the one established in Britain, breeds in north-west central North America and winters south to California, Mexico, Florida and the Carolinas; it is also resident in the West Indies.

NATURALIZED DISTRIBUTION

Europe: British Isles.

EUROPE

British Isles[1]

The Ruddy Ducks now living and breeding in considerable numbers in several southwestern and West Midland counties of England are the descendants of some which escaped from the

Wildfowl Trust's reserve at Slimbridge in Gloucestershire; the first birds (two young) flew away from Slimbridge in the winter of 1952–3, followed by around 20 more in the autumn of 1957, and up to 1963 a total of around 70 juveniles are believed to have escaped.

The earliest reports of Ruddy Ducks in the wild date from 1954, when a single drake was observed at Hingham in Norfolk and another at Carsebreck Loch near Perth in Scotland. In the same year, a party of five 'stifftails' was seen on Aqualate Mere in Staffordshire, but it is uncertain whether or not these birds were *jamaicensis*. Four juvenile Ruddy Duck drakes spent the winter of 1957–8 on Chew Valley Reservoir south of Bristol in Somerset, where they were joined by some females in 1958 and 1959, and a brood of young – the first evidence of breeding in the wild – was seen in 1960.

In the autumn of 1959, Ruddy Ducks began to appear on a number of waters in Staffordshire, and in 1961 breeding took place on Gailey and Belvide reservoirs. Since then, they have flourished, and have continued to increase and to expand their range. The reasons are not far to seek; an abundance of suitable habitats and food, a vacant niche for a freshwater bottom-feeding duck, a congenial climate, a virtual absence of competitors and predators and, in the early years, a continual trickle of reinforcements from Slimbridge, have all played a part in helping them to become established.

Rather surprisingly, however, the breeding population in the lower Severn counties of Somerset and Gloucestershire has remained how (some six to seven pairs), the principal expansion having taken place in the West Midlands, where the birds spread to Shropshire (by 1965), Cheshire (1969 or 1970), Worcestershire (1971), Leicestershire (1973), Warwickshire (1974) and Derbyshire (1975). The small, reedy meres of the West Midlands are now their main breeding strongholds, with three-quarters of all pairs nesting in Staffordshire, Shropshire and Cheshire. In 1978, Ruddy Ducks bred for the first time on the Isle of Anglesey in north Wales, and in the following year in Scotland. From three known breeding pairs in 1961 numbers increased to 6 pairs (in 1965), 10 (1968), 20 (1971) and 35 (1973).

In late summer or early autumn, Ruddy Ducks leave their small reedy breeding waters in the West Midlands and congregate on larger reservoirs such as Belvide, Blithfield, Chew and Blagdon in Staffordshire and Somerset. Smaller numbers winter on other waters. The populations on Anglesey and in Leicestershire seem to be discrete, while a few birds tend to remain in Cheshire, Shropshire, and elsewhere. Hudson (1976) estimated the post-breeding population on these and other waters in 1974 at a minimum of 250 birds, including 45–50 breeding pairs and their offspring; by the following year the winter total had risen to between 300 and 350 (including 50–60 pairs nesting in eight or nine counties, representing an average annual rate of increase of some 25 per cent), and by 1976 and 1977 to 380 and 430–50, respectively. By December 1978 the population had increased to around 770 (an annual rate of increase since 1975 of some 33 per cent), and by February 1981 to around 1,750 – a rate of increase of 50 per cent a year since 1978.

Away from their main breeding and wintering waters Ruddy Ducks have been observed in England and Wales from Berkshire in the south to Yorkshire in the north, and from Glamorgan eastwards to Essex. The most northerly British record is of a drake on the island of Unst in Shetland, and the most westerly a pair that nested on Lough Neagh in Ulster – both in 1974. As Hudson (1978) points out, apparently suitable but so far unexploited habitat exists in Yorkshire, East Anglia, the East Midlands and the Home Counties around London, which may well be colonized as waters in the West Midlands become fully populated.

It was generally believed that a prolonged spell of hard weather would seriously deplete the population of this small duck that lives largely on open water, and seldom visits dry land. In the early years of its colonization of Britain, the Ruddy Duck survived one of the coldest winters of this century (1962–3) with the loss of only two pairs from a total population of six pairs. In the winter of 1978–9 (the hardest since that of 1962–3) a major displacement of the population took place; the Staffordshire waters were abandoned, and most of the birds sought shelter in Somerset, although a few were reported from as far west as Ireland and the Isles of Scilly, and eastwards to Norfolk and Lincolnshire. The rate of mortality during that winter was estimated to be about 13 per cent. In the exceptionally severe winter of 1981–2 (when there was at most a 45 per cent mortality rate) Ruddy Ducks dispersed as far afield as Cornwall, Devon, Dorset and Anglesey. The West Midlands' waters were deserted, but had been reoccupied by the following spring, and the population quickly recovered to its former level. Such dramatic movements and population revivals are, as Vinicombe & Chandler (1982) and Owen, Atkinson-Willes & Salmon (1986) point out, likely to lead to the further spread of the species in Britain, and to the colonization of continental Europe, where individuals were first observed in Belgium in 1979 and in France in 1981–2.

Fear has been expressed that if Ruddy Ducks were to disperse south to the Mediterranean they might compete or hybridize with the White-headed Duck (*Oxyura leucocephala*) – another member of the 'stifftail' tribe – which in Europe may survive only in the Andalucian region of southern Spain, where the population is less than a hundred.

Ruddy Ducks in Britain have increased in numbers and distribution more rapidly over a comparable period of time than any other alien waterfowl – indeed, Vinicombe & Chandler describe their progress as 'a phenomenal population expansion', and Owen et al. predict that 'the species seems destined to become a widespread bird in the western Palearctic'. Ruddy Ducks have been recorded on a total of more than 228 sites in the British Isles, and were admitted to the official British and Irish List in 1971, only a little over a decade after the first pair nested in the wild.

The **White-headed Duck** (*Oxyura leucocephala*), which ranges from the Mediterranean to central Asia and winters south from Egypt to northern India, has drastically declined in much of Europe (where it may survive only in southern Spain) and has disappeared entirely from Italy, Sardinia, Corsica, Yugoslavia and Hungary. In June 1984, 59 eggs were sent from the Wildfowl Trust in England for incubation at a breeding station set up by the Hungarian Ornithological Union at Fulophaza, 160 km south of Budapest. From these eggs, 27 ducklings were reared to maturity, which will eventually be reintroduced to the Kiskunsag National Park. In 1985, a further 40 eggs from the Wildfowl Trust were despatched to Fulophaza.[2]

NOTES

1 Atkinson-Willes 1963; Cramp & Simmons 1977; Hudson 1976, 1978; King 1960, 1976; Lever 1977a; Owen, Atkinson-Willes & Salmon 1986; Sharrock 1976; Vinicombe & Chandler 1982. See also: *British Birds* 72: 492; 73: 257 (1979).
2 *Wildfowl World* (*Magazine of the Wildfowl Trust*) 91: 5 (1984); 92: 16–18; 93: 5 (1985); *The Field*, 1 September (1984); *Oryx* 19: 39 (1985).

Turkey Vulture
(*Cathartes aura*)

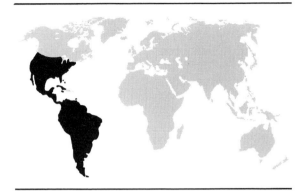

NATURAL DISTRIBUTION

A Nearctic and Neotropical species ranging from southern Canada south to Tierra del Fuego in South America (including Trinidad and Isla Margarita) and the Falkland Islands. In the West Indies it occurs on Cuba, the Isle of Youth, Jamaica and the north-west Bahamas (but may have been introduced to Grand Bahama).

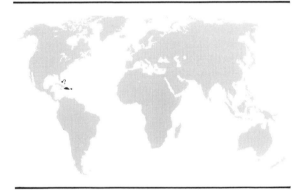

NATURALIZED DISTRIBUTION

North America: West Indies (Puerto Rico, Hispaniola, ?Grand Bahama).

NORTH AMERICA

West Indies[1]

According to Wetmore (1927), Turkey Vultures of the subspecies *C. a. aura* are said to have been introduced by Spanish government agencies from Cuba to Puerto Rico around 1880, where they became established – but increased only slowly, if at all – in the south-west. Wetmore states that

J. Gundlach was positive that there were none on the island in 1874, and they appear to have been first reported in 1899. Wetmore estimated the population in May 1912 at no more than 25, which had doubled a decade later. The American Ornithologists' Union (1983) confirms the species' introduction to, and present establishment in, the island.

Turkey Vultures are believed to have been introduced from Cuba to Hispaniola some time after 1931; they are now well established in the northeastern part of the island (the Dominican Republic), from where they have spread westwards to the Sierra de Oca in the north-central region in Haiti. The American Ornithologists' Union, however, records them on Hispaniola as casual natural visitors from the mainland.

According to Blake (1975), Turkey Vultures have been introduced to Bahama Island (Grand Bahama), though less successfully than to Puerto Rico. However, neither Brudenell-Bruce (1975)

nor Bond (1979) – who gives their Bahamas distribution as 'north-western Bahamas (Grand Bahama, Abaco, Andros; casual on Bimini and New Providence' – make any suggestion that their presence there is the result of human intervention, and the American Ornithologists' Union confirms their status as casual winter visitors on New Providence.

On the mainland, Turkey Vultures are primarily forest dwellers; in Puerto Rico and Hispaniola, however, they occur mainly in open country and the vicinity of large towns – probably as a result of the absence of Black Vultures (*Coragyps atratus*), which occupy these habitats on the continental mainland.

NOTE

1 American Ornithologists' Union 1957, 1983; Bond 1979; Blake 1975; Brudenell-Bruce 1975; Long 1981; Wetmore 1927.

White-tailed Sea Eagle
(*Haliaeetus albicilla*)

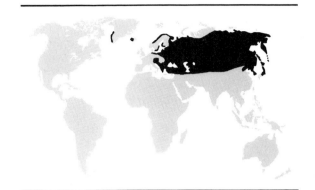

Note: Natural distribution is discontinuous.

NATURAL DISTRIBUTION
Widely but thinly and discontinuously distributed throughout much of Eurasia. Formerly more widespread in Europe (including the British Isles) but has suffered a considerable decline due to persecution, erosion of habitat and, in the Baltic and inland waters of eastern Europe, environmental pollution by pesticides and heavy metals.

NATURALIZED DISTRIBUTION
Europe: British Isles.

EUROPE

British Isles[1]

In prehistoric times the White-tailed Sea Eagle[2] was widely distributed throughout the British Isles. Since the Anglo-Saxon period (*c.* 1,000 years ago), however, when extensive tracts of woodland began to be felled and fenlands drained for agricultural purposes, its habitat in lowland

Britain has been steadily eroded, with a corresponding decline in the species' population. Viable numbers could, however, have survived on the remoter coasts of north-west Scotland and Ireland had not the human population in the nineteenth century increased and partially dispersed to the coast, where changing land-usage brought man and eagle into conflict. As shepherds, crofters[3] and gamekeepers reduced its numbers still further it became increasingly attractive to oologists and skin-collectors. All large raptors are especially susceptible to such persecution due to their relatively long lifespan but slow rate of reproduction, and the White-tailed Sea Eagle was particularly vulnerable because of the accessibility of its eyries and the relative ease with which it could be poisoned with carrion. As a result of human persecution the last native Sea Eagles nested on the English mainland shortly before 1800 (a single pair appears to have survived on the Isle of Man until 1818), in Ireland in 1898 and on the mainland of Scotland in 1901, though a pair is reported to have nested on the Isle of Skye until 1916.

The earliest documented attempt to reintroduce Sea Eagles to Scotland was made in July 1959, when Pat Sandeman released an adult and two young birds from Norway in Glen Etive, Argyll. A month later, the adult was captured while attacking poultry in Appin and despatched to the Edinburgh Zoo. In January 1960, one of the juveniles was killed in a fox trap at Otter Ferry on the shore of Loch Fyne, some 80 km to the south of the point of release, while the other is believed to have been seen on the Mull of Kintyre, over 130 km in the same direction.

A second attempt was made in September and October 1968 when the Royal Society for the Protection of Birds released two pairs of Norwegian eaglets on Fair Isle south of Shetland (owned by the National Trust for Scotland), where Sea Eagles last nested around 1840. Both these attempts failed, almost certainly because the few birds that were released were not reinforced by further liberations in succeeding years.

It was against this background that in 1975 the Nature Conservancy Council, with John Love as Project Officer and with financial assistance from the World Wildlife Fund, the Royal Society for the Protection of Birds, the Scottish Wildlife Trust, and latterly from Eagle Star Insurance,

began a concerted effort to re-establish Sea Eagles in Britain. The attempt was considered both morally and scientifically valid on several grounds. Unlike the Osprey (*Pandion haliaetus*), Sea Eagles do not occur in Britain as migrants and seldom as vagrants, and were thus unlikely to recolonize naturally; vast areas of the west Highlands of Scotland consist of suitable Sea Eagle habitat, and deliberate persecution (though it still occurs) has been reduced as the result of a more enlightened attitude to birds of prey. Moreover, the dissemination of a species' population – the White-tailed Sea Eagle is officially classified as 'vulnerable' in *The ICBP Bird Red Data Book* (King 1981) – is a valuable tool in the hands of the conservationist.

The 10,600-ha Island of Rum[4] (a National Nature Reserve) off the west coast of Scotland was selected as the release site for several reasons. It lies at the heart of the birds' former range and is surrounded by similar suitable habitat. Skye, where the last known British pair probably nested in 1916, is only 13 km distant, and a pair bred on Rum itself only 9 years earlier. Potential prey in the form of Eider Ducks (*Somateria mollissima*), Shags (*Phalacrocorax aristotelis*), Manx Shearwaters (*Puffinus puffinus*), auks (Alcidae), gulls (Laridae) and fish are in abundance, and although there are no sheep on the island, Red Deer (*Cervus elaphus*) – both carcases and grallochs[5] – and feral Goats (*Capra hircus*) provide a ready source of carrion. Sea Eagles are notorious pirates, and some of the species from whom they steal – for example, Otters (*Lutra lutra*), Greater Black-backed Gulls (*Larus marinus*), Herring Gulls (*L. argentatus*), Ravens (*Corvus corax*) and Hooded Crows (*C. corone*) – occur on Rum in considerable numbers. Fulmars (*Fulmarus glacialis*), on the other hand, which have caused the death of some Sea Eagles by clogging their feathers with regurgitated stomach oil, are relatively few. On other islands and on the mainland, Rabbits (*Oryctolagus cuniculus*), Mountain Hares (*Lepus timidus*) and dead sheep are important constituents of the eagles' diet. Norway was again chosen as the source of supply because the Sea Eagle population there (*c.* 450–500 pairs) is the most flourishing in western Europe, which supports in all only around 700–800 pairs distributed between East Germany (100 pairs), West Germany (4–5 pairs in Schleswig-Holstein), Finland (30–40 pairs) and Sweden (100 pairs – of which about two-thirds are spread along the Baltic coast with the remainder in Lapland). The Norwegian population is, moreover, genetically close to the former British race, and seems disinclined to disperse from its natal area.

The Nature Conservancy Council was fortunate in enlisting the assistance of Dr Johan Willgohs (who had provided the Fair Isle birds in 1968), Captain Harald Misund (a Sea Eagle authority from Bodö), and the generous cooperation of the Norwegian authorities. The Royal Air Force agreed to provide transport for the eaglets from northern Norway to Rum, where the first four birds (a male and three females collected, as in subsequent years, by Misund) arrived in June 1975. Table 1 gives details of the arrival and release of eaglets up to 1985. In the decade between 1975 and 1985 (after which introductions ceased), 85 eaglets – mostly aged about 8 weeks – were imported to Rum, where three died before they could be released. After a compulsory month of quarantine and a further short period of acclimatization the remaining 82 were weighed, measured, ringed or wing-tagged and 'hacked'[6] back into the wild. Four females and three males were later found dead. The birds all came from different regions in Norway each year, and were thus genetically variable.

Although most sightings have been within an 80 km radius of Rum, individual eagles have been observed 350 km north in Shetland and over 200 km south on the coast of County Antrim in Northern Ireland.

After the severe winter of 1982 the birds appear to have wandered further afield than in previous years, though sightings in southern and eastern England may well have been of vagrants from the Baltic. At least two have been poisoned at bait probably intended (illegally) for Foxes (*Vulpes vulpes*) or Golden Eagles (*Aquila chrysaetos*), and the flagrant flouting of the law in this respect is a matter of grave concern. Sea Eagles, which are given special protection under Schedule I of the UK Wildlife and Countryside Act, 1981, are, as previously mentioned, especially vulnerable to this form of persecution. This apart, the eagles' survival rate (possibly as high as 60–70 per cent) has been remarkably good, partly due, it is believed, to the absence of competing adults, the apparently increasing tolerance of generally more aggressive Golden Eagles, and a possible reduction in the pollution level of the waters around Rum.

The first British White-tailed Sea Eagle clutch for 67 years was discovered on 6 April 1983. Three days later a second female appeared, and

Table 1 Arrival and release of White-tailed Sea Eagles (*Haliaeetus albicilla*) on the Island of Rum, Scotland, 1975–85

Date	Number imported		Number released		Remarks
	Male	Female	Male	Female	
1975	1	3	0	3	One male died in captivity. Two females released 1975; one found dead Argyll, November
1976	5	5	5	4	Two released 1976; seven released 1979; one female found dead Inner Hebrides 1977; one female died in captivity 1978
1977	2	2	2	2	Three released 1977; one released 1979, found dead Inner Hebrides later same year; one female found dead Skye 1981
1978	4	4	4	3	Four released (two with radios) 1978; one female died in captivity 1979
1979	3	3	3	3	Released 1979
1980	5	3	5	3	Released 1980; one female found dead Inner Hebrides 1982; one male found poisoned Caithness 1981
1981	3	2	3	2	Released 1981
1982	3	7	3	7	Released 1982
1983	3	7	3	7	Released autumn 1983; one died on Rum October 1983
1984	6	4	6	4	Released August 1984
1985	5	5	5	5	Released August 1985

Sources: Love 1983a,b,c (and personal communication, 1985)

for a time all three birds shared incubation. On 14 April, the nest was found to contain two intact eggs and the fragments of at least one other – presumably from a separate clutch. Incubation continued normally until the nest was deserted on 17 May, when it held one damaged and empty egg and the fragments of a second. On 29 April, a new pair was found whose nest contained one egg, but by 15 May this too had been abandoned. Although both breeding attempts failed, due probably to a combination of a spell of inclement weather and the inexperience of young birds, the signs were encouraging. In 1984, two pairs again laid eggs that failed to hatch. In 1985, four pairs laid eggs, of which at least two clutches hatched and one bird fledged successfully in early August – the first White-tailed Sea eaglet to be reared in Britain for 69 years.[7]

NOTES

1 For much of the history and account of the reintroduction to Scotland of the White-tailed Sea Eagle I am indebted to Love, 1983a. Additional references are: Anon. 1984a,b, 1985a,d,g; Collier 1986; R. Dennis 1968, 1969, 1976, 1986 (and personal communication, 1983); Jourdain 1912; Lever 1977a, 1984; J. A. Love 1978, 1980a,b,c,d, 1983b,c (and personal communications, 1983–5); Love & Ball 1979; Nature Conservancy Council 1985; Sandeman 1965; Witherby et al. Vol. 3, 1939; and M. E. Ball, M. Everett and F. D. Hamilton, personal communications, 1983.

2 Sometimes referred to as the 'White-tailed Eagle' or the 'Sea Eagle', the correct appellation is a combination of the two.

3 The joint tenant of a divided farm in Scotland.

4 The correct ancient (Norse or Gaelic) spelling (see *The Times Atlas of the World*, 1972), preferred to the modern but spurious 'Rhum'.

5 The viscera of a deer discarded after shooting.

6 The release of captive-reared fledged birds of prey into the wild.

7 In 1985, it was announced that the Irish Wildbird Conservancy, having witnessed the success of the Nature Conservancy Council's programme, was contemplating the release of White-tailed Sea Eagles on the Blasket Islands off the Dingle Peninsula, County Kerry, where a pair last nested in the 1870s.

Griffon Vulture
(*Gyps fulvus*)

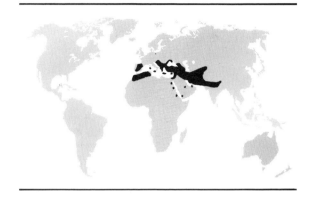

NATURAL DISTRIBUTION

Southern Europe (the Iberian Peninsula, the Ligurian Apennines, Yugoslavia, Romania, Bulgaria, Albania, Greece and Sardinia) and North Africa (Morocco, Algeria and Tunisia) eastwards to central Asia, Afghanistan and north-western India.

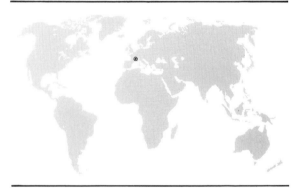

NATURALIZED DISTRIBUTION

Europe: France.

EUROPE

France[1]

Until around 1920, large numbers of Griffon[2] Vultures lived in the Massif Central of southern France; thereafter their numbers steadily declined as a result of deaths caused by shooting and poisoning, for which the slow-breeding birds (which are single-brooded and normally lay only one egg) were unable to compensate by annual recruitment, and by 1940 the population was

extinct. The current project to re-establish them in their former home, now the protected Parc National des Cévennes, is being supervised by Dr Michel Terrasse, Director of Fonds d'Intervention pour les Rapaces.

The site chosen for the reintroduction attempt – above a deep gorge – is unthreatened by agricultural or building development, and local sheep-farming is flourishing. Here three aviaries have been constructed in which the birds are acclimatized before being released; at first the newly freed vultures tend to remain in the neighbourhood of their still-captive brethren, before eventually dispersing. The need to put out food for them, which had originally been envisaged, was found to be superfluous in view of the many sheep carcasses that are available and on which the birds readily feed. Stock for the project has come from the collections of the Zoological Gardens of Paris, La Garenne in Le Vaud (Switzerland), Villars-les-Dombes in Ain (France), and especially from animal rehabilitation centres in the Spanish Western Pyrénées, to which large numbers of vultures are brought for care and attention after being found shot, poisoned, injured, ill or stolen from nests.

Before release, every bird is fitted with a small radio-transmitter (fixed in its rectrices), which is effective for up to 20 km. These transmitters, each of which has a separate frequency, enable researchers to track and quickly locate a possibly ill or injured bird, and to obtain valuable data on foraging territories, dietary preferences, ethology, courtship display, reproduction and interaction with other (potentially competing) scavengers, such as Black and Red Kites (*Milvus migrans* and *M. milvus*), Golden Eagles (*Aquila chrysaetos*), and Ravens (*Corvus corax*). Knowledge thus acquired could also make feasible the reintroduction of another vanished species of the Cévennes, the Egyptian Vulture (*Neophron percnopterus*).

An important factor in the reintroduction programme has been the education of the local human population about the value and importance of these impressive birds. In the 1920s and 1930s, carrion-eating Griffons used often to be seen at the carcasses of sheep, for whose death they were not surprisingly believed to be responsible. Little was then understood by local shepherds about the ecological role of the birds, whose wingspan of up to 2.8 m is an awe-

inspiring and intimidating sight: as a result, so many were killed that, as mentioned above, by 1940 they had disappeared. The education programme, directed at farmers, shepherds, sportsmen, tourists and, especially, children, and consisting of films, slide-shows, meetings, lectures, and newspaper, radio and television reports, was designed to show the birds' value as scavengers of carcasses that would otherwise require burial; to make their return after an absence of 30 years a matter of local pride; and to present them as a tourist attraction. The success of the project, the main chronology of which to the time of writing is described below, won for Michel Terrasse one of the Rolex Awards for Enterprise in 1984. Because of the birds' slow rate of reproduction it is anticipated that the programme will have to continue until the 1990s, with around 10 birds being released annually, before the population becomes fully self-maintaining.

1969. Preliminary study, selection of a site and the construction of the first aviary.

1970. The first four (juvenile) vultures arrived from Spain.

1971. Four more vultures were received from Spain and were released with those imported in the previous year. They remained close to the release site all summer. One was subsequently killed by a hunter and one was electrocuted. The two survivors had disappeared by the end of the year.

1972. Financial responsibility for the project was assumed by the Parc National des Cévennes, with technical advice from Fonds d'Intervention pour les Rapaces. It was decided not to release any more unreliable juveniles nor to remove any birds from the wild, but to take them instead from zoos and private collections.

1977. A second and larger aviary was constructed.

1979. A third aviary was built for breeding.

1978–80. Twenty vultures were held. Three eggs were laid and the first chick hatched in captivity in 1979, followed by another in 1980.

December 1981–January 1982. Twelve adults were freed of which eight survived and adapted to life in the wild.

Spring 1982. Three pairs built eyries in two of

which eggs were laid; the first vulture reared in the wild in the Cévennes for half a century left the nest on 20 September, and joined the eight adults freed in 1981–2. This juvenile remained dependent on its parents until December when it began to feed itself on rubbish-dumps, finally becoming self-supporting in January 1983.

October 1982–April 1983. Nine more adults were released (three in October 1982, three in December 1982 and three in March 1983) of which six became established in the wild, and two immatures aged 3–4 years in March 1983. The last were freed to add variety to the age composition of the population and to test their independence. In April 1983, the wild population comprised 14 adults, 2 immatures, 1 juvenile and 1 chick aged 1 month, and there were 27 birds in the three aviaries. In the spring one bird that had escaped from the aviary in March 1980 or June 1981 returned to the release site accompanied by a wild juvenile; the latter, however, only remained at the site for a month, during which it fed with the other vultures.

Autumn 1983. The two young born in 1982 and 1983 were frequently seen at the release site with their parents. Between September and December, eight more birds were freed in small groups, one of which included the juvenile born in captivity in 1983, together with its paternal parent. In October 1983, there were 25 birds in the wild and in December, 30, of which 14 were adults, 2 were subadults, 12 were immatures and 2 juveniles. There were also 23 in the aviaries.

Spring 1984. Four pulli were hatched – two in captivity and two in the wild.

Autumn 1984. Twelve more captive-bred vultures from Spain, Belgium, and the local colony were liberated, and on 20 November the total wild population numbered 40.

March 1985. Six vultures released, bringing the total population to 43.

April 1985. Six young reared, only one of which was in captivity.

Relatively few birds have died or disappeared after release, but neither have they so far greatly expanded their range in the Grand Causses where, however, they have twice been visited by wild vultures.

The **Bearded Vulture** or **Lammergeier** (*Gypaetus barbatus*) ranges from southern Europe eastwards through the Middle East and central and eastern Asia, south to north-west Africa, eastwards to Egypt, and south through Yemen and Ethiopia to South Africa.

The Bearded Vulture was at one time a widely distributed breeding species in the European Alps, Carpathians, and high montane regions of the Mediterranean, where it has drastically declined since the early nineteenth century. In the Alps, the last known breeding birds were killed in Wallis, Switzerland, in 1886, in Savoie, France, in 1910, and in the Aosta Valley, Italy, in 1913. The present European population of 200–300 survives only in the French and Spanish Pyrénées and in Corsica and Crete, with a few possibly remaining in southern Spain and northern Greece.

In 1978, under the joint auspices of the International Union for Conservation of Nature and Natural Resources and the Frankfurt Zoological Society, a project was inaugurated to reintroduce captive-bred Bearded Vultures to the Swiss, Austrian, French and Italian Alps.[3] In the breeding season of 1982–3, second-generation young began themselves to breed, and it was hoped that the anticipated goal of 10 captive-bred pairs would soon be achieved, when the birds would be released.

NOTES
1 Anon. 1984a; Bagnolini 1982; Brosselin 1971; M. Terrasse 1980a, 1982, 1983, 1984a,b (and personal communication, 1985); and N. Hammond, personal communication, 1984.
2 A variation of Griffin or Gryphon, a mythical creature with the head and wings of an eagle and the body of a lion.
3 Geroudet 1974, 1977, 1981; Holloway & Jungius 1975; Swiss Wildlife Information Service 1981–5; Wackernagel & Walter 1980.

Marsh Harrier
(*Circus aeruginosus*)[1]

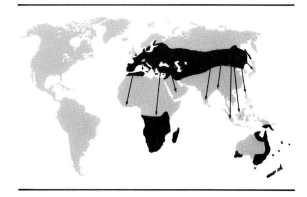

NATURAL DISTRIBUTION
Eurasian, Ethiopian and Australasian regions from the Iberian Peninsula north to southern Sweden and west to Sakhalin Island; north-west and southern-central Africa; southeastern New Guinea, southwestern, southeastern, eastern and northeastern Australia; Tasmania; New Zealand; Norfolk, Chatham, Wallis, Loyalty and Lord Howe islands; New Caledonia, Vanuatu, Fiji, and Tonga (Tofua and Kao).[2] Northern populations winter south in tropical Africa, India and Malaysia.

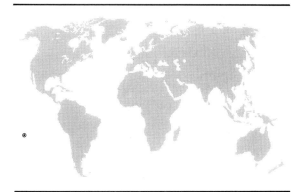

NATURALIZED DISTRIBUTION
Oceania: Society Islands (Tahiti).

OCEANIA

Society Islands (Tahiti)[3]

The Marsh Harrier was introduced in 1883 or 1885 by the German Consul to control rats on Tahiti in the Society Islands from where, appar-

ently without further human intervention, it subsequently spread naturally to other islands in the group. In the early 1900s few were reported, but by about 1920 sightings were being made with increasing frequency.

Holyoak & Thibault (1984) have traced the distribution of the Marsh Harrier in Polynesia. Five or six pairs were established on Maupiti in 1973. Two were seen on Bora-Bora in 1922, and these had increased to an estimated 20 pairs half a century later. On Tupai, there were believed to be two pairs in 1973. The Whitney Expedition noted the presence of Marsh Harriers on Raiatea and Tahaa in 1922, where in 1972–3 they were widespread and abundant; the expedition collected specimens on the former island and on Tahiti and Moorea. Marsh Harriers were seen on a number of occasions on Huahine in 1973. Some were seen in 1921 on Moorea, where in 1972–3 they occurred all over the island, and the population was estimated to number between 35 and 45 pairs. On Tetiaroa, a considerable number were seen in 1921; in 1973, there were thought to be two nesting pairs. On Tahiti, harriers were abundant in the period between 1971 and 1975. In about 1920, a pair was released on Rapa Iti in the Tubuai archipelago, some 1,200 km south-east of Tahiti, but, following complaints from villagers, they were killed a few months later before they could breed.

On Tahiti, Marsh Harriers occur mainly in the mountains below around 1,500 m, and on the plateau of the south-west coast, while on the neighbouring island of Moorea they frequent marshland near the airport at Papetoai and the central plateau region. Throughout the Society Islands harriers hunt in a variety of habitats – bracken-covered hills, montane forests, valleys, plantations, prairies, cultivated land near villages, and sometimes on beaches and rocky reefs. Prey is captured on the ground, in shallow water, in trees or in flight.

Originally introduced to control rats, Marsh Harriers also prey on feral Domestic Fowl (*Gallus gallus*) (q.v.), and have been seen to scavenge on the carcasses of fowl killed on roads. They are believed to be responsible for a decline in the populations of several endemic birds in the Society archipelago. Analysis of regurgitated pellets of harriers on Tahiti and Raiatea shows the remains of rats and mice, which appear to be the main components of their diet, but they also kill Gray-green Fruit Doves (*Ptilinopus purpuratus*) – whose imitated call will often decoy harriers – and White terns (*Gygis alba*). Holyoak & Thibault consider that the rarity of these species, and that of the Tahitian Lory (*Vini peruviana*), the Society Islands Pigeon (*Ducula aurorae*), the Pacific Pigeon (*D. pacifica*), the Spotbill Duck (*Anas poecilorhyncha*) and the Long-billed Reed Warbler (*Acrocephalus caffra*), throughout the Society group can in part be attributed to harrier-predation. Holyoak (1974a) believes that on circumstantial evidence the birds may have been responsible for the extinction of local insular populations of the Tahitian Lory; he indicates that lories were abundant on Bora Bora when only a pair of harriers was present in 1922, but that when the raptors became common about a decade later the lory disappeared.

Conflicting views have been put forward about the presence of Marsh Harriers in the Society archipelago; for example, Bruner (1972) being *pro* and Holyoak (1974a) *anti* their preservation. The situation clearly requires careful monitoring lest populations of rare endemic birds eventually become exterminated.

NOTES

1 Syn. *C. approximans*.
2 According to Watling (1982), the Marsh Harrier's natural colonization of Tonga is relatively recent, and the species may well be expanding its range.
3 Bruner 1972; Holyoak 1974a; Holyoak & Thibault 1984; Long 1981; Thibault 1976; Thibault & Rives 1975; Watling 1982.

Goshawk
(*Accipiter gentilis*)

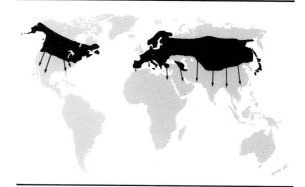

NATURAL DISTRIBUTION
Much of the Holarctic region, but has declined recently in western Europe.

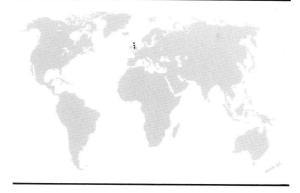

NATURALIZED DISTRIBUTION
Europe: British Isles.

EUROPE

British Isles[1]

In the extensive forests that covered much of Britain in the Middle Ages the Goshawk was probably as common as in continental Europe, and cross-Channel migrations may well have been of frequent occurrence. The species nested in the Scottish Highlands until around the 1880s, but ceased to be a regular breeder in England some years earlier. For long a favourite of falconers, by whom it was protected in the wild and from whom it sometimes escaped to freedom, it slowly declined as a result of de-forestation and the development of the art of shooting flying game (which was accompanied by the persecution of birds of prey) in the eighteenth century, and was the first British raptor to be virtually exterminated. A maximum of three pairs nested in Sussex from at least 1938 (possibly since 1921) until 1951; these may have been the descendants of falconers' birds abandoned during the First World War, or possibly migrants from continental Europe. Up to 1967 there were few other records of nesting in scattered localities, and it was only between 1968 and 1972 that regular breeding in Britain recurred.

Since Goshawks are known to have been decreasing in the Netherlands, France and Belgium (because of poisoning by pesticides) at the time that they were becoming re-established in Britain, natural recolonization from continental Europe seems unlikely, especially as this had failed to occur during the preceding 70 or so years. Some 50 per cent of British falconers' Goshawks escape or are deliberately released (so that the eyases can subsequently be removed from their nests), and those currently breeding in Britain (some of which carry leather anklets, jesses or bells) are almost certainly derived from this source. Moreover, both the geographical distribution and dates of first breeding records are more consistent with the presence of active falconers and known releases than with natural recolonization, and the better established populations (in northwestern rather than southern and eastern districts) are furtherest removed from continental Europe. Kenward (1981) estimated that between 1970 and 1978 about 25 birds a year were successfully re-entering the wild from falconry sources. This would account for the size of the population and for the proliferation of breeding records in new areas in the same period. Marquiss (1981) found that the diversity in sizes of Goshawks breeding in different parts of Britain was consistent with the variation in the source of imported birds – central Europe in the mid-1960s and Fennoscandia (*A. g. buteoides*) in the 1970s – and that those starting to breed in Britain in the latter decade had much longer moulted primaries (comparable to those from Fennoscandia) than would normally be expected from continental birds close to the Channel coast. 'There is thus nothing', Marquiss (1981: 48) concluded, 'in the present evidence which is inconsistent with the view that recent British goshawks have been derived entirely from

falconry sources.' Kenward (1981) clearly concurred with this view: 'It seems', he wrote (p. 306), 'that the return of the goshawk owes most to falconry and little, if anything to natural immigration.'

The failure of the Goshawk to become re-established more rapidly in Britain was not for lack of suitable habitat, since the expansion of commercial forestry during the last half century – especially in the years immediately after the Second World War – helped to provide a protected and relatively undisturbed environment. Moreover, Goshawks are very adaptable in their nesting requirements, breeding freely in small woods and large forests alike, and hunting both in open country and woodland where they take larger prey than their smaller relation the Sparrowhawk (*Accipiter nisus*), with whom, therefore, they do not compete. The only parts of Britain unsuitable for colonization are extensive tracts of open country (such as heathland, moorland, marshes and fens) devoid of trees, and large upland plantations lacking suitable prey, of which the most important are Woodpigeons (*Columba palumbus*), Rabbits (*Oryctolagus cuniculus*) and Moorhens (*Gallinula chloropus*).

In the decade after 1973 at least 53 adult Goshawks are known to have been slaughtered by ignorant gamekeepers, and several eyries were robbed by oologists and falconers. Goshawks are, by nature, largely sedentary birds, and thus generally slow to colonize new areas. They may also have suffered, though probably to a lesser extent than some other birds of prey, from the absorption of toxic organochlorine pesticides with their prey.

The British Goshawk population has increased exponentially from the early 1970s, apart from marked rises in both the overall population and in the number of occupied territories in 1975 and 1977 following peak importation years in 1973 and 1975, and similarly dramatic falls following years of few importations. This seems to confirm the belief that the large numbers of birds imported by falconers in the 1970s materially effected the establishment of a breeding population, especially so when the fluctuation in the number of colonized areas is taken into consideration.

By 1976 there were at least 10 pairs of Goshawks established in the wild in Britain. Four years later the population had increased strikingly to some 60 pairs in 13 separate localities (principally in Scotland and northern England) with a total of 39 known occupied eyries. The reduction in the numbers of Goshawks imported in the 1980s – caused by quarantine expenses and licensing restrictions – resulted in a corresponding reduction in the number released into the wild, and despite their continued persecution Marquiss (1980) believed that the potential rate of reproduction probably outweighed the effects of the release of imported birds at the low level then pertaining. Since 1981, the population has continued to expand, but at a considerably reduced rate. The Wildlife and Countryside Act, 1981, which requires captive hawks to be registered and close-ringed, although it may help to reduce the theft of nestlings could well be responsible for a corresponding increase in the removal of eggs for artificial incubation. By 1983 there were seven areas supporting four or more pairs,

but in only two of the 13 previously inhabited localities had the number of eyries noticeably increased.

Although Marquiss considered that the survival of such a small and localized population, which was subject to a high rate of theft and persecution, was by no means secure, the Goshawk's current widespread but thin distribution, coupled with the fact that the bird tends to make use of alternative nesting sites several kilometres apart in consecutive years (thus making repeated nest-robbery more difficult), should help to ensure its continued – if rather tenuous – presence as a British breeding species.

NOTE

1 Fitter 1959; Hollom 1957; Kenward 1981; Kenward, Marquiss & Newton 1981; Lever 1977a; Marquiss 1981; Marquiss & Newton 1982; Meinertzhagen 1950; Sharrock 1976; Witherby et al. Vol. 3, 1939.

Chimango
Caracara
(*Milvago chimango*)

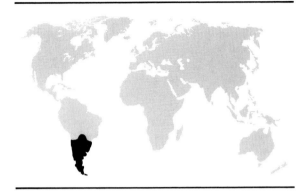

NATURAL DISTRIBUTION
South America from Bolivia, Paraguay, Uruguay, north-central Chile and southeastern Brazil through Argentina as far south as Cape Horn. Southern populations of the form *M. c. temucoensis* winter in northern Argentina.

NATURALIZED DISTRIBUTION
Oceania: Easter Island.

OCEANIA

Easter Island[1]

Chimango Caracaras (? race) were imported to Easter Island (or Rapa Nui) in the South Pacific from Chile in 1928; within 40 years they had overrun the island and were controlling the populations of Chilean Tinamous (*Northoprocta perdicaria*) (q.v.), which had been introduced in 1885, and House Sparrows (*Passer domesticus*) (q.v.), which also arrived from the Chilean mainland in 1928. Like the latter, the Chimango Cara-

cara also feeds on insects associated with the faeces of domestic Cattle (*Bos taurus*) and Horses (*Equus caballus*) and is an efficient scavenger. According to Johnson, Millie & Moffett 1970, it tends to open sores when perching on the backs of cattle in search of ticks, which, as well as injuring the animal, also reduce the value of the hide. Harrisson, who visited Easter Island in 1971, when he estimated the population at not more than 50, considered that, by preying on their young, the Chimango Caracara was having a marked effect on colonies of nesting sea birds; the Red-tailed Tropicbird (*Phaethon rubricauda*) and the Kermadec Petrel (*Pterodroma neglecta*) are among the species to have suffered in this way.

NOTE

1 Harrisson 1971; Holyoak & Thibault 1984; Johnson, Millie & Moffett 1970; Long 1981.

Plain Chachalaca
(*Ortalis vetula*)

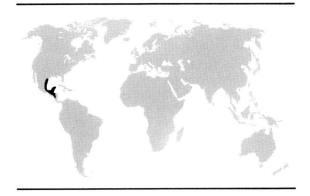

NATURAL DISTRIBUTION
From the lower Rio Grande Valley on the Texan/Mexican border south through tropical eastern and southern Mexico to Honduras; western Nicaragua and northwestern Costa Rica.

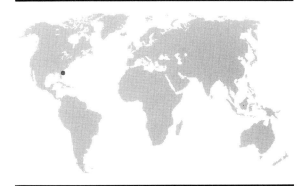

NATURALIZED DISTRIBUTION
North America: USA.

NORTH AMERICA

USA[1]

In 1923, Mr Howard E. Coffin, with the help of

the Bureau of Biological Survey, obtained 42 Plain Chachalacas of the race *O. v. mccalli* (which ranges from southeastern Mexico to southern Texas) from Tamaulipas State in Mexico, which he landed on Sapelo Island off the coast of Georgia. Some of the birds nested successfully in the spring of 1924, and 2 years later Mr Alfred W. Jones of Sapelo Plantation reported that the population had considerably increased and had spread all over Sapelo and onto neighbouring Blackbeard Island. The birds are apparently still established on Sapelo, and possibly also on Blackbeard.

Between 1929 and 1968, small numbers of Plain Chachalacas lived and bred in a semi-wild state in the grounds of the San Diego Zoo in California.

The **Rufous-vented Chachalaca** (*Ortalis ruficauda*),[2] a native of northern South America from northern Colombia to northern Venezuela and the islands of Tobago and Margarita, may have been introduced to Bequia (where it now occurs only in the north) and Union islands (where it is now found only in the west) in the Grenadines by European settlers or the Caribs as early as the late seventeenth century, when it was said to occur also on the island of St Vincent. Delacour & Amadon (1973), on the other hand, suggest that as the species colonized Tobago and Margarita naturally its presence in the Grenadines may not be due to human intervention. Tobago and Margarita, however, lie only 125 and 25 km, respectively, from the nearest point on the South American mainland (the former, moreover, overland via Trinidad), whereas the 175-km flight from Tobago to the Grenadines lies over open water – a long journey for a largely sedentary species.

In 1936, the **Brush Turkey** (*Alectura lathami lathami*), a native of eastern Australia from the Cape York Peninsula in northern Queensland to north of Sydney in New South Wales, was planted in Flinders Chase on Kangaroo Island off the coast of South Australia.[3] Others may have been introduced at a later date to join the first pair, and the birds are known to have survived on the island until at least 1972. The same race was landed on Dunk Island off northern Queensland in about 1935, and may still be established there.

In New Zealand,[4] the Auckland Acclimatization Society received a pair of Brush Turkeys from Sir George Bowen in New South Wales sometime before 1869, which they released unsuccessfully at Kaipara.

In France[5] Brush Turkeys were kept in semi-freedom in a park in Touraine by M. Cornely in 1870–1 and at Bréan-sous-Nappe in Seine-et-Oise by the Marquis d'Hervy of St Denis, but both populations died out during the severe winters of 1888–90.

NOTES

1 Blake 1975; Delacour & Amadon 1973; Gottschalk 1967; Heilbrun 1976; Long 1981; Phillips 1928. See also: *US Department of Agriculture, Bureau of Biological Survey* (1923–4).
2 American Ornithologists' Union 1983; Bond 1979; Delacour & Amadon 1973; Long 1981; Peters 1934.
3 Anon. 1948; Condon 1975; Lees 1972 (in Abbot 1974); Long 1981.
4 Thomson 1922.
5 Etchécopar 1955; Long 1981.

Capercaillie
(*Tetrao urogallus*)

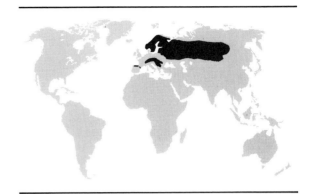

NATURAL DISTRIBUTION
Much of the Palaearctic region apart from eastern Asia, western Europe and the Mediterranean region. Inhabits coniferous forests from Scandinavia south to the Balkans and Carpathians, eastwards to the Altai Mountains and north-west Mongolia. A separate population, *T. u. aquitanicus*, lives in the Pyrenees and Cantabrian Mountains of northern Spain.

NATURALIZED DISTRIBUTION
Europe: British Isles.

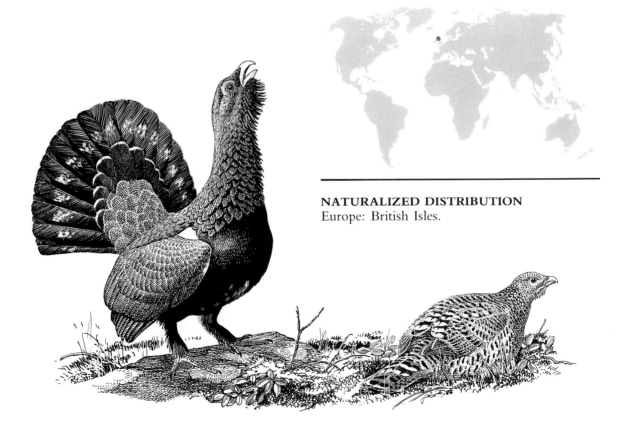

EUROPE

British Isles[1]

There has for long been considerable doubt as to precisely when the last Capercaillie,[2] which was formerly an indigenous species, died out in the British Isles. Witherby et al. (1941: Vol. 5) state that it 'became extinct in Scotland and Ireland about 1760, and England perhaps a century previously'. Pennie (1950–1), however, quotes from Angus (1886) the inscription on a drawing of 'Two coileach-coille, capercailzie, shot on the occasion of a marriage rejoicing in 1785, and which . . . are the last of the native birds heard of in Scotland'. The dates for the last two countries are probably valid, though Capercaillies may have lingered on in Ireland until as late as 1790.

The demise of the indigenous Capercaillie was brought about partially by overshooting, but mainly by the deforestation of its native coniferous woodland habitat in the late seventeenth and early eighteenth centuries; at first this was done to deny a refuge to Wolves (*Canis lupus*),[3] and later to provide timber. The reafforestation programmes of the later eighteenth century came too late to prevent the species' extinction.

Several unsuccessful attempts were made in the nineteenth century to reintroduce Capercaillies to the British Isles. The first took place in Norfolk in about 1823, and was followed by others in Aberdeenshire (1827–31), Perthshire (late 1830s and 1845), Buckinghamshire and Lancashire (1842), Northumberland (1872–7), Yorkshire (1877), and counties Cork and Sligo in Ireland (1879). In the early 1970s, unsuccessful attempts were made to establish the Capercaillie in Grizedale Forest in Lancashire.[4]

The first successful reintroductions were made in 1837–8 at Taymouth Castle, Perthshire, in Scotland, by the Marquess of Breadalbane, who imported 48 Capercaillies from Sweden (although some more recent authors give a different total, this is the (presumably correct) figure given by Lloyd (1867) and Harvie-Brown (1879)). By the autumn of 1839, the population at Taymouth was estimated to number between 60 and 70, and by 1842 (when the first were shot in preparation for a visit by Queen Victoria[5]) the birds were securely established. Twenty years later there were believed to be 1,000–2,000 Capercaillies at

Taymouth, from where 'they have spread over all the more wooded parts of the Highlands as far as Aberdeen'.

The expansion of the Capercaillie in Scotland has been well documented by Harvie-Brown (1879, 1880, 1898), Pennie (1950–1) and others. Table 2 shows the spread of Capercaillies in Scotland until around the turn of the century. The maximum spread of Capercaillies was achieved by about 1914, when they were breeding from Sutherland in the north to Stirling in the south, and from Argyll in the west eastwards to Aberdeen, but thereafter ceased due to extensive timber-felling on private estates, especially during the two World Wars. The general direction of advance from Perthshire until around 1914 was northeastwards and southwestwards along the river valleys, with the hens usually preceding the cocks by several years into new areas, where they hybridized with Black Grouse (*Lyrurus tetrix*) and, less commonly, with Pheasants (*Phasianus colchicus*). One reason for the species' failure to expand its range as mature woodlands with a dry understorey declined, was the tendency to colonize younger plantations, where damp brushwood and shortage of food were responsible for the deaths of many fledglings.

The formation of the Forestry Commission in 1919 helped to ensure the Capercaillie's survival – and that of other forest-dwelling species, such as the Crested Tit (*Parus cristatus*) and Scottish Crossbill (*Loxia curvirostra scotica*) – and the maturation of early plantations encouraged it to re-expand its range. By the late 1930s, Capercaillies were spread over the Tay, Dee and Morayshire regions north to the Dornoch Firth, west into southern Argyll, and south to the Firth of Forth, Stirling, Dunbarton and Lanarkshire.

The Capercaillie's principal winter food, which is also eaten throughout the year, includes buds, shoots, needles, seeds and young cones of Scots Pine (*Pinus sylvestris*), Larch (*Larix decidua*), Douglas Fir (*Pseudotsuga menziessi*) and Sitka Spruce (*Picea sitchensis*), and this has sometimes brought it into conflict with forestry interests. Because these species are also attacked by other animals (e.g. Red and Sika Deer (*Cervus elaphus* and *C. nippon*) and Red Squirrels (*Sciurus vulgaris*)), the degree of damage for which Capercaillies are solely responsible is difficult to ascertain, but in some plantations between 30 and

Table 2 Spread of reintroduced Capercaillies (*Tetrao urogallus*) in Scotland until about 1900

County	First record	Established	Remarks
Isle of Arran	1843	*c.* 1855	Successfully introduced in 1843 (from Taymouth) and 1846 (from Sweden)
Angus	1856	*c.* 1870	Also introduced in 1862 and 1865
Stirlingshire	1856	*c.* 1870	First bred successfully in 1868
Fife	1864	?	Successfully introduced in 1864 and 1874
Dunbartonshire	1867	?	—
Lanarkshire	1868	*c.* 1930	Unsuccessfully introduced in 1860–70, 1902–4 (eggs) and 1929, and successfully in 1930 (from Deeside and Finland) and in 1931
Argyll	1868	*c.* 1875	Unsuccessfully introduced before 1867 (eggs)
Kincardineshire	1870	*c.* 1878	Hatched from eggs brought from Perthshire
Aberdeenshire	1879	*c.* 1897	Unsuccessfully introduced in 1870–3; eggs hatched at Balmoral in 1885 and 1896–7
Inverness-shire	1881	*c.* 1900	Unsuccessfully introduced before 1843 (eggs), and in 1860, 1868, 1873, 1892 and 1894, and successfully in 1895–1900
Morayshire	1884	*c.* 1894	Unsuccessfully introduced in *c.* 1852 (from Norway), 1860, 1878 and 1883, and successfully in 1888 and 1897
Banffshire	*c.* 1886	?	—
Rose-shire	1896	?	Unsuccessfully introduced in 1888 and (?)1899, and successfully in 1910–11, and in 1930 from eggs
Sutherland	?	?	Unsuccessfully introduced in 1870

Sources: Harvie-Brown 1879, 1880, 1898; Lever 1977a; Pennie 1950–1

80 per cent of trees have been effected. Damage is most frequent in early spring when new buds and leading shoots are eaten; recovery from such attacks depends largely on the vigour of the trees, which in an actively growing stand may regenerate successfully within 5 or 6 years, whereas weak plantations are more seriously affected. Normally, however, the damage is not extensive, and the Capercaillie is generally tolerated by the Forestry Commission and most private silviculturists.

Capercaillies are at present confined almost exclusively to the eastern Highlands of east-central Scotland, from the Moray Firth in the north to the upper reaches of the River Forth in the south, being especially abundant in the valleys of the Spey, Don, Dee and Tay. While their natural habitat is old Caledonian forest of Scots Pine (one of the finest remnants of which is the Black Wood of Rannoch in Perthshire, where Capercaillie density has been between 17 and 20 birds per km²), with an understorey of Heather (*Calluna vulgaris*), Bilberry (*Vaccinium myrtillus*), Cowberry (*V. vitis-idaea*) and small trees such as Juniper (*Juniperus communis*), inter-spersed with open glades, the birds now also frequent 20–30-year-old plantations of Larch and Spruce – especially when mixed with Scots Pine. Small discrete populations are established in suitable habitats elsewhere, but Capercaillies seem unable to tolerate the damper maritime climate of the west Highlands coast. The total Scottish population was estimated by Sharrock (1976) to number up to 10,000 pairs, but it is since believed to have declined.

Between 1741 and 1939, several attempts were made to re-establish Capercaillies in parts of mainland Europe[6] (from which they had disappeared due to habitat destruction, overshooting, human disturbance, disease, predators and climatic change) with Scandinavian stock: for example, to Bulgaria in 1900; to Estonia, Latvia, Lithuania and Poland between 1933 and 1939; at Warthegau (formerly western Poland) from 1936–48; to Belgium (where they died out in the Ardennes by about 1820); and to East Jutland and Bornholm in Denmark before the outbreak of the First World War. Most (if not all) the birds were unable to survive in the highly unsuitable intensely cultivated areas in which they were released.

In the 1960s, Capercaillies were reintroduced to the Rossiyskaya Soviet Federated Socialist Republic in the north-central USSR,[7] but with what results is uncertain. Between 1955 and 1965, over 100 birds were restocked in European Russia. Recently, Capercaillies have been introduced to, and have bred in, the Parc National des Cévennes in southern France (Nappee 1981–2). A plan to reintroduce Capercaillies to the Gran Paradiso National Park in Italy was never implemented.

Between 1893 and 1907, large shipments of Capercaillies from Scandinavia arrived in the eastern United States,[8] where several hundred were unsuccessfully released – principally in Maine, Michigan and New York. In 1949 and 1950, 26 were turned down in Wisconsin by the US Fish and Wildlife Service, again without success.

In 1903, 65 (or 52) Capercaillies from Denmark or Sweden were introduced to Algonquin Park, Ontario in Canada:[9] 3 years later 14 from Denmark were released near Cowichan Lake on Vancouver Island and 8 near Bunsen on the mainland of British Columbia, and, in 1907, 23 from Copenhagen were turned down between Whitbourne and Colinet on the Avalon Peninsula of western Newfoundland; these introductions all likewise failed.

The **Willow Grouse** (*Lagopus lagopus*) is a northern Holarctic species ranging in Eurasia from Scandinavia eastward to Kamchatka and Sakhalin Island, and in North America from the Aleutian Islands to Newfoundland. A distinct race, the **Red Grouse** (*L. l. scoticus*), which was at one time considered to be the only species entirely restricted to the British Isles, is established in Ireland, Scotland, Wales, and northern and parts of western England.

In the early 1890s, 70 brace of Red Grouse were released in western Germany[10] at Hoch Venn, Eifel, near the Belgian border, by a textile manufacturer named Scheibler; the planting was successful, but the population has since declined. At about the same time Red Grouse were also successfully turned down at Hautes Fagnes, Ardennes in eastern Belgium.[11] Within a few years, according to Roots (1976), they were

sufficiently well established for up to 20 brace to be shot in a single day, until all shooting was banned. Many were killed during extensive moorland fires in 1911, from which they recovered only to decline again (probably due to disease) in 1930. The remnant population that survives near Botrange is said by Roots to be protected from drainage and afforestation of their open moorland habitat by the Belgian High Venn National Park.

Red Grouse were introduced into Poland between 1933 and 1939 (where, after initial success, they are now believed to have died out), and unsuccessfully in France (in about 1912 and 1939), Norway, Sweden, Denmark, New Zealand (in the 1870s), and in Fiji before 1926. A proposal to introduce them to the Falkland Islands after the Anglo-Argentine War of 1982 was never implemented. Willow Grouse imported from Norway and Canada failed to become established in the United States, and restocking attempts within the Soviet Union appear to have met with mixed results.

The (**Rock**) **Ptarmigan** (*Lagopus mutus*) inhabits the northern areas of the Holarctic region.

Writing of the Faeroe Islands, Williamson (1970: 334, 297) says that 'of several introductions only that of Greenland birds *Lagopus mutus rupestris*[12] at Torshavn in 1890 proved successful [from where they quickly spread to other islands], birds having been seen in recent years in the Norduroyar'. In 1896, Red Grouse were also introduced to the Faeroes, where 'both species apparently succeeded in establishing themselves for some years on Borooy, Kunoy, and Kallsoy', but where Red Grouse have since died out.

Black Grouse (*Lyrurus tetrix*), which are distributed from England, Scotland, and Wales eastwards through Europe to central and western Asia, have been unsuccessfully introduced to Ireland (in the eighteenth and nineteenth centuries), the Soviet Union, Poland, North America and New Zealand. In 1985, a plan was announced to try again to introduce them to Northern Ireland, on the Duke of Abercorn's estate of Baronscourt, County Tyrone.

Black Grouse have also been introduced to the

Gooi Heath in the Netherlands (Taapken 1982), and have been released and bred in the Parc National des Cévennes in southern France (Nappee 1981–2).

NOTES

1 Barclay 1986; Bonar 1907, 1910; Campbell 1906; Davidson 1907; Fitter 1959; Gladstone 1906, 1921a; Grant & Cubby 1972–3; Harvie-Brown 1879, 1880, 1898, 1911; Ingram 1915; Johnstone 1967; Kay 1904; Leckie 1897; Lever 1977a; MacKeith 1916; Mackenzie 1900; Marshall 1907; Menzies 1907; Newlands (in Boitani 1976); Palmar 1965; Pennie 1950–1; Reid 1930; Ritchie 1929; Ross 1897; Sharrock 1976; Witherby et al. Vol. 5, 1941.

2 Variously Capercalze, Capercailze, Capercolly, Caperkelly, Capercaili, Capercaleg, Coileachcoille, etc. The name is probably derived either from the Gaelic *capull* = 'great horse' and *coille* = 'the wood', or from cabher (*coille*) 'old man (of the wood)'.

3 In England the Wolf was hunted to extinction during the reign (1485–1509) of Henry VII; in Scotland in around 1743, and in Ireland in the 1760s.

4 J. C. Cubby, personal communication, 1985.

5 Capercaillies, though classified as game birds (Galliformes), are, because of the resinous flavour of their flesh (due to the predominance of conifers in their diet), virtually inedible.

6 Bobak 1952; Lindemann 1950, 1953; Long 1981; Witherby et al. Vol. 5, 1941.

7 Long 1981; Yanushevich 1966.

8 Bump 1941, 1963; Gottschalk 1967; Long 1981; Phillips 1928.

9 Carl & Guiguet 1972; Long 1981; Phillips 1928; and W. T. Munro, personal communication, 1985.

10 Grzimek 1972; Long 1981; Peterson, Mountfort & Hollom 1954; Roots 1976; Witherby et al. Vol. 5, 1941.

11 See note 11.

12 Howard & Moore (1980) list *rupestris* as confined to northern North America, whereas Peters (Vol. 2) says that it is also found in northwestern Greenland.

Mountain Quail
(Oreortyx pictus)

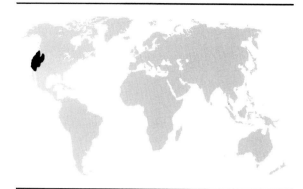

NATURAL DISTRIBUTION

Western USA from Washington and south-western Idaho south to northern Baja California in Mexico (and formerly New Mexico).

NATURALIZED DISTRIBUTION

Europe: ?Greece; North America: Canada; Oceania: ?Hawaiian Islands.

EUROPE

Greece

According to Bohl & Bump (1970), between 1965 and 1968 Mountain Quail from California were sent to the Greek government in exchange for Greek Chukar Partridges (*Alectoris chukar kleini*). Whether the former were released and became established is uncertain.

NORTH AMERICA

Canada[1]

Mountain Quail of the race *O. p. palmeri* (which occurs on the Pacific coast from southwestern Washington to California) were first introduced to Canada in 1860 or 1861 when Charles Wylde released some at his home near Victoria on Vancouver Island, British Columbia. Others were probably liberated at about the same time on the Gulf islands and on the mainland in the lower Fraser Valley where, although Carl & Guiguet (1972) state that the last authentic record of the species was on Vedder Mountain in 1921, Phillips (1928) received a report of some on Sumas Mountain 7 years later. Although both these early attempts eventually failed, from subsequent releases said to have been made in the 1870s and 1880s a sizeable population built up at the southern end of Vancouver Island. In the late 1920s, Phillips reported their presence along the ridges of low mountains that run from Victoria north to the Cowichan Valley at Duncan, but said that they seldom reached Nanaimo.

Half a century later, between 300 and 500 Mountain Quail were established on southern Vancouver Island in small numbers around Durrance Lake, Wark Mountain and Todd Inlet in the hills between Victoria and Sooke harbour in the Highland District, and were occasionally reported from the Malahat near Spectacle Lake, around Cabin Pond on the Goldstream watershed, and from as far north as Mount Sicker and Herd Road near Duncan.

OCEANIA

Hawaiian Islands[2]

In 1929, Mountain Quail from California (of the race *palmeri*) were released on the islands of Hawaii and Kauai, and more may have been imported to these two islands in the 1950s. In 1960, 52 were turned down on the Puu Waawaa Ranch on Hawaii by the owners and the State Division of Fish and Game, followed by a further 36 imported from California in 1961 and 1963. The birds were still present on the ranch in small numbers in the early 1970s.

––––––––––––––––––––

Between 1876 and 1882, well over 400 Mountain Quail were imported to New Zealand[3] by the Auckland and Otago acclimatization societies, which unsuccessfully released them at Matamata, near Lake Omapere, in the Upper Thames District, at Gladbrook, Strath-Taieri and Mataura Bridge, on Venlaw Station and at the foot of the Rock Pillar Range.

––––––––––––––––––––

Phillips traced a considerable number of translocations of Mountain Quail within the United States[4] since 1860–1, to Alabama, Colorado(?), Idaho, Nebraska, Nevada, North Carolina and Oregon, and to Washington, where birds of the form *O. p. palmeri* were released both on the mainland and on San Juan, Whidbey and other islands in the Haro Strait. According to Reilly (1968), only those plantings in western Idaho, central Nevada, eastern Oregon and southeastern Washington on the eastern edge of the species' natural range met with any success.

NOTES

1 Alford 1928; American Ornithologists' Union 1957, 1983; Carl & Guiguet 1972; Davies, Peter & Munro 1980; Godfrey 1966; Guiguet 1961; Long 1981; Phillips 1928; Wylde 1923; and W. T. Munro, personal communication, 1985.
2 Berger 1972; Caum 1933; Lewin 1971; Long 1981; Munro 1960; Walker 1967.
3 Thomson 1922.
4 Carl & Guiguet 1972; Johnsgard 1973; Long 1981; Phillips 1928; Reilly 1968.

California Quail
(*Lophortyx californicus*)

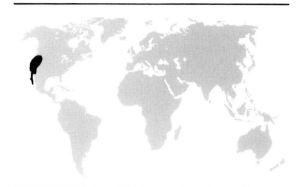

NATURAL DISTRIBUTION
Western USA from southern Oregon and western Nevada south through California to southern Baja California in Mexico.

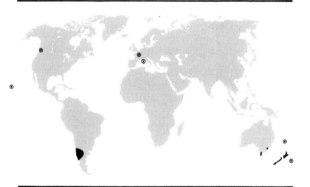

NATURALIZED DISTRIBUTION
Europe: Germany, France; North America: Canada; South America: Chile, Argentina; Australasia: Australia, New Zealand; Oceania: Hawaiian Islands.

EUROPE

Germany; France

According to Niethammer (1963) and Heinzel, Fitter & Parslow (1976), California Quail are currently established in very small numbers

restricted to a few localities in scrubland and open country in parts of Germany. Yeatman (1976, quoted in Cramp 1985) records them as breeding in the wild in one locality on the island of Corsica.

NORTH AMERICA

Canada[1]

The earliest introductions of California Quail in Canada were made on Vancouver Island in British Columbia. Phillips (1928) says they were the nominate subspecies, which ranges from eastern Oregon to Baja California, but, according to the American Ornithologists' Union (1983), they were *L. c. brunnescens* of the Pacific coast from southwestern Oregon to central California. In 1860 or 1861, Charles Wylde released some near his home on the outskirts of Victoria, and at the same time H. M. Peers introduced others, which he had obtained from D. Warbass of San Juan Island (on the United States side of the Haro Strait), to his land at Colquitz Farm, while more were turned down further west at Metchosin. These were followed in the 1870s by further liberations in the same areas by Simon Tolmie, Colonel Prendergast, Major Gillingham and other landowners, and from 1886 into the 1890s more (of the race *L. c. brunnescens*) were released on southern Vancouver Island and across the Straits of Georgia on the lower mainland.

Between 1907 and 1909, A. R. Spalding and H. R. Pooley turned down 30 California Quail on South Pender Island, and others were released on Denman Island, where by the late 1920s Phillips reported that 'flocks of 100 are commonly seen'. In 1908, an unsuccessful introduction was made at Comox on the east coast of Vancouver Island, where a later attempt was more successful. In 1908 and 1910, more were liberated near Nicola south-west of Kamloops in the southern interior of British Columbia, and on the Queen Charlotte Islands.

Lewin (1965) states that California Quail were introduced to the southern Okanagan Valley – well known for its orchards – in 1912 (Phillips says it was to Summerland near the south of Okanagan Lake in about 1910 from Vancouver Island by George N. Gartrell), but Munro & Cowan (1947) suggest that the Okanagan region was populated by natural migrants from Washington (where the species had been recently transplanted) that spread north from Osoyoos. Munro & Cowan suggest further that birds from Nicola dispersing east and south-east via Kelowna and Penticton augmented the population. In all probability, the Okanagan quails were derived from both sources. An open season for shooting was declared in about 1921, when good sport was reported between Summerland and Penticton at the southern end of Okanagan Lake, and by 1923 the birds were abundant south of Naramata. By the late 1920s, Phillips said that California Quail in the Okanagan Valley (where they nested and found shelter beneath orchard prunings) had 'increased wonderfully and now extend north as far as the south end of Woods Lake', and a decade later they were common between Penticton and the US border.

Introductions in the lower Fraser Valley during the First World War by the provincial game warden, A. Bryan Williams, were only partially successful (by the late 1920s a small number only remained about Chilliwack), and those released on the Queen Charlotte Islands and around Vanderhoof near Prince George eventually died out.

By the mid-1950s, California Quail were well established on Vancouver Island – principally on the Saanich Peninsula, near Victoria, and in the south-west around Sooke, from where they ranged sporadically northwards at least as far as Comox. Small numbers still occurred on South Pender Island; although the lower mainland introductions had been largely unsuccessful, a few remained – especially around Ladner, Tsawwassen Beach, Centennial Beach and Beach Grove (on Boundary Bay) south of Vancouver. The species was well established in the southern interior, being particularly abundant in the Osoyoos area near the Canadian/US border at the southern end of the Okanagan Valley; a decade later, around 50,000 California Quail were estimated to occupy some 1,000 km^2 of the Okanagan and Similkameen valleys. Today, between 150,000 and 250,000 are established locally in southern British Columbia – especially on farms and in scrubland on southern Vancouver Island, in the Okanagan Valley, near Keremeos (northwest of Oliver), and between Cache Creek (east of Lillooet) and 20 Mile House. Their main limiting factor seems to be exceptionally heavy winter snowfalls.

SOUTH AMERICA

Chile[2]

According to Swarth (1927), some 'Valley Quail' (a synonym for California Quail) escaped from captivity at Limache near Valparaiso in about, and shortly after, 1864. Around 1870 an unsuccessful attempt was made to establish birds imported from California, USA (of the nominate form) in the Southern Lake region, but from more rewarding plantings made elsewhere at about the same time California Quail were later transplanted to other locations in Chile, such as the Nilahue Valley in Curico Province in 1914, where 5 years later they were said to be increasing and expanding their range. In 1881 or 1882, C. J. Lambert imported large numbers of California Quail from San Francisco, which he released at La Compania in Coquimbo Province, where they multiplied and spread. By the late 1920s, Phillips (1928:20) recorded that California Quail were 'said to be common in the markets of Valparaiso, both dead and alive, and are already important as game'.

Johnson (1965) reported that California Quail were well established from Atacama in the north southwards to Concepción, while Sick (1968) claimed that from Coquimbo they had spread south to Puerto Montt and inland as far as Los Angeles. The present Chilean population may be a combination of the nominate form and *L. c. brunnescens*.

Argentina[3]

California Quail were introduced to Argentina in about 1870, where the race *L. c. brunnescens* is currently established in the provinces of San Juan, Mendoza and Neuquén, and is found eastwards into Córdoba and south to San Carlos de Bariloche in Rio Negro. Since, however, the species' Argentine distribution east of the Andes corresponds closely with that of the Chilean population to the west, and as, moreover, there appear to be no actual records of releases in Argentina, the population in that country may well be derived from the natural dispersal eastwards of birds from Chile.

AUSTRALASIA

Australia[4]

In his anniversary address to the Victoria Acclimatization Society on 24 November 1862, Professor F. McCoy announced that among the various birds that had been released in the Botanic Gardens, Melbourne, were a pair of California Quail. Between 1863 and 1874, a total of 268 were imported from New Zealand to Victoria, where they were released (and their eggs were placed in the nests of native quail) in the Melbourne Botanic Gardens, Ercildoune, Wooling, Shelbourne, Gembrook (a large number in 1872 and 40 more in 1874), on Phillip Island (in 1864), and later on Tasmania and on Huon Island. In 1876, 'American Quail' (possibly California Quail) were introduced to Rottnest Island, Western Australia, by Governor Ord. In 1879 or 1880, the South Australian Acclimatization Society turned a pair out at Pewsey Vale, and in the latter year a number were released at Liverpool Plains, Bathurst, Blue Mountains and elsewhere in New South Wales. At some time before 1919, some California Quail were turned down in Queensland, and other liberations were made in the 1930s and in 1944 in the Prospect region near Sydney, New South Wales. Although the birds bred successfully and became established locally in a number of places, today a remnant survives only near Wonthaggi on the coast of Victoria.

In about 1930, some California Quail were landed on King Island in Bass Strait to replace as a game bird the native Australian, Swamp or Brown Quail (*Synoicus ypsilophorus*), which was declining as the result of increasing human settlement and poor management. The introduced birds became numerous enough for an open season to be declared until public sentiment secured its rescission. In the early 1970s, coveys of up to 30 were reported in open grassland areas, where they remain fairly common. In March 1981, a colony of over 25 was found by T. R. Lindsey[5] near Newcastle on the coast of New South Wales.

In 1895, some California Quail from New Zealand were landed on Norfolk Island where they were soon reported to be abundant; today they remain common in open grassy localities.

New Zealand[6]

According to Hutton (1869), the first California Quail in New Zealand were two pairs released by W. Hay at Papakura near Auckland in 1862. Five years later, the Auckland Acclimatization Society imported 113 (of which 10 were sent to the Waikato and 42 to Nelson), and in 1869 Hutton reported that 'these are now in thousands and have spread for many miles'. The society received a further 14 birds from D. B. Cruickshank in 1870, when Sir George Grey released some on Kawau Island where, according to Thomson (1922), 'they increased to such an extent that in later years the Auckland Society was permitted to net hundreds of them for liberation in the provincial district'.

The second annual report of the Canterbury Acclimatization Society records that at some time before 1865 or 1866 some California Quail were turned down at Brackenfield. In 1867, 1868 and 1871, two, four and 'a large number', respectively, were released by the society, which subsequently purchased 520 birds from its Nelson counterpart and liberated them in various localities. In 1883, they released a further 122, but although 2 years later the birds were reported to be very abundant at Little River, by 1906 Thomson found that 'the Quail seem to be steadily decreasing in most places'. Today, they occur only locally in Canterbury, especially where there are stands of exotic pine plantations in association with gorse and broom and extensive areas of sandy wasteland. They are common in the *Pinus* forests on the coastal sand dunes north of Christchurch and along various watercourses, but rare on the plains where agricultural development has removed suitable cover.

In 1868, the Otago Society released 18 quail at Inch Clutha, where 3 years later they were said to be well established and abundant, and in 1871, 60 were turned down at Waikouaiti and a similar number at Popotunoa (Clinton). At various times between 1881 and 1897 the birds were reported by the society to be numerous around Queenstown, Clutha, Palmerston, Goodwood, on the

Otago Peninsula and near Clyde. Thereafter, they gradually disappeared from Otago Harbour and Dunedin, probably due to predation by Weasels (*Mustela nivalis*) and Stoats (*M. erminea*), which had first been imported from London in 1885 (Lever 1985b), but until at least 1920 were still common and increasing in central Otago.

The Southland Society released a pair of California Quail at Wallacetown in 1873 and 29 in the following year; they appeared to be doing well until about 1890 but thereafter decreased and had disappeared by around the turn of the century.

In 1874 and 1875, the Wellington Society turned down 266 and 118 quail, respectively, which appear to have met with mixed results depending on where they were released. In Taranaki on the west coast (where they first appeared in 1874, having presumably dispersed south from Auckland) the local society imported 60 birds – probably from Nelson – which by 1904 had become 'plentiful in all parts'. On the east coast, California Quail were introduced at an unknown date by the Hawke's Bay Provincial Council, and again later by the local acclimatization society.

California Quail were apparently first introduced to Nelson in 1865 – although where they came from is uncertain – and 3 years later (as mentioned above) the local acclimatization society acquired 42 from their Auckland *confrères*; within little more than a decade the species was better established in Nelson than anywhere else in New Zealand, and large numbers were being shipped to Wellington and the west coast markets for domestic consumption, and frozen or tinned for export as a delicacy to London. The quail's subsequent decline in Nelson was attributed at the time to predation by Stoats and Weasels, and to competition for food with Starlings (*Sturnus vulgaris*) (q.v.), which were first introduced to New Zealand in the 1860s.

As early as 1913 California Quail had become an agricultural pest in some parts of New Zealand. At Te Puke in the Maketu region south of the Bay of Plenty they ate young clover plants and seeds, and in the Waikato district of Auckland they consumed newly sown and germinating turnip seed. Similar reports were received from north of Auckland, from Rotorua and from Nelson, and some farmers resorted to sowing poisoned grass, clover and turnip seeds in an attempt to combat these depredations. Quail were also accused of spreading, through their faeces, the seeds of the Blackberry (*Rubus fruticosus*), which was probably first introduced by the early settlers. More recently, grape and strawberry crops have been damaged, although by way of compensation the birds also consume injurious insects and the seeds of noxious weeds.

As with Pheasants, California Quail seem to have reached their maximum numbers and distribution within about 25 years of their introduction (i.e. mainly between about 1890 and 1900), and to have declined thereafter, due largely to habitat destruction rather than predation by man and introduced mustelids. Thomson and some other contemporary authorities considered that the failure of most Galliformes to become better established in New Zealand was mainly because of competition for food with the increasing numbers of native and introduced passerines. Nevertheless, Wodzicki (1965) described the California Quail as 'widespread and common in North, South and Chatham Islands', and the species is, as Williams (1969) points out, 'the most successful of the Family Phasianidae introduced into New Zealand'. It is now widely distributed there, as the result of natural dispersal and repeated translocations and (often unrecorded) introductions that continued until at least 1945, being found throughout most of North Island and in South Island north and east of the Southern Alps, on some settled offlying islands, and on the Chatham Islands where it was introduced some time before 1900. It is scarce or absent in areas of high precipitation.

In South Island, Williams has found an annual fluctuation in the population, which appears to follow a 4-yearly cycle, the cause of which is unknown. The New Zealand stock is descended from importations of both the nominate subspecies and *L. c. brunnescens*.

OCEANIA

Hawaiian Islands[7]

California Quail (both the nominate subspecies and *L. c. brunnescens*) were first introduced from California to the island of Oahu before 1855; more were subsequently released on all the other larger islands, where according to Walker (1967b) they were well established and a valued game bird by 1865. Munro (1944) records that by 1890 they were 'very common' in open woodland on Hawaii (*californicus*) at around 1,500 m and occurred in 'very large flocks' in *Prosopis chilensis* forest on the coast of Molokai (*brunnescens*). Although they were already well established on Niihau by around the turn of the century, they were later augmented by further importations from California and translocations from Kauai; a small introduction to Lanai, however, apparently failed.

Between 1895 and 1928, the populations on Hawaii and Kauai considerably declined, due mainly to the increasing pressure on grazing by domestic stock and the development of land on the latter for sugar and pineapple plantations. In 1933, Caum found them to be 'quite common' on Hawaii, 'rather common' on Molokai, 'less common to very rare' on Oahu, Maui and Kauai, and absent from Lanai. Munro saw 'a number on Kauai in 1936 and on Niihau in 1939'.

In 1937–8, a dozen pairs were released on Lanai, and until 1940 sporadic importations to the islands continued from California, accompanied by translocations from a game farm on Oahu managed by the Territory Board of Commissioners of Agriculture and Forestry.

In 1946–7, Schwartz & Schwartz (1949) found California Quail extending over nearly 4,700 km² on all the main islands apart from Oahu (from which they were absent or 'very rare') and also on the privately owned Niihau. They ranged from sea level to an altitude of 3,350 m in temperatures from a yearly mean of 75 °F (24 °C) down to 40 °F (4°C), and in areas of annual rainfall between 50 and 150 cm – rising in places to 250 cm. Schwartz & Schwartz estimated the total population to be around 78,000, of which over 62,000 were on Hawaii and nearly 12,000 on Molokai. Seeds were the birds' principal food, and the intensity of grazing by domestic animals and the availability of water their main limiting factors.

Between 1959 and 1961, eight releases totalling 412 quail imported from game farms in Wisconsin and California were made on the Puu Waawaa Ranch on Hawaii, where a decade later the birds were well established and abundant. Zeillemaker & Scott (1976) described the species as local and common on Molokai, Maui and

Hawaii, and local and uncommon on Kauai and Lanai, and as frequenting dry lowland areas. Today, California Quail – known in the islands as *manukapalulu* – of both the introduced subspecies, which on some islands have apparently interbred, are abundant on the leeward (drier) side of Hawaii, Maui, Molokai and Kauai. On Hawaii, they occur from sea level to at least 2400 m on the slopes of Mauna Kea.

In 1912 or 1913, California Quail were released by a Captain Wakelborn (or Wahlbom) on the islands of Masatierra and Masafuera in the Juan Fernández Archipelago[8] off the coast of Chile where, according to Phillips (1928), 'a few years later they were mentioned as doing splendidly'. By the 1930s, they had all but disappeared from Masatierra but were still abundant on Masafuera where, although they later declined due to predation by the large population of introduced Brown Rats (*Rattus norvegicus*) (Lever 1985b), they still occurred in the late 1960s, but have apparently since died out.[9]

In 1935, California Quail were reported to be established in the vicinity of Papeari on Tahiti.[10] In 1938, Guild released some more, which bred successfully in the wild; others were turned down by C. B. Nordhoff. None appear to have survived for long.

In 1917 and 1938, respectively, some California Quail were exported from New Zealand to Fiji[11] and Tonga[12] where, if they were ever released, they failed to become established.

As long ago as 1852, California Quail became temporarily settled around Conflans-sur-Aines in France,[13] and more were unsuccessfully released 2 years later.

In 1906, the government of Natal, South Africa[14] were considering the experimental introduction of California Quail; whether any were subsequently imported and released is unknown.

In England,[15] one or two pairs of California Quail were turned down near Attleborough in Norfolk in the 1850s where they soon disappeared. In 1870, 60 were released at Uckfield in Sussex, and although they were later reported from various parts of the county, breeding was not recorded. In the same year a brace was shot near Bewdley in Worcestershire. In about 1924, several pairs were released or escaped from an aviary at Ballywalter in County Down, Northern

Ireland,[16] and the birds observed at Downpatrick in the same county in 1925 probably came from this source.

Phillips (1928) traced numerous translocations and restockings of California Quail within the United States[17] since 1852 (involving at least four races – *brunnescens*, *californicus*, *catalinensis* (from Santa Catalina Island in the Channel Islands) and *plumbeus*) to Arizona, California (including Santa Rosa and Santa Cruz in the Channel Islands), Colorado, Delaware, Idaho, Illinois, Massachusetts, Maryland, Missouri, Nevada, Long and Gardiners islands, New York, Oregon, Texas, Utah and Washington. None of those in the eastern half of the country were successful, but in the west California Quail have become established in several localities on the periphery of their natural range – especially in parts of Washington, Idaho and Utah.

NOTES

1 Alford 1928; American Ornithologists' Union 1957, 1983; Brown 1868; Carl & Guiguet 1972; Davies, Peter & Munro 1980; Guiguet 1961; Lewin 1965; Long 1981; Munro & Cowan 1947; Phillips 1928; Wylde, 1923; and W. T. Munro, personal communication; 1985. See also: *Forest and Stream* 56: 268 (1901).

2 American Ornithologists' Union 1957, 1983; Barros 1919; Blake 1977; Johnson 1965; Long 1981; Phillips 1928; Sick 1968; Swarth 1927.

3 Long 1981; Olrog 1959; Sick 1968.

4 Blakers, Davies & Reilly 1984; Chisholm 1919, 1950; Condon 1975; Frith 1979; Jenkins 1977; Long, 1981; McCance 1962; McGarvie & Templeton 1974; Pizzey 1980; Rolls, 1969; Ryan 1906; Storr 1965; Tarr 1950.

5 *Australian Birds* 17: 1–26 (1982).

6 Falla, Sibson & Turbott 1979; Hjersman 1948; Hutton 1869; Kinsky 1970; Lever 1985b; Long 1981; Oliver 1930; Thomson 1922, 1926; Williams 1952, 1963, 1969; Wodzicki 1965. See also: *Forest and Stream* 17: 24 (1881).

7 American Ornithologists' Union 1957, 1983; Berger 1981; Caum 1933; Fisher 1951; Hawaiian Audubon Society 1975; Lewin 1971; Locey 1937; Long 1981; Munro 1944; Pyle 1977; Schwartz & Schwartz 1949, 1950a; Walker 1967b, 1981; Zeillemaker & Scott 1976.

8 Hellmayr 1932; Johnson 1965; Long 1981; Phillips 1928; Sick 1968; Skottesberg 1920.

9 W. R. P. Bourne 1983 and personal communication, 1983.

10 Curtiss 1938; Guild 1938; Holyoak 1974a; Long 1981.
11 Long 1981; Williams 1952.
12 See note 11.
13 Long 1981; Phillips 1928.
14 See note 13.
15 Fitter 1959.
16 Fitter 1959.
17 American Ornithologists' Union 1957, 1983; Gullion 1951; Halloran & Howard 1956; Johnsgard 1973; Long 1981; Peters 1934; Peterson 1961; Phillips 1928; Popov & Low 1950.

Gambel's Quail

(Lophortyx gambellii)

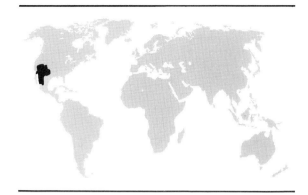

NATURAL DISTRIBUTION

Southwestern USA from southern Nevada, southern Utah, western Colorado and western Texas south through Arizona and New Mexico into northeastern Baja California, central Sonora and northwestern Chihuahua in northern Mexico.

NATURALIZED DISTRIBUTION

Oceania: Hawaiian Islands.

OCEANIA

Hawaiian Islands[1]

Gambel's Quails – known locally as *manuka-palulu* – have been established on the island of Kahoolawe since an introduction by H. A. Baldwin in 1928. From 1958 to 1963, a total of 607 were imported by the State Division of Fish and Game (359 in 1958 from Nevada and 248 between 1959 and 1963 from game farms in Oklahoma and California) for release on Hawaii, where, between 1958 and 1961, 294 were turned down at Puako on the north-west coast. In about 1960, 114 were liberated on Lanai and an unknown number on Maui. Gambel's Quails are still established on Kahoolawe and Lanai. Zeil-lemaker & Scott (1976) record them also on Kauai, Oahu and Maui.

Phillips (1928) traced a considerable number of translocations of Gambel's Quails within the United States[2] since 1885, to Arizona, California, Colorado, Idaho, Kentucky, Massachusetts, New Mexico, Pennsylvania, San Clemente Island (California) and Washington, but only those in north-central Idaho and eastern New Mexico may have been successful.

NOTES

1 American Ornithologists' Union 1957, 1983; Berger 1981; Caum 1933; Hawaiian Audubon Society 1975; Lewin, 1971; Locey 1937; Long 1981; Munro 1944; Peterson 1961; Pyle 1977; Walker 1967b, 1981; Western States Exotic Game Bird Committee 1961.
2 American Ornithologists' Union 1957, 1983; Johnsgard 1973; Long 1981; Phillips 1928; Reilly 1968.

Bobwhite Quail
(*Colinus virginianus*)

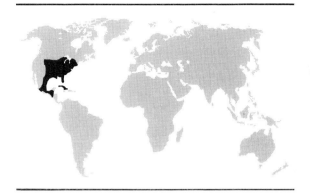

NATURAL DISTRIBUTION

From southern Ontario in southeastern Canada, the Great Lakes and the Dakotas in the USA, west to Colorado and south-east Wyoming, south to eastern Mexico and Guatemala in Central America, and Cuba and the Isle of Youth in the West Indies.

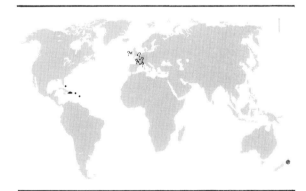

NATURALIZED DISTRIBUTION

Europe: British Isles, France, Germany; North America: West Indies; Australasia: New Zealand.

EUROPE

British Isles[1]

In the nineteenth century, Bobwhite Quail were turned down for sporting purposes on over a dozen separate occasions in the British Isles, principally in England, but also in Scotland (thrice), Ireland (once) and Wales (twice).

The earliest of these introductions was made in Ireland prior to 1813 by General Gabbit. A few years later the Earl of Leicester turned down a

considerable number on his estate at Holkham in Norfolk, where by 1825 the Bobwhite was said to be 'quite a colonized creature, and numerous are the covies, which report says the poachers cannot destroy'. The birds survived in the county until at least 1845.

In the early 1840s, Prince Albert released some Bobwhite Quail in Windsor Great Park in Berkshire, where they remained for about a decade. In 1867, the Prince of Wales (later Edward VII) turned some down at Sandringham in Norfolk, and more were later unsuccessfully introduced to other East Anglian properties.

In 1860, Lord Malmesbury released 16 Bobwhites on his Hampshire estate; 10 years later, Lord Lilford and the Duke of Buccleuch turned some down in Northamptonshire, where they managed to survive until the severe winter of 1880–1. Other plantings were made in Staffordshire and in north Wales in about 1898.

Since the Second World War several attempts have been made to establish Bobwhite Quail in Britain with a view to supplementing the dwindling stocks of the Grey Partridge (*Perdix perdix*) and the alien Red-legged or French Partridge (*Alectoris rufa*) (q.v.).

In 1956, Major Pardoe turned down about 60 near Minsmere on the coast of Suffolk, where they did well until the hard winter of 1962–3; nevertheless, a decade later between two and eight pairs were still breeding successfully, and up to 40 birds were present in winter.

In 1957, 1961 and 1962, well over 100 Bobwhite Quail were unsuccessfully released in East Anglia, and in the late 1960s and 1970s, respectively, more were turned down in counties Cork and Kildare in the Republic of Ireland, and in Gloucestershire, Herefordshire, Wiltshire (and probably elsewhere) in England, and also in Perthshire in Scotland.

In 1964 and again in 1965, 6 Bobwhites were released on Tresco in the Isles of Scilly, where by 1975 the population had increased to between 40 and 50, but had fallen to around 35 by 1976–7. In 1979, when no breeding was confirmed, the population was reported to be rapidly declining – possibly as a result of predation by feral Cats (*Felis catus*). Seven birds were seen in September 1980, but none have been observed thereafter.

In Ireland, the National Association of Regional Game Councils imported 25 pairs of Bobwhite Quail from a game farm in Lancashire,

England, to New Inn, County Tipperary, in January, 1982. In that year and 1983, the progeny of these birds, which were reared at the Lavally Game Farm in Clonmel, were distributed as breeding stock to gun clubs as follows: 1982, 991 birds and 400 eggs to counties Cork, Tipperary, Westmeath, Waterford, Limerick, Longford, Wexford, Monaghan, Cavan, Sligo, Carlow, Louth, and Dublin; 1983, 458 birds to counties Waterford, Limerick, Mayo, Galway, Clare, Offaly and Monaghan. A large number of these birds' progeny have been released (e.g. 800 in Clonmel, County Tipperary, and 500 in 1984 in County Monaghan), but breeding has only been confirmed in Tipperary, Limerick and Wexford.

Fitter (1959: 156), in expressing surprise that Bobwhites in Britain are said to have been killed off by severe wintry weather, claimed that winters in their homeland are much harder. Most of their natural range, however, lies south of 40° N, where the winters are in general far milder than those in Britain. There can be little doubt that harsh winters and cold, wet springs (when breeding success is low, especially on heavy clay soil with poor drainage) have been the main factors that have inhibited Bobwhite Quail from becoming properly established in Britain.

France

Yeatman (1976, quoted by Cramp 1985) records that 65,000 Bobwhite Quail have been released in some 50 French *départements*, where small breeding populations may be forming in humid and bushy country in 71 localities in central and southwestern France.

Germany[2]

Phillips (1928) records that in 1872 about 40 Bobwhite Quail were turned down in Hanover, but with what result is unknown. According to Niethammer (1963) and Heinzel, Fitter & Parslow (1976), Bobwhites are currently established in parts of Germany in very small numbers restricted to a few localities in open and cultivated country and scrub. Rosene (1969), on the other hand, says that introductions in Germany have been unsuccessful.

NORTH AMERICA

West Indies[3]

The Bobwhite Quail occurs naturally in the West Indies on Cuba and the Isle of Youth (where the form is *C. v. cubanensis*) and has been naturalized on Andros, New Providence and Eleuthera in the Bahamas, on Hispaniola and Puerto Rico in the Greater Antilles, and on St Croix in the Virgin Islands. According to Rosene (1969), there have been more attempts to introduce the Bobwhite Quail (mostly from North America) into the West Indies than anywhere else in the world, but due mainly to a marginal habitat and over-shooting the species has now largely disappeared.

Writing of Bobwhites in the Bahamas, Cory (1880: 143) said: 'The inhabitants claim that a number of these birds were imported many years ago from the United States, and have since multiplied so that at the present time they are numerous in the neighbourhood of Nassau.' Today, birds of the Florida subspecies, *floridanus*, occur in pine barrens, thick wooded under-growth, wasteland, fields of rough grass, and farmland, on the islands of New Providence, Andros and Eleuthera.

According to Cory (and confirmed by Wetmore & Swales 1931), Bobwhites must have been introduced to Haiti during the period of French colonial rule (1697–1803), as they were recorded from around Léogane on the south-west coast towards the end of the eighteenth century, where a hundred years later they were said to be abundant. Wetmore & Swales (p. 124) said that they occurred 'along the southern peninsula from a point west of Jérémie through Fonds-des-Negrès east to Port-au-Prince and north and east through the Cul-de-Sac Plain at least as far as Mirebalais and Thomazeau . . . extending inland through the hills to an elevation of 1,200 metres or more'.

Cherrie (1896) records that the Bobwhite Quail was 'introduced into San Domingo [the Dominican Republic] by an American sugar planter by the name of Bass about six years ago. It has increased very rapidly, and now for a good many miles around San Domingo City flocks of from ten to twenty-five are frequently met with.' By the late 1920s, the birds were apparently increasing rapidly, and are now said to be common and widespread throughout the Republic.

According to Gundlach (1878a), Bobwhite Quail (presumably of the form *cubanensis*) were imported from Cuba to Puerto Rico in 1860 by Don Ramón Soler, who released them on his Hacienda Santa Inés near Vega Baja. Although they were said to have been exterminated by around the turn of the century, Bond (1979) indicates that they are still present on the island.

A. and E. Newton (1859) state that the 'Bobwhite had been introduced to St Croix about fifty years ago by one of the Governors and had become very numerous there', where, according to Bond, it still survives. The race imported may have been *C. v. virginianus* of the central and eastern Unites States, though Wetmore (1927) considered it more likely to have been *cubanensis*.

According to Phillips (1928), stock apparently from Florida – and perhaps also from Texas – is said to have been released near Havana, Cuba, sometime before 1923, where hybridization occurred with the native Cuban form.[4]

Lack (1976) says that Bobwhite Quail [of the form *C. v. virginianus*] were introduced to Jamaica[5] in about 1747, where they flourished in the second half of the eighteenth and early nine-teenth centuries, but had nearly died out before 1900. Phillips suggests that the introduction took place in about 1800 (with stock from the east-central States, Virginia, or the Carolinas), and that although the birds were devastated after the introduction in 1872 of the Small Indian Mongoose (*Herpestes auropunctatus*) (see Lever 1985b), they later staged a temporary recovery. Although more were introduced in 1953 the Bobwhite Quail no longer occurs in Jamaica.

In 1886–7, Bobwhites were introduced to Antigua, St Kitts, Guadeloupe and Barbados (and probably also to Martinique), on none of which they now remain.[6]

AUSTRALASIA

New Zealand[7]

In 1898, the Wellington Acclimatization Society imported some 400 Bobwhite Quail from North America, 240 of which were released in the Wellington district, 80 in Otago, 40 in Canterbury and 20 each in Stratford and New Plymouth. In the following year, a further 756 were received, which were distributed as follows: 200 to Auckland, 100 to Wellington, 90 to Canterbury, 70 to Blenheim, 60 to Wanganui, 56 to Waikaremoana, 46 to Otago, 44 to Stratford, 32 to New Plymouth, 30 to Napier, 22 to Southland and 6 to Gisborne. The form imported is believed to have been *C. v. taylori*.

In 1900, the Otago Society reported that 'they were still to be seen in the neighbourhood of where they were liberated, but no young birds have been seen'. Two years later, the Wellington Society stated that 'these birds have so far been a disappointment; reliable information as to their having been seen during the past year is difficult to obtain'. The Pahiatua and Marton subcommittees reported, respectively, that 'they seem to have disappeared' and that they were 'doing well, and they have been seen with young broods'. In the same year, the Taranaki Society was of the opinion that 'Virginian Quail [a synonym for the Bobwhite] are steadily increasing and will, in a year or two, afford good sport', but in 1904 they were obliged to concede that 'Virginian Quail seem to have disappeared'. Although 5 years later the Auckland Society reported in the same terms, some Bobwhites were caught south of Auckland in 1922, and 30 years later some were discovered at Wairoa on Hawke's Bay, and subsequently also inland at Lake Waikaremoana and Waingaroa.

In June and July 1947, the Otago Society imported to Dunedin two separate consignments of 200 eggs each (out of a permitted total of 1,000) from Oakland, California, which were placed in incubators at the society's game farm at Waitati where, of 64 hatched chicks, only 40 survived for as long as a fortnight, and all later died. Today, the Bobwhite Quail, which Wodzicki (1965) described as locally common in North Island', is confined to the Wairoa/Waikaremoana district of Hawke's Bay.

Bobwhite Quail (*C. v. virginianus*) were first introduced to Bermuda[8] from Virginia in the late seventeenth or early eighteenth century, but had died out by around 1840. In 1858 or 1859, more were imported by Richard Darrell, and their descendants were said to be abundant until at least as late as 1900. By the 1940s they were still widely distributed, but remained common only in larger rural areas of Southampton, Warwick, Devonshire, Smith's and Hamilton parishes. Crowell & Crowell (1976) reported that in 1959 they were 'restricted in numbers and localized in distribution', and they are believed to have died out by 1964.

In 1854, 1858, 1861, 1865 and between 1898 and 1900, a large number of Bobwhite Quail were imported from the United States to France,[9] where, according to Phillips (1928), 'some measure of success with them was reported, both in captivity and in a state of freedom'. In 1887, some are believed to have been shipped to Sweden,[10] and in 1901 a consignment of 5,000 was despatched to Count Lewenhaupt's estate at Fosslorjo.

In 1891 (or earlier), an attempt was made 'on quite a large scale' to establish Bobwhites from Kansas, USA in Kashing in eastern China.[11] Apparently, the birds arrived in poor condition after their long journey and the experiment was unsuccessful.

In the early 1960s, Bobwhite Quail were released in Southern Rhodesia (Zimbabwe)[12] and in Natal, South Africa,[13] where Winterbottom (1966) considered they were unlikely to remain without human intervention.

According to Bannerman (1965), an attempt was recently made to introduce Bobwhites to Madeira.

In about 1975, some Bobwhites were released in marshland south of Lima, Peru, but as none were subsequently seen the experiment is presumed to have failed. Since the species is reared for the table in Peru there may well have been other (unrecorded) liberations and/or escapes from captivity. Bobwhite Quail are also said to have been unsuccessfully released in parts of Chile.

Several attempts have been made to establish Bobwhite Quail in Canada,[14] but only those in British Columbia were ever successful. In 1877, some were released in Nova Scotia and Ontario and later others at Winnipeg in Manitoba. In British Columbia, the birds are said to have been present on South Pender Island when the first settlers arrived in 1886, but had apparently disappeared by the turn of the century. In 1899, the British Columbia Forest and Stream Club released 156 at various sites on the southern mainland, and in the following year 130 were liberated near Ashcroft. In 1905 and 1907, 32 and

35, respectively, were turned down near Shuswap and on the Coldstream Ranch near Vernon. Only in the lower Fraser and Okanagan valleys (in the latter especially around Vernon and Osoyoos Lake near the United States border) did the species ever become established, but even there the birds had all disappeared by January 1912. According to Carl & Guiguet (1972), 'several flocks survived near Huntingdon [BC] on the US boundary, but were exterminated in the severe winter of 1947–48'. In 1967–8, N. Milani planted some on his property at Ladner, where they survived only until 1969, and about 20 released on the Reifel Waterfowl Refuge near Vancouver in 1971 failed to survive the following winter. Although the American Ornithologists' Union (1983) indicates that Bobwhite Quail are presently established in southwestern British Columbia, W. T. Munro (personal communication, 1985) says that few if any remain. The race introduced to British Columbia was either pure or hybrid *C. v. virginianus*.

Bobwhite Quail have been introduced to various islands (mainly to Hawaii and Maui) in the Hawaiian[15] group on several occasions since 1906, but have so far failed to establish viable populations. The largest introductions took place between 1959 and 1961 when 108 birds, from game farms in California, New Mexico and Texas, were turned down on the Puu Waawaa Ranch on Hawaii, and in the latter year 90 were released on Maui. The forms imported were *C. v. virginianus* in 1906 and *C. v. ridgwayi* from 1959 to 1961 – the latter from northern and south-central Sonora State in northwestern Mexico.

————————————

Within the United States,[16] Phillips (1928) traced innumerable translocations and restockings of Bobwhite Quail in at least 30 states after 1840: these consisted mainly of captive-bred (with some wild-trapped) stock, and included importations of the race *C. v. texanus* – from northeastern Mexico – which was widely but unsuccessfully introduced and transplanted. Outside their natural range birds of the form *C. v. virginianus* (and hybrids) became established only in parts of Idaho, Montana and Washington, while *C. v. taylori* was successful locally in Idaho, Nevada, Oregon, Washington and northwestern Wyoming.

The **Crested Bobwhite** (*Colinus cristatus*)[17] occurs in central and South America from Guatemala south to Colombia and Venezuela, eastwards to Guyana and northeastern Brazil, and also on Aruba, Curaçao, and Isla Margarita off the coast of Venezuela.

Cassin (1861) said that a specimen of a Crested Bobwhite had been collected by Robert Swift on St Thomas in the Virgin Islands, to which he was told that the species had been introduced some years previously from Venezuela, and where he found the birds to be well established and breeding freely. Skins from St Thomas examined in 1920 were identified as the subspecies *sonnini*, which occurs from eastern Venezuela through Guyana, Surinam and French Guiana into northern Brazil. In 1852, Knox (quoted by Wetmore 1927) considered that 'quail' were very rare on the island, and during his survey of Puerto Rico and the Virgin Islands Wetmore (p. 332) said of the Crested Bobwhite in St Thomas: 'formerly common, present status uncertain'. Although E. R. Blake (1977) confirmed that the species had been introduced on St Thomas, and also on Mustique in the Grenadines, neither C. H. Blake (1975) nor Bond (1979) mention its presence anywhere in the West Indies. The American Ornithologists' Union (1983) indicates that although it has been extirpated on St Thomas, the nominate subspecies survives on Mustique.

NOTES

1 Denny 1844; Fitter 1959; Lever 1977a; Phillips 1928; Sharrock 1976. See also: *Forest and Stream* 25: 103 (1885); *Magazine of Natural History* 4: 16 (1831) and 6: 153 (1833); and *Annals and Magazine of Natural History* 13: 405 (1844).
2 Heinzel, Fitter & Parlsow 1976; Niethammer 1963; Phillips 1928; Rosene 1969. See also: R. Böhm, *Deutsche Akklimatisation (Deutscher Verein Vögelaucht und Akklimatisation)* 5: 17 (1879).
3 American Ornithologists' Union 1957, 1983; Bond 1979; Brudenell-Bruce 1975; Cherrie 1896; Cory 1880; Long 1981; Peters 1934; Phillips 1928; Rosene 1969; Wetmore 1927; Wetmore & Swales 1931. See also: Bowdish 1903.
4 See Barbour 1923. Bond (1979: 65) says that 'Native Cuban quail are very dark, and closely resemble those from Florida'.
5 Lack 1976; Long 1981; Peters 1934; Phillips 1928.
6 Peters 1934; Phillips 1928; Rosene 1969.

7 Falla, Sibson & Turbott 1979; Gurr 1953; Long 1981; Oliver 1930, 1955; Thomson 1922; Westerskov 1956a, 1957a; Williams 1969; Wodzicki 1965.

8 Bourne 1957; Bradlee, Mowbray & Eaton 1931; Crowell 1962; Crowell and Crowell 1976; Hurdis 1897; Reid 1884; Wingate 1965, 1973, and unpublished mimeograph. See also: O. Bangs & T. S. Bradlee, *Auk* 28: 249–57 (1901).

9 Etchécopar 1955; Long 1981; Phillips 1928; Rosene 1969.

10 See note 9.

11 Long 1981; Phillips 1928.

12 Liversidge n.d.; Winterbottom 1966.

13 See note 12.

14 American Ornithologists' Union 1957, 1983; Carl & Guiguet 1972; Long 1981; Munro & Cowan 1947; Phillips 1928; and W. T. Munro, personal communication, 1985.

15 Berger 1972; Lewin 1971; Long 1981; Munro 1960; Walker 1967b; Western States Exotic Game Bird Committee 1961.

16 American Ornithologists' Union 1957, 1983; Bump 1941; Goodrum, 1949; Johnsgard, 1973; Lehmann 1948; Long 1981; Peterson 1961; Phillips 1928; Rosene 1969.

17 American Ornithologists' Union 1957, 1983; C. H. Blake 1975; E. R. Blake 1977; Bond 1979; Cassin 1861; Long, 1981; Wetmore 1927.

Chukar Partridge

(*Alectoris chukar*)[1]

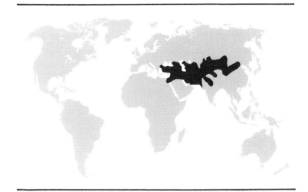

NATURAL DISTRIBUTION

From eastern Greece and Bulgaria, through Asia Minor, Arabia, Iran and northwestern India, to western Mongolia and southern Manchuria in northern China.

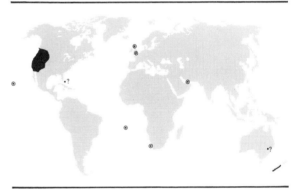

Note: North American distribution is discontinuous.

NATURALIZED DISTRIBUTION

Europe: British Isles; Asia: ?Oman, United Arab Emirates; Africa: South Africa, St Helena; North America: USA, Mexico, Canada, West Indies (?Bahamas); Australasia: ?Australia, New Zealand; Oceania: Hawaiian Islands.

EUROPE

British Isles[2]

Between the two World Wars Chukar Partridges were turned down in Bedfordshire and Surrey in England and in Peeblesshire in Scotland; although these introductions ultimately failed, some of the birds continued to breed until the late 1940s.

Following the decline of the Grey Partridge (*Perdix perdix*), and in the hope that they might become established more easily than the Red-legged or French Partridge (*Alectoris rufa*) (q.v.), several commercial game farms in the early 1970s began rearing for subsequent release both Chukar and Rock Partridges (*A. graeca*).[3] By the late 1970s, a few of the former were established on the South Downs in Sussex and in Kent, and in Scotland in parts of Aberdeenshire and some adjacent counties; *chukar* × *rufa* hybrids have been observed in the south (though these may possibly have been released captive-bred stock), and hybridization between the two species is believed to have occurred in the north. In view of their preference for rocky, semi-desert or alpine habitats, the attempted introduction of these species to the British Isles seems somewhat misconceived.

ASIA

Oman; United Arab Emirates

Chukar Partridges occur in small numbers in lightly cultivated areas and rocky plateaux with some vegetation in mountains of the Musandam Peninsula of Oman, and perhaps also in adjoining areas of the United Arab Emirates. According to Jennings (1981), this isolated population is probably derived from escaped birds that have been imported for food. Gallagher & Woodcock (1980), however, make no such suggestion, and it seems as likely that the birds are derived from natural immigrants that flew across the 75-km wide Strait of Hormuz from southern Iran.

AFRICA

South Africa;[4] Zimbabwe[5]

Three introductions of Chukar Partridges to Table Mountain and Villiersdorp on the South African mainland (involving 30, 50 and 500 birds, respectively, the first of which may have been made by Cecil Rhodes around the turn of the century and the last of which survived, according to Liversidge, for at least 74 years) were unsuccessful, due probably to predation by Wild Cats

(*Felis silvestris*), Black-backed Jackals (*Canis mesomelas*), Meerkats (*Suricata suricatta*), Yellow Mongooses (*Cynictis penicillata*), rodents and egg-eating snakes. In the early 1960s, Chukars were also released – apparently unsuccessfully – in Natal and in Southern Rhodesia (Zimbabwe).

In 1964, six Chukar Partridges were seized by customs officers in Cape Town and despatched to Robben Island in Table Bay – site of a notorious prison camp. When Siegfried (1971) visited the island he saw three separate coveys and estimated the total population to number around 500. P. A. Clancey (personal communication, 1985) wrote of this 'flourishing population' that it is 'racially composite, so derives from game-farm bred stock'.

St Helena[6]

According to Melliss (1870), Chukar Partridges may have been seen on St Helena by the English circumnavigator Thomas Cavendish (1560–92) when he called briefly at the island in 1588, but there is no record of their introduction. Melliss suggests that the birds may have come from northern India (*A. c. chukar*) and says they were abundant on St Helena. In *St Helena, 1502–1938* (1938), Philip Gosse says that Chukars occurred on the island in 1936 – possibly as the result of an introduction from the Persian Gulf, in which case they would presumably be either *A. c. werae* or *A. c. koroviakovi*. By 1949, the population was estimated to number several hundred, but has since considerably declined and is believed to be continuing to decrease.

NORTH AMERICA

USA;[7] Mexico[8]

According to Bump (1941 and 1968), Chukar Partridges have probably been introduced to every state in the USA, but have only become well established in and to the west of the Rocky Mountains.

The first Chukars in the United States are believed to have been five pairs (presumably *A. c. koroviakovi* from southern and eastern Iran, Afghanistan and West Pakistan, but possibly *A. c. chukar* from the Himalayas), shipped from

Karachi in north-west India (now West Pakistan) to Illinois in 1893 by W. O. Blaisdell, who unsuccessfully released some of their offspring near McComb in the following spring. Other early trial plantings that failed were made in Massachusetts and possibly in Maryland and Georgia, but it was not until the 1930s that the species began to be released on a large scale, and by 1953 more than 324,000 had been turned down in nearly every state in the Union.

In 1925, Chukars were imported from India to San Francisco, California, by E. Booth, from whom 3 years later the State Department of Fish and Game acquired five pairs, followed in 1929 by a further five pairs direct from Calcutta, with which they established a breeding stock. Some of their progeny, together with further birds imported from Calcutta, were released in 1932, and by 1936 a total of some 4,600 birds (all presumably *chukar* or *koroviakovi*) had been turned down in 26 counties in 80 sections of the state, where they became established in the Owens River valley and the Mojave Desert, and a breeding stock of over 600 birds remained in captivity.

In 1942–3, the California Department of Fish and Game reared some 22,000 Chukars, nearly 7,000 of which were released in 1947–9. Although Harper, Harry & Bailer (1958) estimated that between 1932 and 1955 some 52,184 farm-reared Chukars of the nominate form were planted in California, the total may have been nearer 85,500. The birds were turned down in almost every county in the state in a wide variety of habitats and climates, ranging from dense stands of timber and brush in warm and damp coastal ranges, through inland mountain regions to hot and arid semi-desert country, and in areas where the annual precipitation ranges from 13–130 cm. The birds prospered most in semi-arid and only lightly cultivated regions, where the annual rainfall is seldom in excess of 25 cm. The trapping and translocation of wild birds to previously unstocked areas began in 1953, and within 2 years some 2,899 Chukars had been liberated in a further seven counties. A shooting season was declared in the state in 1954, and for the first few years the annual take averaged around 4,000 – a figure that had risen dramatically to some 50,000 by 1959.

In 1958, 200 gamefarm-reared birds of the subspecies *A. c. cypriotes* from Turkey or *A. c.* *kurdestanica* from Kurdistan were acquired from New Mexico, and between 1960 and 1968 (when liberations ceased) a total of 8,490 were released by the Department of Fish and Game under the Department of the Interior's Foreign Game Introduction Program, in Madera, San Diego, Siskiyou, Los Angeles, Monterey, Santa Clara, San Benito, San Luis Obispo, Colusa, Kern, Fresno, Stanislaus, Mariposa, Lassen and Tehama counties (see also below under Rock Partridge).

The first of no fewer than 89 recorded introductions of Chukars in Montana took place in 1933, and, by 1940 365 birds had been turned down in 16 counties. After 1950, a further 5,000 were released, and by 1958 the birds had become established locally in the Fromberg/Red Lodge/Bighorn Canyon region south of Billings, where limited shooting was first permitted in 1959.

In November 1934, 50 Chukar Partridges of the Himalayan race were released on the R. L. Douglass Ranch near Fallon in Churchill County, Nevada; these were followed by a further 289 in the centre and west of the state in 1935 (Alcorn & Richardson 1951 suggest that undocumented introductions may have been made previously by private shooting clubs), and by 1941 Chukars had been turned down in most, if not all, counties in Nevada, where they flourished in rugged, semi-desert country at altitudes of between 1,500 and 2,100 m, which compare closely with the 1,800–3,000 m of their range in the Himalayas of Nepal. Alcorn & Richardson say that between 5,000 and 10,000 birds had been released in Nevada by 1951 (many of which were live-trapped wild birds transplanted between 1947 and 1949), and Dorian (1965) estimated the total 2 years later at 6,400, when the birds covered an area of over 100 km^2 – mostly in the west and centre of the state. From 1956 to 1958, many more were released, especially in the south in the Virgin Mountains. The first shooting season was opened in 1947, and by 1963 a total of around 525,000 birds had been killed – a figure that had almost doubled by 1968, making Nevada, in the words of Bohl (1971d), 'the number one chukar state'.

The first introduction of Chukar Partridges to Wyoming was made in 1934 by Judge W. S. Owens of Cody, who by 1941 is believed to have released a total of some 400 birds. In 1938, 55 Chukars were released in Natrona County by a state-owned game farm, which between the following year and 1955 turned down an average of nearly 1,000 birds a year, resulting in the formation of several local populations. In 1954–5, the first wild-trapped Chukars were successfully liberated in parts of southern Wyoming.

The early plantings of Chukar Partridges in Utah were all unsuccessful. In 1935, the Box Elder Wildlife Federation purchased 300 eggs from a breeder in California, which were sent to the Springville Game Farm. In the following year, 76 young birds hatched from these eggs were turned down in Box Elder County – 5 east of Brigham City, 8 east of Mantua, and the remaining 63 on the Connor Springs Ranch. In the same year, eight adults purchased 'from an eastern dealer'[9] were liberated at Connor Springs, where a brood of young was reported a few months later. Within 2 years all 84 birds (and their offspring) had disappeared.

In 1937, William Witney, the manager of the Springville Game Farm, was sent to California to study recent developments in the captive breeding of Chukars. A year later, 50 Springville-reared birds were freed in the Unita foothills east of Brigham City, and a further four pairs on the slopes of what is now the Cedar Breaks National Monument; the birds planted in the Unita range disappeared within a year, while those introduced to the Cedar Breaks – after initially increasing some threefold – survived for only a few years.

In 1940, the Department of Fish and Game acquired 100 Chukars from the Winchester Cartridge Company, which were subsequently released in Sevier, Davis, Utah and Box Elder counties, where they remained for barely a year. In 1940–1, 96 birds from the Springville Game Farm were liberated in Washington County – 38 south of St George, 15 on each of Santa Clara Creek and Gunlock, and 28 at Berry Springs south-west of Hurricane; once again all disappeared after about a year. All 46 liberated in 1941 by the Weber County Wildlife Federation at Arsenal Springs near Weber Canyon also failed to become established. A small number released near the Price Game Farm in 1946, 50 at Mantua and 50 east of Deweyville in 1948, 23 at Parley's Canyon, Salt Lake County, also in 1948, and 13 near Moab on the Green River in 1949 by the Department of Fish and Game, were similarly unsuccessful.

From subsequent plantings near Salt Lake City in 1951–2 – mainly by the Department of Fish and Game from the Price Game Farm – the birds became somewhat tenuously established, and later spread to other parts of the state. The races introduced were *A. c. kurdestanica* and/or *A. c. cypriotes*, and were provided by the Department of the Interior's Foreign Game Introduction Program.

Between 1938 and 1942, around 3,000 Chukar Partridges were successfully introduced to some 18 or 20 counties in Idaho, where the first shooting season was declared in 1949. Between the following year and 1962 a further 25,000 were released, and by 1958 the annual take had reached 69,000.

Chukars were first released successfully in Washington in 1938, and by 1942 a total of 3,962 birds from game farms in California and Colorado had been turned down at 46 sites in 20 counties. Shooting was first allowed in 1949, and by 1951 (when a further 1,879 birds were liberated in 10 eastern counties) a total of 69,080 had been shot. Between 1969 and 1978 (when stockings ceased), 59,155 were released in over 15 counties.

Between 1951 and 1955, 50,000 Chukars were turned down in Oregon with such success that shooting was permitted in 1956, when some 4,000 were harvested. By 1961, a further 26,000 had been released, and the annual take had increased dramatically to almost 38,000. By 1967, the cumulative total was estimated to be around 1,235,000.

In 1957–8, 333 wild-trapped Chukars were liberated with moderate success at Jerome in Arizona and 800 captive-reared birds at Snake Gulch in the same state. At least 8,000 were released in Colorado before 1961, when a further 1,000 were turned down in some western areas. As in Utah, the forms released were *kurdestanica* and/or *cypriotes*, provided by the Foreign Game Introduction Program.

According to King (1968), the Chukar Partridge has been successfully introduced into Florida. An unsigned and undated report (after 1973) entitled 'Southern Hospitality, or the Exotic Invasion of Florida' includes the Chukar in its 'list of Florida exotic species', and says that 'originally introduced from Europe for game farm use in Florida, this species has several small disjunct breeding populations'.

Between 1950 and 1964 (when liberations ceased), 16,621 Chukars of the races *kurdestanica* and/or *cypriotes* were released in New Mexico under the Foreign Game Introduction Program, in the following counties: Eddy, Sierra, Catron, Valencia, Bernalilli, Rio Arriba, Harding, San Juan, Chaves, Santa Fe, Grant, Taos and Hidalgo. By the end of the decade they were said to be 'moderately promising' in the San Juan–Animas–La Plata drainage area in San Juan County, and in the Pyramid Mountains of Hidalgo County.

Unsuccessful attempts to establish the Chukar Partridge in the United States (since 1950 largely by the Fish and Wildlife Service at the instigation of the International Association of Game, Fish and Conservation Commissioners) were made in almost every other state – especially in Kansas (before 1934); in Missouri, where between 1934 and 1937 around 1,900 Himalayan birds were released; in New York, where 25–150 were freed annually by R. L. Gerry on the Aknusti Estate in Delaware County from 1936 to 1939, and in Pennsylvania, where 2,021 were turned down in the same period; in Minnesota, where some 50,000 were released between 1937 and 1941, and a further 34,414 by 1953; in Alaska, where 17 from Wisconsin were released in the Matanusk Valley in 1938; in Tennessee around 1939; in Michigan before 1940; in Wisconsin, where 17,550 were released before 1953; in Nebraska, where 27,842 were freed in some 17 counties between 1964 and 1970, and especially in Alabama, Kentucky, Texas and North Dakota. From 1,368 Chukars planted in western South Dakota a small local population may have become established.

Chukar Partridges in the United States have occupied a niche left vacant by native game birds. In the Great Basin (between the Wasatch and Sierra Nevada mountains), they are found especially on grassy mesas[10] and rocky, sage-covered slopes of arid, rugged canyons in semi-desert montane regions. The introduction of the more lowland Turkish race has helped the species to broaden its range. Chukars are currently established in considerable numbers in Washington, central and eastern Montana, Oregon, northern Idaho, Wyoming, California (south to the mountains of northern Baja California, where they have also been introduced, in Mexico), Nevada, western Utah and south-central Colorado, with smaller populations established in northern Arizona, northern New Mexico, and perhaps in western South Dakota.

The agricultural damage caused by Chukar Partridges in the United States – where in winter and spring they occasionally uproot seedling crops and eat recently sprouted ones and a variety of soft- and stone-fruits – is economically negligible, and is far outweighed by their value as a game bird.

Canada[11]

The first Chukar Partridges in Canada were unsuccessfully released in Nova Scotia sometime before 1934, possibly as early as around the turn of the century. In 1940, A. D. Hitch of Whonock, British Columbia, freed some of the Himalayan race at Alkali Lake and Dog Creek; although this attempt also failed, a further 17 birds were turned down by the Game Commission on the Harper Ranch near Kamloops in 1950, supplemented in the following year by 52 more in the same area, 80 near Savona and 139 near Oliver. Annual introductions in the Okanagan, middle Fraser and Thompson valleys continued to be made until 1955 with stock from Hitch's game farm at Whonock as follows: 1952 (668); 1953 (498); 1954 (500); 1955 (509). By the final year, the birds were sufficiently well established, having increased and spread along rocky stretches of the Thompson and Fraser rivers, for a shooting season to be declared. Although the population suffered a severe setback in the hard winter of 1964–5, scattered coveys are still established in farmland and rugged grassland with low precipitation and little winter snowfall in the Thompson, Fraser, Okanagan and Similakmeen valleys, and around Shuswap Lake between Kamloops and Revelstoke. Chukars have also been sighted near Victoria, although there are no recorded liberations on Vancouver Island. The total British Columbia breeding population is between 5,000 and 7,500 pairs.

A few Chukars that are believed to survive in the valley of Milk River south of Medicine Hat in south-east Alberta may be derived from an undocumented introduction or be migrants from across the US border in western Montana. Chukars have also been introduced, apparently without success, in the prairie country of Saskatchewan.

West Indies (Bahamas)

According to Brudenell-Bruce (1975), Chukar Partridges have been introduced near Rock Sound on the island of Eleuthera in the Bahamas. Bond (1979), however, makes no mention of this introduction.

AUSTRALASIA

Australia[12]

Chukar Partridges of the Himalayan form were unsuccessfully liberated in Victoria in 1864 (23), 1865 (13), 1872 (8) and possibly in 1874. Recently, however, Chukars have been reported to be well established in hilly country with rocky outcrops near Gulgong between the Hunter and Liverpool ranges in east-central New South Wales.

New Zealand[13]

The first Chukar Partridges in New Zealand (14 out of an original consignment of 24 from India – presumably of the Himalayan race – ordered by the Otago Acclimatization Society) arrived in Dunedin on 23 July 1920, where the survivors died shortly after landing. Five years later the Waimarino Society received 62 (out of a shipment of 80), but for some unexplained reason permission to release them was refused and they eventually died in captivity.

In May 1926, two consignments of Chukars of the Himalayan subspecies from Calcutta arrived in New Zealand; in July or early August, 15 pairs were successfully released by Colonel R. B. Neill on behalf of the Ashburton Society at his Barossa sheep station near Mount Somers in the Lake Heron district; and on 2 October, the 24 survivors from a consignment of 28 (which the Otago Society had obtained from the secretary of the Alipore Zoo, near Calcutta, and which had arrived in Dunedin on the SS *Sussex*) were turned down on Isaac Taylor's property in the Hunter Valley at the head of Lake Hawea.

In January 1927, the eight survivors of a shipment of 40 arrived on board the SS *Waihora* in Dunedin, where they died before they could be released. In the following May, 2 (out of a consignment of 50 from Calcutta) were landed in Dunedin, from where 24 were transported to Green Bush in the Hunter Valley, where they were released on 1 September. In September 1928, the Otago Society received 30 (from a shipment of 46 from Calcutta), 13 of which were successfully freed on 2 November in the Floor Creek and 14 in the Northburn Creek on D. Middleton's Lowburn property. In 1929, the Auckland Acclimatization Society imported 28 Chukars from India, 24 of which were unsuccessfully liberated in the Taringamotu Valley near Taumarunui – the first introduction of the species to North Island. Between 1931 and 1933, the same society made five more attempts to establish Chukars in North Island, followed by two more in 1949 and 1950 (when 8 and 13 birds, respectively, the former from Alexandra in central Otago and the latter from that area and from Marlborough) were released at Manaia on the Coromandel Peninsula, but these also failed.

In 1932 and 1933, respectively, 66 out of a shipment of 700 birds of the nominate form from India and 83 from a consignment of 122 of the race *A. c. koroviakovi* from Horbol, Baluchistan (in what is now West Pakistan) arrived in Auckland where the survivors had all died by 1935.

The last documented successful importation of Chukars to New Zealand was made in 1932, when 192 from an original shipment of 200 birds (*A. c. koroviakovi*) from Quetta in Baluchistan were received by the North Canterbury Society; 35 pairs were released at Lake Lyndon, 10 at Lake Taylor, 17 at Hawkeswood, 5 each at Purau and Teddington and 2 at Waipara, the balance of 44 birds being retained for breeding. In 1933, 176 offspring of this breeding stock were released – 25 at Rutherford's in the Mendip Hills, 50 in the Glens of Tekoa on the Upper Hurunui River, 25 on the St Helens Estate, Hanmer, 25 at McAlpines, Craigieburn, 25 at Eskhead on the south branch of the Hurunui River and 26 in the Clarence River Reserve in Marlborough. Thus in 1932–3, a total of 324[14] Chukars were turned down in Marlborough and North Canterbury, and are the ancestors of the birds in those districts today. The North Canterbury Society released the balance of its stock (an unspecified number) in 1936 – half on Mount Herbert on the Banks Peninsula and half near Castle Hill.

Between 1920 and 1933, some 579 Chukars

arrived alive in New Zealand out of a total of 1,338 that left the Indian subcontinent – a low survival rate of only 43 per cent. By 1950, 24 years after the first successful plantings, Chukars were established in South Island from the Wairau River in Marlborough south to Kingston in central Otago, and Wodzicki (1965) described them as locally common in South Island. They are now widely distributed in high country (up to 1,800 m) from Nelson to Otago, mainly east of the Southern Alps, where they favour dry rocky areas with an annual rainfall of less than 65 cm – a habitat and climate very similar to those of their natural range. They do not occur in North Island, but in some parts of South Island they reach a density of one bird per 6 ha.

OCEANIA

Hawaiian Islands[15]

Chukar Partridges of the Himalayan race were introduced on several occasions between 1923 and 1936 to Lanai, Oahu, Molokai and Kahoolawe where they became established. Schwartz & Schwartz (1949) found about 60 on the eastern end of Molokai, near to where they were released, and some 50 on Lanai, which were less static. They considered that although the hot, dry, sparsely vegetated and rocky terrain occupied by the Chukars probably contained enough seed-producing plants to supply the birds' food requirements, the lack of water – especially on Lanai – might be a limiting factor. Seventeen pairs of the Indian race released at Pohakuloa at the base of Mauna Kea on Hawaii in 1949 by the State Division of Fish and Game are said to have multiplied to some 30,000 by 1955; since then the population has declined, but the birds are still common on Big Island. In 1959, Chukars of the Turkish and/or Kurdistan races were transplanted from the US mainland to Kauai, where some still remain. In 1961 76 birds from California were unsuccessfully turned down on the Puu Waawaa Ranch on Hawaii, and in the same year 304 were freed on Maui, Lanai, Molokai, Oahu and Kanai. Chukars are currently well established on Hawaii, Lanai and Maui, locally on Kauai, Molokai and Kahoolawe, and in small numbers (on the leeward slopes of the Waianae Mountains) on Oahu.

In 1950, 250 pairs of Chukar Partridges of the nominate form imported from the United States were unsuccessfully released in France[16] – outside the Alpine range of the native Northern Rock Partridge (*A. graeca saxatilis*) – as follows: 50 pairs in the mouth of the Rhone and in Hérault, 55 pairs in Lot, 25 pairs in the Lower Pyrénées and 10 pairs in the Upper Garonne. The remaining 60 pairs were retained for later introductions at Chambord and Pierrefitte-sur-Sauldre, and for trials at Rabat in Morocco.

In about 1930, F. R. S. Balfour unsuccessfully tried to introduce Chukar Partridges to his estate at Dawyck in Peebleshire, Scotland. At about the same time, Chukars were being kept full-winged at Woburn Abbey by the Duke of Bedford and at nearby Whipsnade Zoo, and also by Alfred Ezra at Foxwarren Park in Surrey. Although the birds bred freely they never became established in the wild.[17]

Chukar Partridges are also said to have been introduced unsuccessfully to the western slopes of the Chilean Andes.

As mentioned above, the closely related **Rock Partridge** (*Alectoris graeca*)[18] was reared on several game farms in Britain in the early 1970s, but so far as is known none ever became established in the wild.

In 1953, 50 Rock Partridges were released in the Crimea in the southern Ukraine, USSR[19] followed by a further 130 in 1961; the birds soon became established along the coast between Alushta and Feodosya and between Bakhchisaray and Sevastopol', where by 1975 the population had increased to around 8,000.

Between 1960 and 1963, some 180 birds were planted near Beregovo, Vinogradov and Svaliany in the Carpathian Mountains in Transcarpathia (the western Ukraine), where by 1970 they had multiplied to about 1,000, but are since believed to have declined.

Thomson (1922) refers to unsuccessful attempts to establish the 'Hungarian Partridge (*Caccabis saxatilis*?)' in New Zealand. Although the 'Hungarian Partridge' is a synonym for the Grey Partridge, Thomson, since he deals elsewhere with the latter species, was presumably referring to the northern race of the Rock Partridge. In 1897, the Wellington, Canterbury, Nelson and some other acclimatization societies jointly imported 20 of these birds, six of which were released by the Hawera Society in the following year. In 1912, the Auckland Society acquired 39, of which 20 soon died; 15 of the survivors were freed at Kaipara and 4 in the Waikato. None of these birds were seen again.

Unsuccessful attempts have also been made to establish Rock Partridges in parts of Germany.[20]

According to Bohl & Bump (1970: 18), between 1965 and 1968 3,126 'Greek chukar partridges (*Alectoris graeca* sp.) obtained from the Government of Greece in exchange for mountain quail' were released, apparently unsuccessfully, in Los Angeles, Madera, Yuba and Santa Clara counties of California, USA. It seems probable that these were Rock rather than Chukar Patridges.

NOTES

1 Some authors still confusingly refer to the 'Chukar Partridge (*Alectoris graeca*)', although the Chukar (*A. chukar*) and the Rock Partridge (*A. graeca*) have been recognized as valid species since 1962 (G. E. Watson, 'Sympatry in Palaearctic *Alectoris* partridges', *Evolution* 16: 11–19), and are geographically distinct except in the Balkans. The latter ranges from the Alps south into Italy and south-west through Yugoslavia into Greece and western Bulgaria. It has only two subspecies – the Northern Rock Partridge (*A. g. saxatilis*) from the Alps and northern Italy, and the Southern Rock Partridge (*A. g. graeca*) from the rest of its range. See also: Bohl, 1971d.

2 Lever 1977a; Sharrock 1976. See also: R. Hudson, *British Birds* 65: 404–5 (1972).

3 See note 1.

4 Liversidge n.d.; Long 1981; Maclean 1985; Siegfried 1971; J. M. Winterbottom 1966, 1978 (and personal communication, 1981).

5 Maclean 1985; Winterbottom 1966.

6 Benson 1950; Haydock 1954; Long 1981; Melliss 1870.

7 Alcorn & Richardson 1951; Aldrich 1947; Allen 1954; American Ornithologists' Union 1983; Bade 1937a,b; Banks 1981; Barnett 1953; Bizeau 1963; Blair 1942; Bohl 1957a, 1968, 1971d; Bohl & Bump 1970; Bossenmaier 1957; Bump 1941, 1968a,b; Bump & Bohl 1964; Burris 1965; Chambers 1965–6; Christensen 1954; Cottam 1956; Cottam, Nelson & Saylor 1940; Dorian 1965; Gabrielson & Lincoln 1959; Gerstell 1940–1; Gottschalk 1967; Greenhalgh & Nielson 1953; Harper, Harry & Bailer 1958; Imhof 1962; Johnsgard 1973; Laycock 1970; Long 1981; Moreland 1950; Nagel 1939, 1945; Nevada Fish and Game Commission 1963; Phillips 1928; Popov & Low 1953; Ruhl 1941; Salter 1953; True 1937; Wells 1953; Western States Exotic Game Bird Committee 1961; Whitney 1971.

8 Peterson & Chalif 1973.

9 It is unclear from Popov's & Low's (1953) account whether they are referring to a dealer in an eastern State or in India.

10 Flat-topped rocky hills with steeply sloping sides.

11 American Ornithologists' Union 1957, 1985; Carl & Guiguet 1972; Davies, Peter & Munro 1980; Godfrey 1966; Guiguet 1961; Long 1981; Peterson 1961; Ritchey & Spalding 1970 (in Carl & Guiguet 1972); and W. T. Munro, personal communication, 1985.

12 Anon. 1977; Long 1981; Ryan 1906.

13 Falla, Sibson & Turbott 1979; Kinsky 1970; Long 1981; Marples & Gurr 1953; Oliver 1955; Williams 1950, 1951.

14 The sixty-ninth annual report of the North Canterbury Acclimatization Society states that 160 Chukars were released in 1932 and 93 in 1933 – a total of only 253.

15 American Ornithologists' Union 1983; Berger 1981; Bump 1968a,b; Caum 1933; Hawaiian Audubon Society 1975; Lewin 1971; Locey 1937; Long 1981; Munro 1960; Pyle 1977; Schwartz & Schwartz 1949; Walker 1967b, 1981; Zeillemaker & Scott 1976.

16 Etchécopar 1955; Long 1981.

17 Fitter 1959 (per G. M. Vevers).

18 See note 1.

19 Dourdine 1975; Long 1981; Yanushevich 1966.

20 Niethammer 1963.

Red-legged Partridge
(*Alectoris rufa*)

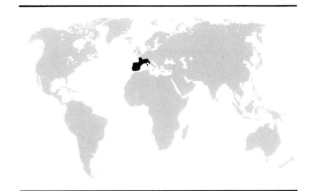

NATURAL DISTRIBUTION

From the Iberian Peninsula north to southern France and lowland Switzerland, eastwards to Corsica and northern and central Italy. Formerly inhabited other parts of Switzerland and Italy, northern France, western Germany and the Channel Islands.

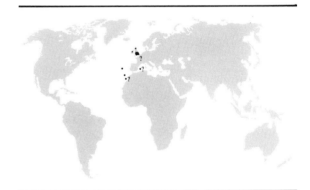

NATURALIZED DISTRIBUTION

Europe: British Isles, ?Germany, ?France, ?Switzerland, ?Belgium, ?the Netherlands, ?Balearic Islands, Azores, Madeira and Porto Santo; Africa: ?Canary Islands.

EUROPE

British Isles[1]

Before they finally became established a number of unsuccessful attempts were made to introduce Red-legged or French Partridges to Britain; these included importations by Charles II to Windsor in Berkshire and Richmond in Surrey in 1673, by the Earl of Rutland to Leicestershire in 1682, and by the Duke of Leeds to Wimbledon in Surrey between 1712 and 1729.

According to Harting (1883), 'In or about the year 1770 several noble sportsmen appear to have combined in importing eggs from France [presumably *A. r. rufa*] and hatching them out under hens on their estates in different parts of the country'. These 'noble sportsmen' included the Earl of Hertford and Lord Rendlesham (both east Suffolk), the Earl of Rochford (Essex) and the Duke of Northumberland. The birds in Suffolk quickly became established, probably because the dry sandy or calcareous soil and a continental climate with the lowest rainfall in Britain provides the optimum habitat and climatic conditions, and the intensively cultivated farmland, heathland and downland of East Anglia is still the species' principal British stronghold.

Other early introductions were made by Sir Harry Fetherstonhaugh in 1776 (unsuccessfully in Sussex), by the Marquess of Hastings in 1820 (unsuccessfully in Worcestershire), and successfully by Lord Alvanley and Lord De Ros in Suffolk in 1823, from where by 1839 Red-legs had crossed into Norfolk and Lincolnshire. Because of the large number of releases after 1830, which continue to this day, it is impossible to say whether the earliest record for each county (when the species was not necessarily established) is the result of natural dispersal or fresh introduction: these include Berkshire in 1809 (though the birds did not become established in the county for many years thereafter); Hertfordshire (1815, established by 1835); Somerset (*c.* 1816); Cambridgeshire (1821, established well before 1883); Kent (1823); Oxfordshire, Yorkshire and Buckinghamshire (all 1835); Sussex (1841); Devon (1844); Huntingdonshire (before 1850, when the birds were said to be well established); Nottinghamshire (1851, from western Lincolnshire); Isles of Scilly (mid-1850s); Wiltshire (1861); Middlesex (1865); Westmorland (the 1860s); Gloucestershire (1881); and Cornwall, Hampshire, the Isle of Wight, Northamptonshire and Rutland (all by 1883). By the late 1930s, Red-legged Partridges were abundant in parts of Yorkshire, the Midlands and in the south-west as far as Somerset, and occurred in smaller numbers in north Wales. In the early 1970s a number of birds were turned down in the Isle of Man.

William B. Baikie and Robert Heddle in *Historia Naturalis Orcadensis* (Edinburgh, 1848) state that Red-legged Partridges were introduced to Orkney, Scotland, by the Earl of Orkney in 1840. At the time of Harting's survey in 1883, the only record on the Scottish mainland was of a single bird shot in Aberdeenshire in 1867. In the early 1970s, a number of more or less successful releases were made north of the Border – in Sutherland, Banffshire, Angus and Kirkcudbrightshire in 1970; in Perthshire, Fife, Dumfriesshire and Stirlingshire in 1973; and in Caithness in 1974. Since then Red-legs have been recorded in Roxburghshire, Kincardineshire, Galloway and Aberdeenshire; in the last-named county they are believed to have hybridized with introduced Chukar Partridges (*Alectoris chukar*) (q.v.) from the Himalayas.

Although Fitter (1959) traced at least a dozen releases in seven Welsh counties, Red-legged Partridges have always been, at best, only very locally distributed in the principality, where they currently occur in parts of Glamorganshire, Brecknockshire, Radnorshire, Montgomeryshire and Denbighshire close to the English border.

According to an apparently contemporary Irish manuscript (per R. J. Knowles), 'In 1767 Thomas Knox of Dungannon, Co. Tyrone, who had a house in France, brought over from there post haste, 72 eggs of the French Partridge. These were set under broody bantam hens on his game preserve. 30 chicks were hatched, of which 18 survived. These were established in Dungannon Park. In 1770 Knox offered his birds for game stocking at 3 guineas a brace.' Since Red-legged Partridges appear on an Irish game list dated 1810, they may have been established in the wild at that time. Two other introductions were made in Ireland – in County Galway – shortly before 1844, but neither appear to have been successful.

The National Association of Regional Game Councils has recently been making further attempts to establish Red-legged Partridges in Ireland. In February 1979 and August 1980, a dozen pairs and 20 birds were obtained respectively from game farms in Worcestershire, England, and in Northern Ireland. The progeny of this nucleus breeding stock, which was kept at New Inn, County Tipperary, and whose eggs were incubated at the Lavally Game Farm in Clonmel, were distributed in summer to gun-clubs as breeding stock and for release as follows:

1979, 282 birds to counties Tipperary, Dublin and Carlow, of which 174 were released and 44 retained as breeding stock; 1980, 601 birds to Tipperary, Dublin, Carlow, Wexford, Louth, Waterford and Limerick, of which 536 were released; more were distributed from Balbriggan Gun Club, County Dublin; 1981, 732 birds to Tipperary, Wexford, Wicklow, Kilkenny, Monaghan, Waterford and Carlow, of which 303 were released and 86 were retained for breeding by the Lavally Game Farm; many more are believed to have been reared and turned down by gun-clubs in 1981.

In spite of considerable dispersal from the release sites in autumn, some birds remained and bred successfully in several counties, including Tipperary, Louth, Dublin and Wexford. In eastern counties – especially in Louth and Dublin, which have the lowest precipitation in Ireland, and where the nucleus of a viable breeding population may be established – Red-legs appeared to be thriving sufficiently for a short open season (1–14 November) to be declared in 1984.

In general, the Red-legged Partridge has not proved as popular a game bird in Britain as the native Grey Partridge (*Perdix perdix*) – mainly because of its tendency to run rather than to fly and when in flight to scatter instead of to pack – and in East Anglia it causes some damage to fields of seedling sugarbeet. In England, the Red-leg population reached a peak around 1930, and then suffered a decline in both numbers and distribution. Since about 1959 this trend has been reversed, and there have been some notable increases – especially in Suffolk and north-west Norfolk – and by the early 1970s the species had reverted to its 1930s distribution. Today, Red-legged Partridges range from southern, south-eastern and eastern England (especially from Lincolnshire south to Hertfordshire and eastwards into East Anglia), northwards to Shropshire and northern Yorkshire; lesser numbers occur west to the Welsh Marches, Somerset, Dorset and eastern Devon, avoiding the heavier and wetter soils of the Weald. Outside this area, localized populations are established in Lancashire and parts of Scotland. Howells (1963) found that the species' distribution coincided with an annual rainfall of less than 90 cm, and that lower precipitation in the breeding season was important for chick survival. The total British population

is estimated to amount to between 100,000 and 200,000 pairs.

Germany; France; Switzerland; Belgium; the Netherlands; Balearic Islands

According to Peters (1934), Witherby et al. (1941: Vol. 5) and Niethammer (1963), the occasional occurrence of Red-legged Partridges (*A. r. rufa*) in northern France, western Germany, Belgium and the Netherlands, and their presence in the Balearic Islands in the Mediterranean, may be the result of introductions, reintroductions and translocations by man. The same may be true of birds in northern and northwestern Spain, northern Portugal and Switzerland. Some authors, however, for example Voous (1960), seem to consider that Red-legs are native to the Balearics.

Until at least the sixteenth century, Red-legged Partridges occurred naturally in the middle Rhine region of western Germany[2] near Bacharach west of Frankfurt. They were at one time resident in much of Switzerland,[3] where they were successfully reintroduced in the eighteenth century and unsuccessfully in this century. In about 1970, 1,530 Red-legs (640 adults and 890 young) were experimentally released in the Hautes-Alpes *département* of southeastern France.[4]

Azores[5]

In the eighteenth century, Red-legged Partridges were introduced to the Azores, where in 1865 they were said to be abundant on Santa Maria, were rare on São Miguel and Terceira, and were not mentioned on any of the other islands. In 1903, Ogilvie-Grant (1905) found them to be numerous on Pico, rare on São Miguel and local on Terceira. They were recorded again on Pico in 1922, and 10 years later were said to be fairly common on Pico and Santa Maria, but had apparently died out on Terceira and São Miguel. Marler & Boatman (1951) saw a small number on Pico, and Bannerman & Bannerman (1966) say that they were rare on Santa Maria and that a few survived on Pico. So far as is known, they have never occurred on Corvo, Flores, Graciosa, São Jorge or Faial.

Madeira and Porto Santo[6]

Red-legged Partridges were probably first introduced to Madeira and Porto Santo from northern Portugal by Prince Henry the Navigator who colonized the islands in 1424–5. In 1851 and 1871, they were said to be scarce on Madeira and were not mentioned at all on Porto Santo, where an attempted introduction around 1850 apparently failed. A second attempt in 1925, when two pairs from the Algarve in southern Portugal (presumably *A. r. intercedens*) were freed on Porto Santo to replace the defunct alien Barbary Partridge (*A. barbara*), was more successful, and the species may still occur on the island. On several occasions prior to 1965 Red-legs of the form *A. r. hispanica* (from northwestern Spain and northern Portugal) were reared and successfully released on Madeira.

AFRICA

Canary Islands[7]

Both Peters (1934) and Bannerman (1963) believe that Red-legged Partridges of the race *A. r. australis* occur on Gran Canaria as the result of human intervention; they appear first to be mentioned there in 1866, but are still only locally distributed.

According to Phillips (1928: 33):

To Lafayette belongs the honour of sending to America the first specimen of a 'French Partridge', which was received by George Washington at Mount Vernon in November 1786. W. O. Blaisdell imported a few pairs into Illinois in 1896, but most of these died. He raised some young from the only pair that he had left and turned them out near Macomb . . . Between 1901 and 1911 only 54 of these birds were imported.

There are records of the release (those of *A. r. rufa* being made under the Department of the Interior's Foreign Game Introduction Program) of at least 32,849 Red-legged Partridges in seven states[8] between 1952 and 1978, as follows: 576 of the form *hispanica* in Colorado (1952–61); 332 *hispanica* in Texas (1955–7) and 3,463 *rufa* (1961–5); 3,216 *rufa* in Oklahoma (1961–8); 6,748 *rufa* in California (1961–70) and 6,237 *hispanica* (1966–74); 11,727 *rufa* in Washington (1961–75);

220 *rufa* in Virginia (1968); and 330 *rufa* in Idaho between 1972 and 1978. At some of the release sites in Texas, Colorado, California, Idaho and especially eastern Washington the birds survived and bred for up to 2 or 3 years before eventually disappearing.

In Australia,[9] Red-legged (and other) Partridges were unsuccessfully turned down at Colac in Victoria in the 1860s or 1870s, and nine birds are believed to have been freed without success in 1873 in bush country near Melbourne.

In New Zealand,[10] the Canterbury Acclimatization Society imported a pair of Red-legged Partridges in 1867, and the Wellington Society's annual report for 1897 stated that in the Rangitikei district the species was increasing. Two years later, 18 birds imported from London were unsuccessfully released on Stewart Island. There must have been other unrecorded introductions, as in 1915 L. F. Ayson told Thomson (1922: 123) that 'they took a hold well in several parts of the Dominion until rabbit-poisoning commenced, and vermin were introduced to destroy rabbits'. More recently, Druett (1983) says that the Auckland Acclimatization Society is currently involved in a programme of breeding and liberating the Red-legged Partridge as a potential upland game bird.

Blake (1975) asserts that Red-legged Partridges have been introduced to Hawaii, but if so the attempt was unsuccessful.

NOTES

1 Fitter 1959; Harting 1883; Howells 1963; Leicester, Earl of 1921; Lever 1977a; Sharrock 1976; Voous 1960; Witherby et al. Vol. 5, 1941.
2 Grzimek 1968.
3 Lueps 1975.
4 Birkan 1971.
5 Bannerman & Bannerman 1966; Long 1981; Marler & Boatman 1951; Ogilvie-Grant 1905 (in Bannerman & Bannerman 1966); Voous 1960.
6 Bannerman 1965; Bernström 1951 and Sarmento 1936 (both in Bannerman 1965); Long 1981; Peters 1934.
7 Bannerman 1963; Long 1981; Peters 1934.
8 Banks 1981; Bohl & Bump 1970; Bump 1957, 1970g; Bump & Bohl 1964; Chambers 1965, 1966; Gottschalk 1967; Harper 1963; Jackson 1957, 1964; Jackson, De Arment & Bell 1957; Kleinschnitz 1957; Long 1981; Phillips 1928; Western States Exotic Game Bird Committee 1961.
9 Long 1981; McCance 1962.
10 Long 1981; Thomson 1922; Williams 1950.

Barbary Partridge
(Alectoris barbara)

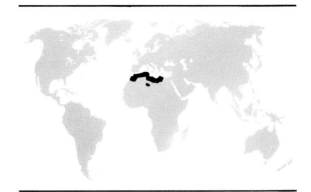

NATURAL DISTRIBUTION

North Africa, from Libya through Tunisia and Algeria to Morocco.

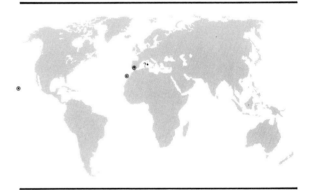

NATURALIZED DISTRIBUTION

Europe: ?Gibraltar, ?Spain, ?Sardinia; Africa: Canary Islands; Oceania: ?Hawaiian Islands.

EUROPE

Gibraltar[1]

Although for many years it has been assumed[2] that the Barbary Partridge was introduced to Gibraltar from North Africa by man, the evidence for this is only circumstantial. In 1749, the Governor's Order Book of General Humphrey Bland authorized the importation of 'game from Barbary' for sporting purposes, and although partridges are not specifically mentioned the possibility must be that some were included to reinforce an already existing stock or as an entirely new game species.

The first mention of Barbary Partridges on the Rock was made by the garrison chaplain, the Revd John White (brother of the celebrated Gilbert, author of *The Natural History of Selborne*) in 1771,[3] when he reported them to be widely distributed. Today, they are confined to the relatively undisturbed open rocky slopes and low scrub of the Upper Rock, Windmill Hill and above Catalan Bay. The population numbers about 30 pairs, and coveys of up to 25 birds form outside the breeding season.

Partridges of the genus *Alectoris* are known to have occurred in Gibraltar during the Würm glaciation in the late Pleistocene (*c.* 50,000 years ago), but further palaeontological research is required before the species can be conclusively identified.

Spain[4]

Barbary Partridges observed in Spain on rocky, arid hillsides with scrub or open woodland in the vicinity of Gibraltar may have migrated from the Rock or have been turned down on their estates by local landowners. Those reported from similar country in Cadiz[5] almost certainly originate in separate introductions.

Sardinia

Although no corroboratory evidence exists, it seems likely that the presence of Barbary Partridges on the island of Sardinia is the result of human intervention.

AFRICA

Canary Islands[6]

Barbary Partridges of the race *A. b. koenigi* have been introduced to Gran Canaria, Hierro, La Palma, Fuerteventura, Lanzarote, Tenerife, Gomera, and some other smaller islands in the Canaries. They were established on Fuerteventura from 1913 until at least 1957, and in 1963 were still present on Tenerife (where they were presumably introduced before 1892 – see next page) and Gomera but had become rare or extinct on Lanzarote.

OCEANIA

Hawaiian Islands[7]

In 1958, Barbary Partridges (*A. b. barbara* of northern Morocco, Algeria and Tunisia) from a game farm in California were unsuccessfully introduced to the Hawaiian Islands. A year later, 104 from the same source were turned down on the Puu Anahulu Ridge of the Puu Waawaa Ranch on Hawaii, and at the same time the Division of Fish and Game freed others in the Kohala Mountains at the extreme northern end of Hawaii. In 1960–1, further releases were made of 321 birds from California, of which 176 were planted on Maui, 68 on Molokai and 77 on Lanai. The current status of Barbary Partridges in Hawaii is uncertain, but a few may survive on the Puu Waawaa Ranch and in the Kohala Mountains.

According to Bannerman (1965: 35), 'Sarmento in *Vertebrados da Madeira* gives 1900 as the year when Barbary Partridges were introduced into Porto Santo [in the Madeira archipelago],[8] remarking that it was very common in Argélia. The bird continued to flourish, [but] for some unexplained reason apparently died out in Porto Santo [by about 1920] and has been replaced [in about 1925] by the Red-legged Partridge [*Alectoris rufa*, q.v.] imported from southern Portugal.' Bernström (1951), who says that only one pair of Barbary Partridges, from Mazagan in Morocco, was imported in 1900, erroneously implies that the species was still resident and breeding on Porto Santo.

Harting (1883, quoted by Fitter 1959: 160), has suggested that Barbary Partridge eggs were often accidentally (and perhaps also fraudulently) imported to England in the eighteenth and nineteenth centuries with those of Red-legs from France, which may account for the few individuals that have been shot. This, of course, presupposes that *A. barbara* had already been imported by game-breeders to France. Barbary Partridge eggs or chicks were, however, deliberately but unsuccessfully imported by the Maharajah Duleep Singh (and possibly by other landowners) to Suffolk, where before they died out they are believed to have interbred with the resident Red-legs.

In about 1929–30, Barbary Partridges were unsuccessfully released at La Capellière in the Île de la Camargue[9] and subsequently on the Îles d'Hyères[10] – both in southern France.

Barbary Partridges have also been unsuccessfully introduced to Italy, Sicily, Malta and Corsica.[11]

Between 1958 and 1968, 5,719 Barbary Partridges from Morocco (presumably *barbara*, but perhaps *spatzi/theresae* from the south) were unsuccessfully released in at least nine counties in California by the Department of Fish and Game under the Department of the Interior's Foreign Game Introduction Program.[12] In the early 1960s, 150 birds freed in Nevada failed to become established, and putative releases in other states were similarly unsuccessful.

In 1868, the Auckland Acclimatization Society imported a pair of Barbary Partridges to New Zealand,[13] and in 1892 the Wellington Society acquired 19 of the form *A. b. koenigi* from Tenerife, 13 of which were liberated on Kapiti Island, where 2 years later a covey including seven young was reported. There are no Barbary Partridges in New Zealand today.

In 1873, some Barbary Partridges were released in Victoria, Australia,[14] where they almost immediately disappeared.

NOTES

1 Cortes, Finlayson et al. 1980.
2 For example, by Lord Lilford, 'Notes on the ornithology of Spain', *Ibis* 2: 173–87, 384 (1866); V. L. Seoane *Revision del Catalago de las Aves de Andalucia* (La Coruna, 1870); F. Bernis, 'Prontuario de la avifauna Espanola, *Ardeola* 1: 11–85 (1954); C. Vaurie, *The Birds of the Palaearctic Fauna (Non-passeriformes)* (H. F. & G. Witherby: London, 1965).
3 R. Holt-White, *The Life and Letters of Gilbert White of Selborne*, 2 vols (John Murray: London, 1901).
4 Cortes, Finlayson et al. 1980; M. Gonzalez-Diez, 'Captura de *Alectoris barbara* en Cadiz', *Ardeola* 4: 193 (1958); E. Trigo de Yarto, 'Notas sobre capturas de aves raras o interesantes', *Ardeola* 6: 367–9 (1960); I. C. T. Nisbet, 'Observacion de perdiz moruna en la provincia de Cadiz', *Ardeola* 6: 382 (1960); J. Brosse & S. Jacquemard-Brosse, 'Notes sur l'avifaune de Gibraltar au moment des migrations d'automne', *Oiseau et la Revue Française d'Ornithologie* 32: 228–39 (1962).
5 Vaurie 1965.
6 Bannerman 1963; Voous 1960.
7 Berger 1972; Bohl 1973; Bohl & Bump 1970; Bump & Bohl 1964; Hawaiian Audubon Society 1975; Lewin 1971; Long 1981; Pyle 1977; Walker 1967b, 1981; Western States Exotic Game Bird Committee 1961.
8 Bannerman 1965; Bernström 1951; Voous 1960; and G. E. Maul, personal communication, 1985.
9 Clegg 1941.
10 Niethammer 1963.
11 Niethammer 1963.
12 Bohl & Bump 1970; Bump & Bohl 1964; Chambers 1965, 1966; Harper 1963; Long 1981; Nevada Fish and Game Commission 1963.
13 Thomson 1922; Williams 1950.
14 Long 1981; Ryan 1906.

Black Francolin
(*Francolinus francolinus*)

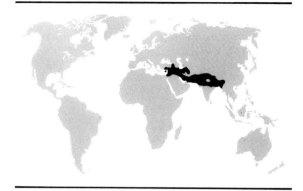

NATURAL DISTRIBUTION

From the eastern Mediterranean (southern Turkey, Cyprus, Syria, Lebanon, Israel and Jordan) to western Burma, north into Nepal and the USSR to the east of the Caspian Sea, and south to the Persian Gulf, the Arabian Sea, north-central India and the Bay of Bengal.

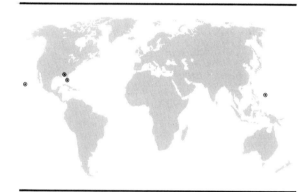

NATURALIZED DISTRIBUTION

North America: USA; Oceania: Marianas (Guam), Hawaiian Islands.

NORTH AMERICA

USA[1]

In 1891, a shipment of nine Black Francolins (formerly known as Black Partridges) from India (presumably *F. f. asiae*) was sent to W. O. Blaisdell of Illinois, but only three survived the journey and they died shortly after landing. Three more were imported in 1911 and a further three in the following year, but what became of them is unknown. Although a few Black Francolins from Baluchistan in West Pakistan – presumably of the race *henrici* or *asiae* – were released (with some Grey Francolins, *Francolinus pondicerianus*) in several southwestern states in 1955, it was not until 1957 that serious efforts began to be made to establish the species in the United States. Between that year and 1974, 11,191 were unsuccessfully released in 10 (mainly southwestern) states as follows: 1,091 in Arkansas between 1960 and 1967; 1,317 in New Mexico (1960–6); 414 in South Carolina (1960–5); 1,896 in Tennessee (1963–8); 2,066 in Virginia (1957–67); 1,632 in California (1970–4); 403 in Alabama (1960–4); 311 in Kentucky (1960–4); 562 in Nevada (1959–64); and 1,499 in Oklahoma (1960–4). Although in some places – especially in the York Prison area of South Carolina, where 30 were released in 1960 and where they bred successfully for about 3 years – the birds managed to survive and initially to increase, their overwintering success rate was generally poor and they eventually all disappeared.

In Florida, where they succeeded in establishing two viable populations, 231 Black Francolins was released (see Table 3). The birds released near Immockalee (6 cocks and 12 hens from Avon Park) were planted in sugar-cane fields surrounded by pine palmettos, fletwoods and sloughs on a ranch near the northern edge of the Big Cypress Swamp, while those turned down in Fisheating Creek (6 cocks and 10 hens from the same source) were freed in sugar-cane

fields in the southeastern portion of the Refuge, some 11 km from Moore Haven. The birds fared best at Belle Glade and at Avon Park, where they were planted in 16.1 ha of Elderberry (*Sambucus simpsonii*) scrub, surrounded by a variety of agricultural crops. Twenty years later, Genung & Lewis (1982) estimated that Black Francolins were established on some 1,036 km^2 of the Everglades agricultural area in Palm Beach County, where they appear to have bred in every year since their release. The first shooting season in Florida was declared in 1964.

Between 1961 and 1973, no less than 3,527 Black Francolins were turned down in Calcasieu and Cameron parishes in southwestern Louisiana, resulting in the establishment of at least one stable population within an 8-km radius of Gum Cove where 311 were released in 1961–2 and where, as in Florida, shooting was permitted in 1964.

The race introduced to the United States was predominantly or entirely *F. f. asiae* from northern India and West Pakistan; some of the birds released were imported direct from the subcontinent and others were bred in captivity in the USA. The majority were turned down under the aegis of the Department of the Interior's Foreign Game Introduction Program.

OCEANIA

Marianas (Guam)[2]

In 1961, under the US Department of the Interior's Foreign Game Introduction Program, 200 wild-caught Black Francolins were released at the Naval Magazine on Guam. Although few sightings from this planting were reported in 1962, by the following year birds were frequently seen up to 16 km from their point of release, and breeding was recorded. In 1967, when the first shooting season was opened on Guam, the birds were apparently continuing to expand their range, and they are now said to be widely distributed in the south of the island.

Hawaiian Islands[3]

According to Walker (1967b), Black Francolins from India were first unsuccessfully introduced

Table 3   Releases of Black Francolins (*Francolinus francolinus*) in Florida, USA, 1960–8

Date	Number	Area
1960 or 1961	40	Avon Park Refuge Game Management Area
1961 or 1962	70	Avon Park Refuge Game Management Area, Highlands County
1962	35 pairs	University of Florida's Agricultural Research and Education Center, Belle Glade, Palm Beach County
1964	18	Immockalee
1964	16	Fisheating Creek Refuge, Glades County
1967	9	Eglin
1968	8	Eglin

Source: Bohl & Bump 1970

to Hawaii in 1958. Between 1959 and 1961, 116 birds from game farms in California and Texas were released at two sites on the Puu Waawaa Ranch on the island. In 1960, a total of 257 were freed on Hawaii, Maui, Kauai and Molokai, 44 of which were planted by the Division of Fish and Game at Kipuka Ainahou, followed in 1962 by a further 491 on three islands, of which 66 were freed by the Division at Kahua in the Kohala Mountains in northern Hawaii. These introductions of wild-caught birds were part of the US Department of the Interior's Foreign Game Introduction Program.

On several islands the birds rapidly dispersed from their points of release and became established on dry agricultural land, in irrigation ditches and in pastures around sugar-cane plantations. The first shooting season was declared in 1967. According to Zeillemaker & Scott (1976), Black Francolins are local and rare on Kauai, and local and uncommon on Molokai, Maui and Hawaii. Berger (1981) describes them as 'well established' on all four islands. Walker (1981) lists them as occurring also on Lanai.

In 1894, 30 Black Francolins were shipped from Karachi in India (now West Pakistan) to Newmore in Ross-shire, Scotland;[4] of the 27 that arrived alive half-a-dozen were released and never seen again, while the remainder survived for only a year or two in captivity.

Black Francolins are said to have been unsuccessfully introduced to the island of Sicily and to Tuscany in northern Italy, and to Valencia in eastern Spain.[5]

In both the Soviet Union[6] and India,[7] Black Francolins have been transplanted on the periphery of their natural range. In the former, a number of unsuccessful translocations were attempted in several regions in the 1880s. According to Yanushevich (1966), in 1932 the forester Tur'evtsev released two cocks and three hens in the Agrichay River valley of the Nukha District of Transcaucasia (a little north of the species' natural range), where by 1947 their progeny were well established throughout the valleys of the Agrichay and Alazani rivers. In India, Black Francolins have been successfully transplanted in the Kutch region of Bombay, slightly south of their natural distribution.

NOTES

1 American Ornithologists' Union 1983; Banks 1981; Bohl & Bump 1970; Bump 1968a,b, 1970b; Bump & Bohl 1964; Bump & Bump 1964; Chambers 1965, 1966; Christensen 1963; Genung & Lewis 1982; Gottschalk 1967; Hart 1967; Long 1981; Murray 1963; Nelson 1972; Nevada Fish and Game Commission 1963; Palermo 1968; Phillips 1928; Robinson 1969; Sims 1963, 1964, 1965; Western States Exotic Game Bird Committee 1961; and L. E. Williams, personal communication, 1980.
2 Bohl 1968; Bump 1968a,b, 1970b; Bump & Bohl 1964; Bump & Bump 1964; Long 1981.
3 American Ornithologists' Union 1983; Berger 1981; Bohl 1968; Bump 1968a,b, 1970b; Bump & Bohl 1964; Bump & Bump 1964; Hawaiian Audubon Society 1975; Lewin 1971; Long 1981; Pyle 1977; Walker 1967b, 1981; Zeillemaker & Scott 1976.
4 Fitter 1959.
5 Niethammer 1963.
6 Long 1981; Yanushevich 1966.
7 Ali 1954 (in Ripley 1961); Long 1981.

Chinese Francolin

(*Francolinus pintadeanus*)

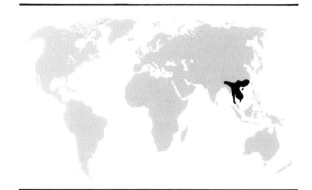

NATURAL DISTRIBUTION

From northeastern India through Indo-China to southern and southeastern China.

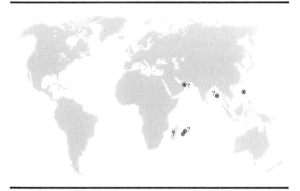

NATURALIZED DISTRIBUTION

Asia: ?Oman, ?Andaman Islands; Africa: ?Madagascar, Mascarenes (?Mauritius, Réunion); Australasia: Philippines.

ASIA

Oman[1]

According to Meinertzhagen (1954), Chinese Francolins that were resident around Muscat in Oman may have been introduced from southern Iran, where they are a popular cagebird. However, neither Jennings (1981) nor Gallagher & Woodcock (1980) mention this species as occurring in the Sultanate, and in any case francolins that escaped in Iran might easily appear in Oman as natural immigrants via the Strait of Hormuz, a flight of barely 75 km.

Andaman Islands

According to Bump & Bump (1964:3), 'F. pinta-deanus, the Chinese Francolin, has taken in . . . the Andamans'.

AFRICA

Madagascar

According to Peters (1934), Chinese Francolins of the nominate form from southeastern China have been successfully introduced to Madagascar.

Mauritius and Réunion[2]

In about 1750, Chinese Francolins (and Grey Francolins, *Francolinus pondicerianus*) from India were introduced for sporting purposes by the French from Indo-China and/or southeastern China to Mauritius and Réunion, where on the former Meinertzhagen (1912) found them mainly on the uplands near Vacoas and Curepipe. By the 1950s they were confined on Mauritius to culti-vated land near watercourses in the higher regions of the central plateau. According to Staub (1976), they still occurred in small numbers on Réunion but had died out on Mauritius.

AUSTRALASIA

Philippines[3]

Chinese Francolins of the nominate form have been successfully introduced from southeastern China to the island of Luzon in the Philippines, where they are established in the vicinity of Manila.

In 1961, Chinese Francolins were introduced from the US mainland to the island of Hawaii,[4] where in the following year 10 birds imported from Hong Kong were released on the Puu Waawaa Ranch. None were ever seen again.

In the Seychelles,[5] where Chinese (and Grey) Francolins are reared in captivity for the table, some occasionally escape but so far as is known have never become established in the wild.

NOTES

1 Long 1981; Meinertzhagen 1954.
2 Barré & Barau 1982; Long 1981; Meinertzhagen 1912; Peters 1934; Rountree, Guérin et al. 1952; Staub 1973, 1976; Watson, Zusi & Storer 1963.
3 Du Pont 1971; Long 1981; Peters 1934.
4 Berger 1972; Lewin 1971; Long 1981; Walker 1967b.
5 Long 1981; Penny 1974.

Grey Francolin
(*Francolinus pondicerianus*)

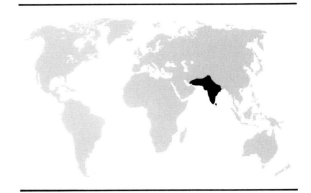

NATURAL DISTRIBUTION
Southeastern Iran, southern Afghanistan, West Pakistan, India (as far north as the Himalayas) and northern Sri Lanka.

NATURALIZED DISTRIBUTION
Asia: ?Oman, ?United Arab Emirates, Andaman Islands; Africa: Mascarenes (Mauritius, Réunion, Rodrigues), Seychelles, Amirante Islands; Oceania: Hawaiian Islands, Marianas (?Guam).

ASIA

Oman; United Arab Emirates

The Makran Grey Francolin (*F. p. mecranensis*) is a common breeding resident in northern Oman, where it is distributed along Al Batinah into the United Arab Emirates, in some wadis in foothills to the north and south of the Hajar Mountains, inland to Al Awaifi, and southwards to the west and east of the Wahiba Sands. Although Gallagher & Woodcock (1980) say that the species was 'probably introduced originally' to Oman, it is possible that it arrived as a natural immigrant via the Strait of Hormuz (a flight of barely 75 km) from southern Iran, where the indigenous form is *mecranensis*.

Andaman Islands[1]

Grey Francolins of the nominate southern Indian race were released at Port Blair on South Andaman in about 1890. Although Abdulali (1967) heard their distinctive *chakeeta chakeeta chakeeta* call at Haddo near Port Blair in 1963–4, he could find no trace of them shortly thereafter. Ali & Ripley (1969), however, say that the birds are still established in the neighbourhood of Port Blair, especially on grassy deforested hilltops.

AFRICA

Mauritius and Réunion[2]

Grey Francolins of the nominate form were introduced by the French from India to Mauritius and Réunion as game birds in about 1750, together with Chinese Francolins (*Francolinus pintadeanus*) (q.v.) from Indo-China and/or southern China. On Mauritius, they soon became abundant and widespread, but by the early 1950s, probably as the result of predation by the introduced Small Indian Mongoose (*Herpestes auropunctatus*) (Lever 1985b), were confined to the rocky coastal plains. By the end of the decade they were precariously established in some of the drier regions, where a few remain today. On Réunion, where some damage to maize seedlings has been reported, the population has declined considerably in recent years due to cyclonic winds and prolonged droughts, but a small number survive on the plain of St Paul.

Rodrigues[3]

Grey Francolins of the nominate subspecies were introduced as game birds to Rodrigues – where they are still common and are shot for sport and food – probably by the French in the eighteenth century or by the British after 1810.

Seychelles[4]

Introduced for sporting purposes to the Seychelles (probably by the French after 1768 or by the British after 1810), where they were at one time abundant and widespread on several islands, Grey Francolins are now confined in the wild to Desroches, though they are reared in captivity for the table (as are Chinese Francolins) on several private estates.

Amirante Islands[5]

Grey Francolins of the nominate subspecies have been introduced to, and still occur on, the Amirante Islands.

OCEANIA

Hawaiian Islands[6]

According to Walker (1967b), the first Grey Francolins (formerly known as Grey Partridges) were imported to Hawaii from India in 1958. In 1959, 1961 and 1965–6, a total of 214 Californian gamefarm-reared birds were released on the Puu Waawaa Ranch on Hawaii, where they quickly became established and spread. In 1961, the Division of Fish and Game turned down 100 at Pohakuloa on the slopes of Mauna Kea, followed in March 1962 by a further 166 at Ahumoa on Mauna Kea, and later by 87 more at Keomuku between Mauna Kea and Puu Hualalai, where they rapidly increased.

Between 1960 and 1962, 1,710 Grey Francolins (of the northern Indian form *F. p. interpositus*) were released in the Hawaiian Islands (see Table 4). Following these liberations, Bump & Bohl (1964: 12–13) reported that the francolins were 'Reproducing on Hawaii and Maui. Seem to be established on Lanai. Most birds have remained in release area but one pair noted 14 miles [22 km] from point of release. Birds found commonly in three different vegetative zones.' By 1963, 'Adults and broods reported from all islands except Kauai. Lanai continues most encouraging, and expansion of range continues. Generally, this species continues to be the most promising import to the State.' The first shooting season was declared in the following year, and

Table 4 Releases of Grey Francolins (*Francolinus pondicerianus*) in the Hawaiian Islands, 1960–2

Date	Number	Island
1960	66	Maui
1960	66	Lanai
1961	115	Hawaii
1961	127	Maui
1961	100	Lanai
1961	100	Kauai
1962	203	Hawaii
1962	239	Maui
1962	259	Lanai
1962	160	Molokai
1962	275	Kauai

Source: Bohl & Bump 1970

today Grey Francolins, which were released under the US Department of the Interior's Foreign Game Introduction Program, are well established in dry open pastureland with some shrub cover on Hawaii, Maui, Molokai, Lanai, and possibly Kauai.

Marianas (Guam)[7]

In 1961, under the US Foreign Game Introduction Program, 188 Grey Francolins of the northern Indian form were released in the Northwest Field area, in Anderson and on Department of Agriculture land near Mangilao on Guam where, according to Bump & Bohl (1964) and Bump (1968a,b), there was some reproduction and they became 'indifferently' established, with little expansion of range.

Between 1954 and 1956, 277 Grey Francolins (*F. p. interpositus*), presented to the United States[8] by the Government of Pakistan, were liberated in southwestern Arizona. From 1959 to 1964, 6,037 birds of the northern Indian form (mostly wild-trapped) were released in three southwestern States by Conservation Commissions under the auspices of the Department of the Interior's Foreign Game Introduction Program, as follows: 2,258 to Nevada (1959–62); 2,574 to New Mexico (1960–4); and 1,205 to Oklahoma (1960–2). Between 1959 and 1968, 5,171 were freed in Texas and, from 1967 to 1975, 2,938 were turned down in California. Although breeding was initially reported near most of the release sites, the birds only became tenuously established in Imperial Valley, California, and 'indifferently' in Texas.

Grey Francolins (presumably of the nominate southern Indian form) may have been imported to Diego Garcia[9] in the Chagos Archipelago from Mauritius or Réunion before 1907. They were still present in 1960 and 1964 but had apparently died out by 1971.

NOTES

1 Abdulali 1964, 1967; Ali & Ripley 1969 (vol. 2:31); Butler 1899; Long 1981; Peters 1934; Ripley 1961.
2 Barré & Barau 1982; Benedict 1957; Gill 1967; Long 1981; Loustau-Lalanne 1962; Meinertzhagen 1912; Rountree, Guérin et al. 1952; Staub 1973, 1976; Watson, Zusi & Storer 1963.
3 Gill 1967; Long 1981; Peters 1934.
4 Long 1981; Penny 1974.
5 Long 1981; Penny 1974; Peters 1934.
6 American Ornithologists' Union 1983; Berger 1981; Bohl & Bump 1970; Bump 1970c; Bump & Bohl 1964; Bump & Bump 1964; Lewin 1971; Long 1981; Pyle 1977; Walker 1967b, 1981; Western States Exotic Game Bird Committee 1961; Zeillemaker & Scott 1976.
7 Bump 1968a, b, 1970c; Bump & Bohl 1964; Bump & Bump 1964; Long 1981.
8 Banks 1981; Bohl 1968; Bohl & Bump 1970; Bump 1968a, b, 1970c; Bump & Bohl 1964; Bump & Bump 1964; Chambers 1965, 1966; Christensen 1963b; Gottschalk 1967; Long 1981; Nevada Fish and Game Commission 1963; Webb 1957; Western States Exotic Game Bird Committee 1961.
9 Bourne 1971; Gadow & Gardiner 1907; Hutson 1975; Long 1981; Loustau-Lalanne 1962.

Erckel's Francolin
(*Francolinus erckelii*)

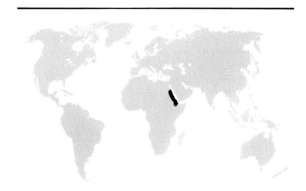

NATURAL DISTRIBUTION
Ethiopia and northeastern Sudan.

NATURALIZED DISTRIBUTION
Oceania: Hawaiian Islands.

OCEANIA

Hawaiian Islands[1]

In November 1957, 38 birds of the nominate (Ethiopian) form of Erckel's Francolin were imported by the Division of Fish and Game from game farms on the US mainland to the island of Hawaii, where they were released on the northwest coast at Puako. In 1958 and 1959, 34 and 117 more, respectively, were turned down near Pohakuloa between Mauna Kea and Mauna Loa, and in 1959–60, a further 107 from game farms in Oklahoma and California were freed on the Puu Waawaa Ranch. In 1960, 353 more were released on seven islands, as follows: on Hawaii (47), Oahu (61), Kauai (37), Molokai (94), Lanai

(40), and 74 were divided between Mauai and Kahoolawe. A year later, a further 51 were liberated on Molokai, and in 1962, 150 more were planted on three (unspecified) islands. None of these releases were made under the US Department of the Interior's Foreign Game Introduction Program. Thus, between 1957 and 1962, 850 Erckel's Francolins were released on seven Hawaiian islands, where they are at present established locally in small numbers in exotic forest and scrub (Guava (*Psidium guajava*), Java Plum (*Eugenia cumini*) and *Eucalyptus*) and mixed native Ohia (*Metrosideros collina*)/Lehua and Koa (*Acacia koa*) woodland on Hawaii, Maui, Molokai, Lanai, Oahu and Kauai.

In 1959–60, 244 Erckel's Francolins were unsuccessfully released by private individuals at three different sites in California, and in 1969, 64 were planted in Washington State where they 'dispersed and disappeared'.[2]

In 1963, the **Red-billed Francolin** (*Francolinus adspersus*),[3] a native of southern Angola, Namibia and Botswana, was introduced to the island of Hawaii; in the following year, four were released on the Puu Waawaa Ranch, where they still occurred in 1965 but are believed to have disappeared soon afterwards. Although most authorities, by omitting to mention them, seem to agree that they are no longer present, the Hawaiian Audubon Society (1975) claimed that they were probably well established and breeding.

In the nineteenth century, the **Bare-throated** or **Red-throated Francolin** (*Francolinus afer*),[4] which occurs naturally in much of southern, southwestern and eastern Africa, was introduced to the island of Ascension in the South Atlantic, where a very small population is established on Green Mountain.

NOTES

1 American Ornithologists' Union 1983; Bump & Bohl 1964; Hawaiian Audubon Society 1975; Lewin 1971; Long 1981; Pyle 1977; Walker 1967, 1981; Western States Exotic Game Bird Committee 1961; Zeillemaker & Scott 1976.
2 Banks 1981; Bump & Bohl 1964; Long 1981; Western States Exotic Game Bird Committee 1961.
3 Berger 1972; Hawaiian Audubon Society 1975; Lewin 1971; Long 1981; Walker 1967b.
4 Long 1981; Stonehouse 1962.

Grey Partridge
(Perdix perdix)

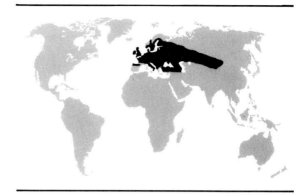

NATURAL DISTRIBUTION

The western Palaearctic, from the British Isles eastwards to the Altai Mountains and Dzungaria in western Mongolia and China, north to Finland and Archangel in the USSR, and south to northern Iberia, the Mediterranean, Turkey and northwestern Iran.

Note: Distribution is discontinuous.

NATURALIZED DISTRIBUTION

North America: USA, Canada.

NORTH AMERICA

USA[1]

The earliest attempt to establish Grey Partridges in the United States (where they are usually known as 'Hungarian Partridges') has been credited to Richard Bache, son-in-law of Benjamin Franklin, who in about 1790 turned some down on his plantation on the Delaware River near the present town of Beverly, New Jersey. In 1877, small numbers were released in California, and before the turn of the century other introductions were made in New Jersey (notably by Pierre Lorillard at Jobstown in 1879), on the south shore of Cape Cod, Massachusetts, by Charles B. Cory in the early 1880s, and in Virginia. Between 1899 and 1912, some 6,000 pairs were unsuccessfully released in Illinois, and during the same period $62,208 was expended in a vain attempt to establish the species in Indiana.

Serious efforts to naturalize Grey Partridges in the United States began in 1900, when 97 were released in Marion County west of Salem in the Willamette Valley, Oregon. In 1913, 218 were freed in several localities in that state, and according to Phillips (1928) in the following year 1,522 were planted in 23 counties. As Schneider (1957) records that in 1913–14 a total of 1,314 birds arrived in two shipments direct from Europe, 426 of those released in that 2-year period were presumably home-reared. Between 1925 and 1932, 401 Grey Partridges were turned down in Oregon, and by 1934 the birds were established successfully over much of the east of the state, but only locally elsewhere. In 1956–7, 1,255 (the progeny of 850 eggs flown in from Denmark in 1949–50) were released in the Willamette Valley in western Oregon, where they were joined by a further 691 between 1969 and 1976.

In 1904 George Gould turned some Grey Partridges down at High Point in North Carolina, where for a time they fared well on a diet of cowpeas planted especially for them.

In 1906, about 250 pairs were released and became established in Spokane County, Washington. Two years later a further 25 pairs were turned down in Columbia County, followed by 200 birds in Lincoln County in 1909, 100 pairs in Columbia County and around 1,000 birds in Chelan County in 1913, and a total of 4,794 between that year and 1915, when the species was established throughout the state – especially east of the Cascade Mountains – and the first shooting season was declared. Between 1969 and 1975, 1,349 were turned down in 13 counties in an 'attempt to upgrade wild stock; not much change reported'. (Banks 1981: 11).

In 1907, Grey Partridges were turned down in Nebraska where they soon disappeared. A further planting in Dawes and Frontier counties in 1969 of 67 imported from Alberta, Canada, was simi-

larly unsuccessful. Large-scale plantings by Gustave Pabst in Waukesha County in southeastern Wisconsin in the following year were more successful, the birds spreading northwards at a rate of 6.5 km a year, and the first shooting season was opened in 1926. Between 1908 and 1913, over 1,400 partridges were released in Connecticut, where they had all disappeared by around 1920.

After their initial introduction in 1877, 35 Grey Partridges were released in California in 1908, followed by a further 2,000 in 1909, which were planted in some 90 localities in five or six counties. Despite repeated introductions in the last half century the species is currently only established in northeastern California near the Oregon border.

In 1909, John C. Phillips unsuccessfully released two lots of Grey Partridges at Wenham, Massachusetts, where they survived for a couple of years but did not breed. Between 1909 and 1940, 17,420 were imported from Europe and liberated in Iowa, where according to Westerskov (1949) the population increased in the north-central part of the state until about 1937–40, but subsequently declined. It was augmented by the release of a further 1,455 birds in Cass and Shelby counties between 1969 and 1972, and Banks (1981: 10) reported that there were 'isolated reports of birds in four southwestern counties by 1978'.

The Grey Partridge was first introduced to Michigan in about 1910, when some 200 birds were released near Saginaw Bay. Eight years later, 100 more were turned down, followed in 1927 by some young birds that H. Jewett allowed to escape, and between 1926 and 1930 by around 600 that were planted near Oxford. According to Dale (1943), between 1910 and 1930 about 1,000 partridges were released over much of southern Michigan. The State Department of Conservation began propagation in 1925 with 105 birds imported from Europe, and in the 1930s a total of 3,297 were liberated in some 40 localities. Although most of the birds disappeared, a small number became established along the southern border.

On 11 November 1911, 120 Grey Partridges imported from Canada were released by the Department of Fish and Game in seven counties in Utah, as follows: in Cache County (4), in Salt Lake (34) , Sevier (8), Tooele (4), Utah (34),

Washington (8) and Weber (28). In April 1917, six pairs were turned down near Santa Clara in Washington County, and in 1920 a further three pairs were freed near St George by Sherman Hardy, followed 2 years later by seven more birds, which were liberated by Vance Tingey several kilometres west of Brigham City in Box Elder County. None of these introductions met with lasting success, though some of the birds planted in 1911 persisted until at least 1915.

In 1923, the Department of Fish and Game turned down 200 pairs of Grey Partridges in Sevier, Uintah, Utah, Salt Lake and Tooele counties, where previous introductions had shown promise. Five years later only two small coveys, in Utah and Uintah, were known to survive, and by 1940 even these had disappeared.

In 1925, a party of 12–15 partridges was released by a private landowner near Santa Clara. In 1938 and again in the following year, the state game warden, Elwin Cloward, freed 50 partridges imported from Alberta, Canada, just east of Richfield. During the next decade, well over a hundred more partridges were released in Utah, but nowhere with permanent success. Grey Partridges in that state today are migrants via the Snake River drainage from Nevada (where they were released at least by 1923) and southern Idaho, where between 1939 and 1942 a total of 924 were transplanted from the north to the southeastern border, from where they spread into Utah by 1948. It is curious that despite repeated attempts to introduce Grey Partridges to Utah their presence there today is entirely due to natural immigration from neighbouring states.

Grey Partridges were first turned down in Montana before 1915 by private landowners, but they did not become widespread until after the Fish and Game Commission acquired 6,000 from Europe between 1922 and 1926, which they released throughout the State – especially in Sheridan County – where the species is today an important game bird.

Attempts to establish Grey Partridges near Batavia in Genesee County, New York State, in 1916, and in northeastern New York in 1921 and 1925, were unsuccessful, and from a total of 27,750 planted between 1927 and 1932 only a handful survived in a few scattered localities. Along the St Lawrence River in the north near the Canadian border they slowly increased until a shooting season was opened in 1952.

In about 1922, Grey Partridges spread south from Saskatchewan and Manitoba in Canada (see below) into North Dakota, where in 1924 an additional 7,500 were released, and by 1942 the state's population was estimated to number between 8 and 10 million.

Between 1926 and 1930, at least 9,806 Grey Partridges, mainly imported from Austria, Hungary and Czechoslovakia, were released in 43 counties of Pennsylvania, where they were subsequently reported to have become established in 31. Further liberations were made in 1931–2 (1,572), 1933 (1,194), 1935 (200), and between 1935 and 1939 when 21,287 wild-caught birds were imported from Europe; the overall cost since 1926 amounted to $131,000. The first shooting season was declared in 1939, but well before 1960 the entire population had died out.

Between 1970 and 1972, 2,056 partridges were released in six counties in Colorado, where they all subsequently disappeared.

From 1950 to 1960, around 6,000 birds were released in western States, including 1,700 in the latter year that had been hatched from eggs imported from Denmark.

Before 1908, less than 8,000 Grey Partridges were imported to the United States; in 1908–9 nearly 40,000 were brought in, and by the mid-1950s – when they had been established for some 20 years in northern and central states – introductions had occurred in at least 42 states. Grey Partridges are now established locally from southern British Columbia, central Alberta, central Saskatchewan, southern Manitoba, southern Ontario, southwestern Quebec, New Brunswick, Prince Edward Island and Nova Scotia south to northeastern California, northern Nevada, western and northern Utah, northern Wyoming, northern South Dakota, northwestern Iowa, northern Illinois, central Indiana, southern Michigan, northwestern Ohio, and northern Vermont and New York. Despite repeated and large-scale introductions in the east coast states, Grey Partridges have never managed to become established east of the Allegheny Mountains. As in Canada, the birds do best in fertile agricultural areas where small grains (and associated insects) provide an abundance of food and cover. Much of the Grey Partridge's success in the northern United States may have been due to the spread of birds from across the Canadian border. Most of the stock released in the former country appears to have been imported from England, Hungary and Czechoslovakia – though, in later years, the birds were acquired mainly from Czechoslovakia, since the race there (*lucida*) is said to be more hardy than the nominate *perdix*.

Canada[2]

Grey Partridges were first introduced to Canada in March 1904 when 57 from England were released by the government on the coast near Vancouver, British Columbia. These were augmented by a further 32 in 1905, followed by 167 more in 1907–8 (which were freed on Vancouver and Sidney islands) and 277 in 1909 (on Vancouver, Saltspring and South Pender Island).

In 1908–9, about 500 partridges were turned down on Vancouver Island by J. L. and A. E. Todd, who also planted 72 on James Island and 32 on Sidney Island in the Haro Strait between Vancouver Island and the State of Washington. In 1909, A. R. Spalding and H. R. Pooley landed 10 on South Pender Island in the same locality, and others were planted on Saltspring Island. According to Phillips (1928), Grey Partridges first arrived in the interior of British Columbia from Washington 'on their own feet' in 1915 (when shooting was first permitted), soon spreading up the Okanagan and Arrow Lakes valleys, where they found the drier climate more to their liking than that of the wetter coastal region.

Phillips records that by the mid-1920s, Grey Partridges were abundant in British Columbia on Lulu Island south of the city of Vancouver, and were increasing and extending their range in the interior, especially in the Okanagan Valley to as far north as Kamloops. Thirty years later Carl & Guiguet (1972) reported that small coveys still occurred on Lulu Island and the neighbouring Sea Island as well as around Ladner and elsewhere, but that in general the birds had not thrived on the lower mainland. On Vancouver Island, a few small coveys remained near Victoria and on the Saanich Peninsula, but here again no sizeable populations had become established. The birds released on James, Sidney and South Pender islands had apparently all disappeared. In much of the interior, the birds declined sharply in 1927,

having been extremely abundant in the Okanagan Valley in 1925–6, but in the mid-1950s were managing to maintain a low population. They were said still to be abundant in the southern interior around Osoyoos – probably as the result of continued infiltration from Washington.

In 1966, a few birds were sighted at Boston Bar between Kamloops and Vancouver, and in 1968–9 small numbers were observed on both sides of the Fraser Canyon from Lillooet north to Empire Valley and possibly to Gang Ranch. Today, between 2,000 and 5,000 remain in farmland and dry grasslands of the lower Okanagan Valley, in the Thompson and Fraser valleys, and on southeastern Vancouver Island. Numbers tend to fluctuate because of the marginal habitat.

In 1908, Fred J. Green imported wild-trapped Grey Partridges at a cost of $3,000 from the plains of Hungary to Alberta on behalf of local sportsmen, where he released 70 pairs in grain fields at High River some 24 km south of Calgary. These were augmented in the following year by a further 95 pairs from the same source, and, according to Phillips (1928), by 42 more pairs in succeeding years. The last planting (of 10 pairs) near Calgary was made in 1914. Phillips records that some time later the Northern Alberta Game and Fish Protection League imported a further 230 birds from Europe; these they released near Edmonton, which had apparently already been reached by dispersants from Calgary some 280 km to the south – a lengthy journey for a largely sedentary species.

From Calgary, Grey Partridges had spread by 1921 over the provincial border to Piapot in neighbouring Saskatchewan, from where in the next year they crossed the US border into North Dakota, and within a further 4 to 5 years had ranged north to township 60, and east to Weyburn and Halbrite. From Edmonton, they spread in the same period 100 km north-west as far as the Pembina River. In Alberta, the first shooting season was opened around 1920.

In 1924, 40 pairs of partridges imported from Czechoslovakia were sent from New York to the Game Protection League of Manitoba, who released them near Warren; these were supplemented in the following year by a further 26 pairs from Alberta, and at the same time 17 pairs were liberated at Neepawa. By the late 1960s Grey Partridges were established in the prairie provinces in southern and central Alberta, south-central Saskatchewan and southern Manitoba where, as in the United States, they flourished on the fertile arable land where small grains (and their associated insects) provide both food and cover.

In eastern Canada, Grey Partridges occur in southern, central and especially eastern Ontario locally north to North Bay on Lake Nipissing, in extreme southwestern Quebec, in southern New Brunswick, on Prince Edward Island and locally in Nova Scotia. There appear to be no records of any introductions in these districts, and the birds in southern Ontario may have come from across the United States border in Michigan. Those in southwestern Quebec are probably the descendants of immigrants from across the St Lawrence in northern New York State, while those in New Brunswick and Nova Scotia and on Prince Edward Island may well be derived from dispersants from Quebec.

In North America, Grey Partridges show a marked preference for arable farmland, where they feed mainly on grain, seeds and insects. Westerskov (1949) considered them to be morphologically well adapted to survive cold winters with limited snowfalls, as occur in the Canadian prairies, but heavy falls of snow cause high mortality. He suggested that the main factor in their successful winter survival in North America has been their acceptance of foods other than the green vegetable matter – principally grass and leaves of clovers (*Trifolium* spp.) and buttercups (*Ranunculus* spp.) – that they consume in Europe.

Thomson (1922) has recorded the liberation of well over 539 Grey Partridges in New Zealand[3] between 1864 and 1911. In the former year, the Nelson Acclimatization Society imported eight, but what became of them is unknown. Between 1867 and 1875, the Auckland Society liberated 86 birds at Mangere, Howick and Lake Takapuna. Details of releases by other societies are as follows: Canterbury (1867–79), 94 at Christchurch and on the Hororata; Otago (1869–1911), 248 south and west of Dunedin, on the Taieri Plain and at Otanomomo and Milton; Southland (1899–1900), 48 on Stewart Island; Wellington (1889–1900), 55 at Upper Hutt, Masterton and Rangitumau; and Taranaki (1894), 8 in the Koru

district. A considerable number were also released by private landowners. Although in some places the birds survived for a year or two, and may even have reared young successfully, they eventually disappeared due, Thomson believed, to phosphorus poison intended for Rabbits (*Oryctolagus cuniculus*), and predation by Marsh Harriers (*Circus aeruginosus gouldi*), Wekas (*Gallirallus australis*), Stoats (*Mustela erminea*) and Weasels (*M. nivalis*), and competition for food from insectivorous birds.

In 1959, two shipments of 150 Grey Partridge eggs arrived in New Zealand from Denmark, from which 115 young were successfully reared to maturity at a game farm at Bulls on the Rangitikei River in North Island; between 1959 and 1968, 8,409 partridges were reared at Bulls, most of which were released at over 70 different sites. From 1964 to 1970, the North Canterbury Acclimatization Society liberated 11,196, few of which were, however, observed during the open season of the latter year. Although in several places, for example on Motiti Island in the Bay of Plenty and at Te Puke, near Bell Block in Taranaki and especially at Oreti Beach in Southland, coveys persisted for several years, they have since apparently died out as the result of contamination by herbicides and insecticides, and predation by feral Cats (*Felis catus*), Stoats, and Black and Brown Rats (*Rattus rattus* and *R. norvegicus*) (Lever 1985b).

Partridges of un-named species have been unsuccessfully introduced on several occasions to Australia.[4] According to Rolls (1969), John Bisdee imported half-a-dozen from England to Tasmania in 1837, which the *Hobart Town Courier* described as 'birds to which the squirearchy are so strongly attached that they will shoot, trap and transport their fellow-creatures for the pleasure of destroying them themselves'. In 1871–2, the Royal Society of Victoria unsuccessfully released some partridges from India, Ceylon (Sri Lanka) and China on Phillip Island and at Gembrook. The annual report for 1875 of the Auckland Acclimatization Society in New Zealand (quoted by Thomson 1922: 121), in referring to the Grey Partridge in that country, says that 'The failure of all previous attempts, both in this colony and in Australia, is by no means encouraging'. Between 1897 and 1912, partridges (?species) were unsuccessfully released in Western Australia. In 1936, 110 partridges imported from England by the Tasmanian Game Protection and Acclimatization Society, in association with the Animals and Birds Protection Board, were liberated in Tasmania at Marrawah (where they survived and bred for a short time), on Garden Island in Norfolk Bay, and at Whiteford and Colebrook.

Grey Partridges of the nominate form were first introduced to Hawaii[5] in 1895 and subsequently on other occasions, but failed to become established.

According to Wood & Wetmore (1926), Grey Partridges may have been (unsuccessfully) introduced to Fiji, and Hellmayr (1932) records that they have been (again unsuccessfully) released in Chile.

The distribution of the Grey Partridge in Europe is much confused by innumerable translocations and restockings for sporting purposes.[6] According to Merikallio (1958), the species may have been successfully introduced to Finland as early as 1750; its appearance in other parts of that country between 1895 and 1898 was probably the result of both further undocumented releases and natural dispersal from the Soviet Union. In the latter country, the central subspecies *P. p. lucida* has been successfully transplanted into northwestern areas, and is generally expanding its range northwards throughout European Russia.[7]

Unsuccessful efforts have been made to establish Grey Partridges in parts of Norway other than the extreme south-east where they occur naturally.

In the British Isles, they have been successfully transplanted to the Isle of Arran (before 1750), and unsuccessfully to other islands, including Shetland (possibly as early as 1742, 'to provide sport for the gentlemen of the county, who ought to have the same pleasures as gentlemen further south'); Gigha (where they survived for a while); Mull (where they were killed by heavy rain and Peregrines, *Falco perigrinus*); Shapinsay, Orkney (1905); the Outer Hebrides; Tiree (where feral Cats and Brown Rats were blamed for their disappearance) and Raasay (before 1904) in the Inner Hebrides; Lundy (where the failure of attempts between 1870 and 1905 was attributed to lack of winter cover from predators – mainly Brown Rats); Lambay, County Dublin (where they also succumbed to Peregrines); and in the

Isles of Scilly. As Fitter (1959: 179) says, 'partridges are suited to a rich agricultural countryside and not to bleak marine islands on our western seaboard'.

According to Witherby et al. (1941: Vol. 5), in France the typical form (which occurs naturally only in the north-east) has been introduced in cultivated districts elsewhere in the country, where the native form is *P. p. armoricana*.

According to du Pont (1971), the **Daurian Partridge** (*Perdix dauuricae*), a native of east-central Asia, Mongolia and northern and central China, has been introduced from northern China (where the form is *P. d. dauuricae*) to the island of Luzon in the Philippines, where it is established in the vicinity of Manila.

Efforts have been made to introduce Daurian Partridges in the Tuvinskaya Oblast of the Soviet Union[8] on the periphery of their natural range in Mongolia, where between 1956 and 1961 some 9,500 were released. In the decade after 1955, over 28,000 Daurian (and Grey) Partridges were liberated in European Russia (especially in the Moscow area) in a vain attempt to replace the Willow Grouse (*Lagopus lagopus*). Both these introductions failed.

In 1923, an unsuccessful attempt was made to introduce Daurian Partridges (*P. d. castaneothorax*) from southern Manchuria to Japan.[9]

The **Madagascar Partridge** (*Margaroperdix madagascariensis*), which is endemic to Madagascar, was introduced to the Mascarene island of Réunion[10] on several occasions in the eighteenth century, where it initially became well established but was said to be declining by the 1940s and 1950s. It still occurs in small numbers in forest ecotone at altitudes of between 400 and 2,200 m. Other Réunion aliens prefer the drier western side of the island.

Madagascar Partridges were also introduced successfully to Mauritius,[11] possibly first by the Dutch[12] in the seventeenth century, but more probably by the French who colonized the island in the eighteenth century, and possibly also again by the British in the nineteenth century. Apparently, the birds did not prosper and were finally exterminated by a severe cyclone in April 1982.

NOTES

1 Allen 1954; American Ornithologists' Union 1957, 1983; Banks 1981; Brown 1954; Bump 1970 d,h; Cottam 1956; Cottam, Nelson & Saylor 1940; Dale 1943; Gerstell 1941; Green & Hendrichson 1938 (in Johnsgard 1973); Gottschalk 1967; Guiguet 1961; Gullion 1951; Gullion & Christensen 1957; Jewett, Taylor et al. 1953; Johnsgard 1973; Laycock 1970; Long 1981; Phillips 1928; Popov & Low 1950; Porter 1955; Schneider 1957; Trueblood & Weigand 1971; Western States Exotic Game Bird Committee 1961; Westerskov 1949; and W. T. Munro, personal communication, 1985.

2 Allen 1954; American Ornithologists' Union 1983; Carl & Guiguet 1972; Cottam 1956; Cottam, Nelson & Saylor 1940; Davies, Peter & Munro 1980; Dexter 1922; Gates 1970 (in Carl & Guiguet 1972); Godfrey 1966; Guiguet 1961; Laycock 1970; Long 1981; Munro & Cowan 1947; Phillips 1928; Smith, Hupp & Ratti 1982; Westerskov 1956a, b, 1966.

3 Falla, Sibson & Turbott 1979; Long 1981; Thomson 1922; Williams 1969; Wodzicki 1965.

4 Littler 1902; Long 1972, 1981; McCance 1962; Rolls 1969; Sharland 1958; Tarr 1950.

5 Berger 1972; Caum 1933; Long 1981; Munro 1960.

6 Voous 1960.

7 G. P. Dement'ev & N. A. Gladkov, *Birds of the Soviet Union*, Vol. 4 (English translation, USNC Clearinghouse for Federal & Technical Information: Springfield, Virginia, 1952), 256–68.

8 Long 1981; Osmolovskaya 1969; Sergeeva & Sumina 1963. See also: Dement'ev & Gladkov (see note 7), pp. 268–75; G. Bump, *The Bearded Partridges* (US Department of the Interior Fish and Wildlife Service, Bureau of Sport, Fisheries and Wildlife, FGL-7, 1970), 4 pp.

9 Kuroda 1937; Long 1981.

10 Long 1981; Meinertzhagen 1912; Rountree, Guérin et al. 1952; Staub 1976; Watson, Zusi & Storer 1963.

11 See note 10.

12 Rountree, Guérin et al. (1952) suggest a seventeenth-century introduction by the Dutch. Although the Dutch built a fort and brought in slaves and convicts they made no permanent settlement on the island, and it seems unlikely that they would have troubled to import game birds.

Common Quail
(*Coturnix coturnix*)

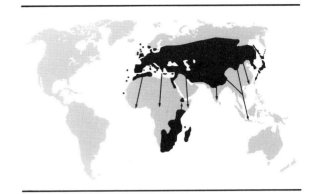

NATURAL DISTRIBUTION

A southern Palaearctic and Ethiopian species, breeding from western Europe eastwards to Japan, north to about 65° N and south to the Azores, Cape Verde, Madeira and Canary Islands, north-west Africa, Corsica, Sardinia, Sicily, Crete, Iran and northern India. Also in southern and eastern Africa, Madagascar, Mauritius (see below) and the Comoros. Northern population winters south to tropical Africa, southern Arabia, India and southern Indo-China.

NATURALIZED DISTRIBUTION

Africa: Mascarenes (?Mauritius, Réunion); Oceania: Hawaiian Islands.

AFRICA

Mauritius and Réunion[1]

According to Rountree, Guérin et al. (1952), the southern Africa and Malagasy subspecies (*africana*) of the Common Quail was introduced to

130

Mauritius in the eighteenth century, although some may have reached there as migrants from Madagascar. The latter is suggested by the omission by Witherby et al. (Vol. 5, 1941) of any mention of introductions when they refer (p. 252) to the presence on Mauritius of a 'resident form'. Since the early 1900s, Common Quail have been introduced to both Mauritius and Réunion (where they may well have been originally imported as early as the eighteenth century) as game birds and for rearing in captivity for food. Most (or all) of those few that occur in Mauritius today are probably escaped cagebirds. On Réunion, they are said to be a successful and abundant game species.

OCEANIA

Hawaiian Islands[2]

The Japanese race (*C. c. japonica*)[3] of the Common Quail was liberated on the islands of Maui and Lanai in 1921. Other islands were later populated either naturally or through unrecorded introductions. In 1944, some were imported to Kauai, and by 1946–7 they occurred on all the larger islands, but were only transitory on Oahu. Schwartz & Schwartz (1949) estimated that the total population numbered 71,880, of which 39,280 were on Hawaii, 20,350 on Maui, 5,470 on Kauai, 5,030 on Lanai and 1,750 on Molokai. The birds range from sea level to an altitude of 2,600 m in mean annual temperatures of between 20 °C and 8 °C, respectively, with an annual rainfall of from 50 to 250 cm. The most flourishing coveys are found below 2,100 m with less than 150 cm of rain a year. They favour the more fertile soil of the smoother and less dissected mountain slopes used for pasturage, and also frequent some pineapple and sugar-cane plantations and market gardens, but avoid forestland and barren lava fields. Although in parts of their natural range Japanese Quail are migratory, in Hawaii there appears to be no seasonal movement. The abandonment of the instinct to migrate is one of the prime requirements for the successful naturalization of a basically migratory species.

At present, Japanese Quail, known locally as *manukapalulu*, are established on Hawaii, Maui,

Molokai, Lanai, Kauai, and possibly on Oahu. In recent years *C. c. japonica* is believed to have interbred with domestic strains released for the training of gun-dogs.

According to Schwartz & Schwartz, in the Far East Japanese Quail, which range from southeastern Siberia and northern China to Korea and much of Japan, are reared in captivity for their flesh, eggs and their song, and the males are trained for cock-fighting. They are also highly regarded as game birds. In parts of southern China, where low winter temperatures are of short duration, the inhabitants are said to carry these birds around in their hands as a source of warmth.

Fitter (1959) traced a dozen attempts between 1862 and 1935 to transplant Common Quail within the British Isles, only one of which – at Rothiemay near Huntly in Banffshire, Scotland, in 1888 – met with even temporary success.

Common Quail were first imported to eastern North America[4] from Sicily and Messina in Italy in 1875, followed 5 years later by a further 5,100. These birds were released in some 16 separate localities in Quebec, Ontario, Massachusetts (189 near Ayer in 1875), Maine (before 1882), Connecticut (before 1879–80, and again in 1913), New Hampshire, New York (before 1881), Vermont (200 in 1877), Pennsylvania (before 1880–1), New Jersey, Virginia and Ohio. Although in several places breeding was reported in the first season, none of the birds returned north after their initial autumn migration: one was killed as far south as Georgia and another in North Carolina, while the capture of others that boarded a ship several hundred kilometres southeast of Cape Hatteras led to speculation that most of the migrating birds had drowned at sea.

Some time before 1904, 200 *C. c. japonica* were released at two sites in the state of Washington, followed in 1923 by a further 500 imported from northern China that were planted in five counties in the same state. From 1900 to 1904, large numbers of the same subspecies from China were released in California.

Between 1955 and 1962, renewed efforts were made to establish vast numbers of *japonica* in the United States – in Missouri (with birds from Japan via California) in 1955, and subsequently in Florida, Illinois (1,498 in 1957–8), Indiana, Kentucky (24,147 between 1957 and 1959), Missouri, Nebraska, New Hampshire, North Carolina, Ohio, Alabama (in the early 1960s), Oklahoma, Texas (1,000 between 1955 and 1957), and Tennessee, where several thousand were released in 1956–7. Between 1956 and 1958, 363,128 Common Quail were turned down by departments of fish and game in some 30 states, and an estimated further 100,000 or more were planted by private sportsmen. Despite this massive release programme, none of the introductions were successful, almost certainly because few if any of the birds returned north from their autumn migration.

In 1862, a dozen 'Madagascar Quail' (presumably *C. c. africana*) were imported to Victoria, Australia,[5] where their subsequent fate is unknown.

According to Thomson (1922), 'Egyptian Quail (species?)' were unsuccessfully released by the Canterbury Acclimatization Society in New Zealand[6] in 1883, and again by Colonel Boscawen before the First World War. These were presumably *C. c. coturnix*, which winters in Egypt.

Newton (1867)[7] refers to the presence in the nineteenth century of a quail (perhaps of this species) in the Seychelles, where it has since died out.

According to Holyoak (1974a), Common Quail were unsuccessfully released on Tahiti[8] in about 1920. They are also said to have been introduced without success on the western slopes of the Chilean Andes.

The **Blue Quail** (*Coturnix chinensis*) (usually known in Britain as the Chinese Painted Quail) is native from India, Malaysia, southern China and Indo-China through the Indonesian islands and Papua New Guinea to Australia, where it occurs in coastal Arnhem Land and from the Cape York Peninsula of Queensland south to Melbourne. In 1894, some birds of the form *C. c. lineata* were introduced from Manila in the Philippines to Guam[9] in the Marianas, where by the mid-1940s they were confined to grasslands in the south of the island.

In 1862, six Blue Quail are believed to have been introduced to Victoria, Australia,[10] where they are more often known as King Quail. Two

years later, 80 were released near Melbourne and 70 on Phillip Island, followed by a further 60 in 1872 and more in succeeding years. Since the birds were imported from China under the designation 'Chinese Quail', they were presumably *C. c. chinénsis*, which is not native to Australia where the indigenous forms are *australis* and *colletti*. 'Chinese Quail' are popular with aviculturists in Australia, and as many Blue Quail in the wild exhibit 'Chinese' characteristics, they may well be descended from aviary escapes (and perhaps also from the nineteenth-century introductions) that have interbred with the endemic forms. Since they are shy and secretive they are not much seen and are sometimes considered uncommon, but are in fact often numerous where there is plenty of suitable habitat in the form of tall, rank and boggy grassland surrounding the margins of marshes and swamps.

The form *C. c. chinensis* was introduced to Mauritius[11] by the French during the first half of the eighteenth century, and, although according to Meinertzhagen (1912) it was still common in the early 1900s, it was virtually exterminated shortly thereafter by the introduced Small Indian Mongoose (*Herpestes auropunctatus*) (Lever 1985b). A few may have survived into the late 1960s, but it is now believed to be extinct. The same form was also imported to Réunion[12] where, although it never became well established, it still occurred in the late 1960s but has probably since died out.

In 1910, Blue Quail from the Far East were released on the island of Kauai in the Hawaiian[13] group, where they are said to have become established. Subsequent introductions, including eight birds that were turned down on the Puu Waawaa Ranch on Hawaii in 1961, apparently failed, though Munro (1960) reported that the species was found on Oahu in the late 1950s. According to later authors, however, *C. chinensis* no longer occurs in Hawaii.

In 1897, 10 'Chinese Quail' were imported from China to New Zealand,[14] but what became of them is unknown.

In 1922 the Australian **Stubble** or **Pectoral Quail** (*Coturnix pectoralis*) was released on Maui and Lanai in the Hawaiian Islands, where it soon disappeared. According to Fisher (1951), some were also freed in the mid-1930s on Niihau, where although Peterson (1961) and Goodwin (1978) indicated that they were said still to occur, Berger (1981) stated that the last record (by Fisher) was in 1947.

Thomson (1922) says that before 1871 this species was imported from Australia to Auckland and Canterbury, New Zealand; in the 1870s, some were released in the Hokianga area of Northland, where they failed to become established.

NOTES

1 Barré & Barau 1982; Long 1981; Rountree, Guérin et al. 1952; Staub 1973, 1976; Watson, Zusi & Storer 1963; Witherby et al. Vol. 5, 1941.
2 American Ornithologists' Union 1983; Berger 1981; Blake 1975; Caum 1933; Long 1981; Munro 1960; Peterson 1961; Pyle 1977; Schwarz & Schwartz 1949; Walker 1967b, 1981; Zeillemaker & Scott 1976.
3 Some authors raise the Japanese race to full specific status.
4 Bump 1970h; Cottam & Stanford 1958; Due & Ruhr 1957; Gottschalk 1967; Imhof 1962; Jackson 1962; Kirkpatrick 1959; Labinsky 1961; Laycock 1970; Long 1981; McAtee 1944; Phillips 1928; Stanford 1957; Stephens 1962; Taylor 1923.
5 Long 1981; McCance 1962.
6 Long, 1981; Thomson, 1922.
7 See also: Gaymer, Blackman et al. 1969.
8 Holyoak 1974a; Long 1981.
9 Long 1981; Mayr 1945; Stophlet 1946; Wetmore 1919 (in Peters 1931).
10 Condon 1975; Long 1981; McCance 1962; Ryan 1906.
11 Long 1981; Meinertzhagen 1912; Peters 1934; Rutgers & Norris 1970; Staub 1976.
12 See note 11.
13 Berger 1972; Blake 1975; Lewin 1971; Long 1981; Munro 1960; Walker 1967, 1981; Zeillemaker & Scott 1976.
14 Long 1981; Thomson 1922.

Brown Quail
(*Synoicus ypsilophorus*)

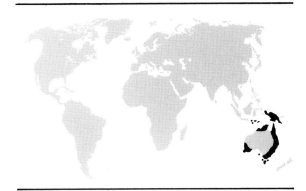

NATURAL DISTRIBUTION
Papua New Guinea, the Lesser Sunda Islands, Indonesia and southwestern, northwestern and eastern Australia, including Tasmania.

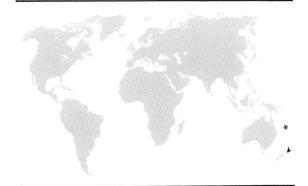

NATURALIZED DISTRIBUTION
Australasia: New Zealand; Oceania: Fiji.

AUSTRALASIA

New Zealand[1]

Two Australian races[2] of the Brown or Swamp Quail – *S. y. ypsilophorus* from southeastern Australia and Tasmania and *S. y. australis* of southwestern Australia and southern Queensland to Victoria – have been introduced to New Zealand. As the species is nomadic, however, it is possible that it may also have arrived as a natural colonist.

In 1866, the Canterbury Acclimatization Society acquired a pair of Brown Quail from Lieutenant-Colonel White, and in 1868 and 1871

they imported a further five and 'a number', respectively, from Australia. According to Williams (1969), more birds that were probably of this species were introduced in 1900 and the early 1930s, but failed to become established.

In 1867, the Auckland Society released four, followed in 1869 by some from Tasmania '(*S. diemenensis*)', and in 1871 by no fewer than 510 from the Australian mainland. According to H. Guthrie-Smith,[3] Brown Quail were introduced privately at Rissington, Hawke's Bay in the 1860s by a Colonel Whitmore. Thomson (1922), however, considered it more likely that they were sent to Hawke's Bay by the Wellington Society (see below).

By 1913, Brown Quail were common in the Bay of Plenty, and by 1916–17 were abundant in the Auckland district, where they were said to be a major factor in the spread of the alien Blackberry (*Rubus fruticosus*) and Gorse (*Ulex europaeus*).

The Otago Society obtained three Brown Quail in 1868 and nine 2 years later, which were unsuccessfully liberated on Green Island south of Dunedin.

In 1872, the Southland Society imported four, which they released at Wallacetown; 25 of their offspring were freed on the Awarua Plains in 1911, and a year later the remainder were unsuccessfully turned down at Mason Bay on the west coast of Stewart Island.

In 1875 and 1876, the Wellington Society released five and 39 Brown Quail, respectively which, according to their annual report for 1885 (quoted by Thomson 1922: 118), 'are rapidly increasing on the West Coast between Waikanae and Manawatu, and on the East Coast of the Wairarapa'. Four years later, Brown Quail in Wellington were 'spreading slowly, but owing to their keeping close to the ground are kept down very much by cats, hawks, and other vermin'. The society's report for 1890 said of the quail that 'they fall an easy prey to cats, rats, etc. They almost disappeared in some of the clearings in the Forty Mile Bush, where formerly there were large bevies'. The Waimarino Society, on the other hand, reported in 1915 that the birds were on the increase.

Thomson (1922: 118) wrote that the Brown Quail was 'almost unknown in the South Island, but is fairly common in many parts of the North Island. I have frequently been told in certain districts that "Native Quail"[4] occur, and have

always found that it is the Australian swamp quail that is referred to.' Oliver (1955) found Brown Quail to be abundant around the Bay of Plenty and further north, and on Three Kings and Mayor islands. They had already been recorded from Mokohinau and Little Barrier islands, but were apparently scarce in Taranaki, Hawke's Bay and Wellington. Wodzicki (1965: 432) said they were 'restricted but locally common, North Island and Three Kings, Poor Knights, Alderman, Mayor, Gt and Little Barrier'. Kinsky (1970) reported them to be widely distributed (especially in the north) in North Island, and present on Three Kings, Poor Knights, Great and Little Barrier, Mayor, Mercury and Alderman islands. Today, Brown Quail are widespread throughout the lowlands of North Island (apart from the south where they are scarce), favouring swamps and the perimeter of tidal marshes. In Northland, they are frequently observed 'dusting' on scrub-bordered tracks. Their presence on offshore islands is probably the result of natural dispersal from the mainland.

OCEANIA

Fiji[5]

According to Watling (1982: 74):

The Swamp quail was introduced and is found only on the dry, leeward sides of Viti Levu and Vanua Levu in Fiji. It inhabits scrub and grassland, especially in and around the extensive sugar-cane growing districts. The date of the Swamp Quail's introduction is not known but it was almost certainly after the introduction [in 1883] of the [Small Indian] mongoose [(*Herpestes auropunctatus*)], whose presence it has been able to survive. However, it is a rare bird and in Viti Levu may well have declined in recent years.

The **Jungle Bush Quail** (*Perdicula asiatica*) ranges from Kashmir and the Himalayas southwards through India to Sri Lanka. According to Meinertzhagen (1912), it was introduced to Mauritius[6] by the French before 1810 (when the island came under British rule) and according to Staub (1976) again in 1905. The birds were confined to the dry plains of the north and north-west, and are believed to have been exterminated shortly after 1912 (when they were described as scarce) by the introduced Small Indian Mongoose (Lever 1985b). A few may survive on the neighbouring mongoose-free island of Réunion,[7] to which they were presumably introduced at the same time as to Mauritius. Two forms are said to have been imported – *P. a. asiatica* from the north of the species' range and *P. a. argoondah* from the south.

NOTES

1 Condon 1975; Falla, Sibson & Turbott, 1979; Kinsky 1970; Long 1981; Oliver 1930, 1955; Thomson 1922, 1926; Williams 1969; Wodzicki 1965.

2 Some authors incorrectly describe them as two separate species – the Swamp Quail (*Synoicus ypsilophorus*) and the Brown Quail (*S. australis*). By some, the genus *Synoicus* is included in *Coturnix*.

3 *Tutira, the Story of a New Zealand Sheep Station* (Blackwood: Edinburgh and London, ·1921).

4 Presumably intended to refer to the extinct *Coturnix pectoralis novaezealandiae*, a race of the Pectoral Quail of Australia and Tasmania.

5 Blackburn 1971; Condon 1975; Long 1981; Mercer 1966; Pernetta & Watling 1978; Watling 1982.

6 Long 1981; Meinertzhagen 1912; Rountree, Guérin et al. 1952; Staub 1976.

7 Long 1981; Staub 1976.

Chinese Bamboo Partridge
(Bambusicola thoracica)

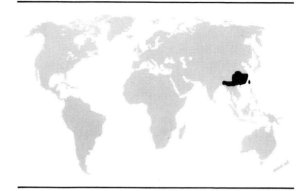

NATURAL DISTRIBUTION
Southern China from southern Shensi (Shaanxi) and Szechwan (Sichuan) to Fukien (Fujian) and Kwangsi (Guangxi); extreme northern Burma; Taiwan.

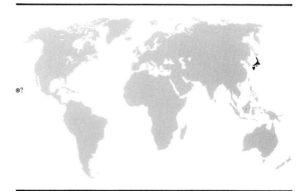

NATURALIZED DISTRIBUTION
Asia: Japan; Oceania: ?Hawaiian Islands.

ASIA

Japan[1]

According to Kuroda (1937), in 1919 Chinese Bamboo Partridges of the mainland nominate form were imported from southern China to Japan, where they were farmed in Tokyo, Hodogaya near Yokohama and elsewhere, before being released in the Kanagawa Prefecture southwest of Tokyo. More are believed to have been introduced in 1920, followed by some of the Taiwanese race *B. t. sonorivox* in 1924. Sakane

(1960) indicates that birds from the Chinese mainland were liberated in about 1930 in the Hyogo Prefecture west of Kyoto on Honshu, where they flourished and became established. A year later some from Taiwan were freed at Kobe west of Osaka on Honshu, and probably also in the Saitama Prefecture at Koshigaya on the northern outskirts of Tokyo.

Although Kaburaki (1940) reported that by the outbreak of the Second World War Chinese Bamboo Partridges were widely distributed in Japan (especially south of the Kwantô district), 20 years later Sakane could find only one small covey of 20 birds near the 1930 release site in Hyogo. Yamashina (1961), however, writing the year after Sakane, claimed that they were breeding not only on Honshu but also on the Seven Islands of Izu Shichito south of Tokyo and on the islands of Shikoku and Kyushu. In 1974, the Ornithological Society of Japan reported that *B. t. thoracica* had spread widely in Honshu, especially southwards from Kanagawa, and that *B. t. sonorivox* was still established in the vicinity of Kobe. The Ornithological Society of Japan's map (1981) shows the species to be well established and breeding widely in Kyushu, Shikoku and southern and western Honshu. The birds eat harmful invertebrates such as locusts, termites and ants, but also cause damage to agricultural crops.

OCEANIA

Hawaiian Islands[2]

In the spring of 1959, 140 wild-trapped Chinese Bamboo Partridges of the mainland form were imported from Japan and released on the island of Maui; a single brood of young was observed in the following year, and by 1961 the birds had dispersed up to 2.5 km from their point of release – their preferred cover being *Acacia decurrens*. In 1961 and 1965, a further dozen, acquired from game farms in Texas and California, were released on Hawaii. Although Lewin (1971) suggested that these latter introductions had

failed and the Hawaiian Audubon Society (1975) reported that the birds were well established only on Maui, Zeillemaker & Scott (1976) and also Walker (1981) recorded their presence on both islands. They may still be established in the Kula region of Maui, although 'none have been reported during the past 10 years'.[3]

According to Phillips (1928), the Bamboo Partridge or *dah chee* was first introduced to the United States[4] from China by A. W. Bush in 1904 or 1905, and between 1922 and 1925, 717 were unsuccessfully released in the state of Washington. In the 1960s and 1970s, 8,616 were turned down in six states, as follows: 645 in Alabama (1962–7); 120 in Arkansas (1962–3); 328 in Missouri (1961–4); 1,735 in Oregon (1962–70); 863 in Tennessee (1963–8); and 4,925 in Washington (1964–75). By 1968, releases in south-eastern states were considered to have failed and were abandoned, but others were continued without apparent success, in Washington and Oregon.

Attempts to establish Chinese Bamboo Partridges in the Rossiyskaya Soviet Federated Socialist Republic in the 1960s, in Bashkirskaya in 1961, in western Siberia, in the Ukraine, and near Moscow since 1956, have all been unsuccessful.[5]

NOTES

1 M. A. Brazil 1985, in press (and personal communication, 1985); Kaburaki 1934, 1940; Kuroda 1937; Long 1981; Ornithological Society of Japan 1974, 1981; Sakane 1960; Yamashina 1961.
2 Berger 1981; Bohl & Bump 1970; Bump 1968a,b; Bump & Bohl 1964; Hawaiian Audubon Society 1975; Lewin 1971; Long 1981; Pyle 1977★; Walker 1967b, 1981; Western States Exotic Game Bird Committee 1961; Zeillemaker & Scott 1976. (★Pyle and some other authors refer to the species as the 'Chinese Bamboo Pheasant'.)
3 A. J. Berger, personal communication 1985.
4 Banks 1981; Bohl & Bump 1970; Bump & Bohl 1964; Chambers 1965, 1966; Long 1981; Phillips 1928; Western States Exotic Game Bird Committee 1961.
5 Long 1981; Yanushevich 1966.

Kalij Pheasant
(*Lophura leucomelana*)

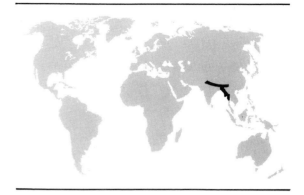

NATURAL DISTRIBUTION
From the Indus River in Pakistan in the western Himalayas eastwards through northern India, Nepal, Sikkim, Bhutan and northeastern Assam, south via the Manipur Hills to Burma and western Thailand.

NATURALIZED DISTRIBUTION
Oceania: Hawaiian Islands.

OCEANIA

Hawaiian Islands[1]

The present population of Kalij Pheasants on the island of Hawaii is descended from a single release in 1962 by L. S. Dillingham and W. Carlsmith, the leaseholders of the state-owned Puu Waawaa Ranch, of 67 birds that had been reared on game farms in Texas and Michigan. These birds were subsequently identified by Lewin & Lewin (1984) as apparently representing intergrades between the White-crested Kalij (*L. l. hamiltonii*) of the western Himalayas and the nominate Nepalese Kalij (*L. l. leucomelana*) – the two most westerly of the nine subspecies from the bird's native range.

Soon after their release, the Pheasants established a small breeding colony in dense stands of exotic Silk Oak (*Grevillea robusta*) woodland immediately above the release site, where they remained for the next 5 years.

Their subsequent dispersal across Big Island was in four directions: by late 1967, they had moved southwards around both sides of Mount Hualalai; by 1971 they had colonized the North Kona coast north of Kailua, from where they moved rapidly southwards by way of the Kahaluu Forest Reserve and the dense ohia (*Metrosideros collina*) forest of the Kaloko Mauka subdivision at between 1,200 and 1,500 m, through the upland forests of South Kona; by the end of the decade a small number had spread around the southern flank of Mauna Loa, and some were occasionally sighted on the southeastern fringe of the Kau Forest.

The eastern half of Hawaii was populated by birds that extended their range eastwards from Puu Waawaa through the dry saddle region (e.g. the Keahou Ranch, the ohia forests along Stainback Highway, the Pohakuloa flats, and the Ainahou Néné (*Branta sandvicensis*) Sanctuary) between Mauna Kea and Mauna Loa. By 1972, the birds had reached the moist windward rainforests containing their preferred dense woodland habitat, including Piha in the Hilo Forest Reserve; from here, by 1973, they had rounded the eastern flank of Mauna Loa, by 1978 had moved southeastwards to the Kulani area, by the following year had spread northwards to the Kalopa Forest on the upper Hamakua coast (which remains their present most northerly

point) and, by 1981, had travelled southwestwards to the eastern edge of the Kau Forest.

Kalij Pheasants on Hawaii spread at a rate of around 8 km a year, and within 14 years most of the mid-elevation forests on the island had been occupied. Although the habitat of the central Kau and Puna forests appears suitable, it had not been colonized at the time of writing (1986), nor had the birds extended their range any further north on the Kona coast than Puu Anahulu, presumably because of the unsuitable dry grasslands to the north. Their absence from the Kohala Mountains in the extreme north of Hawaii similarly appears to be due to the inimical sugar-cane plantations and extensive grasslands north of Kalopa Forest. In 1979, however, six birds were translocated to dense forest with a permanent water supply at Konokoa Gulch north of Kawaihae on the lower western slope of Kohala; although the upper end of the gulch ends in grassland, and does not therefore provide continuous forest cover to the densely wooded central Kohala range, the birds may nonetheless eventually reach and colonize this extensive tract of forest, as they have already proved capable of crossing marginally suitable terrain. Similarly, isolated records of adults near sea level at Ka Lae, Kalapana and Hilo (all at least 24 km from the main portion of the occupied range) suggests that the Kalij's colonization of Hawaii is not yet complete.

Apart from the Spotted Dove (*Streptopelia chinensis*) (q.v.), Kalij Pheasants may now be the most widespread game bird on Hawaii. They are fairly common to abundant in most wooded regions – especially in areas of extensive forest on Mauna Loa and Mauna Kea and in mid-elevation ohia woodlands (such as the Honau-nau Forest Reserve) on the leeward side of the island. Although they occur from sea level to an altitude of 2,450 m, 95 per cent of the birds are established between 450 and 2,150 m. Lewin & Lewin (1984) calculated that the range occupied amounts to around 3,500 km² – one-third of the island's total area.

Although omnivorous in their choice of foods, Kalij Pheasants on Hawaii show a marked preference for (mainly – 63 per cent – exotic) vegetable matter, including, in order of priority, Banana Poka (*Passiflora mollissima*), Thimbleberry (*Rubus rosaefolius*), Gosmore (*Hypochoeris radicata*), Ihi (*Oxalis corniculata*), Guava (*Psidium guajava*),

Kikuyu Grass (*Pennisetum clandestinum*) and Poha (*Physalis peruviana*). Of the Kalij Pheasants collected by Lewin & Lewin, 82 per cent contained the seeds and fleshy fruits of the exotic Banana Poka – the most important plant pest in Hawaii – and 36 per cent contained those of another pest species, the Thimbleberry, both of which, since not all seeds are ground up in the gizzard and thus destroyed, the birds may help to spread. Preferred native species are Tree Fern or hapuu (*Cibotium* sp.), Pukiawe (*Styphelia tameiameiae*), and Hawaiian Raspberry or akala (*Rubus hawaiiensis*). A wide variety of exotic (some 83 per cent) animal food is also consumed, especially Gastropoda – for example, snails (*Oxychilus alliarius*) and slugs (*Limax maximus* and *Arion* sp.) – and a Sowbug (*Parcellio* sp.), an isopod crustacean. Insect food includes beetles (Coleoptera), ants (Hymenoptera), larvae of flies (Diptera) and butterflies (Lepidoptera), and grass-hoppers (Orthoptera). Earthworms (Oligochaeta) and birds' eggs are also eaten.

'The successful colonization of Hawaii Island by Kalij Pheasants', wrote Lewin & Lewin (1984: 644), 'can be thought of as a symptom of a degraded ecosystem, because the birds are in large measure dependant on both exotic plants and animals for food and cover.' Kalij Pheasants are still rapidly expanding their range on the island, and the three remaining large uninhabited areas (Kohala Mountain and the central Puna and Kau forests) will probably soon be colonized. It seems likely that the bird's success on Hawaii, which has been attributed to the ability of this shy woodland species to colonize rainforest areas and other densely vegetated mesic habitats, will lead to its translocation to other islands in the archipelago. The Kalij Pheasant was declared a legal game bird on Hawaii in 1977.

––––––––––––––––––––

In 1926, William J. Mackensen told Phillips (1928) that a few years previously the Connecticut Game Commission had purchased from him five pairs of Black-backed Kalij Pheasants (*L. l. melanota*) – natives of eastern Nepal – which were released somewhere in the state, where they apparently disappeared.

According to Gabrielson & Lincoln (1959) and Burris (1965), a dozen Kalij Pheasants from Wisconsin were unsuccessfully released at Petersburg on Mitkof Island off Alaska in 1941.

In 1962, the US Department of the Interior's Foreign Game Introduction Program, in conjunction with state game departments, imported White-crested Kalij Pheasants (*L. l. hamiltonii*) from the western Himalayas as breeding stock for game-farm production. Between that year and 1976, 6,703 were released as follows: 1,887 in Virginia (1963–76); 2,601 in Tennessee (1964–8); 1,091 in Washington (1966–75); and 1,124 in Oregon (1969–74). Although in some areas (especially in the two western states) the birds survived for several years and bred successfully, no sustained breeding population appears to have resulted from any of these liberations.[2]

According to Bohl (1971a: 4), 'Free roaming white-crested Kalij(?) have existed in the Vancouver, British Columbia, park in recent years'. Blake (1975: 924) says the species is 'Stated to be free in a park in Vancouver, B.C.'.

––––––––––––––––––––

According to Niethammer (1963) and Heinzel, Fitter & Parslow (1976), the **Silver Pheasant** (*Lophura nycthemera*), a native of southern China, Burma, northern Laos, southwestern Kampuchea, North Vietnam, central South Vietnam, Thailand and Hainan, is established in woodlands in parts of Germany. It has been introduced unsuccessfully in England,[3] Scotland,[4] France, the Soviet Union, the United States, Canada, Colombia, New Zealand, (Western) Australia and the Hawaiian Islands. In Britain (e.g. near Chichester, West Sussex, and at Louth, Lincolnshire) and probably in other countries also, Silver Pheasants often succeed in breeding in the wild, but have never established viable populations.

––––––––––––––––––––

The **Cheer Pheasant** (*Catreus wallichii*),[5] which is classified as 'endangered' in *The ICBP Bird Red Data Book* (King 1981), formerly ranged from the Hazara district of Pakistan and Kashmir, India, south-east through Himachal Pradesh and northern Uttar Pradesh along the foothills of the Himalayas to Pokhara in central Nepal. It apparently died out in Pakistan around 1976–7, and may previously have disappeared from Himachal Pradesh, where in 1971 and 1973 two dozen pairs that had been reared by the Pheasant Trust in England were reintroduced to a forest reserve near Simla. In 1978, the World Pheasant Association in England started a campaign to reintroduce Cheer Phesants to Pakistan, where captive-bred birds have been released in the Margalla National Park near Islamabad, Kashmir.

NOTES

1 For much of the information on Kalij Pheasants in the Hawaiian Islands I am indebted to Lewin & Lewin 1984. See also: American Ornithologists' Union 1983; Banks 1981; Berger 1972, 1981; Bohl, 1971a; Bohl & Bump 1970; Bump & Bohl 1961; Hawaiian Audubon Society 1975; Lewin 1971; Lewin & Mahrt 1983; Long 1981; Mull 1978; Paton 1981b; Pratt 1976; Pyle 1977; Walker 1967b, 1981; Zeillemaker & Scott, 1976.

2 Banks 1981; Bohl 1968, 1971a; Bohl & Bump 1970; Bump & Bohl 1961, 1964; Burris 1965; Chambers 1965, 1966; Gabrielson & Lincoln 1959; Gottschalk 1967; Hart 1967; Lewin & Lewin 1984; Long 1981; Phillips 1928; Tuttle 1963.

3 See also Lever 1977a: 353–5.

4 See note 3.

5 Grahame 1980; King 1981; Narwaz 1982; Wayre 1975a.

Red Jungle Fowl
(*Gallus gallus*)[1]

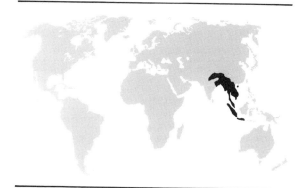

NATURAL DISTRIBUTION

From Kashmir to Assam, Burma and north-eastern India, south and east to Yunnan and Kwangsi (Guangxi) provinces in southern China and Hainan, south through most of Indo-China to Sumatra and Java.

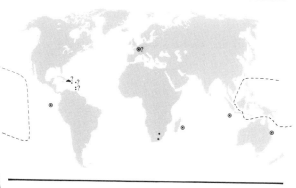

Note: Dotted line indicates Pacific and Indonesian naturalization.

NATURALIZED DISTRIBUTION

Europe: ?France; Africa: South Africa, Réunion; North America: West Indies (?Hispaniola, ?Trinidad, ?Culebra, ?Kick-'em-Jenny, ?Mona); Australasia: Australia, Indonesia, ?Philippines; Oceania: Hawaiian Islands, Polynesia, Micronesia, Melanesia, Galápagos Islands.

EUROPE

France[2]

According to Etchécopar (1955), Jungle Fowl were established in the wild at Cadarache by

143

Inspector-General Muge in about 1930. In 1954, further attempts were made to naturalize the species at Draguingnan and at Aix. Roots (1976: 172) states that 'Red junglefowl have colonized the French countryside around Clères, after being released on the estate of ornithologist Jean Delacour'.

AFRICA

South Africa

Fowl are currently said to be established in the wild in Natal and at Gravelotte in the north-eastern Transvaal.

Réunion[3]

Jungle Fowl are believed to have been introduced to Réunion in the early 1900s. Today, they occur in small numbers only in dense woodland and in cirques[4] on the east coast, and more commonly inland from Bras Panon and in the Liberia region, Eden and the Morne du Bras des Lianes.

NORTH AMERICA

West Indies[5]

Columbus is known to have included Domestic Fowl among the stock he took to Hispaniola on his second voyage in 1493. According to Wetmore & Swales (1931), some were established in the wild near Caracal in 1928. In *Voyage of Discovery and Research* (1847) – quoted by Murphy (1915) – the British admiral, Sir James Clark Ross, records how, *en route* from England to the Antarctic in 1839, he landed two pairs of Domestic Fowl on Trinidad 'to add something useful to the stock of creatures'. According to Bond (1979: 65), 'it is said that feral domestic fowl are thriving on the islet of Kick-'em-Jenny in the Grenadines and on Mona'. They may also occur on Culebra.

AUSTRALASIA

Australia[6]

Jungle Fowl were released in the Plenty Ranges of Victoria probably in the 1860s or 1880s, and a number were established near the railway line at Royal Park until at least 1916. Eleven were planted on Phillip Island in 1866, and others were liberated in Gembrook Reserve in 1870–1, and on Rottnest Island, Western Australia in 1912. These early introductions have all died out.

In about 1880 and 1900, respectively, Japanese guano-traders landed Jungle Fowl on North-West and Heron islands in the Capricorn group off the coast of Queensland at the southern end of the Great Barrier Reef, where they later interbred with Domestic Fowl introduced from the mainland. Before 1969, the Heron Island population was believed to have declined, but in recent years it has apparently increased again. The birds are said to resemble the ancestral type.

Indonesia and Philippines[7]

Red Jungle Fowl may have been introduced to the Malaysian region by the Mongols in the last quarter of the thirteenth century. The first European to see them there appears to have been the English navigator John Davis in 1598, who in *A Ruter . . . for Readie Sailings into the East Indies* (1618) – published in Samuel Purchas' *Purchas his Pilgrimes* (1625) – wrote of the king of Achin in western Sumatra that 'He spends his whole time in eating and drinking with his women, or in cock-fighting'. Sir James Lancaster, a pioneer of the trade between England and the East Indies and appointed to command the East India Company's earliest fleet, observed in 1602 that the natives of the Nicobar Islands 'brought also hennes and coconuts to sell'.

On Java, where Red Jungle Fowl were at one time thought to have been introduced, they were domesticated by at least 1672 when they were seen by Stavorinus. On West Island, in the Cocos (Keeling) group, feral fowl have reverted to their ancestral Red Jungle Fowl plumage, whereas on Horsburgh, Direction and Home islands they have retained more domesticated colour variations. They no longer occur on North Keeling. Elsewhere in the region, fowl are currently established in the wild on Borneo, the Lesser Sunda Islands (including Lombok, Timor and Wetar), Palawan (where they were first noted by Antonio Pigafetta in 1521 – see below), Balabac, Sulawesi, Papua New Guinea, and almost certainly many other islands. Although Delacour suggested that

Jungle Fowl were introduced to the Philippines at a very early date, Parkes (1962) considered that they may be indigenous. Rabor & Rand (1958) found no hybrids there, and suggested that the birds may represent different colonizations or introductions. However that may be, fowl of the form *G. g. gallus* (southern Indo-China, Thailand and Sumatra) are today established in the wild throughout the archipelago.

OCEANIA

Hawaiian Islands[8]

A domesticated form of Jungle Fowl was almost certainly introduced to the Hawaiian Islands from eastern Asia (principally Malaysia), by early Polynesian settlers around AD 500, and Captain James Cook saw some of their descendants (and also *kahilis* – long poles decorated with chicken feathers denoting the sovereignty of Hawaiian kings) when he landed on Kauai in 1778. As elsewhere in the Pacific, Jungle Fowl played a prominent role in the culture of Polynesians who valued them for their feathers, sacrificial purposes, cockfighting and food. The bird may have contributed in no small way to the successful colonization of Hawaii by providing a valuable source of protein for the Polynesians on their long voyages.

After their introduction by European settlers, feral Domestic Fowl freely interbred with wild Jungle Fowl. They were at one time established on all the inhabited islands in the archipelago, but are thought to have died out, except on Kauai, early this century. In 1902, some are said to have been transferred to Lanai, where they survived until at least the 1940s.

Little is known of the former range of the Jungle Fowl in the Hawaiian group except that it included forested land from sea level to an altitude of 2,000 m on all the main islands. The species' extermination everywhere except on Kauai was doubtless caused by overhunting, the deforestation of its preferred habitat, and interbreeding with Domestic Fowl, which tended to reduce the Jungle Fowl's ability to survive in the wild. The introduction in 1881 of the Small Indian Mongoose (*Herpestes auropunctatus*) almost certainly contributed to the birds' decline on all

islands except Kauai and Lanai, where the predator never became established (Lever 1985b).

Between about 1940 and 1950, many introductions of Hawaiian-bred Jungle Fowl (raised from stock obtained from dealers in Thailand and California and of the same subspecies as the former population) were made on Niihau, where they survived until the early 1970s but have since disappeared, and on several other islands: only on Kauai, however, where they generally reinforced the existing population and re-established a new colony in the south-east at Kipu, were they of lasting success.

Schwarz & Schwarz (1949), in their survey of game birds in Hawaii, found that fowl were established in small discrete areas on Kauai totalling 173 km^2. On the windward side of the island, their range lay between 150 and 300 m above sea level where the annual rainfall is from 250 to 500 cm, with mean temperatures of around 20 °C. On the leeward slopes, which supported higher densities, they ranged from 300 to 1,200 m where 125–200 cm of rain fall annually and temperatures average 15–20 °C. The country occupied by the fowl is rugged, comprising largely narrow ridges alternating with small but deep valleys. The soil is too acid to produce cultivated crops but supports a luxuriant forest vegetation. Primarily a forest reserve, the land was used mainly for the maintenance of watershed control for agricultural and domestic irrigation systems. Part of the birds' range that included Kokee was used for human recreational purposes, but only limited grazing of livestock was allowed.

Schwarz & Schwartz reported that the habitat occupied by fowl comprised the peripheral portions of montane forest, where koa (*Acacia koa*) is the dominant tree and ohia (*Metrosideros collina*) the lesser associated species, with some other native and exotic mixed hardwoods. Ground-cover is largely scattered puakeawe with occasional aalii, and alapaio, staghorn, Boston and tree ferns. This habitat is limited, because the forests become denser and wetter and possess fewer food species at higher elevations and more open and/or drier at lower altitudes. Wherever extensions of the forest extend into valleys, and the typical koa/ohia–lehua association is replaced by other species such as kukui and by Guava (*Psidium guajava*), fowl were occasionally found by Schwartz & Schwartz. They suggested a population in 1946–7 of about 1,390 birds, with average densities of between 3 and 15 per km². They indicated that feral Cats (*Felis catus*) and Pigs (*Sus domestica*) were the birds' main predators on Kauai.

In 1963, some Red Jungle Fowl of the subspecies *ferrugineus* were imported from game farms on the US mainland. The Hawaiian Audubon Society (1975) found the birds, known locally as *moa*, to be established and breeding on Kauai and Hawaii. Zeillemaker & Scott (1976) reported their presence on agricultural land and in exotic woodlands (e.g. Guava, Java Plum (*Eugenia cumini*), and *Eucalyptus*) and native montane forest and scrub (e.g. ohia–lehua and koa) on both islands, but less commonly on Hawaii. Although Walker (1981) mentions them only on Kauai, Berger (1981: 177) says they are 'now common in the mountains of Kauai (especially in the Kokee and Alakai Swamp regions), and they are said to exist on Niihau and, in smaller numbers, on Hawaii near human habitation where the birds find some protection from rats and especially mongooses'. The American Ornithologists' Union (1983) lists them as occurring also at Waimea Falls Park on Oahu.

Polynesia, Micronesia and Melanesia[9]

Red Jungle Fowl are known (from archaeological evidence in the Marquesas and Society islands) to have been introduced from eastern Asia (mainly Malaysia) to islands in the South Pacific by early Polynesian voyagers around 3,000 years ago as fighting birds (cockfighting – *faatitoraamoa* – is still a favourite sport in Tahiti) and as a source of food.

The first Europeans to see (presumably domesticated) fowl in the Pacific seem to have been the members of Magellan's voyage of circumnavigation. Antonio Pigafetta, an Italian nobleman from Vicenza who was attached to Magellan's suite, wrote of the natives of the Mariana Islands (where the fleet called in 1521) in his *Primo viaggio intorno al mondo* – known also as *Navigation et découvrement de la Indie supérieure faicte par moi Anthoyne Pigapheta* [*sic*], *Vincentin, chevallier de Rhodes* (*c.* 1524) – that 'their food consists of cocoanuts, bananas, figs, sugar canes, fowls and flying fishes'.

Ball (1933), by examining the works of early explorers, has attempted to trace the status of Domestic Fowl in the Pacific at the time of the arrival of the first Europeans. As mentioned above, they were first reported in the region (in the Marianas) by Magellan's expedition in 1521. They are believed to have occurred on Santa Cruz, north of the New Hebrides (Vanuatu), in 1565, and 30 years later were seen in the Marquesas. Tasman recorded them on Namuka Iki Island (Tonga) in 1643, where Cook also found them in 1773 and again in 1777. In 1765, the English circumnavigator John Byron reported the presence of large numbers on Tinian in the Marianas, where his predecessor Pascoe had also found them in 1742. In 1767, fowl were reported on Méhétia (Tahiti) by Samuel Wallis, who saw them as well on Niuatoputapu Island (north of Tonga) and in the Tuamotu group. Cook also found fowl in the Tuamotus, and on Raiatea (Tahiti), in 1769, and on Tongatapu, Eua Iki (Tonga) and Easter Island (where they had first been reported by Roggeveen when he discovered the island in 1722 and later by Gonzales in 1770) during his second voyage in 1774. Large numbers of fowl were seen by Crozet (one of Marion-Dufresne's officers) on Guam in 1772, and William Bligh found some on Aitutaki in the Cook Islands in 1789.

When Europeans arrived in the Pacific, they carried with them Domestic Fowl from home. Cook probably landed some on Tahiti as early as 1769, and others are believed to have been imported to the Marquesas and elsewhere by Spanish missionaries between 1772 and 1775. Before about the time that the US Antarctic Exploration Expedition of 1838–42, under the command of Charles Wilkes, was in the Pacific, however, Domestic Fowl on most Pacific islands are believed to have been the direct descendants of the original stock introduced from Malaysia. After about 1840, the introduction of European fowl grew apace, and since then the original population has been modified morphologically and genetically by interbreeding with the European birds, and all those now in the wild are hybrids that tend to revert to their ancestral phenotype.

Most of the early references are to fowl kept in captivity by native peoples, but Peale, who sailed with Wilkes on the US expedition, found some *ferae naturae* in the wilder parts of the hinterland of Tahiti, and others in the wild in the

Taioa Valley on Nuku Hiva in the Marquesas were reputedly the descendants of some landed by an English sea captain a few years earlier.

Between 1920 and 1926, feral Domestic Fowl were collected by the Whitney South Sea Expedition from six archipelagos in the south Pacific: the Society Islands (Tahiti, especially in the forests around Papeete, and Moorea and Raiatea); the Marquesas (Ua Huka, Nuku Hiva, Hiva Oa, Mohotani, Tahuata and Eiao); Fiji (Koro, Kio, Makongai, Kambara, Vanua Levu, Viti Levu, Mbalavu and Taveuni); the New Hebrides (Vanuatu) (Efate, Espiritu Santo and Hiw); and on Tubuai and 'Ata, Tonga.

Between 1945 and 1972 various authors reported the presence of freeranging Domestic Fowl of various sizes and plumages on, among others, the following Pacific islands: Mariana, Palau and Caroline islands; Samoa (where they were frequently reinforced by new blood from escaped domestic birds); Tonga; Fiji (especially on islands such as Taveuni that are free from the introduced Small Indian Mongoose, *Herpestes auropunctatus*); the Society Islands (Tahiti, Moorea, Raiatea, Tahoa and Bora-Bora); the Marquesas; the Marshall Islands; the New Hebrides (Vanuatu); New Caledonia (especially on Ile des Pins); Pitcairn and Ocean (Banaba) islands; Îles Gambier (Mangareva, Aukena and Tekava); and in the Tuamotu and Austral (Tubuai) groups.

On Fiji, where feral Domestic Fowl are some-times trapped and redomesticated, Red Jungle Fowl were, according to Pernetta & Watling (1978), originally introduced as a valuable source of protein by aboriginal Melanesian and/or Polynesian settlers. Watling (1982: 73) states that:

The Jungle Fowl . . . is found on many of the larger islands in the region, excluding Viti Levu and Vanua Levu in Fiji where it is now extinct. In Tonga it prob-ably only remains on the smaller uninhabited islands such as 'Ata. . . . In Fiji, Jungle Fowls were common on Viti Levu and Vanua Levu, before the introduction of the mongoose, but have since been lost to these islands as a result of its depredations. On some of the smaller islands they are heavily trapped by Fijians and in danger of extinction. They are shy birds and soon retreat in the face of encroaching agriculture.

According to Holyoak & Thibault (1984), feral Domestic Fowl occur today on Raratonga, Bora-Bora, Raiatea, Huahine, Maiao, Moorea, Tahiti, Rapa, Tubuai, Eiao, Nuku Hiva, Ua Hiva, Ua Pou, Hiva Oa, Tahuata, Mohotani, Fatu Iva, on Mangareva, Aukena and Tekava in the Gambier archipelago, and on Pitcairn. The birds are generally well distributed in secluded forests on Raiatea, Moorea, Tahiti and Rapa, and in most of the Marquesas; on such smaller islands as Raratonga, Eiao and Mohotani the populations are less well established. The birds live princi-pally in forests, to an altitude of 800 m in the Marquesas, and possibly even higher locally in Tahiti. They also occur in reclaimed scrubland (e.g. on Eiao) and rocky areas (e.g. in the Gambier group).

On infertile volcanic islands, more or less wild birds survive in villages and towns, where they feed on scraps of bread, crabs crushed on roads, pulped cocoanuts, fruit and insects. Wild forest-dwelling birds eat insects, seeds and fruit – especially mangoes and guavas; they are generally extremely shy, probably because of continual hunting, and fly strongly and run rapidly when disturbed.

On many islands small populations intermix with domestic birds, and on some islands and on islets with human inhabitants – such as Motu Kotawa near Puka Puka, Eiao and Mohotani – they are carefully preserved. Feral birds closest to the wild type in conformation and coloration are usually found in montane forests such as those on Tahiti and Raiatea, whereas those living near human settlements are more variable in both respects as the result of interbreeding with domesticated stock that are allowed to roam free near villages, and are valued more for their meat than their eggs. Both domesticated birds and especially recaptured wild ones are used for cock-fighting; the latter are caught when defending their territory by the Polynesians who decoy them by imitating their call. Apart from man they are also preyed on by feral Dogs (*Canis familiaris*) and Cats, and Marsh Harriers (*Circus aeruginosus*). Unfortunately, as Holyoak & Thibault point out, feral Domestic Fowl are considered by many ornithologists as of only culinary interest and unworthy of serious scien-tific study, so little is known of the distribution of feral populations.

Galápagos Islands[10]

Feral Domestic Fowl are established on the island of Isabela (Albemarle) where their present range is restricted to parts of the highlands of Sierra Negra near the agricultural settlement of Santo Tómas. From morphological changes (e.g. longer wings and tail and characteristic coloration) and altered behaviour (e.g. the capability of flight and arboreal nesting) it seems probable that they have occurred in this region for many years – perhaps since the end of the nineteenth century.

In 1960, Red Jungle Fowl of the form G. g. murghi (natives from Kashmir to Assam and central India) were imported from Dehra Dun, India into the United States[11] by Alabama, Oklahoma and Virginia. Between 1962 and 1971, 9,582 were released as follows: Alabama, 1,813 (1962–71); Florida, 1,002 (1963–8); Kentucky, 469 (1964–8); Louisiana, 1,151 (1963–7); Oklahoma, 1,093 (1961–7); Tennessee, 566 (1962–6); Georgia, 2,108 (1963–70) and South Carolina, 1,380 (1966–71).[12] Bohl & Bump (1970: 5) said 'Population increase reported from Georgia and South Carolina', and Banks (1981: 13) – after further large-scale liberations in both states – reported that in Bowens Mill, Ben Hill County and Oaky Woods Wildlife Management area, Houston County in Georgia the birds were 'Stable at low population levels 1978' or 'Population stable or declining at very low level in 1978'. In South Carolina, the birds had all disappeared, and it seems improbable that Jungle Fowl are currently naturalized in the United States.

According to Samuel de Champlain,[13] the first Governor of French Canada (quoted by Saunders,[14] p. 393), the Récollet Fathers, who arrived in Quebec in 1615, brought with them, among other stock, 'seven pair of fowl'. These were the first Domestic Fowl to be introduced to Canada, but whether any ever escaped into the wild is unknown. There appear to have been no deliberate attempts to naturalize Red Jungle Fowl in Canada as there have been in the United States.

In 1773, Captain Cook released some Domestic Fowl at West Bay in Queen Charlotte Sound, New Zealand,[15] and although he could find no trace of them there in the following year he was assured by the Maoris in 1777, during his third voyage, that they still occurred in the wild and were also kept in domestication by the local chief. A year later Cook presented the Maoris at Port Nicholson with some 'fowls to take home

and domesticate'. In 1814, the Revd Samuel Marsden imported Domestic Fowl from Sydney, Australia to the Bay of Islands, and thereafter they were acquired widely by the Maoris (who may have obtained them previously from early whalers) from whom many escaped into the bush. According to Thomson (1922: 110), 'in recent years these wild fowl have been exterminated'. In 1840, Sir James Clark Ross's expedition landed some fowl on the Auckland Islands, and 25 years later Captain Norman released some on Campbell Island; in both cases they failed to become established.

According to Bourne (1971), fowl are reported to have become feral on Poule Isle in the northerly Peros Banhos group of the Chagos Archipelago in the Indian Ocean, where they are now believed to have died out.

Benson, Beamish et al. (1975), quoting Ridgeway (1895), say that fowl were probably introduced by man to Îles Glorieuses north of Madagascar between 1882 and 1893. They were abundant on Grande Glor in 1895, and a few still occurred in 1906–8, but by 1970–1 they had apparently been exterminated.

Melliss (1870) states that at that time large numbers of Red Jungle Fowl (of the form G. g. bankiva from Java) were being reared in captivity on St Helena in the South Atlantic, and that some escaped and became established in the wild. Haydock (1954), however, does not mention their presence there in the 1950s.

According to Johnstone (1982), in the Southern Ocean Domestic Fowl have been imported to the Chatham and Falkland islands[16] and to Îles Kerguelen, and have occurred on Tristan da Cunha since 1810; they were present on Marion Island between 1950 and 1967, and at one time also on Gough and Macquarie islands. Whether any became feral is uncertain.

In England,[17] unsuccessful attempts have been made to establish Red Jungle Fowl in the New Forest, Hampshire; Whipsnade, Bedfordshire; Foxwarren Park, Surrey; and Elveden Hall, Suffolk.

NOTES

1 The Red Jungle Fowl is the ancestor of the Domestic Fowl. It was probably bred in captivity in southeastern Asia in prehistoric times – certainly before 1400 BC. The species is known to have been

domesticated in the Indus Valley by around 2500 BC, and by 1500 BC had spread to central and northwestern Europe.

2 Etchécopar 1955; Long 1981; Roots 1976.

3 Barré & Barau 1982; Long 1981; Staub 1976.

4 Bowl-shaped hollow at the head of a valley or on a mountainside.

5 Bond 1979; Long 1981; Murphy 1915; Wetmore & Swales 1931.

6 Blakers, Davies & Reilly 1984; Jenkins 1977; Kikkawa & Boles 1976; Lavery 1974; Long 1981; McBride, Parer & Foenander 1969; McCance 1962; Pizzey 1980; Ryan 1906; Servénty 1948; Tarr 1950.

7 Ball 1933; Delacour 1947; Long 1981; Mayr 1945; Parkes 1962; Peters 1934; Rabor & Rand 1958; Stokes, Sheils & Dunn 1984; Stresemann 1936.

8 American Ornithologists' Union 1983; Ball 1933; Berger 1981; Fisher 1951; Hawaiian Audubon Society 1975; Long 1981; Munro 1960; Peterson 1961; Pyle 1977; Schwartz & Schwartz 1949; Walker 1967b, 1981; Zeillemaker & Scott 1976.

9 Armstrong 1932; Ball 1933; Delacour 1966; Halloran & Halloran 1970; Holyoak, 1974a,b; Holyoak & Thibault 1984; Lancan & Mougin 1974; Long 1981; Mayr 1945; Mercer 1966; Pearson 1962; Pernetta & Watling 1978; Watling 1982; Williams 1960; Yaldwyn 1952.

10 B. Barnett, personal communication, 1982.

11 Banks 1981; Bohl & Bump 1970; Bump, 1968a,b; Bump & Bohl 1964; Chambers 1965, 1966; Gottschalk 1967; Kays 1972; Keeler 1963; Long 1981; Robinson 1969.

12 Other states are believed to have been involved in the release programme, but details are lacking.

13 Samuel de Champlain, *Works*, ed. H. P. Biggar (Champlain Society: Toronto, Canada, 1922–33), 1: 277–8, 301–2.

14 R. M. Saunders, 'The first introduction of European plants and animals into Canada', *Canadian Historical Review*, 388–406 (1935).

15 Thomson 1922.

16 Woods (1975) does not mention the presence of feral Domestic Fowl in the Falkland Islands.

17 Fitter 1959.

Common Pheasant
(Phasianus colchicus)

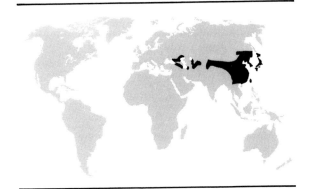

NATURAL DISTRIBUTION

A southern Palaearctic and northeastern Oriental species, with numerous races: in eastern Europe it occurs in parts of Transcaucasia and on the northern slopes of the Caucasus Mountains; in Asia it is found from northern Asia Minor north to the Aral Sea, Semipalatinsk, Mongolia and Manchuria, eastwards to Ussuriysk, Korea, Japan and Taiwan, and south to Tonkin, Burma, south-western China, Tibet, Sinkiang, the Pamirs, and northern Afghanistan and Iran.

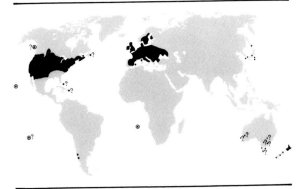

NATURALIZED DISTRIBUTION

Europe: British Isles, continental Europe; Asia: Japan; Africa: ?St Helena; North America: USA, Mexico, Canada, West Indies (?Dominican Republic, ?Bahamas (Eleuthera)); South America: Chile; Australasia: Australia; New Zealand; Oceania: Hawaiian Islands, Society Islands (Tahiti).

EUROPE

British Isles[1]

For many years it was generally accepted that the Common Pheasant (*Ph. c. colchicus* from the southwestern slopes of the Caucasus Mountains and the basin of the Phasis (Rioni) River near Colchicus[2] (Kutais) in Georgia and Armenia) was first introduced to Britain by the Romans. In 1933, however, Dr P. R. Lowe announced that bones discovered in a Romano-British midden at Silchester in Berkshire, which had previously been thought to be those of Pheasants, were in fact those of ordinary domestic fowl. The earliest documentary evidence of Pheasants in Britain occurs in a manuscript (in the British Museum) of about 1177, which contains details of rations specified by the Earl of the East-Angles and West-Saxons (later King Harold II) for the canons' household at the monastery of Waltham Abbey in Essex in 1058–9. This document shows that Pheasants were certainly known in Britain, if only in captivity, before the time of the Norman Conquest, having perhaps been introduced in the early years of the reign (1042–66) of the Saxon king, Edward the Confessor, and evidence exists that they began to become established in the wild shortly thereafter. In a charter of 1089, the Bishop of Rochester in Kent assigned to the monks of that city, among other provender, 16 Pheasants from four separate manors,[3] and two years later a licence was granted to the Abbot of Malmesbury to kill wild Hares and Pheasants. Thomas à Becket is said to have eaten Pheasant on the day of his murder, 29 December 1170, and in 1249 the Sheriff of Kent was commanded to produce two dozen Pheasants for a feast for Henry III.

Exactly when the Pheasant became established in the wild in the English countryside is uncertain. From the twelfth century onwards, the species began to appear with increasing frequency in English literature, and by about 1320, if no earlier, Pheasants were apparently sufficiently well established to be regarded as game, and by the late fifteenth century they were given legal protection by the Crown.

The earliest reference to Pheasants in Scotland appears to have been made by Bishop Lesley, who in *De Origine Moribus et rebus gestis Scotorum*

(1578), recorded that, though 'common with other nations, they are scarce with us'. Pheasants were first introduced to Ireland at some date before the late 1580s, when a number were exported from that country to Pembrokeshire in Wales.

Some 31 races of the Common Pheasant have been described, at least five of which have been introduced to Britain. *Ph. c. colchicus* was followed in 1768 by the Chinese Ring-necked Pheasant (*Ph. c. torquatus*) from eastern China. In 1898, the Prince of Wales's Pheasant (*Ph. c. principalis*) from southern Turkestan and northwestern Afghanistan and the Mongolian Pheasant (*Ph. c. mongolicus*) from Kirgizskaya and Chinese Turkestan, were released on the Island of Bute off the west coast of Scotland (and the former also in Norfolk and Kent) by Colonel Sutherland and Lord Rothschild. Pallas's Pheasant (*Ph. c. pallasi*) from southeastern Siberia and central Manchuria was liberated in Norfolk before 1930, and *Ph. c. satscheuensis* (western Kansu) in Kent in 1942. The Green or Japanese Pheasant (*Ph. (c.) versicolor*) was first imported by the Earl of Derby for his menagerie in Cheshire in about 1840. A melanistic mutant has been named '*tenebrosus*', and a buff or cream-coloured mutant has been called, for no apparent reason, the 'Bohemian' Pheasant. All these forms have freely interbred (many, but not all, of the present stock of cocks showing some trace of the *torquatus* white neck-ring) and it is now certain that there are no pure pheasants in Britain today, where the population is annually supplemented by birds reared by man for sporting purposes. Their high economic and recreational value more than compensates for the small amount of agricultural damage they do, though they are considered by the British Sugar Corporation to be a significant pest from May to July of seedling sugarbeet in East Anglia.

Yapp (1983) attempted to prove that, far from having been introduced to England in the second half of the eleventh or in the twelfth century, the Common Pheasant was not 'well-known or feral in England before the fourteenth century'. He based his opinion on the alleged mistranslation, over a period of many years, of the word *fasianus* from medieval Latin manuscripts, and claimed that 'The earliest certain and good pictures of Pheasants [are] in an English manuscript . . . dated 1396–1407'. Yapp's theory (and it is no

151

more) is of interest, but further research is required before its validity can be assessed.

Continental Europe

Highly prized for sporting purposes and its decorative qualities, the Pheasant is an almost ubiquitous species in suitable habitats in continental Europe where, as in the British Isles, the population is constantly reinforced by man.

Common Pheasants were traditionally introduced to Europe by Jason and the Argonauts when, in about 1300 BC, they brought some back with them from Colchis to Greece on board the *Argo* on their return from searching for the Golden Fleece. In *The Pheasant* (Fur and Feather Series, 1895), A. J. Stuart-Wortley wrote: 'from the evidence of a crowd of classical writers . . . I am convinced that Martial was correctly informed when he wrote: "*Argiva primum sum transporta carina; Ante mihi notum nil nisi Phasis*[4] *erat*".' Stuart-Wortley later quotes Raimondi of Brescia who said '*O quanto noi dobbiamo d'obligo a gli Argonauti*'.

From Greece, Common Pheasants were introduced to Italy, and thence by the Romans to southern France and Germany, though the precise dates of their arrival are uncertain. As in the British Isles, other races were subsequently imported and the European population (which now occurs from southern Norway, Sweden and Finland southwards throughout western Europe – including parts of the western USSR – apart from Portugal and southern and western Spain) is now composed largely, if not entirely, of hybrids.

Niethammer (1963) suggested the following dates for the arrival of Common Pheasants in Europe: Germany and Czechoslovakia in the eleventh century; Austria (1414); Hungary (fifteenth/sixteenth century); northern France (1530); Corsica (sixteenth century); Calabria and Rumania (seventeenth century); Switzerland (?1642); Sicily, Belgium and Norway (eighteenth century); Sweden (1740); and Finland (1901–3). *Ph. c. torquatus* and *mongolicus* arrived on Isla Procida off Naples in 1759, and were introduced elsewhere in Italy by 1775.

In France,[5] Japanese Pheasants were first introduced in about 1850, and were later followed by *P. c. formosanus* from Formosa (Taiwan), and

around the turn of the century by *mongolicus* imported by the German animal dealer Carl Hagenbeck. Delacour (1951) records that some Korean Pheasants (*Ph. c. karpowi*) were bred in captivity at Clères in 1926 and subsequently unsuccessfully released. According to Etchécopar (1955), the melanistic mutant (so-called '*tenebrosus*') was introduced to France with considerable success around 1930.

In Norway,[6] the first Chinese Ring-necked Pheasants (*Ph. c. torquatus*) were turned down at Baerum near Oslo in 1875–6. At present, Pheasants are established in Norway only in cultivated regions of Ostfold, Akershus and Vestfold in the extreme south-east.

Pheasants were first introduced to Finland[7] in 1901 by the industrialist K. Fazer, who 2 years later established a game farm near Helsinki from where Pheasants were subsequently despatched to landowners in other parts of the country. Immediately after the Second World War, the Finnish Pheasant population probably amounted to only a little over 600 birds, but by around 1957 it was estimated to number in excess of 20,000 – all in the extreme south. As in the British Isles, the comparatively minor agricultural damage caused by Pheasants is more than compensated by their great economic and recreational value.

ASIA

Japan[8]

According to Kuroda (1922), Pheasants (presumably the Korean race *Ph. c. karpowi* – natives of southern Manchuria and Korea) were introduced in the Middle Ages to Tsushima and Urishima islands in the Korea Strait. In 1919, 1923 or 1924 (accounts differ), Korean birds were introduced from that country to the plains and mountains near Tsushima west of Nagoya on Honshu and also on Kyushu, where they hybridized with the native Japanese Pheasant (*Ph. (c.) versicolor*). In 1930, others from the same source were released at Oshamambe and Hidaka on Hokkaido where *versicolor* does not occur, and have done well in those parts where mild winters ensure their survival. In 1965 or 1966, Korean Pheasants were also liberated on Hachijo Jima and Miyake Jima.

AFRICA

St Helena

According to T. H. Brook in his *History of the Island of St Helena* (1808: 37–8, quoted by Gladstone 1923), Ring-necked Pheasants were introduced to St Helena by Fernando Lopez, a Portuguese who went to live on the island in 1513. Melliss (1870) records their presence there in 1588, and says that they were abundant at the time of his visit. Benson (1950) counted nearly 100 in 1949, and Haydock (1954), who reported damage to potato crops, estimated the population at almost 75 pairs.

NORTH AMERICA

USA[9]

The first, albeit unsuccessful, attempt to establish Pheasants in North America is recorded in Chapter 601 of the Colonial Laws of New York, passed on 1 November 1733 and entitled 'An act to preserve the breed of English Pheasants in this Colony'. This reveals that the late Governor, Colonel John Montgomerie (who died in office on 1 July 1733) had placed 'about half a dozen couple of [pinioned] English Pheasants' on Nutten Island (now Governor's Island, near the Statue of Liberty in Upper New York Bay, and not, as Allen (1956) points out, the island of the same name off the south coast of Long Island). The birds apparently increased and spread to nearby Nassau (now Long) Island, where Montgomerie's successor, Governor William Crosby, sought their protection for a period of 5 years to 1 December 1738. A penalty of 10 shillings or 5 days in jail was prescribed for anyone disturbing or destroying birds or their eggs, though the Governor himself was permitted to shoot them and to give them and their eggs away – a privilege that was also accorded to the recipients. After Crosby's death in 1736, this law was not re-enacted, and there is no further record of this introduction.

Similarly, some Pheasants sent from France by the Marquis de Lafayette as a gift to George Washington in 1786 also failed to become permanently established. Four years later, Benjamin Franklin's son-in-law, Richard Bache,

released some Pheasants imported from England on his estate near Beverly on the Delaware River, New Jersey; Roots (1976: 163) incorrectly refers to this liberation as 'the first in the New World'. In the early years of the nineteenth century, 'a rich landowner of that time' (Phillips 1928: 42) released some on the Passaic River opposite Belleville in the same state; both these introductions failed, as did others by William Upshire in Accomac County, Virginia, and on several estates along the James River. According to Jeremy Belknap in *The History of New Hampshire* (1793), quoted by Allen, 'The late Governor Wentworth brought several pairs of pheasants from England, and let them fly in his woods, at Wolfeborough; but they have not since been seen'.

Allen expressed some surprise that these early introductions to New York and New Jersey were unsuccessful, since climatic conditions there are comparable to those in England: the probable reasons for their failure were that too few birds were released; that once in the wild they were not reinforced by further liberations; and poaching.

Almost a century was to pass before the first successful introduction of Pheasants was made in North America. In 1877, a lawyer and politician in the State of Oregon, Judge Owen Nickerson Denny, was appointed to the post of US Consul in Shanghai. On 28 January 1881, Denny wrote to A. H. Morgan in his home state:

I mentioned in my last letter that it was my intention to try and stock our State with some of the finest varieties of game pheasants found in China, and to this end I have been collecting them for some months past.

I am sending by the ship *Otago* out of Port Townsend [Washington State], Captain Royal commanding, about 60 Mongolian pheasants to be turned loose in various sections of the state. . . .

These birds are delicious eating and very game and will furnish fine sport.[10]

This consignment of Pheasants (accompanied by 'Mongolian sand grouse' and 'Chefoo partridges') was packed in small wicker baskets which, in the rough weather encountered in the Pacific, proved quite inadequate for the needs of the birds. According to Phillips (1928: 44), the shipment, which cost Denny some $300, 'reached Olympia [Washington State] safely, but owing to bad management the birds did not reach their destination in Portland [Oregon] alive'.

Undaunted by this initial failure, in the

following year Denny despatched to his brother John in Oregon on the barque *Isle of Bute* a further 28 wild-caught Ring-necked Pheasants (10 cocks and 18 hens)[11] in a 7-m² bamboo cage lined with gravel and planted with bushes and shrubs, with plentiful supplies of grain and charcoal. This shipment arrived safely at Portland, Oregon via Olympia, on 13 March 1882, and was released near the Dennys' home on Peterson Butte in Willamette Valley where, according to Laycock (1970), Judge Denny's wife, Gertrude, wrote to her sister-in-law, that 'He thinks that perhaps the folks there will protect them for the sake of the Denny family, til they get a good start in the country'. Two years later, when the Consul-General (as he then was) and his wife returned home from Shanghai, 'Denny pheasants', as they had come to be known, were already spreading naturally far and wide from their point of release, and had soon colonized an area of around 65 by 300 km, while large numbers were being trapped (most of which had been stocked from Willamette Valley) for translocation to more distant parts of Oregon and other northwestern States.

In Washington, the first Pheasants were planted in 1883 or 1885 in the west of that state, through the good offices of Judge Denny, and other birds from Oregon were turned down in several localities in the early 1890s and in the east between 1898 and 1900. Pheasants appearing in northern Washington in 1922 are believed to have crossed the Canadian border from British Columbia; in the same year at least 100,000 birds were shot in Washington, and in the next few years large numbers of gamefarm-reared birds and eggs were distributed throughout the state, including to San Juan Island in Puget Sound. In neighbouring Idaho, Pheasants were first introduced at Kemiah in 1903, although the State Legislature had provided for their protection as early as 1899. In southern Idaho, the first Pheasants were turned down near Buhl in 1907, and in neighbouring Montana before 1895. In the latter state, some 7,000 birds were released and several thousand eggs distributed between 1909 and 1929; although Pheasants were reported to be abundant in some localities by 1926 and shooting was allowed 2 years later, the Wildlife Restoration Division trapped and translocated 5,677 wild birds to uncolonized areas between 1941 and 1948.

The first shooting season for Pheasants in North America was declared in Willamette Valley, Oregon in 1891, when some 50,000 birds were killed; a year later the harvest had increased to between 250,000 and 500,000. Washington followed suit shortly afterwards, but Idaho not until 1916. In most of Oregon, hens received full protection in 1937, in Washington in 1941 and in Idaho in 1945, although they could be shot during the open season wherever they were causing damage. In the last state, an authorized game farm opened as early as 1908 but closed down – presumably due to lack of demand – in the following year. In Oregon, Gene Simpson of Corvallis started to rear Pheasants commercially in the early 1900s for large-scale stocking of adjacent states. In 1911, Simpson's farm (which he continued to manage until 1939) was leased to the state, and became probably the earliest of the large state-controlled game farms.

In northwestern states, Pheasants occur from sea level to an altitude of over 1,500 m in the Upper Klamath Basin of southern Oregon, and in areas with an annual precipitation of 300 cm at Forks on the Olympic Peninsula of Washington to 12.7 cm at Yakima in the centre of the state. At one point in the Sinlahekin Valley, in north-central Washington, the ranges of Pheasants and Mountain Goats (*Oreamnos americanus*) overlap. The most thriving populations occur in a few isolated regions of the Willamette Valley in Oregon, but Allen estimated that most of the region supported some 10 birds per 100 acres (40 ha).

The earliest (unsuccessful) attempts to establish Pheasants in California were made by private landowners on the coast near San Francisco Bay in the late 1870s and early 1880s. The success of Denny's introduction in Oregon in 1882 stimulated interest in California, and in 1889 the State Board of Fish Commissioners purchased 140 at $10 a pair, which they released in Monterey, Sacramento, Marin and Nevada counties in San Joaquin Valley. By 1898, they had acquired a further 710 birds (most of which came from Oregon although at least one was imported from Hong Kong) and these were released at several sites in the north and centre of the state. Some, though not all, of these introductions were successful, and the biennial report of the Board of Fish Commissioners for 1899–1900 (quoted by Allen) stated that 'nides[12] of young birds have been seen in Humboldt, Santa Clara and Fresno Counties'. The Board's next two reports expressed cautious optimism about the future of Pheasants in California and disclosed that the largest population occurred in Santa Clara, with around 1,000 on the Morrow Ranch near San Jose, and lesser numbers in Fresno, Humboldt, Santa Cruz and Kern counties.

In 1905, the Commissioners discontinued the introduction of Pheasants on the grounds of expense, and no further releases were made by California until a state game farm was established near Hayward in Alameda County in 1908, with a nucleus of breeding stock mainly from Oregon and Pennsylvania. During the next decade, no fewer than 4,183 Common Pheasants were reared and released in at least 31 counties, and the game farm, its objective achieved, was closed down in 1918. By 1916, it was estimated that there were between 7,000 and 8,000 Pheasants in California, of which 2,000 were in Santa Clara County with smaller populations in Humboldt, Inyo, Siskiyou, Santa Cruz, Tulare, Lake and Napa counties. The sole colony of *torquatus* reported consisted of 200–300 birds near Williams in the Sacramento Valley, Colusa County, where J. S. Hunter, formerly Chief of the Bureau of Game Conservation, saw adults with two nides in 1916. This, Allen reports, was the first published record of Pheasants established in what later became their most important area in California.

During the next few years, some local populations increased considerably; in parts of Santa Clara Valley ranchers reported the destruction by mowers of large numbers of nests, and widespread damage to crops in Owens Valley, Inyo County, resulted in the declaration of an open season in 1925. In the early 1920s, when Pheasants were first reported from the deltas of the Sacramento and San Joaquin rivers, some 5,000 were released by private landowners – mostly in Owens and Round valleys, Inyo County, with a few in San Diego County and around Modesto in Stanislaus County. Demands for further stocking encouraged the Fish and Game Commission to open another state game farm in 1925 at Yountville, from which over 3,000 birds were released in the following year. Until 1952, there was a growing trend towards increased production resulting in more and larger releases, with a peak liberation in 1951 of no fewer than 107,000; by 1955 over one million

Pheasants had been stocked throughout California, of which 583,878 were planted between 1926 and 1949.

The earliest local shooting season in the state was declared in Inyo and Mono counties from 1 to 7 December 1925, with a possession and season limit of six brace. Although many birds were reported they were overshot, and the experiment was not repeated in the following year. The first state-wide open season was declared from 15 to 20 November 1933 (when Sacramento Valley held the largest population) with a daily and possession limit of two cocks. The same regulations were renewed annually until 1941, when the season's limit was reduced from 10 to 8 cocks per gun, and thereafter they varied each year to provide 10 days in 1942, 15 in 1943 and 1944 and 6 in 1945. Bags were limited to 2 per day and a total of 10 per season, except in 1943–4 when 4 cocks were permitted on the opening day. During the 1950s, the season gradually became stabilized, with 10 days' shooting allowed and a limit of 2 cocks a day and 10 overall. The season was designed to coincide with the brief period which usually occurs towards the end of November between the completion of the rice harvest and the arrival of heavy rainstorms, thus ensuring access by guns to the state's densest Pheasant populations in the rice-growing region of the Sacramento Valley (which by the 1950s was providing nearly 50 per cent of the state's annual harvest of 500,000 birds) and most of the best shooting is to be found in California's fertile and well-irrigated Central Valley.

Ring-necked Pheasants in California range from 60 m below sea level in the Imperial Valley along the Mexican border (where, with their extension into Baja California, they are probably the most southerly population in North America, and where in summer game-farm incubators have to be kept at a lower temperature than the outside air) up to the Great Basin area of the north-east at altitudes of over 1,200 m with sub-zero winter temperatures, where arid sagebrush is replaced by fertile farmland. The state's population can be split into a trio of natural subdivisions: these are the temperate irrigated Central and Imperial valleys, the upland Great Basin region and the Pacific coastal valleys.

Central Valley, which is situated, as its name implies, in the heart of California and stretches for about 70 km from the Coast Range to the Sierras and from Redding around 600 km south to the Tehachapi Mountains, comprises the Sacramento and San Joaquin valleys – an area of diversified agriculture on rich alluvial soil irrigated by the Sacramento and San Joaquin rivers. Imperial Valley is basically similar to the southern portion of San Joaquin Valley. The Sacramento Valley rice-belt, which bestrides the Sacramento River, in Butte, Glenn, Colusa, Sutter, Yolo and Sacramento counties, supports the largest and most flourishing Pheasant population in California. The triangular delta between Sacramento, Stockton and the northeastern tip of San Francisco Bay – a southern extension of the rice-belt – provides a marginal habitat; unsuitable orchards, vineyards, barley, wheat, cotton and alfalfa fields in some parts of the San Joaquin Valley are only thinly populated, with low to medium densities in irrigated districts near Merced and between Mendota and Gustine. Some heavy populations, however, occur near Oakdale in the northeastern San Joaquin Valley in the vicinity of undulating land adjoining the western Sierras, which provides pasturage for sheep and cattle, arable land for barley, rice, alfalfa and corn (for silage), and orchards and vineyards.

Some 80 km west of the Colorado River a fertile agricultural belt surrounded by desert lies astride the United States/Mexican border. Over half of this area, which in California stretches north to the Salton Sea, forms Imperial Valley, whose cultivated land ranges from sea level to 70 m below. Only small populations of Pheasants exist on its 325,000 ha, which grow mainly winter vegetables, alfalfa, flax, barley, wheat and sugarbeet. The earliest recorded release of Pheasants in Imperial Valley was made by the Division of Fish and Game in 1926, and between that year and 1928 a total of 450 were turned down; the rate of stocking increased after 1948 when the valley acquired its own state-run game farm, but the birds have never fared very well in the excessively hot and arid climate.

There are two general regions in California that are related climatically and partly geographically to the Great Basin; these are the northeastern area consisting of eastern Siskiyou and Modoc and Lassen counties, and Owens Valley in Mono and Inyo counties. Habitats here are similar to those in eastern Oregon, Idaho and

Nevada. The land rises to an altitude of over 1,200 m, and is surrounded by semi-arid sagebrush clad mountains with harsh sub-zero winters; between 150 and 500 mm of the low annual precipitation falls as medium to light snow from October to March, and agriculture is based on the raising of livestock and the production of grain. Pheasants occur principally around Tule Lake near the Oregon border and in parts of the mixed farmland of Honey Lake Valley in Lassen County. Owens Valley, at a height of 1,200 m east of the Sierra Nevada in Inyo County, which was one of the first places in California where Pheasants were stocked and had the state's earliest open season in 1925, today supports very few birds. Small numbers are also found in some of the more level valleys of the Sierra Nevada that are similar to those of the Great Basin.

On the coastal belt of California Pheasants are only lightly distributed – particularly in the south. The greater part of the population is centred on Eureka, Humboldt County, where the habitat is similar to that in Oregon. In general, the coastal strip has dry summers and wet winters, with an annual rainfall between October and March that varies from 100 to 130 cm near the Oregon border to 25 cm near Mexico, and produces mainly barley and wheat. The largest coastal Pheasant populations were formerly in the grain-growing Salinas and Santa Clara valleys, but since their changeover to orchards and salad vegetables, respectively, Pheasants have declined.

In the arid southwestern states, Pheasants are well established in Utah and eastern Colorado, and less so in Nevada, New Mexico, Arizona, Oklahoma and Texas. The earliest private releases, in New Mexico in 1872 and Colorado in 1875, both failed, but were followed by more successful attempts in Colorado (24 birds at four separate sites) in 1885 and in 1894, and Utah (c. 1890), and by further failures in Oklahoma (1909), Arizona (1912), New Mexico (1916), Nevada (before 1917), and finally Texas (1939). In Colorado, the earliest release by the state was made in 1901, and shooting was first permitted in 1929. Since then, shooting has occurred annually, and between 1957 and 1961 a total of more than 206,000 were shot.

Pheasants were first introduced to Utah[13] in about 1890 by the Hon. M. H. Walker, who released them on his farm at the mouth of Big

Cottonwood Canyon near Salt Lake City.[14] The source of these birds is unknown, but it appears that they must have been successful, as they were given protection by the Territorial Legislature in 1894.[15] Walker and his brother turned down more Pheasants on their farm in 1898, when birds from the earlier release were said to be increasing.

On 1 March 1893, 'English and Chinese pheasants' (presumably *colchicus* and *torquatus*) were liberated on Antelope Island in Great Salt Lake by John E. Dooly, Senr.[16] Where these birds came from is unknown, but the planting was presumably successful, as they were being shot on the island between about 1895 and 1905 when, or shortly afterwards, they disappeared.

In 1900, the first introduction was made in the Uintah Basin near Vernal; a decade later, Pheasants in this locality were said to be increasing and expanding their range. By 1914, Pheasants were found in Utah in significant numbers only in Salt Lake (where they had been well established for at least a decade and were causing damage in market gardens), Weber, Utah and Uintah counties. A 7-day open season was declared in these counties in 1917 and 1918, with a bag limit of two cocks a day and four per season; some 300 birds were shot in Salt Lake County alone during this 2-year period.

In 1921, the Utah Fish and Game Department acquired 200 gamefarm-raised Pheasants from various parts of the United States, from which 1,000 birds had been reared in a state game farm at Springville by the following year. In 1923–4, 5,064 Pheasants and 1,540 eggs were despatched from Springville to several counties in the state. In the latter year, a 10-day open season was authorized in Salt Lake County, and, although 3,000 birds are said to have been killed, the overall population was apparently unaffected. In 1925, 4,868 Pheasants were liberated in Utah, and between 1926 and 1940 the State Fish and Game Department annually reared and released over 5,000 birds from Springville and a second farm built at Price. An open season was declared in 10 counties in 1927 and 1928, when an estimated 100,000 birds were shot, and by 1935, when they were said to be increasing throughout the state, shooting was permitted in 15 counties: 5 years later, a further five counties held an open season, and in the following year around 150,000 birds were killed in Utah, where they were then well established wherever there was suitable habitat.

The number of birds released annually by the State Fish and Game Department had increased to around 8,000 by 1943 and to 28,000 by 1948. By 1950, Pheasants were established and breeding well in most agricultural regions (about 3 per cent) of Utah.

Thriving Pheasant populations in the south-west occur only in eastern Colorado (especially along the South Platte River from Denver to the Nebraska border but also up to an altitude of 2,300 m on the eastern slopes of the Rocky Mountains west of Denver) and in Utah, where they are most abundant in northern and central areas and in the Uintah Basin in the north-east. Smaller numbers are found in Nevada, mainly in irrigated valleys around Reno and Carson City; Arizona; New Mexico (where the first successful introduction was in 1932); and in the panhandles of Oklahoma and Texas on the fringe of the species' range in the south-west.

In the plains and prairie-lands, state game departments began distributing Pheasant eggs between 1905 and 1915, and later South Dakota, Iowa, Nebraska and North Dakota caught and translocated wild birds to unstocked areas; unaccountably, most early attempts to naturalize Pheasants in this region were unsuccessful.

In 1900 or 1901, the fences of William Benton's game farm at Cedar Falls, Iowa, were blown down, allowing 2,000 Pheasants to escape, and a decade later the Conservation Commission began distributing eggs and poults. Sporadic introductions in Kansas up to 1925 all failed, but between that year and 1940 over 18,000 birds were released and 100,000 eggs were distributed. From 1934 to 1951, the Department of Mines and Natural Resources turned down 5,000 Pheasants in Manitoba, where severe winters are the principal limiting factor. In 1905, 70 pairs of Pheasants were acquired from Illinois and Wisconsin by the Conservation Department of Minnesota, where a decade later a state game farm was established, which, by the mid-1950s, had released 691,600 birds and distributed 96,578 eggs. The first open season in Minnesota was declared in 1924. In Nebraska, where only 1,000 Pheasants were introduced, some 40,000 wild birds were trapped and translocated in 1926–7, and a state game farm was not established until shooting was allowed almost throughout the state. Pheasants released on a somewhat random basis in North Dakota between 1910 and the early 1930s failed to become established, and only succeeded after wild-trapped birds were translocated from South Dakota between 1929 and 1934. In Missouri, Pheasants became established as the result of the release of birds and distribution of eggs from about 1904 to 1933.

In South Dakota, which supports the largest Pheasant population in the region and probably in the whole of North America, early plantings were all made privately, and no game farms were ever set up. In 1891, a local newspaper announced that N. L. Witcher was importing to Sturgis some Pheasants from Oregon, which, given protection for a few years, he anticipated would 'drive out the vulgar native grouse, which are not really game birds' (quoted by Laycock 1970: 28). Nothing more was heard of Witcher's birds (either because they never arrived or did not receive the required protection), so in 1898 Dr A. Zetlitz of Sioux Falls acquired some Pheasants from Illinois. This consignment, according to Laycock (p. 28), 'numbered half a dozen ringnecks, plus a few assorted golden and silver pheasants'. In the following spring, Zetlitz released 10 (presumably ringnecks) in Minnehaha County, where they survived for only a few years. Zetlitz liberated more in 1903 and these, reinforced by further private plantings in the next few years, apparently settled down and became established.

In 1911, the South Dakota game department acquired 200 pairs of Pheasants from an out-of-state game farm, and during the First World War 7,000 were released at a cost of $20,000, enabling an open season to be declared in 1919. Within 8 years, between 1.5 and 2 million birds were being harvested annually. In *Fifty Million Pheasants in South Dakota* (1941), J. W. Cluett, director of the state's Department of Game, Fish and Parks (quoted by Laycock 1970: 29), estimated 'that since the first open season . . . approximately 20,000,000 pheasants have been *legally* killed in South Dakota'. At that time, some 1.5 million Pheasants were being shot annually in the state without causing any apparent diminution in the population, and in 1943 – when the state's Pheasant population was estimated to be a staggering 60 million – the State Legislature adopted the Pheasant as its 'state bird'.

Until at least 1950, regular stocking continued in some (though not all) states; 6,000 12-week-old chicks, for example, were released in that

year in Iowa, and in Minnesota 73,793 young birds, 3,186 adults and 42,177 day-old chicks were distributed to sportsmen and landowners, while Nebraska and Kansas were releasing Pheasants at an average rate of 10,000–15,000 and 20,000 a year, respectively. By this time, stocking had been discontinued in North and South Dakota and in Missouri. The most flourishing populations – in the north-central parts of the region – are derived from a relatively small number of introductions that were made in suitable habitats, where repeated plantings were not required. Before 1905, less than 500 Pheasants were introduced in the northern prairie states, yet between 1940 and 1950 over 82 million were killed in North and South Dakota, Nebraska, Iowa and Minnesota – a staggering rate of increase on the continent's central grasslands. 'Environmental changes appear to have been an important factor in bringing about the pheasant population fluctuations and shifts in the plains and prairie pheasant island; but some other factor or factors also appear to have exerted an influence.'[17]

Between 1860 and 1910, the Great Lakes States came under increasingly intensive cultivation; fertile land was cleared of timber, and the production of wheat was superceded by that of corn and by dairy-farming. Small and intensively cultivated farms, together with an increased demand for sporting facilities from a rapidly growing urbanized human population, caused a rapid decline in the native Prairie Chicken (*Tympanuchus cupido*) westwards through the grasslands of the Lakes States. The pressure for increased grazing was responsible for a reduction in the size and numbers of small commercial forestry plantations – favoured habitats of the Ruffed Grouse (*Bonasa umbellus*). Most of the land that had once been suitable for these two native species was transformed into good Pheasant country, and the decline of the natives may well have hastened the introduction of the aliens, which in the Lakes States in the nineteenth century were all made by private landowners or sportsmens' organizations.

In Ohio, it is apparent that Pheasants were first introduced before the turn of the century, since the State Fish and Game Report for 1900 refers to the presence of a 'pheasantry' near Van Wert; that, and another near Celina set up in 1896, were among the first in the United States, and from them birds were released – though without success – from 1893 to 1896. By 1903, however, repeated plantings in a number of areas had succeeded in establishing Pheasants in 10 counties.

In 1893, A. G. Baumgartel, who ran a sportsmens' club near Holland, Michigan, purchased a nucleus breeding stock from which he subsequently reared up to 200 birds annually, some of which were released (the first in the state) in March 1894 or 1895. They were reinforced by others in later years, and although breeding in the wild was reported all the birds disappeared, possibly due to poaching, when the project was abandoned in 1899. Between 1917 and 1925, the state conservation department released 35,000 birds and distributed 222,000 eggs to shooting-clubs and private landowners, and by the latter year the species was sufficiently well established for an open season to be declared.

Schorger (1947) points out that although the large Pabst plantings in southern Wisconsin did not begin until 1911, 'pheasants were liberated much earlier than has been assumed' – that is, according to reports in local newspapers, by at least 10 individuals or groups after 1891.

The first Great Lakes State-sponsored releases on record were made in Indiana in 1908, Illinois (1910), Michigan (1918), Ohio (1919) and Wisconsin (1929). Leopold (1933) estimated that in Indiana, Illinois, Ohio, Michigan, Minnesota, Missouri and Wisconsin between 1900 and 1930 (when the species had become firmly established), no fewer than 224,436 Pheasants were reared at a cost of $750,000, and that 742,000 eggs were distributed by game farms at a cost of $150,000: by 1950, some 2.4 million birds had been stocked in these seven states.

In Ohio, the coastal strip along the southern shore of Lake Erie was the first to be colonized, and natural expansion of range from this area accounts for most of the state's population, though some rough country in the south and east remains unoccupied in spite of natural spread and artificial stocking.

Two years after the establishment of a state-run game farm in Michigan, Pheasants began to be widely distributed, with such success that an open season was declared in 1922; up to 1947 around 5,000 were being released annually.

Although the earliest state-sponsored liberation in Indiana was made as early as 1908, the programme was not in full swing until about 1930, when a few districts in the north and east supported viable populations. Similarly, although in Illinois Pheasants were first turned down by the state as early as 1910, most of the 35 or so releases before 1928 (the earliest of which took place in the 1890s) were made privately in the west and south along the Mississippi River. After the state-release programme got under way in 1928, the main Pheasant populations built up in the north-east near Lake Michigan, whence they spread westwards and southwards in the following decade but became established only locally in central, western and southern counties. By 1953, a total of 1.5 million Pheasants had been released in Illinois, and, since then, repeated attempts have been made to establish them in southern districts.

Although by the 1950s Wisconsin had one of the largest state-run game farms in North America, some of its earlier plantings were made with wild-trapped birds translocated from other states. Adult birds, day-old chicks and eggs were widely distributed; between 1931 and 1937 (when 5,700 were reared) some 250,000 day-old birds were despatched by the state to sporting organizations and private individuals, and by the 1950s this figure had increased to some 160,000 per annum. The Pheasants introduced to the Great Lakes States, where the main limiting factors are climate, predation, farming practices and over-shooting of hens, came from China (presumably *torquatus*), England and continental Europe.

Apart from the rich agricultural parts of New Jersey, Pennsylvania and New York the north-eastern seaboard states provide, in general, unsuitable Pheasant habitats.

The unsuccessful eighteenth-century introductions in New York and New Jersey have already been discussed: after the first attempt in New York in or before 1733 no further plantings appear to have been made until 1877, when a number were unsuccessfully released in Central Park, New York City. Between 1886 and 1891, 4,120 were liberated by J. L. Breese in Tuxedo Park in the lower Hudson Valley, where, although there is no evidence that the birds were ever properly established or breeding, Phillips (1928) records that large shoots were held in 1890 and 1891. The first recorded successful liberation was in 1892–3, when 275 cocks and 300 hens were planted on 1,200-ha Gardiner's Island at the eastern end of Long Island. By the turn of the century, the post-breeding population numbered almost 5,000, and 300–400 cocks were being shot each season. In the early 1900s, Pheasants gradually became established on Long Island as the result of plantings on various properties possibly reinforced by natural dispersal from Gardiner's Island. Pheasants released privately in the State of New York came from two main sources – the Pleasant Valley Fish Hatchery (sic) near Bath where over 1,000 were reared between 1897 and 1904, and the Wadsworth Estate near Geneseo in the Genesee Valley, where 350 were reared and stocked in 1903. By 1905, Pheasants were well established throughout the fertile Ontario lowland of western New York. Between 1897 and 1939, state authorities turned down 595,056 birds and distributed 3,519,179 eggs to groups and private individuals, and by 1941 up to 500,000 were being harvested each year.

After two earlier failures by Pierre Lorillard in northern New Jersey in about 1880, Pheasants imported from England were turned down in 1887 by Rutherford Stuyvesant on his Tranquility Game Preserve at Allamuchy, where, according to Phillips, they were established and breeding by the early 1890s.

Between 1892 and 1895, several hundred Pheasants were imported from England to Pennsylvania by private landowners, by whom they were released with some success in Lehigh and Northampton counties; further small private introductions were made in New Jersey from the late 1890s until 1915 when the State Game Commission started its own programme, and between the latter year and 1925 some 49,000 were turned down. Three years later, Phillips recorded that at least 50,000 were being shot during the brief open season then prevailing. Shortly before 1938, some 30,000 incubator-reared Pheasants (and Bobwhite Quail, *Colinus virginianus*) were released in Pennsylvania. Between 1949 and 1964, 3,000 were unsuccessfully liberated near Centre Hall, but the release of a further 1,006 wild-trapped birds in the same area during the next 2 years resulted in the establishment of a viable population.

In Massachusetts, Pheasants were also first released in the 1890s, and, although by 1906 they were apparently more or less established, stocking recommenced between 1907 and the outbreak of the First World War. According to

Phillips (1928: 42), 'some of the early stock introduced into Massachusetts and probably other Eastern States, purchased from Vernier de Guise, of New Jersey, was very nearly pure, old dark-necked English pheasants, or *P. colchicus*'. Phillips himself released some birds at North Beverly, Massachusetts, in 1897–8. From Massachusetts, Pheasants spread northwards into New Hampshire, southwestern Maine and southern Vermont. On Great and Egg islands off the south coast of Cape Cod, Phillips records that Pheasants were unsuccessfully released in the 1880s by C. B. Cory.

The earliest recorded releases in New Hampshire (the results of which are unknown) were made by private individuals in 1893 and 1895, and in the latter year also by the Fish and Game Commission. By 1912, Pheasants were reported in some numbers around Mount Vernon and in the region of Brookline, and thereafter they increased so rapidly that in 1918 the Fish and Game Department was forced to buy grain for supplementary winter feeding. Three years later, state authorities began their own stocking programme.

Pheasants first appeared in Maine as dispersants from Massachusetts and New Hampshire before 1897; in that year, five pairs were released and nides were observed during the next 3 years, but all the birds apparently disappeared during the severe winter of 1899–1900. Some, however, must have survived (or there may have been further releases or dispersals from adjoining states) as they gradually spread into Cumberland County, and from 1912 onwards were regularly observed around Portland. By 1920, Pheasants were increasing considerably in southern Maine, and 6 years later horticultural damage was reported in York County. From the 1920s, the state assumed a major role in Pheasant-stocking, and by 1931 birds had been planted in all coastal and some inland counties.

The first (privately organized) introduction of Pheasants in Rhode Island was made in 1894, and it was not until 1925 that the state began to take an active part in the stocking programme.

New York was the first of the eastern states to establish a game farm (at Sherbourne in 1909) and, in 1910, 1,200 birds and 6,500 eggs were distributed to shooting-clubs and private individuals. By the end of the First World War, 20,000 birds were being reared per year, and according to the annual report of the New York Conservation Committee for 1918 all suitable habitats in the state had been occupied. By 1930, up to 40,000 or more birds were being released annually, and a decade later this figure had increased to over 90,000. Pennsylvania established two small game farms in 1929, where the combined production never exceeded 30,000, and later farms were also started in Maine, New Hampshire, Massachusetts, Maryland and New Jersey. Most of the early nucleus breeding stock was imported from England, Germany and elsewhere in Europe.

By the mid-1950s, Pheasants in New England were established in Maine only along the coastal belt and in larger river valleys. In New Hampshire, they were mainly in the valley of the Merrimack River, along the coast, and in the narrow Connecticut River Valley. In Vermont, Pheasants occurred only near agricultural land on the eastern shore of Lake Champlain and discontinuously in the valley of the Connecticut River. Post-breeding populations in Massachusetts totalled around 60,000, most of which were to be found intermittently in Bristol County and in the Connecticut and Concord River valleys. In Connecticut, where the post-breeding total may have amounted to 100,000, most of the birds lived in the valley of the Connecticut River. In New York, the most flourishing populations (about 50 per 40 ha) occurred in the two northwestern counties of Erie and Niagra, with lesser numbers (10–20 per 40 ha) in the Erie/Ontario lowlands, about 10 per 40 ha in parts of Ulster and Dutchess counties, and between 1 and 5 per 40 ha in the Mohawk and Hudson valleys.

In Pennsylvania, Pheasants were widely distributed, occurring in the highest densities (about 50 per 40 ha) in the fertile farmlands south and east of the Blue Ridge Mountains. They were also abundant west of York, east of York to the New Jersey line, and south to the border with Maryland. Along the western border with Ohio, Pheasants were established southwards from the Pymatuning Reservoir almost to New Castle, and from the southern shore of Lake Erie to the Ohio River, eastwards to the mountain foothills and south into Washington County. They were also to be found in the Conemaugh and Loyalhanna valleys east of Pittsburgh, and in the river valley south of Williamsport to the confluence with the Susquehanna River and along that

river from the New York border south to Scranton.

In New Jersey, Pheasants were established in the three northern farmland counties of Hunterdon, Somerset and Warren, while small numbers were scattered in the north of Delaware, Maryland and West Virginia. In Rhode Island the post-breeding population numbered between 10,000 and 12,000.

According to Phillips, there have been many unsuccessful attempts to naturalize Pheasants in the southeast – in Virginia, North and South Carolina, Georgia, Tennessee and Alabama. In the first-named state, large numbers of birds were planted in 1906 and again in 1913 (when some were also liberated in Alabama), and on Jekyl Island off the coast of Georgia and on the mainland around Thomasville a number were released before 1888. As late as the 1950s, 20,000 were turned down over an 8-year period in Kentucky.

Between 1934 and 1942, several unsuccessful attempts were made to establish Pheasants in Alaska – well to the north of the species' natural (and naturalized) range. In the former year, 225 were released in the extreme south at Sitka and Goddard Hot Springs on Baranof Island; in 1936 and again 3 years later 100 and a dozen, respectively, were planted on the mainland at Ketchican and, probably in the former year, some were released further north at Cordova. Five hundred transplanted from Minnesota were turned down further west near Palmer in the Matanuska Valley in 1938–9, and others at Fairbanks (the first away from the coast) and on Wrangell Island in the south in 1936 and 1952. On the latter, there was also a release of 32 in 1940. In 1939 and 1940, 75 and 60, respectively, were liberated in the south at Petersburg, and in the latter year 85 were turned down at Kenai Lake south of Anchorage, while in 1942 46 were released in the south at Haines. A few managed to survive at Manuska until at least 1952, probably only because of the relatively large number that were released.

The earliest Pheasants imported to the United States came from China and England and were exclusively *colchicus* and *torquatus*. The Mongolian subspecies *mongolicus* was released (in California) probably around 1894, and, according to Phillips, the Prince of Wales's Pheasant (*principalis*) first in 1906. The Japanese or Green Pheasant (*Ph. (c.)*

versicolor) was liberated in Colorado as early as 1882 and in Oregon by 1885.

In the United States, Pheasants fare best in northern agricultural areas. In general, viable populations became established during the 1920s and 1930s, and by the start of the latter decade most of the more suitable habitats, apart from some in the Great Lakes States, had been colonized. By the 1950s, they seldom occurred in the east south of the thirty-ninth parallel near the southern border of Pennsylvania, and most were found north of a line from the northern tip of Chesapeake Bay to Chicago (apart from the three northwestern counties of Ohio), and were rare in the warm and humid south-east. In the west, too, the majority of birds occurred north of a line between San Francisco and the Colorado/New Mexico border, though a few ranged as far south as northern Mexico. According to Leopold (1933), this southern limit of the Pheasant's distribution in North America coincides almost exactly with the end of the glaciers' advance during the last Ice Age. Pheasants require a certain amount of calcium in their diet for their eggs to hatch successfully, and food grown in areas over which glaciers have passed is richer in calcium than that grown in non-glacial areas. Furthermore, high (southern) temperatures during incubation are known to reduce the hatching success rate of Pheasants' eggs. The largest more-or-less continuous area of Pheasants in North America was established in the northern Great Plains States of Nebraska, Iowa, Minnesota, South Dakota and, especially, in North Dakota.

In the south and west of their range, Pheasant populations are governed by the availability of water: few are found in arid regions (except in parts of Washington and Oregon), but they can be abundant in fertile irrigated valleys. By the 1960s, they occurred in varying numbers in all states west of Arkansas, but only in low densities south of Colorado. In the east, too, their distribution was discontinuous: they were found, again in irregular numbers, in the Great Lakes States and in all eastern states north of, and including parts of, Maryland. Average populations lived in parts of Wisconsin, Illinois, Michigan, Ohio, Pennsylvania and New York, and lesser numbers in the New England states and in northern New Jersey. In general, however, few of the northeastern populations

were comparable to those in the irrigated valleys of the west. In the Midwest, Indiana and southern Illinois, in spite of fertile land that grows good corn crops, supported relatively few Pheasants. Throughout their range, cold and wet springs result in high chick mortality, and hot and dry summers cause early mowing, which kills many nesting birds.

The populations and annual harvest of birds in individual states have fluctuated considerably. That the species' potential rate of reproduction is considerable is shown by an interesting experiment conducted in 1937 by Einarsen (1942 and 1945). In that year the Co-Operative Wildlife Research Unit of Corvallis, Oregon, released two cocks and six hens (*Ph. c. torquatus*) on the 161-ha Protection Island in Puget Sound, which comprised 48 ha of grain crops, 19 ha of sand quarries and 94 ha of grass-covered sand dunes, open pastureland and small woods. No upland game lived on the island, but to simulate a degree of natural predation Einarsen turned loose a couple of tom Cats (*Felis catus*). Despite predation by the Cats and by Cooper's Hawks (*Accipiter cooperii*) and Great Horned Owls (*Bubo virginianus*), by 1941 the Pheasant population had erupted to well over 1,540 (an annual increase of some 277 per cent), giving a ratio of more than nine birds per hectare. A year later the figure had risen to 2,000 – a ratio of nearly 12 birds per hectare.

In 1945, there were estimated to be between 30 and 40 million Pheasants spread over 130,000 km^2 of South Dakota; this is a density of something over 2 per hectare, and on the Sandlake Waterfowl Refuge in the same year the figure was over 10 per hectare; yet by 1948, the state's average density had fallen to 30 per 40 ha. In Michigan in 1944, about 1.4 million out of a post-breeding population of 4 million were killed over an area of 65,000 km^2; this is an average of 23 per 40 ha but ranged from about 75 per 40 ha in Genesse County down to only 5–6 in marginal habitats. In Wood County, Ohio, the population and harvest per 40 ha in 1937 was 40 birds and 14 cocks, respectively. The 1948 post-breeding population on the McManus Ranch in the Sacramento Valley of California amounted to about 125 per 40 ha. In Pennsylvania, the 1915 harvest was 796; 7 seven years later, after large-scale releases of gamefarm-reared birds, it was about 20,000, and shortly thereafter the annual kill had multiplied tenfold. By the late 1920s, the rate of increase had slowed down, but by the early 1930s, between 250,000 and 290,000 birds were being shot annually. The harvest rose still further between 1937 and 1941, when it amounted to 537,990, but subsequently declined, in line with that of other states, to a low of 213,000 in 1946, only to rise again by 1954 to an estimated 450,000. In recent years the pattern has been similarly fluctuating.

The release of Pheasants in the United States continued into the 1970s, both in their established range and also in new localities, under the auspices of the Foreign Game Introduction Program (FGIP) of the Department of the Interior's Fish and Wildlife Service. Many of these later introductions were made with hitherto untried subspecies and hybrids. Although the project was officially terminated in 1970, some of the participating states still held stocks of birds obtained under the auspices of FGIP, and the release of these birds and their progeny continued with mixed results until at least 1978. Table 5

gives details of releases of Pheasants made in the United States under the FGIP between 1960 and 1978. Between 1960 and 1978, 341,261 Pheasants were released in the United States under FGIP, as follows: Tennessee (1960–8), 49,228; Pennsylvania (1962–8), 46,576; Texas (1966–78), 46,535; New York (1968–71), 24,566; Virginia (1961–4), 22,182; Indiana (1964–75), 20,936; Oklahoma (1961–70), 19,483; New Mexico (1960–8), 17,201; Missouri (1961–71), 15,809; Idaho (1966–74), 13,539; Iowa (1962–78), 13,358; Washington (1965–75), 10,569; Kentucky (1961–72), 10,512; Maryland (1961–71), 7,988; California (1965–8), 6,678; Arizona (1966–70), 3,970; Utah (1964–7), 3,717; Alabama (1960–9), 2,987; South Carolina (1961–8), 1,055; Florida (1961–8), 936; Louisiana (1964–78), 836; Georgia (1963–6), 712; Nevada (1962–8), 643; Colorado (1971–2), 478; Arkansas (1962–8), 428; and Illinois (1963–4), 339. Of this total, some 142,339 (41.7 per cent) were planted in Tennessee, Pennsylvania and Texas. In addition, considerable numbers were released outside FGIP; for example, 84,505 in Minnesota between 1965 and

Table 5 Releases of Pheasants (*Phasianus colchicus*) in the United States, 1960–78

State	Years	Subspecies/Hybrid	Natural range	Number released
Alabama	1960–8	West Iranian (*talischensis*)	SW and S Caspian Sea	2,906
	1969	East Iranian (*persicus*) and/or *talischensis*	SW Transcaspia and SW and S Caspian Sea	81
Arkansas	1962–8	West Iranian (*talischensis*) × Chinese Ring-neck (*torquatus*)	SW and S Caspian Sea and E China	428
Arizona	1966–70	Afghan White-winged (*bianchii*)	Pamir and Hindukush Mts	3,970
California	1965–8	Afghan White-winged (*bianchii*)	Pamir and Hindukush Mts	6,678
Colorado	1971–2	Afghan White-winged (*bianchii*)	Pamir and Hindukush Mts	478
Florida	1961–8	West Iranian (*talischensis*) × Chinese Ring-neck (*torquatus*)	SW and S Caspian Sea and E China	936
Georgia	1963–6	West Iranian (*talischensis*) × Chinese Ring-neck (*torquatus*)	SW and S Caspian Sea and E China	712
Idaho	1966–74	Japanese (*versicolor* or *robustipes*)	Japan	13,539
Illinois	1963–4	Korean Ring-neck (*karpowi*)	S Manchuria and Korea	339
Indiana	1964–8	West Iranian (*talischensis*) × Chinese Ring-neck (*torquatus*)	SW and S Caspian Sea and E China	8,685
	1964–75	Korean Ring-neck (*karpowi*)	S Manchuria and Korea	12,251
Iowa	1962	West Iranian (*talischensis*) × Chinese Ring-neck (*torquatus*)	SW and S Caspian Sea and E China	155
	1962	East Iranian (*persicus*)	SW Transcaspia	42
	1962–3	East Iranian (*persicus*) × Chinese Ring-neck (*torquatus*)	SW Transcaspia and E China	200

Continued

Table 5 (continued)

State	Years	Subspecies/Hybrid	Natural range	Number released
Iowa (*cont.*)	1969–78	Chinese Ring-neck (*torquatus*)	E China	12,961
Kentucky	1962–6	West Iranian (*talischensis*)	SW and S Caspian Sea	331
	1961–6	West Iranian (*talischensis*) × Chinese Ring-neck (*torquatus*)	SW and S Caspian Sea and E China	3,344
	1962–6	East Iranian (*persicus*)	SW Transcaspia	401
	1961–6	East Iranian (*persicus*) × Chinese Ring-neck (*torquatus*)	SW Transcaspia and E China	2,253
	1966–72	Korean Ring-neck (*karpowi*)	S Manchuria and Korea	3,250
	1967–72	Japanese (*versicolor* or *robustipes*)	Japan	933
Louisiana	1966	West Iranian (*talischensis*)	SW and S Caspian Sea	53
	1978	West Iranian (*talischensis*) × Chinese Ring-neck (*torquatus*)	SW and S Caspian Sea and E China	50
	1978	Chinese Ring-neck (*torquatus*)	E China	78
	1964–7	Japanese (*versicolor* or *robustipes*)	Japan	655
Maryland	1961–8	East Iranian (*persicus*) × Chinese Ring-neck (*torquatus*)	SW Transcaspia and E China	2,304
	1965–7	East Iranian (*persicus*) × West Iranian (*talischensis*)	SW Transcaspia and SW and S Caspian Sea	491
	1969–71	West Iranian (*talischensis*) × Chinese Ring-neck (*torquatus*)	SW and S Caspian Sea and E China	5,104
	1969	Japanese (*versicolor* or *robustipes*)	Japan	89
Missouri	1964–71	West Iranian (*talischensis*)	SW & S Caspian Sea	3,123
	1961–5	East Iranian (*persicus*)	SW Transcaspia	1,653
	1959–61	East Iranian (*persicus*) × Chinese Ring-neck (*torquatus*)	SW Transcaspia and E China	1,633
	1962–71	Korean Ring-neck (*karpowi*)	S Manchuria and Korea	7,473
	1967–8	Korean Ring-neck (*karpowi*) × West Iranian (*talischensis*)	S Manchuria and Korea and SW and S Caspian Sea	1,927
Nevada	1963–8	Afghan White-winged (*bianchii*)	Pamir and Hindukush Mts	415
	1962–5	Afghan White-winged (*bianchii*) × Chinese Ring-neck (*torquatus*)	Pamir and Hindukush Mts and E China	228
New Mexico	1960–8	Afghan White-winged (*bianchii*)	Pamir and Hindukush Mts	17,201
New York	1968–71	Korean Ring-neck (*karpowi*)	S Manchuria and Korea	13,683
	1968–71	Japanese (*versicolor* or *robustipes*)	Japan	10,883
Oklahoma	1962–70	West Iranian (*talischensis*)	SW and S Caspian Sea	4,011
	1963–70	East Iranian (*persicus*)	SW Transcaspia	3,177
	1964–8 and 1970	Afghan White-winged (*bianchii*)	Pamir and Hindukush Mts	3,816
	1961–4, 1967 and 1970	Afghan White-winged (*bianchii*) × Chinese Ring-neck (*torquatus*)	Pamir and Hindukush Mts and E China	5,294
	1969	East Iranian (*persicus*) × Chinese Ring-neck (*torquatus*)	SW Transcaspia and E China	847
	1969–70	West Iranian (*talischensis*) × Chinese Ring-neck (*torquatus*)	SW and S Caspian Sea and E China	2,338
Pennsylvania	1962–8	Korean Ring-neck (*karpowi*)	S Manchuria and Korea	5,010

Continued

Table 5 (continued)

State	Years	Subspecies/Hybrid	Natural range	Number released
Pennsylvania (*cont.*)	1963–7	Korean Ring-neck (*karpowi*) × Chinese Ring-neck (*torquatus*)	S Manchuria and Korea and E China	41,566
South Carolina	1961–8	West Iranian (*talischensis*)	SW and S Caspian Sea	1,055
Tennessee	1964–8	West Iranian (*talischensis*)	SW and S Caspian Sea	1,369
	1961–8	West Iranian (*talischensis*) × Chinese Ring-neck (*torquatus*)	SW and S Caspian Sea and E China	26,382
	1964–5	East Iranian (*persicus*)	SW Transcaspia	502
	1960–3	East Iranian (*persicus*) × Chinese Ring-neck (*torquatus*)	SW Transcaspia and E China	15,650
	1962–5	Japanese (*versicolor* or *robustipes*)	Japan	2,264
	1962–4	Japanese (*versicolor* or *robustipes*) × Chinese Ring-neck (*torquatus*)	Japan and E China	3,061
Texas	1967	West Iranian (*talischensis*)	SW and S Caspian Sea	12
	1966–78	Chinese Ring-neck (*torquatus*)	E China	5,935
	1967–8	Chinese Ring-neck (*torquatus*) × ?	E China	276
	1966–73	Afghan White-winged (*bianchii*)	Pamir and Hindukush Mts	7,494
	1968–73	Korean Ring-neck (*karpowi*)	S Manchuria and Korea	5,396
	1966–78	East Iranian (*persicus*) × Chinese Ring-neck (*torquatus*)	SW Transcaspia and E China	27,422
Utah	1964–7	Afghan White-winged (*bianchii*)	Pamir and Hindukush Mts	3,717
Virginia	1961–6	West Iranian (*talischensis*)	SW and S Caspian Sea	1,589
	1961–4	East Iranian (*persicus*)	SW Transcaspia	1,930
	1969–76	East Iranian (*persicus*) and/or West Iranian (*talischensis*)	SW Transcaspia and/or SW and S Caspian Sea	12,060
	1959–62	East Iranian (*persicus*) × West Iranian (*talischensis*)	SW Transcaspia and SW and S Caspian Sea	417
	1968 and 1973–6	Korean Ring-neck (*karpowi*)	S Manchuria and Korea	438
	1960–74	Japanese (*versicolor* or *robustipes*)	Japan	5,748
Washington	1965–75	Japanese (*versicolor* or *robustipes*)	Japan	10,569

Sources: Banks 1981; Bohl & Bump 1970; Bump & Bohl 1964; Chambers 1965

1969. Bump & Bohl (1964) and Bohl & Bump (1970) summed up the distribution and status of the various races of Pheasants in the United States as follows:

West Iranian (*talischensis*). Doing well in Virginia by 1963 when birds had been reported from more than 40 counties. Near one release site in Kentucky, 57 nides were observed in the same year. Survival and reproduction apparent in South Carolina, Florida, Alabama, Tennessee and Arkansas, but declining in Missouri. *Ph. c. talischensis* was being widely crossed in captivity with northern Ring-necks (*torquatus*) to try to produce a bird likely to thrive south of the Ring-neck range and north of the Gulf States, where temperatures approximate those of *talischensis*'s native range, that is between 35 °C in summer and −3 °C in winter. By 1970, there was continuing evidence of survival and increase in parts of Virginia and also in Oklahoma, but South Carolina, Florida, Alabama, Tennessee and Arkansas reported 'fair to discouraging' results. Some states were releasing Korean (*karpowi*) or Ring-neck × West Iranian hybrids, which in Virginia were proving more adaptable than the pure subspecies.

East Iranian (*persicus*). Although in 1964 the birds were surviving and breeding well in

Missouri and Iowa they appeared to be doing less well than *talischensis* in Virginia, Kentucky and Tennessee. By 1970, 'poor to discouraging' results with little reproduction were reported in most states, apart from one evolving population in Virginia. Hybrids apparently fared better than pure-bred birds.

Korean (*karpowi*). By 1963 reproducing in Pennsylvania, and by 1970, when they were being reared on game farms in seven states from New York to Texas, 'excellent wild reproduction' was reported in Pennsylvania and in Missouri, with relic populations elsewhere. Korean × West Iranian and Korean × northern Ring-neck hybrids appeared to be unsuccessful.

Afghan White-winged (*bianchii*). Reproducing well in Oklahoma and Missouri (where 66 nides were reported in one locality) by 1963. In the following year, shooting was permitted in New Mexico and in 1966 in Nevada. In California, the birds were breeding successfully in several localities, including Imperial Valley. Evaluation was continuing in release areas of higher precipitation in Oklahoma and in limited habitats of southwestern Utah.

Japanese (*versicolor* or *robustipes*). Originally introduced, according to Phillips, unsuccessfully by the Colorado State Sportsmens' Association in about 1882, and again by Judge Denny (5 cocks and 17 hens) in 1885, when they were placed on Protection Island in Puget Sound, Washington. Further introductions in the 1960s resulted in 'fair to good abundance' in eastern Virginia and reproduction in Tennessee by 1963. Results in other states were so far inconclusive, though some failures were confirmed. By 1970, Eastern Shore populations in Virginia were 'definitely evolving', but birds released elsewhere in that state appeared to be interbreeding with Ring-necks, and were thought to be producing mutants or sterile offspring, while in five other states results were as yet undetermined.

The American Ornithologists' Union (1983: 136) described Pheasants in the United States as widely established from 'northern Minnesota, northern Wisconsin, central Michigan . . . south, at least locally, to southern interior California, . . . Utah, southern New Mexico, northern and southeastern Texas, northwestern Oklahoma,

Kansas, northern Missouri, southern Illinois, central Indiana, southern Ohio, Pennysylvania, northern Maryland, New Jersey and North Carolina (Outer Banks)'. In some areas where they are especially abundant Pheasants may have an inhibiting effect on stocks of the native Bobwhite Quail (e.g. in Iowa and Wisconsin) and Prairie Chicken (e.g. in eastern South Dakota). As in Europe, the relatively small amount of agricultural and horticultural damage Pheasants cause in the United States (where growing corn (maize), grains, potatoes, melons, tomatoes and strawberries are sometimes locally effected) is vastly outweighed by their economic and recreational value.

Mexico[18]

From Imperial Valley in southern California Pheasants have dispersed into northern Baja California, where they are established in the Mexicali Valley east of Lake Salada. This population is probably the most southerly in North America.

Canada[19]

In 1882, C. W. R. Thompson acquired 20 *colchicus* Pheasants from Lord Ernest Hamilton in England which he imported to Victoria on Vancouver Island, British Columbia, where they all subsequently died. In the following year, Thompson imported a further 25 birds from China, which he released at Esquimalt where they became established. Phillips (1928)[20] states that when the first shooting season opened on Vancouver Island, before 1888, around 1,000 birds (all cocks) were killed. In 1886, Edward Musgrave freed a dozen Chinese birds on Saltspring Island, and 4 years later a further 20 from the same source on Prevost Island. In the same year, the Mainland Protective Association released 20 birds at Point Grey, and 3 years later a further 23 at Ladner near the mouth of the Fraser River. According to Carl & Guiguet (1972), between 1890 and 1900 a total of 82 Pheasants were turned down in various localities in British Columbia, including some on Pender Island and five Japanese *versicolor* on Jedidiah Island.

In 1908, 28 *mongolicus* Pheasants were imported

for breeding to Chilliwack, where a year later 275 were released. In 1909, the British Columbia Game Commission made its first planting – with *torquatus* birds imported from Shantung Province, China – and a year later the commission assumed responsibility for future rearing at and stocking from the province's game farm at Saanich on Vancouver Island. This was closed down in 1933, but until 1954 thousands of Pheasants were acquired annually from commercial breeders and released in various localities, including the southern interior (where the first open season was declared in 1896), on the Queen Charlotte Islands, and in the northern interior near Vanderhoof. Pheasants near Tlell on Graham Island in the Queen Charlotte archipelago were, until at least the 1960s, the most northerly population in North America.

Elsewhere in Canada, according to Phillips, sporadic attempts, all of which failed, were made to establish Pheasants in New Brunswick (before 1925), Nova Scotia (before 1893), on Prince Edward Island in the Gulf of St Lawrence (before 1925), and probably in parts of Quebec. In the mid-1920s, large numbers were released in Manitoba. In the late 1950s a few pairs were released near St John's, Newfoundland, where some survived until at least 1968.

In the relatively mild climate of southern Ontario, Pheasants were first released prior to 1892; as a result of further sporadic plantings and the establishment of a Provincial pheasantry, they were sufficiently abundant on the Niagara and Magra peninsulas and in the Point Pelee area for a fortnight's open season to be declared in 1910. Their range limitation in this region is, as in northern Wisconsin and Michigan, governed by the availability of food in winter. According to Clarke & Braffette (1946)[21]:

Anything up to 50 inches [127 cm] of snowfall may be thought of as optimum conditions for pheasants . . . the isopleth determining the northward growth of seed corn almost exactly agrees with the 50 inch snowfall line . . . the areas having at least 50 percent of the occupied land in crops are the best regions for pheasants. Anything less than 50 percent would seem to be deficient in food supply for the birds.

In southern Ontario, where they are most abundant along the shores of Lakes Erie and St Clair and on Pelee Island (and in general elsewhere in North America), Pheasants' distribution coincides closely with the 50-inch snowfall line.

Pelee Island,[22] most southerly land in Canada, consists of 4,000 ha of fertile farmland derived from reclaimed marshes in the western end of Lake Erie, some 30 km north of Marblehead, Ohio. In 1927, three dozen Pheasants from the Ontario mainland were landed on Pelee Island.[23] Five years later, the population had multiplied to an estimated 20,000, and damage to farm crops was being reported. Although Clarke (1947) estimated the population in 1934 at between 50,000 and 100,000, Stokes (1954) believed that the 1950 level of 38,000 suggests a total of no more than 50,000 in 1934. However that may be, the population was large enough to cause serious crop damage, and many clutches of eggs were destroyed by irate farmers. Stokes records that the islanders are said to have killed 'wagonloads' of birds during the first few years after shooting was allowed, and that 'one hunter succeeded in shooting his limit from an armchair!'. The population remained high until 1938 but apparently fell in 1939–40, only to recover again by 1942 but once more declined between 1943 and 1945; in 1946, Clarke estimated the post-breeding population at around 10,000; by 1949–50, this figure had risen to 37,000, and in the latter year 12,000 hens were shot in an attempt to reduce damage to crops. Hard winters and cold, wet springs, coupled with overshooting of hens (especially during the economic depression of the early 1930s but also – out of season – into the 1940s) were the probable reasons for the species' decline. The fall in the population in 1943 followed large bags in the 1942 and 1943 shooting seasons (about 10,000 birds in each), plus a 142-cm winter snowfall in 1942–3 (compared to an average of 81 cm) and 17.5 cm of rain in the following May and 12.2 cm in July. The recovery between 1947 and 1949 was associated with mild winters and springs and a ban on the shooting of hens. In 1947, the Pelee Island Pheasant Project, sponsored by the Wildlife Management Institute and Ontario Department of Lands and Forests, was formed to monitor the future status of Pheasants on the island.

Pelee Island, half of which lies below lake level, is one of Ontario's most prosperous agricultural areas, and its clay soil is almost identical to that which supports heavy Pheasant populations in Michigan's 'Thumb' between lakes Michigan and Huron. Since there are few cattle on the island little grass is grown for hay, so few nesting hens are killed by mowers. Soyabeans (75 per cent), grain (15 per cent), corn or maize (5 per cent) and tobacco (3 per cent) are the principal crops. Woodlands, wasteground, marshes, roads, field headlands, rough pastures and ditches which provide shelter, nesting sites and a source of food cover some 20 per cent of the island. Although such predators as feral Cats (*Felis catus*) and Dogs (*Canis familiaris*), Brown Rats (*Rattus norvegicus*), squirrels (*Sciurus* spp), Fox Snakes (*Elaphe vulpina*), Common or American Crows (*Corvus brachyrhynchos*), Common Grackles (*Quiscalus quiscula*), Cooper's (*Accipiter cooperii*), Sharp-shinned (*A. striatus*), Red-tailed (*Buteo jamaicensis*), Rough-legged (*B. lagopus*) and Marsh (*Circus cyaneus*) Hawks, do occur on Pelee, there are no Red Foxes (*Vulpes (fulva) vulpes*), Striped Skunks (*Mephitis mephitis*), North American Mink (*Mustela vison*), Weasels (*M. nivalis*), Raccoons (*Procyon lotor*) or Virginia Opossums (*Didelphis virginiana*). The Pheasants' decline in the early 1940s is unlikely to have been caused by predation, which may, however, have hindered their recovery. Nest desertion and shortage of food when the population becomes too large may be the birds' main limiting factors, while the fact that they are on an island from which dispersal is well-nigh impossible may account for their phenomenal success. Stokes suggested that Pelee Island, which in 1950 had a legal bag of over 22,000 (220 per 40 ha), offered arguably the finest Pheasant shooting in North America.

Pheasants are currently established in Canada in Nova Scotia, New Brunswick, and on Prince Edward Island, and in southern Quebec, southern Ontario (as far north as St Joseph's Island in Lake Huron), southern Manitoba (especially near Winnipeg), central Saskatchewan, central Alberta and British Columbia (perhaps including the Queen Charlotte Islands), and possibly in Newfoundland. In British Columbia, between 10,000 and 15,000 occur mainly in the Kamloops/Okanagan/Osoyoos area west to Cache Creek, in the West Kootenays, at Alkali Lake in the Cariboo, throughout the arable farmland of the lower mainland, on southeastern Vancouver Island, on islands in the Fraser River, and in the Thompson Valley. Numbers in British Columbia have declined in recent years as a result of changes in husbandry. According to Guiguet (1961), three races – *colchicus*, *torquatus* and *mongolicus* – have been imported to Canada.

West Indies

In the 1950s, Chinese Ring-necked Pheasants (*torquatus*) were introduced for sporting purposes to the Dominican Republic by Ramfis Trujillo. They were overshot before they had an opportunity of becoming properly established, but a few pairs still apparently survive in the hills on the Alcoa Project near Cabo Rojo.

Brudenell-Bruce (1975) says that Ring-necked Pheasants were introduced (before 1959) at Hatchet Bay on the island of Eleuthera in the Bahamas. Bond (1979) makes no reference to this introduction.

SOUTH AMERICA

Chile[24]

According to Sick (1968), Pheasants have probably been introduced to several countries in South America but have only ever become established in Chile. Pheasants from England were imported to that country as the founder stock of an avicultural collection by C. J. Lambert in 1886 or 1887. Two pairs released in a park at La Compania, 16 km from Bahia de Coquimbo, had by 1897 increased in numbers and spread up to 25 km inland. This population eventually died out, but a second shipment of birds from Germany in 1914 became locally established in the provinces of Valdivia and Cautin, where Johnson (1965) estimated the population to number around 1,000. The present status and distribution of Pheasants in Chile is uncertain; according to Goodall (1946–57), they then survived only on Pichi Colcuman Island in Lago de Ranco in the Andean foothills of Valdivia Province. Blake (1977), however, says that as well as on Pichi Colcuman, Pheasants also occur in the wild further north on a farm at Allipen in Cautin Province.

AUSTRALASIA

Australia[25]

According to Jenkins (1959), Pheasants imported from England were released in Victoria on several occasions in or before 1855 (including 71 on Phillip Island and 4 at Sandstone and on Churchill Island), and they were apparently spreading shortly thereafter. Balmford (1978) records that several were imported in 1858, when birds released previously were said to be breeding, and 11 and a larger number in two shipments in 1859. The Victoria Zoological and Acclimatization Society released 8 Pheasants (on Phillip Island) in 1864, 30 in 1870, 15 in 1871, 70 in 1872 and more than 100 in 1873, and distributed large numbers of eggs to individuals and shooting clubs, while many more birds were released in the colony by private landowners. Although they initially did well where they were protected by man, none of these introductions was of long-standing.

On Tasmania, both Chinese and melanistic mutant '*tenebrosus*' Pheasants were liberated in about 1882 but failed to become established. In the mid-1940s, others were released at Sandford, Carlton, Cambridge and elsewhere, and before the end of the decade were reported to be thriving at Cambridge. In the early 1960s, attempts were made to establish Pheasants on Bruny Island off the south coast of Tasmania as well as elsewhere on the Tasmanian mainland.

On King Island at the western end of Bass Strait between Tasmania and Victoria, Pheasants were released by the Tasmanian Game Protection and Acclimatization Society in about 1910. On Flinders Island, at the eastern end, they were introduced around 1959 and again in the 1960s, though as Tarr (1950) points out, there may have been earlier but unrecorded releases since a single bird was found before 1959.

In South Australia, Pheasants (about 50 according to a local newspaper) were turned down at Echunga and elsewhere in the Mount Lofty Ranges by the Upland Game Association in 1961. In spite of vigorous opposition from conservationists, who even petitioned the Government to prohibit further releases, the association later claimed to have liberated more than 500 birds in various parts of the state, and in the 1960s the association had planted some 600 birds over a 3-year period on Fleurien Peninsula near Adelaide. According to Vincent (1971, in Abbott 1974), a single bird was released on Kangaroo Island off the coast of South Australia, though for what purpose is unknown. Tarr reported that a few Pheasants may have been

freed in the Hawkesbury district of New South Wales in 1944.

Pheasants were unsuccessfully liberated on the mainland of Western Australia by the Acclimatization Committee at some time between 1897 and 1912 and in 1905 and/or 1912 on Rottnest Island. In January 1928, H. A. Pearse, on behalf of the Zoological Gardens at South Perth, landed a cock and three hens on Rottnest Island, where they became established. According to Chisholm (1950), Pheasants have also been introduced to the Onslow district of Western Australia.

On Rottnest Island, Pheasants were described as 'widespread' by Jenkins (1959) and as 'a moderately common resident' by Storr (1965). On King Island, Chisholm in 1950 said they were 'common and widespread'. Blakers, Davies & Reilly (1984) show Pheasants as established between 1977 and 1980 in Western Australia (both on Rottnest Island and the mainland), Victoria, southern and western New South Wales, and on King and Flinders islands and Tasmania. Pizzey (1980) says they are present on Rottnest, King and (more recently) Flinders islands, in Tasmania, in the southern tablelands of New South Wales, possibly in the Australian Capital Territory (Canberra), and in the Mount Lofty Ranges of South Australia. Private releases in the bush continue to be made from captive-bred stock.

New Zealand[26]

The first Pheasants introduced into New Zealand were a cock and three hens imported from England by a Mrs Wills, a passenger on the *London*, in 1842. Others were landed in the following year by a Mr Petre, but nothing further was heard of either shipment.

The earliest successful liberation of Pheasants in New Zealand seems to have been made in 1845 by Walter Brodie at Mongonui where, although they were soon increasing in numbers, they did not stray far from their release site. Subsequently, until 1869, more birds were turned down at Tauranga, Tolago Bay, Raglan, Kawau, Bay of Islands and Napier.

James Hay informed Thomson (1922: 111) that Pheasants were first imported to Banks's Peninsula 'by Messers Smith and C. H. Robinson in the "Monarch" in 1850. Mr Robinson gave Mrs

Sinclair one pair. She kept them in a wire-house, but one having escaped, the other was let out. Instead of remaining in Pigeon Bay, the birds went straight over the hill to Port Levy in the early spring of 1851,' where they rapidly increased and from where some returned to Pigeon Bay in 1857.

In 1853, Sir Edwin Dashwood imported some Pheasants from England to Nelson, where they multiplied and spread to the Waimea Plains and adjacent districts. A few years later two unsuccessful attempts were made to establish Pheasants in this area by Henry Redwood, but in each case only a single bird arrived safely from England.

The Otago Acclimatization Society turned down 4 Pheasants in 1865, 36 in 1866, 6 in 1867, 12 in 1868, 100 in 1869, 13 in 1870, 10 in 1874 and 12 again in 1877. Six years after the initial release they were reported to be increasing rapidly in Otago, and by 1877 were 'abundant from Oamaru to Invercargill; many shooting licences have been granted' (Thomson, p. 111).

In 1865, some Pheasants were imported from England to Christchurch by the Prime Minister, Sir Frederick Weld. Two years later the Canterbury Acclimatization Society imported four, followed by 30 in 1868; by 1871 they were said to be 'thoroughly established, and needing no further importations' (Thomson, p. 111). In 1867 and 1868, the Auckland Acclimatization Society imported seven and two Pheasants, respectively, and in 1869 a Mr Wentworth released a number on the Hokonuis.

All these releases were of Common Pheasants (*Ph. c. colchicus*) imported from England.

Captain F. W. Hutton told Thomson that the first shipment of Chinese Ring-necked Pheasants (*torquatus*) were two dozen imported from that country on the barque *Glencoe* by Thomas Henderson in 1851. The only survivors that reached Auckland alive, five cocks and two hens, were released at Waitakere. Five years later, Henderson imported a further consignment from China on the schooner *Gazelle*, the half-a-dozen survivors of which were also liberated at Waitakere. These 13 birds, most of which were cocks, seem to have been the only Ring-necks released in Auckland, where they slowly increased and where large numbers were shot in 1865. They were first noted in the Waikato in 1864–5, and by 1869 were very common from Auckland through the Waikato and Thames

almost to Taupo. In the same year, they arrived at Whangarei but were reported only infrequently further north. In the Auckland Society's annual report for 1874–5 (quoted by Thomson 1922: 112) it is said that 'the Chinese pheasant is the common bird of this Province'.

In 1874 and 1875, the Wellington Acclimatization Society imported 20 and 4 Chinese Ring-necked Pheasants, respectively; these shipments to Auckland and Wellington were the only nineteenth-century ones of *torquatus* that Thomson could trace. Many birds (though whether *colchicus, torquatus* or hybrids is not always certain), were, however, distributed to other acclimatization societies: thus Otago received three *torquatus* from Auckland in 1864 followed by a further 15 in 1877, of which 7 were despatched to Oamaru and 5 to Tapanui. In 1867, the Canterbury Society acquired three Ring-necked Pheasants which they used as the founder-stock of a pheasantry from which in the following year they sold 40 birds to members at £2 a pair. 'In the tussock-covered land of Canterbury they throve specially well', James Drummond wrote to Thomson (p. 115), 'and the large Cheviot Estate, then held by the Hon. W. Robinson, was soon stocked with them. . . . The society continued to import pheasants for a considerable time. It bred about a hundred birds in a year.' By 1869, both *colchicus* and *torquatus* were said to occur 'in thousands' on the Cheviot Hills Station, and the society's report for 1871 said that Pheasants were 'thoroughly established and needing no further importations'. Nevertheless, according to Williams (1969), 19 (the survivors of a shipment of 49) were imported to Canterbury in 1880.

In 1869–70, the Southland Society obtained large numbers of both *colchicus* and *torquatus* from other societies, which they released in various localities (including five on Stewart Island), and in 1874 they liberated four of the latter at Wallacetown.

In 1879 and 1880, the Nelson Acclimatization Society obtained 20 and 18 Ring-necked Pheasants, respectively, from their Auckland *confrères*, which they released in Maitai Valley. A further five were liberated in Atawhai Valley in 1882, followed in 1898 by 20 more imported from England: these were distributed between Aniseed Valley, Wakapuaka, Hope, Pokororo and Eares Valley; those at Wakapuaka and

Pokororo were later reinforced by 20 birds transferred from Hawke's Bay. Between 1912 and 1945, over 400 Pheasants were planted in various localities, including Golden Downs, Thorpe, Woodstock, Baton, Stanley Brook, Pokororo, Wai-iti Valley, Redwoods Valley, Moutere, Motueka Valley and Waiwhero, and between the latter year and 1956 more were released in the same areas by private individuals.

Although Thomson considered that the Common Pheasant never established itself so readily in New Zealand as the Chinese Ringneck, there can be little doubt, as Thomson himself stated, that by 1871 birds of both races were abundant and widely distributed. According to Westerskov (1955a), their success was 'associated with bush burns and the weed tangles following the burns', but Oliver (1955) suggested that fires may have been responsible for the destruction of many Pheasant eggs and chicks.

From the 1880s, for several reasons, the population began to decline. The enormous increase in the number of Rabbits (*Oryctolagus cuniculus*), which had been introduced from England some 30 years earlier (Lever 1985b), led to the use of phosphorus-poisoned grain (which was equally accessible to birds) as a controlling agent. Small insectivorous songbirds (especially Starlings (*Sturnus vulgaris*) q.v., imported in 1867–8 and in later years) rapidly increased and became serious competitors for food. The importation around 1882 of Stoats (*Mustela erminea*) and Weasels (*M. nivalis*) (Lever 1985b) introduced a new threat into the hitherto virtually predator-free environment. In some areas, too, poaching was rife. 'In the South Island, and in those parts of the North Island where rabbits abounded', wrote Thomson (1922: 114), 'the history of the naturalisation of the pheasant seemed to be that at first the birds increased rapidly and became very common, then their increase stopped, their numbers decreased and finally in 25 years they were all but exterminated.' In Otago, Pheasants virtually disappeared between 1882 and 1892; they were reported to be decreasing in Wellington in 1885–8, and were scarce around Christchurch by 1890. In those parts of North Island uninfested by Rabbits, however, Pheasants remained fairly abundant, though less so than in earlier years.

To try to make good their losses many of the acclimatization societies revived their stocking programmes in the 1890s: thus in 1895 seven hens and two cocks from Auckland were released in Otago between Waihola and the coast. Two years later, 22 birds (the survivors of a shipment of 32 from London) were retained for breeding at Milton and/or Clinton. In 1899, a further consignment of 21 arrived from England and were held for breeding, while more than 80 home-reared birds were released. Liberations continued in Otago until at least 1914–15, but none seem to have met with lasting success.

On Stewart Island, where Rabbits had died out and where Ferrets (*Mustela furo*), Stoats and Weasels did not occur, the Southland Society planted 16 Pheasants in 1895, 48 in 1901, 37 in 1902, 36 in 1904, 16 in 1907, 105 in 1909 and 47 in 1910. Again, none of the birds released survived for long.

Members of the Wellington Society reared Pheasants for several years, but with only mixed success. In 1897, in partnership with some other societies, they imported 40 from England, and in 1905 they acquired four pairs from the Government. In 1907, they reared 430; in 1908, 347 (*colchicus* × *torquatus* hybrids); in 1910, 230; in 1912, more than 300; and doubtless large (but unspecified) numbers in the intervening years. Most were released, but appear to have succumbed to Stoats and Ferrets. The Nelson Society reintroduced Pheasants in 1912 and in succeeding years, and by 1915 they were reported to be thriving, as they were also in Taranaki.

In 1922, Thomson (p. 116) wrote:

In spite of all the efforts which have been put forth during the last half-century, pheasants are not very common anywhere in the North Island, and are extremely rare in the South. Poisoned grain, ferrets, stoats, weasels, wild cats, hawks [which were preserved because they preyed on Rabbits], wekas [*Gallirallus australis*] and poachers have all been blamed for this failure [but] . . . the diminution of their food supplies caused by the vast increase of all kinds of small birds has been the chief agent.

The introduction in 1892 of the insectivorous European Hedgehog (*Erinaceus europaeus*), which is now virtually ubiquitous in New Zealand (Lever 1985b), posed yet another threat to the beleaguered Pheasant.

Competition with other species for winter food not only caused the death through starvation of many Pheasants but rendered the survivors unfit for spring reproduction. The offspring of those birds that did nest successfully found a shortage of insect life on which to feed, again partially through competition from alien Passerines, and were preyed on by introduced California Quail (*Lophortyx californicus*) (q.v.).

According to Westerskov, by the early 1960s several hundred thousand Pheasants had been turned down in New Zealand; most were *colchicus* or *torquatus*, but with an admixture from 1923 of the Mongolian race (*mongolicus*) and from 1938 of melanistic mutants ('*tenebrosus*'). As in the British Isles and North America, the present stock are all hybrids, many of the cocks retaining at least a trace of the neck-ring. Although in many areas populations are self-maintaining, elsewhere they are reinforced by annual releases. Wodzicki (1965: 432) considered Pheasants to be 'widely distributed and common, North and South Islands', whereas Kinsky (1970) found them 'irregularly distributed'. They flourish most in the coastal scrub of North Island between 34° and 40° S, with lesser numbers in Nelson, Canterbury and Otago.

Although Thomson reported much damage by Pheasants to such crops as young grass, sprouting maize, potatoes, carrots, beans, peas, barley, wheat and many kinds of fruit (which was compensated for by the consumption of great quantities of injurious insects), today only minor local damage to market gardens and young maize is sometimes reported.

OCEANIA

Hawaiian Islands[27]

According to Walker (1967b), the Mongolian Pheasant (*mongolicus*) was first introduced to Hawaii in 1865, the Chinese Ring-neck (*torquatus*) in about 1875, the Japanese Pheasant (*versicolor*) before 1900, the Common Pheasant (*Ph. c. europaeus*)[28] in 1959, and melanistic mutants ('*tenebrosus*')[29] in 1960. (Elsewhere in the same paper, however, Walker says that 'by 1865 Chinese Ring-necked Pheasants . . . were well established and provided considerable sport shooting'.) Both Japanese and Chinese Ring-necked Pheasants were released on all the larger islands, and were subsequently reinforced by further liberations of birds acquired from dealers on the US

mainland, the territorial game farm on Oahu, and possibly also directly from Japan and China.

Schwarz & Schwartz, (1949 and 1951b) found Pheasants on Molokai, Hawaii, Lanai, Maui, Kauai and Oahu (Niihau was uncensused). All suitable habitats were occupied, and only areas with a high precipitation associated with dense rainforests and barren, dry, regions devoid of vegetation at low elevations and on high mountain tops were uncolonized. Pheasants ranged from sea level to an altitude of 3,000 m; from tropical regions to others where sub-zero temperatures were common; in areas with an annual rainfall of between 25 and 760 cm; on recent lava soil and on deep loam; in forested and grassland areas and in desert and other infertile country; in pineapple and sugar-cane plantations and in market gardens; and in all varieties of topographical conditions. They flourished most on medium to rich soils with a moderate rainfall, a permanent supply of water, and open cover interspersed with plenty of food species.

The only two regions supporting concentrations of pure Japanese Pheasants were the windward slopes of Mauna Kea and Mauna Loa on Hawaii; Ring-necks and hybrids also occurred, but Schwartz & Schwartz found the ratios to be approximately 3 Japanese : 1 hybrid : 1 Ring-neck. Where Japanese birds occurred elsewhere, the ratio was around 2 hybrids : 2 Ring-necks : 1 Japanese; regions with the latter population composition occurred near Japanese concentrations on Hawaii and locally on other islands. As was to be expected, the rate of hybridization increased progressively towards the periphery of each species' concentration.

Japanese Pheasants were found to thrive most on gently sloping land with richer soils in damp – frequently misty – and open forests. Although they occurred at all elevations in the Ring-necks' range, their main concentrations lay between 1,200 and 2,300 m, where the mean annual temperatures are between 10° and 15 °C, with a rainfall of between 320 and 50 cm at low and high altitudes, respectively. High densities occurred where cover consisted of scattered clumps of koa trees (*Acacia koa*) interspersed with grassy meadows with mixed herbaceous growth; smaller numbers frequented open grasslands, sugar-cane plantations and less-open forests. Overgrazing by mammals, which had transformed much of the forest into grassland, had improved Japanese Pheasant habitat, but on already open land heavy grazing seemed likely to inhibit tree regeneration which would reduce the species' preferred range. 'We believe', wrote Schwartz & Schwartz (1949: 29), 'the green [Japanese] pheasant is decreasing through hybridization since its more restricted distribution and lower numbers tend to favor the ring-neck.'

In 1946–7, Schwartz & Schwartz censused the Pheasant population in the Hawaiian Islands at 70,340, divided as follows: Hawaii 35,190, Maui 12,590, Kauai 11,540, Oahu 7,160, Molokai 2,410 and Lanai 1,450. They reported that Pheasants sometimes caused local damage to such crops as sweet potatoes, tomatoes and young corn (maize), but that the species was (1949: 26) 'the most important game bird in the Hawaiian Islands because of its wide distribution, sporting qualities and table value', while the 'brilliantly-colored pelt is sought for certain feathers used in making leis which are commonly worn on hatbands'.

Munro (1960) said that Chinese Ring-necks were well established on most islands, especially on Lanai, but that in line with the prediction of Schwartz & Schwartz, Japanese Pheasants (and *mongolicus*) seemed to have largely disappeared through hybridization with *torquatus*. Peterson (1961) reported that the Japanese Pheasant was still established on Kauai, Molokai, Lanai, Maui and Hawaii, that *colchicus* (which had been imported 2 years earlier) occurred locally on all the larger islands, and that hybrids were not uncommon. Between 1959 and 1966, 44 *torquatus*, 119 *colchicus*, 73 melanistic mutants ('*tenebrosus*'), and 8 Japanese birds were imported from game farms on the US mainland and released on the Puu Waawaa Ranch on Hawaii. The Hawaiian Audubon Society (1975) said that Ring-necks occurred in open grasslands on all the main islands, and pure Japanese birds probably only on the slopes of Mauna Kea and Mauna Loa on Hawaii. Common Pheasants were also present on Hawaii, but their current status was uncertain. Zeillemaker & Scott (1976) described Ring-necks as common on Oahu, Molokai, and Maui, uncommon on Kauai and Hawaii, and of indeterminate status on Lanai, while Japanese Pheasants were local and uncommon on Hawaii and local and rare on Oahu and Maui. Walker (1981) said that the Ring-necked Pheasant – known locally as *kolohala* – was to be found on Hawaii, Maui, Molokai, Lanai, Oahu and Kauai, and Japanese Pheasants on all the above except Oahu.

Society Islands (Tahiti)[30]

Guild (1938) records that sometime previously he had released Ring-necked Pheasants on Tahiti, where they were soon established and breeding. More were liberated on several subsequent occasions, especially in the region of Taravao. Monsieur J. P. Vernoux told Holyoak & Thibault (1984) that some hens had been seen in 1975.

Ring-necked Pheasants released on Bermuda[31] in the nineteenth century apparently enjoyed only limited success.

Since 1970 a shooting club has been releasing small groups of Ring-necked Pheasants at an altitude of 1,800 m in the foothills of the Andes 50 km east of Lima in Peru, where large numbers have been shot, but no reproduction in the wild has so far been observed. In 1974, some Pheasants were liberated somewhere east of Yauca and Chala in the Department of Arequipa some 450 km south of Lima.

In September 1959, 80 Ring-necked Pheasants were released on a private estate near El Volcán in Chiriquí, Panama, where they were all shot before 1965.

Meinertzhagen (1912) records that Ring-necked Pheasants from St Helena were introduced to Mauritius in about 1880 but died out shortly thereafter.

According to Bernström (1951) and Bannerman (1965), Common and Ring-necked Pheasants have been introduced unsuccessfully to the islands of Madeira and/or Porto Santo. The former were breeding on Madeira in 1687, but died out shortly thereafter. The latter were introduced unsuccessfully from England before the First World War, and again in 1936.

Ring-necked Pheasants introduced to Pitcairn Island[32] around 1935 were all soon killed off by the islanders.

In July 1945, 57 Mongolian Pheasants were introduced jointly by the US Navy and the California Fish and Game Commission to Guam in the Marianas for sporting purposes, where, not surprisingly, they were soon shot out.

In the early 1900s, Pheasants from England were released in the Knysna and Bredasdorp districts of Cape Province in South Africa,[33] where they remained for several years. In 1927, others from the Rooipoort game farm near Kimberley were freed on land owned by the Rhodes Fruit Farm Company in Western Province. In 1931–2, the Game Conservator of Zululand in Natal imported some Pheasants to the Hluhluwe Game Reserve, where about 20 were subsequently reared and released; a few of their descendents remained in the district until at least 1962. Two clutches of eggs were placed in the nests of wild Helmeted Guineafowl (*Numida meleagris coronata*), and most hatched successfully. Although Pheasants were unsuccessfully introduced to the Cape on a number of subsequent occasions, few other attempts appear to have been made to naturalize upland game birds in South Africa, probably because of the great variety and former abundance of native species.

In the Soviet Union,[34] Common Pheasants have been translocated both within and without their natural range. They were established in previously unoccupied parts of Transcaucasia in 1890 and in the northern Caucasus after 1930. Attempts to introduced Pheasants to Moldavia between 1949 and 1961, to the Rossiyskaya Soviet Federated Socialist Republic from 1960 to 1964, and to western Siberia and the Ukraine, either failed altogether or were only partially successful. In the last named region, some Ring-necks from Czechoslovakia were successfully turned down in 1958 in the Biryuchiy Peninsula on the western shore of the Sea of Azov. Between 1953 and 1963 other, but unsuccessful, attempts were made in various parts of the Ukraine – especially in Odessa – including one release involving 445 birds. From 1955 to 1965, over 9,000 Pheasants were liberated in European Russia, including some 500 in 1958–9 near Moscow, but these failed to become established. Most of the successful transplantations in the Soviet Union were apparently made with the northern Caucasian and west Caspian form, *Ph. c. septentrionalis*.

In 1910–11 or 1912, unsuccessful attempts were made to naturalize Pheasants on Cyprus,[35] and again in 1952, at Troödos, Paphos, Aghirda, Athalassa, Kouklia, Lanaca and elsewhere.

According to Hachisuka & Udagawa (1951),

some Pheasants of the local form, *Ph. c. formosanus*, were in 1929 translocated to Kashoto (Hwoshaotao) on Taiwan where, after initially becoming established, they were later exterminated.

NOTES

1 Cramp & Simmons 1977; Dunning 1974; Fitter 1959; Gladstone 1921b, 1923, 1924, 1926; Lever 1977a, 1978, 1979b; Lowe 1933; Matheson 1963; O'Gorman 1970; Pernetta & Handford 1970; Sharrock 1976; Tozer 1974; Wayre 1969; Witherby et al. Vol. 5, 1941; Yapp 1983.

2 Hence the generic and specific scientific names given to the bird by Linnaeus in his *Systema Naturae* (1758) (*phasianus* = native of Phasis). This district represents its topo-typical locality.

3 An Old English territorial unit, originally of feudal lordship.

4 See note 2.

5 Delacour 1951; Etchécopar 1955; Long 1981.

6 Haftorn 1966; Long 1981; Myrberget 1976.

7 Long 1981; Merikallio 1958.

8 Brazil 1985; Kaburaki 1934, 1940; Kuroda 1922; Long 1981; Ornithological Society of Japan 1974; Sakane 1960.

9 For much of the history of the Pheasant in North America I am indebted to Allen (1956). Other references are: Allen 1954, 1962; American Ornithologists' Union 1957, 1983; Anon. 1890; Banks 1981; Bohl 1970a,b, 1971a; Bohl & Bump 1970; Bump 1941, 1963, 1968,a,b 1970e; Bump & Bohl 1964; Burger 1964; Burriss 1965; Chambers 1965, 1966; Christensen 1963b, 1967; Colson 1968; Cottam 1956; Einarsen 1942, 1945; Ellis & Anderson 1963; Gabrielson & Lincoln 1959; Gerstell 1938; Gigstead 1937; Gottschalk 1967; Greely, Labisky & Mann 1962; Hart 1967; Janson, Hartkorn & Greene 1971; Laycock 1970; Leopold 1933; Long 1981; McAtee 1945; McNeel 1973; Nelson 1963; Phillips 1928; Popov & Low 1950; Robinson 1969; Roots 1976; Ruhl 1941; Sandfort 1963; Schorger 1947; Shaw 1908; Shields & Neudahl 1970; Silverstein & Silverstein 1974; Tuttle 1963; Wandell 1949; Wollard, Sparrowe & Chambers 1977.

10 Quoted by Laycock (1970) from an article in the September 1964 issue of the *Oregon Historical Quarterly* by Virginia C. Holmgren. As Laycock points out, Denny was almost certainly mistaken in describing his birds as 'Mongolian pheasants' (*mongolicus*), since their natural range is well over 3,000 km west of Shanghai. They were doubtless *torquatus* from eastern China. Phillips (1928) says the shipment consisted of 70 birds.

11 Phillips says this consignment totalled 100 pairs.
12 Nide = a brood of young pheasants.
13 For much of the information on Pheasants in Utah I am indebted to Popov & Low (1950).
14 J. Sharp, Report of the State Fish and Game Warden for 1897–8, *Deseret News* (Salt Lake City, Utah), 4–39 (1899), quoted by Popov & Low (1950: 15).
15 *Deseret Evening News*, 16 March 1894 (quoted by Popov & Low).
16 *Deseret Evening News*, 1 March 1893 (quoted by Popov & Low).
17 Kimball, Kozicky & Nelson, in Allen 1956.
18 American Ornithologists' Union 1957, 1983; Long 1981; Peterson & Chalif 1973.
19 Allen 1956; American Ornithologists' Union 1957, 1983; Carl & Guiguet 1972; Cottam 1956; Davies, Peter & Munro 1980; Godfrey 1966; Guiguet 1961; Laycock 1970; Long 1981; Phillips 1928; Roots 1976; Tuck 1968; and W. T. Munro, personal communication, 1985.
20 See also *Forest and Stream* 31: 453 (1888).
21 Quoted by McCabe, MacMullen & Dustman, in Allen 1956.
22 For the history of Pheasants on Pelee Island I am indebted to Clarke (1947) and Stokes (1954).
23 According to Laycock (1970), Frank Vorhees of the Ohio Division of Conservation released 100 Pheasants from the Wellington Game Farm on Pelee Island in exchange for a like number of Bass.
24 Blake 1977; Goodall, Johnson & Philippi 1951–7; Hellmayr 1932; Johnson 1965; Long 1981; Sick 1968.
25 Balmford 1978; Blakers, Davies & Reilly 1984; Chisholm 1950; Condon 1975, 1978; Frith 1979; Green 1969 (in Condon 1975); Jenkins 1959, 1977; Littler 1902; Long 1972, 1981; Pizzey 1980; Ryan 1906; Serventy 1948; Sharland 1958; Storr 1965; Tarr 1950; Vincent, 1971 (in Abbott 1974).
26 For much of the early history of Pheasants in New Zealand I am indebted to Thomson (1922). Other references are: Falla, Sibson & Turbott 1979; Kinsky 1970; Lever 1985b; Long 1981; Oliver 1955; Thomson 1926; Westerskov 1955a,b, 1957b, 1962, 1963; Williams 1969; Wodzicki 1965.
27 American Ornithologists' Union 1957, 1983; Berger 1981; Caum 1933; Hawaiian Audubon Society 1975; Lewin 1971; Long 1981; Munro 1960; Peterson 1961; Pyle 1977; Schwartz & Schwartz 1949, 1951b; Walker 1967b, 1981; Zeillemaker & Scott 1976.
28 'Ph. c. *europaeus* (Bulgaria) has been described as differing very slightly from *Ph. c. colchicus*'; Witherby et al. 1941 (Vol. 5: 240).
29 See Delacour 1951 and Goodwin 1982a.
30 Guild 1938; Holyoak 1974a; Holyoak & Thibault 1984; Long 1981.
31 Bourne 1957; Crowell 1962; Crowell & Crowell 1976; Long 1981; D. B. Wingate 1973 (and personal communication, 1981).
32 Holyoak & Thibault 1984; Long 1981; Williams 1960.
33 Liversidge n.d.; Long 1981; Siegfried 1962; and P. A. Clancey and J. M. Winterbottom, personal communications, 1981.
34 Anon. 1959; Long 1981; L'vov 1962; Nazarenka & Gurskii 1963; Osmolovskaya 1969; Shlapak 1959; Yanushevich 1966.
35 Bannerman & Bannerman 1971; Long 1981; Niethammer 1963.

Reeves's Pheasant
(Syrmaticus reevesii)[1]

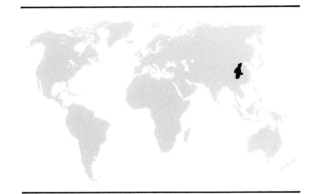

NATURAL DISTRIBUTION
Mountainous regions of northern and central China, including western Hopeh (Hebei), Shansi (Shanxi), southwestern Shensi (Shaanxi), Hupeh (Hubei), western Honan (Henan), Anhwei (Anhui), and northwestern Szechwan (Sichuan).

NATURALIZED DISTRIBUTION
Europe: France, Germany; Oceania: ?Hawaiian Islands.

EUROPE

France; Germany

Despite Roots's claim (1976: 166–7) that Reeves's Pheasants have 'successfully colonized forested areas in France, Hungary, Czechoslovakia and Austria', they are currently believed to be established in continental Europe[2] only in northern France (from plantings made before 1955) and in parts of Germany.

OCEANIA

Hawaiian Islands[3]

Reeves's Pheasants, imported from a game farm on the US mainland, were first released in Hawaii in 1957. In 1959, 1960, 1964 and 1966, 180 from game farms in California, Michigan and Wisconsin were planted on the Puu Waawaa Ranch on Hawaii where, although most soon disappeared, Lewin (1971) reported that a few remained around the release site. In the autumns of 1960 and 1961, 548 from a game farm in California were liberated on Maui, Lanai, Oahu, Molokai, Hawaii and Kauai. Bump & Bohl (1964: 29) defined their status as follows: 'Kauai and Hawaii release holding their own; others doubtful. Broods observed on Kauai and Hawaii. Unbanded adults seen on Hawaii and Molokai. Species holding its own on several of the release areas; but is nowhere indicating establishment. Small broods reported from Molokai and Oahu; adults from the original releases were seen, in excellent condition on Hawaii and Kauai.' They summarized the position by saying (p. 4) that Reeves's Pheasant 'is maintaining itself in Hawaii'.

Although Walker (1967b: 10) listed the species as 'not known to be established in Hawaii', Bohl & Bump (1970: 6) said that it 'occurs locally on three islands in Hawaii', and the Hawaiian Audubon Society (1975) stated that Reeves's Pheasants were established on Kauai, Molokai and Lanai, though their status was uncertain. Zeillemaker & Scott (1976), Pyle (1977), Walker (1981) and Berger (1981), however, make no reference to their presence on any of the islands, so their current status must be in some doubt.

According to Phillips (1928), Reeves's Pheasants may have been introduced in the 1880s by Rutherford Stuyvesant to his estate in New Jersey in the United States.[4] In 1907–9, 422 were imported, and in 1914, 20 were released in Yakima County, Washington, where in the following year they were mentioned in the game laws of the state, and were said still to survive there 4 years later. In 1931–3 and 1947–9, at least 233 and 815, respectively, were released unsuccessfully in New York and California. In 1940 and 1947, 3 and 47 Reeves's Pheasants from Wisconsin were turned down near Kenai Lake on the south coast of Alaska, where they all eventually succumbed to the severe winters.

Between 1954 and 1977, 35,698 Reeves's Pheasants were released in eight states both within the Department of the Interior's Foreign Game Introduction Program and independently, without the establishment of any permanent viable populations, as follows: Ohio (1954–61), 22,735; Kentucky (1959–63), 7,674; Washington (1969–77), 3,721; Iowa (1963–9), 3,377; Tennessee (1964–6), 768; Missouri (1964–7), 678 (including 19 wild birds imported from France); Arkansas (1959–60), 247; and Virginia (1960–2), 219. In addition, 1,210 Reeves's × Chinese Ring-neck (*Phasianus colchicus torquatus*) hybrids were liberated in Ohio in 1960–1. According to Korschgen & Chambers (1970), whose findings were largely confirmed by Stephens (1966 and 1967), the failure of Reeves's Pheasants to become established in the United States is due to their vulnerability to predators; a lack of inherent wildness; their monogamous habits; and their poor reproductive success and chick survival rate.

In New Zealand,[5] the Wellington Acclimatization Society imported nine Reeves's Pheasants in 1897, and 2 years later more were brought in by the Wanganui Society and released on the Wanganui River, where they apparently soon disappeared.

The earliest reference to Reeves's Pheasant in western literature is to be found in the journal (dictated to Rusticiano or Rustichello of Pisa while imprisoned in Genoa in 1298) of Marco Polo, of which the original English translation is as follows: 'There be plenty of Feysants and very greate, for one of them is as big as 2 of ours, with tails of eight, 9 and tenne spans[6] long, from the Kingdom of Erguyl or Arguill, the West side of Tartary.'

The first Reeves's Pheasant to reach Europe was one presented in 1831 to the Zoological Society of London, where the species bred successfully in 1867.

In the British Isles[7] in 1870, Lord Tweedmouth released a pair of Reeves's Pheasants, which he had imported from Peking (Beijing), at Guisachan (Cougie) at the western end of Strathglass, Inverness-shire in Scotland. After a further four cocks had been introduced, the birds bred freely – over 20 being reared successfully in the first year – but were inclined to wander, some flying over 30 km north to Strathconan. Nevertheless, according to Gray (1882, quoted by Sharrock 1976: 451) on Guisachan 'more than 100 had been shot in the course of a single season, and the birds were found to be as hardy as (the young indeed more so than) the commoner varieties of pheasant'. Gray considered that 'It was not too much to expect that in a very few years it would become thoroughly naturalised, and be found in considerable numbers all over the country.' In 1892, a dozen cocks were counted at Guisachan, and by the middle of the decade the species was said to be well established on that estate and on the adjacent one of Balmacaan.

In the last quarter of the nineteenth century, Reeves's Pheasants were released in England by Lord Lilford at Lilford Hall in Northamptonshire, by the Duke of Bedford at Woburn Abbey in Bedfordshire, and by other landowners at Tortworth in Gloucestershire and Bedgebury in Kent. In Scotland, they were turned down at about the same time at Duff House and Pitcroy in Aberdeenshire, at Tulliallan in Fife, at Mount Stewart on the Isle of Bute by the Marquess of Bute, and in Kirkudbrightshire. In Ireland, Colonel Edward H. Cooper unsuccessfully liberated some at Markree Castle in County Sligo. In all these localities (apart from Ireland), Reeves's Pheasants at first bred successfully, and these, albeit temporary, successes with the species belie Roots's assertion (1976: 166) that 'several attempts to establish it in the British Isles failed completely'.

In this century, Reeves's Pheasants have been released in the British Isles as follows: in Dorset and Ross-shire where, although populations survived in the wild until at least the mid-1950s, none were present by the end of the following decade; at Elveden Hall near Thetford in Suffolk in 1950 by the Earl of Iveagh; near Louth in Lincolnshire (where they are shot annually, but seldom breed) since about 1955; at Megginch Castle, Errol, Perthshire, in the mid-1960s by Captain Humphrey Drummond; in Morayshire (70) and Cumberland in 1969; in Inverness-shire, where in 1969–70 more than 50 were turned out in Kinveachy Forest, where they were apparently breeding in the wild by 1973–4; at West Ashby in Lincolnshire, since about 1970; at West Dean, near Chichester in West Sussex; in Dumfriesshire; at Woburn Abbey in Bedfordshire, where numbers have been declining in recent years; and doubtless elsewhere. Although on at least some of these properties Reeves's Pheasants have bred in the wild, they seem never to have succeeded in establishing viable naturalized populations, and in December 1983 the British Ornithologists' Union Record Committee reported that 'It is believed that all Game Conservancy and other attempts at introduction have failed'.[8]

Reeves's Pheasants, which favour hilly and densely wooded country, would, were they to become established, fill a vacant habitat niche unoccupied by any other British game bird. Although their fast, high flight makes for difficult shooting, they are not universally popular among landowners because of the pugnacity of the cocks and their tendency to interbreed with other pheasants. Their failure to become permanently established in the British Isles may be, as Sharrock (1976) suggests, because the cocks, which often spread far from their release site and lack the far-carrying call of other pheasants, become too dispersed for successful pairing.

NOTES

1 The species is frequently, but incorrectly, referred to as 'Reeve's' or the 'Reeve' Pheasant. It is named after John Reeves (1774–1856) who, while in the service of the East India Company in China, sent back many specimens of fauna and flora to England.
2 Bump 1958a, 1964, 1968a,b; Etchécopar 1955; Heinzel, Fitter & Parslow 1972; Niethammer 1963; Roots 1976; Thomson 1964.
3 Berger 1981; Bump & Bohl 1964; Hawaiian Audubon Society 1975; Lewin 1971; Long 1981; Walker 1967b; Western States Exotic Game Bird Committee 1961.
4 Banks 1981; Bohl & Bump 1970; Bump 1941, 1958a, 1968a, b; Bump & Bohl 1964; Edminster 1937; Korschgen & Chambers 1970; Long 1981;

Phillips 1928; Seibert & Donohoe 1965; Stephens
1966, 1967.
5 Long 1981; Thomson 1922.
6 Span = *c.* 22.5 cm (*c.* 8.75 in).
7 Blank 1970; Fitter 1959; Gray 1882; Lever 1977a;
Roots 1976; Sharrock 1976.
8 *Ibis* 126: 443 (1984).

Lady Amherst's Pheasant
(Chrysolophus amherstiae)

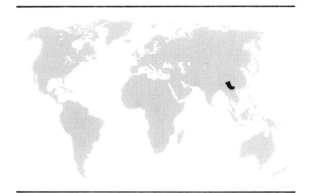

NATURAL DISTRIBUTION
Upland regions of southwestern China (Szechwan (Sichuan), Yunnan and western Kweichow (Guizhou)) and neighbouring parts of Tibet and upper Burma.

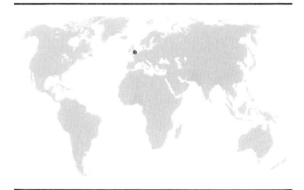

NATURALIZED DISTRIBUTION
Europe: British Isles.

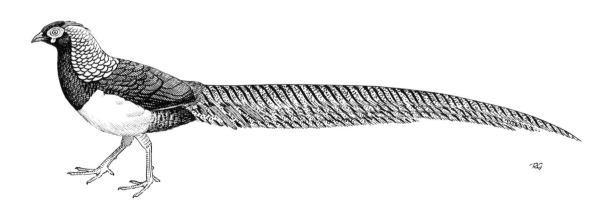

EUROPE

British Isles[1]

Lady Amherst's Pheasant[2] was first introduced to England in 1828, but because of the small number imported from China there is no record of successful breeding until 1871. Thereafter, a captive-bred stock was built up, but, according to Sharrock (1976), an initial shortage of hens resulted in early crossing with the closely related Golden Pheasants (*Chrysolophus pictus*) (q.v.), so that pure *amherstiae* became somewhat uncommon.

The earliest attempts to establish the species in the wild were made in about 1895 by the Marquess of Bute at Mount Stewart on the Isle of Bute, and at around the same time by the Duke of Bedford (with Lady Amherst's × Golden hybrids) at Cairnsmore near Newton Stewart in Wigtownshire, and with pure-bred stock at Woburn in Bedfordshire. Subsequently, Lady Amherst's Pheasants were released by Lord Montagu of Beaulieu in the Beaulieu Manor woods in Hampshire in 1925; in Richmond Park, Surrey, in 1928–9 and 1931–2; in Whipsnade Park, Bedfordshire, in the 1930s; and by the Earl of Iveagh at Elveden Hall near Thetford in Suffolk in 1950.

At Cairnsmore (and on Bute, in the Beaulieu Manor woods and at Elveden, where Lady Amherst's Pheasants were released with Golden Pheasants) the latter soon obliterated *amherstiae* characteristics. At Woburn[3] and Whipsnade, however, the former thrived and spread, and their descendants form the principal population in Britain today in private and state forestry plantations in south Bedfordshire and neighbouring parts of Buckinghamshire and Hertfordshire. Smaller numbers have occurred around Exbury in Hampshire since the 1950s, and in north-west Norfolk (and perhaps elsewhere in that county) since the early 1970s.

In view of their readiness to interbreed, it is unfortunate, as Sharrock points out, that in Britain populations of Golden and Lady Amherst's Pheasants tend to overlap, and the position has been exacerbated by the release of the former into areas already occupied by the latter and vice versa. In 1971, some Lady Amherst's Pheasants were found hybridizing in Galloway with Golden Pheasants; these may have been the descendants of the original introduction or recently released birds. It is to be hoped that any future liberations of either species will be made where the other does not already occur.

In the Far East, where in parts of China their range overlaps that of the Golden Pheasant, Lady Amherst's Pheasants inhabit rocky mountain slopes, forests, woodland and scrub at higher altitudes (between 2,000 and 4,000 m) than their congener. In England, they live in deciduous forests, young coniferous plantations, or mixed woodland with dense undergrowth, especially Bramble (*Rubus fruiticosus*) and Rhododendron (*Rhododendron ponticum*). Introduced for ornamental rather than sporting purposes, Lady Amherst's Pheasant is generally disliked by gamekeepers and landowners because of its skulking habits and tendency, when disturbed, to run rather than to fly, but is sometimes tolerated because of the beautiful plumage of the cock. Loss of identity through hybridization with Golden Pheasants is the main problem that Lady Amherst's Pheasants have to face in Britain, where the population (which is not, even now, completely pure, and could degenerate still further if more Golden Pheasants are released in Bedfordshire as they have been several times since 1949) is in the region of 100–200 pairs. The species was admitted to the British and Irish List in 1971.

Phillips (1928: 41–2) says that in the United States 'No records of any attempted plantings of the Amherst pheasant have been found, though a few birds doubtless have been liberated. . . . Hybrids between this and the golden pheasant were, it is believed, set out by Alexander Forbes on Naushon Island, Mass., a few years ago.'

According to Sick (1968), attempts by shooting clubs and the Ministry of Agriculture to establish Lady Amherst's (and other) Pheasants in Colombia did not succeed.

Thomson (1922: 110) records that the 'Diamond Pheasant (probably Lady Amherst's Pheasant)' was imported to New Zealand in 1907 (when the Otago Acclimatization Society had a pair at Opoho) but so far as is known none were ever released.

In the Hawaiian Islands,[4] Lady Amherst's Pheasants, imported from game farms in the United States in 1931 and 1932, were released on

Oahu in 1932 and on Hawaii in the following year, but never succeeded in becoming established.

NOTES

1 Cheng 1963; Delacour 1965; Fitter 1959; Lever 1977a; Sharrock 1976; Thomson 1964; Wayre 1969.
2 Sometimes incorrectly referred to as the 'Amherst' Pheasant, the species is named after the first wife of William Pitt Amherst, 1st Earl Amherst of Arracan (1773–1857), who in 1816 was sent as an envoy to the Emperor of Japan and in 1823 was appointed Governor-General and Viceroy of India.
3 According to M. C. Thompson, steward of the Bedford Estates (personal communication, 1985), Lady Amherst's Pheasants at Woburn have 'declined severely in recent years', and in 1984 more were released to supplement the surviving stock.
4 Berger 1981; Caum 1933; Long 1981; Munro 1960; Schwartz & Schwartz 1951; Walker 1967b.

Golden Pheasant
(*Chrysolophus pictus*)

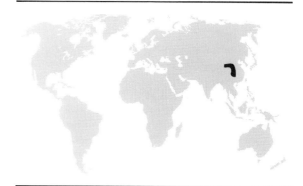

NATURAL DISTRIBUTION
Mountainous regions of central China from southeastern Tsinghai (Qinghai) and southern Kansu (Gansu) southwards to Szechwan (Sichuan) and central Hupeh (Hubei).

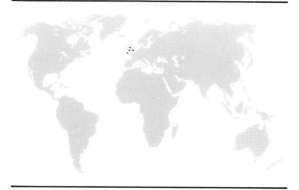

NATURALIZED DISTRIBUTION
Europe: British Isles.

EUROPE

British Isles[1]

The first Golden Pheasant in captivity in Britain was a single bird in the collection of Eleazar Albin, who described it in his *History of Birds*

(1731–8). The earliest mention of a specimen in the wild refers to a bird seen in Norfolk in 1845.

In the 1880s, Golden Pheasants imported from China were released on several private estates in the west Highlands of Scotland, where they appear to have fared best on the island of Gigha. Golden Pheasant × Lady Amherst's Pheasant (*Chrysolophus amherstiae*) (q.v.) hybrids (whose offspring later reverted to pure Golden characteristics) were turned down in about 1895 at Cairnsmore near Newton Stewart in Wigtownshire by the Duke of Bedford, and pure-bred stock at Monreith in the same county by Sir Herbert Maxwell, Bt in 1902. Others were freed in 1895 by the Marquess of Bute at Mount Stewart on the Isle of Bute, where they interbred with the closely related *Chrysolophus amherstiae* (released at the same time) and with Common Pheasants (*Phasianus colchicus*) (q.v.). In England, Golden Pheasants were freed at Tortworth in Gloucestershire in the 1890s; in the Beaulieu Manor woods in Hampshire by Lord Montagu of Beaulieu in 1925 where, as on Bute, they hybridized with Lady Amherst's Pheasants planted at the same time; at Sevenoaks in Kent before 1942; at Whipsnade in Bedfordshire several times since 1949; and near Bournemouth in Hampshire. On several occasions since the late 1890s Golden Pheasants have been introduced to estates in East Anglia, notably at Elveden Hall near Thetford in the Brecks of Suffolk by the Earl of Iveagh in and before 1950. They have also been turned down, by the Williams-Bulkeley family, on the Isle of Anglesey off the coast of north Wales.

The triangle formed by Kirroughtree Forest, Penninghame and Creetown in Wigtownshire and Kirkudbrightshire in south-west Scotland (Galloway), and the Brecklands of west Norfolk and west Suffolk – especially between Thetford and Brandon and in Thetford Chase – are the principal strongholds of Golden Pheasants in Britain today. Smaller numbers occur on Tresco (between 5 and 10) in the Isles of Scilly (where two pairs were released in 1975); on Anglesey; in Cardrona Forest in Peebles-shire; in the Sandringham/Wolferton area of north-west Norfolk (since 1967); and perhaps also elsewhere.

The Golden Pheasant's natural habitat in the central uplands of China is bushes, bamboo thickets and similar low but dense scrub on rocky slopes and in valleys. In Britain, on the other hand, it frequents coniferous woodlands – especially forestry plantations – and sometimes mixed coniferous/deciduous woods. In Galloway, where they are believed to be descended from the Duke of Bedford's introduction in 1895, Golden Pheasants have increased and spread in recent years following extensive afforestation, and are most numerous in 15–30-year-old stands of Scots Pine (*Pinus sylvestris*) and Larch (*Larix decidua/kaempferi*). In the Brecklands, too, Golden Pheasants thrived after the planting of softwoods on extensive tracts of heathland.

Although Golden Pheasants were originally introduced for sporting purposes they provide poor shooting due to their inclination, when alarmed, to run rather than to fly, and the alleged pugnacity shown by the colourful cocks towards other pheasants makes them generally unpopular with gamekeepers. They are today regarded solely as an ornamental species.

In the Far East, where in places the Golden Pheasant's distribution coincides with that of the closely related Lady Amherst's Pheasant, the two species tend to live allopatrically at different altitudes. In Britain, however, they interbreed freely wherever their ranges overlap. They are reared all over the country in garden aviaries as well as on large estates, and small numbers are often turned down (or escape) in entirely unsuitable habitats – such as open farmland with little or no cover – where they are soon destroyed or from which they become dispersed. 'It may well be', wrote Sharrock (1976: 148), 'that predation, not least by man, is a contributory factor to the tendency for small introductions to fail in unprotected environments.' Sharrock estimated the population of Golden Pheasants, which because of their skulking habits are difficult to assess quantitatively, at between 500 and 1,000 pairs. The species was admitted to the British and Irish List in 1971.

Etchécopar (1955) records that Golden Pheasants were released for sporting purposes before 1939 near Compiégne and at Livry in France where they were soon shot out.

According to Palmer (1899), Golden Pheasants may have been kept in some of the old deer parks of Maryland in the United States[2] in the late seventeenth century, and Phillips (1928) suggests that some may later have been stocked in deer parks along the James River in Virginia. If this is not so, probably the first of these 'overgorgeous birds' (as Phillips described them) to reach North America was a pair presented by the Marquis de Lafayette to George Washington at Mount Vernon, Virginia, in November 1786. In 1883 (possibly as early as 1857), around 100 were released in the state of Washington. In about 1885, 11 cocks and 15 hens, imported by Judge Owen Denny from China (see p. 154), were placed on Protection Island near Port Townsend in that state, and at around the same time others were released on Goat Island in San Francisco Bay, California. Some time before 1909, some were freed on Arsenal Isle near Moline in Illinois, and others are believed to have been liberated near Lynn Haven, Virginia. In 1930, 16 were turned down in the southern Willamette Valley of Oregon, and between 1900 and 1948, about 100 were stocked on the King Ranch in Texas. In none of these localities did the birds persist for more than a year or two.

In Canada, Phillips records that some Golden Pheasants were released near Nanaimo on Vancouver Island, British Columbia, some time before 1928, where a few were later shot and the rest disappeared.

Sick (1968) reported that attempts by the Ministry of Agriculture and shooting clubs to establish Golden (and other) Pheasants in Colombia were unsuccessful.

According to Thomson (1922), between 1867 and 1907 more than 10 Golden Pheasants were imported to New Zealand by the acclimatization societies of Auckland, Canterbury, Wellington and Otago, but so far as is known none were ever released.

Although Golden Pheasants freed on Tahiti by Eastham Guild (1938) were reported to be breeding shortly thereafter they soon disappeared.

In the Hawaiian Islands,[3] Golden Pheasants were first released in 1865, and possibly also in 1867 and 1870 and again after 1932 when a game farm was established on Oahu. These, and more recent attempts to naturalize the species, were all unsuccessful.

Between 1930 and 1940, a Mr Chaplin made repeated attempts to naturalize Golden Pheasants in the Jonkershoek Valley, South Africa,[4] where a few remained until at least 1942.

NOTES

1 Cheng 1963; Delacour 1965; Fitter 1959; Harvie-Brown & Buckley 1892; Lever 1977a; Maxwell 1905; Thomson 1964; Sharrock 1976; Wayre 1969.
2 Gottschalk 1967; Lehmann 1948; Long 1981; Palmer 1899; Phillips 1928.
3 Berger 1972; Long 1981; Munro 1960; Schwartz & Schwartz 1951; Walker 1967b.
4 Siegfried 1962.

Common Peafowl
(*Pavo cristatus*)

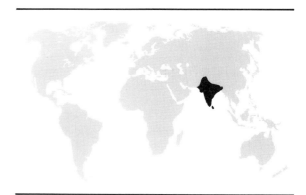

NATURAL DISTRIBUTION
Pakistan, India north to the Himalayas, Nepal, Bangladesh and Sri Lanka.

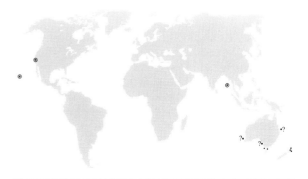

NATURALIZED DISTRIBUTION
Asia: Andaman Islands; North America: USA; Australasia: Australia; New Zealand; Oceania: Hawaiian Islands.

ASIA

Andaman Islands

According to Abdulali (1964 and 1967), Peafowl were introduced to Ross Island off Port Blair on South Andaman in about 1868, where Hume (1873) reported that they had flourished, although introductions to the South Andaman mainland had been unsuccessful. The birds on Ross Island were destroyed by the invading Japanese in 1940, but after the archipelago's liberation more were imported, and there is now a small semi-feral population.

NORTH AMERICA

USA[1]

A small colony of Peafowl is established in the vicinity of Palos Verdes Estates, Rolling Hills, and Portuguese Bend in southern California. It is believed to be descended from birds that escaped or were released from captive flocks introduced in the 1920s, though when this occurred is unknown. In 1973, the population numbered between 20 and 30 adults plus an indeterminate number of subadults, and 2 years later at least 15 were counted. They are reported to roost in pines, to be thoroughly wild and completely independent of man.

AUSTRALASIA

Australia[2]

In Victoria, Peafowl were released on Gembrook Reserve in 1870–1 with Guineafowl (*Numida meleagris*) (q.v.) and Red Jungle Fowl (*Gallus gallus*) (q.v.); in the former year at least 10 were also turned out in the bush near Melbourne, while four were liberated with Guineafowl at Cape Liptrap in 1872 and probably more in the bush a year later.

Young Peafowl reared in the Zoological Gardens of South Perth were freed in various parts of Western Australia (especially at Gingin and Pinjarra) before 1912, but by 1959 a small number survived only in the vicinity of the latter, 80 km south of Perth. In about 1912, and probably again in 1915 or 1917, some were landed on Rottnest Island, where about 50 (one account says up to 100) were established in dense cover in 1965. Before the 1950s Peafowl were said to occur near Onslow in the north-west and possibly in other parts of Western Australia, while a few semi-feral birds were maintained near Northam.

Elsewhere in Australia, feral Peafowl have been established in several localities. In 1950, they were reported from East and West Sister islands and Prime Seal Island in the Furneaux group in Bass Strait; from Tasmania; in the Blackall and Gladstone districts of Queensland; and on the headwaters of the Snowy River (and, semi-feral, in the Finley and Deniliquin districts) in New South Wales. Since about 1972, individual birds have been seen at Porky Beach and at Loorana on King Island in Bass Strait, where a flock of a dozen was observed at Pass River later in the decade. In 1975, feral Peafowl were reported from Murray's Lagoon on Kangaroo Island off the coast of South Australia, and in the following year were said to be breeding on Heron Island in the Capricorn group at the southern end of the Great Barrier Reef off the Queensland coast. Today, feral Peafowl probably occur only on islands in the Furneaux group and on King Island in Bass Strait, and perhaps also on Rottnest, Heron, and Kangaroo islands though isolated semiferal populations are frequently found on the mainland near human settlements.

New Zealand[3]

The first Peafowl in New Zealand were imported by a Mr Petre in 1843. Twenty-four years later the Otago Acclimatization Society introduced two, and elsewhere private individuals and dealers brought in others at around the same time, some of which, particularly in North Island, escaped into the bush where they became established. Thomson (1922), who was told that Peafowl were formerly to be found in several places in the Hawke's Bay area and that they were once numerous in the valleys of the Turakina and Wangahu rivers, reported that they had since died out, probably through competition for food, especially insects, with introduced

Passerines: they still occurred, however, in bush districts inland from Wanganui.

Oliver (1930 and 1955) recorded that in 1862 Peafowl were introduced at Waimarama, Hawke's Bay, and that in the 1950s colonies survived there and at Gisborne, Mahia, Wairoaiti, Tutira and on the Wanganui River between Tokomaru and Longacre. Wodzicki (1965) said that Peafowl were established locally in North Island, and Kinsky (1970) recorded them at Marohemo and south Kaipara heads in Northland, and at Opotiki, Wanganui, Hawke's Bay and Gisborne. Falla, Sibson & Turbott (1979) indicated that several feral populations occurred in North Island from Kaipara to Wanganui and Hawke's Bay.

OCEANIA

Hawaiian Islands[4]

On which island in the Hawaiian group Peafowl were first introduced is uncertain. All authorities agree that they were imported by Mrs Frances Sinclair in (or about) 1860, though Schwartz & Schwartz (1949), who say they were first seen in that year on Kauai, add a caveat that some may have been brought in at an earlier date. Fisher (1951) states that they were released on the island of Hawaii in the 1860s and on Niihau in the 1890s. Another account claims that they were first introduced, to Niihau, in about 1860, and that from there some were later transferred to the Kalalau Valley on Kauai and thence by Charles Grey to Lanai, where they disappeared during the construction of Lanai City. In 1909, two birds (presumably a pair) were released on the Puu Waawaa Ranch on Hawaii, where they bred successfully and became quite common in ohia (*Metrosideros collina*) forest where Passion Flower vines (*Passiflora* sp.) that festoon the trees provide an abundance of cover. Although they did not spread far from their release site some were later distributed to other leaseholders on the island.

Peafowl were reported to be plentiful on Kauai in 1936 and on Niihau in the early 1940s. In 1946–7, Schwartz & Schwartz estimated the population on Oahu, Maui, Molokai, Kauai and Hawaii to be 530, and indicated that on Niihau the birds were 'abundant'. They occurred on the

various islands in small discrete colonies near their original release sites, and ranged over areas of up to 15.5 km² in extent from sea level to an altitude of 1,500 m in annual precipitations of between 50 and 100 cm. At sea level, they were found in the algaroba flats, near sea level in the kukui/guava (*Psidium guajava*)/Java plum (*Eugenia cumini*) association, and in mamani forests at higher elevations. Dense brushy, grassy or herbaceous undergrowth and, in forested habitats, Passion Flower vines, provided plenty of cover. Although thickly vegetated areas were used for roosting and shelter, small openings in the bush and the forest ecotone were extensively visited for feeding and for nuptial display by the cocks. Feral Pigs (*Sus domestica*) and Small Indian Mongooses (*Herpestes auropunctatus*) seemed to be the most important predators (Lever 1985b).

Peterson (1961) reported that Peafowl remained established in small and scattered areas on Niihau, Kauai, Oahu, Molokai, Maui and Hawaii. The Hawaii Audubon Society (1975) considered that Peafowl were probably only well established and breeding on Oahu, Maui and Hawaii. Zeillemaker & Scott (1976) indicated that they were locally rare on Hawaii and perhaps occurred on Kauai, whereas Walker (1981) listed them as present on Hawaii, Maui, Molokai and Oahu. Berger (1981) said they occurred on all the main islands except Lanai, whereas the American Ornithologists' Union (1983: 136) lists them as 'presently established on Oahu and Hawaii, doubtfully so on Molokai and Lanai'. Confusion over the Peafowl's status in Hawaii may have arisen because of the difficulty in differentiating between free-ranging but semi-domesticated stock on ranchland and truly feral flocks in more remote forested regions.

Wetmore & Swales (1931) suggest that Peafowl may have been established in the wild on the Neyba plains in the Dominican Republic towards the end of the eighteenth century. They are recorded there in 1798 and again in 1810, but apparently not thereafter.

According to Bernström (1951) and Bannerman (1965), Peafowl were introduced (probably by Prince Henry the Navigator, who colonized the islands in 1424–5) to Madeira – where they bred in the wild until 1455 – and/or Porto Santo, but died out shortly thereafter.

Holyoak (1974a) says that in the Society Islands feral Peafowl were established on Raiatea in about 1920 and that they were also introduced on Tahiti, but have since died out on both islands.

Peafowl that at one time lived in the wild on St Helena (Melliss 1870) have long since disappeared.

According to Liversidge (n.d.) Peafowl have been unsuccessfully introduced to South Africa.

Whistler (1923) records that the presence of Peafowl in the Sind region of Pakistan and in adjacent desert areas is apparently the result of translocations by human agency. Ticehurst (1924) said that they then occurred at Bobi near Mirpur Khas, at Umarkot, near Sukkur on the Indus, and in a semi-feral state at Sehwan – all probably as the result of separate transplantations by man, since the Thar Desert effectively prevents any

natural extension of range in this area. According to Ali & Ripley (1968–74), Peafowl are currently established in a semi-feral state in various parts of Sind, including around Hyderabad, Mirpur Khas, Umarkot and Sehwan.

NOTES

1 Blake 1975; Hardy 1973; Heilbrun 1976; Long 1981.
2 Balmford 1978; Blakers, Davies & Reilly 1984; Chisholm 1950; Hobbs 1961; Jenkins 1959, 1977; Kikkawa & Boles 1976; Lavery 1974; Long 1972, 1981; McGarvie & Templeton 1974; Pizzey 1980; Ryan 1906; Serventy 1948; Storr 1965; Tarr 1950.
3 Falla, Sibson & Turbott 1979; Kinsky 1970; Oliver 1930, 1955; Thomson 1922; Wodzicki 1965.
4 American Ornithologists' Union 1957, 1983; Berger 1981; Bryan 1958; Caum 1933; Fisher 1951; Hawaiian Audubon Society 1975; Lewin 1971; Long 1981; Munro 1944; Peterson 1961; Pyle 1977; Schwartz & Schwartz 1949; Walker 1967b, 1981; Zeillemaker & Scott 1976.

Helmeted Guineafowl

(Numida meleagris)[1]

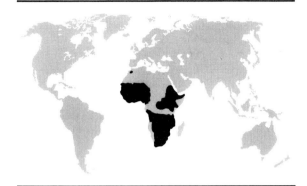

NATURAL DISTRIBUTION

Most of Africa except the extreme north (where it occurs only in parts of central Morocco) and the south-west. Has declined in many areas because of overshooting.

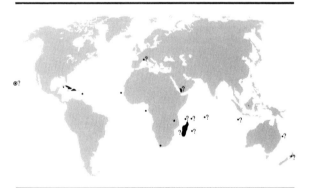

NATURALIZED DISTRIBUTION

Europe: ?France; Asia: ?Yemen; Africa: South Africa, Mozambique, ?Madagascar, ?Comoros, Mauritius, Agaléga Islands, Cape Verde Islands, Annobón Island; North America: West Indies; Australasia: ?Australia, ?New Zealand; Oceania: Cocos (Keeling) Islands, ?Hawaiian Islands, ?Chagos Archipelago.

EUROPE

When the Guineafowl was first imported to Europe is uncertain, but it is known to have been domesticated by both the ancient Greeks (who knew it as *meleagrides*) and by the Romans, whose writers, Varro and Columella, mention it in their works (both entitled *De re rustica*[2]) published,

respectively, about 54 BC and in the middle of the first century AD. There is, however, no evidence of the species' continuous domestication since that period, and it was probably reintroduced to Europe by Portuguese traders from west Africa in the late fifteenth or early sixteenth century, when it was known in England as the 'Tudor Turkey'. It was not, however, apparently well known in Europe until around the middle of the sixteenth century, when the English physician, John Caius, sent a description and drawing, with the name *Gallus mauritanus*, to Konrad Gesner, the German–Swiss naturalist, who published both in his *Paralipomena* in 1555.

France[3]

Although Guineafowl were released for shooting in France many years ago, attempts to establish them were not continued, as they proved unsatisfactory game birds. Heinzel, Fitter & Parslow (1976: 100), however, state that they are 'found S France', though their map does not indicate any location(s).

ASIA

Yemen[4]

According to Meinertzhagen (1954), Guineafowl were probably introduced to the Arabian Peninsula. Today they are found only in the extreme northwestern regions of the People's Democratic Republic of Yemen (South Yemen) and in the Republic of Yemen as far north as Wadi Itwad in Asir Tihama. Since, however, the race in Yemen, *N. m. meleagris*, is the same as occurs on the other side of the Red Sea in Africa, the birds may well be descended from natural immigrants from Ethiopia, barely 50 km away across the Bab al Mandab at the mouth of the Red Sea.

AFRICA[5]

South Africa; Mozambique

Guineafowl have been shot out over much of their former range in Africa, but domesticated birds of the race *N. m. mitrata* (the Mitred Guineafowl), which occurs from southern Kenya to Zimbabwe and in Madagascar, were successfully reintroduced from Europe and South Africa in some areas; for example, around Cape Town and Stellenbosch in the southwestern Cape Province, probably as long ago as the late nineteenth century, and on Likoma Island in Lake Niassa, Mozambique in 1912. Liversidge (n.d.) put the feral South African population at a maximum of 1,000.

Madagascar and Comoros[6]

Although Landsborough Thomson (1964) claims that Guineafowl occur in the Malagasy Republic and in the Comoros group probably as the result of human intervention, neither Rand (1936) nor Milon, Petter & Randrianasolo (1973) suggest that on Madagascar they are other than indigenous.

According to Benson (1960), birds of the race *N. m. mitrata* have probably been introduced to the islands of Grande Comore, Anjouan and Mayotte in the Comoros archipelago, where they were first collected in 1843 and were said to be abundant in 1876. Again, however, the possibility must be that they are native to the islands.

Mauritius and Rodrigues[7]

Guineafowl of the race *N. m. mitrata* are said to have been introduced from Madagascar to Mauritius in the early eighteenth century, where Bernardin de Saint Pierre saw some in 1769. Despite predation by the introduced Small Indian Mongoose (Lever 1985b), a few were reported to survive in the Black River Gorges area of Mauritius until at least 1970.

Staub (1976) records that P. Marragon, the Civil Agent for Rodrigues, wrote to the Council of the Mascarenes in August 1803 strongly advocating the importation of Guineafowl to Rodrigues; this probably took place shortly afterwards, as the birds were said to be abundant on the island by 1864. Between 1967 and 1976 they were deliberately exterminated because of the damage they caused to the island's maize crop.

Agaléga Islands[8]

Guineafowl were introduced to the Agaléga Islands in the Indian Ocean shortly after their settlement by the French in 1818. They were said to be abundant in the wild by 1837, and a few may have survived in some grassland areas until at least 1963. According to Guého & Staub (1983), they have now disappeared as a result of predation by feral Dogs (*Canis familiaris*) and Black Rats (*Rattus rattus*), which escaped from the wreck of the *Mathilde* on 5 September 1891.

Cape Verde Islands[9]

In 1461, Prince Ferdinand of Portugal, brother of King Alphonso V, populated the hitherto uninhabited Cape Verde Islands (which had been discovered in 1456 by the Venetian navigator Alvise Cadamosto) with slaves imported from Guinea on the coast of West Africa, and it seems likely that Guineafowl of the race *N. m. galeata* from that area were brought in at the same time. They were apparently seen on Sal by the English buccaneer William Dampier who visited the islands in 1683, were reported to be abundant on Maio in 1709, and were observed on São Thiago by Charles Darwin in 1832. According to Bannerman & Bannerman (1968), they were found by Bolle on São Nicolau, São Vincente Fogo, Maio and São Thiago in about 1856, and had recently been reintroduced to Brava where they had previously died out. In 1873, Henry Moseley found Guineafowl on Santo Antão, São Vincente, São Nicolau, Brava, Fogo and especially on São Thiago where, he wrote in *Notes by a Naturalist on H.M.S. Challenger* (1879), 'we met with several flocks of wild galinis, which are abundant on the island'. Barboza du Bocage (1898) found Guineafowl on São Thiago, São Nicolau, São Vincente, Santo Antão, Brava and Boa Vista in 1898, and Murphy (1924) saw them on Fogo. Guineafowl now occur on most of the islands mentioned above apart from São Vincente and Brava.

Annobón Island[10]

Guineafowl are established in the wild – probably as introduced aliens – on Annobón Island off the coast of Gabon south of the Gulf of Guinea. In the early 1960s, they were common on cultivated land in the north, where they have maintained their numbers for over a century. They have apparently never been domesticated on the island, so the present population, if the species has been introduced by human agency and is not a natural immigrant from West Africa, must be descended from deliberate releases.

NORTH AMERICA

West Indies[11]

According to Wetmore (1927) and Bond (1979), the Guineafowl was first introduced from West Africa to the West Indies as early as 1508. (Writing in 1836, Karl Ritter said that the species was introduced to the Antilles in about 1500 – a claim later repeated by Wetmore – but this assertion is unsubstantiated.) The Guineafowl is now domesticated throughout the region and would, as Bond remarks, doubtless have become feral on many islands had it not been for predation by the introduced Small Indian Mongoose (*Herpestes auropunctatus*). It occurs in the wild in most lowland areas of Hispaniola where it is preyed on by feral Cats (*Felis catus*), on Cuba, on the Isle of Pines (Youth), and on Barbuda where it is regarded as an important game species.

On Hispaniola, the Guineafowl was well established and widespread by the eighteenth century. P.-F.-X. Charlevoix records its presence in the wild in his *Histoire de l'ile Espagnole ou de S. Domingue* (1733),[12] and M. L. E. Moreau Saint-Méry, in *A Topographical & Political Description of the Spanish Part of Saint-Domingo* (1798), says that it was found in many different localities. E. Descourtilz reported that Guineafowl were common thereabouts when he visited Port-au-Prince in 1799, and William Walton, the British agent in San Domingo from 1802–9, wrote in his report on the Spanish colonies (published in 1810) that Guineafowl were so common on the Neiba plains of the south coast that they fetched only one *real* in the local market. Christy (1897) found them abundant and widespread both in domestication and the wild, and Danforth (1929) reported that they were common in woods by the Yaqui River near

Monte Cristi and that a few were to be seen at La Vega, San Juan, L'Archahaie, St Marc and Les Salines. Wetmore & Swales (1931) found them in many areas – mainly in Haiti. Although Guineafowl are still well established in the Dominican Republic, their numbers are rapidly decreasing due to overshooting and predation by the introduced Mongoose. Indeed, as Phillips (1928: 11) remarks: 'Where that obstreperous animal, the mongoose, is present, it preys extensively on guinea fowl and keeps their numbers much in check.'

Bond reports that Guineafowl are also established on Cuba eastwards from Las Villas Province, on the nearby Isle of Youth in the Gulf of Batabanō, and on Barbuda in the Leeward Islands (which, according to Phillips, 'was made into a sort of game preserve more than 200 years ago'), where the Moroccan race *N. m. sabyi* has been established in the wild since before 1889.

Elsewhere in the West Indies, Guineafowl have been unsuccessfully introduced as game birds on Gonave Island off the west coast of Hispaniola. On Jamaica, they apparently flourished in the eighteenth and nineteenth centuries but died out sometime after 1928. In Puerto Rico, they were reported in mountainous areas in 1836, 1869 and 1878; in 1911–12, Wetmore was told that some could still be found in natural forest on Cerro Gordo and Monte del Estado above Maricao, in Caguana near Barros, and on El Yunque de Luquillo, but by about 1927 he considered that they had died out. Phillips, however, states that they still occurred in the wild on the island in 1928, so the probability is that, as in Jamaica, they died out shortly thereafter. Guineafowl are certainly no longer 'firmly established' on Jamaica and Puerto Rico as claimed by Roots (1976). On Barbados, Guineafowl were common in domestication in 1889, but whether any were ever released or became feral is unknown. In 1700, a pair was unsuccessfully freed on the island of Trinidad.

AUSTRALASIA

Australia[13]

Ryan (1906) records that some 170 Guineafowl were unsuccessfully released at Gembrook

Reserve in 1870–1, and at Cape Liptrap, Lillydale and elsewhere in Victoria in 1872–3. Several hundred were held in captivity in Western Australia before 1912, where their offspring were allowed to range free in the hope that they would become established in the wild. Although by the 1920s they were said to be thriving in some coastal districts where they were repeatedly augmented by further introductions, they eventually died out. A small number turned down on Rottnest Island off the coast of Western Australia likewise failed to become established.

Between 1960 and 1970, Guineafowl were released on Heron Island in the Capricorn group at the southern end of the Great Barrier Reef off the Queensland coast, where they are now said to be tenuously established and breeding.

New Zealand[14]

The Revd R. Taylor informed Thomson (1922) that Guineafowl were first introduced to New Zealand by early missionaries who landed some at the Bay of Islands. In the early 1860s, Guise Brittain and Cracroft Wilson imported some from India, which they presented to the Canterbury Acclimatization Society, and in 1864 they gave half-a-dozen to a Mr H. Redwood of Nelson. Three years later, the Otago Society distributed 23 among a number of private landowners, but nowhere in South Island did Guineafowl become established – probably because of the severe winters.

In North Island, they were released in several localities by private individuals, but by the 1920s were only established at Aberfeldy, some 65 km inland from Wanganui. A few were subsequently reported from further north in the Waikato River region. Today, some are thought to survive in the wild in rough country with scrub and wooded gullies in parts of south-central North Island.

OCEANIA

Cocos (Keeling) Islands

According to Stokes, Sheils & Dunn (1984), a feral pair of Guineafowl established for several years near the Transmitter on West Island, apparently derived from domestic stock belonging to the Clunies-Ross family on Home Island.

Hawaiian Islands[15]

Since 1874, Guineafowl have escaped from domesticity or have been released on several Hawaiian islands (including a considerable number on Lanai in 1914), but in most places have failed to become established. Schwartz & Schwartz (1949) found about 500, whose numbers were gradually decreasing, on Lanai, Molokai, Maui, Kauai and Hawaii, and believed that these lingering flocks would disappear within a few years. A small number, however, are believed to survive on private property on the island of Hawaii (and, according to Walker (1981), on Maui, Molokai and Lanai) but their exact status is unknown.

Chagos Archipelago[16]

Gadow & Gardiner (1907) found a small number of feral Guineafowl on Takamaka, Fouquet and Anglaise islands in the Chagos group in 1907. Although Loustau-Lalanne (1962) saw none when he visited the islands in 1960 or 1961, Bourne (1971) heard reports of them on Salomon Island. It seems possible that a few may remain on some of the less-frequented islands in the archipelago.

Guineafowl have been domesticated in the United States[17] since the early days of colonization, but have never shown any signs of reverting to the wild. Between 1886 and 1890, some were unsuccessfully released in Tuxedo Park in New York State by the Tuxedo Park Club, and in about 1890 between 40 and 50 were turned down as game birds on Jekyl Island, Georgia, again without success. In the early 1900s a few Guineafowl became temporarily established in California, but there were no further reports of 278 released in the southern Willamette Valley of Oregon in 1929–30. A small number were turned down in Georgia and California in 1942, where they succeeded in becoming established for only a short time.

Guineafowl (of the subspecies *N. m. galeata*)

may have been seen on St Helena[18] by the English circumnavigator Thomas Cavendish when he landed briefly on the island in 1588. In 1870, they occurred in both domesticity and in the wild, but are believed to have died out by the turn of the century.

Guineafowl of the same race as on St Helena were probably introduced to Ascension[19] in the South Atlantic in about 1815 when, following the incarceration of Napoleon on St Helena, the island was garrisoned by the British. By the 1830s they were sufficiently well established to allow some 1,500 to be shot in a single day, and by 1864 they were still abundant enough to be shot under licence. Their extirpation towards the end of the century was probably caused by excessive shooting.

The American Ornithologists' Union (1983), which says that Guineafowl still occur on Ascension, indicates that they are also established on Trindade off the coast of Brazil.

Guineafowl (*N. m. galeata*) were introduced from the coast of Guinea to Madeira and Desertas (on both of which they bred in the wild until at least 1579) and possibly also to Porto Santo,[20] but died out soon afterwards.

In 1906, Mr T. Bell introduced Guineafowl to Raoul Island[21] in the Kermadecs, where within 3 years they had disappeared. The species has also been turned down without success in several localities in Germany.[22]

NOTES

1 The Helmeted Guineafowl is the ancestor of the domestic variety.
2 Vol. 8, ch. 2; vol. 3.
3 Etchécopar 1955; Heinzel, Fitter & Parslow 1972; Long 1981; Niethammer 1963.
4 Long 1981; Meinertzhagen 1954.
5 Liversidge, n.d.; Long 1981; Mackworth-Praed & Grant 1952–73.
6 Benson 1960; Landsborough Thomson 1964; Long 1981; Milon, Petter & Randrianasolo 1973; Rand 1936.
7 Benedict 1957; Gill 1967; Long 1981; Rountree, Guérin et al. 1952; Staub 1973, 1976.
8 Guého & Staub 1983; Long 1981; Watson, Zusi & Storer 1963.
9 Bannerman & Bannerman 1968; Barboza du Bocage 1898; Long 1981; Murphy 1924.
10 Fry 1961; Long 1981.
11 Bond 1979; Christy 1897; Danforth 1929, 1934; Feilden 1889; Lack 1976; Long 1981; Murphy 1915;

Peters 1934; Phillips 1928; Roots 1976; Wetmore 1927; Wetmore & Swales 1931. See also: *Osprey* 4: 21 (1899); *Forest and Stream* 20: 68 (1883) and 54: 149 (1900).
12 Vol. 1: 38–43.
13 Kikkawa & Boles 1976; Lavery 1974; Long 1972, 1981; Ryan 1906; Storr 1965.
14 Falla, Sibson & Turbott 1979; Oliver 1930, 1955; Thomson 1922; Wodzicki 1965.
15 American Ornithologists' Union 1957, 1983; Berger 1981; Hawaiian Audubon Society 1975; Long 1981; Munro 1960; Schwartz & Schwartz 1949; Walker 1967b, 1981; Zeillemaker & Scott 1976.
16 Bourne 1971; Gadow & Gardiner 1907; Long 1981; Lousteau-Lalanne 1962.
17 Bump 1941; Gottschalk 1967; Gullion 1951; Long 1981; Phillips 1928.
18 Haydock 1954; Long 1981; Melliss 1870; Peters 1934.
19 Long 1981; Stonehouse 1962.
20 Bannerman 1965; Bernström 1951; Long 1981.
21 Long 1981.
22 Niethammer 1963.

Common Turkey
(*Meleagris gallopavo*)

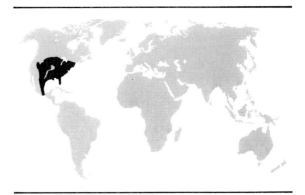

Note: Original natural distribution.

NATURAL DISTRIBUTION

Formerly much of central, northeastern and eastern USA and extreme southeastern Canada, south to southern Mexico. Now confined naturally to southern USA south to central Mexico, but distribution greatly extended by widespread reintroduction and restocking.

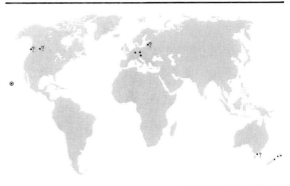

NATURALIZED DISTRIBUTION

Europe: ?Germany, ?Poland, ?Austria, ?USSR; North America: ?Canada; Australasia: ?Australia, New Zealand; Oceania: Hawaiian Islands.

EUROPE

The Turkey,[1] which is now domesticated virtually throughout the world, seems to have been first described in *La Natural Hystoria de las Indias*[2] (?1526 or 1527) by the Spanish historian Oviedo y Valdés, who says that shortly after the subjugation by Cortez and his *conquistadors* of

New Spain (Mexico) in 1521, it was taken from domestication there to islands in the Caribbean and to Castilla del Oro (Darien).

Precisely when the species first arrived in Europe is uncertain. It may possibly have been brought back to England by John Cabot in 1498 or by one of his successors early in the sixteenth century, but the oft-quoted distich ('Hops, and Turkies, Carps and Beer came into England all in a year') by Sir Richard Baker in his *Chronicle* (1643: 298) cannot be relied on, since although Hops may have been imported to England in the year traditionally referred to (1524), Carp (*Cyprinus carpio*) are known to have been introduced before 1496 (see Lever 1977a). Although Turkeys were first introduced to Germany in about 1530, the earliest documentary evidence of their presence in England is a constitution drawn up by Archbishop Cranmer in 1541, which names the 'Turkey-cocke' as one of the 'greater fowles' of which a priest was permitted 'but one in a dishe', and its association with the Crane (*Grus grus*) and (Mute) Swan (*Cygnus olor*) makes the possibility of confusion with the Guineafowl (see note 1) unlikely. Furthermore, the relatively low price of the two adult Turkeys and four chicks provided at a feast for the serjeants-at-law in 1555[3] suggests that the species was by that time widely established, and by 1573[4] Turkeys were already a feature of 'Christmas husbandrie fare'. Both cock and hen were figured for the first time by Pierre Belon in his *L'Histoire de la Nature des Oyseaux* (1555: 249), as was the cock in the same year by Konrad Gesner in *Historia animalum*.

Germany;[5] Poland; Austria; USSR

Turkeys were first seen in Germany around 1530, and were being bred in domestication in the region of the Lower Rhine at least as early as 1571. When feral populations first became established is uncertain, but the species has a long history in German sporting lore. One of the main shooting areas was in the valley of the River Donau (Danube), where small populations survived until the outbreak of the Second World War, during which they appear to have been exterminated. In about 1959–60 (and also probably on previous occasions), several hundred eggs were imported from Pennsylvania in the United States in an attempt to re-establish feral popu-

lations in various parts of (West) Germany, and between 1959 and 1966, 127 adult birds were also imported. The results of these reintroductions are uncertain, but in the mid-1960s small populations are known to have survived in Kottenforst, Buschhoven and Boenning Hardt in the Rhineland, and Aliev & Khanmamedov (1966) refer to the species as a valued game bird reared successfully for many years around Hanover in West Germany, and in Pomerania (on the East Prussian/Polish border), as well as in Austria and the Latviya SSR of the USSR. The same authors also claim that 'interesting experiments' have been conducted with Turkeys in Transcaucasia. Recent (but unconfirmed) reports suggest that feral Turkeys may have died out in Germany except where the species is regularly stocked. According to Niethammer (1963), feral Turkeys were first established in Czechoslovakia in 1870, France in 1875, Austria in 1880, Hungary in 1885, Poland in 1901 and Sweden in 1930.

NORTH AMERICA

Canada[6]

Although the wild Turkey was formerly a native of extreme southeastern Canada its reintroduction some 4,000 km west of its previous range may reasonably be treated here as an introduction.

In 1910, two pairs were released on James Island, British Columbia, by Sir Richard McBride and some colleagues who had acquired the island for sporting purposes. The birds soon became established and bred – some of their progeny dispersing to nearby Sidney Island – but had apparently been shot out by 1929. Around a dozen were planted unsuccessfully on South Pender Island in 1931, and between 30 and 40 on Sidney and Prevost islands before 1954. In 1961 and 1962, J. Todd turned down 10 and 12, respectively, on Sidney Island, and by 1972 a small population, which was not open to shooting, had become established. According to W. T. Munro, however, (personal communication, 1985), all these introductions seem eventually to have failed. A few birds, believed to have been released in the United States, are occasionally seen along the British Columbia border.

In 1962, some Turkeys (probably *merriami* – see below) that had been wild-caught in South Dakota, USA, were liberated in the Alberta portion of the Cypress Hills Provincial Park on the Alberta/Saskatchewan border, where within a year the population had increased to around 50. According to the American Ornithologists' Union (1983: 141), they are presently established in Canada locally in 'southern Alberta, southern Saskatchewan, southwestern Manitoba and southern Ontario (probably)'.

AUSTRALASIA

Australia

In January 1928, Turkeys from the South Perth Zoo were unsuccessfully released on Rottnest Island, Western Australia. Others landed at a later date on Prime Seal Island in the Furneaux group in Bass Strait fared better, and according to Tarr (1950) were still established there.

New Zealand[7]

Thomson (1922) records that feral Turkeys were settled in various parts of New Zealand, including the Erewhon estate in the Kaimanawa Range; behind Kaikoura in Marlborough (where, however, they seldom moved far from the homesteads from which they had strayed); inland from Wanganui and, until about 1890, in the region of Hawke's Bay and near Bealey in the Waimakariri River valley. Thomson considered that the bird's decline could be largely attributed, as in the case of Pheasants (*Phasianus colchicus*) (q.v.) and Peafowl (*Pavo cristatus*) (q.v.), to competition for food (especially insects) with introduced songbirds. According to Oliver (1955), feral Turkeys of the form *M. g. mexicana* (from northern and central Mexico) were tenuously established near homesteads in Hawke's Bay, Canterbury and Nelson provinces and in the Chatham Islands in 1890, and 60 years later were apparently well settled in Wellington, Marlborough and Hawke's Bay. Wodzicki (1965: 432) recorded them as 'Locally common, North and South Islands', as also did Falla, Sibson & Turbott (1979).

OCEANIA

Hawaiian Islands[8]

According to Locey (1937), Turkeys were first imported to Hawaii – as game birds – from China in 1788. Feral Turkeys in the Hawaiian Islands today, however, are reputedly descended partly from free-ranging domestic stock imported from Chile in 1815. Before 1938 they were said to be abundant, but between that date and 1941 the birds suffered a serious decline probably due, according to Schwarz & Schwartz (1949), to an outbreak of blackhead (*Histomonas*) which often becomes epidemic in large concentrations of domestic birds. The same authors were told in 1946–7 that feral Turkeys were abundant on Niihau (where over the years thousands are said to have been released), but estimated that probably less than 200 were found elsewhere, most of which were in the vicinity of ranches at altitudes of between 600 and 1,500 m on the leeward side of Hawaii.

In 1958, the State Division of Fish and Game released some Turkeys at Omaokoili near Pohakuloa in the Mauna Kea Game Management Area on Hawaii. These were augmented in 1961 by some wild Eastern Turkeys (*M. g. silvestris* from southeastern USA), which were obtained from the King Ranch in Texas, and by 37 more a year later. On the Puu Waawaa Ranch, also on Hawaii, a dozen birds (possibly Merriam's Turkeys, *M. g. merriami*, from southwestern USA and northwestern Mexico) imported from a game farm in California, 103 *silvestris* from a New York game farm and 28 of the Rio Grande form (*M. g. intermedia*) of northern Texas to northeastern Mexico (including some captive-reared stock acquired from a Texan game farm and some wild birds captured on the King Ranch) were released in 1959, 1960 and 1961–2, respectively. In 1960–1 (and probably in subsequent years), small numbers of the Rio Grande subspecies were also released on Kauai, Molokai, Lanai and Maui; by the latter year they were reported to be breeding on Hawaii and Molokai, surviving on Lanai, but declining on Mauai and Kauai.

The present status of feral Turkeys in the Hawaiian Islands is uncertain. Walker (1967b) listed both *gallopavo* and *intermedia* as established but not open to shooting: Berger (1972) confirmed the presence of *intermedia*, while in

1975 the Hawaiian Audubon Society said that feral Turkeys were probably established and breeding on Kauai, Oahu, Molokai, Lanai and Hawaii. Zeillemaker & Scott (1976) reported that the 'Common Turkey' was local and rare on Kauai and Oahu, local and uncommon on Molokai, Lanai and Maui, and locally common on Hawaii, where it inhabited exotic Guava (*Psidium guajava*), Java Plum (*Eugenia cumini*) and Eucalyptus (*Eucalyptus* sp.) woodland and scrub. Pyle (1977) confirmed the presence in the islands of *gallopavo*, while Walker (1981) stated that although the 'Domestic Turkey' occurred only on Hawaii, the Rio Grande subspecies – known locally as *pelehu* – was also to be found on Maui, Molokai and Lanai. The American Ornithologists' Union (1983) listed them as present on Niihau, Lanai, Maui and Hawaii.

For much of the eighteenth century George II maintained a flock of 2,000 or 3,000 semi-feral Turkeys for shooting in Richmond Park, Surrey, England.[9] Such a large concentration of game proved an irresistible attraction to local poachers, and affrays between them and royal gamekeepers became so frequent that the flock was eventually dissolved by George III.

In 1866, J. Gilmour of Poltalloch in Argyllshire, Scotland,[10] acquired three wild Turkeys from Lake Huron in Canada, which successfully reared 17 young in the following year; more were imported to Poltalloch in succeeding years, and by 1892 the semi-feral flock there (despite the dispersal of some to other Scottish estates) had increased to around 200, but later died out. In the 1870s, the Duke of Argyll imported some Canadian Turkeys to his seat at Inverary where, although at first they did well, all eventually disappeared. In the following decade, some wild Turkeys were released in woods at Invergarry on Loch Oich in Inverness-shire, where they bred successfully for a number of years but received supplementary food in winter.

In the 1890s, the Earl of Ducie released Turkeys in coverts at Tortworth in Gloucestershire, but found that they drove out his Pheasants. Between the two World Wars the Earl of Iveagh liberated Turkeys in Warren Wood on his Elveden Hall estate in Suffolk, where they eventually disappeared. In the late 1950s, Bruce Campbell told Fitter (1959) that Turkeys were then established in the wild on the Earl of Home's property, The Hirsel, in Berwickshire.

In 1982, a dozen Turkey eggs were imported from the United States to County Limerick in the Republic of Ireland by a member of the National Association of Regional Game Councils. Six of these hatched successfully, and three cocks and two hens were reared to maturity. In 1983, their progeny comprised eight hens and three cocks, and in the following year young birds were distributed among landowners in several counties, including Cork (where 10 were released), Donegal (at Brownhall, Ballintra), Sligo, and Clare, where eight were turned down. In addition, eggs were widely distributed, and birds were released in several other counties in 1985.

Before the Second World War, semi-feral North American Turkeys and Australian **Brush Turkeys** (*Alectura lathami*) bred in the grounds of Whipsnade Zoo and at Woburn Park in Bedfordshire, where they died out in the early 1940s for lack of supplementary winter feeding.

According to Wetmore & Swales (1931), Baron de Wimpffen, on his visits to Saint (Santo) Domingo on Hispaniola in 1788–90, reported that 'Turkeys, which the Jesuits seem only to have domesticated for themselves, have run wild again'. Bond (1979: 65) says that 'The North American Turkey was introduced on Andros [Bahamas] in 1954, but is probably not established there as a feral species'.

Wood & Wetmore (1926) suggest that the Turkey may have been introduced (unsuccessfully) in Fiji.

As a result of relentless persecution and extensive deforestation of their woodland habitat, Turkeys disappeared from much of their native range following European settlement of North America.[11] In the century or so after 1813 they vanished from at least a dozen states, and their present distribution (which is more widespread than it was around the turn of the century and includes areas where they were unknown within historic times) is the result of repeated reintroduction, restocking and stocking – allied to considerable habitat improvement – with transplanted wild or captive-bred stock. The following details are culled largely from Hewitt (1967).

The first recorded translocations were made in the late 1870s with birds reared by J. D. Caton at Ottawa, Illinois. Some were released on Santa Cruz Island off the coast of California in 1877, where they survived for a decade, and others unsuccessfully in Pennsylvania in 1879, in Wisconsin in 1887, in California in 1888 and in New York before 1893. By the mid-1920s other attempts, most of which failed, had been made in Pennsylvania, California, Oregon, Washington, Maryland, Virginia, Wisconsin, Arizona, Minnesota, Massachusetts, New York, and on Grand Island in Lake Superior and Naushon Island in Buzzards Bay.

After about 1925 the reintroduction and restocking of Turkeys grew apace, especially in the 1950s and 1960s when transplanted wild-trapped birds (mainly *silvestris* or hybrids) largely supplanted the use of captive-bred stock. By 1967 efforts had been made to establish or re-establish Turkeys in some 41 states, in at least 28 of which a degree of success was reported. Of particular interest is the fact that in several states (including Washington, Minnesota, Nebraska, Montana, North and South Dakota, Oklahoma and California, and possibly Utah, Idaho, Wyoming, Oregon, Arizona and South Dakota) Turkeys have become established outside their previous natural range. The Eastern Turkey (*silvestris*) is re-established in north-central Michigan, central Wisconsin, southeastern Massachusetts and Ohio, and has become established outwith its former range in south-central North Dakota and south-western Okalahoma. The Rio Grande Turkey (*intermedia*) is established north of its native range in west-central North Dakota and re-established in northern, central and eastern Texas, and in Kansas and Oklahoma. Plantings of *intermedia* failed in Alabama, Georgia, South Carolina and Mississippi, and apparently also in California, Iowa, Nebraska, Ohio and South Dakota. Merriam's Turkey (*merriami*) has become established in northern Montana, southwestern North Dakota, south-central California, north-central Nebraska, and west-central South Dakota, and re-established in eastern Utah, southwestern Texas, southeastern Arizona, the coastal ranges of south-central California, central Wyoming and southwestern South Dakota. Although Walker (1949) indicated that the wild Turkey in the United States was in a precarious position its future, now seems assured at least in the foreseeable future.

NOTES

1 The name 'Turkey' is believed to be derived either from the misapprehension that it was from that country, or by its inhabitants, that the bird was first introduced to Europe, or from its repeated gobbling call note which has been rendered onomatopoeically as *turk, turk, turk*. The name was originally applied, by several sixteenth-and seventeenth-century authors who curiously confounded the two species, to the Guineafowl (*Numida meleagris*) and even Linnaeus in his *Systema Naturae* (1758) confusingly gave to the Turkey the generic name *Meleagris*.

2 Ch. 36. Oviedo includes both curassows (Cracidae) and turkeys in the same category – pavos (peafowl) – but carefully distinguishes between them, pointing out *inter alia* that the cock of the latter makes a wheel (*hacen la rueda*) of his tail, though this is neither as large nor as impressive as that of the 'Spanish Pavo'. Samuel Purchas, in *Purchas his Pilgrimes* (1625), quotes from Oviedo's 1526 or 1527 work and also from an expanded version published in 1535.

3 Sir William Dugdale, *Origines Juridiciales* (1666), 135.

4 Thomas Tusser, *Hundreth Good Pointes of Husbandrie* (1573).

5 Frank 1970; Heinzel, Fitter & Parslow 1976; Kauffman 1962; Lindzey 1967; Long 1981; Niethammer 1963; Zeuner 1963.

6 American Ornithologists' Union 1957, 1983; Carl & Guiguet 1972; Godfrey 1966; Long 1981; MacDonald & Jantzen 1967; and W. T. Munro, personal communication, 1985.

7 Falla, Sibson & Turbott 1979; Long 1981; Oliver 1955; Thomson 1922; Wodzicki 1965.

8 American Ornithologists' Union 1957, 1983; Berger 1972, 1981; Blake 1975; Bryan 1958; Burger 1954a,b; Caum 1933; Fisher 1951; Hawaiian Audubon Society 1975; Lewin 1971; Locey 1937; Long 1981; Peterson 1961; Pyle 1977; Sakai & Scott 1984; Schwartz & Schwartz 1949; Walker 1967b, 1981; Western States Exotic Game Bird Committee 1961; Zeillemaker & Scott 1976.

9 Fitter 1959.

10 Fitter 1959.

11 American Ornithologists' Union 1957, 1983; Bailey & Rinell 1967; Bump 1941; Burger 1954a,b; Glazener 1967; Greene & Ellis 1971; Lee & Lewis 1959; Long 1981; MacDonald & Jantzen 1967; Phillips 1928; Popov & Low 1950; Powell 1967; Schorger 1942; Shaffer & Gwynn 1967; Walker 1949; Wilson & Lewis 1959.

Weka
(*Gallirallus australis*)

NATURAL DISTRIBUTION

Gisborne and Poverty Bay (and perhaps parts of Central Auckland and Northland) on North Island, New Zealand, and from Nelson and north Marlborough to Fiordland and western Otago in South Island. Also on Stewart Island.

NATURALIZED DISTRIBUTION

(see over)

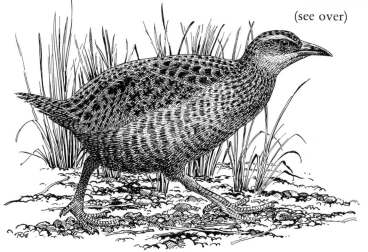

NATURALIZED DISTRIBUTION

Australasia/Oceania: ?Macquarie Island, Chatham Islands, Open Bay Islands, Motunui Island, Jacky Lee Island, Big Solander Island, Codfish Island, Kapiti Island, ?Kawau Island.

AUSTRALASIA/OCEANIA

Macquarie Island[1]

According to Sir Walter Lowry Buller (in Oliver 1955), Wekas may have been first introduced to Macquarie Island (discovered in 1810) by Captain Gilroy as early as 1830. The first documented importation of these rails, however, was made in 1867 by sealers and whalers, who brought in Stewart Island Wekas (*G. a. scotti*) as a source of food. More (believed to be of the nominate subspecies from northern and western South Island) were introduced in 1872 by Captain Prinz, master of the *Sarah Pile*, and others in 1874 and 1879 by Mr (later Sir) Thomas Elder, a Scottish-born South Australian pastoralist.

Macquarie Island, which lies some 1,150 km south-west of Stewart Island in the Southern Ocean, measures some 30 km from north to south and averages 4–5 km from west to east. It consists of a 250-m high plateau, surrounded by precipitous tussock-clad slopes fringed by shingle beaches and raised coastal terraces.

Although Scott (1882) found Wekas to be scarce on the island, Hamilton (1894) reported that they had 'increased and multiplied in a most extraordinary way', and occurred in coastal tussock grassland below the plateau all round the island except in the extreme north.

According to Brothers & Skira (1984), who visited Macquarie Island in 1976, 1979 and 1983, and from whom much of the following is derived, two colour phases were introduced – the normal chestnut form (which now predominates) and a darker one. Almost all the birds found by Brothers & Skira occurred in tussock grassland (*Poa foliosa* and Macquarie Island Cabbage, *Stilbocarpa polaris*) on the coastal terraces (especially in the north-west), covering a total area of some 50 km². A few birds were discovered in low coastal valleys up to 100 m above sea level and 1 km inland (e.g. at Green Gorge on the east coast), and the small number that ventured onto the high plateau were found feeding in or near tussock grassland rather than on the more open herbfield. Brothers & Skira estimated the total population in 1979 at up to 500.

Wekas on Macquarie Island appear to breed from August to November, building their nests in the middle of the base of clumps of tussock-grass. Clutches of up to four eggs are laid, and more than one brood is sometimes raised. Chick mortality seems to be high, the main predators being feral Cats (*Felis catus*) and Great Skuas (*Stercorarius* (*Catharacta*) *skua lonnbergi*), both of which also sometimes try to kill adult Wekas; some eggs may be taken by Black Rats (*Rattus rattus*).

The preferred foods of Wekas on Macquarie Island are vegetation, molluscs, insects and arachnids, and to a lesser extent mammals and birds. Although few Rabbits (*Oryctolagus cuniculus*) are eaten, House Mice (*Mus musculus*) and Black Rats may be important food items because of their size and abundance.

The relative scarcity of Wekas on Macquarie Island until at least the early 1880s was due to a combination of their own low fecundity and heavy predation by feral Cats. The population explosion that occurred by about 1890 was probably triggered by the introduction of Rabbits between 1870 and 1880. The rapid increase and dispersal of Rabbits relieved the pressure of predation on Wekas, whose prospects were further enhanced by the abundance of burrow-nesting petrels and other birds as a readily accessible source of food.

Although Brothers & Skira claim (p. 145) that 'the presence of Wekas on Macquarie Island for over a century has had a disastrous effect on the native fauna', the individual roles played by Wekas, Cats and Black Rats in exterminating, between 1880 and 1891, the endemic ground-nesting Macquarie Island Parakeet (*Cyanoramphus novaezeelandiae erythrotis*) and, by 1894, the Macquarie Island Banded Rail (*Rallus philippensis macquariensis*), and in extirpating from the main island such burrow-nesting species as the Blue Petrel (*Halobaena caerulea*), Fairy Prion (*Pachyptila turtur*), Grey Petrel (*Procellaria cinerea*) and Common Diving Petrel (*Pelecanoides urinatrix*) – all of which still nest on nearby stacks that are inaccessible to predators – are difficult to determine. Most reports implicate Cats and tend partially to exonerate Black Rats and Wekas, though the last-named do prey to a limited extent on Sooty Shearwaters (*Puffinus griseus*) and White-headed Petrels (*Pterodroma lessoni*). Antarctic Prions (*Pachyptila desolata*), which used formerly to nest in the tussock grassland occupied by Wekas, are now confined to the high plateau herbfield where Wekas seldom occur.

Brothers & Skira believe that the distribution and numbers of Wekas on Macquarie Island have been directly related to those of Rabbits. Although as recently as the early 1970s Wekas were to be found in suboptimum habitat (which has been further degraded by the small population of Rabbits) in the south of the island, Brothers & Skira saw few south of Green Gorge. The Weka population has tended to be highest where that of Rabbits is also greatest, both providing an abundant source of food for Cats, and in habitats unsuitable for both Cats and Rabbits. Thus where the number of Rabbits is low, predation of Wekas by Cats increases. The introduction to Macquarie Island in 1978 of the European Rabbit Flea (*Spilopsyllus cuniculi*) as a vector for myxomatosis, resulted in a marked decline in the number of Rabbits and an increase in predation by Cats on Wekas, which in October 1983 Brothers & Skira (p. 154) reported to be 'rare in all areas'. As a result of an attempted eradication programme by the Tasmanian National Parks and Wildlife Service, Wekas (and Cats) may soon be eliminated from Macquarie Island, if indeed this has not already occurred.

Chatham Islands[2]

According to Peters (1934), Wekas of the form *australis* have been introduced to the Chatham Islands. Atkinson & Bell (1973), who say that two subspecies of Weka were formerly present, state (p. 385) that 'The Weka now on Chatham and Pitt Islands is the Buff Weka (*Gallirallus australis hectori*) of eastern South Island, which was introduced to the Chathams in 1905. This subspecies is probably extinct on the mainland'. On Chatham Island, feral Cats, Black Rats and Wekas may be jeopardizing the survival of the endangered endemic Chatham Island Taiko or Magenta Petrel (*Pterodroma magentae*), a burrow-nesting gadfly petrel dramatically rediscovered, after a gap of 111 years, in 1978.

Wekas have done so well on the Chathams that in February 1962 16 were reintroduced from the islands to Arthur's Pass National Park in Canterbury, South Island, where they are now re-established and thriving.

Open Bay Islands, Motunui Island, Jacky Lee Island, Big Solander Island and Codfish Island (South Island);[3] Kapiti Island and Kawau Island (North Island)[4]

According to Atkinson & Bell (1973), Wekas of the form *scotti* originally occurred naturally only on parts of the New Zealand mainland and on Stewart Island. In the early 1900s, birds of this race were introduced by sealers and mutton-birders[5] as an additional source of food to several offshore islands, including Open Bay Islands off the coast of Westland, Big Solander and Jacky Lee Island in Foveaux Strait, and Codfish Island off the northwestern coast of Stewart Island. On Motunui Island (2 km north-east of Jacky Lee) Wekas appear to be hybrids between introduced *scotti* and *australis*.[6] On all these islands they have been implicated in the predation of various species of burrow-nesting petrels and of the Banded Rail (*Rallus philippensis*), which is a common species on those islands where Wekas do not occur. By the outbreak of the Second World War, Fairy Prions had considerably declined — allegedly due to predation of their young by Wekas — and Blackburn (1968) reported heavy Weka predation of Mottled (or Scaled) Petrels (*Pterodroma inexpectata*) on Codfish Island, where they were presumed to have been responsible for the earlier eradication of an extensive colony of Cook's Petrels (*P. cookii*).

According to Falla, Sibson & Turbott (1979), the Wekas on Kapiti Island are believed to be hybrids between *greyi* (the North Island form) and *scotti*, in which case one or both may have been introduced. Oliver (1955) records that *hectori* is said to have been introduced by Sir George Grey in 1863 to Kawau Island in the Hauraki Gulf, where it became well established.

Oliver states that after the wreck of the *Grafton* in 1864, Wekas were reputedly released on Auckland Island, but if so they failed to become established.

By about 1940, North Island Wekas[7] had become confined to the Gisborne area on the East Coast, where local damage by pecking was reported to tomatoes, melons and pumpkins, domestic poultry yards were robbed, and plants uprooted in search of insects.[8] To reduce local Weka depredation, and as a conservation measure, a number of attempts[9] have been made to re-establish the species in its former haunts by catching birds near Poverty Bay and releasing them at, among other places, the Pararaki River, Aorangi Range and the Orongorongo Research Station, Rimutaka Range (13 in 1958); Whatarangi, Palliser Bay (40 in December 1966), and near the Matakitaki Stream, Cape Palliser (40 in February 1968), followed by others in the same areas in 1969; at Rawhiti, Bay of Islands (149 between 1966 and 1971); in the Russell Forestry Unit, 30 km south of Rawhiti (32 in 1967); and at South Kaipara Head, where 32 were liberated in 1968 and a similar number in the following year. Only at Whatarangi, Matakitaki and Rawhiti were the attempted reintroductions successful; near the last named a population of about 100 appears to have become established on the 16-km coastal strip between Cape Brett and Whangaruru North Head south of the Bay of Islands.

According to Mackworth-Praed & Grant (1962), the form *meridionalis* of the almost cosmopolitan **Moorhen** or **Common Gallinule** (*Gallinula chloropus*) was successfully introduced to St Helena in the South Atlantic in about 1930.

Peterson (1961) and Berger (1972) record that unsuccessful attempts have been made to re-establish the Hawaiian form *sandvicensis* – which now occurs locally only on Kauai, Oahu and Molokai – on Maui and Hawaii.

According to Wace & Holdgate (1976), flightless moorhens found on Tristan da Cunha in the South Atlantic (where the endemic *Gallinula n. nesiotis* was exterminated in the late nineteenth century by visiting sealers and whalers in search of food) may be the descendants of the **Gough Island Moorhen** or **Coot** (*G. n. comeri*) introduced in the early 1950s.

Condon (1975) says that the **Purple Gallinule** or **Swamphen** (*Porphyrio porphyrio*), a native of southern Europe and Africa, Asia and much of the Far East, Australia and New Zealand, has been introduced to Argentina.

The occurrence on Mauritius, where it is now extinct, of the form *madagascariensis* was possibly the result of an introduction before 1812 from Madagascar, though Newton & Newton (1861) considered it was 'probably aboriginal'.

The forms *poliocephalus* (Iraq to Thailand and the Andaman and Nicobar islands) and *melanotus* (southern New Guinea and eastern Australia) have been unsuccessfully introduced in the Hawaiian Islands.

According to Watson, Zusi & Storer (1963), the **Madagascar Button Quail** (*Turnix nigricollis*) may have been imported to the island of Réunion; Staub (1976) says that it was introduced at an early date, and both authors state that it is still established there.

Although Button Quail could have reached Îles Glorieuses by natural dispersal from Madagascar (a distance of around 90 km), Benson, Beamish et al. (1975) say that Penny (1974) considered that they must have been introduced by human agency, presumably for sporting purposes. Scrub-clearance and tree-felling in recent years have provided improved habitat for the birds, which prefer open grasslands, light brush and cultivated land, and in 1970–1 the population was estimated to number some 300 pairs.

According to Rountree, Guérin et al. (1952), Button Quail from Madagascar were successfully introduced to Mauritius before 1669. Meinertzhagen (1912) indicates that they had been introduced (? again) shortly before that date. They have since died out on the island.

In 1985, the International Crane Foundation presented three captive-bred pairs of the **Eastern Sarus Crane** (*Grus antigone sharpii*), a species which has largely disappeared from its native range of eastern Assam and Burma to southern

Indochina, to the Royal Forestry Department of Thailand; the offspring of these birds, which will be bred in captivity at Bang Phra, will be released in the Bang Phra Wildlife Sanctuary wetland east of Bangkok.[10]

NOTES

1 Brothers & Skira 1984; Carrick 1957; Falla, Sibson & Turbott 1979; Hamilton 1894; Jenkin, Johnstone & Copson 1982; Johnstone 1982; Lever 1985b; Long 1981; Oliver 1955; Peters 1934; Scott 1882; Taylor 1979; Watson 1975.

2 Atkinson & Bell 1973; Blackburn 1968; Falla, Sibson & Turbott 1979; Johnstone 1982; Lever 1985b; Long 1981; Peters 1934.
3 Atkinson & Bell 1973; Johnstone 1982; Long 1981.
4 See note 3.
5 'Muttonbird' = Short-tailed Shearwater (*Puffinus tenuirostris*).
6 R. J. Nilsson, unpublished report, 1985.
7 Falla, Sibson & Turbott 1979; Long 1981; Pracy 1969; Robertson 1976.
8 Carroll 1963.
9 Carroll 1963.
10 Anon. 1985b,c.

Chestnut-bellied Sandgrouse

(*Pterocles exustus*)

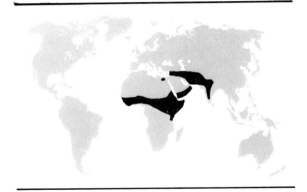

NATURAL DISTRIBUTION

Africa, from Senegal eastwards through the Sudan to Ethiopia, Somalia and Egypt, south through Kenya to northern Tanzania; southern Arabia, and Asia from the Mediterranean to India.

NATURALIZED DISTRIBUTION

Oceania: Hawaiian Islands (Hawaii).

OCEANIA

Hawaiian Islands[1]

Chestnut-bellied Sandgrouse of the Asian race, *hindustan*,[2] were first introduced to the Hawaiian Islands in 1961, when 140 were released on Hawaii, 137 on Molokai and 118 on Kauai. On Kauai, the birds dispersed up to 24 km from their release site, but subsequently (as on Molokai) disappeared. In 1962, a further 401 were liberated on Hawaii, of which 104 were turned down at Ahumoa (2,135 m), 266 on the south side of Puu Hualalai (1,830 m) and Hale Laau, and 31 at

Pohakuloa (1,980 m), where Bump & Bohl (1964: 20) claimed the experiment (involving the release of 796 birds) was the 'most successful to date'.[3] Elsewhere on Hawaii, the birds were said by Lewin (1971) to have disappeared by 1966, and Walker (1967b: 10) lists them as having been introduced but 'not known to be established'. The Hawaiian Audubon Society (1975), however, considered that Sandgrouse might still occur on Hawaii, but that their status on the island was uncertain. Zeillemaker & Scott (1976) indicated that the species was established but rare on lowland and dry agricultural land and pastures on Hawaii. Although Pyle (1977) made no mention of them, Walker (1981) listed Sandgrouse as present on Hawaii. According to A. J. Berger (personal communication, 1985), 'a population estimated to be in the low hundreds [is] in the Waimea plains area of the island of Hawaii'. The birds had previously been overlooked because they had dispersed to the Waimea plateau, where they now range from Waimea 16 km south to the Waikaloa Road, and the same distance from west to east. The habitat consists of managed cattle pastureland, dominated by exotic herbs and grasses. Limited shooting is permitted.

The US Department of the Interior's Foreign Game Introduction Program, as Paton, Ashman & McEldowney (1982) point out, required for this planting in the Hawaiian Islands a sedentary species like the Sandgrouse which was capable of withstanding such environmental and climatological extremes as cold, summer droughts, a minimum food supply, and limited water, because the annual rainfall on the release sites in the central plateau on Hawaii between Mauna Kea, Mauna Loa and Hualalai averages only 38 cm. A factor that could inhibit Sandgrouse from more readily becoming established in Hawaii may be, as Bump (1968a,b) points out, that although the habitat where the birds were released is not dissimilar from that of their range in India and Pakistan – desert flats where vegetation and water are often very scarce – the temperature is in general somewhat cooler.

According to Gottschalk (1967), Sandgrouse have been released in the United States[4] on several occasions since 1881, when some were turned down in Oregon and Washington. In desert areas of Moapa, Pahrump and Pahranagat valleys in southern Nevada,[5] 991 Sandgrouse of the race *hindustan*, which had been caught in the Thar Desert on the India/Pakistan border, were released in 1960, followed by a further 1,648 in Moapa, Virgin and Pahrump valleys in 1961. Few overwintered near the release sites, the majority dispersing south at the onset of cooler winter weather, and two ringed birds were recovered nearly 1,300 km south at Navajao, Sonora, in northwestern Mexico. None of these introductions, nor some apparently made in the late 1960s, were successful, probably because, as to a lesser extent in Hawaii, winter temperatures tend to fall too low.

In Australia,[6] Sandgrouse were liberated at Melbourne, Victoria, in 1863, and on Phillip Island (10) in 1864 and several more in 1872, but all soon disappeared.

NOTES

1 American Ornithologists' Union 1983; Berger 1981; Bump 1968a,b; Bump & Bohl 1964; Hawaiian Audubon Society 1975; Lewin 1971; Long 1981; Paton, Ashman & McEldowney 1982; Pyle 1977; Walker 1967b, 1981; Western States Exotic Game Bird Committee 1961; Zeillemaker & Scott 1976.

2 According to Berger (1981: p. 240), the subspecies imported was *erlangeri* – a native of southwestern Saudi Arabia.

3 According to Paton, Ashman & McEldowney (1982), the total released in 1961–2 was 725 (493 on Hawaii, 118 on Kauai and 114 on Molokai).

4 Bump 1968a,b; Bump & Bohl 1964; Chambers 1965; Christensen 1963a; Gottschalk 1967; Long 1981; Nevada Fish and Game Commission 1963.

5 Chambers (1965) refers to releases made in New Mexico.

6 Long 1981; Ryan 1906.

Feral Pigeon
(*Columba livia*)

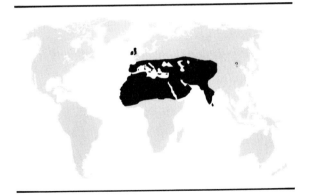

Note: Map shows original distribution of wild Rock Dove.

NATURAL DISTRIBUTION
The Rock Dove (which is the ultimate ancestor of the Feral Domestic Pigeon) was originally confined to coastal and inland cliffs of the western Palaearctic and northern Ethiopian regions and to those of the Indian subcontinent. Its present distribution is confused by extensions of range through hybridization with feral stock.

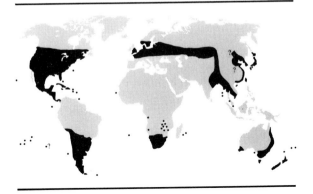

Note: Map shows discontinuous distribution of Feral Pigeon only outside natural range of wild Rock Dove.

NATURALIZED DISTRIBUTION[1]
Virtually cosmopolitan. Europe: British Isles; Eurasia north to around 60° N and east to 90° E; Asia: much of Southeast Asia, Korea, Inner Mongolia, China (Manchuria and on the coast south to Hong Kong), Taiwan, Hainan, Japan, Singapore, Malaysia, Andaman and Nicobar islands; Africa: South Africa, Angola, Mozambique, Zambia, Zimbabwe, Morocco, Algeria, Tunisia, Libya, Niger, Chad, Guinea, Sierra Leone, Ghana, Togo, Benin, Nigeria, Egypt,

Sudan, Mascarenes (Mauritius, Réunion), Cape Verde Islands, St Helena; North America: USA, Canada, Mexico, Bermuda, Bahamas, West Indies (including Cuba, Jamaica, Puerto Rico, St Croix, Trinidad and Antigua); Central America; South America (especially Argentina, Brazil, Uruguay, Chile, Peru and Bolivia), Juan Fernández Islands; Australasia: Australia, New Zealand, Norfolk Island; Oceania: Hawaiian Islands, Polynesia, ?Easter Island, ?South Georgia, Galápagos Islands, and probably elsewhere.

EUROPE

British Isles[2]

Feral Pigeons in the British Isles, which are found wherever man has constructed large enough urban communities for them to dwell in, are the descendants of native Rock Doves that were first captured and domesticated probably by Neolithic people; some were released or escaped from medieval dovecotes when meat became more readily available through improved methods of preservation and distribution. Yet until the agricultural revolution of the early nineteenth century, semi-domesticated dovecote pigeons continued to play an important part in the rural economy – the birds being allowed to fly free to find their own food in the fields during the day but returning to the safety of the dovecote at night.

Ritchie (1920) has traced the stages of the domestication of the Rock Dove in Scotland; the coastal breeding caves of the wild 'doos' became the earliest natural 'doocots', additional artificial nesting holes being constructed in them by man: such 'doocaves' can still be seen on the coasts of Berwickshire and Fife. As the wild Rock Doves gradually became accustomed to breeding in artificial nests in their seaside caves, they were captured and transported to man-made 'doocots' inland. Ritchie could find no evidence of when this practice started, but it was evidently well established by the first half of the fifteenth century when severe penalties were imposed on those convicted of 'the breaking of dowcattes'.

There seems little reason to doubt that much the same process occurred elsewhere in the British Isles; dovecotes are known to have been constructed in England by the Normans in the late eleventh and early twelfth centuries, and in his *De legibus et consuetudinibus Angliae* (compiled between 1235 and 1259), Henry de Bracton included doves among wild animals in England that had been 'tamed and by habit return'.

When domesticated pigeons first reverted to the wild is uncertain, but by the late fourteenth century they are known to have been nesting on St Paul's Cathedral in London since the bishop complained that the windows were being broken by people throwing stones at the birds. Three centuries later, when on 2 September 1666 Samuel Pepys wrote in his *Diary* that during the Great Fire of London 'the poor pigeons were loth to leave their houses, but hovered about the windows and balconys till they were, some of them burned, their wings, and fell down', the birds appear to have been well established and widespread in the capital.

The study of feral domestic species has for long been a much neglected branch of ornithology. Gompertz (1957), in her pioneer field work on the Feral Pigeons of London, describes her surprise at the disdainful attitude towards her subject shown by many ornithologists. Thus, there is little information as to when Feral Pigeons settled in other cities and towns and in the country, but it was in all probability at around the same time as in London.

Wherever Feral Pigeons and wild Rock Doves have come into contact since earliest times they have tended to interbreed, and in the present century occasional lost racing pigeons that have failed to return to their lofts have joined flocks of Rock Doves and feral birds; this interbreeding must have greatly influenced the genetic composition of many wild populations, and while urban and inland rural colonies of Feral Pigeons are entirely descended from escaped or released domestic (or semi-domesticated racing) stock, many coastal ones are composed of hybrids, and only on a few of the more remote seaside cliffs do any pure Rock Doves remain today.

Feral Pigeons occur in a bewildering variety of plumages: 'blue' (which resembles the wild Rock Dove, but in which birds derived from domestic or racing stock have the thicker bill and more prominent white cere common to many domestic and semi-domesticated strains) and 'blue chequer' (in which the wing coverts are spotted with black) are the most common, while especially in urban populations melanism, albinism and even erythrism are not unusual. Most Rock Doves, which are naturally dimorphic, have normal grey plumage on the back and characteristic double black wing-bars; the latter feature also often occurs in feral birds, thus increasing the difficulty in differentiating between pure and hybrid populations.

Feral Pigeons on the coastal cliffs of England, Wales, the Isle of Man and southern Scotland feed and nest as did their Rock Dove ancestors and indeed are, as Sharrock (1976) points out, their latter-day ecological substitutes. In Ireland, Feral Pigeons are fairly widespread, particularly in the eastern half. Rural maritime populations, which usually behave as truly wild birds, nest colonially on ledges or crevices in seaside caves, and occasionally among boulders or on sheltered cliff faces, while inland colonies breed in old or ruined buildings; urban Feral Pigeons nest on window-ledges and crannies in buildings that act as surrogates for seashore caves and cliffs. Feral Pigeons are especially notable for their extended breeding season; eggs can be laid throughout the year, each pair producing an average of five clutches. According to Sharrock, about 25 per cent of rural pairs, and a rather higher proportion of urban ones, nest in winter; melanic morphs are more likely to be all-seasons breeders than those with wild-type coloration, which tends to explain the prevalence of melanics in urban populations.

EURASIA[3]

Rock Doves are known to have been domesticated in the eastern Mediterranean (possibly first in Egypt) and the Middle East some 5,000 years ago, and numerous dovecotes – some of great antiquity – are scattered across Europe and southwestern Asia as far east as Iran.

The history of the establishment of populations of Feral Pigeons in continental Europe and Asia is likely to be much the same as in the British Isles. In many parts of Europe their numbers apparently increased considerably after the Second World War. Throughout Eurasia, they are today in suitable (mostly inland) localities at least as far north as 60° N and east to 90° E. They are common residents in much of Southeast Asia apart from Malaya and Vietnam,

and occur also in Korea and Inner Mongolia; in parts of China (especially Manchuria and coastal regions south to Hong Kong); on the Japanese islands of Kyushu, Honshu, Shikoku and Hokkaido, and on Taiwan and Hainan. In Thailand (where they are believed to have been introduced many years ago from India), Feral Pigeons are widely established near human settlements. Populations in Korea, Manchuria and on Honshu are probably descended almost exclusively from escaped or released domestic birds, while those elsewhere in northern China and in Mongolia may have an admixture of wild Rock Dove stock. In Malaysia, isolated populations occur in the Batu Caves north of Kuala Lumpur in Selangor, and (since about 1960) around the docks and city of Singapore, where they are fed by shopkeepers and various religious groups to propitiate the gods.

Andaman and Nicobar islands

Kloss (1903) refers to an introduction of domestic pigeons to Car Nicobar in 1898 where he saw numbers of them 2 years later. Abdulali (1967) says that feral birds are established around Nancowry on Camora Island in the Nicobars and at Port Blair on South Andaman.

AFRICA[4]

South Africa; Angola; Mozambique; Zambia; Zimbabwe

Domesticated pigeons from Holland were first introduced to Cape Town in April 1654 by the then Governor, Jan van Riebeeck, and by the middle of the following century dovecotes had been constructed on several farms in the Cape. Racing pigeons did not appear until the 1890s, when the British imported some for carrying despatches during the Boer War. From both of these sources, birds must from time to time have been lost to the wild, though as in other parts of the world precisely when this happened is uncertain. In 1969, the Percy FitzPatrick Institute of African Ornithology circulated a questionnaire which, together with personal observations made by Brooke (1981), revealed the presence of Feral Pigeons in the following countries and towns in southern Africa: **South Africa**. *Bophuthatswana*: Mafeking. *Cape Province*: Alice, Bellville, Beaufort West, Cape Town, Citrusdal, Cradock, De Aar, Dordrecht, Douglas, East London, Elliott, Franschhoek, Fraserburg, George, Goodwood, Graaff-Reinet, Griekwastad, Hopetown, Kimberley, King William's Town, Knysna, Kuruman, Loxton, Malmesbury, Matatiele, Milnerton, Mossel Bay, Napier, New Bethesda, Oudtshoorn, Paarl, Parow, Port Elizabeth, Queenstown, Rawsonville, Simonstown, Somerset East, Stellenbosch, Strand, Uitenhage, Vanrhynsdorp, Vredenburg, Wellington, Wolseley, Worcester, Wynberg. *Natal*: Durban, Estcourt, Glencoe, Ladysmith, Newcastle, Pietermaritzburg, Port Shepstone, Stanger, Umtentweni, Verulam, Westville. *Orange Free State*: Allanridge, Bethlehem, Bethulie, Bloemfontein, Hertzogville, Kroonstad, Paul Roux, Reddersburg, Senekal, Virginia, Vrede, Welkom. *Transvaal*: Alberton, Benoni, Bethal, Boksburg, Braamfontein, Carletonville, Coligny, Delareyville, Germiston, Heidelberg, Johannesburg, Kempton Park, Klerksdorp, Krugersdorp, Lichtenburg, Lydenburg, Makwassie, Middleburg, Modderfontein, Nelspruit, Nylstroom, Orkney, Pietersburg, Potchefstroom, Pretoria, Springs, Standerton, Stilfontein, Vanderbijl Park, Vereeniging, Verwoerdburg, Volksrust, Warmbad, Wolmaransstad. *Transkei*: Umtata. **Angola**: Luanda, Lubango (formerly Sa da Bandeira). **Mozambique**: Beira. **Zimbabwe**: Bulawayo, Fort Victoria, Gatooma, Gwelo, Que Que, Salisbury (Harare), Umtali. **Zambia**: Lusaka and other large towns and on the Copperbelt, where they breed freely but are not spreading.

In southern African towns Feral Pigeons roost communally at night, and by day forage in the surrounding countryside and, on the coast, on beaches in the intertidal zone. They are seldom resident outside urban areas, an exception being the cliffs north of Port St Johns on the northern Transkei coast. In captivity, *Columba livia* can hybridize with its close South African relation the Speckled (Rock) Pigeon (*C. guinea*), and where both occur together in the wild – for example in Cape Town and Grahamstown – there may be interspecific competition for food and nesting sites.

Elsewhere on the continent, Feral Pigeons appear to be established in much of northwestern Africa (including Morocco, northern Algeria, Tunisia, western Libya, Niger, Chad, Guinea, Sierra Leone, Ghana, Togo, Benin and Nigeria, but excluding Mauretania, Mali, Western Sahara, southern Algeria, Liberia and the Ivory Coast) and in most of Egypt and northern Sudan.

Mauritius and Réunion[5]

Domesticated pigeons were probably introduced to Mauritius from Europe in about 1715, when the island came under the control of the French East India Company. Previously confined to the St Denis, Port Louis and Signal Mountain areas, feral birds now occur throughout the island, though principally near human settlements.

Cape Verde Islands

Escaped domestic pigeons are recorded as nesting on cliffs on São Nicolau and São Thiago before 1856, where Henry Moseley[6] saw them in abundance during the voyage of HMS *Challenger* in 1873.

St Helena[7]

Both domesticated and Feral Pigeons are said to have been abundant on St Helena by around 1870. Some were released by troops stationed on the island after the First World War, and their descendants were apparently plentiful near Jamestown in 1938, where a few remained a decade later. By the mid-1950s, several hundred were established and breeding in the north-east on the ledges of Cat Hole at Heartshape Waterfall.

NORTH AMERICA

USA[8]

Although documentary evidence is lacking, domesticated pigeons were probably first imported to the United States by early settlers in 1621; their feral descendants are today established in suitable habitats throughout the country apart from Alaska where, according to Heilbrun (1976), they have been found only in Sitka on

Baranof Island and in Anchorage. In general, they frequent urban and suburban areas where they forage in public parks, sometimes cultivated farmland and coastal cliffs, but seldom wilderness regions.

Research, largely carried out in the United States, has shown that pigeons (among other birds, especially parrots (Psittacidae)) are responsible for the spread of several noxious diseases, including psittacosis or ornithosis, cryptococcal meningitis (caused by the fungus *Cryptococcus neoformans*), histoplasmosis, toxoplasmosis and encephalitis. In addition, Feral Pigeons damage and deface buildings with their faeces, may weaken mortar by pecking it for its lime content, block gutters and downpipes with their nesting material, reduce the yield of agricultural crops (especially grain) through their depredations, and compete with domestic fowl for food. Strenuous attempts have been made to eradicate them in cities and towns in the United States (and indeed almost throughout the world) using a variety of methods (e.g. shooting, trapping, poisoning, nest destruction, the use of stupefying and/or contraceptive baits, and electrified wires on roosting sites), but all have been of no avail.

Canada[9]

According to Marc Lescarbot,[10] 'pigeons' were first introduced to New France by Poutrincourt in 1606. Feral birds are today established in urban, and to a lesser extent rural, areas of southern Canada to about 52° N. A few colonies occur away from human settlements – for example in British Columbia where in May 1966 some were found nesting on cliffs along the eastern side of the southern Okanagan Valley from Osoyoos to Vaseux Lake. In the prairie Provinces, according to Roots (1976), spillages at rail terminals and grain elevators provide Feral Pigeons with a valuable source of winter food.

Mexico

According to Peterson & Chalif (1973), Feral and semi-feral Pigeons occur in many Mexican towns and perhaps also in some canyons and cliffs; they are, however, scarce or absent in Yucatán and Campeche.

Bermuda[11]

Domestic pigeons were first introduced to Bermuda early in the eighteenth century. Feral birds are still uncommon, but a few colonies nest on some of the more precipitous coastal cliffs such as those at Highpoint in Southampton Parish, along the South Shore, and on Abbott's Cliffs on Harrington Sound. The species is not, as claimed by Crowell & Crowell (1976: 56) 'reaching pest proportions' on the islands.

West Indies[12]

Bond (1979: 101) records that 'The domestic Rock Dove . . . occurs [in the West Indies] as a semi-feral species'; islands it has colonized include Cuba, Jamaica, Puerto Rico, St Croix, Trinidad and Antigua. According to Heilbrun (1977), the Feral Pigeon has been recorded on the island of Eleuthera in the Bahamas.

CENTRAL AMERICA

Feral Pigeons are currently established in many towns and cities in most countries of Central America.

SOUTH AMERICA

Argentina; Brazil; Uruguay; Chile; Peru; Bolivia

Most large urban areas in South America, especially those in the south, support populations of Feral Pigeons;[13] in Argentina and Chile they now occur as far south as Isla Grande, Tierra del Fuego, where one was shot at Bahia Buena Suceso as long ago as 1915, and where in 1960 some were observed near Ushuaia, Argentina – the most southerly town in the world – on the northern shore of the Beagle Channel. Those in towns and villages in the foothills and heights of the Andes in Peru, and on the coast, are said to be descended from birds imported by the Spanish conquistadors under Pizarro in the sixteenth century.

Between 1969 and 1975, H. E. M. Dott (personal communication, 1986) observed Feral Pigeons in the Bolivian towns of Villa Busch, Montero and Santa Cruz (all in the department of Santa Cruz); Villa Montes (Tarija); Sucre (Chuquisaca); La Paz (La Paz); Cochabamba (Cochabamba); Oruro (Oruro); and Potosí (Potosí). The last-named town – the highest of these localities – lies at an altitude of 4,100 m. Only in the centre of La Paz, however, at an elevation of 3,750 m, was the species common. Dott also noticed isolated pairs (though perhaps of Domestic, rather than Feral, Pigeons) on tiny, isolated roadside dwellings in the same departments, sometimes far removed from any town or village. 'Thus *C. livia* is widespread but not abundant in Bolivia', says Dott (personal communication, 1986), 'from low to high altitudes, but [was] not noted in the humid Andean slopes or foothills, or in Beni Department [in the north].'

In the central plazas and streets of La Paz and Cochabamba cities, the native Eared Dove (*Zenaida auriculata*) is abundant and breeding; since in central La Paz *C. livia* has begun to infiltrate the Eared Dove's habitat, any future increase of the former in the capital or in Cochabamba might well have an effect on the native species. The indigenous Bare-faced Ground Dove (*Metriopelia ceciliae*) also roosts and nests on buildings in semi-arid parts of Cochabamba, La Paz, Oruro, Chuquisaca and Potosí departments; since, however, it prefers town suburbs and villages to city centres it is likely to be less affected than *auriculata* by any increase in *livia*.

Dott describes the colours of Feral Pigeons in Bolivia as including dark, patched dark and white, and brownish-pink with dark or white.

Juan Fernández Islands[14]

Domestic pigeons were introduced to Masatierra Island (Robinson Crusoe) in the Juan Fernández group many years ago – possibly by the first colonist in 1572, a Spanish pilot after whom the islands (which he had discovered in 1563) were named. Sick (1968) remarks that only on Juan Fernández in the South American region has the Feral Pigeon reverted to its Rock Dove ancestors' wild habitat.

AUSTRALASIA

Australia[15]

Although (as in the case of the United States) documentary evidence is lacking, it seems likely that domestic pigeons were originally brought to Australia by the First Fleet in 1788. The earliest recorded liberation was at Cape Liptrap, Victoria, before 1873. Feral birds are now established in many of the larger cities and towns and in some suburban and rural areas over most of the continent (especially in the east and south-east), and according to Frith (1979) occasionally (e.g. near Victor Harbour in South Australia, where they nest in rock crevices on cliff-faces and forage on agricultural land) also well away from human settlements, and occur in vast numbers in the wheat-lands of that state. Frith records that Feral Pigeons have been found breeding on the ground in gull (Laridae) colonies on islands off the coast of New South Wales, and in holes in trees on maritime pastoral land in the same state. They occur as far north as Townsville and the Atherton Shire in Queensland (where they are said to have been first introduced in the nineteenth century), and in the south on Kangaroo Island (where they were first recorded in 1967) and on Tasmania.

Long (1972) has traced the spread of pigeons in Western Australia. They were probably first introduced by the early settlers, and were well enough established on Rottnest Island by 1890 to warrant their destruction because of pollution of the rainwater supply. In 1951, they occurred in Perth and Fremantle and in some nearby rural districts, and a decade later were reported on Garden Island and in several country towns and on farms throughout the Perth metropolitan area. They have since been found nesting in native Gum trees (*Eucalyptus* spp.) at Nangeenan, Moora, Trayning and Yorkrakine Rock, and in bush at North Baandee and east of Kununoppin. Surveys by Long in 1968–9 showed that Feral Pigeons were widespread in the metropolitan and adjacent areas from Fremantle to Midland and Armadale, and also occurred in 77 country towns throughout the state.

New Zealand[16]

As in North America and Australia, pigeons were probably first brought to New Zealand by early settlers – according to Wodzicki (1965: 432) in about the 1850s. Thomson (1922), who said that they were feral in many parts of New Zealand, recorded their presence at Lake Wakatipu; on the Rock and Pillar Range from Middlemarch to Waipiata in Strath-Taieri; on the Galloway Station in central Otago; in the Duntroon district inland from Oamaru; in the Dunstan Range; and around Napier. In some places – for example, Lake Wakatipu and Strath-Taieri – Feral Pigeons appeared to contain 'a strain of nearly every pigeon tribe. Some make an attempt to "tumble" . . . they are of all colours, and apparently of all breeds, and several of them have the "tumbling" habit' (Thompson 1922: 134). Oliver (1955) said that pigeons were then feral in most cities and country districts throughout New Zealand, and on sea cliffs on the south coast of Banks Peninsula in Canterbury. Wodzicki (1965) reported them to be 'Restricted but abundant, North and South Islands', while Kinsky (1970) said they occurred 'Especially in parts of Hawke's Bay, Marlborough, Canterbury, Otago, and all major cities'. Falla, Sibson & Turbott (1979) recorded that in some places, notably on the west coast of Auckland, in Hawke's Bay and on the Banks Peninsula, Feral Pigeons have reverted to their Rock Dove ancestors' sea cliff habitat.

Norfolk Island

Smithers & Disney (1969) say that small numbers of Feral Pigeons are well established around buildings and nest colonially in caves in coastal cliffs on Norfolk Island.

OCEANIA

Hawaiian Islands[17]

Domesticated pigeons were first introduced to the Hawaiian group in 1796 during the reign of King Kamehameha I. Formerly abundant on all islands except Kauai (they occurred, according to Munro (1944), in 'immense flocks on Hawaii in 1891' and also on Molokai in the early 1900s), Feral Pigeons declined shortly thereafter due to a combination of factors, including overshooting at their common roosting and nesting sites;

changing land-usage, which greatly decreased their feeding range; and probably parasitic tapeworm infestation, which reduces the rate of successful breeding.

During their 1946–7 survey, Schwartz & Schwartz (1949) assessed the total population at approximately 2,550, of which the vast majority (2,300) were on Hawaii, with around 100 each on Lanai and Molokai and 50 on Oahu. The birds were found to roost and nest at all seasons on sheltered coastal cliffs, in rocky gulches, and in collapsed lava tubes to an altitude of 3,000 m on the slopes of Mauna Kea on Hawaii. Temperatures within this range vary from an annual mean of 5–20 °C, and rainfall, which seems to affect the birds' feeding range more than their choice of roosting and nesting sites, from under 50 cm to 200 cm.

Schwartz & Schwartz found that the birds' diet consisted of 77 per cent seeds, 7 per cent fruit and, unusually, 16 per cent animals, including the larvae and pupae of cutworms (*Agrotis ypsilon*), the larvae of wireworms (*Conoderus exsul*) and the shells of snails (*Succinea konaensis*). As pigeons feed on better pastures and in cultivated fields (apart from sugar-cane plantations), patterns of land-usage, soil and climate dictate the distribution of their feeding grounds. Corn (*Zea mays*) is especially attractive, and pigeons cause damage to the newly planted crop and also during and after its harvest. Other favoured foods include the seeds of Maltese Thistle (*Centaurea melitensis*) and the seeds and fruits of Akia (*Wikstroemia phillyraefolia*). Wherever corn-fed poultry are reared, Feral Pigeons often gather in large flocks. Some predation of eggs and squabs occurs in those roosting and nesting sites accessible to Small Indian Mongooses (*Herpestes auropunctatus*), Black and Brown Rats (*Rattus rattus* and *R. norvegicus*), and man.

Peterson (1961) found Feral Pigeons to be established locally on Hawaii, Molokai, Oahu, Lanai, and on Midway some 2,500 km northwest of Hawaii. The Hawaiian Audubon Society (1975) reported them to be well established and breeding on all these islands (with the possible exception of Midway) and also present on Kauai and Maui. Zeillemaker & Scott (1976) recorded them on agricultural land and pastures and in residential and community parks on Oahu and Molokai (where they were common), on Kauai, Maui and Hawaii (uncommon) and on Lanai where they were said to be local and uncommon. Walker (1981) listed them as occurring on Hawaii, Molokai, Lanai and Oahu.

Polynesia[18]

In eastern Polynesia, where Feral Pigeons are established locally in the Cook, Society, Tubuai, Tuamotu and Marquesas groups, they were reported by Holyoak & Thibault (1984) on the following islands: **Palmerston** – some were observed in the village in 1973; **Rarotonga** – birds probably from the Society Islands some-times arrive on the coast; **Bora Bora** – around 70 were counted near the village of Vaitape in 1972; **Raiatea** and **Tahaa** – although they were not recorded in 1920 a few small colonies were seen in 1972 and 1973; **Huahine** – some were noted in 1973; **Moorea** – although absent in 1921 they were established locally in 1972 and 1973; **Tahiti** – introduced in the [early] nineteenth century and very common in Papeete and on the coast [they were not, however, mentioned by Wilson (1907) nor by the Whitney Expedition, but were later referred to by Curtiss (1938)]; **Tubuai** – present in small numbers on the coasts; **Îles Gambier** (**Mangareva**) – small groups observed on the cliffs [of Mount Duff] in 1971; **Nuku Hiva** – a small semi-domesticated flock was seen in 1975; **Ua Huka** – collected in the south in 1922 and very common on the cliffs in 1975; **Ua Pou** – observed in the village in 1975; **Hiva Oa** – reported for the first time in 1958, some semi-domesticated and wild colonies were seen in 1975; **Tahuata** – fairly well distributed on the cliffs in 1975. Holyoak (1974a) estimated that in the Society Islands 10 per cent of the population has 'wild type' Rock Dove plumage, 30 per cent are darkly chequered (with many black markings on the wing coverts), 50 per cent are mainly dusky or black, and the remaining 10 per cent are principally white, reddish or cinnamon.

In western Polynesia, the Feral Pigeon 'is not a recent arrival, for it was certainly present soon after the turn of the century and there is evidence that it may have first arrived with missionaries as early as the 1840s' (Watling 1982: 78). In Fiji, the birds are locally common on all the larger islands, being especially abundant around Suva on Viti Levu and in several villages on Taveuni.

In Samoa, a small flock of 20 was first observed on Savaii in 1972.

As elsewhere throughout the world, Feral Pigeons in Polynesia are centred on towns and villages and obtain their food directly or indirectly from man. In Papeete, they eat bread, fruit, vegetables and rubbish gleaned especially from the market and port. In the rest of the Society Islands, they feed around the coconut plantations. Although in the Marquesas some remain near villages and in coconut groves others – on Ua Huka, Hiva Oa and Tahuata – live on coastal cliffs and feed on grain grown in the drier areas. In Fiji, they are confined almost entirely to urban and suburban areas, where they eat mainly grain and food refuse; they only rarely stray onto agricultural land and have not colonized smaller islets or coastal cliffs. In general, the most truly wild flocks seem to be those in the Gambier Archipelago and in the Marquesas.

Throughout Polynesia, Feral Pigeons are believed to breed the year round. In Papeete and in neighbouring villages, they nest on buildings; in the Marquesas, some populations breed in holes in coastal cliffs and on an islet near Tahuata; elsewhere, Holyoak & Thibault believe there may be some competition for nesting places with the indigenous Blue-gray Noddy (*Procelsterna cerula*). In Fiji and in other islands in western Polynesia, Feral Pigeons nest on window-ledges, under the eaves of houses, or in makeshift dovecotes.

Easter Island

Pigeons are believed to have been introduced to Easter Island (Rapa Nui) in the same year (1928) as the Chimango Caracara (*Milvago chimango*) (q.v.) and House Sparrow (*Passer domesticus*) (q.v.).

South Georgia

Watson (1975) reported that Feral Pigeons were established at the whaling station on South Georgia in January 1968.

Galápagos Islands

In the Galápagos Islands, Feral Pigeons have been recorded on all the inhabited islands (i.e. Santa Cruz, Isabela, San Cristóbal and Floreana).[19]

The critically endangered **Pink Pigeon** (*Columba* (= *Nesoenas*) *mayeri*)[20] is endemic to the island of Mauritius where its future is threatened by habitat destruction and by the predation of its nests by introduced Crab-eating Macaques (*Macaca fasicularis*) and Black Rats (*Rattus rattus*) (Lever 1985b). In March 1984, a pair of captive-reared birds were reintroduced to Mauritius in the Botanic Gardens at Pamplemousses, under the joint auspices of the International Council for Bird Preservation and the Jersey Wildlife Preservation Trust, as the first step in an attempt to increase the wild population which was then estimated to number between 15 and 20 birds.

NOTES

1 In order to present a complete overall picture, the establishment of Feral Pigeons in the native range of the Rock Dove has been included, even though the former are not, strictly speaking, 'naturalized' there (see pp. xiii–xiv).

2 Fitter 1959; Gompertz 1957; Goodwin 1954; Lever 1977a; Ritchie 1920; Sharrock 1976; Witherby et al. Vol. 4, 1940.

3 Brazil 1985 and in press; Etchécopar & Hue 1978; Goodwin 1970; King, Dickinson & Woodcock 1975; Long 1981; Ornithological Society of Japan 1981; Peters 1937; Ringleben 1960; Voous 1960.

4 For information on Feral Pigeons in southern Africa I am principally indebted to Brooke (1981). See also: Winterbottom 1978.

5 Long 1981; Meinertzhagen 1912; Rountree, Guérin et al. 1952; Staub 1976.

6 *Notes by a Naturalist on HMS Challenger* (London, 1879).

7 Benson 1950; Haydock 1954; Long 1981; Melliss 1870.

8 American Ornithologists' Union 1957, 1983; Cooke & Knappen 1941; Elton 1958; Hardy 1973; Heilbrun 1976; Laycock 1970; Levi 1941; Long 1981; Morris 1969; Peterson 1961; Phillips 1928;

Roots 1976; Schorger 1952; Silverstein & Silverstein 1974.

9 Carl & Guiguet 1972; Godfrey 1966; Long 1981; Roots 1976; Schorger 1952.

10 *History of New France*, ed. W. L. Grant (Champlain Society: Toronto, 1907–14), Vol. 2: 266, quoted by R. M. Saunders, 'The first introduction of European plants and animals into Canada', *Canadian Historical Review*, 392 (1935).

11 Bourne 1957; Crowell 1962; Crowell & Crowell 1976; D.B. Wingate 1973 (and personal communication, 1981).

12 American Ornithologists' Union 1957, 1983; Bond 1979; Heilbrun 1976, 1977; Holland & Williams 1978; Long 1981.

13 H. E. M. Dott 1986 (and personal communication, 1986); Goodwin 1970; Humphrey, Bridge et al. 1970; Long 1981; Olrog 1959; Sick 1968.

14 Johnson 1967; Long 1981; Sick 1968; and W. R. P. Bourne, personal communication, 1983.

15 Abbott 1974; Balmford 1978; Blakers, Davies & Reilly 1984; Condon 1962; Frith 1979; Lavery 1974; Lavery & Hopkins 1963; Long 1971, 1972, 1981; McGill 1960; Serventy & Whittell 1951, 1962; Storr 1965.

16 Falla, Sibson & Turbott 1979; Kinsky 1970; Long 1981; Oliver 1955; Thomson 1922, 1926; Williams 1969; Wodzicki 1965.

17 Berger 1981; Bryan 1958; Caum 1933; Elton 1958; Hawaiian Audubon Society 1975; Levi 1941; Long 1981; Munro 1944; Peterson 1961; Pyle 1977; Schwartz & Schwartz 1949; Walker 1967b, 1981; Zeillemaker & Scott 1976.

18 Curtiss 1938; du Pont 1972; Holyoak 1974a, 1979; Holyoak & Thibault 1984; Lancan & Mougin 1974; Long 1981; Pernetta & Watling 1978; Thibault 1976; Thibault & Rives 1975; Watling 1982; Wilson 1907.

19 C. A. Valle, personal communication, 1986.

20 Delacour 1959; King 1981; Lever 1985b; Meinertzhagen 1912. See also: S. A. Temple, 'Wildlife in Mauritius today', *Oryx* 12: 584–90 (1974) and S. A. Temple, *World Wildlife Yearbook, 1974–75* (World Wildlife Fund: Morges, Switzerland, 1975), 210-12.

Madagascar Turtle Dove
(*Streptopelia picturata*)

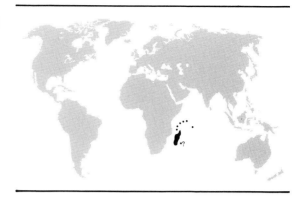

NATURAL DISTRIBUTION

Madagascar; Mauritius (? introduced); Îles Glorieuses (? natural colonist or introduced;? now extinct); Anjouan (Comoros Islands); Aldabra; Assumption (? now extinct); Amirantes; Seychelles; Diego Garcia (Chagos Archipelago).

NATURALIZED DISTRIBUTION

Africa: Mauritius (?native); Réunion, Seychelles and Amirantes (non-native races); Îles Glorieuses, (?introduced or natural colonist; ?now extinct), Agaléga Islands; Oceania: Diego Garcia (Chagos Archipelago; ?endemic race).

AFRICA

Mauritius[1]

Although Rountree, Guérin et al. (1952) point out that Carié (1916) suggested that Madagascar Turtle Doves may have been natives of Mauritius, most other authorities seem agreed that the species occurs there as the result of an early intro-

duction from Madagascar (*S. p. picturata*). Although apparently at one time abundant, Meinertzhagen (1912) reported them as scarce – a status which they appear to have retained into the 1950s, when they were said to be local and confined to remote wooded regions. Staub (1976), however, reported them to be widespread.

Réunion[2]

The nominate form *S. p. picturata* has been introduced to Réunion (probably from Mauritius) where it is scarce except in the south-east around Saint Philippe.

Seychelles[3]

From Mauritius or Madagascar *S. p. picturata* has been introduced to the Seychelles where, except on Cousin, Cousine and possibly Frigate, it has displaced or diluted the blood of the smaller endemic race *S. p. rostrata*, which is in danger of extinction. According to Newton (1867), the birds were established but uncommon on Mahé, where they were believed to have been introduced by the local Inspector of Police in about 1850. Diamond & Feare (1980) record them as breeding regularly on all the main islands except Marianne.

Amirantes[4]

On 23 September 1967, I.S.C. Parker collected two female Madagascar Turtle Doves on St Joseph's Atoll in the Amirantes, which were believed to represent a recent introduction by man from the Seychelles. These specimens may be *picturata* × *rostrata* hybrids. The introduced birds have interbred with *aldabrana* (an endemic race of Aldabra Island from which it was presumably imported) and probably also with the endemic Amirantes race *saturata*.

Penny (1974, quoting Benson) suggests that Madagascar Turtle Doves first arrived in the Seychelles and Amirantes (and possibly also in the Chagos Archipelago) as 'excess food stores on a pirate ship', and that they were helped in

becoming established by the comparative rarity of the endemic subspecies. According to the *Encyclopaedia Britannica*, 'there is a strong tradition, probably well founded, that [these islands] had been from Arab times a rendezvous of the pirates and corsairs who infested the high seas between South Africa and India'.[5]

Îles Glorieuses[6]

In 1883 the first specimen of a Madagascar Turtle Dove was collected in the Îles Glorieuses, where Ridgeway (1895) believed that the species had been introduced by man. Benson (1970) and Penny (1974), however, suggest that the birds may have arrived as natural colonists from Aldabra Island, some 250 km to the north-west. The subspecies has been named *coppingeri*. As there are no records for it on the islands after 1906 it is presumably now extinct.

Agaléga Islands

According to Guého & Staub (1983), Madagascar Turtle Doves were introduced to the Agalégas at an early date (probably shortly after their settlement by the French in 1818) from the Mascarenes, and are now present in small numbers.

OCEANIA

Chagos Archipelago (Diego Garcia)[7]

Although Loustau-Lalanne (1962) records the apparent absence of Madagascar Turtle Doves on Diego Garcia in the Chagos Archipelago in 1907, they were well established all over the island (especially near Pointe Est) by the early 1960s. Documentary evidence is lacking, but the species may have been introduced from the Seychelles. Bourne (1971), however, considers that the birds on Diego Garcia are an endemic race, *S. p. chuni*, and points out that Ripley (in Bourne 1971) disagrees with Benson (1970) who says that the birds are hybrids between *picturata* and *comores*, the latter being endemic to Anjouan in the Comoros group.

NOTES

1 Carié 1916; Long 1981; Meinertzhagen 1912; Peters 1937; Rountree, Guérin et al. 1952; Staub 1976.

2 Barré & Barau 1982; Long 1981; Peters 1937; Staub 1973, 1976.

3 Benson 1970; Diamond & Feare 1980; Gaymer, Blackman et al. 1969; Long 1981; Newton 1867; Penny 1974; Peters 1937.

4 Benson 1970; Long 1981; Penny 1974.

5 Vol. 23: 752 (1926).

6 Benson 1970; Benson, Beamish et al. 1975; Long 1981; Penny 1974; Ridgeway 1895.

7 Benson 1970; Bourne 1971; Hutson 1975; Long 1981; Loustau-Lalanne 1962.

Collared Dove

(Streptopelia decaocto)

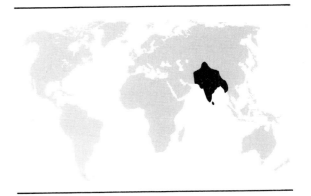

NATURAL DISTRIBUTION[1]

Originally probably restricted to the drier regions of central and southern Asia – Afghanistan, India, Burma, Sri Lanka and western China (Chinese Turkestan) – from where in early times it colonized naturally (and/or was perhaps introduced to) Iran, and thence westwards via the Near East to Turkey, possibly as early as the sixteenth century but certainly by the early 1700s.

In Europe (apart from western Turkey), Collared Doves were first recorded in Bulgaria in 1853, and from the end of the century until about 1930, when they began to expand their range rapidly and dramatically northwestwards, they were established only in Turkey and tenuously in parts of the Balkans (Albania, Bulgaria and Yugoslavia). They were first reported in the last named (at Belgrade) in 1912, and reached southern Hungary in 1930, Romania in 1933, Czechoslovakia in 1936, Romania (Bucharest) and Austria in 1938, Greece in 1939, southern Germany in 1943, Italy in 1944, the Netherlands in 1947, Denmark in 1948, Sweden and Switzerland in 1949, Poland and France in 1950, and Belgium, Norway, the USSR (Moldavia) and England (Lincolnshire) in 1952 – thus spreading over 1,600 km in under 20 years. They arrived in Luxembourg in 1956, Northern Ireland (County Down) in 1960, eastern Iceland (Lodmundàrfjord) in 1964 and the Faeroe Islands (Thorshavn) in 1970.

According to Hudson (1965), Collared Doves were not breeding in Europe west of Hungary, Czechoslovakia and Austria in 1940. Breeding was first confirmed in the Netherlands in 1949, Sweden (Scania) in 1951, England (Norfolk), Switzerland and Norway in 1955, France in 1956,

Scotland (Morayshire) in 1957, Ireland (Dublin and Galway) in 1959, Wales (Pembrokeshire and Cardiganshire) in 1961, the Isle of Man in 1964, Shetland in 1965, southern Finland in 1968, and the Faeroes and southern Iceland in 1971.

'The colonization of Britain and Ireland', wrote Sharrock (1976: 246), 'has been one of the most dramatic events witnessed by present-day ornithologists, but is just one stage in an even more dramatic range-extension northwestwards across Europe. . . . When Collared Doves reached [the British Isles] they found an ecological niche not filled by any other bird and, in the absence of competition, proceeded to demonstrate the potential for geometric population increase that is presumed to be inherent in all species. During their first decade they increased and spread at the incredible rate of 100% per annum.'

By the early 1970s, the Collared Dove was established throughout Europe apart from Iceland, Scandinavia (north of about 69° 30' N), and the Iberian Peninsula. According to Mayr (1956b), its expansion in northern Europe was assisted by an amelioration in climatic conditions and an increase in its preferred habitat through the spread of agriculture.

In Africa, the Collared Dove is replaced in Ethiopia, Sudan and Somalia, and from Senegal to Chad and the Central African Republic by the African Collared or Pink-headed Dove (*Streptopelia roseogrisea*). In Arabia, birds in Yemen are likely to be *roseogrisea* and those in Oman *decaocto*.

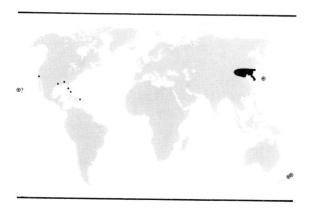

NATURALIZED DISTRIBUTION[2]
Asia: ?China; ?North and South Korea; Japan; North America: USA; West Indies; Australasia: New Zealand; Oceania: ?Hawaiian Islands.

ASIA

China; North and South Korea[3]

According to Stresemann & Nowak (1958) (with whom Goodwin (1970) agrees), Collared Doves were shipped from India to northern China where they escaped and became established, spreading westwards into eastern Inner Mongolia, north into central Manchuria, and south into North and South Korea where, however, Gore & Won (1971) recorded them only on Hong-do Island and some islands off the southwestern coast. Vaurie (1961), on the other hand, considers it more probable that the birds arrived in northeastern China by natural extension of range and/or introductions from (western) Inner Mongolia and/or western China. He points out that the subspecies in northeastern China (*stoliczkae* according to Howard & Moore (1980), but *decaocto* according to Stresemann & Nowak (1958)) is the same as that which occurs in Chinese Turkestan.

Japan[4]

In the eighteenth or early nineteenth century (certainly before about 1830), Collared Doves from China were imported as cagebirds to the island of Honshu, where they escaped and became established. Fisher (1953) records that by 1875 they were abundant in the Kwanto region near Tokyo, but were greatly reduced in numbers through overshooting by the end of the century. By 1925, they were known to occur only in the Saitama and Chiba prefectures, where they were almost exterminated after the Second World War, and by the late 1950s only a few score survived near Koshigaya north of Tokyo. According to the Ornithological Society of Japan (1981), Collared Doves are at present confined to the Kanto Plain in Saitama where, however, they are apparently increasing.

NORTH AMERICA

USA[5]

The earliest record of a free-flying Barbary Dove (usually known in the United States, where it is a favourite of aviculturists by whom it has often been released or from whom it has escaped, as the Ringed Turtle Dove) was of an individual noted in Buena Park, Los Angeles, California, in 1909. The species was first observed in Central Park in 1921, where 5 years later a flock of 25 had become established, and by 1929 20 pairs had colonized Pershing Square where one pair bred successfully. In the late 1920s, further populations became established in other parks and gardens in the urban centre of Los Angeles (e.g. in the grounds of the Central Library and in Olvera Street. Although Cooke & Knappen (1941) indicated that the birds were susceptible to predation by hawks, Hardy (1973) considered that the population, which he estimated to number several hundred, was apparently stable. By the late 1950s, Barbary Doves had been reported in California from as far east as San Bernardino and Redlands and northwards from most of the San Fernando Valley; by the mid 1970s they ranged from at least Pasadena to Redlands and south to the Palos Verdes Hills. This extension of range may have been the result of natural dispersal from the city centre or could represent recruitment to the population through further escapes and/or releases from dealers or private aviaries.

Barbary Doves are also established locally in parts of southern and central Florida (e.g. Winter Park in Orange County and in Pinellas County on the west coast at St Petersburg). They appear to be rapidly colonizing suburban Alabama, where by 1978 they were found in Athens, five suburbs of Birmingham, Auburn, Montgomery, Hayneville, and in Mobile where they first bred at Springhill, and the Houston region of eastern Texas.

West Indies

According to Lack (1976), as long ago as 1863–4 'domestic doves (*S. risoria*)' sometimes associated in Jamaica with native White-winged Doves (*Zenaida asiatica*), but there are no subsequent records of their occurrence on the island. Bond (1979: 101) states that 'in the West Indies . . . locally, Old World turtle doves (*Streptopelia*) occur as a semi-feral species'. In his index (p. 254), this is expanded to '*Streptopelia risoria*' – the Barbary Dove. The islands to which they

have been introduced include New Providence in the Bahamas and Puerto Rico.

AUSTRALASIA

New Zealand[6]

The Canterbury Acclimatization Society imported the first Collared Doves to New Zealand in 1866; others were introduced by the Nelson and Auckland Societies in 1867, and for at least the next 50 years many more were brought in by dealers and private individuals by whom they were often released around homesteads and dwellings. In 1916, E. F. Stead told Thomson (1922: 133) that 'there is a fairly large number in the (Christchurch) domain. People have turned them out in their gardens in various parts of the city, and they stop about and do fairly well, but they do not seem to increase'. 'The same', Thomson adds, 'is true of suburban gardens about Dunedin.' These South Island populations did not long persist.

In North Island, a colony of feral Barbary Doves has been established for some years around Whakatane on the Bay of Plenty. In 1971, Stidolph (1974) found two Barbary Doves at Masterton, where some 30 or so were present in the following year. A feral population, probably the result of deliberate releases, seems to have become established in Masterton Park and in the western suburbs of the town where there are plenty of trees and shrubs.

OCEANIA

Hawaiian Islands[7]

Collared (or Barbary) Doves introduced to the island of Kauai in 1920, to Oahu in 1928 and later elsewhere, failed to become established. In 1961, 11 were released on the Puu Waawaa Ranch on Hawaii, where a few may remain around the ranch buildings.

According to McGill (1948), the earliest report of an escaped Collared (or Barbary) Dove in the wild in Australia came from the suburban area of Sydney, New South Wales, in August 1946. Long (1981) states that a small colony of 15 that became established in the Wattle Grove area near Perth in Western Australia in 1975 was destroyed by the state's Agriculture Protection Board. According to Paton & Barrington (1985), Barbary Doves are from time to time reported in the wild in and around Adelaide and on Eyre Peninsula, South Australia.

Before the successful invasion of England by Collared Doves in 1952 several attempts had previously been made to naturalize Barbary Doves in central London. Many were made by, or at the instigation of, the indefatigable Frank Finn, while on leave from the Indian Museum in Calcutta. In April 1896, a single bird was seen in a garden in Brixton, and 3 years later a pair was said to be breeding on Duck Island in St James's Park. In March 1902, another pair was seen in the same park, and in July 1905 yet another was reported in a different Brixton garden. In *Ornithological and Other Oddities* (1907), quoted by Fitter (1959: 220), Finn claimed that a few Barbary Doves had 'long been living and breeding in St. James's Park, though the public do not often see them'. The last recorded occasion when Barbary Doves were observed in the park was in May 1916, when a pair reared two young on Duck Island. More recently escaped Barbary Doves have become established in Lancashire and elsewhere, where they may have interbred with Collared Doves. Hudson (1972) indicates that although Collared Doves can be a local nuisance in Britain when they are abundant, particularly where grain is stored or processed, they have not yet become an economically significant national pest.

NOTES

1 Ennis 1965; Fisher 1953; Hudson 1965, 1972; Langseth 1965; Leys 1964; Long 1981; Mayr 1965b; Ojala & Sjöberg 1968; Reuterwall 1956; Sharrock 1976; Stresemann & Nowak 1958; Vaurie 1961; Voous 1960.

2 The domesticated Barbary Dove (*S. risoria*) is descended from the African Collared or Pink-headed Dove (*S. roseogrisea*), which, except in plumage (*risoria* is normally a more creamy buff or white in colour), it closely resembles. Except where all authorities are in agreement, no attempt has been made here to distinguish between introductions of *decaocto* and *risoria*, since accounts of which species was involved often differ. D. Goodwin (personal communication, 1985) considers that, at least in the United States, it seems likely that all pre-1940 records of introductions of 'Ringdoves' and 'Collared Doves', refer, unless clearly stated otherwise, to Barbary Doves.

3 Goodwin 1970; Gore & Won 1971; Long 1981; Stresemann & Nowak 1958; Vaurie, 1961.

4 Brazil 1985 and in press; Fisher 1953; Long 1981; Ornithological Society of Japan 1974, 1981; Taka-Tsukasa & Hachisuka 1925; Udagawa 1949; Voous 1960; Yamashina 1961.

5 American Ornithologists' Union 1957, 1983; Blake 1975; Cooke & Knappen 1941; Cottam 1956; Gottschalk 1967; Grinnell 1929; Hardy 1973; Heilbrun 1976; Imhof 1978; Long 1981; Owre 1973; Willett 1933.

6 Falla, Sibson & Turbott 1979; Long 1981; Stidolph 1974; Thomson 1922.

7 Berger 1972; Lewin 1971; Long 1981; Walker 1967b.

Spotted Dove

(Streptopelia chinensis)

NATURAL DISTRIBUTION

Sri Lanka, India, Pakistan and Burma south through Malaysia to Sumatra, Java, the Lesser Sunda Islands, Borneo and Palawan, northwards to Yunnan in southern and central China, Taiwan and Hainan.

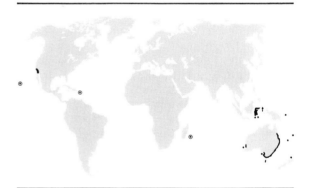

NATURALIZED DISTRIBUTION

Africa: Mauritius; North America: USA, Mexico, ?West Indies; Australasia: Australia, New Zealand, Indonesia (Sulawesi, Moluccas and some small islands in the Flores Sea), New Britain; Oceania: New Caledonia, Hawaiian Islands, Fiji.

AFRICA

Mauritius[1]

The race *suratensis* (India) or possibly *tigrina* (Burma to Palawan, Borneo and Sumatra) of the Spotted Dove was introduced to Mauritius from Bengal[2] by Cossigny de Palma in 1781. A specimen was described as early as 1834, and

Meinertzhagen (1912) found the birds to be common on the island where they remain today both widespread and abundant.

According to Roots (1976), Spotted Doves of the Indonesia race (*tigrina*) are also established on the nearby island of Réunion.

NORTH AMERICA

USA and Mexico[3]

Spotted Doves of the form *S. c. chinensis* have for many years been imported by aviculturists from eastern China to the United States. The species was first recorded in the wild in 1917 when a dead bird was found in Los Angeles, California, where subsequent enquiries revealed that it was a common resident in North Hollywood. Within 6 years it was abundant in much of the Los Angeles basin, and a decade later had spread west to the suburb of Santa Monica, south to Inglewood, north to Pasadena, and to Alhambra. The speed with which the population increased can be gauged from the ringing records made by Harold Michener at Pasadena (quoted by Cooke & Knappen 1941): the first Spotted Dove was trapped and ringed in December 1933, 33 were ringed in 1934, 76 in 1935, 256 in 1936, 404 in 1937 and 483 in 1938.

By about 1940, Spotted Doves had spread eastwards over the coastal plains south of the San Gabriel Mountains, were to be found in Los Angeles and Orange counties, and had been recorded at Palm Springs in San Bernardino County eastwards to Redlands in Riverside County; by 1946 they had spread as far north as Lancaster and Bakersfield. Reuther (1951) considered that this expansion may have been assisted by further releases and/or escapes. By the 1960s, the birds had extended their range northwards to Santa Barbara and Santa Maria, eastwards to Pear Blossom, south-east to Palm Springs, and south to Oceanside and San Diego; a few years later they had spread further southeast from Palm Springs to the Salton Sea. By the early 1970s, the population appeared to have stabilized and its rate of expansion to have decreased; deserts and an absence of large trees (of which *Eucalyptus* are a favourite) appear to inhibit any further extension of range in an east-

erly direction. The American Ornithologists' Union (1983) described the birds as occurring primarily from Santa Barbara and Bakersfield south to San Diego and the Salton Sea, and in the Tijuana region of extreme northwestern Baja California, Mexico. Although in its optimum suburban habitats the Spotted Dove seems to outnumber the smaller native Mourning Dove (*Zenaida macroura*), there is apparently little evidence of interspecific competition, nor between Spotted Doves and White-winged Doves (*Z. asiatica*) or Band-tailed Pigeons (*Columba fasciata*).

West Indies

Blake (1975) indicates that Spotted Doves have been introduced to the West Indies. Although Bond (1979: 101) states that 'in the West Indies . . . locally, Old World turtle doves (*Streptopelia*) occur as [a] semi-feral species', in his index the only member of the genus listed is *risoria* – the Barbary Dove. The American Ornithologists' Union (1983: 255), however, says that 'a small population persists on St Croix, in the Virgin Islands (introduced in 1964)'.

AUSTRALASIA

Australia[4]

The offspring of eight Spotted Doves of the nominate form from eastern China, imported to the Botanic Gardens in Melbourne by the Victoria Acclimatization Society in 1866, were released near Melbourne and at Cape Liptrap in 1870, 1872 and (16) in 1874. Twenty more were liberated in the Botanical Gardens at Adelaide in South Australia in 1881, where they apparently failed to become established, and the present population there is descended from some that escaped from Adelaide Zoo when their aviary was destroyed by a storm in 1931. Spotted Doves (and Laughing Doves (*Streptopelia senegalensis*) q.v.) in Perth, Western Australia, are descended from stock deliberately released at Northam, Yatheroo and Dardanup by the South Perth Zoo in and after 1898. There is no record of Spotted Doves ever having been liberated in Sydney, New South Wales, but since the Victoria Acclimatization Society is known to have provided other species for release there, Spotted Doves may well have been included. Chisholm (1926) reported that they were common in the city at that time, and had spread inland as far as the Blue Mountains; 6 years later between 50 and 100 pairs were established in the Royal Botanic Gardens. Frith & McKean (1975) believe that all these southern populations are probably derived from stock originally obtained from Melbourne.

Little evidence exists to document the species' early spread in southern Australia, where until the 1930s Spotted Doves were regarded as a novelty in many country towns. Ryan (1906) reported them to be spreading around Port Phillip, Victoria, in tea-tree scrub 'which offers them capital cover', and by the 1950s they were established within a radius of 150 km of Melbourne. In South Australia, they dispersed northwards and southwards from Adelaide to Clare and Victor Harbor, respectively; they were first noted on Dudley Peninsula in about 1951, on Kangaroo Island in March 1953, in the Mount Lofty Ranges and the Barossa Valley in 1961, and on Eyre Peninsula in 1966. In northeastern New South Wales they appeared at Lismore in 1935, by 1941 had spread over 30 km downstream along the Richmond River, and by 1952 were colonizing surrounding dairy farms and cattle yards. By 1964, they had spread to the coastal sugar-cane fields 30 km to the east, and the population was more or less continuous – especially in urban areas – 160 km north to Brisbane in southern Queensland and 270 km or more south at least as far as Kempsey. They were seldom, however, seen west of the Great Dividing Range.

In Western Australia, Spotted (and Laughing) Doves were established in Perth and its environs before 1912, and until at least 1920 were being recaptured for translocation to other parts of the state, where they apparently flourished wherever pine trees were available for nesting. Although in 1929 they were reported to have spread 'far and wide', they seem in fact not to have ventured much beyond the Perth metropolitan area, but since the mid-1930s have been slowly but steadily expanding their range. Spotted Doves were first observed on Rottnest Island off Perth around 1937, but until 1951 remained more or less confined to Perth and its suburbs, the most distant record at that time being 230 km south on the coast at Busselton. By 1958, Spotted

Doves were being reported at several places along the eastern railway line to Wooroloo (60 km from Perth), sporadically as far south as Quindalup (190 km), and occasionally elsewhere such as at Dongara, Kalgoorlie and Katanning: by 1967, they were established in Western Australia as far east as Wooroloo and south to Quindalup and Katanning, and in at least some places are continuing to expand their range.

According to Mr W.D. Armstrong, sometime Speaker of the Queensland Legislative Assembly (quoted by Chisholm 1919 and Jenkins 1977):

The Indian Dove *Turtur ferrago* was introduced to Queensland early in 1912. My nephew the present Lord Huntingfield was then with his regiment in India and sent me 26 pairs, 16 pairs of which survived the journey. I kept 4 pairs at Adare, Gatton . . . the others I gave to Mr Bailey the then Curator of the Brisbane Botanic Gardens . . . they soon became independent.

These birds, which within a year were reported to be well established in the grounds of the University of Queensland, were either *S. c. suratensis* or the reddish peninsular Indian race of the Rufous or Eastern Turtle Dove (*Streptopelia orientalis*). The reason given for their introduction was 'that our beautiful gardens lacked the pleasing music created by bird life'.

The Spotted Doves in northern Queensland are descended from stock released at Gordonvale in the 1940s. Although some were present in Townsville on the coast 250 km south of Gordonvale in 1926, they were not subsequently reported there until 1965, and their earlier occurrence may have been the result of an unrecorded release. Early records elsewhere in northern Queensland came from Cairns (25 km north of Gordonvale) and Innisfail (50 km south) in 1945; from Babinda (1950–4); from MacKay (on the coast midway between Gordonvale and Brisbane) in 1959; and from Mareeba (35 km north-west) and Atherton (50 km south-west) in 1964. Since McKay is some 575 km south of Gordonvale the presence of Spotted Doves there as early as 1959 may be attributable to an undocumented local release.

By the 1970s, Spotted Doves were well established in Perth; in Adelaide and many adjacent rural areas; in parks and gardens in Melbourne; in some of the larger provincial cities of Victoria; and in Sydney and Brisbane. In the south and in Western Australia they were found principally in urban environments, but in Queensland also occurred along creeks and in coastal scrub on partially cleared land, as well as in highly cultivated agricultural districts as far north as Mossman, nearly 100 km from Gordonvale. They had not, however, penetrated the unbroken *Eucalyptus* forests or the rainforest. The populations in Western Australia and South Australia are discrete, while that centred on Melbourne and in southern Victoria is probably separate from the one based on Sydney. The Sydney/Brisbane population is now continuous along the coast between the two cities, and extends respectively south and north of them both: the north Queensland population based on Gordonvale is also discrete.

Pizzey (1980) summed up the Spotted Dove's distribution as follows: within their range the birds were common and well established in urban areas, and were spreading in settled and agricultural regions of the coastal east and south-east from around Cooktown in northern Queensland to parts of Eyre Peninsula and Kangaroo Island in South Australia. They ranged inland in New South Wales to approximately the Moree/Gunnedah/Albury area; in central Victoria north to the Murray River; in South Australia upstream on the Murray at least as far as Loxton, and northwards to Port Augusta; and in Western Australia from Perth 325 km north to Dongara, with isolated populations (presumably arising from separate introductions) at Kalgoorlie (525 km east of Perth) and Katanning (250 km south-east), and on Rottnest and other offshore islands. On Tasmania, populations were centred on Hobart (where the species was said to be common in 1918) and Launceston.

Apart from those imported to Brisbane from Indian in 1912 (which were presumably *suratensis*), the source and identity of many of the early introductions are unknown. Frith (1979), however, considered that both *chinensis* (eastern China) and *tigrina* (Burma and Malaysia) were involved, since a large number of samples examined in Perth, Adelaide, Melbourne and Sydney by the Commonwealth Scientific and Industrial Research Organization's Division of Wildlife Research revealed typical examples of both races and innumerable intergradations. At Innisfail in northern Queensland there are believed to be pure *tigrina* birds.

In rural habitats in eastern Australia, the Spotted Dove lives sympatrically with the similarly sized native Bar-shouldered Dove (*Geopelia humeralis*). Where the former is abundant, however, the latter is now uncommon – a change in status of the two species typified near Lismore in northeastern New South Wales. As mentioned above, Spotted Doves first appeared in Lismore in 1935, when the Bar-shouldered Dove was the common dove of the open country; by 1952, the two species were numerically equal, but by 1970 the former had almost entirely supplanted the latter due, it is assumed, at least in part to interspecific competition (Frith 1979). Near Adelaide and on the outskirts of Melbourne, Spotted Doves may also be replacing the small native Barred Dove (*Geopelia striata*) with which it competes for food and habitat. In Western Australia, Spotted Doves have been accused of spreading the stickfast flea (*Echidnophaga gallinaceae*), and especially in the east of the country are said to damage germinating horticultural and silvicultural crops.

New Zealand[5]

According to Thomson (1922: 135), the Otago Acclimatization Society had two 'Indian Doves (? *Turtur ferrago*) [see above] in their aviary at Dunedin in 1907'. Wodzicki (1965: 432) said that the 'Malay Spotted Dove' (*tigrina*) was introduced to New Zealand early in the present century, and that by 1965 it was 'locally abundant, North Island'. As elsewhere, the species is a favourite with aviculturists in New Zealand, to which large numbers have been imported from Southeast Asia. In recent years, Spotted Doves have become established and common in wooded gardens and parks in the city and suburbs of Auckland from Albany (though they are uncommon on the North Shore) south to Papakura and Karaka.

Indonesia[6]

The form *tigrina* has been successfully introduced to several eastern Indonesia islands, including Celebes (Sulawesi), the Moluccas and some small islands in the Flores Sea south of Sulawesi. They were imported to the first-named from Java around 1835, and a century later were reported to be established on the northern Minahassa Peninsula, in the centre of the island and on the southern peninsula near Makassar.

New Britain

According to Mayr (1945), the form *tigrina* has also been imported to New Britain where it is naturalized in the extreme north around Rabaul.

OCEANIA

New Caledonia

Delacour (1966) says that in 1939 *tigrina* was introduced from South-east Asia to New Caledonia, where it occurs in many villages and cultivated areas but has been much reduced in numbers by shooting in Noumea.

Hawaiian Islands[7]

Spotted Doves (of the nominate subspecies) are believed to have been first introduced to Hawaii from China in 1788, and according to Caum (1933) they were 'very common' on Oahu in 1879; Schwartz & Schwartz (1949) say they were well established in the archipelago before 1900, and according to Fisher (1951) they had colonized Niihau from Kauai (where they were introduced around 1890) by about 1930. They were introduced to Maui, Hawaii, Molokai and Lanai also in about 1890, and Caum states that by 1933 they were widely distributed throughout the islands.

During their 1946–7 study of game birds in Hawaii, Schwartz & Schwartz found Spotted Doves of the nominate form on all the main islands – mainly from sea level to 1,200 m, in mean annual temperatures of between 20 °C and 15 °C, respectively; on Hawaii, however, they sometimes reached 2,400 m, where the mean annual temperature is around 5 °C. Rainfall throughout this range varies from less than 25 cm to 250 cm annually, though in a few places it may reach 625 cm. Preferred habitats appeared to be dense wooded thickets of algaroba or kiawe (*Prosopis chilensis*) in coastal regions below 900 m,

where annual mean temperatures lie between 20 °C and 17 °C and rainfall varies from under 50 cm to around 150 cm. The birds occurred in pineapple and sugar-cane plantations, pastures, waste land, market gardens, around homesteads, in urban areas and in clearings in *Eucalyptus* and ironwood (*Casuarina* sp.) groves, but dense forests and barren lava fields were unoccupied. This range was shared with the more recently introduced Barred Dove (*Geopelia striata*) (q.v.), although the larger Spotted Dove extended to higher altitudes, tolerated a greater rainfall and occurred in more heavily timbered areas. This distribution, Schwartz & Schwartz considered, was governed by temperature, rainfall and the pattern of vegetation. They censused the various islands' populations as follows: Hawaii, 31,570; Kauai, 10,470; Lanai, 3,470; Maui, 16,730; Molokai, 13,990; Oahu, 12,450 – a total of 88,680.

The diet of Spotted Doves in Hawaii was found to consist of seeds (77 per cent) and fruit (23 per cent). In the 1940s, the birds were said to be decreasing not, Schwartz & Schwartz contended, due to competition for food with the Barred Dove as was generally supposed (though Schwartz & Schwartz concede that in arid areas or in times of drought competition for fruit may be of significance), but more probably as a result of heavy parasitism by tapeworms, which inhibit nutrition and thus breeding success. Light predation of adults, juveniles and eggs by the introduced Small Indian Mongoose (*Herpestes auropunctatus*), and of juveniles and eggs by arboreal Black and Polynesian Rats (*Rattus rattus* and *R. exulans*) and introduced Common Mynahs (*Acridotheres tristis*) was not considered significant.

In 1961, eight Spotted Doves from a game farm in California were released on the Puu Waawaa Ranch on Hawaii, where Schwartz & Schwartz indicated a low-density population in 1946–7 of 1–25 birds per 2.5 km².

Walker (1967b) lists Spotted Doves as established and open to public shooting in Hawaii. Zeillemaker & Scott (1976) say that they are common residents in agricultural land and pastures, exotic forests and scrubland (Guava (*Psidium guajava*), Java Plum (*Eugenia cumini*) and *Eucalyptus*) and indigenous mixed ohia (*Metrosideros collina*) and koa (*Acacia koa*) woodland) on Kauai, Oahu, Molokai, Lanai, Maui and Hawaii; Walker (1981) lists them as also occurring on

Kahoolawe. They are found from sea level to an altitude of 2,400 m (mainly below 1,200 m), and are said to be relatively tame in urban areas but more wary in country districts. They cause little harm except the spread through their faeces of such plants as the alien Lantana (*Lantana camara*). Few later introductions of Columbidae to Hawaii (with the exception of the Barred Dove) have succeeded in the face of competition from this well-established species.

Fiji[8]

Around the turn of the century, Spotted Doves of the race *tigrina* were imported as cagebirds from Australia to Viti Levu in Fiji where, according to Watling (1982), they were first recorded as being established in 1923; 30 years later they were said to occur on all the main islands, including Nukulau and the coasts of Taveuni. Watling (pp. 79–80) says that in Fiji the Spotted Dove:

can become a serious pest of sorghum or lodged rice, though of the latter it more commonly feeds on fallen grain after harvest. . . . it is usually encountered in suburban gardens, villages and agricultural land, although it sometimes ventures into grass clearings in forested areas. . . . it is found on the larger islands, and some of the smaller islands closeby. . . . It is now a very common species in most man-modified habitats.

According to Fitter (1959), around the turn of the century the Duke of Bedford successfully acclimatized the Malay race (*tigrina*) of the Spotted Dove in the park of Woburn Abbey in Bedfordshire, England, where, however, they had to be fed throughout the winter and were preyed on by Sparrowhawks (*Accipiter nisus*).

NOTES

1 Benedict 1957; Condon 1975; Long 1981; Meinertzhagen 1912; Roots 1976; Rountree, Guérin et al. 1952; Staub 1976.

2 One account says that the birds may have come, not later than the early nineteenth century, from southern China, in which case the race would presumably have been *vacillans* (southeastern Yunnan) or *forresti* (northeastern Burma to northwestern Yunnan).

3 American Ornithologists' Union 1983; Blake 1975; Cooke & Knappen 1941; Gottschalk 1967; Hardy 1973; Long 1981; McLean 1958; Reuther 1951; Storer 1934; Willett 1933.

4 Blakers, Davies & Reilly, 1984; Boehm 1961; Bravery 1970; Chisholm 1919; Colebatch 1929; Condon 1962, 1968, 1975; Frith 1972, 1979; Frith & McKean 1975; Jenkins 1959, 1977; Kingsmill 1920; Lavery 1974; Le Souef 1912; Long 1972, 1981; McGill 1960; Pizzey 1980; Ryan 1906; Sedgwick 1958, 1976; Serventy & Whittell 1951, 1962; Storr 1965; Tarr 1950; White 1946.

5 Falla, Sibson & Turbott 1979; Kinsky 1970; Long 1981; Oliver 1955; Thomson 1922; Williams 1953; Wodzicki 1965.

6 Delacour 1947; Delacour & Mayr 1946; Goodwin 1970; Long 1981; Meyer 1879; Peters 1937; Ripley 1961; Stresemann 1936.

7 American Ornithologists' Union 1957, 1983; Bancroft 1982; Berger 1981; Bryan 1958; Caum 1933; Fisher 1951; Hawaiian Audubon Society 1975; Lever 1985b; Lewin 1971; Locey 1937; Long 1981; Munro 1960; Peterson 1961; Pyle 1977; Schwartz & Schwartz 1949, 1951c; Walker 1967b, 1981; Zeillemaker & Scott 1976.

8 Blackburn 1971; Gorman 1975; Holyoak 1979; Long 1981; Mayr 1945; Mercer 1966; Parham 1954; Pernetta & Watling 1978; Turbet 1941; Watling 1982.

Laughing Dove
(*Streptopelia senegalensis*)

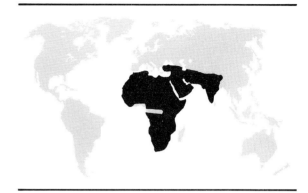

NATURAL DISTRIBUTION
Most of Africa (apart perhaps from the south-eastern Ivory Coast, southern Ghana, Equatorial Guinea, Gabon, Congo and parts of western Zaire) through the Near East, the southwestern USSR, Arabia and Asia Minor to India and extreme northwestern China.

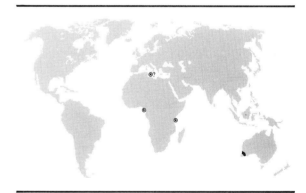

NATURALIZED DISTRIBUTION
Europe: ?Malta; Africa: Principe Island, ?Mafia Island; Australasia: Australia.

EUROPE

Malta

According to Goodwin (1970), Laughing Doves have been introduced (presumably *S. s. phoenicophila* from northwest Africa) to the island of Malta, where they are believed now to have died out.

AFRICA

Príncipe Island

Snow (1950) states that the local race (*S. s. thomé*) of the Laughing Dove was introduced around 1905 from the Portuguese island of São Tomé in the Gulf of Guinea to another Portuguese island, Príncipe, 100 km or so to the northeast, where it is now common in settled areas and also occurs in plantations.

Mafia Island

Mackworth-Praed & Grant (1957) consider that Laughing Doves (of the nominate form) may have been introduced to Mafia Island off the coast of Tanzania.

AUSTRALASIA

Australia[1]

In 1898–9, Laughing Doves of the nominate form (and Spotted Doves (*Streptopelia chinensis* q.v.) were released from the South Perth Zoo at Northam, Yatheroo and Dardanup near Perth in Western Australia. Both species became established in the city and its suburbs before 1912, and until at least 1920 were being recaptured for transference elsewhere in the state, where they seem to have done well wherever pine trees were available for nesting. Although in 1929 they were reported to have spread 'far and wide', they seem in fact not to have ventured much beyond the Perth metropolitan area, but since the mid-1930s have been slowly but steadily extending their range. Laughing Doves spread more rapidly and further than *chinensis*; they reached Rottnest Island around 1930 (some 7 years in advance of their congener), and by 1958 were established in several places in the wheat-belt between Geraldton and Tambellup eastwards to Beacon and Merredin, with discrete populations at Kalgoorlie and Esperance. In the late 1970s, they reached both Cue and Mount Magnet east of Geraldton. Pizzey (1980) recorded them east to about Southern Cross (325 km from Perth), north to Geraldton (375 km) – occasionally to Shark Bay

(750 km) – and 400 km south to Albany; isolated populations (presumably arising from separate introductions) were centred on Kalgoorlie and Esperance (respectively, 525 km east and 575 km south-east of Perth), with others on Rottnest and Garden islands off the Perth coast.

Elsewhere in Australia, Laughing Doves were reported in the 1940s at Toowoomba west of Brisbane in southern Queensland (and possibly also across the border in New South Wales) where they failed to become established.

According to Goodwin (1970), Laughing Doves have been successfully translocated locally outside their natural range in Israel, Syria, Jordan, Lebanon and Turkey. Vaurie (1961) quotes Heim de Balzac (1926) that Laughing Doves had been translocated to, and were then common at, El Golea in southern Algeria.

The **Red-eyed Dove** (*Streptopelia semitorquata*) is a common native of most of Africa (apart from the south-west) south of the Sahara.

In September 1933, birds imported from Beira in Mozambique (presumably therefore *S. s. australis*) were released at Elgin in southwestern Cape Peninsula, South Africa.[2] Others that had been reared in captivity elsewhere in the Cape were also liberated, but since much of the western Cape has since been colonized naturally from the east, it is uncertain whether the present stock are the descendants of introduced birds or natural immigrants.

The status and present distribution of the **Javanese Collared Dove** (*Streptopelia bitorquata*) is uncertain. It has been recorded on Sumatra, Java, the Lesser Sunda Islands (Bali, Lombok, Sumbawa, Flores, Solor and Timor), and Palawan, and in northern Borneo, the Philippines and the Marianas.[3] Only in the last (where the form is *S. b. dusumieri* from the Philippines and Borneo) has it certainly been introduced by human agency; until at least the mid-1940s it was abundant in rice fields, grasslands and open country in the south, but now survives in small numbers only on Saipan, Rota and Guam.

Although documentary evidence is lacking, Javanese Collared Doves probably occur on

Sumatra[4] as the result of human intervention. Their status as indigene or alien in Borneo[5] is in doubt; the only recent record is of two birds on Si-Amil Island off Semporna on the north-east coast in 1962, so the species may now be extinct on the island.

Thomson (1922) records that five 'Java Doves' imported to New Zealand by the Otago Acclimatization Society in 1867 were subsequently given to a Mr Fred Jones, by whom they were released on Green Island where they soon disappeared. Others were brought in by the Nelson Society in the same year and eight by the Wellington Society in 1875, but what became of them is not known. 'Java Dove' is the name usually given by bird-dealers to the all-white variety of the Barbary Dove (*S. risoria*).[6]

The **Red-collared Dove** (*Streptopelia tranquebarica*) is found in India, Sikkim and eastern Nepal, and from northern Tibet to Indo-China and the northern Philippine Islands.

It was recorded once in Singapore in 1940, but not again until 1980.[7] A population estimated at some 200, believed to be descended from escaped cagebirds, is currently established around the boundary of the airport, where the presence of juveniles implies successful breeding. A recent record of an evidently wild bird at sea suggests that occurrences on the Malay Peninsula are the the result of natural dispersal.[8]

NOTES

1 Blakers, Davies & Reilly 1984; Colebatch 1929; Frith 1979; Jenkins 1959, 1977; Kingsmill 1920; Le Souef 1912; Long 1972, 1981; Pizzey 1980; Sedgwick 1958; Serventy 1948; Serventy & Whittell 1951, 1962, 1967; Storr 1965; Tarr 1950.
2 Long 1981; Mackworth-Praed & Grant 1962; Winterbottom 1956.
3 Delacour & Mayr 1946; Long 1981; Mayr 1945; Peters 1937; Ralph & Sakai 1979; Stophlet 1946.
4 Delacour 1947; Goodwin 1970; Long 1981; Smythies 1960.
5 Goodwin 1970; Gore 1968; Long 1981; Smythies 1960.
6 D. Goodwin, personal communication, 1985.
7 C. J. Hails, personal communication, 1985.
8 D. R. Wells, personal communication, 1986.

Barred Dove

(Geopelia striata)

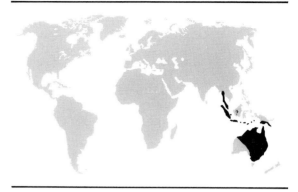

NATURAL DISTRIBUTION

From extreme southeastern Burma (southern Tenasserim) and southern Thailand south through Malaysia to Sumatra, Java, and the Lesser Sunda Islands (Bali, Lombok, Sumbawa, Flores, Solor and Timor), eastwards to Tanimbar and Kai Besar islands and southern New Guinea; also northern, and most of the eastern half of, Australia.

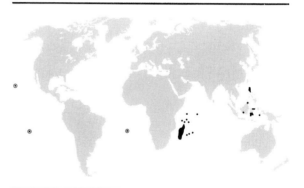

NATURALIZED DISTRIBUTION

(see over)

NATURALIZED DISTRIBUTION

Africa: St Helena, Madagascar, Mascarenes (Mauritius, Réunion, Rodrigues), Agaléga Islands, Seychelles, ?Cosmoledo Island; ?Farquhar Islands; Îles Glorieuses; Australasia: Borneo, Philippines, Sulawesi, Ambon; Oceania: Hawaiian Islands, Society Islands, Chagos Archipelago.

AFRICA

St Helena[1]

According to Peters (1937), Barred Doves of the form *G. s. striata* (southern Burma, southern Thailand and Malaysia) have been introduced to the island of St Helena in the South Atlantic. Melliss (1870), who says that this introduction was made with stock from New South Wales in Australia (where the subspecies is *tranquilla*), reported the birds to be widespread and abundant. In the late 1940s, Barred Doves were common in upland areas and in Jamestown, and in 1952–3 were noted as still widely distributed and plentiful.

Madagascar[2]

Barred Doves of the nominate form have been successfully introduced to the Malagasy Republic. Rand (1936) says that although they were at one time abundant they had apparently died out before 1936. Forty years later, however, Staub (1976) found them once more to be common in lowland areas. Presumably either Rand was mistaken or the present population is the result of a more recent introduction.

Mauritius[3]

Meinertzhagen (1912) says that Barred Doves were introduced to Mauritius from the Malay Peninsula around 1750. According to Benedict (1975) and Staub (1976), they were imported from the Sunda Islands and Malaysia by Cossigny de Palma in 1781. They reached (or were transferred to) Round Island off Mauritius before 1860, and later appeared also on nearby Flat Island. They are now widespread and common on Mauritius.

Réunion

Watson, Zusi & Storer (1963) say that the Barred Dove has been introduced to, and is abundant on, the island of Réunion.

Rodrigues

According to Staub (1973 and 1976), Barred Doves were introduced to Rodrigues in 1764; Gill (1967) found them to be abundant and reported that they had also spread to some small offlying islands.

Agaléga Islands

According to Guého & Staub (1983), Barred Doves – probably introduced from the Mascarenes – are well established on both Île du Nord and Île du Sud in the Agalégas.

Seychelles[4]

Several authorities state that the nominate form of the Barred Dove was imported to the Seychelles from India via Mauritius, perhaps by early Indian traders; as, however, the species does not occur in India, the ultimate source of these birds was probably southern Burma. Newton (1867) found them to be well established in lowland areas. Together with the introduced Common Mynah (*Acridotheres tristis*) (q.v.) and the Madagascar Fody (*Foudia madagascariensis*), Barred Doves comprise the bulk of the coastal plateau avifauna of Mahé and Praslin. The last named is now one of the commonest land birds, especially near settlements, in the archipelago, where Diamond & Feare (1980) record it as breeding regularly on Mahé, Praslin, Silhouette, La Digue, Felicité, Marianne, Frégate, Aride, Cousin, and Cousine.

Cosmoledo Island

Penny (1974) says that Barred Doves were probably introduced to Cosmoledo Island, where they are now common.

Farquhar Islands

Although Watson, Zusi & Storer (1963) found Barred Doves to be abundant around settlements on Farquhar Island (Providence Bank), Penny (1974) reported this introduced species to be rather scarce. Two years later, however, C. J. Feare (personal communication, 1986) found it to be common on North Island (especially around the settlement) but less common on South Island

Îles Glorieuses

Benson, Beamish et al. (1975) were told by M. Penny that in 1969 a local meteorologist, H. Desramais, had introduced Barred Doves to Îles Glorieuses, where a few survived until at least 1971.

AUSTRALASIA

Borneo

Smythies (1960) says that the small number of Barred Doves surviving in southern Borneo are the descendants of birds released by local tribesmen. In 1965, two pairs were introduced to Tanjong Aru, Kota Kinabalu, on the coast of Sabah in northern Borneo (now, with Sarawak, a part of East Malaysia) where Gore (1968) reported that they were established.

Philippines

Whitehead (1899) suggested that Barred Doves, which are a favourite cagebird in the region, may have been introduced by man to the Philippines where, however, he collected them between 1893 and 1896 only on Luzon and Samar. Du Pont (1971) states that Barred Doves from Borneo have since been imported to Lubang, Luzon, Mindoro and Verde.

Sulawesi; Ambon

According to Peters (1937), Barred Doves of the nominate form have probably been introduced to Sulawesi and to Amboina (Ambon) in the Moluccas; Stresemann (1936) recorded them in

south-central Sulawesi and also on the southern peninsula, and Escott & Holmes (1980) reported them at Gorontalo (on the south coast of the Minahassa Peninsula) in extreme northern Sulawesi.

OCEANIA

Hawaiian Islands[5]

Barred Doves of the nominate form and of two subspecies (*tranquilla* from south-central Australia and *placida* from northern Australia) were introduced in 1922, together with Bar-shouldered Doves (*Geopelia humeralis*) of southern New Guinea and northern and northeastern Australia, to Oahu by the Honolulu City Council and to Kauai by Mrs Dora Isenberg, and also to Maui and Molokai. The last-named species failed to become established, but, according to Munro (1944), *tranquilla* and/or *placida* was transferred to (or colonized naturally) Lanai in 1922, where they flourished until 1926 but within 2 to 3 years had disappeared. By 1935–7, the nominate form was established on all the main islands except Hawaii, to which, according to Munro, it had only recently been transferred, but which Schwartz & Schwartz (1949), in their reconnaissance of the game birds of the archipelago, say was probably colonized naturally from Maui between 1935 and 1938. By the late 1940s, Barred Doves were established in all suitable habitats on the larger islands except on Hawaii, where they were found only on the Kona coast and in a few places in North Kohala. Schwartz & Schwartz censused the population as follows: Hawaii, 7,840; Kauai, 52,090; Lanai, 10,380; Maui, 44,610; Molokai, 51,900; Oahu, 69,900 – a total of 236,720.

Barred Doves in Hawaii were found to range from sea level to an altitude of 900 m (occasionally 1,200 m) where mean annual temperatures vary from 20 °C to 15 °C, respectively. Although they occurred in areas with an annual precipitation as high as 380 cm, the most flourishing populations were established in drier and warmer conditions below 900 m, where rainfall varies from less than 50 cm to 150 cm per annum and where the mean annual temperature is around 20 °C. The densest populations were found in some coastal regions of Molokai and

Oahu. Only small numbers occurred in those areas where suitable food is seasonal or in short supply, and where water is largely unavailable and roosting cover sparse. The birds were found in urban and suburban districts, in pineapple and sugar-cane plantations, in market gardens and on pastures and waste land, but seldom on barren lava fields or in dense forests. Barred Doves shared this range with introduced Spotted Doves (*Streptopelia chinensis*) though the latter (larger) species occurred at higher elevations, was more tolerant of damp conditions and ventured into more heavily timbered woodland.

Barred Doves' diet in Hawaii was found to consist almost entirely (97 per cent) of seeds, with small amounts of Lantana fruit (*Lantana camara*), Pineapple root (*Ananas comosus*), and the seed pods and leaves of algaroba or kiawe (*Prosopis chilensis*). Although this diet coincided to some extent with that of Spotted Doves, Schwartz & Schwartz found little evidence of significant interspecific competition for food (other, perhaps, than for fruit in arid areas or in times of drought), since they tended to feed on plants at different stages of cultivation or succession and, when feeding synchronously, to utilize different species. Predation of adults, young and eggs by introduced Small Indian Mongooses (*Herpestes auropunctatus*), feral Cats (*Felis catus*), arboreal Black and Polynesian Rats (*Rattus rattus* and *R. exulans*) and alien Mynahs was, as in the case of Spotted Doves, considered to be insignificant.

In 1961–2, 18 Barred Doves were released on the Puu Waawaa Ranch on Hawaii, where although Schwartz & Schwartz indicated that the species did not occur at the time of their survey, it had since become established.

Walker (1967b) listed Barred Doves as established and open to public shooting on Hawaii. Zeillemaker & Scott (1976) indicated that they were abundant on agricultural land and pastures and in residential and community parklands on Kauai, Oahu, Molokai, Lanai and Maui, and that they were common on Hawaii. Walker (1981) lists them as occurring also on Kahoolawe.

Society Islands[6]

Barred Doves were first released, unsuccessfully, on the island of Tahiti by Eastham Guild in 1938 – ostensibly to replace the apparently dying-out endemic Grey-green Fruit Dove (*Ptilinopus purpuratus chrysogaster*). A further 21, introduced at Paea from Kauai in the Hawaiian Islands by W. A. Robinson in 1950 (one account says not until between 1962 and 1967), had, by 1971–4, colonized maritime areas of Papara on the south coast to Arue on the north coast via the entire west coast – including Punaauia and suburbs west of Papeete – and by 1975 were established and common continuously along the coast from Arue to Papeari. By the end of the decade, they had been observed on two occasions on the neighbouring island of Moorea, and Holyoak & Thibault (1984) considered that a new population might be evolving on that island. On Tahiti, where they occur singly, in pairs or in small flocks, they frequent coastal areas, gardens and cultivated land, and feed on small seeds gleaned from grasslands, gardens, waste ground and roadside verges.

Chagos Archipelago[7]

From the Seychelles, Barred Doves were in 1960 introduced by a Seychellois immigrant, Raymond Mein, to the Chagos Archipelago, where in that year a party of 14 was observed by Loustau-Lalanne (1962) at Pointe Este. According to Hutson (1975), local islanders reported in 1975 that in about 1966 some 16 birds had been landed on Diego Garcia, where 4 died in captivity and the remaining 12 were released. Since Barred Doves had been seen some 6 years previously, Hutson considers this report suspect, though there may well have been more than one introduction. By 1971, the birds had dispersed from Pointe Este but were nowhere common.

Fitter (1959) says that around the turn of the century the Duke of Bedford found that the northern Australia form (*placida*) of the Barred Dove could be acclimatized in the park of Woburn Abbey in Bedfordshire, England, if predation by Tawny Owls (*Strix aluco*) could be controlled.

Three pairs of the south-central Australian form (*tranquilla*) of the Barred Dove were released on

Kangaroo Island off the coast of South Australia in September 1937, followed by a further five pairs in February 1940. Several were reported on the island by members of the Ralph Tate Society in 1941, but there seem to be no further records of them thereafter.[8]

In Thailand, where they occur naturally in the south, Deignan (1945) recorded that Barred Doves (presumably of the nominate form) were transferred from Java by H. H. the late Chao Kaeo Nawarat na Chiang Mai to the north of the country, where they were released and became locally established east of the town of Mae Khao. According to Lekagul & Cronin (1974), they have also been liberated within the last 60 years in central Thailand, and Deignan (1963) reported that they were firmly entrenched on the northern plateau and on the central plains around Bangkok (Krung Thep).

According to Owre (1973: 495), the **Inca Dove** (*Scardafella inca*), a native of the southwestern United States and northern Central America, bred at Key West in 1965–6, and may have gained a foothold in southern Florida.

D. B. Wingate (personal communication, 1981) says that the **Common Ground Dove** (*Columbina passerina bahamensis*) was 'probably introduced [to Bermuda[9]] as a caged bird from the Bahamas in the 1600s or 1700s because no specific mention was made of small doves by the first settlers'. The species is currently uncommon in Bermuda.

According to Webster (1975), the **Emerald Dove** (*Chalcophaps indica*), a native of India, Southeast Asia, Indonesia and northern and eastern Australia, has been introduced by man to Hong Kong, where small numbers are resident and breed in the Tai Po Kau Forestry Reserve, and others have been noted in several parts of the New Territories.

Munro (1944) and Walker (1967b) record that in 1924 Emerald Doves were unsuccessfully introduced from Singapore to Oahu in the Hawaiian Islands.

Thomson (1922: 135) says that in 1867 the Auckland Acclimatization Society imported to New Zealand two 'New Caledonia Green Doves' (presumably this species) and subsequently a further four, but what became of them is not known.

The **Australian Crested Dove** (*Ocyphaps lophotes*), which inhabits most of the continent, was unsuccessfully released on Oahu, Molokai and Lanai in the Hawaiian Islands in 1922 (Munro 1944; Walker 1967b). In 1964, eight were freed on the Puu Waawaa Ranch on Hawaii, where, according to Lewin (1971), they had spread within 3 years some 7 km from their release site. They are not, however, referred to by Zeillemaker & Scott (1976), Pyle (1977), Berger (1981) or Walker (1981), so they have presumably now disappeared.

According to Fitter (1959), Australian Crested Doves were acclimatized around the turn of the century in the park of Woburn Abbey in Bedfordshire, England, by the Duke of Bedford, by whom they were fed during winter and where they were preyed on by Sparrowhawks (*Accipiter nisus*). They are also said at one time to have been acclimatized in France.

Phillips (1928: 47) states that in the United States this species 'appears to have escaped [before 1925] and established itself in a small way at Berkeley, California, in the trees and shrubbery near the Claremont Hotel at the edge of the town', where Cooke & Knappen (1941) say that 'Reports indicate that the colony is not increasing noticeably, if it is still in existence'. It is not referred to by Hardy (1973).

In 1876–7, the Wellington Acclimatization Society imported a dozen Crested Pigeons from Australia to New Zealand, where 'they were seen for some months afterwards, and then disappeared' (Thomson 1922: 132). The Melbourne Zoo sent six to the Canterbury Society in 1883 and 4 years later 10 (of which five were set free) were imported by the Auckland Society, but the species never became established in New Zealand.

In September 1937, a dozen birds of the nominate form (central and east-central Australia) were released at Flinders Chase on Kangaroo Island[10] off the coast of South Australia, followed by a further pair in February 1940. A number were observed on the island in 1966 and a small population now seems to be established.

According to Brudenell-Bruce (1975), the **White-bellied Dove** (*Leptotila jamaicensis*) – a native of the West Indies (Jamaica, Grand Cayman and St Andrew), Mexico (the Yucatán Peninsula and adjacent islands) and the Bay Islands off Honduras – was introduced from Jamaica (where the nominate form occurs) to New Providence in the Bahamas (where it is now an uncommon resident) as part of a programme to restock the island with birds destroyed by a series of hurricanes in the late 1920s. Bond (1979) confirms that the species has been introduced to New Providence.

NOTES

1 Benson 1950; Haydock 1954; Long 1981; Melliss 1870; Peters 1937.
2 Long 1981; Peters 1937; Rand 1936; Staub 1976. See also: A. Grandidier, *Histoire Naturelle de Madagascar; Oiseaux* (1879), 470.
3 Benedict 1957; Long 1981; Meinertzhagen 1912; Newton 1861; Rountree, Guérin et al. 1952; Staub 1973, 1976; Vinson 1950.
4 Barré & Barau 1982; Diamond & Feare 1980; Gaymer, Blackman et al. 1969; Long 1981; Newton 1867; Penny 1974.
5 American Ornithologists' Union 1957, 1983; Berger 1981; Bryan 1958; Caum 1933; Hawaiian Audubon Society 1975; Lewin 1971; Locey 1937; Long 1981; Munro 1944; Peterson 1961; Pyle 1977; Schwartz & Schwartz 1949, 1950b, 1951a; Walker 1967b, 1981; Zeillemaker & Scott 1976.
6 Guild 1938; Holyoak 1974a; Holyoak & Thibault 1984; Long 1981; Montgomery, Gagné & Gagné 1980; Thibault & Rives 1975.
7 Bourne 1971; Hutson 1975; Long 1981; Lousteau-Lalanne 1962; Penny 1974.
8 Abbott 1974; Anon. 1948; Cleland 1942; Condon 1948a, 1962, 1968; Long 1981.
9 See also: Bourne 1957 (quoting Verrill 1901–2); Crowell 1962; Crowell & Crowell 1976; Wingate 1973.
10 Anon. 1948; Condon 1948, 1962, 1968; Long 1981.

Mourning Dove
(*Zenaida macroura*)

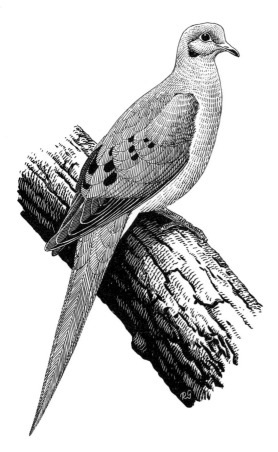

NATURAL DISTRIBUTION
North America from around 50° N south to Panama; the Bahama Islands and the Greater Antilles east to Culebra and Vieques.

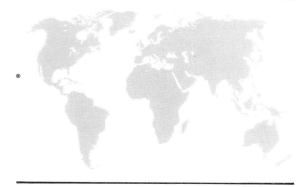

NATURALIZED DISTRIBUTION
Oceania: Hawaiian Islands.

OCEANIA

Hawaiian Islands[1]

Mourning Doves of the form *Z. m. marginella* (natives of western North America and Central America) were introduced to the island of Hawaii in 1929 or 1930 – 'Possibly imported directly from native country' (Walker 1967b: 11). In 1962, 1964 and 1965, 168 from a Californian game farm were released on the Puu Waawaa Ranch on Hawaii, where a few years later they were reported to be established locally around the ranch buildings.

Walker (1967b) lists the species as having 'been introduced . . . but not known to be established';

the Hawaiian Audubon Society (1975) states that it may be established but that its current position is poorly known; but Zeillemaker & Scott (1976) make no mention of it at all. Pyle (1977: 112, 118) lists it as 'a new introduction; apparently established and breeding, but for less than 25 years', whereas Walker (1981) lists it as an established game species. Berger (1981) and the American Ornithologists' Union (1983) say that Mourning Doves are presently established in the North Kona region on Hawaii.

Although according to Crowell (1976), the first Mourning Dove was recorded on Bermuda[2] as long ago as 1884, it was not until 1954–8 that the islands were colonized naturally – presumably by birds of the eastern North American form *Z. m. carolinensis*. According to Crowell & Crowell (1976), Mourning Doves only became widely distributed when more open habitat was created by the destruction of the native Bermuda Cedars (*Juniperus bermudiana*) by a scale insect, *Carulaspis minima*, accidentally introduced in a cargo of nursery plants around 1946. In 1960, Mourning Doves were still established only locally in Bermuda, but a decade later were abundant and widespread. Wingate (1973: 3) described them as 'now one of the commonest landbirds on the island'.

According to Liversidge (n.d.), the Mourning Dove has been unsuccessfully introduced to South Africa.

In 1961 and 1965, approximately 40 **White-winged Doves** (*Zenaida asiatica*), which range from the southwestern United States south through Central America to northwestern South America, of the race *Z. a. mearnsi*[3] from a game farm in the United States were released on the Puu Waawaa Ranch on Hawaii, where Lewin (1971) indicated that they were established around the ranch buildings. As with *Z. macroura*, their current status on Hawaii is uncertain. Although Walker (1967b: 11) lists them as having 'been introduced . . . but not known to be established', the Hawaiian Audubon Society (1975) indicated that the species might have been successful, but that its then status was poorly

known. Zeillemaker & Scott (1976), Pyle (1977), Berger (1981) and Walker (1981), however, do not refer to it at all.

According to Fisk (1968) and Owre (1973), White-winged Doves from Venezuela (presumably *Z. a. meloda* transferred from western South America) and Mexico (*mearnsi* or *asiatica*) were imported privately to Florida in the United States,[4] where they were bred in captivity between 1954 and 1959 when 25 were released near Homestead, Dade County in the extreme south of the state. By 1968, no fewer than 200 were regularly returning for food to their release site, and they were observed over an area of more than 100 km².

Lovett E. Williams, however, (personal communication, 1981) wrote as follows:

According to Frank Williams who released the birds there accidentally, this population resulted from approximately seven pairs liberated in the early 1960s. (Despite the fact that Frank Williams is still available to provide such information, there is some disagreement in the literature already concerning the method of liberation, date, and number of birds involved.) I estimate the 1980 population of White-winged Doves in south Florida to be approaching 10,000 and spreading rapidly along the east coast of Florida northward. The Florida Game & Fresh Water Fish Commission has transplanted some of these birds from south Florida into citrus grove habitat farther north in the State, and some of these transplants have been successful. This was undertaken because, in our view, the man-made conditions of citrus culture are ideal White-winged Dove habitat as indicated by the occupation of such habitat in its natural range in the western U.S. and by the established population of south Florida.

Blake (1975) indicates that the White-winged Dove has been transplanted into western Cuba.

NOTES

1 American Ornithologists' Union 1983; Berger 1981; Bryan 1958; Caum 1933; Hawaiian Audubon Society 1975; Lewin 1971; Long 1981; Pyle 1977; Walker 1967b, 1981.
2 Crowell 1962; Crowell & Crowell 1976; Wingate 1973.
3 According to Walker (1967b: 11), the native range of *mearnsi* is 'C. America. Howard & Moore (1982: 142) say that it is found in the southwestern United States and western Mexico, and on the Tres Marias Islands south of Golfo de California.
4 Fisk 1968; Long 1981; Owre 1973; and L. E. Williams, personal communication, 1981.

Kuhl's Lory
(Vini kuhlii)

NATURAL DISTRIBUTION
Rimatara Island, Tubuai Archipelago.

NATURALIZED DISTRIBUTION
Oceania: Line Islands (Teraina, Tabuaeran and
?Kiritimati).

OCEANIA

Line Islands[1]

Kuhl's Lories are said to have been introduced
from Rimatara to Washington (Teraina) and
Fanning (Tabuaeran) in the Line group by islanders,
from whom they later escaped or by
whom they may have been deliberately released.
They are believed to have become established
before 1798, and are now common on both
islands. In December 1957, 6 were transferred
to Christmas island (Kiritimati) at the southern
end of the archipelago, where they were released
at London on the north-west coast. Two were
seen in the following July, and three early in

1959, and a few are thought still to occur on the island.

The **Tahitian Lory** (*Vini peruviana*)[2] is a native of most of the Cook and Society islands, and perhaps also of those of western Tuamotu. It is believed to have been transferred to Aitutaki in the Cook archipelago by early Polynesian settlers. The species disappeared from Tahiti in the Society group before 1937, when an unsuccessful attempt was made to re-establish it by Eastham Guild.

The **Ultramarine Lory** (*Vini ultramarina*) is an endemic of some (but not all) of the Marquesas Islands. In 1964, several were noted in the verdant interior valley of Vaipae'e village on Uahuka, where caged *pihiti* (the bird's local name), imported from Uapou, had been released some years earlier. The birds have since increased and spread, representing a significant expansion of this rare bird's range (Decker 1980).

The **Musk Lorikeet** (*Glossopsitta concinna*) occurs naturally in eastern and southeastern Australia and Tasmania. According to Corfe (1977), the species was first observed in Western Australia at Alfred Cove, a suburb of Perth, in September 1975, where breeding was confirmed shortly thereafter, but where they are since believed to have died out.

The **Blue-streaked Lory** (*Eos reticulata*), which is endemic to Kepulauan Tanimbar, Indonesia, has, according to Salvadori (1905–6) and Peters (1937), apparently been transported by man to the islands of Tual, Kepulauan Kai (Ewab) and Damar, Kepulauan Barat Daja, in the south Banda Sea. T. Silva (personal communication, 1985) suggests that liberated lories and lorikeets (?spp.) may also be established elsewhere in Indonesia.

The **Rainbow Lory** (*Trichoglossus haematodus*) – a native of the Lesser Sunda Islands, the southern Moluccas, New Guinea, Vanuatu, the Bismark, Solomon, Admiralty, Ninigo, New Caledonia and Loyalty archipelagos, and northern, eastern and southeastern Australia and Tasmania – has become successfully established in Perth, Western Australia, over 2,000 km west of its nearest natural range. For some years, perhaps since the early 1960s, a small colony of up to nine individuals, believed to be the descendants of escaped cagebirds, has existed in the King's Park in the University of Western Australia. Smith (1978) records that the birds have been seen up to 38 km south of Perth at Safety Bay, and a recent report suggests that a population of around 50 may be established in the Hollywood area. The subspecies concerned is thought to be *moluccanus* from eastern Australia and Tasmania.

Fear has been expressed that if the Rainbow Lory were to become numerous in Western Australia it might cause damage to agricultural crops and compete for food and nesting holes with indigenous parrot species.

According to Watling (1982), the scarlet feathers of the **Collared Lory** (*Phigys solitarius*) – a species endemic to the Fijian Islands – were at one time highly prized by Tongans and Samoans for decorating the edges of mats, and a flourishing trade grew up, both in feathers and live birds which were kept in captivity in Samoa for periodic plucking; escaped lories were frequently to be seen in Samoa where, however, they appear never to have succeeded in becoming established.

NOTES
1 Bachus 1967; Forshaw 1980; Gallagher 1960; Long 1981; Peters 1937.
2 Amadon 1942; Forshaw 1980; Guild 1938; Holyoak 1974a,b; Long 1981.

Sulphur-crested Cockatoo
(*Cacatua galerita*)

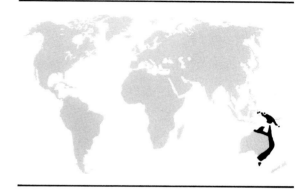

NATURAL DISTRIBUTION
Northern, eastern and southeastern Australia from the Kimberleys in Western Australia to Victoria and Tasmania; New Guinea and some nearby islands to the north and east, and the Aru Islands.

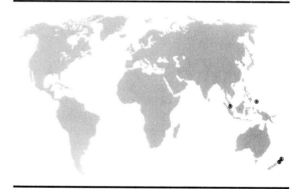

NATURALIZED DISTRIBUTION
Asia: Singapore; Australasia: New Zealand,[1] Indonesia (Palau Archipelago, Seram Laut, Gorang Laut).

ASIA

Singapore

Although Madoc (1956) states only that escaped Sulphur-crested Cockatoos are occasionally found in the wild in Singapore, C. J. Hails (personal communication, 1985) says they have been resident and breeding on the island for more than 40 years, where Lesser Sulphur-crested (see below) may well also occur.

AUSTRALASIA

New Zealand[2]

According to Wodzicki (1965), the Sulphur-crested Cockatoo was first liberated in New Zealand in 1920. Since, however, Thomson (1922: 137) stated that 'This species is frequently to be seen on the Waitakerei Ranges, where it appears to have established itself', it seems probable that the birds were released some years earlier. Reports of Sulphur-crested Cockatoos in Nelson at about the same time were found to be based on the presence of 'one tame bird which frequently flew over the town screeching'.

From the 1920s onwards considerable numbers of Sulphur-crested Cockatoos were imported from Australia to New Zealand, where escaped birds established colonies near Auckland and at Wellsford, Hunua Hills, Glen Murray and Fordell, and in Turakina Valley, Hunterville, Waikato and Wainuiomata. In some places they damaged haystacks by pulling them apart to get at the seed heads.

Wodzicki (1965: 432) described the birds as 'Locally common, North Island'. Five years later Kinsky (1970) said that Sulphur-crested Cockatoos were established at Fordell, Hunterville and on the western side of the lower Waikato Valley, and that they also occurred at North Kaipara Heads, Auckland, and in Wainuiomata Valley, Wellington.

Falla, Sibson & Turbott (1979) recorded them as well established in limestone country between the lower Waikato and Raglan, and in the watersheds of the Turakina and Rangitikei on the southwestern coast of North Island, with a small colony in Wainuiomata Valley. Although most of the population is almost certainly descended from escaped cagebirds, recruitment from time to time by natural immigrants from southeastern Australia (where, as in New Zealand, the form present is *C. g. galerita*), cannot be discounted.

Indonesia (Palau, Seram Laut and Gorang Laut)[3]

Sulphur-crested Cockatoos of the New Guinea form (*C. g. triton*) have been introduced to the Palau Islands, where in about 1950 they were apparently breeding and spreading. The same race is said to have been introduced to Ceramlaut (Seram Laut) and Goramlaut (Gorang Laut) in the Moluccas.

Both Munro (1944) and Berger (1981) say that the Sulphur-crested Cockatoo has been released or has escaped in the Hawaiian Islands, but has never become naturalized.

Wingate (1985) states that Sulphur-crested Cockatoos have been observed making nests in Bermuda.

In Western Australia,[4] 2,000 km from their nearest natural range, escaped or deliberately released Sulphur-crested Cockatoos were first noted, at Mandurah, south of Perth, in 1935. In 1956, a pair was observed at Kalamunda, where three birds were seen in 1963; later reports were from West Swan (several in 1964), Coolup (15–16 in 1972), Pinjarra (24 in 1972), Byford (11 in 1972–3), Guildford (18–23 in 1975), Pinjarra-Coolup (16–20 in 1975), Mundijong (10–12 in 1975), Peel Inlet (28 in 1975), Bullsbrook (1976), Carrabungup (14 in 1976) and Pinjarra (25–35 in 1976). The birds may now be established from Coolup to the Perth metropolitan area, north to Bullsbrook and as far south as Harvey. They are known to be breeding at both Pinjarra and Guildford, where flocks of, respectively, about 100 and 60 were counted in 1979. The race transplanted seems to be *C. g. galerita* of eastern Australia.

The **Lesser Sulphur-crested Cockatoo** (*Cacatua sulphurea*), a native of Sulawesi, the Sunda Islands and islands in the Flores and Java seas, has been successfully introduced to Singapore and Hong Kong. In the former, Rowley (in Forshaw 1980) reported that small parties appeared to be established in the Botanic Gardens, and T. Silva, (personal communication, 1985) says that some were seen on Sentosa Island in 1983. In Hong Kong, Webster (1975) recorded the presence – but not the breeding – of up to 30 birds in Happy Valley and the grounds of Hong Kong University, while Viney (1976) counted 13 at Victoria Barracks, 21 each in Happy Valley and the university, and 6 on Stonecutters Island (Ngon Shun Chau) west of Kowloon, where breeding was strongly suspected. According to Webster, most of the birds are of the form *citrinocristata*[5] (from Sumba Island), perhaps with an admixture of another race.

The **Salmon-crested Cockatoo** (*Cacatua moluccensis*), a native of Seram, Saparua and Haruku in the southern Moluccas, may have been translocated by man to Ambon (Amboina) in the same archipelago.

Forshaw (1980) says that **Goffin's Cockatoo** (*Cacatua goffini*) has been transplanted from Kepulauan Tanimbar in Indonesia to Tual Island in Kepulauan Kai (Ewab).

The **Little Corella** (*Cacatua sanguinea*), a native of southern New Guinea, northwestern Queensland, and western, northwestern and east-central Australia, is resident (and presumably breeds) on St John's Island, 5 km south of Singapore.

The **Long-billed Corella** (*Cacatua tenuirostris*) occurs naturally in Australia in two discrete populations, of which one (*pastinator*) is in the south of Western Australia and the other (*tenui-rostris*) in southeastern South Australia, western Victoria and adjacent parts of New South Wales.

According to Condon (1975), a few of the latter were in the 1950s transplanted to Buckland Park, Port Gawler north of Adelaide, where their descendants remain, and a flock of between 7 and 11 has been recorded in West Gippsland, Victoria;[6] both these areas are outside the species' natural range. McGarvie & Templeton (1974) say that two birds that had probably been released from captivity were seen at Reekara on King Island in Bass Strait on several occasions in 1968–70: they could well, however, have been natural immigrants from Victoria.

NOTES

1 In New Zealand the species is sometimes known as the White Cockatoo (*Kakatoe galerita*). The White Cockatoo is, however, a different species, *Cacatua alba*.
2 Falla, Sibson & Turbott 1979; Forshaw 1980; Kinsky 1970; Long 1981; Oliver 1930, 1955; Thomson 1922; Williams 1975; Wodzicki 1965.
3 Forshaw 1980; Long 1981; Ripley 1961.
4 Long 1981.
5 T. Silva (personal communication, 1985), however, says that *sulphurea* and *citrinocristata* are so distinct that they should not be regarded as conspecific (as they are treated by, e.g., Howard & Moore 1980).
6 T. Silva, personal communication, 1985.

Red-shining Parrot
(*Prosopeia tabuensis*)

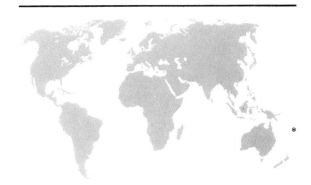

NATURAL DISTRIBUTION
Fijian Islands.

NATURALIZED DISTRIBUTION
Oceania: Tonga ('Eua).

OCEANIA

Tonga[1]

According to Watling (1982: 92):

There is little doubt that the range of the Red-breasted Musk Parrot [= Red-shining Parrot] has been extended by human agency. As with the Collared Lory [*Phigys solitarius*; see under Kuhl's Lory], there was a considerable trade with the Samoans and Tongans for its red feathers and there is documented evidence of live parrots being taken to Tonga in the eighteenth century. Either it was purposely introduced to the islands of 'Eua and Tongatapu there, or escaped birds became naturalised there. The population on Tongatapu has died out, with the widespread clearance of natural habitat for agriculture, but it still thrives on 'Eua.

There is some uncertainty attached to the taxonomy

of this species. The type specimen [*P. t. tabuensis*] was collected [in 1777] by Captain Cook's naturalists from the introduced population in Tonga. This population cannot be safely distinguished from that one on the island of Gau [Ngau, Fiji] and they are classified as the same race. It seems unlikely, however, that the Tongan birds are the descendants from the Gau birds alone, it is more probable that both populations which form the nominate subspecies, are in fact a mixture of two or more races.

Red-shining Parrots (known locally as *koki*) are at present common on 'Eua in inland forests, in deep and thickly wooded gullies, and in forest ecotone in the east of the island. They also occur in plantations and in coastal forests. Rinke (1986a) estimated the population at 1,000 (± 50 per cent).

The birds' principal food item on 'Eua among some 30 food plants identified by Rinke (1986b) is the Nutmeg (*Myristica hypargyraea*), which fruits continuously. Rinke considers that depredations claimed by islanders on such crops as bananas, pawpaws and corn, is exaggerated.

Red-shining Parrots breed in old hollow trees in densely forested areas. In easily accessible parts of the island their success rate is claimed by Rinke to be virtually nil; chicks are removed from their nests by Tongans shortly before fledging, and sometimes even adults are captured in their nesting holes while feeding their offspring. Young birds are usually kept as pets, but on a diet of cooked starchy tubers of Taro (*Colocasia antiquorum*), yams (*Dioscorea* sp.) and Sweet Potatoes (*Batatas batatas*), seldom survive in captivity for as long as 6 months. Adults are normally killed and eaten, their feathers being used in the decoration of *Pandanus* mats.

As a result of the rapidly increasing deforestation of all readily accessible areas, coupled with direct depredation by the island's native population, Rinke considered that Red-shining Parrots on 'Eua will continue to decline, except perhaps in deep and inaccessible ravines and in precipitous parts of the east coast.

In Fiji,[2] the form *P. t. splendens*, which Watling says is restricted (contrary to a popular Fijian legend) to Kadavu (Kandavu) and the neighbouring island of Ono, was introduced to Viti Levu and to the westerly Yasawa Group probably by early Melanesian or Polynesian (or

possibly by nineteenth-century European) colonists. It was apparently at one time much commoner on Viti Levu than it is today, and it may possibly be declining. According to Mayr (1945), this form has also been introduced to the island of Ovalau where, however, Watling says that the species does not occur. Primarily a bird of forest or secondary scrub associations, the Red-shining Parrot also frequents the environs of villages and gardens.

Meyer's Parrot (*Poicephalus meyeri*) ranges from southern Chad and northeastern Cameroon eastwards to western Ethiopia and south through central and eastern Africa to northern South West Africa (Namibia). An isolated population of the northern Mozambique and Transvaal subspecies, *P. m. transvaalensis*, in the eastern Cape Province, South Africa,[3] is probably descended from escaped aviary birds.

The **Eclectus Parrot** (*Eclectus roratus*) is a native of Indonesia where it is distributed in the Moluccas, Lesser Sunda Islands, Tanimbar, Kai, Biak and Aru islands, New Guinea and its offlying islands, the Cape York Peninsula in northeastern Queensland (Australia), the Admiralty Islands, the Bismark Archipelago and the Solomon Islands. Ripley (1951) reported a single bird on Aulupsechel (Auluptagel) Island and a flock of 10 on another island in the Palau Archipelago; these were presumably escaped cagebirds and, according to Forshaw (1980), were probably of the Kai Island and New Guinea race, *E. r. polychloros*. The latter author says that the same form has also been introduced to the Goram or Gorong Islands, off the southeastern tip of Seram. According to Berger (1981), Eclectus Parrots have from time to time escaped from captivity in the Hawaiian Islands but have never become established in the wild.

The **Blue-naped Parrot** (*Tanygnathus lucionensis*) of Indonesia ranges from the Philippine Islands south to Palawan Island and the Sulu Archipelago. The species' status on Mantanani Besar off the northwestern coast of Sabah, North Borneo, and on the Si-Amil Islands (south-east of Semporna and east of Tawau on the southeastern coast) is uncertain. Between 30 and 100 were counted on the latter in 1962. They may have been introduced by traders from the Sulu Archipelago.[4]

The **Great-billed Parrot** (*Tanygnathus megalorynchos*) ranges south in Indonesia from Talaut and Sanghir islands and the northern Moluccas to Tanimbar Island, and westwards through the Lesser Sunda Islands. According to Hachisuka (1934), the nominate form *T. m. megalorynchos* of Talaut and Sanghir islands and the northern and central Moluccas may have been introduced by human agency to Balut Island – the most southerly of the Philippine group.

The **Chestnut-fronted Macaw** (*Ara severa*), which ranges from eastern Panama to northern Bolivia and central Brazil, and from eastern Venezuela to the Guianas and northwestern Brazil, has for several years been breeding in scattered localities around Miami in Dade County, southeastern Florida, in the United States, where the population is estimated to number at least 50.[5]

According to Lack (1976), reports by Sir Hans Sloane,[6] Patrick Broune,[7] Philip Gosse[8] and W. T. March[9] that may refer to the **Blue and Yellow Macaw** (*Ara ararauna*), which ranges from eastern Panama to Paraguay and southern Brazil, suggest that the species may once have been indigenous or naturalized on Jamaica. Some *ararauna* have recently been seen in the wild in Puerto Rico[10] where, however, no breeding is so far known to have occurred.

NOTES

1 See also: Forshaw 1980; Mayr 1945; Peters 1937; Rinke 1986a,b; Watling 1986.
2 Forshaw 1980; Holyoak 1979; Mayr 1945; Watling 1982.
3 Clancey 1965 (in Forshaw 1980); Long 1981; Mackworth-Praed & Grant 1957–74; Roberts 1940.
4 Gore 1968; Kloss 1930 (in Forshaw 1980); Long 1981; Thomson 1966 (in Forshaw).
5 O. T. Owre, personal communications, 1980 and 1985.
6 *Voyage to Islands of Madera, Barbadoes, Nieves, St Christopher and Jamaica* (1707).
7 *Civil and Natural History of Jamaica* (1756 and 1789).
8 *Birds of Jamaica* (1847).
9 'Notes on the birds of Jamaica', *Proceedings of the Philadelphia Academy of Natural Sciences*, 62–72 (1864).
10 T. Silva, personal communication, 1985.

Crimson Rosella
(Platycercus elegans)

NATURAL DISTRIBUTION
From northeastern Queensland to southeastern South Australia, including Kangaroo Island.

NATURALIZED DISTRIBUTION
Australasia: New Zealand, Norfolk Island.

AUSTRALASIA

New Zealand[1]

In 1910, a small consignment of Crimson and Eastern Rosellas (*Platycerus eximius*) that had been refused entry to New Zealand were released off Otago Heads on the southeastern coast of South Island. Small populations of both species (and of hybrids) still survive in hill country near Dunedin, where before 1930 damage to orchards was being reported. This, however, is said to have been more than compensated for by the birds' destruction of the larvae of the Golden-haired Blowfly (*Calliphora laemica*), which was introduced from Australia before 1874. Since

1963–4, a few Crimson Rosellas that escaped from local aviculturists have been established and breeding in the north-west suburbs of Wellington on North Island.

Norfolk Island[2]

Crimson Rosellas of the form *P. e. elegans*, which range from southeastern Queensland to south-eastern South Australia, have been introduced to Norfolk Island where they were well established and abundant by at least the late 1960s, and where interspecific competition for food and nesting sites has probably been responsible for the decline of the endemic race of the Red-fronted Parakeet or Green Parrot (*Cyanoramphus novaezelandiae cookii*).

According to Forshaw (1969), Crimson Rosellas have been unsuccessfully released on Lord Howe Island.

In the mid-1960s Crimson Rosellas were either deliberately released or escaped from captivity near Perth in Western Australia. A pair was sighted at Darlington in 1966–7 and one at Kelmscott in 1975, and a single bird is reported to have been seen in January 1980.[3]

NOTES

1 Falla, Sibson & Turbott 1979; Hamel 1970; Kinsky 1970; Long 1981; Oliver 1930; Thomson 1922.
2 Forshaw 1980; Long 1981; Smithers & Disney 1969.
3 Long 1981.

Eastern Rosella

(Platycercus eximius)

NATURAL DISTRIBUTION

From southeastern Queensland to southeastern South Australia and Tasmania.

NATURALIZED DISTRIBUTION

Australasia: New Zealand.

AUSTRALASIA

New Zealand[1]

Frequently imported to New Zealand by aviculturists before the early 1920s,[2] escaped or deliberately released Eastern Rosellas were occasionally to be seen in North Island in the neighbourhood of Auckland, where before about 1930 they were said to be established in the Waitakere Range. Wodzicki, who said that the subspecies introduced was *P. e. eximius* of southeastern Australia, described the birds (1965: 433) as 'locally common, North and South Islands'. Falla, Sibson & Turbott (1979) found them to be well established in North Island around Manukau Harbour and Whangaroa near Auckland, but rare south of Auckland where they were, however, slowly spreading north, with a smaller population (some of which are Crimson Rosella (*P. elegans*) × *P. eximius* hybrids) in hills near Dunedin in South Island, where damage to orchards was being reported before 1930. Kinsky (1970) said that in North Island escaped Eastern Rosellas were well established and spreading throughout Northland from Awanui south to the lower Waikato (Waingaro), and were also to be found in Wairarapa, Waikanae and the upper Hutt Valley, while in South Island they occurred mainly between the Waikouaiti River and the Waipori Gorge in Otago. Falla et al. (1979: 166–7) said that birds which had escaped into the Waitakeres were now 'strongly established between Raglan and Houhora; increasing south of Auckland and extending their range eastwards. There appear to be expanding pockets on Coromandel and north of Wellington.

Prefer open or lightly timbered country . . . In the South Island a small population surviving in the hills near Dunedin is said to include hybrids between Eastern (*P. eximius*) and Crimson Rosellas (*P. elegans*)'.

According to Forshaw (1969), a population of Eastern Rosellas in the Mount Lofty Ranges near Adelaide (well to the west of the species' natural range in South Australia) is probably descended from escaped aviary birds.

NOTES

1 Falla, Sibson & Turbott 1979; Forshaw 1980; Hamel 1970; Kinsky 1970; Long 1981; Oliver 1930, 1955; Rostrum 1969; Thomson 1922; Wodzicki 1965.
2 For the arrival of Eastern Rosellas in New Zealand in 1910 see under Crimson Rosella (*P. elegans*).

Budgerigar
(*Melopsittacus undulatus*)

NATURAL DISTRIBUTION

Widely distributed throughout arid inland regions of Australia, but rare or absent in the Cape York Peninsula (Queensland), northern Arnhem Land (Northern Territory), east of the Great Dividing Range (Queensland and New South Wales), and in the extreme south-west of Western Australia; in parts of the west and south-west its range extends to the coast; it also occurs on several offshore islands, but not in Tasmania.

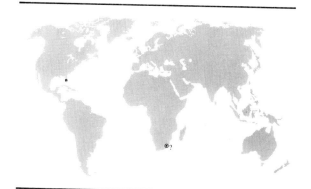

NATURALIZED DISTRIBUTION

Africa: ?South Africa; North America: USA.

AFRICA

South Africa[1]

Several attempts were made in the early 1960s to naturalize Budgerigars in South Africa. T. B. Oatley (personal communication, 1981) wrote as follows:

253

There is, or used to be, a flock of budgerigars living in evergreen forest (an unlikely habitat) at Umbogintwini, south of Durban [Natal]. The area is the site of a large A.E. & C.I. factory with a large housing estate for its employees. This flock evidently persisted solely on the strength of escapee recruitment and probably relied largely on bird table seeds for its food supply.

According to Liversidge (n.d.), this population, which never amounted to more than 20 individuals, died out after surviving for only about 3 years.

NORTH AMERICA

USA[2]

Between 1925 and 1940, some 240,000 Budgerigars were imported from Australia as cagebirds to the United States – most of which were consigned to California and Florida – where they soon became the most popular species kept by American aviculturists, and where a number inevitably from time to time escaped.

In 1956, an ex-USAF officer, Anthony J. Shank, acquired a pair of Budgerigars (to which he is believed to have later added at least a further two dozen pairs) that were kept in a large aviary built round an Australian Pine tree in Parsley Trailer Park at Reddington Shores near St Petersburg on the west coast of central Florida. A few years later, when the population had considerably increased, the birds were released into the trailer park, where they were soon nesting freely in Australian Pines, 'punk' (decayed) timber and nesting boxes provided by local residents.

Thereafter, many more Budgerigars (perhaps as many as 3,000) escaped or were purposely liberated by those in the holiday business wanting to provide a novel tourist attraction (e.g. by the Edison Estate at Fort Myers, which in 1959 allowed 'homing' flocks to roam), by bored pet owners and, especially, by breeders who reared birds either professionally for sale to pet shops or as a hobby, and who needed to dispose of undesirable colour phases. By about 1962, several thousand free-flying birds were established in the vicinity of St Petersburg, where they were regarded as an unusual attraction by holidaymakers. Frequent recruitment to the population from these sources continues to the present day.

By 1975–6, Budgerigars were apparently well established in Florida from New Port Richey to Englewood (respectively, 50 km north, and double that distance south, of St Petersburg) on the Gulf of Mexico, while a few were reported from as far north as Cedar Key, 150 km from St Petersburg, and at Port Charlotte and Punta Gorda a little to the south of Englewood. The population in St Petersburg was estimated to number some 3,000. On the east coast, Budgerigars were reported to be established at Cocoa, Dade County, and in 1977 at Jacksonville near the border with Georgia.

In the autumn of 1977, a questionnaire on Budgerigar sightings was circulated among 130 representatives of the Florida Audubon and Florida Wildlife Societies and the State Game and Fresh Water Fish Commission: the results collated from the 50 per cent response to this questionnaire indicated, according to Shapiro (1980: 8) that:

the budgerigar is abundant in Ft Lauderdale and Ft Pierce on the east coast, and ranges extensively from Spring Hill in the north down to Sanibel Island [south of Port Charlotte] on the west coast. Very few sightings were noted in the interior or northern part of the state. The heaviest concentrations appear to be near Venice [80 km south of St Petersburg], St Petersburg, Seminole, Largo [just north of St Petersburg] and Holiday. All the major known releases and escapes have occurred in these 'hot spots'. It may be that range expansion from these points of introduction has been in a predominantly north–south direction, and the sightings in Spring Hill and Sanibel represent the current limits of the range.

Wenner & Hirth (1984) summarized the distribution and status of Budgerigars in Florida in 1977–8 as follows: they were confined to residential areas, breeding in colonies of 100 or more on the Gulf coast from Hudson to Fort Myers, with transient flocks extending north to Spring Hill and south to Sanibel Island and Naples. On the Atlantic coast, they bred near Fort Pierce, Port St Lucie, and Fort Lauderdale, with transient flocks occurring from Miami and West Palm Beach to north of Fort Pierce. Flocks of 30 or more occurred sporadically as far north as Gainesville (especially in winter), with occasional individuals being sighted in the Panhandle north of Gainesville and in the Jacksonville area. Budgerigars were absent from the interior, apart from small colonies in Winter Park, and they were unknown in the Keys. The densest concentrations occurred from Charlotte to Citrus counties in New Port Richey, Clearwater, St Petersburg, Largo, Seminole, Sarasota, Bradenton, Venice, Englewood and Port St Lucie.

A combination of factors has contributed to the successful establishment of the Budgerigar in Florida. Young cocks may produce spermatozoa within 60 days of leaving the nest, and this rapid sexual development – a physiological adaptation to their arid homeland environment – enables young birds to reproduce quickly in optimum conditions. Breeding can take place at any season, and may be stimulated by heavy rainfall preceding a period of abundant food in conjunction with optimum temperatures and photoperiod; several broods may be reared annually. Their ability to survive for considerable periods without water enables Budgerigars to devote more time to the important search for food, of which in Australia the seeds of Spinifex (*Triodia* spp.) and Mitchell Grass (*Astrebla* sp.) are especially favoured.

Although Budgerigars in urbanized Florida are the descendants of domesticated stock, they retain the adaptability and opportunism that characterize their wild Australian ancestors. They breed freely in nest boxes and readily visit bird tables for oats, millet and canary seed, which more than compensate for the shortage of natural nesting cavities and wild seeding grasses, of which the seeds of Bahia-grass (*Paspalum* spp.) are sometimes eaten. Indeed, the provision of artificial nesting sites and food and the protection accorded them by man (similar to that given to the Ring-necked Parakeet (*Psittacula krameri*) in Britain) are, perhaps, the most important factors in the Budgerigar's successful colonization of Florida.

Such rapidly growing trees as Eucalyptus (*Eucalyptus* sp.), Silk Oak (*Grevillea robusta*) and Australian Pine (all aliens from Australia) and native Live Oak (*Quercus virginiana*) provide roosting sites and shelter for Budgerigars in their dense foliage, and Shapiro (1979) records that telephone cables, television aerials, lamp posts and shopping centre signs are also utilized. Droughts, which in Australia are responsible for the death of large numbers of Budgerigars, are unknown in Florida where there is an abundant supply of water, and the species' natural nomadic

habits have helped it steadily to expand its range. The rate of expansion, however, has been retarded by the birds' strong tendency to nest at high densities, and by the abundance of nesting and roosting sites and food near the points of release.

The Budgerigar's ability to spread further both within and without Florida, and its present and future influence on the native ecosystem are, as Shapiro points out, unknown. Although biotic and climatic factors of southern Florida have favoured the naturalization of many exotic tropical species, more temperate conditions north of Lake Okeechobee (27°N) have effectively prevented their northward expansion. This natural inhibition, however, does not apply in the case of the adaptable and aggressive Budgerigar, which can survive 20–35 nights of frost a year in northern Florida, and may thus have the physiological potential to expand into southern Texas and Mexico.

Budgerigars in Florida compete for food and/or nesting sites with such native species as the Purple Martin (*Progne subis*), Red-bellied Woodpecker (*Melanerpes carolinus*) and Mourning Dove (*Zenaida macroura*), and with the alien House Sparrow (*Passer domesticus*) (q.v.). Localized damage to citrus trees in urban and suburban gardens has been reported, but were Budgerigars to spread into the state's interior they could become a serious threat to millet and, perhaps, rice crops. The numbers and colonial roosting habits of the alien Starling (*Sturnus vulgaris*) (q.v.), which has successfully colonized most of the United States, cause environmental problems (in the form of excessive noise, accumulations of guano on buildings used for roosting, and interference with air-traffic control) that could be mirrored by the Budgerigar. The possibility of the transmission of parasites and/or diseases to native species and to humans cannot be ignored.

The Budgerigars' main controlling agents in Florida are Red-shouldered Hawks (*Buteo lineatus*), Red-tailed Hawks (*B. jamaicensis*) and domestic Cats (*Felis catus*). Control by man, were it ever to be attempted, is likely to prove ineffectual for two main reasons; first, because of the already large population and the species' high rate of reproduction which would quickly make good any losses, and, second, because of the opposition from local residents that such a campaign would inevitably arouse. Shapiro recounts how a woman in St Pierce asked the State Game and Fresh Water Fish Commission to shoot a Red-shouldered Hawk which was killing Budgerigars in her garden: 'ironically', wrote Shapiro, 'it is the hawk that is the protected species'.

Since no official census of Budgerigars in Florida has yet been made, the state-wide total remains unknown; although distribution is patchy even within colonized areas, the fact that some roosts have been estimated to hold upwards of 8,000 individuals (with an increasing preponderance of wild-type, light-green birds) indicates that where they do occur overall numbers can be very high, and the species is rapidly becoming one of the commonest birds in coastal Florida.

Elsewhere in the United States, Budgerigars are frequently observed in the wild, but have seldom become established; in California, according to Hardy (1973), a colony lived (but is not known to have bred) for a number of years in natural cavities in Sycamore trees (*Platanus racemosa*) along the arroyo[3] in lower Topanga Canyon inland from Malibu Beach. Escaped Budgerigars in Puerto Rico are believed rapidly to succumb to the island's excessive heat and humidity.

Numerous attempts have been made to naturalize Budgerigars in Britain,[4] but none have ever met with lasting success. Many aviculturists keep flocks of free-flying 'homing' birds that are allowed out of their aviaries during the day, returning to them at night to roost. Some occasionally fail to 'home', while others are deliberately released, and colonies which have bred in the wild have become temporarily established locally (e.g. at Margaretting in Essex, in Windsor Great Park in Berkshire, at Beaulieu in the New Forest in Hampshire, near Downham Market in Norfolk, and at Fenstanton in Huntingdonshire). The most recent (and by far the most successful) population, which in 1975 was estimated to number over 100 birds, was formed in 1971 on Tresco in the Isles of Scilly (from where the birds spread to some other neighbouring islands), where they died out during the hard winter of 1975–6. Since the species seems unable to survive permanently in this most temperate climate in Britain it is unlikely to do so elsewhere.

In several countries in continental Europe, Budgerigars have from time to time become temporarily acclimatized in the wild – on one occasion even in the Swiss Alps.

In Japan (Kaburaki 1934 and Brazil 1985) and Hong Kong (Webster 1975), escaped or deliberately released Budgerigars are frequently observed in the wild and sometimes breed successfully, but fail to maintain themselves.

In South America, according to Sick (1968), Budgerigars have escaped or have been freed on several occasions in Colombia and Brazil (and probably also elsewhere) but have never become permanently established.

Thomson (1922: 136) records that 'at an early date' unsuccessful attempts were made to naturalize Budgerigars in Canterbury, New Zealand, and that 'every bird-dealer has brought numbers into the country for sale'. In 1871, two (or two pairs) were released by the Auckland Acclimatization Society, but failed to become established.

In the Hawaiian Islands,[5] Budgerigars frequently escape or are deliberately released from avicultural collections. In 1970, four were seen at Diamond Head on Oahu where some were still present in 1973; their subsequent status, however, is uncertain.

According to Gallagher & Woodcock (1980: 190), 'ex-captive parrots occur occasionally in Oman, such as the Budgerigar, but there is no evidence of their naturalization'.

On several occasions, Budgerigars have been unsuccessfully released in the Society Islands. (Holyoak & Thibault 1984).

NOTES

1 Liversidge n.d.; J. M. Winterbottom 1966, 1978 (and personal communication, 1981); and T. B. Oatley, personal communication, 1981.
2 For much of the information on Budgerigars in the United States, I am indebted to A. E. Shapiro 1979, 1980 (and personal communication, 1980). See also: American Ornithologists' Union 1983; Anon. 1980; Blake 1975; Bull 1973; Bull & Ricciuti 1974; Cooke & Knappen 1941; Fisk & Crabtree 1974; Forshaw 1980; Hardy 1973; Heilbrun 1976, 1977; King 1968; Lever 1984b; Lipp 1963; Long 1981; O'Keefe 1973; Owre 1973; Phillips 1928; Wenner & Hirth 1984; Wyndham 1978.
3 Watercourse, gully or channel.
4 Fitter 1959; Lever 1977a, 1984b; Sharrock 1976. See also: British Trust for Ornithology Records Committee Report, *Ibis* 120: 411 (1978).
5 Berger 1981; Blake 1975; Hawaiian Audubon Society 1975; Long 1981; Munro 1944; Pyle 1977.

Grey-headed Lovebird
(*Agapornis cana*)

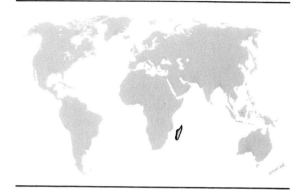

NATURAL DISTRIBUTION
Confined to coastal regions and the south-west of Madagascar.

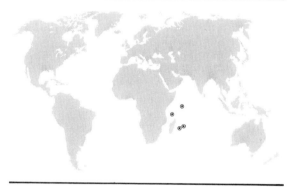

NATURALIZED DISTRIBUTION
Africa: Seychelles, Comoros, Mascarenes (Réunion, Rodrigues).

AFRICA

Seychelles[1]

Grey-headed Lovebirds were introduced to the island of Mahé in the Seychelles in 1906 where they became abundant. In the 1930s, they were still very common, especially in Gordon Square in Port Victoria, but thereafter suffered a serious decline (for reasons unknown) and are now rare except in Victoria, Port Launay, Anse la Mouche, and Anse Boileau in the west, where they feed mainly on the seeds of Elephant Grass (*Panicum maximum*). A small number, descended from a separate introduction, also occur on the island of Silhouette, 22.5 km west by north of Mahé.

Comoros

According to Peters (1937) and Benson (1960) birds of the nominate form of coastal Madagascar have probably been introduced to the Comoros archipelago, where Benson found them to be well established and quite common in cultivated regions and in open country on Anjouan and Mayotte, and in lesser numbers also on Grand Comore and Moheli.

Réunion

Grey-headed Lovebirds have been released frequently on the island of Réunion, where Watson, Zusi & Storer (1963) recorded the presence of flocks of up to 30 birds; Gill (1967), however, could only find them in small numbers, and Staub (1976) reported them as rare.

Rodrigues and Mauritius[2]

Grey-headed Lovebirds of the nominate subspecies were first described on Rodrigues and Mauritius in 1725,[3] where they are said to have been imported as cagebirds from Madagascar by the Dutch in the early seventeenth century. At one time abundant on Mauritius, they were much reduced in numbers by a cyclone in April 1892, and 20 years later were reported to be scarce. Apparently, they disappeared altogether prior to the mid-1950s. On Rodrigues, where Watson et al. (1963) found them to be not uncommon, large numbers have been killed because of the damage they cause to maize crops, and they are today rare.

The same subspecies was introduced, possibly from the Comoros archipelago, to the islands of Zanzibar and Mafia,[4] where, however, they apparently died out between 1913 and 1930.

According to Clancey (1964, in Forshaw

1980), Grey-headed Lovebirds of the nominate subspecies may have been unsuccessfully introduced to Natal, South Africa, in the late 1880s.

The **Nyasa Lovebird** (*Agapornis lilianae*), a native of northwestern Mozambique to eastern Zambia, has, according to Benson & White (1957, in Forshaw 1980), been successfully translocated to Lundazi in the latter country, and is reported by Clancey (1965, in Forshaw) sometimes to have escaped from aviculturists in South West Africa (Namibia).

The **Rosy-faced** or **Peach-faced Lovebird** (*Agapornis roseicollis*) is a native of southern Angola, South West Africa (Namibia) and the northwestern Cape Province of South Africa. In the 1960s, it was deliberately translocated or accidentally introduced to Middelburg in the Transvaal, and in the following decade to Fish Hoek in the Cape Peninsula and to Durban. According to Liversidge (n.d.), a population of around 30 became established in one of these (unspecified) areas for a period of some 5 years after its introduction, and was (? in the 1960s) said to be increasing.

In Western Australia, a small colony is said to have been established in Perth in the mid-1960s, and since at least the early 1970s there have been sporadic reports of individuals in South Australia in and around Adelaide, on the Eyre Peninsula, and at Yankalilla in the Mount Lofty Ranges (Paton & Pollard 1985).

NOTES

1 Diamond & Feare 1980; Gaymer, Blackman et al. 1969; Penny 1974.
2 Benedict 1957; ·Benson 1960; Gill 1967; Long 1981; Mackworth-Praed & Grant 1952–73; Meinertzhagen 1912; Peters 1937; Rountree, Guérin et al. 1952; Staub 1976; Watson, Zusi & Storer 1963.
3 *Relation de l'Île Rodrigues* (Archives Nationales, Fonds des Colonies), C4.12(48).
4 Ellis 1975; Mackworth-Praed & Grant 1952–73; Peters 1937.

Fischer's Lovebird and Masked Lovebird
(*Agapornis fischeri* and *A. personata*)

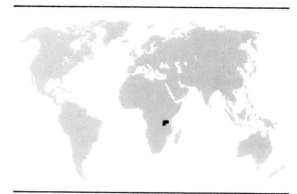

Note: Map shows combined distribution.

NATURAL DISTRIBUTION
Northern Tanzania (*fischeri*), and northeastern Tanzania from Arusha and the Serengeti Plains to Lake Rukwa (*personata*).

Note: Map shows combined distribution.

NATURALIZED DISTRIBUTION
Africa: Kenya.

AFRICA

Kenya[1]

Fischer's and Masked Lovebirds, introduced by aviculturists to Kenya from northern Tanzania (where in the mid-1920s they were widely trapped for export as cagebirds to Europe), escaped from captivity and were established and breeding in the former country by the mid- to late 1960s. Zimmerman (1967) reported that 'several recently secured bird specimens represent

additions to the known avifauna of Kenya'; these included a Fischer's Lovebird from Isiolo in the Northern Frontier District north of Mount Kenya – one from a flock of 8–10 seen in 'lush acacia woodland' that were believed to have escaped from aviculturists at Nanyuki or Meru – respectively, 60 km south-west and 30 km south of Isiolo. Masked Lovebirds colonized residential areas of the capital, Nairobi (where Cunningham van Someren (1969 and 1975) admits to having 'lost birds'), where they feed largely on the seeds of the Australian exotic *Grevillia robusta*, and have been seen at Mwea-Tebere in the Aberdare (Nyandarua) Mountains of western Kenya, while Fischer's Lovebirds settled mainly around Lake Naivasha where they feed and roost in waterside *Acacia* trees. Since about 1970, both species have also become established on the coast around Mombasa (especially at Nyali Beach), where 20 *personata* were reported in 1972 and 6 *personata* and 30–40 *fischeri* in 1974, when they were said to be interbreeding – frequently in the commandeered nests (in Coconut, Borassus and Dom Palms) of the Palm Swift (*Cypsiurus parvus*). In some parts of Kenya, damage to grain crops (especially millet) by these two species has been reported.

Fischer's and Masked Lovebirds that escaped at Namanga in Kenya near the Tanzanian border failed to become established, possibly due to the absence of suitable grasses as a source of food.

According to Bull (1973), Masked Lovebirds that from time to time escaped into parks in the New York City area have never become permanently established.

As well as being exported from Tanganyika (Tanzania) to aviculturists in Europe in the mid-1920s, Fischer's and Masked Lovebirds were translocated to Dar-es-Salaam and Tanga on the Tanganyikan coast, where they were established and breeding in the wild by around 1928, *personata* being the commoner species in Dar-es-Salaam (where a large number were released) and *fischeri* more abundant in Tanga. In 1938–9, *personata* had spread past Kisiju, over 50 km south of Dar-es-Salaam, and inland to Nzaza more than 30 km to the south-west; in the latter year a further 200 *personata/fischeri* escaped or were released in Dar-es-Salaam to swell the stock of birds already there.

Before 1948, some Fischer's Lovebirds escaped from Mr A. C. Robbie of Muholola Farm south of Saranda in Tanzania, where they soon disappeared.

Since, as Cunningham van Someren (1975) says, 'these new feral populations have been able to adapt to a very diverse range of conditions, coastal to Kenya highlands, where hitherto they were unknown', it seems strange that neither has succeeded in spreading north naturally from their ranges on the interior plateau of northern Tanzania.

NOTE
1 Barlass 1975; Cunningham van Someren 1969, 1975; Elliott 1970; Ellis 1975; Forshaw 1980; Long 1981; Mackworth-Praed & Grant 1957; Williams & Arlott 1982; Zimmerman 1967.

Ring-necked Parakeet
(*Psittacula krameri*)

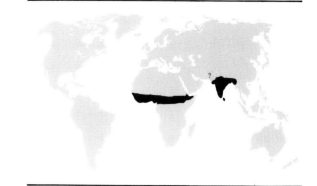

NATURAL DISTRIBUTION
From Senegal and Guinea in west Africa eastwards to northern Uganda, Sudan and northern Ethiopia and Somalia. A separate population exists from Pakistan (and possibly eastern Afghanistan) through India, Nepal and Bangladesh to central Burma and Sri Lanka.

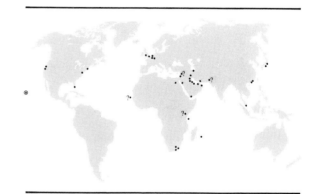

NATURALIZED DISTRIBUTION
Europe: British Isles, West Germany, Belgium, the Netherlands; Asia: ?Lebanon, Israel, Arabia (Iraq, ?Kuwait, Bahrain, ?Qatar, United Arab Emirates, Oman, People's Democratic Republic of Yemen (Aden), Saudi Arabia and Iran), ?Afghanistan, Singapore, Hong Kong, Macau, Japan; Africa: ?Cape Verde Islands, Egypt, ?Kenya, Zanzibar, South Africa, Mauritius; North America: USA; Oceania: Hawaiian Islands.

EUROPE

British Isles[1]

Between 1969 and 1971, a population of Ring-necked Parakeets became established in Surrey, Kent and Essex in the southwestern, southern, southeastern and eastern outer suburbs of London, and also around Gravesend in Kent. Breeding was first confirmed (in Croydon and near Langley Park in Surrey) in 1971, although it may possibly have occurred as early as 1969 near Southfleet in Kent; in 1973, parakeets first nested successfully in Greater London, and in Bromley, Beckenham and Margate in Kent. Since then, they have spread from Gravesend to towns on the Medway, and are seen regularly all over the Isle of Thanet. Elsewhere in southern England, free-flying Ring-necked Parakeets (believed to be strays from a 'homing' flock near Marlow in Buckinghamshire) became established near Wraysbury in that county and around Old Windsor in Berkshire in 1972, and subsequently also in adjacent parts of the Thames Valley.

In northwestern England, a second population is established around the southern suburbs of Greater Manchester (where breeding was first recorded in 1974), extending westwards to Merseyside (Liverpool) where the first nest was found in 1980.

By 1983, Ring-necked Parakeets had been recorded from 50 counties in England, Scotland and Wales (but from none in Ireland), and breeding had been confirmed in England – in Berkshire (at least once), Kent, Surrey, Sussex (since 1974), Norfolk, Greater London, Greater Manchester, Merseyside and West Yorkshire (at least once) – and on at least one occasion in Clwyd (formerly Denbighshire) in north Wales.

The success of the Ring-necked Parakeet in becoming established in Britain is due at least partially to its ready acceptance of food, which includes mixed seeds, dried fruits, nuts (especially peanuts), coconut and fat, provided by surburban households (who generally regard it with the same favour shown to the Budgerigar (*Melopsittacus undulatus*) in Florida in the United States). Most birds are thus able to survive all but the harshest winters. The majority of parakeets occur in gardens (45 per cent according to Hawkes 1976) and parks, where damage to the buds and blossom of a variety of trees and shrubs, and to

plums, pears and – especially – apples has been recorded. Whole apples are seldom consumed, up to four bites only being normally taken from each fruit. The current population is not large enough to cause serious economic damage, but were parakeets to increase in numbers and spread the potential harm they could do to agricultural, horticultural and orchard crops – especially in a farming and fruit-growing county such as Kent – would be considerable. In India, where Ring-necked Parakeets are regarded as serious pests, Simwat & Sidhu (1973) recorded significant losses (in some cases up to a third of the crop) to growing maize, sorghum, pearlmiller, sesame, wheat, barley, Indian mustard, groundnuts, mangoes, guavas, figs, grapes, peaches, jambalona, sunflowers, gram, sarson and pomegranates, and also to stored grain. In Sudan, Cunningham van Someren (1969) says that parakeets cause considerable damage to fields of sorghum around Sennar on the Blue Nile.

Since breeding (almost entirely in the old nestholes of Greater Spotted Woodpeckers (*Dendrocopos major*) and Green Woodpeckers (*Picus viridis*)) takes place before that of most British birds, parakeets compete advantageously with such hole-nesting species as Great Tits (*Parus major*), Nuthatches (*Sitta europaea*) and Tree Sparrows (*Passer montanus*). Another potential problem, were the population to increase dramatically in the densely populated urban environment in which it is presently established, is the risk to man from psittacosis.

Three separate sources have been suggested as the origin of Ring-necked Parakeets in Britain; they may have come from free-flying 'homing' flocks that failed to return to their aviaries; they may have escaped from pet shops or exotic bird farms (since London is one of the main centres of commercial aviculture), or they may have been deliberately turned loose by members of ships' companies in London and Liverpool when they realized that importation would be delayed by a long and expensive period of quarantine. In all probability, each of these sources has contributed to the present population, which B. Hawkes (personal communication, 1984), who conducted a 4-year survey of the species on behalf of the British Trust for Ornithology, in 1982 estimated to number about 1,000, of which some 300 were in Greater London, 200 in Kent, 110 in Surrey, 70 in Sussex, 18 or more in Berkshire and 24 in

Greater Manchester. In 1983, the Ring-necked Parakeet was added to category C of the official British and Irish List; this covers birds introduced by man which breed regularly in the wild and seem able to maintain a viable population without further introductions.

West Germany[2]

In 1967, half-a-dozen Ring-necked Parakeets were at liberty in the grounds of Köln Zoo, where breeding took place 2 years later. Thereafter, the population rapidly increased, and by 1983 numbered between 250 and 300, including 50 breeding pairs. New breeding colonies have been formed at Brühl (four pairs since 1979) and Erfstadt a few kilometres south-west of Köln, and at Bonn (where nesting was first confirmed in 1979), and probably also at Wiesbaden and between Leverkusen and Düsseldorf, where around 100 were counted in 1979.

Belgium

Cramp (1985) says that small populations of Ring-necked Parakeets have been established in Brussels (since about 1970) and Antwerp.

The Netherlands[3]

In 1975–6, colonies of free-flying Ring-necked Parakeets became established in The Hague (about 30), Rotterdam, and Amsterdam, Zeeland. Although breeding may first have taken place as early as 1968 (before the colonies became properly established), it was not confirmed until 1980. The population has risen from between 40 and 50 in 1977 to several hundred in 1981, and is probably now self-supporting.

ASIA

Lebanon

According to Forshaw (1980), there are unconfirmed reports of free-flying Ring-necked Parakeets in Lebanon.

Israel[4]

Ring-necked Parakeets first escaped from the zoo in Tel Aviv and from private aviculturists in about 1960 (one account says not until 1969). Since then, they have increased and spread over most of the coastal plain and the Galilee and Jordan valleys, where they are now well established and breeding.

Arabia

Gallagher & Woodcock (1980:190) say that the Ring-necked Parakeet 'has been introduced into Iraq, Iran, Arabian Gulf, N. Oman, Aden, E. Africa, U.K., etc.'. According to Jennings (1981: 71 and 131), 'the origin of the Gulf population is obscure but is probably at least partially derived from escaped cage birds as it is commonly for sale in the markets . . . occurs in flocks of up to forty . . . movements within Gulf are erratic'. In Arabia, Silsby (1980: 75) says of Ring-necked Parakeets that 'in all probability they were originally escaped cage birds which have bred and multiplied'.

More cautiously, Forshaw (1980) suggests that the species may have been introduced to Iran, Iraq and Kuwait but that further evidence is necessary before this can be confirmed. The many scattered populations in Arabia could conceivably be relics (perhaps reinforced by recent escapes from captivity) of a formerly more widespread distribution in which the African and Asian populations were united.

Iraq[5]

Between 1938 and 1952, free-flying Ring-necked Parakeets were seen quite frequently in the vicinity of Baghdad; in 1959, some were reported at Karradah Sharqiyah, and others have been seen at Al Kut. Marchant (in Forshaw 1980) indicates that the small number of records suggests a declining local colony, probably derived from escaped birds.

Kuwait; Bahrain; Qatar; United Arab Emirates

Ring-necked Parakeets are breeding residents in Bahrain, the United Arab Emirates, and on the

Musandam Peninsula on the Arabian Gulf.[6] In Qatar, they occur in small numbers as irregular passage migrants and perhaps also as breeding residents. In Kuwait, where they may have bred near Al Ahmadi, they appear mainly as winter visitors.

Oman[7]

In Oman, Ring-necked Parakeets are breeding residents on Al Batinah on the Gulf of Oman, especially near Al Khaburah and Suwaiq (Suwayq Dajjah), and are vagrants or scarce visitors to Masirah on the Arabian Sea. The subspecies introduced has been variously described, as in Egypt, as *borealis* (from western Pakistan and northern India to central Burma) or *manillensis* from southern India and Sri Lanka.

People's Democratic Republic of Yemen (Aden)[8]

In 1962, at least 22 pairs of Ring-necked Parakeets were estimated to be established in Tawahi, the Crescent (the shopping centre of Aden), Crater, Ma'alla and 12 km north at Shaykh Uthmān in the Democratic Republic of Yemen.

Saudi Arabia[9]

In Saudi Arabia, Ring-necked Parakeets occur in Hijaz (Hejaz) on the Red Sea, and probably breed in the Eastern Province south of Kuwait on the Arabian Gulf.

Iran[10]

In Iran, free-flying Ring-necked Parakeets have been observed in city gardens of Tehran and at Bandar Abbas on the Strait of Hormuz.

Afghanistan[11]

Small flocks of 12–15 Ring-necked Parakeets recorded in Kabul and Jalalabad near the border with Pakistan could be escaped cagebirds or natural dispersants.

Singapore

Medway & Wells (1976) say that escaped Ring-necked Parakeets have bred on the island of Singapore, where small numbers are currently established and breeding.[12]

Hong Kong and Macau[13]

Ring-necked Parakeets of the form *P. k. borealis* (western Pakistan and northern India to Burma) in Hong Kong and Macau may represent a natural extension of range or, more probably, are descended from escaped cage birds introduced before 1903, when they were first seen in the wild. A decade later they were established as common breeding residents in Hong Kong, and in the mid-1970s were still quite abundant and widespread, especially in the north of Hong Kong and on the Mong Tseng Peninsula. Recently, flocks of up to 30 have been seen in the vicinity of Homantin and Kowloon Tong.

There are unconfirmed reports of the presence of Ring-necked Parakeets elsewhere in south-eastern China, where Gallagher & Woodcock (1980) say that *P. k. borealis* breeds, and in parts of Indo-China.

Japan

According to Brazil (1985 and in press), in Japan Ring-necked Parakeets breed in Tokyo and in Kanagawa, Aichi and Hiroshima prefectures on Honshu, and in Ehime Prefecture on Shikoku.

AFRICA

Cape Verde Islands

According to Mackworth-Praed & Grant (1970: 405), the Ring-necked Parakeet was 'probably introduced' to the Cape Verde Islands. It is, however, not mentioned by Bannerman & Bannerman (1968).

Egypt[14]

Ring-necked Parakeets (at one time described variously as *borealis* or *manillensis*) escaped from

Giza Zoo (on the west bank of the Nile) between 1901 and 1908, and in some places are said to have been abundant before 1912, when others were released (or escaped) in the Egyptian delta. Three years later they were reported to be well established and numerous in and around Cairo, and, between 1916 and 1919, 127 were destroyed in the gardens of Giza Zoo. A decade later, however, they were still common locally near Cairo and at El Giza, and were occasionally reported at Helwan (15 km south of Cairo) and at the Delta Barrage. In 1971 and 1979–81, Goodman (1982) counted 50 and flocks of 35 and 40, respectively, in the grounds of Giza Zoo, and, by 1981, Ring-necked Parakeets had spread to the Gezira Sporting Club at Zamalek (4 km from Giza Zoo), where flocks of up to 15 were seen and breeding was confirmed. There are now estimated to be several hundred birds established in and around Giza and Cairo.

In 1971, a single Ring-necked Parakeet was seen at Bahig (190 km north-west of Giza) – presumably the result of a separate release. Goodman has identified the subspecies established in Egypt as *manillensis* from southern India and Sri Lanka.

Kenya[15]

In 1969, Ring-necked Parakeets were found to be breeding – in holes in the hardwood tree *Brachylaena hutchinsii* – in the Nairobi National Park in southern Kenya. They may have been birds that escaped from a dealer who imported some from India in about 1961, or others lost by a private aviculturist who obtained stock from the same source more recently. It has, however, also been suggested that these birds, believed to be of the nominate form that ranges from West Africa to northern Uganda and the southern Sudan, could represent a natural southeasterly extension of range.

Zanzibar

According to Mackworth-Praed & Grant (1957), Ring-necked Parakeets of the race *P. k. borealis* were introduced to the island of Zanzibar at an unknown date (certainly before 1935 when they were described as scarce), where they are said still

to be slowly increasing and expanding their range in the vicinity of Zanzibar town.

South Africa[16]

T. B. Oatley (personal comunication, 1981) wrote as follows:

As far as I am aware, there are two separate flocks [of Ring-necked Parakeets] maintaining themselves in Natal: one is in the Burman Bush (a relic forest patch) at Durban and the other at Sordwana Bay on the Zululand coast (see *Bird Atlas of Natal* by Cyrus and Robson, 1980).

The Durban flock must have originated from aviary escapes as the species is easily bred in captivity and widespread in aviaries in built-up areas. Indeed the Durban flock is probably still periodically augmented by new escapes, but they are also breeding as they have been seen visiting bird feeding tables in surrounding suburban gardens with immature birds accompanying the adults.

The likelihood is that the other population at Sordwana Bay also originated from escapes. The Sordwana Bay camping site is heavily patronised by fishermen and their families in the school holiday periods, but is a rural area and there are no known parrot breeders' aviaries within more than 100 miles [160 km]. I think it is unlikely that the birds have extended their range down the east coast of Africa from Zanzibar (see Vincent, 1972). . . . It is much more likely that these birds were also escapes from cages – 'pets' of some of the 4,000 well-to-do people who crowd into the area for a week or so four times a year.

There is nothing to indicate that these two populations are, or are likely to become, so numerous as to have an impact on local species. The Durban population does well on local feeding trays, and neither group lives in agricultural areas where cereal crops might provide a significant food source.

Around Durban, an adult Ring-necked Parakeet was present on the Berea for several weeks in 1969, while a pair seen at Red Hill in July 1974 was followed by the appearance of several others on the coast in the early winter of 1975. The birds have since bred successfully at Tugela Mouth, around Durban Bay and near Pietermaritzburg. Flocks of up to 30 are now not uncommon, and there is some tendency to spread inland.[17]

According to Vincent (1972), Ring-necked Parakeets were first observed around Sordwana Bay in Tongaland in September 1970, where a month later up to 60 were counted in a single flock. An immature bird collected for Vincent was identified as of the same race – *borealis* – as that established in Zanzibar. The birds in north-eastern Zululand, which occur singly or in flocks mainly in parks and gardens but also in lightly wooded areas and coastal bush, could, Vincent considered, either represent an extension of range south from the coast of Tanzania via Mozambique (a total distance of some 2,600 km from Zanzibar) or be derived from another hitherto unrecorded introduction somewhere to the south of Zanzibar.

According to Weissenbacher & Allan (1985), flocks of adult Ring-necked Parakeets accompanied by juveniles have been recorded in and around Johannesburg since 1970. In September 1984, a flock of between five and eight was observed attending two nest cavities in willow (*Salix babylonica*) trees at Gillooly's Farm, some 10 km west of the city centre, in an area of flat mown lawns with scattered copses and rows of exotic *Eucalyptus* and willows. One nest, from which an adult was flushed, was later found to contain at least two eggs, while near the other (the branch in which it was built having fallen to the ground) were discovered two dead chicks. This was the first confirmed breeding attempt by this species in the Transvaal. Despite their presence in this area for at least the past 15 years, the birds remain scarce and local.

In the 1860s, Ring-necked Parakeets are said to have been accidentally introduced to Cape Town, where they later died out.

Mauritius[18]

Although Gallagher & Woodcock (1980) say that races of the Ring-necked Parakeet other than *P. k. borealis* occur naturally across central Africa and in Mauritius and southern India, most other authors seem agreed that the birds in Mauritius, where the form is *borealis*, occur as a result of human agency. According to Carié (1916), some escaped from an aviary in Grand Port Louis in about 1886, where they rapidly increased and became established in native lowland forest (especially the Macabé Forest) in and around the Black River Gorges in the south-west, nesting mainly in holes in Indian Mahogany (*Terminalia catappa*). In this habitat, Ring-necked Parakeets live sympatrically with the closely related and gravely endangered endemic Mauritius or Echo Parakeet (*Psittacula echo*), formerly considered only a subspecies of *krameri*: although Ring-necked and Echo Parakeets do not apparently interbreed, the former (and the introduced Common Mynah (*Acridotheres tristis*) q.v.), do compete with the native species for nesting sites. At present, Ring-necked Parakeets are confined to coastal plains in the south and south-east of the island and to the Alma-Quartier Militair and Pamplemousses areas, where damage to maize crops has been reported.

NORTH AMERICA

United States[19]

In 1972, Ring-necked Parakeets of the subspecies *manillensis* (peninsular India and Sri Lanka) appeared to be establishing a viable population in suburban north Dade County, Florida, where free-flying birds may have existed for over a decade and the presence of immatures suggested successful breeding. At least 37 were counted in Dade County in 1976, when a party of seven was also reported in St Augustine in northeastern Florida.

A small number of Ring-necked Parakeets, which may have become established in 1956, were breeding in the Highland Park district of Los Angeles in California until 1963, when they disappeared. A decade later, there was an unconfirmed report of a pair breeding at Solvang in Santa Barbara County, and in the following year a pair is known to have nested successfully in a cemetery in Los Angeles County, and another in Vasona Park, Los Gantos, in Santa Clara County, where within a few years a colony of perhaps 15–20 became established. In 1976, two Ring-necked Parakeets were shot at Cucamonga in the same state, where a flock of up to 16 birds may have been present. Blake (1975) indicates that the same subspecies (*manillensis*) that occurs in Florida has been introduced to California, where the birds are rigorously controlled.

In New York, free-flying Ring-necked Parakeets have often been reported; before 1974, a small group existed for several years based on the Bronx Zoo, and a party of up to half-a-dozen frequented the Bronx/Westchester region in

1975–6. The species is said also to have occurred since 1973 at Hampton, Virginia.

OCEANIA

Hawaiian Islands[20]

Munro (1960) indicated that Ring-necked Parakeets that had escaped from captivity had from time to time been noted in the Hawaiian Islands where, although they have occurred periodically (and may have nested) on Oahu for more than 50 years, they seem never to have become permanently established. In the 1970s, about 30 were observed near Kalaheo in southern Kauai. In 1981, Paton, Griffin & McIvor (1982) saw Ring-necked Parakeets in Hanapepe Valley and near Kukuiolono Park on Kauai, and in the same year discovered a nest in an ohia tree (*Metrosideros polymorpha*) on Hawaii – the first confirmed breeding of any psittacid in the archipelago. Breeding populations may now be established on Kauai, Oahu and Hawaii, where the birds could become an agricultural pest were they to increase and spread.

———————————

Beavan (1867) says that Colonel R. C. Tytler released several pairs of Ring-necked Parakeets that he had obtained in Calcutta (presumably, therefore, *borealis*) at Port Blair on South Andaman Island[21] in the Bay of Bengal during the period (1789–91) of the penal colony, and that although the majority were recaptured by the convicts some apparently became briefly established in the surrounding jungle.

———————————

The **Moustached Parakeet** (*Psittacula alexandri*) ranges from northern India and Nepal through Indo-China to southern China and Hainan; it also occurs on the islands of Java, Bali, the Andamans, Simalur, Lasia, Babi, Nias, Karimon Java and Kangean.

Birds of the nominate form (Java and Bali) have been introduced to southern Borneo[22] where they still occur only locally, and others of unknown race to Penang Island[23] off the west coast of Malaya where their present status is uncertain. Moustached Parakeets that from time

to time escape from captivity on Singapore Island,[24] Malaya, are believed to have nested in the wild but have never become well established.

———————————

In the 1970s, the **Plum-headed Parakeet** (*Psittacula cyanocephala*), a native of India and Sri Lanka, is said to have been successfully introduced to Johannesburg, South Africa.

———————————

According to Gallagher & Woodcock (1980: 190), ex-captive parrots occur occasionally in Oman, such as the **Large Indian** (or Alexandrine) **Parakeet** (*Psittacula eupatria*), native from eastern Afghanistan to Indo-China, and of southern India, Sri Lanka and the Andaman Islands, 'but there is no evidence of their naturalisation'.

NOTES

1 Anon. 1974b; Cramp 1985; Cunningham van Someren 1969; England 1970; Fitter 1959; Goodwin 1983; B. Hawkes 1976 (and personal communication, 1984); Hudson 1974; Lever 1977a, 1978, 1979, 1980a, 1981; Sharrock 1976; Simwat & Sidhu 1973. See also: *Ibis* 126: 441(1984).
2 Cramp 1985; and B. Hawkes, personal communication, 1984.
3 Cramp 1985; Taapken 1981; Teixeira 1979.
4 Cramp 1985; and B. Hawkes, personal communication, 1984.
5 Cramp 1985; Forshaw 1980; Gallagher & Woodcock 1980; Long 1981; Marchant 1963 (in Forshaw); Marchant & Macnab 1962; Moore & Boswell 1956.
6 Cramp 1985; Forshaw 1980; Gallagher & Woodcock 1980; Jennings 1981; Long 1981; Meinertzhagen 1954; Silsby, 1980.
7 de Schauensee & Ripley 1953 (in Forshaw); Forshaw 1980; Gallagher & Woodcock 1980; Long 1981; Vaurie 1965 (in Forshaw).
8 Ennion 1962; Gallagher & Woodcock 1980; Long 1981.
9 Jennings 1981; Silsby 1980.
10 Forshaw 1980; Gallagher & Woodcock 1980.
11 Long 1981; Niethammer & Niethammer 1967 (in Forshaw 1980); Puget 1970 (in Forshaw).
12 C. J. Hails, personal communication, 1985.
13 Forshaw 1980; Gallagher & Woodcock, 1980; Herklots 1940 (in Forshaw); Long 1981; Vaughan & Jones 1913; Webster 1975.
14 Cramp 1985; Etchécopar & Hüe 1964 (in Forshaw 1980); Flower 1933; Flower & Nicholl 1908; Goodman 1982; Hachisuka 1924; Haensel 1975;

Long 1981; Meinertzhagen 1930; Nicholl 1912; Vaurie 1965 (in Forshaw).

15 Cunningham van Someren 1969; Forshaw 1980.

16 Anon. 1976a; P. A. Clancey 1976a,b (and personal communication, 1981); Lever 1982b,c; Liversidge n.d.; Morris 1982; Murray & Murray 1984; Patten 1982; Sinclair 1981; Vincent 1972; Weissenbacher & Allan 1985; J. M. Winterbottom 1978 (and personal communication, 1981); and T. B. Oatley, personal communication, 1981.

17 P. A. Clancey, personal communications, 1981 and 1985.

18 Benedict 1957; Carié 1916; Forshaw 1980; Gallagher & Woodcock 1980; King 1981; Long 1981; Meinertzhagen 1912; Rountree, Guérin et al 1952; Staub 1976. See also: S. A. Temple, 'Wildlife in Mauritius today', *Oryx* 12: 584–90(1974); and *World Wildlife Yearbook, 1974–75* (World Wildlife Fund:

Morges, Switzerland, 1975), 210–12.

19 American Ornithologists' Union 1983; Blake, 1975; Bull 1973; Hardy 1964, 1973; Heilbrun 1976, 1977; Long 1981; Ogden 1972 (in Owre); Owre 1973; Shelgren, Thompson & Palmer 1975.

20 American Ornithologists' Union 1983; Berger 1981; Blake 1975; Hawaiian Audubon Society 1975; Long 1981; Munro 1960; Paton, Griffin & McIvor 1982; Pyle 1977.

21 See also: A. Alcock, *A Naturalist in Indian Seas* (John Murray: London, 1902); A. L. Butler, 'Birds of the Andamans and Nicobars', *Journal of the Bombay Natural History Society* 12: 386–403, 555–71, 684–96 (1899); 13: 144–54 (1900).

22 Forshaw 1980; Long 1981; Smythies 1960.

23 King, Dickinson & Woodcock 1975; Long 1981.

24 Gibson-Hill 1952; Long 1981; Medway & Wells, 1976.

Brown-throated Conure
(Aratinga pertinax)

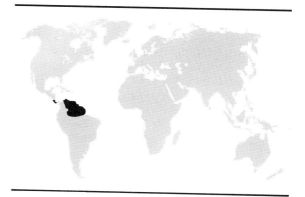

NATURAL DISTRIBUTION
South America from northern Colombia and northern Venezuela south through Guyana, Surinam and French Guiana to north-central Brazil, and the islands of Curaçao, Bonaire, Aruba, Tortuga, Margarita and Los Frailes. A discrete population occurs in western Panama.

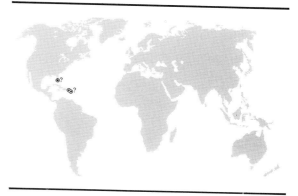

NATURALIZED DISTRIBUTION
North America: ?USA, West Indies (St Thomas, Virgin Islands).

NORTH AMERICA

USA

According to Owre (1973: 494), the Brown-throated Parakeet (= conure) 'is reported to have bred[1] at Key West, Florida [in 1970–1] and there are increasing reports of the species in the Miami area'.

269

West Indies[2]

As early as 1892, Graf von Berlepsch (quoted by Salvadori, 1905–6) indicated that Brown-throated Conures[3] had been introduced to St Thomas in the Virgin Islands; this must have taken place before 1860 when a number of specimens were collected. The species was later reported to be common, but was nearly exterminated by hurricanes in 1926 and 1928. By the early 1960s, when the population had recovered to around 400, the birds had extended their range to much of the island, being most numerous in the east. Although Bond (1979) and the American Ornithologists' Union (1983) say that Brown-throated Conures were introduced to St Thomas from Curaçao, T. Silva (personal communication, 1985) states that they have not been introduced, but have probably arrived as storm-borne vagrants. From St Thomas, the birds have recently spread to eastern Puerto Rico, Culebra, and St John. The form on St Thomas is the same as that on Curaçao – *A. p. pertinax*.

The **Orange-fronted Conure** (*Aratinga canicularis*) of west-central Mexico south to western Costa Rica has, according to Owre (1973: 494), been 'reported from throughout the Miami area [Florida, USA] and from northward along the Atlantic Coastal Ridge', where breeding[4] is suspected. Heilbrun (1976 and 1977) reported that some still occurred in Dade County in southern Florida in 1976–7. Others have been recorded in the wild elsewhere in the United States (e.g. at Santa Ana in southern Texas and in the New York City area), and T. Silva (personal communication, 1985) has 'heard credible reports of it in the drier parts of Puerto Rico (e.g. Fajardo)'.

The American Ornithologists' Union (1983) states that the **Hispaniolan Parakeet** (*Aratinga chloroptera*) has been introduced to, but is not certainly established in, southern Florida and Puerto Rico. T. Silva (personal communication, 1985) says that the species occurring in the wild in Puerto Rico is not *chloroptera* but the northern South American **White-eyed Conure** (*Aratinga leucophthalmus*).

The nominate subspecies of the **Mitred Conure** (*Aratinga mitrata*), which ranges from central Peru to northwestern Argentina, has bred successfully on the island of Puerto Rico.[5]

The **Green Conure** (*Aratinga holochlora*) – a native of Mexico, Nicaragua and Guatemala – established in the Everglades west of Palm Beach and Lake Worth in Florida, USA, where the colony was believed to have existed since at least 1919 (perhaps since around the turn of the century), has probably died out. The species has also nested successfully in the wild near Corpus Christi, Texas.[6]

According to Liversidge (n.d.), the 'Black Headed Conja' (?**Dusky-headed Conure** (*Aratinga weddellii*) from western Amazonia or **Black-capped Conure** (*Pyrrhura rupicola*) from Peru, Brazil and Bolivia) and the 'Jendya Conja' (**Jandaya Conure** (*Aratinga jandaya*)) from northeastern Brazil have been unsuccessfully introduced to South Africa.

NOTES

1 For nesting habits and the feeding of nestlings see under *Amazona ochrocephala* (Yellow-crowned Amazon).

2 American Ornithologists' Union 1983; Blake 1975; Bond 1979; Forshaw 1980; Leopold 1963 (in Forshaw); Long 1981; Nicholls 1943 (in Forshaw); Peters 1937; Salvadori 1905–6.

3 Referred to as 'Caribbean Parakeets' by Blake (1975) and Bond (1979).

4 See note 1.

5 T. Silva, personal communication, 1986.

6 T. Silva, personal communication, 1986.

Nanday Conure
(*Nandayus nenday*)

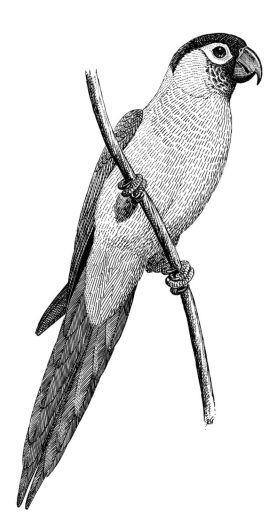

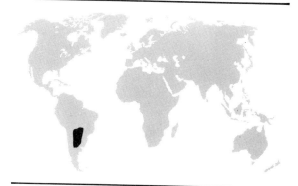

NATURAL DISTRIBUTION
Southeastern Bolivia, Paraguay and northern Argentina.

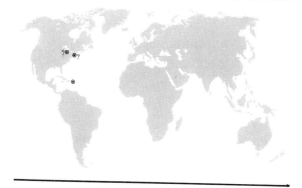

NATURALIZED DISTRIBUTION
North America: ?USA, ?Canada, West Indies (Puerto Rico).

NORTH AMERICA

USA and Canada[1]

Hardy (1973: 507–8) says that 'this South American species has been observed for several years in Loma Linda, San Bernardino County [California]. . . . Local residents reported that two adult birds had been released in 1968 and that they had subsequently been seen with one and then four additional birds thought to be their offspring.' Fisk & Crabtree (1974), who saw four birds in the same district in 1972, say that the colony is derived from birds that escaped from captivity in Yucaipa in 1969. Since then, the population has fluctuated, but was said by Shelgren, Thompson & Palmer (1975) to be stable at between two and five birds. Nanday Conures have been seen in recent years in Pasadena (8–10 birds), West Los Angeles (4–6) and the Palos Verdes Peninsula (2) – all in Los Angeles County – and three that escaped from a roadside zoo near Moss Landing in Monterey County in 1975 were still there 6 years later.

Bull (1973 and 1974) stated that Nanday Conures have escaped into the wild in parts of northern New Jersey (where breeding may have occurred), and that flocks of between 20 and 200 have been reported from around Detroit in Michigan and from across the Canadian border near Windsor, Ontario. Successful breeding has also been reported near Corpus Christi, Texas.[2]

According to the American Ornithologists' Union (1983: 783), 'a small population has apparently become established in recent years at Coney Island, Brooklyn, New York'.

West Indies (Puerto Rico)

According to T. Silva (personal communication, 1985), Nanday Conures are not uncommon in Puerto Rico, where in Mayaguez they associate with White-fronted Amazons (*Amazona albifrons*) and Hispaniolan Amazons (*A. ventralis*).

Three Nanday Conures were observed on Oahu in the Hawaiian Islands in 1973 and one in 1974, but none subsequently.

The **White-eared Conure** (*Pyrrhura leucotis*) is a native of northern Venezuela and eastern Brazil; according to Forshaw (1980), some 20 birds of the nominate form (of eastern and southeastern Brazil), which had been confiscated and later released by fauna authorities in 1971, became well established and quite common in the Botanic Gardens of Rio de Janeiro where, however, they had died out by 1977.[3]

In the early 1930s, an *emigré* Scottish shepherd, Mr John Hamilton, released parrots on some small islands off West Falkland. Since other animals that he introduced at around the same time are known to have come from the extreme south of South America, it seems probable that the parrots, too, came from this region; if this is so the species is likely to have been the **Patagonian Conure** (*Cyanoliseus pathogonus*) or **Austral Conure** (*Enicognathus ferrugineus*); so far as is known the birds never became established in the Falklands.

NOTES
1 Bull 1973, 1974; Fisk & Crabtree 1974; Hardy 1973; Long 1981; Shelgren, Thompson & Palmer 1975.
2 T. Silva, personal communication, 1986.
3 Ridgely 1981.

Monk Parakeet
(*Myiopsitta monachus*)

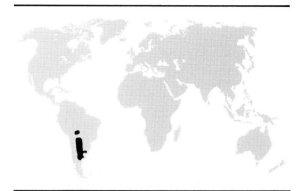

NATURAL DISTRIBUTION
Central and southeastern Bolivia, Paraguay, southern Brazil, northern, central and western Argentina, and Uruguay as far south as the Rio Negro.

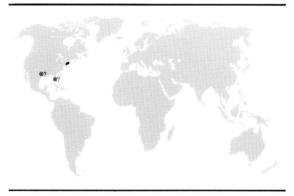

NATURALIZED DISTRIBUTION
North America: USA, West Indies (Puerto Rico).

NORTH AMERICA

USA[1]

Monk or Quaker Parakeets have for many years been a favourite cage bird of amateur aviculturists in the United States; in 1968, 11,745 were imported legally from South America, followed by a further 8,611 in 1969, 14,271 in 1970 and 29,598 in 1971–2 – a total for the 5-year period of 64,225. Further importations were banned in 1972 because of a fear that the birds might introduce Newcastle disease, but two years later this restriction was lifted and importations were recommenced.

The earliest reports of free-flying Monk Parakeets in the United States date from 1967, when some were observed in the wild in the New York metropolitan area, where in 1970 eight nests were found. Near Miami in Florida breeding was recorded in or before 1969. Two years later, a pair bred north of Lansing in Shiawassee County, Michigan, and in 1972 nesting was reported from Columbus, Ohio; Owosso, Michigan; Norman, Oklahoma; Asheville, North Carolina; Northwood, North Dakota; Omaha, Nebraska; and San Fernando Valley, California. Sightings were made in Bradford County, Pennsylvania, at Seaford, Virginia, and in Illinois and Minnesota. In 1973, birds were reported at Huron, Ohio and at Plymouth, Indiana, and were found to be breeding in Dallas, Texas. By the following year, they were said to occur in the wild from Texas, Alabama and Florida in the south northwards to Wisconsin and Cape Elizabeth in Maine.

In southern California, the authorities of the San Diego Zoo irresponsibly released 15 Monk Parakeets in Balboa Park in November 1971; as a result of complaints by local residents and the State Department of Agriculture all but two were subsequently recaptured. A year later, free-flying birds were seen in Los Angeles, Sacramento, San Diego and Orange counties; in the last-named, a flock of 11 (including nine apparent immatures) was reported at Anaheim near Disneyland and another of nine on a golf course in Santa Ana, and breeding was reliably reported in the San Fernando Valley. In 1974, Monk Parakeets were being observed also in San Bernardino, Sonoma, Santa Barbara and Fresno counties. Between 1972 and 1977, some 43 were reported in the wild in California, where between May 1974 and June 1977 at least 17 were killed by county personnel.

In Florida, Monk Parakeets dispersed from their initial nesting site near Miami, and by 1973 were widely but thinly distributed north of the Tamiami Canal, sometimes occurring in association with Canary-winged Parakeets (*Brotogeris versicolurus*).

In Chicago, Illinois, several small flocks totalling some 20–30 birds are breeding in the wild, but T. Silva (personal communication, 1985) suspects that many die during severe winters.

In New York, Monk Parakeets became established in the wild around Binghamton, Waterloo, Owego and Watertown before 1971; by 1973, when all five boroughs of New York City had been colonized, 200 or more were said to be established in the New York City/New Jersey area, with more in southeastern New York where, however, they are since believed to have died out. Others had penetrated upstate as far west as Buffalo and north to Plattsburg near the Canadian border, as well as into adjacent parts of Connecticut and south into Maryland.

All free-flying Monk Parakeets in the United States have been birds that had been deliberately released (including in 1969 a dozen allegedly while in transit at John F. Kennedy Airport, New York) or had accidentally escaped from avicultural collections following the large-scale importations of 1968–72.

By 1973, the popular press was claiming that there were some 4,000–5,000 free-flying Monk Parakeets at large in the United States. Although it is true that by 1975 they had been sighted in the wild in at least 30 states – Keffer (1974a) said in '50% of the 50 United States' – the overall population was far less than the press had claimed; indeed, only 367 were 'confirmed' and 163 killed between 1970 and 1975.

In 1973, the fear of interspecific competition between the progressively increasing aliens (which were reproducing most successfully in the New York metropolitan area) and native species, coupled with the potential risk to man of ornithosis and of Newcastle disease to domestic poultry, allied to the possibility of depredation of agricultural and orchard crops, led to the inauguration of a euphemistically termed 'retrieval' (i.e. eradication) campaign organized by state authorities in cooperation with the national Fish and Wildlife Service. That this operation (which was helped by the species' conspicuous and communal nests/roosts) had an effect is apparent from the reduction in range subsequently reported (by Heilbrun 1976 and 1977), when birds were seen only in Brooklyn and the Lower Hudson, New York; in Lisle Arboretum, Illinois; in Dallas, Texas; and in Fort Lauderdale, Dade County, Tampa and West Palm Beach in Florida. The American Ornithologists' Union (1983: 269) described Monk Parakeets as 'established in the north-eastern United States from southern New York and Connecticut south to New Jersey, with individual reports south and west to Kentucky and Virginia, but the present distribution in

North America is very local and its status in doubt . . . possibly also in Texas (Austin) and southern Florida (Dade County and Key Largo, present status in doubt)'.

The Monk Parakeet is unique in being the only parrot of over 330 species to construct its nest (which is used also for roosting) of sticks, and is one of the few to breed communally. The nest-cum-roost is a huge, globular construction of woven twigs – often more than a metre high and up to the same distance wide – with, in South America, up to a dozen or more individual nests inside, which several pairs of birds, linked by strong behavioural bonds, combine to build. In South America, these structures are usually erected between 7 and 10 m from the ground in tall bushes or trees, and sometimes in *Opuntia* cactus. In the United States, all nests found in California have been in exotic species of palms, but elsewhere the birds have been more eclectic; the spaces between gutters and drainpipes on buildings, window airconditioners, underneath eaves, steel girders, grain elevators, utility poles, the top of a microwave tower over 30 m high, a broken floodlight, a church bell tower and a construction crane – as well as trees – have all been utilized. Frequently, several nests are constructed in close proximity.

In South America, the Monk Parakeet is primarily a lowland species, favouring areas of low precipitation (*c.* 50 cm a year) such as open forests, riverine and savannah woodland, dry *Acacia* scrub, palm groves, farmland and orchards, where it feeds on grain, seeds (especially sunflower), corn (maize), sorghum, millet, rice, fruit (mainly pears, grapes, apples, peaches and citrus species) and insects. Although primarily a sedentary species, Monk Parakeets will travel long distances to reach fields of ripening grain. Losses to a wide variety of agricultural and orchard crops in South America range from 2 per cent to 45 per cent. In Argentina, where they are regarded as a major pest, Monk Parakeets are, in spite of the slaughter of vast numbers by trapping, poisoning, shooting and nest-burning, responsible for an estimated $10 million worth of damage a year.

In the United States, Monk Parakeets are almost omnivorous, eating beetles, grasshoppers, seeds of pine, spruce, sunflower and grasses, *Acacia* and *Mimosa* pods, corn (maize), wheat, sorghum, barley, oats, hemp, *Eucalyptus* buds, passion-vine fruit, and wild and cultivated fruits including citrus species, tomatoes, figs, apricots, apples, persimmons, loquats, pears, plums, grapes, mulberries, peaches and cherries. They prefer urban and suburban rather than rural habitats, where their habit of visiting bird tables in winter for a supplementary diet of butter, cheese, suet, bread, raisins and commercial wild-bird seed may, as in the case of the Ring-necked Parakeet (*Psittacula krameri*) in England, help them to survive the northern winter.

The potential damage Monk Parakeets could cause were they to become widely established in the United States, where both climate and habitat in southern and mid-Atlantic states appear to be suitable, is readily apparent; in California it was calculated in 1972 that depredation to agricultural and orchard crops could exceed $2 million annually – a figure computed by assuming only 0.1 per cent damage to crops whose annual value then amounted to $2 billion. The indigenous but now extinct Carolina Parakeet (*Conuropsis carolinensis*) at one time ranged as far north as North Dakota, Wisconsin, the Great Lakes and New York and, according to Bull & Ricciuti (1974), readily turned when the opportunity arose from its usual diet of wild seeds and fruits to cultivated varieties. Furthermore, although Monk Parakeets are most abundant in the subtropical part of their natural range they easily adapt to sub-zero winter temperatures in the temperate zone, and their survival in the northeastern United States, where winters are colder than in any of their homelands, has been greatly assisted by the readiness with which they accept food from man.

West Indies (Puerto Rico)[2]

Monk Parakeets have been introduced to the island of Puerto Rico, where they nest in coconut palms on the coast in and near the capital city of San Juan, and are said to number several thousand and to be ubiquitous.[3]

In October 1936, 31 Monk Parakeets were released in the grounds of Whipsnade Zoo in Bedfordshire, England,[4] where they survived for several years before being recaptured following complaints of damage to local orchards. They have also been at liberty on a number of occasions in the park of the Duke of Bedford's nearby Woburn Abbey estate. Monk Parakeets are not, *pace* Keffer (1974a), at present naturalized in the British Isles, where the species present is the Ring-necked Parakeet (*Psittacula krameri*).

In the Netherlands, Monk Parakeets are said by Bull (1973) to have bred in the wild in the city parks of Amsterdam.

According to Blake (1975) and Berger (1976), free-flying Monk Parakeets have been observed in the Hawaiian Islands, but have never become established.

In 1984, a pair of Monk Parakeets successfully reared one young at Nyeri in Kenya[5] – the first-known wild breeding record for that country.

The Ornithological Society of Japan's map (1981) indicates that Monk Parakeets have nested successfully in the wild at Osaka on Honshu.

Wingate (1985) records that Monk Parakeets have been observed building nests in Bermuda.

Monk Parakeets have also been reported from the metropolitan area of Barcelona, Spain.

NOTES

1 Anon. 1974a; Banks 1977; Banks & Clapp 1972; Brown & Forbes 1973; Bull 1971, 1973, 1975; Bull & Ricciuti 1974; Bump 1971; Bump 1971 (in Briggs and Hough 1973); Clapp 1975; Clapp & Banks 1973; Davis 1974; Freeland 1973; Hardy 1973; Heilbrun 1976, 1977; Keffer 1974a; Keffer, Davis & Clark 1974; Long 1981; Neidermyer & Hickey 1977; O'Keefe 1973; Owre 1973; Rockwell (in Briggs & Hough 1973); Ryan 1972; Schubert 1973; Simpson 1974; Trimm 1972, 1973.
2 Forshaw 1980; Long 1981; Neidermyer & Hickey 1977.
3 T. Silva, personal communication, 1985.
4 Fitter 1959; Lever 1977a.
5 A. and S. Braguine, personal communication, 1984.

Green-rumped Parrotlet
(*Forpus passerinus*)

NATURAL DISTRIBUTION

Northern Colombia, northern Venezuela and Trinidad south through Guyana, Surinam and French Guiana to northern, north-central and north-eastern Brazil.

NATURALIZED DISTRIBUTION

North America: West Indies (Jamaica, Barbados, ?Curaçao, ?Tobago).

NORTH AMERICA

West Indies (Jamaica, Barbados, Curaçao and Tobago)[1]

Bond (1979:113) says that the Green-rumped Parrotlet was introduced near Old Harbour, Jamaica, in about 1918; since then it has steadily expanded its range, and is 'now widespread in rather open country in lowlands on the southern side of the island'. It also occurs, according to Lack (1976), in natural forests, and in some cultivated localities at slightly higher altitudes.

Green-rumped Parrotlets were introduced to Barbados during the early years of the present century, according to Bond (1979), but are now 'rare and evidently decreasing . . . recently reported from Christchurch and St. Philip'.

Voous (1957, in Forshaw 1980) says that Green-rumped Parrotlets were reported on Curaçao in 1954–5, where they may now be established. Whether they were introduced by human agency or appeared as natural immigrants from Venezuela (a flight of only 75 km) is unknown.

According to Ffrench & Ffrench (1966), a pair of Green-rumped Parrotlets found breeding in the wild on Tobago had certainly been introduced as cagebirds from Trinidad; since then, Ffrench (1973) says that several more have been imported to Tobago, where they may now be established. Possible recruitment to the population by natural dispersants from Trinidad, a little over 35 km to the south-west, cannot be discounted.

Bond (1979) and the American Ornithologists' Union (1983) say that the Green-rumped Parrotlet has been unsuccessfully introduced to Martinique.

NOTE

1 American Ornithologists' Union 1957, 1983; Bond 1979; Lack 1976; Long 1981.

Canary-winged Parakeet
(*Brotogeris versicolurus*)

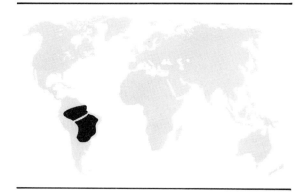

NATURAL DISTRIBUTION
Southeastern Colombia and eastern Ecuador eastwards to southern French Guiana, south through Brazil, Bolivia and Paraguay to northern Argentina.

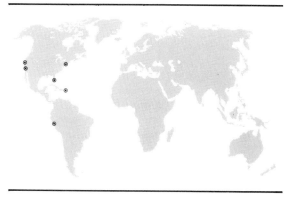

NATURALIZED DISTRIBUTION
North America: USA, West Indies (Puerto Rico); South America: Peru.

NORTH AMERICA

USA[1]

Between 1968 and 1970, a total of 123,721 Canary-winged Parakeets were imported as cage-birds into the United States (32,477 in 1968, 37,150 in 1969 and 54,094 in 1970), and those now apparently well established in the wild in central (Pinellas County) and southern Florida, tenuously near San Francisco in California, and perhaps also on Long Island, New York, are birds that subsequently escaped from captivity or were deliberately released.

In Florida, a flock of 50 free-flying Canary-winged Parakeets was counted at a roost in South Miami as early as 1969. Others were later reported from Upper Matecumbe Key and from the western Everglades, the Everglades National Park, and the Tamiami Trail. In 1970, a small number were observed at Fort Lauderdale, where 2 years later spring flocks of between 40 and 50 were recorded. In December 1972, nearly 700 Canary-winged Parakeets – some in immature plumage – were counted at a roost in Coconut Grove, and the total population in the Miami metropolitan area was estimated to number between 1,500 and 2,000. In 1975, they were recorded at Sarasota, Bradenton, Fort Lauderdale and in Dade County, and in the following year (when 394 were counted in Dade County) also in Naples and Tampa. In 1976, when flocks of several hundred were to be seen around Miami and the species was said to be the commonest parrot in Florida, a single bird was reported at Cape Charlotte on the Gulf of Mexico. Canary-winged Parakeets in Florida are sometimes seen in association with Monk or Quaker Parakeets (*Myiopsitta monachus*). Nests are usually constructed by burrowing into the decaying leaf stalks around the trunks of exotic palms,[2] and depredations on mangoes and other fruits grown in suburban gardens have caused some concern. O. T. Owre says that Canary-winged Parakeets had become 'noticeably more abundant' in Florida in the 1970s, and that the population may now number at least 2,000, and possibly many more.[3]

In California, where Canary-winged Parakeets are said to be locally common on and near the Palos Verdes Peninsula, Los Angeles, a small party of between 10 and 12, which later disappeared, was reported at Pedley in Riverside County in 1971. A year later, when a flock of around 30 was counted at Point Fermin on the coast in San Pedro, southern Los Angeles, and another, where breeding was suspected, in Averill Park, 41 Canary-winged Parakeets were censused during the Audubon Society Christmas Bird Count. Although, according to Bull & Ricciuti (1974), between 40 and 80 were breeding in the San Pedro area by 1974, and Shelgren, Thompson & Palmer (1975) said that a considerable number were nesting in the San Pedro/Palos Verdes Peninsula vicinity, only 29 were counted on the latter in 1976.

Outside the Los Angeles area, Canary-winged Parakeets were recorded in 1973–4 in the Hollywood Hills. Further north, a pair was seen in 1973 at San Mateo, south of San Francisco, and another at Bakersfield in Kern County in the following year. In 1977, a colony of 15 was established at San Francisco and another of only 8 (a fall of 21 since the previous year) on the Palos Verdes Peninsula, Los Angeles. Favourite foods of Canary-winged Parakeets in California include the fruit of such exotic trees as Avocado (*Persea americana*), Primrose Tree (*Laguneria pattersoni*) and Rusty-leaf Fig (*Ficus rubiginosus*), as well as the buds of orange trees (*Citrus* sp.). The birds in California are of the subspecies *chiriri* (northern Bolivia and northern Argentina to eastern and southern Brazil).

According to Bull (1973), flocks of up to 50 Canary-winged Parakeets have been seen on the eastern end of Long Island, New York, where they have successfully overwintered, and on one occasion some were reported from north of Long Island Sound in eastern Connecticut.

West Indies (Puerto Rico)

Bond (1979) says that Canary-winged Parakeets have been introduced to Puerto Rico, where Forshaw (1980) states that a population of several hundred is apparently well established. According to T. Silva (personal communication, 1985), the subspecies is *chiriri* and the population numbers several thousand. They breed in termite nests, some of which may be occupied by more than one pair.

SOUTH AMERICA

Peru[4]

Some time after 1964, Canary-winged Parakeets became established in the wild around the city of Lima, and possibly also in some nearby rural areas. Flocks of up to 10, derived from birds that have escaped from local markets where they are frequently for sale or from private aviculturists, have been recorded.

The **Orange-chinned Parakeet** (*Brotogeris jugularis*) ranges from southwestern Mexico to northern and southeastern Colombia and western and northwestern Venezuela. In 1970, seven were counted in the Dade County (Florida, USA) Christmas Bird Census; Owre (1973: 494) said that they were 'in increasing evidence about Miami'; and Bull & Ricciuti (1974: 54) recorded them as one of the 'members of the parrot family flying free in parts of the United States'. A small number were recorded in Dade County in the 1975 and 1976 Christmas Bird Counts.[5] Free-flying individuals are also from time to time reported in the New York City area. The species has been imported to Hawaii[6] where it has occasionally escaped from captivity on Oahu but has never become established.

According to Blake (1975), the **Tui Parakeet** (*Brotogeris sanctithomae*), a native of central, western and northeastern Brazil, southeastern Colombia and northeastern Peru, has been intro-duced to Florida, USA. Since the species is very rare in aviculture, T. Silva (personal communication, 1985) questions this identification.

NOTES

1 American Ornithologists' Union 1983; Banks & Clapp 1972; Bull 1973; Bull & Ricciuti 1974; Clapp 1975; George 1971 (in Owre 1973); Gore & Doubilet 1976; Hardy 1973; Heilbrun 1976, 1977; Long 1981; Ogden 1969 (in Owre 1973); O'Keefe 1973; O. T. Owre 1973 (and personal communication, 1980); Shelgren, Thompson & Palmer 1975; Shroads 1974; Stevenson 1971 (in Owre 1973).
2 For nesting habits and the feeding of nestlings see under *Amazona ochrocephala* (Yellow-crowned Amazon).
3 Personal communications, 1980 and 1985.
4 American Ornithologists' Union 1983; Forshaw 1980; Koepcke 1970 (in Forshaw 1980); Long 1981.
5 Bizet 1971 (in Owre 1973); Bull, 1973; Heilbrun 1976, 1977; Owre 1973.
6 Berger 1972; Munro 1960.

Green-cheeked Amazon
(*Amazona viridigenalis*)

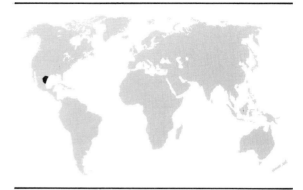

Northeastern Mexico from Nuevo León and Tamaulipas south to northern Veracruz.

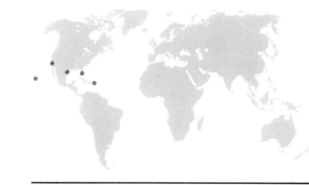

NATURALIZED DISTRIBUTION
North America: USA, West Indies (Puerto Rico); Oceania: Hawaiian Islands.

NORTH AMERICA

USA[1]

Between 1968 and 1972, well over 2,000 Green-cheeked Amazons were imported legally as cage-birds into the United States (and others probably entered illegally), where some inevitably escaped. According to Owre (1973: 494), the species (also known as the Red-crowned Parrot) 'is the most abundant of the amazons now present in south-eastern Florida. These have been reported from the Florida Keys and are commonly seen throughout metropolitan Miami and in Fort Lauderdale. In November 1972 the author counted 32 in a flock feeding in casuarina [*Casuarina* sp.] trees (exotic to Florida) on the University of Miami campus.' Here, in May of the following year, Owre discovered a nest containing two eggs in a hollow in a casuarina.[2] In 1975–6, the birds were still present in Fort Lauderdale, Dade County, and in West Palm Beach, and in the latter year four were reported from near Lantana, south of West Palm Beach. Owre (personal communication 1980) says that in southeastern Florida 'Amazon parrots are increasing in numbers locally'. Some have hybridized with Yellow-crowned Amazons (*Amazona ochrocephala oratrix*) (q.v.).[3]

Hardy (1973: 509) said that in California, where in 1963 he saw a pair or more in north Pasadena near Orange Grove Boulevard and in El Molino Avenue, Green-cheeked Amazons were 'very rare and very local'. The birds are believed to have escaped or been deliberately released during a serious fire that ravaged the Bel-Air district of west Los Angeles in 1961. According to the American Ornithologists' Union (1983), they are currently established and breeding in the San Gabriel Valley, Los Angeles County.

In southern Texas, Green-cheeked Amazons were reported in 1973 in the Rio Grande Delta and also at Madero, and 2 years later a flock of half-a-dozen was said to have been living in Brownsville for more than a year.

West Indies (Puerto Rico)

T. Silva (personal communication, 1985) says that Green-cheeked Amazons that have escaped from captivity are breeding in the wild in Puerto Rico.

OCEANIA

Hawaiian Islands[4]

Since 1970, a small colony of Green-cheeked Amazons – descended from escaped cagebirds – has been established on the island of Oahu.

The **Mexican Lilac-crowned Amazon** (*Amazona finschi*), which is closely related to the Green-cheeked Amazon (with which, according to the American Ornithologists' Union 1983, it constitutes a superspecies), has been introduced to, and may be established in, Los Angeles County in southern California.

The **Hispaniolan Amazon** (*Amazona ventralis*) is, according to Howard & Moore (1980), restricted to the island of Hispaniola, though Bond (1979) and the American Ornithologists' Union (1983) list it also as occurring on Grande Cayemite, Gonâve and Saona.

According to Forshaw (1980), birds captured in the Dominican Republic for sale to aviculturists were refused entry to Puerto Rico, and could not be returned to their country of origin for fear of prosecution; they were accordingly set free off the port of Mayaguez at the western end of Puerto Rico, to which many of them flew and where several hundred are now well established and breeding. Bond says that Hispaniolan Amazons are also reported to have been introduced to Culebra, some 30 km off the eastern end of Puerto Rico, where they may, however, be natural colonists. On at least one occasion in Puerto Rico *ventralis* has hybridized with the introduced **Yellow-winged Amazon** (*Amazona aestiva xanthopteryx*), a native of eastern Brazil, northern and eastern Bolivia, Paraguay, and northern Argentina. Ironically, *ventralis* is declining in its natural range in Hispaniola, but increasing on Puerto Rico.

According to the American Ornithologists' Union (1983), the Hispaniolan Amazon has also been introduced to, and is established on, St Croix and St Thomas in the Virgin Islands.

The **Red-lored Amazon** (*Amazona autumnalis*) is a native of eastern Mexico south to western Ecuador, western Colombia and northwestern Brazil. Hardy (1973) records that from about 1968 to at least 1973 two of these birds lived in the business centre of San Bernardino, California, USA, while another (or the same) two were reported by Fisk & Crabtree (1974) in the residential district of Loma Linda, San Bernardino.

The **White-fronted Amazon** (*Amazona albifrons*), which occurs naturally from northwestern Mexico to northwestern Costa Rica, may, according to Owre (1973), have been breeding at that time in Coral Gables in southeastern Florida, USA, where the same author also reported seeing the free-flying **Orange-winged Amazon** (*Amazona amazonica*), a native of Colombia east to French Guiana (including Trinidad and Tobago), south to northern Bolivia and eastern Brazil. Small numbers of the latter species are also established and breeding in the San Juan area of Puerto Rico.[5]

NOTES

1 American Ornithologists' Union 1983; Banks & Clapp 1972; Clapp 1975; Clapp & Banks 1973; Hardy 1973; Heilbrun 1976, 1977; Long 1981; O. T. Owre 1973 (and personal communication, 1980); Robertson 1972 (in Owre 1973); and T. Silva, personal communication, 1985.

2 For nesting habits and the feeding of nestlings see under *Amazona ochrocephala* (Yellow-crowned Amazon).

3 T. Silva, personal communication, 1985.

4 American Ornithologists' Union 1983; Blake 1975; Hawaiian Audubon Society 1975; Long 1981; Pyle 1976–8.

5 American Ornithologists' Union 1983; and T. Silva, personal communication, 1985.

Yellow-crowned Amazon
(*Amazona ochrocephala*)

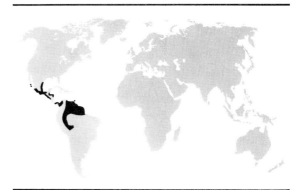

NATURAL DISTRIBUTION
From central Mexico (including Las Tres Marias Islands) south through Panama (including Las Perlas Islands) and Trinidad to the Amazon basin (including Marajo Island), as far west as eastern Peru.

NATURALIZED DISTRIBUTION
North America: ?USA, West Indies (Trinidad, Puerto Rico).

NORTH AMERICA

USA[1]

A serious fire in the Bel-Air district of west Los Angeles, California, in 1961, which destroyed many private aviaries and caused the owners of others to release their stock, is believed to be the origin of many of that city's free-flying Yellow-crowned Amazons. Hardy (1973: 508) reported them to be 'locally fairly common at all seasons . . . in flocks of from two to three to an estimated 30 individuals' over a wide area. A colony of between 2 and about 20 had, since around 1963, been established on either side of Orange Grove Boulevard within a few square kilometres of the intersection with El Molino Avenue in Pasadena. Hardy reported what appeared to be concentrations of the birds in Glendale (four in 1970–1), Alhambra (about 30 in 1970), Pepperdine College (three in 1962), north Pasadena (along Orange Grove Boulevard), Westwood, west Los Angeles, Lomita, San Bernardino, Brentwood, Altadena, Glendora, Ontario, Pomona and Loma Linda.

Preferred foods of Yellow-crowned Amazons in California include Walnuts (*Juglans regia*), the bark of Camphor trees (*Cinnamomum camphorum*), and the fruit and seeds of oranges and tangerines (*Citrus* spp.). Hardy considered that the presence of many exotic species of fruit-bearing trees was undoubtedly a major factor in the survival of the birds in the Los Angeles basin.

The appearance of green-headed subadults as early as 1973 provided strong circumstantial evidence of successful breeding – probably in natural crevices in accumulations of dead fronds on exotic species of palm – though no nest had so far been found. As Hardy pointed out, cavity-nesting *Amazona* parrots (and those of the related genera *Brotogeris* and *Aratinga*) seem to be both relatively inactive and secretive around the nest. They feed their young – by regurgitation – only a few times a day and spend long hours away from and on the nest (thus entailing few visits), from which the young finally emerge almost fully fledged, closely resembling (except, in the case of *A. ochrocephala*, in colour) their parents. Moreover, since feeding by regurgitation also takes place between adults, this activity is not conclusive evidence of breeding.

Elsewhere in the United States, Yellow-crowned Amazons have successfully overwintered in New York, and in 1973 and 1976 respectively small numbers were observed in the Rio Grande Delta and at Southmost Palms in southern Texas. T. Silva (personal communication, 1985) has also seen Yellow-crowned Amazons of the subspecies *oratrix* (southern and southwestern Mexico) in Miami, Florida, where some have hybridized with Green-cheeked Amazons (*A. viridigenalis*) (q.v.).

West Indies (Trinidad and Puerto Rico)

The nominate form of the Yellow-crowned Amazon occurs naturally from western Colombia to Surinam and northern Brazil and on the island of Trinidad. On the last-named, where it is now rare, it has long been kept in captivity by aviculturists from whom, according to Ffrench (1973), it sometimes escapes and reverts to the wild.

Blake (1975) lists *A. ochrocephala* as having been introduced to Puerto Rico; according to T. Silva (personal communication, 1985), the subspecies established is *oratrix*.

Berger (1972) records that in 1969–70 Yellow-crowned Amazons of the race *A. o. auropalliata* (southern Mexico to northwestern Costa Rica) were observed around the base at Diamond Head on Oahu in the Hawaiian Islands, where they apparently failed to become established.

Writing about five **anis** (*Crotophaga* sp.) in the Galápagos Islands in 1980, D. C. Duffy said that 'rumour has it that these birds were deliberately introduced in the vague hope that they might control ticks on cattle'.[2] P. Kramer, however, considered that 'anis seem to have become or are becoming established in the islands. My guess is that they are independent immigrants'.[3]

NOTES
1 Bull 1973; Bull & Ricciuti 1974; Fisk & Crabtree 1974; Hardy 1973; Heilbrun 1976; Long 1981.
2 *Noticias de Galápagos* 33 (1981).
3 *Biological Journal of the Linnean Society* 21: 255 (1984).

Barn Owl
(*Tyto alba*)

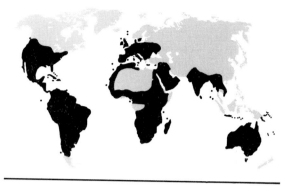

NATURAL DISTRIBUTION
Virtually cosmopolitan; Europe (including Corsica, Sardinia, Sicily, Malta, Crete, Cyprus and the Balearic Islands), Africa (including the Azores, the Canaries, Madeira, the Cape Verde Islands, the Comoros and Madagascar), Arabia, India, Sri Lanka, Burma, northern and central Thailand, Vietnam, Java, the Lesser Sunda Islands, southeastern New Guinea and some adjacent Melanesian islands, Australia, the USA, extreme southern Canada, the West Indies, and Central and South America, including the Galápagos Islands.

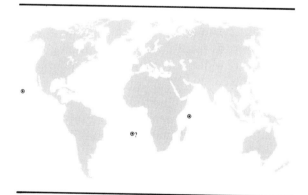

NATURALIZED DISTRIBUTION
Africa: Seychelles, ?St Helena; Oceania: Hawaiian Islands.

AFRICA

Seychelles[1]

In 1949, Barn Owls of the African race *T. a. affinis* were unsuccessfully imported from East Africa to Île Platte (most southerly of the Seychelles) in an attempt to control crop damage caused by introduced Black Rats (*Rattus rattus*)(Lever 1985b). Others from South Africa released on Mahé by the Department of Agriculture in 1951–2 quickly became established, and have since spread to most of the larger islands in the archipelago where, according to Diamond & Feare (1980), they breed regularly on Mahé, Praslin, Silhouette, Cousin and Cousine, and are especially common on the last named. In 1976, they were found also on Aride.[2]

As a biological form of rat control, Barn Owls proved singularly ineffective, preferring to prey instead on more easily captured native birds. On Mahé, Praslin, La Digue and Silhouette, they have contributed to the near eradication of the local race, *Gygis alba monte*, of the White or Fairy Tern, which elsewhere occurs only in Madagascar and the Mascarenes. Diamond & Feare record that on Cousin and Aride (and presumably also on other islands) they take White Terns, Black Noddies (*Anous tenuirostris*), Audubon's Shearwaters (*Puffinus lherminieri*) and Bridled Terns (*Sterna anaethetus*), and doubtless other species. They have also been implicated in the reduction or extinction of the following endemic Seychellois birds: the Sunbird (*Nectarinia dussumieri*), Magpie Robin (*Copsychus sechellarum*), Paradise Flycatcher (*Terpsiphone corvina*), Black Parrot (*Coracopsis nigra barklyi*), Turtle Dove (*Streptopelia picturata rostrata*), Blue Pigeon (*Alectroenas pulcherrima*), White-Eye (*Zosterops modesta*), Bare-legged Scops Owl (*Otus insularis*), Fody (*Foudia sechellarum*), Brush Warbler (*Nesillas (Bebrornis) sechellensis*) and Kestrel (*Falco araea*). The last-named species, which has been preyed on by feral Cats (*Felis catus*) and Black Rats and has suffered loss of habitat through the replacement of native forest by coconut plantations, has been subjected to fierce competition for nesting and roosting sites by the larger and more aggressive Barn Owl.

Largely as a result of the findings of the 1964 Bristol University Expedition, a bounty was placed on the Barn Owl's head in the Seychelles, where the consequences of its introduction to control rats are comparable, albeit on a lesser scale, to those of the Small Indian Mongoose (*Herpestes auropunctatus*) introduced for the same purpose in the West Indies (Lever 1985b).

St Helena[3]

A species of owl, which may have been the Barn Owl, is believed to have been introduced to St Helena from South Africa by the island's earliest Agricultural Officer (presumably as a form of pest control) some time before 1937 when breeding was confirmed. **African Scops Owls** (*Otus senegalensis latipennis*) or **White-faced Scops Owls** (*O. leucotis granti*) may also occur on St Helena. As the island lies less than 2,000 km from the African mainland, and as both Barn and Scops Owls are partially migratory, the natural arrival of both species is not impossible.

OCEANIA

Hawaiian Islands[4]

In April, June and October 1958, 15 Barn Owls of the North American subspecies *T. a. pratincola* were imported from California by the State Department of Agriculture and released at Kukuihaele on Hawaii, in an attempt to control damage caused to sugarcane plantations by introduced Black Rats. Between April 1959 and June 1963, a further 71 from California and Texas were turned down, including 36 at Kukuihaele; 18 on 10 June 1959 at Kilohana, 2 on 3 November 1961 in the Waimea Valley, 4 on 10 May 1963 at Mana, and 4 on 4 June 1963 in the Kekaha Sugar Company's plantations – all on Kauai. Others were planted at Hauula on Oahu, and on the Molokai Ranch in western Molokai.

Tomich (1962) reported that on Hawaii Barn Owls had spread from the Hamakua coast 'at least 24 miles [38.6 km] toward Hilo (Laupahoehoe) and 5 miles [8 km] toward Kohala (Waimanu Valley)', and had also been seen near Puu Waawaa 'some 30 miles [48 km] southwest of Kukuihaele'. Although by June 1965 27 of the 28 owls released on Kauai had been found ill, injured or dead, some 35 sightings of live and apparently healthy birds in 1965–6 indicated that they were established and breeding over much of Kauai, especially around Kilohana and in lowland areas. Unfortunately, as Tomich points out, the 'imported owls were not banded so they cannot be distinguished from those which may have hatched'. 'This', Berger (1981) rightly concludes, 'seems another example of the haphazard way in which introductions are still being made in Hawaii.'

In 1971, Tomich examined 104 regurgitated Barn Owl pellets,[5] of which 91 contained only the remains of alien House Mice (*Mus musculus*) – some holding bones of as many as nine separate mice. Only nine pellets included remnants of Black Rats, and as Berger has said, 'the known spread of the Barn Owl in Hawaii to grazing land and into forested areas suggests . . . that this species has done no more good in controlling rats in the sugarcane fields than did the mongooses'.

Zeillemaker & Scott (1976) recorded Barn Owls in agricultural land and pastures and introduced (Guava (*Psidium guajava*), Java Plum (*Eugenia cumini*) and *Eucalyptus*) and native ohia (*Metrosideros collina*) and koa (*Acacia koa*) forests on Kauai, Molokai and Hawaii (where they were uncommon), on Oahu (rare), and possibly also on Lanai and Maui. They also occur on Kahoolawe.

In view of the damage wrought by Barn Owls on the avifauna of the Seychelles, and the potential harm they could cause to small endemic birds and to the Hawaiian Owl (*Asio flammeus sandvicensis*), the local race of the Short-eared Owl, their introduction to the Hawaiian Islands seems particularly ill-judged.

In December 1899 the Otago Acclimatization Society imported seven Barn Owls from London to New Zealand,[6] which were liberated at West Taieri where they soon disappeared. Individuals of the Australian form *T. a. delicatula* (presumably natural vagrants) have been recorded at Westland on the west coast of South Island in 1947, at Haast in 1955 and at Runanga in 1960. From subfossil evidence it seems possible that Barn Owls may once have been part of the indigenous avifauna of New Zealand.

When the SS *Makambo* grounded on Lord Howe Island[7] (600 km off the east coast of Australia) in 1918, Black Rats swam ashore and were soon devastating the island's birdlife (Lever 1985b). Between 1922 and 1930, 100 owls of three species were released in an unsuccessful attempt to eradicate the rats; these were Barn Owls of the Australian and possibly the American races, the **Tasmanian Masked Owl** (*Tyto novaehollandiae castanops*) and the **Boobook Owl** (*Ninox novaeseelandiae boobook*) from eastern Australia. Barn Owls are said to have died out by 1936,[8] and the only known surviving species, the Masked Owl, has had no apparent effect on the rat population but preys instead on the local race (*candida*) of the White or Fairy Tern and on other sea birds.

According to Condon (1975), the Barn Owl is probably a natural colonist in Tasmania, where it was first recorded in 1910 and is today rare.

Wingate (1973) says that the Barn Owl was 'first recorded on Bermuda in 1931 and [is] now fairly common and very valuable as a rat predator. Barn Owls breed and roost in holes of coastal cliffs and caves throughout the Island'. The birds almost certainly arrived in Bermuda as natural colonists from the eastern United States – a distance of around 1,000 km.

Why Barn Owls should have succeeded so well in controlling rats in Bermuda but failed in the Seychelles and Hawaii (where they were introduced for that specific purpose) is uncertain; it may be that the greater size and more varied habitats of the two latter archipelagos gave them the opportunity to disperse into areas where the abundance of small birds offered easier (and less retaliatory) prey.

NOTES

1 Blackman 1965; Diamond & Feare 1980; Lever 1985b; Long 1981; Penny 1974; Roots 1976. (Roots, p. 139, incorrectly says that Barn Owls were 'liberated on the Seychelles during the nineteenth century'.) See also: Fisher, Simon & Vincent 1969 and King 1981.
2 C. J. Feare, personal communication, 1986.
3 Benson 1950; Haydock 1954; Long 1981.
4 American Ornithologists' Union 1983; Au & Swedberg 1966; Berger 1981; Blake 1975; Long 1981; Peterson 1961; Pyle 1976, 1977; Roots 1976; Tomich 1962; Zeillemaker & Scott 1976.
5 All but the largest prey of owls is normally swallowed whole without being picked or plucked; the

indigestible parts, such as bones, fur and feathers, are subsequently disgorged in the form of pellets.

6 Condon 1975; Falla, Sibson & Turbott 1979; Long 1981; Thomson 1922.

7 Hindwood & Cunningham 1950; Lever 1985b; Long 1981; McKean & Hindwood 1965; Recher & Clark 1974; Roots 1976.

8 The American Ornithologists' Union (1983), however, indicates that Barn Owls of both forms are still established on Lord Howe Island where, since there is apparently no evidence of inter-breeding, the Australian birds may constitute a separate species, *Tyto delicatula* (Gould 1837).

Great Horned Owl
(*Bubo virginianus*)

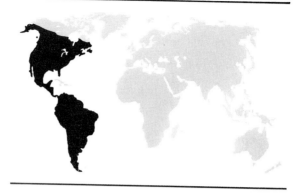

NATURAL DISTRIBUTION
The entire Nearctic and Neotropical regions south of about 55° to 65° N, apart from the West Indies and some other offshore islands.

NATURALIZED DISTRIBUTION
Oceania: Marquesas Islands.

OCEANIA

Marquesas Islands[1]

In his journal for December 1927, Mgr. Le Cadre records that he had acquired eight Great Horned Owls from San Francisco (presumably, therefore, either *B. v. saturatus* or *B. v. pacificus*) at a price of $8 '*combattre l'invasion des rats*' on the island of Hiva Oa – largest of the more southerly Mendaña group in the Marquesas archipelago. The owls have become fairly abundant on Hiva Oa, but fortunately have not gained access to the neighbouring islands of Tabuata (Tahuata) and Mohotani (Motane).

In their natural range, Great Horned Owls occur in a wide variety of habitats from taiga to deserts and forests; on Hiva Oa, they frequent both coastal regions and the hinterland up to an altitude of at least 1,000 m. They are believed to nest on cliff faces and are not shy in approaching settled areas to capture domestic poultry; elsewhere on Hiva Oa they have probably been responsible for the decline of the nominate subspecies of the endemic White-capped Fruit Dove (*Ptilinopus dupetithouarsii*). Although mainly nocturnal, they sometimes emerge from their perches among rocks or in trees and visit villages in broad daylight. Their nocturnal call is a series of between three and eight deep ululations.

The **Eagle Owl** (*Bubo bubo*) occurs throughout most of the Palaearctic region and in India and China. Since before 1964 captive-bred birds of the nominate European subspecies have been reintroduced to montane forests at Kilsbergen, Närke, in southern Sweden,[2] and since 1971 others have been released in the Vosges and Jura Mountains of Alsace, where the species disappeared in the early 1900s. Eagle Owls have also been reintroduced in the northern Eifel Mountains of West Germany.

NOTES

1 Holyoak & Thibault 1984; Peters 1940.
2 Broo 1978; Curry-Lindahl 1964; Long 1981; Wayre 1966.

Little Owl
(Athene noctua)

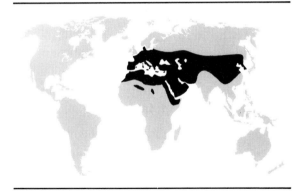

NATURAL DISTRIBUTION

The entire Palaearctic region north to around 57° N in Denmark in western Europe and to about 45–50° N in Manchuria in northeastern China; also northeastern Africa (eastern Sudan, northeastern and eastern Ethiopia and Somalia), parts of the Sahara Desert and Arabia.

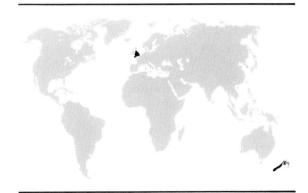

NATURALIZED DISTRIBUTION

Europe: British Isles; Australasia: New Zealand.

EUROPE

British Isles[1]

According to Linn (1979: 9), 'The Little Owl . . . [is] recorded from interglacial deposits in the British Isles'. The first, but unsuccessful, attempt to establish (or re-establish) it was made in 1842 or 1843 by Charles Waterton, an eccentric but engaging naturalist, who released five that he had brought back from Italy in his park at Walton Hall in Yorkshire. Liberations in Sussex and

Norfolk in 1876 also failed, but E.G.B. Meade-Waldo achieved limited success with some 40 birds that he freed in Kent between 1874 and 1880, which were followed by a further 25 in 1896 and again in 1900.

Principal credit, however, for the naturalization of the Little Owl in Britain belongs to that great ornithologist Lord Lilford, who between 1888 and 1890 successfully turned down a considerable number from Holland (*A. n. vidalii*) in the grounds of his estate near Oundle in Northamptonshire. Little Owls released in Hertfordshire and Yorkshire in about 1890 and in the latter county again around 1905 failed to become established, but others freed in Sussex in 1900–1, in Essex in 1905 and 1908, and in Hampshire and Yorkshire, met with some success.

Although initially Little Owls were slow in gaining a foothold in Britain (by the turn of the century they were breeding regularly only in Kent, Northamptonshire, Bedfordshire and Rutland), their subsequent spread – partially accelerated by the successful post-1900 plantings – was remarkably rapid. By 1910, they had travelled west as far as the River Severn and north to the River Trent, and by the following decade occurred in every county of England and Wales south of the River Humber apart from Cornwall and west Devon in England and Caernarvonshire and northern Denbighshire in north Wales, which were, however, colonized by about 1930 at the same time as north Yorkshire, Durham and southern Northumberland. Westmorland, Cumberland and northern Northumberland were reached in the 1940s and early 1950s. Even as late as the early 1970s, however, there were few breeding records from Scotland (none of which were north of Midlothian) and the species has still not colonized either the Isle of Man or Ireland.

While Little Owls were still spreading north in the 1940s they were apparently declining in some southern and western counties, possibly as a result of some exceptionally harsh winters during that decade. Between 1956 and 1965, they also noticeably decreased in southeastern England, perhaps due to contamination of their prey by long-residual toxic pesticides. By the 1970s, they seemed to be staging a modest recovery in the west, but in the south were apparently still less abundant than in the early 1950s.

During the 1930s, when the Little Owl was rapidly expanding its range, it was roundly condemned by ill-informed gamekeepers, landowners and farmers, and even by such respected biologists as C. B. Ticehurst, T. A. Coward and Professor James Ritchie, because of its alleged predation on game-bird chicks and domestic poultry. As a result of these accusations, the newly formed British Trust for Ornithology commissioned Alice Hibbert-Ware in 1936 to make a detailed study of the Little Owl's diet.[2] She found that the bulk consisted of (largely injurious) insects, with lesser numbers of other invertebrates, mammals (including such pests as introduced House Mice (*Mus musculus*), Brown Rats (*Rattus norvegicus*) and young Rabbits (*Oryctolagus cuniculus*)) and small birds; game-bird chicks and domestic poultry were only very rarely taken. Indeed, of the 60 or so alien vertebrates at present naturalized in the British Isles, the Little Owl is the only one that can be regarded as actively beneficial to man.

A major factor that contributed to the success of the Little Owl in becoming established in the British Isles (on the northwestern edge of its natural range) was the existence of an empty ecological niche for a mainly diurnal and largely insectivorous small bird of prey.

AUSTRALASIA

New Zealand[3]

In 1906, the Otago Acclimatization Society imported 28 Little Owls from Germany[4] (presumably *vidalii* or *noctua*), half of which were released at Ashley Downs, Waiwera, and half at Alexandra. In the following year, a further 39 were brought in and turned down at Alexandra, and in 1908, when several of the birds introduced in 1906 were reported to have bred successfully, a third consignment of 80 was distributed to various localities including Rotorua where a pair was released but soon disappeared; this last was the only recorded liberation in North Island. In 1910, a fourth shipment of 72 birds arrived in New Zealand, 14 of which were released and the remainder sold to farmers and orchardists by whom they were liberated in North Canterbury and elsewhere.

By about 1915–16, Little Owls were reported to be established in a number of districts, including Wendon, Pyramid Hill, Skippers, Wyndham, Galloway Station in Central Otago, the Taieri Plain, Kaitangata, Invercargill and Hawera. Thomson (1922: 140) reported that Little Owls had become 'firmly established in the south portion of the South Island [where] they are now quite common round Dunedin'.

Little Owls were released in New Zealand to prey on the various species of alien birds that had been introduced to control insect pests but which were, instead, themselves proving a nuisance in crop-growing districts of Otago. Although by 1909, according to Thomson (p. 138), 'several fruit growers in Central Otago reported them as having proved already a great boon to their orchards' – a marked contrast to the attitude shown to the species in England – the relief seems to have been short-lived because, despite the continued presence of Little Owls, small birds are still a nuisance to orchardists, horticulturists and farmers in both Otago and Canterbury. Although Oliver (1955) suggested that Little Owls may have been implicated in the considerable decline of such native birds as Collared Grey Fantails (*Rhipidura fuliginosa*), Bellbirds (*Anthornis melanura*), Tomtits (*Petroica macrocephala*) and Grey Flyeaters (*Gerygone igata*), Marples's (1942) study of their diet revealed that, as in the British Isles, insects are the major constituent, and that small birds comprise only about 8 per cent of the total food intake. Williams (1969: 443) nevertheless considered that 'The contribution of Little Owls to the useful destruction of insects is as doubtful as their alleged useful effects in abating the small bird nuisance'. According to Druett (1983), there is evidence that Little Owls in New Zealand have flourished at the expense of the native Boobook Owl or Morepork (*Ninox novaeseelandiae*), with which they compete for food.

By 1955, Oliver reported that Little Owls were abundant from central Canterbury south to Foveaux Strait, had spread into North Canterbury and had been recorded in Nelson and Marlborough and on Stewart Island. Wodzicki (1965: 433) described them as 'widely distributed and common, South Island'. Kinsky (1970) reported Little Owls to be widespread throughout South Island (including Marlborough) east of the ranges, and that they were spreading into Westland. Sometime before 1966, some were taken to North Island, where they were shortly afterwards recorded at Butterfly Creek (Wellington), Te Marua, Otaki, Ohau, Waitohu, Palmerston North and as far north as Rotorua. Falla, Sibson & Turbott (1979) said that Little Owls were established in South Island east of the main range from Puysegur Point in Southland northwards to Marlborough and Golden Bay, and that they had recently colonized Westland where they were probably increasing; their status in North Island is uncertain.

NOTES

1 Ainslie 1907; Blathwayt 1902, 1904; Bradshaw 1901; Burton 1973; Buxton 1907; Ellison 1907; Fitter 1959, 1967; Hibbert-Ware 1937–8; Lever 1977, 1982a, 1985c; Lilford 1895, 1903; Marples 1907; Ritchie 1920; Roots 1976; Scott 1967; Sharrock 1976; Steele-Elliot 1907; Waterton 1871; Witherby et al. Vol. 2, 1938; Witherby & Ticehurst 1908. See also: R. Aldington, *The Strange Life of Charles Waterton* (Evans: London, 1949), 156–7.
2 See also: W. E. Collinge, 'The food and feeding habits of the Little Owl', *Journal of the Ministry of Agriculture* 28: 1022–31 (1921–2).
3 Falla, Sibson & Turbott 1979; Kinsky 1970, 1973; Long 1981; Marples 1942; Oliver 1955; Thomson 1922, 1926; Williams 1969, 1973; Wodzicki 1965.
4 Hence the alternative name in New Zealand of 'German Owl'.

Edible-nest Swiftlet
(*Collocalia inexpectata*)

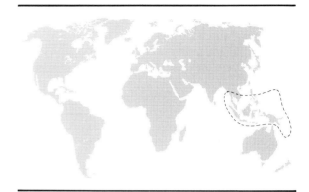

Note: Dashed line encloses the species' approximate natural range; the western extremity is uncertain.

NATURAL DISTRIBUTION
Because of problems of classification, the natural distribution of this species is uncertain. It probably ranges eastwards from the Andaman and Nicobar islands through southern Burma, Tenasserim, Thailand, Malaysia, Palawan, the southern Philippines, Con Ton Island, Annam and Tonkin to the Marianas in the north and the Sunda Islands in the south, and may extend further east to include New Guinea, the Solomon Islands, and New Caledonia.

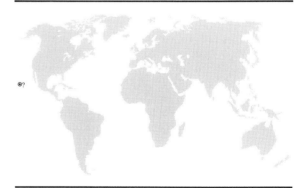

NATURALIZED DISTRIBUTION
Oceania: ?Hawaiian Islands.

OCEANIA

Hawaiian Islands[1]

On 15 May 1962, between 125 and 175 Edible-nest Swiftlets[2] were released, for aesthetic purposes and for no better reason than that the Apodidae are not represented in the Hawaiian archipelago, in the lower Niu Valley on Oahu by David Woodside of the State Division of Fish and Game. According to Bowles (1962):

The birds were collected by mist net on Guam [in the Marianas, where the local subspecies is *bartshi*] and flown to Hawaii where they were released in one large mass at about 3.0 p.m. All of the birds survived the trip. There was also a broken egg found in the crate. A previous sample of 12 birds had been thoroughly studied for parasites etc. and all tests showed negative. The project was sponsored and paid for by the Hui Manu [Bird Society] organization in Honolulu.

On 29 January 1965, Woodside freed a further 200 – also from Guam – at Waimen Falls in Waimea Valley on Oahu, where they all disappeared. In November 1969, however, a group of half-a-dozen was seen in the North Halawa Valley, where later a colony of some 25 was found. Berger (1981) records that two were seen near the summit of the Pali in Moanalua Valley in August 1975, and in the following June two more were noted in North Halawa Valley, where several were reported in September 1977. In January 1978, old nests were discovered in a cave in the upper North Halawa Valley, and in the following July two birds were seen on the Manana trail.[3] Samuelson (1985) reported a sighting in Kahaluu Valley. The species' present status on Oahu is uncertain.

All members of the Apodidae possess considerably enlarged salivary glands; the nests of *Collocalia* swiftlets of the Indo-Australasian region are constructed primarily of saliva, which agglutinates nests to the walls and roofs of caves; it is these nests, the most prized of which are those built by *C. inexpectata*, that are eaten by man, mainly as 'bird's-nest soup'.[4]

According to Sick (1968), unsuccessful attempts have been made to re-establish large numbers of **hummingbirds** (Trochilidae) in Brazil (Volieren), and since 1956 also in Peru, Ecuador and Venezuela.

NOTES

1 Berger 1981; Blake 1975; Bowles 1962; Donaggho 1970; Hawaiian Audubon Society 1975; Long 1981; Pyle 1977; Samuelson 1985.

2 The nomenclature of this species is confusing; it has been variously described as *C. inexpectata*, *C. vanikorensis*, *C. esculenta*, *Aerodramus fuciphagus*, or the Gray Swiftlet (*A. vanikorensis*).

3 *Elepaio* 39:18 (1979).

4 N. Langham, 'Breeding biology of the Edible-nest Swiftlet *Aerodramus fuciphagus*', *Ibis* 122: 447–61 (1980); Lord Medway, 'The antiquity of trade in edible birds' nests', *Federations Museums Journal*, series 2, 27: 36–47 (1963); C. C. Wang, 'The composition of Chinese edible birds'-nests and the nature of their proteins', *Journal of Biological Chemistry* 49: 429–38 (1921).

Laughing Kookaburra

(Dacelo novaeguineae)[1]

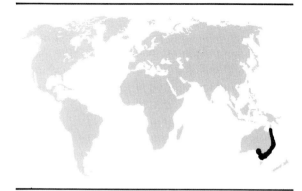

NATURAL DISTRIBUTION

Eastern Australia from the central Cape York Peninsula in northern Queensland south through New South Wales to Victoria, and westwards to the Eyre Peninsula in South Australia.

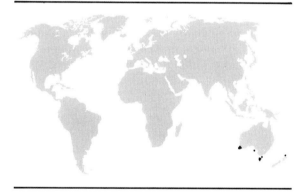

Note: Map includes successful translocations in and around Australia.

NATURALIZED DISTRIBUTION

Australasia: New Zealand.

AUSTRALASIA

New Zealand[2]

According to Thomson (1922), the Canterbury Acclimatization Society acquired two pairs of Laughing Kookaburras (largest of the kingfishers) from a Mr Wilkin in 1864, but what became of them is unknown. Thomson also says (p. 137) that, in *Station Life in New Zealand* (London, 1870:16), Lady Barker states that on her voyage from Melbourne to New Zealand on the *Albion* in 1865 one of her fellow-passengers was travelling with a consignment of birds – 'chiefly laughing jackasses';[3] again, there is no record of what happened to them. In 1866 and 1869, the Otago Society liberated four and two, respectively, near the Silverstream, where they remained for a time but eventually disappeared. In 1867, the Nelson Society imported some and a year later the Auckland Society received one from a Dr Stratford – but once more their fate is unrecorded. In 1876 and 1879, 14 and 1 Laughing Kookaburras, respectively, were released by the Wellington Society; one was seen as late as 1885 but apparently none thereafter.

In the early 1860s, Sir George Grey released some Laughing Kookaburras on Kawau Island in Hauraki Gulf, Central Auckland, where according to Thomson they all died. In 1916, however, Thomson was told that a few were still to be found on the east coast near Auckland, and Oliver (1930 and 1955) indicates that Sir George Grey's introduction was the only successful one in New Zealand, and that from Kawau some crossed to the nearby mainland coast where they were common in the late 1920s; by the mid-1950s, they were apparently established in North Auckland from Whangarei to the Waitakerei Ranges and also on Kawau Island. Wodzicki (1965: 433) described Laughing Kookaburras as 'Locally rare, North Island', and Kinsky (1970) found them to be established on Kawau Island and on the adjacent mainland – principally between Auckland and Whangarei. Falla, Sibson & Turbott (1979) said that a small but apparently fairly stable population survived among the creeks and islands between Cape Rodney and the Whangaparaoa Peninsula along the western coast of the Hauraki Gulf. Wanderers are also sometimes seen on Little Barrier Island. Some may also occasionally arrive naturally as wind-blown vagrants from Australia.

———————————

According to Blackburn (1971), Laughing Kookaburras were unsuccessfully introduced to Fiji before 1926.

———————————

On the Australian mainland, Laughing Kookaburras have been successfully transplanted to the south-west of Western Australia, and also to Kangaroo and Flinders islands (off the coast of South Australia and in Bass Strait, respectively), and to Tasmania.

Serventy & Whittell (1951, 1962 and 1967) and Long (1972 and 1981) have traced the establishment of Laughing Kookaburras in Western Australia.[4] The earliest release took place before 1896 (Roots (1976:138) incorrectly says 1898) when some were seen in the Mullewa area. Between 1897 and 1912, several hundred were obtained from Victoria by the Director of the Zoological Gardens in South Perth and from the state's Acclimatization Society, by whom they were apparently released in several areas. They were well established in several places before 1912, and by the 1920s were becoming fairly common between the Darling Range and the coast. By the mid-1960s, they had spread into forested districts in the south-west from Albany (380 km southeast of Perth) and Bald Island in the south northwards to Jurien Bay – 200 km north of Perth. Beyond Moora, Bolgart and the Great Southern Railway they occurred only as occasional wanderers, but were from time to time reported further inland – for example, from Kellerberrin, Nangeenan, Lakes Grace and Holt, Holt Rock, Gnowangerup, Borden, Dangin and Kweda: at the last two places they may now be established – as they have recently become at Dudinin east of Wickepin – and may soon colonize Ravensthorpe. According to Serventy & Whittell, Laughing Kookaburras were probably independently transplanted to the Mingenew and Irwin districts where they have been seen as far south as Arramel (32 km south of Dongarra), and at Stockyard and Cockleshell gullies. In Western Australia, Kookaburras are alleged to kill small native birds and domestic poultry chicks.

In January 1926, two pairs of Laughing Kookaburras were released on Kangaroo Island,[5] where their descendants are known to have survived until at least 1969 and where some probably still remain.

According to Condon (1975), the Laughing Kookaburra has been transplanted from the mainland to Flinders Island.

In 1902, W. McGowan released some Laughing Kookaburras in Tasmania[6] where they failed to become established; 3 years later, others were successfully liberated in several parts of northern Tasmania and on Waterhouse Island off the north-east coast, from where they have spread to eastern and southern Tasmania.

NOTES

1 Synonymous with *Dacelo gigas*.
2 Falla, Sibson & Turbott 1979; Kinsky 1970; Long 1981; Oliver 1930, 1955; Roots 1976; Thomson 1922; Williams 1973; Wodzicki 1965.
3 A synonym for Kookaburra.

4 See also: Glauert 1956; Jenkins 1959, 1977; Kingsmill 1920; Le Souef 1912; Roots 1976.
5 Anon. 1948; Basten 1971 (in Abbott 1974); Long 1981.
6 Jenkins 1959, 1977; Long 1981; Pollard 1967; Ridpath & Moreau 1965; Roots 1976.

Great Kiskadee
(*Pitangus sulphuratus*)

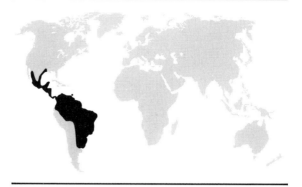

NATURAL DISTRIBUTION

Southern Texas and northern Mexico south through central America to Colombia, Venezuela, Trinidad, the Guianas, northeastern Peru, eastern Ecuador, northern, eastern and central Brazil, Bolivia, Paraguay and northern Argentina from La Pampa and Mendoza east to Buenos Aires.

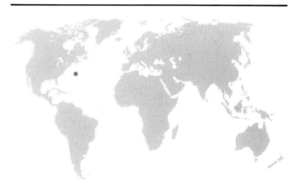

NATURALIZED DISTRIBUTION

North America: Bermuda.

NORTH AMERICA

Bermuda[1]

The introduction of the Great Kiskadee to Bermuda is a classic example of the folly of releasing one animal as a biological controlling agent of another without having previously carried out preliminary research into the likely consequences.

In 1905, a West Indian lizard, *Anolis grahami*, was introduced to Bermuda from Jamaica by the then Director of Agriculture 'to control the Mediterranean fruit fly'. In about 1946, a scale insect, *Carulaspis minima*, was accidentally imported in a cargo of nursery plants; within 3 years it had killed almost half the islands' endemic Bermuda Cedars (*Juniperus bermudiana*), and by 1951, 85 per cent had been destroyed. In an attempt to save the remaining trees, the Bermuda government imported predatory Coleoptera (ladybirds, *Coccinella* spp.) and parasitic Hymenoptera, which it was hoped would prey on the scale insects and aphids. By then, unfortunately, *Anolis grahami* was so abundant that, with the help of two other alien lizards, *A. roquet* from Barbados and *A. leachii* from Antigua (believed to have been released from British naval ships in about 1940), and two species of ant (which were themselves in turn eaten by lizards), they prevented the introduced insects from becoming established.

On the recommendation of F. J. Simmonds of the Commonwealth Bureau of Biological Control, and in spite of protestations from island conservationists, some 200 Great Kiskadees – large Tyrant Flycatchers – from the Port of Spain area of Trinidad (*P. s. trinitatis*) were released between April and mid-summer 1957 near the Aquarium and in the Botanic Gardens on Bermuda by the Department of Agriculture and Fisheries, in the hope that they would control the lizards. The fact that Kiskadees are adaptable, generalized, opportunistic and catholic feeders was apparently either overlooked or ignored. The birds dispersed from their release sites into nearby mangrove swamps, sheltered valleys with watercourses and places with plenty of shade trees, where they multiplied rapidly, became widely distributed, and within a decade were Bermuda's third or fourth most abundant and, with their striking plumage and harsh call, most conspicuous bird.

A survey carried out in the early 1960s showed that *Anolis* lizards formed a minor (less than 10 per cent) part of the Kiskadees' diet, which comprised mainly berries, vegetables, fish, and eggs of native birds. A decline in such terrestrial species as the endemic White-eyed Vireo (*Vireo griseus bermudianus*) (known locally as the 'Chick-of-the-village'), the Eastern Bluebird (*Sialia sialis*) and the alien Common Cardinal (*Cardinalis cardinalis*) that occurred at about this time was attrib-

uted at least partially to competition for food and to predation of their eggs and young by Kiskadees, although probably it was largely the result of habitat loss from urban development. Because of their noisy and raucous call (which has been likened to the French '*Qu'est-ce qu'il dit?*', from which is derived the bird's onomatopoeic name), Kiskadees are regarded as an environmental nuisance, and their depredations on soft fruits makes them a pest to orchardists in Bermuda, where they were removed from the list of protected birds in 1963.

In the summers of 1973 and 1974, Dr David E. Samuel conducted a second survey of the Kiskadee's feeding habits. Analysis of the contents of 57 stomachs revealed the remains of noctuid (owlet moth) larvae in 7, Surinam cherries in 14, seeds of the Chinese Fan Palm in 7, and intertidal organisms in 6; some crabs and gastropods were also present – but no lizards. Alleged predation of fish (*Gambusia* sp.) released in mangrove swamps to control mosquito larvae was also reported. The 1975–7 population was estimated at between 40,000 and 60,000 (with a density of up to 8–10 pairs per hectare), which a decade later had increased to around 100,000, spread over the islands' 54.5 km².

The **Superb Lyrebird** (*Menura (superba) novaehollandiae*),[2] a native of southeastern Australia from southeastern Queensland to eastern Victoria, has been successfully transplanted to Tasmania. Accounts differ as to the precise numbers involved and the dates they were transferred: between 1934 (when some were released in the southwest slightly east of Five Mile Post on the road between the entrance to the Mount Field National Park and Lake Dobson) and 1949, 11 pairs of the nominate form were imported from Victoria (13 of which were brought in between 1934 and 1941), of which one died in captivity. Half-a-dozen were freed at Hastings in the southeast in 1945, and the remaining pair in the National Park. By 1943–4, the birds were well established in both localities, and in the early 1960s were said to be spreading slightly.

NOTES

1 American Ornithologists' Union 1983; Blake 1975; K.L. Crowell 1962 (and personal communication, 1981); Crowell & Crowell 1976; Long 1981; D. E.

Samuel 1975 (and personal communication, 1981);
D. B. Wingate 1973 (and personal communication, 1981).
2 Long 1981; Pollard 1967; Ridpath & Moreau 1965; Sharland 1944; Slater 1974; Wall & Wheeler 1966.

Skylark
(*Alauda arvensis*)

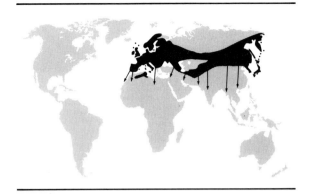

NATURAL DISTRIBUTION
From northern Scandinavia south to the Iberian Peninsula in western Europe, and from the British Isles eastwards through the southern and central USSR, · Asia Minor, western Siberia, central Asia, northern Iran and Afghanistan, and northwestern India to China, Taiwan, Sakhalin Island, Korea, Japan and the Kuril and Ryukyu islands. Also in north-west Africa (northern Morocco, Algeria, Tunisia and northwestern Libya). In parts of their range Skylarks migrate south in winter. Following land clearance for agricultural purposes, Skylarks have greatly expanded their range on the southern edge of the taiga[1] in western Siberia.[2]

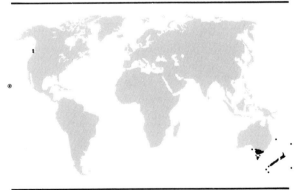

NATURALIZED DISTRIBUTION
North America: Canada, USA; Australasia: Australia, New Zealand; Oceania: Hawaiian Islands.

NORTH AMERICA

Canada[3]

According to Scheffer (1935 and 1955), Chinese immigrants may have unsuccessfully introduced Skylarks to the Fraser River delta in British Columbia before the turn of the century. In the autumn of 1903 (some accounts say in the previous year), the Natural History Society of British Columbia – with financial support from the Provincial government and private individuals – released 100 pairs of the nominate form imported from England (Cooke & Knappen 1941 say 99 birds) at Duncan, Colwood, North Saanich, Beacon Hill, Cedar Hill, and the Jubilee Hospital near Victoria on southern Vancouver Island. In April 1913, a further 49 birds were liberated in the same general localities, 34 of which were planted at Rithet's Farm, 9 at Lansdowne Road and 6 at Cadboro Bay. Others are said to have been freed at about the same time on the lower mainland at the mouth of the Fraser River. In 1908 or 1910, G. W. Wallace released some more on the Saanich Peninsula of southern Vancouver Island, and in 1919 Mrs E. A. Morton is said to have turned down five at Oak Bay.

Skylarks apparently did no more than maintain their numbers on Vancouver Island until about 1925, but thereafter they increased and by the end of the decade had become quite common. By 1935, they were, according to Cooke & Knappen (1941: 180–1), 'as abundant as any of the other small birds in the occupied area around Mount Tolmie and Mount Douglas . . . [but] are not yet numerous enough to spread to adjoining sections'. In the following year, when the population was said to number 219, a colony was found at Sidney, some 27 km north of Victoria. Twenty years later, when their numbers were about the same, Skylarks had colonized suitable habitats around Victoria and on the Saanich Peninsula.

By 1962, when they had become established over a low snowfall area of some 8,000 ha, the population had increased fivefold. In the later 1960s, when much of the Skylarks' habitat was lost to urban development, especially around Victoria, the birds suffered a decline. Today, a few hundred survive only in grasslands around the University of Victoria campus, on the Rithet Estate, in the vicinity of the airport, along the eastern side of the McHugh Valley, near Duncan and in a few other localities on the Saanich Peninsula; from time to time, one or two are reported from Sidney Island. Severe winters with long-lying snow take a heavy toll of the depleted population.

According to Cooke & Knappen (1941: 180), Skylarks were unsuccessfully liberated at Montreal, Quebec in eastern Canada; no further information seems available.

USA

Although there have been many attempts by man to naturalize the Skylark in the United States the only established colony is derived from natural dispersants from the introduced population in British Columbia, Canada. On 15 August 1960, Skylarks were first observed on San Juan Island, Washington State,[4] some 18 km east of the Saanich Peninsula on Vancouver Island on the opposite side of Haro Strait. In May 1970, breeding by some of the dozen pairs present was first confirmed on the south coast of San Juan, where in 1972 a total of 63 was counted of which 27 were displaying males. From San Juan, Skylarks seem likely to spread to other islands in the archipelago (including Waldron, Orcas, Shaw, Lopez and Blakely), and thence across Rosario Strait to Cypress, Lummi, Guemes, Fidalgo and Whidbey, islands, and even to the Washington mainland – a distance from San Juan of only 33 km – where fear has been expressed that they could become as serious an agricultural pest as in New Zealand and the British Isles.

Although elsewhere in the United States[5] some of the numerous attempts to naturalize Skylarks nearly succeeded, all eventually failed. Table 6 gives details of the principal introductions – all of birds believed to have been imported from England. According to Palmer (1899), many more undocumented introductions were probably made around New York, and the population on Long Island may from time to time have been reinforced. Phillips (1928) records that between 1900 and 1914 at least 5,000–7,000 Skylarks arrived in New York. Cooke & Knappen (1941) refer to other releases made in Cambridge, Massachusetts; Bergen and Passaic counties, New Jersey; Detroit, Michigan; and Centreville and St Louis, Missouri. Blake (1975)

Table 6 Principal introductions of Skylarks (*Alauda arvensis*) to the United States, 1851–1908

Date	Number	Introduced by	Released at	Remarks
1851	?	Mr Bateman	Near Cincinnati, Ohio	Disappeared
1852	48	Trustees of Greenwood Cemetery	Long Island, New York	Disappeared
1853	?	John Gorgas	In Delaware Bay off Wilmington, Delaware, and ? at Washington, DC	Disappeared after a year or two
1870s	?	?	Near Cincinnati, Ohio	Breeding in 1878 but disappeared before 1882
1871 or 1874	50 pairs	Henry Reiche	Brooklyn, New York	Settled near Brooklyn and at Newtown and Canarsie but eventually died out
1880 (December)	200	I. W. England	74 survivors at Ridgewood, New Jersey, in May 1881	Settled near Brooklyn and at Flatbush, Long Island; bred for 20–30 years but then died out
1889 and 1892	*c.*50 pairs	Portland Oregon Song Bird Club (Society for the Introduction of European ? at Washington, DC	Portland, Molalla and Waldo Hills, Oregon, and Milwaukee, Wisconsin	Bred at Portland, Salem and Gresham until *c.*1908 and in 1896 were common in the Umpqua Valley, Douglas County, and in Marion and Washington counties, but eventually disappeared
1896	75 pairs +	Game Warden Mackenzie	George W. Cozzens's ranch near San Jose, California	Died out after a year
1908	*c.*200	?	Santa Cruz County, California	Apparently not seen again

Source: Phillips 1928

lists the Skylark as an 'introduction'; and an 'invader' in Alaska.

AUSTRALASIA

Australia[6]

The Skylark seems to have been introduced to Australia at the instigation of Edward Wilson, editor of the *Melbourne Argus* and founder in 1861 of the Acclimatization Society of Victoria, to supplement the native Singing Bushlark (*Mirafra javanica*), which he disparagingly described as 'a bird somewhat resembling the Skylark in size and colour, which flutters upwards while it sings; but its song is little better than a sort of melancholy croak'.[7] The poet Richard Horne, appointed Commissioner for Crown Lands in Melbourne in 1852, actually suggested that Australian birds did not lack the ability to sing but merely required teaching, and an anonymous contributor to the *Argus*, who may have been Horne but is suspected of being a (presumably) tongue-in-cheek Wilson, wrote that 'the powers of our indigenous songsters might be improved. They have voices, but have never been taught to use them'.[8]

In 1854, the *Argus* reported that Robert Morrice, 'a settler of many years standing,' had recently received a shipment of 150 songbirds from England, and that seven Skylarks from this consignment had been released in the Barrabool Hills near Geelong,[9] some 60 km south-west of Melbourne. In January 1856, an unnamed dealer imported no fewer than 800 songbirds (including Skylarks) to Australia, followed 3 months later by a second shipment that was landed in Sydney, New South Wales. More were imported to Melbourne by a bird dealer named Brown in January and November of the following year on board the *Sydenham*, and in January and December 1858 a dealer named Neymaler landed some at Melbourne, as did a Mr Rushall from the *Norfolk* in October of the same year. Some of these birds may have been released by private individuals in the 1850s, since Skylarks were reported in and around Melbourne in 1855 (perhaps wanderers from Geelong), 1857 and 1858. Others were subsequently turned down by the Royal Zoological and Acclimatization Society of Victoria as follows: 1860 (7 in July); 1862 (6 in the Melbourne Botanic Gardens, according to Professor F. McCoy in his anniversary address to the society on 24 November of that year); 1863 ('a small lot'); 1864 (some on Phillip Island); 1867 (80); ?1866 (32); 1870 and 1872 (30 each); and 1873–4 (about 100). Many of the later releases were made at Mount Ridley near Melbourne. As early as 1864, the Victoria Acclimatization Society reported that among other naturalized birds 'the Skylark may now be considered thoroughly established', and Ryan (1906) said that the birds were 'well established in the district around Melbourne', where they were slowly increasing and spreading. Tarr (1950) reported that Skylarks were fairly widespread in Victoria.

Skylarks were first imported to South Australia in July 1862, and 18 were freed in parks around Adelaide and at Enfield in 1879. Shortly afterwards, 22 pairs were released at Dry Creek north of Adelaide and a further nine pairs at Enfield. In 1881, 147 were set free at various localities near Adelaide and three dozen were released 75 km north at Kapunda. Skylarks are said to have been turned down by the South Australia Acclimatization Society on many occasions after 1889, and by the late 1940s were well established on the Adelaide Plains.

In New South Wales, Skylarks were introduced near Sydney in 1866, 1870–2 and 1883, when 70 from a shipment of 200 from Canterbury in New Zealand were despatched to the Blue Mountains, Maneroo, Ryde and elsewhere. By the late 1940s they were common along the New South Wales littoral and westwards to some inland areas. In 1963, they were reported from Lord Howe Island off the New South Wales coast.

In 1869, the *Flying Cloud* from England landed several species of birds (including Skylarks, which were released unsuccessfully) in Queensland, as were others in Western Australia by the Acclimatization Committee before 1912.

Skylarks may have been released in Tasmania in 1862 or 1872, and some are known to have been planted between about 1887 and 1892. Three dozen imported from New Zealand in

1899 by a Mr Talbot of Malahide were reported at the 1907 Annual General Meeting of the North Tasmania Acclimatization Society to be established in several localities, including Invermay, East and West Tamar, at Ormley near Avoca, and at Cataract Cliffs. By about 1902, Skylarks were said to be common at Risdon and Glenorchy near Hobart, and by the late 1940s were established in many agricultural districts, especially in southern Tasmania, and on King and Flinders islands in Bass Strait.

Frith (1979: 193) reported that the Skylark was:

now widespread in south-east South Australia, Tasmania, most of Victoria, and the southern New South Wales coast and tablelands. It avoids the drier inland. It lives mainly in well-cultivated lands and long-established pastures. It has successfully invaded the coastal heaths of New South Wales. Throughout its range it lives side by side with the Singing Bushlark and [Richard's] Pipit (*Anthus novaeseelandiae*). All three birds have superficially similar habitat needs, but it is not known if the Skylark provides competition for either of the native species.

Pizzey (1980) reported Skylarks to be common in Tasmania, in southeastern South Australia and around Adelaide, on Kangaroo Island, and throughout most of Victoria, but less common in the Riverina and east coast tablelands of New South Wales. Although largely migratory in the Northern Hemisphere, Skylarks in Australia appear to be sedentary, nomadic or only partially migratory, which may be one reason for their successful naturalization.

New Zealand[10]

According to Thomson (1922), Skylarks were introduced to New Zealand as follows: 20 by the Nelson Acclimatization Society sometime before September 1864; 4 by the Otago Society in 1867, 35 in 1868, 61 in 1869, and others by private dealers; 13 by the Canterbury Society in 1867 and 18 in 1871; 10 by the Auckland Society in 1867 and 52 in 1868 (by 1873 they were considered to be well established in the provincial district); 52 by the Wellington Society in 1874 and 56 in 1875. In 1879, 70 were released on Stewart Island, where although they were seen for a while at the head of Paterson Inlet they eventually disappeared. According to Oliver (1955), Skylarks were introduced to the Chatham Islands by L. W. Hood towards the end of the nineteenth century.

Although Thomson says that the earliest release in Canterbury took place in 1867, Williams (1969) points out that since the second annual report of the Acclimatization Society, published in mid-1866, lists Skylarks with 'other English and Australian birds turned out in various parts the previous season', 1865 is more likely to have been the year of release; perhaps these were the half-a-dozen birds that Williams says arrived from England in 1863 but whose subsequent fate is unrecorded. In 1875, Williams continues, 300 Skylarks were freed by the Society in South Canterbury at a cost of 15s. each. Two hundred out of a shipment from England in 1880 were forwarded to Australia 3 years later, which suggests that the birds were already well established in Canterbury, and 2 years later Skylarks and Goldfinches (*Carduelis carduelis*) from England were exchanged for Australian Black-backed Magpies (*Gymnorhina tibicen*) and Wonga-wonga Pigeons (*Leucosarcia melanoleuca*).

Thus, in the 15 years between 1864 and 1879, at least 691 Skylarks (and probably many more) were released in New Zealand by the various acclimatization societies, and others were doubtless liberated by home-sick settlers so that, as Thomson (1922: 140) wrote, 'The introduction of this bird was general throughout New Zealand. . . . In every part they increased rapidly and spread throughout the whole country, but they confine themselves to cultivated districts, and are not found in the bush or open mountain country.'

Palmer (1899) said that Skylarks 'are chiefly of interest in this connection, because in their native home they are almost universally considered beneficial, but in New Zealand (where they have been introduced) they have developed traits which render them far from desirable additions to the fauna of that island'. This is confirmed by Thomson, who wrote (1922: 140–1) that 'next to the [House] sparrow [(*Passer domesticus*) q.v.] the Skylark is considered by farmers to be the most destructive of the small birds which have been introduced into New Zealand. They are particularly destructive in spring, when they pull wheat and other grains out of the ground just as they are springing. They also uproot seedling cabbage, turnip and other farm plants.'

Although, as Palmer said, in their native range Skylarks were at one time 'almost universally considered beneficial', such is unfortunately no longer the case. In the British Isles,[11] where the tendency towards larger fields may have favoured them, Sharrock (1976: 280) pointed out that:

At first sight this may seem an unlikely bird to be dubbed an agricultural pest, but the Skylark has become just that to some specialist farmers. From time to time, during the last 50 years or so, there have been reports of grazing Skylarks damaging seedlings of arable crop plants such as lettuces and peas; but recent reports from areas where sugar-beet is the main crop are more serious. Formerly, beet seeds were sown continuously in drills, and the young plants thinned out at a later stage (after the period of vulnerability to bird damage) to leave the more healthy ones. Since the early 1970s, however, a more usual procedure in mechanised farming has been the precision drilling of single seeds in pelleted form, properly spaced out; with fewer sugar-beet seedlings available for grazing, bird damage inevitably affects plants which should provide the grower with his crop, reducing the yield in patches over a very wide area which may total some thousands of hectares annually (Dunning, 1974).

Wodzicki (1965: 433) reported Skylarks in New Zealand to be 'widely distributed and common, North, South and Stewart Islands and Raoul [Kermadecs], Chatham and Auckland Islands'. Kinsky (1970) found them throughout the main and outlying islands and on the Chatham, Auckland, Campbell and Kermadec islands. The last three groups were colonized naturally – the last-named apparently in 1946. According to Falla, Sibson & Turbott (1979), Skylarks are established on the main islands in all types of open habitats up to 1,600 m, and on the Chatham, Auckland and Kermadec islands. Their status on Campbell Island is uncertain. Some flocking and local movements occur in autumn, but there is no evidence yet of migration which, as in Australia, may help to explain the species' successful naturalization. In Auckland, loose flocks are still present in spring when local birds are paired and males are singing territorially.

OCEANIA

Hawaiian Islands[12]

Skylarks of the nominate form[13] were first introduced to the Hawaiian Islands from England in

1865, when 10 were released on high tableland at Leilehua on Oahu, where they were joined in 1870 by others despatched from New Zealand by the Hon. A. S. Cleghorn; in the latter year some were also freed on Kauai by Mrs Frances Sinclair. Later importations of Skylarks from New Zealand were released at Moiliili on Oahu, from where some were subsequently transferred to Kauai, Maui (1886), Molokai (1917), Lanai (1917) and Hawaii (1902). Henshaw (1904) said that the introductions on Oahu had been a 'great success' and had encouraged the release of Skylarks on the windward side of Hawaii where, however, 'their fate is at present unknown'; Henshaw also believed that Skylarks occurred 'in small numbers on Maui', and Bryan (1907) found them to be 'common on the grass lands' of Molokai.

According to Fisher (1951), Skylarks were liberated on Niihau before 1920 by Francis Sinclair who 'later took some of his stock to Kauai for release there'. By 1936, Skylarks were said to be fairly common on Lehua Island (to which they had presumably flown from Niihau), and in 1947 Fisher found small numbers to be widely distributed on the latter island.

The American Ornithologists' Union (1957) reported that Skylarks were established on Hawaii, Oahu and Lanai; Peterson (1961) found them to be widespread on Niihau, Maui and Hawaii, local on Oahu, Molokai and Lanai, and scarce on Kauai. Berger (1972) reported them to be common in suitable open habitat on Hawaii, Maui and Lanai, slightly less so on Oahu, and rare or absent on Kauai, where they seem to have died out around 1938. The Hawaiian Audubon Society (1975) said that Skylarks were established on all the main islands of the group but were most common on Hawaii and Maui – especially on the grassy slopes of Mauna Kea and Mauna Loa on the former and of Haleakala on the latter. Zeillemaker & Scott (1976) recorded Skylarks as local and uncommon on cultivated land and pastures on Oahu and Lanai, uncommon on Molokai, common on Maui and Hawaii, and accidental visitors or vagrants on Kauai. The American Ornithologists' Union (1983) described them as established on the main islands from Niihau eastwoods. On Kauai, Skylarks are regarded as a nuisance to newly planted lettuces, and their range throughout the archipelago has been adversely effected by the growth of pineapple and sugar-cane plantations.

NOTES

1 Coniferous forest lying between the treeless Arctic tundra and the treeless plains of the steppes.
2 E.g. Voous 1960.
3 Blake 1975; Brooks & Swarth 1925 (in Carl & Guiguet 1972); Carl & Guiguet 1972; Cooke & Knappen 1941; Long 1981; Phillips 1928; Scheffer 1935, 1955; Sprot 1937; Stirling & Edwards 1962; and W. T. Munro, personal communication, 1985. See also: *Rochester Post* (New York), 9 April (1913) and *Canadian Field-Naturalist* 39: 175 (1925) (both in Phillips 1928).
4 Blake 1975; Bruce, 1961; Long 1981; Wahl & Wilson 1971; Weisbrod & Stevens 1974.
5 American Ornithologists' Union 1957, 1983; Blake 1975; Cleaveland 1865 (in Murphy 1945); Cooke & Knappen 1941; Cottam 1956; Gottschalk 1967; Long 1981; Palmer 1899; Pfluger 1896 (in Jewett & Gabrielson 1929); Phillips 1928; and W. T. Munro, personal communication, 1985.
6 Balmford 1978; Blakers, Davies & Reilly 1984; Condon 1962; Frith 1979; Hardy 1928; Harman 1963a; Jenkins 1977; Le Souef 1912; Littler 1902; Long 1972, 1981; McGill 1960; McKean & Hindwood 1965; Pizzey 1980; Rolls 1969; Ryan 1906; Tarr 1950; Williams 1953; Wilson 1858.
7 *Transactions of the Philosophical Institute of Victoria* (1857), quoted by Frith (1979).
8 Quoted by Balmford (1978: 243).
9 Several authors, e.g. Frith (1979), Hardy (1928) quoting Wilson (1858), and Williams (1953), say that this first release took place in 1850.
10 Falla, Sibson & Turbott 1979; Kinsky 1970; Long 1981; Oliver 1955; Palmer 1899; Thomson 1922, 1926; Williams 1953, 1969, 1973; Wodzicki 1965.
11 Dunning 1974; Edgar 1974; Hardman 1974; Sharrock 1976.
12 American Ornithologists' Union 1957, 1983; Berger 1981; E. H. Bryan 1958; W. A. Bryan 1908; Caum 1933, 1936; Fisher 1951; Hawaiian Audubon Society 1975; Henshaw 1904; Long 1981; Munro 1944; Peterson 1961; Phillips 1928; Pyle 1977; Zeillemaker & Scott 1976.
13 According to Munro (1944), the race *A. a. japonica* (Japan and the Ryukyu Islands) was unsuccessfully introduced in 1934.

Red-whiskered Bulbul

(*Pycnonotus jocosus*)

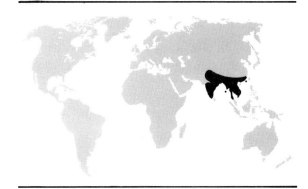

NATURAL DISTRIBUTION
India, Nepal, Bangladesh, Burma, the Andaman Islands, southern China, Thailand, northern Malaya, southern Indo-China and North Vietnam.

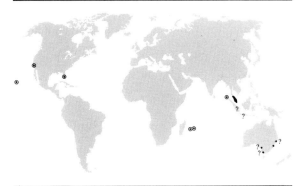

Note: Presence in southern Malaya probably a result of escaped transplanted stock.

NATURALIZED DISTRIBUTION
Asia: Nicobar Islands, ?Java and Sumatra; Africa: Mascarenes (Mauritius, ?Réunion); North America: USA; Australasia: Australia; Oceania: Hawaiian Islands.

ASIA

Nicobar Islands[1]

Red-whiskered Bulbuls (*P. j. whistleri*) have been introduced from Port Blair in the Andaman Islands to the Nicobars, where they are now common on Trinkat and Camorta islands and perhaps also on Nancowry, but are believed not to occur elsewhere.

Java and Sumatra

According to Long (1981), the Red-whiskered Bulbul may have been introduced to Java and Sumatra where it is a popular cagebird.

AFRICA

Mauritius; Réunion

Red-whiskered Bulbuls of the race *P. j. emeria* (eastern India, Burma and southwestern Thailand) have been introduced to, and are now established on, the island of Mauritius.[2] They first arrived in Port Louis on the sailing ship *C.J.S.* (belonging to the firm of Charles Jacobs & Sons) in about 1891, when some were given by the master, Gabriel Reynard, to a local resident; in the following year their cage was destroyed in a cyclone and the birds were apparently killed. Others imported by Reynard in or shortly after 1892 escaped from their aviary, multiplied rapidly, and by 1911 were distributed throughout Mauritius, where Meinertzhagen (1912) reported them to be causing damage in orchards, and where they are now widespread and abundant.

On 27 December 1972, the Mauritian newspaper, *Le Cernéen* (quoted by Staub 1976), reported the presence on Réunion of Red-whiskered Bulbuls that had been introduced by a tourist from Mauritius.

NORTH AMERICA

USA

The escape into the wild of the Red-whiskered Bulbul in Florida[3] resulted, as Owre (1973) has pointed out, in the naturalization of a new family of Passeriformes in the Western Hemisphere.

In late July or early August 1960, a number of these birds (believed to have been between 5 and 10 pairs) that had been imported from Calcutta in eastern India (where the form is *P. j. emeria*[4] and the climate is not dissimilar to that of southeastern Florida) escaped from Alton Freeman's Miami Rare Bird Farm in the suburb of Kendall in Dade County, where they first nested in a Croton (*Croton* or *Codiaeum* sp.) hedge in the following April, and from where by that autumn some had ventured as far afield as Princeton, 56 km south-west of Miami. In August 1963, a flock of 23 was counted in Kendall, and by the following year the population had increased to between 35 and 50.[5] During their first decade in the wild there was an annual increment of some 30–40 per cent in the total population to a little under 250 by the winter of 1969–70, when some 8.2 km^2 of suburban Kendall had been colonized. By 1973, the population had doubled to around 500, and since then the birds have continued to increase and to expand their range in a southerly direction.

Several demographic and ecological changes, which have been described by Owre and apply also to some other alien birds, have contributed to the successful naturalization of the Red-whiskered Bulbul in southeastern Florida. Fifty years ago the Atlantic Coastal Ridge, a narrow and slightly elevated strip of land extending from north of Palm Beach to south of Homestead that forms the eastern edge of the Everglades basin with, on its seaward edge, mangrove swamps and beaches bordering the Atlantic, was still largely covered with pseudoclimax pineland and climax tropical hammock.[6] Drainage of the Everglades and dredging of the mangroves was already under way, and since then there has been an enormous increase (tenfold between 1930 and 1970) in the region's human population. The native flora has all but been replaced by urban/suburban development replanted with gaudy exotic flowers, ornamental trees and edible fruits, and even native shade (and roosting) trees have been superseded by alien species. Much of southeastern Florida is now virtually devoid of native plants, and this 'disturbed' environment has become, in Owre's words (1973: 492), 'preconditioned for exotic invasion' (analogizing the 'preadaptation' shown by some successful invaders to a new environment), while the subtropical climate ensures the flowering and fruiting of more than 1,000 species of exotic zoochrous trees and shrubs (providing nectar, fruit and seeds to some of which most alien birds are accustomed) at all seasons. This permanent supply of food is augmented by the large number of birdtables in suburban gardens and these have played an important part in the successful establishment of many alien species.

The Red-whiskered Bulbul, which as Carleton & Owre (1975) point out has been called a 'species of civilization',[7] was already conditioned to a man-modified habitat, and in Florida found an environment not unlike that in its native range. Being, like another Florida alien, the Budgerigar (*Melopsittacus undulatus*) (q.v.), relatively harmless and visually and vocally attractive to man, Red-whiskered Bulbuls are both fed and jealously protected by local residents. Furthermore, as Carleton & Owre indicate, the bulbuls' communal roosting habit is of great importance to a pioneering species in a new environment. Young of the year join adults in these assemblies, which can serve as 'information centres'[8] in the search for food, help to synchronize breeding, and afford protection from predation.

Carleton & Owre found Red-whiskered Bulbuls roosting in Figs (*Ficus benjamina*) from southern Asia, tall African Napier Grass (*Pennisetum purpurem*), an exotic species of *Acalypha*, a Mango (*Mangifera indica*) from tropical Asia, and exotic palms. Because of the conformation of their mouth, the size of food they can easily mandibulate and crush is limited. They feed mainly on small drupaceous fruits, berries and syconia of over two dozen exotic species – for which they compete with the native Northern Mockingbird (*Mimus polyglottos*). To a lesser extent they feed on nectar from blossoms, flower parts, growing shoots and small insects. In the first-named category, the Brazilian Holly or Pepper (*Schinus terebinthifolius*), a small tree or shrub that has been widely disseminated by birds throughout southeastern Florida to the disadvantage of native plants, is of primary importance. The syconia of figs also form a significant part of the bulbuls' diet; although two species of fig (including the common *Ficus aurea*) are native to southern Florida, 19 aliens have been planted, including *F. benghalensis* and *F. indica* that bulbuls feed on in India. Seven species of *Lantana*, the drupaceous seeds of which are much favoured by bulbuls in India, occur in Dade County where, as Carleton & Owre point out, as with *Ficus* the birds have encountered a food generically, and in some cases specifically, the same as in their native range. Bulbuls also feed extensively on the drupes of the exotic *Jasminum fluminense* and on those of some of the nine other alien jasmines (Oleaceae) established in the region, on the berries of *Cestrum diurnum*, and on other jessamines (Solanaceae). The largest fruits they consume are the fleshy pomes of over-ripe Asian Loquats (*Eriobotrya japonica*).

In captivity, bulbuls readily accept the fruits of Wild Coffee (*Psychotria undata*), Florida Holly or Dahoon (*Ilex cassine*), French Mulberry (*Callicarpa americana*), Marlberry (*Ardisia escallonoides*) and Virginia Creeper (*Parthenocissus quinquefolia*), which, though largely absent from suburbia, would be encountered if bulbuls were to spread into rural habitats. Although throughout much of their native range Red-whiskered Bulbuls are reported to be something of a nuisance to orchardists and horticulturists, Carleton & Owre found no evidence to suggest primary damage in Florida to citrus or other large fruits of commercial significance such as mangoes[9] and avocados, though bulbuls will enlarge holes previously made by such agricultural pests as Red-bellied Woodpeckers (*Melanerpes carolinus*), and possibly squirrels (Sciuridae) and insects. In laboratory conditions, they ate Mulberries (*Morus rubra*) and crushed Barbados Cherries (*Malphigia punicifolia*) that are consumed by man. Bulbuls have also been seen to eat a tropical Indian Raspberry (*Rubus albescens*), introduced to Florida in 1948.

Plants visited, apparently for nectar, florets and/or insects, include Bottlebrush (*Callistemon lanceolatus*), Cajeput (*Melaleuca quinquenervia*), Coconut Palm (*Cocos nucifera*), Woman's Tongue (*Albizzia lebbeck*), Cecropias (*Cecropia palmata*) and Umbrella or Octopus Trees (*Brassaia actiniphylla*). Insects eaten include *Cycloneda sanguinea* (Coccinellidae), tropical web-spinners (Embryoptera), dipterans and hemipterans: foliage caterpillars such as the Mahogany Web (*Macolla thrysisalis*) are also favoured.

The reluctance of bulbuls to expand their range in Florida has been attributed to their apparent traditional attachment, outside the breeding season, to communal roosts. In view of the paucity of potential predators, however (which may include Hispid Cotton Rats (*Sigmodon hispidus*), feral Cats (*Felis catus*), Blue Jays (*Cyanocitta cristata*), American Kestrels (*Falco sparverius*) and Black Snakes (*Coluber constrictor*)), 'no obvious ecological factors exist', wrote Carleton & Owre (1975: 55), that will prevent colonization of the entire tropical zone of southeastern Florida'.

In about 1968, some Red-whiskered Bulbuls

became established in the Los Angeles County Arboretum (Arcadia) and in Huntington Gardens and San Marino, California,[10] where they are a favourite local cagebird and frequent escaper. Although they are welcomed by residents of southeastern Florida, attempts have been made by the Los Angeles County Department of Agriculture to dislodge them in California, where by January 1972 a total of 47 had been killed – a figure that by 1977 had risen to 84. Nests in California are usually built near water in trees such as oaks (*Quercus* sp.), and in the Arboretum bulbuls have been seen eating the fruit of the Paperbark Mulberry (*Broussonetia papyrifera*). In 1975, a single bird was seen as far away as the Pasadena/San Gabriel Valley.

AUSTRALASIA

Australia[11]

Red-whiskered Bulbuls (presumably of the nominate form) imported from China by the New South Wales Zoological Society in 1880 (Roots 1976 incorrectly says 1885) apparently disappeared. Others introduced about the turn of the century were more successful, and deliberately released and/or escaped birds became established around Sydney. Some were reported at Homebush in 1902 and at Double Bay in 1917, where they increased and were reported to be causing some damage to peas, figs and strawberries. They were nesting at Hunters' Hill in 1919 and at Wahroonga 2 years later, and by about 1920 were apparently common in the Sydney suburbs, where by 1933 flocks of up to 100 were proving a nuisance in soft-fruit orchards. By 1950, when they were common throughout most of the county of Cumberland, they had spread up to 100 km from Sydney, and a decade later were said to be abundant within 150 km north, south and west of that city, including the Royal National Park, the Wollongong area and the Blue Mountains. Frith (1979: 188) said that in Sydney the Red-whiskered Bulbul 'is now very abundant in city and suburban gardens and has colonized some nearby semi-rural districts. In the city it is considered a pest of orchards and gardens . . .

[and] is nowhere so numerous as in street plantings of native figs when these are fruiting.' In compensation, it destroys vine moth larvae and other injurious invertebrates and, according to Gregory-Smith (1982), has been recorded as a foster-parent of the native Pallid Cuckoo (*Cuculus pallidus*). Although, as Frith points out, it seems unlikely that the birds will be able to spread very far north of Sydney through the sandstone gullies and *Eucalyptus* forests where there is little fruit, were they ever to reach the coastal rainforests, where wild figs and other soft fruits are plentiful, they could theoretically travel north from there at least as far as southern Queensland.

In Victoria, Red-whiskered Bulbuls were first reported at Ashfield in 1915–16 and at Geelong and in city gardens in Melbourne in 1948, where a decade or so later they were said to be 'fairly well established'.

In South Australia, there were sporadic reports between 1943 and 1945 of Red-whiskered Bulbuls in northern Adelaide and in Westbourne Park. Although Roots claimed that they were established in Adelaide, and Long (1981: 298) said that at that time the species was 'still common around Adelaide, Sydney and Melbourne', Blakers, Davies & Reilly (1984) do not show the Red-whiskered Bulbul as occurring in Adelaide.

Pizzey (1980) described the Australian distribution of the species as follows: in New South Wales, common and widespread in the Sydney area with an apparently recent extension of range to the Lower Hunter Valley, and also established (presumably from a separate release and/or escape) at Coffs Harbour 450 km north of Sydney; in Victoria, a smaller colony exists in and around the suburb of South Yarra; in South Australia, birds have been reported since 1979 at Hackham, Murray Bridge (where a small population may be established), Stirling, Waterfall Gully and Beaumont (all near Adelaide), but are known to have bred successfully only at Enfield in December 1983. Blakers, Davies & Reilly (1984: 358) describe Red-whiskered Bulbuls as 'now present on the coast from Lake Macquarie to the Shoalhaven River, and west to the Blue Mountains'. It is noteworthy that whereas in Florida the Red-whiskered Bulbul is at present an almost exclusively suburban species, in New South Wales, where it seems to be slowly spreading, it has ventured into rural parks, thickets and heavily timbered gullies.

OCEANIA

Hawaiian Islands[12]

Although all bulbuls are in the 'prohibited entry' category of the Hawaii State Department of Agriculture, several species have been imported illegally. In the autumn of 1965, two Red-whiskered Bulbuls were seen on the Lower Makiki Heights on Oahu, where several were reported a year later, two dozen were present in 1967, and one pair nested twice in 1971. Four were observed on several occasions in the autumn of 1967 at Pacific Heights, where seven were counted at Christmas in the following year. Since then, they have spread to Kaimuki and the Punchbowl areas and along the length of Manoa Valley. All the birds are believed to be descended from a single escape or release. Zeillemaker & Scott (1976) record the Red-whiskered Bulbul as local and uncommon in residential districts and community parklands on Oahu, where by 1979 they occurred from Hawaii Kai to Pearl City Heights. They feed mainly on the fruits of the Date Palm (*Phoenix dactylifera*), Papaya (*Carica papaya*), Mango (*Magnifera indica*), Autograph Tree (*Clusia rosea*), Loquat (*Eriobotrya japonica*), Avocado (*Persea americana*), Octopus Tree (*Brassaia actiniphylla*) and Mock Orange (*Murraya exotica*). They have also been seen gathering nectar from Coconut Palms (*Cocos nucifera*) and Bottlebrush (*Callistemon lanceolatus*) trees.

In Malaya,[13] Red-whiskered Bulbuls seldom occur naturally south of northern Kedah and southern Kelantan. They are a favourite cagebird of the region, and populations in the suburbs of Kuala Trengganu, Ipoh and Kuala Lumpur (where they were said to be spreading in 1962–3), and on the islands of Penang and Singapore (where they were first reported in about 1924), are probably derived from escaped translocated stock. As might be expected, the race established in southern Malaya appears to be *P. j. pattani* from Thailand, northern Malaya and southern Indo-China.

NOTES

1 Abdulali 1964, 1967; Long 1981; Osmaston 1933; Peters 1960; Ripley 1961; Roots 1976.
2 Long 1981; Meinertzhagen 1912; Peters 1960; Roots 1976; Rountree, Guérin et al. 1952; Staub 1976.
3 American Ornithologists' Union 1983; Ali & Ripley 1968–74; Banks & Laybourne 1968; Blake 1975; Carleton 1971; Carleton & Owre 1975; Deignan 1945; Fisk 1966; Gore & Doubilet 1976; Gottschalk 1967; King 1968; Long 1981; Owre 1973. (See also an untitled and undated typescript annotated 'From: some endangered and exotic species in Florida, part 2, compiled by D. F. Jackson, D. Stoll and N. Cooper. Florida International University, Miami', 205–23.)
4 Fisk (1966) suggests that the form present in Florida may be *P. j. pyhrrotis*, which is found in northern India and Nepal.
5 Fisk (1966: 10) claims that the population had increased to 'perhaps 100 roosting in a flock'.
6 An area with deep, rich soil, and hardwood vegetation.
7 E. C. S. Baker, *The Fauna of British India including Ceylon and Burma*, 2nd edn (Taylor and Francis: London, 1935), 1: 395.
8 P. Ward & H. Zahavi, 'The importance of certain assemblages of birds as "information centres" for food finding', *Ibis* 115: 517–34 (1973).
9 Gore & Doubilet (1976), however, say that Red-whiskered Bulbuls in Florida do eat mangoes.
10 Blake 1975; Hardy, 1973; Heilbrun 1976; Long 1981; Roberson & Keffer 1978.
11 Blakers, Davies & Reilly 1984; Chaffer 1933; Condon 1962; Frith 1979; Gregory-Smith 1982; Hindwood & McGill 1958; Long 1981; McGill 1960; MacPherson 1921, 1923; Paton 1985; Pizzey 1980; Roots 1976; Tarr 1950; Thomson 1964.
12 American Ornithologists' Union 1983; Berger 1975d, 1981; Blake 1975; Hawaiian Audubon Society 1975; Heilbrun 1976; Long 1981; Pyle 1977; Zeillemaker & Scott 1976.
13 Long 1981; Madoc 1956; Medway & Wells 1976; and C. J. Hails, personal communication, 1985.

Red-vented Bulbul
(*Pycnonotus cafer*)

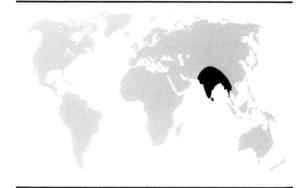

NATURAL DISTRIBUTION

From Pakistan, India, Nepal and Sri Lanka eastwards through the Himalayas to Bangladesh, northern, central and southern Burma and extreme western Yunnan in China.

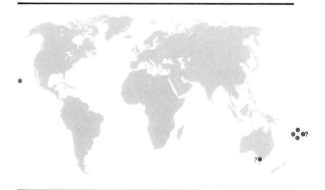

NATURALIZED DISTRIBUTION

Australasia: ?Australia; Oceania: Hawaiian Islands, Fiji, Tonga, Samoa, ?Society Islands (Tahiti).

AUSTRALASIA

Australia[1]

Red-vented Bulbuls are recorded as breeding in the wild in Sydney and Melbourne as long ago as 1917; a few may still survive in the suburbs of the latter city, although none are said to have been reported since October 1942.

OCEANIA

Hawaiian Islands[2]

On 10 October 1966, a flock of at least half-a-dozen Red-vented Bulbuls was seen at Waipahu on the island of Oahu: these birds may have escaped from captivity while in transit at Honolulu International Airport, but were more probably deliberately (and illegally) released in the previous autumn at the same time as Red-whiskered Bulbuls (*Pycnonotus jocosus*). By June 1967, they had been reported from near Fort Shafter, in Kailua, and at Bellows Air Force Station at Waimanalo, and later spread to Manoa Valley and the Moanulua Gardens. They are now more widely distributed on Oahu than *jocosus*, but like their congener are confined to residential areas. Zeillemaker & Scott (1976) described their status on Oahu as 'uncommon'. Berger (1981: 193), however, said that 'This abundant species now occurs from Hanauma Bay and Koko Crater to Waipahu and Wahiawa on the leeward side of Oahu and from Waimanalo to Laie on the windward side. It will not take many years before the species is found throughout the island.'

Fiji[3]

Watling (1978b: 109; 1982: 100) has traced the introduction of the Red-vented Bulbul to Fiji; it was first imported in about 1903, and

can be linked with the arrival of indentured Indian labour around that period. As with the early English settlers in New Zealand, who brought with them many English birds for sentimental reasons, so the Indian immigrants might be expected to have brought the Bulbul, because it holds a special place in Indian poetry, folklore and literature. Most of Fiji's Indian immigrants came from Uttar Pradesh with large numbers from Bengal and Bihar . . . areas which coincide with the distribution of *P. c. bengalensis* [the race established in Fiji]. Possibly the strongest reason for the immigrants bringing the Bulbul to Fiji was its widespread use as a fighting bird. Fighting birds were fed on a special diet and highly prized by their owners. During the fight the adversaries were tethered on a T-shaped perch by a cord fastened to a soft string around the body to prevent them escaping. Heavy bets were placed and occasionally fights continued until the death of one of the combatants occurred. Although animal fighting is now prohibited in India, Bulbul fighting still continues as a popular rural sport in some provinces. The sport is not practised in Fiji today.

At present, Red-vented Bulbuls in Fiji are common only on the main island of Viti Levu and on some small offlying islands such as Beqa; on the former they are abundant in both agricultural and residential habitats, are often seen in clearings and patches of immature secondary seral associations (such as floodplains, river banks and landslips) in forests, and occasionally venture into mature woodlands. These are much the same habitats as are occupied in India. Lesser numbers occur on Ovalau and Wakaya, and a small colony exists at Waiyevo on Taveuni; these may have become established through natural dispersal or by deliberate introductions. Red-vented Bulbuls are absent from Vanua Levu, Kadavu, and the Yasawa and Mamanuca groups, and are believed not to occur on Vatulele, Lakeba, Ono, Gau and several islands of the Lau group.

Red-vented Bulbuls in Fiji have been accused of contributing to the exodus of indigenous species into 'bush' habitats, of spreading noxious weeds, and of being a serious agricultural pest. Watling (1979), who examined each of these charges in detail, pointed out that since bulbuls have been established for a considerable time, and because no accurate records exist of the status of native birds in the nineteenth century, it is impossible to compare the position of the latter before the arrival of the former: even if data were available comparisons would be of doubtful validity in view of the great increase in man-modified habitats in the period when bulbuls were becoming established. That bulbuls are aggressive and successful colonists there can be no doubt. Pernetta & Watling (1978) recorded assaults, in descending numbers, on the following species in the Sigatoka Valley on Viti Levu: Common Mynah (*Acridotheres tristis*), Polynesian Triller (*Lalage maculosa*), Jungle Mynah (*A. fuscus*), Wattled Honeyeater (*Foulehaio carunculata*), Grey-backed White-Eye (*Zosterops lateralis*), Red Avadavat (*Amandava amandava*), Spotted Dove (*Streptopelia chinensis*) and Vanikoro Broadbill (*Myiagra vanikorensis*). The White-breasted Wood Swallow (*Artamus leucorhynchus*), the White-collared Kingfisher (*Halcyon chloris*), the two mynahs and, especially, the honeyeater were themselves seen to initiate attacks on bulbuls.

Four of the eight species assaulted by bulbuls are themselves naturalized aliens (the two mynahs, the dove and the avadavat); this led Pernetta & Watling to conclude that interspecific aggression between alien bulbuls and indigenes does not occur sufficiently often to account for the presence of the latter primarily in forested habitats; this is more likely to be the result of the notorious ability of exotics, and inability of natives, to adapt to man-modified habitats.

The Red-vented Bulbul, which has been called an 'opportunistic frugivore', would provide serious competition for food with native fruit-eating species were their feeding strategies and locations not very different. Bulbuls feed mainly on the fruits of alien invasive weeds found in immature secondary growth and on cultivated land, whereas indigenous frugivores tend to prefer native or aboriginally introduced fruits growing in forested areas. The exception, the White-throated Pigeon (*Columba vitiensis*), seems to be the only native species with which bulbuls directly compete for food.

Although primarily associated with 'disturbed' agricultural and residential environments, bulbuls do frequently enter immature secondary growth in forested areas, where they find two of their principal food resources – the primary colonist scrubby weeds Prickly Solanum (*Solanum torvum*), scattered mainly by White-throated Pigeons, and *Piper aduncum*, disseminated by fruit bats (*Pteropus* spp). On cultivated land, bulbuls find such other introduced invasives as Guava (*Psidium guajava*), Lantana (*Lantana camara*), Cape Gooseberry (*Physalis angulata*) and Wild Passion Flower (*Passiflora foetida*). The seeds of these weeds (some of which are natives of India) are spread not only by bulbuls but also by several other birds, as evidenced by their abundance on a number on bulbul-free islands. It seems probable, however, that the distribution of bulbuls is largely dependant on the presence of these plants, because ecological restrictions, rather than topographical barriers such as sea crossings, are acknowledged to be the determinants in the composition of insular avifaunas. Only on Viti Levu and Ovalau are the bulbuls' three favourite food plants – *Piper aauncun*, Prickly Solanum and Cape Gooseberry – found growing abundantly together; all but one of the other larger islands lack at least two of these weeds; the exception is Vanua Levu on which *Piper aduncum* and Prickly

Solanum gained a foothold in the mid-1970s; this, if they spread as expected, would enable the bulbuls to colonize that island.

Although a small colony of Red-vented Bulbuls near Auckland in New Zealand was eradicated in 1954–5 because of their reputation as an agricultural nuisance, and Berger (1975d) claimed that in Fiji bulbuls were 'considered a serious pest on fruit trees and in vegetable gardens', Watling found that in the Sigatoka Valley – the most important vegetable growing area of Fiji – agricultural crops comprised less than 3 per cent of the birds' diet. Some damage was caused to tomatoes, egg plants (aubergines), brassicas and such pulse plants as cowpeas, pigeon peas and longbeans, but this was considered of only limited economic significance, and the birds much preferred to feed on introduced weeds such as the Cape Gooseberry.

Tonga[4]

Red-vented Bulbuls in Tonga (probably, as in Fiji, *bengalensis*) are all descended from a single pair that was released or escaped from captivity on the island of Niuafo'ou in 1928 or 1929; in the 1940s some of their descendants were transferred by Prince Tungi to Tongatapu to control insect pests, from where they spread naturally to 'Eua, a distance of some 20 km. Although not mentioned by Mayr (1945) as occurring in Tonga in 1945 they were said by Dhondt (1976a) to be abundant on Tongatapu 30 years later. In 1976, Watling (1978b) found them to be widespread on the island, which is entirely lacking in extensive tracts of natural habitat, but much less common than on Fiji.

Samoa[5]

According to Watling (1982), there is an unconfirmed report, which is not corroborated by German Colonial Government records, that the Red-vented Bulbul first occurred in Western Samoa 'as a self-introduction' in 1912, and that it was liquidated on the orders of the Governor of the time, a Dr Solf. In view of the species' home range its appearance in Samoa as a natural colonist seems unlikely.

In 1943, some Red-vented Bulbuls (*bengalensis*)

were despatched from Fiji to a bird dealer in New Caledonia on board a US troopship; *en route*, however, the vessel was diverted to Apia on Upolu in Western Samoa, where the birds were subsequently released by the marines. By at least 1963, when some were seen in Pago Pago (but probably by the late 1950s), they had made the 75-km sea crossing (or had been transferred) to Tutuila in American Samoa, where they were said to be abundant in 1965. Strangely, they were unrecorded on Savai'i – only 15 km from Upolu – until 1974. Red-vented Bulbuls are today common in residential and agricultural (but not in natural) habitats on Upolu and Tutuila, but less so on Savai'i.

Society Islands

Bruner (1979) records that in March of that year the Red-vented Bulbul was first recorded on Tahiti, in the residential area of Patutoa, Papeete, where she considered that it would probably become established.

In October 1952, some Red-vented Bulbuls of the form *bengalensis* escaped, or were deliberately released, from a ship in Auckland Harbour, New Zealand;[6] they became temporarily established in the suburbs of that city, where they are known to have bred at Stanley Bay and Remeura in 1954, when the population was estimated to have increased to around fifty. Shortly afterwards, they were successfully eradicated by the Department of Agriculture on the grounds that they 'had undoubtedly proved to be something of an agricultural and orchard pest in Fiji'.[7]

The **White-eared Bulbul** (*Pycnonotus aurigaster*) is a native of Burma, Thailand, North Vietnam, southern Indo-China, southern China and Java. Before the mid-1930s, the subspecies *P. a. aurigaster*, an endemic of Java, was successfully introduced to, and became established at, Medan on the northeast coast of Sumatra.[8]

Between 1923 and at least 1950, a small colony of *P. a. aurigaster*, the free-flying descendants of escaped cagebirds imported from Java, was established in suburban Singapore,[9] where C. J. Hails (personal communication, 1985) has said they were dying (or had died) out.

According to Stresemann (1936), White-eared Bulbuls were introduced to Celebes (Sulawesi), where they became established on the southern peninsula.

Escott & Holmes (1980) say that in May 1977 small groups of the **Yellow-vented Bulbul** (*Pycnonotus goiavier*), a native of southeastern Thailand, southern Indo-China, Malaysia, Sumatra, Java, Bali, Lombok, Borneo and the Philippine Islands, were observed at Ujung Pandang in southern Sulawesi, where they were presumably introduced. They could, however, equally well be natural colonists from Borneo.

NOTES

1 Blakers, Davies & Reilly 1984; Lendon 1952; Le Souef 1918; Long 1981; Slater 1974; Watling 1978a.
2 American Ornithologists' Union 1983; Bancroft 1981a; Berger 1975d, 1981; Blake 1975; Hawaiian Audubon Society 1975; Heilbrun 1976; Long 1981; Pyle 1976; Watling 1978b, 1982; Williams 1983a, b; Zeillemaker & Scott, 1976.
3 Bahr 1912; Berger 1975d; Gorman 1975; Long 1981; Mayr 1945; Mercer 1966; Parham 1954; Pernetta & Watling 1978; Peters 1960; Turbet 1941; Watling 1977, 1978b, 1979, 1982.
4 Dhondt 1976a; Long 1981; Mayr 1945; Pernetta & Watling 1978; Watling 1978b, 1982.
5 Ashmole 1963; Armstrong 1932; Clapp & Sibley 1966; Dhondt 1976a, 1977; Keith 1957; Long 1981; Mayr 1945; Pernetta & Watling 1978; Watling 1978b, 1982.
6 Falla, Sibson & Turbott 1979; Kinsky 1970; Long 1981; Oliver 1955; Roots 1976; Turbott 1956; Watling 1978b.
7 Watling 1978b (but see also under Fiji).
8 King, Dickinson & Woodcock 1975; Kuroda 1933–6; Long 1981; Peters 1960. See also: K. W Dammerman & C. B. Kloss *Treubia* 13(3–4): 344 (1931).
9 Gibson-Hill 1952; Long 1981; Medway & Wells 1976; Peters 1960.

Northern Mockingbird
(*Mimus polyglottos*)

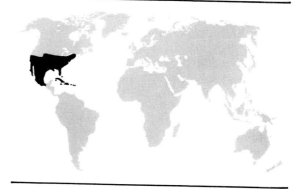

NATURAL DISTRIBUTION

From north-central California eastwards to central New Jersey in the USA, south to the Isthmus of Tehuantepec in southern Mexico. In the West Indies, in the Bahamas and Greater Antilles (including the Cayman Islands) east to the Virgin Islands. Occurs casually further north in the USA, and according to Godfrey (1966) has been spreading slowly north into parts of south-central and southeastern Canada. In the early twentieth century it spread eastward in the Virgin Islands, reaching St Thomas in 1916, St John around 1927 and later Anegada (Robertson 1962).

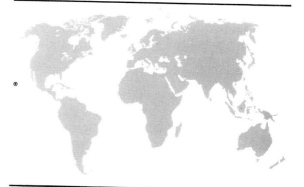

NATURALIZED DISTRIBUTION

Oceania: Hawaiian Islands.

OCEANIA

Hawaiian Islands[1]

Caum (1933), writing of *M. polyglottos*, said that 'since 1928 a number of these birds, imported from the mainland by private individuals, osten-

sibly as game birds [*sic*], have been intentionally liberated in Honolulu [on Oahu]'. Munro (1944) confirms this date. Berger (1981: 194), however, does not mention this introduction, but says that 'the Hui Manu [Bird Society] released birds on Oahu in 1931, 1932 and 1933, and on Maui in 1933 (*Elepaio* 21: 81). There seem to be no further records of introductions.'

According to Munro, mockingbirds first reached Hawaii by 1936, and by the late 1950s were established on Maui (where they appeared first in 1933), and occurred locally on Oahu, Molokai (first in 1951) and Lanai, and occasionally on Hawaii. In 1959, on Maui Udvardy (1961) found mockingbirds to be 'very common residents . . . in all the dry, kiawe-[*Prosopis chilensis*] covered habitats that I visited'. In the same year, Hawaii was colonized with birds from Maui. Shortly afterwards they appear to have spread to all the larger islands as well as to some of the lesser ones to the north-west, such as Nihoa, Tern in the French Frigate Shoals (about October 1960) and Necker around 1966. Although Richardson & Bowles (1964) indicate that mockingbirds may have been introduced to Kauai (where in 1961 they were locally common on the south coast and appeared to be spreading rapidly) Berger (1975f) considered that they probably arrived naturally (perhaps around 1946) from Oahu. In 1972, the same author reported mockingbirds to be 'well established on Kaui, Oahu, Molokai, Lanai, Maui and Hawaii'. Zeillemaker & Scott (1976) recorded them as common on Maui, uncommon on Kauai, Oahu, Molokai, Lanai and Hawaii, and as occurring as accidental vagrants only in the northwestern islands of the Hawaiian Islands National Wildlife Refuge (Pearl and Hermes Reef, Lisianski and Laysan islands, Maro Reef, Gardner Pinnacles, French Frigate Shoals, and Necker and Nihoa islands) and on Kaula Rock. They also occur on Kahoolawe. Mockingbirds prefer dry lowland cultivated areas, pastures, exotic forests and scrubland (Guava (*Psidium guajava*), Java Plum (*Eugenia cumini*) and *Eucalyptus* sp.), and residential districts and community parklands.

According to Bourne (1957), Northern Mockingbirds (of the nominate form from the central, eastern and southeastern United States) were introduced to Bermuda in 1893; they appear to have flourished until about 1914 but thereafter declined and eventually disappeared. Long (1981: 304) says that the birds 'exhausted the food supply after only a short period of establishment'. This seems unlikely in view of the species' varied diet, which includes insects, grubs, pollen, nectar, fruit, berries and seeds.

Benson (1950) states that American mockingbirds (? *M. polyglottos*) are said to have been introduced to the island of St Helena where, after apparently becoming temporarily established, they eventually died out (see also below under *M. gilvus*).

Guild (1938) unsuccessfully released a number of Northern Mockingbirds on Tahiti.

According to Phillips (1928: 52), 'The famous American mocking bird was at one time a common cage bird, and there have no doubt been many attempts to introduce it on the north Pacific coast and in other parts [of the United States][2] outside its normal range.' These include birds translocated from Louisiana to San Francisco, California, in 1891; three pairs released by the Society for the Introduction of Useful Song-Birds into Oregon in the spring of 1892 at Milwaukee, where they apparently bred in the following year; and 40 pairs freed by the Portland, Oregon, Club in the spring of 1895, which survived for about a year.

Peters (1960) says that the form *M. p. orpheus* (the Bahamas and Greater Antilles) was successfully translocated to the island of Barbados in the Lesser Antilles, where it was later eradicated.

The **Tropical Mockingbird** (*Mimus gilvus*) ranges from southern Mexico south to Guatemala, Honduras and El Salvador, and from Colombia and Venezuela south through Guyana, French Guiana and Surinam to northern and eastern Brazil; it also occurs on Martinique, the Windward Islands, Trinidad and Tobago.

In Panama, where de Schauensee (1964) says Tropical Mockingbirds were introduced, Ridgely (1976) indicates that they were first reported in 1932; they are now said to be common throughout the Canal Zone and have spread east to Tocumen and Portobelo and west as far as La Chorrera and Boca del Rio, in Colón and Panamá provinces.

In the second half of the nineteenth century, the form *M. g. tolimensis* (western and central Colombia) was, according to Sick (1967), successfully translocated from the Magdalena division of northwestern Colombia to the Cauca division in the south-west.

Peters (1960) reports that the race *M. g. antillarum* (Martinique and the Windward Islands) was translocated to Barbados and Nevis in the Lesser Antilles where, after becoming temporarily established, it has since been eradicated.

On Trinidad and Tobago (where the subspecies is *tobagensis*), Tropical Mockingbirds are, according to Ffrench (1976), apparently a recent arrival. In 1931 on Trinidad, they were confined to St Augustine, but by 1956 had spread to Port of Spain, Piarco and oil company residential districts in the south of the island. They now occur on Trinidad in the Northern Range, on the east coast as far north as Toco, at Caroni, Orapouche, Bocas and Comuto, and on Chacachacare Island between Trinidad and Venezuela, and are apparently also common on Tobago. They are presumably the descendants of natural colonists from Venezuela, where the subspecies is *melanopterus*.

According to Melliss (1870), 'South American mockingbirds' (? sp.) were introduced to the island of St Helena; if this is so they failed to become permanently established (see also above under *M. polyglottos*).

NOTES

1 American Ornithologists' Union 1983; Berger 1972, 1975f; Blake 1975; Caum 1933; Dunmire 1961; Hawaiian Audubon Society 1975; Long 1981; Munro 1944; Pyle 1977; Richardson & Bowles 1964; Udvardy 1961; Zeillemaker & Scott 1976.
2 Jewett & Gabrielson 1929; Long 1981; Phillips 1928. See also: Anon., *Oregon Naturalist* 2: 23 (1895).

Dunnock
(*Prunella modularis*)

NATURAL DISTRIBUTION

Europe (including the British Isles but excluding the southern half of the Iberian Peninsula, Mediterranean coastal regions, most of Italy, the Balkans and extreme northern Scandinavia) eastwards into the central European USSR and south into Turkey, northern Iran, Lebanon and the Caucasus. Some birds winter in north-west Africa (Algeria and Tunisia), the Mediterranean, Israel and Egypt. According to Voous (1960), the Dunnock has considerably expanded its breeding range in Scandinavia during the present century.

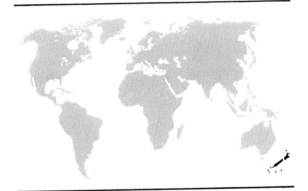

NATURALIZED DISTRIBUTION

Australasia: New Zealand.

AUSTRALASIA

New Zealand[1]

Thomson (1922: 148) quotes from Dr Arthur S. Thomson's *The Story of New Zealand* (2 vols, London, 1859) where it is claimed that 'Mr [Walter] Brodie, the settler who introduced pheasants [in 1845], sent out, in 1859, 300 sparrows for the purpose of keeping the caterpillars in check'. Thomson was unable to verify this claim, but pointed out that Brodie had lived at Mongonui in North Auckland, where Hedge Sparrows[2] were then unknown.

The Auckland Acclimatization Society acquired a single Hedge Sparrow from England (where the subspecies is *occidentalis*) in 1867, 2 in 1868, 7 in 1872, 19 (out of a shipment of 80) in 1874 and 18 in 1875. The first nests were discovered in 1873, and the birds soon became established. The Otago Society released 18 in 1868 and 80 in 1871, while their fellows in Canterbury introduced one in 1867, 8 in 1868, 9 in 1869, 41 in 1871 and 19 in 1872. A further shipment of 11 was landed at Christchurch in 1875, where some were sold and the remainder turned out in the society's gardens. In 1878, 72 pairs of 'hedge chanters' were ordered from England but there is no record of their arrival in Canterbury.

Thomson also quotes Drummond (1907) who claimed that:

It was Captain Stevens who brought the first hedge-sparrow to the colony, and it is claimed to the Southern Hemisphere. It came in the 'Matoaka' together with the first house-sparrows. It was the only survivor of a consignment. For a long time it was an object of interest in the Society's grounds in Christchurch, many people journeying to the gardens to see the stranger.

Thomson said that he was unaware of the source from which Drummond acquired his information, which he claimed was not included in the Canterbury Society's annual reports. In this, however, he was apparently mistaken, as Williams (1969: 444) states that 'the solitary dunnock's arrival' is referred to in the report published in May 1867. Could there, perhaps, have been confusion with the single bird procured by the Auckland Society in the same year?

In 1876, Walter Shrimpton liberated some Hedge Sparrows in the Hawke's Bay area, and the Wellington Society introduced 4 in 1880, 26 in 1881 and 20 in 1882; thereafter, the birds apparently spread rapidly and widely throughout New Zealand.

'Here perhaps', wrote Williams, 'is the only introduced bird about which no ill is spoken . . . their diet, which is predominantly of insects, ensures their popularity or, perhaps more accurately, their uncritical acceptance.' In this sentiment Williams was echoing Thomson, who said of the Hedge Sparrow that 'It is the one bird against which no word of complaint has ever been raised'. In Thomson's time Hedge Sparrows had not yet penetrated into undisturbed bush country but were, according to Philpott (1918), established in smaller areas of bush, in suburban gardens and in shrubby groves up to an altitude of 900 m. As most nests are built quite close to the ground, Thomson believed that predation by introduced Stoats (*Mustela erminea*) and feral Cats (*Felis catus*) was probably a controlling factor.

Wodzicki (1965: 433) said that Hedge Sparrows were 'widely abundant and common, North, South, Stewart and Raoul [Kermadec], Chatham and Auckland Islands'. Kinsky (1970) reported them to be generally distributed on the main islands and on Kapiti and other nearby offshore islands, and that they had spread also to Stewart, Snares (by 1948) and Campbell islands (probably before 1907). Falla, Sibson & Turbott (1979) found Hedge Sparrows to be a most successful colonizer and well established in all kinds of cover (including coastal mangrove swamps, saltmarshes, parkland, gardens, exotic forests and subalpine scrub) between sea level and 1,600 m; they have spread to most offshore islands (including Three Kings, Little Barrier, Hen, Kapiti, Solander, Codfish, Stewart, Raoul, the Chathams, the Antipodes, Snares and Aucklands) and into the subantarctic as far as Campbell Island – 700 km south of the New Zealand mainland. On distant islands, Hedge Sparrows are believed to breed on Campbell, the Antipodes, the Chathams, and perhaps elsewhere.

According to Phillips (1928) Hedge Sparrows, among other species, are said to have been released unsuccessfully in Cincinnati in the United States in 1872–4.

NOTES

1 Drummond 1907; Falla, Sibson & Turbott 1979; Kinsky, 1970; Lever 1985b; Long 1981; Oliver 1930, 1955; Philpott 1918; Thomson 1922, 1926; Williams 1953, 1969, 1973; Wodzicki 1965.
2 The Dunnock was, until quite recently, known as the Hedge Sparrow. In describing the species' introduction to New Zealand the earlier appellation has been retained.

White-rumped Shama
(*Copsychus malabaricus*)

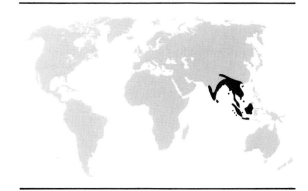

NATURAL DISTRIBUTION

India, Nepal, Sri Lanka, the Andaman Islands, Burma, Bangladesh, Thailand, Indo-China, Hainan, Malaysia, Borneo, Java and Sumatra.

NATURALIZED DISTRIBUTION

Oceania: Hawaiian Islands.

OCEANIA

Hawaiian Islands[1]

White-rumped Shamas of the form *C. m. indicus* (Nepal, Assam and northeastern India), imported via San Francisco by Alexander Isenberg, were released on the island of Kauai in 1931, where by 1960 Richardson & Bowles (1964) found them to be a 'moderately common resident locally, usually in inhabited lowland areas' where they showed 'much adaptability to habitats varying widely in vegetation and aridity'. In 1940, more were freed by the Hui Manu ('Bird Society') in the Nuuanu Valley and on the Makiki Heights

on Oahu, where some were observed at Pauoa Flats in 1948, in the upper Manoa Valley in the following year, and at Tantalus in 1950. Berger (1972) reported Shamas to be 'fairly common in suitable wet habitats on Oahu: upper Manoa Valley, Tantalus, upper Nuuanu Valley, along the Koolau Range to the Aiea loop trail, as well as along the slopes of the Pali'. The Hawaiian Audubon Society (1975) found them to be fairly common in the upper valleys on the ridges of the Koolau Range. A year later, Zeillemaker & Scott (1976) described Shamas as common on Kauai and uncommon on Oahu in exotic forests and scrub (i.e. Guava (*Psidium guajava*), Java Plum (*Eugenia cumini*) and *Eucalyptus* sp.). Berger (1981: 196–7), however, said that 'The Shama is common on both the windward and leeward sides of Oahu. The birds prefer areas of lush vegetation, but they also occur on the Manoa campus of the university, at the Makiki nursery, occasionally at Kapiolani Park, the Na Laau arboretum on Diamond Head, and even in the residential areas of Kailua.'

The **Magpie Robin** or **Dyal** (*Copsychus saularis*) occurs naturally from Pakistan, India, Bangladesh, Sri Lanka and the Andaman Islands eastwards to southern China, Hainan, southern Thailand, Malaysia, Sumatra, Java, Borneo, the Greater Sunda Islands and the Philippines.

In 1922, a pair of the form *C. s. prosthopellus* (southern and eastern China and Hainan), imported from Hong Kong, was released by Mrs Dora Isenberg on Kauai in the Hawaiian Islands.[2] Ten years later more were freed on Kauai and on Oahu by the Hui Manu, and others of the same race were liberated on Oahu in about 1950. A decade later, Magpie Robins were reported to occur along the Manoa Stream in the upper Manoa Valley and on Tantalus on Oahu. Zeillemaker & Scott (1976) recorded them as local and rare on Oahu and of 'undetermined abundance' on Kauai in the same habitats as *C. malabaricus*. They are not referred to by Pyle (1977), and the American Ornithologists' Union (1983: 785) says that 'there is no evidence of establishment; there have been no reliable reports since 1967'.

NOTES

1 American Ornithologists' Union 1983; Ali & Ripley 1968–74; Berger 1972, 1981; Blake 1975; Harpham 1953; Hawaiian Audubon Society 1975; Long 1981; Munro 1960; Pyle 1977; Richardson & Bowles 1964; Zeillemaker & Scott 1976.

2 American Ornithologists' Union 1983; Berger 1972, 1981; Blake 1975; Bryan 1958; Caum 1933; Hawaiian Audubon Society 1975; Long 1981; Peterson 1961; Zeillemaker & Scott 1976.

Blackbird
(*Turdus merula*)

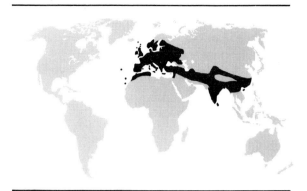

NATURAL DISTRIBUTION

The Palaearctic Region, occurring in Europe from the British Isles eastwards to the central USSR and north to around 63° N in Norway; in the Atlantic in Madeira, the Azores and the Canary Islands; in North Africa in Morocco, Algeria and Tunisia; and from Asia Minor eastwards through India, Sri Lanka and northern Burma to central-southern China, northern Vietnam and central Laos.

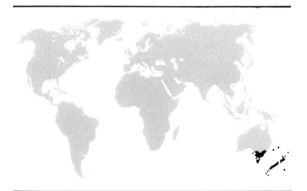

NATURALIZED DISTRIBUTION

Australasia: Australia, New Zealand.

AUSTRALASIA

Australia[1]

Table 7 gives details of introductions of Blackbirds to Australia. Between the 1860s (when they were valued at 50*s.* each) and the 1880s, Blackbirds were released on some 50 occasions in Australia, mainly in Victoria (in the Melbourne

Table 7 Introductions of Blackbirds (*Turdus merula*) to Australia, 1857–82

Date	Number	Locality	Remarks
1857 (January)	?	Melbourne, Victoria	Imported by a dealer named Brown
1857 (August)	72 (including Song Thrushes, q.v.)	Melbourne, Victoria	Shipped on the *Severn* from England
1858 (January)	?	Melbourne, Victoria	Imported by a dealer named Neymaler
1858 (October)	?	Melbourne, Victoria	Imported by a Mr Rushall from England on the *Norfolk*
1858 (December)	?	Melbourne, Victoria	Imported by Neymaler
1860s	?	Hobart, Tasmania	Said to have become established
1862–3	?	Melbourne, Victoria	
1862 (after)	?	Sydney, New South Wales	
1863	?	Adelaide, South Australia	
1864	6	Botanic Gardens, Melbourne, Victoria	
1866	17	Botanic Gardens, Melbourne, Victoria	
1869	?	Brisbane, Queensland	Shipped on the clipper *Flying Cloud* from England; failed to become established
1872	22	Botanic Gardens, Melbourne, Victoria	
1872	'A few'	Near Sydney, New South Wales	Apparently failed to become permanently established; present population is probably derived from an aviary release in 1940
1879	4	Mount Lofty, Adelaide,	Released by South Australia Acclimatization Society
1881	?	Beaumont and Torrens Park,	
1882	At least 45	South Australia (and ? Tasmania)	

Sources: see note 1

Botanic Gardens, on Phillip Island, at Western Port and at Gembrook) and in the Royal Park near Sydney in New South Wales. In his anniversary address to the Victoria Acclimatization Society on 24 November 1862, Professor F. McCoy said that 18 Blackbirds (among other species) had so far been liberated in the Botanic Gardens in Melbourne; 2 years later the society claimed that Blackbirds, *inter alia*, 'may now be considered thoroughly established', and by 1913 they were said to be 'breeding freely' in Victoria.

By the mid-1920s, Blackbirds were established in the Botanic Gardens at Sydney in New South Wales (where they later died out, and were introduced again in 1940) and at Albury near the border with Victoria. Twenty-five years later they had become widespread and fairly abundant in South Australia on the Adelaide Plains, around Mount Lofty, at Victor Harbour, at Coorong (Salt Creek), and near Mount Gambier north-

wards to Oodnatta, as well as on the mainland of Victoria and on Mud Island in Port Phillip Bay. They appeared on Kangaroo Island (South Australia) in 1947, at Canberra and on Flinders Island (where they may have been introduced around 1930) in Bass Strait around 1949, at Deniliquin (New South Wales) in 1954, at Doveton in 1957, and at Dareton in 1959. By the turn of the decade they were established in citrus orchards along the Murray River in New South Wales, in the Riverina, on the central tablelands, at Baroonga, Tocumwal, Mathoura, Tooleybuc and Goodnight, in the Sunraysia district, and in coastal regions north to Sydney. They appeared at Broken Hill in 1975–6, at Cobar in 1976, and at Armidale in 1977.

Blackbirds appear first to have been recorded as breeding in the wild in Tasmania in about 1918; they reached Port Davey in the south-west around 1937–8, and by the late 1940s were widely distributed. A decade later they were established on the coast at Recherche, Bound Bay, Spain Bay, Point Eric, Cox Bight and Moth Creek, but did not reach Bicheno on the east coast until the early 1960s.

Williams (1953) suggests that Blackbirds were probably introduced to Norfolk Island some 1,500 km east of Brisbane, by man around 1939; they were reported to be abundant there in the late 1960s. On Lord Howe Island, where they were first noted in 1953 and where by the late 1950s they were widely but sparsely distributed, Blackbirds are believed to be natural immigrants from New Zealand, some 1,300 km to the south-east.

Initially, Blackbirds in Australia spread only slowly from their centres around Melbourne and Adelaide. After the Second World War they began to expand their range more rapidly, and had soon colonized most of the southeastern mainland, Tasmania and islands in Bass Strait, but until the early 1960s were still uncommon in much of New South Wales. Frith (1979: 187) described the Blackbird as 'now widespread in Tasmania. On the mainland its present range extends from Adelaide and the Mount Lofty Ranges, South Australia, throughout the southeast of that State, along the Murray River, throughout Victoria except the arid scrubs of the north-west, and irregularly throughout southern New South Wales to as far north as Goulburn [97 km north-east of Canberra]. It is still slowly extending its range [and] . . . is most numerous in towns, gardens and well-established horticultural districts. In Tasmania and Victoria, however, it has invaded the bush and lives successfully in the moister forests.' Pizzey (1980) found Blackbirds to be common and widespread in Tasmania and in most of Victoria and South Australia except in the mallee; to occur as occasional visitors in the Flinders Range; to be established in eastern New South Wales north and west to Cobar and west along the Murray River and watercourses of the southern Riverina, and in vineyards and citrus orchards as far as Waikerie/Moorook in South Australia.

In horticultural areas, Blackbirds are a serious pest to growers of soft fruit – especially grapes, cherries and figs. In Victoria, their diet includes the fruits of the native *Pittosporum undulatum* and *Exocarpos cupressiformis*, which they seem to be spreading into new areas. Their impact, if any,

on such native species as White's Thrush (*Zoothera dauma*) in the wet forests of Tasmania is, as Frith points out, as yet unknown.

New Zealand[2]

In about 1862, the Nelson Acclimatization Society imported 26 Blackbirds to New Zealand, but what became of them is unrecorded. The Otago Society released a pair at Dunedin in 1865, 6, also at Dunedin (in 1867), 39 (1868), 21 (1869) and 70 (1871). A decade later the society reported, with a trace of embarrassment, that Blackbirds were 'now exceedingly numerous and we regret to say are found to be rather partial to cherries and other garden fruits'.

In 1865, the Canterbury Society acquired a pair, which had been landed at Lyttleton, from Captain Rose of the *Mermaid*, who at the same time sold 'a number of songbirds' to the society for £18. These two Blackbirds were presumably those referred to in the society's report for 1866 as having been released, with other English and Australian species, in the previous year. In 1867, the Canterbury Society obtained a further 46 Blackbirds, which Captain Stevens had landed from the *Matoaka* at Lyttleton, and in the following year they acquired 152 more. The annual report for 1871 stated that Blackbirds (and Song Thrushes (*Turdus philomelos*) q.v.) 'have not increased as well as expected, and it is much to be feared have been killed by cats'. In the same year,[3] a Mr R. Bills imported a shipment of 62 on behalf of the society, which obtained a further 95 in 1872 and 117 more in 1875; 40 of this last consignment were liberated at Levels, Otipua, Waimate, Otaio, Geraldine, Albury and 'the back of Timaru' in South Canterbury.

The Auckland Society introduced 8 Blackbirds in 1865, about 30 in 1867, 132 in 1868 (when they were 'considered to be thoroughly acclimatized'), and released a considerable number more in 1869. Ten years later, Blackbirds were first liberated on Stewart Island, where by about 1920 they were, according to Thomson (1922: 146), 'seen every breeding season near settlements'.

Many of New Zealand's offshore islands have been colonized by Blackbirds naturally from the mainland. According to Williams (1953), they reached Campbell and the Chatham and Auckland islands around the turn of the century, the

Snares in 1907 and the Kermadecs in 1910. Drummond (1907) said that they had 'taken up their residence on the lonely Auckland Islands', and Thomson stated that they were increasing on the Chatham Islands. By the mid-1950s, Blackbirds had also been reported from Three Kings, Poor Knights, Hen, Little Barrier, Mayor, Karewa, Kapiti and Solander islands.

In South Island's Southland, according to Philpott (1918):

unlike the thrush the blackbird is to be found in the heart of the big bushes. I have met with the bird wherever I have gone, and found it as common on the Hunter Mountains at 3000 feet [900 m] elevation, as in the bush near Invercargill. . . . The spread of succulent-fruited plants is probably accomplished to a greater extent by blackbirds than by any other species.

According to Thomson, the spread of the Blackbird (and Song Thrush) in North Island was almost certainly from Auckland, and he quotes H. Guthrie-Smith[4] who suggested that they dispersed via the coast of the Gulf of Thames, the Coromandel Peninsula, down the Bay of Plenty, round the East Cape and on to Hawke's Bay. Guthrie-Smith found Blackbirds in the heart of the forest country, and Thomson saw no reason why, since the intervening strip of bush was comparatively narrow, they (and Song Thrushes) should not have spread over from the Thames Valley direct to the east coast. Although Blackbirds were 'rare or altogether wanting' north of Whangarei in North Island, elsewhere Thomson described them around 1920 as 'now one of the commonest of our introduced birds in very many parts of New Zealand'. Oliver (1955) found Blackbirds to be distributed throughout both North and South islands, while a decade later Wodzicki (1965: 433) described them as 'widely distributed and abundant, North, South, Stewart, and Raoul, Chatham, Campbell, Snares and Auckland Islands'. Kinsky (1970) said that Blackbirds had colonized the two main islands and all outlying islands (including Stewart, the Kermadecs, Chatham, Snares, Aucklands and Campbell), while Falla, Sibson & Turbott (1979) reported them to be one of New Zealand's commonest birds, occurring on the mainland from sea level to an altitude of around 1,400 m and on many offshore islands from the Kermadecs to Campbell Island.

The wide dispersal of the Blackbird in New Zealand (an important factor in its successful naturalization) is due largely to the introduction of the partially migratory nominate form, *T. m. merula*, of western Europe. Its favourite habitats are gardens, parks and farmland, but it also occurs in large stands of dense native forest and bush that are shunned by the closely related Song Thrush. Apart from their depredation of soft fruits,[5] Thomson reported that Blackbirds in New Zealand also sometimes attack and kill such native species as the Tui or Parson Bird (*Prosthemadera novaeseelandiae*) – a variety of honeyeater – and Smithers & Disney (1969) suggested probable competition on Norfolk Island with the Island Thrush (*Turdus p. poliocephalus*).

Among other species, Blackbirds were introduced by Cecil Rhodes to South Africa[6] between 1898 and 1902 but failed to become permanently established; Liversidge (n.d.) indicates that a maximum population of perhaps 100 birds survived for 38 years before dying out.

In the United States,[7] a dozen Blackbirds were set free in Greenwood cemetery on Long Island, New York, towards the end of 1852, and 16 pairs by the Portland, Oregon, Society for the Introduction of European Songbirds in May 1889, followed by a further 19 pairs in 1892. In spite of initial optimistic reports none of these liberations were permanently successful.

Blackbirds (among other songbirds) from England were released on St Helena[8] in 1852 and again in the early 1900s, but failed to become established.

According to Wood & Wetmore (1926), Blackbirds from England were unsuccessfully liberated in about 1925 on Kanathea Island in the eastern Lau Group, Fiji.

In the spring of 1972, 106 young Blackbirds of the nominate form were transported by air from Poznan in western Poland 1,000 km east to the Ukranian SSR (where the form is *T. m. aterrimus*) and freed in the grounds of Kiev Zoo; about half settled within a radius of 5 km of the zoo where they bred successfully in 1973 and are now considered to be established.

In western Europe,[9] the Blackbird was formerly a woodland or forest-edge species, and it is only in the past 150–200 years that it has spread into fields, hedgerows, commons, heaths and suburban – even urban – parks, squares and gardens. In Italy and southern Europe, urban gardens were colonized probably in the late eighteenth century, in northern France, the Netherlands and central and southern Germany in the first half of the nineteenth century, in the region of the River Elbe in northwestern Germany around 1875, in Denmark in about 1890, in Mecklenburg in north-central Germany around the turn of the century, in Norway shortly after 1910, and in southern Finland in the early 1920s. In parts of southeastern Europe, the Blackbird is still mainly a species of woodlands or forest ecotone.

NOTES

1 Balmford 1978; Blakers, Davies & Reilly 1984; Chisholm 1918, 1926; Coleman 1939; Condon 1962; Cooper 1947; Dove 1919; Frith 1979; Green &
Mollison 1961; Hobbs 1961; Jenkins 1977; Long 1981; McKean & Hindwood 1965; Pizzey 1980; Rolls 1969; Ryan 1906; Smithers & Disney 1969; Snow 1958; Tarr 1950; Thomas 1965; Williams 1953.

2 Drummond 1907; Falla, Sibson & Turbott 1979; Kinsky 1970; Long 1981; Oliver 1955; Philpott 1918; Snow 1958; Thomson 1922; Williams 1953, 1969, 1973; Wodzicki 1965.

3 Williams (1969) says that this shipment was made in 1873.

4 *Tutira, the Story of a New Zealand Sheep Station* (Blackwood: Edinburgh and London, 1921).

5 For the diet of Blackbirds in New Zealand see under Song Thrush (pages 333–4).

6 Liversidge n.d.; Long 1981; Siegfried 1962; J. M. Winterbottom 1966, 1978 (and personal communication, 1981).

7 Cleaveland 1865 (in Murphy 1945); Long 1981; Phillips 1928. See also: *Forest and Stream* 8: 262 (1877).

8 Benson 1950; Long 1981; Melliss 1870.

9 Sharrock 1976; Snow 1958.

Song Thrush
(*Turdus philomelos*)

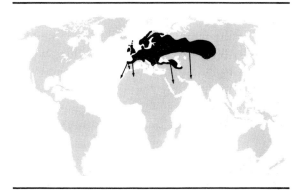

NATURAL DISTRIBUTION
Eurasia, from the British Isles eastwards through Europe (apart from northern Scandinavia, Portugal and most of Spain) to central Asia. Winters south to the Iberian Peninsula, the Canary Islands, north Africa, Arabia and south-western Asia.

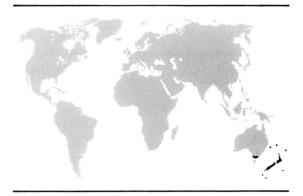

NATURALIZED DISTRIBUTION
Australasia: Australia, New Zealand.

AUSTRALASIA

Australia[1]

Table 8 gives details of introductions of Song Thrushes to Australia. In his anniversary address to the Victoria Acclimatization Society on 24 November 1862, Professor F. McCoy said that 24 Song Thrushes (among other species) had so far been released in the Botanic Gardens in Melbourne, and 2 years later the society announced that Thrushes, *inter alia*, 'may now be

Table 8 Introductions of Song Thrushes (*Turdus philomelos*) to Australia, 1856–1936

Date	Number	Locality	Remarks
1856 (April)	?	Sydney, New South Wales or Melbourne, Victoria	
1857 (January)	?	Melbourne, Victoria (Botanic Gardens and Royal Park)	Imported by a dealer named Brown
1857 (August)	72 (including Blackbirds, q.v.)	Melbourne and Phillip Island, Victoria	Shipped on the *Severn* from England
1858 (January)	?	Melbourne, Victoria (Botanic Gardens and Royal Park)	Imported by a dealer named Neymaler
1858 (October)	?	Melbourne, Victoria (Botanic Gardens and Royal Park)	Imported by a Mr Rushall from England on the *Norfolk*
1858 (December)	?	Melbourne, Victoria (Botanic Gardens and Royal Park)	Imported by Neymaler
?1859	48	Melbourne, Victoria (Botanic Gardens)	Reported to be breeding in 1860
?1860	37	Melbourne, Victoria (Botanic Gardens)	
1860	7 pairs	Melbourne, Victoria	
1863	'A small lot'	Melbourne, Victoria (Botanic Gardens)	
1864	2 pairs	Phillip Island, Victoria	Released by Victoria Acclimatization Society
c.1864–5	49	Botanic Gardens, Melbourne (18); Yarra Bend; Sandstone and Churchill islands; Geelong, Victoria	Released by Victoria Acclimatization Society
1866	6	Royal Park, near Sydney, New South Wales	
1869	?	Brisbane, Queensland	Shipped on the clipper *Flying Cloud* from England; failed to become established
1872	28	Botanic Gardens, Melbourne, Victoria	
1872	'A small lot'	'near Sydney', New South Wales	Failed to become established
1879–80	?	Adelaide, South Australia	Failed to become established
1880	12	Gembrook, Victoria	Released by Victoria Acclimatization Society
?1900–5	?	New South Wales	Failed to become established
1935 or 1936	?	Canberra	Introduced from New Zealand, despite protests to the Minister of Internal Affairs; bred at Red Hill in 1937, but apparently died out by 1939

Sources: see note 1

considered thoroughly established'. The birds slowly multiplied and expanded their range until by the turn of the century they were to be found all round the city of Melbourne and its suburbs, but had yet to spread into the surrounding countryside. By the late 1940s, Song Thrushes were fairly common in parks and gardens in Melbourne and had spread to Sherbrooke Forest, Macedon, Geelong (where some had been planted in 1865), Belgrave and possibly Ararat. Frith (1979: 187) described the Song Thrush as 'quite common in Melbourne and is widespread in small numbers in towns and heavily developed districts in southern Victoria generally. It has disappeared elsewhere'. Pizzey (1980), who found Song Thrushes to occur in Melbourne and elsewhere in Victoria including Warragul, parts of the Mornington Peninsula, Dandenong and Yellingbo to the east, Macedon to the north and Werribee, Geelong and Lorne in the south-west, described them as usually rather rare and local near human habitation.

According to Williams (1953), Song Thrushes probably arrived on Norfolk Island around 1913 and on Lord Howe Island in about 1929 – on both as natural immigrants from New Zealand, respectively 750 km to the south and 1,300 km to the south-east. On the former island, they were present and breeding in the early 1960s and were 'common' in 1969; on the latter, about 50 were counted in 1959 and they were recorded as breeding there a few years later.

New Zealand[2]

Song Thrushes were first introduced to New Zealand around 1862,[3] when the Nelson Acclimatization Society imported and released five. These birds disappeared, and the subsequent colonization of Nelson was probably the result of natural dispersal from Canterbury where, according to the Acclimatization Society's annual report for 1866, 'thrushes' (which Williams (1969: 443) assumes to refer to *philomelos*), were already present. A further three dozen from England were landed in Canterbury in 1867, followed a year later by two dozen more. The society's report for 1870 (quoted by Thomson 1922: 143), however, states that 'they have not increased so well as expected, and it is much to be feared have been killed by cats'. More were accordingly imported in 1871 and (in the care of a Mr R. Bills) in 1875, some of which were sold for 15s. each, while others were released in Christchurch Gardens and 20 in native bush at Bluecliffs, Four Peaks and 'at the back of Timaru'. Twenty more pairs were imported in 1878 and an additional four dozen pairs in 1880, but it was not until around the turn of the century that Song Thrushes became firmly established in the province.

The Otago Society imported 2 in 1865, 4 in 1867, 49 in 1868, 48 (from Mr J. A. Ewen in London in the charge of Mr Bills) in 1869 and 42 in 1871. These birds quickly established themselves in native bush in the vicinity of Dunedin, where they found a more suitable habitat than the comparatively open country of North Canterbury. In their annual report for 1881 (quoted by Thomson 1922: 143), the Otago Society stated that 'thrushes, we are glad to find, are becoming more plentiful in the neighbourhood', adding, somewhat naively, that 'they are blamed for destroying fruit'.

In 1867, the Auckland Society imported 30 Song Thrushes followed by a further 95 in 1868, and these, too, rapidly became established. The Wellington Society acquired eight in 1878, but what became of them is unknown.

On New Zealand's offshore and outlying islands, Song Thrushes have been recorded from Poor Knights, Hen, Little Barrier, Three Kings, Kapiti, D'Urville, Raoul (Kermadecs, before 1910), the Chathams (before 1922), the Antipodes, Campbell, Snares (around the turn of the century), Stewart, Codfish, the Aucklands and Macquarie: they are said to breed on Three Kings, Raoul, the Chathams, Campbell, the Aucklands and Snares, and probably on some others also.

In Southland on South Island, according to Philpott (1918):

The song-thrush does not appear to penetrate far into the big forests, nor to spread into unsettled areas. In the coastal forest of Fiord County they are seldom to be heard, though plentiful enough about the settlements of Tuatapere and Papatotara. Nor does the bird favour the mountains; I do not think I have ever heard one above the bush-line (about 3,000 feet) [*c.* 900 m].

In North Island, Thomson considered that Song Thrushes (and Blackbirds (*Turdus merula*)) almost certainly spread east and south from Auckland.[4] 'At the present day', wrote Thomson (1922: 143), 'thrushes are found from one end of New Zealand to the other in enormous abundance. They are responsible, along with blackbirds, for continual and serious depredations in orchards.' As with Blackbirds, the cultivated fruits most affected include cherries, plums, apricots, currants, raspberries, boysenberries, grapes, gooseberries, strawberries and apples. Other alien plants eaten and spread by Song Thrushes and Blackbirds include the fruit or seeds of the noxious Blackberry (*Rubus fruiticosus*), Sweetbriar Roses (*Rosa rubiginosa*), Cape Fuchsia (*Leycesteria formosa*), Elderberries (*Sambucus nigra*),

Ink-weed or Poke-weed (*Phytolacca octandra*) and Barberries (*Berberis vulgaris*). On the credit side, Song Thrushes and Blackbirds consume large quantities of injurious insects and snails.

By the 1930s, Song Thrushes were established throughout New Zealand except in densely forested habitats; Wodzicki (1965: 433) reported them to be 'widely distributed and abundant, North, South, Stewart, and Raoul, Chatham, Campbell, Snares and Auckland Islands'. Kinsky (1970) said that, in addition to North and South islands, they had colonized all outlying islands including Stewart, the Kermadecs, the Chathams, Snares, the Aucklands and Campbell. Today, Song Thrushes are one of the commonest birds in New Zealand, being widely distributed, according to Falla, Sibson & Turbott (1979), in gardens, parks and farmland and in some open forested areas on the two main islands, and on offlying groups from the Kermadecs in the north to Campbell Island in the south. They are, perhaps, slightly less successful as colonizers of distant offshore islands than the more adventurous and aggressive Blackbird.

––––––––––––––––––––

Winterbottom (1981) wrote that in South Africa[5] the Song Thrush was 'introduced by Cecil Rhodes to Cape Town at the turn of the century and [was] fairly common until *c.* 1936. No records since 1947 and probably extinct'. This is confirmed by Liversidge (n.d.), who indicates that a possible maximum of around 100 survived (at Newlands on the Cape Peninsula) for 47 years before dying out.

In the United States[6] towards the end of 1852, the Trustees of the Greenwood cemetery on Long Island, New York, acquired several species of songbirds from England, which they unsuccessfully released; among them were a dozen thrushes, which were probably *philomelos*. According to the records of the Society for the Introduction of European Songbirds, of Portland, Oregon (quoted by Phillips 1928: 52), 'Thirty-five pairs of song thrushes [were] liberated in 1889 to 1892 (and increased)'. In May 1893, 15 'gray' song thrushes[7] were liberated in New York City, and a further 25 pairs of thrushes from England were subsequently released by the Portland Bird Club. As with Blackbirds, despite initial optimism none of these plantings met with lasting success.

It seems probable that Song Thrushes were among the songbirds from England recorded by Benson (1950) as having been unsuccessfully released on the island of St Helena in the early years of this century.

––––––––––––––––––––

The **Island Thrush** (*Turdus poliocephalus*) occurs on many islands in Indonesia and the Pacific from Sumatra and Taiwan to Fiji and Samoa. Between 1885 and 1900, birds from Christmas Island (where the form is *T. p. erythropleurus*) were released on Pulo Luar (Horsburgh) in the Cocos (Keeling) archipelago in the Indian Ocean; by the 1940s, they had spread to South Island (Atas) and to West Island (Panjang) and were plentiful on all three.[8]

NOTES

1 Balmford 1978; Blakers, Davies & Reilly 1984; Chisholm 1950; Frith 1979; Jenkins 1977; Lamm & White 1950; Long 1981; McGill 1960; McKean & Hindwood 1965; Pizzey 1980; Rolls 1969; Ryan 1906; Smithers & Disney 1969; Tarr 1950; Williams 1953.

2 Falla, Sibson & Turbott 1979; Kinsky 1970; Long 1981; Oliver 1930; Philpott 1918; Thomson 1922, 1926; Williams 1953, 1969, 1973.

3 Thomson (1922: 142) says 'about 1872'. Since he (1926) and other later authors give the date as 1862, the former is presumably either a misprint or was subsequently revised.

4 For their route see under Blackbird (page 329).

5 Liversidge n.d.; Long 1981; Mackworth-Praed & Grant 1962–3; Siegfried 1962; J. M. Winterbottom 1966, 1978 (and personal communication, 1981); and P. A. Clancey, personal communication, 1981

6 Cleaveland 1865 (in Murphy 1945); Jewett & Gabrielson 1929; Long 1981; Phillips 1928. See also: *Forest and Stream* 8: 262 (1877) and *Oregon Naturalist* 3: 32–154 (1896).

7 These may perhaps have been Clay-coloured Thrushes (*Turdus grayi*) from central and northern South America.

8 Gibson-Hill 1949; Long 1981; Van Tets & Van Tets 1967.

Melodious Laughing Thrush

(Garrulax canorus)

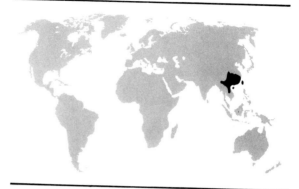

NATURAL DISTRIBUTION
Southern China (especially in the valley of the Yangtze (Jinsha Jiang) River, northern Indo-China, Hainan, and Taiwan.

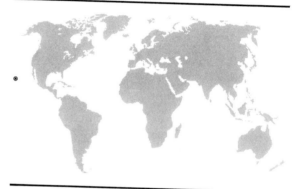

NATURALIZED DISTRIBUTION
Oceania: Hawaiian Islands.

OCEANIA

Hawaiian Islands[1]

The Melodious Laughing Thrush (known also as the Chinese Thrush or Hwa-Mei) was introduced as a cagebird to the island of Oahu by Chinese immigrants in the late nineteenth century. According to Caum (1933), 'a number obtained their freedom at the time of the great fire in the Oriental quarter of Honolulu in 1900, and took to the hills behind the city'. More – of the nominate subspecies – were subsequently imported from China and released on Maui in 1902 and on Molokai and Hawaii in 1909, and in 1918 birds on Oahu were trapped and translocated to Kauai. By around 1930 Caum found them to be 'well established' on Oahu.

According to Munro (1960), the Melodious Laughing Thrush, a bird of the scrub layer, soon became widespread and abundant, and succeeded in penetrating deeper into the forests than any other introduced species; by the early 1940s, however, it was apparently decreasing locally, but by the late 1950s/early 1960s it had staged a recovery, and was described as common on Kauai, local on Oahu and Hawaii, and scarce on Molokai and Maui. Ord (1967) reported it to be 'abundant on Hawaii, Maui and Oahu, from 400 feet [120 m] up to the tree limit'. Richardson & Bowles (1964) found it also to be common on Kauai, where it occurred from sea level to an altitude of 1,400 m, in montane forest, in humid forested valleys, and in barren and arid canyons of the south Na Pali coast. It was equally at home in introduced Lantana (*Lantana camara*), *Malastroma*, blackberry, and *Albizzia* forests, and in dense native woodland with a high annual rainfall in the Alakai Swamp region where, and in Kokee, it was especially common.

The Hawaiian Audubon Society (1975) reported that the Melodious Laughing Thrush occurred on all the main islands apart from Lanai, and was common on Kauai. A year later, Zeillemaker & Scott (1976) described its habitat as introduced forest and scrubland (Guava (*Psidium guajava*), Java Plum (*Eugenia cumini*) and *Eucalyptus* sp.) and native mixed ohia (*Metrosideros collina*) and koa (*Acacia koa*) forest, and its status as common on Kauai, uncommon on Hawaii, and rare on Oahu, Molokai and Maui. On the last-named island it had been reported to be fairly common below about 1,000 m in the Kipahulu Valley in 1945.

In 1941, an unsuccessful attempt was made to introduce the Melodious Laughing Thrush to Woodside, California, USA.[2]

The **Greater Necklaced Laughing Thrush** (*Garrulax pectoralis*[3]) occurs naturally from Nepal eastwards to southeastern China and Hainan, and south to southeastern Burma, western Thailand, northern Laos and North Vietnam.

In 1919, birds of this species were introduced

by Mrs Dora Isenberg via San Francisco to Kauai[4] in the Hawaiian Islands, and around 1950 others (probably from Kauai) are said to have been released on Oahu.[5] On the former island, some were reported on the east coast near Lihue in 1959, and by 1964 they were apparently sparsely distributed in the Wailua Homesteads region, where a flock of half-a-dozen was noted in March 1967. Two were seen near Kapaa on the east coast of Kauai in July 1970, and 19 at Lihue in 1976. The species' present status on Kauai is uncertain, but Zeillemaker & Scott (1976) described it as locally uncommon in introduced forests and scrubland (Guava, Java Plum and Eucalyptus). It seems now to be established in the Huleia Valley (including the National Park) and the Wailua Valley (including the House Lots area).

A pair of the **White-crested Laughing Thrush** (*Garrulax leucolophus*), a native of the western Himalayas eastwards to southwestern China and Indo-China (and western Sumatra), that had presumably escaped from captivity was reported (by Berger 1972) to have bred in 1969 at Diamond Head on Oahu in the Hawaiian Islands.

The **White-browed Laughing Thrush** (*Garrulax sannio*) occurs naturally in eastern Assam, northeastern Burma, northern Laos, North Vietnam, northern Indo-China, southern and southwestern China and on Hainan.

Although King, Dickinson & Woodcock (1975) list the species as a . natural vagrant to Hong Kong, Webster (1975) suggests that it may have been introduced there by aviculturists from whom it subsequently escaped, and that it has probably been established and breeding in the wild in at least two areas on the island since the early 1970s. Why these birds should be considered introduced aliens rather than natural colonists from the nearby Chinese mainland (where the form is *G. s. sannio*) is unclear.

The **Grey-sided Laughing Thrush** (*Garrulax caerulatus*)[6] occurs naturally from the eastern Himalayas through Assam, Burma and Yunnan to Fukien (Fujian) in eastern China.

Caum (1933) reported that five unidentified

laughing-thrushes were released on Oahu in the Hawaiian Islands in 1928. Some were seen in 1949, 1950, 1954 and 1960, but it was not until 1978 that the species was identified by Taylor & Collins (1979), although the American Ornithologists' Union (1983: 786) enters the caveat that 'the specific identification of the recent report has not been verified'.

NOTES

1 American Ornithologists' Union 1983; Berger 1981; Blake 1975; Caum 1933; Elton 1958; Hawaiian Audubon Society 1975; Long 1981; Munro 1960; Ord 1967; Peterson 1961; Pyle 1977; Richardson & Bowles 1964; Zeillemaker & Scott 1976.
2 Isenberg & Williams, *Avicultural Magazine* 53(2): 48–50 (1946), quoted by American Ornithologists' Union (1957).
3 Until recently, it was generally believed by, for example, Caum (1933) and Blake (1975), that the second species of laughing-thrush naturalized in Hawaii was the White-throated (*Garrulax albogularis*) or Lesser Necklaced (*G. moniliger*). In 1976, however, C F. Zeillemaker, in a letter to *Elepaio* (journal of the Hawaiian Audubon Society; 36: 113–14), indicated that the second species was in fact the Greater Necklaced Laughing Thrush (*G. pectoralis*).
4 American Ornithologists' Union 1983; Berger 1981; Blake 1975; Caum 1933; Hawaiian Audubon Society 1975; Heilbrun 1976; Long 1981; Peterson 1961; Pyle 1977; Richardson & Bowles 1964; Zeillemaker & Scott 1976.
5 Bryan 1958.
6 American Ornithologists' Union 1983; Berger 1981; Caum 1933; Taylor & Collins 1979.

Red-billed Leiothrix
(*Leiothrix lutea*)

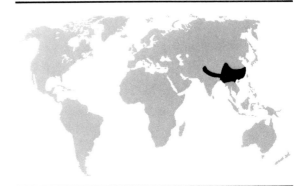

NATURAL DISTRIBUTION
From the western Himalayas eastwards through southwestern and northeastern Burma and southern Assam to northwestern Yunnan, northeastern Vietnam and southern, southeastern and central China.

NATURALIZED DISTRIBUTION
Asia: ?Hong Kong; Oceania: Hawaiian Islands.

ASIA

Hong Kong[1]

The Red-billed Leiothrix or Pekin Robin is a popular cagebird in Hong Kong, where the numerous records of its occurrence in the wild from many parts of the island may be of escaped birds or of natural colonists from mainland China.

OCEANIA

Hawaiian Islands[2]

Although according to Caum (1933), the Red-billed Leiothrix was first introduced to the Hawaiian Islands (on Kauai) via San Francisco by Mrs Dora Isenberg in 1918, the Territorial Board of Agriculture and Forestry's records (and Fisher & Baldwin 1947) indicate that as early as 1911 37 of the nominate form[3] were imported as cage-birds from southeastern China, followed by others in 1913, 1915 and 1917, some of which are believed to have escaped and to have become established in the wild before 1918. In 1928 and 1929, more were brought in from the Far East via San Francisco by Mr W. H. McInerny who released them on Oahu, and in that year and the following one others were imported by the Board of Agriculture direct from the Far East and set free on Oahu, Molokai, Maui, Hawaii and Kauai.

Caum said that the Red-billed Leiothrix 'occurs in rather large flocks on Kauai and is reported to be breeding on Molokai, Maui and Hawaii'. By the end of the Second World War, the species was established, breeding and extending its range on those islands and had spread (or been introduced) to Oahu. In about 1968, however, although no accurate census was taken, the population on Oahu appeared to be drastically declining.

The Red-billed Leiothrix favours damp areas in native and introduced forest with, since it seldom rises more than 5 m from ground level, a dense understorey for cover. It ranges to an altitude of at least 2,400–2,700 m, but seldom occurs below 120 m or in areas with less than 100 cm of annual rainfall; indeed, because it bathes and drinks frequently, the presence of permanent standing water may be a governing factor in its distribution. It eats both plant and animal matter, including the fruits of Thimbleberry (*Rubus rosaefolius*), Strawberry Guava (*Psidium cattleianum*) and over-ripe Papaya (*Carica papaya*), the corolla and small buds of flowers, and flies (Diptera), ants (Hymenoptera), larvae (Lepidoptera) and small molluscs (Mollusca). It has been identified as a vector of the endoparasite *Plasmodium vaughani*, which is responsible for outbreaks of avian malaria, and has been accused of causing some damage to fruit and vegetable crops.

Berger (1972) described the Red-billed Leiothrix as widely distributed on all the main Hawaiian islands, but apparently least common on Kauai where it was first deliberately introduced. The Hawaiian Audubon Society (1975) found it to be declining at lower elevations on Hawaii and Oahu but still present on all the main islands. Zeillemaker & Scott (1976) said that it occurred in introduced forest and scrubland (i.e. Guava (*Psidium guajava*), Java Plum (*Eugenia cumini*) and Eucalyptus sp.), in native mixed Ohia (*Metrosideros collina*) and koa (*Acacia koa*) woodland, and in Mamane (*Sophora chrysophylla*)/Naio (*Myoporum sandvicense*) scrub on Hawaii (where it was widespread and abundant); on Oahu (numerous in the Koolau and Waianae mountain ranges); on Maui (common in the damp forests on Haleakala and in the west of the island); on Molokai (uncommon in mountain valleys at Mapulehu); on Lanai (uncommon); and possibly on Kauai. According to the American Ornithologists' Union (1983: 566), the birds are 'now common on Molokai, Maui and Hawaii, formerly common but now rare on Kauai and Oahu'. A. J. Berger (personal communication, 1985) said that 'the species is now almost rare on [Oahu], but still is doing very well on the other island'. Large flocks of up to 100 strong are occasionally reported.

————————————

In April 1905, 2 years after his retirement as Deputy Superintendent of the Indian Museum at Calcutta, Frank Finn turned out some 30 'Pekin Robins' in St James's Park, London, followed shortly afterwards by a further 15 in Regent's Park. Two months later he claimed that they were flourishing and would soon become established. In *Ornithological and Other Oddities* (1907), however, he was forced to admit that his experiment had failed. Other attempts to naturalize the Red-billed Leiothrix in England,[4] such as that by the Duke of Bedford at Woburn Abbey in Bedfordshire, where for several years a small flock lived and nested in a dense thicket of Wild Privet (*Ligustrum vulgare*), were also ultimately unsuccessful.

In 1898, 13 Red-billed Leiothrixes were unsuccessfully released, probably by a M. Thiebaux, on a 34-ha property near Meaux, 40 km east of Paris.[5]

Phillips (1928: 49) wrote that he had 'known

of Japanese robins (Liothrix) [*sic*] living successfully in a free state [in the USA] during summer'.

According to Sick (1968), the Red-billed Leiothrix has been released, probably without success, in Colombia.

Le Souef (1912) records that 'The Pekin nightingale' (probably *Leiothrix lutea*) had been liberated in Western Australia by the Acclimatization Committee, but had failed to become established.

NOTES
1 Long 1981; Viney 1976; Webster 1975.

2 American Ornithologists' Union 1983; Ali & Ripley 1968–73; A. J. Berger 1981 (and personal communication, 1985); Blake 1975; Caum 1933; Elton 1958; Fisher & Baldwin 1947; Hawaiian Audubon Society 1975; Long 1981; Pyle 1977; Richardson & Bowles 1964; Zeillemaker & Scott 1976.

3 According to Ali & Ripley (1968–73), the race introduced to Hawaii is *calipyga* of the eastern Himalayas. This seems unlikely if the birds were imported from southeastern China.

4 Fitter 1959; Goodwin 1956; Niethammer 1963.

5 Etchécopar 1955; Niethammer 1963.

Japanese Bush Warbler
(*Cettia diphone*)

NATURAL DISTRIBUTION

From Sakhalin Island and the adjacent mainland of the USSR south through Manchuria, Japan and Korea to east-central China; winters in southern China.

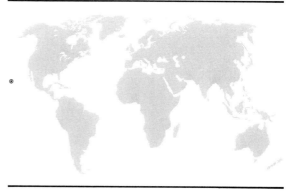

NATURALIZED DISTRIBUTION

Oceania: Hawaiian Islands.

OCEANIA

Hawaiian Islands[1]

Japanese Bush Warblers (known in Japan as *Uguisu*) were first released to control insect pests on the island of Oahu by the Territory of Hawaii Board of Agriculture and Forestry in 1929. Between 1930 and 1941, some 116 more were freed on Oahu by the Hui Manu ('Bird Society') and the Honolulu Mejiro Club. According to Berger (1977), some of these releases were made in the Nu'u-anu Valley, and others 'in bushes of gardens of the F. J. Lowrey residence, Old Pali

Road'. Although the birds are said to have been doing fairly well in 1937, it was another decade before the first nest was discovered on Oahu. By 1956, they were slowly extending their range, and were found in damp areas in the Koolaus, such as Poamoho, Kawailoa, Kipapa, Waiawa, Pupukea and Kaunala, but were more common in the upper Pa Lehua section of the Waianae Mountains.

Berger (1972) said that the birds occurred 'along the Poamoho trail, Aiea loop trail, St Louis Heights trail, and in Moanalua Valley in the Koolau Range, and along the Pe Lehua trail north to Peacock Flats in the Waianae Mountains', where they inhabit dry, luxuriant forest understorey, and where they have apparently increased in both numbers and range since the 1960s. Because they are shy and secretive birds they may well occur in valleys and on mountain ridges where they have not yet been seen. Zeillemaker & Scott (1976) recorded the species as 'uncommon' in introduced forests and scrub (Guava (*Psidium guajava*), Java Plum (*Eugenia cumini*) and *Eucalyptus* sp.) and native mixed ohia (*Metrosideros collina*) and koa (*Acacia koa*) forests on Oahu. Berger (1981: 198) said that on Oahu the Japanese Bush Warbler 'occurs in the Waianae Range from Peacock Flats in the north to Pa Lehua in the south. In the Koolau Range the species is found from Waialae Iki Ridge to Waimea Valley and Pupukea, as well as on the windward side of the Pali as far north as Kahuku (*Elepaio* 38: 56). The birds are common at the Makiki nursery in Honolulu and in Moanalua Valley. Bush Warblers were heard on Molokai in 1979 (*Elepaio* 40: 27), and on Lanai [and Maui] in 1980 (*Elepaio* 41: 77).'

According to Long (1981), the **Madagascar Grass Warbler** or **Cisticola** (*Cisticola cherina*) may have been deliberately introduced by human agency to the neighbouring islands of Cosmoledo and Astove (where it is now abundant), but more probably colonized them naturally after about 1940.

NOTE

1 American Ornithologists' Union 1983; Berger 1972, 1975c, 1977c, 1981; Blake 1975; Carothers & Hansen 1982; Caum 1933; Conant 1980; Gossard 1956; Hawaiian Audubon Society 1975; Long 1981; Munro 1960; Peterson 1961; Pyle 1977, 1979; Zeillemaker & Scott 1976.

Varied Tit
(*Parus varius*)

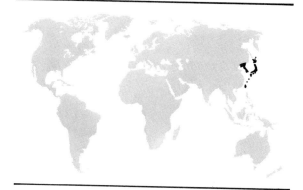

NATURAL DISTRIBUTION
Extreme southeastern Manchuria, Korea, Japan (including the Amami, Ryukyu and Izu islands) and Taiwan.

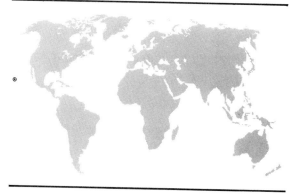

NATURALIZED DISTRIBUTION
Oceania: ?Hawaiian Islands.

OCEANIA

Hawaiian Islands[1]

The Varied or Japanese Tit (known also as the *yamagara*) was first released on the island of Kauai by Mrs Frances Sinclair in about 1890. Some (of the nominate form) imported from Japan were freed, also on Kauai, by Mrs Dora Isenberg in 1905 and 1907, and in the former year others were brought to the same island via Germany by Richard Isenberg. More Varied Tits, also from Japan, were planted on Oahu, Maui and Hawaii in 1928 and 1929 and on Oahu by the Hui Manu ('Bird Society') in 1930 and 1931.

On Maui and Hawaii, they seem to have disappeared by 1938, but Caum (1933) referred to their presence in the Kokee area on Kauai. During the 1940s their numbers diminished, and by the end of the following decade they survived, according to Peterson (1961), very locally only on Kauai and along some forest trails on Oahu. Ord (1967) confirmed their existence in the Kokee region, and Berger (1972) said that they appeared to be fairly well established in the vicinity of Kokee, but that on Oahu they occurred only on the Aiea Trail and, less commonly, on the Poamoho Trail in the Koolau Mountains. Although the Hawaiian Audubon Society (1975) expressed uncertainty about the status of Varied Tits on these two islands, and Pyle (1977) makes no mention of them, Zeillemaker & Scott (1976) indicate that they were local and uncommon in native mixed ohia (*Metrosideros collina*) and koa (*Acacia koa*) forests on Oahu, and possibly also on Kauai. In December 1976, however, Zeillemaker told Berger (1981) that he was sure the species no longer occurred on Kauai, and the latter believes that the population on Oahu has also probably died out. The American Ornithologists' Union (1983: 516), however, believed that 'small numbers may persist in the Kokee area of Kauai and the Koolau Mountains of Oahu'.

According to Munro (1960), the Varied Tit replaced some extinct endemic insectivorous birds as a predator of forest pests. It was one of the few species that penetrated indigenous forests in preference to colonizing man-made habitats.

NOTE

1 American Ornithologists' Union 1957, 1983; Berger 1981; Blake 1975; Caum 1933; Elton 1958; Hawaiian Audubon Society 1975; Long 1981; Munro 1960; Ord 1967; Peterson 1961; Phillips 1928; Zeillemaker & Scott 1976.

Grey-backed White-eye

(Zosterops lateralis)

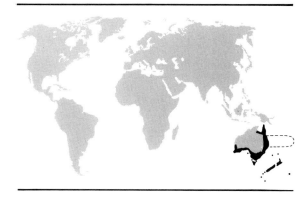

Note: Dashed line encloses distribution in archipelagos from the Great Barrier Reef eastwards to Fiji. Map includes range as natural colonist of New Zealand.

NATURAL DISTRIBUTION

Littoral and adjacent regions of Australia from around 25° S in Western Australia through South Australia, Victoria, Tasmania and New South Wales to the Cape York Peninsula and the Gulf of Carpentaria in northern and western Queensland; islands of the Great Barrier Reef eastwards through New Caledonia and Vanuatu to Fiji. (A natural colonist of New Zealand.)

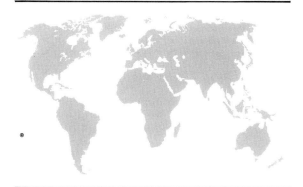

NATURALIZED DISTRIBUTION

Oceania: Society Islands.

OCEANIA

Society Islands[1]

Grey-backed White-eyes of the nominate form[2] were first introduced (from New Zealand)[3] to the Society Islands in about 1937 by Guild (1938), who released some on Tahiti where they were

345

first reported by King (1958); they are now widely distributed and abundant on Tahiti, from where they have since colonized other islands in the archipelago. Their present status and the date (in parentheses) of their first appearance on the various islands are as follows: Moorea, very common (1971); Huahine, uncertain (1972); Raiatea, widespread (1972); Tahaa, widely distributed (1973); Bora Bora, uncommon on the main island and occurs also on some small islets (1971); Maupiti, at Paumea only (1973). They may also have colonized Mehetia, which has not, however, been visited by an ornithologist for many years, and possibly also Tupai. In 1973, some were unsuccessfully released on Tetiaroa.

On Tahiti, Grey-back White-eyes live in woodland habitats, gardens, plantations, lowland forests and mountains as high as the summit of Mont Orohena (2,241 m) – the highest point on the island – though they are, perhaps, more frequently seen at lower altitudes. On Moorea, they occupy the same range of habitats as on Tahiti, while on the main island of Bora Bora and on the smaller islets they are established in coconut groves and reclaimed bushland. On Raiatea, they had apparently not yet reached the mountain forest by 1973.

Grey-backed White-eyes in the Society Islands eat small fruits, segments of larger fruits, small seeds, nectar, probably flower pollen, and insects, including bugs (Homoptera), small larvae (Lepidoptera) and lacewings (Neuroptera).

A simple but well constructed cup-shaped nest made of vegetable matter is built in the fork of a bush or tree at a variety of altitudes – for example, in orange trees at sea level on Moorea and in *Metrosideros collina* at 800 m on Tahiti – in which are laid two or three (sometimes four) pale-blue eggs that hatch after 10–11 days' incubation. The young leave the nest some 9–12 days after hatching. From observations made in the Society Islands it appears that the birds moult synchronously, and that the period corresponds to that of birds in New Zealand. Since breeding is strictly seasonal in New Zealand it seems probable that it is the same also in the Society Islands.

The nominate form of the Grey-backed White-eye first appeared in New Zealand[4] (in Otago and Southland) as a natural immigrant from the mainland of Australia or Tasmania[5] in 1832. Breeding was reported in 1850, and by 1856 the species had spread to Waikanae in Wellington and to Nelson, by 1860 to Otago, by 1863 to Wanganui, by 1865 to Auckland and by 1867 to the Bay of Islands. It has since become widely established and common on both the main islands, on Stewart Island and on other islands as far offshore as Campbell Island in the south, the Chathams in the east, and Norfolk in the north where it was first recorded (presumably as an immigrant from Australia or New Zealand) in 1904.

The status of *Zosterops* on Lord Howe Island,[6] between Australia and New Zealand, is confused. *Zosterops l. lateralis* is said to have been introduced (probably from New South Wales) in 1924 and the Slender-billed White-eye (*Z. tenuirostris*) and/or the White-chested or Norfolk Island White-eye (*Z. albogularis*) from Norfolk Island in 1931 or 1936. These populations, an endemic species—the Robust Silvereye (*Z. strenua*)—and *Z. l. tephropleura* (which may have been endemic or could, since it is said to have closely resembled *Z. l. lateralis*, have evolved on Lord Howe), may all now be extinct.

NOTES

1 For much of the information on Grey-backed White-eyes in the Society Islands, I am indebted to Holyoak & Thibault 1984. Other sources are: Bruner 1972; Guild 1938; Holyoak 1974a; Jouanin 1962; King 1958; Long 1981; Thibault 1976.

2 According to Holyoak & Thibault (1984), *Z. l. lateralis* nests in Tasmania and on islands in Bass Strait, and winters in Victoria, eastern New South Wales and southeastern Queensland: it is the race that has colonized New Zealand. Howard & Moore (1980), however, say that the resident form in Tasmania is *Z. l. halmaturina*.

3 Long (1981: 336) misquotes Guild (1938) as saying that the birds he imported to Tahiti came from Tasmania (see note 2).

4 Falla, Sibson & Turbott 1979; Holyoak & Thibault 1984; Long 1981; Smithers & Disney 1969; Wodzicki 1965.

5 See note 2.

6 McKean & Hindwood 1965.

Japanese White-eye

(*Zosterops japonica*)

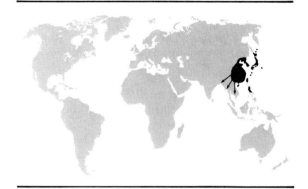

NATURAL DISTRIBUTION

Eastern and southern China, Taiwan, Hainan, the mainland of Japan and its adjacent islands, the northern Philippines, and extreme southeastern Manchuria and Korea; winters south to Burma, North Vietnam, Thailand and Laos.

NATURALIZED DISTRIBUTION

Oceania: Hawaiian Islands.

OCEANIA

Hawaiian Islands[1]

According to Caum (1933), Japanese White-eyes (sometimes known as Mejiros) were imported to Hawaii from Japan in 1929[2] by the Territorial Board of Agriculture and Forestry who released them on Oahu. Later introduction on Oahu were made by the Hui Manu ('Bird Society'), by the Board of Agriculture, and by private individuals. At least 252 were released on the island of Hawaii in June 1937, and the Hui Manu probably planted some also on Maui, Molokai and Lanai. By 1933, Mejiros were said to be established on Oahu and possibly also on Kauai, and by at least the late 1950s they had colonized all the main islands.

The Japanese White-eye is known to be a host both to the endoparasite *Plasmodium vaughani*, which causes avian malaria, and also to bird pox (which is spread by the accidentally introduced tropical mosquito *Culex pipiens quinquefasciatus*), against which native species have no resistance. It is this lack of inbuilt immunity, rather than direct interspecific competition (e.g. for food), that has resulted in a serious decrease and/or the extermination of some endemic Hawaiian honeycreepers (Drepanididae) and of some other native species in Volcanoes National Park. Limited damage to orchard fruit has been reported, but injurious insects are also eaten.

According to Zeillemaker & Scott (1976), Japanese White-eyes in Hawaii occur in a variety of habitats, including introduced forests and scrub (i.e. Guava (*Psidium guajava*), Java Plum (*Eugenia cumini*) and *Eucalyptus* sp.), native mixed ohia (*Metrosideros collina*) and koa (*Acacia koa*) forest, residential and community parklands, and agricultural land and pastures. Berger (1981: 198–9) described the species as

now certainly the most abundant land bird in the Hawaiian Islands. It occurs on all of the islands and is found from sea level to tree line on Maui and Hawaii. It occurs in very dry areas (e.g. Kawaihae, Hawaii) and very wet areas (300 or more inches [760 cm] of rain a year). There is virtually nowhere that one can go in Hawaii without seeing these birds.

The subspecies known to have been introduced to the Hawaiian Islands is the nominate one, which occurs naturally on the main Japanese islands from Honshu to Kyushu, and on islands in the Korea Strait between southern Japan and South Korea. It is possible that one or more other subspecies are also present.

According to the American Ornithologists' Union (1983), the Japanese White-eye has been introduced to the Bonin Islands (Ogasawara Gunto) where, as on the Izu Islands, the subspecies is *stejnegeri*. Its presence on these islands may, however, be a result of natural dispersal.

The endemic **Christmas Island White-eye** (*Zosterops natalis*) was introduced between 1885 and 1900 to Pulo Luar (Horsburgh) in the Cocos (Keeling) group in the Indian Ocean.[3] Until at least the late 1940s, it was apparently confined to Pulo Luar (where it was abundant) but may, like the Island Thrush (*Turdus poliocephalus*),[4] have since spread to other islands (such as West) in the archipelago. On Pulo Luar in 1982, it remained abundant only in remnants of the original forest vegetation along the shoreline of the lagoon.

The **Noisy Miner** (*Manorina melanocephala*) is a native of Australia where it ranges from southeastern South Australia through Victoria, Tasmania and New South Wales to eastern and north-central Queensland. It is recorded as having been introduced to, and is said to be established on, the Olu Malau (Three Sisters) group in the southeastern Solomon Islands.[5]

According to F. W. Hutton's *Catalogue of the Birds of New Zealand* (1871), quoted by Thomson (1922), Noisy Miners had previously been imported from Victoria, Australia, to Nelson and Canterbury in New Zealand. The Otago Society released 80 near Palmerston in 1880, where they disappeared after a couple of years. (See also under Common or Indian Mynah (*Acridotheres tristis*), page 496.)

The **Black Drongo** (*Dicrurus macrocercus*) ranges from southeastern Iran and Afghanistan through India, Sri Lanka, Burma, Thailand, Laos, Vietnam and Malaysia north to China and Taiwan and south to Bali and Java.

In 1935, the Taiwanese race (*D. m. harterti*) was introduced by the Japanese to Rota Island in the southern Marianas, from where it appears to have spread without human assistance to Guam – over 100 km to the south; it is now widespread and abundant on both islands, where it may have been responsible for the decline of several small passerines.[6]

A population of 100–200 **Oriental White-eyes** (*Zosterops p. palebrosa*)—natives of India, Sri Lanka, Bangladesh, Nepal and Bhutan—in San Diego, California, USA, was reduced to around a dozen in the early 1980s by netting and shooting.

NOTES

1 American Ornithologists' Union 1957, 1983; Berger 1981; Blake 1975; Caum 1933; Fisher 1951; Guest 1973; Hawaiian Audubon Society 1975; Jarvis 1980; Keffer 1978; Long 1981; Munro 1960; Pyle 1977; Richardson & Bowles 1964; Zeillemaker & Scott 1976.
2 According to M. Keffer, L. Davis, D. Clark et al., 'An evaluation of the pest potential of the genus *Zosterops* (White Eyes) in California', California Department of Food and Agriculture Special Service Unit Publication, 22 pp. (1976), some local avicultural dealers are known to have released *Z. japonica* in the Hawaiian Islands in 1928.
3 Gibson-Hill 1949; Long 1981; Stokes, Sheils & Dunn 1984; Van Tets & Van Tets 1967.
4 See p. 334.
5 French 1957; Galbraith & Galbraith 1962.
6 Baker 1951; Long 1981; Peters 1962; Ralph & Sakai 1979; Ripley 1961.

Yellowhammer
(*Emberiza citrinella*)

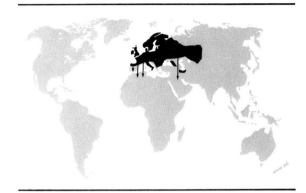

NATURAL DISTRIBUTION

Eurasia, from the British Isles eastwards to Siberia, north to about 65°–70° N, and south in Europe to northern Spain and Portugal, Yugoslavia and Hungary. Winters south to southern Spain, Portugal, Morocco, Algeria, Tunisia and Iran.

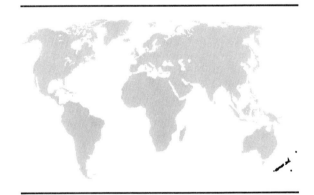

NATURALIZED DISTRIBUTION
Australasia: New Zealand.

AUSTRALASIA

New Zealand[1]

Thomson (1922) lists the following introductions of Yellowhammers (probably of the nominate subspecies) to New Zealand: by the Nelson Acclimatization Society, 3 in 1862; by the Auckland Society, 8 in 1865, 4 in 1867, 5 in 1868, an unspecified number in 1869, 16 (out of a shipment of 148) in 1870, and 312 in 1871; by the Canterbury Society, 1 in 1867 and 34 in 1871; and by the Otago Society, 8 in 1868 and 31 in 1871. Williams (1969) adds that according to the Canterbury Society's records nine dozen were ordered in 1872, and 40 were released in various parts of South Canterbury in 1875. Four years later, 32 were freed on Stewart Island, where they soon disappeared.

Thomson (1922: 176) records that Yellowhammers 'quickly spread all over New Zealand, and today are common from Foveaux Strait [between South and Stewart Islands] to the extreme north of the North Island', becoming established wherever grain and grass seeds were available.

On offshore islands, Yellowhammers were recorded on the Chatham Islands in 1910, on the Kermadecs around 1946, on Lord Howe Island about 1949, and on Three Kings, Mokohinau, Little Barrier, Kapiti, Codfish, Campbell and the Aucklands before 1955. Williams (1973) recorded them as breeding only in the Kermadecs and Chathams.

Wodzicki (1965: 433) described Yellowhammers as 'widely distributed and common, North, South, Stewart and Raoul [in the Kermadecs], and Chatham Islands'. Kinsky (1970) recorded them as having spread to the above mentioned islands, and as appearing as stragglers on others. Falla, Sibson & Turbott (1979) found Yellowhammers to be widely distributed on the two main islands in all kinds of open country from beaches, saltings and marshes at sea level to alpine tussock grass at 1,600 m. In the south, they breed regularly on the Chatham Islands, and have appeared as vagrants on even more remote subantarctic islands, while in the north they have bred on Raoul in the Kermadecs. Large flocks sometimes assemble in winter.

Thomson's account of the Yellowhammer's history in New Zealand suggests, as Williams (1969) points out, that this is another example of a species becoming rapidly established, reaching a high population density shortly thereafter, and then declining permanently from its peak of abundance, in a classic sigmoid curve.

In Thomson's time (1922: 176), Yellowhammers were 'destroyed wholesale as noxious pests in all grain-growing areas', and Oliver (1955) claimed that, because of their consumption of grain and newly sown grass seeds, they were one of the most damaging introductions to New Zealand. In the British Isles, however, their destruction of injurious insects and consumption of weed seeds is generally considered to outweigh any damage they may cause to crop seeds, and Williams (1969) says that complaints of their depredations in New Zealand are nowadays less common.

Frith (1979) records that the Victoria Acclimatization Society of Australia unsuccessfully released 15 Yellowhammers near Melbourne in 1863, followed by a similar number in 1864. According to Jenkins (1977), some may also have been freed without success in various parts of New South Wales in 1880.

Phillips (1928) states that in the United States Yellowhammers were among several species released unsuccessfully in Oregon in the late nineteenth century by the Portland Song Bird Club.[2]

NOTES

1 Falla, Sibson & Turbott 1979; Kinsky 1970; Long 1981; Oliver 1930, 1955; Thomson 1922, 1926; Williams 1953, 1969, 1973; Wodzicki 1965.
2 Long (1981: 464) quotes Phillips (1928) incorrectly as saying that Yellowhammers were released by the Cincinnati Acclimatization Society between 1872 and 1874.

Cirl Bunting
(*Emberiza cirlus*)

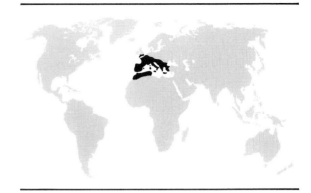

NATURAL DISTRIBUTION
Central and southern Europe (including south-western England) from northern France, Belgium, southwestern Germany, Switzerland, Yugoslavia and Bulgaria south to the Mediterranean, the Balearic Islands, Sicily, Corsica, Sardinia and Crete, eastwards to Turkey and western Transcaucasia. Also resident in northern Morocco, Algeria and Tunisia in North Africa.

NATURALIZED DISTRIBUTION
Australasia: New Zealand.

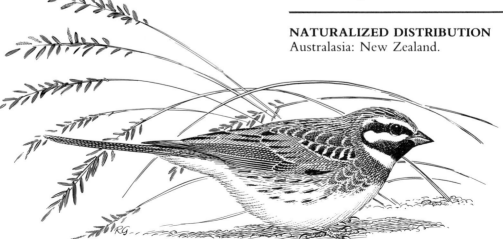

AUSTRALASIA

New Zealand[1]

Thomson (1922 and 1926) was able to trace only three recorded importations of Cirl Buntings (of the nominate subspecies) to New Zealand – in 1871, when 7 were brought in by the Otago Acclimatization Society, in 1879 when 18 were unsuccessfully released on Stewart Island, and in 1880 or 1881 when 4 were introduced by the Wellington Society. Since, however, Thomson once discovered several Cirl Buntings in a cage allegedly containing only Yellowhammers (*Emberiza citrinella*) – the females and young of which quite closely resemble those of *E. cirlus* – it seems probable that others may have been unwittingly imported.

The birds freed in South Island in Otago and in North Island in Wellington seem at once to have increased and spread; from the latter, they had reached Taranaki by 1916, where they were said to be common and to occur in flocks along the coast at Hawera and elsewhere. Their appearance was, however, Thomson reported, very erratic; at one time they considerably increased in Otago, reaching the MacKenzie country by 1875, and then, unaccountably, drastically declined.

Williams (1953) said that the Cirl Bunting had a restricted distribution in New Zealand and was nowhere common. Oliver (1955) records the species as occurring at Tauranga, Hawke's Bay,

Manawatu, Wairarapa, Hutt Valley, Wellington, Canterbury, Otago and on Resolution Island off the coast of Southland. Wodzicki (1965: 433) described Cirl Buntings as 'locally rare, North and South Islands'. Kinsky (1970) said they were established locally possibly in Taranaki, and in Hawke's Bay, Wellington, Nelson, Marlborough, North Westland, Canterbury and Otago. Falla, Sibson & Turbott (1979) found them to be widely distributed in open country but rather rare, except perhaps in a few favoured localities, such as the limestone country east of the Southern Alps in the north and east (e.g. near Oamaru on the coast of Otago) of South Island, and in the southern half of North Island. Small nomadic flocks assemble in autumn and winter and may cross the Cook Strait between the two main islands.

It seems likely that climatic factors are the Cirl Bunting's main limiting factor in New Zealand; it may be significant that in southern England, where it is on the northern edge of its range, it appears most at home on the lower slopes of the limestone downland escarpment, mainly below an altitude of about 90 m (sometimes at sea level), and often with a southerly aspect.

NOTE

1 Drummond 1907; Falla, Sibson & Turbott 1979; Kinsky 1970; Long 1981; Oliver 1930, 1955; Sharrock 1976; Stidolph 1933; Thomson 1922, 1926; Williams 1953, 1969, 1973; Wodzicki 1965.

Yellow Grass
Finch

(Sicalis luteola)

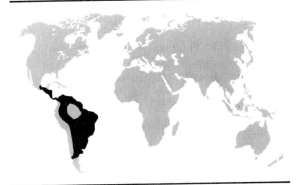

NATURAL DISTRIBUTION
Southwards from southern Mexico through central America to most of South America north of about 40° S, but not west of the Andes.

Note: Not known to be naturalized on all islands within dashed line.

NATURALIZED DISTRIBUTION
North America: West Indies (Barbados, the Grenadines, Mustique, St Lucia, Guadeloupe, St Vincent, Antigua, Martinique, Marie Galante).

NORTH AMERICA

West Indies (Barbados, the Grenadines, Mustique, St Lucia, Guadeloupe, St Vincent, Antigua, Martinique and Marie Galante)[1]

Pinchon (1963) says that Yellow Grass Finches (also commonly known as Grassland Yellow Finches), according to Peters (1970) of the nominate subspecies from Colombia, Venezuela, Guyana and Brazil, were introduced to the island of Barbados around the turn of the century, where Bond (1928) – who then named the species *Sycalis arvensis luteiventris* – found them to be abundant on the windward side in 1926.

From Barbados, Yellow Grass Finches arrived naturally in the Grenadines, Mustique and southern St Lucia, and by 1945 had reached Martinique. Guth (1971) saw a party of 15 at Beauport (Port Louis) on Grande-Terre, Guadeloupe, and 20 north-west of Morne à l'Eau on Basse-Terre in 1969. Kirby (in Bond 1972) found them on St Vincent in 1972, where Lack, Lack et al. (1973), who noted several on the Arnos Vale airfield, were told they had arrived after a severe hurricane. Between 1977 and 1982, Barré & Benito-Espinal (1985) saw some on Grande-Terre, lesser numbers on Martinique, and two (at Folle Anse, Grand Bourg) on Marie Galante, where the species had not been previously recorded. Yellow Grass Finches are continuing their northwards spread in the Caribbean from the Windward Islands, appearing, for example, on Antigua in 1973 (Holland & William in Bond 1980), but seem not as yet to have reached the most northerly Leeward Islands nor the Greater Antilles.

Barré & Benito-Espinal found that in Guadeloupe, Martinique and Marie Galante, Yellow Grass Finches live in open country, large meadows in dry areas, and in dense but fairly low bushes, entering tangled thickets only for roosting and resting. Very small paddocks or enclosures between sugar-cane fields remain unoccupied. This may explain why the species has failed to colonize the intensively cultivated and wooded island of Basse-Terre, and why on Martinique and Grande-Terre the populations are localized and relatively small; Barré & Benito-Espinal saw 60 in St Anne on the former in December 1983 and a maximum of 30 near the airport on the latter in the following September. Yellow Grass Finches breed in the wet season and in the early part of the dry season; the nest, built of grasses, is constructed in a tuft of herbage near the ground.

NOTE

1 Barré & Benito-Espinal 1985; Bond 1928, 1972, 1979, 1980; Guth 1971; Holland & William (in Bond 1980); Kirby (in Bond 1972); Lack, Lack et al. 1973; Peters 1970; Pinchon 1963; Pinchon & Benito-Espinal 1980.

Saffron Finch
(*Sicalis flaveola*)

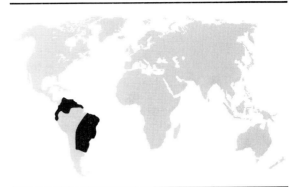

NATURAL DISTRIBUTION

South America, where it occurs in Colombia, Venezuela, the Guianas, Trinidad, southwestern Ecuador, northwestern Peru, northeastern and southeastern Brazil, southeastern Bolivia, Paraguay, Uruguay and northern Argentina.

NATURALIZED DISTRIBUTION

North America: West Indies (Jamaica, Puerto Rico, ?Tobago); Central America: Panama; Oceania: Hawaiian Islands.

NORTH AMERICA

West Indies (Jamaica,[1] Puerto Rico and ?Tobago)

Saffron Finches are believed to have been introduced to the Black River area on the south-west coast of Jamaica by the Revd J. M. Shakespeare in about 1823 – certainly well before 1847. According to Lack (1976), they were widely distributed in lowland cultivated districts with

short grass and scattered trees, especially near houses, but did not occur in native woodlands. Bond (1979) says that they are found in open country and gardens in Kingston, Mandeville and Moneague. As these finches are popular cagebirds in Jamaica, it is likely that the naturalized population, which may originally have been derived from escaped pets, is continually replenished.[2]

According to Ffrench (1973) and Blake (1975), some Saffron Finches (presumably of the nominate subspecies from Trinidad) were transferred in 1958 to Charlotteville on the neighbouring island of Tobago, where their present status is uncertain.

T. Silva (personal communication, 1985) has seen Saffron Finches at Bacardi in Puerto Rico.

CENTRAL AMERICA

Panama[3]

A pair of Saffron Finches (almost certainly escaped cagebirds – perhaps from a vessel passing through the canal) were seen at Gatun in central Panama in July 1951. The species is now locally common in residential areas and parks along the Caribbean coast of the Canal Zone, from Gatun Dam to Gatun and Coco Solo, and individuals are sometimes reported elsewhere.

OCEANIA

Hawaiian Islands[4]

Saffron Finches, presumably escaped or released cagebirds, appear to have been established in the Hawaiian Islands since 1965, when some were seen in a garden on the slopes of Diamond Head, Oahu, where they have since been observed annually, and from where they have spread to adjacent districts. The Hawaiian Audubon Society (1975) reported that they frequented Kapiolani Park on Oahu, and the area between Kona and Kamuela on Hawaii. Zeillemaker & Scott (1976) list them as local and rare in residential and community parklands only on Oahu. A. J. Berger (personal communication, 1985) says there are 'several small populations in widely

scattered locations on Oahu: e.g., Kapiolani Park in Honolulu; Radford Terrace near Pearl City; near Salt Lake. Also at several locations on Hawaii: Kamuela, the Puuwaawaa Ranch, Hualalai Mountain, Kailua–Kona region; 100 birds seen in one day at the Puuwaawaa Ranch.' On the last-named island, Saffron Finches are believed to have been deliberately released before 1966.[5] Breeding in Hawaii was first confirmed in 1977.

The **Common Diuca Finch** (*Diuca diuca*), which ranges south from northern Chile, northern Argentina, and Uruguay to about 50° S, was imported in 1928 to Easter Island (Rapa Nui) in the South Pacific, where despite predation by introduced Chimango Caracaras (*Milvago chimango*) (q.v.), Johnson, Millie & Moffett (1970) found it still to be surviving in 1968. According to Holyoak & Thibault (1984), the subspecies present is believed to be *D. d. crassirostris* from northern Chile and Argentina.

The **Cuban Grassquit** (*Tiaris canora*) is endemic to the island of Cuba and possibly to the Isle of Youth, though it may have been originally transferred to the latter by human agency. The **Yellow-faced Grassquit** (*T. olivacea*) ranges south from eastern Mexico through Central America to western Colombia and western and northwestern Venezuela; it also occurs on Cozumel and Holbox Islands off the coast of Yucatán (Mexico), and in the Caribbean in the Greater Antilles from Cuba and the Cayman Islands eastwards to Puerto Rico, Vieques and Culebra.[6]

In March 1963, an aircraft carrying a consignment of some 600 Cuban Grassquits and other species from Cuba to a European zoo made a forced landing in Nassau on New Providence in the Bahamas.[7] Some 200 birds died because of this delay, and most of the survivors – including 300 Cuban Grassquits, some Yellow-faced Grassquits, some Indigo Buntings (*Passerina cyanea*) (which winter in the Bahamas from eastern North America) and other species – were released. Three years later, the two grassquits were said to be fairly common in Nassau and eastern New Providence, where they still apparently survive, and where fear has been expressed that they may hybridize with the native Black-faced Grassquit (*T. b. bicolor*).

Yellow-faced Grassquits, presumably escaped or released cagebirds, were first seen at Pacific Palisades on Oahu in the Hawaiian Islands in August 1974.[8] Zeillemaker & Scott (1976) described them as local and uncommon on agricultural land and in pastures on Oahu, where at least 40 were seen in October 1978.[9] They have also been observed on Manana and Kipapa trails in the North and South Halawa Valleys,[10] and in Lanikai.[11] A. J. Berger (personal communication, 1985) says that 'a small population (no estimate of numbers) continues to survive in the Koolau mountains of Oahu'.

Blake (1975) lists both the **Puerto Rican Bullfinch** (*Loxigilla portoricensis*) and the **Lesser Antillean Bullfinch** (*L. noctis*) as having been translocated to St John in the Virgin Islands. The present status of the former is not known. The importation of the latter is confirmed by Raffaele & Roby (1977), who say that it was first seen in April 1971, and that by January 1972 the population had increased to about 100. The possibility of natural colonization from Anguilla, Antigua or Barbuda (where the subspecies is *ridgwayi*) cannot be ignored.

NOTES

1 Allen 1962; Blake 1975; Bond 1979; de Schauensee 1970; Lack 1976; Long 1981.
2 Roots (1976: 175) claims that 'The South American Saffron Finch thrives on Barbados, St Lucia and Martinique'. In fact, it is the (South American) Yellow Grass Finch (*S. luteola*) that is established on these (and other) Caribbean islands.
3 De Schauensee 1970; Heilbrun 1977; Long 1981; Peters 1968; Scholes 1954.
4 American Ornithologists' Union 1983; Berger 1981; Hawaiian Audubon Society 1975; Long 1981; Pyle 1976, 1977; Zeillemaker & Scott 1976.
5 *Elepaio* 39: 20, 75.
6 American Ornithologists' Union 1983; Blake 1975; Bond 1971, 1979; Lack 1973, 1976; Long 1981; Peters 1968.
7 American Ornithologists' Union 1983; Blake 1975; Bond 1971, 1979; Brudenell-Bruce 1975; Long 1981; Peters 1968.
8 *Elepaio* 35: 65.
9 *Elepaio* 38: 106.
10 *Elepaio* 39: 20.
11 *Elepaio* 35: 92.

Red-crested Cardinal

(Paroaria coronata)

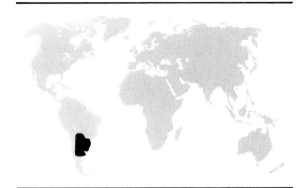

NATURAL DISTRIBUTION

Eastern Bolivia, Paraguay, southeastern Brazil, Uruguay, and northern Argentina.

NATURALIZED DISTRIBUTION

Africa: ?Agaléga Islands; North America: ?USA; Oceania: Hawaiian Islands.

AFRICA

Agaléga Islands

Red-crested Cardinals that had escaped from aviaries were at one time numerous on the Agaléga Islands in the Indian Ocean, but had become rare by about 1924. In 1981, Guého & Staub (1983) could find only a single individual, on Île du Nord. The decline, they believed, was caused by interspecific competition with the introduced Madagascar Fody (*Foudia madagascariensis*) (see page 473).

NORTH AMERICA

USA

Owre (1973) first saw free-flying Red-crested Cardinals in the grounds of Crandon Zoo on Biscayne Key off Miami in southern Florida in 1965. Subsequently, there were scattered reports of the birds from Coconut Grove and elsewhere in Dade County. In the spring of 1973 some were seen in Fort Lauderdale, and Owre believed that they might well be breeding in Dade and Broward counties. O'Keefe (1973: 47) listed them as having 'become part of Florida's birdlife'.

OCEANIA

Hawaiian Islands[1]

Between 1928 and 1931, Red-crested Cardinals, imported from Brazil via San Francisco, California, were turned out on the island of Oahu by Mr William McInerny and the Hui Manu ('Bird Society'), and others were later planted on Kauai by Mrs Dora R. Isenberg.

The species' subsequent history in the Hawaiian Islands is somewhat confused. According to Peterson (1961), the birds were then widespread on Oahu and local on Kauai and Maui; Richardson & Bowles (1964), on the other hand, were unable to find any on Kauai in 1960. Some were seen on Molokai and on Maui in 1967. In about 1970 there were said to be a few on Kauai and Molokai, and perhaps also on Maui. Berger (1972) described them as common in parts of Hawaii 'as well as in such drier areas on Leeward Oahu as the Coast Guard Air Station at Barber's Point, at Waikiki, and in the Koko Head region around Hanauma Bay'. According to the Hawaiian Audubon Society (1975), they occurred in lowland dry bush country, thickets and urban areas on all the larger main islands, although they were uncommon on Oahu where, however, Heilbrun (1976) indicated that there had been some recent expansion of range in the south. Zeillemaker & Scott (1976) described them as local and uncommon on Kauai and Molokai, common on Oahu and local and rare on Maui, in exotic woodlands and scrub (i.e. Guava

(*Psidium guajava*), Java Plum (*Eugenia cumini*) and *Eucalyptus* sp.), and in residential and community parklands. The American Ornithologists' Union (1983) indicates that they are common on Oahu, are also established on Molokai, and occur locally on Kauai, Lanai, Maui and Hawaii. According to Berger (1981: 216), on Kauai the Red-crested Cardinal:

has been reported at Lihue, Poipu Beach, Wailua Valley, and the Hanapepe salt ponds. . . . single birds [were seen] near Naha and in the Manele-Hulopoe Bay area of Lanai during 1976. There appear to be no records of the introduction of the Red-crested Cardinal to Maui or Hawaii, but the species has been seen in the Kona area. . . . The Red-crested Cardinal is a common nesting bird on the Manoa campus of the University of Hawaii (annual rainfall about 41 inches [104 cm]), as well as in such drier areas on Leeward Oahu as at Barber's Point, at Waikiki, and in the Koko Head region around Hanauma Bay.

Summing up, Berger (personal communication, 1985) described the Red-crested Cardinal as 'very common in all lowland areas of Oahu; uncommon on Kauai; uncommon on Molokai; reported once from Lanai'. There seems to be little conflict with Common Cardinals (*Cardinalis cardinalis*), even though both species exist sympatrically in urban areas.

According to Winterbottom (1966), some Red-crested Cardinals that had escaped from captivity bred in the wild in 1957 at Hermanus in the Western Cape, South Africa; they subsequently appeared to become established near Durban in Natal, where Liversidge (n.d.) indicates that a maximum population of six survived for only a couple of years. Others introduced to Randburg in the Transvaal in the 1970s have also died out.

The **Yellow-billed Cardinal** (*Paroaria capitata*) occurs in south-central Brazil, southeastern Bolivia, Paraguay, and north-central Argentina.

The species was first recorded in Kailua-Kona on the island of Hawaii in November 1973,[2] although it may have been present since as long ago as 1930, following introduction by the Hui Manu ('Bird Society'). Since about 1975, small flocks of up to a dozen or so have been sighted in coastal thickets in the North Kona district – at the City of Refuge, at Opaeula, and Aimakapa ponds, and at Honokohau. Up to 20 birds have been counted at Honokohau and 10 at Opaeula pond.[3] Breeding was first confirmed in 1976. The bird is not listed by Zeillemaker & Scott (1976), but is included by Pyle (1977: 112) as a 'resident foreign introduced species'.

NOTES

1 Bancroft 1981b; Berger 1981; Blake 1975; Bryan 1958; Caum 1933; Collins 1976; Hawaiian Audubon Society 1975; Heilbrun 1976; Long 1981; Munro 1960; Ord 1967; Peterson 1961; Richardson & Bowles 1964; Pyle 1977; Zeillemaker & Scott 1976.

2 *Elepaio* 34: 95.

3 *Elepaio* 39: 20.

Common Cardinal
(*Cardinalis cardinalis*)

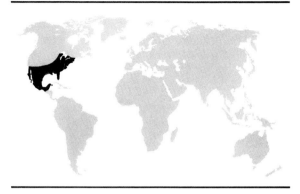

NATURAL DISTRIBUTION

The USA and southern Canada westwards from Connecticut and southern Ontario to south-eastern South Dakota, south to southern Florida and the Gulf of Mexico, west from northern Texas to southeastern California, south through Mexico (including Baja California, and Tiburon, Tres Marias, Cerralvo and Cozumel Islands) to Belize in British Honduras, and Lake Petén Itzá in Guatemala.

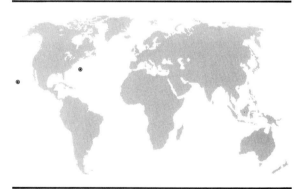

NATURALIZED DISTRIBUTION

North America: Bermuda; Oceania: Hawaiian Islands.

NORTH AMERICA

Bermuda[1]

According to J. R. Bartram in *The Cage Birds of Bermuda* (1879),[2] Common Cardinals (of the nominate subspecies) were probably introduced to Bermuda from Virginia, USA by early settlers in about 1700. 'Formerly abundant throughout the Island', wrote Wingate (1973), 'it was rapidly displaced from the built-up areas by the introduction of the House Sparrow [*Passer domesticus*]. It remained common, however, in rural areas up until the 1950s when the loss of the cedar forest [*Juniperus bermudiana*], the introduction of the Kiskadee [*Pitangus sulphuratus*] and establishment of the Starling [*Sturnus vulgaris*], and the increase of urbanization, all contributed to a drastic reduction of its numbers.'

OCEANIA

Hawaiian Islands[3]

Common Cardinals of various subspecies imported via San Francisco, California, were released on the island of Oahu by Mr William McInerny in 1929 and by the Hui Manu ('Bird Society') in 1931, on Kauai by Mrs Dora R. Isenberg in 1929, and between those dates at Hilo on Hawaii. On all three islands they were well established before 1940, and from Kauai had spread to Niihau, where they were abundant, before about 1950. They first appeared on Maui in 1949, on Molokai in 1951, and on Lanai in 1957.

In Hawaii, the Common Cardinal breeds throughout the year, enabling it to raise more broods than it does during the March to September nesting season in its natural range. It multiplied rapidly, and was soon reported to be damaging fruit crops. According to Peterson (1961), Common Cardinals were then well established in lowland and residential areas on most, if not all, the larger islands. Berger (1972) reported them to occur in both wet and dry regions on all the main islands to an altitude of around 2,300 m; they were especially common in lowland areas of kiawe or algaroba (mesquite) (*Prosopis chilensis*). Zeillemaker & Scott (1976) described them as common in exotic woodland and scrub (i.e. Guava (*Psidium guajava*), Java Plum (*Eugenia cumini* and *Eucalyptus* sp.), native mixed ohia (*Metrosideros collina*) and koa (*Acacia koa*) forests and other habitats, on Kauai, Oahu, Molokai, Lanai, Maui and Hawaii. Berger (1981: 219) said that the Common Cardinal

is now found on all the main islands. It is common in some lowland areas, and has moved upward into the mountains. . . . The Cardinal is a characteristic bird in many residential areas, and it is found in a wide variety of other habitats. Richardson and Bowles (1964) found the Cardinal near sea level, in the very dry regions of the Na Pali Coast, at Kokee State Park, and in the exceedingly wet forest of the Alakai Swamp at an elevation of 4,000 feet [1,200 m] along the trail to Mt Waialeale.

Although both species exist sympatrically in urban areas, there seems to be little competition with Red-crested Cardinals (*Paroaria coronata*) (q.v.).

Common Cardinals are believed to have been introduced to the island of Tahiti[4] in about 1950–2; although at one time said to be widely distributed and abundant, they were apparently declining by the early 1970s when Bruner (1972) described them as being confined to Punaauia and Paéa and to the remoter parts of Tautira. This distribution partially coincides with that of the Crimson-backed Tanager (*Ramphocelus dimidiatus*), which Bruner does not mention. This led Holyoak & Thibault (1975) to suggest, despite the lack of similarity between the two species, that the birds referred to by Bruner were not *cardinalis* but *dimidiatus*. This assessment they subsequently confirmed (Holyoak & Thibault (1984). (See also below.)

Long (1981) says that 'Virginia cardinals' (presumably *cardinalis*) were probably released unsuccessfully in Victoria, Australia, in the 1860s or 1870s.

Several races of the Common Cardinal have been repeatedly translocated since about 1880 from various parts of the United States to southwestern California. Miller (1928) quotes Lyman Belding (*Land Birds of the Pacific District*, 1890: 175) that half-a-dozen were transplanted from Missouri to Galt in Sacramento County, where they remained for several years In 1972, when about 20 breeding pairs were established in an area of some 80 ha of eastern Los Angeles,[5] Hardy (1973: 511) described them as living in 'riparian thicket on both sides of the San Gabriel River in the Whittier Narrows area (including especially the Nature Preserve of the County of

Los Angeles), near South El Monte, California'. Hardy reported that the colony appeared to be stable.

In eastern North America, the Common Cardinal has been extending its range slowly northwards for the past century and a half. It reached Michigan in 1837 (where a century later it was ubiquitous), Wisconsin – via the Mississippi Valley – around the turn of the century, first bred in Canada (at Point Pelee, Ontario) in 1901, and has been extending its range in southeastern South Dakota since 1904.

The range of the **Crimson-backed Tanager** (*Ramphocelus dimidiatus*) extends from Panama in Central America (including Coiba Island and the Perlas archipelago) south to northern and western Colombia east of the Andes, and northwestern Venezuela.

Eastham Guild, an American resident of Tahiti, records (1938 and 1940) that he had previously imported some Crimson-backed Tanagers – in about 1930, according to Holyoak & Thibault (1984), who say that in 1974 the species was established in small numbers in the Punaauia, Paéa and Taravao areas. Bruner (1979: 92), quoting Holyoak & Thibault (1975), says that it is 'now a common bird in [those] districts'. Which subspecies was introduced has not been determined. Thibault & Rivers (1975) found that in Tahiti the birds are restricted to gardens and coastal plantations, where they live mainly on fruit, including bananas. They are normally seen only singly or in pairs, actively fluttering about in vegetation.

It has been alleged, though on what evidence is uncertain, that the Crimson-backed Tanager in Tahiti was at one time erroneously recorded as the Scarlet Tanager (*Piranga olivacea*) – a native of eastern North America that winters south in northwestern South America; this error is said to have arisen through possible confusion (e.g. by Guild 1938, and Long 1981) between *R. dimidiatus* and *R. bresilius* (the Brazilian Tanager), which to aviculturists is often known as the 'Scarlet Tanager'. Holyoak (1974a) says that *olivacea* was introduced unsuccessfully to Tahiti in the 1960s, and Guild (1938) states that he had previously released *bresilius* there, which he refers to as the 'Scarlet Tanager'.

The **Blue-grey Tanager** (*Thraupis episcopus*) is distributed from southeastern Mexico through Central America (including the Perlas archipelago) southwards in South America (including Trinidad and Tobago) to northern Peru, northern Brazil and northern Bolivia.

According to Gottschalk (1967: 128), Blue-grey Tanagers had 'very recently . . . apparently become acclimated in the vicinity of Miami, Florida, USA, after escaping from aviaries'. This statement was amplified by Owre (1973), who quoted I. V. Arnold[6] as saying that the species had first been seen in the wild – feeding on the fruit of the exotic evergreen tree Sapodilla (*Achras sapote*) – in Hollywood, Broward County, in the previous year. Nesting was first recorded by D. R. Paulson & H. M. Stevenson[7] in 1961, and King (1968) described the birds as having been 'successfully introduced into the state'. By 1971, the population in northern Dade County was apparently increasing, and several were also seen in south Miami, where the species' continued presence was reported by Heilbrun (1976). The American Ornithologists' Union (1983), however, says that in recent years it has apparently disappeared.

In the late 1970s, a small number of Blue-grey Tanagers – probably escaped cagebirds that had been brought from Iquitos in northeastern Peru (where the local subspecies is *caerulea*) – were established around the city of Lima.

Guild (1940) recorded his importation of Blue-grey Tanagers to the island of Tahiti, where although they initially bred successfully they subsequently disappeared.

The **Red-legged Honeycreeper** (*Cyanerpes cyaneus*) ranges southwards from southeastern Mexico through Central America to South America (including Trinidad and Tobago) as far south as Bolivia and southeastern Brazil.

Although de Schauensee (1964) suggests that the species' presence on the island of Cuba is the result of human intervention, Bond (1979) indicates that it occurs there naturally.

Guild (1938 and 1940) states that he released Red-legged Honeycreepers on Tahiti, where although they at first bred successfully they later died out.

NOTES

1 American Ornithologists' Union 1957, 1983; Bourne 1957; K. L. Crowell 1962 (and personal communication, 1981); Crowell & Crowell 1976; D. B. Wingate 1973 (and personal communication, 1981); and D. E. Samuel, personal communication, 1981.

2 I am grateful to Dr David B. Wingate (personal communication, 1981) for drawing this reference to my attention.

3 American Ornithologists' Union 1957, 1983; Berger 1981; Blake 1975; Bryan 1958; Caum 1933; Fisher 1951; Hawaiian Audubon Society 1975; Long 1981; Munro 1960; Peterson 1961; Pyle 1977; Richardson & Bowles 1964; Zeillemaker & Scott 1976.

4 Bruner 1972; Holyoak 1974a; Holyoak & Thibault 1975, 1984; Long 1981.

5 Blake (1975: 925) says they were transplanted to Pasadena.

6 *Florida Naturalist* 34:44–5 (1961).

7 *Audubon Field Notes* 16: 398–404 (1962).

Spotted-breasted Oriole

(*Icterus pectoralis*)

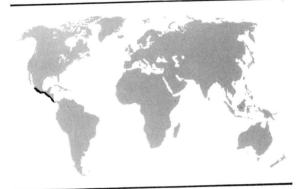

NATURAL DISTRIBUTION
Western Central America, from southwestern Mexico through southern Guatemala, El Salvador, western Honduras, and western Nicaragua, to northwestern Costa Rica.

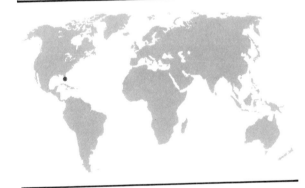

NATURALIZED DISTRIBUTION
North America: USA.

NORTH AMERICA

USA[1]

The Spotted-breasted Oriole was one of the first exotic birds to breed in the wild in suburban Miami, southern Florida, where Brookfield & Griswold (1956) found escaped cagebirds nesting along the Miami River in September 1949. By 1956, they ranged north and south for more than 40 km; by May 1961, they had reached Hypoloxo Island in Broward County, and by the following year had spread to West Palm Beach,[2] 120 km north of Miami.

Six years later, when King (1968) described them as having been 'successfully introduced into the state', Spotted-breasted Orioles were established in Palm Beach, Broward and Dade counties in southeastern Florida; also in 1968, W. B. Robertson[3] reported them at Pine Island in Everglades National Park, some 65 km south of Miami, and in the following year two were noted by C. and L. Walkinshaw[4] at Lake Wales in central Florida, 240 km to the north. By 1973, when O'Keefe claimed they had 'become part of Florida's birdlife', Owre reported that Spotted-breasted Orioles were appearing in Florida, albeit irregularly, somewhat north of the Tropical Zone. In October 1975, a flock of 47 was counted at Palm Beach, and others were seen at Stuart, some 55 km to the north.

Living largely on fruit and nectar, Spotted-breasted Orioles presumably exploit a wide range of fruiting and flowering plants and shrubs – tropical and subtropical, native and exotic – which are cultivated in suburban districts well into northern Florida: their further northwards expansion is thus unlikely to be inhibited by lack of suitable foods. According to Peters (1968), the subspecies introduced to Florida is the nominate one, *I. p. pectoralis*, which in Central America occurs north of southern Nicaragua.

NOTES

1 Brookfield & Griswold 1956; Heilbrun 1976; King 1968; Long 1981; O'Keefe 1973; Owre 1973; Peters 1968.
2 H. M. Stevenson, *Audubon Field Notes* 15: 402–5 (1961), and 16: 21–5 (1962).
3 *Audubon Field Notes* 22: 516–20 (1968).
4 *American Birds* 24: 246–7 (1970).

Troupial
(Icterus icterus)

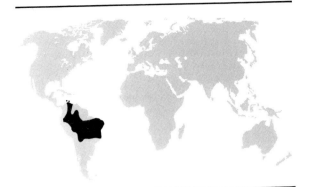

NATURAL DISTRIBUTION
South America, from northern and eastern Colombia and northern and western Venezuela (including the islands of Aruba and Curaçao), south through eastern Ecuador, eastern Peru and southwestern Guyana to northern and eastern Bolivia and southwestern Brazil.

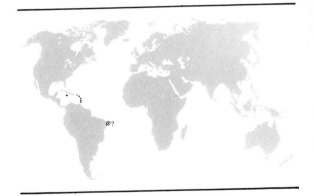

NATURALIZED DISTRIBUTION
North America: West Indies (?Jamaica, Puerto Rico, Mona, St Thomas (including Water Island), St John, Antigua, Dominica, Grenada, ?Trinidad); South America: ?Isla de Itamaracá (Brazil).

NORTH AMERICA

West Indies[1]

Authorities differ concerning the precise status (and subspecies) of the Troupial in the West Indies. The birds were first reported to be breeding near the coast at Quebradillas in north-western Puerto Rico by Gundlach around 1878 (quoted by Wetmore 1927). Bowdish (1903) found them to be popular cagebirds on Puerto Rico, where although he seems not to have seen any himself he was told that in some places they were established in the wild. Herklots (1961) says that birds of the nominate subspecies (from eastern Colombia and northwestern Venezuela) had been introduced to, and were established on, Puerto Rico, Jamaica and St Thomas (including Water Island); Herklots, Allen (1962) and de Schauensee (1970) state that the birds probably came from Curacao, where the subspecies is *ridgwayi*. Allen said that on Puerto Rico the Troupial was an uncommon local resident of long standing (perhaps even a native species), and that the birds have also occurred on other islands in the Caribbean, including St John, Antigua, Dominica and Grenada.

On Puerto Rico, where the Troupial is still a popular pet, the population is continually augmented by escaped cagebirds. It is probably scarce on all other islands to which it has been introduced, which Blake (1975) lists only as St Thomas, Mona and Jamaica. On Jamaica Lack (1976) says that it was at one time partially naturalized, but later died out. Finally, Bond (1979: 220) describes the Troupial as having been 'introduced (apparently) and established in Puerto Rico and St Thomas, including Water Island; also reported from Jamaica, St John, Antigua, Dominica and Grenada (escaped cage-birds?). Recently introduced on Mona'. The birds occur in 'semi-arid woodland and mangrove swamps,

chiefly in southwestern Puerto Rico (e.g. Guánica State forest) . . . and east and south coasts of St Thomas . . . numerous near Guánica'. The subspecies established on Puerto Rico and St Thomas is, according to Peters (1968), *I. i. ridgwayi*. Reports of Troupials on the island of Barbuda may have arisen through the misidentification of Carib Grackles (*Quiscalus lugubris*).

Ffrench (1976) said that Troupials seen on Trinidad in 1932 may have been natural immigrants from Venezuela. Others seen in suburban districts on the island between 1964 and 1966, on the other hand, were probably escaped cagebirds.

SOUTH AMERICA

Isla de Itamaracá (Brazil)[2]

Sick (1968) says that Troupials of the eastern Brazilian subspecies *I. i. jamacaii* have occurred on Isla de Itamaracá north of Recife (Pernambuco) since 1927–9. Whether they arrived as natural colonists or were introduced by human agency is unknown.

NOTES

1 Allen 1962; Blake 1975; Bond 1979; Bowdish 1903; de Schauensee 1970; Ffrench 1976; Gundlach 1878 (in Wetmore 1927); Herklots 1961; Lack 1976; Long 1981; Peters 1968.
2 Long (1981) erroneously indicates that this island is off the coast of Venezuela.

Shiny Cowbird
(*Molothrus bonariensis*)

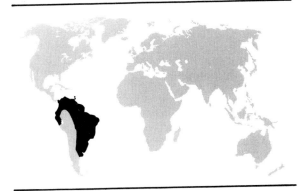

NATURAL DISTRIBUTION
South America, from eastern Panama through Colombia, western and southwestern Ecuador, eastern and western Peru, northern Venezuela, Trinidad, Tobago, the Guianas and northern Brazil, south to eastern Bolivia, Paraguay, Uruguay, and northeastern and east-central Argentina.

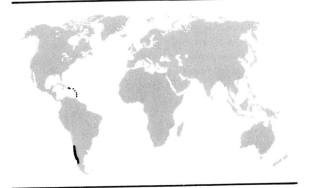

NATURALIZED DISTRIBUTION
North America: ?West Indies (Lesser Antilles, Puerto Rico, Hispaniola); South America: Chile.

NORTH AMERICA

West Indies (Lesser Antilles, Puerto Rico and Hispaniola)[1]

The first specimen of a Shiny Cowbird in the West Indies was collected on Vieques Island, 10 km east of Puerto Rico, by E. Newton in 1860. For many years there were no reports of any further sightings on Vieques, but in 1934 some were seen on St Croix, 65 km to the southeast. In 1955, Shiny Cowbirds appeared on the island of St John, 60 km north of St Croix, and in the same year (possibly as early as the 1940s) at Cabezas de San Juan in northeastern Puerto Rico; a decade later they had spread to western Puerto Rico, from where they reached Mona Island, 70 km to the west, in 1971 or 1972, and the Dominican Republic, a further 70 km westwards, at around the same time. By the late 1970s they were well established on the south coast of the republic around the capital, Santo Domingo, and also on parts of the eastern and northern coasts, from where they appear to be spreading.

In 1899, Shiny Cowbirds were found on Carriacou in the Grenadines in the southern Lesser Antilles, from where they have spread slowly northwards through the Windward Islands, reaching Grenada (in the south) in 1901, Barbados in 1916 (probably an introduction), St Vincent (1924), St Lucia (1931), Martinique (1948 or 1949), and Marie Galante and Antigua in the southern Leeward Islands in 1959. (None, however, were seen on Antigua between 1972 and 1977 by Holland & Williams (1978).)

Bond (1979: 215) said of the species that it was 'a rather recent arrival in the West Indies, but now well established in Lesser Antilles north to Martinique, and in Puerto Rico and Hispaniola; also recorded from Mona, Vieques, Culebra and several of the Virgin Islands'. The subspecies present in the West Indies is apparently *M. b. minimus*, which also occurs in the Guianas and northern Brazil, so the possibility of natural colonization (as implied by Blake (1975), who describes the species as an 'invader' from Grenada to Martinique, Antigua, Puerto Rico, the Virgin Islands and Hispaniola) cannot be ignored, even though it is a popular cagebird in the region.

New World cowbirds are parasitic species, filling the role of Old World cuckoos (Cuculidae) by depositing their eggs in the nests of other – usually smaller – birds such as grackles (Icteridae) and mockingbirds (Mimidae). Brood parasitism by Shiny Cowbirds of the endemic Yellow-shouldered Blackbird (*Agelaius x. xanthomus*) on Puerto Rico and on Mona Island (where the local subspecies is *monensis*), is said to be one of the factors responsible for the Blackbird's marked decline on both islands and official classification in *The ICBP Bird Red Data Book* (King 1981) as 'vulnerable'. On Hispaniola, Shiny Cowbirds are believed to parasitize the endemic Black-cowled Oriole (*Icterus d. dominicensis*), and, in the Lesser Antilles, endemic warblers (*Dendroica* spp.), St Lucia Orioles (*Icterus laudabilis*) and Martinique Orioles (*I. bonana*) also suffer.

SOUTH AMERICA

Chile[2]

Shiny Cowbirds were first occasionally reported in central Chile before 1877; between 1906 and 1914, large numbers were imported to the country as cagebirds, and by 1910–12 sizeable flocks were established near Machalí. By the mid-1960s, they were numerous from Copiapó in Atacamá Province in the north to Aisén Province in the south, that is between 27° S and about 47° S. The population is much more likely to be descended from escaped or deliberately released cagebirds than from natural immigrants from Argentina, to whom the Andes would have proved a well-nigh insuperable barrier. The subspecies established is the nominate one, *M. b. bonariensis*, from central South America.

The **Western Meadowlark** (*Sturnella neglecta*) ranges southwards from southern Canada through the whole of the United States west of a line between Lake Ontario and Louisiana.

Western Meadowlarks imported to the Hawaiian Islands[3] from San Francisco, California, were released in 1931 on Kauai by Mrs Dora R. Isenberg, and on Oahu by the Hawaiian Board of Agriculture and Forestry. Three years later, others were freed on Niihau, and at about the same time some were also placed on Maui. They seem to have become established only on Kauai, where Berger (1981: 206) reported them to be 'fairly common but highly localized, being found near Kekaha, Lihue, Kapaa, and Kilauea'. They are said also to have occurred near Hanalei. Zeillemaker & Scott (1976) described them as 'common' in cultivated land and fields only on Kauai. Pyle (1977) confirmed their presence as an introduced species 'long-established and breeding'.

Thomson (1922) records that in 1869 the Auckland Acclimatization Society imported a pair of Western Meadowlarks from California to New Zealand, 'but they did not increase'.

The **Carib Grackle** (*Quiscalus lugubris*) occurs in northeastern South America from northeastern Brazil through the Guianas to northern Venezuela and eastern Colombia, and on the islands of Trinidad, Margarita, Los Testigos, Los Hermanos and Los Frailes, and in the West Indies from Grenada and Barbados in the southern Lesser Antilles northwards through the Windward Islands to Montserrat and Guadeloupe.

According to Peters (1968), the Barbados subspecies, *Q. l. fortirostris*, was transplanted between 1912 and 1914 to Barbuda, Antigua, and possibly also to St Kitts. Blake (1975) indicates that it has also been introduced to St Martin. On Antigua, where Danforth (1934) recorded them as 'introduced and locally common', Holland & Williams (1978) found Carib Grackles to be abundant. Bond (1979: 216) described the species as 'introduced on Barbuda, Antigua, St Kitts and possibly on St Martin', and as occurring only in settled districts. This distribution is confirmed by the American Ornithologists' Union (1983).

Carib Grackles first appeared on the island of Tobago, according to Ffrench (1973), in about 1905, but whether as natural immigrants or an introduction from Trinidad is uncertain.

The **Great-tailed Grackle** (*Quiscalus mexicanus*) ranges from the southern United States southwards through Central America to Peru and Venezuela.

Primarily birds of the tropical coastal lowlands, large numbers of Great-tailed Grackles occur in the 4,500-km^2 temperate Valley of Mexico – a subdivision of the Anáhuac Plateau in the central Mexican highlands – at altitudes of over 2,000 m. These birds are probably all descended from some that, according to information given by

Aztec Indians to a sixteenth-century Spanish Franciscan friar, Bernardino de Sahagún (Sahagún [1577] 1963, quoted by Haemig 1978),[4] were translocated to the Aztec city of Tenochtitlán (near the present site of Mexico City) from the provinces of Cuextlan and Totonacapan (in what is now the northern half of the state of Veracruz, several hundred kilometres to the east) by the Aztec Emperor Auitzotl (reigned 1486–1502). Auitzotl has been described as an innovative and imaginative ruler, under whom the Aztec empire greatly expanded and all forms of culture achieved new heights of excellence. It seems entirely appropriate, as Haemig points out, that such an energetic and creative leader should conceive the idea of introducing a tropical coastal bird into the central Mexican highlands.

According to Sahagún, the Great-tailed Grackle was known to the Aztecs as the *Teotzanatl* – the 'divine' or 'marvellous grackle'. A name such as this, Sahagún continues, was given to a bird that was rare, unusual or esteemed, and was bestowed on the Great-tailed Grackle because it had hitherto been unknown in Tenochtitlán.

Since it is known that pre-Columbian Indians made extensive use of feathers in the decoration of head-dresses, clothing and ceremonial articles, and that to this end there was a considerable traffic and trade in exotic birds, it seems probable that Great-tailed Grackles were translocated to the central Mexican highlands for this purpose.

In Tenochtitlán, the grackles were, interestingly, allowed to range free, being fed and protected, at the command of the Emperor, by the local inhabitants. According to Sahagún, they multiplied rapidly and spread far and wide, even becoming a pest in some areas, and are now one of the commonest birds on the altiplano. The subspecies established in the Valley of Mexico, *Q. m. mexicanus*, is the same as that found in Veracruz, giving added credence to Sahagún's account.

NOTES

1 American Ornithologists' Union 1957, 1983; Blake 1975; Bond 1979; Holland & Williams 1978; King 1981; Long 1981; Peters 1968; Post & Wiley 1976, 1977a,b; Robertson 1962.
2 Friedman 1929; Hellmayr 1932; Johnson 1967; Long 1981; Peters 1968.
3 American Ornithologists' Union 1957, 1983; Berger

1981; Blake 1975; Bryan 1958; Caum 1933; Hawaiian Audubon Society 1975; Heilbrun 1976; Long 1981; Munro 1960; Peterson 1961; Pyle 1977; Zeillemaker & Scott 1976.

4 As Haemig points out, among the avifauna of Latin America are several species with unusual disjunctive distributions. Certain populations of these birds may be separated from others of their kind by thousands of kilometres of apparently suitable habitat, suggesting a non-natural colonization. In the past, these discrete colonies have usually been attributed to the survival of relict populations or to the arrival of storm-borne waifs. Haemig propounds the intriguing possibility that they may, however, be descended from birds imported by pre-Columbian Indian traders. These include the Green Jay (*Cyanocorax yncas*), Vermilion Flycatcher (*Pyrocephalus rubinus*), Melodious Blackbird (*Dives dives*), Chinampas Grackle (*Quiscalus palustris*), Military Macaw (*Ara militaris*) and Mexican Parrotlet (*Forpus cyanopygius*). All, as Haemig says, seem likely to have been sought-after by Indian feather-merchants.

Chaffinch
(*Fringilla coelebs*)

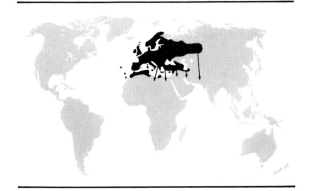

NATURAL DISTRIBUTION

The Western Palaearctic, from the Azores, Madeira, the Canary Islands and the British Isles eastwards through Europe and North Africa to the Middle East and Central Asia. Winters south to North Africa, Iraq, central Iran and Afghanistan.

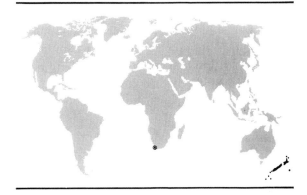

NATURALIZED DISTRIBUTION

Africa: South Africa; Australasia: New Zealand.

AFRICA

South Africa[1]

The endemic British subspecies of the Chaffinch (*F. c. gengleri*) is believed to have been introduced from England to South Africa by Cecil Rhodes in 1898. It has not spread far and remains confined to gardens and exotic (e.g. Cluster Pine (*Pinus pilaster*) and oak (*Quercus* sp.)) plantations on the lower slopes of Table Mountain on the northern Cape Peninsula, where it is most abundant in Newlands and Kenilworth but occurs from Sea Point to Plumstead, Tokai and Hout Bay. Liversidge (n.d.) indicated a possible maximum population of around 100 and said that it was decreasing, and Maclean (1985: 774) describes it as established 'only in Cape Town area from Kloof Nek to Tokai and Cape Peninsula'.

Siegfried (1962) suggested that the failure of Chaffinches to become more widely established in South Africa is probably because they have been unable to adapt to the native vegetation, and their eggs and young are undoubtedly preyed on by alien Grey Squirrels (*Sciurus carolinensis*). In South Africa, Chaffinches do not form large single-sex flocks outside the breeding season as they tend to do in Britain and continental Europe.

AUSTRALASIA

New Zealand[2]

Table 9 gives details of the importations by acclimatization societies of Chaffinches of the British subspecies (*gengleri*) from England to New Zealand. Many more were brought in by private aviculturists and bird-dealers. In Canterbury, Chaffinches soon became established, especially in exotic pine plantations but seldom in indigenous woodlands or above the treeline. Until at least around 1920 a bounty was given for their destruction in such grain-growing areas as South Canterbury. In Otago, they became abundant around Dunedin but later declined, according to Thomson (1922), through eating poisoned grain put out for Rabbits (*Oryctolagus cuniculus*). Even after trapping was substituted for poisoning in Otago, and other small passerines considerably increased, the Chaffinch remained for some time 'a comparatively rare bird'. Elsewhere, it spread only slowly, but by about 1920, Thomson continues (1922: 170), was 'common throughout both the islands, and very abundant in some parts, especially from Taupo [in central North Island] northwards', to the upper limit of the bush line at around 900 m.

In 1879, 70 Chaffinches were freed on Stewart Island, where although they were seen for a while around the head of Paterson Inlet they had all

Table 9 Introductions by acclimatization societies of Chaffinches (*Fringilla coelebs*) to New Zealand, 1862–77

Date	Number	Introduced by	Remarks
1862–4	23	Nelson AS★ (SI)†	
1864	'Several'	Auckland AS (NI)‡	Released
1865–6	?	Canterbury AS (SI)	
1867	45	Auckland AS (NI)	Released; said to be 'thoroughly acclimatized' in 1868
1867	11	Canterbury AS (SI)	Released in the society's gardens where they became established
1868	5	Canterbury AS (SI)	Released; by 1870–1 said to be 'thoroughly established and to need no further importations'
1868	68	Auckland AS (NI)	
1868	27	Otago AS (SI)	Released
1869	'a considerable number'	Auckland AS (NI)	
1869	6	Otago AS (SI)	Released
1871	'a further lot'	Canterbury AS (SI)	
1871	66	Otago AS (SI)	Released
1874	70	Wellington AS (NI)	Released
1876	36	Wellington AS (NI)	Released
1877	20	Wellington AS (NI)	Released; 'A few more' freed in subsequent years

Sources: see note 2
★ AS, Acclimatization Society; †SI, South Island; ‡NI, North Island

disappeared before the outbreak of the First World War. They reappeared on Stewart Island before 1930, and spread to other New Zealand offshore islands as follows: Mayor and Kapiti (before 1930); the Snares (before 1948); Three Kings, Mokohinau, Little Barrier, Codfish, the Aucklands and Campbell (before 1955); and Macquarie and the Chathams (before 1965); they bred on Three Kings, the Chathams, the Antipodes, Campbell and the Aucklands before 1973.

By 1965, Chaffinches in New Zealand, according to Wodzicki (1965: 433), were 'widely distributed and abundant, North, South, Stewart and Chatham, Campbell, Snares, Auckland and Macquarie Islands'. Williams (1969: 446) said that the Chaffinch is 'sometimes suggested as the most widespread and perhaps even the commonest of all birds in New Zealand'. Falla, Sibson & Turbott (1979) certainly regarded the Chaffinch as New Zealand's most abundant finch; they found it to be evenly distributed, wherever there are trees and shrubs, up to an altitude of 1,400 m, and reported that it had penetrated into bush and forests as no other finch had succeeded in doing. It also frequents gardens, parks and agricultural land, and has proved an energetic colonist of nearby offshore and distant subantarctic islands, breeding as far south as Campbell Island. Although Chaffinches in New Zealand cause a limited amount of damage to grain, apricot, peach, apple and nectarine crops, their most significant ecological impact may be to affect the natural regeneration of some alien pines through their consumption of seeds.

Phillips (1928) records several unsuccessful attempts to naturalize Chaffinches in the United States; Joshua Jones freed some in Central Park, New York, in 1878; the Portland Song Bird Club released 40 pairs in Oregon in 1889, 20 pairs in 1907, and a further 20 at a later date; at least 30 or 40 pairs were planted in New York City for several years before 1893, and a small number around San Francisco, California, in the 1890s. None became established.

Similarly, in Australia[3] Chaffinches were introduced unsuccessfully. In April 1856 (Balmford 1978) and January 1857 (Rolls 1969), consignments of songbirds, which included Chaffinches, arrived in Sydney, New South Wales, and (through a bird dealer named Brown) in Melbourne, Victoria, respectively. Le Souef (1890) records that in February 1863, 130 'small birds, principally sparrows and chaffinches' arrived in Melbourne on the *Relief*, where 40 of the latter were liberated later in the same year, 220 in 1864 and 235 in 1872. Although in 1864 the Victoria Acclimatization Society announced in its annual report (quoted by Rolls) that 'the chaffinch . . . may now be considered thoroughly established', the claim was somewhat premature since the birds later died out. Three Chaffinches reported by Jenkins (1977) to have been released by the Acclimatization Society of South Australia in 1879 or 1880 soon disappeared.

According to Sharrock (1976: 430), 'The [natural] range of the Chaffinch has shifted northwards in Europe during the period of climatic amelioration in the past 50 years, at the expense of the Brambling (*Fringilla montifringilla*)'. A parallel extension of range northwards into western Siberia in the same period is recorded by Voous (1960).

NOTES

1 Hogg 1982; Knock, Pringle & Martin 1976; Lever 1985b; Liversidge n.d.; Long 1981; Mackworth-Praed & Grant 1963; Maclean 1985; Roberts 1940; Robinson 1953; Rowan 1952; Schmidt, Longrigg & Pringle 1976; Siegfried 1962; Wattel 1971; J. M. Winterbottom 1966, 1978 (and personal communication, 1981); and P. A. Clancey and J. Vincent, personal communications, 1981.
2 Falla, Sibson & Turbott 1979; Kinsky 1970; Lever 1985b; Long 1981; Oliver 1930, 1955; Thomson 1922, 1926; Williams 1953, 1969, 1973; Wodzicki 1965.

Canary
(Serinus canaria)

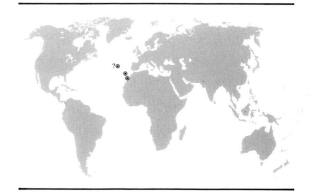

Note: Presence in Azores may be a result of human intervention or natural colonization.

NATURAL DISTRIBUTION
Western Canary Islands (including Gran Canaria, Tenerife, La Palma, Gomera and probably Hierro) and Madeira; ?Azores.

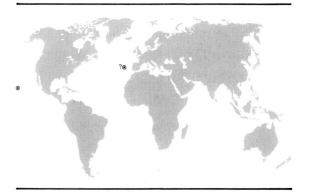

Note: Presence in Azores may be a result of human intervention or natural colonization.

NATURALIZED DISTRIBUTION
Europe: ?Azores; Oceania: Hawaiian Islands.

EUROPE

Azores

Whether the Canary's presence in the Azores, where it is now widespread and abundant on all the islands, is the result of human intervention or natural colonization is, according to Bannerman & Bannerman (1966), uncertain.

OCEANIA

Hawaiian Islands[1]

In March 1909, Mr Daniel Morrison, manager of the Commercial Pacific Cable Company, bought a pair of Canaries from the crew of the SS *Siberia* in Honolulu harbour on Oahu, which he later transported to Sand Island in the Midway group. In February and April 1910, 10 young hatched in Morrison's aviary and these, together with a further two males that arrived from Honolulu in July, were released later in the same year.[2] Breeding in the wild began in December 1910, and in the first season some 60 birds were reared successfully. Because Morrison's employers would not permit the introduction of potential predators, such as Domestic Cats (*Felis catus*), to the Midway Islands, the Canaries succeeded in becoming established, within a few generations reverting to a wild-type whitish, brownish or intermediate plumage. At first they tended to nest on the ground, but later in introduced Ironwood trees (*Casuarina* sp.). In May 1945, Fisher & Baldwin counted about 30 on Sand Island, where 3 years later Bailey (1956) also found a few, adding that since his previous visit in 1913 'the ironwoods had grown to tall trees, probably giving the canaries safe places to nest, while the Laysan Finches [*Loxioides/Psittirostra cantans*], low nesting species, could not escape the rats'. The Hawaiian Audubon Society (1975) stated that the birds were well established and breeding. In July 1978 a flock of 73 was counted on Sand Island.[3]

Zeillemaker & Scott (1976) record Canaries as uncommon in coastal areas and wetlands and in exotic woodland and scrub, such as Guava (*Psidium guajava*), Java Plum (*Eugenia cumini*) and *Eucalyptus*. Their presence was confirmed by Pyle (1977).

Fitter (1959) refers to one of the few (perhaps the only) deliberate attempt to naturalize Canaries in Britain, when in 1939–40 R. M. Lockley introduced six pairs to the island of Skokholm off the Pembrokeshire coast of Wales; they bred successfully in the wild and increased to around 50, but were then decimated by migrant Sparrowhawks (*Accipiter nisus*).

According to Zeuner (1963), Canaries became temporarily established on the Italian island of Elba in the sixteenth century, when a vessel carrying large numbers of them sank off the coast.

Crowell & Crowell (1976) say that Canaries were imported to Bermuda by Portuguese immigrants from the Azores (or Madeira) – probably in the 1930s. Alternatively, they may have arrived in the same shipment of cagebirds that resulted in the establishment of the Goldfinch (*Carduelis carduelis*) (q.v.) in the late nineteenth century. Whether these were wild or domesticated birds is not recorded. They seem to have reached peak abundance in the 1940s, but thereafter to have declined, due probably to a combination of the loss of the native Bermuda Cedar (*Juniperus bermudiana*) forest, interspecific competition from the alien House Sparrow (*Passer domesticus*) (q.v.) and Goldfinch, and increasing urbanization. They died out around 1966–70.[4]

The earliest deliberate attempt to establish Canaries in Australia was made by the Victoria Acclimatization Society, who released 18 near Melbourne. The date of release is variously given as 1859 (2 years before the society was founded) by Jenkins (1977), 1862–9 (by Balmford 1978) and 1872 (by Ryan 1906). These birds were presumably the descendants of some imported by a dealer named Neymaler, in a consignment of various songbirds, in January 1858. This planting, like many succeeding ones, was unsuccessful.

Thomson (1922) says that efforts by private aviculturists to establish Canaries in New Zealand were frustrated by feral Cats (*Felis catus*).

According to Holyoak & Thibault (1984), Canaries have been unsuccessfully released on Raratonga in the Cook Islands.

After the Budgerigar (*Melopsittacus undulatus*), the Canary is the world's most popular cagebird (Ellis, in Mason 1984). In many countries it frequently escapes from captivity or is deliberately released, but seldom becomes established for more than a limited period. This may be, as Thomson (1922) suggested, because the domesticated variety (which is the one almost invariably involved) is an 'artificial' and inbred bird that would require several generations in the wild to re-acquire its natural defensive mechanism. It is noteworthy that the only certainly naturalized population (on Sand Island) evolved in a once predator-free environment. It would be an interesting experiment to release wild birds from the Canary Islands, Madeira or the Azores, in an apparently suitable alien habitat.

NOTES

1 American Ornithologists' Union 1957, 1983; Bailey 1956; Berger 1981; Blake 1975; Bryan 1912b; Ellis (in Mason 1984); Fisher & Baldwin 1945; Hawaiian Audubon Society 1975; Long 1981; Munro 1960; Peterson 1961; Pyle 1977; Zeillemaker & Scott 1976.

2 One account says 14 birds were released whereas another says only 11.

3 *Elepaio* 39: 76.

4 D. B. Wingate, personal communication, 1984 and unpublished mimeograph.

Yellow-fronted Canary
(*Serinus mozambicus*)

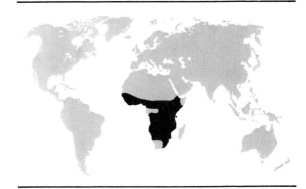

NATURAL DISTRIBUTION

Most of Africa south of the Sahara apart from eastern Ethiopia, Somalia, Equatorial Guinea, Gabon, Congo, and Western Cape Province, South Africa.

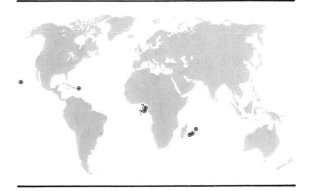

NATURALIZED DISTRIBUTION

Africa: Mascarenes (Mauritius, Réunion, Rodrigues), ?São Tomé, ?Annobón; North America: West Indies (Puerto Rico); Oceania: Hawaiian Islands.

AFRICA

Mauritius, Réunion and Rodrigues[1]

Yellow-fronted Canaries of the nominate form (Kenya to Zambia and Mozambique) were introduced to Mauritius, Réunion and – according to Jean Vinson[2] – Rodrigues, probably from the coast of Mozambique, by the French East India Company around the middle of the eighteenth century, possibly in about 1764. On Mauritius, where they were formerly a serious pest of cereal crops, they frequent coastal groves of *Casuarina* sp. which furnish both seeds for food and shelter, and lowland areas on Réunion. On all three Mascarene islands they are today well established and common.

São Tomé; Annobón

According to Peters (1968), Yellow-fronted Canaries of the southwestern Zaire and northern Angola subspecies *S. m. tando* have probably been introduced to the Portuguese island of São Tomé and the Spanish island of Annobón in the Gulf of Guinea: the possibility of natural colonization from the West African mainland, however, cannot be ruled out.

NORTH AMERICA

West Indies (Puerto Rico)

According to the American Ornithologists' Union (1983), Yellow-fronted Canaries have been introduced to, and are established in, north-eastern Puerto Rico.

OCEANIA

Hawaiian Islands[3]

The Yellow-fronted Canary was first recorded at Koko Head on Oahu in 1964, where breeding was confirmed in about 1977. Zeillemaker & Scott (1976) record the species as local and rare in residential and community parklands on that island. Berger (1981: 221) said that on Oahu 'the species is now a common resident in the Diamond Head–Kapiolani Park region of Waikiki; it has also been seen at Kawela Bay near the Kuilima hotel, some 30 miles [48 km] from Diamond Head (*Elepaio* 38: 106)'.

Although the Yellow-fronted Canary was probably released on the Puu Waawaa Ranch on Hawaii before about 1960, it was not until December 1977 that the first birds in the wild (a flock of 11 in the mamane (*Sophora chrysophylla*)/naio (*Myoporum sandvichense*) forest on

Mauna Kea) were reported. At first they were confined to the eastern, southern and western slopes of Mauna Kea, from Puu Laau to Puu Kahinahina, between 2,100 and 2,800 m. At about the same time some were also seen at Halepohaku (2,900 m), and flocks of 18 and 37 were counted between Puu Kole and Puu Kaupakuhale. 'Large numbers' were seen on Hualalai Mountain in June 1978.[4] By 1981 they had spread to the damp ohia (*Metrosideros collina*) forest at 1,280 m on Stainback Highway.

Yellow-fronted Canaries of the nominate form (Peters 1968), collected on Desroches in the Amirante Islands in 1884 and 1892 were, Penny (1974) believed, the descendants of birds introduced by human agency. They could, however, have arrived in the islands as natural immigrants from coastal Tanzania. According to C. J. Feare (personal communication, 1986), they died out before 1976.

In about 1929, H. Bruins-Lich unsuccessfully released Yellow-fronted Canaries, imported from South Africa where the form is *S. m. granti*, on the island of St Helena in the South Atlantic (Haydock 1954).

Guild (1938) states that he had unsuccessfully released 'Cape Canaries' on the island of Tahiti. These were probably *S. mozambicus* but could perhaps have been the Yellow-crowned Canary, *S. canicollis* (see below).

The **Yellow-crowned Canary** (*Serinus canicollis*) ranges southwards in Africa from eastern Zimbabwe to the eastern Transvaal, Zululand and Natal, and to southern Cape Province, South Africa.

According to Le Gentil (1780), quoted by Meinertzhagen (1912: 90), 'It was imported to Mauritius and Réunion from the Cape of Good Hope during the last war, partly as an experiment and partly as a present to the ladies. It is one of the most pernicious presents ever made to the island, as it eats all the crops and increases without effort.' On Mauritius,[5] the birds were eventually eradicated by farmers and the great cyclone of 1892. On Réunion,[6] Yellow-crowned Canaries of the nominate subspecies have flourished, and are now well established in scrubland and cultivated areas (where they are something of a pest to grain, fruit and vegetable crops) from around 600 m to the lower limit of the *Philippia* heath at 1,800–2,000 m.

Huckle (1924), quoted by Haydock (1954), refers to the presence of Yellow-crowned Canaries on the island of St Helena in the South Atlantic. None remain there today.

———

The **Yellow Canary** (*Serinus flaviventris*) ranges southwards in Africa from South West Africa (Namibia), Botswana, Lesotho, southwestern Transvaal and the Orange Free State to Cape Province, South Africa.

Melliss (1870), who refers to the presence of large numbers of the canary *Crithagra butyracea* on St Helena, may have been referring to this species. More recently, Haydock (1954) says that around 1929 H. Bruins-Lich imported Yellow Canaries of the form *S. f. marshalli* (northwestern Cape Province and Transvaal) to the island. Peters (1968), however, says that it is the nominate form (from the Western Cape Province) that has been introduced.

In the nineteenth century, Yellow Canaries were also released on Ascension Island, where Stonehouse (1962) estimated the population at a minimum of 100–200 birds.

NOTES

1 Decary 1962; Long 1981; Mackworth-Praed & Grant 1955–63; Meinertzhagen 1912; Peters 1968; Rountree, Guérin et al. 1952; Staub 1976; Watson, Zusi & Storer 1963.

2 J. Vinson, 'Quelques rémarques sur l'Île Rodrigues et sur la faune terrestre', *Royal Society of Arts and Sciences of Mauritius* 2: 263–77 (1965).

3 American Ornithologists' Union 1983; Berger 1977b, 1981; Blake 1975; Hawaiian Audubon Society 1975; Long 1981; Paton 1981; Pyle 1976, 1977; Van Ripper 1978; Zeillemaker & Scott 1976.

4 *Elepaio* 39: 76.

5 Benedict 1957; Decary 1962; Long 1981; Meinertzhagen 1912; Peters 1968; Rountree, Guérin et al. 1952; Staub 1976; Watson, Zusi & Storer 1963.

6 See note 6.

Greenfinch
(Carduelis chloris)

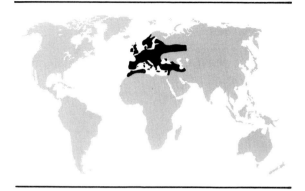

NATURAL DISTRIBUTION
Much of the western Palaearctic, from the British Isles eastwards to about 60° E in the USSR, north to around 70° N in Norway, and south to North Africa and the Middle East.

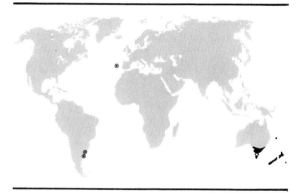

Note: Distribution in Australia is discontinuous. Occur as vagrants only on several New Zealand subantarctic islands.

NATURALIZED DISTRIBUTION
Europe: Azores; South America: Uruguay, Argentina; Australasia: Australia, New Zealand.

EUROPE

Azores

Marler & Boatman (1951) reported the presence in the Azores of small numbers of Greenfinches only on the island of Pico. Bannerman & Bannerman (1966), who say that Greenfinches (according to Peters (1968) of the southern Europe and North African subspecies *C. c. aurantiventris*) were introduced to the Azores, presumably from Portugal, around 1890, found a few only on Terceira and on the largest island in the group, São Miguel.

SOUTH AMERICA

Uruguay

According to Cuello & Gerzenstein (1962), Greenfinches first bred successfully in the wild in Uruguay at Montevideo in 1929. By 1960 they were, according to Armani (1983), very abundant on the coastal zone in the departments of Canelones (especially at La Paloma) and Maldonado, especially at Punta Ballena. Sick (1968) indicates that they had been established in a limited area near the south coast for some 40 years, but had not yet spread north across the Rio Yaguarón (Jaguarão) into Rio Grande do Sul in southern Brazil. Armani reported adults in winter as far north as Durazno, Sarandi Grande and Minas between 1979 and 1981, and near Juan L. Lacaze in the department of Colonia in 1980.

Argentina

Greenfinches are believed to have been introduced to Argentina in about 1900. Armani (1983) reported them to be well established and abundant in 1961 between Mar de Ajo and Necochea, Mar del Plata, and by 1980 the population had noticeably increased in Pinamar, Chapadmalal and Miramar. Nesting has been observed at Punta Inoio, Mar de Ajo, Pinamar, Villa Geisel, Mar del Plata and Necochea, south to Reta and Tres Arroyos. In the winter of 1982, small groups of up to half-a-dozen appeared at Villalonga, Ramos Hejia, General Villegas, Pehuajo, Azul and Coronel Pringles, and in the following September three cocks and four hens were observed at Bahia Blanca. The vegetation and climate in the provinces of Buenos Aires, La Pampa and Rio Negro are very similar to those of the species' natural range in Europe, and the vast fields of sunflowers and the numerous wild seeding plants of Buenos Aires provide an abundant supply of food.

AUSTRALASIA

Australia[1]

It seems probable that Greenfinches (of the European nominate subspecies) were included in the consignment of 800 songbirds imported to Australia from England in January 1856, and/or in other shipments that arrived in Sydney, New South Wales, in the following April and, through a dealer named Neymaler, at Melbourne, Victoria, in January 1858. Of these, according to Ryan (1906), 50, 40 and 20 were released near Melbourne in 1863, 1864 and 1872, respectively. Jenkins (1977) says that 20 were freed in the Royal Park, Melbourne, in 1863, but whether these were additional to, or were included in, Ryan's figure of 50 is unclear. The birds did fairly well, and by the early 1900s were established near the metropolis and in tea-tree scrub around Port Phillip. In 1879–80 (and probably earlier), seven pairs of Greenfinches were liberated near Adelaide in South Australia, and in the latter year some 'Green linnets' (presumably this species) were freed at Maneroo and Bodalla, south of Sydney, New South Wales, where they were said to be flourishing in 1896. It is reasonable to assume that these attractive little birds were also subsequently translocated to various other localities.

In New South Wales, Greenfinches had spread south and west to Albury, on the border with Victoria, and to Bathurst and a few other districts by about 1910. Tarr (1950) confirmed their presence in Albury, reported them to be fairly common in Sydney and in the Melbourne metropolitan area, and said that elsewhere in Victoria they had been recorded in Coleraine, Daylesford, Geelong, Caramut, Ballarat and Inglewood. By the following decade, they had spread west to Orange in New South Wales, and in southeastern South Australia were well established and common near Adelaide, in the Mount Lofty Ranges, and south to Victor Harbour.

In Tasmania, Greenfinches were first recorded, presumably as natural immigrants from Victoria via King Island in Bass Strait, at Marrawah in the extreme north-west in 1945. Before the end of the decade, a few had spread to nearby Stanley and Robbins islands, and in November 1951 some were observed in the south-west at Port Davey inlet. Before 1958, they had extended their range along the north coast as far east as Launceston. In Bass Strait, a small number of Greenfinches were noted on Flinders Island in 1948, and McGarvie & Templeton (1974) reported that flocks of over 100 occurred annually in April and May on King Island.

According to Williams (1953), Greenfinches first arrived on Norfolk Island, presumably as natural colonists from New Zealand, in about 1939, and are now apparently established and breeding.

Frith (1979: 192) described the Greenfinch in Australia as 'common around Adelaide and the adjoining hills, but not elsewhere in South Australia. It is well distributed through the southern half of Victoria but is only common locally. It is present in small numbers in a few places in south-east New South Wales.' Pizzey (1980) found the species to be well established, but apparently discontinuously. In New South Wales, it occurred in parts of Sydney, including Botany Bay, intermittently westwards to Orange and south-west to between the ACT and Albury. In Victoria, Greenfinches were widely but patchily distributed over much of the state – especially along the coast – except in the mallee region of the north-west. In Tasmania, they occurred in the north, the east and in the midlands, and on the west coast had been recorded as far south as between the Henty River and Strahan; again, as in Victoria, they were most abundant on the coast. They were common on King Island, but less so on Flinders Island, where they occurred only locally. In South Australia, they were established throughout much of the coastal south-east, and as far north as Adelaide and the Mount Lofty Ranges.

As Frith points out, the Greenfinch has proved a less successful colonist in Australia than has the closely related Goldfinch (*Carduelis carduelis*). In Eurasia, where their distribution is not dissimilar, the two species tend to live sympatrically in agricultural land, gardens and pastures. The Greenfinch, however, favours well-wooded farmland with an abundance of shrubs, whereas the Goldfinch prefers open, rough and neglected fields, roadside verges and weed-infested wasteland. In Australia, there seem to be similar habitat preferences. Greenfinches colonize permanent leys and gardens and parks where exotic European trees and shrubs predominate; they have also become established coastally in native tea-tree thickets. Goldfinches, on the other hand, have settled in open pastureland, creek banks and neglected roadside verges overgrown with tall weeds – especially Black Knapweed (*Centaurea nigra*) and thistles (*Carduus/Cirsium* spp.).[2] They also favour areas where artichokes and sunflowers are extensively grown. Goldfinches are found, too, in stands of pines, poplars and jacarandas in city parks and gardens. Neither species has successfully invaded native *Eucalyptus* forest.

Frith could find no evidence that either species was a serious competitor with native ones for food, habitat or nesting sites, nor a significant economic pest. In the east of their Australian range, Goldfinches cause some damage to apricot buds, but also kill injurious apple moths. Both birds build their nests mainly in introduced trees and shrubs, and feed largely on the seeds of alien weeds. There seems little doubt, Frith concluded, that the Goldfinch in Australia (and probably the Greenfinch also) has occupied a hitherto vacant niche of principally man-made habitats. Although in Eurasia there are many differences in the diet, behaviour and movements of the two species, there seems no indication why, in Australia, the former has expanded its range so much more than the latter.

New Zealand[3]

According to Thomson (1922), the Nelson Acclimatization Society imported five Greenfinches to New Zealand in 1862, but what became of them is unrecorded. Drummond (1907), however, quoted by Thomson (1922: 174), said that:

the first greenfinches about which I have been able to secure any information, were liberated in Christchurch in 1863, where a pair were purchased at auction for five guineas. They soon nested, but the only occupant at first was one little greenfinch. Before the warm summer days had passed, however, a second family of five was reared, and in the following winter a flock of eight was seen daily. In the next year, late in the autumn, more than twenty were flushed from a little patch of chickweed, and it was not long before the birds had spread so widely that their note became a well-known sound in Canterbury.

Elsewhere, according to Thomson, Drummond gives the date of this introduction as 1866, but says that there is no record of it in the society's records. The birds soon became widely distributed in Canterbury, reaching the Mackenzie district by about 1870.

The only other liberations of Greenfinches recorded by Thomson were 'several' by the Auckland Acclimatization Society in 1865, 18 in 1867 and 33 in 1868, when they were 'considered to be thoroughly acclimatized'; in the last year, a further 8 were freed by the Otago Society.

As Williams (1969) points out, there is some confusion about the introduction of Greenfinches to New Zealand because of the variety of vernacular names used for the species. Thus, the Canterbury Acclimatization Society reported that by 1865 'linnets' had been introduced to 'various parts', and that in 1866–7, 20 were held in the society's gardens. In 1867 or 1868 a small number were sold, and in the latter year flocks were said to be established in the gardens, while others were reported to have bred successfully at Rangiora. The same society's annual report for 1870 states that 'green linnets' (presumably *chloris*) were among those species considered to be so well established that no further releases were necessary. 'Brown linnets', the same report continues, were to be introduced, and 'grey linnets', were not yet properly established. The former, presumably *Acanthis cannabina*, were apparently part of a shipment of assorted songbirds landed in Christchurch by a Mr R. Bills early in 1875, and later in the same year 30 'brown linnets' and a like number of Greenfinches (specifically named) were released in various parts of South Canterbury at a cost of 10s. each.

By about 1920, Thomson recorded, Greenfinches were especially abundant in all settled regions of both main islands, where they were a pest to ripening grain crops and, in such fruit-growing areas as Central Otago, to apricots, cherries, peaches and plums. It was to combat their depredations, and those of other frugivorous aliens, that Little Owls (*Athene noctua*) were imported to New Zealand from 1906. In 1918, Thomson was informed that in Southland Greenfinches were then considerably less common than they had been before the turn of the century, probably due to the replacement of cereal crops by dairy-farming and stock-raising.

Thomson recorded that Greenfinches had spread to the Chatham Islands by about 1920, Oliver (1930) that they had reached Kapiti Island, and (1955) that they occurred on Little Barrier, Stewart, Auckland and Campbell islands. Williams (1953) found the birds to be common in settled districts. Wodzicki (1965: 433) reported Greenfinches to be 'widely distributed and common, North, South, Stewart and Chatham and Campbell Islands'. Kinsky (1970) stated that they occurred on the Chatham Islands and had straggled to the Kermadecs, Snares and Campbell islands. Williams (1973) said that they had been recorded as breeding on Chatham and Campbell islands, but not yet on the Kermadecs, Auckland or Snares. Falla, Sibson & Turbott (1979) found Greenfinches to be widely but unevenly distributed in New Zealand, where in some places they were locally abundant to around 600 m. They had colonized Chatham Island naturally, but occurred only as vagrants on many other subantarctic islands, and were in general not persistent colonists of offshore islands.

Greenfinches in New Zealand favour mainly open country, farmland, scrub and exotic – especially Pine (*Pinus pinaster*) – forests. In winter, they feed mainly on the pine seeds they extract from fir-cones; they also eat the seeds of several noxious alien weeds. Large flocks gather in late autumn, winter and early spring, particularly in coastal urban areas. Although Greenfinches are destructive to cereal, vegetable, fruit and flower crops, they also destroy injurious insects and grubs.

––––––––––––––––––––––––––

Phillips (1928) reported that Greenfinches had probably been released near Boston, Massachusetts, USA, where one was caught in Weston in 1880. Both he and Jewett & Gabrielson (1929)[4] say that 15 pairs of Greenfinches were unsuccessfully liberated in Oregon by the Portland Song Bird Club between 1889 and 1892. Phillips also states (1928: 60) that 'linnets of some kind' were introduced without success in British Columbia, Canada, by the Natural History Society of Victoria.

Benson (1950) refers to the unsuccessful introduction or five 'green linnets' to the island of St Helena.

––––––––––––––––––––––––––

Sharrock (1976: 412) reports that:

During this century, Greenfinches have expanded their [natural] range in Britain and Ireland and increased in numbers. Several of the western Scottish islands and the Isles of Scilly have been colonized and there have been increases and extensions of range in Cornwall, western Mayo, western Donegal and northern Scotland. This range extension has been assisted by increased planting of commercial woodland . . . There has been some evidence of a decline in Ireland since about the early 1960s, however, and this appears to be continuing. . . . The inner suburbs and central urban parts of such large cities as London have been colonized during the 20th century, and this may have been encouraged by increased garden feeding during the winter.

NOTES

1 Balmford 1978; Blakers, Davies & Reilly 1984; Chisholm 1919, 1926; Condon 1962; Frith 1979; Jenkins 1977; Long 1981; McGarvie & Templeton 1974; McGill 1960; Peters 1968; Pizzey 1980; Roots 1976; Ryan 1906; Sharland 1958; Smithers & Disney 1969; Tarr 1950; Wakelin 1968 (in Smithers & Disney 1969); Williams 1953.

2 Hence their soubriquet of 'Thistle Finch'.

3 Drummond 1907; Falla, Sibson & Turbott 1979; Gillespie 1982a, b; Kinsky 1970; Long 1981; Oliver 1930, 1955; Thomson 1922; Williams 1953, 1969, 1973; Wodzicki 1965. See also: *Timaru Herald* 10 July (1930), quoted by Williams (1969).

4 Quoting Pfluger in the *Oregon Naturalist* 3: 32–154 (1896).

Goldfinch
(*Carduelis carduelis*)

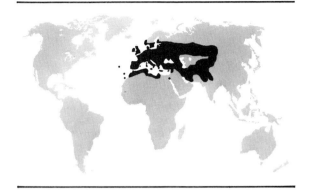

NATURAL DISTRIBUTION
Much of the western Palaearctic, from the British Isles eastwards to between 75° and 80° E in the USSR, north to between 60° and 65° N in Scandinavia and the USSR, south to North Africa, Israel, Iran, Afghanistan and Baluchistan.

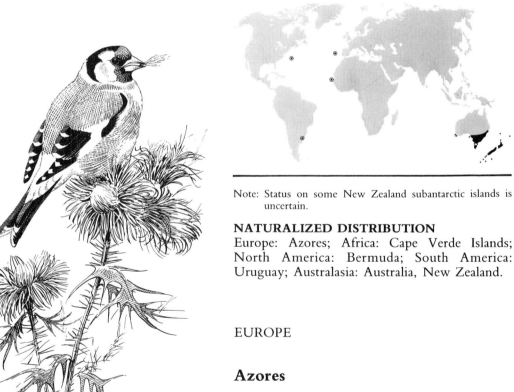

Note: Status on some New Zealand subantarctic islands is uncertain.

NATURALIZED DISTRIBUTION
Europe: Azores; Africa: Cape Verde Islands; North America: Bermuda; South America: Uruguay; Australasia: Australia, New Zealand.

EUROPE

Azores

Goldfinches were first recorded in the Azores in 1903, where they are believed to have been imported from Madeira (where the subspecies is *C. c. parva*) around 1890. They are said to occur in small numbers on São Jorge, Faial (Fayal), São Miguel, Terceira and Pico (Bannerman 1965; Bannerman & Bannerman 1966; Marler & Boatman 1951).

AFRICA

Cape Verde Islands

Bannerman & Bannerman (1968) say that in 1964 Goldfinches (probably of the form *parva*) that had been imported to Porto Praia on São Tiago (largest of the Cape Verde Islands) were established and breeding in gardens there and in the suburb of Fazenda.

NORTH AMERICA

Bermuda[1]

From the early nineteenth century Goldfinches were imported as cagebirds to Bermuda, where an escaped individual was reported in the wild as early as 1849 by Hurdis (1897), who wrote (quoted by Wingate, unpublished work): 'Had I not been aware of a recent importation of many of these birds from the island of Madeira, and of the escape of one or two at the time of landing, I should indeed have been puzzled to account for its appearance'. The main source of the present population, however, seems to have been the deliberate release of a large number of various songbirds (including Goldfinches) from a disabled steamship off the port of St George's around 1885.[2] Within a decade, small charms[3] were established throughout the island, and by the outbreak of the First World War the Goldfinch was said to be Bermuda's fourth most abundant bird. By 1919, it was already considered by some authorities to have established sufficient differentiation to entitle it to subspecific rank.

The Goldfinch is still a common Bermudan resident, feeding among the seed-cones of exotic *Casuarina*[4] trees and on the seeds of such annuals as sow-thistle, sea-marigold and seaside goldenrod. It seems to have filled a niche left vacant by the extinction of a native finch at the time of human settlement, and has had no apparent ecological effects in Bermuda.[5]

Despite the Goldfinch's known introduction to Bermuda, the population there was described in 1913 as an endemic subspecies, differing from the British one (*britannica*) in having a darker plumage. This difference was finally explained by Austin (1963), who identified the Bermudan population as *C. c. parva* (from Madeira, the Canary Islands and the Azores, where it was probably not introduced – from Madeira – until around 1890). A few individuals of the British subspecies may also have been imported from time to time.

SOUTH AMERICA

Uruguay

Cuello & Gerzenstein (1962) and Sick (1968) record that Goldfinches were established and breeding in the 1960s in Montevideo and elsewhere in the department of Canelones in southern Uruguay. Armani (1984) reported that the birds ranged from the departments of Maldonado and Lavalleja east of the capital as far west as the department of Soriano. Between 1960 and 1975, Armani regularly observed Goldfinches in pineland bordering the road to Carrasco Airport, and also in the Lecoq zoological park, where the population has always been highest.

Lecoq is an extensive park planted with eucalyptus, pines, mimosas and willows, with wide tracts of grassland and clumps of trees and thickets, little maintained and seldom visited by man. In the park, Goldfinches are extremely common, especially in large eucalyptus trees near the entrance, and in pines and eucalyptus bordering the lake, where they breed between late October and March.

Elsewhere in Uruguay, Armani has observed Goldfinches near the village of Campana, not far from Ombues de Lavalle, Colonia; near Rio San Salvador, close to Castillos, in Soriano; on the road between Solis and Minas, Lavalleja; and near Lago del Sauce. In winter, they have been reported from as far afield as Paysandú and Tacuarembó, respectively north-west and north-east of Montevideo. There are unconfirmed reports in Uruguay of hybridization between Goldfinches and native Hooded Siskins (*Carduelis m. magellanicus*).

Although, during a sojourn of more than 5 years in Argentina, Armani failed to observe a single Goldfinch, individuals are occasionally reported at La Plata, Buenos Aires; these are probably storm-borne vagrants from Montevideo, a distance across the Rio de la Plata of only 150 km, or, according to Sick (1968), cagebirds that have escaped from visiting ships. An attempted introduction is believed to have taken place at Colonia in about 1900 (see also under House Sparrow, *Passer domesticus*).

AUSTRALASIA

Australia[6]

Table 10 gives details of introductions of Goldfinches to Australia. It seems not unreasonable to suppose that these attractive little birds were also later translocated to various other localities.

In Victoria, Goldfinches were well established and common by the turn of the century near Melbourne and Geelong, and in thick vegetation around Port Phillip. They had colonized the area between Winchester and Colac by 1904, and 2 years later were reported from Pine Plains in the mallee. They had spread to Castlemaine by 1913, and to Carraragarmungee (between Beechworth and Wangaratta) and Genoa (in the extreme eastern corner of Gippsland near the border with New South Wales) by 1915. By 1928, they were reported to have spread up to 65 km north of Bendigo, and it seems probable that all suitable habitats in the state were colonized during the following decade.

In New South Wales, Goldfinches were established in Sydney in 1886, had reached Goulburn by 1913, and before 1920 had crossed the Victoria border from Carraragarmungee, Wangaratta, Beechworth and Genoa. They were established and common in Duntroon and Tuggranong in the ACT and at Boree, south of Armidale before 1922. Later in the decade, they were noted at Tumbarumba, Sofala, Bega, Armidale, Tamworth and Glen Innes, and in Canberra before 1929. By the outbreak of the Second World War they were well established in townships along the western railway as far as Dubbo, and stragglers had penetrated further north still to Gilgandra.

From northern New South Wales, Goldfinches

spread naturally into southern Queensland, although their presence on Stradbroke Island off the coast of Brisbane before 1925 may have been due to escaped cagebirds. They were recorded at Stanthorpe in 1917, at Brisbane in 1919 and around Hamilton in 1932.

Goldfinches colonized Kangaroo Island off the coast of South Australia between about 1910 and 1920, and by 1923 had spread to Mount Remarkable.

Long (1972) has traced the introduction of Goldfinches into Western Australia. Some are known to have been released before 1912, and a few were observed in the Perth suburb of Graylands between 1927 and 1930. Others were seen in the gardens of the Supreme Court in Perth in 1933, and by 1948 small numbers had become locally distributed in several suburban areas. During the early and mid-1960s they continued gradually to expand their range, and by 1967 were widespread in the metropolitan district and surrounding localities west of the Darling Scarp. By the end of the decade they ranged from Wanneroo and Upper Swan south to beyond Armadale, Forrestdale and Bibra Lake, with a small discrete colony as far south as Rockingham. Outwith the metropolitan area they were found to be established at Albany (380 km to the south-east) from 1955 until at least 1969. Since the late 1960s, Goldfinches have declined in Western Australia, probably through a combination of disease, shortage of food as a result of land development, predation, trapping for the cagebird trade, and direct attacks from the aggressive native Singing Honeyeater (*Meliphaga virescens*). Today, a few Goldfinches probably survive only in Albany and Perth.

In Tasmania, Goldfinches are said to have been established since the early 1880s. By the turn of the century, they were abundant around Hobart, Derwent Valley, New Norfolk, Glenora and Macquarie Plains, and on the north coast near Latrobe and Davenport.

Smithers & Disney (1969) record the presence of adult and young Goldfinches around the Melanesian Mission on Norfolk Island, where they probably arrived as natural immigrants from New Zealand.

Tarr (1950) found Goldfinches to be widely distributed in suitable habitats throughout both New South Wales (especially around Sydney) and Victoria. In South Australia, they were estab-

Table 10 Introductions of Goldfinches (*Carduelis carduelis*) to Australia, 1827–1912

Date	Number	Locality	Introduced by	Remarks
1827*	'Several'	Hobart, Tasmania	The vessel *Wansted*	
? January and April 1856	? (Part of a shipment of 800 songbirds)	Melbourne, Victoria, and Sydney, New South Wales	?	
? January 1857	?	Melbourne, Victoria	A dealer named Brown	
November 1857	'Several pairs'	Melbourne, Victoria	The vessel *Sydenham*	
October 1858	?	?	Mr Rushall via the *Norfolk*	
1862	?	Adelaide, South Australia	South Australia AS†	
1863	34	Melbourne, Victoria	Victoria AS	Released
1863	12	Kerang (250 km north of Melbourne) and New South Wales	Victoria AS	Released
1864	20	Melbourne, Victoria	Victoria AS	Released
1879	43+	Adelaide, South Australia	South Australia AS	Released
1880	32	Maneroo, Bodalla, Ryde, Blue Mountains, New South Wales	From New Zealand	Released; some shot near Ashfield c.1886
c.1880	?	Hobart and Launceston, Tasmania	?	
1881	110	Adelaide, South Australia	South Australia AS	Released; more 'repeatedly' freed in the 1880s
Between 1899 and 1912	?	Perth, Western Australia	Western Australia AS	Released

Sources: see note 6
* According to W. Lawson, in *Blue Gum Clippers and Whale Ships of Tasmania* (Georgian House, Melbourne, 1949). Jenkins (1977) indicates a (later ? 1880 or 1883) introduction from New Zealand
† AS, Acclimatization Society

lished on the Adelaide Plains, from the Mount Lofty Ranges to Victor Harbour, on the south Yorke Peninsula and on Kangaroo Island, around Tantanoola, north to Clare, and east to the border with Victoria. In Queensland, they were confined to the Darling Downs and to some coastal resorts around Brisbane, and in Western Australia to the metropolitan area of Perth. They were common on agricultural land in Tasmania, and occurred also on King and Flinders islands in Bass Strait.

Long (1970) reported Goldfinches to be widespread in most cultivated areas and grasslands of southeastern Queensland, New South Wales, South Australia (excluding the far north but including Kangaroo Island), Tasmania, King and Flinders islands, and the metropolitan area of Perth in Western Australia, west of the Darling Scarp.

In 1979, Frith wrote (p. 192):

The Goldfinch has been very successful and has spread throughout Victoria and south-east South Australia; it has reached Tasmania and is now very common there. In New South Wales it has occupied all the south-eastern part of the State. It is established in south-east Queensland. In New South Wales and Queensland it is more common on the cooler tablelands than the coast, but is very numerous also in some irrigated inland districts. In Western Australia so far it has limited distribution in Perth and its immediate surroundings and near Albany.

(For Frith's assessment of the interaction in Australia between the Goldfinch, the Greenfinch (*Carduelis chloris*) and native species, for the habitat preferences of the two aliens, and for their diets and economic importance, see page 385.)

Pizzey (1980) found Goldfinches, which in Australia are locally nomadic in autumn and winter, to be widespread in suitable habitats south from the Brisbane area and the Darling Downs in southern Queensland, through eastern and southern New South Wales inland as far as Moree/Gilandra/Lake Cargelligo, and from southwestern New South Wales to the arid country north of Balranald and Wentworth, extending to the highlands of the north-east, the southern tablelands, and the alpine zone of the south-east. In Victoria, Goldfinches were virtually ubiquitous, being especially numerous along the littoral and in the western plains. In Tasmania (where they have been recorded at an altitude of 1,200 m on Mount Wellington), Goldfinches were widely distributed in the east, but in the west occurred mainly in settled districts. They were also established on most of the islands in Bass Strait. In southeastern South Australia, they were found as far north as about the Barrier Highway, south to the Yorke and southern Eyre peninsulas and Kangaroo Island. In Western Australia, they were confined to Perth and Albany.

New Zealand[7]

According to Thomson (1922), the Nelson Acclimatization Society imported 10 Goldfinches to New Zealand in 1862;[8] what became of them is unknown. Subsequently, releases were made as follows: by the Otago Society, 3 (in 1867), 30 (1868), 54 (1869) and 31 (1871); by the Auckland Society, 11 (1867) and 44 (1871); by the Canterbury Society, an unknown number in 1865, 95 (1871, or 1873), 60 (1872), and 'a number' early in 1875; by the Wellington Society, 1 (1877), 52 (1880), 22 (1881) and 103 (1883).

Drummond (1907) records that in Canterbury Goldfinches had reached the Mackenzie country by 1875 and West Oxford by 1880, and 3 years later had increased so greatly that a number were shipped to Australia, together with some Skylarks (*Alauda arvensis*) (q.v.), in exchange for Black-backed Magpies (*Gymnorhina tibicen*) and Wonga-wonga Pigeons (*Leucosarcia melanoleuca*).

Thomson (1922: 173) says that 'The birds appear to have at once established themselves at all the centres, and to have quickly spread. They are now extraordinarily abundant in all parts of New Zealand.'

By about the turn of the century, Goldfinches had straggled to such offshore islands as the Antipodes, Snares, Aucklands and Campbell, and by 1910 had also been recorded on Chatham and the Kermadecs. Before about 1920 they were established on Chatham and the Aucklands, and by the end of the following decade had also been observed on Kapiti, Stewart, Three Kings, Mokohinau and Little Barrier islands. In 1956, a single specimen was collected on Macquarie Island, nearly 900 km south-west of South Island.

Wodzicki (1965: 433) found Goldfinches to be 'common, widely distributed, and abundant, North, South, Stewart, and Chatham, Raoul [Kermadecs], Antipodes, Snares, and Auckland Islands'. Kinsky (1970) confirmed that the birds had spread to many outlying islands, including Chatham, Auckland, Campbell and the Antipodes, and had straggled to the Kermadecs, Snares and Macquarie. Williams (1973) said that Goldfinches had bred on Chatham, Campbell, the Antipodes and the Snares, but not so far on some of the other islands such as Three Kings, the Kermadecs and Macquarie.

Falla, Sibson & Turbott (1979) reported that Goldfinches were established and abundant over large portions of both main islands to above the treeline at an altitude of about 1,000 m, but were relatively uncommon in Westland. They were natural colonists of the Kermadecs and appeared as vagrants on subantarctic islands as far south as Campbell Island, though they seemed to breed only sparingly away from the mainland.

In winter, large flocks up to 2,000 strong often frequent coastal saltings, especially in the north, where they feed on succulent annual glassworts (*Salicornia* spp.). At other seasons they inhabit open country and farmland, where they live on (and help to spread) the seeds of Tree Lupins (*Lupinus arboreus*), thistles (*Carduus/Cirsium* spp.) and other weeds. In some areas, they are locally a minor pest of grain, rape, and strawberry and other fruit crops, but also kill injurious insects. The young are sometimes preyed on by Sacred Kingfishers (*Halcyon sancta vagans*) and Long-tailed Koels (*Urodynamis* (*Eudynamis*) *taitensis*).

Goldfinches are now said to be more abundant in New Zealand than in the British Isles.

In view of the many occasions on which large numbers of Goldfinches have been planted in many localities in the United States,[9] it may seem strange that, as Gottschalk (1967: 128) says, they 'have always disappeared'. Indeed, as long ago as 1928 Phillips (p. 57) expressed his surprise that 'the bird did not finally succeed, after surviving for so many years in the Eastern States, especially about New York and Boston'. Their failure is, however, readily explained: climatic factors, rather than a lack of suitable habitat, are likely to be the species' controlling factor in the eastern United States; more than three-quarters of British Goldfinches (which greatly increase in numbers in hot, dry summers, when there is an abundance of seeding plants) regularly migrate in autumn to milder regions of western and southern Europe.

Table 11 gives details of the principal introductions of Goldfinches (of the British subspecies

C. c. britannica) to the United States. From these, and perhaps other unrecorded plantings (and possibly from aviary escapes), reports of Goldfinches came from Liberty and La Grange, Missouri (1906 and 1907); Buffalo, New York (1929); Milwaukee, Wisconsin, (1935); Manchester, Massachusetts, and Larkspur and Elk Valley, California (1935–40); Hanover, New Hampshire (1937); Ithaca, New York (1940); and from Long Island, New York (until development in the mid-1950s destroyed their natural habitat), where more were apparently released as recently as 1976, but where, according to the American Ornithologists' Union (1983: 753), 'the population is very low or possibly extirpated'.

As mentioned above, Goldfinches spread naturally from the United States to Toronto, Ontario, Canada[10] in 1887. In 1908 and 1910, Mr G. H. Wallace released some unsuccessfully on the Saanich Peninsula of Vancouver Island, British Columbia. In 1913, more were freed in Victoria by the city's natural history society, but these, too, failed to become established. A single bird seen in New Brunswick sometime before 1966

Table 11 Principal introductions of the British subspecies of Goldfinch (*Carduelis c. britannica*) to the United States, 1846–1907

Date	Locality	Introduced by	Remarks
1846	Brooklyn, New York	Thomas Woodcock	Seen in 1847 in Greenwood Cemetery on Long Island, and in Brooklyn suburbs
1852	Greenwood Cemetery, Long Island, New York	Cemetery Trustees	Four dozen released
1870	St Louis, Missouri	?	
1872–4 (and ?1870)	Cincinnati, Ohio	Cincinnati Acclimatization Society	Disappeared
1872–4	Mt Auburn Cemetery, Cambridge, Massachusetts	Society for Acclimatization of Foreign Birds	Breeding freely in eastern Massachusetts and New Haven, Connecticut, in the 1880s and 1890s; present until *c*.1900; spread north to Toronto, Ontario, Canada, in 1887
1879	Hoboken, New Jersey	?	Crossed Hudson River to Central Park, New York, in 1879; common there until the 1890s, and present until 1936; spread to Long Island in 1889, and survived there until *c*.1900
1889–92	Portland, Oregon	Portland Song Bird Club	40 pairs freed; 'became plentiful'
c.1891	Near San Francisco, California	?	Disappeared
1899	Boston, Massachusetts	?	
1907 (and after)	Portland, Oregon	Portland Song Bird Club	'At least 20, and probably 40, more pairs'

Source: Phillips 1928

is more likely to have been an escaped pet than a dispersant from Long Island, USA.

In *Ornithological and Other Oddities* (1907), Frank Finn, formerly curator of the Indian Museum in Calcutta (quoted by Winterbottom 1956b), said that a British soldier, returning from the Boer War in 1902, brought back with him from South Africa two Goldfinches that he had caught on the hills of Heidelberg in the Transvaal. Their origin is unknown.

Sharrock (1976: 414) wrote of the Goldfinch in the British Isles:

During the 19th century, a serious and widespread decrease was reported over Britain and Ireland, which has been attributed to the catching of huge numbers[11] for sale as cage-birds. Following the banning of this practice in Britain in 1881 and in Ireland since 1930, marked revivals were recorded, with a return to many former areas at the edge of the range in Scotland and a spread into western Ireland and Scilly.

The **Lesser Goldfinch** (*Carduelis psaltria*) occurs naturally from the western and south-central United States south through Mexico and Central America to northwestern South America. Blake (1975) lists it has having been introduced to Cuba in the West Indies. Bond (1979: 226) says that it has been 'recorded [since before 1966] from Habana Province and once from Santiago de Cuba . . . probably introduced from Yucatán' [in southeastern Mexico, where the local subspecies is *C. p. jouyi*]. The American Ornithologists' Union (1983) implies that it may since have disappeared.

Although Lesser Goldfinches occur naturally in Panama, Ridgely (1976) considers that most of those appearing in the Canal Zone are escaped cagebirds.

The endangered **Red Siskin** (*Carduelis cucullatus*) of northeastern Colombia and northern Venezuela has been introduced to, and is breeding in the wild in, southeastern Puerto Rico.[12]

NOTES

1 American Ornithologists' Union 1957, 1983; Austin 1963, 1968; Blake 1975; Blakers, Davies & Reilly 1984; Bourne 1957; K. L. Crowell 1962 (and personal communication, 1981); Crowell & Crowell 1976; Hurdis 1897; Phillips 1928; Reid 1884; D. B. Wingate 1973 (and personal communication, 1981, and unpublished mimeograph); and D. E. Samuel, personal communication, 1981. See also *Auk* 13: 238 (1896); 18: 255 (1901); 21: 391 (1904); *Osprey* 5: 85 (1901).

2 Phillips (1928) says in 1884 and 1893; Austin (1968) says in 1893.

3 The collective noun for a small flock of Goldfinches.

4 Introduced to replace the native Bermuda 'cedar' (*Juniperus bermudiana*), which was all but eradicated by the accidental importation of scale insects (*Carulaspis minima*) in a shipment of nursery plants in the mid-1940s.

5 D. B. Wingate, personal communication, 1981.

6 Balmford 1978; Barret 1922; Blakers, Davies & Reilly 1984; Bourke 1957; Brown 1950; Cheyney 1915; Chisholm 1915, 1919, 1924, 1925, 1926; Condon 1962; Cooper 1947; Edwards 1925; Fletcher 1909; Frith 1979; Goodwin 1978; Jack 1952; Jenkins 1959, 1977; Lawrence 1926; Le Souef 1903, 1912; Littler 1902; Long 1967b, 1970, 1972, 1981; Middleton 1965; Norton 1922; Pizzey 1980; Rolls 1969; Roots 1976; Ryan 1906; Sedgwick 1957; Serventy 1948; Serventy & Whittell 1951, 1962; Smithers & Disney 1969; Tarr 1950; White 1923; Williams 1953; Wilson 1928; Wright 1925.

7 Drummond 1907; Falla, Sibson & Turbott 1979; Grant 1983; Keith & Hinds 1958; Kinsky 1970; Long 1981; Oliver 1930, 1955; Thomson 1922, 1926; Williams 1953, 1969, 1973; Wodzicki 1965.

8 Long (1981: 452) says that 'In 1862 the Nelson Acclimatisation Society liberated 118 birds'. The author has been unable to trace any other reference to this release.

9 Adney 1886; American Ornithologists' Union 1957, 1983; Austin 1968; Cleaveland 1865 (in Murphy 1945); Cooke & Knappen 1941; Cottam 1956; Gottschalk 1967; Hix 1905; Jewett & Gabrielson 1929; Jung 1936; Long 1981; Mills 1937; Montagna 1940; Nichols 1936; Palmer 1899; Phillips 1928; Shadle 1930; Sharrock 1976; Wetmore 1964. See also: *Oregon Naturalist* 3: 32–154 (1896).

10 Carl & Guiguet 1972; Godfrey 1966; Long 1981; Phillips 1928.

11 In the 1850s, for example, more than 130,000 a year were reputedly being caught near Worthing, Sussex.

12 American Ornithologists' Union 1983, and T. Silva, personal communication, 1985; see also King 1981.

Redpoll
(*Acanthis flammea*)

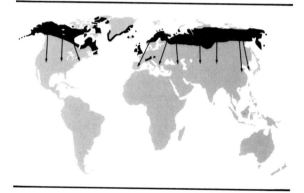

NATURAL DISTRIBUTION

A circumpolar Holarctic species, ranging eastwards from Alaska in the western USA through North America and Eurasia to the Chukotskiy Poluostrov Peninsula in the eastern USSR; winters south to central North America and Eurasia.

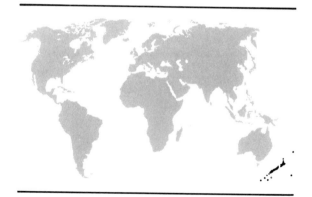

NATURALIZED DISTRIBUTION
Australasia: New Zealand.

AUSTRALASIA

New Zealand[1]

The Nelson Acclimatization Society acquired two Redpolls – the sole survivors of a larger shipment – in 1862; what became of them is unknown.

In late 1867 or early 1868, the Canterbury Society received a consignment of Redpolls from England, the 14 survivors of which were sold or released in the society's gardens in the latter year; the annual report for 1868 notes that 'the redpoles

395

[*sic*] turned out in the Gardens have settled in a body at Timaru'. In 1872, Canterbury acquired a further 50, and in the following year[2] liberated 120 more. In 1875, a Mr R. Bills brought in another 120 Redpolls from England in a shipment of assorted songbirds (valued at £329), which were sold (for 15*s.* a pair), distributed or released in the Christchurch Gardens and in some 40 or so other localities in South Canterbury.

In 1868, the Otago Society imported 10 Redpolls, followed 3 years later by a further 71; these all dispersed from Dunedin to high moorland country nearby.

A single Redpoll (presumably the only survivor of a larger consignment) was received by the Auckland Society in 1871, followed a year later by an additional 209, which were freed at various sites south of Auckland. Finally, the Wellington Society imported two in 1875.

The Redpoll seems to have become established and increased rapidly in New Zealand. Thomson (1922: 172) wrote that the species was 'not commonly seen about the towns or in thickly settled districts, but is abundant in both islands, especially in open upland country at moderate elevations. It is common in the back country near Dunedin'. Four years later, Thomson (1926) reported that Redpolls were common in high, open country from the Foveaux Strait (between South and Stewart islands) northwards to Auckland, especially in Southland, Otago and Canterbury in South Island, and along the west coast of North Island between Wellington and Taranaki. So numerous did the birds become that as many as 500 could be caught in a single day in Southland, where, according to Philpott (1918), they were frequently seen above the tree line at around 900 m. Philpott reported that in Southland Redpolls fed on the seeds of Toe-toe grass (*Arunda conspicua*) and in coastal sand dunes on those of *Juncus* rushes and other plants; in summer, Thomson found that the birds consumed large numbers of green flies (*Aphis* spp.) and the seeds of flowering grasses, and reported that in winter they frequently assembled in huge flocks.

On offlying islands, Redpolls are believed to have reached Campbell and the Snares around 1907, were first recorded as vagrants on Macquarie in 1912 and on Lord Howe (where they seem since to have disappeared) in 1913 (Williams 1953). Oliver (1930) reported them on Kapiti, Stewart and Campbell islands, and (1955)

also on Three Kings, the Chathams, the Snares and the Aucklands.

Williams (1953) described Redpolls in New Zealand as widely distributed and locally common. Wodzicki (1965: 433) reported them to be 'widely distributed and abundant, North, South, Stewart, and Chatham, Campbell, Auckland, and Macquarie Islands.' Kinsky (1970) said that they had spread to many offshore islands, including the Kermadecs, Aucklands, Campbell, the Snares, Chatham and Macquarie. Williams (1973) stated that the Redpoll bred on the Antipodes, Aucklands and Snares, and on Chatham and Campbell islands, and probably also on Macquarie, but was not known to do so on Three Kings or the Kermadecs. Falla, Sibson & Turbott (1979) found Redpolls to be well distributed and abundant in a wide variety of habitats, in South Island rising to an altitude of 1,600 m; in the north of North Island they were relatively uncommon, but some bred on sun-baked gumlands in Northland near the coast around Parengarenga Harbour, and among sand dunes and broken scrub along parts of the west coast of Auckland. Further south, Redpolls were more plentiful on the Volcanic Plateau, and bred freely above the bush line in the ranges, especially in Egmont, and in the south of North Island. They had colonized naturally most of New Zealand's subantarctic islands (including Macquarie), and were possibly the commonest passerine on Campbell Island.

As with several other birds there is some doubt as to which subspecies of the Redpoll was (or were) introduced to New Zealand. From a sample of only about 35 specimens, Westerskov (1953a) concluded that only the Lesser Redpoll (*A. f. cabaret*), which is the resident subspecies in the British Isles, had been imported. Stenhouse (1960), from a sample of about 170 specimens, some of which were collected in Canterbury, decided that both *cabaret* and the nominate Mealy Redpoll (*A. f. flammea*) – an autumn and winter visitor to Britain – were established and interbreeding. It may be significant, as Williams (1969) points out, that the 1868 annual report of the Canterbury Society specifically states that the birds imported from England in 1867 or 1868 included Mealy Redpolls. There is no apparent evidence of the subspecies imported in subsequent shipments, but as they all originated in England they could have been *cabaret* and/or *flammea*. Wodzicki (1965), however, refers only to the presence of *cabaret*, which, as it is the resident subspecies in Britain, seems likely to have been the one most frequently imported.

At one time the Redpoll – one of New Zealand's commonest and most widespread birds – was regarded as one of the few alien species that had not become an economic pest, and by killing turnip greenfly and other insects was sometimes actually beneficial. Now, however, it is known that in some fruit-growing regions such as central Otago it can be a significant nuisance to orchardists, destroying the buds, blossom and mature fruit of apricots and other varieties. Even though large numbers have been killed by shooting, trapping and poisoning, efforts to reduce the damage appear to have been unavailing.

NOTES

1 Bull 1966; Falla, Sibson & Turbott 1979; Hawkins 1962; Kinsky 1970; Laycock 1970; Long 1981; Oliver 1930, 1955; Philpott 1918; Stenhouse 1960; Thomson 1922, 1926; Westerskov 1953a; Williams 1953, 1969, 1973; Wodzicki 1965.
2 Thomson (1922) says in 1871; Williams (1969) says in 1873.

House Finch
(Carpodacus mexicanus)

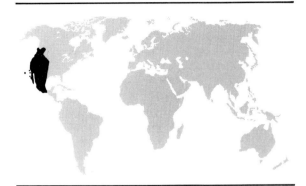

NATURAL DISTRIBUTION
Western North America, from southern British Columbia, Canada (since the 1930s), south to Oaxaca and Veracruz in southern Mexico, and eastwards to north-central and southeastern Wyoming, western Nebraska, western Kansas, western Oklahoma and central Texas, USA. Also present on the Pacific islands of San Clemente, Los Coronados, San Benito and Guadaloupe. On the mainland the species seems to be spreading slowly eastwards.

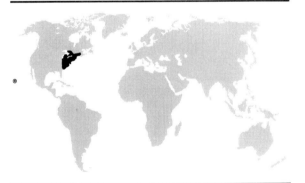

NATURALIZED DISTRIBUTION
North America: (Eastern) USA, (Eastern) Canada; Oceania: Hawaiian Islands.

NORTH AMERICA

(Eastern) USA; (Eastern) Canada

Although the House Finch is a native of western North America its establishment in the east, nearly 2,500 km from its nearest natural range, justifies its consideration here as a naturalized species.

The eastern population of House Finches in North America[1] is descended from birds liberated on western Long Island, New York, in 1940, by one or more dealers[2] in cagebirds (by whom they were known as 'Hollywood Finches' or 'Red-headed Linnets') when they were informed that the species was protected by federal law. The first wild House Finch in the east was seen at Jones Beach on Long Island on 11 April 1941. In March of the following year, a party of seven was observed near a silvicultural nursery at Babylon, some 19 km north-east of Jones Beach. On 28 May 1943 a nest (the first recorded in the east) containing four chicks was found, and within a few months the colony had increased to about a dozen; by July 1944, it had grown to around 18, several of which were young birds.

Thereafter, the population multiplied rapidly – to 24 by 1945, to 38 by 1946 and to over 50 by the late summer of 1947. The birds may have suffered a severe setback at Babylon after a heavy fall of snow in the winter of 1947–8, although a marked increase at this time in colonies at Hewlett and Lawrence (respectively 37 and 42 km to the west) and at Westbury (19 km north-east of Hewlett) – at all of which colonies had existed since at least 1944 – suggests the possibility of dispersal from Babylon. By the summer of 1948 several dozen were again present at Babylon, and these had increased to around 70 by the winter of 1949–50.

By 1950–1 there were increasingly frequent reports of House Finches from outside the Babylon/Hewlett/Westbury/Lawrence area – for example, at Riis Park, Idelewild, Williston, Roslyn and Wyandanch – suggesting a degree of peripheral expansion.

On 18 May 1948 came the first authenticated record of a House Finch away from Long Island – at Tarrytown, New York – followed by others at Ridgewood, New Jersey (1949), at Bedford and Armonk, New York (1951), and in Greenwich, Connecticut, where between 20 and 30 were noted in the winter of 1951–2.

By 1951 all four of the original colonies were thriving, and were showing small increases from the numbers of spring 1949. It was estimated that there were about 70 at Babylon, 35 at Westbury, 30 at Lawrence, 90 at Hewlett, 30 in Connecticut and perhaps 25 elsewhere – a total of around 280. Five years later, House Finches were well established and breeding throughout southwestern

Suffolk and southern Nassau counties, and had also bred in Greenwich, Fairfield County, and southwestern Connecticut. They first nested in New Jersey in 1959 and in Pennsylvania (at Columbia) in 1962. In February 1963 they were recorded for the first time in North Carolina, where breeding was confirmed at Charlotte in 1975. By 1968 they were widely distributed throughout New Jersey, and had spread north to Massachusetts and south to South Carolina, where they first appeared (in Greenville) in 1966, and where breeding was confirmed in 1979. Within a decade they had bred as far west as Cleveland, Ohio, and as far north as Brunswick, Maine,[3] and had spread northwards to Ontario and Quebec in southern Canada and southwards to Birmingham, Alabama, while isolated reports came from even more distant localities. The American Ornithologists' Union (1983: 746) described them as breeding

from Illinois, Indiana [since the early 1980s], southern Michigan, southern Ontario, southern Quebec, New York, Vermont, Massachusetts, and (probably) Maine and southern New Brunswick south to Missouri, Tennessee, Georgia and South Carolina, and wintering south to Mississippi and Alabama, and north to southern Wisconsin.

The House Finch's rapid expansion of range southwards and westwards seems to be continuing, and it may well be that the eastern population will eventually join up with the western one, which seems to be spreading slowly eastwards.

In the western United States, House Finches occur in a wide variety of habitats with an adequate supply of water, food – in the form of low-growing seeding and fruiting plants – and roosting and nesting sites above ground level. In the east, they have colonized similar habitats that meet these minimum requirements. They feed largely on weed and grass seeds, on the seeds of Mouse-ear Chickweed (*Cerastrum* sp.), on the fruits and berries of flowering shrubs, and in winter on the berries of Sumac (*Rhus* sp.) and on sunflower seeds, hemp, millet, rape and cracked corn provided at birdtables.

In the west, House Finches are serious pests of apricots, cherries, peaches, pears, nectarines, plums, avocados, grapes, apples, figs, strawberries, blackberries, and raspberries – eating both the buds and maturing fruit – and also cause lesser damage to maize, lettuce, broccoli, flax, tomato and other crops. Palmer (1972), who says that in California House Finches affect more than 20 different crops, states that they and Starlings (*Sturnus vulgaris*) are the two main bird pests of agriculture and horticulture in the state. Whether House Finches will become a pest of similar proportions in the east remains to be seen.

There seems to be little interspecific conflict with, for example, such species as Purple Finches (*Carpodacus purpureus*) or House Sparrows (*Passer domesticus*), with neither of which House Finches appear to compete for either food or nesting or roosting sites.

The House Finch in eastern North America has undergone a dramatic morphological change since its first appearance in the wild in 1941. According to Aldrich & Weske (1978: 528):

It has been assumed that the liberated birds were from California. Specimens of the new eastern population resemble most closely those from western California [*C. m. frontalis*] in size but differ from them in having relatively smaller legs and feet. In color, eastern birds resemble House Finches from northeastern Colorado and southeastern Wyoming, as well as those from eastern Washington and northern Idaho. On the basis of historical and size evidence we conclude that the eastern House Finch population is descended from California stock but has differentiated from it in color and size after liberation in the east. The change took place rapidly, as two specimens taken 9 and 11 years after introduction showed differences from California birds that now characterize the eastern population. The case of the House Finch parallels that of the House Sparrow (*Passer domesticus*) in its rapid evolutionary change after introduction and spread into new environments.

Several climatic and associated vegetational differences from California were encountered by eastern House Finch pioneers. The lower temperatures have not selected for larger size in the new eastern population as was the case with House Sparrows that moved into colder climates, and no other environmental factor or combination of factors including substrate aspect is the obvious cause of differentiation in eastern birds from their California ancestors.

OCEANIA

Hawaiian Islands[4]

According to Caum (1933), House Finches (of the subspecies *frontalis*), probably from San Fran-

cisco, California, were imported as cagebirds to the Hawaiian Islands before 1870 (perhaps as early as 1859), where some soon escaped and/or were released and became established in the wild.

As early as the turn of the century, McGregor (1902) found House Finches to be extremely common on Maui. Zeillemaker & Scott (1976) described them as abundant on Kauai and Hawaii, and common on Oahu, Molokai, Lanai and Maui, in agricultural and pastureland, introduced forests and scrub of Guava (*Psidium guajava*), Java Plum (*Eugenia cumini*) and *Eucalyptus*, mixed native ohia (*Metrosideros collina*) and koa (*Acacia koa*) woodland, residential and community parklands, and in some other habitats, including urban areas. On Hawaii and Maui they also occur in high ranching country and forestlands, but are uncommon in the depths of near-virgin rainforests. They are abundant in partly cutover mixed ohia–koa forests, and in the mamani–naio (*Sophora chrysophylla*) forest on Mauna Kea on Hawaii. They also occur on Niihau, and have straggled casually west to Nihoa. Although primarily seed-eaters in the islands (on Mauna Kea large flocks feed on the alien European Spear Thistle (*Cirsium vulgare*) – known locally as *pua kala*), their love of overripe fruit – especially Papaya (*Carica papaya*) – has earned them the nickname of *ainikana* ('papaya bird'). They have also become something of a pest to other fruits and some vegetables.

As long ago as 1911, Joseph Grinnell drew attention to an interesting change in coloration of House Finches in Hawaii, where in most the pink or red of *frontalis* has been replaced by yellow or orange. The islands' birds have also differentiated so markedly from the mainland forms in other morphological characteristics that at one time they were considered to be a distinct subspecies – *mutans*. The discovery by Brush & Power (1976), however, that yellow coloration in House Finches can be caused by nutrition or physiological deficiencies, finally invalidated this claim.

The **Laysan Finch** (*Loxioides/Psittirostra cantans*) is endemic to the islands of Laysan (the nominate subspecies) and Nihoa (*ultima*) in the Hawaiian group. From these two islands, birds have been translocated to Sand, Midway, Eastern and Oahu, to Southeast Island in Pearl and Hermes

Reef, and to Tern and East islands in French Frigate Shoals.[5]

In or before about 1891, some Laysan Finches of the nominate subspecies were translocated from Laysan Island to Midway by the sons of a resident, one Captain Walker. These, it is presumed, died out.

In May 1905, Mr Daniel Morrison, manager of the Commercial Pacific Cable Company on Midway Island, obtained same Laysan Finches from Max Schlemmer, manager of a German chemical company on Laysan Island, which he released on Sand Island in the Midway group, where they promptly disappeared. In the following September, Morrison received a further consignment of birds from a Captain Piltz on Laysan Island, which were despatched to a Mrs Colley on Midway. These were, however, eventually released on nearby Eastern Island, as there were said to be too many feral Cats (*Felis catus*) on Midway. On Eastern Island, the finches rapidly increased, and in January and May 1910 a number were transferred by Morrison to Midway, where they flourished and increased before eventually dying out around 1944. Large numbers were also freed in Honolulu on Oahu, where they soon disappeared.

In March 1967, 108 Laysan Finches were transferred from Laysan Island by employees of the US Bureau of Sport, Fisheries and Wildlife, and released on Southeast Island in Pearl and Hermes Reef, where by 1970 they had multiplied to about 350 and by 1974 had further increased to around 500. At the same time, members of the Bureau transplanted 42 of the *ultima* subspecies from Nihoa to French Frigate Shoals, where 32 were freed on Tern Island and the remainder on East Island; on the former only six were surviving in 1970–4, and on the latter they disappeared soon after their release.

NOTES

1 Aldrich 1982; Aldrich & Weske 1978; American Ornithologists' Union 1983; Bock & Lepthien 1976; Brush & Power 1976; Breckenridge 1984; Elliott & Arbib 1953; Grimm & Shuler 1967; Hamel & Wagner 1984; Heller & Wise 1982; Jackson 1981; Katholi 1967; Kricher 1983; Long 1981; Moore 1939; Palmer 1972; Paxton 1974; Peters 1968; Potter 1964a,b; Pyle 1977; Quay 1967; Tallman 1982; Toups & Hodges 1981; Wise & Cooper 1982; Woods 1968.
2 K.L. Crowell (personal communication, 1981) says that House Finches were 'released from Macy's Department Store 40 years ago'.
3 The reference by M. Lohoefener to nesting in northwestern Kansas (*Kansas Ornithological Society Bulletin* 28: 9–10 (1977)), clearly represents an extension of range of the western (natural) population rather than, as implied by Long (1981: 458), of the eastern population.
4 Aldrich 1982; American Ornithologists' Union 1983; Berger 1981; Blake 1975; Bryan 1958; Caum 1933; Grinnell 1911; Hawaiian Audubon Society 1975; Hirai 1975; Long 1981; McGregor 1902; Moore 1939; Munro 1960; Phillips 1928; Pyle 1977; Zeillemaker & Scott 1976.
5 Berger 1981; Bryan 1912; Caum 1933; Hawaiian Audubon Society 1977; Lever 1985b; Long 1981; Munro 1960; Peters 1962; Peterson 1961.

Red-cheeked Cordon-bleu
(*Uraeginthus bengalus*)

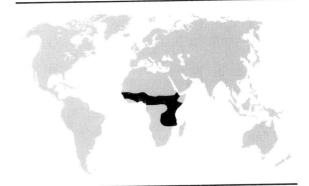

NATURAL DISTRIBUTION
Senegal, Guinea and the Gambia eastwards to the Sudan and Ethiopia, south through Uganda, Kenya and Tanzania to eastern Angola, Zambia and southern Zaire.

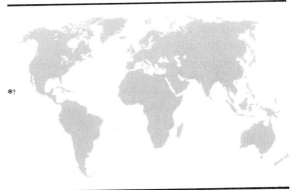

NATURALIZED DISTRIBUTION
Oceania: ?Hawaiian Islands.

OCEANIA

Hawaiian Islands[1]

In about 1965, Red-cheeked Cordon-bleus[2] were deliberately released or accidentally escaped on Oahu in the Hawaiian Islands, where between 30 and 50 were counted in the Diamond Head area in the winter of 1976–7. Zeillemaker & Scott (1976) said they were local and rare in dry lowland areas on Oahu, and Pyle (1977) described them as 'apparently established and breeding'. The American Ornithologists' Union (1983) said that on Oahu they were nearly, if not

quite, extinct, and that they have also occurred on Hawaii.

According to Bannerman & Bannerman (1968), Red-cheeked Cordon-bleus of the nominate form (western, north-central and eastern Africa) were introduced to São Vincente in the Cape Verde Islands before 1924 (when specimens were collected), but have since died out.

Guild (1938) records that he liberated some birds of this species in Tahiti, where shortly afterwards they bred successfully but where they have since disappeared.

The (**Southern** or **Angolan**) **Cordon-bleu** (*Uraeginthus angolensis*) ranges from Angola, the southern Congo, southern Zaire and southern Tanzania, south to the Transvaal and north-eastern Cape Province, South Africa. It does not occur in South West Africa (Namibia), southern Botswana or the Western Cape. Snow (1950) and Peters (1968) record that in the first half of the present century Cordon-bleus of the nominate form (southwestern Zaire, northern Angola and northwestern Zambia) were introduced to the Portuguese islands of São Tomé and Príncipe in the Gulf of Guinea. It is possible, however, that the birds on these islands are natural wind-blown colonists from the African mainland, although this would have involved a flight of well over 1,000 km.

Several individuals of this species appeared in the wild on Oahu in the Hawaiian Islands[3] at the same time as *bengalus*, where they apparently became established in the Kapiolani Park – Diamond Head area, in and around the Na Laau Arboretum, and later possibly also at Hualalai on Hawaii. They are not, however, referred to by Zeillemaker & Scott (1976), by Pyle (1977) nor by the American Ornithologists' Union (1983), so they have presumably since disappeared.

In 1929 and 1938, respectively, Cordon-bleus were unsuccessfully released on the South

Atlantic island of St Helena by H. Bruins-Lich (Haydock 1954), and on Tahiti in the South Pacific by Eastham Guild (Guild 1938). Those imported to the former came from South Africa, where the races are *cyanopleurus* and *niassensis*.

Cordon-bleus of the subspecies *niassensis* (eastern Tanzania, southeastern Zaire to Zimbabwe and the Transvaal) were translocated from the Tanzanian mainland to, and later escaped or were freed on, the Tanzanian island of Zanzibar[4] before 1934, when several were collected. Their present status on Zanzibar is uncertain.

The **Blue-capped Cordon-bleu** (*Uraeginthus cyanocephala*) is confined to southern Ethiopia, southern Somalia, Kenya, and northern and central Tanzania. In about 1965, at the same time as *bengalus* and *angolensis*, some *cyanocephala* were released or escaped into the wild on Oahu in the Hawaiian Islands,[5] where they remained until at least 1975, but have since probably died out. They are not referred to by Zeillemaker & Scott (1976), by Pyle (1977) nor by the American Ornithologists' Union (1983).

Berger (1981: 208) concludes his account of the genus in the Hawaiian Islands by saying that 'One or more species of the Cordon-bleu group was liberated on the Puuwaawaa ranch on Hawaii and can be seen there and in adjacent areas'.

NOTES

1 American Ornithologists' Union 1983; Berger 1981; Donaggho 1966; Hawaiian Audubon Society 1975; Long 1981; Pyle 1976, 1977; Ralph & Pyle 1977; Zeillemaker & Scott 1976.
2 There seems to be some confusion as to which species of Cordon-bleu has occurred in the wild in Hawaii, but Berger (1981) claims to have seen all three.
3 Berger 1981; Blake 1975; Hawaiian Audubon Society 1975; Heilbrun 1976, 1977; Long 1981.
4 Long 1981; Mackworth-Praed & Grant 1955–61; Pakenham 1939; Peters 1968.
5 Berger 1981; Blake 1975; Hawaiian Audubon Society 1975; Heilbrun 1976; Long 1981; Pyle 1976.

Orange-cheeked Waxbill
(*Estrilda melpoda*)

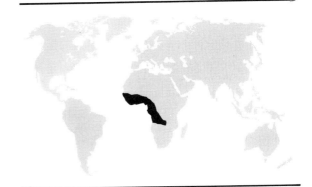

NATURAL DISTRIBUTION
Senegal and the Gambia eastwards to the Central African Republic and northern Zaire, south through western Zaire and the Congo to northern Angola.

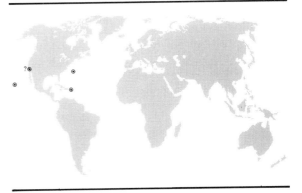

NATURALIZED DISTRIBUTION
North America: ?USA, Bermuda, West Indies (Puerto Rico); Oceania: Hawaiian Islands.

NORTH AMERICA

USA

Orange-cheeked Waxbills, almost certainly escaped aviary birds, were first noticed in the wild in southern California in 1965, where 3 years later breeding was reported. The population, which was based on Averill Park, San Pedro – from where occasional excursions were made to nearby Peck Park – apparently never numbered more than around 15–20, and according to Hardy (1973) was declining, possibly because of the clearance of vegetation in Averill Park. Waxbills are so popular with aviculturists, Hardy adds, that it is surprising more escapes are not reported. Those that have been seen (some of which may occasionally have nested in the wild) probably succumb to competition from native seedeaters and to predators.

Bermuda

Orange-cheeked Waxbills – escaped or deliberately released cagebirds – were first noted in Bermuda feeding on saw-grass sedge, panicum and foxtail grasses, in marshes in Devonshire and Paget parishes in the mid-1970s. Breeding was confirmed towards the end of the decade, and by the early 1980s the birds had spread to several other localities, including Pembroke Marsh, Tucker's Town and Ferry Point, St George's. As they have been observed feeding, with introduced Goldfinches (*Carduelis carduelis*) (q.v.) and migrant Indigo Buntings (*Passerina cyanea*), high up in alien and now widespread Casuarina trees (*Casuarina* sp.), their future in Bermuda seems assured.[1]

West Indies (Puerto Rico)[2]

Orange-cheeked Waxbills of the nominate form (Senegal and the Gambia to northern Zaire, northern Angola and Zambia) were imported to Puerto Rico (presumably as cagebirds) before 1874, when they were found to be established and breeding on the western coastal plain from Anasco to Mayagüez and Cabo Rojo, from where by the mid-1920s they had spread along the south coast to Yauco. Bond (1979) says that they frequent marshes, acacia thickets, cane fields, pastures and gardens in the west of the island.

OCEANIA

Hawaiian Islands[3]

In October 1965, a small flock of eight Orange-cheeked Waxbills – almost certainly escaped pets – was sighted along the Na Laau trail on the Ewa slope of Diamond Head on the island of Oahu, where 30 were counted at the following Christmas. Only six were seen in 1966, but between 1967 and 1969 more than 20 were reported annually, and the birds were considered to be slowly increasing. Zeillemaker & Scott (1976) list the species as local and rare in dry lowland residential and community parklands on Oahu, and Pyle (1977) confirmed that it was apparently established and breeding.

Guild (1938) reported that in that year he liberated some Orange-cheeked Waxbills in Tahiti, where they bred successfully. They have since died out on the island.

The **Lavender Waxbill** or **Lavender Firefinch** (*Estrilda caerulescens*)[4] is a West African species, ranging from Senegal southwards to Nigeria, and eastwards to the western Central African Republic, southwestern Chad, and northern Cameroon.

In about 1965, some Lavender Waxbills escaped from captivity or were released on Oahu in the Hawaiian Islands,[5] where they became established in the Kapiolani Park–Diamond Head area, and by 1976–7 had increased to between 30 and 50. Zeillemaker & Scott (1976) described them as local and uncommon in dry lowland residential and community parklands on Oahu, and Pyle (1977) confirmed that they appeared to be established and breeding. Two years later, Ashman & Pyle (1979) reported that in the previous year some were found to be established on a small portion of the Puu Waawaa Ranch on Hawaii.

NOTES

1 D. B. Wingate, personal communications, 1984 and 1985.
2 American Ornithologists' Union 1983; Biaggi 1963; Blake 1975; Bond 1971, 1979; Long 1981; Peters 1968; Raffaele 1983; Wetmore 1927.
3 American Ornithologists' Union 1983; Berger 1981; Blake 1975; Hawaiian Audubon Society 1975; Long 1981; Pyle 1976, 1977; Zeillemaker & Scott 1976.
4 Long (1981: 408–9) incorrectly identified the species as *E. perreini*.
5 American Ornithologists' Union 1983; Ashman & Pyle 1979; Berger 1981; Blake 1975; Hawaiian Audubon Society 1975; Long 1981; Pyle 1976, 1977; Ralph & Pyle 1977; Zeillemaker & Scott 1976.

Common Waxbill
(Estrilda astrild)

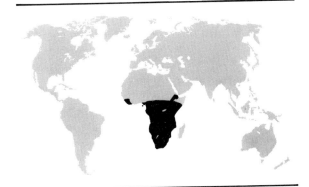

NATURAL DISTRIBUTION

Africa south of between 5° and 7° N, with a northerly extension into eastern Sudan and western Ethiopia, and an apparently discrete population in Sierra Leone and Liberia.

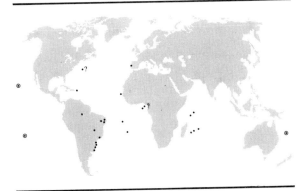

NATURALIZED DISTRIBUTION

Europe: Portugal; Africa: Mascarenes (Mauritius, Réunion, Rodrigues), Seychelles, Amirante Islands, Cape Verde Islands, São Tomé, ?Príncipe, Ascension, St Helena; North America: ?Bermuda, West Indies (Puerto Rico); South America: Brazil; Oceania: Hawaiian Islands, Society Islands (Tahiti), New Caledonia.

EUROPE

Portugal

According to Vincente (1969), who is followed by Long (1981), the waxbill naturalized in Portugal is the Black-rumped Waxbill (*Estrilda troglodytes*). Peters (1968), Heinzel, Fitter &

Parslow (1976) and Goodwin (1982b), however, have correctly identified the species as *E. astrild*. In August 1964, about 100 – believed to have been descended from birds that had escaped from a private aviary – were reported around Lagóa de Óbidos on the coast of Portugal some 100 km north of Lisbon. In 1965 and 1966, nests were found, young were seen, and the population had increased threefold. Thereafter, the birds began to spread and continued to multiply; in 1967, several hundred were noted between Óbidos and Vau, 200 at the railway station in Óbidos, some to the south at Galeota, and in November others at Ponta da Erva, 70 km south of Óbidos. In late 1968, a number were seen at Pinteus, 60 km south of Óbidos, and by the following year the population had increased to around 1,000. All observations of this seed- and insect-eating species have been made in marshy localities, with an abundance of reed beds and watercourses.

AFRICA

Mauritius, Réunion and Rodrigues[1]

Common Waxbills of the nominate form (natives of southern Botswana, western Cape Province, western Transvaal, the Orange Free State and Natal to the Limpopo and Orange rivers, South Africa) were imported as cagebirds to Mauritius in the eighteenth century, where they are now fairly widespread and abundant. From Mauritius, they were introduced to Rodrigues around 1764 and to Réunion, on both of which they are now widely distributed and common.

Seychelles[2]

Jean Baptiste de Malavois, who retired as military commandant of the Seychelles in 1788, said that Waxbills were then very common and an agricultural pest on the island of Mahé, to which they may have been imported as cagebirds from Africa by the wives of the first settlers some 20 years previously. They have since been largely displaced by another seed-eating alien, the Madagascar Fody (*Foudia madagascariensis*) (q.v.), which was introduced around 1860, and by a decline in cultivated seed crops and by the drainage of pastures for plantations. They are

now locally common only in wettish grasslands along the western coast of Mahé, and on the grassy plateau of La Digue. Some authorities have suggested that they could be natural colonists from the east African mainland or from Zanzibar (where the form is *E. a. minor*); if this were so they should, as Penny (1974) points out, have diverged morphologically and in plumage from the African race, whereas in fact they are identical, suggesting a recent arrival.

Amirante Islands

Common Waxbills (of the nominate form, according to Peters 1968) have been introduced, perhaps from the Seychelles, to the Amirantes, where they once occurred on Desroches but are now confined to Alphonse.

Cape Verde Islands

Bannerman (1949) records that in 1865 a mail-steamer carrying a consignment of Common Waxbills, which a French bird-dealer was shipping from Goree to Europe, was wrecked on the island of São Vincente, allowing several hundred to escape. A century later, Bannerman & Bannerman (1968) found them to be abundant on São Tiago and on Brava and recent colonists of Fogo, but to have disappeared some time ago from São Vincente, and also from Sãnto Antão (the most northerly and westerly island in the group), where some had been present in 1924. The form in the Cape Verdes, where damage to tomato crops has been reported, is *jagoensis*, which also occurs in western Angola.

São Tomé; Príncipe

Common Waxbills are said to have been introduced by human agency to both São Tomé and Príncipe in the Gulf of Guinea, where, however, according to Peters (1968) they now occur only on the former. Bourne (1955 and 1966a) says that the subspecies present is *jagoensis* (western Angola and the Cape Verdes), whereas Howard & Moore (1980) indicate the existence of an endemic form *sousae*. The birds could well, however, have been natural immigrants from Gabon on the west African mainland, where the race is *rubriventris*.

Ascension; St Helena

Common Waxbills were imported to Ascension (and probably at the same time to St Helena) by British Royal Marines after the islands were garrisoned to guard Napoleon Bonaparte in 1815. On the former, Stonehouse (1962) estimated the population at between 300 and 400. On the latter, where Melliss (1870) found them to be widespread and abundant, doubts have been expressed about the identity of the subspecies involved: Haydock (1954) compared specimens collected in 1952–3 with several African races, and found them to resemble closely the nominate form rather than a separate endemic one, *sanctaehelenae*, as had been suggested; Bourne (1955) and Peters (1968) considered, respectively, that the subspecies was *jagoensis* and *astrild*.

NORTH AMERICA

Bermuda

In the early 1970s, Common Waxbills, descended from escaped or deliberately released cagebirds, became established in large fodder crop fields at St Luke's farm in Southampton parish. Although they at first bred successfully, and by the end of the decade had increased to around 50–60, the change in husbandry from fodder grass to vegetables (following the cessation of dairy farming) caused them to decline, and the survivors may no longer be breeding.[3]

West Indies (Puerto Rico)

Blake (1975) lists the Common Waxbill as having been introduced to Puerto Rico – probably after about 1960. Its presence there is confirmed by the American Ornithologists' Union (1983).

SOUTH AMERICA

Brazil

According to Mitchell (1957), quoting Santos (1948), Common Waxbills may have been first introduced to Brazil early in the reign (1822–31) of Emperor Dom Pedro I. Sick (1968) says that they were certainly there before 1870, and that they continued to arrive (though whether carried deliberately or as stowaways is unclear) on slavers from west Africa until the dethronement of Emperor Dom Pedro II and the creation of the Republic in 1889. According to Oliveira (1980), they were introduced to Porto Allegre, Rio Grande do Sul, in 1930–1.

In Brazil, Waxbills have only become naturalized in association with man: for example, at Vitória, Espirito Santo, after 1940; in the Botanical Gardens of Rio de Janeiro before 1957; in Salvador, Bahia, and Brasilia since at least 1964; at Recife, Pernambuco, in Manaus, and perhaps also at Meceio, Algoas, in 1967; and in Belo Horizonte, Minas Geraes, in 1968. Sick (1966) states that the species introduced was originally but erroneously believed to be the Black-rumped Waxbill, *E. troglodytes*.

OCEANIA

Hawaiian Islands

In January 1981, Ord (1982) correctly identified between 18 and 24 Common Waxbills in the Kuilima area on Oahu where, according to the American Ornithologists' Union (1983), they are now established.

Society Islands (Tahiti)[4]

Imported to Tahiti between 1908 and 1919, Common Waxbills are now abundant in coastal regions, especially around Pamatai and Punaauia, but are less common in inland valleys, where they have been partially displaced by the alien Red-browed Waxbill (*Aegintha temporalis*) (q.v.). In November and December 1920, the Whitney expedition collected 22 Common Waxbills on Tahiti, and some were successfully released on the island by Eastham Guild in 1938. Unknown on Moorea in 1921, Common Waxbills have since become abundant along the coast. On both islands they frequent unwooded and grassy habitats, gardens, dense vegetation in plantations, thickets, and the borders of littoral coconut groves; they also occur in the hills to an altitude of 750 m. They feed almost exclusively on small seeds of grasses, rushes (*Juncus* sp.), and noxious dicotyledon plants; some rice is also taken. They are most often seen in small flocks actively hunting for food in low-growing shrubs, or perching in bushes or the lower branches of trees.

New Caledonia

Mayr (1945) records the introduction of Common Waxbills to New Caledonia, where Delacour (1966) found large numbers in gardens and on cultivated land. Their presence is confirmed by Holyoak & Thibault (1984).

According to Peters (1968), the nominate form of the Common Waxbill has been introduced to the island of Madagascar, where it has since died out.

Reichenow (1908) found Common Waxbills in the Comoros archipelago in 1903, where,

according to Benson (1960) and Peters (1968), they have now disappeared.

Although Guého & Staub (1983) were told that Common Waxbills occurred on Agaléga Atoll, they saw none there during their visit in 1981.

According to Mayr (1945), either *E. astrild* or *Aegintha temporalis* (the Red-browed Waxbill) was at one time established on Viti Levu in the Fijian Islands. Neither species is mentioned by Pernetta & Watling (1978) nor, apparently, by any other authorities.

NOTES

1 Benedict 1957; Gill 1967; Long 1981; Meinertzhagen 1912; Peters 1968; Rountree, Guérin et al. 1952; Staub 1976; Watson, Zusi & Storer 1963.
2 Crook 1961; Fisher, Simon & Vincent 1969; Gaymer, Blackman et al. 1969; King 1981; Long 1981; Newton 1867; Penny 1974.
3 D. B. Wingate, personal communications, 1984 and 1985.
4 Guild 1938; Holyoak 1974a; Holyoak & Thibault 1984; Thibault & Rives 1975; and J. C. Thibault, personal communication, 1980.

Black-rumped Waxbill

(*Estrilda troglodytes*)

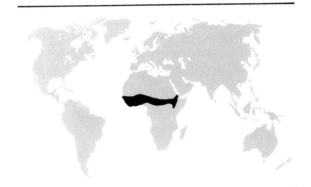

NATURAL DISTRIBUTION
From Senegal eastwards across Africa to central Sudan and northwestern Ethiopia, south to northwestern Uganda and northern Zaire.

NATURALIZED DISTRIBUTION
North America: West Indies (Guadeloupe, Puerto Rico); Oceania: Hawaiian Islands.

NORTH AMERICA

West Indies

Barré & Benito-Espinal (1985) were informed that Black-rumped Waxbills have been established on Basse-Terre, Guadeloupe, since at least the late 1960s, where they also occur in smaller numbers on Grande-Terre. On both islands, Black-rumped Waxbills live sympatrically with Red Avadavats (*Amandava amandava*) (q.v.), with which they share the same habitat requirements. The greater abundance of *troglodytes* than of *amandava* on Basse-Terre and vice versa on Grande-

Terre may be partly a result of interspecific competition, but may also be explained by the more recent arrival of *troglodytes* on Grande-Terre from west-central Basse-Terre.

On Guadeloupe, Black-rumped Waxbills feed largely on *Panicum maximum*, an exotic introduced many years ago from Africa that has colonized roadside verges and abandoned cane fields. Through interspecific competition, they (and other alien Estrildidae) may be having an adverse effect on the less-aggressive and prolific native Black-faced Grassquit (*Tiaris bicolor*).

The American Ornithologists' Union (1983) and Raffaele (1983) say that Black-rumped Waxbills are also established on the island of Puerto Rico.

OCEANIA

Hawaiian Islands[1]

On the island of Oahu, Black-rumped Waxbills (and other finches) accidentally escaped or were deliberately released in about 1965, and are now established and slowly increasing in the Kapiolani Park – Diamond Head region. Zeillemaker & Scott (1976) record *troglodytes* as local and uncommon in dry lowland residential and community parklands on Oahu, and Pyle (1977) lists them as 'apparently established and breeding'. The American Ornithologists' Union (1983) says

that they occur in small numbers on Oahu and also on Hawaii.

According to Cortes, Finlayson et al. (1980: 20), in Gibraltar 'single waxbills, and groups of up to five, have been seen on the Rock almost annually since 1975'. Those fully identified have proved to be Black-rumped Waxbills (*Estrilda troglodytes*). There is an unconfirmed record of two **Crimson-rumped Waxbills** (*E. rhodopyga*) on the Rock on 17 December 1979. 'It is possible', Cortes, Finlayson et al. wrote, 'that waxbills are consolidating their presence in Iberia as populations derived from released or escaped cagebirds (Heinzel et al. [1976] mention *E. astrild*) and that those seen in Gibraltar are wanderers from these populations.'

Guild (1938) records that in that year he released Black-rumped Waxbills on the island of Tahiti where, although they at first bred successfully, they have since died out.

As mentioned elsewhere, waxbills introduced to Portugal and Brazil and erroneously reported to be *E. troglodytes* have since been correctly identified as *E. astrild*.

NOTE
1 American Ornithologists' Union 1983; Berger 1981; Blake 1975; Hawaiian Audubon Society 1975; Long 1981; Ord 1982; Pyle 1976, 1977; Zeillemaker & Scott 1976.

Red Avadavat
(*Amandava amandava*)

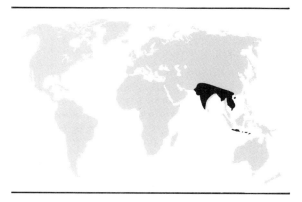

Note: Distribution in Indo-China may be discontinuous.

NATURAL DISTRIBUTION
Western Pakistan, India, Nepal and Burma eastwards to Yunnan in southwestern China, Hainan, Indo-China, Java, Bali and the Lesser Sunda Islands.

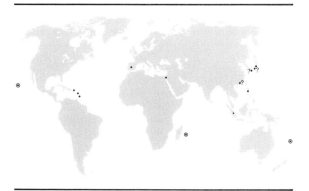

NATURALIZED DISTRIBUTION
Europe: Spain; Asia: Japan, ?Hong Kong; Africa: Egypt, Réunion; North America: West Indies (Guadeloupe, Martinique, Puerto Rico); Australasia: Philippines, Sumatra; Oceania: Hawaiian Islands, Fiji.

EUROPE

Spain[1]

In Spain, Red Avadavats were noted for the first time in the wild in Arganda, some 15 km southeast of Madrid, in 1974, where they were still present and breeding a decade later. In the Extre-

madura region, south-west of Madrid, the species was first captured in the wild in 1978. Red Avadavats are now known to be breeding in large numbers in marshland along the rivers of the Guadiana basin from a point 10 km south of Badajoz (less than 5 km from the Portuguese border) to beyond Villanueva de la Serena, a distance of some 110 km. They breed from August to November, before the onset of the autumnal rains. Although the population in January 1984 was estimated to number some 4,000, Red Avadavats, which nest in swampy ground and are mainly granivorous, do not seem to be competing with any native species. The birds are still increasing and expanding their range, and may soon spread over the border into eastern Portugal.

ASIA

Japan

According to Kaburaki (1940), the Red Avadavat was imported as a cagebird to the Japanese island of Honshu, where it was then established in the wild in the Gihu, Aiti, Tokyo, Saitama and Tiba prefectures. The Ornithological Society of Japan (1974) reported that although there seemed to have been few recent records, the birds were still apparently breeding in Honshu, and their 1981 map shows probable breeding also on Kyushu and Shikoku. According to Brazil (1985, in press, and personal communication, 1985), the most notable sites for the Red Avadavat are at Oi-koen and Tamagawa near Tokyo, and 'from Kanto southwards it has become quite common in its preferred habitat of tall grasses and reeds of marshes, river banks and rough land, with flocks of up to 200 reported'.

Hong Kong

The precise status of the Red Avadavat in Hong Kong has not been determined. Dove & Goodhart (1955) saw some at Mai Po in 1953, and Webster (1975) reported that flocks of up to 35 were regularly to be found – and probably bred – on the Mai Po marshes, at Long Valley, and occasionally elsewhere. These may have been escaped or released pets or natural vagrants from the Chinese mainland, where the resident subspecies is *flavidiventris*.

AFRICA

Egypt

Meinertzhagen (1930) records that Red Avadavats, which had presumably escaped or been released from captivity, were first recorded in the Delta area of Egypt in 1905. They were later also found inland at El Faîyum by Hachisuka (1924). Nicoll (see Meinertzhagen) apparently told Hachisuka that from at least 1914 to 1924 they were common and breeding in several localities (e.g. near El Gîza, Inshâs el Raml, Bilbeis, and around the Delta Barrage) within a 30-km radius of Cairo. This is confirmed by Raw, Sparrow & Jourdain (1921). Thereafter, for some unexplained reason, they disappeared, although some were noted by Meinertzhagen at Luxor in 1928. In 1975, Safriel reported their reappearance 4 km south-west of Ismâ'ilîya towards El Wasifîya and Abu Suweir on the western bank of the Suez Canal.

Réunion; Mauritius

According to Rountree, Guérin et al. (1952) and Benedict (1957), Red Avadavats were imported as aviary birds to Mauritius at an early date (perhaps by the first French settlers in 1715), and survived until they were annihilated by the cyclone of 1892, or around 1896 (Staub 1976). Rountree (1951) received an unsubstantiated report of an apparently flourishing colony in part of the west coast savannah; this, however, is not referred to by Staub. Red Avadavats were also imported at an early date to Réunion (possibly by the early colonists in 1664 or later from Mauritius), where they are now established but rare.

NORTH AMERICA

West Indies (Guadeloupe, Martinique and Puerto Rico)[2]

Red Avadavats were probably originally introduced to the island of Guadeloupe as cagebirds by the British or French in the eighteenth century. In recent times, they were first seen in the wild in about 1965 in the vicinity of Pointe-à-Pitre on the south-west coast of Grande-Terre. A couple of years later they appeared on the Baie de Fort-de-France on the west coast of Martinique, where they became established from Le Lamentin in the north southwards to Rivière-Salée and the Usine Petit-Bourg.

Red Avadavats are currently the most widespread exotic on Guadeloupe, where they have probably colonized the whole of Grande-Terre and the west-north-west of Basse-Terre. They favour low-lying damp areas, the edges of ponds, roadside verges and the borders of fields. They generally occur in pairs or small family groups, though sometimes in flocks of up to 50 individuals. They feed largely on *Panicum maximum*, an exotic imported from West Africa many years ago that has taken over disused sugar-cane fields (in which Red Avadavats are believed to nest) and roadside verges. As with other alien Estrildidae, Red Avadavats on Guadeloupe probably compete, to the latter's disadvantage, with the less-pugnacious and prolific indigenous Black-faced Grassquit (*Tiaris bicolor*).

Raffaele (1983) and T. Silva (personal communication, 1985) say that the Red Avadavat is a common introduced species on the island of Puerto Rico.

AUSTRALASIA

Philippines

Delacour & Mayr (1946) and du Pont (1971) say that Red Avadavats that escaped from captivity became established in the environs of Manila on the island of Luzon.

Sumatra

Delacour (1947) and Ali & Ripley (1968–74) state that the Red Avadavat has been introduced to the island of Sumatra. According to Peters (1968), the subspecies there is *A. a. punicea* – a native of Indo-China, Java and Bali. The possibility of natural colonization from Java, however, cannot be ruled out.

OCEANIA

Hawaiian Islands[3]

Red Avadavats are believed to have been imported as pets to the island of Oahu in the Hawaiian archipelago in the first decade of the present century, and to have been established for many years in and around Pearl Harbor, where, however, Caum (1933), reported them as 'nowhere particularly common'. More may have been brought in by the Hui Manu ('Bird Society') between 1930 and 1968. Ord (1963) estimated the population at around 100. The Hawaiian Audubon Society (1975) reported that some were established in grassland near sugar-cane plantations on the Waipio Peninsula in Pearl Harbor, where, however, they are much less abundant in the West Loch area than the more recently imported Black-headed Mannikin (*Lonchura malacca*) (q.v.). Zeillemaker & Scott (1976) listed Red Avadavats as local and uncommon in agricultural and pastureland (away from the peninsula) on Oahu; Pyle (1977) confirmed their presence as a long-established and breeding resident. Berger (1981: 209) said that the species 'has now begun to increase its range on Oahu'.

Fiji[4]

Red Avadavats are believed to have been first imported to Fiji sometime before 1906 by the Hon. Mr Remenschneider, when they became established in the suburbs of Suva on the south coast of Viti Levu. Pernetta & Watling (1978) record them as common in agricultural, urban, suburban and grassland habitats on the main islands. Watling (1982: 132), in his definitive work on the birds of the region, says the species is 'a bird of open country, agricultural land and gardens, but also found at the forest edge, or in substantial clearings. An exotic bird naturalised on Viti Levu and Vanua Levu [where] . . . it is common [Mercer (1966) and Holyoak (1979) claim that it occurs only in small numbers] and usually seen in small groups; on occasions – especially on the way to the communal roost – large flocks are sometimes formed. The subspecies is probably *A. a. flavidiventris* [southwestern China, Burma and the Lesser Sunda Islands].' Mercer (1966) says that depredations on seedling rice have been recorded; Watling, on the other hand, states that although Red Avadavats are 'especially partial to the seeds of Jungle Rice *Echinochloa colenum*' those of cultivated varieties are very rarely taken.

In France, Yeatman (1976) records that Red Avadavats survived for several years in the wild near Orléans before eventually dying out in 1974.

According to Hume (1880), Red Avadavats were then abundant on Singapore Island, to which they had presumably been imported (Delacour 1947 and Gibson-Hill 1949c). They were still common in 1924, but thereafter seem to have disappeared. Large numbers continued to be imported as pets after the Second World War, and those occasionally seen in the wild are probably birds that have escaped or been released. Peters (1968) records the subspecies introduced as *punicea*.

In the nineteenth century, Red Avadavats were imported to the Comoros group,[5] where specimens were collected on Mayotte in 1884 and on Mohéli (five) in 1904, but where the birds have since died out.

Legge (1874) says that Red Avadavats of the nominate subspecies imported from Bengal, India, to Ceylon (Sri Lanka), escaped and became established in Colombo, where they subsequently disappeared.

According to Beavan (1867), 25 Red Avadavats were released by Colonel R. C. Tytler at Port Blair on South Andaman Island at the time of the establishment there of a penal colony in 1858, but Hume (1873) said they had by then all disappeared.

Guild (1938) records that in that year he released some Red Avadavats on Tahiti, where they nested successfully shortly thereafter but eventually died out.

The **Green Avadavat** (*Amandava formosa*) is a native of central India. According to Ripley (1961), a colony of escaped birds was at that time established at Lahore in Pakistan.

The **Zebra Finch** (*Poephila guttata*) occurs throughout Australia, except in the extreme south-west and along the south-east coast, and in the Lesser Sunda Islands.

Pearson (1962) records that at some time before 1962 four Zebra Finches were imported from Australia (where the subspecies is *castanotis*) to Nauru Island north-east of Papua New Guinea, where, as he saw half-a-dozen in grassland in the interior, the birds were apparently breeding. Zebra Finches (and the endemic **Cocos Island Finch** (*Pinaroloxias inornata*) have also been recorded from the Tuamotu Islands northeast of the Society group.

On Tahiti in the Society archipelago, Guild (1938) records that Zebra Finches released by him in that year bred successfully in the wild. They subsequently died out.

According to Thomson (1922), the Wellington Acclimatization Society imported a dozen Zebra Finches to New Zealand sometime before 1885; what became of them is unknown.

In September 1937, an attempt was made to establish Zebra Finches on Kangaroo Island[6] off the coast of South Australia, when a dozen were unsuccessfully transferred from the mainland to Flinders Chase.

NOTES

1 de Juana 1985; de la Cruz, da Silva et al. 1981; de Lope, Guerrero & de la Cruz 1984; de Lope, Guerrero et al. 1985; Equipos del Centro de Migración 1974.

2 Barré & Benito-Espinal 1985; Pinchon 1976; Pinchon & Benito-Espinal 1980; Raffaele 1983; and T. Silva, personal communication, 1985.

3 American Ornithologists' Union 1983; Berger 1981; Blake 1975; Bryan 1958; Caum 1933; Hawaiian Audubon Society 1975; Long 1981; Munro 1944; Ord 1963; Peterson 1961; Pyle 1976, 1977; Zeillemaker & Scott, 1976.

4 Gorman 1975; Holyoak 1979; Long 1981; Mercer 1966; Parham 1954; Pernetta & Watling, 1978; Turbet 1941; Watling 1982; Wood & Wetmore 1926.

5 Benson 1960; Long 1981; Milne-Edwards & Oustalet 1888; Reichenow 1908.

6 Abbott 1974; Anon. 1948; Condon 1962; Long 1981.

Red-browed Waxbill
(*Aegintha temporalis*)

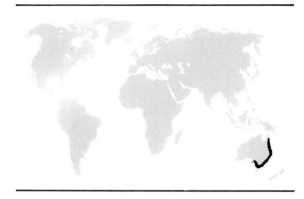

NATURAL DISTRIBUTION
Southern and eastern coastal Australia, from the Mount Lofty Ranges and Kangaroo Island in South Australia, eastwards and northwards through Victoria and New South Wales to approximately Princess Charlotte Bay on the Cape York Peninsula of northern Queensland.

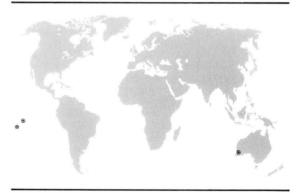

Note: Population in Western Australia is descended from transplanted stock.

NATURALIZED DISTRIBUTION
Oceania: Society and Marquesas islands.

OCEANIA

Society and Marquesas islands[1]

Red-browed Waxbills of the nominate subspecies, which is widely distributed in eastern Australia from coastal New South Wales to coastal central Queensland, have been introduced to the Society Islands and to the Marquesas: the

following details are taken largely from Holyoak & Thibault (1984).

Tahiti: seen for the first time in 1899; 3 years later a specimen was collected which is now in the B. P. Bishop Museum in Honolulu, Hawaii; in 1920–1, the Whitney expedition found the species to be locally abundant and collected 28; more were released by Eastham Guild in 1938; the birds are today still very common. **Moorea**: three specimens were collected by the Whitney expedition in 1921, but none were seen by Holyoak in 1972; today they are widespread and abundant. **Mohotani**: reported for the first time as recently as August 1975, when several pairs were discovered nesting in *Casuarina* groves. **Nuku Hiva**: not seen by the Whitney expedition in 1920, but apparently present in 1958, when the species is referred to by King (1958) as *Taeniopygia castanotis* – the former name of the Zebra Finch; on all available evidence, however, the species present on Nuku Hiva and Hiva Oa (see below) is, as on other Polynesian islands, actually *A. temporalis*; large numbers were seen in 1971 and again in 1975. **Ua Huka**: not reported in 1920 by the Whitney expedition, but occurred in 1971–5 near Hane. **Ua Pou**: not observed by the Whitney expedition in 1920, but present in small numbers between 1971 and 1975. **Hiva Oa**: introduced, according to diocesan archives, to Atuona in 1936; again described by J. E. King in 1958 as *T. castanotis*, but actually *A. temporalis*; the species was common in 1971–5. **Tahuata**: not seen in 1920 by the Whitney expedition but present in 1975.

In the Society and Marquesas islands, Red-browed Waxbills frequent mainly lawns, thickets and shrubs, especially in groves of *Casuarina* trees; they are sometimes also found in woodland ecotones. On the Toovii plateau on Nuku Hiva they occur up to an altitude of 800 m, and to 700 m on the fern-covered hills of Tahiti. Although in the Marquesas they are largely confined to littoral regions, on Tahiti they are more commonly found in valleys up to 6 km inland than on the coast, where they are apparently replaced by the introduced Common Waxbill (*Estrilda astrild*) (q.v.).

Red-browed Waxbills in the Society and Marquesas islands feed mainly on small seeds from grasses and other herbaceous vegetation, taken either from the ground or from growing plants, and, probably, as in Australia, on insects. Generally tame and easy to approach, they occur in the breeding season in pairs or small groups, but at other times associate in larger flocks of up to 15 individuals, often in the company of alien Chestnut-breasted Mannikins (*Lonchura castaneothorax*) (q.v.). On Mohotani, and probably elsewhere, a favourite nesting site seems to be *Casuarina* trees.

According to Thomson (1922), the Otago Acclimatization Society imported four Red-browed Waxbills into New Zealand in 1867 and the Auckland Society a further four in 1871; what became of them is unknown.

Mayr (1945) records that either Red-browed or Common Waxbills were at one time established on the island of Viti Levu, Fiji. Neither species is referred to by Pernetta & Watling (1978) nor by Watling (1982), so they must have since disappeared.

Mayr also states that Red-browed Waxbills were introduced to New Caledonia, where they were said to be common in grasslands in the mid-1940s. Since Delacour (1966) does not refer to them, they have presumably died out.

According to Dell (1965), Red-browed Waxbills were found to be well established in orchard clearings in Darling Range gullies east of Perth, Western Australia, in 1958. Long (1972) reported them to occupy a limited area from Bickley, Hackett Gully and the Dell to the edge of the escarpment towards Helena Valley and Darlington. They are now, according to Long (1981: 417), 'reported to be relatively scarce'.

NOTE
1 Guild 1938; Holyoak 1974a; Holyoak & Thibault 1984; King 1958; Long 1981; Thibault & Rives 1975; Townsend & Wetmore, 1919.

Bronze Mannikin
(*Lonchura cucullata*)

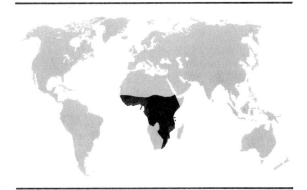

NATURAL DISTRIBUTION
Southern Africa from around 12°–15° N, apart
from eastern Ethiopia, Somalia, southern Angola,
Namibia, western Botswana and western South
Africa, but including the east coast islands of
Zanzibar and Mafia, and São Tomé and Príncipe
in the Gulf of Guinea.

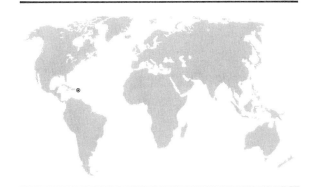

NATURALIZED DISTRIBUTION
North America: West Indies (Puerto Rico).

NORTH AMERICA

West Indies (Puerto Rico)[1]

Exactly when Bronze Mannikins (of the nominate form, which ranges eastwards from Senegal
to the Sudan and south to Uganda) first arrived
– presumably as cagebirds – in Puerto Rico is
uncertain. They may have been imported from
West Africa on board Spanish slave-ships at any
time between 1530 (or earlier) and 1820 when,
under British influence, the trade was aban-

doned.[2] When they first became established in the wild is likewise unknown. A specimen was collected on the island by Robert Swift in 1864 or 1865, and another in 1866. They were reported to be locally common in 1903, and further specimens were obtained in 1920. Seven years later they were apparently a common resident on the coastal lowlands, especially in the extreme south-west around Cabo Rojo, where flocks numbering several hundred were reported. According to Bond (1979), Bronze Mannikins (known locally as, *diablitos*) are especially common in the capital, San Juan, and have spread eastwards to Vieques Island. They favour open, lowland coastal areas, especially along streams, and the borders of pastures and lawns, and are rare in the hills. They cause significant economic damage in rice fields.

Bronze Mannikins were first recorded in the Comoros, on Anjouan where they were said to be common, in 1876, and several were collected there and on Mayotte in 1884 and 1886. They are now abundant on those two islands and also on Grande Comore and Mohéli. According to Benson (1960), the subspecies present is *L. c. scutata*, which occurs on the nearby east African mainland in Tanzania and Mozambique; as they are seldom kept as pets in the Comoros the population is thus probably the result of natural colonization.

Bronze Mannikins, first recorded on the Spanish island of Fernando Póo (Bioko) in the Gulf of Guinea in 1929, were found by Fry (1961) to be fairly common. Although they may have been imported by man they are more likely to be natural colonists from Cameroon on the west African mainland.

In 1938, Guild (1938) unsuccessfully released some Bronze Mannikins on the island of Tahiti.

The **Warbling Silverbill** (*Lonchura malabarica*) has two discrete populations: *L. m. cantans* and *L. m. orientalis* occur in Africa from Senegal eastwards to Somalia and south to northern Tanzania, and also across the Red Sea in southern Yemen, whereas the nominate form ranges from Oman eastwards across the Persian Gulf to the Himalayas of northern India, and south to Sri Lanka.

In 1967, 104 Warbling Silverbills of the African subspecies *cantans* were imported as cagebirds to the island of Hawaii.[3] They were first reported in the wild by Berger (1975e), who (1981: 209–10):

found a large population on the leeward slope of Kohala Mountain (Hawaii) during 1974. This species later was found at Pohakuloa; flocks totalling 'hundreds of birds' were seen in both North Kohala (Mahukona) and South Kohala (Waikoloa) during February 1978. . . . It is assumed that this species was first liberated on the Puuwaawaa ranch, but no details are available. During December 1978, some 40 silverbills were found in kiawe thickets below Ulupalakua, Maui (*Elepaio* 39: 89) and several were seen on Lanai during 1979 (*Elepaio* 40: 119). . . . Like the other species of waxbills and finches, the silverbill is primarily a seed-eating bird. Hence, the tremendous populations of these birds will make impossible the growing of small grain crops on Hawaii.

Four Warbling Silverbills were found at Lua Makika on Kahoolawe in 1980 (Conant 1983), others were seen on west Molokai in 1981, 15 on Molokini in 1983, several on Oahu in 1984 (Conant 1984), and the species was reported on Kauai in 1985.

According to the American Ornithologists' Union (1983), a pair of Warbling Silverbills nested successfully on Merritt Island, Florida, USA, in June 1965,[4] but they failed to become established.

NOTES

1 American Ornithologists' Union 1983; Blake 1975; Bond 1971, 1979; Bowdish 1903; Cory 1889; Long 1981; Peters 1968; Raffaele 1983; Wetmore 1927; Wetmore & Swales 1931.
2 Long (1981: 427), following Wetmore (1927) and Wetmore & Swales (1931), says that the Bronze Mannikin's introduction to Puerto Rico is believed to 'date back to the French colonisation'. Puerto Rico was, however, under Spanish rule from 1509

until it was seized by the United States in 1898, and was never colonized by the French. See also: H. A. Raffaele, *Quarterly Review of Biology* 57: 206–7 (1982).

3 American Ornithologists' Union 1983; Berger 1975e, 1981; Conant 1983, 1984; Hawaiian Audubon Society 1975; Long 1981; Pyle 1976, 1977; Zeillemaker & Scott 1976.

4 *American Birds* 19: 537 (1965), where they are listed as '*Euodice cantans*'.

Nutmeg Mannikin
(Lonchura punctulata)

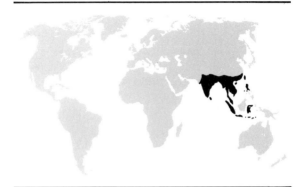

NATURAL DISTRIBUTION

India, southern Nepal, Bhutan, Bangladesh, Assam, Burma and Sri Lanka, eastwards to Yunnan in southern China, Taiwan, and Hainan, south through Thailand, Indo-China, the Philippines (Luzon and Mindoro), Malaysia, Sumatra, Java, the Lesser Sunda Islands, Sulawesi and Timor, eastwards to Tanimbar Island in the southern Banda Sea.

NATURALIZED DISTRIBUTION

Asia: ?Singapore, Yap Island, Palau Islands; Africa: Mascarenes (Mauritius, Réunion); North America: West Indies (Guadeloupe, Puerto Rico, Hispaniola); Australasia: Australia; Oceania: Hawaiian Islands.

ASIA

Singapore

Although Ward (1968) considered that Nutmeg Mannikins, which are abundant in gardens on

421

Singapore Island where they appear to be increasing, are the descendants of escaped cage-birds, they could equally well be natural colonists from the mainland of Malaya. In either event, since they are not mentioned by Robinson & Chasen (1927–39), they are presumably a relatively recent arrival.

Yap Island

Ralph & Sakai (1979) reported that Nutmeg Mannikins have been introduced to, and are common on, Yap Island in the Carolines.

Palau Islands

Marshall (1949) found Nutmeg Mannikins breeding in grassland on Babelthuap Island (largest of the Palau archipelago), where he believed they had been recently introduced, and Ripley (1951) saw a flock on Koror Island immediately to the south. Peters (1968) records the form present as *L. p. cabanisi*, which is endemic to the Philippines, so natural coloniz-ation of the Palau Islands – where the birds are now said to be rare – cannot be ruled out.

AFRICA

Mauritius; Réunion

According to Meinertzhagen (1912), Nutmeg Mannikins were introduced to Mauritius from Java (where Howard & Moore (1980) list the race as *nisoria*) in about 1800. They were found by Meinertzhagen to be well established, by Benedict (1957) to be increasing, and by Staub (1976) to be fairly common. On Réunion, where the date of their introduction has apparently not been recorded, Watson, Zusi & Storer (1963) described them as becoming rare, and Staub as very rare. Peters (1968) says that the form present on both islands is *topela*, which Howard & Moore list as occurring in southern China, Thailand and Indo-China. So far as is known, Nutmeg Mannikins have never been introduced to the island of Rodrigues.

NORTH AMERICA

West Indies (Guadeloupe, Puerto Rico and Hispaniola)

Barré & Benito-Espinal (1985) say that on the island of Guadeloupe in the Lesser Antilles Nutmeg Mannikins seem at present confined to clearings and moist cultivated slopes on the windward side of Basse-Terre, although they may recently have also gained a foothold at Abymes in the west of Grande-Terre. Like other alien Estrildidae they seem likely to become established in this dry region where, as on Basse-Terre, there is an abundance of *Panicum maximum* (an exotic imported many years ago from West Africa that has invaded roadside verges and aban-doned sugarcane fields) on which they feed. In January 1984, Barré & Benito-Espinal saw 120 feeding on Sorghum (*Sorghum alepense*) at Duclos, and in the following December around 100 on a rice field on Mont Lézard. Experimental rice cultivation at Roujol has in some places suffered over 90 per cent depredation from Nutmeg Mannikins, and it seems likely that the birds could cause extensive harm to cereal crops cultivated on a large scale on Guadeloupe.

Nutmeg Mannikins in Guadeloupe breed in the rainy season (August–October) during the main fruiting period of *Panicum maximum*. They construct their nests between 2 and 8 m from the ground in the dense foliage of such species as *Euphorbia lactea*, *Panicum*, Mangoes (*Mangifera indica*) and small palm trees. Interspecific compe-tition with Nutmeg Mannikins (and other exotics) on Guadeloupe may be adversely affecting the less-prolific and aggressive native Black-faced Grassquit (*Tiaris bicolor*).

According to Bond (1979: 239), 'Many exotic species have recently been introduced in Puerto Rico, including the Scaly-breasted Munia [Nutmeg Mannikin] (*Lonchura punctulata*) . . . [and] in the Dominican Republic as well'. On the former island the species is common.[1] As in Guadeloupe, considerable economic damage by Nutmeg Mannikins to fields of rice has been reported on both Puerto Rico and Hispaniola.

AUSTRALASIA

Australia[2]

Nutmeg Mannikins first appeared near Brisbane in southern Queensland around 1937 (having possibly escaped in about 1930) where, in spite of large populations of native Chestnut-breasted Mannikins (*Lonchura castaneothorax*), they became established in long grass and rank herbage along the banks of the Brisbane River. From here they spread slowly 100 km north to Noosaville and the Noosa River by 1961, west through the Darling Downs, 65 km north-west to Esk by 1955–6, and later 160 km south through *Eucalyptus* forest to the cane fields and extensive swampy grasslands of the Tweed, Richmond and Clarence rivers in New South Wales.

In 1951 and 1954, Nutmeg Mannikins that had escaped from aviaries became established in and around Townsville, Ingham and Rockhampton in northern and central Queensland, where they found an ideal habitat with a similar climate to that of much of their natural range. In the latter year, they appeared in Innisfail and Mackay, and by 1960 and 1961; respectively, they had spread 300 and 450 km north through the grasslands and cane fields of the coastal lowland belt to Cairns and Cooktown. They first appeared in Atherton, south of Cairns, in 1964, when they were said to be one of the commonest birds in the coastal towns of northern Queensland.

Nutmeg Mannikins were first seen in Sydney, New South Wales, in 1947, when they were reported to be 'breeding in fair numbers' in the Metropolitan area, and although a decade later they were increasing their numbers and range they had still not spread outside the county of Cumberland. Frith (1979) found them to be fairly common in a few localities, but said that they had not as yet penetrated the inhospitable sandstone scrub and *Eucalyptus* forests north of Sydney to the apparently suitable habitats of the Hunter and other coastal rivers. They were first reported inland at Mudgee in 1979 by Kurtz (1980), who also recorded them as well dispersed on the Cumberland Plain, and as present at Grafton, Lismore, Casino and Murwillumbah in the northern coastal region; at Taree on the central coast; at Windsor (a flock of 50) and Wilberforce (70) near Sydney; and at Moruya on the south coast. In South Australia, Watmough (1981)

found a group of half-a-dozen at Felixtow in 1978 and a similar number at Paradise (both north-eastern suburbs of Adelaide) in the following year.

Nutmeg Mannikins in Australia multiplied rapidly and in some places became very abundant. Along the 200-km stretch of the Queensland coast between Ingham and Cairns, where in 1960 they were said to be already as numerous as the extremely common Chestnut-breasted Mannikin, Frith found a decade later that in some localities the exotic species actually outnumbered the indigene. Although the success of the former has usually been assumed to have taken place at the expense of the latter, Frith was unconvinced by this explanation. He pointed out that to some extent the two species occupy separate ecological niches. The native is well adapted to life in the rice paddies and cane fields of northern Queensland, and to pastureland and waterside reedbeds, but is not a commensal of man. The alien, on the other hand, exploits a wider range of habitats and has a broader-based diet, breeds throughout the year, is double or treble brooded, lays a larger (seven or more) clutch of eggs (native finches breed but twice a year and tend to lay no more than half-a-dozen eggs), and lives and nests freely in settled as well as rural areas, giving it an inbuilt advantage. It has also been suggested that Nutmeg Mannikins – a vigorous species – compete for territory, and in some places have displaced, native Red-browed Waxbills (*Aegintha temporalis*), Double-barred Finches (*Poephila bichenovii*) and Zebra Finches (*P. guttata*). Again, Frith points out that since each of these species have different habitat and food requirements and a generally diverse ecology from those of the genus *Lonchura*, serious interspecific competition seems highly unlikely.

Slater (1974) described the Nutmeg Mannikin's Australian range as stretching from Sydney northwards along the New South Wales and Queensland coasts to Cooktown. Pizzey (1980), who believed that in Queensland and coastal northeastern New South Wales Nutmeg Mannikins may be displacing related grass-finches such as the Chestnut-breasted Mannikin, said that the former was now locally common and in some places abundant coastally from Moruya, 250 km south of Sydney on the coast of southern New South Wales, northwards along some 3,000 km of coast to Cooktown in northern Queensland,

and inland to the Miles – Meandarra area 300 km west of Brisbane in southern Queensland. This distribution is confirmed by Blakers, Davies & Reilly (1984). The subspecies established in Australia has been identified by Peters (1968) as *L. p. topela*.

OCEANIA

Hawaiian Islands[3]

Nutmeg Mannikins of the form *L. p. topela* were imported to Hawaii by Dr William Hillebrand around 1865. Writing in 1933, Caum said that the species 'does considerable damage to green rice . . . [and] is not particularly common in districts where rice is not grown'. Sorghum crops also suffered considerable depredations. Although these crops are no longer grown commercially in Hawaii, Ricebirds (as the species is sometimes known) are common in wide range of habitats, such as residential areas, agricultural land and pastures, forests and woodland ecotone, lowlands and dense bush, in both arid and wet areas from sea level to 2,300 m, on all the main islands, where they feed on the seeds of grains, grasses, rushes and weeds. According to Berger (1981: 211):

The species seems to be highly erratic, indicated by its seasonal and annual distribution: it is present in large numbers in certain areas during one year and scarce or even absent in others. . . . On the island of Hawaii, I have found the Ricebird from sea level to at least 7,500 feet [2,300 m] on Mauna Kea. On Maui, I have seen the species at sea level and near Paliku cabin in Haleakala Crater. I have found the Ricebird to be common in dry regions where the rainfall averages 20 inches [50 cm] or less annually: . . . By contrast, I have found the Ricebird in extremely wet areas.

Similarly, on Kauai, Richardson & Bowles (1964) found Nutmeg Mannikins

under extremely diverse conditions, as along the uppermost Koaie River (3,750 feet) [1,150 m] and in dry Milolii Canyon near sea level. They were common usually in high-grass clumps along roads or by clearings in the Kokee region, and also in the grasses beside the innumerable roads of sugarcane fields. Ricebirds appear to occur in virgin forest areas rarely, except along open stream beds, . . . roads and jeep trails.

In the West Loch area of Pearl Harbor on Oahu Nutmeg Mannikins are, however, now outnumbered by the more recently introduced Black-headed Mannikin (*Lonchura malacca*) (q.v.). Zeillemaker & Scott (1976) describe the former as a common introduced resident, especially on agricultural land and pastures and in residential and community parklands, on Kaui, Oahu, Molokai, Lanai, Maui and Hawaii. It also occurs on Kahoolawe.

According to Gaymer, Blackman et al. (1969), Nicoll claimed to have found a Nutmeg Mannikin on Mahé in the Seychelles in 1906. None have been seen there since.

Thomson (1922) records that in 1868 the Auckland Acclimatization Society of New Zealand acquired eight 'Nutmeg Sparrows' or 'Cowry Birds' from a Miss Wright; what happened to them is not known.

Guild (1938) unsuccessfully released Nutmeg Mannikins in that year on the island of Tahiti.

The American Ornithologists' Union (1983) records that pairs of Nutmeg Mannikins nested successfully in Florida, USA, at Cocoa Beach in 1964[4] and on Merritt Island,[5] but failed to become established.

According to Brazil (1985 and in press), the Nutmeg Mannikin is well established and breeding in Okinawa, where it may have arrived naturally from China as a typhoon-blown waif.

Brazil (1985 and in press) also records the breeding on Okinawa of the **White-rumped Munia** (*Lonchura striata*), a native of India, Nepal, Burma, Sri Lanka, southern China and Indo-China, and of the **Pale-headed Mannikin** (*L. maja*) of southern Thailand, Malaysia, Sumatra, Java and Bali. The latter may also breed north of Osaka on Honshu (Ornithological Society of Japan 1981). In April 1984, a single individual of *maja* was seen in a flock of *punctulata* of Roujol on Guadeloupe in the Lesser Antilles by Barré & Benito-Espinal (1985).

The **Javanese Munia** (*Lonchura leucogastroides*) is confined to southern Sumatra, Java, Bali and Lombok. C. J. Hails (personal communication, 1985) reports it to be the most abundant munia on Singapore Island, where it was first introduced in 1922 and is now widely distributed, occurring in small flocks of up to 10 or so, mainly in wooded gardens, scrubland, and clearings in woodland, and along the banks of reservoirs.

NOTES

1 T. Silva, personal communication, 1985.
2 Bell 1961; Blakers Davies & Reilly 1984; Bravery 1970; Frith 1979; Immelman 1970; Kurtz 1980; Lavery 1974; Lavery & Hopkins 1963; Long 1981; McGill 1960; Peters 1968; Pizzey 1980; Slater 1974; Tarr 1950; Watmough 1981.
3 American Ornithologists' Union 1983; Berger 1981; Blake 1975; Caum 1933; Hawaiian Audubon Society 1975; Long 1981; Munro 1960; Peters 1968; Pyle 1976, 1977; Richardson & Bowles 1964; Zeillemaker & Scott 1976.
4 *American Birds* 18: 504–5 (1965).
5 Ibid. 19: 537 (1965).

Black-headed Mannikin
(*Lonchura malacca*)

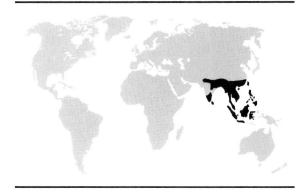

NATURAL DISTRIBUTION

Northern India and eastern Nepal eastwards through Bangladesh, Assam and Burma into Yunnan in southern China, Taiwan, and Hainan, south through Thailand, Indo-China, Malaysia, Sumatra, the Philippines, Palawan, Borneo, Sulawesi and Java. An apparently discrete population (of the nominate form) occurs in southern India and Sri Lanka.

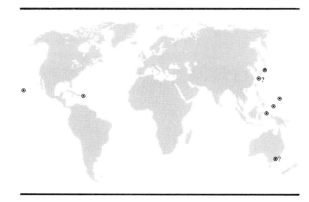

NATURALIZED DISTRIBUTION

Asia: ?Japan; North America: West Indies (Puerto Rico); Australasia: ?Australia, ?Moluccas (Halmahera), Palau Islands (Babelthuap and ?Koror); Oceania: Hawaiian Islands, Marianas (Guam).

ASIA

Japan

Kaburaki (1934 and 1940) reported that Black-headed Mannikins of the form *L. m. atricapilla* (northeastern India, Bangladesh, Assam and Burma) were introduced to Japan 'before the Restoration' (i.e. prior to 1871), and that they were established around Tokyo and in a few nearby localities until at least the late 1930s. The Ornithological Society of Japan (1974) considered that they were still established in the wild and breeding locally, and their 1981 map shows breeding on Honshu north-west of Osaka, at Niigata, and at Tokyo. M. A. Brazil (personal communication, 1985) believed that they were breeding also on Okinawa in the Ryukyu Islands; if so, they presumably arrived as natural immigrants from Taiwan. Especially in winter they frequent harvested rice fields.

NORTH AMERICA

West Indies (Puerto Rico)

The Black-headed Mannikin is a common introduced bird in Puerto Rico,[1] where it is frequently to be seen perching on tall grass-heads. It is said to cause considerable damage in rice fields.

AUSTRALASIA

Australia[2]

Escaped Black-headed Mannikins of the subspecies *atricapilla* were reported by Tarr (1950) and McGill (1960) to have been breeding in small numbers in Centennial Park, Sydney, New South Wales, in 1929, at Long Neck Swamps in 1937, and at Dee Why Swamps in 1948. From here they spread to other localities around Sydney, where they came into contact with the closely related native Chestnut-breasted Mannikin (*Lonchura castaneothorax*), which is here near the southern extremity of its range and occurs only in small numbers. The present status of the Black-headed Mannikin in Australia is uncertain; although Blakers, Davies & Reilly (1984) say that it has not been reported from around Sydney since 1960, other authorities state that the birds, which are seldom seen, occur in long grass and reeds among scattered bushes and trees, where they normally form small close-knit flocks that feed on the seeds of weeds and grasses. In August 1977, a single bird was sighted at Nowra, 125 km south of Sydney.

Moluccas (Halmahera)

According to Ripley (1961) and King, Dickinson & Woodcock (1975), Black-headed Mannikins have been successfully imported to the island of Halmahera – largest of the Moluccas – where Peters (1968) has identified the race present as *jagori* (the Philippines, Palawan, Borneo and northern Sulawesi). In view of the proximity of its native range, however, the possibility of natural colonization cannot be ignored.

Palau Islands (Babelthuap and ?Koror)

Ripley (1951) discovered Black-headed Mannikins of the endemic Javan subspecies *ferruginosa* established on Babelthuap – largest of the Palau Islands – and on Koror, immediately to the south, and suggested the possibility of a hybrid population. According to Ralph & Saki (1979), they are still abundant on Babelthuap.

OCEANIA

Hawaiian Islands[3]

Imported to the Hawaiian Islands as a cagebird between 1936 and 1941 (privately and by the Hui Manu or 'Bird Society'), Black-headed Mannikins were first reported to be breeding in the wild by Udvardy (1960), who saw 10 adults and 15 juveniles near West Loch in Pearl Harbor on Oahu on 26 April 1959. (Udvardy was told that the Black-headed Mannikins that he saw in two pet shops in Honolulu in the same year had been imported from Calcutta, India, where the subspecies is *atricapilla*.) Ord (1963) judged the population to number between 400 and 500. In March 1972, an estimated 900 were counted in the vicinity of West Loch.[4] The species was then more abundant than either the Red Avadavat (*Amandava amandava*) (q.v.) or the Nutmeg Mannikin (*Lonchura punctulata*) (q.v.) in the West

Loch area, where it frequented mainly kiawe or mesquite (*Prosopis chilensis*) thickets and open grassland dividing sugar-cane plantations. Elsewhere it favoured golf courses, grassy roadside verges ·and weedy headlands of cane fields.

In May 1970, Berger (1981) found Black-headed Mannikins of the nominate form (which are confined to southern India and Sri Lanka) near the Waikiki aquarium in Honolulu. The Hawaiian Audubon Society (1975) reported that the birds appeared to be established primarily in the grassy lowlands of the Waipio Peninsula in Pearl Harbor, from where they seemed slowly to be spreading inland; by 1977, they had been reported 24 km north of Pearl Harbor, and also at Laie on the north coast of Oahu, the latter almost certainly representing birds of separate origin. Zeillemaker & Scott (1976) described Black-headed Mannikins as local and uncommon in dry lowland agricultural land and pastures only on Oahu. In the same year, the species was found to be apparently well established also on the island of Kauai, where in the following year between 40 and 50 were counted near Poipu Beach. Were they to become abundant in the Hawaiian Islands and to continue to increase their range, Black-headed Mannikins could become a serious pest to agricultural crops.

Marianas (Guam)

Ralph & Saki report that Javan Black-headed Mannikins have been imported to the island of Guam – most southerly of the Marianas – where they are abundant.

Guild (1938) recorded that in 1938 he unsuccessfully liberated Black-headed Mannikins on Tahiti in the Society Islands.

According to the American Ornithologists' Union (1983), a pair of Black-headed Mannikins bred successfully in 1965 on Merritt Island, Florida, USA,[5] but failed to become established.

NOTES

1 American Ornithologists' Union 1983; Raffaele 1983; and T. Silva, personal communication, 1985.
2 Blakers, Davies & Reilly 1984; Long 1981; McGill 1960; Tarr 1950. See also: A. Rogers, *Australian Birds* 13: 1–21 (1978).
3 American Ornithologists' Union 1983; Berger 1981; Blake 1975; Bryan 1958; Hawaiian Audubon Society 1975; Long 1981; Ord 1963; Pratt 1977; Pyle 1976, 1977; Ralph & Pyle 1977; Udvardy 1960; Zeillemaker & Scott 1976.
4 *Elepaio* 38: 56
5 *American Birds* 19: 537 (1965).

Chestnut-breasted Mannikin
(*Lonchura castaneothorax*)

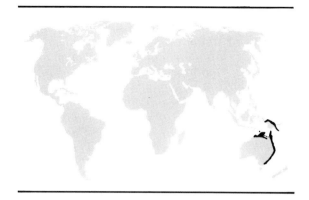

NATURAL DISTRIBUTION

Eastern coastal Australia from southern New South Wales to the Cape York Peninsula of northern Queensland, and northern Australia from the Gulf of Carpentaria and its offshore islands in the Northern Territory westwards through Arnhem Land (including Melville Island) to about Derby in Western Australia. (The northern population may be discrete from that on the Cape York Peninsula.) Also in northern, northwestern, central and southwestern New Guinea.

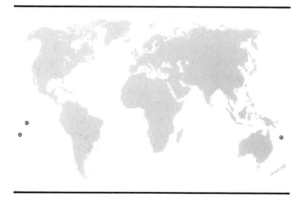

NATURALIZED DISTRIBUTION

Oceania: Society and Marquesas islands, New Caledonia.

OCEANIA

Society and Marquesas islands

Chestnut-breasted Mannikins of the nominate form (eastern Queensland and New South Wales) have been widely introduced in French Polynesia;[1] the following details are taken largely from Holyoak & Thibault (1984).

Tahiti: introduced in the late nineteenth century, specimens were first collected in 1899 and again by the Whitney expedition (34) in 1920; in 1938, Guild (1938) successfully released some more; the species is now widely distributed. **Moorea**: established before 1921 (when 16 were collected by the Whitney expedition); the birds are now widespread. **Tetiaroa**: introduced in 1973 but not found by Holyoak (1974a). **Maiao**: a total population of under 200 was found in 1973. **Huahine**: present in 1972. **Raiatea**: found by Holyoak in 1972. **Tahaa**: present in 1973. **Bora Bora**: introduced towards the end of the nineteenth century, specimens were collected for the first time in 1899; the birds were numerous in 1971–2. **Maupiti**: a few were seen in 1973. **Mopelia**: small numbers were found near the settlement in 1973. **Makatea**: several dozen pairs were seen in the village in 1973. **Nuku Hiva**: not found by the Whitney expedition in 1920; seen for the first time in 1971. **Ua Huka**: also noted for the first time in 1971. **Ua Pou**: again not reported by the Whitney expedition in 1920, but seen for the first time in 1971. **Hiva Oa**: introduced, according to the diocesan archives, in 1936, but not mentioned again (by King) until 1958. **Tahuata**: the Whitney expedition found none in 1920; reported for the first time in 1975. **Mohotani**: three birds were sighted in April 1975, but were not found during later visits; they were probably vagrants from a neighbouring island. **Fatu Iva**: present in 1975; the local inhabitants believed they had been introduced between about 1955 and 1960.

It seems that in French Polynesia the Chestnut-breasted Mannikin's range of habitats is more diverse than in Australia: in the latter country, it frequents grasslands, reedy swamps, watercourses and mangroves whereas in the former it is widespread on bracken-covered hill slopes in the interior, in pastures and gardens, on cultivated and wasteland, in forest ecotones and in coconut plantations. On Tahiti, the birds range from sea level to an altitude of 700 m and to 800 m on Nuku Hiva, but are more common in the lowlands, especially in areas exposed to humid winds. They feed by perching on reed stems and on various herbaceous plants, and by picking seeds from flowerheads, which they pull within reach with their beaks, and then seize with their feet while they extract the seeds. Although in Australia they are rarely seen on the ground, on Tahiti they frequently perch on short swards. On Raiatea, they have been seen eating *Casuarina* seeds up to 15 m from the ground. Very gregarious throughout the year Chestnut-breasted Mannikins form large flocks outside the breeding season that in French Polynesia may contain 50–100 individuals, and often associate with other Estrildidae – especially introduced Red-browed Waxbills (*Aegintha temporalis*). Juveniles tend to form separate flocks from adults. In a group the birds fly fast and straight, but individuals tend to have a somewhat undulating flight.

New Caledonia

According to Delacour (1966) and Pizzey (1980), Chestnut-breasted Mannikins from northern Australia (*castaneothorax* or *assimilis*) have been successfully imported to New Caledonia, where they are now common in gardens and on cultivated land.

In *The Jubilee History of Nelson, from 1842 to 1892* (Nelson, 1892), quoted by Thomson (1922), Lowther Broad states that six 'Australian sparrows' (presumably *L. castaneothorax*) had been imported to New Zealand and released in Nelson sometime before September 1864. In the same year, a dozen sent from Sydney, New South Wales, by a Mr Wilkin, were unsuccessfully turned down by the Canterbury Acclimatization Society. In 1867, the Auckland Society freed 25, which in their annual report of the following year they claimed were 'considered to be thoroughly acclimatized'. A further pair freed in 1871 disappeared, and there are no Chestnut-breasted Mannikins in New Zealand today.

Chestnut-breasted Mannikins may have become established in two places in Australia well outside their natural range.

On 23 September 1933, Dr. A. M. Morgan (1933) discovered a manniken nest containing four chicks at Hope Valley Reservoir in South Australia. Nothing more was heard of them until, in late autumn 1971, Eckert (1975) saw a small flock near Black Swamp in the same state, followed a year later by another (? the same) small group some 5 km away on the Endersby property at Finniss. In the same year, a dead juvenile was picked up, and on 28 May 1973, when a small party again visited the Endersby property, an immature male was collected. Whether the 1970s birds were descended from those found in 1933 or, as seems more likely, represent a later aviary escape is unknown, but Eckert believed that a small number were established and breeding in grasslands and the reedy margins of swamps in the Finniss–Black Swamp area. 'The Chestnut-breasted Finch [Mannikin]',

he wrote, 'has now occurred sufficiently in a feral state to justify inclusion on the South Australia list as an introduced species.'

Kolichis (1978) records that between 1973 and at least 1977 small flocks of Chestnut-breasted Mannikins (presumably escaped cagebirds) were observed in the Perth suburb of Osborne Park in Western Australia, where, however, they had apparently not yet bred.

NOTE

1 Guild 1938; Holyoak 1974a; Holyoak & Thibault 1984; King 1958; Long 1981; Peters 1968; Pizzey 1980; Thibault 1976; Thibault & Rives 1975; Townsend & Wetmore 1919.

Java Sparrow
(*Padda oryzivora*)

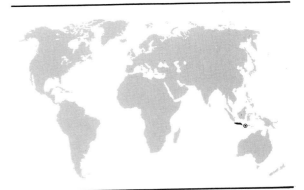

NATURAL DISTRIBUTION
Java and Bali.

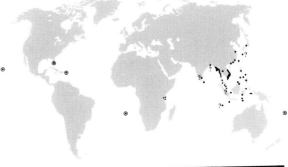

NATURALIZED DISTRIBUTION
Asia: China, Hong Kong, Taiwan, Japan, South Vietnam, West Malaysia (Malaya, Penang Island, Singapore), Thailand, Burma, ?India, Sri Lanka; Africa: East Africa (Tanzania, Zanzibar, Pemba Island), St Helena; North America: USA, West Indies (Puerto Rico); Australasia: East Malaysia (Borneo), Sumatra, Indonesia (Sulawesi, Moluccas, Lesser Sunda Islands), Philippines, Christmas Island, ?Cocos (Keeling) Islands; Oceania: Hawaiian Islands, Fiji.

ASIA

China[1]

Precisely when Java Sparrows, which in the Far East are usually known as Paddy Birds or Rice Birds[2], were first introduced as cagebirds[2] to China is unrecorded; since, however, they are known to have been transported from that country to Japan at least from the seventeenth century, their arrival in the former must have been at an early date. As a result of both deliberate releases and aviary escapes they have for long been naturalized in various parts of (mainly coastal) southern China. Swinhoe (1860) saw some at Amoy (Xiamen) in southern Fukien (Fujian) Province, and others were recorded in 1891 as far north as Shanghai in southern Kiangsu (Jiangsu) Province, and in 1892 in the south around Swatow (Shantou) in northern Kwangtung (Guangdong) Province. La Touche (1925–34) found Java Sparrows in scattered localities along the Kiangsu coast north of Shanghai, and in the south in Fukien, in Swatow, and further south in Kwangtung.

Hong Kong[3]

In Hong Kong, where they are still a favourite cagebird, Java Sparrows seem first to have been recorded by Swinhoe (1861). Nowadays, small numbers are seen in most years, but in 1975 a flock of around 150 was reported near Sek Kong.

Taiwan

According to Horikawa (1936), the people of Formosa (Taiwan) then had a practice (called *hojo*) of releasing Java Sparrows (and other small birds) as an offering to the dead; birds found in such places as the suburbs of T'ain-nan, Kaohsiung and the capital, T'ai-pei (Kuroda 1937), are probably the descendants of such liberations, reinforced by latter-day aviary escapes of this popular cagebird.

Japan[4]

During the period of the Tokugawa Shōgunate (1598–1867), Java Sparrows, imported from China, were widely kept in Japanese aviaries. Kuroda (1937) quotes a description of the species in the seventeenth-century *Honho Shokkan* ('Handbook of Japanese Foods'), and also says that the *Wakum Sho* ('Dictionary of the Japanese Language'), published in the following century, states that the birds were a recent arrival from overseas. Until at least the mid-1930s large

numbers continued to be imported from abroad by aviculturists, from whose aviaries many subsequently escaped.

In this century, a flock of 30–40 Java Sparrows was established in 1913 at Haneda, between Yokohama and Tokyo, and before 1937 a mass escape took place from crates in Yokohama docks after the arrival of a shipment from Shanghai. In the latter year, small flocks were reported on agricultural land at Minami Miyagi-cho, Adachiku, Tokyo, where they were said to be significant pests in paddy fields. Although Kaburaki (1934 and 1940) recorded that Java Sparrows were then widely distributed in Japan, Kuroda (1937) found that in many places local populations were of only short duration. Although according to Brazil (1985, and personal communication, 1985), Java Sparrows have been seen in southern Honshu in flocks of 200–300 (and perhaps also on Okinawa), breeding may not occur annually.

South Vietnam

In the mid- to late 1920s, Java Sparrows were established in the residential suburbs of Saigon (Ho Chi Minh City), large flocks were seen on the south coast in Nha Trang (Delacour & Jabouille 1927), and some were collected further south in Phan Rang (Delacour & Jabouille 1931). Today, according to Wildash (1968), Java Sparrows are widely distributed throughout the country, to which large numbers have been imported over the years as pets.

West Malaysia (Malaya, Penang Island and Singapore)[5]

Java Sparrows were imported from Java to Singapore Island in the 1840s after the annexation of the latter in 1819 by Sir Stamford Raffles on behalf of the British East India Company. They were certainly established in the wild there before 1879 when they were recorded by Kelham (1881); Ward (1968) believed that from around 1850–1950 they were fairly common (being described as the commonest bird on the island in the 1920s), but that thereafter they declined due to habitat loss.

In Malaya, Java Sparrows were probably

introduced to Kuala Lumpur before 1910, and perhaps at about the same time to Georgetown, the capital of Penang Island, and to Alor Star (or Alor Gajah). By the late 1930s they seem to have been established locally in several localities.

On both Singapore Island and in Kuala Lumpur the Java Sparrow is a mainly urban species, living sympatrically with the native Tree Sparrow (*Passer montanus*). Before the Second World War it thrived on a diet of rice and grain intended for domestic fowl, but declined after the invasion of the Japanese, when rice and other foodstuffs were in short supply. After the cessation of hostilities it seems to have staged something of a recovery – especially on farmland and in settled areas – but is now seen only occasionally, although sometimes in flocks 20–30 strong.[6] Whether the population is self-sustaining or depends for its survival on new recruitment is unknown.

Although frequently imported as pets, Java Sparrows have only ever enjoyed local success in the wild on the Malayan Peninsula. Medway & Wells (1976) recorded colonies in, from north to south and all on or near the west coast, Kangar (Perlis State), Alor Star (Kedah), Georgetown (Penang Island), Ipoh (Perak), Kuala Lumpur (Selangor), Seremban (Negri Sembilan), Malacca and on Singapore Island. They say that only in the northern states of Perlis and Kedah do Java Sparrows live and breed in open country, paddy fields, scrub and grassland, and that elsewhere they are found solely in settled areas, where the population is probably augmented by recurrent recruitment from escaped cagebirds. According to Keffer (1972b). Java Sparrows also occur in the Rhio archipelago (Kepulaun Riau) south of Singapore.

Thailand[7]

At some time before 1938, Java Sparrows were introduced to, and are still established around, the city of Bangkok in the central plains of Thailand.

Burma[8]

Java Sparrows occurred in the wild in Tenasserim and in Arakan Yoma (both in southern Burma) by the late nineteenth century and 1912, respectively. They are at present well established in both Tenasserim and in western Burma.

India[9]

Java Sparrows are known to have been established in the wild in India at Madras before 1910 and in Calcutta by 1931. Although populations seldom if ever become permanently established, a few small local ones, which rarely spread far, may still occur in various localities.

Sri Lanka[10]

Since before 1870, Java Sparrows have been established in the wild in the capital, Colombo, where they are constantly augmented by escaped cagebirds. A few other small colonies are found elsewhere in Sri Lanka where, as in India, they neither increase greatly nor spread.

AFRICA

East Africa (Tanzania, Zanzibar and Pemba Island)[11]

Vaughan (1932) quotes the English explorer, Sir Richard Burton in *Zanzibar: City, Island and Coast* (1872), as saying that Java Sparrows were landed on that island by a Captain Ward, the master of a whaling-ship out of Salem, Massachusetts, USA, around 1857. From there they crossed the 40-km wide Zanzibar Channel to the Tanzanian mainland probably in the 1930s (certainly before 1957), and the 50 km of open sea to Pemba Island to the north. They are now well established on Zanzibar Island, especially in Zanzibar town, and on Pemba are something of a pest in rice fields.

St Helena[12]

According to Melliss (1870), Java Sparrows were a recent introduction (as cagebirds) to St

Helena, where he reported them to be fairly common in the wild. They remained quite abundant until at least the 1930s, but by the early 1950s had apparently declined, probably because of reduction in the area of cultivated seed crops.

NORTH AMERICA

USA

According to Phillips (1928: 56), 'small numbers of Java Sparrows were liberated in Central Park, N.Y., by Joshua Jones in 1878' – apparently without success. Subsequently, the US Bureau of Biological Survey permitted the species' importation only on the strict understanding that none were to be released; as Phillips points out, however, as large numbers continued to be brought in, it is probable that from time to time some were freed or managed to escape.

Owre (1973) reported that Java Sparrows, which have for long been favoured by aviculturists in Miami, Florida, were first noted in the wild in northern Coral Gables as long ago as 1960. They are often to be found sharing the communal roosts of the alien House Sparrow (*Passer domesticus*), in which Owre saw some for the first time in 1966: between 1968 and 1969 the population at one such roost increased threefold from 50 to 150. By the early 1970s, Java Sparrows were established and breeding over an area of several square kilometres in both residential and downtown districts, where they seemed to suffer little if any competition from *domesticus*. More recently, Heilbrun (1976) reported the presence of Java Sparrows in Dade County. The situation in southern Florida has not altered greatly in the past decade.[13]

West Indies (Puerto Rico)

Blake (1975) lists the Java Sparrow as having been introduced to Puerto Rico in the West Indies. This is confirmed by Bond (1979), who says that the species is established in the capital San Juan. According to T. Silva (personal communication, 1985), it is common, especially around El Moro.

AUSTRALASIA

East Malaysia (Borneo)[14]

It seems probable that Java Sparrows have occurred in the wild in various parts of (mainly northern) Borneo since before about 1860. They are said to have been imported to Labuan Island off the coast of Sabah by the Governor, the Hon. Hugh Low, before 1889, when they were reported to be abundant in some places and to be damaging paddy fields, but not to have spread to the mainland. They are still common on Labuan, where they continue to plunder rice paddies in competition with such native Estrildidae as Dusky Mannikins (*Lonchura fuscans*), White-headed Mannikins (*L. leucogastra*) and Black-headed Mannikins (*L. malacca*). They are also found in smaller numbers on the coast at Tuaran and at Kinabalu – both in Sabah.

Sumatra

Long (1981), following Riley (1938), includes Sumatra in the Java Sparrow's natural range. Most authorities, however, seem agreed that it was originally restricted to the islands of Java and Bali from where it was introduced to (or perhaps colonized naturally) Sumatra (where its present distribution is uncertain) many years ago. Keffer (1972b) lists it as also present on Billiton (Belitung) Island off the south-east coast of Sumatra.

Indonesia (Sulawesi, Moluccas and Lesser Sunda Islands)[15]

On Sulawesi (Celebes), Java Sparrows seem first to have been noted in the wild in 1913 by Stresemann (1936), who confirmed their presence on the southern peninsula and on the eastern (seaward) end of the northern Minahassa Peninsula. They still apparently occur in Sulawesi in a few scattered localities.

According to King, Dickinson & Woodcock (1975), Java Sparrows have been introduced to, and still occur in, the Moluccas and Lesser Sunda Islands: in the latter, they are known to have been established in the wild on Lombok by at least 1933. Keffer (1972b) says they are also to be found on Kangean Island north of Lombok.

Philippines[16]

Java Sparrows have occurred in the wild in the Philippines since before 1933. By the mid-1940s they had become established around Manila on the island of Luzon, and have since colonized many other islands in the archipelago.

Christmas Island[17]

Java Sparrows are believed to have been first imported to Christmas Island in the Indian Ocean between about 1913 and 1923. By the 1940s they were fairly common in settlements along the north coast, and by the mid-1960s occurred in this area in flocks of up to 50. Over the years the population has been frequently supplemented by further cagebird escapes.

Cocos (Keeling) Islands

Gibson-Hill (1949a), quoting from J. Holman's *A Journey Round the World* (London, 1846: 382), says that Java Sparrows were apparently imported to the Cocos (Keeling) Islands before 1828. Wood-Jones (1909) reported them to be common there, and in 1941 Gibson-Hill found them abundant on Pulo Tikus (Direction) and in lesser numbers on Pulo Luar (Horsburgh) and Pulo Selma (Home) – the only three inhabited islands – where they probably supplemented their diet with grain put out for domestic fowl. According to Stokes, Sheils & Dunn (1984), they are since believed to have died out.

OCEANIA

Hawaiian Islands[18]

Caum (1933) states that Java Sparrows may have been introduced to Hawaii by Dr William Hillebrand in about 1865, and again around 1900 (Phillips (1928: 56) says 'at least 25 or 30 years ago, but apparently did not prosper'). Further shipments of this popular cagebird have been imported over the years, and the first bird in the wild was observed in the grounds of the Bernice P. Bishop Museum in Honolulu on Oahu in July 1964, followed by a further two at Fort Shafter

in August of the following year. Java Sparrows seem first to have bred successfully in the wild in late 1968 or early 1969 on the slopes of Diamond Head in eastern Honolulu, where some may have been deliberately released in 1967. 'The increase in numbers and the range expansion since that time', wrote Berger (1981: 212), 'have been phenomenal.' By 1972 the population had increased to more than 60, and within a further 2 years had spread into the upper Manoa Valley. In the following year, Java Sparrows were reported by the Hawaiian Audubon Society (1975) to have expanded their range from Kapiolani Park to Makiki and Kalihi. In 1976, when the population had risen to 231, Zeillemaker & Scott listed Java Sparrows as local and rare in dry lowland residential and community parklands on Oahu, where they are said to be noticeably susceptible to ornithosis or psittacosis. By 1984 they were believed to be still expanding their range rapidly on Oahu, and were gaining a foothold on Hawaii.

Fiji[19]

Watling (1982: 132) states that 'the Java Sparrow was first collected in Fiji by the artist-naturalist, William Belcher, in 1925. . . . [it] is restricted to south-east Viti Levu, the Savusavu area of Vanua Levu and several pockets in Taveuni. It is found only in [wet] agricultural and suburban habitats. . . . Within its restricted range, it is a common bird, but for some reason has been unable to spread further'.

In about 1750, Java Sparrows were introduced as cagebirds from Malaya to the island of Mauritius,[20] where they escaped and became established. Within some 15 years they had multiplied to such an extent that flocks of 200–300 were causing serious damage to grain crops. In 1771, a bounty was placed on their heads, and in 1804 it was suggested that sparrow-hawks (*Accipiter* sp.) be imported as a form of biological control. The killing of large numbers by farmers, a diminution of their food supply and, finally, the great cyclone of 1892, eventually succeeded in eradicating them from Mauritius.

According to Lydekker, Johnston & Ainsworth-Davis,[21] Java Sparrows were also introduced, presumably from Mauritius, to the island of Réunion, where they have since become extinct.

Mackworth-Praed & Grant (1955) include the Seychelles among the places to which Java Sparrows have been introduced.

Reichenow (1908), quoted by Benson (1960), saw Java Sparrows on the island of Mayotte in the Comoros archipelago in 1903 but not in 1906–7, when they had presumably died out.

Liversidge (n.d.) lists the Java Sparrow as an unsuccessful introduction to South Africa.

Java Sparrows, though whether in captivity or flying free is uncertain, are recorded by Balmford (1978) in the Melbourne Botanic Gardens in Victoria, Australia, in 1856. In 1863, 20, 35 and 200 were released by the Victoria Acclimatization Society at Ballarat, in the Botanic Gardens and in the Royal Park, respectively, leading the society to claim in its annual report of the following year (quoted by Rolls 1969), that 'the Java Sparrow . . . may now be considered thoroughly established'. The species has since died out in Australia.

According to Thomson (1922), the Nelson Acclimatization Society imported some Java Sparrows to New Zealand in 1862, and in 1867 the Auckland Society acquired half-a-dozen from a Captain Forsyth; what became of them is unknown.

NOTES

1 Cheng 1963, 1976; Kuroda 1937; La Touche 1925–34; Long 1981; McClure 1974; Riley, 1938; Swinhoe, 1860.

2 A striking aberration with pure white plumage occurs in captivity, and occasionally in the wild.

3 King, Dickinson & Woodcock 1975; Long 1981; Swinhoe 1861; Webster 1975.

4 Kaburaki 1934, 1940; Kuroda 1913, 1937; Long 1981; Ornithological Society of Japan 1974; Uchida 1937.

5 Bucknill & Chasen 1927; Delacour 1947; Gibson-Hill 1949a; Glenister 1951; Kelham 1881; Kuroda 1933–6; Long 1981; Madoc 1956; Medway & Wells 1976; McClure 1974; Oxley, 1849; Ridley 1898; Riley 1938.

6 C. J. Hails, personal communication, 1985.

7 Deignan 1963; King, Dickinson & Woodcock 1975; Lekagul & Cronin 1974; Long 1981; Riley 1938.

8 Hopwood (1912); King, Dickinson & Woodcock 1975; Kuroda 1933–6; Long 1981; Smythies 1953. See also: Blandford 1890: 182; R. Lydekker, H. Johnston & J. R. Ainsworth-Davis, *Harmsworth Natural History* (Harmsworth: London, 1910), 2: 980.

9 Ali & Ripley 1968–74; Kuroda 1937; Law 1932; Long 1981; Ripley 1961; Wait 1931. See also: Lydekker, Johnston & Ainsworth-Davis (note 8 above).

10 Henry 1955; King, Dickinson & Woodcock 1975; Long 1981; Phillips, 1966.

11 Long 1981; Mackworth-Praed & Grant 1957–60; Pakenham 1936, 1939, 1943, 1945, 1959; Riley 1938; Vaughan, 1930, 1932. See also: Lydekker, Johnston & Ainsworth-Davis (note 8 above).

12 Haydock 1954; Long 1981; Mackworth-Praed & Grant 1960; Melliss 1870; Riley 1938.

13 O. T. Owre, personal communication, 1981.

14 Gore 1968; Long 1981; Sharpe 1889; Smythies 1960.

15 King, Dickinson & Woodcock 1975; Kuroda 1933–6, 1937; Long 1981; Stresemann, 1936.

16 Delacour 1947; Delacour & Mayr 1946; Du Pont 1971; Kuroda 1933–6; Long 1981; Riley 1938.

17 Chasen 1933; Gibson-Hill 1947; Long, 1981; van Tets & van Tets 1967; Watson, Zusi & Storer 1963.

18 American Ornithologists' Union 1983; Berger 1975a, 1981; Blake 1975; Bryan 1958; Caum 1933; Hawaiian Audubon Society 1975; Long 1981; Phillips 1928; Pyle 1976, 1977; Throp 1969; Zeillemaker & Scott 1976. See also: R. L. Pyle, *American Birds* 38: 431 (1984).

19 See also: Gorman 1975; Holyoak 1979; Long 1981; Mercer 1966; Parham, 1954; Pernetta & Watling 1978; Turbet 1941.

20 Benedict 1957; Decary 1962; Long 1981; Meinertzhagen 1912; Rountree, Guérin et al. 1952. (Both Decary and Meinertzhagen quote from Le Gentil (1781).) See also: Lydekker, Johnston & Ainsworth-Davis (note 8 above).

21 See note 8.

House Sparrow
(*Passer domesticus*)

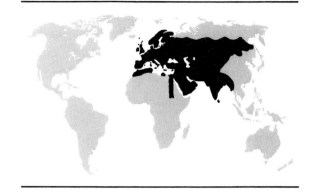

NATURAL DISTRIBUTION
The Palaearctic Region from the British Isles eastwards to the Amur Oblast in the eastern USSR, northwards in Europe to northern Scandinavia and to south of the Arctic Circle in the USSR, south to southern Europe, north-west Africa, Egypt, Sudan, Arabia, India, Bangladesh and southern Burma. The species has considerably extended its range eastwards naturally in the past 200 years (formerly it occurred in Eurasia only as far north as central Scandinavia, east to the Caspian and Aral seas, in the Near East, India and Burma), but is still absent from Vietnam and Indo-China and from most of China and Mongolia.

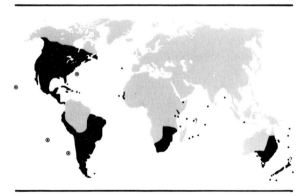

Note: Distribution, especially in southern Africa and South America, is discontinuous.

NATURALIZED DISTRIBUTION
Europe: Azores; Asia: Java, ?Maldive Islands, Andaman Islands; Africa: South Africa, [Botswana, Namibia, Zimbabwe, Zambia, Malawi, Zaire], Mozambique, Senegal, [Mauretania, The Gambia], Tanzania (including Zanzibar), Kenya,

?Somalia, Cape Verde Islands, Comoros, ?Seychelles, Amirante Islands, Mascarenes (Réunion, Mauritius, Rodrigues); North America: USA, Canada, [Mexico, Guatemala, El Salvador, Costa Rica, ?Belize, ?Honduras, ?Nicaragua, Panama], Bermuda, West Indies (Cuba, ?Jamaica, ?St Thomas, [Puerto Rico, Hispaniola], Bahamas); South America: Argentina, [Uruguay], Brazil, Chile, Peru, [Paraguay, Ecuador, ?Colombia, ?Venezuela, Bolivia, Falkland Islands, Juan Fernández Islands]; Australasia; Australia, New Zealand, [Norfolk Island]; Oceania: Hawaiian Islands, New Caledonia, ?Vanuatu, Easter Island, Chagos Archipelago.

Note. Countries that have been colonized by natural extension of range of naturalized populations are enclosed within square brackets.

EUROPE

Azores

According to Agostinho (1963), 'some tens of sparrows, brought from Portugal, were set free at Lajes Airport on Terceira in 1960'. By 1982, the entire island had been colonized, and since then the birds have spread to all the other inhabited islands except Santa Maria and Corvo. House Sparrows were, according to Le Grand (1983, and personal communication to J. D. Summers-Smith), established and breeding on Graciosa, São Jorge, Pico, and Faial by 1970; they arrived on São Miguel in 1972 or 1973, and on Flores a decade later. Summers-Smith (in preparation) estimates the breeding population in the archipelago in 1984 at between 50,000 and 60,000.

ASIA

Java

According to Summers-Smith (1963), quoting Meinertzhagen (1958), the House Sparrow was introduced to Java after 1885, where it seems to have become established in some settled areas.

Maldive Islands

According to Ash (1984b), the House Sparrow in the Maldives 'is a recent immigrant which is now established on one island (Malé) and is a potential pest if it should spread to other islands on which millet is grown'. Whether it occurs on Malé as a natural or shipborne immigrant is uncertain.

Andaman Islands

According to Abdulali (1964), Mr O. H. Brookes imported about six House Sparrows to Ross Island in the South Andamans in 1882, followed by 20 more in 1895. They probably came on the mail steamer from Rangoon in Burma, in which case they would have been of the subspecies *indicus*. Abdulali reported them to be quite common at Port Blair on the South Andaman mainland, and to occur also at Choldhari.

AFRICA

South Africa[1]

Two forms of the House Sparrow have been imported to South Africa, and various dates have been suggested for their introduction. Summers-Smith (1963), in his definitive monograph on the species, says that in about 1890 birds of the nominate form (Europe and northern Asia) were released at East London in the Eastern Cape and others of the form *P. d. indicus* (southern Afghanistan, Pakistan, India, Bangladesh and Burma) at Durban in Natal. Mackworth-Praed & Grant (1963), on the other hand, say that *indicus* was first liberated in 1893 and again in 1897, and that the nominate form, imported from Surrey, England, in 1914, was planted at East London. Clancey (1963) indicated that the birds released at Durban were probably imported in the late nineteenth century by immigrants from India, and suggested (to Harwin & Irwin 1966) that the East London population arose from released cagebirds translocated from Durban; this, as Harwin & Irwin point out, is unlikely, in view of the certainty that the original stock at East London was of the nominate form.

Winterbottom (1965) says that the introduction at East London took place in 1927 (but told Harwin & Irwin that it was in 1907), and (1966) that an attempted introduction at Cape Town by Cecil Rhodes in 1902 (the date also given by Gebhardt 1959) was 'frustrated' – presumably by the statesman's death on 26 March of that year. Siegfried (1962) claims that the House Sparrow was introduced at Durban in about 1900 and at East London in 1927, and, finally, Courtenay-Latimer (1942 and 1955) states that the East London release was not made until 1930.

'The extension of range [of the House Sparrow in South Africa], wrote Summers-Smith (1963: 186), 'has been less spectacular than in other parts where it has been liberated.' The *domesticus* birds at East London, which seem to have been almost or even entirely sedentary, interbred with *indicus*, which dispersed and/or was translocated from Durban, to produce offspring with dual characteristics; these were subsequently superseded by others with the appearance of the normally more-dominant *indicus*. It is thus, as Harwin & Irwin point out, birds of the latter form that have colonized the region. 'From Durban', Summers-Smith continues, 'the House Sparrow has spread over all Natal and into Transvaal and Orange Free State; from East London a spread has taken place along the coastal regions of Cape Province joining up in the north with the birds from Durban.' This expansion was at first gradual and steady rather than dramatic – it took about half a century, for example, for the whole of Natal to become occupied.

To quote Summers–Smith again (p. 188): 'When it is considered how sedentary the House Sparrow is in most parts of its range it is not surprising that the dispersal is rather variable. This is particularly the case when the suitable habitats are separated by even quite short distances of unsuitable country.' Indeed, the species' acquired ability in southern Africa to disperse for a considerable way over ecologically inimical terrain to establish populations in new localities has, perhaps, been the most important element in its colonization of the region. Another factor has been the difference in the density of the human population (on which the species is largely dependant) between the southern African region and that pertaining in most of its natural range, where even today its distribution is some-

what patchy; again, the bird's adaptability – through a gradual modification of the original genotype – has enabled it to become eventually a successful colonist. Yet another possible factor, referred to by Harwin & Irwin (1966), has been its readiness to associate with such nomadic natives as the Red-billed Quelea (*Quelea quelea*). A possible inhibiting element, on the other hand, in the early years of the House Sparrow's expansion, may have been interspecific competition with the indigenous Cape Sparrow (*Passer m. melanurus*) and possibly with the Grey-headed Sparrow (*P. griseus stygiceps*).

In the northern Cape Province, the Transvaal and elsewhere, the major dispersal that led to the colonization of Botswana, Mozambique, Zimbabwe (where some are said to have been released in Salisbury (Harare) in 1957) and Zambia (see below) appears to have begun in the late 1940s or early 1950s. As previously mentioned, it was not until some 50 years after its introduction that the House Sparrow colonized Natal from its point of release in Durban. In 1949, it crossed the Drakensberg Mountains to Bethlehem, 930 km to the north-west, by 1953 had spread over the whole of the Orange Free State and the central and southern Transvaal, and in 1954 appeared at Mankaiana in Swaziland. By 1965, House Sparrows had increased their range explosively 1,600 km or more south-west to the Cape Peninsula, north-west to Great Namaqualand, and north into Zambia. Some early records for individual localities in South Africa up to 1964 are listed in Table 12.

Today, according to Winterbottom (1978: 975), the House Sparrow 'has spread virtually throughout the Republic of South Africa', including, according to Liversidge (n.d.), 'even into desert situations where humans and houses provide protection, food and nesting sites'. J. Vincent (personal communication, 1981) says that the species is 'now very widespread throughout southern Africa . . . It is a commensal of man, and extremely common in urban areas and on farms. . . . The main ecological effect of the species has been to oust the local species, *Passer melanurus*, from much of its former habitat, particularly from the urban areas and from farms. It is also fairly aggressive and tends to discourage some of the other indigenous birds, particularly where it is very common.' Winterbottom

Table 12 Records of House Sparrows (*Passer domesticus*) in South Africa up to 1964

Date	Locality	Province
By 1950	Fort Beaufort, King William's Town and Butterworth	Cape Province (from Durban)
*c.*1950	Pretoria, Vanderbijl Park and Vereeniging	Transvaal
1951	Richard's Bay	Natal
1950s	Southern Zululand	Natal
1954–62	Johannesburg (outer suburbs to city centre)	Transvaal
1952 (April)	Nylstroom	Transvaal
1953	Northam	Transvaal
1953 (December)	Waterval-Boven	Transvaal
1956 (or before)	Mafeking	Transvaal
1957 (July)	Skukuza, Kruger National Park	Transvaal
1959 (September)	Letaba	Transvaal
1959	Springfontein, Bloemfontein and Kroonstad	Orange Free State
1961 (May)	Shingwedsi	Transvaal
1962	Port Nolloth, Olifantshoek and Kuruman	Cape Province
1964	Cape Town	Cape Province

Sources: see note 1

(personal communication, 1981), on the other hand, says that 'The Sparrow has been accused of ousting our indigenous *P. melanurus* in farms and villages but the evidence is contradictory and inconclusive'.

Following their introduction to South Africa in the late nineteenth century, House Sparrows have been extending their range naturally northwards during the last hundred years. 'The first major movement that was to lead to the colonization of Bechuanaland [Botswana], Moçambique [see below], Rhodesia [Zimbabwe] and Zambia', wrote Harwin & Irwin (1966: 6, from whom much of the following information is derived), 'seems to have taken place in the early 1950s or possibly even somewhat earlier.'

In Botswana, House Sparrows were established at Lobatsi and Ramah by 1956, at Molepolole, Palapye, Mahalapye, Francistown and Pitsani in 1958, at Gaberones by January 1960, on the Botswana side of the Tuli Circle in 1963, and at Lothlekane and Rakops in November of the following year (Cole 1962; Markus 1958; Vernon 1962). According to Harwin & Irwin (p. 7), 'One of the major dispersal routes would appear to have been centred along the line of rail in eastern Bechuanaland . . . the unevenness of the spread indicates the probability of westerly dispersal [also] from the adjacent Transvaal.'

'Three main routes of invasion appear to have been involved in the colonization of Rhodesia', wrote Harwin & Irwin (p. 8): 'Through the northern Transvaal via Louis Trichardt and Messina to Beit Bridge, on the Limpopo; through eastern Bechuanaland through the Sul do Save [Mozambique] to Malvernia on the Rhodesian border and probably sporadically through the eastern Transvaal.' The exact date of the species' natural arrival in the country has never been ascertained, but the release of some by aviculturists seems to have played little part in its subsequent establishment. The following dates give some indication of the House Sparrow's spread in Zimbabwe: Bulawayo by 1956 or earlier; Harare in 1957 (when some are said to have been deliberately released but from where they spread only slowly); Beit Bridge, Nyamandhlovu and Gwelo (1959); Plumtree (1960); Essexvale, Somabula, Que Que, Loretto Mission, Silobela and Karoi in northwestern Mashonaland (1961); Woolandale, Gwanda, Lupane on the main Victoria Falls road, Dett, Main Camp, Wankie National Park, Bannockburn on the Gwelo/Lourenço Marques (Maputo) railway, Gutu, Selukwe, Beatrice and Marandellas (1962); Bembesi, Filabusi, Fort Victoria, Triangle, Sinoia, Banket, near Mtoroshanga in the Umvukwes, Headlands, Rusape, Mayo Police Camp and Umtali (1963); Umniati, Fort Rixon, Nkai, Tjolotjo, near Concession and Seki, Binga on the south shore of Lake Kariba and Sentinel Ranch on the Limpopo (1964). In 1965, House Sparrows first appeared at Kezi in Matabeleland, Belingwe, Manyoli Ranch, West Nicholson, Gatooma, Enkeldoorn, Shabani, Sipolilo in northern Mashonaland (where they may have occurred since 1963), Inyanga Village, east of Umtali at the Forbes border post, Odzi, Birchenough Bridge in the Sabi Valley, Chipinga and Hippo Valley. 'By the end of 1965', wrote Harwin & Irwin (p. 10), 'the House Sparrow was found throughout Rhodesia, even if still only patchily distributed.'

Sparrows first crossed the Zambesi from Zimbabwe into Zambia in February or March 1965, when some appeared at Livingstone in the Libuyu and Maramba townships. In October, a pair was seen at Kalomo, and a month later others began frequenting the grounds of the Victoria Hotel in Lusaka. In December 1966, a pair was present for a short time at Ngoma in Kafue National Park, and in the same month others appeared at Ndola in the Copperbelt, where 30 were seen the following year, when some were also reported at Kitwe. House Sparrows were first seen in the south of the Eastern Province in 1971 – possibly the result of a spread northwards in neighbouring Malawi rather than from the west via the Luangwa Valley. A year later some were observed in the Northern Province at Mbala, only 23 km from the Tanzanian border. Harwin & Irwin believed that colonization of Zambia is as likely to have been via the Zambezi Valley as along railway lines, and that in urban environments competition with the indigenous Grey-headed Sparrow is inevitable.

From Zambia (or northern Mozambique), House Sparrows crossed the border into Malawi, where they were first seen at Chileka in mid-1967, at Blantyre by 1968, and at Chikwawa and Balaka in 1969. After an apparent spread northwards, they reached Dedza in 1970, Lilongwe (1971), Namitete (1973) and Bana (1974). By 1975, they were still uncommon in Zomba but very abundant in Lilongwe, where they have steadily increased since 1972, when the establishment of the capital was followed by an extensive building programme (Benson & Benson 1977). From Malawi, House Sparrows have crossed the border in the extreme south of Zaire.

In South West Africa (Namibia), Uys (1962) records that House Sparrows first appeared in the previous year at Grunan. According to Winterbottom (1971), they had reached Swakopmund, Gobabeb, Etemba and Gobabis by 1968, and by May of the following year had arrived at Heliordor near Otavi and were continuing their northward expansion. These birds presumably represent a northerly extension of range from the Western Cape Province of South Africa.

Mozambique[2]

According to Da Rosa Pinto (1959), House Sparrows of the nominate subspecies were introduced to Lourenço Marques (Maputo) in southern Mozambique by a Portuguese immigrant in late 1955, where they spread rapidly until 4 years later they were 'found throughout the squares and gardens of the city'. Da Rosa Pinto added that House Sparrows had also become widely established in the Sul do Save; these, Harwin & Irwin considered, were probably *indicus* birds, which as early as 1951 were established at Richard's Bay, 160 km north of Durban, by 1954 had spread into Swaziland, and would probably have crossed the border into southern Mozambique at about the time that *domesticus* was introduced to Maputo. An alternative source for the colonization of the Sol do Save could have been the Kruger National Park in the northeastern Transvaal, which was colonized between 1957 and 1961. By September 1960, House Sparrows had reached Malvernia on the border with Zimbabwe, nearly 450 km north of Maputo, where they were widely distributed and breeding in considerable numbers along the railway line.

In northern Mozambique, *indicus* birds were established in Tete before April 1967, where they had probably arrived from Salisbury (Harare) in northeastern Zimbabwe – a distance of some 200 km.

Senegal; Mauretania; The Gambia

Ndao (1980) records the arrival of House Sparrows (presumably as shipborne stowaways) in Dakar, Senegal, around 1970. Since then they have spread 100 km inland up the Sénégal River to Podor, as well as to Kaolack and Diourbel, and northwards as far as Nouakchott on the coast of Mauretania, and south to Banjul, The Gambia. So far, according to M.Y. Morel (personal communication to J. D. Summers-Smith), the birds are confined to European-style towns.

Tanzania and Kenya[3]

The status of the House Sparrow in Tanzania and Kenya is uncertain. On Zanzibar Island (Tanzania) in 1929 it was, according to Vaughan (1930), restricted to the capital, and this is confirmed by Pakenham (1943). From Zanzibar, some later crossed the Zanzibar Channel (probably by ship) to Dar-es-Salaam on the Tanzanian mainland. Summers-Smith (1963: 186) says that '*indicus* birds were introduced from Bombay to Zanzibar about 1900 and are still confined to the city', while Williams & Arlott (1982: 383) state that 'The Indian race of the House Sparrow . . . is an introduced species recorded from Mombasa, Kenya and Zanzibar. Present status unknown but no recent records'. Away from the Tanzanian coast, House Sparrows from Zambia have crossed the border into the extreme south of Tanzania.

In Mombasa, House Sparrows have been reported from time to time since at least 1950. In 1978, Summers-Smith (in preparation) saw a single female there, and records that P. L. Britton found a pair in April of the following year. Ash & Colston (1981) recorded the discovery of a small colony near the railway station, which they considered was the result of a new introduction, rather than the descendants of previous importations. In May, 1981, a small group of 25–30 was seen at the Old Terminal of Mombasa Airport; by the following October the birds had increased and spread to Moi Avenue and the grounds of the Manor Hotel, and by December to Mombasa Hospital. Since then, House Sparrows have spread inland along the Mombasa/Nairobi road, and by 1984 were within 150 km of the capital (M.-Y. Morel, personal communication to J. D. Summers-Smith).

Somalia[4]

According to Mackworth-Praed & Grant (1960), House Sparrows of the north-east African race, *P. d. niloticus*, occur at Berbera on the Gulf of Aden coast of the Somali Republic, where they were 'probably introduced'. In December 1981, a male and two females (of the form *indicus*) appeared in Mogadishu (Muqdisho) (Ash & Miskell 1983). The origin and fate of these birds are unknown. In 1980, a *Passer domesticus* × Somali Sparrow (*P. castanopterus*) hybrid was seen at Hal Hambo, 31 km south-west of Mogadishu Ash & Colston (1981) believed that this was a result of a mating of the native species with a shipborne *domesticus*.

Cape Verde Islands

Bannerman & Bannerman (1968) say that House Sparrows were presumably imported to the Cape Verde Islands sometime before 1924, when a dozen were collected on São Vincente. Bourne (1966) suggested that they may have arrived accidentally in cargo vessels from Europe between 1922 and 1924. In 1965, they were common in central Mindelo and the Porto Grande on São Vincente, but seemed to occur on no other islands in the group. Summers-Smith (1984) found them still present when he visited São Vincente in 1983, but they were restricted to the town and impoverished farmland to the south. On São Vincente, House Sparrows have hybridized with Spanish Sparrows (*P. hispaniolensis*), which arrived, presumably naturally, around 1951. The latter seem now to have died out.

Comoros

In the Comoros archipelago, House Sparrows were first recorded on Grande Comore in 1879, in settled areas of Mohéli in 1903 (Grote 1926), and on the islet of Pamanzi off Mayotte in 1943 where, according to Summers-Smith (1963), they were introduced by occupying troops. The form (or forms) established seems to be in some doubt; Benson (1960) says it is *arboreus* (= *rufidorsalis*); Peters (1962) that both *indicus* and *rufidorsalis* (from along the upper Nile in the Sudan) have been introduced; Mackworth-Praed & Grant (1963) that *indicus* and *arboreus* are present; Watson, Zusi & Storer (1963) that the race is *arboreus*; and Summers-Smith (1963: 185) that 'These birds . . . have been identified as belonging to the subspecies *rufidorsalis*'. Watson et al. indicate that House Sparrows are common on Grande Comore, in settled areas on Mohéli and on Pamanzi. Summers-Smith says that on the latter 'they still occupy only one village. They are said to have been introduced to Anjouan but must have died out . . . The distribution on the two islands where they have been for some time is interesting: . . . on Mohéli they are present in every village, while on the Grand Comoro they are found in only one; C. W. Benson . . . could not detect any difference between the islands to account for this.'

Seychelles

House Sparrows seem to have been first noted in the Seychelles in 1965 when Penny (1974) saw a flock of about 20 behind the post office in Port Victoria on Mahé. According to Gaymer, Blackman et al. (1969), the subspecies may have been *arboreus* (= *rufidorsalis*). J. D. Summers-Smith (personal communication, 1985) searched for them unsuccessfully in Victoria in 1974.

Amirante Islands

According to Gaymer, Blackman et al. (1969), the House Sparrow was then established and common on the islands of Alphonse and D'Arros in the Amirantes. Penny (1974: 110–11) says that 'presumably it was introduced from Africa, probably by accident in a shipload of rice. It occurs and breeds on Desroches, Resource, St Joseph, D'Arros and probably other islands in the Amirantes'. In 1976, C. J. Feare (personal communication, 1986) found House Sparrows breeding on Desroches, mainly around the settlement.

Réunion, Mauritius and Rodrigues[5]

According to Summers-Smith (1963), House Sparrows of the Indian race have been present on the island of Réunion since 1845. Coquerel,[6] quoted by Staub (1976: 73), claims they were imported from France. Rountree, Guérin et al. (1952) say that the same form was imported to Mauritius (presumably from Réunion) between about 1859 and 1867, and Summers-Smith says that it has certainly been there since 1885. According to Meinertzhagen (1912: 89), 'the story goes that a British soldier brought a single pair [of *domesticus*] out from home with him as a souvenir of the old country, but that he died at Port Louis [Mauritius], and on his dying request the birds were liberated'. The newspaper *Le Cernéen* for January 1926 (quoted by Staub) states, on the other hand, that the birds came from India. Although the form on Mauritius is known to be *indicus*, Meinertzhagen's account could well have some foundation, since in South Africa (see above) the genes of *domesticus* were swamped by those of the apparently more dominant Indian race. In about 1930, the House

Sparrow was also introduced to the island of Rodrigues where, as on Réunion and Mauritius, it is common and ubiquitous.

NORTH AMERICA

USA and Canada[7]

House Sparrows were first introduced to the United States (where they are frequently known as English Sparrows) by Nicolas Pike, Director of the Brooklyn Institute of New York, in the hope, according to Barrows (1889: 294), that 'they would control a palgue of "the hanging worm" or measuring worm'[8] (*Eunomos subsignarius*) that was defoliating trees. According to Pike, quoted by Laycock (1970: 68–9):

It was not till [the autumn of] 1850 that the first eight pairs were brought from England to the Brooklyn Institute. . . . early in the spring of 1851 they were liberated, but they did not thrive. I went to England in 1852 . . . on my arrival in Liverpool I gave the order for a large lot of Sparrows and song birds to be purchased at once. They were shipped on board the steam-ship *Europa*, if I am not mistaken . . . Fifty Sparrows were let loose in the Narrows [between Staten Island and Brooklyn], according to instructions, and the rest on arrival were placed in the tower of Greenwood Cemetery chapel . . . In the spring of 1853 they were all let loose in the grounds of Greenwood Cemetery, and a man hired to watch them. They did well and multiplied.

Until at least well into the 1880s large numbers of House Sparrows (some 1,600 of which were importations from Europe, and were therefore of the nominate subspecies) were released in more than 100 urban centres in 39 states and 4 Canadian provinces in parcels of between 5 and 1,000 birds. 'In many of the cases', wrote Barrows (1889), 'it is positively known that the sparrows were brought to this country from the Old World [at least 19 shipments of several hundred each], and mainly, if not entirely, from Great Britain and Germany. But no sooner had they become fairly numerous . . . than people began to take them to other places, sometimes in large numbers, but more often only a few pairs at a time.'

Table 13 gives details of those introductions of House Sparrows to North America that are known to have been made with stock imported

Table 13 Introduction of House Sparrows (*Passer domesticus*) of European stock to North America, 1851–81

Date	Number	Locality	State/Province	Remarks
1851	8 pairs	Brooklyn	New York	By Nicolas Pike
1852	50 (? pairs)	The Narrows	New York	By Nicolas Pike
1853	?	Greenwood Cemetery, Brooklyn	New York	By Nicolas Pike
1854	?	Portland	Maine	By Colonel William Rhodes of Quebec, Canada
1858	?	Portland	Maine	By Thomas Amory Deblois
1858	?	Peace Dale	Rhode Island	By Jos. Peace Hazard; from Liverpool, England; some escaped when landed at Boston, Massachusetts; failed
1858	?	Boston	Massachusetts	Accidental escape of birds *en route* to Rhode Island
1860	12	Madison Square	New York	By Eugene Schieffelin,* to kill caterpillars infesting the square's trees
1864	?	Central Park	New York	
1864, 1865 or 1866	?	Montreal and Quebec	Quebec	
1865–9	c.100	Rochester	New York	
1866	200	Union Park	New York	
1867	40 pairs	New Haven	Connecticut	
1867	?	Galveston	Texas	By European immigrants
1868–9	20+	Boston Common	Massachusetts	
1868 or 1869	1,000	Philadelphia	Pennsylvania	Released 'by the civic authorities'; largest single planting in North America
1869	20	Charleston	Massachusetts	
1869	20 pairs	Cleveland and Cincinnati	Ohio	
1873 or 1874	30	Salt Lake City	Utah	By European (? German) immigrants
1874	6 pairs	Strathroy	Ontario	By L. H. Smith, at a cost of $1 each; by October 1886 'in thousands' in Strathroy and 'plentiful in every town, city and village in this part of Ontario'†
1875	?	Fort Howard, Green Bay, and Sheboygan (6)	Wisconsin	
1875	?	Akron	Ohio	
c.1875	?	Halifax	Nova Scotia	
1881	?	?	New Brunswick	
1881	5	Iowa. City	Iowa	

Sources: Barrows 1889; Phillips 1928

* Schieffelin, the founder and first president of the American Acclimatizaton Society and of the Friends of Shakespeare Movement, was an eccentric drug manufacturer who conceived the whimsical notion of introducing to North America all the birds mentioned by Shakespeare

† Barrows 1889

direct from Europe. Apart from the early plant-ings, the spread of House Sparrows from the points of release averaged some 40 km in the first 5 years, 80 km after 10 years and over 160 km after 15 years – a remarkable rate of expansion. That this rapid extension of range was at least in part triggered by the species' equally extraordi-nary increase in numbers is suggested by the following extract from the *Topeka* (Kansas) *Journal* of about 1890:

In 1864, F. W. Giles conceived the idea of importing some of these birds. He shipped in all 28 of them. They were confined in cages at his place in Topeka until all but 5 had died. At last the 5 were turned loose. . . . the following fall there were 12 birds. The second season found 60, the third summer about 3,000 [*sic*!]. Then they increased so fast that no account could be kept, and in the twenty-five years which followed they spread all over the west.

Doughty (1978) has traced in some detail the establishment and spread of the House Sparrow in North America. The vast growth of urban-ization and the human population in the second half of the nineteenth and early twentieth centuries was of material assistance to the highly commensal Sparrow. In the 50 years between 1860 and 1910 the overall population increased from 31 to 92 million and the urban population from 6 to 42 million. Thus the percentage of city dwellers during the period rose from 19.3 per cent to 45.6 per cent. The rate of urbanization rose sharply after 1850 from 4 per cent in the decade 1860–70 to 7 per cent between 1880 and 1890, and there was at the same time a corre-sponding growth in the size of cities and towns – first of the established ports and townships of the Atlantic seaboard and then of the newer ones of the Midwestern States. The construction of urban parks and gardens, and the preponderance of horse-drawn transport which ensured a continual source of food for Sparrows (especially in winter) through grain spilled from nosebags and droppings, also greatly helped Sparrows to become established.

Most Sparrow introductions in the United States occurred in the decade after 1864, and urban colonies established in such cities as Brooklyn, New York, Boston and Philadelphia became the source of supply both for trans-locations by man to other states and, as urban habitats became overcrowded, for the natural expansion of the species into rural districts.

From the early releases in the 1850s in New York, Maine, Rhode Island and Massachusetts Sparrows spread westwards throughout those states, and by the following decade had reached the six central mid-western states in the Mississippi drainage system and Texas and South Carolina. Colonization of the four north-central states, of a further six in the south, of three between the Mississippi River and the Rocky Mountains, and of California occurred – as the result of releases and/or natural expansion – during the next decade. By 1870, Sparrows had gained a toehold in some 20 states, in the District of Columbia, and in one (or perhaps two) Canadian provinces, stretching as far south as Columbia, South Carolina, Louisville, Kentucky and Galveston, Texas, west to St Louis, Missouri, and Davenport, Iowa, and north to Montreal in Canada. By the middle 1880s, they were established in some 35 states and 5 terri-tories,[9] including nearly all the region east of the Mississippi River (except for parts of Florida, Alabama and Mississippi), as well as portions of eight western states. Sparrows thus occurred in North America from southern New Brunswick south to southern Georgia, central Alabama and Mississippi, west to eastern Arkansas, Kansas and Nebraska, north-central Iowa and southeastern Minnesota, and north to northern Wisconsin, upper Michigan, Ontario and Quebec. Extensive and flourishing populations were also established around New Orleans, Louisiana, Salt Lake Valley, Utah, the San Francisco Bay region and the lower Sacramento and San Joaquin River valleys in California. 'Forty years after its intro-duction', wrote Wing (1943), who said that the species spread fastest in the 25–30 years after its first introduction (and estimated the total early 1940s population at not more than 150 million distributed over some 9.5 million km²), 'the Sparrow had completed its conquest of America.'

The widespread establishment of Sparrows came about, firstly, through their deliberate translocation for nostalgic reasons by European immigrants – for example, to Galveston, Texas in 1867, to San Francisco, California around 1871, and to Salt Lake City, Utah about 1873; secondly, through their habit, like that of their congener the Tree Sparrow (*P. montanus*), of riding the paddleboats that regularly plied the major river systems; and, thirdly, by natural dispersal along railway tracks and highways that formed arterial routes between urban communities, and on which the birds found plenty of food from the spillage from boxcars on freight trains and carts. They were further helped by the deliberate provision of extra food and of nesting boxes by man, the destruction of potential predators, and legal protection in the late 1880s in some 20 states.

'The marvellous rapidity of the Sparrow's multiplication', wrote Barrows (1889: 21–2), 'the surpassing swiftness of its extension, and the prodigious size of the area it has overspread are without parallel in the history of any bird. . . . We can never know how many separate introductions were made, nor how many thousands of individuals were introduced, but it is certain that the number of places thus supplied is much greater than has been supposed.'

Between 1870 and 1875, Sparrows were expanding their range at a rate of some 260 km² a year, and in the decade from the former year had extended their distribution by an additional 37,500–41,000 km² or more. Between 1880 and 1885, this had increased to a staggering 260,000 km² a year – a total for the period of some 1.3 million km². By 1883, about a third of the United States had been overrun, and 3 years later it was estimated that Sparrows were established over nearly 2.6 million km² of North America, including more than 370,000 km² of Canada; in the following year, a further 1.25 million km² was occupied. Palmer (1899) reported that only three states (Montana, Nevada and Wyoming) and three territories (Alaska, Arizona and New Mexico) appeared to remain uninfested, and in Ohio, Illinois, Michigan and Utah Sparrows were officially declared a pest, and a bounty system was introduced.

In the great new urban conurbations the aggressive and commensal Sparrow held a distinct advantage over more retiring and peaceful natives (a common relationship between introduced adventives and indigines in a man-modified environment), to such an extent that the Federal bird census of 1916–20 showed the species to be the commonest breeding bird (8.7 per cent of the population) in north-central states.

By 1898, Sparrows had crossed the Great Plains to Colorado in the eastern foothills of the Rocky Mountains, and when Abbott (1903) described them as 'ubiquitous' in the United States, only small pockets (e.g. in central Nevada, southern California, parts of the southwest and the northern Rockies) remained uninfested, and even here Sparrows were established locally by 1915.

Between 1910 and 1930, there is evidence of a decline in the Sparrow population in eastern North America that paralleled a similar decline in the use of horse-drawn transportation and thus the supply of, especially, winter food from manure and spillage. The number of horses in Denver, Colorado, for example, according to Doughty, fell by some 33 per cent between 1907 and 1917, and that in New York City dropped below 100,000 by 1919 and continued to decline rapidly thereafter. As a corollary the number of motor cars rose from a mere 8,000 in 1900 to 458,377 by 1910.

Even without the benefit of hindsight it seems extraordinary, in view of the House Sparrow's known destructiveness in England where organizations to destroy it were in existence as early as 1744, that the species' deliberate introduction to North America could ever have been contemplated, let alone countenanced. Dr B. H. Warren, speaking before the Microscopical Society in West Chester, Pennsylvania in 1879 (quoted by Laycock 1970: 73), was one of the first to recognize the House Sparrow as a serious threat, when he begged his audience 'to lend their aid, and speedily too, that some means may be devised for the blotting out of this unlooked-for bane'. This sentiment was echoed by Barrows (1889) who wrote: 'It is only within the past year that we have come to realize something of the magnitude of the "craze" which led so many people to foster and distribute this serious pest.' This judgement was expanded by Palmer (1899: 98):

The damage which it does in destroying fruit and grain, in disfiguring buildings in cities and towns, and in driving away other birds, makes it one of the worst of feathered pests. The rapidity with which it increases in a new locality is scarcely more remarkable than the persistency and care which have been displayed in introducing it into foreign lands, in spite of the warnings of persons familiar with its habits. . . . The true character of the bird is now so well known that it is unnecessary to dwell on its injuries to fruit and grain, the nuisance it has become in large cities, and the extent to which it has replaced native birds. The ill-directed care and energy expended on introducing and fostering it thirty years ago are largely responsible for the marvelous rapidity of its distribution.

It was the strictures of Warren, Barrows, Palmer, and like-minded people that persuaded Congress in 1900 to pass the Lacey Act prohibiting the further importation of exotic fauna into the United States.

Research both before and after enactment of the Lacey Act revealed the extent to which House Sparrows had become a pest. They failed to destroy infestations of geometrid insects and, especially, the hairy larvae of the White-marked Tussock-moth (*Orgyia leucostigma*), and their aggressive behaviour may inhibit such native insectivores as Northern Mockingbirds (*Mimus polyglottos*), Robins (*Turdus migratorius*), Northern Orioles (*Icterus galbula*), Yellow-billed Cuckoos (*Coccyzus americanus*) and Black-billed Cuckoos (*C. erythropthalmus*). With some others – especially Purple Martins (*Progne subis*), Tree Swallows (*Tachycineta bicolor*), Cliff Swallows (*Petrochelidon pyrrhonota*), Eastern Bluebirds (*Sialia sialis*), House Wrens (*Troglodytes aedon*) and Purple Finches (*Carpodacus purpureus*) – they also compete for non-insect foods and nesting sites and whose eggs and nestlings they destroy. Altogether, the US Department of Agriculture has recorded harassment by House Sparrows of more than 70 native species.

House Sparrows also came increasingly to be regarded, through their consumption of, and damage to, stored and standing grain, estimated as amounting to some 2 kg per bird per year, as an economic threat to farmers. This was a potentially serious problem, since the area under grain had more than tripled from 21 million ha in the 1860s to over 74 million ha by the end of the century. Corn (maize) was the largest single crop, amounting to 12 million ha in 1866 and to some 38.5 million by 1900. The area planted with wheat and oats remained, respectively, about a half and a third that of corn; rye and buckwheat continued to account for between 607,000 and 809,000 ha and 405,000 ha, respectively, for most of the same period. Judd (1901) concluded that House Sparrows were 'undoubtedly a most destructive pest' of these and other crops, such as sorghum, barley and rice; of the buds and blooms of such fruits and vegetables as pears, plums, grapes, cherries, currants, apples, strawberries, raspberries, blackberries, tomatoes and peas; of commercially grown blossoms, which they deflower; and also that they were responsible for the spread among domestic poultry of cestode and nematode parasites that cause Newcastle disease and avian influenza. Inside and outside buildings, House Sparrows foul stored food, block gutters, downpipes and drains with nesting material, and damage brickwork with their droppings. The only benefit they confer by way of compensation is the destruction of large numbers of the introduced alfalfa weevil. It is little wonder that, as Skinner (1905) points out, when the ancient Egyptians invented the art of writing they chose the Sparrow as the hieroglyph denoting 'enemy'.

As the destruction of Sparrows began in the United States, they found a ready market in the restaurant trade where they were known euphemistically as 'reed-birds'; Laycock (1970) records that in 1887 House Sparrows were fetching $1 a hundred in Albany, New York.

Many of the arguments raised against Sparrows were, however, as Doughty (1978) points out, foolishly anthropomorphic in origin, contrasting, for example, 'brave, hardy and industrious New World citizens' with 'dirty over-sexed, quarrelsome and noisy immigrants'. Even so eminent an ornithologist and distinguished army surgeon as Elliott Coues could write (1878) of their mating behaviour: 'I am not a delicate woman, nor yet a squeamish man, to be shocked by their perpetual antics during the spring and summer; being something of an anatomist I can stand it without embarrassment; but all are not thus constituted' (!).[10]

Sparrows nevertheless managed to retain some protagonists – described disparagingly by Coues as 'old fogies', 'quasi-ornithologists' and 'silly people' – such as Dr Thomas M. Brewer, zoologist, friend and near-contemporary of Audubon, who claimed that by their consumption of injurious insects and the seeds of noxious plants House Sparrows, on balance, were more beneficial than detrimental.

Doughty suggests that the antagonism shown to Sparrows was a reaction to aliens by xenophobic natives displaying an excess of chauvinism at a time when human immigrants were flooding the United States in the late nineteenth and early twentieth centuries – for example, 10 million between 1860 and 1890 – when economic depression, high unemployment, urban industrial blight and social unrest were all blamed on immigrants who, like Sparrows, usually lived in urban centres. 'Problems of an evolving society', wrote Doughty, 'were translated as cultural differences as Americans lost confidence in the process of assimilation and opted for isolationism.'

Following the decimation of many species of birds through the demands of the millinery trade in the late nineteenth century, the Protection of Birds and their Nests and Eggs Act was enacted for all non-game species. Under Section 7, however, the House Sparrow was specifically excluded from this Act, which by 1902 had been adopted by 31 states, 4 Canadian provinces and the District of Columbia – most of which lay east of the Mississippi and north of the Ohio and Potomac rivers – of which 30 specified the Sparrow in their list of noxious species.

The carnage of the First World War induced absurd comparisons between the slaughter of men in Europe and that of House Sparrows in North America that are today difficult to comprehend. Neltje Blanchan,[11] quoted by Doughty, suggested that killing Sparrows might 'Prussianize our children [who] might just as well grow up in Berlin' (!). However, as Doughty says, 'It was certain that Sparrows had no redeeming qualities . . . the conflict in Europe and social and economic problems at home deserved more the public's attention than Sparrows did . . . the English Sparrow had become North America's most successful avian immigrant.'

In western Canada, House Sparrows are believed to have crossed the border into British Columbia, Alberta and Saskatchewan soon after their establishment in Washington, Montana and North Dakota towards the end of the nineteenth century. By the late 1930s, they had spread along the railroads north to the limits of cultivation. Summers-Smith (1963: 177–8) described the species' distribution in Canada as follows:

In the east, the Gaspé peninsula and the Magdalen Islands are occupied but on the north bank of the St Lawrence it is not found east of Baie Comeau and the bird does not breed on Newfoundland or Anticosti Island, though isolated birds have been recorded from the latter. It breeds regularly along the line of the railway from Quebec to Winnipeg with isolated occurrences further north, for example at Moose Factory and Churchill on Hudson Bay; to the west it has been reported breeding north to The Pas in Manitoba and across about the same latitude to Lac La Biche in Alberta, with isolated records from as far north as

Chipewyan, Alberta and Fort Smith and at 62° N on the Mackenzie River thirty miles [48 km] from Fort Simpson in North Western Territory. In the Rockies it occurs at Banff and Jasper Parks but on the west coast it does not extend much north of Vancouver and the southern part of Vancouver Island. So far it has not been recorded from Alaska, though it has pushed along the Alaskan highway from Dawson Creek to Fort Nelson.

Twenty years later, however, Summers-Smith (in preparation) was able to refer to the sighting in June 1981 of four or five birds at Anchorage Airport in Alaska,[12] but with no evidence yet of establishment or breeding.

A significant variation in size in individuals from geographically distinct areas led Johnston & Selander (1964) to conclude that the House Sparrow in North America is realizing an evolutionary potential by rapid morphological changes after establishment in new and environmentally different localities. The development of this most interesting phenomenon (which, incidentally, has probably been more closely studied in the case of the House Sparrow than in that of any other naturalized animal) is fully discussed by, among others, Packard 1967; Selander & Johnston 1967; Johnston & Selander 1971, 1973a,b; Johnston & Klitz 1977; and Hamilton & Johnston 1978. It has not, however, so far led to the description of any new races (Summers-Smith, in preparation).

Throughout North America, adult House Sparrows fall prey to Cooper's Hawks (*Accipiter cooperii*), Sharp-shinned Hawks (*A. striatus*), Red-shouldered Hawks (*Buteo lineatus*), Swainson's Hawks (*B. swainsoni*), Marsh Hawks or Hen Harriers (*Circus cyaneus*), Screech Owls (*Otus asio*), Snowy Owls (*Nyctea scandiaca*) and feral Cats (*Felis catus*), while grackles (*Quiscalus* spp.) and Red-headed Woodpeckers (*Melanerpes erythrocephalus*) prey on eggs and nestlings. Heavy and prolonged winter snow, however, seems to be House Sparrows' principal – albeit temporary – controlling factor in North America.

From the southwestern United States – where they were present at Tombstone, Arizona, in 1904, at Brownsville, Texas, in 1905 and San Diego California in 1913 – House Sparrows probably crossed the border into Mexico[13] early in this century; by 1930 they had spread as far south as San Luis Potosí in the east and

Guadelajara and central Baja California in the west, and by 1938 had reached Alvarado on the Gulf and Chilpancingo, the capital of Guerrero State, in the west. A decade later they arrived in Tuxtla Gutiérrez, the capital of Chiapas State near the border with Guatemala,[14] where between 10 and 25 were first seen in the central plaza of Quezaltenango, 70 km from the Mexican border at an altitude of 2,350 m in the volcanic highlands, in 1970. They appeared in Chichicastenango-Alden before 1973, and in late 1974 a party of eight was counted at Lake Atitlan, Cerro de Oro, in south-central Guatemala, which had increased to 30 a year later and to 50 in the following year. From Guatemala, House Sparrows spread south to La Paz, El Salvador, by 1972; to Cartago in central Costa Rica by 1975; to Concepción in Chiriquí, the westernmost province of Panama, in 1976; and more recently to eastern Panama Province.

In Costa Rica,[15] House Sparrows extended their range rapidly; by early 1976 they were established and breeding in some numbers in the cities of San José, Cartago and Nicoya, and probably also in Liberia, suggesting an original invasion via the Guanacaste lowlands. By 1980, they were firmly entrenched in all the main cities on the central plateau, and probably in most of the towns of the Pacific lowlands, from Puntarenas northwards, and had been recorded in Turrialba, San Isidro, Palmar Norte, and possibly Golfito. They appear to be dispersing into new areas and starting colonies in groups rather than as pairs or individuals.

House Sparrows are presumably also present, as Summers-Smith (in preparation) points out, in Belize, Honduras, and Nicaragua, although there appear as yet to be no published records for those countries. It seems probable that House Sparrows travelling south through Central America will eventually join up with those working their way northwards through Ecuador and Colombia from the northwestern coast of South America.

Today, according to the American Ornithologists' Union (1983: 764–5), House Sparrows are established in North and Central America

from southern Yukon, central and southeastern British Columbia, southwestern Mackenzie, northwestern and central Saskatchewan, northern Manitoba, northern Ontario, southern Quebec (including Anticosti and Magdalen Islands) and Newfoundland south throughout southern Canada, the continental United States, and

most of Mexico to Veracruz, Oaxaca and Chiapas, locally in Central America (where range expanding rapidly in recent years) south to Panama (east to central Panamá province).

Bermuda

According to D. B. Wingate (personal communication, 1981), the House Sparrow in Bermuda was a 'Deliberate introduction in 1870 and 1874 "for house fly control in the towns". The first introduction of a few birds was to St Georges by the mayor Mr W. C. J. Hyland. The second involving about 50 birds was to Hamilton. Both introductions were imported from New York, USA [where the birds are of the nominate form] . . . The Sparrow rapidly increased to abundant before 1900 and has largely displaced the Eastern Bluebird (*Sialia sialis*) as a cavity nester. It is now the most abundant land bird on Bermuda.'[16]

In 1876, House Sparrows were among several birds afforded legal protection in Bermuda, where fines of between 5*s*. and £1 were levied for their destruction. By 1883, however, the former had increased so much and were causing such damage that a bounty was offered 'to encourage the destruction of sparrows'.

Until after the Second World War Bermuda relied exclusively on horse-drawn transport and this, as in North America, undoubtedly contributed to the House Sparrow's successful establishment on the island. It is, perhaps, most common on Front Street in Hamilton, where the author has frequently seen it feeding in the docks and on the droppings of waiting carriage-horses. The total 1985 population was estimated at around 120,000 – the same as that of the alien Starling (*Sturnus vulgaris*) (q.v.).

West Indies[17]

Cuba

Spanish monks are said to have introduced House Sparrows to Havana, Cuba, in 1850 and again in the late 1890s. Today they are widespread throughout the island, occurring especially in such large towns as Havana and Camagüey. The form established throughout the West Indies appears to be the nominate *domesticus*.

Jamaica

According to Lack (1976), House Sparrows were

introduced to Annotto Bay on the north-east coast of Jamaica around 1903. Summers-Smith (1963: 180) said that they 'are also present in the north of Jamaica from Port Antonio to Port Maria', respectively 35 km east and 17 km west of Annotto Bay. Lack, on the other hand, indicates that they spread only a short distance from their point of release, have since declined and were last recorded in 1966.[18] Lack saw none when he visited Jamaica in 1971, but Bond (1979: 223) says of the species that 'On Jamaica [it] occurs in and near Annotto Bay'.

St Thomas; Puerto Rico; Hispaniola

On St Thomas in the Virgin Islands a small colony of House Sparrows was established in the only town on the island, Charlotte Amalie, in 1953. Bond (1979: 223) says that they are now 'Perhaps extirpated on St Thomas'. From St Thomas, House Sparrows are said to have been introduced (or to have dispersed) in 1978 to the neighbouring islands of Puerto Rico and Hispaniola. On the former, they are common in Ponce on the south coast, from where they are said to be spreading.[19]

Bahamas

In the Bahamas, an unsuccessful attempt was made to introduce House Sparrows to Nassau on New Providence – 'within the last few years', according to a report of 1877 quoted by Palmer (1899), and in 1875, according to Summers-Smith (1963). They were reported to have been wiped out there by a hurricane in 1909 (Gebhardt 1959).

In 1956 or June 1959 (accounts differ), numbers of House Sparrows were seen in open country, mangrove swamps and coppice in and around Nassau, and since then others have been reported from the islands of Grand Bahama and Eleuthera. These birds probably came as shipborne stowaways from Florida, USA, and their descendants still occur on Grand Bahama and New Providence, and on islands as far north as Walker Cay.

SOUTH AMERICA

Argentina[20]

In 1872 or 1873,[21] Mr E. Bieckert released 20 cages[22] of House Sparrows in Buenos Aires in an unsuccessful attempt to control a harmful psychid moth *Oiketicus kirbyi*.[23] More are believed to have been liberated shortly thereafter, and by 1898 they were reported to have dispersed over a radius of 'fifty leagues' (about 240 km) from Buenos Aires. By 1909 they had reached Risistencia in Chaco Province, 800 km north of Buenos Aires, and by 1917 had spread north to Las Palmas and south to Cabo San Antonio. By the end of the decade House Sparrows were established throughout settled regions of the country and were beginning to spread into unsettled areas. They were recorded at Rio Negro, Puerto Horno, Maquinchao and Huanuluan in 1920–1, at Aimaicha in Tucuman Province, Santa Fé, and Concepción in Corrientes Province in 1926, and a decade later had spread to Bahia Blanca on the coast and westwards along the railway to Zapala in Neuquén Province in the foothills of the Andes. By the autumn of 1957 House Sparrows had penetrated as far south as Ushuaia, the capital of Tierra del Fuego, at 54° 50′ S the most southerly town in the world, and were shortly thereafter established throughout most of Argentina.

Uruguay[24]

According to Summers-Smith (1963: 180), 'By the end of the 19th century the House Sparrow was advancing across the border [from Argentina] into Uruguay'. There is also believed to have been at least one deliberate introduction at Colonia around 1900 of birds imported from Buenos Aires across the Rio de la Plata (see also under Goldfinch). By 1913 House Sparrows were said to be common throughout the country.

Brazil[25]

Summers-Smith (1963: 180) says that the House Sparrow was introduced 'to Brazil in 1903, with the hope that it would combat a caterpillar that was attacking the ornamental shrubs that were planted during the modernisation of the capital, Rio de Janeiro': his map, however, (p. 181), shows the year as 1905 – the same date as that given by Sick (1957). Smith (1973), on the other hand, says they were introduced to Rio de Janeiro in 1906 to combat mosquitoes, and that 4 years later some were transplanted to southern Brazil by the Mayor of Bagé near the Uruguayan border, where they rapidly became established in Rio Grande do Sul.

In northern Brazil, Summers-Smith records that some House Sparrows were seen in Belém on the Rio do Para, just south of the Equator, in 1927, where they had apparently died out 2 years later. Muller (1967) gives the date of their arrival as 1928 (as shown on Doughty's 1978 map), and Sick (1968) says that although they could have been storm-blown from the south they are more likely to have arrived on board ship.

In recent years House Sparrows have expanded their range rapidly in Brazil: they reached Rio das Mortes, Mato Grosso (via the Paraguay River) in 1954; Distrito Federal, Brasília and Côrrego Bley, Espírito Santo in 1959; Goiás, east of Brasília and Recifé, Pernambuco (where they were released to kill noxious insects in parks) in 1963; Uruçui, Floriano, and Rio Parnaiba, Piani in 1964–5, Teófilo Otoni, Minas Gerais in 1965; and Fortaleza, Ceará in 1968. Summers-Smith recorded that by the early 1960s the southern states of Rio Grande do Sul, Santa Caterina, Parana, São Paulo, Rio de Janeiro, Espírito Santo, Minas Gerais, and parts of Goiás and Mato Grosso had been colonized. In São Paulo state, House Sparrows have been found to be the hosts of the first instar nymphs of *Triatoma sordida* – a vector of Chagas' disease, which can be fatal to man. The construction of roads in central Brazil since 1957 has probably helped the House Sparrow's northward spread. Between 1959 and about 1964, the birds extended their range some 800 km along the Belém/Brasília highway to Imperatriz and Marabá on the Tocantins River in, respectively, Maranhão and Pará states. In the latter town, a flourishing population had become established by 1971, and by 1979 numbers had increased to around 800. House Sparrows subsequently first appeared in Brazilian Amazonia as follows: at Itinga (1973); at Itupiranga on the Tocantins River (1974); at Salinópolis on the Pará coast (1976); at Mosqueiro on the Pará River, at Castanhal (Pará), and at Belém, the capital of Pará (1978); at São Caetano de Odivelas at the mouth of the Pará River, in São Luis on the coast of Maranhão (where about 1,000 were established), and at Vila Rondon (1979).

As Smith (1980) points out, House Sparrows have been invading Brazilian Amazonia along two fronts – via the Atlantic coast and the highways of the interior. Their rate of expansion has been faster along the coast, from which they have also moved inland. They are most conspicuous in the public squares of the various towns and cities which they have invaded, where for roosting they favour Mango (*Mangifera indica*) and Jackfruit (*Artocarpus heterophyllus*) trees, and feed on rice kernels, grass seeds, manioc bread, the fruit and flowers of Cashew (*Anacardium occidentale*), and small insects. They are relatively shy of man, which contributes to their survival.

Chile[26]

House Sparrows were introduced to Chile in 1904 by Señor A. Cousino, in 1915 by a Frenchman at Los Andes and Rio Blanco in Aconcagua, central Chile, and in 1918 at Punta Arenas on the Strait of Magellan – according to Summers-Smith (1963), probably by monks from Buenos Aires. They spread rapidly and by 1951 were established from Tierra del Fuego and Chiloé Island north to Arica on the Peruvian border, which they reached in about 1940.

Peru[27]

According to Leck (1973), House Sparrows were introduced to parks in Lima in 1951, where within 20 years they outnumbered the native Rufous-collared Sparrow (*Zonotrichia capensis*), and Summers-Smith says they were translocated to Callao, 12 km west of Lima, in 1953. The same author records that 10 years later the Lima/Callao population had joined up with Sparrows that spread north from Chile around 1950–1, and west from Bolivia. The species is now common in southwestern Peru, with flocks ranging through farmland, and has now spread to all coastal regions, but is still less abundant in the north.

Paraguay[28]

Wetmore (1926) records that House Sparrows (presumably from northeastern Argentina) were first noted in Asunción, capital of Paraguay, in

1920; they are now established throughout most of the country.

Ecuador[29]

According to Ortiz-Crespo (1977), House Sparrows reached Guayaquil in Ecuador (presumably from northern Peru) in 1969, and Esmeraldas, 1° N of the Equator, in 1977, from where by now they may have crossed the border into neighbouring Colombia. Summers-Smith (in preparation), however, searched for them unsuccessfully in Maracaibo and Caracas, Venezuela, in 1983.

Bolivia[30]

Dott (1986), who lived and travelled in Bolivia in 1969–71 and 1974–5 and from whom much of the following is derived, has traced the spread of House Sparrows in Bolivia which, as he points out, has taken place virtually without documentation.

Although according to Summers-Smith (1963) House Sparrows first appeared in the south of the country in 1928, Eisentraut (1935) says that the first record is of a few pairs in the south at Villa Montes in 1930. More were seen in Villa Montes and three other southern localities in 1936, which strongly suggests that Bolivia was colonized by birds crossing the border from Argentina and, perhaps, Paraguay in the middle to late 1920s. Thereafter, they may have spread steadily northwards, but although Summers-Smith says that they reached the capital, La Paz, in west-central Bolivia, in the early 1950s, according to Dott they had still not penetrated to central Bolivia by that date.

By 1969–75 the distribution of House Sparrows had altered dramatically. Many widely distributed new localities – mostly at low or mid elevations, but a few at high altitudes – had been invaded. By 1969 House Sparrows were widespread and common throughout the city and environs of Cochabamba where, however, they occurred only singly or in small parties of up to 10. In Tarija, Sucre, Villa Montes, Villa Abecia, Las Carreras and Camargo (which Dott visited mainly in 1974), House Sparrows were well established and abundant on and around the

buildings, but were not observed in large flocks or in rural areas.

On the sparsely vegetated and very cold high altiplano, Dott saw House Sparrows in 1970 and 1975 only in small numbers in the mining community of Oruro and in La Paz (where their presence in the residential zone of Irpavi was first confirmed in 1981 by Serrano Priego & Cabot Nieves 1983) – both at an altitude of around 3,750 m, and where in winter night-time temperatures fall regularly to between −10 °C and −20 °C. These may be the highest altitudes at which House Sparrows have ever succeeded in becoming established. In the capital, Dott found them solely in and around the railway station, which strongly suggests that they arrived there (and possibly also in Oruro, which is situated on the same line that connects with Cochabamba) by train. It is, as Dott points out, unlikely that House Sparrows could have crossed unaided some 200 km of antiplano or mountain.

In the lowlands, Dott found House Sparrows to be thoroughly established and abundant in and around Santa Cruz by 1969 and in Montero in 1975. Yet in settlements but a short distance from these towns House Sparrows occurred only irregularly; in 1975, they were, for example, fairly common in Portachuelo, less numerous in Buena Vista, and present but uncommon in Buen Retiro. In towns and villages at a greater distance from Santa Cruz and Montero, Dott searched for House Sparrows in vain.

Elsewhere in Bolivia, in the humid and tropical Andean foothills and in the extensive northern and eastern lowlands, Dott found House Sparrows only in Trinidad, the principal town of Beni department, and in the large village of Magdalena, in both of which they were well established but not numerous in 1974; how they reached these two isolated localities is uncertain, but it seems unlikely that they arrived unaided.

House Sparrows in Bolivia are thus currently established in towns and villages scattered over about 50 per cent of the country. These are located mainly in the tropical and semi-arid slopes of the Andes in southern and central Bolivia (Cochabamba, Chuquisaca and Tarija departments) and in the lowlands in the city of Santa Cruz and adjacent townships. They have reached only two centres on the high antiplano, in both of which they are fairly uncommon. They have not so far been recorded from the humid Andean descents, nor from most of the vast northern and eastern lowlands, apart from two isolated localities. As they do not occur anywhere in Bolivia away from human habitation, there are large areas of this sparsely populated country that have yet to be invaded. Although Dott was unable to trace any case of Bolivians deliberately carrying House Sparrows from one part of the country to another, it seems probable that in many instances the birds have used man as an unwitting means of transportation – whether by road, rail, river or air.

By 1963 Summers-Smith recorded that House Sparrows (of the nominate form) were established over most of the southern half of South America south of 12°–15° S, including most of Argentina, Chile, Uruguay, Paraguay, parts of Brazil, and western Peru. In the past two decades, they have extended their range northwards into northern Bolivia and Ecuador, and are continuing to spread in both the west and east of the continent. Their history in South America is, as Summers-Smith points out, confused by a combination of natural dispersal, translocations within individual countries, introductions from one country to another, and importations from Europe – the last coinciding with massive immigration of western Europeans into Brazil, Uruguay, Argentina and Chile around the turn of the century.

In southern South America, House Sparrows have expanded their range in climatic conditions not very different from those of their European range, while in the north they are becoming established in localities that require considerable metabolic adaptation, of which, as Kendeigh (1976) (among others) has pointed out, they have proved themselves well capable. In Bolivia, they live in a wide range of climatic conditions, varying from the semi-arid and humid tropical to the sub-zero montane. In Amazonia, Brazil, which House Sparrows have colonized naturally, Smith (1980) noted that earlier efforts by man to introduce them had been unsuccessful. This, as Dott points out, suggests that time is necessary for metabolic adjustment, and/or that advantage was taken of the provision of improved man-made habitats; the latter is an essential feature of the species' establishment in both Bolivia and Brazil.

Although Dott noticed no interspecific competition between House Sparrows and native South American species, the former are reported to compete for food and, especially, nesting sites with Rufous-collared Sparrows (see under Peru), Saffron Finches (*Sicalis flaveola*), Pale-legged Horneros (*Furnarius leucopus*), Bare-faced Ground Doves (*Metriopelia ceciliae*), Hooded Siskins (*Carduelis magellanicus*), Palm Tanagers (*Thraupis palmarum*) and Diuca Finches (*Diuca diuca*).

Falkland Islands[31]

According to Bennett (1926), House Sparrows first arrived in the Falkland Islands – in the town of Stanley on East Falkland – in 'November 1919 via assisted passages on four different steamers from Montevideo', Uruguay. Hamilton (1944) said that about 20 arrived on a whaling factory ship in late October 1919, and in later years they were probably joined by more from other visiting ships. Although Bennett stated that 'by 1924 they had spread over the islands', Hamilton claimed that they were only established in Stanley; a few managed to reach a small settlement some 48 km away, where they were all destroyed by the manager, who thought they were ejecting the endemic Black-throated Finch (*Melanodera m. melanodera*). By about 1960 House Sparrows had spread westwards 22 km to Fitzroy and 96 km to Darwin, and 48 km north-west to Teal Inlet. Woods (1975) noted that they had reached Green Patch – also on East Falkland.

In 1958–9, about half-a-dozen House Sparrows became established on West Point Island off West Falkland, over 160 km west of Stanley, and in late October of the latter year three pairs appeared on nearby Carcass Island. Since they were unknown on the mainland of West Falkland, the origin of these birds is uncertain: they could have been a result of further importations on whaling or other ships from the South American mainland, or even have been storm-borne vagrants from the coast of Argentina; alternatively, they might have travelled from Stanley on inter-island mail or cargo vessels, or have been natural dispersants. According to R. Woods (personal communication, 1985):

The West Point colony reached at least 50 individuals by 1980, but declined to very few after the settlement was uninhabited for only one month, September 1980. Since then, few have been seen, but I saw at least 3 birds in October 1983 and saw signs of one nest under eaves. The small colony, probably about 10 birds, survived on Carcass Island at least till January 1984 and breeding occurred in the 1983/84 season.

Today, according to Woods (1975: 205), the House Sparrow in the Falkland Islands is 'numerous only in Stanley, due to its inability to adapt itself to an environment away from man'.

Juan Fernández Islands

According to Summers-Smith (1963: 182), 'The spread to the Juan Fernández group took place in a similar way [as to the Falklands – presumably by ship from Valparaiso, Chile] about 1943 and it is now present on both Mas-a-tiera and Mas-a-fuera'. W. R. P. Bourne (personal communication, 1983) saw 'a few dozen' in the town of São Juan Bautista on the former (Robinson Crusoe Island) in 1983.

AUSTRALASIA

Australia[32]

The earliest attempt to naturalize House Sparrows in Australia was made on 24 November 1862[33] when the *Suffolk* sailed from England with a cargo of 60 (or 60 pairs), all of which died *en route*. A second shipment a few weeks later was more successful, and 19 Sparrows were safely offloaded from the *Princess Royal* at Melbourne, Victoria in January 1863. On 9 June, a third consignment of 130 'small birds, principally Sparrows and Chaffinches', arrived in Melbourne from England on the *Relief*. On 15 September of the same year, 80 House Sparrows were released in Royal Park in the Melbourne Botanic Gardens by the Secretary of the Victoria Acclimatization Society, Mr George Sprigg – hence the early nickname for the birds of 'Spriggies'; a further 40 were freed in October by the Superintendent of Pentridge Stockade (gaol), Colonel Champ, and on 3 November the Society proudly announced that 'a pair of English Sparrows have built a nest in the Park [the Melbourne

Zoological Society Gardens] . . . and have hatched off some young ones'. Two years later, a pair of schoolboys who discovered a House Sparrow's nest at Warrnambool, 240 km south-west of Melbourne, were fined the then considerable sum of £5 for taking the eggs.

In March 1864,[34] 125 House Sparrows were liberated at Boroondara by Mr J. O'Shannasy – the first outside Melbourne – who was given them on condition that he would 'take special care of the Sparrows to be liberated in his plantations'. In the same year, the Victoria Acclimatization Society announced that, together with other songbirds, 'the Sparrow . . . may now be considered thoroughly established'. Six freed at Ballarat in 1865 quickly settled down; 'another lot' was released at an unspecified locality in 1866; and in 1867 yet more at Tower Hill, Maryborough, St Arnaud, Benalla, Heathcote, Kyneton, Portland, Warrnambool, Barwon Park near Geelong (by Mr Thomas Austin), Beechworth, Daylesford, Somerton, Winchelsea, Meredith, Gisborne, Castlemaine, Ararat (14 in October) and on the Murray River – all bred in the Royal Zoological Park, Melbourne.

Although in 1867 it was reported that at Flemington Sparrows were destroying caterpillars and injurious insects, in the following year complaints were received of damage to fruit trees in Collins Street, Melbourne, and two recent immigrants, the Revd O. Mackie and Count de Castelnau, issued a statement that 'these birds have always been found to be most destructive in France'. As a result, in 1871 Dr L. L. Smith introduced and carried an amendment to the Game Act to exclude House Sparrows (and Common Mynahs (*Acridotheres tristis*), q.v.) from its protection – thus in effect declaring them pests. Nevertheless, a year later a further shipment of 100 Sparrows arrived from England and these were released in various localities.

In Adelaide, South Australia, House Sparrows were first liberated, as in Victoria, in 1863, and although according to Jenkins (1959) they stoutly denied it, more were probably released later by the Acclimatization Society. Some were reported at Magill, near Adelaide, in 1868, at Mount Gambier in 1874 and on Kangaroo Island in 1893.

At least one pair of House Sparrows was despatched from Melbourne to Sydney, New South Wales, in 1863, where on 9 February it was announced that eggs were being incubated. Some of the subsequent fledglings were translocated to Murrurundi by a Dr Gordon early in 1865, where they nested successfully later in the same year. The present population has been augmented by dispersal northwards from Victoria.

In Tasmania, some House Sparrows were imported to Hobart and/or Launceston from Melbourne in 1863 or 1867 (in the belief, so it is said, that they were Tree Sparrows (*Passer montanus*), q.v.) and from Adelaide 3 years later, and quickly became established. (Summers-Smith's map (1963: 184) indicates that the birds were introduced to Launceston between 1861 and 1871.)

A shipment of House Sparrows from England that arrived in Brisbane, Queensland, on the *Flying Cloud* in 1869 all died shortly afterwards. In 1875, permission was refused to introduce some to Champion Island in Torres Strait between the Cape York Peninsula and New Guinea. The state's present population is derived from natural emigration from northern New South Wales.

The earliest record of House Sparrows in Western Australia was in 1897 when a party of five was shot in Perth. When the Adelaide to Perth railway was being constructed between 1912 and 1917 the engineers employed a man to kill any Sparrows that tried to follow the lines and glean scraps from the railhead camps. Nevertheless, in about 1914 some managed to cross the border from South Australia at Eucla, and by 1918 had spread 58 km west to Mundrabilla Station where they died out in the following year. Stringent precautions by the Agriculture Protection Board of Western Australia (especially at seaports and along the Trans-Australia Railway), the presence of the Nullarbor Plain and the change from horse-drawn to motorized transportation have together combined so far to prevent House Sparrows from becoming established in the state.

Ryan (1906) reported that House Sparrows had spread 'well over Victoria, also in southern New South Wales and in South Australia, as well as in Tasmania and the intervening islands' – usually following human settlement. Tarr (1950) found them to be abundant throughout New South Wales and in many parts of Victoria; in Queensland they had reached as far north as Rockhampton, and in South Australia ranged north to Marree and west to Tarcoola; they were also common in settled districts of Tasmania and on King and Flinders islands in Bass Strait. A decade later, House Sparrows were found to be well established and breeding on Kangaroo Island (South Australia), and had spread as far south as Moth Creek on Tasmania. In Queensland, they were first recorded in Atherton in October 1965 and had spread to Tolga and Kairi before the end of the decade; by 1978 they were breeding on islands in the Torres Strait.

According to Frith (1979: 190), the House Sparrow 'now extends from the eastern edge of the Nullarbor Plain throughout South Australia, except the most arid parts, throughout Tasmania, Victoria, New South Wales and Queensland to as far north as Mount Isa at least in the inland and to Cairns on the coast. . . . it has failed to cross the deserts to colonize the Northern Territory'. Pizzey (1980) found House Sparrows to be common and well established in eastern Australia and on some offshore and Great Barrier Reef islands, from Cooktown, Queensland inland to Mount Isa–Bedourie, and in nearly all of New South Wales and Victoria; they are widespread in eastern Tasmania but in the west occur mostly in settled regions and are established on most islands in Bass Strait; in South Australia, they range north to the Oodnadatta/William Creek/Mount Willoughby area (via the railway line to Alice Springs), and west to beyond Tarcoola (in good seasons to Nullarbor Station, where they have bred), and have colonized Kangaroo Island and some smaller coastal islets. They have yet, however, to traverse the Nullarbor Plain in sufficient numbers to become established in Western Australia, although there is some evidence that they are continuing to spread both westwards and northwards.

Especially in Victoria, and to a lesser extent also in Queensland, House Sparrows consume considerable amounts of food on large-scale poultry farms in autumn and winter. In districts where cereal crops are cultivated they eat growing and stored grain (especially wheat and maize), and fruit (particularly cherries, apricots and plums) in orchards and vegetables (mainly tomatoes and peas) in market gardens. In urban areas they deface (and damage) buildings with their droppings, block gutters, drains and downpipes with nesting material, and destroy germinating seedlings. (For the interaction between House Sparrows and Tree Sparrows see p. 466.)

New Zealand[35]

Thomson (1922: 148) quotes from Dr Arthur S. Thomson's *The Story of New Zealand* (2 vols, London, 1859) that 'Mr Brodie, the settler who introduced pheasants, sent out, in 1859, 300 sparrows, for the purpose of keeping the caterpillars in check'. Thomson mentions this in his account of the 'Hedge-Sparrow (*Accentor modularis*)'[36] but Long (1981), quoting Hargreaves (1943), takes it to refer to the House Sparrow. Whichever the species was it seems soon to have disappeared.

The earliest authenticated introduction of the House Sparrow to New Zealand was of a single bird imported by the Nelson Acclimatization Society in 1862. Two years later, according to Thomson, the Society imported a further shipment, of which again only one survived the voyage from England. In 1871, half-a-dozen were successfully released at Stoke where they quickly became established. According to Sir Walter Lowry Buller, in *A History of the Birds of New Zealand* (London, 1873), more were brought in by the Wanganui Society in 1866.

In 1864, the Canterbury Society issued to prospective immigrants from England a list of birds and the prices per pair they were prepared to offer for them; this included 15*s.* for House Sparrows. Three years later the Society released 40 – many of which bred successfully at Kaiapoi in the following year – and in their annual report for 1871 claimed that the birds were 'thoroughly established and need no further importations'.

The Auckland Provincial government were rather more generous, offering in the same year 30*s.* per pair; this enabled the Auckland Society to release 2 (out of an original shipment of 72 brought out by the *Viola* from Glasgow, Scotland) in 1865 and 47 in 1867, and by the following year to 'consider them thoroughly acclimatized'. In 1868, the Otago Society liberated 3, followed by a further 11 in 1869.

These appear to be the only recorded introductions (made mainly for nostalgic reasons but also to combat caterpillars and insects in the grain fields of South Island and the orchards of North Island) of House Sparrows (all of which were of the nominate form) to New Zealand, where according to Thomson (1922: 167), they 'very quickly increased in all parts until they became a very serious pest'.

That at least some of the acclimatization societies became embarrassed in later years by the recklessness of their predecessors in importing such an acknowledged pest is shown by their naive denials that any such introductions were ever made. In 1889, only 25 years after they had been offering to purchase House Sparrows from immigrants, the Canterbury Society, for example, quoted by Thomson (p. 165), said: 'we most deliberately deny ordering or introducing this questionable bird, but we well remember the devastations made by the caterpillars and grubs previous to their advent' – adding, somewhat ingenuously, 'even if the Society had brought in Sparrows they would not be to blame'.

House Sparrows colonized, naturally or more probably by ship, the Chatham Islands around 1880[37], Campbell Island in about 1907 (Summers-Smith's map (1963: 184) indicates between 1900 and 1907, and 'extinct 1946–51'), Great and Little Barrier, Poor Knights, Kapiti and Stewart islands by around 1930, the Snares in about 1948 (Summers-Smith's map indicates between 1907 and 1948), and Three Kings, Mokohinau, Mayor, Karewa, Codfish and the Auckland islands by 1955. (Summers-Smith's map indicates that they colonized the Aucklands between 1907 and 1946.) Wodzicki (1956) suggested a recent occupation of White Island in the Bay of Plenty, where Summers-Smith's map indicates an arrival between 1925 and 1947. Wodzicki (1965: 433) described the House Sparrow as 'widely distributed and abundant, North, South, Stewart and Chatham, Auckland, Snares and Campbell Islands'. Kinsky (1970) confirmed Wodzicki's distribution, and Williams (1973) said that House Sparrows were breeding on the Chathams, Snares, Aucklands and Campbell islands, but not apparently on Three Kings. Falla, Sibson & Turbott (1979) said that House Sparrows were widely distributed throughout New Zealand, not always (as elsewhere) in association with man. In the north, where little grain is grown, they frequent saltings and mangrove swamps, and have followed man to offshore islands.

As elsewhere, House Sparrows in New Zealand have long been regarded as a serious pest, and as early as 1882 the Small Birds Nuisance Act was passed in an attempt to control them. They attack such grain crops as barley, oats, wheat and linseed at the time of sowing, at germination and when ripe. They eat the buds and blossoms of apples, nectarines, grapes and peaches, and the mature fruits of strawberries, grapes, apples, raspberries, cherries, pears, plums and peaches. Dawson (1970) estimated the average grain loss through House Sparrow depredation at about 5 per cent, rising in some crops to as high as 20 per cent. Apart from feral and domestic house Cats (*Felis catus*), House Sparrows' main controlling agents in New Zealand are, according to Thomson, Marsh Harriers (*Circus aeruginosus gouldi*), Sacred Kingfishers (*Halcyon sancta vagans*), Long-tailed Koels (*Urodynamis* (*Eudynamis*) *taitensis*) and Golden Bronze Cuckoos (*Chrysococcyx* (*Chalcites*) *lucidus*).

Norfolk Island

According to Williams (1953), the House Sparrow colonized Norfolk Island around 1939. Summers-Smith's map (1963: 184) indicates that they arrived sometime between 1913 and 1939. As Norfolk lies some 1,400 km east of Australia and 750 km north of New Zealand it seems probable that they arrived on board ship. Smithers & Disney (1969) found them in abundance in villages, around homesteads and in adjacent pastures.

OCEANIA

Hawaiian Islands[38]

The earliest reference to House Sparrows in Hawaii that Thrun (1909) was able to trace was to 'a further supply' in May 1859 – signifying a previous introduction before that date. In July 1871, nine imported from New Zealand were released in Honolulu on Oahu, where 8 years later they were said to be numerous. As late as 1902, they were not reported from outside Honolulu, and their subsequent appearance on other islands in the group around 1917 was almost certainly the result of further unrecorded importations (probably from San Francisco) and/or translocations.

Peterson (1961) said that House Sparrows (of the nominate form) were established on all the main islands with the possible exception of Niihau; Summers-Smith (1963: 183) recorded them as 'present on all of the inhabited islands in

the group', while Zeillemaker & Scott (1976) reported them to be common in residential and community parklands on Oahu, Molokai, Lanai, Maui and Hawaii, uncommon on Kauai (and Niihau), and to occur as accidental vagrants on Kure and Midway Atolls.

As Berger (1981) points out, the House Sparrow has not enjoyed the same spectacular success in Hawaii that it had on the North American mainland. This is no doubt due largely to the more tropical climate and different habitat. It is most abundant in urban areas and in the country occurs only near settlements. Three out of a group of nine House Sparrows caught on Oahu were found to be infected with the malarial parasite *Plasmodium cathemerium* – the first record for this species from any Pacific island.

According to Johnston & Selander (1964) and Selander & Johnston (1967), House Sparrows in Hawaii exhibit marked differences in plumage from European and North American mainland populations. In Hawaii, the dark markings are less distinct, there are few if any fine streaks on the underparts, and the legs and feet are usually pale buff instead of dark brown. The general overall colour is rufous-buff, which is especially strong on the breast and flanks.

New Caledonia[39]

Palmer (1899) reported the presence of House Sparrows on New Caledonia, where they are now abundant in villages and towns. Precisely how or when they were introduced does not seem to have been recorded.

Vanuatu

Cain & Galbraith (1957) recorded the existence of House Sparrows in the New Hebrides; exactly when or how they arrived is again unknown.

Easter Island[40]

In 1928, House Sparrows were introduced from Chile to Easter Island (or Rapa Nui) where they soon became thoroughly established, finding a ready source of food in the insects and seeds from the droppings of feral Cattle (*Bos taurus*) and

Horses (*Equus caballus*). They nest and roost in caves in the sea-cliffs, and are preyed on by Chimango Caracaras (*Milvago chimango*) (q.v.), which were introduced from Chile in the same year. Why these two species were imported (presumably deliberately) to Easter Island has not been established, although the latter is an efficient scavenger.

Chagos Archipelago

According to Bourne (1971), House Sparrows were first recorded on the islands of Salomon and Peros Banhos in the northern Chagos group in 1905, where the Percy Sladen Trust expedition of that year was informed they had been imported from Mauritius. Loustau-Lalanne (1962) and Hutson (1975) found them still to be common on these two islands, but absent from Diego Garcia. The form established is presumably *indicus*.

———————————

According to Hagerup (1891) and Salomonsen (1950), House Sparrows of the nominate form were unsuccessfully introduced from Denmark to Ivigtut, a cryolite mining area north of Frederikshåb in coastal southwestern Greenland, around 1880. Long's map (1981: 377) indicates a failed introduction in south-central Iceland, but he does not mention it in the text, and the author has been unable to trace any reference to it.

According to Watling (1982), 'The House Sparrow has been recorded once in Suva, Fiji, almost certainly arriving on a cargo ship'.

Ashford (1978) mentions the sighting of four House Sparrows in the grounds of the Central Veterinary Laboratory in Kila Kila, a suburb of Port Moresby in Papua New Guinea, in 1976, where they disappeared after January of the following year.

Although House Sparrows were apparently present on the Agaléga Islands in the Indian Ocean around 1924, Guého & Staub (1983) found no trace of them during their visit in 1981.

In the Philippines, House Sparrows have been unsuccessfully released, according to the American Ornithologists' Union (1957), in Manila on the island of Luzon.

Benson (1950) says that 26 'London sparrows' were unsuccessfully imported to the island of St

Helena in the South Atlantic in the twentieth century. Melliss (1870), however, says that he introduced the birds in November 1820, and that they succeeded in becoming temporarily established in the capital, Jamestown.

According to Watson (1975), House Sparrows introduced to South Georgia in the Southern Ocean failed to become established.

———————————

In the past 200 years House Sparrows have greatly extended their natural distribution in Europe; as Sharrock (1976: 442) points out, their willingness to adapt to food sources provided by man 'explains their spread and increase in England two centuries ago, and through Scotland during the nineteenth century', where they reached Sutherlandshire in the extreme northwest around 1900. 'With the advance of the crop line in northern Europe and Siberia during the climatic amelioration of this century', Sharrock continues, 'the species spread northwards via the railway lines and the Norwegian coastal steamer routes.'

Summers-Smith (1963) has traced the House Sparrow's spread northwards and eastwards in Eurasia. In Europe, it crossed the Arctic Circle in Sweden in 1840 and in Norway in 1858, and reached Finmark (where it became permanently established in 1887) in the 1850s, the Lofoten Islands in 1872, Troms in 1879, Arkhangel'sk in 1882 and Peisenfjord on the Russian/Norwegian border in 1899.

In Siberia, House Sparrows travelled on grain-barges up the Ob', reaching Berezova (64° N) in 1876, and later settled on the Poluostrov Yamal at more than 70° N – their most northerly point. In the Petchora Valley, they reached 68° N in 1880, and birds that had probably been translocated from Tobolsk 3 years earlier were established at Obdursk (66° N) in 1897. In the Yenisei Valley, they arrived at Worogowo (61° N) by 1840, and crossed the Arctic Circle 30 years later. They reached Aleksandrovka in 1919 and became established in Murmansk on the Poluostrov Kol'skiy by 1923. In these northerly latitudes, House Sparrows were doubtless helped in their expansion of range by river transport, and their survival is considered to be largely dependent on food provided by man.

Eastwards, Sparrows began to spread along the Irtysh Valley following the start of cultivation there around 1800; they had penetrated as far east as Irkutsk west of Lake Baikal by the second half of the nineteenth century (Southern (1945) says not until 1910) and by 1929 (according to Southern not until 1932) had reached Nikolay-evsk-na-Amure at the mouth of the River Amur opposite Sakhalin Island at 141° E – their most easterly point. This eastward spread has followed land cultivation, the extension of roads, and the construction of the Trans-Siberia railway.

Southwards, House Sparrows had spread in the west to Kazakh in Azerbaydzhan by the 1840s, and later in the east to Ulan Bator and villages along the River Selanga in northern Mongolia; their dispersal further south into China has been inhibited by the Gobi Desert.

In the House Sparrow's natural range, Summers-Smith forecast a further spread in Siberia and from the Amur region of the Soviet Union south through Manchuria and Korea into China. Roots (1976) seems to have anticipated this expansion when, in discussing the House Sparrow, he describes how in China nearly three million were killed in the winter of 1955 (!). These were mainly Tree Sparrows (*P. montanus*), which are widespread throughout China, perhaps with some Saxaul Sparrows (*P. ammodendri*) and Cinnamon Sparrows (*P. rutilans*) – but certainly no *domesticus*.

Summers-Smith (1963, *passim*) summed up the results of House Sparrow introductions and the future of naturalized populations throughout the world as follows:

The outstanding thing about these introductions has been their extraordinary success. The main reason for this has been the lack of competition from native species. No bird of any other genus has exploited and adopted man-made urban habitats to anything like the extent of the House Sparrow and thus there were no real competitors. . . . It is interesting that the House Sparrow appears to have been less successful in its African introductions than in other parts of the world. [Written in 1960, before the species' major African expansion.] Here is the one place where members of the genus *Passer* were already established: . . . In North and South America the pattern of spread appears to have been very similar: first the cities and larger towns were occupied and from these the birds infiltrated to the villages and populous farming areas. The main factor responsible was most probably the transportation of grain. . . . In North America, the limit in the north is already the limit of cultivation . . . to the

south it is probable that the bird will continue to spread southwards in Central America. In South America . . . consolidation of that area of the sub-continent already occupied . . . [and] a further extension of range on the west coast . . . It seems improbable . . . that the House Sparrow will for long be denied entry to Western Australia but extensions in other parts of Australasia appear unlikely. Further spread is to be expected in South Africa despite competition from related species . . . In the last hundred years its range has more than doubled [to some 32 million km²] and at present it occurs on about a quarter of the earth's surface, being found from 6° to 70° in the northern hemisphere and from 12° to 55° in the southern, and a wide variety of habitats from sea level up to as high as fifteen thousand feet [4,600 m].

NOTES

1 Benson & Benson 1977; P. A. Clancey 1963, 1964 (and personal communication, 1981); Cole 1958; Courtenay-Latimer 1942, 1955; Daniels 1954; Dowsett 1971, 1976; Gebhardt 1959; Harwin & Irwin 1966; Liversidge n.d.; Long 1959, 1981; Mackworth-Praed & Grant 1963; Maclean 1985; Markus 1960; Meiklejohn, Hodgson & Hodgson 1966; Newton-Howes 1966; Roots 1976; Siegfried 1962; Summers-Smith 1963; Thomas 1971; Thomson & Aspinwall 1971; Tuer 1969; Van Bruggen 1960; Vierke 1970; Wetmore 1957; J. M. Winterbottom 1959–61, 1962, 1965, 1966, 1978 (and personal communication, 1981); and J. Vincent and S. Wolff, personal communications, 1981.

2 Da Rosa Pinto 1959; Harwin & Irwin 1966; Long 1981; Payne & Payne 1967.

3 Ash & Colston 1981; Gebhardt 1959; Long 1981; Mackworth-Praed & Grant 1960; Pakenham 1943, 1945, 1959; Peters 1962; Summers-Smith 1963; Vaughan 1930, 1932; Williams & Arlott 1982.

4 Ash 1983; Ash & Colston 1981; Ash & Miskell 1983; Long 1981; Mackworth-Praed & Grant 1960; Peters 1962; Summers-Smith 1963.

5 Barré & Barrau 1982; Benedict 1957; Long 1981; Mackworth-Praed & Grant 1963; Meinertzhagen 1912; Palmer 1899; Peters 1962; Rountree, Guérin et al. 1952; Staub 1973, 1976; Summers-Smith 1963; Watson, Zusi & Storer 1963.

6 In Berlioz, *Oiseaux de la Réunion*, p. 68.

7 For much of the history of House Sparrows in the United States and Canada I am indebted to Doughty 1978; other references are Abbott 1903; American Ornithologists' Union 1957, 1983; Anderson 1934; Barrows 1889; Blake 1975; Bryant 1916; Calhoun 1947; Carl & Guiguet 1972; Coues 1878, 1879, 1890; Eastbrook 1907; Elton 1958;

Flieg 1971; Gebhardt 1959; Gentry 1878; Hamilton & Johnston 1978; Jarvis 1980; Jefferson 1985; Johnston & Klitz 1977; Judd 1901; Kalmbach 1930, 1940; Laycock 1970; Long 1981; McKinley 1960; Murphy 1978; Packard 1967; Palmer 1899; Phillips 1928; Pindar 1925; Robbins 1973; Roots 1976; Samuel 1969; Selander & Johnston 1967; Silverstein & Silverstein 1974; Skinner 1905; Southern 1945; Stoner 1939; Summers-Smith 1963; Weaver 1939, 1943; Wetmore 1964; Wing 1943a, 1956; and K. L. Crowell, personal communication, 1981.

8 The larvae of the Snow-white Linden moth.

9 Term applied to a region before its admission to the Union as a state.

10 Coues, as Doughty points out, was repeating the opinions of Georges-Louis Leclerc, Comte de Buffon, in his *Histoire Naturelle, Générale et Particulière*, tome 4: *Histoire des Oiseaux* (1812) and those in Gentry 1878.

11 *New Country Life* 32: 82 (1917).

12 C. R. Cole, personal communication.

13 Alvarez del Toro 1950; Gebhardt 1959; Wagner 1959.

14 Land 1970; Peterson & Chalif 1973; Thurber 1972.

15 Campos Ramirez & Morúa Navarra 1983; Reynolds 1982; Reynolds & Stiles 1982; Stiles & Smith 1980.

16 See also Blake 1975; Bourne 1957; Crowell & Crowell 1976; Long 1981; Palmer 1899; Peters 1962; Roots 1976; Summers-Smith 1963; Wingate 1973; and K. L. Crowell, personal communication, 1981.

17 Blake 1975; Bond 1979; Brudenell-Bruce 1975; Doughty 1978; Lack 1976; Laycock 1970; Long 1981; Palmer 1899; Peters 1962; Phillips 1928; Roots 1976; Summers-Smith 1963.

18 *Goose Board Broadsheet* CI, 7: 22 (1966).

19 T. Silva, personal communication, 1986, per José Santiago.

20 de Schauensee 1971; Frisch 1981; Gibson 1918; Johnson 1967; Long 1981; Olrog 1959; Summers-Smith 1963; Wetmore 1926.

21 An anonymous account says that House Sparrows were first introduced (? unsuccessfully) to Argentina by European farmers around 1820.

22 Summers-Smith (1963: 180) says that 'about twenty pairs' were released in 1872.

23 Summers-Smith (1963) gives the name of the moth as *Oeceticus platensis*.

24 de Schauensee 1971; Summers-Smith 1963; Wetmore 1926.

25 Carvalho 1939; de Schauensee 1971; Doughty 1978; Frisch 1981; Gliesch 1924; Johnson 1967; Long 1981; Müller 1967; Ortiz-Crespo 1977; Roots 1976; Sick 1957, 1959, 1967, 1968, 1971; Smith 1973, 1980; Summers-Smith 1963.

26 Doughty 1978; Frisch 1981; Goodall, Johnson &

Philippi 1946; Johnson 1965, 1967; Long 1981; Sick 1968; Summers-Smith 1963; Wetmore 1926.

27 de Schauensee 1971; Hughes 1970; Johnson 1967; Koepcke 1952, 1961, 1970; Niethammer 1956; Parker, Parker & Plenge 1982; Summers-Smith 1963.

28 de Schauensee 1971; Summers-Smith 1963; Wetmore 1926.

29 Ortiz-Crespo 1977.

30 See also: Bond & de Schauensee 1942; Eisentraut 1935; Niethammer 1953, 1956; Serrano Priego & Cabot Nieves 1983.

31 Bennett 1926; Cawkell & Hamilton 1961; Doughty 1978; Hamilton 1944; Long 1981; Peters 1962; Summers-Smith 1963; Wetmore 1926; R. Woods 1975 (and personal communication, 1985).

32 Blakers, Davies & Reilly 1984; Bravery 1970; Condon 1962; Cooper 1947; Frith 1979; Gebhardt 1959; Green & Mollison 1961; Helms 1898; Jenkins 1959; Lavery 1974; Le Souef 1958; Lindley-Cohen 1898; Littler 1902; Long 1964, 1972, 1981; Palmer 1899; Pescott 1943; Pizzey 1980; Rolls 1969; Ryan 1906; Sage 1957; Serventy & Whittell 1962; Slater 1970; Summers-Smith 1963; Tarr 1950; Wheeler 1960; Williams 1953.

33 One account claims that House Sparrows were first imported to Victoria in the 1850s, but that there is no record of any liberations.

34 Hardy (1928) says that Sparrows from China and Java were also liberated in the St Kilda district of Melbourne in 1864. These birds were in fact Tree Sparrows (*Passer montanus*) (q.v.).

35 Dawson 1970; Falla, Sibson & Turbott 1979; Forbes 1893; Gebhardt 1959; Hargreaves 1943; Kinsky 1970; Long 1981; Oliver 1930, 1955; Palmer 1899; Peters 1962; Prescott 1943; Roots 1976; Stead 1927; Summers-Smith 1963; Thomson 1922, 1926; Williams 1953, 1969, 1973; Wodzicki 1956, 1965. See also: *Report of the New Zealand Department of Agriculture, Division of Botany*, 8 (1897).

36 Now the Dunnock (*Prunella modularis*).

37 *Ibis*, 543 (1893). Summers-Smith's map (1963: 184) indicates that the Chathams were colonized between 1893 and 1901; Forbes (1893) indicates invasion before that date.

38 American Ornithologists' Union 1957, 1983; Berger 1981; Blake 1975; Bryan 1958; Caum 1933; Doughty 1978; Hawaiian Audubon Society 1975; Johnston & Selander 1964; Long 1981; Palmer 1899; Peters 1962; Peterson 1961; Pyle 1977; Roots 1976; Selander & Johnston 1967; Summers-Smith 1963; Thrun 1909; Zeillemaker & Scott 1976.

39 Delacour 1966; Leach 1928; Long 1981; Palmer 1899; Phillips 1928; Landsborough Thomson 1964.

40 Holyoak & Thibault 1984; Johnson, Millie & Moffett 1970; Lever 1985b; Long 1981; Sick 1968.

Tree Sparrow
(*Passer montanus*)

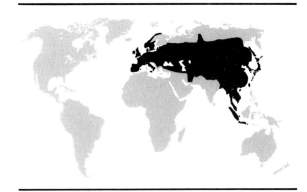

NATURAL DISTRIBUTION

Most of Eurasia (apart from southern Iran and Turkey, the Middle East, and India) south of the tundra and taiga zones, including Malaysia, Indo-China, Indonesia (including Sumatra, Java and Bali), Hainan, Sakhalin Island, Taiwan, Japan and the Ryukyu Islands.

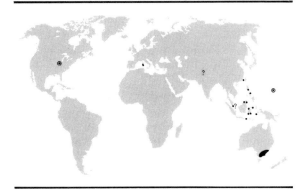

NATURALIZED DISTRIBUTION

Europe: Sardinia (Italy); Asia: ?India, ?Singapore, Pescadores Islands (P'eng-hu Lieh-tao); North America: USA; Australasia: Australia, Philippines, Lesser Sunda Islands, Moluccas, Sulawesi (Celebes), Borneo; Oceania: Marianas.

EUROPE

Sardinia (Italy)

According to Voous (1960), 'the Tree Sparrow seems to have been introduced [to Sardinia] by man'. This, according to J. D. Summers-Smith (personal communication, 1985), is likely to have

been by ship from Naples, where the birds occur in the town centre.

ASIA

India

Raju & Price (1973) reported a small isolated population of Tree Sparrows from the Eastern Ghats in Andra Pradesh. The origin of these birds, believed to be of the form *malaccensis* (the southern Himalayas, Nepal, Burma and Assam, eastwards to Yunnan, and south through Thailand, Indo-China, Hainan and Malaysia to Sumatra, Java and Bali), is unknown, but they may well represent an introduction by man. Price (1979) estimated the population at under 500, and considered that it was dying out.

Singapore

Although Robinson & Chasen (1927) claim that Tree Sparrows may have been among the first birds introduced to Singapore after its occupation by Sir Stamford Raffles on behalf of the East India Company in 1819, Ward (1968) plausibly suggests that the species could already have been established in small native villages in Malaya and Singapore before European colonization, having spread southeastwards down the Malay Peninsula, perhaps on coastal trading vessels, in the sixteenth and seventeenth centuries. From the Malay Peninsula, Tree Sparrows spread southwards to Sumatra, Java and Bali. Although some authorities (e.g. Voous 1960) have suggested that this extension of range has been a result of introductions, the continuous spread is, as Summers-Smith (in preparation) points out, quite consistent with natural dispersal.

Pescadores Islands (P'eng-hu Lieh-tao)

According to Horikawa (1936) – repeated by Hachisuka & Udagawa (1951) – Tree Sparrows were released on the Pescadores Islands (P'eng-hu Lieh-tao) in the Tai-Wan Hai-Hsia (Formosa Strait) between Taiwan and mainland China by a Chinese named Rosuirin around 1728. The form in the Pescadores (where Tree Sparrows now occur on the islands of Yü-weng Tao, P'eng-hu tao, Pa Chao Hsü and Ta Hsü) is said by Peters (1962) to be *dilutus*, which ranges from Transcaspia south to northeastern Iran, through Afghanistan, northern Baluchistan and western Pakistan, eastwards through Uzbekistan, Tadzhikistan, Sinkiang, Lake Balkash, northern Mongolia and Manchuria, and south through mainland China.

NORTH AMERICA

USA[1]

On 20 April 1870, a bird-dealer named Kleinschmidt and Mr Carl Daenzer, editor of the *Anzeiger des Westerns* (a German-language daily newspaper) released between 20 and 32[2] Tree Sparrows (which had been imported from Germany and were therefore of the nominate form) in Layfayette Park in suburban residential southern St Louis, Missouri. The birds quickly became established, apparently because the presence of breweries started by the German immigrant population provided an abundant source of grain. On 24 April 1871, an individual was reported from an area of St Louis well away from the release site, and numbers were observed in the environs of the city by James C. Merrill in 1875.

In 1877, when Tree Sparrows were well established in the city and were breeding in nesting boxes provided especially for them, the larger and more aggressive House Sparrow (*Passer domesticus*) (q.v.) arrived in downtown St Louis, and forced Tree Sparrows to disperse outside the city limits. Since, however, in Europe (though not elsewhere in their natural range) the latter prefer rural and suburban habitats to an urban environment, they soon became re-established in considerable numbers in Tower Grove Park and Shaw's Garden (the Missouri Botanical Garden). Here they remained until in the 1890s encroachment by man and *domesticus* compelled them to move once again; by this time the population had grown to such an extent that several separate flocks had formed and these settled in various suburban districts – especially in parts of St Charles and St Louis counties and at Creve Coeur Lake, from where they spread 50 km westwards to Washington on the Missouri River; this area was not, however, fully colonized until the mid-1930s.

Around the turn of the century small flocks began crossing the Mississippi River into western Illinois, where they became established in Alton, Grafton, East St Louis and Belleville. By 1922, Tree Sparrows had been reported from the six Illinois counties nearest to St Louis (i.e. Madison, Jersey, Calhoun, St Clair, Hersey and Monroe); 3 years later they began to appear as irregular visitors in Fulton County, Kentucky, some 220 km south-east of St Louis, and were first observed in Boone and Calhoun counties in the same state in April 1934. Like their congener, the House Sparrow, they are believed to have travelled on board the steamship paddleboats that regularly plied the Mississippi River.

In the winter of 1938–9, a colony of about 90 Tree Sparrows became established near Horseshoe Lake, Illinois (where small numbers had occurred since 1934), from where the birds later spread throughout St Louis and St Charles counties. After the Second World War, Tree Sparrows began to appear more frequently outside an 80-km radius of St Louis (e.g. at Hannibal in Marion County, Missouri, 140 km to the north-west, and at Jacksonville in Morgan County, Illinois, 130 km to the north). They first nested at Hannibal in 1946 and in the following year at Hull 16 km to the east in Illinois. In about 1953, eight pairs were seen at Mauvaiterre, south-east of Jacksonville.

During the 1950s the centre of the population gradually moved from Horseshoe Lake to Grand Marias State Park, East St Louis. At the beginning of the decade there were some 250 Tree Sparrows at the former and only half this number in the latter; by 1957 the ratio had been reversed, the population at the former having dwindled to 137 whereas in the latter there were three separate flocks of 175, 150 and 25, respectively. By the end of the decade the birds had become rare or had disappeared entirely from their former haunts, and were slowly dispersing in a north and northeasterly direction. At this time they occurred principally in Charles County in east-central Missouri and in Jacksonville, Springfield, Calhoun and St Clair in western Illinois.

Between 1959 and 1962 Tree Sparrows spread 175 km north from St Louis up the Mississippi River to Quincy and south to Modoc, and 140 km north-east up the Illinois to Virginia in Cass County (where they were breeding in 1964) and to Beardstown; by the end of the decade they were established along the Illinois between Hardin and Beardstown (a distance of some 100 km), and eastwards to Jacksonville and Springfield in Sangamon County. Although on the Missouri River they had still penetrated no further west than Washington, some localities from which they had disappeared had been recolonized (e.g. Affton, Grafton, Alton, Godfrey and Belleville). It is interesting to note that almost a century after its introduction the Tree Sparrow's expansion of range was still closely associated with major river systems.

Flieg (1971) found that the species' spread has followed a well-defined pattern; when flocks disperse in spring the birds scatter and territorialize over a wide area, those individuals occurring in most densely populated localities spreading furtherest to provide adequate space for each breeding pair. This, Flieg considered, together with the build-up of dense populations in Baden and St Charles County, coupled with increasing urbanization, could well account for the birds' northern and northeastern expansion to Quincy and Beardstown via the Mississippi and Illinois rivers, which provide natural dispersal routes on steamboats where grain is grown in the fertile bottomlands.[3] The colonies in Jacksonville and Springfield could have originated in a spread eastwards from the Illinois River and/or a cross-country dispersal from the large concentrations (e.g. at East St Louis) in the Illinois American bottomlands. The relatively low-density populations in urban areas and in southern parts of the species' Missouri distribution required little if any more space for breeding than for overwintering. The greatest expansion in this area (westwards up the Missouri River to Washington) took place in the mid-1930s.

The preferred habitat of the Tree Sparrow in the United States is agricultural land (both arable and stock) rich in food, nesting sites and winter roosts, and its distribution in the Missouri River delta in St Charles County, the Illinois American bottomlands around East St Louis, the high bottomlands between the Mississippi and the Illinois, and the extensive flatland between Jacksonville and Springfield includes much of the most fertile in eastern Missouri and southern Illinois. In contrast, the hilly and densely populated country of Missouri south of St Louis, much of it forested with oak and hickory, is unsuitable for agriculture and thus inimical to Tree Sparrows. The reclamation of vacant land in St Louis itself (resulting in a diminution in the supply of seed-producing weeds) has undoubtedly contributed to the decline of the species in that city.

In autumn and winter in rural and suburban districts Tree Sparrows form flocks up to 300 strong, from which in spring mated pairs disperse throughout the breeding colony area, nesting between early April and mid August in small colonies. Urban residents usually winter in pairs or occasionally in small flocks, and breed in smaller areas than do rural and suburban birds. Preferred nesting sites are cavities between 4 m and 10 m from the ground in such trees as American Elm (*Ulmus americana*), Maple (*Acer saccharinum*), Black Willow (*Salix nigra*) and Sweet Gum (*Liquidambar styraciflua*).

The Tree Sparrow's distribution in the United States is discontinuous because of an absence of unbroken suitable habitat. Wilhelm (1959), mostly from counts of winter flocks, estimated the total population to be around 1,500. Twelve years later, Flieg (1971) put the total at about 2,500, distributed over some 22,000 km^2 (i.e. less than nine birds per km^2), of which, however, he estimated that only some 25 per cent of land was actually occupied. Flieg reported that the birds ranged from Washington, Missouri, and Modoc, Illinois, northwards to Springfield, Beardstown, Quincy and Bloomington – the last-named some 90 km north-east of Springfield – and that a single bird had recently been taken in Milwaukee, Wisconsin, more than 300 km north of Bloomington. Barlow (1973), who estimated the population at around 25,000, found the birds to be spreading slowly north of a line between Springfield in central Illinois and Hannibal in northeastern Missouri. The American Ornithologists' Union (1983) described them as established in east-central Missouri and western Illinois, with a straggler reported in western Kentucky (Lone Oak).

AUSTRALASIA

Australia[4]

The minutes of the Victoria Acclimatization Society for 24 March 1863 state that 'between 30 and 40 Chinese Sparrows [the vernacular name of the subspecies *saturatus*] have been received from Mr G. W. Rusden', who is thanked 'for selecting and bringing out [from China] under his personal supervision some valuable Chinese birds'. Some of these were released on 7 and 20 October of the same year in, respectively, the Botanic Gardens in Melbourne and in the Pentridge Stockade (prison) by the Superintendent, Colonel Champ. The first proceedings of the Zoological and Acclimatization Society of Victoria record that 20 'Chinese Sparrows' were released in the same year in the St Kilda district of Melbourne, where they first nested in the following December. Altogether, more than 40 Tree Sparrows were released in Victoria in 1863, 40 (including some *malaccensis* from Java) at St Kilda and Ballarat in 1864, a few possibly in 1870, and 70 in 1872. In 1864, the Victoria Acclimatization Society announced that, among other species, 'the Chinese Sparrow . . . may now be considered thoroughly established'. Some sent from Melbourne to Sydney, New South Wales, quickly settled down, whereas others imported to Tasmania in the 1860s apparently disappeared.

By the turn of the century, Tree Sparrows had spread to Junee in New South Wales (midway between Melbourne and Sydney), and by the outbreak of the First World War were fairly common in and around Wangaratta, Victoria (200 km north-east of Melbourne), and in most of the townships of the Riverina in New South Wales. In 1933 they were described as occurring in the Wellington region, 240 km north of Junee and 640 km north-east of Melbourne, and by the late 1940s were common at Albury and had spread to Tumbarumba. Although as late as the mid-1950s they were still most abundant in and around Melbourne, they were beginning to spread along the Melbourne–Sydney railway. In the second half of the decade they became established at Tocumwal, Wagga Wagga, Cootamundra and Moama in New South Wales, and in some northern Victoria towns such as Shepparton and Cobran, and in Orbost in the south-east were said to occur in the same numbers as House Sparrows. Elsewhere, Long (1972) records that in Western Australia two Tree Sparrows that had arrived on a boat from south-east Asia in 1966 were shot in Geraldton, and that 4 years later a single bird was shot in the Perth suburb of Palmyra in the same state.

Today, Pizzey (1980) records Tree Sparrows as established from Melbourne and towns of central and northeastern Victoria to southern New South Wales (where they are fairly common in open habitats and tablelands of the southern Riverina, especially between Moama and Albury), northeastwards to Sydney, Newcastle and the Hunter River Valley where they are rare. In Victoria, where they shun dense highland forests, they have been recorded as far west as Dimboola (300 km north-west of Melbourne) and in New South Wales west to between Wagga Wagga and Cowra (around 300 km south-west of Sydney), with recent extensions further west to Weethalle and Hay. Summers-Smith (in preparation) records them as far north in New South Wales as Wellington. According to Keve (1976), who examined only a small sample, the Australian population includes the nominate form (Europe, western, northern and northeastern Asia and Asia Minor), *saturatus* and *catellatus*.[5]

The Tree Sparrow in Australia has not been as successful a colonist as its congener the House Sparrow, and seldom do local populations of the former approach those of the latter. The habitat preferences of the two species vary sharply from one part of their range to another. In Europe, for example, although they also occur sympatrically, *montanus* is in general a bird of rural habitats whereas *domesticus* is largely a commensal of man, while elsewhere in its natural range the Tree Sparrow is an urban species. In Australia, according to Frith (1979), the position is still apparently developing. The House Sparrow spread rapidly after its introduction and soon colonized the most favourable habitats: Tree Sparrows are expanding their range much more slowly, and are probably suffering from inter-specific competition with their well-established, larger and more abundant and aggressive relations. In general, *domesticus* is closely associated with man, while *montanus* is more usually found in suburban and rural areas; in some townships of northern Victoria and southern New South Wales, however, Tree Sparrows are now

well established and, as previously mentioned, occur in more or less equal numbers as House Sparrows.

The interaction of the two species with each other and with native birds is uncertain. In urban areas both *montanus* and *domesticus* are significant economic pests of horticultural seedling crops; in the countryside they compete for food with domestic poultry and consume large quantities of growing, stacked and stored grain.

Philippines

Whitehead (1899) collected and recorded the presence of Tree Sparrows, which he believed had been imported by the Chinese before the middle of the century, in Manila on the island of Luzon and in Cebu City on Cebu between 1893 and 1896. Delacour & Mayr (1946) reported them to be well established and common in and around Manila and in other settled parts of Luzon, and also on Cebu. According to Parkes (1959) and Du Pont (1971), the subspecies on Luzon is *saturatus* (Sakhalin Island, South Korea, Japan and Taiwan) and was imported from Japan or Taiwan, whereas that on Cebu is *malaccensis*, and came from the Malay Peninsula. Du Pont says that the latter form has also been recorded on the island of Negros a few kilometres west of Cebu.

Lesser Sunda Islands and Moluccas

Vaurie, in Peters (1962), says that Tree Sparrows of the race *malaccensis* have been introduced to, and seem to be established on, the islands of Ambon (south of Seram in the Moluccas) and Lombok in the Lesser Sunda Islands; on the latter, Summers-Smith (in preparation) suggests that they may occur as natural colonists from Bali.

Sulawesi (Celebes)

Tree Sparrows (according to Peters (1962) of the same form as in the Lesser Sunda Islands) have been introduced to Sulawesi, where Stresemann (1936) indicates that they were then restricted to the southern peninsula. Since then they have become widely distributed; Escott & Holmes

(1980) reported them at Ujung Pandang in the south, from Donggala (the port of Palu) on the northwestern coast, and at Manado at the tip of the northern Minahassa Peninsula.

Borneo

Although Tree Sparrows are said by Vaurie (in Peters 1962) to have occurred in Borneo as early as the 1950s, no specific localities are mentioned. Gore (1964) reported that early in that year a group of three or four had arrived in the port of Sandakan in northeastern Sabah. By the following September, a small breeding colony had become established in the dockland area, from where the birds began to spread to other parts of the town. Smythies (1981) recorded Tree Sparrows in Sarawak in 1965; Gore (1968) found a small colony on Labuan Island off the southwestern coast of Sabah in 1966; Harrisson (1970 and 1974) saw some in Brunei in 1969 and in Sabah in 1973. It has been suggested (e.g. by Medway & Wells 1976) that these birds probably arrived as stowaways on vessels from Hong Kong and/or Singapore, where the subspecies are respectively *saturatus* and *malaccensis*: so far, however, no taxonomic study has been made to determine the birds' source of origin (Summers-Smith, in preparation).

'The discontinuous nature of these occurrences, both in space and time', wrote Summers-Smith, 'suggests that they are the result of introductions rather than a natural spread of range, probably involuntarily as ship-borne immigrants.'

OCEANIA

Marianas

According to Ralph & Sakai (1979), Tree Sparrows have been introduced to the Marianas, where they are common on the islands of Saipan and Rota and uncommon on Guam. Summers-Smith (in preparation) considers it most likely that they are of the form *saturatus*.

———————————

Thomson (1922) records that in New Zealand the Otago Acclimatization Society released two Tree Sparrows in 1868, and that the Auckland Society freed three in the same year and a further nine in 1871, none of which were heard of again.

According to Bourne (1957), an unsuccessful attempt was made in the nineteenth century to introduce Tree Sparrows (recorded by Peters (1962) as of the nominate form) to Bermuda.

Abdulali (1964) records an unsuccessful introduction of Tree Sparrows from Moulmein in Burma to the Andaman Islands by Colonel R. C. Tytler in about 1860.

———————————

The **Spanish Sparrow** (*Passer hispaniolensis*) occurs naturally from the Mediterranean region of southwestern Europe and North Africa eastwards through Turkey, the Caucasus, Iran and Transcaspia to Turkestan and Afghanistan. The species' origin in the Canary and Cape Verde islands is uncertain.

In the Canaries,[6] Spanish Sparrows arrived (possibly as shipborne stowaways) in the early nineteenth century. Between about 1820 and 1830 they were confined to Fuerteventura and Lanzarote, from where they spread to Gran Canaria before 1856; they arrived on Tenerife between 1871 and 1887 – probably as a deliberate introduction around 1880. According to Meade-Waldo (1893), they failed to become established, but 12 years later Von Thanner (1905) found them abundant in Santa Cruz on La Palma. By 1949 they had spread to Gomera, and today occur on all the aforementioned islands; on some they have both driven the native Rock Sparrow (*Petronia petronia*) from settled areas and have become a pest of growing crops, but are themselves regarded by the human inhabitants as something of a culinary delicacy.

Spanish Sparrows were first recorded in the Cape Verde Islands[7] (on São Nicolau and São Thiago) in 1865, from where by 1898 they had apparently spread to Brava, Fogo, Boa Vista and Maio. They seem to have died out on Brava before 1951, but are now established on all the other inhabited islands apart from São Vincente, where although they were once said to be especially common in and around Mindelo, they are now believed to have died out.

Bannerman (1965) records that following a period of prolonged easterly gales in 1935 Spanish Sparrows (of the nominate form) arrived as wind-blown vagrants from southern Spain or

North Africa on the island of Madeira, where they became established in the capital, Funchal, whence they have since spread slowly east and west along the south coast.

NOTES

1 For much of the information on Tree Sparrows in the United States I am indebted to Flieg 1971; other references are American Ornithologists' Union 1957, 1983; Barlow 1973; Baumgartner 1984; Bennitt 1932; Blake 1975; Cooke & Knappen 1941; Cottam 1956; Gault 1922; Jones 1942; Long 1981; McKinley 1960; Musselman 1950, 1953; Phillips 1928; Pindar 1925; Robbins & Barlow 1973; Roots 1976; Wetmore 1964; Widmann 1907; Wilhelm 1959. See also: *Forest and Stream* 5: 372 (1876); *Bulletin of The Nuttall Ornithological Club* 2: 73 (1877); 5: 121, 191 (1880); *Auk* 6: 326 (1889); 26: 322 (1909); *US Department of Agriculture (Division of Economics) Ornithological Bulletin* 2: 184 (1888).

2 A letter from Daenzer dated 4 February 1888, Phillips (1928), Cooke & Knappen (1941) and Wetmore (1964) all say that 12 pairs of Tree Sparrows were released. Barlow (1973) gives the number freed as 20. Twenty pairs of House Sparrows (*P. domesticus*) (q.v.) and some Old World finches were liberated at the same time.

3 Low-lying alluvial land along a river.

4 Blakers, Davies & Reilly 1984; Frith 1979; Hobbs 1961; Keve 1976; Le Souef 1958; Long 1972, 1981; McGill 1960; Pizzey 1980; Rolls 1969; Roots 1976; Ryan 1906; Sage 1956; Tarr 1950; Williams 1953.

5 Type locality England: Kleinschmidt 1935. This race is not recognized. (J. D. Summers-Smith, personal communication, 1985.)

6 Bannerman 1953, 1963; Cullen, Guiton et al. 1952; Lack & Southern 1949; Long 1981; Meade-Waldo 1893; Von Thanner 1905.

7 Alexander 1898, Bannerman 1953; Barboza du Bocage 1898; Bourne 1955, 1966; Fea 1898–9; Keulemans 1866; Long 1981; Voous 1960.

Village Weaver

(Ploceus cucullatus)

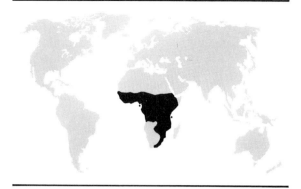

NATURAL DISTRIBUTION

Africa south of about 15° N apart from eastern Ethiopia, eastern Somalia, northern Angola, South West Africa (Namibia), western Botswana and western South Africa.

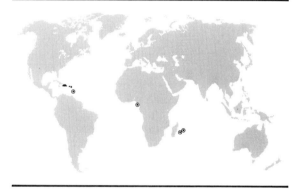

NATURALIZED DISTRIBUTION

Africa: ?São Tomé Island, Mascarenes (Mauritius, Réunion); North America: West Indies (Puerto Rico, Haiti, Dominican Republic, Saona, Martinique).

AFRICA

São Tomé Island

According to Peters (1962), the nominate form of the Village Weaver that ranges from Senegal eastwards to Cameroon, Chad and on Fernando Póo Island (Bioko), probably occurs on São Tomé in the Gulf of Guinea as a result of human intervention; it could well, however, have arrived on the island as a natural immigrant from Guinea or Gabon on the West African mainland.

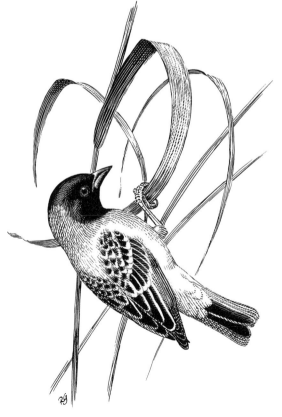

Mauritius and Réunion[1]

Village Weavers of the race *spilonotus* (southern Mozambique and eastern South Africa) were apparently imported from the latter country to Mauritius in about 1886 where they were released in the north near Cap Malheureux, and to Réunion at an unknown date by a Mr Beylier. They were found to be increasing on the former in the 1950s and common in lowland regions on the latter in the following decade, but had not so far spread to Rodrigues. On both Mauritius and Réunion they have become a pest to seed crops.

NORTH AMERICA

West Indies (Puerto Rico, Haiti, Dominican Republic, Saona and Martinique)[2]

Precisely when Village Weavers (of the nominate form) were first introduced to the West Indies is unknown. They may have been brought as cage-birds to Hispaniola from West Africa on Spanish slavers at any time after 1512. According to Moreau de Saint-Méry (1797–8),[3] some had previously been imported from Senegal and elsewhere in West Africa to the town of Cap Francaise in Haiti where they were placed in a number of large aviaries, and where Fitzwater (1971) claimed that a colony was established near Tron Caiman as early as 1783. In 1927, a small population was found at Cul-de-Sac in Haiti, and by about 1930 the birds were local residents in both Puerto Rico and Haiti, especially near Port d'Estere, Thomazeau between Port-au-Prince and L'Arcahaie, and a few years later a small breeding colony was found in Haiti north of Trouin.

In the 1960s, the Village Weaver population on Hispaniola (where the species is known locally as Madame Sara or the Fauvette Warbler) increased dramatically to such an extent that serious damage to rice crops was reported. Although many birds are poisoned and shot annually, they still occur in flocks up to several hundred strong that kill trees by defoliating them for nesting material, and are serious pests in rice plantations, where crop losses of up to a fifth have been reported. Bond (1979: 224) described the species'

habitat and range as 'chiefly fairly open lowland country in Haiti, in particular the Cul-de-Sac plain, including Port-au-Prince. Has in recent years become widespread in Hispaniola . . . and [on] Saona Island'.

On the island of Martinique in the Lesser Antilles, where they have occurred since before 1963 and where they are now well established in the region of Prêcheur, Village Weavers are first known to have bred successfully before 1980. They have yet to be recorded on Guadeloupe or on any other islands in the Lesser Antilles.

According to Bannerman & Bannerman (1968), Village Weavers of the nominate form were introduced to Praia on southern São Thiago in the Cape Verde Islands before 1924, but have since apparently died out.

The **Black-headed** or **Yellow-backed Weaver** (*Ploceus melanocephalus*) occurs naturally from Senegal to Benin, Niger, Chad, Nigeria, the Central African Republic, Zaire, Zambia, the northeastern Sudan, and western Uganda, Kenya and Tanzania. According to Snow (1950), a *Sitagra* sp. was introduced to São Tomé in the Gulf of Guinea between 1909 and 1928, where it became fairly abundant. Peters (1962) says that the form that may have been imported is *P. m. capitalis* of Nigeria, southern Chad and the Central African Republic.

The **Baya Weaver** (*Ploceus philippinus*) ranges from Pakistan eastwards to southwestern China, Malaysia, Sumatra, Java and Bali. From time to time, for example in 1970 (Webster 1975), small groups (which could be either escaped or deliberately released cagebirds or natural immigrants from the Chinese mainland) appear on Hong Kong Island and near Ping Shan, but have not been known to breed.

Berger (1972) reports that since 1965 Baya Weavers have escaped or have been unsuccessfully released on Oahu in the Hawaiian Islands.

Wingate (1985) records that the South African **Masked** or **Cape Weaver** (*Ploceus capensis*), which may have been introduced unsuccessfully to Mauritius in 1892 (Meinertzhagen 1912), has been observed building nests in Bermuda.

NOTES

1 Benedict 1957; Carié 1916; Long 1981; Peters 1962; Rountree, Guérin et al. 1952; Staub 1976; Watson, Zusi & Storer 1963.

2 American Ornithologists' Union 1957, 1983; Barré & Barau 1982; Barré & Benito-Espinal 1985; Blake 1975; Bond 1964, 1971, 1972, 1979; Fitzwater 1971; Long 1981; Pinchon 1963, 1976; Pinchon & Benito-Espinal 1980; Raffaele 1983; Wetmore & Lincoln 1933; Wetmore & Swales 1931.

3 *Description de la Partie Française de Saint-Dominique*, Vol. 1: 300 and Vol. 2: 426.

Madagascar Fody
(*Foudia madagascariensis*)

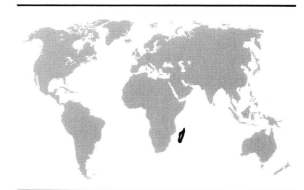

NATURAL DISTRIBUTION
Madagascar.

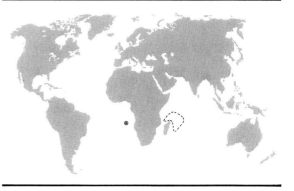

Note: Not naturalized on all islands within dashed line.

NATURALIZED DISTRIBUTION
Africa: Mascarenes (Mauritius, Réunion, Rodrigues), Seychelles, Amirante Islands, Farquhar Atoll, Providence Group, Comoros, Agaléga Islands, ?Assumption, ?Aldabra, ?Cargados Carajos, ?Îles Glorieuses, St Helena; Oceania: Chagos Archipelago.

AFRICA

Mauritius; Réunion; Rodrigues

According to Moreau (1966),[1] the Madagascar Fody was established on the island of Mauritius before 1775 and was released on Rodrigues around 1865. On the former, where it is now widespread and abundant, it tends to disperse inland in summer when grasses (Gramineae) are in seed. On the latter (and on Réunion, where

the date of its arrival is apparently unrecorded), it is common in native forests. Although Newton (1959) could find no evidence of interspecific competition between Madagascar Fodies and the endangered endemic Mauritius Fody (*Foudia rubra*), Temple, Staub & Antoine[2] considered that there may be some seasonal rivalry for food. On Rodrigues, competition from *F. madagascariensis* (coupled with extensive destruction of forest habitat in the 1960s) may well be an important factor in the decline of the endemic and endangered Rodrigues Fody (*F. flavicans*). Moreau points out that the Madagascar Fody is one of the most successful naturalized birds on islands around Madagascar.

Seychelles[3]

Madagascar Fodies were first introduced to the island of Mahé around or before 1860 (certainly before 1865): Penny (1974: 116) cites a possibly apocryphal story of 'two neighbours who were in dispute over the ownership of a plot of land where one of them was growing rice. The frustrated party, to gain revenge on his rival, sent to Mauritius for some cardinals,[4] which were known to be a plague of rice fields, and released them into his neighbour's territory. From that day to this, it has been well-nigh impossible to grow rice in Mahé'. From Mahé, the birds colonized naturally (or were introduced to) Praslin before 1904 (probably in 1902), Frigate before 1939, Cousin after 1940 (one account says not until the late 1950s) and Cousine in 1958. Today, Madagascar Fodies breed regularly and are abundant and widespread on all the larger islands, especially in settled areas, and on some have largely displaced an earlier seed–eating introduction, the Common Waxbill (*Estrilda astrild*) (q.v.), which may have been introduced as long ago as 1768. On the other hand, Crook (1961) considered that interspecific competition with the rare Seychelles Fody (*Foudia sechellarum*) had played no part in the reduction in range of the endemic species, since both seem to have adopted separate ecological niches that differ from their original ones. On 27-ha Cousin, for example, over 1,000 *sechellarum* live in native woodland, whereas about 50 *madagascariensis* occupy more disturbed habitats. (See also below under Seychelles Fody.)

Amirante Islands; Farquhar Atoll; Providence Group

According to Moreau (1966) and Penny (1974), the Madagascar Fody has colonized – or has been introduced to from the Seychelles (in some cases perhaps accidentally) – most of the cultivated Amirante Islands, where it was first recorded (on Desroches) in 1882, and Farquhar Atoll. In 1976, C. J. Feare (personal communication, 1986) found the species to occur as follows: Amirantes: breeding on Eagle and Desroches, but absent from Desnoeufs, Marie Louise, Etoile, Boudeuse and African Banks. Farquhar: common and breeding, even on the tiny islets of the atoll rim. Providence Group: present, with males in red breeding plumage on Cerf, and breeding in small numbers on Providence; about 100 present and breeding on St Pierre – an island that formerly supported a vast breeding colony of seabirds, but where, since devastation of the habitat by guana extraction activities, the Madagascar Fody is now the only breeding species.

Comoros[5]

Madagascar Fodies were first collected on the island on Mohéli in 1864 (and again in 1869) and on Mayotte in 1888, from where they spread to Grande Comore and Anjouan probably after 1906–7. Benson (1960) believed that they may originally have reached the archipelago, where they are now established on all islands, as natural colonists.

Agaléga Islands

According to Guého & Staub (1983), the relatively recent introduction of the Madagascar Fody to the Agaléga Islands (where it is now common on both Île du Nord and Île du Sud) has resulted, through interspecific competition, in the almost total disappearance of the introduced Red-crested Cardinal (*Paroaria coronata*), which was already rare on the islands by 1924.

Assumption; Aldabra; Cargados Carajos

According to Long (1981: 393), 'The Madagascar Weaver[6] is believed to have been introduced and to have become established on these islands but details appear to be lacking'. The author has been unable to trace any reference to these alleged introductions.

Îles Glorieuses

Benson, Beamish et al. (1975) suggest that Madagascar Fodies probably occur as natural colonists on Îles Glorieuses where, however, it is possible that they were introduced.

St Helena[7]

Two dates have been suggested for the introduction of Madagascar Fodies to St Helena; 1673, when the British East India Company assumed control from the Dutch and were declared 'the true and absolute lords and proprietors' of the island, or 1815, when it was strongly garrisoned by British troops guarding Napoleon Bonaparte. Of these alternatives, the latter seems the more likely, since cagebirds that had presumably escaped or been deliberately released were not recorded in the wild until Melliss (1870) found them to be common. In 1952–3, Haydock (1954) reported them to be fairly abundant in both littoral and highland areas, where they have become something of an agricultural pest.

OCEANIA

Chagos Archipelago[8]

The Madagascar Fody was first recorded on the island of Diego Garcia in 1884 by Finsch (1887), when it was said to be abundant. Although 2 years later Saunders (1886) found the species to be rare, in 1899 several were collected on the island where, however, none were reported by the Percy Sladen Trust expedition of 1905. Bourne (1971) found fodies on Île du Coin, Peros Banhos in 1957, and Loustau-Lalanne (1962) and Hutson (1975) reported them to be well estab-

lished on Diego Garcia and scarce on Perhos Banhos and Salomon; a few were also seen by Hutson on Île Grande Barbe.

The **Seychelles Fody** (*Foudia sechellarum*)[9] is a rare endemic of the Seychelles archipelago, where although it was originally found on at least Marianne, La Digue, Praslin, Frigate, Cousin and Cousine, it now survives only on the three last-named rat-free islands. Five birds translocated by the British Seychelles Expedition in August 1965 to D'Arros in the Amirantes were still alive 3 years later, but, according to Penny (1974), have not been seen since. As mentioned above, competition with the alien Madagascar Fody (*F. madagascariensis*) is not considered by Crook (1961) to have been a factor in the reduced distribution of the native species in the Seychelles, since each occupies a separate ecological niche that differs from its original one.

NOTES

1 Other references are: Barré & Barau 1982; Benedict 1957; Cheke 1985; Crook 1961; Fisher, Simon & Vincent 1969; King 1981; Lever 1985b; Long 1981; Moreau 1960; Newton 1959; Peters 1962; Rountree, Guérin et al. 1952; Staub 1973, 1976; Watson, Zusi & Storer 1963. See also: S. A. Temple, J. J. F. Staub & R. Antoine, 'Some background information and recommendations on the preservation of the native flora and fauna of Mauritius', unpublished report submitted to the Mauritius Government (1974).
2 See under note 1.
3 Crook 1961; Diamond & Feare 1980; Fisher, Simon & Vincent 1969; Gaymer, Blackman et al. 1969; King 1981; Lever 1985b; Long 1981; Newton 1867; Penny 1974.
4 The species is also known as the Red Fody, Madagascar Cardinal or Madagascar Weaver.
5 Benson 1960; Crook 1961; Long 1981; Milne-Edwards & Oustalet 1888.
6 See note 4.
7 Crook 1961; Haydock 1954; Long 1981; Melliss 1870.
8 Bourne 1971; Finsch 1887; Hutson 1975; Long 1981; Loustau-Lalanne 1962; Peters 1962; Saunders 1886.
9 Crook 1961; Fisher, Simon & Vincent 1969; Gaymer, Blackman et al. 1969; King 1981; Lever 1985b; Long 1981; Newton 1867; Penny 1974.

Red Bishop
(*Euplectes orix*)

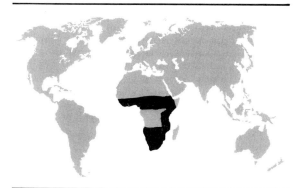

NATURAL DISTRIBUTION

Africa south of about 12° N apart from Somalia, southern parts of Zambia, Zaire, and northern Angola and South West Africa (Namibia).

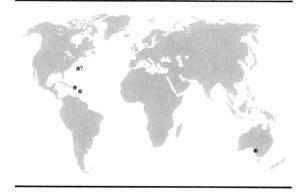

NATURALIZED DISTRIBUTION

North America: ?Bermuda, West Indies (Martinique, Puerto Rico); Australasia: ?Australia.

NORTH AMERICA

Bermuda

In the early 1970s, Red Bishops, descended from escaped or deliberately released cagebirds, became established in large fodder crop fields at St Luke's farm in Southampton parish. Although they at first bred successfully in stands of Cow Cane (*Arundo donax*), and by the end of the decade had increased to around 50–60, the change in husbandry from fodder grass to vegetables (following the cessation of dairy farming) caused them to decline, and the survivors may no longer be breeding.[1]

West Indies (Martinique and Puerto Rico)

In October 1982, Barré & Benito-Espinal (1985) saw a party of four male Red Bishops at Carère on the island of Martinique, where they believed that the species was established and spreading in the vicinity of Duclos, inland from the town of Fort-de-France. Two years later Bon-Saint-Côme (1984) reported a flock of about 50 near Lareinty, and several pairs at Gaigneron.

The Red Bishop is a common introduced bird in the rice fields and sugar-cane plantations on the island of Puerto Rico.[2]

AUSTRALASIA

Australia[3]

Red Bishops – escaped or deliberately released cagebirds – were first reported in the wild at Wood's Point near Paradise some 40 km south of Adelaide on the Murray River in South Australia in 1926, where 3 years later they were found to be breeding. In 1933, a small colony of some 15–20 birds had become established in reed-beds in the Murray Bridge/Tailem area along the Murray River where, although none have been reported since 1976, a small number may possibly survive. In South Australia isolated sightings of Red Bishops were reported in Hope Valley in 1932, at McLaren Flat (1933), Noarlunga, Cape Finnis and Lake Alexandrina (1936), and at Berri (north-east of Adelaide) in 1941; in New South Wales some were seen at Kuringai and in the Turramurra district north of Sydney in 1944; in none of these areas do any survive today.

———————————————

In about 1965, Red Bishops that had presumably escaped or had been deliberately released from aviaries appeared in the wild on Oahu in the Hawaiian Islands, where according to Pyle (1976 and 1977) they remained in small numbers until at least 1973. As Berger (1972), who says the birds were of the form *franciscana* (Senegal to Ethiopia, Uganda and Kenya), and Blake (1975) only record the species as having been 'introduced', and as it is not referred to at all by

Zeillemaker & Scott (1976), it has presumably now disappeared.

According to Haydock (1954), an unsuccessful attempt was made around 1929 by H. Bruins-Lich to establish Red Bishops of the nominate form (imported from South Africa) on the island of St Helena.

———————————————

The **Golden Bishop** (*Euplectes afer*) occurs over much the same range as its congener *E. orix* except that it is present in west-central Africa but absent from western South Africa.

Berger (1972) says that birds of the nominate subspecies (the so-called Napoleon Weaver, which ranges from Senegal to Chad and the Central African Republic) escaped or were released on Oahu in the Hawaiian Islands around the same time as *orix*, where a few survived until at least 1972. The Hawaiian Audubon Society (1975) suggested that the species may then still have been established, but since, as with the Red Bishop, it is again only referred to by Berger (1972) and Blake (1975) as an 'introduction', and is ignored by Zeillemaker & Scott (1976) and Pyle (1977), it must be presumed to have now died out.

According to Brazil (1985 and in press), the Golden Bishop has been found breeding in the Chiba, Kanagawa and Hyogo prefectures of Japan. The 'Napoleon Weaver' is also a common bird in the rice fields of Puerto Rico.[4]

———————————————

An unsuccessful attempt was made by Guild (1938) to establish 'orange weavers' (?sp.) in Tahiti.

———————————————

The **White-winged Widow Bird** or **White-winged Wydah** (*Euplectes albonotatus*) ranges in Africa from the southern Sudan south to the eastern Cape Province of South Africa, and from Cameroon south through the Congo to Angola.

A number are believed to have escaped or been released in Australia[5] from the wreck of the *Malabar* in 1931, when they became established in swampy grassland along the Hawkesbury River north of Sydney, New South Wales. In 1967, about 50 were reported, and some were seen again in the following year. Although Frith (1979) believed that the colony had died out, it is possible that a few may still be established around Windsor on the Hawkesbury River.

Haydock (1954) records that around 1929 an unsuccessful attempt was made by H. Bruins-Lich to naturalize White-winged Widow Birds of the nominate form, imported from South Africa, on St Helena in the South Atlantic.

The **Pin-tailed Wydah** (*Vidua macroura*) is a resident of Africa (apart from Somalia) south of about 15° N, including some east and west coast offshore islands.

In June 1962, the species was first reported in the wild in the Hawaiian Islands[6] near the Waikiki Aquarium on Oahu. In the early 1970s a number became established locally in the Kapiolani Park–Diamond Head area and in the Na Laau Arboretum on Oahu, where, although breeding is known to have occurred, the host of this parasitic species has not been recorded. According to Zeillemaker & Scott (1976), Pin-tailed Wydahs were then still local and uncommon in dry lowland residential and community parklands. Pyle (1977) lists them as 'apparently established and breeding', but the American Ornithologists' Union (1983) says that they have not become established.

Blake (1975) and the American Ornithologists' Union (1983) say that the Pin-tailed Wydah has been introduced to, and is established in, Puerto Rico, where it is widespread but uncommon.

Milne-Edwards & Oustalet (1888) recorded the presence of Pin-tailed Wydahs on the island of Mayotte in the Comoros archipelago north-west of Madagascar, where three were collected in 1903 and a further 10 in 1906–7. None, however, have been reported since then, and, according to Benson (1960), the species has died out.

NOTES

1 D. B. Wingate, personal communications, 1984 and 1985.
2 Raffaele 1983; and T. Silva, personal communication, 1985.
3 Blakers, Davies & Reilly 1984; Condon 1948b, 1962; Frith 1979; Jenkins 1977; Lendon 1948; Long 1981; Morgan 1933; Tarr 1950.
4 Raffaele 1983; and T. Silva, personal communication, 1985.
5 Frith 1979; Lane 1975; Long 1981; McGill 1960; Tarr 1950.
6 American Ornithologists' Union 1983; Berger 1981; Blake 1975; Hawaiian Audubon Society 1975; Heilbrun 1976, 1977; Long 1981; Pyle 1976, 1977; Zeillemaker & Scott 1976.

European Starling
(*Sturnus vulgaris*)

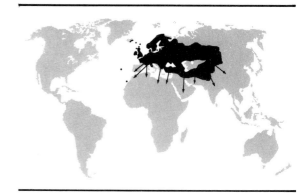

NATURAL DISTRIBUTION
A Palaearctic species occurring from the British Isles, the Azores and the Canaries, eastwards to Lake Baikal in the USSR, north to northern Scandinavia, and south to southern France, central Italy, northern Greece, Turkey and northern Iran, Afghanistan and Pakistan. In much of Europe, it has considerably extended its range in the present century, but is currently declining in the north. Winters south in the Iberian Peninsula, northern Africa, Egypt, Iraq, Arabia, southern Iran, Nepal, northern and eastern India and extreme northwestern China.

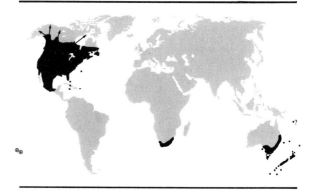

Note: Occurs in Bahamas and Cuba as winter visitor; natural colonist of Bermuda, Fiji and Tonga.

NATURALIZED DISTRIBUTION
Africa: South Africa; North America: USA, Canada, Mexico, West Indies (Jamaica, ?Puerto Rico); Australasia: Australia, New Zealand.

AFRICA

South Africa[1]

Meinertzhagen (1952) records that on 14 January 1899 he gave the former Prime Minister of South Africa, Cecil John Rhodes, shortly before he sailed from Southampton for Cape Town, 18 Starlings that had been caught at a winter roost on his father's estate at Mottisfont in Hampshire, England, and this has since been generally accepted as the date of the only known shipment of Starlings to South Africa.

Basing his argument on Sir Lewis Michell's authoritative biography of Rhodes,[2] R. K. Brooke (personal communication, 1981) convincingly disputes Meinertzhagen's date. As a busy politician, Rhodes would have had little opportunity to concern himself with other matters until, after the disastrous Jameson Raid, he resigned the premiership in January 1896. Thereafter, he made several visits to England (in 1899 arriving at Southampton on 14 January – the day Meinertzhagen says that he left), and according to Michell the only dates on which he could have returned to South Africa with a consignment of winter-caught Starlings were 3 April 1897, 21 April 1900 and 18 January 1902. Early records of Starlings in South Africa make the last two dates unlikely – and in any case Rhodes was dying by 1902. 'I therefore believe', wrote Brooke, 'that the introduction took place in 1897: the birds arrived on 20 April [the voyage normally took 17 days] in Table Bay Harbour and were probably released the next day at Groote Schuur at Rondebosch.' In support of his claim, Brooke draws attention to Sclater,[3] who says that he was informed that Rhodes brought Starlings to Cape Town in 1898, and that at the time of writing the birds were well established on the inhabited slopes of Table Mountain and that they had been reported in Stellenbosch on the interior side of the Cape Flats. This precise report of hearsay within a decade of the event, Brooke contends, supports his belief that the birds arrived in April 1897. Although it may seem strange that Meinertzhagen could have been mistaken, Brooke's argument is remarkably persuasive.

Whatever the exact date of their arrival, the Starlings, which Colonel Meinertzhagen suggested were probably winter visitors to Britain from continental Europe, seem to have settled down well in the South West Cape. By at least 1905 they had reached Wynberg, some 16 km from Cape Town, and within a further 2 years had colonized Robben Island (now the site of a notorious prison camp) in Table Bay.

By 1910, Starlings had spread eastwards across the Cape Flats to Gordon's Bay and Stellenbosch at the foot of the Hottentots' Holland Mountains, which for some years seem to have acted as a barrier to their further advancement. They reached Worcester, to the north-east, before 1922, and Elgin to the east in the same year. By the end of the decade, they had dispersed from one or both of these centres along the Breede Valley to Riversdale where, however, they seem at first to have occurred only locally and in small numbers since they were not recorded in Heidelberg, only 32 km west of Riversdale, until 1942. Two years previously Starlings had arrived on the banks of the Great Brak River, but surprisingly were not observed at Mossel Bay until 1953. They reached Knysna in 1944 or 1945, George in 1948, Plettenberg Bay in 1951 and Port Elizabeth possibly by 1953. By 1949, large flocks occurred on the Cape Flats and elsewhere in the South West Cape.

Their dispersal northwards from Cape Town through the Swartland is less well documented. They reached Darling around the turn of the century and Velddrift, at the mouth of the Berg River, between 1926 and 1928. In the latter year they arrived at Redlinghuis and Ceres (probably from Worcester), from where by 1953 they had spread to the Cold Bokkeveld. The Olifants River Mountains impeded their expansion inland, but they arrived at Citrusdal around 1944 and at Clanwilliam some 6 years later. Winterbottom & Liversidge (1954) recorded their most northerly locality as at Kleinvlei, 19 km north of Clanwilliam, where they arrived in 1952.

Starlings' colonization of the Breede Valley between Worcester and Swellendam is also not well documented. Although they are believed to have reached Kogmanskloof near Montagu by at least 1940 they were not observed at Robertson for a further 5 years, suggesting an invasion via the river further east – possibly from Riversdale. Alternatively, they may have come over the Rivier Zonder End Mountains from Elgin (bypassing Villiersdorp) or have colonized Kogmanskloof from Worcester, subsequently backtracking to Robertson. Other dates for the first arrival of Starlings in the South West Cape are, to the north, Tulbagh (1920) and Hoop en Vitkoens (1953); to the east, Somerset West (1910), Heidelberg (1942), River Sonderend (1943), Tradouw's Pass (1947) and Barrington and Ladismith (1953); and to the south-east, Hermanus (1938), Port Beaufort (1942) and Cape L'Agulhas (1944).

The early 1950s distribution and status of Starlings in the South West Cape, as recorded by Winterbottom & Liversidge (1954), is summarized in Table 14. By the early 1950s, the Starling was thus established in the South West Cape along the coast from Graafwater and Clanwilliam south and east to Plettenberg Bay, inland to a line running through Citrusdal, the southern border of the Cold Bokkeveld, Orchard (near De

Table 14 Distribution and status of European Starlings (*Sturnus vulgaris*) in the South West Cape, South Africa in the early 1950s

Area	Distribution and status
Aliwal North	Present since 1942–4
Barkly West	Uncertain
Barrydale	Possibly since 1949
Bellville	Generally distributed and common
Bredasdorp	Resident in Bredasdorp and Napier; common in Potberg Valley
Caledon	Elgin (since *c.*1922); Grabouw (before 1922); Hermanus (before 1938, probably before 1934, common by 1944); Villiersdorp (since 1943)
Cape Town	Generally distributed and common
Ceres	Common since *c.*1928; also recorded at Prince Alfred Hamlet and at Hoop en Uitkoms on the Cold Bokkeveld
Clanwilliam	Uncommon but breeding at Citrusdal since *c.*1944 and at Clanwilliam since *c.*1950. A few at Craig Royston since *c.*1949; reported from Graafwater and Kleinvlei
Fort Beaufort	Uncertain
George	At George since 1948 and at Great Brak River since *c.*1940; recorded in 1952 on the Avontuur road beyond the Outeniqua Mountains north of George
Heidelberg	Present since 1943–4

Continued

Table 14 (*continued*)

Area	Distribution and status
Knysna	Patchily distributed in Knysna since 1944–5; first nested 1947; fairly common between the Klein River and De Vlugt; first reported at Plettenberg Bay in 1951, and nested in 1952; at Barrington since 1953
Ladismith	Since 1953; also between Ladismith and Barrydale
Malmesbury	Present at Hopefield, Malmesbury, Mooreesburg and Velddrift. Breeding in Langebaan–St Helena Bay area; in the Darling area present since 1900 and generally distributed
Montagu	Present for many years in limited urban areas; no record of breeding; present at Kogmanskloof since at least 1940
Mossel Bay	Two pairs seen in 1953
Paarl	Generally distributed; numerous and breeding at Franschhoek, Paarl and Wellington
Piquetberg	At Redlinghuis since *c.*1928; also recorded at Kapiteinskloof, Saner and Piquetberg
Port Elizabeth	Present by at least 1954
River Sonderend	Present and breeding since 1943
Riversdale	Common at Melkhout-Kraal and at Riversdale where they first arrived in 1930
Robertson	Uncommon; first recorded in 1945
Simonstown	Common in urban areas
Somerset West	Generally distributed and common at Faure, Gordon's Bay (first bred 1914) and Strand; less common at Somerset West (since 1910)
Stellenbosch	Present in the Blauwklip River valley in small flocks since before 1940; arrived at Groot Drakenstein *c.*1924 and at Stellenbosch (common) *c.*1910
Swellendam	Uncertain; recorded at Port Beaufort at the mouth of the Breede River in 1942, at Swellendam and the Tradouws Pass in 1947 and at Storms Vlei in 1948
Tulbagh	Generally distributed but uncommon; first recorded *c.*1920
Worcester	First recorded before 1922; also at Orchard in the Hex River valley
Wynberg	Nested on the Wetton road in 1903 or 1905; generally distributed and common

Source: Winterbottom & Liversidge 1954

Doorns), Robertson, Montagu, Barrydale, Ladismith and the Outeniqua Mountains. The area occupied lay almost exclusively below the 600 m contour and had a relatively dense European human population.

From the South West Cape, Starlings gradually began to spread into the Eastern Cape. They were first confirmed as breeding in Uniondale in 1955 (possibly in the previous year), having probably arrived from the south-west via the Kamnasie River valley (where they were first noted in 1952) rather than from Oudtshoorn in the west where none were recorded until 1956.

In Humansdorp, Starlings are known to have been established (and probably breeding) in both urban and rural areas by 1960. In Uitenhage in 1956, a pair usurped the hole of a Red-breasted Wryneck (*Jynx ruficollis*) on Amanzi Estate; by 1960, Starlings were breeding in the town and were regularly seen on the sewage disposal works and in various parts of the surrounding countryside.

In the Port Elizabeth Division, a single Starling was seen at Sea View in March 1954, and 3 years later (or less) breeding probably took place at Deal Party Estate. By the autumn of 1960, Starlings were widespread and breeding in Port Elizabeth and in the residential suburbs of Walmer, Skoenamakers Kop, Swartkops and Redhouse.

Starlings were first recorded in Grahamstown in October 1958, when a pair was observed nesting, and at King William's Town in April 1961. In the following year, the Department of Agriculture and Technical Services reported that Starlings had been released in East London and in Durban, Natal, and that they were established throughout the Cape Province: they were not, however, recorded at East London until 1966, at Gonubie Mouth and Keisammahoek until 1969, and at Kei Mouth and Seymour until 1970. 'From Cape Town', wrote Winterbottom (1978: 975), 'the Starling . . . has penetrated a considerable distance northward into the Karoo, even to the Orange River at its mouth. However, its establishment in the Karoo seems rather insecure and it is liable to retreat thence during a drought'. Maclean (1985: 666) described the Starling as occurring in the 'western, southwestern, southern, eastern and northeastern Cape, Karoo, and southern Natal (to Durban); northward expansion apparently slowing down towards Natal'. P. A. Clancey (personal communication, 1985) wrote that although 'singletons have occurred in Durban, it seems not to breed any further to the north-east than Umtata in the Transkei. Competition from the [Common] Indian Myna *Acridotheres tristis* is too great in these parts.'

Although Starlings appear to be non-migratory in the Western Cape (where, however, considerable flocks gather on the Cape Flats in winter), there is evidence of some seasonal movement in the Eastern Cape. One of the birds' favourite habitats is wattle-groves bordering large permanent vleis:[4] their food includes grasshoppers, hairy caterpillars and the arils[5] of rooikrantz (*Acacia cyclops*); in orchards along and under the Hottentot's Range some depredation to soft fruit occurs, but in compensation injurious insects are also eaten, sometimes being 'hawked' – swallow-like – on the wing. Although the nominate form was presumably the one introduced, Meinertzhagen records that an individual taken at Stellenbosch in 1949 had a purple head and ear-coverts similar to those of *S. v. menzbieri*[6] of Krasnoyarsk.

Colonization by Starlings of new areas in South Africa was not by emigration from over-populated groups (as is normally the case with many other species) but rather by the casual arrival of a single pair that bred and then departed, followed in the succeeding year by the appearance of several pairs that nested at the same site; there then followed a simple increase in the colony which appeared proportionate to the rate of successful breeding. According to Liversidge, colonization has been by 'long jumps' rather than from township to township, with intervening areas being occupied later. Although initially slow to spread, and an almost exclusively urban species, the Starling has now moved into the interior and is found throughout the Cape in areas of intensive cultivation around European-style farmsteads as well as in villages and towns. Indeed, 'No factor other than the occupation of human habitation', wrote Liversidge (1962: 15), 'is evident in the spread of the species'. Feare (1984) considered that further expansion northwards into cultivated parts of East Africa was possible, but that a similar extension of range in the south-west would probably be prevented by the Namib and Kalahari deserts.

NORTH AMERICA

USA, Canada and Mexico[7]

In view of the subsequent history of the Starling in the United States it is a matter of some surprise that several early introductions failed completely.

As early as the winter of 1872–3,[8] (and again in succeeding years) Starlings are believed to have been unsuccessfully liberated by the Acclimatization Society of Cincinnati, Ohio, and in July 1877 more were released without success in Central Park, New York, by the American Acclimatization Society, and at about the same time possibly also in Tuxedo Park. The records of the Portland (Oregon) Song Bird Club reveal that some 35 pairs were freed near that city in 1889 and 1892, and that although they initially 'increased remarkably well' only a few survived by the turn of the century.

The Starling's reputation as a mimic was the indirect cause of its introduction to the United States. In Shakespeare's Henry IV occurs the line 'Nay, I'll have a starling shall be taught to speak nothing but 'Mortimer''".[9] In the 1880s, an eccentric New York drug manufacturer, amateur ornithologist and Shakespearian, Eugene Schieffelin, conceived the bizarre idea of introducing to the United States all the birds referred to by the Bard. Accordingly, 40 pairs (of the nominate form) imported from England were planted in Central Park in 1890 and a like number in the following year (Phillips 1928).[10] Breeding began almost immediately, the first nest being discovered, appropriately, under the eaves of the American Museum of Natural History; by 1893–4, flocks up to 50 strong were being reported, and by the following year Starlings were common in many districts of New York City and had spread to Long Island where 3 years later they were said to be abundant. In 1895, Frank M. Chapman[11] summed up the Starling's introduction to, and status in, the United States as follows:

This Old-World species has been introduced into Eastern North America on several occasions, but only the last importation appears to have been successful. The birds included in this lot, about sixty in number, were released in Central Park, New York city, in 1890, under the direction of Mr Eugene Schieffelin. They seem to have left the park and established themselves in various favourable places in the upper part of the city. They have bred for three successive years in the roof of the Museum of Natural History and at other points in the vicinity. In the suburbs about the northern end of the city they are frequently observed in flocks containing as many as fifty individuals. These birds are resident throughout the year, and as they have already endured our most severe winters, we may doubtless regard the species as thoroughly naturalized.

In 1897, Starlings were released at Springfield, Massachusetts, and at Allegheny, Pennsylvania, and at around the same time also at Bay Ridge, New York, and perhaps elsewhere, but nowhere seem to have met with lasting success. The Central Park birds, however, continued to flourish, although initially they increased and expanded their range only slowly, dispersing no more than 40 km in their first decade. Thereafter, they spread explosively, and by 1908 their range included Connecticut, New Jersey and southeastern Pennsylvania. By 1916, they had crossed the Allegheny Mountains to West Lafayette, Ohio, and in the following year appeared in Savannah, Georgia. Their rate of expansion then declined, following heavy mortality in the severe winter of 1917–18, and by around 1920 the population was showing signs of stabilization. They reached Alabama in 1918, Kentucky (1919), Louisiana (1921), Illinois and South Carolina (1925), Texas (1926), Oklahoma (1929), northern Mississippi and Iowa (1930), Minnesota (1932), Arkansas and South Dakota (1933), Missouri (1934), Nebraska and Wyoming (1937), New Mexico, Colorado and Nevada (1938), North Dakota, Montana and Utah (1939), Idaho (1941), California (1942), Oregon and Washington (1943) and Arizona (1946).

The spread of Starlings in the United States was steady and concentric from their point of release in New York – non-breeding pioneer winter parties of half-a-dozen or so often reconnoitering in advance of the main population that arrived some 5 years later. By 1938, they had extended their range to 103° W and were breeding as far west as the Mississippi and probably in eastern Texas. By 1940, they had spread some three-quarters of the way to the west coast, where they were first seen on 10 January 1942 at Tule Lake in Siskiyou County, California, and in the following year north of Pullman in Whitman County, Washington, and at Malheur National Wildlife Refuge in Harney County, Oregon.

Cooke & Knappen (1941) recorded Starlings as breeding south to northern Florida, as far north as the northern bank of the St Lawrence River, east to the eastern end of Anticosti Island, Quebec, and as far west as eastern South Dakota, Nebraska and Kansas. Outside the breeding season winter migrants had been recorded from as far afield as Montana, Salt Lake City, Utah, Denver, Colorado and Albuquerque, New Mexico. Wing (1943) estimated the area occupied by Starlings at some 7 million km² and the total population at up to 50 million.

By 1952–3, Starlings were found throughout southern Canada and in the whole of the United States apart from southern Florida and north-eastern New Mexico. They were breeding widely in both countries north-east of a line extending from south-central British Columbia, north-eastern Oregon and northern Utah to southern Mississippi; south-west of this line they occurred mainly as winter migrants. They were first recorded in Alaska, at Juneu airport in the south-east, on 17 April 1952, having probably spread from the Burns Lake region or the Queen Charlotte Islands of northern British Columbia; a decade later three Starlings were reported from Fort Yukon north of the Arctic Circle, and breeding was first recorded in Alaska at St Petersburg, in 1963. In 1974, a group of four was seen in the north-west at Kotzebue on the Chukchi Sea, and single birds at Homer and Cordova in the south. Four years later Starlings were breeding in the Alaskan interior at Fairbanks.

By the mid-1950s – when the population was estimated at well over 50 million – colonization of the United States and central-southern Canada was virtually complete; Starlings could then be found, if only on migration outside the breeding season, almost throughout the former country, though they were, perhaps, not yet fully entrenched on parts of the Pacific coast. As Elton (1958: 26) wrote, 'In zoogeographical terminology, a purely Palaearctic species . . . has become Holarctic within half a century'.

In Canada, unsuccessful attempts were made to establish Starlings in Quebec in 1875, 1889 and 1892. Emigrants from the northeastern United States seem first to have appeared, at Niagara Falls, Ontario, in the autumn of 1914, and on 1 December of the following year at Halifax, Nova Scotia. Thereafter they spread to Betchouane,

Quebec by April 1917, to Brockville, Ontario (1918), Toronto, Ontario (1922), Grand Manan Island, New Brunswick (autumn, 1924), Tignish, Prince Edward Island (late 1930 or early 1931), York Factory, Manitoba (11 May 1931), Camrose, Alberta (late 1934), Tregarva, Saskatchewan (spring 1937), and Tomkins, Newfoundland on 9 June 1943, where by 1956 they were established and breeding over an area of some 5,200 km². In British Columbia, Starlings were first recorded at Williams Lake in 1945–6; in the late winter of 1946–7, some were seen at Oliver in the southern Okanagan Valley (where they may have come north from Washington or west from Alberta) and on the coast at Bella Coola at the head of Burke Channel. They first nested in the Province in 1948, and by 1950 were well established and breeding in xerophytic forest areas of the Okanagan Valley and the southern Rocky Mountains trench, in the open 'parklands' of the Cariboo, and in the extensive grasslands around Nicola Lake. By 1953, they had been recorded from as far west as the Queen Charlotte archipelago and Vancouver Island; 5 years later, Carl & Guiguet (1958) reported that 'a large population winters in Vancouver City on the lower mainland', and by the end of the decade Starlings were widely distributed and common throughout most of British Columbia. In 1969, a single individual penetrated as far north as Inuvik, south of the Beaufort Sea, in the Northwest Territory.

Starlings may have crossed the border from southern Texas into northeastern Mexico as early as 1935; 3 years later, in December, a number were seen at Anaxhuac east of Nuevo Laredo, and a party of 10 was observed at Santa Lucia between Laredo and Monterrey in December 1939. In 1946, a flock estimated at 500 was counted at Nuevo Laredo, and 2 years later some were noted at Linares, Nuevo Léon. By the early 1970s, Starlings had reached Guanajuato, northern Veracruz and Yucatán, from where they are still spreading southwards.

The American Ornithologists' Union (1983: 586) described the Starling's North American distribution as follows:

breeds from east-central and southeastern Alaska, southern Yukon, northern British Columbia, southern Mackenzie, central Saskatchewan, northern Manitoba, northern Ontario, northern Quebec, southern Labrador and Newfoundland south to northern Baja California [Mexico], southern Arizona, southern New Mexico, southern Texas, the Gulf coast and southern Florida (to Key West), and *winters* throughout the breeding range and south to Guanajuato, Veracruz, the Bahama Islands (south to Grand Turk, and eastern Cuba). . . . Reported casually in the Hawaiian Islands (Oahu, possibly also Hawaii), on Bermuda [but see below], and in the summer north to western and northern Alaska, northern Mackenzie and Southampton Island; an individual recorded in Panama (Canal Zone) was questionably a natural vagrant.

After several failures and a slow start the explosive spread of the Starling in North America has been little short of phenomenal. It is even more remarkable because, as Feare (1984) points out, it has taken place on a continental land mass that already possessed several indigenous birds (e.g. such members of the New World Oriole family, Icteridae, as blackbirds (*Agelaius*), grackles (*Quiscalus*) and cowbirds (*Molothurus*)) with similar ecological requirements, rather than on an island or archipelago where adventives might be expected to be successful. The Starling's colonization of North America seems to have been helped by three main factors: first, although the bird's Eurasian range suggests that it is adaptable to a wide variety of habitats and climates, it is naturally a lowland species, seldom being found above 600 m, whereas in North America it seems equally at home in the Great Plains region, much of which lies at over 1,500 m and in places rises to more than 2,100 m; second, it competes successfully with such other hole-nesting birds as Wood Duck (*Aix sponsa*), Eastern Bluebirds (*Sialia sialis*) and Red-headed Wood-peckers (*Melanerpes erythrocephalus*); finally, in contrast to introductions to other countries, at least some of the founder stock imported to the United States was, or later became, migratory, thus assisting natural dispersal. Indeed, the movement of Starlings in North America is, as would be expected, in general similar to that in Europe. Some populations remain sedentary while others migrate, and a few apparently migrate in certain years but not in others. Migration occurs from mid-February to late March and again between late September and November. Topographical features determine migration routes – the birds flying north–south or north-east–south-west on the Atlantic seaboard, while west of the Appa-lachians they tend to travel north-east–south-west.

Although, following human settlement westward, the Starling's overall distribution initially advanced more rapidly in southern and south-central states, it extended its breeding range more rapidly in the north. Within 80 years of its introduction it was, according to Feare, one of the most numerous birds in North America, with a breeding range that extended from Arctic Canada to subtropical Mexico. Although the Starling's geographical distribution may now have stabilized, the population density in some areas seems still to be increasing. Dolbeer & Stehn (1979), who found that between 1968 and 1976 the breeding population doubled in southwestern states and that in California it increased by 19 per cent, also noted decreases in density (although no contraction of range) in some states. They suggested that numbers would continue to rise in the former area (and in some other places, especially in Michigan), and that agricultural damage would intensify.

Starlings have been recognized as an agricultural pest since at least the 1920s, and the good they do by probing the ground for insects, grubs, wireworms and Japanese beetles (in summer up to 90 per cent of their food may consist of small invertebrates) is far outweighed by their depredations on fruits, berries, corn (maize), grain, rice and seeds, and millions of dollars are spent annually in efforts to control their numbers. In urban areas, the accumulated guano of huge roosting murmurations damages buildings and fosters histoplasmosis; Starlings can also transmit other diseases such as avian tuberculosis, toxoplasmosis, psittacosis, cryptococcal meningitis, avian malaria and Newcastle disease. Several aircraft crashes have been attributed to damage caused by Starlings being sucked into jet engines. Attempts at control, by shooting, trapping, poisoning, the use of contraceptive baits, fireworks, automatic exploders, the broadcasting of distress calls and ultrasonic sound, and electrifying (or applying jelly-like substances, e.g. 'Roost No More' to) window ledges, and even stuffed owls (!), have met with only limited success.

West Indies (Jamaica[12] and ?Puerto Rico)

Starlings were liberated near Annotto Bay on the north-east coast of Jamaica in 1903–4. Although Taylor (1953) records that they were not established at the release site in the 1940s, he says that in 1947 flocks of between 200 and 300 were encountered in the Parish of St Ann some 55 km to the west. Bond (1979) reported them from Brown's Town, some 60 km to the west, in 1949, and others were noted in the Castleton Botanical Gardens 42 km away in 1951 and on the coast at Ocho Rios 40 km from Annotto Bay in 1952. Although initially they spread only slowly, in recent years, according to Lack (1976), they have increased their range more rapidly, and are now widely distributed in pastureland with scattered trees in lowland areas and in some mid-elevations, but seldom occur in natural habitats.

Bond (1979: 180) says that the Starling 'has become well established in Jamaica . . . [in] open, farming country, chiefly in the hills'. Jamaica has been less cleared of native forest than some other West Indian islands and this, rather than the tropical climate, may have inhibited the species' expansion on the island.

According to the American Ornithologists' Union (1983), the Starling has also been introduced to, and is established on, Puerto Rico (see also page 484).

AUSTRALASIA

Australia[13]

Table 15 gives details of introductions of Starlings (believed to have all been of the nominate

Table 15 Introduction of European Starlings (*Sturnus vulgaris*) to Australia, 1856–81

Date	Number	Locality	Remarks
*c.*1800*	75	Hobart, Tasmania	Imported by Dr E. L. Crowther from New Zealand
1856 (April)	?	Sydney, New South Wales, or Melbourne, Victoria	
1857 (January)	?	Melbourne, Victoria	Imported by a dealer named Brown
1858 (January)	?	Melbourne, Victoria	Imported by a dealer named Neymaler
1860	6	Phillip Island, Victoria	
1862	44	Melbourne, Victoria	
1863	36	Melbourne and/or Phillip Island, Victoria	
1864	6	Melbourne, Victoria	
1865	120	Melbourne, Victoria	
1866	6	Phillip Island, Victoria	
1866	15	Melbourne, Victoria	
1860s	?	Adelaide, South Australia	By the Acclimatization Society
1869	14	Brisbane, Queensland	Imported by the Queensland Acclimatization Society with other species from England on the *Flying Cloud*; most died soon after arrival
1871	*c.*20	Melbourne, Victoria	
1880	?	Sherwood Scrubs, New South Wales	Probably from Victoria; reported to be breeding in 1883
*c.*1880	?	Victoria	From New Zealand
1881 (and after)	89	Black Hills and Torrens Park, near Adelaide, South Australia	By the Acclimatization Society; spread rapidly and established on Eyre Peninsula by the end of the century

Sources: see note 13
* This is the date given by Littler (1901), but since Starlings were not introduced to New Zealand until 1862, it is presumably a misprint for 1860, or more probably, 1880

subspecies) to Australia. In his anniversary address delivered to the Victoria Acclimatization Society on 24 November 1862, Professor F. McCoy said that eight Starlings (part of the Zoological Society's stock which had been transferred to the Acclimatization Society) had, together with other songbirds, been released in the Botanic Gardens in Melbourne, where two years later the society reported that they 'may now be considered thoroughly established'. Nevertheless, in about 1880 more were imported to Victoria from New Zealand – largely on the advice of Edward Wilson, sometime editor of the *Argus* newspaper and founder in 1861 of the Acclimatization Society of Victoria, who, according to Jenkins (1977), said 'I think . . . that it [the Starling] is one of the most useful birds in the world' (!); as a result, by 1885 'large flocks' were established in Royal Park and in the grounds of the university, and by 1906 the entire southern portion of Victoria had been colonized.

In South Australia, Starlings rapidly increased, were common in some places as early as 1894, and had spread to the Eyre Peninsula by about 1900 and to Kangaroo Island before 1910. In the Riverina region of New South Wales, Starlings were still very rare in 1906 when, according to Frith (1979: 194), local residents were reported to 'long for their arrival to help them to battle against the huge armies of locusts and caterpillars that often infest those districts'. Twenty years later, Starlings were established throughout settled areas of New South Wales, and by the middle 1940s had become serious horticultural pests in the Riverina. Colonization of Queensland (where Starlings were first recorded at Stanthorpe in 1919) is believed to have been the result of natural spread from New South Wales. On Tasmania, Starlings had dispersed to Sorrel by the end of the century and by the early 1900s were common in and around Hobart, but had spread little beyond Sandy Bay, 6 km away; to the north they had penetrated to Bridgewater and had been recorded from up to 32 km inland.

Tarr (1950) reported Starlings to be established in cultivated regions throughout most of New South Wales, Victoria and Tasmania, and on King and Flinders islands in Bass Strait. In Queensland, they were common along the coast between Brisbane and Maryborough – a distance of some 225 km. In South Australia, they were abundant on Eyre Peninsula and on Kangaroo Island, but probably occurred no further north than Port Augusta – 275 km from Adelaide.

Pizzey (1980) found Starlings well established in much of southern and eastern Australia and on many coastal islands from Eyre Peninsula and Kangaroo Island to about the Tropic of Capricorn (23°28′ S) in Queensland: in the latter state, where they range inland to around Roma, occasional records since the late 1970s from as far north as Innisfail, Cairns, Port Douglas, the Iron Range on Cape York Peninsula and even from Cape Moresby in Papua New Guinea suggest the possibility of a coastal extension of range northwards. Starlings also occur, presumably as natural immigrants, on Lord Howe Island (since 1924), and have been common on Norfolk Island (where they are believed to have first appeared around 1913) since at least the late 1960s. They are widespread and abundant virtually throughout New South Wales, Victoria, Tasmania and islands in Bass Strait; in South Australia they are found north to the Oodnadatta–Birdsville Track north of Lake Eyre, and west to Ooldea on the southern fringe of the Great Victoria Desert, 275 km east of the border with Western Australia. Reports from around Nullarbor Station on the Bight coast in western South Australia (where 2,000 were destroyed in 1980–1) and from near Eucla in Western Australia (where the species was officially proscribed by the Bureau of Agriculture as early as 1895) and even from as far west as Esperance (700 km west of the South Australia border) suggest the probability of a gradual expansion westwards. The destruction of a single Starling near Esperance in 1970 led to the discovery and eradication of two small breeding colonies in the vicinity where, however, others were reported in 1976 and 1982. An influx of Starlings from South Australia in the spring of 1984 resulted in the destruction of some 600 birds between Eucla and Mundrabilla. Although further spread away from the coast in this area is likely to be inhibited by the arid interior, and the Great Victoria Desert has hitherto proved an effective barrier to invasion from the south-east of the apparently suitable intensively cultivated south-west of Western Australia, the construction of townships along the south coast of Australia may, as Feare (1984) points out, enable Starlings to 'leap-frog' their way into Western Australia (as, indeed, has been occurring intermittently since 1976), despite efforts to prevent them by the Agricultural Protection Board of Western Australia.

The preferred habitats of Starlings in Australia are settled areas and intensively (and, to a lesser extent, lightly) cultivated land, and in Victoria, New South Wales, South Australia, Tasmania and coastal Queensland most of these habitats have already been occupied. Although, according to Frith (1979), Starlings have not so far invaded *Eucalyptus* forests, they can live in considerable numbers in *Eucalyptus* woodland, in riverine timber belts, and around swamps on open inland plains – in some places in relatively unaltered native habitats.

As elsewhere, Starlings in Australia are sedentary, migratory, nomadic and dispersive; as an example of the last, Pizzey (1980) cites the case of an individual ringed at Oatlands on Tasmania on 12 September 1959 and recovered at Brisbane, Queensland, on 11 October – a flight of 1,960 km in 29 days at an average speed of 67.6 km per day.

Until around the turn of the century, Starlings in Australia were regarded somewhat ambiguously, being considered a pest in South Australia but protected in Victoria. Cleland (1910) seems to have been the first to see the species in its proper perspective: 'Though useful to a slight extent, [the Starling] does much more harm than good. . . . Unquestionably starlings feed greatly on cultivated fruits and on cultivated grains during the season when these are available. . . . its virtues are unquestionably less than its defects, and no encouragement whatever should be given to its appearance in any part of the country.' Starlings in Australia damage fruit, corn, vegetable crops and newly seeded fields and, with House Sparrows (*Passer domesticus*) (q.v.), in autumn and winter in Victoria consume vast amounts of grain used on large commercial poultry farms. They carry and transmit parasites and diseases, contaminate buildings and kill trees with their droppings, and compete for food and, especially, nesting sites with native species – particularly parrots (Psittacidae) and some waterfowl (Anatidae) in the interior where suitable sites are limited.[14] In compensation, Starlings kill locusts, larvae, wireworms, blowflies, cutworms and sheep and cattle ticks. In winter, they form huge murmurations up to 20,000 strong that are preyed on by Brown Goshawks (*Accipiter fasciatus*) and Little Falcons (*Falco longipennis*).

New Zealand[15]

Thomson (1922) records that Starlings were introduced to New Zealand in an attempt to combat plagues of insects that occurred in the late 1850s and early 1860s (see Table 16). Thus between 1862 and 1883 a total of 653 Starlings were introduced to New Zealand by acclimatization societies, and many more were imported during this period by private individuals. As early as 1870 Starlings were reported in some parts to be 'becoming very numerous', and Mr C. Hutchins told Thomson (p. 155) that 'when I arrived in Napier from England in 1875, there were only four starlings in the town. They increased rapidly . . . and after eleven years they were there in hundreds of thousands'. Thirty-six years later Thomson said that Starlings were 'abundant in most parts of the country, and . . . the noise they make when roosting can be heard, literally for miles'.

Table 16 Introduction of European Starlings (*Sturnus vulgaris*) to New Zealand, 1862–83

Date	Number	Acclimatization Society
*c.*1862	17	Nelson
1865	12	Auckland
1867	3	Otago
1867	20	Canterbury
1867	15	Auckland
1868	81	Otago
1868	82	Auckland
1869	85	Otago
1871	40	Canterbury
1877	60	Wellington
1878	90	Wellington
1881	14	Wellington
1882	100	Wellington
1883	34	Wellington

Source: Thomson 1922

On New Zealand's offshore islands Starlings were introduced to the Chathams by Mr L. W. Hood before the turn of the century; they were first recorded on Campbell Island around 1907, on the Kermadecs (before 1910), on Macquarie (about 1930), on the Snares (1948) and on the Antipodes in 1952. Oliver (1955) reported them on Three Kings, Kermadecs, Mokohinau, Hen, Great and Little Barrier, Poor Knights, Mayor,

Kapiti, Karewa, the Chathams, Stewart, the Snares, Auckland, Campbell and Macquarie. Wodzicki (1965:434) said that Starlings were 'widely distributed and abundant, North, South, Stewart and Raoul [Kermadecs], Chatham, Snares, Auckland, Campbell, and Macquarie Islands'. Kinsky (1970) confirmed their presence on the Chathams, Kermadecs, Snares, Aucklands, Campbell and Macquarie islands, and Williams (1973) added that they nested on Three Kings, the Kermadecs, Chathams, Antipodes, Campbell, Auckland and Macquarie islands, but not apparently on the Snares. Falla, Sibson & Turbott (1979) said that Starlings were one of the most familiar birds in New Zealand, occurring in all habitats except dense bush at altitudes over 1,200 m, and that they were common on the Kermadecs and Chathams and had even colonized remote subantarctic Macquarie and Campbell. They have recently become established on Cavalli Island (Motuharakeke) off the east coast of Northland.

As in Australia, it was not for some years after its establishment that the Starling's status as a pest was recognized in New Zealand. Drummond (1906) claimed that 'there is hardly any limit to the good words said of the starling. It is frequently described as the only introduced bird worth having'. As the species became more numerous and widespread this extravagant encomium became modified. It was found that the birds' communal roosts created unwelcome noise and defaced and damaged buildings; that they competed successfully for food and nesting sites with native species; that they damaged a variety of grain and fruit crops, including pears, plums, peaches, grapes, cherries, currants and strawberries, and that they ate considerable numbers of beneficial Bumble Bees (*Bombus* spp.) and Hive or Honey Bees (*Apis mellifera*). Starlings also eat, and disseminate through their droppings, the seeds and fruits of several noxious plants. By way of compensation they eat some injurious invertebrates, such as army worms, the larvae of crane flies, click beetles, and sheep and cattle ticks. Indeed, Moon (1979) claimed that the Starling in New Zealand is 'regarded as a beneficial species to gardening and farming' except in forested areas, and Feare (1984) said that its successful colonization of New Zealand has been assisted by the provision of nesting boxes, as it is widely believed that Starlings help to control grassland insect pests. In sheep-farming districts, where natural nesting sites are in short supply, Starlings are encouraged to breed by the provision of a box on nearly every fence post.

In 1954, 58 Starlings were transplanted outside their natural range in the Soviet Union near Ulan-Ude in the Buryat ASSR, south-east of Lake Baikal, where although breeding occurred in the following year they disappeared shortly thereafter.

'Although the Starling became established in Bermuda in the mid-1950's', wrote D. B. Wingate (personal communication, 1981), 'and increased rapidly to become the second most abundant bird [after the House Sparrow (*Passer domesticus*)] by the mid-1960s, it was not deliberately introduced. Vagrants began arriving from the North American continent as early as 1929 after the species had begun to increase in North America. But it did not begin breeding on Bermuda until after the cedar [*Juniperus bermudiana*] forest had died from an introduced scale insect [*Carulaspis minimia*] epidemic in the late 1940s.' The total 1985 population was estimated at around 120,000 – the same as that of the introduced alien House Sparrow (q.v.). Competition for nesting sites between Starlings and the native Eastern Bluebird (*Sialia sialis*) has contributed to a decline of the latter in Bermuda since the 1960s.

Starlings were first recorded in the Bahamas[16] in 1956, and have since been reported from Nassau on New Providence, on Grand Bahama and on Eleuthera, southwestwards to Grand Turk in the Turks Archipelago. According to Roots (1976: 132), 'the Bahama race of the red-bellied woodpecker [*Melanerpes superciliaris bahamensis*] has become very rare since the introduced starling commandeered its tree holes'. Starlings have, however, never been introduced to the Bahamas, where they occur solely as winter visitors (mainly mid-October to mid-March) from the United States.

Starlings also occur as winter visitors in north-eastern Cuba,[17] especially on the coast in the vicinity of Gibara.

In November 1949, five Starlings flew ashore from a vessel out of Falmouth, England, near

Lago de Maracaibo, Venezuela,[18] but were not seen again. Although much of South America[19] is likely to be unsuitable for Starlings they could well become established in some of the more temperate towns in the foothills of the Andes and perhaps also in Tierra del Fuego.

According to the American Ornithologists' Union (1983: 586), Starlings are also 'reported casually in the Hawaiian Islands (Oahu, possibly also Hawaii)',[20] where they were first recorded – presumably as natural vagrants from the west coast of North America – as recently as July 1979. Were they to become permanently established, they would probably compete for breeding sites with native hole-nesting species, but would be unlikely to compete with them for food because of differing dietary requirements.

Exactly when Starlings first arrived on Ono-i-Lau,[21] a tiny islet lying some 368 km south-east of Suva on Viti Levu in the Fijian archipelago, is uncertain. Some Fijians believe that they appeared in 1922 or in the later 1920s, while others contend that they did not occur there before 1948. Pernetta & Watling (1978) suggest that they may have arrived around 1930. When first discovered in 1951, a population numbering around 1,000 adults was well established and widely distributed on Ono-i-Lau, and also occurred on Tuvana-i-Tholo and Tuvana-i-Ra to the south, on Votua (several hundred), 129 km north-north-east, and on Doi. Hill (1952) suggested, in the absence of any documented introduction, that the birds came as natural immigrants from the Kermadecs, some 1,200 km to the south, which they colonized from New Zealand before 1910, and which support the nearest population to Fiji. Alternatively, they might possibly have arrived on board ship from Australia or New Zealand. Pernetta & Watling found Starlings to be locally abundant in agricultural areas and villages on Ono-i-Lau and Votua. In the absence of competing Common Mynahs (*Acridotheres tristis*) (q.v.), they are also common on the island of Tongatapu in Tonga – especially in the capital, Nuku'alofa. Attempts to eradicate the Starling in Fiji and Tonga were unsuccessful, but so far the species has not spread as was initially feared. 'It is probable', wrote Watling (1982: 102), 'that tropical conditions do not suit it and it will remain restricted to the southernmost islands in the region.'

According to Cain & Galbraith (1957), Starlings have been reported from the New Hebrides (Vanuatu), 1,150 km north of Norfolk Island and 1,300 km west of Ono-i-Lau.

The **Black-winged Starling** (*Sturnus melanopterus*) is confined to the islands of Java, Bali and Lombok.

Escaped cagebirds have occurred from time to time since around 1920 on the island of Singapore, where at least one pair has bred successfully.[22] A small population is presently established on St John's Island, 5 km south of Singapore, where it is assumed to be breeding. These birds are believed to have been released by smugglers in an attempt to evade the authorities.

NOTES

1 For much of the early history of the Starling in South Africa, I am indebted to Winterbottom & Liversidge 1954 and Liversidge 1962. Other references are: Cyrus & Robson 1984; Feare 1984; Gebhardt 1954; Howard 1907; Liversidge n.d.; Long 1981; Mackworth-Praed & Grant 1963; Maclean 1985; Meinertzhagen 1952; Peters 1962; Quickelberge 1972; Roots 1976; Siegfried 1962; Van der Merwe 1984; J. M. Winterbottom 1955a, b, 1957a, b, 1966, 1978 (and personal communication, 1981); and R. K. Brooke, P. A. Clancey and J. Vincent, personal communications, 1981. See also: *The Ostrich* 9: 9(1938); 14: 156(1943); 16: 157–68; 214–7 (1945); 22: 202 (1951); 23: 23, 129–30, 220–21 (1952); 25: 89–96 (1954); 26: 46, 136, 157 (1955); 28: 124 (1957); 29: 19–22, 49 (1958); 31: 173 (1960); 33: 75 (1962); and W. L. Sclater, *Annals of the South African Museum* 3 (8): 303–87 (1905).
2 *The Life of the Rt Hon. Cecil John Rhodes 1853–1902*, 2 vols (Arnold: London, 1910).
3 See under note 1, p. 366.
4 Hollows in which water collects during the rainy season.
5 The fleshy cup surrounding the seeds of some plants.
6 *S. v. menzbieri* is not mentioned by D. Amadon (in J. L. Peters's *Check-list of Birds of the World* (1962)), and C. Vaurie (*American Museum Novitates* No. 1694: 16) argues that it is anteceded by *poltaratskyi*, which is the currently accepted subspecific name for the purple-headed forms from western Siberia. (C. J. Feare, personal communication, 1985.)
7 American Ornithologists' Union 1957, 1983; Anderson 1934; Ballard 1964; Blake 1975; Carl & Guiguet 1972; Coffey 1959; Coleman 1974, 1977;

Cooke 1925; Cooke & Knappen 1941; Cottam 1956; Dickerson 1938; Dolbeer & Stehn 1979; Elton 1958; Feare 1984; Forbush 1920; Godfrey 1949; Guiguet 1952a, b, c; Howard 1959; Imhof 1962; Jarvis 1980; Jewett & Gabrielson 1929; Jung 1945; Kalmbach 1922, 1928, 1932; Kalmbach & Gabrielson 1921; Kessell 1953, 1957; Laycock 1970; Long 1981; Mills 1943; Moore 1984; Palmer 1899; Peters 1962; Peterson & Chalif 1973; Phillips 1928; Quaintance 1946, 1949, 1951; Ricklefs & Smeraski 1983; Roots 1976; Sealy 1969; Silverstein & Silverstein 1974; Stewart 1964; Tousey & Griscom 1937; Tuck 1958; Wing 1943a; Wood 1924; Yocum 1963.

8 Laycock (1970: 77) says that 'trial introductions were hopefully, but unsuccessfully carried out in Massachusetts and New Jersey in 1844'.

9 Part I, act 1, scene 3.

10 Other accounts say, respectively, that 60 pairs, 60 birds and 20 birds were released in 1890.

11 *Handbook of Birds of Eastern North America* (Appleton: New York), quoted by Feare (1984: 38).

12 Bond 1979; Long 1981; Taylor 1953.

13 Anon. 1985h; Balmford 1978; Blakers, Davies & Reilly 1984; Chisholm 1926; Cleland 1910; Condon 1962; Cooper 1947; Douglas 1972; Feare 1984; Frith 1979; Jenkins 1929a, 1977; Kinghorn 1933a,b; Lavery 1974; Littler 1901; Long 1972, 1981; McKean & Hindwood 1965; Morris 1969; Palmer 1899; Peters 1962; Pizzey 1980; Rolls 1969; Roots 1976; Ryan 1906; Smithers & Disney 1969; Tarr 1950; Thomas 1957; Williams 1953.

14 As early as 1876–82, A. Newton, in W. Yarrell's *A History of British Birds* (4th edn, vol. 2), was predicting that where introduced abroad Starlings would contribute to the destruction of native species.

15 Collinge 1919, 1920–1; Drummond 1906; East & Pottinger 1975; Falla, Sibson & Turbott 1979; Feare 1984; Kinsky 1970; Long 1981; Moon 1979; Oliver 1955; Palmer 1899; Thomson 1922, 1926; Williams 1953, 1969, 1973; Wodzicki 1965.

16 Bond 1979; Long 1981; Taylor 1953.

17 American Ornithologists' Union 1983; Bond 1979; Lack 1976; Long 1981.

18 American Ornithologists' Union 1983; Scott 1950.

19 Sick 1968.

20 American Ornithologists' Union 1983; Elliott 1980; A. Berger, personal communication, 1985.

21 Carrick & Walker 1953; Dhondt 1976a; Hill 1952; Long 1981; Manson-Bahr 1953; Mercer 1966; Pernetta & Watling 1978; Watling 1982.

22 C. J. Hails, personal communication, 1985.

Common Mynah
(*Acridotheres tristis*)

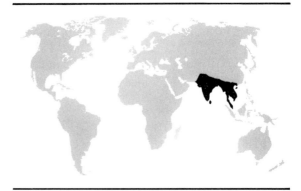

Note: Map includes natural extension of range in Indo-China, which may have been assisted by escapes from captivity.

NATURAL DISTRIBUTION

From Afghanistan, India, Nepal, Sri Lanka and Burma eastwards to Hainan and southern China; in this century it has expanded its range naturally southwards through Thailand, Laos, Cambodia, North and South Vietnam, and Malaya as far south as Singapore.

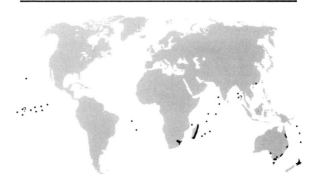

NATURALIZED DISTRIBUTION[1]

Asia: Hong Kong, Andaman and ?Nicobar islands, Laccadive and Maldive islands; Africa: South Africa, Madagascar, Mascarenes (Mauritius, Réunion, Rodrigues), Seychelles, Agaléga Island, Comoros, St Helena, Ascension; Australasia: Australia, New Zealand; Oceania: Hawaiian Islands, Fiji, ?Samoa (Tutuila), Polynesia (Cook, Tubuai, Society, Tuamotu and Marquesas islands), Solomon Islands, ?Vanuatu, New Caledonia, Chagos Archipelago.

491

ASIA

Hong Kong[2]

The Common Mynah was first reported in Hong Kong in January 1952, where a small population, presumably derived from escaped cagebirds, is established and breeding on the Mong Tseng Peninsula, and perhaps also elsewhere.

Andaman and Nicobar islands[3]

According to Beavan (1867), Common Mynahs were introduced as scavengers to Port Blair on South Andaman Island by Colonel R. C. Tytler shortly after the establishment there of a penal colony in 1858. Palmer (1899) indicates that they were introduced to the Andamans before 1873, whereas Wood (1924) says that they were released on Ross Island in about 1880, where Hume (1873) said they had greatly increased but had not crossed the 400 m of open water to Port Blair where, however, by the turn of the century they were one of the commonest bird species. Abdulali (1964) said that they were then common in suitable areas throughout the South Andamans. They were apparently common in the harbour on Nancowry Island and on Camorta Island in the neighbouring Nicobar archipelago around the turn of the century (Butler 1899 and Richmond 1903), but were not found there by Abdulali (1967).

Laccadive and Maldive islands

According to Ali & Ripley (1968–74), Common Mynahs probably occur in the Laccadive and Maldive archipelagos, on some islands of which they are abundant, as the result of introduction by human agency. They are absent, however, from Addu Atoll in the extreme south.

AFRICA

South Africa[4]

According to a report in the *Natal Mercury* of 25 November 1932, three pairs of Common Mynahs imported from Mauritius (where they were said to be adept in destroying injurious insects, including the cane-borer of sugar cane) were released by a M. Leon St Guillaume from the top of a double-decker, horse-drawn tram in Point Road, Durban, in 1888. Kent (1927) says that 'About the year 1900 a dealer in birds on the Point Road, allowed several pairs to escape from captivity. Those finding a happy environment soon established themselves and bred rapidly. Today Mynahs are known in several Natal towns.' According to J. Vincent (personal communication, 1981), this latter introduction coincided with the arrival in Durban of immigrants from India. Since the Mynahs of Mauritius are of the nominate form (Afghanistan, India and Southeast Asia) and those in South Africa have been identified as *A. t. tristoides* (central and northern Burma and Nepal) either the earlier introduction did not take place or, more probably, the birds eventually died out; in either case the population in South Africa today would seem to be descended from those that escaped around the turn of the century.

By the 1950s Common Mynahs had become established over most of Natal, and had spread to Johannesburg, Bramley (around 1938), Germiston, Pretoria and the Witwatersrand in the Transvaal, to the Orange Free State, and to Cape Province, where they first appeared at Kimberley (where they have since died out) in 1964. Mynahs are now established throughout Natal and the Witwatersrand and in much of the Transkei, are locally common in the Transvaal Highveld, and appear to be spreading down the coast through Cape Province. 'The species has been extremely successful', wrote J. Vincent (personal communication, 1981), 'although it occurs exclusively in association with man – mainly in urban areas and to a lesser extent on farms. . . . The ecological effects of mynahs is mainly to chase other bird species away. They are very aggressive when breeding and will not tolerate smaller birds in their territory, apart from being omnivorous and usurping the niches of others.' Maclean (1985: 667) described Mynahs as occurring in 'Natal, Transkei, Johannesburg, Pretoria (not established)'. In some areas Mynahs have been accused of causing damage to soft-fruit crops.

According to Kent (1927), 'In nests examined during the latter part of the nesting season it is usual to find many bird lice *Mallophaga*. They breed up to abnormal numbers during the warm weather, and are shaken or cleaned off by the birds when they leave the nest. They then start to wander from the environs of the nest and occasion much alarm owing to the resemblance they bear to blood-sucking lice.' Liversidge (1975) records that an outbreak of dermatitis (with eruptive lesions similar to scabies) in Oribi Military Hospital in Pietermaritzburg in 1945 was only brought under control when a Mynah's nest in the ward containing sarcoptes itchmites (*Ornithonyssus (Liponyssus) bursa*) was discovered and destroyed.

Madagascar[5]

Common Mynahs of the nominate form have been introduced to the Indian Ocean island of Madagascar to control grasshoppers and other insects on at least two occasions – first towards the end of the eighteenth century and later in 1875 at Tamatave on the east coast of Grande Île by the then French Consul, Alfred Grandidier. In 1863, Maillard (quoted by Decary 1962) said that although at first regarded as the 'saviour of agriculture', Mynahs were soon found not only to be eating few insects but to have become a pest in the soft-fruit orchards which they had been imported to protect. Milon, Petter & Randrianasolo (1973) quoted Grandidier as saying that the descendants of his birds had become abundant around Tamatave by 1879, and Decary states that 6 years later Mynahs were common there and at Pointe à Larrée.

By 1930 Mynahs were well established and plentiful between Tamatave and Brickville, and had been recorded in the north at Maroantsetra and at Fénérive. Eighteen years later they had spread inland towards Tananarive as far as Rogez and Mouneyres. By 1952 they had colonized Vatomandry, Mananjary, Manakara and Vohipeno on the east coast, as well as much of the intervening country, and in the following year a small population became established at Maroantsetra; by the early 1970s Mynahs were established and common at Farafangana and inland towards Ihosy.

The spread of Mynahs on Madagascar has been helped both by translocations for insect control and also by the deliberate release and/or accidental escape of cagebirds belonging to the Malagasy, among whom the species is a favourite pet. In 1957–8, several pairs were turned down at Ambanja on the north-west coast of Sambirano, and more recently on the nearby island of Nossi Bé. In 1969, some were observed on Baobab trees (*Andansonia digitata*) in Sisal (*Agave* spp.) plantations at Amboasary and Berenty.

Mauritius, Réunion and Rodrigues[6]

In 1755 or 1759, Desforges-Boucher, then Governor-General of Île de France (Mauritius) and Réunion,[7] and the intendant, Pierre Poivre, introduced Common Mynahs (of the nominate form) from the Coromandel coast of southeastern India to the islands in an attempt to control a plague of locusts (*Nomadacris septemfasciata*) that were ravaging the cereal crops on which the Mascarenes settlers were dependent. (Meinertzhagen (1912) says they were introduced in the mid-eighteenth century by Count Mahé de la Bourdonnais, who was Governor of the Île de France from 1735 to 1740, and who died in 1753.) Possibly because the birds affected their crops more than the locusts, the Mynahs were all destroyed by the settlers, and more had to be imported in 1762 and/or 1767. By about 1770, according to Commerson (quoted by Staub 1976), they had considerably increased and were destroying large numbers of locusts on both islands. This is confirmed by Charles Grant, in *The History of Mauritius* (1801) quoted by Meinertzhagen, who wrote: 'The Isle of France was formerly exposed to the ravages of locusts. None of these noxious insects, however, have been seen here since the year 1770. It is pretended that the Martin, a kind of bird brought here from India, which has multiplied in a very extraordinary manner, has destroyed them.'

On Mauritius, where they are now the most abundant bird species, Common Mynahs compete successfully for nesting sites with the endangered endemic Mauritius or Echo Parakeet (*Psittacula echo*). On the neighbouring island of Rodrigues, where they were presumably introduced at around the same time, Mynahs were also reported – by the Civil Agent, Philibert Marragon, in 1795 – to be killing large numbers of locusts.

Seychelles[8]

Common Mynahs of the nominate form were probably first imported to the Seychelles from Mauritius by the then Governor of the latter, Count Mahé de la Bourdonnais, to control insect pests and/or as a cagebird shortly after the establishment of the first settlement there in about 1742, and possibly again around 1830. Newton (1867) found Mynahs to be the most abundant bird on Mahé, and they are today still the commonest species there and in the lowlands and lower hills on all the main islands except Aride and Cousin, where some predation on the eggs of White Terns (*Gygis alba*) has been recorded. More than a century ago Newton suggested that competition with Mynahs had been responsible for the decline of the now endangered Seychelles Magpie Robin (*Copsychus sechellarum*). The chief predator of the latter, however, may be the endemic skink *Mabuya wrightii*.

Although Bourne (1966b) records that in the neighbouring Amirantes Mynahs were 'abundant' on the island of Desroches (and also that there were 'many' on Coetivy in the Seychelles), C. J. Feare (personal communication, 1986) was unable to find any in the Amirantes, Providence or Farquhar islands when he visited them in 1976.

Agaléga Island[9]

The existence of large numbers of blackbeetles (cockroaches), ants, flies, mosquitoes and scorpions on Agaléga Island prompted the introduction of Common Mynahs of the nominate form from Mauritius as controlling agents before 1871 – probably by Auguste Le Duc around 1827–30. Although the birds suffered a sharp decline in 1912 (possibly as a result of a severe cyclone in the preceding year), Cheke & Lawley (1983) found them still to be abundant during their visits to the island in 1974–8.

Comoros

According to Voeltzkow (quoted by Benson 1960), who saw Mynahs in the Comoros in 1914 and 1917, they had previously been released by a French planter named Regoin on the island of Anjouan, where they were first recorded in 1906–7 but were apparently absent from Grande Comore and Mayotte. Benson found Common Mynahs of the nominate form to be established and common on Grande Comore, Mohéli, Mayotte and Anjouan.

St Helena[10]

Common Mynahs were introduced to St Helena in the South Atlantic either in 1815 when the island was garrisoned by a contingent of British Royal Marines to guard Napoleon Bonaparte, or possibly not until 1885; they quickly became established and are now the most abundant landbird there and on adjacent islands. Although Benson (1950) has suggested that the birds appeared to him more like Hill Mynahs or Southern Grackles (*Gracula religiosa*) (q.v.) – natives of India and southeastern Asia which were apparently introduced to St Helena in 1829 – specimens collected by Haydock (1954) have been definitely identified, according to Holyoak & Thibault (1984), as *A. tristis tristoides*. Some damage to fruit crops has been reported on St Helena.

Ascension

Common Mynahs were imported to control insects on Ascension shortly after its colonization by a garrison of British Royal Marines in 1815. According to Stonehouse (1962), a population of some 400 existed in the late 1950s.

AUSTRALASIA

Australia[11]

Ryan (1906) and Jenkins (1977) together record the release of over 320 Common Mynahs on at least seven occasions in Victoria in the decade after 1862, as follows: over 100 – at a cost of £1 each – in the Melbourne metropolitan area in 1862; 42 'Indian mino birds' in late 1862 or early 1863; 40 in 1864; 20 in Royal Park and some on Phillip Island in 1865; 'another small lot' (?50) in the Botanic Gardens in 1866; and 70 in 1872. The last release was made even though in the previous year Dr L. L. Smith had introduced and carried an amendment to the Game Act removing Mynahs and House Sparrows (*Passer domesticus*) (q.v.) from its protection, thus effectively declaring them pests.

In New South Wales, where in contrast they appeared on a list of protected species in 1880, Mynahs were probably introduced to Sydney by the Acclimatization Society at about the same time as in Victoria – though the reason for their introduction is not known. Mynahs caught in the precincts of St Patrick's cathedral in Melbourne were translocated in or about 1883 at the request of the Victoria Sugar Company, Hamleigh Company and Gairloch Company, to northern Queensland, to control a plague of locusts and cane beetles that were laying waste the fields of sugar cane. Most were released on the Herbert and Johnstone Rivers plantations and some at Townsville where, although they successfully colonized other local townships they had little effect on the insects. In 1918, some Mynahs were released at Cairns by a Mr B. Robinson, who also liberated eight at Toowoomba in the Darling Downs, and in about 1920 others are believed to have been freed by the Hon. A. J. Thynne in the Biddeston area, where they first nested in 1921–2.

Mynahs were released, apparently unsuccessfully, near Hobart, Tasmania, in the early 1900s, but it was not until after 1914 that they are believed to have arrived on the island naturally from Victoria. In South Australia, Mynahs were first recorded on the outskirts of Adelaide (at Blair, Athol and Enfield) in 1957 – though whether as escaped cagebirds or the result of a deliberate release is uncertain.

In New South Wales, Mynahs had spread to Ryde by about 1884 and were common in the suburbs of Sydney by 1896, but did not begin to spread outside the city until the late 1930s or early 1940s. A decade later they were established and common south of Sydney Harbour, and were reported to occur north of the Parramatta at Lane Cove and North Ryde. They were recorded in the Thirroul area in 1960, were breeding at Wollongong (75 km south of Sydney) in the following year, and by 1964 were well established at Lane Cove and North Ryde. By the mid-1970s Mynahs were firmly entrenched along the coast between Sydney and Wollongong, had been observed inland at Marulan and

Marrangaroo and north at Tweed Heads, and were still apparently expanding their range. Hone (1978) reported Mynahs to be widespread in urban areas (where they breed more freely than in rural environments) of eastern New South Wales, with three or four separate populations based on Sydney, Canberra (where some were introduced in the late 1960s), Newcastle and in the north-east. Hone was uncertain whether the Sydney and Newcastle populations were contiguous or discrete, and was unable to account for the lapse of time between the species' introduction (after which it did little more than maintain itself, except perhaps at Ryde) and eventual expansion: interspecific competition for food and nesting sites with introduced European Starlings (*Sturnus vulgaris*) (q.v.), House Sparrows (q.v.) and Feral Pigeons (*Columba livia*) (q.v.), an alien environment, climatic variation, and their generally sedentary disposition, may have been contributory factors.

In the past century, the developed area of Sydney and the city's human population have both greatly increased, with a corresponding enlargement of the habitat suitable for the commensal Mynah. An important factor in the species' dispersal has been the growth in road and rail transport that has provided 'corridors' to towns hitherto uncolonized. During the breeding season Mynahs are strongly territorial so this dispersal has probably occurred mainly in spring, when birds of the previous year seek unclaimed territories. Hone believed that the Mynah's distribution in New South Wales will probably expand considerably as more suitable habitats become available in coastal resorts, in Hunter Valley and on the tablelands of Goulburn, Bathurst and elsewhere, and that birds from southern Queensland may colonize towns in northeastern and northwestern New South Wales.

In Victoria, where as early as 1864 the Acclimatization Society claimed that, with other songbirds, 'a most active and interesting bird, the Indian mino, may now be considered thoroughly established', Mynahs had colonized Melbourne and some of the larger neighbouring townships by the turn of the century, but away from these areas at first spread only slowly. In Queensland, Mynahs were recorded in the Atherton shire in 1931 (where they now occur in all but dense rainforest areas), were established and common in the sugar plantations and at Cairns in the mid-1940s (when some were also seen for the first time in the south-east), and in urban areas of Townsville by the early 1960s.

Frith (1979: 194) said of the Mynah that it

is now strongly established in the cities and towns of south-east Victoria, in Sydney, and in north Queensland from Townsville to Cairns. It appeared in Adelaide in 1957 but does not seem to be thriving (Condon 1968). It appeared in south-east Queensland in about 1945, and since 1960 occasional birds turn up in north-east New South Wales. The early introductions in Tasmania apparently failed, but Indian Mynas have been seen in the northern part of the island in the last decade. There seems little doubt that the species is still increasing its range.

Pizzey (1980) described the Common Mynah as occurring in many urban and agricultural regions of eastern Australia; it is well established in coastal northeastern Queensland from around the Mossman–Atherton tablelands south to Mackay, and in the south-east from the Darling Downs to the Brisbane area, where it is believed to be a relatively recent arrival. Mynahs are also firmly settled along the littoral of northeastern New South Wales, in the Newcastle–Sydney–Illawarra region at least as far inland as the Blue Mountains Plateau, and since the late 1960s in the ACT. In Victoria, Mynahs are also well entrenched and are becoming increasingly widespread, having dispersed from Melbourne eastwards to Orbost, west to Geelong and Ballarat, through central Victoria, and to the Murray Valley between Cobden and Swan Hill, where they are, however, as yet rare. In Tasmania, Mynahs were reported near Launceston on 1967, and, as reported by Frith, have since been noted elsewhere in the north of the island. In South Australia a small colony may persist in the northern suburbs of Adelaide, where Mynahs were first reported in 1957, and where they are actively controlled. Where they occur in Australia Mynahs are mainly urban scavengers, very commensal, in general locally common and often very abundant, and largely sedentary. In Queensland, damage to fruit, especially figs, has been reported, and the species' habit of nesting in holes and crevices in buildings can make them a local nuisance. Because of the habitats Mynahs occupy they seldom come into conflict with native species. The birds imported to Victoria came from India and/or Afghanistan, and are therefore of the nominate form.

New Zealand[12]

Common Mynahs of the nominate form seem first to have been introduced to the South Island of New Zealand in 1870 when a Mr F. Banks presented 18 'Indian Minaul [sic] birds', which he had imported from Melbourne, Australia, to the Canterbury Acclimatization Society. According to Captain F. W. Hutton, writing in 1890 (quoted by Thomson 1922: 159), 'A few used to be about Christchurch, but they have disappeared before the starlings'. In 1916, Mr Edgar T. Stead told Thomson that 'In the early nineties there were a few minahs nesting in some houses on the North Belt (Christchurch), but there are now none left, and there have not been any for fifteen years at least.'

In Otago, some Common Mynahs were imported in the early 1870s to Dunedin by a Mr Thomas Brown, where although they nested for several years in the First Church steeple and on a few neighbouring houses they had all died out before 1890.

In 1916, a Mr F. G. Gibbs of Nelson told Thomson that 'Minahs were imported in the seventies. I remember that they were very plentiful in the streets when I arrived in 1877, but a few years later they disappeared. As they were very tame, they were shot down by boys in large numbers, and may have been exterminated in this way.'

In North Island, the Wellington Acclimatization Society released 30 Common Mynahs in 1875 and 40 in 1876, and more were freed by the Hawke's Bay Society in 1877. Their subsequent spread does not seem to have been traced in detail, but they were abundant around Napier in Hawke's Bay by 1890 when they began also to increase on Tutira. In 1912, they were said to be fairly plentiful in buildings in Tuparoa, where they had become a pest to soft fruits and new-sown leys; Thomson (1922) reported that although uncommon around Wellington they had spread up the coast to Wanganui and New Plymouth, throughout Taranaki (where they were quite common, though less so than around the turn of the century), eastwards to Wairarapa, and to Napier where they occurred in thousands. 'One of the most remarkable things about them', wrote Thomson (p. 159), 'is their increase after their first introduction, and then their subsequent diminution, and – in some districts – their ultimate disappearance. The latter appears to have been due, either directly or indirectly, to the starlings, the increase of the latter coinciding with the decrease of the former' – as might be expected with the weaker of two closely related species sharing the same ecological niche.

Probably as a result of this interspecific competition, Mynahs seem to have spread only slowly in New Zealand. In 1947, they were confined to five towns in the Wairarapa, were abundant in parts of Hawke's Bay, were uncommon in the Manawatu south of Wanganui, and in the north were apparently spreading from Waikato to Auckland. By 1953 they were established from Wanganui north to Auckland, and by the end of the decade had reached the Bay of Islands on the north-east coast. Wodzicki (1965: 434) described the birds as 'widely distributed and abundant in northern half of North Island', where they had penetrated as far north as Doubtless Bay. Kinsky (1970) found Mynahs established in Northland, Auckland, Waikato, Bay of Plenty, Taranaki, Gisborne, Hawke's Bay, Volcanic Plateau and northern Wairarapa, that is north of about 40° S. South of a line between Wanganui and Waipukurau, Mynahs were local and rare, and in the Hutt Valley and in Marlborough and Nelson (where two were seen in 1956) in South Island they appeared only as infrequent stragglers. Falla, Sibson & Turbott (1979) said that Mynahs were firmly established over much of North Island, where they were common north of Wanganui and in southern Hawke's Bay, and were increasing on Volcanic Plateau where they first became established in the mid-1940s. At Mamuka and Kaingaroa, they ascend to over 600 m and to more than 900 m on Desert Road. Occasionally, flocks reach such offshore islands as Little Barrier in Hauraki Gulf, where they are quickly eradicated by wildlife conservation authorities.

Mynahs in New Zealand frequent open country, forest ecotone and coastal foreshores, and in many places are the characteristic bird of roadside verges and rubbish tips. They prey on the eggs and nestlings of the alien Feral Pigeon (*Columba livia*) (q.v.) and the indigenous Silver Gull (*Larus novaehollandiae scopulinus*) and Southern Black-backed or Kelp Gull (*L. dominicanus*), and also on those of small native and introduced birds, with some of whom – for example, House Sparrows (*Passer domesticus*) (q.v.), Starlings

(*Sturnus vulgaris*) (q.v.) and Blackbirds (*Turdus merula*) (q.v.) – they also compete for food and nesting sites. Where Mynahs come into contact with man they have been accused of causing damage to apricots, apples, pears, strawberries and gooseberries. By way of compensation they also kill numbers of injurious insects, including sheep and cattle ticks.

Hone considered that the Mynah's preference for the milder northern parts of North Island suggests their inability to breed satisfactorily further south. Their spread northwards, according to Hone, has been gradual and recent and their southern boundary has correspondingly now moved north to well above 40° S. Baker & Moeed (1979) described adaptive differentiation in New Zealand Mynahs, with (contrary to Bergmann's Rule) larger birds in the warmer northern regions.

OCEANIA

Hawaiian Islands[13]

According to Caum (1933), the Common Mynah was 'introduced from India[14] in 1865 by Dr William Hillebrand to combat the plague of army worms [*Laphygma exempta* or *Cirphis unipuncta* and cutworms (*Spodoptera* spp.)] that was ravaging the pasture lands of the islands. It has spread and multiplied to an amazing extent; reported to be abundant in Honolulu in 1879, it is now extremely common throughout the Territory'. It was introduced to (or colonized) the other main islands around 1883. Frings & Frings (1965) estimated that there were roosts of more than 4,000 birds in two trees in Hololulu. Berger (1972: 203) said that Common Mynahs were 'common to abundant in lowland areas of the inhabited islands, being most common in residential areas and in the vicinity of human habitation in outlying districts . . . and the birds may be encountered at almost any elevation . . . up to at least 8,000 feet [2,400 m]'. Zeillemaker & Scott (1976) found Common Mynahs in abundance on Kauai, Oahu, Molokai, Lanai, Maui and Hawaii, where they occur mainly in agricultural country and pasturelands, residential and community parks, in introduced forests and scrub (i.e. Guava (*Psidium guajava*), Java Plum

(*Eugenia cumini*) and *Eucalyptus*), and in native mixed ohia (*Metrosideros collina*) and koa (*Acacia koa*) forests. They were first recorded on Niihau in the 1870s, and on Kure and Midway Atolls in 1974; on the latter, they had increased to several hundred by mid-1980.

Although Phillips (1928) claimed that the Common Mynah had become a pest in Hawaii, Caum and Berger agree that it played little or no part in the extermination of endemic birds and, since it shuns dense forest, does not – contrary to Roots's (1976: 134) claim that Mynahs 'increase only at the expense of those native birds coming into competition with them' – seem to compete for food or nesting sites with any surviving species. Many do, however, act as hosts of bird mites (*Ornithonyssus* (*Liponyssus*) *bursa*) that invade buildings, and at least in Honolulu often harbour a parasitic ocular nematode (*Oxyspirura mansoni*), which also occurs on exotic game birds, the Red-crested Cardinal (*Paroaria coronata*) (q.v.) and the House Sparrow (*Passer domesticus*) (q.v.). The malarial infection *Plasmodium circumflexum* has also been found in Common Mynahs in Hawaii. As J. E. Alicata has said,[15] 'there is thus good reason to believe that wild birds serve as reservoir hosts from which infection can be acquired'. As well as killing insects, Mynahs also feed extensively on such cultivated fruit as avocados, papayas, mangoes, guavas and especially figs.

In 1858, the ornamental plant Lantana (*Lantana camara*) was introduced to Hawaiian gardens from Mexico (where it is harmless), and before long Mynahs, and Spotted Doves (*Streptopelia chinensis*) (q.v.), were eating the berries (which were ignored by native species) to such an extent that correlative fluctuations were noticed in the abundance of fruits and Mynahs – the latter spreading the seeds until rank growths of *Lantana* became an agricultural nuisance on those islands where they occurred. Elton (1927) traced an interesting sequence of events that followed: several species of insects were imported to Hawaii in an attempt to check the growth and spread of *Lantana*, and some (in particular an agromyzid fly) destroyed so much seed that *Lantana* noticeably declined. A corresponding decrease in the number of Mynahs, which were largely dependent on *Lantana* berries for food, enabled the army worm and cutworm larvae in the sugar-cane plantations and grasslands – which Mynahs had been intro-duced to control – to stage a comeback. It was then found that as Lantana was destroyed it was replaced by other alien shrubs, some of which were more difficult to eradicate.

Laycock (1970) has graphically described efforts made by the Royal Hawaiian Hotel on Waikiki Beach to discourage Mynahs from roosting in a pair of Banyan trees (*Ficus* (*benghalensis*) *indica*) in its forecourt, where their noise and droppings were annoying guests; forbidden by the government to kill the birds, the hotel authorities tried jerking the limbs on which the birds perched with ropes, hoisting caged cats into the branches, setting off fireworks, and broadcasting distress calls and high-frequency sound waves; the birds largely ignored these distractions, and hotel guests complained that the fireworks disturbed them more than the birds and that the high-frequency waves caused their false teeth to vibrate!

Recently, Byrd (1979) indicated that the Common Mynah in Hawaii may be a significant predator of the eggs of the local race of the Wedge-tailed Shearwater (*Puffinus pacificus cuneatus*), since in his study area on Kilauea Point on Kauai some 23 per cent of eggs laid by Shearwaters were destroyed by Mynahs.

Fiji[16]

Most of the early references to Mynahs in Fiji name the species as the Bank Mynah (*Acridotheres ginginianus*) – a native of Pakistan and northern India; these references are certainly in error, since the only species known to have been imported to the archipelago are the Common Mynah and Jungle Mynah (*A. fuscus*) (q.v.).

Although Wood & Wetmore (1926) suggest that the Common Mynah may have been introduced to Fiji as early as 1876, most authorities consider it was probably first imported (with the Jungle Mynah) from India between about 1890 and 1900 to control Orthoptera insects in sugarcane plantations, in which, according to Stoner (1923), it was fairly ineffective. The species' spread was probably assisted by the East Indian population among whom Mynahs were a favourite pet, which they carried about with them on their interisland travels in cages, from which they sometimes escaped or were deliberately released. Thus by the 1920s Common

Mynahs, which were removed from the list of protected species in 1923, were plentiful on several of the inhabited islands, and although many died on Viti Levu in the severe hurricane of 1931, within 20 years they had recovered to their former numbers. Pernetta & Watling (1978) found Mynahs to be common commensals of man in agricultural, suburban and urban habitats on the main islands, where they lived on insects, fruit and refuse. Watling (1982: 105) said:

The Common Mynah was introduced to Fiji in about 1890 to control insect pests of the emerging sugar industry. It is a very common bird throughout its range in the region . . . The Common Mynah, together with other introduced birds, is frequently accused of driving the indigenous birds 'into the bush'. . . . it is far more likely that it is the inability of the native birds to adapt to man-modified habitats which restrict them to forested areas. . . . [Common Mynahs] are restricted to the larger islands of the group and some of those close offshore, as well as Vatulele and Lakeba.

Predation on the emergent stems of commercially valuable ground nuts and on the eggs and young of terns (*Sterna* spp.) and noddies (*Anous* spp.) has been reported in Fiji.

Samoa

The Common Mynah was first reported in American Samoa on the island of Tutuila in 1980. Whether it is established there is uncertain. (See also under Jungle Mynah (*A. fuscus*), page 504.)

Polynesia (Cook, Tubuai, Society, Tuamotu and Marquesas islands)

Holyoak (1974a) found Common Mynahs in Polynesia to be common in urban areas, on cultivated land, in lowlands and upland regions to an altitude of 1,000 m on Tahiti, Moorea and Raiatea, probably present on Huahine but absent from Bora Bora, and of indeterminate status on other islands.

Holyoak & Thibault (1984)[17] have traced the distribution of Common Mynahs on islands in the region as follows. **Aitutaki**: not seen by Townsend in 1899; in 1973 well distributed, having been introduced, according to the local population, some years previously. **Manuae**: fairly common in 1973 on the islets of Manuae and Auotu. **Atiu**: well distributed in 1973. **Mauke**: abundant near human habitation and in plantations. **Rarotonga**: introduced from Tahiti between 1905 and 1920 (Syme 1975 says from New Zealand in the 1920s to control insect pests); in 1922 they were reported to be abundant; in 1973 they were the commonest coastal bird occurring, according to Turbott (1977), throughout cultivated areas, in valleys and on tidal flats and airfields. **Mangaia**: introduced, according to the islanders, in 1952–4, by 1973 they were very common. **Palmyra**: a dozen were released in the 1940s, and a single bird was seen in 1953. **Rurutu**: a few were observed by the Whitney expedition in 1921. **Tubuai**: the Whitney expedition found the species fairly common near human settlements and collected three specimens; in 1974 it was plentiful in coastal areas and on grasslands of the interior. **Bellingshausen**: introduced several years ago. **Scilly**: not recorded by the Whitney expedition, but found in limited numbers near settlements in 1973. **Mopelia**: unrecorded by the Whitney expedition, but found in restricted numbers near human habitation on the main islet in 1973. **Raiatea** and **Tahaa**: not found by the Whitney expedition, but very common in 1972–3. **Huahine**: not present at the time of the Whitney expedition, but frequently seen in 1972–3. **Moorea**: the birds first appeared on the island (where the Whitney expedition found them to be common) early in the century, following either an introduction by man or emigration from Tahiti. **Tahiti**: introduced between 1908 and 1915 (to control wasps, according to Bruner 1972), the species was already well distributed at the time of the Whitney expedition; between 1971 and 1975 it was found in all coastal areas and at lower elevations; on Tahiti, Common Mynahs eat a variety of cultivated fruits, especially in the street markets of Papeete, where, according to Holyoak, they were formerly eaten by the inhabitants. **Hao** and **Mururoa**: introduced around 1971 and present in small numbers. **Nuku Hiva**: a few were released around 1971 but were killed shortly afterwards. **Hiva Oa**: 16 introduced around 1918 had increased within 3 years to an estimated 1,000; the species is today very common in coastal regions and occurs in lesser numbers at higher altitudes.

In Polynesia, Common Mynahs colonized some islands very quickly, but a sea crossing of only a few kilometres can be enough to hinder their progress; thus they have spread all over Hiva Oa but have failed to reach Tahuata only 3 km away. They live near human settlements, in coconut groves, in plantations and on the ecotone of secondary forests, they prefer open habitats, are less often found in dense woodland, and seldom ascend above 500–700 m. Introduced to control destructive insects, Common Mynahs mainly eat fruit (both cultivated and wild), berries, copra, insects (caught in vegetation, on the ground, especially the larvae of Lepidoptera and Hymenoptera, and occasionally in flight), household refuse, and biting parasites (especially ticks) from the backs of cattle. Common Mynahs have – through their aggressive nature, competition for food and nesting sites, and the dissemination of avian malaria – contributed in no small way to the diminution, perhaps even in some cases to the extinction, of some native birds, especially such hole-nesting ones as lorys (*Vini* spp.) and kingfishers (*Halcyon* spp.). It is also possible that, by robbing their nests, Common Mynahs have been responsible for the decline on Hiva Oa of the Red-moustached Fruit Dove (*Ptilinopus mercieri tristrami*) and the Marquesas Warbler (*Acrocephalus mendanae mendanae*), and of the Long-billed Reed Warbler (*A. caffra caffra*) on Tahiti and *A. c. longirostris* on Moorea.

Solomon Islands[18]

Common Mynahs of the nominate form have been successfully introduced to Guadalcanal, Russell and the Olu Malau (Three Sisters) islands in the southeastern Solomon group.

Vanuatu

According to Mayr (1945), Common Mynahs may have been introduced successfully to some islands in the New Hebrides (Vanuatu).

New Caledonia

Delacour (1966) records that introduced Common Mynahs were common in villages, gardens and cultivated land in New Caledonia.

Chagos Archipelago[19]

In 1905, Common Mynahs that had escaped from captivity were established in considerable numbers on Egmont Atoll in the Chagos group, from where by around 1953 they had spread to Diego Garcia. In the same year, 15 are said to have been shipped from Mahé in the Seychelles to the Chagos Archipelago, but all died before reaching their destination. A second consignment of a dozen birds from Agaléga Island in 1954 or 1955 was apparently more successful. Some were seen on Diego Garcia in 1960, and 4 years later the species was one of the commonest birds on the island. In 1967, flocks of between 40 and 60 were frequently reported, and the birds were recorded as still abundant on the island in the mid-1970s.

In July 1930, a small flock of some half-a-dozen Common Mynahs was discovered in the environs of Los Angeles in California, USA,[20] where they were destroyed before they could cause damage to figs, grapes and other fruits in the region. The species was said to be established and breeding in the Los Angeles area in 1949 but, if so, it has since died out.

As recently as the turn of the century Common Mynahs in Southeast Asia[21] did not occur naturally south of the Tropic of Cancer; since then, birds of the nominate form have colonized the entire mainland region, largely by a natural extension of range from the north-west as a result of increasing cultivation and urbanization following deforestation, perhaps helped by the release or escape of cagebirds. Some dates for their appearance in various countries are as follows. Burma: first noted in the south at Pakchan estuary in 1919. Thailand: fairly common, according to Lekagul & Cronin (1974), in northern villages by 1914; they had reached Phatthalung in the south by 1929, and by 1937 were widely distributed near human habitation; today they are common in the vicinity of Bangkok and on the central plains, where they were rare in the 1920s. Malaya: although still rare in the north in 1930 they had reached Province Wellesley by the following year, were common in Taiping in Perak in 1932 and had arrived at Kuala Lumpur, Selangor, a year later; they had spread to Kuala Trengganu on the east coast by 1948, but were still local and scarce in the north-east 4 years later, though widespread at Trengganu by 1957. Singapore: first recorded in 1936, Mynahs were established and breeding by the following decade, and are now common.

NOTES

1 Roots (1976: 134) claims that the Indian (or Common) Mynah is also established in 'Japan, central western North America [and] Luzon in the Philippine Islands'. In fact, the species successfully introduced to North America (in British Columbia, Canada) and in Manila in the Philippines is the Crested Mynah (*Acridotheres cristatellus*), which was also introduced to Japan before 1957 where it has since almost certainly died out.

2 King, Dickinson & Woodcock 1975; Long 1981; Webster 1975.

3 Abdulali 1964, 1967; Ali & Ripley 1968–74; Beavan 1867; Butler 1899; Hume 1873; King, Dickinson & Woodcock 1975; Long 1981; Palmer 1899; Richmond 1903; Wood 1924.

4 Bigalke 1964; Calder 1953; Holyoak & Thibault 1984; Kent 1927; Liversidge 1975, n.d.; Long 1981; Mackworth-Praed & Grant 1963; Maclean 1985; Peters 1962; Roberts 1940; Roots 1976; Siegfried 1962; Summers-Smith 1963; Van Nierop 1958; J. M. Winterbottom, 1966, 1978 (and personal communication, 1981) and P. A. Clancey, J. Vincent and S. Wolff, personal communications, 1981.

5 Benson 1960; Decary 1962; Long 1981; Milon, Petter & Randrianasolo 1973; Rand 1936; Van Someren 1947.

6 Benedict 1957; Benson 1960; Decary 1962; Gill 1967; King 1981; Long 1981; Meinertzhagen 1912; Milon, Petter & Randrianasolo 1973; Palmer 1899; Penny 1974; Rountree, Guérin et al. 1952; Staub 1976; Watson, Zusi & Storer 1963. See also:

Mémoire sur l'Île Rodrigues, Mauritius Archives TB 5/2: 1–17 and Jerdon 1863: 326.

7 According to Decary (1962), Common Mynahs were introduced to Réunion in 1755.

8 Benson 1960; Diamond & Feare 1980; Fisher, Simon & Vincent 1969; Gaymer, Blackman et al. 1969; King 1981; Long 1981; Newton 1867; Penny 1974; Ripley 1961; Roots 1976.

9 Cheke & Lawley 1983; Guého & Staub 1983. See also: Bojer 1871.

10 Benson 1950; Gosse 1938; Haydock 1954; Huckle 1924; Long 1981.

11 Anon. 1969; Blakers, Davies & Reilly 1984; Chisholm 1919, 1926, 1950; Condon 1968; Frith 1979; Hone 1978; Jenkins 1977; Lavery 1974; Lavery & Hopkins 1963; Long 1981; Pizzey 1980; Rolls 1969; Roots 1976; Ryan 1906; Sefton & Devitt 1962; Sharland 1958; Summers-Smith 1963; Tarr 1950; Walker 1952; White 1946.

12 Baker & Moeed 1979; Cunningham 1948; Falla, Sibson & Turbott 1979; Hone 1978; Kinsky 1970; Long 1981; Oliver 1955; Peters 1962; Summers-Smith 1963; Thomson 1922, 1926; Wodzicki 1965. See also: H. Guthrie-Smith *Tutira, the Story of a New Zealand Sheep Station* (Blackwood: Edinburgh and London, 1921).

13 American Ornithologists' Union 1957, 1983; Bancroft 1984; Berger 1972, 1981; Blake 1975; Byrd 1979; Caum 1933; Eddinger 1967; Elton 1927, 1958; Fisher 1951; Laycock 1970; Long 1981; Munro 1960; Palmer 1899; Peterson 1961; Phillips 1928; Pyle 1977; Richardson & Bowles 1964; Zeillemaker & Scott 1976.

14 According to Palmer (1899), the birds were imported from China.

15 *Parasites of Man and Animals in Hawaii* (Karger: Basel, 1969).

16 Blackburn 1971; Gorman 1975; Long 1981; Lyon-Field 1938; Mercer 1966; Parham 1954; Pernetta & Watling 1978; Stoner 1923; Watling 1975, 1978a, 1982; Wood & Wetmore 1926.

17 See also: Bruner 1972; Holyoak 1974a; Syme 1975; Turbott 1977.

18 Cain & Galbraith 1956, 1957; French 1957; Galbraith & Galbraith 1962; Long 1981.

19 Bourne 1971; Hutson 1975; Long 1981; Loustau-Lalanne 1962.

20 Laycock 1970; Long 1981; Miller 1930; Willett 1930.

21 Chasen 1924; Gibson-Hill 1949b,c; Long 1981; Madoc 1956; Medway & Wells 1976; Peters 1962; Ward 1968.

Jungle Mynah and White-vented Mynah

(*Acridotheres fuscus* and *A. javanicus*)

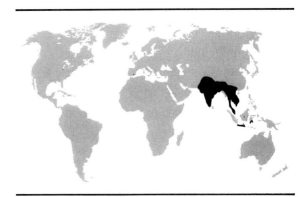

Note: Map shows combined distribution.

NATURAL DISTRIBUTION
From India, Burma and northeastern Assam eastwards to northern and central Malaysia, Java and southern Sulawesi (combined distribution).

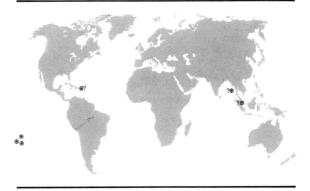

Note: Map shows combined distribution.

NATURALIZED DISTRIBUTION
Asia: Singapore, (southern) Malaya, ?Andaman Islands; North America: ?West Indies (Puerto Rico); Australasia: Sumatra; Oceania: Fiji, Samoa, Tonga.

ASIA

Singapore and (southern) Malaya[1]

The early records of these two species are very confused; for shedding light on the problem I am indebted to C. J. Hails (personal communication, 1985).

At one time two subspecies, *Acridotheres f. javanicus* and *A. f. torquatus*, were recognized,[2] both being known as the Buffalo Mynah. Later taxonomists divided them into two full species, *A. javanicus* (the White-vented Mynah) and *A. fuscus* (sometimes *A. mahrattensis*), for which they retained the vernacular name of Buffalo (or Jungle) Mynah. This nomenclature all recent authors on birds of the region accept.

The only author to have recognized both species in Singapore appears to be Gibson-Hill, and Hails could find no other evidence for the presence there of two species or races. Thus, when Ward (1968) referred to *A. fuscus* he was almost certainly alluding to what is now known as *A. javanicus*. There are no known skins of *fuscus* from Singapore in the ex-Raffles Museum collection, all those contained therein coming from northern Malaya. There are, however, Singapore skins of *javanicus* dating from 1920 and 1921, and these probably represent the species' earliest appearance on the island. If *fuscus* had also occurred it would almost certainly have been included in the collection, which contains all other species known to have been present in Singapore at the time. The natural range of *fuscus* extends only as far south as Malacca, some 240 km north of Singapore, and there have been no records of the species in the latter within at least the past 15–20 years.

There are thus two alternatives; either *fuscus* at one time occurred in Singapore where it was only recognized by Gibson-Hill (*fuscus* and *javanicus* are very similar in appearance, and are difficult to differentiate in the field), and has either since died out or has been absorbed, by interbreeding, with *javanicus*; or *javanicus* was the species referred to, and the literature subsequently became confused by changes in nomenclature.

Hails believes that the second alternative is the more probable; he points out that since the natural range of *fuscus* does not extend as far south as Singapore, its presence there would have involved the prior introduction of another very similar *Acridotheres* species, and that the absence of *fuscus* skins from Singapore in the Raffles Museum collection must be significant. The dates of *javanicus* skins pre-date Gibson-Hill's published records by some years, so he was clearly not fully aware of the situation. Furthermore, the likelihood of two subspecies remaining separate on one small island must be very remote.

At present, White-vented Mynahs of the nominate subspecies are widespread and very common on the island of Singapore, where in both urban and rural habitats they outnumber the Common Mynah (*A. tristis*) by a ratio of around two to one, and from where they have spread south to Tandjungpinang Island south of the strait of Singapore, and in 1973 north across the Johor Strait to Johor Baharu on the mainland. D. R. Wells (personal communication, 1986) says that since then their numbers have rapidly increased north of the causeway, until by 1985 they were by far the most common mynah in southern Johor, and had spread 120 km up the west coast from Johor Baharu to within 30 km of the Malacca state border. The statement by Medway & Wells (1976) that they occur on Penang Island, however, appears to be in error (Wells 1983).

The continental subspecies (*A. j. grandis*) has recently extended its range naturally southwards to the southern suburbs of Kuala Lumpur, where it first appeared in March 1983. Although breeding has yet to be recorded its numbers (though not its distribution) have greatly increased, and it seems now to be thoroughly established and to be more than holding its own in competition with the Common and Jungle mynahs and with the Crested Mynah (*A. cristatellus*).[3] The birds share communal roosts in shade trees with *tristis* and cause some local problems for housing-estate residents, but do not appear to be competing with any native species.

Andaman Islands

According to Beavan (1867), who said they were flourishing and had spread to Ross Island, Jungle Mynahs (of the nominate form) from Burma were introduced to Port Blair on South Andaman by Colonel R. C. Tytler soon after the establishment of a convict settlement there in 1858. Whether any remain today is uncertain.

NORTH AMERICA

West Indies (Puerto Rico)

According to the American Ornithologists' Union (1983: 786), the White-vented Mynah 'has been introduced in recent years in Puerto Rico

(Bayamón area); criteria for establishment will likely be met in the next few years'.

AUSTRALASIA

Sumatra

Ripley (1961) says that 'Orange-billed Jungle Mynas (*A. javanicus*)' have been introduced to the island of Sumatra, where Delacour (1947) describes them as *A. f. javanicus*.

OCEANIA

Fiji[4]

Most of the early reports of Mynahs in Fiji refer to the Bank Mynah (*A. ginginianus*) of Pakistan and northern India; as the only species known to have been imported to the islands are the Jungle Mynah and the Common Mynah (*A. tristis*) these references are clearly mistaken.

According to Pernetta & Watling (1978), the Jungle Mynah was introduced to Fiji from India (Lyon-Field (1938) said possibly from Burma) in about 1890 at the same time as the Common Mynah, to combat orthopterous pests in sugar-cane plantations. Lyon-Field reported numerous attempts, which were only partially successful, to translocate large numbers from Viti Levu to Vanua Levu and other nearby islands. Although Blackburn (1971) said that Jungle Mynahs were common only on Viti Levu and Nukulau, Pernetta & Watling found them to be abundant in agricultural, urban, suburban and scrub areas on all the main islands with the exception of Taveuni.

In his definitive work on the avifauna of the region, Watling (1982: 106) said that the Jungle Mynah 'is found only on Viti Levu and its offshore islands and on Vanua Levu – although on the latter island it is very rare – in Fiji. . . . Jungle Mynahs were introduced to Viti Levu in about 1900, but not until after 1938 did they become established on Vanua Levu, where they have not flourished. It was purportedly introduced to control Armyworm, which can be a pest to many crops.' In Fiji, Jungle Mynahs, although primarily insectivorous, do not remove

parasites from the backs of cattle and horses, on which they perch solely to detect insects disturbed by the animals' feet. They frequently eat fruit and also nectar – especially from the flowers of the African Tulip Tree (*Spathodea campanulata*). Jungle Mynahs, despite their name, prefer such man-modified habitats as pastures, parks and gardens in urban and suburban districts, and lightly wooded areas, but also venture quite frequently into denser forests.

Although earlier reports tended to exonerate Mynahs from causing agricultural damage in Fiji (or even claimed that, by their destruction of injurious insects, they were actually beneficial to farmers), Watling (1975) recorded serious attacks on the plumules[5] of commercially valuable ground-nut crops.

Samoa[6]

Dhondt (1976b) reported the presence of small flocks of Common Mynahs since at least 1972 in the suburbs of Apia on the island of Upolu in Western Samoa. Watling (1978a), however, found no trace of this species on Upolu in January of that year, but instead saw small local-ized groups of Jungle Mynahs, generally in association with horses or cattle on playing fields or pastureland, which are believed to have arrived around 1970.

Tonga

Rinke (1986a) says that 'the Jungle Mynah has recently colonized the island of Niuafo'ou, apparently without human assistance, and may compete with the lories [the Blue-crowned Lory (*Vini australis*)] for nesting sites. Mynahs are likely to spread through the islands of Fiji, Tonga and Samoa by natural means as their population numbers are very high on certain Fiji islands. Hurricanes, which often occur in this region, may aid their dispersal'. (See also Rinke, 1986b.)

Exactly when Jungle Mynahs first appeared on Niuafo'ou is uncertain, but since they are not referred to in Tonga by Watling (1982), it was presumably after that date.

————————————

Ripley (1961) says that 'Orange-billed Jungle

Mynas' were introduced to Christmas Island in the Indian Ocean around 1904, where according to Chasen (1933) they apparently disappeared shortly afterwards.

NOTES

1 Chasen 1925; Gibson-Hill 1949b,c, 1950, 1952; Long 1981; Medway & Wells 1976; Ward 1968; D. R. Wells, 1983 (and personal communication, 1986); and C. J. Hails, personal communication, 1985.

2 Howard & Moore (1980) still recognize both subspecies, whereas Gruson (1976) includes *javanicus* in *fuscus*.

3 D. R. Wells, personal communication, 1986.

4 Blackburn 1971; Long 1981; Lyon-Field 1938; Mercer 1966; Parham 1954; Pernetta & Watling 1978; Turbet 1941; Watling 1975, 1978a, 1982.

5 The rudimentary stem of an embryo plant.

6 Dhondt 1976b; Long 1981; Potter 1981; Watling 1978a, 1982.

Crested Mynah
(*Acridotheres cristatellus*)

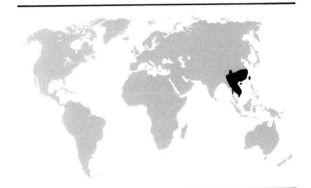

NATURAL DISTRIBUTION
From Bangladesh, eastern Burma and Thailand eastwards to central and southern China, Taiwan and Hainan, south through Indo-China.

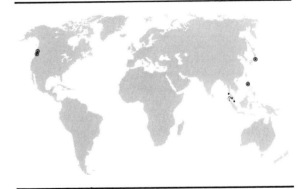

NATURALIZED DISTRIBUTION
Asia: Malaya, Japan; North America: Canada, ?USA; Australasia: Philippines.

ASIA

Malaya (Penang, Singapore and ?Kuala Lumpur)[1]

Since at least 1920, Crested Mynahs of the subspecies *A. c. brevipennis* from Hainan and Indo-China, presumably the descendants of escaped or released cagebirds, have been established and common in and around Georgetown on Penang Island off the west coast of Malaya (where they frequent open country, orchards, paddy fields, coconut groves, parklands and suburban gardens) and in rural and agricultural areas, where they live sympatrically with Common and Jungle Mynahs (*A. tristis* and *A. fuscus*).

A single Crested Mynah first appeared in Singapore in 1983, where in the following year a pair bred on the university campus. A second pair nested in 1985, and a further two individuals were sighted. These birds, presumably released or escaped pets, may eventually succeed in multiplying into a viable breeding population. It is believed that the Singapore birds may be of a different form to those established in Penang.

Since a solitary Crested Mynah was shot in Kuala Lumpur in July 1978, small numbers have been observed along the Kelang River in the south of the city; in 1985, however, D. R. Wells (personal communication, 1986) could find only one pair, and was uncertain of the species' status.

Japan

According to Brazil (1985 and in press), the Crested Mynah 'breeds in Tokyo and has been recorded quite widely in Japan – some may even be wild birds from Taiwan'.

NORTH AMERICA

Canada and USA[2]

Crested Mynahs are currently established in Canada only in and around the city of Vancouver in British Columbia. 'Little appears to be known', wrote Phillips (1928: 55), 'as to how the bird arrived in Vancouver; the introduction dates from about 1894 and may or may not have been accidental.' Cumming (1925) says that in the late nineteenth century large numbers of 'Chinese Starlings' (as the species was then sometimes known) were being imported under the trade name of 'Hill Mynahs' from the Far East to England (where in Liverpool they fetched 12*s.* each) and other European countries. 'It is supposed', Phillips continued, 'that birds escaped from some ship touching at this port [Vancouver] or that some irate skipper had tired of his noisy passengers and put them ashore at the first port of call.' One story claims that a large wicker cage consigned to a Japanese resident of Vancouver

broke open in transit, permitting the birds it contained to escape, while another suggests that 'an oriental resident' of Vancouver deliberately released some Mynahs for sentimental reasons. Grinnell (1921) said that the 'Chinese Starling' 'is frequently brought in to North America from the Orient as a cage bird' – so the opportunities for its escape or release would have been boundless.

However and whenever the species arrived in Vancouver its presence was first confirmed in 1897 when two pairs were reported by a city resident; this date was subsequently confirmed by T.P.O. Menzies, Secretary-Curator of the City Museum of Vancouver, and by A. Brooks and H. S. Swarth.[3] It was not, however, until 1904 that the first specimens were collected – by F. Kermode near the Vancouver waterfront. A few years later a small number crossed the Strait of Georgia to Vancouver Island, while occasional individuals were reported in Washington and Oregon across the border in the United States.

Before about 1920, when a winter roost estimated to number 1,200 formed at the intersection of Carroll and Cordova streets, Crested Mynahs occurred in Vancouver only in small numbers. By 1921, however, they had become the dominant city land bird, and had expanded their range over an area of some 1,035 km² including North Vancouver, across the Burrard Inlet, on Sea and Lulu islands in the Fraser River delta, in New Westminster, and in Coquitlam in the east and Ladner in the south.

By 1925, when the population in Vancouver had multiplied to between 6,000 and 7,000, the direction of dispersal was generally southeastwards, where land had been cleared along the Pacific highway. Two years later, when Crested Mynahs were especially abundant on the North Shore, the Vancouver-based population had risen to some 20,000, and wanderers had spread 80 km south to Bellingham in Washington, where they subsequently became established in small numbers at Lake Washington, at Juanita Bay, and near Seattle. Phillips (1928) summed up the bird's distribution and status as follows:

the city of Vancouver is its main stronghold. It is common in the outskirts of the town and breeds abundantly even in the down-town districts. In the summer it spreads out into rural districts . . . They have begun to destroy a good deal of fruit, especially cherries, blackberries and apples. . . . they are advancing steadily towards the Washington line at the rate of a mile or two a year . . . . There are already many thousands . . . The advance so far is certainly to the south. The birds seem to suffer from cold weather and will probably be confined to the immediate coast.

Despite Phillips's prognostication, by 1930 Crested Mynahs had extended their range 80 km inland from Vancouver as far as Chilliwack, although their primary stronghold remained Greater Vancouver and cultivated land adjoining the mouth of the Fraser River. An individual seen at Portland, Oregon, in February 1922 or 1924, a flock of a dozen near Lake Washington on the Sammamish River in August 1929, and half-a-dozen at Juanita Bay near Seattle in August 1933, almost certainly derived from separate introductions.

By the mid-1950s Crested Mynahs were mostly restricted to urban habitats in the Vancouver area, where they had considerably declined, to rural districts around the city and New Westminster, and to houses and adjoining pastureland on Lulu Island and, to a lesser extent, on Sea Island. Small numbers were occasionally reported in Victoria, Nanaimo, Union Bay, Alert Bay and Courtenay on Vancouver Island.

In 1959, only two doubtful sightings were made of Crested Mynahs on the North Shore and none south of the South Arm of the Fraser River, though some were observed as far east as the eastern edge of New Westminster, and many on Lulu Island and a considerable number on Sea Island. The aggregate population was put at around 2,500, so the actual figure was probably less, indicating a sharp decline since the zenith in the mid-1920s. The birds assembled in large roosts in winter, but spread out through built-up districts in the breeding season (April to July) – as they do in central and southern China where, however, the mean daily temperatures for the period average some 12–15 °C higher than in Vancouver. In Canada, Crested Mynahs do not nest colonially, favouring crevices and holes in buildings and trees – especially dead conifers and hemlocks.

Mackay & Hughes (1963) estimated the populations of the main roosts in Vancouver and New Westminster in 1959–60 as follows: Lapointe Pier (600); Connaught Bridge (500); Sir Guy Carleton School (150); Collingwood United Church (20); and Russell Hotel, New Westminster (60) – a total of 1,330. There were also about 800 birds on Lulu Island, where there appeared to be no large roost. Since Lulu lies some 6.5 km from the nearest Vancouver city roost and the two populations seem to be discrete, the total number of Crested Mynahs in British Columbia may have been in the region of 2,130. By the mid-1960s the birds were confined, apart from a small colony at Nanaimo on the east coast of Vancouver Island, to the Greater Vancouver area localities to which they remain restricted today. (Roots (1976: 134), who wrongly refers to the birds as Indian (Common) Mynahs,[4] estimated the total population at 'no more than 3,000' – almost certainly an exaggeration – and said that 'the species is fairly well established in metropolitan Vancouver, the western Fraser Delta, on Lulu Island and southern Victoria Island'.)

For some years after its arrival it was feared that if it became widely established the Crested Mynah could become a serious pest to soft-fruit orchardists along the Pacific coast. Its failure to do so has been attributed to several factors, including competition for nesting sites with the alien Starling (*Sturnus vulgaris*) (q.v.) and an unfavourable climate and environment that are responsible for the rearing of only a single brood. The birds in British Columbia have been identified as of the nominate form.

AUSTRALASIA

Philippines[5]

Wood (1924), quoting from Whitehead (1899), says that 'Le Martin' was imported on at least three occasions between 1849 and 1852 to Manila by the Spanish Governor-General, Martinez, to control locusts on the island of Luzon in the Philippines. By 1893–6 the birds, which are of the nominate form from central and southern China and eastern Burma, had not spread far from the purlieus of Manila, and by 1924 had still only colonized a few townships near the capital. Du Pont (1971) recorded that they had spread south to Negros. The species' present status in the Philippines is uncertain.

According to Brazil (1985 and in press), the **Bank**

Mynah (*Acridotheres ginginianus*), which is confined naturally to Pakistan and northern India, breeds in Japan in Tokyo and Kanagawa.

NOTES

1 Gibson-Hill 1949b,c; Long 1981; Medway & Wells 1976.
2 American Ornithologists' Union 1957, 1983; Anderson 1934; Blake 1975; Carl & Guiguet 1972; Cooke & Knappen 1941; Cumming 1925; Godfrey 1966; Grinnell 1921; Guiguet 1952b; Jewett, Taylor et al. 1953; Keffer 1972a; Kelly 1927; Kermode 1920; Laycock 1970; Long 1981; Mackay & Hughes 1963; Munro 1921, 1922, 1930; Phillips 1928; Roots 1976; Scheffer & Cottam 1935; Wood 1924; Young 1922, 1925.
3 *A Distributional List of the Birds of British Columbia*, no. 17 (Cooper Ornithological Club, 1925).
4 Munro & Peter (1981: 5) also mistakenly refer to the species as the Common Mynah.
5 Delacour & Mayr 1946; Du Pont 1971; Long 1981; Peters 1962; Roots 1976; Whitehead 1899; Wood 1924.

Hill Mynah
(*Gracula religiosa*)

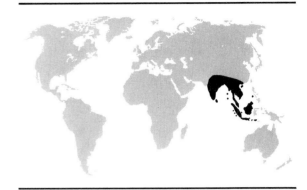

NATURAL DISTRIBUTION
From India and Nepal through Burma and Thailand to extreme southern China and Hainan, south through Indo-China, Sri Lanka, the Andaman and Nicobar islands to Malaysia, Sumatra, Kepulauan Mentawai, Java, Bali, Borneo, Palawan and the Lesser Sunda Islands.

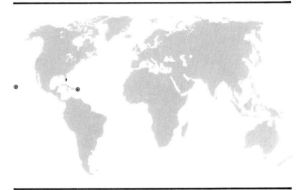

NATURALIZED DISTRIBUTION
North America: USA, West Indies (Puerto Rico); Oceania: Hawaiian Islands.

NORTH AMERICA

USA[1]

The Hill Mynah or Southern Grackle has for long been a favourite of aviculturists in the United States. In 1972, escaped cagebirds were established locally in a narrow coastal strip of southeastern Florida, from Homestead at least as far north as Boynton Beach in Palm Beach County – a distance of some 125 km – and breeding was

reported in many localities in Palm Beach, Broward and Dade counties.

In India, this species lives largely on berries and fruit – particularly those of *Ficus* spp. – so its potential as a horticultural pest in southern Florida, where it has been seen to oust woodpeckers (Picidae) from their nesting holes, must be considerable. O. T. Owre (personal communications, 1981 and 1985) says that since his 1973 publication 'Some species are noticeably more abundant, e.g. . . . the Hill Myna . . . [which] 'remains a common breeding bird throughout urban areas of southeastern Florida'.

West Indies (Puerto Rico)

According to the American Ornithologists' Union (1983), the Hill Mynah has been introduced to, and is established on, the island of Puerto Rico, from where it appears as a casual vagrant on Mona and Vieques.

OCEANIA

Hawaiian Islands[2]

In 1960, three Hill Mynahs escaped from a pet shop in Honolulu on Oahu, followed a year later by a further five; these birds settled in the Upper Manoa Valley, from where they spread to Tantalus, the State Forestry Division Nursery in Makiki Valley, Kahana Valley, and to the Mokuleia County Park on the north-west coast where they became established. In November 1965, a flock of a dozen was seen in the Lyon Arboretum of the University of Hawaii, and a single bird in the Woodlawn region of Manoa Valley in October of the following year. Zeillemaker & Scott (1976) record the species as local and rare in introduced forests and scrublands (i.e. Guava (*Psidium guajava*), Java Plum (*Eugenia cumini*) and *Eucalyptus* sp.) on Oahu, and of indeterminate status on Kauai.

Hill Mynahs of the nominate form (natives of Malaysia, Sumatra, Java, Bali and Borneo) were introduced to Christmas Island[3] in the Indian Ocean around 1923, from where they disappeared within a decade.

The Hill Mynah is said to have been introduced to the island of St Helena[4] in the South Atlantic in 1829 and to have been common in Jamestown and upland areas until at least 1870. Although Benson (1950) has indicated that the Mynahs established on St Helena seemed to him like *G. religiosa*, they have since been positively identified as *Acridotheres tristis tristoides*, so *religiosa*, if it was indeed introduced, has presumably since died out.

Reports of Hill Mynahs introduced to the Chagos Archipelago are based on mistaken identity – the species established there being the Common Mynah (*A. tristis*) (q.v.).

Records of Hill Mynahs on the island of Hong Kong[5] (e.g. at Pokfulam, on the Peak, in the New Territories, at She Shan, at Victoria Barracks, at Ho Man Tin, at Fanling and on Stonecutters Island) have usually been assumed to be of escaped cagebirds. They could equally, however, be of immigrants from the Chinese mainland, where the local race is *intermedia*. No viable population has so far become established, but Webster (1975) has suggested that this could eventually happen.

NOTES
1 Ali & Ripley 1972; American Ornithologists' Union 1983; Blake 1975; Gore & Doubilet 1976; Heilbrun 1976; Long 1981; O. T. Owre 1973 (and personal communications, 1981 and 1985). See also: H. W. Kale, *Audubon Field Notes* 25: 752 (1972).
2 American Ornithologists' Union 1983; Berger 1981; Blake 1975; Donaggho 1966; Hawaiian Audubon Society 1975; Long 1981; Moulton & Pimm 1983; Pyle 1977; Walker 1967a; Zeillemaker & Scott 1976.
3 Chasen 1933; Long 1981; Peters 1962.
4 Benson 1950; Huckle 1924; Long 1981; Melliss 1870.
5 King, Dickinson & Woodcock 1975; Long 1981; Webster 1975; Viney 1976.

Black-backed Magpie
(*Gymnorhina tibicen*)

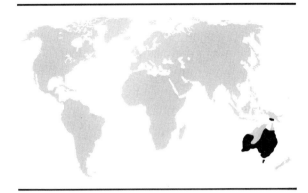

NATURAL DISTRIBUTION
Much of Australia (including parts of eastern Tasmania) and central-southern New Guinea.

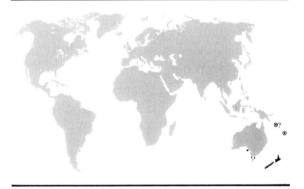

Note: Map includes translocations to Australian islands.

NATURALIZED DISTRIBUTION
Australasia: New Zealand; Oceania: ?Solomon Islands, Fiji.

AUSTRALASIA

New Zealand[1]

In 1864, the Canterbury Acclimatization Society released eight Black-backed Magpies (also known as Australian or White-backed Magpies)[2] of the nominate form which they had imported from Victoria, Australia, in an attempt to combat insect pests, followed by a further 4 in 1866, 32 in 1867 and 7 in 1868 – all from the same source. In their annual report for 1866, the society reported that the birds released in 1864 were 'doing well'. At about the same time the society acquired 18 from Tasmania (where the subspecies is *G. t. hypoleuca*), from where, in 1870, Mr E. Dowling imported a large number, which were liberated at Glenmark. Two dozen more were introduced to Canterbury in 1871, an unknown number costing £84 in 1874, and in 1883 a pair was received from Australia by the society in exchange for Skylarks (*Alauda arvensis*)(q.v.) and Goldfinches (*Carduelis carduelis*) (q.v.). According to Thomson (1922: 151), 'The birds soon established themselves in the provincial district, and are now fairly common'. Around 1920 they spread as far south of the Waitaki as the Horse Ranges. McCaskill (1945) recorded their first occurrence in various parts of Canterbury as follows: Greta Valley, Motunau (1876); Waimate (about 1900); Cheviot (about 1905); Lyndhurst (about 1915); Bluecliff (about 1918); Mount White (1924); Craigieburn (1929); Glenthorne Station between the Harper and Wilberforce rivers (1930 or earlier); Cass (1931); and Okains Bay (1939). Williams (1969: 450) said that their 'occupation of suitable areas of Canterbury has been virtually complete for many years, though [their] numbers may still be increasing in some areas'.

In the five years between 1865 and 1869 the Otago Society imported 3, 20, 32, 20 and 6 Black-backed Magpies, respectively.[3] Thomson reported that although they initially seemed to be doing well, and were nesting at Inch-Clutha and in Dunedin, they subsequently vanished before reappearing from Canterbury in the north; by 1918–19 they had been reported from as far south as Hampden and Moeraki.

Sir George Grey introduced some Black-backed Magpies to Kawau Island in Hauraki Gulf probably before 1867 (possibly as early as 1861), and in the former year and in 1870 the Auckland Society acquired 10 and 1, respectively. 'They very quickly became numerous', wrote Thomson of Grey's birds, 'and spread to the mainland.' In 1874, no fewer than 260 were imported by the Wellington Society, by whom they were presumably released.

'These birds are fairly common in many parts of the North Island', Thomson wrote in 1922 (p. 151), 'from Wellington to north of Whangarei, but their numbers vary a good deal.' They were less common in Taranaki than in former years, but in the forest ecotone inland from Wanganui they were abundant. Four years later, Thomson (1926) reported them to be fairly common between Wellington and Whangarei in North Island, and common north of Timaru in north Canterbury, South Island.

By the mid-1940s *G. t. hypoleuca* was established in the Hokianga region of Northland to the Hunua Hills, and from Taranaki, Lake Taupo and the Waiapu River south to Cook Strait. In South Island, it occurred from the Kaikoura Peninsula in Marlborough south to Otago. By about 1950 birds of the nominate form were established in North Island at Karaka near Auckland, in the Turakina/Wangaehu district, in Hunterville and Raumati, from Clive and Hastings to Waipukurau, between Dannevirke and Woodville, and at Pahiatua and Wairarapa: in South Island they were found at Waiau in Marlborough and in the Kaikoura/Cheviot region, but were nowhere abundant.

Wodzicki (1965: 434) described the status of both races as 'Restricted but common, North and South Islands'. Five years later, Kinsky (1970) found birds of the nominate form to be established at Hawke's Bay and Turakina, and interbreeding with *hypoleuca* at Foxton and Levin. In South Island, they occurred in the Cheviot/Kaikoura district and perhaps also in Rangiora. The *hypoleuca* form was established in North Island from Wellington to Taranaki, and in the Tongariro National Park, Volcanic Plateau, Bay of Plenty and Waikato, and occasionally in Northland and on Great and Little Barrier islands: in South Island it was found from Nelson and Marlborough to Southland – mainly east of the Southern Alps.

According to Falla, Sibson & Turbott (1979), the nominate form was formerly known only from north of Canterbury in South Island, whence it spread northwards into Marlborough. It was first identified in North Island at Hastings in 1946, and 30 years later was widely distributed in the Hawke's Bay region and in some places to the south, while stragglers had been reported from as far north as Manukau and Kaipara in Central Auckland. The *hypoleuca* subspecies is widely distributed in both North and South

Islands – to an altitude of 1,000 m in the Tongariro National Park in the former and in the latter on the eastern side of the Southern Alps. In many areas, such as on the Volcanic Plateau, it is still spreading as more land is claimed for sheep farming, but is absent from most of Northland and Southland and from the west side of the Alps. Occasional wanderers are reported from offshore islands – especially Kapiti and Little Barrier.

Black-backed Magpies have proved aggressive and successful colonists in New Zealand, favouring open grasslands, agricultural land and shelterbelts, as well as urban and suburban parks and wooded gardens. Although they sometimes prey on the eggs and young of small birds and on lizards and bees, they also destroy injurious insects and mice.

OCEANIA

Solomon Islands

According to Cain & Galbraith (1956 and 1957), Black-backed Magpies of the nominate form were introduced before 1945 to Guadalcanal in the Solomon Islands, where some were seen between Honiara and Tenaru in 1955 or 1956 and in grassland near the Tenaru River around 1960. Whether any survive today is uncertain.

Fiji[4]

According to Watling (1982: 95):

On Taveuni, the Australian Magpie is a common bird which was first introduced in the 1880s to control the Coconut Stick Insect (*Graeffea crouani*), which can on occasions be a serious pest of coconut palms. There have been at least two and probably more, separate introductions from Australia. One of which, in 1916, was organized by the Agriculture Department who charged planters £1.00 a pair. Some of these birds went to plantations on islands other than Taveuni, certainly to Vanua Levu and probably also to Viti Levu, but only on Taveuni are they established,[5] although they are frequently seen on the southern coast of Vanua Levu.

On Taveuni the birds are restricted to lowland plantations – mainly in the north-west – where they eat fruit, seeds, domestic refuse, carrion, grubs, worms and, on occasion, small vertebrates, as well as phasmid insects, and nest in the forks of large trees or in the crowns of coconut palms. Both the nominate form and the subspecies *hypoleuca* have been introduced to Fiji, where they freely interbreed.

_____

Campbell (1906) records that in the previous year he had introduced nine Black-backed Magpies of the nominate form from Australia to Nuwara Eliya in south-central Ceylon (Sri Lanka); nothing more seems to have been heard of them.

_____

In about 1850, Black-backed Magpies (presumably of the nominate form) were translocated by a Mr Calman to Kangaroo Island off the coast of South Australia; *G. t. tibicen* or *hypoleuca* is also believed to have been introduced to King and Flinders islands in Bass Strait.[6] According to Storr (1965), the Western Australia form, *dorsalis*, has been introduced on a number of occasions without lasting success to Rottnest Island.

NOTES

1 Falla, Sibson & Turbott 1979; Kinsky 1970; Long 1981; McCaskill 1945; McIlroy 1968; Oliver 1930; Thomson 1922, 1926; Williams 1969; Wodzicki 1965.
2 Williams (1969: 451) says: 'Black-backed magpies (*Gymnorhina tibicen*) have, as far as is known, never been intentionally introduced [to New Zealand] but have been brought in among white-backed magpies [*Gymnorhina hypoleuca*] and are reported by Oliver [1955] to interbreed with them.' In fact, *hypoleuca* is the eastern Victoria and Tasmania subspecies of *G. tibicen*.
3 One account says that 111 birds (not 81) were imported to Otago between 1865 and 1869.
4 Blackburn 1971; Long 1981; Pernetta & Watling 1978; Turbet 1941; Watling 1982.
5 According to Turbet (1941), they were then also established in the Lau Islands south-east of Taveuni.
6 Abbott 1974; Campbell 1906; Long 1972, 1981; Morgan 1929.

Greater Bird of Paradise
(Paradisaea apoda)

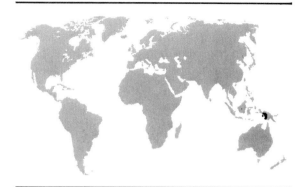

NATURAL DISTRIBUTION
Southern New Guinea and the Aru Islands.

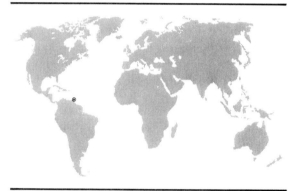

NATURALIZED DISTRIBUTION
North America: West Indies (?Little Tobago).

NORTH AMERICA

West Indies[1]

In the late nineteenth century thousands of Greater Birds of Paradise were slaughtered annually for their plumes, which were then in great demand by milliners in London, Paris and New York. In an attempt to save the species from extinction, Sir William Ingram, Bt, a well-known newspaper proprietor, organized and equipped an expedition to the Aru Islands off the coast of Dutch New Guinea in 1909, which succeeded in capturing 47 or 48 immature birds of unknown sex of the nominate subspecies; these were brought back to the 182-ha hilly island (highest point, 137 m above sea level) of Little

Tobago in the West Indies, which had been purchased by Sir William as a sanctuary, where they were released in September of the same year. Three more were added in 1912. Several soon died, and by 1913 only between 16 and 30 were known to survive. In the early 1920s, when up to 15–16 were sometimes seen together, an unsuccessful attempt was made by a Mr Luban to capture the survivors for translocation to Florida, USA.

After Sir William's death in 1924, Little Tobago was presented by his three sons to the government of Trinidad and Tobago, on condition that it should remain a sanctuary in perpetuity, with a warden appointed to care for the Birds of Paradise.

Initially the birds spread over most of the island – occasionally even making the short flight to the neighbouring island of Tobago where, however, they never became established. Because of the dense vegetation on Little Tobago, which is similar to that in the birds' native range, no accurate census has ever been possible. According to Guppy (1931), there were only a few surviving at that time, and in 1955 the population was judged to number only 11. Gilliard (1958), who spent 3 weeks of that year on the island, estimated the population (which after half a century of isolation was still identical in behaviour and plumage to that on the Aru Islands) to number between 15 and 35, which he believed might be the maximum the island could support. In 1965–6, following a severe hurricane 2 years previously, Dinsmore (1967), during a stay of 10 months on the island, found a maximum of seven (four of which were males), and concurred with Gilliard's estimation of the maximum sustainable population.

Although no Bird of Paradise nest has ever been found on Little Tobago, the birds have in the past undoubtedly bred successfully. Their principal foods on the island include Papaya (*Coccothrinax* sp.), Parrot Apple (*Clusia* sp.), 'wild cherry' (probably *Bursera* sp.), 'wild plum' (probably *Spondias monbin*), *Carica* spp., bananas, insects, young birds and eggs. They live mostly in deciduous seasonal forest canopy.

The decline (and possible extinction) of the Greater Bird of Paradise on Little Tobago has been attributed to a combination of factors: these include a shortage of food and water; unsuccessful dispersal to Tobago; predation; interspecific competition with native birds; hurricane Flora of 1963, which destroyed much of their habitat, and may have blown some of them out to sea; human disturbance; too small an initial stock (a common reason for the failure of animals to become naturalized); disease; inbreeding; and genetic drift. There seem to have been no records of the birds on the island in recent years.

NOTE

1 Baker 1922, 1923; Dinsmore 1967, 1969, 1970a,b, 1972; Ffrench 1973; Gilliard 1958; Guppy 1931; Herklots 1961; Ingram 1911, 1913, 1915, 1917, 1918, 1943, 1956; Long 1981; Peters 1962; Scott 1967; Tomlinson 1981; Westermann 1953.

Tufted Jay
(*Cyanocorax dickeyi*)

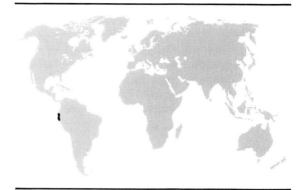

Note: Natural distribution of possible ancestor, the White-tailed Jay (*Cyanocorax mystacalis*) (after Hardy 1969 and Haemig 1979).

NATURAL DISTRIBUTION

[Of possible ancestor, the White-tailed Jay (*C. mystacalis*).] Between Guayaquil and Trujillo in coastal southwestern Ecuador and northwestern Peru.

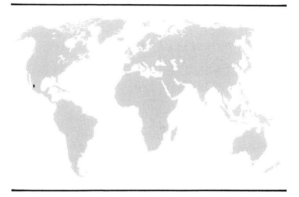

Note: After Crossin 1967 and Haemig 1979.

NATURALIZED DISTRIBUTION

North America: Mexico (Nayarit, Durango and Sinaloa).

NORTH AMERICA

Mexico

The Tufted or Painted Jay occupies a minute range of barely 6,200 km^2 in the barranca[1] country of the Sierra Madre Occidental in central Nayarit, southwestern Durango and southeastern

517

Sinaloa in western Mexico. Some 4,000 km north of its close congener, the possibly conspecific White-tailed Jay, the range of the Tufted Jay represents one of the most remarkable avian disjunctions in the western hemisphere. For long regarded as a relict population or as descended from storm-borne waifs, Haemig (1979),[2] from whom much of the following information on the species is derived, argues persuasively for a pre-Columbian introduction by man.

First made known to science as recently as 1934, when eight were collected by Chester Lamb in the barranca country east of Mazatlán in southern Sinaloa, the Tufted Jay was found by Moore (1935) most closely to resemble taxonomically the South American White-tailed Jay – a member of a genus (with the exception of the Green Jay (*C. yncas*)) not otherwise found north of Guatemala. The two species are very similar in appearance, the Tufted being slightly larger, with a longer crest, slightly darker blue on its back, a little more white on its tail, and larger supraorbital spots than its South American congener. Most of these differences, however, can, as Haemig points out, be attributed to the Tufted Jay's lengthy geographic isolation and its gradual morphological adaptation (thus conforming to Bergmann's[3] and Gloger's[4] ecogeographic rules), and crest length in jays frequently varies considerably between different age groups and geographic populations of the same species.

The relict theory holds that *Cyanocorax* jays, similar to the Tufted and White-tailed, were at one time distributed continuously from Mexico to South America, and that the Central American populations eventually died out through interspecific competition with White-throated Magpie Jays (*Calocitta formosa*), Brown Jays (*Psilorhinus morio*), and *Cissilopha* spp. and *Cyanolyca* spp. jays, which then replaced them. The last surviving Tufted Jays – in western Mexico – thus became separated by some 4,000 km from their South American congeners.

The species with which the Tufted Jay was last reputedly in contact, the Black-chested Jay (*Cyanocorax affinis zeledoni*) of southern Costa Rica and Panama, differs, however, markedly from both *C. dickeyi* and *mystacalis*, and from the affinity aspect it appears more probable that it was with *mystacalis* that *dickeyi* was last in contact. Moreover the relict theory cannot

account for the absence of the Tufted Jay, and the species that supposedly supplanted it, from other apparently suitable barranca habitats in western Mexico, where the only jay is Steller's Jay (*Cyanocitta stelleri purpurea*), with which the Tufted Jay, in its tiny range, exists sympatrically. There is no evidence that jays similar to the Tufted or White-tailed ever inhabited Central America or the country between their present disjunctive populations; the former, like the Dwarf Jay (*Cyanolyca nana*) and the White-throated Jay (*Cyanolyca mirabilis*), occupies a restricted range probably because of the difficulty experienced by a sedentary species in dispersing from a precipitous montane habitat.

The storm-carried waif theory holds that in the distant past a small flock of White-tailed Jays was blown by high winds from South America northwards to western Mexico, where they subsequently evolved into today's Tufted Jays. Even were the prevailing wind in the region a southerly one (instead of the North-East Trade), the enormous distance involved, coupled with the fact that the Humboldt Current, which originates in Antarctica and runs northwards along the west cost of South America, making the entire eastern Pacific south of 5° N (around central Colombia) far too cold for the creation or maintenance of hurricanes, effectively negates this hypothesis.

A third possibility, for which Haemig argues convincingly, is introduction by man. The Tufted Jay's restricted and disjunctive distribution; the fact that in western Mexico it does not occur below 1,200 m, whereas the White-tailed Jay is a bird of the tropical lowlands; the species' poor reproductive success which hinders dispersal, and its apparent maladaptation to its montane barranca environment – are all strongly suggestive of a man-induced origin.

If, however, the Tufted Jay is a pre-Columbian exotic, why is it found in remote and mountainous western Mexico rather than in the centre and south of the country, where the principal imperial cities were situated? Haemig elegantly answers this apparent conundrum by pointing out that as recently as the 1950s a large number and a wide variety of artifacts that covered a timespan of many centuries were unearthed in various sites in western Mexico; these were stylistically unlike any of those found in the rest of Mesoamerica, but bore a striking similarity to objects of the same kinds from coastal Ecuador and Peru. Some appear to be entirely absent from the intervening countries of South and Central America, while those that do occur there are still found principally in western Mexico and northwestern South America. The fact that articles showing many distinctive styles have been discovered in both regions (rather than only a few, which might indicate convergent evolution) has led anthropologists to believe in some form of cultural contact between the two areas – perhaps for millennia before the arrival of the Spanish *conquistadores*; much of such intercourse, probably from as early as around 1500 BC, was probably through ship-borne trade, but some at least may well have been as a result of small-scale emigration from South America. Such emigration is further suggested by the burgeoning in western Mexico about AD 900 of a flourishing, varied and sophisticated copper metallurgical industry, which produced wares stylistically similar to those made in Ecuador and Peru, and apparently owed nothing to local invention. Similarities in metal artifacts other than copper, such as gold, have also been noted between western Mexico and northwestern South America.

As previously mentioned, a thriving trade and traffic in colourful feathers is known to have existed in the pre-Columbian era,[5] and what more natural than that immigrants to western Mexico from northwestern South America should have brought with them not only artifacts and a knowledge of metallurgy, but also White-tailed Jays, whose vivid plumage and engaging character would have enabled them to fill a dual role as both a source of feathers for ornamental and ritual purposes and as a pet? As Haemig (1979: 86) concludes, the Tufted Jay is probably neither a relict species nor a storm-carried waif, 'but rather is simply part of a general pattern of South American artifacts left in western Mexico by ancient man'.

The **Azure-winged Magpie** (*Cyanopica cyana*) occurs in central, east-central and northeastern Asia, Korea, Manchuria, eastern, northern, and western China, and Japan, with a discrete European population in western Spain and Portugal.

The presence of a disjunctive subspecies (*cooki*) in the Iberian Peninsula has led to speculation that it might occur as a result of introduction by man. According to Goodwin (1976a: 172) and personal communication, 1986:

This theory is usually discounted on the grounds that there are distinct racial differences between the far-eastern and Iberian forms . . . These differences are, however, not very great . . . it cannot be considered impossible that the differences of the Iberian Azure-winged Magpie could have arisen subsequent to introduction, if this took place long ago.

A more cogent objection to the introduction theory is that, contrary to popular opinion, successful introductions of birds to new areas . . . seem only to have been achieved where quite large numbers of individuals in good condition have been liberated together. . . . It seems unlikely either that so many Azure-winged Magpies were once imported into Iberia or that a considerable number of both sexes escaped or were liberated or, alternatively, that the escape of only a few individuals would have led to their establishing their species.

That the Azure-winged Magpie may be a declining species that once inhabited a much larger range is suggested by the fact that within its present ranges it is absent from many areas that appear suitable. At least in the Far East this seems unlikely to be due to persecution by man, its patchy distribution seems due to rather rigid habitat and/or temperature requirements (Dos Santos 1968).

[The range of] the Chough [*Pyrrhocorax pyrrhocorax*] is of interest in this connection. Were the Chough to become extinct in the central parts of its range and in the western parts north of the Pyrenees (and in central Europe and the British Isles it may well be in the process of so-doing) its range would then show similar disjunction to that of *Cyanopica*.

NOTES

1 Ravine with steeply sloping sides.
2 See also: Amadon 1944; Brodkorb 1972; Crossin 1967; Darlington 1938; Haemig 1978; Haffer 1975; Hardy 1969; Moore 1935, 1938; Sahagùn [1577] 1963.
3 The tendency for the body size of the subspecies of homoiothermic animals to increase as the mean temperature of their environment decreases.
4 The tendency for the pigmentation of the subspecies of homoiothermic animals to become darker as the mean temperature and humidity of their environment increases.
5 See p. 372.

House Crow
(*Corvus splendens*)

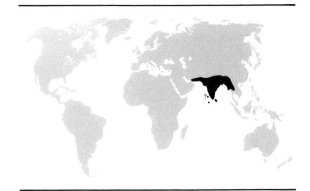

NATURAL DISTRIBUTION
From southern Iran through Afghanistan, Pakistan, India, Sri Lanka, the Laccadive (?introduced) and Maldive islands, Nepal, Bhutan and Assam eastwards to southern Burma, Thailand (?introduced in the south-west), and western Yunnan in southern China.

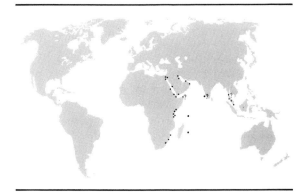

Note: After Goodwin 1976a; Meininger, Mullié & Bruun 1980; and Bijlsma & Meininger 1984.

NATURALIZED DISTRIBUTION
Asia: Arabia (Oman, United Arab Emirates, Saudi Arabia, Bahrain, Kuwait, People's Demo-

cratic Republic of Yemen (Aden), Israel, ?Jordan, ?Laccadive Islands, Malaysia (Malaya and Singapore), ?Thailand; Africa: South Africa, Mozambique, Kenya, Tanzania (including Zanzibar and Pemba islands), Sudan, ?Somalia, Ethiopia, Djibouti, Egypt, Mauritius, Seychelles.

ASIA

Arabia (Oman, United Arab Emirates, Saudi Arabia, Bahrain, Kuwait and People's Democratic Republic of Yemen (Aden))[1]

According to Gallagher & Woodcock (1980: 35 and 270), the House Crow was probably introduced by man to northern Oman where it is a 'common resident in parts of Musandam, along Batinah to Muscat, and at Qurayat, occasionally to Masirah; most resemble *C. s. zugmayeri* [Sind and Baluchistan, Pakistan] or intergrades with *C. s. splendens* [peninsular India]'. Jennings (1981: 90) adds that the species 'is an abundant resident in the villages of the east coast of the United Arab Emirates, Musandam and near Ras al Khaimah town but never very far inland'; a few also occur at Dhaid and, since 1977, at Dubai. Silsby (1980: 87) says that the species is also an 'occasional visitor to Hejaz, Bahrain and Kuwait'. In Saudi Arabia, House Crows are found in Jeddah on the Red Sea coast, where they were introduced in 1978.

Although Ripley (1961) says that the House Crow's status in Muscat is uncertain, Peters (1962) states that the resident form there, *C. s. zugmayeri*, seems to have been introduced; when this took place is uncertain, but Meinertzhagen (1924 and 1954) – who believed that the population might be a natural one – reported the appearance of occasional birds in the early 1920s. Although the House Crow is non-migratory, it is possible that these eastern Arabian populations represent a natural extension of range westwards – perhaps by storm-carried vagrants – across the Persian Gulf and the Gulf of Oman from southern Iran.

As early as 1866 (and again in 1892), Barnes (1893) reported the presence of 'crows' (which he described as *culminatus*[2] in Aden (People's Democratic Republic of Yemen), where he was informed that House Crows had been introduced in the middle 1840s by an officer of the Bombay Infantry, whose religion allegedly required that the bodies of its dead adherents should be consumed by crows (!). Yerbury (1886) noted three 'crows' in Aden which he believed had been imported. By the late 1940s House Crows were, according to Browne (1950), fairly well established in Aden, where between October and May flocks of up to 30 were not uncommon – especially in gardens at Crater. Although Meinertzhagen (1954) recorded that in Aden 'only a few pairs remain', Smith (1956) found them to be 'now very common, especially at Sheikh Othman' [Shaykh 'Uthmān]. Three years later, Sage (1959) saw a dozen at Steamer Point in Aden Town and others elsewhere, and by the early 1960s the House Crow was, according to Ennion (1962), established as a common breeding resident 'throughout the Colony at Sheikh Othman. Not elsewhere'. Clarke (1967) confirmed the status of the House Crow as 'now a common bird' in Aden.

According to Ash (1984a), the main increase in numbers and distribution of House Crows in Aden appears to date from the early 1970s, when they spread out from their strongholds in Crater and Khormaksar, though it was not until 1979 that they reached Dar Saad on the outskirts of Sheikh Othman, where they had been very common for more than 20 years.

Since 1982, the population and range of the birds have increased dramatically; their recent arrival inland at Lahej in southern Yemen is likely to have been via villages along the road, while their spread eastwards to Zinjibār on the southern Yemen coast in Abyan, which dates from 1981 to 1982, and nearby Jaar (1983), may have been a result of natural spread or of transportation by vehicle or coastal vessel. Their earlier appearance further east at Al Mukallā in Hadramaut, where they were first seen in 1978 or 1979, suggests a separate arrival from the east by sea. Although House Crows did not multiply as rapidly in Al Mukallā (where in 1984 Ash estimated the population at around 100) as in Aden, their dispersal from the former presumably accounted for their appearance in Ash Shihr in 1983, where in the following year there was a colony of 15 or 16.

In Aden in late 1984, Ash counted flocks of 400 and 600 birds, and estimated a roost at

Sheikh Othman to number some 5,000; his own calculation of the total Aden population was at least 50,000, but other figures quoted to him varied between 10,000 and 2 million. The subspecies present in Aden and Yemen is apparently *protegatus* from Sri Lanka.

House Crows in Aden are regarded as serious pests, complaints against them including the destruction of domestic refuse bags and the dissemination of their contents; damage to electric wiring and the disorientation of television aerials; the depositing of excrement and the spread of disease; excessive noise as a result of their high numbers; the destruction of fruit, domestic poultry and drying fish, and, allegedly, of newborn calves, kids and lambs; predation on the eggs and young of small native birds; and the obstruction – by 'mobbing' – of such valuable scavengers as Black Kites (*Milvus migrans aegyptius*) and Egyptian Vultures (*Neophron percnopterus*).

The expansion in numbers and distribution of House Crows in Aden and southern Yemen is a result of the increasing availability and amount of domestic refuse, which is the birds' principal food source. To control their numbers, an improvement in the method of refuse collection and hygiene, and nest destruction during the peak nestling season in May, have been suggested by Ash, augmented, if necessary, by shooting and poisoning.

Israel and Jordan[3]

Krabbe (1980) records that in Israel the first pair of House Crows was seen in 1976 in Elat at the head of the Gulf of Aqaba, where they are now breeding annually. From Elat, they have been seen crossing the gulf to Aqaba in Jordan, where, too, they may now be breeding.

Laccadive Islands

According to Ali & Ripley (1972), House Crows may have been introduced to the Laccadive Islands where, as in the neighbouring Maldives, the resident form is *C. s. maledivicus*. They may, however, occur there naturally or as self-colonists from the Maldives.

Malaysia (Malaya and Singapore)[4]

Authorities differ as to when House Crows of the Sinhalese subspecies (*protegatus*) were introduced to Malaya: Ward (1968) says there has been a breeding colony there since 1898, Delacour (1947) and Medway & Wells (1976) say that birds were imported in January 1903, while Gibson-Hill (1949b,c) and Madoc (1956) state that the introduction was made around 1919 to combat a plague of caterpillars that were ravaging coffee plantations.

Although House Crows may have reached Malaya as stowaways on board ship both previously and subsequently, the earliest deliberate introduction by man is described in detail by Willey, Treacher et al. (1903).

In 1902, the resident Governor-General of the Federated Malay States, Mr W. H. Treacher, wrote to the Colonial Secretary in Ceylon at the request of a 'prominent planter' on Penang, Mr E. V. Carey, to ask whether some House Crows could be shipped to the island, 'in the hope and expectation that they might prove beneficial in keeping down the numbers of caterpillars which occasionally devastate estates in this country'. On 28 December 1902, six dozen birds were shipped from Colombo on board the SS *Austria* bound for Penang, where 56 arrived safely and in good condition on 2 January 1903; these birds were all released before the end of the month.

From Klang, Selangor, where several were freed and where they soon became established, House Crows spread only slowly, probably not reaching Port Swettenham on the coast until the mid-1950s. In 1953–4, a small number were seen arriving on Penang Island, over 250 km to the north, where they remained for several months. A decade later they seemed to be extending their range in Selangor, since some were reported north of Kapar in the north and in southern Sembilan in the south. In the last 20 years colonies have become settled in Kuala Lumpur, at Prai, Province Wellesley (where they were well established in 1967), and at Georgetown, Penang. Single birds were observed at Cape Rachado in March 1969 and at Batu Berendam, Malacca (some 250 km south of Klang) in February 1972. According to Medway & Wells (1976), the birds at Prai and Georgetown may originally have arrived by ship, and the colony at Klang may have received reinforcements in the same manner;

as, however, House Crows are strong fliers, the birds at Prai (some 500 km south of their nearest breeding range) and Georgetown may be descended from dispersants from Thailand in the north and/or from Klang in the south.

From the latter, where they are now very common, House Crows had extended their range by the mid-1970s north to Jeram, south to Banting, and inland to Kuala Lumpur. The spread north along the Selangor state coast continues, and the birds are now established in the town of Kuala Selangor. Southwards from the nucleus in Kelang town (south-west of Kuala Lumpur) stragglers have been reported from as far down the coast as Malacca. The Kelang population now numbers around 20,000 and that in Kuala Lumpur between 4,000 and 6,000, although attempts to control the birds induce fluctuations. In the north, crows from the population centred on Penang, Prai and Butterworth have recently been recorded as far inland as the town of Kulim.[5]

In 1948, a small colony of House Crows became established in the docks of Singapore – where they had presumably arrived by ship – and where 20 years later between 200 and 400 roosted outside Gate No. 3 at Tanjong Pagar. Gibson-Hill (1952) suggested that this population may be derived from escaped cagebirds or from pets released during the Japanese occupation in the Second World War, but Ward (1968) considered that the founder stock could have arrived from Klang (over 650 km to the north) or even from Burma – a flight of at least 1,250 km. From Singapore, House Crows have crossed the Johor Strait to Johor Baharu town on the mainland. Anecdotal accounts led C. J. Hails (personal communication, 1985) to believe that the population may be declining, possibly as a result of improved hygienic conditions. Nevertheless, as D. R. Wells (personal communication, 1986) points out, 'further spread is certain and eradication out of the question'.

Thailand

Peters (1962) suggests that the presence of House Crows of the form *C. s. insolens* (which occurs also in southern Burma and western Yunnan) in southwestern Thailand may be the result of an introduction by man; Lekagul & Cronin (1974),

however, describe them only as a rare resident and make no reference of any introduction.

AFRICA

South Africa[6]

On 14 September 1972, two House Crows were seen approaching the South Pier in Durban, Natal, from an east-northeasterly direction. On 18 October, they were joined by three more birds, but all five disappeared shortly afterwards and none were seen again until 24 December, when two were noted at the Old Fort. Reports about their behaviour varied – Sinclair (1974: 189) stating that they were 'at all times very wary and unapproachable' whereas Clancey (1974: 32) found them to be 'relatively confiding'. Breeding was first recorded in October 1975. The origin of these birds – believed to be of the nominate subspecies – has not been determined, but they were presumably either escaped or deliberately released cagebirds or natural or shipborne dispersants south of Zanzibar[7] (see below). When they first arrived in Durban, House Crows were concentrated on the beachfront, where they fed on scraps left by fishermen, day trippers, and patrons of the local drive-in cinema. Attempts by the Natal Parks Board to eradicate them were unsuccessful. 'The House Crow', wrote P. A. Clancey (personal communication, 1981), 'is now well established in [western] Durban (flocks of up to 60 in non-breeding season), and has travelled [450 km] south to East London [first in November 1975] and the Cape (Cape Town) [1,400 km].' According to J. Vincent (personal communication, 1981), 'the population in Durban [estimated in 1982 at over 200] has remained very restricted in numbers and locality. No influence on other species has been recorded'. Clancey (personal communication, 1985) said that he had not heard of breeding beyond the confines of the Indian residential districts of west metropolitan Durban, although individuals have been recorded inland between Durban and Pietermaritzburg (Cato Ridge).

Mozambique

P. A. Clancey (personal communication, 1985) wrote that in the 1950s he was sent the skin of a crow collected somewhere in Mozambique (subsequently identified as *C. splendens*) by the then director of the museum in Lourenço Marques (Maputo), Dr A. A. da Rosa Pinto, but that it had proved impossible to determine if a viable population existed. It now seems that there is a thriving colony of breeding House Crows on Inhaca Island in Algoa Bay off Maputo in southern Mozambique, and that more probably occur on other coastal islands further north, such as Bazaruto, south of Beira, 'where ravens (*sic!*) were recorded in the 1950s'.

Kenya[8]

According to Britton (1980), House Crows were first recorded in Kenya on the coast at Mombasa in 1947, from where Mackworth-Praed & Grant (1960) reported that they had spread some 6 km north along the coast to Nyali. In his first (1963) edition, Williams (p. 230) described the House Crow as 'now common at Mombasa'. By 1972, the birds had extended their range some 16 km north to Mtwapa and 20 km inland to Mazeras, and 5 years later small numbers had reached the coastal resort of Kilifi, nearly 60 km north of Mombasa. Britton (1980: 123) suggested that 'recently established disjunct populations at Malindi and Watamu [on the coast further north of Mombasa] are probably derived from birds released locally'. In his revised edition (1982: 398), Williams said that House Crows were 'now abundant along the Kenya coast'

In January 1985, J. S. Ash and C. J. Feare found House Crows to be very common in and around Mombasa, where although they subsist largely on garbage (which is certainly what maintains their numbers), they seem to have increased at the expense of such native species as weavers (Ploceidae) and sunbirds (Nectariniidae). Away from the coast, Ash and Feare found House Crows as far inland as Mariakani, 35 km from Mombasa. They suspected that hearsay records from Voi (about 170 km inland) referred to the Cape Rook (*Corvus capensis*).[9]

Tanzania[10]

Between 1893 and 1895 House Crows of the nominate subspecies from Bombay were released as urban scavengers of offal in the town of Zanzibar by Sir Gerald Porter and a Dr Charlesworth. Others were subsequently introduced for the same purpose to the neighbouring island of Pemba where, according to Pakenham (1979), they no longer occur. More were imported from Bombay in India as garbage scavengers to Zanzibar in the 1890s, where they became well established in the capital and from where they have spread into rural areas and to the coast of Tanzania around Dar-es-Salaam. In March 1981, C. J. Feare (personal communication, 1986) found House Crows feeding with native Pied Crows (*Corvus albus*) in the abattoirs at Tanga (on the coast opposite Pemba Island), from where there seem to be no other records. Williams (1963: 230 and 1982: 398) described the species respectively as 'abundant on Zanzibar Island' and 'abundant . . . in northeastern Tanzania; also on Zanzibar Island'.

In Kenya and Tanzania, where it is still slowly increasing and spreading, the House Crow is destroying the nests, eggs and young of both native wild birds, such as Morning Warblers (*Cichladusa arquata*), Mousebirds (*Colius* spp.), Golden Palm Weavers (*Ploceus bojeri*), *Camaroptera* spp. and Rufous Chatterers (*Argya rubiginosa*), and – since it is a close commensal of man – domestic poultry, and is becoming a nuisance to growing farm crops and soft fruits. In compensation it also eats locusts and termites. In some places it seems to be displacing the Pied Crow as an urban scavenger. Attempts have been made to eradicate House Crows from Zanzibar, but to no avail.

Sudan, Somalia and Ethiopia[11]

Precisely when House Crows were first introduced – probably from India – to Port Sudan on the Red Sea coast is unrecorded. Meinertzhagen (1949) saw a flock of 40 in the public gardens there in 1941, and a few years later Cave & MacDonald (1955) found a considerable number nesting on the girders of the harbour bridge and feeding in the gardens. Williams (1963 and 1982) records the species as common in the area.

Davis (1951) refers to the arrival by ship on Cape Guardafui in the Somali Republic in November 1950 of four House Crows from Colombo, Sri Lanka.

According to Urban & Brown (1971) and Boswall (1971), House Crows have occurred in Massawa on the Red Sea coast of Ethiopia since at least 1968.

Djibouti

According to Clarke (1967), House Crows probably spread some 240 km south-west from Aden to Djibouti City in the French Territory of the Afars and Issas (Djibouti) before May 1958 (Long (1981: 351) erroneously quotes Clarke as saying that they came from Port Sudan). More than 25 were counted in Djibouti in 1975, and Welch & Welch (1984) found them to be 'extremely numerous, many hundreds, around Djibouti City'. They have also been recorded from Obock on the opposite coast of Golfe de Tadjoura.

Egypt[12]

Meininger, Mullié & Bruun (1980) have traced the establishment of the House Crow as a breeding resident in Egypt, where Goodwin (1976a) said the species had successfully colonized Port Tewfiq, Suez. It is first known to have occurred there in 1945, but may have been present as long ago as 1922. In April 1967, several were seen at Ismâ'ilîya at the head of the Great Bitter Lake, where others were reported a decade later. In 1978, at least 50 were observed in Suez – mostly near the harbour. Although some showed behaviour indicative of nesting, no proof of breeding could then be found.

On 8 January and 9 February 1979, 10 and 58 House Crows, respectively, were seen in Suez, where in the following November Sherif M. Baha el Din found two occupied nests in a tree in a small garden near the harbour. During their visits to Suez in December 1979 and January 1980, Meininger et al. saw House Crows in flocks of between 20 and 40, concentrated near the local slaughterhouse, where they fed on offal in the company of Cattle Egrets (*Bubulcus ibis*). On 4 May 1980, Sherif Baha el Din discovered a breeding colony of 20–30 pairs in a large garden at Port Tewfiq, where the birds are now considered to be thoroughly established. Bijlsma & Meininger (1984) estimated the population at

Suez, where the species is the only abundant avian scavenger, and in surrounding areas at between 800 and 850.

On 13 August 1979, Sherif Baha el Din found two adults feeding four recently fledged young at Râs Ghârib on the Gulf of Suez, some 160 km south-east of Suez, where Meininger et al. saw two on 19 January 1980. On 22 June 1980, Sherif Baha el Din reported another two in the harbour at Safâga on the Red Sea coast, some 200 km south of Râs Ghârib. They have also been observed at Ain Sukhna.

Mauritius[13]

According to J. D. Shuja (personal communication to C. J. Feare), House Crows were first imported to Mauritius by immigrants from India when the island came under British rule in 1810. Meinertzhagen (1912) recorded that some were introduced from India to Port St Louis around 1910 [*sic*]. By about 1920 a small colony appears to have been established in the meat market of Port St Louis. Some birds (for example, a pair that accompanied the SS *Ikauna* from Colombo to Mauritius in November 1950) have made the voyage from India and Sri Lanka as natural shipborne dispersants, being treated *en route* as pets by the crew, and it seems probable that some continue to arrive from time to time in this way.

Benedict (1957) claimed that House Crows no longer occurred in Mauritius. Staub (1976), however, stated that a flock of around 100 frequent high ficus and 'African Sausage' trees of the Jardin de la Compagnie and Jardin de la Plaine Verte and the abattoir in Port Louis, where they are useful scavengers, are increasing, and have spread north to Grand Baie and south to Mahebourg. Shuja reported that since the late 1970s the birds have multiplied and spread inland, and are now established in Rose Hill, Beau Bassin, and on the verges of Quatres Bornes, where they are said to be becoming something of a pest, and to be destroying the eggs and young of native species.

Seychelles

Feare & Watson (1984) record that between 29 April and 4 May 1970 a House Crow travelled on a ship out of Bombay bound for the Seychelles where, on approaching Mahé, it flew off to St Anne Island. This is the earliest record of the species in the archipelago. In October 1978 Feare saw a single individual on Bird Island, and at the same time a further three were observed in the port area of Mahé after the arrival of a cargo vessel from India. Since then, House Crows have been reported at Mont Fleuri, Moyenne Island, Sunset Hotel, La Retraite rubbish dump (where 11 were counted in 1985), and on a housing estate at Machabee. Breeding has been confirmed on Silhouette, but nests and eggs have always been successfully destroyed. Pressure is currently being exerted for an attempt to be made to eradicate House Crows in the Seychelles before they become properly established; were they to succeed in doing so, native birds – many of which are already endangered – would almost certainly be affected.

Crows (? sp.) have frequently arrived in Australia[14] (especially Western Australia and Victoria) on board ship from India, but have never succeeded in becoming established. The earliest known record dates from about 1900, when an unidentified crow arrived in the country on a ship out of Colombo, Ceylon (Sri Lanka).

The earliest record in Western Australia dates from 1926 when three birds landed in Fremantle off the SS *Naldera* from London via Colombo; one survived until February 1928. On 22 August 1942, Captain J. L. Ruddiman found six on board his vessel after leaving Cochin on the west coast of India; one pair built a nest of ropes' ends and cotton waste near the engine, and the group was last seen on 5 September in sheds on the North Wharf of Fremantle. Between 1926 and 1950 about 15 House Crows are known to have arrived in Western Australia; from 1950 to 1967 they came in regularly on ships from India, and at least 30 were destroyed by the authorities.

In May 1959, three were reported to have flown ashore at Geelong, Victoria, off the MV *Tavince* from Colombo. In April 1963 more were found at large in the Werribee district south-west of Melbourne.

In about 1860, Colonel R. C. Tytler imported some House Crows to the penal colony of South Andaman[15] to scavenge on the settlement's refuse; the birds, however, seem soon to have disappeared.

As Meininger, Mullié & Bruun (1980) point out, the House Crow lives exclusively as a close commensal of man, as close as, if not closer than, the House Sparrow (*Passer domesticus*), and no population is known to exist away from man. The species' occurrence at Aden, Port Sudan, Elat, Aqaba, Suez, Ismâ'ilîya and elsewhere, may well be the result of transportation by ship, as has several times been reported between Sri Lanka and Australia and Africa. The fact that the former localities are all situated on important sea routes tends to support this presumption.

NOTES

1 Ash 1984a; Barnes 1893; Browne 1950; Bundy & Warr 1980; Clancey 1974; Clarke 1967; Ennion 1962; Gallagher & Woodcock 1980; Jennings 1981; Long 1981; Meinertzhagen 1924, 1954; Meininger, Mullié & Bruun 1980; Peters 1962; Ripley 1961; Sage 1959; Silsby 1980; Smith 1956; Stanford 1973; Walker 1981; Warr 1978; Yerbury 1886.

2 *Corvus macrorhynchos culminatus* is the southern Indian and Sri Lankan subspecies of the Jungle Crow.

3 Krabbe 1980; Meininger, Mullié & Bruun 1980.

4 Delacour 1947; Gibson-Hill 1949b,c, 1952; Long 1981; Madoc 1956; Medway & Wells 1964, 1976; Meininger, Mullié & Brunn 1980; Ward 1968.

5 D. R. Wells, personal communication, 1986.

6 P. A Clancey 1974 (and personal communications 1981 and 1985); Liversidge, n.d.; Meininger, Mullié & Bruun 1980; Mowat 1980; Oatley 1973; Sinclair 1974, 1981; and J. Vincent and J. M. Winterbottom, personal communications, 1981.

7 A specimen of *C. s. splendens* found on the coast of Mozambique in the 1950s was believed to have arrived naturally from Zanzibar.

8 Britton 1980; Clancey 1974; Mackworth-Praed & Grant 1955; Meininger, Mullié & Bruun 1980; Williams 1982 (and 1963). See also: *Bulletin of the East African Natural History Society*, August and November (1972).

9 C. J. Feare, personal communication, 1986.

10 Clancey 1974; Long 1967, 1981; Mackworth-Praed & Grant 1955; Meininger, Mullié & Bruun 1980; Pakenham 1943, 1949, 1959, 1979; Vaughan 1930; Williams 1982 (and 1963).

11 Ash 1977, 1984a, 1985; Boswall 1971; Cave & MacDonald 1955; Clancey 1974; Davis 1951; Long 1981; Mackworth-Praed & Grant 1955;

Meinertzhagen 1949; Meininger, Mullié & Bruun 1980; Urban & Brown 1971; Williams 1963, 1982.

12 Goodwin 1976a; Meininger, Mullié & Bruun 1980; Meininger, Mullié et al 1979.

13 Ali & Ripley 1972; Benedict 1957; Clancey 1974; Long 1981; Meinertzhagen 1912; Meininger, Mullié & Bruun 1980; Rountree, Guérin et al. 1952; Staub 1976.

14 Blakers, Davies & Reilly 1984; Gibson 1961; Hylton 1927; Jenkins 1959; Long 1967a, 1972, 1981; McGill 1949; Meininger, Mullié & Bruun 1980; Robinson 1950; Ruddiman 1952; Smith 1967.

15 Ali & Ripley 1972; Beavan 1867; Long 1981.

Rook

(Corvus frugilegus)

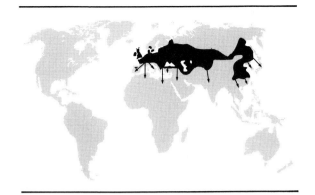

Note: Distribution in Mongolian region uncertain.

NATURAL DISTRIBUTION

In Europe and the Middle East from the British Isles eastwards to eastern Siberia, north to the White Sea, western Finland and extreme southern Norway and Sweden, south to the southern USSR, northern Iran, northeastern Iraq and Turkey, Bulgaria, Yugoslavia, Germany and northern France. In the Far East from the eastern USSR, Mongolia and Manchuria south to central-southern China. Winters south to the Iberian Peninsula, north-west Africa, Egypt, northern Arabia, southern Iran, northwestern India, southeastern China, South Korea and Japan.

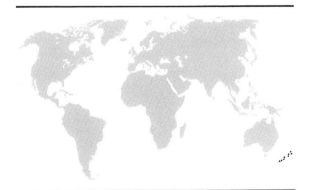

NATURALIZED DISTRIBUTION
Australasia: New Zealand.

AUSTRALASIA

New Zealand[1]

Rooks were first introduced to New Zealand in 1862 when three were released in Nelson where, after remaining for a few years, they eventually disappeared. Others seem to have been liberated at about the same time in Canterbury, since a local newspaper of April 1870 (quoted by Thomson (1922: 152)), referring to the presentation of a single bird to the Canterbury Acclimatization Society, states that 'The rooks first imported into the province by Mr Watts Russell, some years ago, were all killed by cats'. According to Drummond (1907), there were Rooks in Christchurch in 1868, but he does not say whether in the wild or in captivity. Thomson records that three dozen were shipped from London in 1871, but that only five[2] survived the voyage to be released in the society's gardens in Christchurch in the following year. These birds, said the society's report for 1871, quoted by Williams (1969: 449), should prove 'of great value to agriculture' – a somewhat provocative claim. According to Williams, 20 more pairs were ordered in 1872 and 1873, of which about 30 were freed in the society's gardens in 1874. (Thomson (1922) says that 35 were released in the gardens in March 1873, and (1926) that others were imported in 1875.) It was these two shipments, says Williams, that were the founding stock of the Rook population in Canterbury.

The first rookery in Canterbury was built in Cathedral Square, Christchurch, in 1872, and by 1885 at least three more had been formed – three in or near Cathedral Square and one at Fendalton. In 1890, Captain F. W. Hutton told Thomson (1922: 154) that 'these birds are well naturalized about Christchurch, but do not now increase much; possibly owing to poisoned grain'. By the turn of the century, the only occupied rookery near Christchurch was that at Fendalton, and by 1916 Thomson found that although Rooks were quite common south of Christchurch they were very local, and had spread little from their point of release. Three years later Thomson was told by A. H. Cockayne that although Rooks had formerly been abundant in Dean's Bush at Riccarton, Christchurch, they were now rare.

In the mid-1920s the trees in Christchurch in which the Rooks used to roost began to die, forcing the birds gradually to disperse inland, until by around 1950 they were building some 24 km west of the coast, and at least 13 rookeries had been constructed over an area of more than 155 km². By the mid-1950s there were 19 occupied rookeries over about 260 km², and by the end of the following decade others had been formed at Peel Forest and on Banks Peninsula east of Christchurch. Bull (1957), who lists 41 rookeries that were constructed at various times in and around Christchurch as well as three in the Peel Forest area and a similar number on Banks Peninsula, estimated that by 1947 the Christchurch population had increased some seven- to tenfold from the 1926 total of 1,000. 'This fairly rapid increase in the population', Bull continues, 'does not appear to have been maintained, for the 1956 estimate falls within the range of those made in 1947.' This, Williams says, is also true of the rookeries censuses made in 1947, 1955 and 1956 that suggested that around 1,700 nests existed in those 3 years. Widespread poisoning between 1956 and 1967 reduced this population to barely 700.

Although, according to Williams, the Rook had one of the most limited distributions of any alien bird in Canterbury, Bull considered that early attempts at control actually assisted the species' dispersal. By the late 1960s, as a result of the destruction of nests, Rooks were less common around Christchurch than for many years, but were still relatively common on Banks Peninsula where their destruction of agricultural and silvicultural pests such as the 'grass-grub' *Odontria* (*Costelytra*) *striata* precluded their disturbance.

In 1869, the Auckland Acclimatization Society imported a pair of Rooks, followed in 1870 by a further 64. Initially, the birds had some difficulty in becoming established, since the society's annual report for 1872, quoted by Thomson (1922: 152), states that 'eight nests were built in the Gardens, but unhappily a night review of the volunteers took place just as incubation commenced, when the firing caused the majority of the rooks to forsake the nests, so that only three small broods were hatched. In January a severe epidemic broke out amongst them which destroyed several.' A year later, a few pairs nested, but the society's report for 1874 concluded that 'they are not doing so well. The young have died' – perhaps because the climate was too hot for them.

According to Bull & Porter (1975), Rooks were introduced to the Hawke's Bay area to control insect pests on at least two occasions in the early 1870s: in 1872 and 1873 some may have been released in the vicinity of Big Bush (near Mangateretere north-east of Hastings), and in October of the following year a shipment of 72 for the Hawke's Bay Acclimatization Society arrived at Napier on the *Queen Bee*. Thomson reported that although the birds increased only slowly in North Island they had, by around 1920, spread to Hawke's Bay, Hick's Bay and Lake Taupo.

By the late 1950s there were five discrete populations of Rooks in New Zealand, two of which were in North Island (at Hawke's Bay and in southern Wairarapa) and three in South Island (at Christchurch, on Banks Peninsula and in Peel Forest). Although, according to Bull, only one of these colonies was certainly descended from nineteenth-century plantings, at least some of the others may have resulted from liberations rather than natural dispersal.

The Rook has not proved an adventurous colonizer in New Zealand, and even 80 years after its introduction had only achieved a very local distribution. This may have been due at least in part to widespread persecution on account of its alleged pest status, although, as mentioned above, Bull considers that the reverse may be true. Between 1965 and 1969, however, the breeding population in the Hawke's Bay area doubled when control measures were relaxed and the cultivated acreage increased. It took Rooks at Hawke's Bay 96 years to spread from Napier to Woodville, a distance of only some 130 km, and they have only dispersed at a rate of 1.3–3.1 km per year southwards, and even less northwards. Wodzicki (1965: 434) described Rooks as 'Locally common, North and South Islands'. Kinsky (1970) found them to be established at Hawke's Bay, in southern Wairarapa and in Canterbury, and said that they had spread to Tolaga Bay (north of Gisborne), Miranda (on the Firth of Thames), Cloverlea, Manawatu (Wellington) and the Awhitu Peninsula. R. E. R. Porter told McLennan & MacMillan (1983) that the population based on Hawke's Bay – by far the largest in New Zealand – was in 1976 estimated to number 26,000. Falla, Sibson & Turbott (1979) said that Rooks were well established in two North Island districts (Hawke's Bay and southern Wairarapa) and in three in South Island (Christchurch, Banks Peninsula and Peel Forest). The most southerly rookery is near Sutton in Otago and the most northerly one on the Firth of Thames. Both Williams (1973) and Falla et al. say that Rooks have been recorded on the Chatham Islands, some 860 km east of Christchurch. In North Island, Rooks are currently well established in the Hawke's Bay area, and rookeries have been constructed in several localities near Auckland and Wellington; in South Island, they persist at West Melton, Sunnyside, Banks Peninsula and Geraldine.

As early as 1917 Rooks in New Zealand acquired a bad reputation as a pest, being accused in the Hawke's Bay area of eating walnuts, sprouting oats and wheat, and even (presumably sickly) adult sheep. They also sometimes severely damage other cereal crops (especially maize) pumpkins, potatoes and peas. In compensation they eat many injurious insects including, in the Hawke's Bay area, the 'grass grub' *Costelytra zealandica* (the larvae of an indigenous scarabaeid beetle that eats the roots of a number of pasture plants) but sometimes seriously damage the herbage when probing the topsoil. They have mainly been controlled (since as early as 1915) by shooting, nest destruction, tree felling at rookeries, trapping and poisoning. According to Bull & Porter (1975), intensive trials of poisons by the Pest Destruction Board using DRC-1339 were begun in Hawke's Bay in 1971, and within 2 years some 16,000 Rooks had been accounted for. McLennan & MacMillan (1983: 139) point out, however, that 'controversy over whether Rooks are on balance beneficial or harmful to agriculture has persisted for some 50 years, but cannot be resolved until the significance of their predation on insect pests is assessed'.

In 1894, 80 Rooks were introduced from Lancashire, England, to Vivebrogård, Himmerland, Denmark, to control an outbreak of Cockchafers (*Melolontha vulgaris*), where they bred and subsequently spread to most of northern Jutland.[3]

The **New Caledonian Crow** (*Corvus moneduloides*) is endemic to New Caledonia and to some of the islands in the Loyalty group. Mayr (1945) records that sometime previously this species had been translocated to the island of Maré (most southerly of the Loyalty Islands) where it was hitherto unknown. According to Delacour (1966), it is a serious predator of the eggs, young and adults of some endemic birds – especially pigeons and doves such as the White-throated Pigeon or Metallic Wood Pigeon (*Columba vitiensis hypoenochroa*), the Emerald Dove (*Chalcophaps indica sandwichensis*) and the New Caledonia or Giant Pigeon (*Ducula goliath*) – and also of domestic poultry. In New Caledonia, the crow is a protected species.

The **Common** or **American Crow** (*Corvus brachyrhnchos*) is a North American species occurring between about 60° N and 30° N, with a southerly extension into southern Florida.

According to Phillips (1928: 56), 'For some untold reason the common crow of the Eastern States was introduced about 1876 into Bermuda, where for a time it became abundant. Later it was nearly exterminated but has continued to exist in small numbers ever since.[4] D. B. Wingate (personal communication, 1981), however antedates this introduction by 38 years: 'Although Bermuda had a native crow when the islands were first settled', he writes, 'this was apparently exterminated. The present crow population originated from a pet pair of crows introduced from Halifax, Nova Scotia by Lady Paget wife of Admiral Sir Charles Paget in 1838.' Because of the damage crows cause to agricultural and horticultural crops, they are unprotected in Bermuda (Wingate 1973), where the total 1985 population was estimated at around 500.

The **Jackdaw** (*Corvus monedula*) is a Eurasian species, occurring from western Europe eastwards to northern and central Asia, and south to western India.

Payn (1948) says that the ancient colony of Jackdaws in the city of Tunis in Tunisia, and the small number 350 km away in Constantine in eastern Algeria, are both probably descended from escaped cagebirds. The race established in North Africa is *C. m. cirtensis*.

According to Voous (1960) and Sharrock (1976), both the Jackdaw and Rook are typical of the steppe fauna of central Europe and Russia, and it seems probable that they spread to western Europe naturally from those regions. In recent times the Jackdaw has further expanded its European range, especially northwards into Fenno-Scandia, probably as a result of increased cultivation in forested regions and perhaps climatic amelioration.

Thomson (1922) records that Jackdaws were unsuccessfully introduced to New Zealand by the Otago Acclimatization Society in or before 1867 and by the Canterbury society between 1868 and 1871 or 1872.

In November 1984, a flock of Jackdaws arrived, probably as transatlantic ship-borne stowaways, on the north coast of the Gulf of St Lawrence off Port Cartier, Quebec, Canada, where 52 were subsequently killed.

Between March 1984 and April 1985, other Jackdaws were reported from Block Island (Rhode Island, USA); Nantucket Island, Massachusetts; Brier Island and Bon Portage Island, Nova Scotia; Miquelon Island (off Newfoundland); Whitby, near Toronto; and Lewisburg, Pennsylvania. These birds were all found to be of the western and central European subspecies *spermologus*, which also occurs in the British Isles. Apart from an escaped cagebird in Florida in the winter of 1962–3, these are the first authentic records of the species in the New World. These birds may only have failed through human interference from establishing themselves as a breeding species in the wild in North America, where there is a vacant niche for a medium-sized crow.[5]

In 1970, a programme was started to reintroduce the **Raven** (*Corvus corax*), which ranges over most of the Holarctic region, to Belgium.[6] In 1973, 50 birds (mostly yearlings) were liberated in the southern and northeastern Ardennes; most settled down near the release sites, where nesting was suspected in 1979 and confirmed in the following year. By 1981, there were some 8–10 breeding pairs, and the birds were considered to be established.

There has also been a recent attempt to reintroduce Ravens to Sumava, Czechoslovakia.[7]

The **Common Magpie** (*Pica pica*)[8] is an

Holarctic species, occurring over much of the Palaearctic and western Nearctic Regions, as well as in the northern Oriental Region. The Chinese form *sericea* (which occurs also in Korea, Burma and northern Indo-China) was reputedly brought back to the northern part of the Japanese island of Kyūshū by the Great Taicoon or *Sei-i-tai-shogun*, Hideyoshi, on returning from his successful invasion of Korea in 1598. It is still confined to northwestern Kyūshū where it is locally common in Kumamoto, Fukuoka, Saga and Nagasaki. Occasional disruption to tele-communications are reported through the construction of bulky nests on telegraph poles, and some damage to agricultural crops has also occurred; in compensation, however, injurious insects and carrion are also eaten.

The **Red-billed Blue Magpie** (*Urocissa erythro-rhyncha*) ranges from the Himalayas eastwards to China and south to northeastern Burma, Assam, Laos, North Vietnam, Kampuchea, Hainan and northern Thailand.

In 1965, five were sold by a pet shop to an aviculturist in Honolulu on Oahu in the Hawaiian Islands, where they were placed in an open-air aviary in Kahaluu Valley; here they remained until feral Dogs (*Canis familiaris*) broke down the wire of their enclosure in late 1965 or 1966, permitting them to escape. By mid-1970 they had become established in the wild, and several adults and young were seen in the Kahana Valley, up to 16 km from their point of escape. Because of their size and liking for fruit it was feared that they could become a serious pest were they to increase and spread. A. J. Berger (personal communication, 1985) said that 'the few escaped birds were collected by members of the State Division of Forestry and Wildlife', and that none remain.

NOTES

1 Bull 1957; Bull & Porter 1975; Coleman 1971; Drummond 1907; Falla, Sibson & Turbott 1979; Kinsky 1970; Long 1981; McLennan & MacMillan 1983; Oliver 1955; Porter 1979; Purchas 1980; Stead 1927 (in Coleman 1971); Thomson 1922, 1926; Williams 1953, 1969, 1973; Wodzicki 1965.
2 Williams (1969: 449) says four.
3 Moller 1980.
4 See also: *Auk* 32: 229 (1915).
5 Mead 1986; Smith 1986.
6 Delmotte & Delvaux 1981; Delvaux 1978; Maury & Delvaux 1974.
7 Vodak 1980.
8 Brazil 1985, in press; Kaburaki 1934; Long 1981; Ornithological Society of Japan 1974, 1981; Peters 1962; Voous 1960; Yamashina 1961.

Appendix

The following two species have been included because, although not strictly 'naturalized' as defined in the Preface, they are classic examples of the important role that the introduction and translocation of animals can play as a means of wildlife conservation.

Hawaiian Goose (*Branta sandvicensis*)

Although extensively hunted by Polynesians in the craters of Mauna Loa, Mauna Kea and other volcanoes during their flightless moult period, some 25,000 endemic Hawaiian Geese or Nénés (*Branta sandvicensis*)[1] survived until the end of the eighteenth century on the sparsely vegetated lava flows that cover much of the volcanic slopes on the islands of Hawaii and Maui. Predation by European settlers, who arrived in the early nineteenth century, and by introduced Black and Brown Rats (*Rattus rattus* and *R. norvegicus*), feral Cats (*Felis catus*), Dogs (*Canis familiaris*) and Pigs (*Sus domestica*), and Small Indian Mongooses (*Herpestes auropunctatus*), together with loss of habitat to agriculture and competition for grazing from introduced Goats (*Capra hircus*) (Lever 1985b), had restricted the Hawaiian Goose by about 1850 to the wilder parts and higher elevations of both islands. By the turn of the century it had disappeared from Maui and was rare even in mountainous regions of Hawaii; by the early 1940s barely 50 (wild and captive) Nénés remained; by 1949 only 42 survived (of which 30 were held in captivity); and by 1952 the entire world population is believed to have numbered about 30. The subsequent reintroduction of the Néné to Hawaii and Maui is a classic example of the value of breeding endangered species in captivity.

In 1918, an Hawaiian aviculturist, Herbert C. Shipman, established a captive flock of Nénés at Keaau near Hilo on Hawaii, where by the late 1940s 43 goslings had been reared successfully. In 1927, a similar venture was started by the Hawaiian Board of Agriculture and Forestry who reared a number of birds before disbanding the flock in 1935.

In 1949, the Board of Agriculture established a new flock of Nénés at Pohakuloa on the slopes of Mauna Kea on Hawaii, and in the following year Sir Peter Scott's Wildfowl Trust at Slimbridge in Gloucestershire, England, started to rear Nénés imported from Hawaii. During the next 30 years some 1,200 goslings were reared at Slimbridge, of which 200 were reintroduced to the Haleakala crater on Maui (first in 1962), and by 1970 around 800 had been bred at Puhakuloa.

The first reintroduction of Hawaiian Geese back into the wild was made in 1960, and by the end of the decade 498 had been planted in three separate localities; by 1975 a total of 1,061 had been freed on Hawaii and 391 on Maui.

From its nadir of 30 in 1952, the world population of wild and captive Hawaiian Geese increased to about 100 by 1957, to about 200 (1959–60), to 427 (1962), to over 500 (1966), to a little under 1,000 by 1970, and to over 1,000 by 1975, of which at least 600 were living free. In the wild, some 300 at present occur between 1,525 and 2,440 m on the slopes of Mauna Loa, Mauna Kea and Hualalai on Hawaii (where they occupy an area of some 3,100 km^2), and 125 at the eastern end of the Haleakala crater on Maui. There are also 12 breeding pairs and 2 unpaired females at Pohakuloa. Although thanks to its tameness and fecundity the future of the Hawaiian Goose in captivity seems assured, and in the wild the birds are afforded complete protection by both federal and state legislation, 'The future of the species in the wild is', according to *The ICBP Bird Red Data Book* (King 1981), 'still in jeopardy until it can be shown that reproduction is sufficient to offset losses from all sources'. The Néné is officially classified by the International Union for Conservation of Nature and Natural Resources as 'vulnerable'.

NOTE

1 American Ornithologists' Union 1957, 1983; Anon. 1976c; Baldwin 1945; A. J Berger 1978, 1981 (and personal communication, 1985); Devick 1982; Fisher, Simon & Vincent 1969; Gaselee 1963; Hawaiian Audubon Society 1975; Kear 1981, 1985; Kear & Berger 1980; King 1981; Lever 1985b; Long 1981; Mills 1978; Peterson 1961; Ripley 1965; Scott 1985; Smith 1952; Stone 1983; Walker 1970.

Saddleback
(*Creadion carunculatus*)

Widespread and abundant throughout New Zealand at the time of European settlement in the early nineteenth century, the endemic Saddleback or Tieke (*Creadion carunculatus*) rapidly declined following the arrival of introduced predators on the two main islands, and by the early 1900s the North Island subspecies (*C. c. rufusater*) survived only on 484-ha Hen Island in Hauraki Gulf, and the South Island nominate form only on Big South Cape Island (911 ha) and on Solomon Island – both off the south-west coast of Stewart Island. In the words of *The ICBP Bird Red Data Book* (King 1981), the Saddleback's 'relocation program has been one of the classic success stories in the short history of management of endangered species'.

In about 1962, Black Rats (*Rattus rattus*) became established on Big South Cape and Solomon Islands and by about 1964 or 1965 they had exterminated five species of birds on the former, three of which were endemic (Lever 1985b). In 1964, the New Zealand Wildlife Service successfully translocated 36 Saddlebacks from Big South Cape to two neighbouring predator-free islands, and subsequent introductions of these birds' progeny to other nearby islands resulted, within a decade, in a total population of the nominate form of about 200.

North Island Saddlebacks were at the same time successfully reintroduced from Hen Island (where there was a flourishing population of around 500 pairs) to other islands in and near Hauraki Gulf, and by the late 1970s the population had doubled. Table 17 gives details of the various translocations of Saddlebacks in New Zealand. Except where indicated on the table most of these translocations have been successful, and flourishing populations of both North Island and South Island Saddlebacks have become re-established on a number of islands; these have all been declared reserves, and the cessation of agricultural activities and burning has caused the vegetation to regenerate, resulting in the growth of coastal scrub woodland and understorey that is the Saddleback's natural habitat. The releases on Kapiti Island in 1981–3 are, according to I. A .E. Atkinson (personal communication, 1985), the first time that the New Zealand Wildlife Service has attempted to establish Saddlebacks on islands infested with Brown Rats (*Rattus norvegicus*), and is proving much more difficult than anticipated.

R. J. Nilsson (unpublished report, 1985) has summarized the progress made by the New

Table 17 Translocation of Saddlebacks (*Creadion carunculatus*) on South Island (1964–84) and North Island (1925–83), New Zealand

Date	Number	Locality	Remarks
South Island Saddleback			
1964	21	Big or Stage Island (south-west of Stewart Island)	
1964	15	Kaimohu Island (south-west of Stewart Island)	
1965 and 1969	30 and 17	Inner Chetwode Island, Cook Strait	Failed
1969	16	Betsy Island (south-west of Stewart Island)	
1972	20	Womans Island (north-east of Stewart Island)	
1972	19	North Island (north-east of Stewart Island)	
1974 and 1976	23 and 22	Putauhina Island (south-west of Stewart Island)	
1978	38	Kundy Island (south-west of Stewart Island)	
1980 and 1982	34 and 38	Maud	Failed
1981	20	Motunui Island	Transferred from Womans Island (9) and North Island (11); all but two were first year juveniles not more than five months old; believed to have bred in 1982 and to be thriving
1984	41	Putauhina Island	
North Island Saddleback			
1925	4 pairs	Little Barrier Island (Hauraki Gulf)	Killed by rats and feral cats
1925	4 cocks, 5 hens	Kapiti Island (Wellington)	Introduced by the Department of Internal Affairs; died out by 1931 as a result of predation by rats and feral cats
1950	6	South Cove, Big Chicken Island (Hauraki Gulf)	Two or more seen in 1953; none thereafter: too few birds released
1964	23	Middle Chicken Island (Hauraki Gulf)	Breeding in 1965, when 22 adults were seen with 7 young
1966	29	Red Mercury Island (Hauraki Gulf)	
1968	29	Cuvier Island (Hauraki Gulf)	
1968	25	Fanal Island (Hauraki Gulf)	Apparently failed
1971	21	Big Chicken Island (Hauraki Gulf)	
Before 1979	?	Middle Chicken, Marotiri and four of the Kawhihi Islands (Hauraki Gulf)	From Middle Chicken Island the birds have flown 150 m to Coppermine Island
?	?	Stanley Island (Mercury Group)	Apparently successful
?	?	Little Barrier Island (Hauraki Gulf)	

Continued

Table 17   *(continued)*

Date	Number	Locality	Remarks
North Island Saddleback *(cont.)*			
?	?	Tiritiri Island (Whangaparoa Peninsula)	
1981, 1982 and 1983	100, 94 and 50	Kapiti Island (Wellington)	Heavy predation by Brown Rats
1983	16	Motukawanui Island (Cavalli group, north of Bay of Islands)	Three pairs reared young in 1984

Sources: Atkinson & Bell 1973; Fisher, Simon & Vincent 1969; King 1981; Long 1981; Merton 1965a, b, 1973, 1975a, b; Mills & Williams 1979; Newman 1980; R. J. Nilsson (unpublished report to the Director of the NZ Wildlife Service, 1985); Skegg 1964; Williams 1973, 1976; and I. A. E. Atkinson, personal communication, 1985. See also *Oryx* 19: 176 (1985)

Zealand Wildlife Service in re-establishing the South Island Saddleback; the populations on the various islands to which it has been introduced are as follows: Big (50); Kaimohu (30); Betsy (12); Womans (20); North (20); Putauhina (20); Kundy (60); and Motunui (40) – a total of 252. On the last named 48-ha island there are indications that the thriving population may represent the most successful liberation of the species to date in the southern region. On Motunui, the forest structure consists mainly of various species of hardwood shrubs, interspersed with extensive tangles of *Muelenbeckia complexa* and Supplejack (*Ripogonum scandens*). Saddlebacks on this island appear to be exclusively canopy feeders, and one of the principal reasons for their success is the variety and abundance of autumnal berries, such as *Aristotelia serrata*, *Myrsine chathamica*, *Ripogonum scandens*, *Schefflera digitata*, *Fuchsia excorticata*, *Pittosporum tenuifolium colensoi* and *Coprosma lucida*. The nearby 30-ha island of Jacky Lee (2 km south-west of Motonui)

supports a hardwood vegetation similar to that of its larger neighbour, and if cleared of introduced Stewart Island Wekas (*Gallirallus australis scotti*) and found to be free from rats, would provide a promising site for the translocation of Saddlebacks and other endangered species.

The policy of cropping successful populations of Saddlebacks to provide a founding stock for transference to other islands has provided a valuable safety-factor for the two races; both have also been bred in captivity – the former in the Mount Bruce Native Bird Reserve at Wairarapa, where eight birds were introduced between 1964 and 1968, and the latter by a private aviculturist.

The current official status of the New Zealand Saddleback is 'recovering'. *The ICBP Bird Red Data Book* concludes its account of the species by saying: 'The officers of the New Zealand Wildlife Service who so capably carried out the management plan outlined above, deserve the congratulations of all conservationists for their work.'

Bibliography

The published material on naturalized birds is extensive. Only the more important references are given here, the principal ones being marked with an asterisk★.

A

Abbott, C. 1903. European birds in America. *Bird Lore* 5: 163.

Abbott, I. 1974 causes The avifauna of Kangaroo Island and of its impoverishment. *Emu* 74: 124–34.

Abdulali, H. 1964 and 1967. Birds of the Nicobar Islands, with notes on some Andaman birds. *Journal of the Bombay Natural History Society* 61: 483–571; 64: 139–90.

Adams, J. S. 1971. Black Swans at Lake Ellesmere. *Wildlife Review* 3: 23–5.

Adams, R. T. 1971. The Partridge in New Zealand. *Wildlife Review* 3: 4–8.

Adney, E. T. 1886. Naturalization of the European Goldfinch in New York City and vicinity. *Auk* 3: 409–10.

Agostinho, J. 1963. Variations dans l'avifauna des Açores. *Alauda* 31: 305–6.

Ahlbom, B., von Essen, L. & Fabricius, E. 1973. Kanadagåsen fortsätter att expandera. *Svensk Jakt* 111: 224–30.

Ainslie, D. 1907. The Little Owl in Bedfordshire. *Zoologist*, 353.

Alcorn, J. R. & Richardson, F. 1951. The Chukar Partridge in Nevada. *Journal of Wildlife Management* 15: 265–75.

Aldrich, J. W. 1947. *The Hungarian and Chukar Partridges in America.* US Department of the Interior Fish and Wildlife Service, Wildlife Leaflet No. 292 (10 pp.).

———. 1982. Rapid evolution in the House Finch (*Carpodacus mexicanus*). *Journal of the Yamashina Institute for Ornithology* 14: 179–86.

Aldrich, J. W. & Weske, J. S. 1978. Origin and evolution of the eastern House Finch population. *Auk* 95: 528–36.

Alexander, B. 1898. An ornithological expedition to the Cape Verde Islands. *Ibis*, series 7, 4: 74–118.

Alford, C. E. 1928. Field notes on the birds of Vancouver Island. *Ibis*, series 12, 4: 181–210.

Ali, S. & Ripley, S. D. 1968–75. *Handbook of the Birds of India and Pakistan, together with those of Bangladesh, Nepal, Bhutan and Sri Lanka*, 10 volumes. Oxford University Press: Bombay and London.

Aliev, F. F. 1970. Acclimatization of mammals and birds in the Caucasus. *International Union of Game Biologists* 9: 167–9.

Aliev, F. F. & Khanmamedov, A. I. 1966. Results and prospects of the acclimatization of birds in Transcaucasia. In A. I. Yanushevich ed., *Acclimatization of Animals in the USSR* (*Proceedings of the conference on the acclimatization of animals in the USSR, Frunze, 10–15 May, 1963*), 33–4. Israel Program for Scientific Translations: Jerusalem.

Allan, P. S. 1939. Starlings in New Mexico. *Auk* 56: 477–8.

Allen, D. L. 1954. *Our Wildlife Legacy*. Funk & Wagnalls: New York.

★————. ed. 1956. *Pheasants in North America*. Stackpole Company: Harrisburg, Pennsylvania; Wildlife Management Institute: Washington, DC.

————. 1962. *Pheasants Afield: the Pheasant in North America – History, Habits and Future*. Collier: New York.

Allen, R. P. 1962. *Birds of the Caribbean*. Thames & Hudson: London.

Alvarez del Toro, M. 1950. English Sparrows in the Chiapas. *Condor* 52: 166.

Amadon, D. 1942. Birds collected during the Whitney South Sea Expedition: notes on some non-passerine genera. *American Museum Novitates* No. 1176: 1–21.

————. 1944. The genera of Corvidae and their relationships. *American Museum Novitates* No. 1251: 1–21.

American Ornithologists' Union 1957 and 1983. *Check-List of North American Birds*. 5th and 6th editions. Lawrence, Kansas

Anderegg, R., Frey, H. & Müller, H. U. 1983. Reintroduction of the Bearded Vulture or Lammergeier *Gypaetus barbatus aureus* to the Alps. *International Zoo Yearbook* 23: 35–41.

Anderson, R. M. 1934. Effects of the introduction of exotic animal forms. *Proceedings of the 5th Pacific Science Congress, Victoria and Vancouver, June 1933*, 769–78. University of Toronto Press: Toronto.

Andrle, R. F. & Axtell, H. H. 1961. Cattle Egrets in Mexico. *Wilson Bulletin* 73: 280.

Angus, W. C. 1886. The Capercaillie. *Proceedings of the Natural History Society of Glasgow*, n.s., 1: 380.

Anon. 1873. Introduction of European birds in the United States for economic purposes. *Zoology*, series 2, 8: 3696. (See also *Nature*, 14 August 1873.)

————. 1874. The introduction of singing birds into the country [USA]. *Forest & Stream* 2: 264.

————. 1881. Zoological miscellany. *Journal of the Cincinnati Society of Natural History* 4: 339.

————. 1890. Chinese Pheasants in America. *Forest & Stream* 35: 28.

————. 1936. Chukar Partridge – new success in state. *California Conservation* 1: 10–11.

————. 1942. Should we introduce exotic game birds? *Wildlife Conservation* 6: 3, 15.

————. 1944. The Chukar Partridge in Wisconsin. *Passenger Pigeon* 6: 41–2.

————. 1946. White Swans, *New Zealand Bird Notes* 2: 16.

————. 1948. Flinders Chase, Kangaroo Island. *South Australian Ornithologist* 18: 76–7.

————. 1949. Conduct Wisconsin tests with European grouse. *Wisconsin Conservation Bulletin* No. 35.

————. 1954. Brown Francolins may give international flavor to hunting. *Arizona Game & Fish Department Wildlife News* 1: 6.

————. 1956. *The Coturnix Quail*. Ohio Division of Wildlife, Leaflet No. 1.

————. 1959. [Pheasants near Moscow, USSR.] *Okhota i Okhotnich'e Khozyaistvo* 6: 56 [in Russian].

————. 1961a. *Annual Report of the Western States Exotic Game Bird Committee, 8th May 1960–April 1961*.

————. 1961b. [Mockingbirds in Hawaii.] *Elepaio* 21: 81.

————. 1962. *The Foreign Game Introduction Program*. US Department of the Interior Fish and Wildlife Service, Conservation Leaflet.

————. 1963a. Parakeet city – a tourist attraction. *Florida Naturalist* 36: 18.

————. 1963b. Status of the foreign game introduction program. *Transactions of the 28th North American Wildlife & Natural Resources Conference*, 240–7.

————. 1963c. Nevada exotic game bird introductions fruitful so far, hold promise for the future. *Nevada Wildlife (Nevada Fish and Game Commission)* 3: 1–5.

————. 1967. *Towards a New Relationship of Man and Nature in Temperate Lands. Part III. Changes due to Introduced Species.* (*Proceedings of the 10th IUCN Technical Meeting, Lucerne, June 1966.*) IUCN Publications n.s. No. 9 (259 pp.). Morges.

————. 1968. Problems in species' introductions. *IUCN Bulletin* 2(7): 70–1.

————. 1969. Indian Mynas in Canberra. *Canberra Bird Notes* 5: 3–4.

————. 1972. Paradiesvögel [Bird of Paradise in South America]. *Gefiederte Welt* 96: 242.

————. 1974a. Pest evaluation – Monk Parakeet. California Department of Food & Agriculture. Mimeograph (23 pp.).

————. 1974b. Parakeets run wild in south-east England. *New Scientist* 63: 119.

————. 1976a. A catalogue of birds of the South African sub-region. Ring-necked Parakeet. *Durban Museum Novitates* No. 21: 45–6.

————. 1976b. *Exclusion and Detection Manual*. California Department of Food & Agriculture (37 pp.).

————. 1976c. Nene restoration project, 1st July 1972–30th June 1975. Hawaii State Department of Lands and Natural Resources. *Elepaio* 36: 104–8.

————. 1977. A new bird. *Royal Australasian Ornithologists' Union Atlas Newsletter* 4: 4.

————. 1980. Parakeets [Budgerigars] established in Florida. *Outdoor News Bulletin of the Wildlife Manage-*

ment Institute, Washington, DC 34: 3.

———. 1982. More on Big Island Cattle Egrets. *Elepaio* 43: 19–20.

———. 1984a. France – Griffon Vulture project earns award. *Birds (Magazine of the Royal Society for the Protection of Birds)* 10: 60.

———. 1984b. Return of Sea Eagles to Britain. *Oryx* 18: 67.

———. 1984c. [Restoration of Aleutian Island Canada Goose.] *The Philadelphia Inquirer* (25 November). (Quoted in *Oryx* 19: 115 (1985).)

———. 1984d. Fragile cargo: rescue mission. *Wildfowl World* 91: 5.

———. 1985a. Returning a lost species [Sea Eagle]. *Country Life* 178: 152.

———. 1985b. New blood for Sarus Crane captive stock. *Oryx* 19: 38.

———. 1985c Thailand to reintroduce Sarus Crane. *Oryx* 19: 171.

———. 1985d. Historic hatching. *Oryx* 19: 239.

———. 1985e. Griffon Vulture colony survives third spring in Cevennes. *World Birdwatch (Newsletter of the International Council for Bird Preservation)* 7: 4.

———. 1985f. Surrey's Chinese residents [Mandarin]. *Country Life* 177: 502.

———. 1985g. White-tailed Eagle. *Birds (Magazine of the Royal Society for the Protection of Birds)* 10: 11.

———. 1985h. Starlings. *Agriculture Protection Board of Western Australia, Annual Report for the year ending June 1985*, 20.

Armani, C. G. 1983. [The Greenfinch (*Carduelis chloris*), a new Fringillidae in South America? *Oiseau et La Revue Française d'Ornithologie* 53: 294–6 [in French].

———. 1984. [The Goldfinch (*Carduelis carduelis*) in South America.] *Oiseau et La Revue Française d'Ornithologie* 54: 271–2 [in French].

Armstrong, J. S. 1922. *Handlist to the Birds of Samoa*. Bale & Sons, Danielsson: London.

Ash, J. S. 1977. Four species of birds new to Ethiopia and other notes. *Bulletin of the British Ornithologists' Club* 97: 4–9.

———. 1983. Over fifty additions of birds to the Somalia list including two hybrids, together with notes from Ethiopia and Kenya. *Scopus* 7: 54–79.

———. 1984a. Report of the UNEP ornithologist/ecologist on the advice to the Government of the Peoples' Democratic Republic of Yemen on 'Combating the Crow Menace'. United Nations Environmental Programme (UNEP/84/0189). Mimeograph (31 pp.).

———. 1984b. Vertebrate pest management (bat and crow control): report prepared for the Government of the Maldives. Food and Agriculture Organization (TCP/MDV/2307): Rome (11 pp.).

———. 1985. Two additions to the Somalia list: Greater Frigatebird *Fregata minor* and Indian House Crow *Corvus splendens*. *Scopus* 9: 108–10.

Ash, J. S. & **Colston, P.** 1981. A House × Somali Sparrow *Passer domesticus* × *castanopterus* hybrid. *Bulletin of the British Ornithologists' Club* 101: 291–4.

Ash, J. S. & **Miskell, J. E.** 1983. Birds of Somalia, their habitat and distribution. *Scopus*, Special Suppl. No. 1 (97 pp.).

Ashby, E. 1919. Introduction of birds. *Emu* 19: 1–73.

Ashford, R. W. 1978. First record of the House Sparrow for Papua New Guinea. *Emu* 78: 36.

Ashman, P. & **Pyle, P.** 1979. First records of Lavender Fire-finch on Hawaii. *Elepaio* 40: 12.

Ashmole, M. J. 1963. *Guide to the Birds of Samoa*. Pacific Scientific Information Centre, Bernice P. Bishop Museum: Honolulu.

Atkinson, I. A. E. & **Bell, B. D.** 1973. Offshore and outlying islands. In G. R. Williams ed., *Natural History of New Zealand: an Ecological Survey*, Ch. 15, 372–92. A. H. & A. W. Reed: Wellington.

Atkinson-Willes, G. ed. 1963. *Wildfowl in Great Britain*. Nature Conservancy: London.

Au, S. & **Swedberg, G.** 1966. A progress report on the introduction of the Barn Owl (*Tyto alba pratincola*) to the island of Kauai. *Elepaio* 26: 58–60.

Austin, O. L. 1963. On the American status of *Tiaris canora* and *Carduelis carduelis*. *Auk* 80: 73–4.

———. 1968. ed. A. C. Bent's life histories of North American cardinals, grosbeaks, buntings, towhees, finches, sparrow and allies. *US National Museum, Smithsonian Institution Bulletin* No. 237 (parts 1–3).

Australian Acclimatization Societies. *Annual Reports.*

B

Bach, R. N. 1964. The status of the Pheasant and Hungarian Partridge in North Dakota. *North Dakota Outdoors* 9: 3–4.

Bachus, G. J. 1967. Changes in the avifauna of Fanning Island, central Pacific, between 1924 and 1963. *Condor* 69: 207–9.

Bacon, P. J. 1980. A possible advantage for the 'Polish' morph of the mute swan. *Wildfowl* 31: 51–2.

Bade, A. 1935. Mr Chukar—now a naturalized Californian. *Game Breeder and Sportsman* 39: 118, 143.

———. 1937a. The Chukar Partridge in California. *California Fish and Game* 23: 233–6.

———. 1937b. The Chukar Partridge in California. *Transactions of the North American Wildlife Conference* 2: 485–9.

Bagnolini, C. 1982. Réintroduction du Vautour Fauvre dans les Cévennes. *Fonds d'Intervention pour les Rapaces, Newsletter* No. 9: 18–19.

Bahr, P. 1912. Notes on the avifauna of the Fiji Islands. *Ibis*, series 9, 6: 282–314.

Bailey, W. & **Rinell, K. T.** 1967. Management of the Eastern Turkey in the northern hardwoods. In

O. H. Hewitt ed., *The Wild Turkey and its Management*, 261–302. Wildlife Society: Washington, DC.

Baker, A. J. & **Moeed, A.** 1979. Evolution of the introduced New Zealand populations of the Common Myna. *Canadian Journal of Zoology* 57: 570–84.

Baker, H. D. 1922. Little Tobago, Bird of Paradise island. *Bulletin of the Pan-American Union* 54: 344–7.

———. 1923. Birds-of-Paradise at Little Tobago Island. *Bird-Lore* 25: 295–302.

*Baker, H. G.** & **Stebbins, G. L.** 1965. The genetics of colonizing species. *Proceedings of the First International Union of Biological Sciences, Symposium on General Biology.* Academic Press: New York.

Baker, R. H. 1951. *The Avifauna of Micronesia, its Origin, Evolution and Distribution.* Publication No. 3. University of Kansas, Museum of Natural History (359 pp.).

Baldwin, P. H. 1945. The Hawaiian Goose, its distribution and reduction in numbers. *Condor* 47: 27–37.

Balham, R. W. 1952. Grey and Mallard Ducks in the Manawatu district, New Zealand. *Emu* 52: 163–91.

Balham, R. W. & **Miers, K. H.** 1959. *Mortality and Survival of Grey and Mallard Ducks banded in New Zealand.* Wildlife Publication No. 5. New Zealand Department of Internal Affairs.

Ball, S. C. 1926. Concerning the introduction of foreign birds into Hawaii. *Proceedings. of the Hawaiian Academy of Sciences 1st Annual Meeting,* 28–9. Special Publication No. 11. Bernice P. Bishop Museum: Honolulu.

———. 1933. Jungle Fowls from Pacific Islands. *B. P. Bishop Museum Bulletin* No. 108 (121 pp.).

Ballard, J. 1964. Starlings: they can be controlled. *American Fruit Grower* 84: 22–3, 38.

*Balmford, R.** 1978. Early introductions of birds to Victoria. *Australian Bird Watcher* 7: 237–48. (Reprinted in *Victorian Naturalist* 98: 96–105 (1981).)

Bancroft, J. 1981a. Observations at a nest of a Red-vented Bulbul. *Elepaio* 42: 42–3.

———. 1981b. Nesting observations of the Red-crested Cardinal on Oahu. *Elepaio* 42: 63–4.

———. 1982. Observations of the Zebra Dove and Spotted Dove on Oahu. *Elepaio* 43: 39–40.

———. 1984. Observations of the Common Myna. *Elepaio* 44: 74–5.

Banks, R. C. 1970. Birds imported into the United States in 1968. *US Department of the Interior Fish and Wildlife Service, Special Scientific Report (Wildlife)* No. 136.

———. 1977. Wildlife importations into the United States, 1900–1972. *US Department of the Interior Fish and Wildlife Service, Special Scientific Report (Wildlife)* No. 200.

———. 1981. Summary of foreign game bird liberations, 1969–1978. *US Department of the Interior Fish*

and *Wildlife Service, Special Scientific Report (Wildlife)* No. 239.

Banks, R. C. & **Clapp, R. B.** 1972. Birds imported into the United States in 1969. *US Department of the Interior Fish and Wildlife Service, Special Scientific Report (Wildlife)* No. 148.

Bank, R. C. & **Laybourne, R. C.** 1968. The Red-whiskered Bulbul in Florida. *Auk* 85: 141.

Bannerman, D. A. 1949. *The Birds of Tropical West Africa* Vol. 7. Oliver & Boyd: London.

———. 1953. *The Birds of West Equatorial Africa.* Oliver & Boyd: London.

———. 1963. *The Birds of the Atlantic Islands*, Vol. 1. *History of the Canary Islands and Salvages.* Oliver & Boyd: London.

———. 1965. *Birds of the Atlantic Islands*, Vol. 2. *History of the Birds of Madeira, the Desertas and Porto Santo Islands.* Oliver & Boyd: London.

Bannerman, D. A. & **Bannerman, W. M.** 1966. *Birds of the Atlantic Islands*, Vol. 3. *History of the Birds of the Azores.* Oliver & Boyd: London.

———. 1968. *Birds of the Atlantic Islands*, Vol. 4. *History of the Birds of the Cape Verde Islands.* Oliver & Boyd: London.

———. 1971. *Handbook of the Birds of Cyprus and Migrants of the Middle East.* Oliver & Boyd: Edinburgh.

Barbour, T. 1923. *Birds of Cuba.* Memoirs of the Nuttal Ornithological Club No. 6. Cambridge, Mass.

———. 1943. *Cuban Ornithology.* Memoirs of the Nuttal Ornithological Club No. 9. Cambridge, Mass.

Barclay, H. J. & **Bergerud, A. T.** 1975. Demography and behavioural ecology of California Quail on Vancouver Island. *Condor* 77: 315–23.

Barclay, R. 1986. Restoring the Cock to the woods. *Country Life* 180: 178.

Barlass, J. C. 1975. Introduced Lovebirds in Mombassa. *Avicultural Magazine* 81: 55–6.

Barlow, J. C. 1973. Status of the North American population of the European Tree Sparrow. In S. C. Kendeigh ed., *Symposium on the House Sparrow and European Tree Sparrow in North America,* 10–23. Ornithological Monograph No. 14. American Ornithologists' Union: Lawrence, Kansas.

Barnes, H. E. 1893. On the birds of Aden. *Ibis*, series 6, 5: 57–83.

Barnett, D. C. 1953. Chukar Partridge introductions in Washington. In *Proceedings of the 32nd Annual Conference of the Western Association of State Game and Fish Commissioners, 15–17 June, 1952,* 154–61.

Barrau, J. & **Devambez, L.** 1957. Some unexpected results of introductions in New Caledonia. *La Terre et La Vie* 104: 324–34.

Barré, N. & **Barau, A.** 1982. *Oiseaux de la Réunion.* St Denis.

Barré, N. & **Benito-Espinal, E.** 1985. Oiseaux granivores exotiques implantés en Guadeloupe, à Marie-Galante et en Martinique (Antilles françaises). *L'Oiseau et la Revue Française d' Ornithologie* 55: 235–41.

Barret, C. L. 1922. Birds around a homestead. *Emu* 21: 257–61.

———. 1926 Introduction of British birds. *Victorian Naturalist* 43: 190–91.

Barrington, D. C. 1985. Recent sighting and evidence of breeding of Red-whiskered Bulbuls. *South Australian Ornithologist* 29: 151.

Barros, R. 1919. [California Quail in Chile.] *Revista Chilena de Historia Natural* 23: 15–16 [in Spanish].

Barros-Valenzuela, R. 1964. Varias aves cuya aclimatacion convendria al Chilena. *Boletín de la Academia Chilena de Ciencias Naturales* No. 49: 109–12.

Barrows, W. B. 1889. The English Sparrow (*Passer domesticus*) in North America, especially in its relation to agriculture. *US Department of Agriculture, Division of Economics, Ornithology and Mammalogy Bulletin* No. 1: 1–606.

Bartholomew, J. 1929. Capercaillie in west Stirling. *Scottish Naturalist*, 61.

Baskett, T. S. 1947. Nesting and production of the Ring-necked Pheasant in north-central Iowa. *Ecological Monograph* No. 17: 1–30.

Bates, M. 1956. Man as an agent in the spread of organisms. In W. L. Thomas et al. eds, *Man's Role in Changing the Face of the Earth* (*Proceedings of an International Symposium, Princeton, 1955*), 788–804. Cambridge University Press: Cambridge.

Bathgate, A. 1897. Notes on acclimatisation in New Zealand. *Transactions of the New Zealand Institute* 30: 266–79.

———. 1903. The Sparrow plague and its remedy. *Transactions of the New Zealand Institute* 36: 67–79.

Baumgartner, A. M. 1942. Some notes on the Starling (*Sturnus vulgaris*). *Indiana Audubon Yearbook* 20: 10–14.

———. 1984. Sex and age characteristics of American Tree Sparrow. *Passenger Pigeon* 46: 143–5.

Bavin, C. R. 1977. Wildlife importations. *Proceedings of the 57th Annual Conference of the Western Association of State Game and Fish Commissioners*, 241–6.

Beavan, R. C. 1867. The avifauna of the Andaman Islands. *Ibis* 3: 314–34.

Behle, W. H. 1954. Changing status of the Starling in Utah. *Condor* 56: 49–50.

Belhnap, J. 1952. The Hungarian Partridge in New York State. *Kingbird* 2: 80–2.

Bell, H. L. 1961. The introduced Spice Finch in north-eastern Queensland. *Emu* 61: 94–6.

Benedict, B. 1957. The immigrant birds of Mauritius. *Avicultural Magazine* 63: 155–7.

Bennett, A. G. 1926. A list of the birds of the Falk-lands Islands and dependencies. *Ibis*, series 12, 2: 306–33.

Bennett, G. 1862. *Acclimatisation: its Eminent Adaptation to Australia.* Acclimatisation Society of Victoria: Melbourne.

Bennett, G. 1982. Turkeys – five provinces, not four. *Birdfinding in Canada* 10: 13.

Bennitt, R. 1932. *Checklist of the Birds of Missouri.* University of Missouri Studies, Vol. 8. Columbia.

Benson, C. W. 1950. A contribution to the ornithology of St Helena, and other notes from a sea voyage. *Ibis* 92: 75–83.

———. 1960. The birds of the Comoro Islands: results of the British Ornithological Union Centennial Expedition, 1958. *Ibis* 103: 5–106.

———. 1970. An introduction of *Streptopelia picturata* into the Amirantes. *Atoll Research Bulletin* 136: 195–6.

Benson, C. W. & **Benson F. M.** 1977. *The Birds of Malawi.* Montford Press: Linbe, Malawi.

Benson, C. W., Beamish, H. H., Jouanin, C., Salvin, J. & **Watson, G. E.** 1975. The birds of the Isles Glorieuses. *Atoll Research Bulletin* 176: 1–30.

Benson, C. W., Brooke, R. K., Dowsett, R. J. & **Irwin, M. P. S.** 1971. *The Birds of Zambia.* Collins: London.

Berger, A. J. 1972. Hawaiian birds, 1972. *Wilson Bulletin* 84: 212–22.

———. 1975a. The Java Sparrow in Hawaii. *Elepaio* 36: 14–16.

———. 1975b. History of the exotic birds in Hawaii. *Elepaio* 35: 60–5, 72–80.

———. 1975c. The Japanese Bush Warbler on Oahu. *Elepaio* 36: 19–21.

———. 1975d. Red-whiskered and Red-vented Bulbuls on Oahu. *Elepaio* 36: 16–19.

———. 1975e. The Warbling Silverbill, a new nesting bird in Hawaii. *Pacific Science* 29: 51–4.

———. 1975f. The Mockingbird on Hawaii Island. *Elepaio* 35: 139.

———. 1977a. Nesting seasons of some introduced birds in Hawaii. *Elepaio* 38: 35–8.

———. 1977b. Nesting of the Yellow-fronted Canary on Oahu. *Elepaio* 37: 128.

———. 1977c. Nesting of the Japanese Bush Warbler. *Elepaio* 37: 148.

———. 1977d. Nesting seasons of some introduced birds in Hawaii. *Elepaio* 38: 35–8.

———. 1977e. *The Exotic Birds of Hawaii.* Island Heritage: Norfolk Island, Australia.

———. 1978. Reintroduction of Hawaiian Geese. In S. A. Temple ed., *Endangered Birds – Management Techniques for Preserving Threatened Species*, 339–44. University of Wisconsin Press: Madison.

*———. 1981. *Hawaiian Birdlife.* University Press of Hawaii: Honolulu. (1st edn, 1972.)

Bergman, G. 1956. [Introduction of the Greylag Goose.] *Suomen Riista* 10: 121–8 [in Finnish].

Bernström, J. 1951. Check-list of the breeding birds of the archipelago of Madeira. *Boletin do Museu Municipal do Funchal* 5: 64–82.

Berruti, A. 1973. [House Crows in South Africa.] *Natal Bird Club News Sheet* 215: 4; 219: 2; 223: 4.

Biaggi, V. 1963. The first record for Puerto Rico of the nests of the Scarlet-cheeked Weaver Finch. *Wilson Bulletin* 75: 91.

————. 1970. *Las Aves de Puerto Rico.* Universidad de Puerto Rico: San Juan.

Bijleveld, M. ed. 1979. Meeting on the reintroduction of the Bearded Vulture into the Alps. *Report of Proceedings of the International Union for Conservation of Nature 1979*, 103. 1UCN: Morges.

Bijlsma, R. G. & Meininger, P. L. 1984. Behaviour of the House Crow *Corvus splendens* and additional notes on its distribution. *Le Gerfaut* 74: 3–13.

Bikalke, R. C. 1964. Indian Mynas (*Acridotheres tristis*) in Kimberley. *Ostrich* 35: 60.

Bingham, M. G. 1971. House Sparrows recorded from Eastern Province, Zambia. *Zambian Ornithological Society Newsletter* 1: 3.

Birkan, M.G. 1971. Success factor as regards releases of farm-raised Grey Partridges, *Perdix perdix* L. *Transactions of the 10th Congress of the International Union of Game Biologists*, 356–8.

Birkhead, M. 1985. Birds that have come to stay. *The Field* 266: 48–9.

Bizeau, E. 1963. Chukar Partridge in Idaho. *Idaho Wildlife Review* 15: 3–4.

Blackburn, A. 1968. The birdlife of Codfish Island. *Notornis* 15: 51–65.

————. 1971. Some notes on Fijian birds. *Notornis* 18: 147–74.

Blackburn, B. 1932. The Starling. *Victorian Naturalist* 49: 156.

Blair, F. D. 1942. The Chukar Partridge in Minnesota. *The Conservation Volunteer* 4: 16–20.

Blake, C. H. 1961. Notes on the history of the Cattle Egret in the New World. *Chat* 25: 24–7.

★————. 1975. Introductions, transplants, and invaders. *American Birds* 29: 923–6.

————. 1977. *Manual of Neotropical Birds*, Vol. 1. University of Chicago Press: Chicago and London.

Blaker, D. 1971. Range expansion of the Cattle Egret. *Ostrich* 10: 27–30.

★**Blakers, M., Davies, S. J. J. F. & Reilly, P. N.** 1984. *The Atlas of Australian Birds.* Royal Australasian Ornithologists' Union: Moonee Ponds, Victoria.

Blanford, W. T. ed. 1890. *The Fauna of British India, including Ceylon and Burma*, Vol. 2 (by Oates, E. W.). Taylor & Francis: London.

Blank, T. H. 1970. Reeve's Pheasant. *Game Conservation Annual Review, 1969–70*, 81–2.

Blathwayt, F. L. 1902 and 1904. The Little Owl in Lincolnshire. *Zoologist*, 112, 74.

Blignaut, J. 1958. European Starling, *Sturnus vulgaris,*
at Uniondale. *Ostrich* 29: 49.

Blurton-Jones, N. G. 1956. Census of breeding Canada Geese, 1953. *Bird ·Study* 3: 153–70.

Blyth, E. 1867. The ornithology of India: a commentary on Dr Jerdon's *Birds of India. Ibis* series 2, 3: 1–48.

Bobak, A. W. 1952. *Das Auerhuhn.* Die neue Brehm Bucherei: Leipzig.

Bock, C. E. & Lepthien, L. W. 1976. Growth in the eastern House Finch population, 1962–71. *American Birds* 30: 791–2.

Boehm, E. F. 1961. Indian Turtledove extends its range in South Australia. *Emu* 61: 55.

Bohl, W. H. 1957a. Chukars in New Mexico, 1931–57. *New Mexico Department of Game and Fish Bulletin*, 1–69.

————. 1957b. A study of the introduction, release and survival of Asiatic game birds. New Mexico Department of Game and Fish, Job Completion Report W-58-R-5 (84 pp.).

————. 1964. A study of the Japanese Green and the Korean Ring-necked Pheasant. *US Department of the Interior Fish and Wildlife Service, Special Scientific Report (Wildlife)* No. 83 (65 pp.).

————. 1968. Results of foreign game introductions. *Transactions of the 33rd North American Wildlife and Natural Resources Conference*, 389–98.

————. 1970a. *The Green Pheasants.* US Department of the Interior Fish and Wildlife Service, Bureau of Sport, Fisheries and Wildlife FGL-13 (4 pp.). Government Printing Office: Washington, DC.

————. 1970b. *The South Korean Ring-necked Pheasant.* US Department of the Interior Fish and Wildlife Service, Bureau of Sport, Fisheries and Wildlife FGL-15 (4 pp.). Government Printing Office: Washington. DC.

————. 1971a. *The Kalij Pheasants.* US Department of the Interior Fish and Wildlife Service, Bureau of Sport, Fisheries and Wildlife FGL-18 (4 pp.). Government Printing Office: Washington, DC.

————. 1971b. *The White-winged Pheasants.* US Department of the Interior Fish and Wildlife Service, Bureau of Sport, Fisheries and Wildlife FGL-21 (4 pp.). Government Printing Office: Washington, DC.

————. 1971c. *The Rock Partridges.* US Department of the Interior Fish and Wildlife Service, Bureau of Sport, Fisheries and Wildlife FGL-23 (4 pp.). Government Printing Office: Washington, DC.

————. 1971d. *The Chukar and Great Partridges.* US Department of the Interior Fish and Wildlife Service, Bureau of Sport, Fisheries and Wildlife FGL-24 (4 pp.). Government Printing Office: Washington, DC.

————. 1973. *The Barbary, Arabian Black-head and Philby's Partridges.* US Department of the Interior

Fish and Wildlife Service, Bureau of Sport, Fisheries and Wildlife FGL-28 (4 pp.). Government Printing Office: Washington, DC.

Bohl, W. H. & **Bump, G.** 1970. Summary of foreign game bird liberations, 1960–1968, and propagations 1966–1968. *Department of the Interior, Fish and Wildlife Service, Special Scientific Report (Wildlife)* No. 130 (61 pp.).

★**Boitani, L.** ed. 1976. *Reintroductions: Techniques and Ethics.* World Wildlife Fund: Rome.

Bojer, W. 1871. Avifauna of Agaléga. *Transactions of the Royal Society of Arts and Sciences of Mauritius*, series B, 5: 132–40.

Bolen, E. G. 1971. Some views on exotic Waterfowl. *Wilson Bulletin* 83: 430–4.

Bon-Saint-Côme, M. 1984, Un nouveau venu à plumes: l'Ignicolore [*Euplectes oryx*]. *France-Antilles* (27 October).

Bonar, H. N. 1907. Capercaillie in Midlothian. *Annals of Scottish Natural History*, 51–2.

——. 1910. Capercaillie in East Lothian. *Annals of Scottish Natural History*, 120.

Bond, J. 1928. On the birds of Dominica, St Lucia, St Vincent and Barbados. *Proceedings of the Academy of Natural Sciences of Philadelphia* 80: 523–45.

——. 1948. Origin of the bird fauna of the West Indies. *Wilson Bulletin* 60: 207–29.

——. 1964–1980. *Supplements to the Checklist of the Birds of the West Indies (1956).* Academy of Natural Science of Philadelphia: Lancaster, USA.

——. 1979. *Birds of the West Indies.* Collins: London. (1st edn, 1960.)

Bond, J. & **de Schauensee, R. M.** 1942. The birds of Bolivia, Part 1. *Proceedings of the Academy of Natural Sciences of Philadelphia* 94: 307–91.

Bond, R. M. 1957. The Cattle Egret in Jamaica, British West Indies. *Condor* 59: 269.

Booth, E. S. 1948. Starlings in Washington State. *Condor* 50: 165.

Bossenmaier, E. F. 1957. The status of the Chukar Partridge in Wyoming. *Proceedings of the 37th Annual Conference of the Western Association of State Game and Fish Commissioners*, 234–8.

Boswall, J. 1971. Notes from coastal Eritrea on selected species. *Bulletin of the British Ornithologists' Club* 91: 81–4.

Bourke, P. A. 1957. Introduced birds of New South Wales. *Emu* 57: 263–4.

Bourne, W. R. P. 1955. The birds of the Cape Verde Islands. *Ibis* 97: 508–56.

——. 1957. The breeding birds of Bermuda. *Ibis* 99: 94–105.

——. 1966a. Further notes on the birds of the Cape Verde Islands. *Ibis* 108: 425–9.

——. 1966b. Observations on islands in the Indian Ocean. *Sea Swallow* 18: 40–3.

——. 1971. The birds of the Chagos Group, Indian Ocean. *Atoll Research Bulletin* 149: 175–207.

——. 1983. New Zealand ornithological survey of Juan Fernandez, South Pacific. *Ibis* 125: 595.

Bowdish, B. S. 1903. Birds of Porto Rico. *Auk* 20: 10–23.

Bowles, J. 1962. The Guam Edible Nest Swiftlet. *Elepaio* 23: 14–15.

Bradlee, T. S., Mowbray, L. M. & **Eaton, W. F.** 1931. A list of birds recorded from the Bermudas. *Proceedings of the Boston Society of Natural History* 39: 279–82.

Bradshaw, C. J. 1901. A Little Owl at Henley. *Zoologist*, 476.

Bravery, J. A. 1970. Birds of the Atherton Shire, Queensland. *Emu* 70: 49–63.

Brazil, M. A. 1984. The mysterious and controversial Mute Swan. *Kakko* 33: 3–5 [in Japanese].

——. 1985. [Exotic birds in Japan.] *The Japan Times* (Wild Watch, 28 June).

——. In press. *The Birds of Japan: A Checklist.*

Bready, M. B. 1929. *The European Starling on his Western Way.* Knickerbocker Press: New York.

Breckenridge, W. J. 1941. The Starling, a universal alien. *The Conservation Volunteer* 3: 10–13.

——. 1984. House Finch in Hennepin County. *Loon* 56: 64.

Breese, P. L. 1959. Information on Cattle Egret, a bird new to Hawaii. *Elepaio* 20: 33–4.

Briggs, J. N. & **Haugh, J. R.** 1973. Habitat selection in birds with consideration of the potential establishment of the Parakeet (*Myiopsitta monachus*) in North America. *Kingbird* 23: 1–9.

Britton, P. L. ed. 1980. *Birds of East Africa.* East Africa Natural History Society: Nairobi.

Brodkorb, P. 1972. Neogene fossil jays from the Great Plains. *Condor* 74: 347–9.

Bronson, W. S. 1948. *Starlings.* Harcourt, Brace & Co.: New York.

Broo, A. 1978. Project Eagle Owl, south west. In T. A. Geer ed., *Birds of Prey Management Techniques*, 104–20. British Falconers' Club: Oxford.

Brooke, R. K. 1964 and 1966. Distribution of Feral Rock Doves (*Columba livia*). *Honeyguide* 43: 2–3; 48: 12.

——. 1973. European Starling (*Sturnus vulgaris*). *Ostrich* 44: 131–2.

——. 1976. Morphological notes on *Acridotheres tristis* in Natal. *Bulletin of the British Ornithologists' Club* 96: 8–13.

★——. 1981. The Feral Pigeon – a 'new' bird for the South African list. *Bokmakierie* 33: 37–40.

——. 1983. On the introduction of the Indian Mynah in Harare. *Honeyguide* 116: 15.

——. 1985. Bibliography of alien birds in southern and south-central Africa. Unpublished computer printout by the Percy FitzPatrick Institute of African Ornithology, University of Cape Town.

Brooke, R. K., Lloyd, P. H. & **de Villiers, A. L.** 1986. Review of invasive alien terrestrial vertebrate species in South Africa. In I. A. W. MacDonald & F. J. Kruger eds, *Ecological Synthesis of South African Biological Invasions (Proceedings of a Symposium of the South African National Programme for Ecosystem Research)*. Oxford University Press: Cape Town.

Brookfield, C. M. & **Griswold, O.** 1956. An exotic new oriole settles in Florida. *National Geographic Magazine* 109: 261–4.

Brosselin, M. 1971. Réintroduction du Vautour Fauvre dans les Causses de Lozère et d'Aveyron. *Le Courrier de la Nature* 18: 74–6.

Brothers, N. P. & **Skira, I. J.** 1984. The Weka on Macquarie Island. *Notornis* 31: 145–54.

Brown, A. G. 1950. The birds of Turkeith, Victoria. *Emu* 50: 105–13.

Brown, C. P. 1954. Distribution of the Hungarian Partridge in New York. *New York Fish and Game Journal* 1: 119–29.

Brown, C. R. 1981. The impact of Starlings on Purple Martin populations in unmanaged colonies. *American Birds* 35: 266–8.

Brown, L. & **Forbes, J.** 1973. Monk Parakeet meeting, Albany, New York; memorandum to participants. US Department of the Interior, Bureau of Sport, Fisheries and Wildlife (6 pp.).

Brown, L. H., Urban, E. K. & **Newman, K. B.** 1982. *The Birds of Africa*, Vol. 1, Academic Press: London and New York.

Brown, R. 1868. Synopsis of the birds of Vancouver Island. *Ibis*, n.s., 4: 414–27.

Browne, P. W. P. 1950. Notes on the birds observed in South Arabia. *Ibis* 92: 52–65.

Bruce, J. A. 1961. First record of the European Skylark on the San Juan Islands, Washington. *Condor* 63: 418.

Brudenell-Bruce, P. G. C. 1975. *Birds of New Providence and the Bahama Islands*. Collins: London.

Bruner, A. 1979. Red-vented Bulbul now in Tahiti. *Elepaio* 40: 92.

Bruner, P. L. 1972. A field guide to birds of French Polynesia. *Pacific Scientific Information Centre, Bernice P. Bishop Museum, Honolulu Bulletin* No. 93.

Brush, A. F. & **Power, D. M.** 1976. House Finch pigmentation: carotenoid metabolism and the effect of diet. *Auk* 93: 725–39.

Bryan, E. H. 1940. A summary of the Hawaiian birds. *Proceedings of the 6th Pacific Science Congress, California, 1939* 4: 185–9. University of California Press: Berkeley.

———. 1958. *Checklist and Summary of Hawaiian Birds*. Books About Hawaii: Honolulu.

Bryan, W. A. 1908. Some birds of Molokai. *Occasional Papers of the Bernice P. Bishop Museum* No. 4: 133–76.

———. 1912a. Introduction of birds into Hawaii. *Proceedings of the Hawaiian Entomological Society* 2: 169–75.

———. 1912b. The introduction and acclimatization of the Yellow Canary on Midway Island. *Auk* 29: 339–40.

———. 1915. Introduced birds. In *Natural History of Hawaii*, Ch. 22. Honolulu.

Bryant, H. C. 1916. The European House Sparrow and its control in California. *California Fish and Game Commission Teachers' Bulletin* No. 7.

Buckland, F. 1861. The acclimatisation of animals. Paper read before Society of Arts, London. Acclimatisation Society of Victoria: Melbourne (Victorian Pamphlet No. 32, La Trobe Library, Victoria).

Buckman, C. A. 1967. The rugged Ring-necked Pheasant of Minnesota. Unpublished report, Minnesota Department of Conservation, Division of Game and Fish (23 pp.).

Bucknill, J. A. 1913. A third contribution to the ornithology of Cyprus, *Ibis*, series 10, 1: 2–14.

Bucknill, J. S. & **Chasen, F. N.** 1927. *Birds of Singapore Island*. Government Printer: Singapore.

Bull, J. 1971. Monk Parakeets in the New York City region. *Linnean Society Newsletter* No. 25: 1–2.

———. 1973. Exotic birds in the New York City area. *Wilson Bulletin* 85: 501–5.

———. 1975. Introduction to the United States of the Monk Parakeet – a species with pest potential. *Bulletin of the International Council of Bird Preservation* No. 12: 98.

Bull, J. & **Ricciuti, E. R.** 1974. Polly want an apple? *Audubon* 76: 48–54.

Bull, P. C. 1957. Distribution and abundance of the Rook (*Corvus frugilegus* L.) in New Zealand. *Notornis* 7: 137–61.

———. 1966. Introduced birds. *Notornis* 13: 122–3.

———. 1973. The Starling: friend or foe? *New Zealand Agricultural Journal* 127: 55–9.

Bull, P. C. & **Gaze, P. D.** 1972. Bird distribution mapping scheme. *Notornis* 19: 267–70.

Bull, P. C. & **Porter R. E. R.** 1975. Distribution and numbers of the Rook (*Corvus frugilegus* L.) in the North Island of New Zealand. *New Zealand Journal of Zoology* 2: 63–92.

Bull, P. C., Gaze, P. D. & **Robertson, C. J. R.** 1978. *Bird Distribution in New Zealand: A Provisional Atlas 1969–1976*. Ornithological Society of New Zealand: Wellington.

Buller, W. L. 1872–3. *A History of the Birds of New Zealand*. Voorst: London.

Bump, G. 1940. The introduction and transplantation of game birds and mammals into the state of New York. *Proceedings of the 5th North American Wildlife Conference*, 409–20.

———. 1951. Game introductions – when, where and

how. *Transactions of the 16th North American Wildlife Conference*, 316–26.

———. 1952. How shall foreign game be introduced? *Atlantic Naturalist* 7: 112–17.

———. 1957. Foreign game introductions into the southeast. *Proceedings of the llth Annual Conference of the Southeastern Association of Game and Fish Commissioners*, 17–20.

———. 1958a. Special field report on wild Reeves Pheasants in France. Unpulished report, US Department of the Interior Bureau of Sport, Fisheries and Wildlife, Washington DC (4 pp.).

———. 1958b. New birds for old. *Colorado Outdoors* 7: 1–6.

———. 1958c. History and analysis of tetraonid introductions into North America. *Journal of Wildlife Management* 27: 855.

———. 1968a. *Foreign Game Investigation: Federal–State Co-operative Program*. US Department of the Interior Fish and Wildlife Service Publication No. 49 (14 pp.). Government Printing Office: Washington, DC.

———. 1968b. Exotics and the role of the State–Federal foreign game investigation program. *Proceedings of a Symposium on Introduced Exotic Animals: Ecological and Socioeconomic Considerations*, 5–8. Caesar Kleberg Research Program in Wildlife Ecology, Texas A & M University: College Station.

———. 1970a. Acclimatization of game animals in the United States. *Transactions of the 9th International Congress of Game Biologists, Moscow, September 1969*, 136–40 [in English with Russian summary].

———. 1970b. *The Black Francolins*. US Department of the Interior Fish and Wildlife Service, Bureau of Sport, Fisheries and Wildlife. FGL-1 (4 pp.). Government Printing Office: Washington, DC.

———. 1970c. *The Gray Francolins*. US Department of the Interior Fish and Wildlife Service, Bureau of Sport, Fisheries and Wildlife FGL-2 (4 pp.). Government Printing Office, Washington, DC.

———. 1970d, *The Eastern Gray Partridges*. US Department of the Interior Fish and Wildlife Service, Bureau of Sport, Fisheries and Wildlife FGL-8 (4 pp.). Government Printing Office, Washington, DC.

———. 1970e. *The Manchurian Ring-necked Pheasant*. US Department of the Interior Fish and Wildlife Service, Bureau of Sport, Fisheries and Wildlife FGL-9 (4 pp.). Government Printing Office: Washington, DC.

———. 1970f. *The Coturnix or Old World Quails*. US Department of the Interior Fish and Wildlife Service, Bureau of Sport, Fisheries and Wildlife FGL-10 (4 pp.). Government Printing Office, Washington, DC.

———. 1970g. *The Red-legged Partridges*. US Department of the Interior Fish and Wildlife Service, Bureau of Sport, Fisheries and Wildlife FGL-16 (4 pp.). Government Printing Office, Washington, DC.

———. 1970h. *The Western Gray or Hungarian Partridges*. US Department of the Interior Fish and Wildlife Service, Bureau of Sport, Fisheries and Wildlife FGL-17 (4 pp.). Government Printing Office: Washington, DC.

———. 1971. *The South American Monk, Quaker, or Grey-headed Parakeet*. US Fish and Wildlife Service, Bureau of Sport, Fisheries and Wildlife, Wildlife Leaflet No. 496.

Bump, G. & **Bohl, W. H.** 1961. Red Jungle Fowl and Kalij Pheasants. *US Department of the Interior Fish and Wildlife Service, Special Scientific Report (Wildlife)* No. 62 (41 pp.).

———. 1964. Summary of foreign game bird propagation and liberations 1960–1963. *US Department of the Interior Fish and Wildlife Service, Special Scientific Report (Wildlife)* No. 80 (48 pp.).

Bump, G & **Bump, J. W.** 1964. A study and review of the Black Francolin and Gray Francolin. *US Department of the Interior Fish and Wildlife Service, Special Scientific Report (Wildlife)* No. 81.

Bump, G & **Robbins, S.** 1966. *The Newcomers: Birds in our Lives*, 343–53. US Fish and Wildlife Service. Government Printing Office: Washington, DC.

Bundy, G. & **Warr, E.** 1980. A check-list of birds of the Arabian Gulf States. *Sandgrouse* 1: 4–49.

Burger, G. V. 1954a. The status of introduced wild Turkeys in California. *California Fish and Game* 40: 123–45.

———. 1954b. Wild Turkeys in central coastal California. *Condor* 56: 198–206.

———. 1964. Survival of Ring-necked Pheasants released on a Wisconsin shooting preserve. *Journal of Wildlife Management* 28: 711–21.

Burris, O. E. 1965. Game transplants in Alaska. *Proceedings of the 45th Annual Conference of the Western Association of State Game and Fish Commissioners, Anchorage, Alaska, 7–8 July 1965*, 93–104.

Burton, J. A. 1973. *Owls of the World*. Peter Lowe: London.

Buss, I. O. 1946. *Wisconsin Pheasant Populations*. Wisconsin Conservation Department Publication No. 326, A-46 (148 pp.).

But'ev, V. T. & **Zhuravlev, M. N.** 1975. Unpremeditated introduction of the Indian Starling. *Priroda, Akademiya Nauk SSSR, Moskva* 7: 88–9.

Butler, A. L. 1899. Birds of the Andaman and Nicobar Islands. *Journal of the Bombay Natural History Society* 12: 386–403, 555–71, 684–96.

Buxton, P. A. 1907. The spread of the Little Owl in Hertfordshire. *Zoologist*, 430.

Byrd, G. V. 1979. Common Mynah predation of Wedge-tailed Shearwater eggs. *Elepaio* 39: 69–70.

Byrd, G. V., Zeillemaker, C. F & Telfer, T. 1980. Population increases of Cattle Egrets on Kauai. *Elepaio* 41: 25–8.

C

Caccamise, D. F., Lyon, L. A. & Fischl, J. 1983. Seasonal patterns in roosting flocks of Starlings and Common Grackles. *Condor* 85: 464–81.

Cahalane, V. H. 1955. Some effects of exotics on nature *Atlantic Monthly* 10: 176–85.

Cahn, A. R. 1938. Climatographic analysis of the problems of introducing three exotic game birds into the Tennessee Valley and vicinity. *Transactions of the 3rd North American Wildlife Conference*, 807–17.

Cain, A. J. & Galbraith, I. C. J. 1956. Field notes on birds of the eastern Solomon Islands. *Ibis* 98: 262–95.

————. 1957. Birds of the Solomon Islands. *Ibis* 99: 128.

Calaby, J. H. 1977. Changing the face of a continent. *Australian Natural History* 19: 62–5.

Calder, D. 1953. Distribution of the Indian Mynah. *Bokmakierie* 5: 4–6.

Calhoun, J. B. 1947. The role of temperature and natural selection in relation to the variations in the size of the English Sparrow in the United States. *American Naturalist* 81: 203–28.

Calman, W. T. 1931. Discussion on the introduction of alien species. *Proceedings of the Linnean Society of London* 142: 6, 11–14, 17–20.

Cameron, D. D. 1981. Ferals that failed. *Noticias Galápagos* 33: 21–2.

Campbell, B. & Lack, E. eds. 1985. *A Dictionary of Birds.* T. & A. D. Poyser: Calton, Staffordshire.

Campbell, H. 1906. Introduction of Australian Magpies to Ceylon. *Emu* 5: 231–2.

Campbell, H. 1956. Pheasants in New Mexico. *New Mexico Wildlife* 1: 5.

Campbell, J. M. 1906. Capercaillies in Ayrshire. *Annals of Scottish Natural History*, 186.

Campbell, M. L. 1973. How the Chukar got its start in Wyoming. *Wyoming Wildlife* 37: 26–9.

Campbell, W. S. 1943. The English Sparrow in Australia. *Victorian Naturalist* 60: 9–11.

Campos Ramirez, R. G. & Morúa Navarra, A. P. 1983. Distribution of the House Sparrow (*Passer domesticus*) in Costa Rica: three new localities. *Brenesia* 21: 409–10 [in Spanish, with English abstract].

Cant, G. 1962. The House Finch in New York State. *Kingbird* 12: 68–72.

Carié, P. 1910. Notes sur l'acclimatation du Bulbul (*Otocompsa jocosa* L.). *Bulletin de la Société Nationale d'Acclimatation de France*, 462–74.

————. 1916. L'acclimatation a l'île Maurice: mammiferes et oiseaux. *Bulletin de la Société Nationale d'Acclimatation de France*, 1–62.

Carl, G. C. 1952. Alien animals on Vancouver Island. *Victoria Naturalist* 9: 7–10.

Carl, G. C. & Guiguet, C. J. 1972. *Alien Animals in British Columbia.* Handbook No. 14 (94 pp.). British Columbia Provincial Museum: Victoria. (First published 1958.)

Carleton, A. R. 1971. Studies on a population of the Red-whiskered Bulbul in Dade County, Florida. Unpublished MSc thesis, University of Miami.

Carleton, A. R. & Owre, O. T. 1975. The Red-whiskered Bulbul in Florida, 1960–1961. *Auk* 92: 40–57.

Carlquist, S. 1980. *Hawaii: A Natural History.* Pacific Tropical Botanical Garden: Hawaii.

Carlson, C. E. 1941. The Hungarian Partridge in Minnesota. *The Conservation Volunteer* 2: 41–4.

————. 1946. Status of Pheasants [in USA], 1946. *The Conservation Volunteer* 9: 30–3.

Carothers, J. H. & Hansen, R. B. 1982. Occurrence of the Japanese Bush Warbler on Maui. *Elepaio* 43: 17–18.

Carvalho, J. C. M. 1939. O pardal [House Sparrow] em Minas Gerias e a possibilidade de sua extinção. *O Campo* 10: 34–5.

Carrick, R. 1957. The wild life of Macquarie Island. *Australian Museum Magazine* 12: 255–60.

Carrick, R. & Walker, C. 1953. Report on the European Starling, *Sturnus vulgaris*, at Oni-i-Lau. *Transactions and Proceedings of the Fiji Society, 1951–1954* 5: 51–8.

Carroll, A. L. K. 1963. Food habits of the North Island Weka. *Notornis* 10: 289–300.

Cassin, J. 1861. Catalogue of birds from the island of St Thomas, West Indies. *Proceedings of the Academy of Natural Sciences of Philadelphia, 1860*, 374–9.

★Caum, E. L. 1933. The exotic birds of Hawaii. *Occasional Papers of the Bernice P. Bishop Museum* No. 10: 1–55.

————. 1936. Notes on the fauna and flora of Lehua and Kaula Islands. *Occasional Papers of the Bernice P. Bishop Museum* No. 21: 2–17.

Cave, F. O. & MacDonald, J. D. 1955. *Birds of the Sudan.* Oliver & Boyd: Edinburgh and London.

Cawkell, E. M. & Hamilton, J. E. 1961. The birds of the Falkland Islands. *Ibis* 103a: 1–26.

'C. H.' 1952. Buntings, the latest bird introduction by the Hui Manu. *Elepaio* 13: 25–6.

Chaffer, N. 1933. The Bulbul. *Emu* 33: 136–7.

Chalbreck, R. H., Dupuie, H. H. & Belsom, D. J. 1975. Establishment of a resident breeding flock of Canada Geese in Louisiana. *Proceedings of the 28th Annual Conference of the Southeastern Association of Game and Fish Commissioners*, 442–55.

Chalmers, C. E. 1972. Cattle Egret in the Gippsland area [of Victoria, Australia]. *Emu* 72: 180–1.

Chamberlain, M. 1889. Some account of the birds of southern Greenland from the mss. of A. Hagerup. *Auk* 6: 291–7.

Chambers, G. D. 1965–6. *Summary of Foreign Game Bird Propagation, 1964 and 1965, and Liberations, 1960–1964 and 1960–1965.* Missouri Conservation Commission.

Chapman, F. M. 1925. The European Starling as an American citizen. *Natural History* 25: 480–5.

Chasen, F. N. 1924. On the occurrence of certain alien birds in Singapore. *Journal of the Malayan Branch of the Royal Asiatic Society* 2: 68–70.

———. 1925. Further remarks on the birds of Singapore Island. *Singapore Naturalist* 5: 71–3.

———. 1933. Notes on the birds of Christmas Island, Indian Ocean. *Bulletin of the Raffles Museum* 8: 55–87.

Cheel, E. 1934. Effect of the introduction of exotic plants and animals on Australian plant life. *Proceedings of the 5th Pacific Science Congress, Victoria and Vancouver, June 1933* 1: 791–6. University of Toronto Press: Toronto.

Cheke, A. S. 1985. *Observations on the Surviving Endemic Birds of Rodriguez.* Report of the British Ornithologists' Union Mascarene Islands Expedition. Cambridge University Press: Cambridge.

Cheke, A. S. & **Lawley, J. C.** 1983. Biological history of Agaléga, with special reference to birds and other land vertebrates. *Atoll Research Bulletin* 273: 65–108.

Cheney, G. M. 1915. Birds of the Wangaratta district, Victoria. *Emu* 14: 199–213.

Cheng Tso-hsin ed. 1963. *Chung-Kuo Ching-Chi Tung-wu Chich-Niao Lei (China's Economic Fauna: Aves).* Science Publication Society: Peking.

———. 1976. *Distributional List of Chinese Birds.* Science Publication Society: Peking.

———. 1978–9. *Fauna Sinica: Aves,* Vols 2 (Anseriformes) and 4 (Galliformes). Science Press, Academia Sinica: Peking.

Cherrie, G. K. 1896. [Introductions to North America.] *Field Columbia Museum of Ornithology,* series 1: 1–26.

Chisholm, A. H. 1915. The Mallacoota excursion. *Emu* 14: 126–34.

———. 1919. Introduced birds of Queensland. *Emu* 19: 60–2.

———. 1925. Spread of the Goldfinch. *Emu* 25: 93.

———. 1950. Birds introduced into Australia. *Emu* 50: 97–100.

Chisholm, E. C. 1924. The avifauna around Tumbarumba, New South Wales. *Emu* 24: 102–6.

———. 1926. Birds introduced into New South Wales. *Emu* 25: 276–9.

Christensen, G. C. 1954. The Chukar Partridge in Nevada. *Nevada Fish and Game Commission Biological Bulletin* No. 1: 1–77.

———. 1961. Preliminary results from Nevada's participation in the foreign game introduction program. *Proceedings of the 41st Annual Conference of the Western Association of State Game and Fish Commissioners,* 130–5.

———. 1963a. Sandgrouse released in Nevada found in Mexico. *Condor* 65: 67–8.

———. 1963b. Exotic game bird introductions into Nevada. *Nevada Fish and Game Commission Biological Bulletin* No. 3.

———. 1967. The status of Nevada's exotic game bird program. *Proceedings of the Annual Conference of the Western Association of State Game and Fish Commissioners, Honolulu, Hawaii, 16–20 July 1967,* 84–93.

———. 1970. The Chukar Partridge: its introduction, life history and management. *Nevada Department of Fish and Game Biological Bulletin* No. 4 (82 pp.).

Christensen, G. C. & **Bohl, W. H.** 1964. A study and review of the Common Indian Sandgrouse and the Imperial Sandgrouse. *Department of the Interior Fish and Wildlife Service, Special Scientific Report (Wildlife)* No. 84 (71 pp.).

Christensen, R. 1963. A short history of 'John Ringneck'. *South Dakota Conservation Digest* 30: 12–14.

Christisen, D. M. 1951. *History and Status of the Ring-necked Pheasant in Missouri.* Missouri Conservation Commission (66 pp.).

Christy, C. 1897. Field notes on the birds of San Domingo. *Ibis* 3: 317–42.

Clancey, P. A. 1960. The Indian Mynah: is it guilty of driving the indigenous birds away? *Natal Bird Club News Sheet* 64: 1–2.

———. 1963. The House Sparrow on the Atlantic seaboard of the Cape. *Ostrich* 34: 168.

———. 1964. *The Birds of Natal and Zululand.* Oliver & Boyd: Edinburgh.

———. 1966. The Indian Mynah. *Bokmakierie* 18: 37.

———. 1974. The Indian House Crow in Natal. *Ostrich* 45: 31–2.

———. 1976a. Roseringed Parakeet in Natal and Zululand. *Albatross (Newsletter of the Natal Bird Club)* 241: 5.

———. 1976b. A catalogue of birds of the South African sub-region. *Durban Museum Novitates* 11: 46.

Clapp, R. B. 1975. Birds imported into the United States in 1972. *US Department of the Interior Fish and Wildlife Service, Special Scientific Report (Wildlife)* No. 193.

Clapp, R. B. & **Banks, R. C.** 1973. Birds imported into the United States in 1970 and 1971. *US Department of the Interior Fish and Wildlife Service, Special Scientific Reports (Wildlife)* Nos 164 and 170.

Clapp, R. C. & **Sibley, F. C.** 1966. Notes on the birds of Tutuila, American Samoa. *Notornis* 13: 157–64.

★**Clark, A. H.** 1949. *The Invasion of New Zealand by People, Plants and Animals: The South Island.* Rutgers University Press: New Brunswick.

Clarke, C. H. D. 1947. Pelee Island Pheasant shoot. *Sylva* 3: 45–55.

Clarke, C. H. D. & **Braffette, R.** 1946. Ring-necked Pheasant investigations in Ontario, 1946. Ontario Department of Lands and Forests. Mimeograph.

Clarke, G. 1967. Bird notes from Aden Colony. *Ibis* 109: 516–20.

Clegg, W. E. 1941. Birds of the Île de la Camargue and the Petite Camargue. *Ibis*, 14th series (suppl.), 5: 556–609.

Cleland, J. 1910. The Australian fauna and flora and exotic invasions. *Journal of Natural History of the Scientific Society of Western Australia* 3: 12–18.

———. 1942. Birds seen on Kangaroo Island by members of the Ralph Tate Society. *South Australian Ornithologist* 16: 19–21, 31–3.

Coffey, B. B. 1959. The Starling in eastern Mexico. *Condor* 61: 299.

Cole, D. T. 1958. House Sparrows in Mafeking. *Ostrich* 29: 87.

———. 1962. House Sparrows in the Northern Cape and Bechuanaland. *Ostrich* 33: 54–5.

Colebatch, H. 1929. *The Story of 100 Years: Western Australia 1829–1929*, Ch. 30. Government Printer: Perth.

Coleman, E. 1939. Notes on the increase of the Blackbird. *Emu* 38: 515–21.

Coleman, J. D. 1971. The distribution, numbers and food of the Rook, *Corvus frugilegus* L., in Canterbury, New Zealand. *New Zealand Journal of Science* 14: 494–506.

———. 1972. The breeding biology of the Rook, *Corvus frugilegus* L., in Canterbury, New Zealand. *Notornis* 19: 118–39.

———. 1974. The use of artificial nest sites erected for Starlings in Canterbury, New Zealand. *New Zealand Journal of Zoology* 1: 349–54.

———. 1977. The foods and feeding of Starlings in Canterbury. *Proceedings of the New Zealand Ecological Society* 24: 94–109.

Coleman, S. 1949. The Chukar Partridge in Nevada. *Proceedings of the 29th Annual Conference of the Western Association of State Game and Fish Commissioners*, 135–8.

Collier, R. 1986. Return of the Sea Eagle. *Bird Watching* (August): 30.

Collinge, W. E. 1919. The plague of Starlings. *Nature Review* 434: 252–7.

———. 1920–21. The Starling – is it injurious to agriculture? *Agriculture* 27: 1114–21.

Collins, M. S. 1976. South American Cardinal populations on the Big Island [Hawaii]. *Elepaio* 37: 1–2.

Colson, R. B. 1968. New Pheasant introductions – a progress report. *Wildlife Conservation* 23: 2–4.

Conant, P. 1980. Japanese Bush-warbler on Lanai. *Elepaio* 40: 169.

Conant, S. 1983. Kahoolawe birds – including first Warbling Silverbill record. *Elepaio* 44: 63–5.

———. 1984. First Oahu record of the Warbling Silverbill. *Elepaio* 44: 116–17.

Condon, H. T. 1948a. Birds introduced onto Kangaroo Island. *South Australian Ornithologist* 18: 78.

———. 1948b. The introduced Grenadier Weaver or Red Bishop bird. *South Australian Ornithologist* 19: 1.

———. 1962. A handlist of the birds of South Australia. *South Australian Ornithologist* 23: 6–8. (Revised edition, 1968; South Australian Ornithological Association: Adelaide.)

———. 1975. *Checklist of the Birds of Australia*, Vol. 1. *Non-passerines*. Royal Australasian Ornithologists' Union: Melbourne.

Cooke, M. T. 1925 and 1928. Spread of the European Starling in North America. *US Department of Agriculture Circular* Nos 36 (7 pp.); 40 (10 pp.).

*Cooke, M. T. & **Knappen, P.** 1941. Some birds naturalized in North America. *Transactions of the 5th North American Wildlife Conference*, 176–83.

Cooper, H. M. 1947. Some notes on Kangaroo Island birds. *South Australian Ornithologist* 18: 48.

Cooper Ornithological Society 1957. *Checklist of the Birds of Mexico*, Part 2. University of California: Berkeley.

Cooper, W. T. & **Forshaw, J. M.** 1977. *The Birds of Paradise and Bower Birds*. Collins: Sydney.

Corfe, B. 1977. Musk Lorikeets at Alfred Cove. *Western Australian Naturalist* 13: 209.

Cortes, J. E., Finlayson, J. C., Garcia, E. F. J. & **Mosquera, M. A.** 1980. *The Birds of Gibraltar*. Gibraltar Bookshop.

Cory, C. B. 1880. *Birds of the Bahama Islands*. Published by the author: Boston, Mass.

———. 1881. List of the birds of Haiti. *Bulletin of the Nuttall Ornithological Club* 6: 151–5.

———. 1889. *The Birds of the West Indies*. Estes & Lauriat: Boston, Mass.

Cottam, C. 1929. Status of the Ring-necked Pheasant in Utah. *Condor* 31: 117–23.

———. 1941. European Starlings in Nevada. *Condor* 43: 293–4.

———. 1950. The effect of uncontrolled introductions of plants and animals. *Proceedings and Papers of an International Technical Conference on the Protection of Nature, Lake Success, New York, August 1949*, 408–13. Unesco: Paris.

———. 1956. The problem of wildlife introductions – its successes and failures. *Proceedings of the 46th Convention of the International Association of Game, Fish and Conservation Commissioners*, 1–37, 94–111.

Cottam, C. & **Standford, J. A.** 1959. Coturnix Quail in America. *Proceedings of the 48th Convention of the International Association of Game and Fish Conservation Commissioners*, 111–19.

Cottam, C., Nelson, A. L. & **Saylor, L. W.** 1940.

The Chukar and Hungarian Partridges in America. US Department of the Interior Biological Survey, Wildlife Leaflet No. BS-159 (6 pp.).

Cottam, C., Sooter, C. A. & **Griffiths, R. E.** 1942. The European Starling in New Mexico. *Condor* 44: 182.

Coues, E. 1878. The ineligibility of the European House Sparrow. *American Naturalist* 12: 499–505.

———. 1879. On the present status of *Passer domesticus* in America, with special reference to western states and territories. *Bulletin of the United States Geological Survey*, 175–93.

Coues, W. P. 1890. *Passer domesticus* in Cape Breton. *Auk* 7: 212.

Councilman, J. J. 1974. Breeding biology of the Indian Mynah in city and aviary. *Notornis* 21: 318–33.

Courtenay-Latimer, M. 1942. English House Sparrow introduced into South Africa at East London. *Ostrich* 13: 181.

———. 1955. The English Sparrow at East London. *Bokmakierie* 7: 32.

Cramp, S. ed. 1985. *The Birds of the Western Palaearctic*, Vol. 4. Oxford University Press: Oxford.

Cramp, S. & **Simmons, K. E. L.** 1977, 1979 and 1982. *The Birds of the Western Palaearctic*, Vols 1–3. Oxford University Press: Oxford.

Crook, J. H. 1961. The fodies (Ploceinae) of the Seychelle Islands. *Ibis* 103a: 517–48.

Crosby, G. T. 1972. Spread of the Cattle Egret in the Western Hemisphere. *Bird Banding* 43: 205–12.

Crossin, R. S. 1967. The breeding biology of the Tufted Jay. *Proceedings of the Western Foundation of Vertebrate Zoology* 1: 265–99. Los Angeles.

Crowell, K. L. 1962. Reduced interspecific competition among the birds of Bermuda. *Ecology* 43: 75–88.

Crowell, K. L. & **Crowell, M. R.** 1976. Bermuda's abundant, beleaguered birds. *Natural History* 85: 48–56.

Cuello, J. & **Gerzenstein, E.** 1962. Las aves del Uruguay. *Comunicaciones Zoologicas del Museo de Historia Natural de Montevideo* 6: 1–91.

Cullen, J. M., Guiton, P. E., Horridge, G. A. & **Peirson, J.** 1952. Birds of Palma and Gomera. *Ibis* 94: 68–84.

Cumming, R. A. 1925. Observations of the Chinese Starling (*Ethiopsar cristatellus*). *Canadian Field-Naturalist* 39: 187–90.

———. 1932. Birds of the Vancouver district. *Murrelet* 13: 3–15.

Cunningham, J. M. 1948. Distribution of the Myna in New Zealand. *Notornis* 3: 57–64.

———. 1951. Position of the Mynah in 1950. *Notornis* 4: 66–7.

———. 1954. Further notes on the distribution of the Myna. *Notornis* 5: 210.

Cunningham van Someren, G. R. 1969. Escapes of

Psittacula krameri and *Agapornis* spp. breeding in Kenya. *Bulletin of the British Ornithologists' Club* 89: 137–9.

———. 1975. *Agapornis fischeri* Reichenow in Kenya? *Auk* 92: 370–1.

Curry-Lindahl, K. 1964. The reintroduction of Eagle Owls in Sweden. *Annual Report of the Norfolk Wildlife Park, 1964*, 31–3.

Curtiss, A. 1938. *A Short Zoology of Tahiti.* Guide Press: New York.

Cuthbertson, M. B. 1952. Meet the Mynahs. *African Wildlife* 6: 64–6.

Cutten, F. E. A. 1966. Clutch size and egg dimensions of the Black Swan, *Cygnus atratus*, at Lake Ellesmere, Canterbury, New Zealand. *Emu* 65: 223–5.

Cyrus, D. & **Robson, N.** 1980. *Bird Atlas of Natal.* University of Natal Press: Pietermaritzburg.

———. 1984. Pending invasion into Natal of European Starlings. *Albatross* 275: 4.

D

Dale, F. H. 1941. Judgement suspended on Hungarian Partridge projects in Michigan. *Michigan Conservationist* 10: 6–7.

———. 1943. History and status of the Hungarian Partridge in Michigan. *Journal of Wildlife Management* 7: 368–77.

Danforth, S. T. 1929. Notes on the birds of Hispaniola. *Auk* 46: 358.

———. 1934. The birds of Antigua. *Auk* 51: 364.

Daniel, M. J. 1976. An imported fauna. *Australian Natural History* 18: 370–3.

Daniels, T. S. 1954. House Sparrows in the Eastern Cape. *Ostrich* 25: 37–8.

Darlington, P. J. Jr. 1938. The origin of the fauna of the Greater Antilles, with discussion of dispersal of animals over water and through the air. *Quarterly Review of Biology* 13: 274–300.

Da Rosa Pinto, A. A. 1959. Alguns novos records de aves para o Sul do Save e Moçambique, incluindo o de um genero novo para a sub-regiao da Africa do Sul, com a descricao de novas sub-especies. *Boletim da Sociedade de Estudos de Moçambique* 118: 15–25.

Davidson, J. 1907. Capercaillies in Moray. *Annals of Scottish Natural History*, 52.

Davies, A. K. 1985a. The British Mandarins – outstripping the ancestors? *British Trust for Ornithology Newsletter* 136: 10.

———. 1985b. A place for Mandarins. *Birds (Magazine of the Royal Society for the Protection of Birds)* 10: 12–14.

Davies, R. G., Peter, S. J. L. & **Munro, W. T.** 1980. *Preliminary Upland Game Bird Management Plan for British Columbia.* Fish & Wildlife Department, Ministry of Environment.

Davis, D. E. 1950. The growth of Starling *Sturnus vulgaris* populations. *Auk* 67: 460–5.

Davis, L. R. 1974. The Monk Parakeet: a potential threat to agriculture. *Proceedings of the 6th Vertebrate Pest Conference, 5–7 March, Anaheim, California,* 253–6.

Davis, M. 1951. Ocean vessels and the distribution of birds. *Auk* 68: 529–30.

Dawson, D. G. 1970. Estimation of grain loss due to Sparrows (*Passer domesticus*) in New Zealand. *New Zealand Journal of Agricultural Research* 13: 681–8.

Day, A. M. 1949a. A new look at exotics. *Field and Stream* 54: 54–5, 145–7.

———. 1949b. Introduction of exotic species. *Proceedings of the 38th Convention of the International Association of Game and Fish Conservation Commissioners,* 138–44.

Dearborn, N. 1912. The English Sparrow as a pest. *US Department of Agriculture, Farmers' Bulletin* No. 493.

Decary, R. 1962. Sur des introductions imprudentes d'animaux aux Mascareignes et à Madagascar. *Bulletin du Muséum National d'Histoire Naturelle* 34: 404–7.

Decker, B. 1980. The probable introduction of the Uapou Blue Lorikeet [*Vini ultramarina*] to Uahuka, Marquesas. *Elepaio* 41: 8.

Deignan, H. G. 1945. The birds of northern Thailand. *Bulletin US National Museum, Smithsonian Institution* No. 186.

———. 1963. Checklist of the birds of Thailand. *Bulletin, US National Museum, Smithsonian Institution* No. 226.

de Juana, E. 1985. Avadavat (*Amandava amandava*) [in Spain]. *British Birds* 78: 345.

Delacour, J. 1947. *Birds of Malaysia.* MacMillan: New York.

———. 1954–64. *Waterfowl of the World,* 4 vols. Country Life: London.

———. 1965. *The Pheasants of the World.* Country Life: London. (First published 1951.)

———. 1966. *Guide des Oiseaux de la Nouvelle Calédonie et de ses Dependances.* Delachaux et Niestlé: Neuchâtel.

Delacour, J. & **Amadon, D.** 1973. *Curassows and Related Birds.* American Museum of Natural History: New York.

Delacour, J. & **Jabouille, P.** 1927. Recherches ornithologiques dans les Provinces du Tranninh (Laos) de Thua-Thien et de Kontoum (Annam). *Archives d'Histoire Naturelle de la Sociétié Nationale et d'Acclimatation de France* 3: 1–216.

———. 1931. *Les Oiseaux de l'Indochine Française,* 4 vols. Exposition Coloniale Internationale: Paris.

Delacour, J. & **Mayr, E.** 1946. *Birds of the Philippines.* MacMillan: New York.

de la Cruz, C., da Silva, E., Perdigon M., Alcantud, V., Vázquez, F., Carbajo, F. & **Lope, F.** 1981. Bengali Rojo (*Estrilda amandava*). *Ardeola* 28: 165.

Dell, J. 1965. The Red-browed Finch, *Aegintha temporalis,* in Western Australia. *Western Australia Naturalist* 9: 160–9.

de Lope, F., Guerrero, J. & **de la Cruz, C.** 1984. [A new species of bird in the Iberian Peninsula: *Estrilda (Amandava) amandava.*] *Alauda* 52: 312 [in Spanish].

de Lope, F., Guerrero, J., de la Cruz, C. & **da Silva, E.** 1985. [Some aspects of the biology of the Red Avadavat in the basin of the Guadiana, Spain.] *Alauda* 53: 167–80 [in Spanish].

Delmotte, C. & **Delvaux, J.** 1981. La réintroduction du Grand Corbeau (*Corvus corax*) en Belgique, première nidification en liberté. *Aves* 18: 108–18.

Delvaux, J. 1978. A propos de la réintroduction du Grand Corbeau (*Corvus corax*) en Belgique. *Aves* 15: 196.

Dennis, R. 1964. Capture of moulting Canada Geese on the Beauly Firth. *Wildfowl Trust 15th Annual Report,* 71–4.

———. 1968 and 1969. Sea Eagles. *Fair Isle Bird Observatory Report* 21: 17–21; 22: 23–9. (See also *Scottish Birds* 9: 173–235 (1976).)

———. 1986. When perseverance pays off: the return of the Sea Eagle. *Country Life* 179: 388–9.

Denny, H. 1844. Bobwhite Quail in Norfolk. *Annals of the Magazine of Natural History* 13: 405–6.

de Pinto, O. 1933. O pardal [House Sparrow] em sua relaçôes com a agricultura. *Boletim de Biologia, São Paulo,* n.s., 1: 15–20.

de Ridder, M. 1982a. L'actualité ornithologique: la perruche à collier [Ring-necked Parakeet]. *Naturalistes Belges* 63: 174–9.

———. 1982b. [Alexander's parakeet: an advantage or a nuisance?] *Wielewaal* 48: 240–2, 370.

de Schauensee, R. Meyer. 1964. *The Birds of Colombia and Adjacent Areas of South and Central America.* Livingston: Narberth, Pennsylvania for Academy of Natural Sciences of Philadelphia.

———. 1966–70. *The Species of Birds of South America and their Distribution.* Livingston: Narberth, Pennsylvania for Academy of Natural Sciences of Philadelphia.

———. 1970. *A Guide to the Birds of South America.* Livingston Publishing Company: Wynnewood, Pennsylvania.

———. 1978. *A Guide to the Birds of Venezuela.* Princeton University Press: Princeton, New Jersey.

———. 1984. *The Birds of China.* Oxford University Press: Oxford.

Despeissis, A. J. 1906. A Starling scare. *Journal of Agriculture of Western Australia* 13: 238–40.

D'Evelyn, F. 1908. The English Sparrow question. *Journal of the South African Ornithologists' Union* 4: 131–2.

Devick, W. S. 1982. Status of the Nene populations on Hawaii and Maui between 1985 and 1980. *Proceedings of the Hawaii Volcanoes National Park Scientific Conference* 4: 60

De Vos, A. & **Petrides, G. A.** 1967. Biological effects caused by terrestrial vertebrates introduced into non-native environments. *Proceedings of the 10th IUCN Technical Meeting, Lucerne, June 1966*, 113–19. IUCN Publications, n.s. No. 9. Morges.

Dexter, J. S. 1922. The European Gray Partridge in Saskatchewan. *Auk* 39: 253–4.

Dhondt, A. A. 1976a. Bird notes from the Kingdom of Tonga. *Notornis* 23: 4–7.

———. 1976b. Bird observations in western Samoa. *Notornis* 23: 29–43.

———. 1977. Breeding and postnuptial molt of the Red-vented Bulbul in western Samoa. *Condor* 79: 257–60.

Diamond, A. W. & **Feare, C. J.** 1980. Past and present biogeography of central Seychelles birds. *Proceedings of the 4th Pan-African Ornithological Congress*, 89–98.

Diamond, J. M. & **Veitch, C. R.** 1981. Extinctions and introductions in the New Zealand avifauna: cause and effect? *Science* 211: 499–501.

Dickerson, L. M. 1938. The western frontier of the European Starling in the United States as of February, 1937. *Condor* 40: 118–23.

Dilks, P. J. 1974. Diet of Feral Pigeons (*Columba livia*) in Hawkes' Bay, New Zealand. *New Zealand Journal of Agricultural Research* 18: 87–90.

———. 1975. The breeding of the Feral Pigeon (*Columba livia*) in Hawkes' Bay, New Zealand. *Notornis* 22: 295–301.

Dinsmore, J. J. 1967. Ecology and behaviour of the Greater Bird of Paradise on Little Tobago Island. Unpublished MSc thesis, University of Wisconsin.

———. 1969. Dual calling by Birds of Paradise. *Auk* 86: 139–40.

———. 1970a. History and natural history of *Paradisaea apoda* on Little Tobago Island, West Indies. *Caribbean Journal of Science* 10: 93–100.

———. 1970b. Courtship & behaviour of the Greater Bird of Paradise. *Auk* 87: 305–21.

———. 1972. Avifauna of Little Tobago Island. *Quarterly Journal of the Florida Academy of Science* 35: 55–71.

Dolbeer, R. A. & **Stehn, R. A.** 1979. Population trends of Blackbirds and Starlings in North America, 1966–1976. *US Department of the Interior Fish and Wildlife Service, Special Scientific Report (Wildlife)*, No. 214 (99 pp.).

Donaggho, W. 1941. A report of ornithological observations made on Kauai. *Elepaio* 2: 52.

———. 1966. Indian Hill Mynah in Hawaii. *Elepaio* 26: 110–11.

———. 1970. Observations of the Edible Nest Swiftlet on Oahu. *Elepaio* 30: 64–5.

Donnelly, B. G. 1966. First arrival of the House Sparrow at Port Elizabeth. *Bee-eater* 17: 2.

———. 1974. House Sparrow : new distributional data. *Ostrich* 45: 137–8.

Dorian, H. 1965. The economic value of the Chukar Partridge to Nevada. *Proceedings of the Annual Conference of the Western Association of State Fish and Game Commissioners, Anchorage, Alaska, 7–8 July, 1965*, 55–6.

Dorst, J. 1964. L'introduction d'espèces animales et leur impact sur l'environment tropical. In *The Ecology of Man in the Tropical Environment (Proceedings of the 9th IUCN Technical Meeting)*, 245–53. IUCN Publications, n.s. No. 4. Morges.

Dorward, D. F. 1957. The Night-Heron colony in the Edinburgh Zoo. *Scottish Naturalist* 69: 32–6.

Dos Santos, J. R. 1968. The colony of Azure-winged Magpies in the Barca d'Alva region. *Cyanopica* 1: 1–28.

Dott, H. E. M. 1986. The spread of the House Sparrow *Passer domesticus* in Bolivia. *Ibis* 128: 132–7.

*★***Doughty, R.** 1978. The English Sparrow in the American landscape: a paradox in nineteenth century wildlife conservation. *University of Oxford School of Geography, Research Paper* No. 19 (36 pp.).

Douglas, G. W. 1972. Ecological problems caused by introduced animals and plants. *Victoria's Resources* 14: 1–6.

Dourdine, A. D. 1975. Acclimatization of the Rock Partridge (*Alectoris graeca*) in the Crimea and in Transcarpathia. *Transactions of the 10th Congress of the International Union of Game Biologists*, 361.

Dove, H. S. 1919. The Blackbird in Tasmania. *Emu* 19: 70.

Dove, R. S. & **Goodhart, H. J.** 1955. Field observations from the colony of Hong Kong. *Ibis* 97: 311–40.

Dowsett, R. J. 1971 and 1976. The spread of the House Sparrow in Zambia. *Bulletin of the Zambian Ornithological Society* 3: 50–2; 8: 2–6.

*★***Druett, J.** 1983. *Exotic Intruders: the Introduction of Plants and Animals into New Zealand.* Heinemann: Auckland.

Drummond, J. 1906. Introduced birds. *Transactions of the New Zealand Institute* 39: 227–52

———. 1907. Dates on which introduced birds have been liberated or have appeared in the different districts of New Zealand. *Transactions and Proceedings of the New Zealand Institute* 39: 503–8.

Due, L. A. & **Ruhr, C. E.** 1957. The Coturnix Quail in Tennessee. *Migrant* 28: 48–53.

Du Mont, P. A. 1945. The invasion of the Starling into Iowa. *Iowa Bird Life* 14: 30–3.

Dunmire, W. W. 1961. *Birds of the National Parks in*

Hawaii. Hawaii Natural History Association: Honolulu.

Dunning, R. A. 1974. Bird damage to sugar beet. *Annals of Applied Biology* 76: 325–35.

Du Pont, J. E. 1971. *Philippine Birds*. Monograph Series No. 2. Delaware Museum of Natural History. Greenville : Delaware.

———. 1972. Notes from western Samoa, including the description of a new parrot-finch (*Erythrura*). *Wilson Bulletin* 84: 375–6.

Duvigneaud, P. 1949. The introduction of exotic species. *Unesco International Technical Conference on Nature*. Mimeograph.

E

East, R. & **Pottinger, R. P.**1975. Starling predation on grass grub populations in Canterbury. *New Zealand Journal of Agricultural Research* 18: 417–52.

Eastbrook, A. H. 1907. The present status of the English Sparrow problem in America. *Auk* 24: 129–34.

Eaton, W. F. 1924. Decrease of the English Sparrow in eastern Massachusetts. *Auk* 41: 604–6.

Eckert, J. 1975. Feral Chestnut-breasted Finches in South Australia. *South Australian Ornithologist* 27: 23.

Edberg, R. 1962. Våra Kanadagäss. *Jaktsignalen* 19: 16–21.

Eddinger, R. C. 1967. A study of the breeding behaviour of the Mynah (*Acridotheres tristis* L.). *Elepaio* 28: 1–5, 11–15.

Edgar, W. H. 1974. Observations on Skylark damage to sugar beet and lettuce seedlings in East Anglia [England]. *Annals of Applied Biology* 76: 335–7.

Edminster, F. C. 1937. The Reeves Pheasant in New York. *Transactions of the 2nd North American Wildlife Conference* 2: 490–3.

Edwards, H. V. 1925. Birds of a New South Wales garden. *Emu* 24: 282–6.

Ehrhorn, E. M. 1925. Bird introductions into Hawaii. *Hawaiian Board of Agriculture and Forestry Report for 1924*, 42–3.

Eikhoudt, H. 1973. Nijlganzen boven Friesland [Egyptian Geese in the Netherlands]. *Vanellus* 26: 202–5.

Einarsen, A. S. 1942. Specific results from Ring-necked Pheasant studies in the Pacific northwest. *Transactions of the 7th North American Wildlife Conference*, 130–8.

———. 1945. Some factors affecting Ring-necked Pheasant density. *Murrelet* 26: 2–9.

Eisentraut, A. 1935. Biologische Studien im bolivianischen Chaco, VI, Beitrag zur Biologie Vogelfauna. *Mitteilungen aus dem Zoologischen Museum in Berlin* 20: 367–443.

Elkins, W. A & **Nelson, U. C.** 1957. Wildlife introductions and transplants in Alaska. *Science in Alaska, 1954*, 29–30.

Elliott, B. G. 1980. First observation of the European Starling in Hawaii. *Elepaio* 40: 100–1.

Elliott, H. 1970. Birds of the world: lovebirds. *Bird World* 4: 1236–9.

Elliott, H. N. 1964. Starlings in the Pacific northwest. *Proceedings of the 2nd Vertebrate Pest Control Conference, 4–5 May 1964, Anaheim, California*, 29–39.

Elliott, J. J. & **Arbid, R. S.** 1953. Origin and status of the House Finch in the eastern United States. *Auk* 70: 31–7.

Ellis, J. A. & **Anderson, W. L.** 1963. Attempts to establish Pheasants in southern Illinois. *Journal of Wildlife Management* 27: 225–39.

Ellis, M. 1975. Birds introduced into East Africa. *Avicultural Magazine* 81: 115–16.

Ellison, A. 1907. Little Owls breeding in Hertfordshire. *Zoologist*, 430.

Ellwood, J. 1971. Goose conservation. *Wildfowlers' Association of Great Britain and Ireland Report and Yearbook, 1970–1971*, 59–60.

★**Elton, C. S.** 1927. *Animal Ecology*. Sidgwick and Jackson: London.

★———. 1958. *The Ecology of Invasions by Animals and Plants*. Methuen: London.

England, M. D. 1970. Escapes. *Avicultural Magazine* 76: 150–2.

———. 1974. A further review of the problem of 'escapes'. *British Birds* 67: 177–97, 393–4.

Ennion, H. E. 1962. Notes on birds seen in Aden and the Western Aden Protectorate. *Ibis* 104: 560–62.

Ennis, T. 1965. The arrival and spread of the Collared Dove (*Streptopelia decaocto*) in Northern Ireland. *Irish Naturalists' Journal* 15: 63–7.

Equipos del Centro de Migracíon y de la Cátedra de Cordados. 1974. Capturas y observaciones reiteradas de Bengali Amandava (*Estrilda (Amandava) amandava*) en las cercanías de Madrid. *Ardeola* 20: 385–6.

Escott, C. J. & **Holmes, D. A.** 1980. The avifauna of Sulawesi, Indonesia; faunistic notes and additions. *Bulletin of the British Ornithologists' Club* 100: 189–94.

Etchécopar, R. D. 1955. L'acclimatation des oiseaux en France au cours des 100 dernières années. *La Terre et La Vie* 102: 42–53.

Etchécopar, R. D. & **Hüe, F.** 1964. *Les Oiseaux du Nord de l'Afrique de la Mer Rouge aux Canaries*. N. Boubée: Paris.

———. 1978. *Les Oiseaux de Chine, de Mongolie, et de Corée: Non-Passereaux*. Les Editions du Pacific: Tahiti.

F

Faber, L. A. 1946. The history of stocking and

management of the Ring-necked Pheasant in the state of Iowa. *Iowa Conservationist* 5: 73, 75, 78, 81, 84, 93; 6: 97, 103.

Fabricius, E. 1970. A survey of the Canada Goose (*Branta canadensis*) in Sweden. *Zoologisk Revy* 32: 19–25.

———. 1982. Kanadagåsens förekomst och ekologie. *Vår Fågelvarld*, Suppl. 9: 53–6.

———. 1983a. [Canada Geese in Sweden.] *Fauna och Flora* 75: 205–21 [in Swedish, with English summary].

———. 1983b. [The Canada Goose in Sweden.] *Statens Naturvårdsverket Report* No. 1678 (85 pp.) [in Swedish, with English summary].

Falla, R. A., Sibson, R. B. & Turbott, E. G. 1979. *A Field Guide to the Birds of New Zealand.* Collins: London.

Farley, F. L. 1935. The European Starling (*Sturnus vulgaris*) in Alberta. *Canadian Field-Naturalist* 49: 119.

Fea, L. 1898–9. Dalle Isole del Cabo-Verde. *Bollettino della Società Geologica Italiana*, series 2, 11: 356–68, 537–52; 12: 7–26, 163–74, 302–12.

Feare, C. J. 1979. Ecology of Bird Island, Seychelles. *Atoll Research Bulletin* 226: 1–29.

———. 1984. *The Starling.* Oxford University Press: Oxford.

Feare, C. J. & Watson, J. 1984. Occurrence of migrant birds in the Seychelles. In D. R. Stoddart ed., *Biogeography and Ecology of the Seychelles Islands*, 559–74. W. Junk: The Hague.

Feilden, H. W. 1889. On the birds of Barbados. *Ibis*, series 6, 1: 477–503.

Ferguson, A. D. 1913. Introductions of foreign game birds into the southern San Joaquin and Tributary section. *California Division of Fish and Game, Game Bulletin* 1: 35–40.

Fetherston, K. F 1949. A study of the Ring-necked Pheasant on Pelee Island, Ontario. Unpublished thesis, Cornell University (170 pp.).

Ffrench, R. P. 1976. *A Guide to the Birds of Trinidad and Tobago.* Harwood Books: Pennsylvania (first published 1973; Livingston: Wynnewood, Pennsylvania).

Ffrench, R. P. & Ffrench, M. 1966. Recent records of birds in Trinidad and Tobago. *Wilson Bulletin* 78: 5–11.

Fichter, G. 1970. The new nature of Florida. *Florida Wildlife* (December): 10–15

Field, L. B. 1938. Mynah birds. *Fiji Agricultural Journal* 9: 19–22.

Finsch, O. 1887. Ein Besuch auf Diego Garcia im Indischen Ozean. *Deutsche Geographische Blatter, Bremen, 1887*, 30–42.

Fisher, H. I. 1948. The question of avian introductions in Hawaii. *Pacific Science* 2: 59–64.

———. 1951. The avifauna of Niihau Island, Hawaiian Archipelago. *Condor* 53: 31–42.

Fisher, H. I. & Baldwin, P. H. 1945. A recent trip to Midway Islands, Pacific Ocean. *Elepaio* 6: 11–13.

———. 1947. Notes on the Red-billed Leiothrix in Hawaii. *Pacific Science* 1: 45–51.

Fisher, J. 1953. The Collared Turtle Dove in Europe. *British Birds* 46: 153–81.

Fisher, J., Simon, N. & Vincent, J. 1969. *The Red Book – Wildlife in Danger.* Collins: London.

Fisk, E. J. 1966. A happy newcomer in a fruitful land. *Florida Naturalist* 39: 10–11.

———. 1968. White-winged Doves breeding in Florida. *Florida Naturalist* 41: 126.

Fisk, L. H. & Crabtree, D. M. 1974. Black-hooded Parakeet: new feral breeding species in California. *American Birds* 28: 11–13.

Fitter, R. S. R. 1950. Man's additions to the British fauna. *Discovery* 11: 58–62.

★———. 1959. *The Ark in Our Midst.* Collins: London.

———. 1964. *Naturalized Birds.* In A. Landsborough Thomson ed., *A New Dictionary of Birds*, 505–7. Nelson: London.

———. 1967. Animal introductions and their ecological effects in Europe. *Proceedings of the 10th IUCN Technical Meeting, Lucerne, June 1966*, 177–80. IUCN Publication, n.s. No. 9. Morges.

Fitzwater, W. D. 1971. The Weaver Finch of Hispaniola. *Pest Control* 39: 19.

Fleischer, R. C. 1982. Clutch size of Costa Rican House Sparrows. *Journal of Field Ornithology* 53: 280–1.

Fletcher, J. A. 1909. Stray feathers: Cleveland, Tasmania, notes. *Emu* 9: 95.

★**Flieg, G. M.** 1971. The European Tree Sparrow in the western hemisphere – its range, distribution and life history. *The Audubon Bulletin (Illinois Audubon Society)* 157: 2–10.

Flower, S. S. 1930. The European Starling in North America. *Ibis*, series 12, 6: 373–4.

———. 1933. Notes on some birds in Egypt. *Ibis*, series 13, 3: 34–46.

Flower, S. S. & Nichol, M. J. 1908. *Wild Birds of the Giza Gardens 1898–1908.* Government of India: Cairo.

Flux, J. E. C. & Flux, M. M. 1981. Population dynamics and age structure of Starlings (*Sturnus vulgaris*) in New Zealand. *New Zealand Journal of Ecology* 4: 65–72.

Fog, M. 1973. *Kanadensisk gås i Europa.* Vildtbiologisk Station: Kalø.

Forbes, H. O. 1893. Birds inhabiting the Chatham Islands. *Ibis*, series 6, 5: 521–46.

Forbes, J. E. & Brown, L. P. 1974 The New York Monk Parakeet retrieval program. *Transactions of the Northeastern Fish and Wildlife Conference, 25–28 February 1974*, 1–8.

Forbes-Watson, A. 1972. Birds naturalized in East Africa. *East Africa Natural History Society Bulletin*, 144–5.

Forbush, E. H. 1916. *The Starling.* Massachusetts State Department of Agriculture Circular No. 45 (23 pp.).

Forshaw, J. 1969. *Australian Parrots.* Lansdowne: Melbourne.

———. 1980. *Parrots of the World.* Lansdowne: Melbourne.

Frank, H. 1970. Über die Einburgerung von Wild-puten [Wild Turkey]. *Proceedings of the 8th International Congress of Game Biologists,* 382–6.

Frazier, F. P. 1964. New records of Cattle Egrets in Peru. *Auk* 81: 553–4

Freeland, D. B. 1973. Some food preferences and aggressive behaviour by Monk Parakeets. *Wilson Bulletin* 85: 332–4.

French, W. 1957. Birds of the Solomon Islands. *Ibis* 99: 126.

Friedman, H. 1929. *The Cowbirds: a Study in the Biology of Social Parasitism.* Charles Thomas: Springfield, Illinois.

Frings, C. & **Frings, S.** 1965. Random jottings about Mynahs. *Elepaio* 26: 48–9.

Frisch, J. D. 1982. *Aves Brasileiras,* Vol. 1. Dalgas-Ecoltec Ecologia Técnica e Comércio: São Paulo.

Frisch, S. & **Frisch, J. D.** 1964. *Aves Brasileiras.* Irmãos Vitale S. A.: São Paulo.

Frith, H. J. 1952. Notes on the pigeons of the Richmond River, New South Wales. *Emu* 52: 89–99.

★———. 1979. Acclimatization. In H. J. Frith, *Wildlife Conservation,* 137–95. Angus and Robertson: Sydney. (First published 1973.)

Frith, H. J. & **McKean, J. L.** 1975. Races of the introduced Spotted Turtledove, *Streptopelia chinensis* (Scopoli), in Australia. *Australian Journal of Zoology* 23: 295–306.

Froggatt, W. W. 1912. The Starling: a study in agricultural zoology. *Agricultural Gazette of New South Wales* 23: 610–16.

Frost, P. 1983. Birds and man. *Bokmakierie* 35: 26–32.

Fry, C. H. 1961. Notes on the birds of Annobon and other islands in the Gulf of Guinea. *Ibis* 103a: 267–76.

Fuller, C. 1909. The English Sparrow. *Natal Agricultural Journal* 7: 76–80.

Fuller, W. A. 1955. First record of the Starling in North West Territories. *Canadian Field-Naturalist* 69: 27.

G

Gabrielson, I. N. & **Lincoln, F. C.** 1959. *The Birds of Alaska.* Stackpole: Harrisburg, Pennsylvania; Wildlife Management Institute: Washington, DC.

Gabrielson, N. & **Kalmbach, E. R.** 1921. Economic value of the Starling in the United States. *US Department of Agriculture Bulletin* No. 868.

Gadow, H. & **Gardiner, J. S.** 1907. The Percy Sladen Trust Expedition to the Indian Ocean. Aves; with some notes on the distribution of land-birds of the Seychelles. *Transactions of the Linnean Society of London, Zoology* 11–12: 103–10.

Galbraith, I. C. J. & **Galbraith, E. H.** 1962. Land birds of Guadalcanal and the San Cristoval group, eastern Solomon Islands. *Bulletin of the British Museum (Natural History), Zoology Series* No. 9.

Galbreath, D. S. & **Moreland, R.** 1953. The Chukar Partridge in Washington. *Washington State Game Department Biological Bulletin* No. 11 (54 pp.).

Gallagher, M. D. 1960. Bird notes from Christmas Island, Pacific Ocean. *Ibis* 102: 489–502.

Gallagher, M. & **Woodcock, M. W.** 1980. *The Birds of Oman.* Quartet Books: London.

Gaselee, J. 1963. The precious Né-né. *Animals* 1: 15–18.

Gault, B. T. 1922. *Check List of the Birds of Illinois.* Illinois Audubon Society: Chicago.

Gaymer, R., Blackman, R. A. A., Dawson, P. G., Penny, M. & **Penny, C. M.** 1969. Endemic birds of the Seychelles. *Ibis* 111: 157–76.

Gebhardt, E. 1944. *Passer d. domesticus* in Südamerika. *Ornithologische Monatsberichte* 52: 95–8.

———. 1954. Die gegenwärte Verbreitung von Haussperling, Star und Buchfink [House Sparrow, Starling and Chaffinch] in Südafrika. *Journal für Ornithologie* 95: 58–60.

———. 1959. Europäische Vögel in überseeischen Ländern. *Bonner Zoologische Beiträge* 10: 310–41.

Gentry, T. E. 1878. *The House Sparrow at Home and Abroad.* Claxton, Remsen & Haffelfinger: Philadelphia.

Genung, W. G. & **Lewis, R. H.** 1982. The Black Francolin in the Everglades agricultural area. *Florida Field Naturalist* 10: 65–9.

George, W. 1971. Canary-winged Parakeets. *Florida Naturalist* 44: 25–6.

Gerhart, J. D. 1976. Indian Myna (*Acridotheres tristis*) – new distributional data. *Ostrich* 47: 222.

Geroudet, P. 1974. Premiers pas vers la réintroduction du Gypaète Barbu [Bearded Vulture] dans les Alpes. *Nos Oiseaux* 32: 300–10.

———. 1977. The reintroduction of the Bearded Vulture in the Alps. In R. D. Chancellor ed., *Report of the Proceedings of World Conference on Birds of Prey, Vienna, 1975,* 392–7. International Council for Bird Preservation: Cambridge.

———. 1981a. Notes sur le statut actuel du Gypaète Barbu *Gypaetus barbatus* en Europe et autour de la Mediterranée. In *Rapaces Mediterranée,* 73–5. Colloque d'Evisa en Corse.

———. 1981b. La perruche à collier [Ring-neck parakeet], un souci nouveau? *Nos Oiseaux* 36: 37.

Gerstell, R. 1937. The status of the Ring-necked Pheasant in Pennsylvania. *Transactions of the 2nd North American Wildlife Conference,* 505–11.

———. 1938. An analysis of the reported returns obtained from release of 30,000 artificially propagated Ring-necked Pheasants and Bobwhite Quail. *Transactions of the 3rd North American Wildlife Conference*, 724–9.

———. 1940. The Hungarian and Chukar Partridges – their status in Pennsylvania. *Pennsylvania Game News* 11: 3, 32.

———. 1941. The Hungarian and Chukar Partridges in Pennsylvania. *Transactions of the 5th North American Wildlife Conference*, 405–9.

Gibson, A. R., Baker, A. J. & Moeed, A. 1984. Morphometric variation in introduced populations of the Common Myna (*Acridotheres tristis*): an application of the jackknife to principal component analysis. *Systematic Zoology* 33: 408–21.

Gibson, D. D. & Hogg, N. D. 1982. Direct recovery in Alaska of California-banded Cattle Egret. *American Birds* 36: 335.

Gibson, E. 1918. Further ornithological notes from the neighbourhood of Cape San Antonio, Province of Buenos Aires. Part 1. Passerines. *Ibis*, series 10, 6: 363–415.

Gibson, J. D. 1961. Colombo Crows in Victoria. *Emu* 61: 244–5.

Gibson-Hill, C. A. 1947. Field notes on the birds of Christmas Island, Indian Ocean. *Bulletin of the Raffles Museum* 18: 87–165.

———. 1949a. The birds of the Cocos–Keeling Islands, Indian Ocean. *Ibis* 91: 221–43.

———. 1949b. Annotated checklist of the birds of Malaya. *Bulletin of the Raffles Museum* 20: 1–299.

———. 1949c. A checklist of the birds of Singapore Island. *Bulletin of the Raffles Museum* 21: 132–83.

———. 1950. Myna matters. *Malay Nature Journal* 5: 58–75.

———. 1952. Notes on the alien birds recorded from Singapore Island. *Bulletin of the Raffles Museum* 24: 241–57.

Giglioli, H. 1881. Notes on the avifauna of Italy. *Ibis* 4: 181.

Gigstead, G. 1937. Habits of the Wisconsin Pheasant. *Wilson Bulletin* 44: 28–34.

Gill, E. L. 1952. The European Starling in the Cape. *Ostrich* 23: 129–30.

Gill, F. B. 1967. Birds of Rodriguez Island, Indian Ocean. *Ibis* 109: 383–90.

Gillespie, G. D. 1982a. Greenfinch (*Carduelis chloris*) feeding behaviour and impact on a rapeseed crop in Oamaru, New Zealand. *New Zealand Journal of Zoology* 9: 481–6.

———. 1982b. Factors affecting daily seed intake of the Greenfinch (*Carduelis chloris*). *New Zealand Journal of Zoology* 9: 295–300.

Gilliard, E. T. 1958. Feathered dancers of Little Tobago [Greater Bird of Paradise]. *National Geographic Magazine* 114: 328–440.

Ginn, W. E. 1961. Ring-necked Pheasant becomes naturalized. *Outdoor Indiana* 14: 16–17.

———. 1962. The Ring-necked Pheasant in Indiana: history, research and management. *Bulletin of the Indiana State Department of Conservation* No. 6 (107 pp.).

Gladstone, H. S. 1906. Capercaillie in Ayrshire. *Annals of Scottish Natural History*, 116.

———. 1921a. The last of the indigenous Scottish Capercaillie. *Scottish Naturalist*, 169–77.

———. 1921b. A 16th century portrait of the Pheasant. *British Birds* 15: 67–9.

———. 1923–4. Introduction of the Ring-necked Pheasant to Great Britain. *British Birds* 17: 36–7; 18: 84.

———. 1926. Birds mentioned in the Acts of the Parliaments of Scotland, 1124–1707. *Transactions and Journal of the Proceedings of the Dumfries and Galloway Natural History and Antiquarian Society*, series 3, 12: 10–46.

Glauert, L. 1956. Problems of conservation. (c) Introduction of exotics. In: Fauna conservation in Western Australia. *Western Australia Fisheries and Fauna Bulletin* No. 1.

Glazener, W. C. 1967. Management of the Rio Grande Turkey. In O. H. Hewitt ed., *The Wild Turkey and its Management*, Ch. 15, 453–92. Wildlife Society: Washington, DC.

Glenister, A. G. 1951. *The Birds of the Malay Peninsula, Singapore and Penang*. Oxford University Press: London and Kuala Lumpur.

Gliesch, R. 1924. O pardal europeo [House Sparrow], Estudo sôbre sua divulgação, especialmente no Estado do Rio Grande do Sul. *Egatea* 9: 1–8.

Godfrey, R. 1930. Indian Myna and English Starling in Natal. *Blythswood Review* 7: 174–5.

———. 1930. Alien birds in South Africa. *Blythswood Review* 11: 327–8.

Godfrey, W. E. 1949. European Starling reaches the Pacific coast. *Canadian Field-Naturalist* 63: 165.

———. 1966. *The Birds of Canada*. National Museum of Canada, Bulletin No. 203 (Biological series No. 73). Bryant Press: Toronto. (Reprinted 1974 by Information Canada: Ottawa.)

Gompertz, T. 1957. Some observations on the Feral Pigeon in London. *Bird Study* 4: 2–13.

Goodall, J. D., Johnson, A. W. & Philippi, R. A. 1946–57. *Las Aves de Chile, su Conocimento y sus Costumbres*. Platt Establecimentos Gráficos: Buenos Aires.

Gooding, C. D. & Walton, C. R. 1963. The Sparrow invasion of 1962. *Journal of Agriculture of Western Australia* 4: 412–18.

Goodman, S. M. 1982. The introduction and subspecies of Rose-ringed Parakeet in Egypt. *Bulletin of the British Ornithologists' Club* 102: 16–18.

Goodrum, P. 1949. Status of the Bobwhite in the

United States. *Transactions of the 14th North American Wildlife Conference*, 359–67.

Goodwin, D. 1952. The colour varieties of Feral Pigeons. *London Bird Report* (1951) 16: 35–6.

———. 1954. Notes on Feral Pigeons. *Avicultural Magazine* 60: 190–213.

———. 1956. The problems of birds escaping from captivity. *British Birds* 49: 339–49.

———. 1970. *Pigeons and Doves of the World*. British Museum (Natural History): London.

———. 1976a. *Crows of the World*. British Museum (Natural History): London; Cornell University Press: Ithaca.

———. 1976b. On some characters of Rock and Feral Pigeons. *Pigeon Science & Genetics Newsletter* 2: 9–14.

———. 1978. *Birds of Man's World*. British Museum (Natural History): London.

———. 1982a. On the status of the Green Pheasant. *Bulletin of the British Ornithologists' Club* 102: 35–7.

———. 1982b. *Estrildid Finches of the World*. British Museum (Natural History): London; Oxford University Press: Oxford.

———. 1983. Notes on feral Rose-ringed Parakeets. *Avicultural Magazine* 89: 84–93.

Gore, M. E. J. 1964. A new Borneo bird [*Passer montanus*]. *Journal of the Sabah Society* 2: 109.

———. 1968. Checklist of the birds of Sabah, Borneo. *Ibis* 110: 165–96.

Gore, M. E. J. & **Won, P.** 1971. *The Birds of Korea*. Taewon Publishing Co.: Seoul, Korea; Charles E. Tuttle: Tokyo.

Gore, R. & **Doubilet, D.** 1976. Florida, Noah's Ark for exotic newcomers. *National Geographic Magazine* 150: 538–58.

Gorman, M. L. 1972. The origin of the avifauna of urban and suburban Suva, Fiji. *Fiji Agricultural Journal* 34: 35–8.

———. 1975. Habitats of the land birds of Viti Levu, Fiji Islands. *Ibis* 117: 152–61.

———. 1979. *Island Ecology*. Chapman & Hall: London.

Gossard, G. 1956. The Japanese Bush Warbler in Hawaii. *Elepaio* 17: 2–3.

Gosse, P. 1938. *St Helena, 1502–1938*. Cassell: London.

Gottschalk, H. 1972. Chaffinches. *Cape Bird Club Newsletter* 102: 3.

Gottschalk, J. S. 1966. Our experiences with exotics. *Virginia Wildlife* 27: 14–15, 18–21.

———. 1967. The introduction of exotic animals into the United States. *Proceedings of the 10th IUCN Technical Meeting, Lucerne, June 1966*, 1–29. IUCN Publications n.s. No. 9. Morges.

Graczyk, R., Fedorenko, A. P., Loskot, V. M. & **Chuprin, S. L.** 1975. Introduction of the Blackbird into Kiev Ukrainian-SSR, USSR, from Poznan, Poland. *Vestnik Zoologii* 3: 29–32.

Graham, S. A. & **Hesterberg, G.** 1948. The influence of climate on the Ring-necked Pheasant. *Journal of Wildlife Management* 12: 9–14.

Grahame, I. 1980. Re-introduction of captive-bred cheer pheasants *Catreus wallichi*. *International Zoo Yearbook* 20: 36–40.

Gramlich, F. 1980. The Cape Elizabeth Monk Parakeets. *Maine Quarterly Audubon Magazine*.

Grant, A. 1983. Predation of Goldfinch (*Carduelis carduelis*) by New Zealand Kingfisher (*Halcyon sancta*). *Notornis* 30: 318.

Grant, G. S. 1982. Common Mynahs attack Black Noddies and White Terns on Midway Atoll. *Elepaio* 42: 97–8.

Grant, J. 1949. The European Starling in the Canadian Rockies. *Canadian Field-Naturalist* 63: 117.

Grant, W. & **Cubby, J.** 1973. The Capercaillie reintroduction experiment at Grizedale [England]. *Wildfowlers Association of Great Britain and Ireland, Report and Yearbook 1972–1973*, 96–8.

Grasby, W. C. 1906. Beware of the Starling. *Western Australian* (22 February).

Gray, R. 1882. The introduction of Reeve's Pheasant into Scottish game preserves. *Proceedings of the Royal Society of Edinburgh* 7: 239.

Greely, F., Labisky, R. F. & **Mann, S. H.** 1962. Distribution and abundance of Pheasants in Illinois. *Illinois Natural History Survey, Biological Notes* 47: 1–16.

Green, R. H. & **Mollison, B. C.** 1961. Birds of Port Davey and the south coast of Tasmania. *Emu* 61: 223–36.

Green, R. J. 1984. Native and exotic birds in a suburban habitat. *Australian Wildlife Research* 11: 181–90.

Green, W. E. & **Hendrickson, G. O.** 1938. The European Partridge in north-central Iowa. *Iowa Bird Life* 8: 18–22.

Greene, R. & **Ellis, R.** 1971. Merriam's Turkey. In T. W. Mussehl & F. W. Howell eds, *Game Management in Montana*, Ch. 20, 167–73. Montana Fish and Game Department: Helena.

Greenhalgh, C. M. 1954. Some possible factors in Chukar introductions into Utah. *Proceedings of the 33rd Annual Conference of the Western Association of State Game and Fish Commissioners, 1–3 June, 1953*, 147–9.

Greenhalgh, C. M. & **Nielson, L. R.** 1953. Chukar introductions into Utah. *Proceedings of the 32nd Annual Conference of the Western Association of State Game and Fish Commissioners*, 165–7.

Gregory-Smith, R. 1982. Bird species introduced to Australia. *Adjutant* 12: 51–9.

Grimm, W. C. & **Shuler, J.** 1967. First sight record of House Finch in South Carolina. *Chat* 31: 45–6.

Grinnell, J. 1906. Foolish introductions of foreign birds. *Condor* 8: 58–9.

———. 1911. The linnet of the Hawaiian Islands: a problem in speciation. *University of California Publication (Zoology)* No. 7: 179–95.

———. 1921. 'Chinese Starling' (*A. cristatellus*) in Vancouver, British Columbia, Canada. *Condor* 23: 170.

———. 1925. Risks incurred in the introduction of alien game birds. *Science* 61: 621–3.

———. 1929. Ringed Turtle Dove at large in Los Angeles. *Condor* 31: 130–1.

———. 1930. McAtee on naturalizing birds. *Condor* 32: 133–4.

———. 1936. Further note on the status of the Skylark on Vancouver Island. *Condor* 38: 122.

Grinnell, J., Bryant, H. C. & **Storer, T. I.** 1918. *The Game Birds of California.* University of California Press: Berkeley.

Grote, H. 1926. Der Haussperling der Komoren-Insel Moheli. *Ornithologische Monatsberichte* 34: 147–8.

Groves, F. W. 1956. Report of the committee on the introduction of exotic animals. *Proceedings of the 46th Annual Convention of the International Association of Game and Fish Conservation Commissioners,* 77–85.

Gruson, E. S. 1976. *Checklist of the Birds of the World.* Collins: London.

Grzimek, B. 1972. *Animal Encyclopaedia: Birds,* Vol. 7, Part 1. Van Nostrand Reinhold: London.

Guého, J. & **Staub, F.** 1983. Observations botaniques et ornithologiques à l'atoll d'Agaléga. *Proceedings of the Royal Society of Arts and Sciences of Mauritius* 4: 15–110.

Guest, S. J. 1973. A reproductive biology and natural history of the Japanese White-eye (*Zosterops j. japonica*) in urban Oahu. *Island Ecosystems Technical Report* No. 29 (95 pp.).

Guiguet, C. J. 1952a. European Starling. *Victoria Naturalist* 9: 22.

———. 1952b. Another record of the Crested Mynah on Vancouver Island. *Victoria Naturalist* 9: 52–3.

———. 1952c. The European Starling on Vancouver Island. *Canadian Field-Naturalist* 66: 37.

———. 1961 and 1983. *The Birds of British Columbia.* 4. *Upland Game Birds.* 2. *Sparrows and Finches.* Handbook No. 42, series 10 (122 pp.). British Columbia Provincial Museum, Department of Recreation and Conservation: Victoria.

⋆**Guild, E.** 1938. Tahitian aviculture: acclimatisation of foreign birds. *Avicultural Magazine,* series 5, 3: 8–11.

———. 1940. Western Bluebirds in Tahiti. *Avicultural Magazine,* series 5, 5: 284–5.

Gullion, G. W. 1951. Birds of the southern Willamette Valley, Oregon. *Condor* 53: 129–49.

———. 1956. The current status of the Starling in Nevada. *Condor* 58: 446.

———. 1965. A critique concerning foreign game bird introductions. *Wilson Bulletin* 77: 409–14.

Gullion, G. W. & **Christensen, G. C.** 1957. A review of the distribution of gallinaceous game birds in Nevada. *Condor* 59: 128–38.

Gundlach, J. 1878a. [Bobwhite Quail in Puerto Rico.] *Journal für Ornithologie* 26: 161.

———. 1878b. Apuntes para la Fauna Puerto-Riqueña. Aves. *Anales de la Sociedad Española de Historia Natural* 7: 141–234, 343–422.

Gunther, R. T. 1917. Note on the acclimatisation of the Black Swan. *Ibis,* series 10, 5: 241–4.

Guppy, P. L. 1931. Colonization of *P. apoda* on Little Tobago. *Avicultural Magazine,* series 4, 9: 5–8.

Gurney, J. H., Russell, C. & **Coues, E.** 1885. *The House Sparrow.* Gurney and Jackson: London.

Gurr, L. 1953. A recent attempt to introduce Virginian Quail into New Zealand. *Notornis* 5: 164.

———. 1954. A study of the Blackbird, *Turdus merula,* in New Zealand. *Ibis* 96: 225–61.

Guth, R. W. 1971. New bird records from Guadeloupe and its dependencies. *Auk* 88: 180–2.

Guthrie, D. 1903. Canada Geese in the Outer Hebrides. *Annals of Scottish Natural History,* 119.

Gwynn, A. M. 1953. Some additions to the Macquarie Island list of birds. *Emu* 53: 150–2.

H

Hachisuka, M. U. 1924. Notes on some birds from Egypt. *Ibis,* series 11, 6: 771–3.

———. 1934. *The Birds of the Philippine Islands, with Notes on the Mammal Fauna,* Part 3. H. F. & G. Witherby: London.

Hachisuka, M. & **Udagawa, T.** 1951. Contribution to the ornithology of Formosa. *Quarterly Journal of the Taiwan Museum* 4: 1–180.

Haddon, M. 1984. A re-analysis of hybridization between Mallards and Grey Ducks in New Zealand. *Auk* 101: 190–1.

Haemig, P. D. 1978. Aztec Emperor Auitzotl and the Great-tailed Grackle. *Biotropica* 10: 11–17.

⋆———. 1979. Secret of the Painted Jay. *Biotropica* 11: 81–7.

Haensel, J. 1975. Ornithologische Eindrücke Während eines Studienaufenthalts in Agypten im Herbst 1971. *Beiträge zur Vogelkunde* 21: 312–22.

Haffer, J. 1975. *Avifauna of Northwestern Colombia, South America.* Bonner Zoologische Monographien No. 7. Zoologisches Forschungsinstitut und Museum Alexander Koenig: Bonn.

Haftorn, S. 1966. *Våre Fugler.* Mortensen: Oslo.

Hagerup, A.T. 1891. *The Birds of Greenland.* Little, Brown: Boston, Mass.

Halazon, G. 1949 and 1950. Progress reports: studies of the introduction, release and survival of Capercaillie and Black Grouse. *Wisconsin Wildlife Research*

Quarterly Progress Reports 8(3): 92–7; 8(4): 92–7.

Halloran, A. F. & **Halloran, A. G.** 1970. Feral chickens of French Polynesia. *Proceedings of the Oklahoma Academy of Science* 49: 169–70.

Halloran, A. F. & **Howard, J. A.** 1956. Aransas Refuge wildlife introductions. *Journal of Wildlife Management* 20: 460–1.

Hamel, J. 1970. Hybridization of Eastern and Crimson Rosellas in Otago. *Notornis* 17: 126–9.

Hamel, P. B. & **Wagner, S. J.** 1984. Status of the House Finch in South Carolina, including discovery of two nests in Clemson. *Chat* 48: 5–7.

Hamerstrom, F. N. 1936. A study of the nesting habits of the Ring-necked Pheasant in north-west Iowa. *Iowa State College Journal of Science* 10: 173–203.

Hamilton, A. 1894. Notes on a visit to Macquarie Island. *Transactions of the New Zealand Institute* 27: 559–79.

Hamilton, J. E. 1944. House Sparrows in the Falkland Islands. *Ibis* 86: 553–4.

Hamilton, S. & **Johnston, R. F.** 1978. Evolution in the House Sparrow. 6. Variability and niche width. *Auk* 95: 313–23.

Hancock, J. & **Elliott, H.** 1978. *The Herons of the World*. London Editions: London.

Hankla, D. J. 1968. Summary of Canada Goose transplant program on nine national wildlife refuges in the south east, 1953–65. In R. L. Hine & C. Schoenfeld eds, *Canada Goose Management*. Dembar Educational Research Service Inc.: Madison, Wisconsin.

Hanson, C. L. 1963. Exotic game bird introduction program in Ohio: a preliminary evaluation. *Game Research, Ohio* 2: 205–14.

Hanson, H. G. 1946. The Pheasant in Oklahoma. *Oklahoma Game and Fish News* 2: 8–9.

Hardman, J. A. 1974. Biology of the Skylark. *Annals of Applied Biology* 76: 337–41.

Hardy, A. D. 1928. Skylarks and Nightingales in Australia. *Emu* 27: 300–1. (See also *Melbourne Argus*, 7 January, 1928.)

Hardy, J. W. 1964. Ringed Parakeets nesting in Los Angeles, California. *Condor* 66: 445–7.

——. 1969. A taxonomic revision of the New World jays. *Condor* 71: 360–75.

*——. 1973. Feral exotic birds in southern California. *Wilson Bulletin* 85: 506–12.

Hargreaves, A. 1943. Introduction of Sparrows. *Victorian Naturalist* 60: 96.

Harman, I. 1963a. Skylark 'centenary'. *Australian Aviculturist*, 72.

——. 1963b. A dandy among British finches: the Goldfinch. *Australian Aviculturist*, 113.

——. 1963c. A sturdy Britisher: the Greenfinch. *Australian Aviculturist*, 122.

Harper, H. T. 1963. The Red-legged Partridge in California. *Proceedings of the 43rd Annual Conference*

of the Western Association of State Game and Fish Commissioners, 193–5.

Harper, H. T., Harry, B. H. & **Bailer, W. D.** 1958. The Chukar Partridge in California. *California Fish and Game* 44: 5–50.

Harpham, P. 1953. Tantalus bird notes: the Shama Thrush. *Elepaio* 13: 74–6.

Harrison, J. 1952. The distribution of the Peat Partridge, *Perdix perdix sphagnatorum*, in North-West Germany. *Bulletin of the British Ornithologists' Club* 72: 53–4.

Harrisson, T. 1970. Birds from the rest house verandah, Brunei. *Journal of the Brunei Museum* 2: 269–78.

——. 1971. Easter Island, a last outpost. *Oryx* 11: 2–3.

——. 1974. The Tree Sparrow in Borneo (East Malaysia and Brunei): a population explosion? *Malayan Nature Journal* 27: 171.

Hart, D. 1967. Evolving Pheasant populations. *Virginia Wildlife* 28: 10–11.

Hart, F. E. 1943. Hungarian Partridges in Ohio. *Ohio Conservation Bulletin* 7: 4–5, 26.

Harting, J. E. 1883. The local distribution of the Red-legged Partridge. *The Field* 61: 130–1.

Harvie-Brown, J. A. 1879. *The Capercailzie in Scotland*. David Douglas: Edinburgh.

——. 1880. The Capercaillie in Scotland. *Scottish Naturalist*, 289–94.

——. 1898. Capercaillie in south-east Lanarkshire. *Annals of Scottish Natural History*, 118.

Harvie-Brown, J. A. & **Buckley, T. E.** 1892. *A Vertebrate Fauna of Argyll and the Inner Hebrides*. David Douglas: Edinburgh.

Harwin, R. M. 1952. Birds introduced into the Transvaal. *Wits Bird Club News Sheet* 3: 1. (Republished 1984 in *Wits Bird Club News* 127: 10.)

——. 1959. House Sparrow in Southern Rhodesia. *Rhodesian Ornithological Society Bulletin* 29: 4.

——. 1960. House Sparrow in the eastern Cape. *Ostrich* 31: 27.

*Harwin, R. M.** & **Irwin, M. P. S.** 1966. The spread of the House Sparrow, *Passer domesticus*, in south-central Africa. *Arnoldia* 2: 1–17.

Harwin, R. M., Bromley, F. C., Freer, J., Last, J., Grabandt, C. & **Reed, R. A.** 1952. House Sparrow (*Passer domesticus*). *Ostrich* 23: 136.

Haverschmidt, F. 1947 and 1950. Cattle Egret in Surinam, Dutch Guiana. *Auk* 64: 143; 67: 380–1.

——. 1951. The Cattle Egret, *Bubulcus i. ibis*, in British Guiana. *Ibis* 93: 310–11.

——. 1953. Cattle Egret in South America. *Audubon Magazine* 55: 202–4.

——. 1958. Cattle Egret in Surinam, Dutch Guiana. *Ardea* 45: 168–76.

Hawaiian Audubon Society. 1975. *Hawaii's Birds*. Hawaiian Audubon Society: Honolulu.

Hawaiian Division of Fish & Game. 1961, 1962 and 1966. Experimental introduction of foreign game birds and mammals. Project Nos W-5-R-12, 13 and 17 (Job No. 50).

Hawkes, B. 1976. The invasion of the Asians [Ring-necked Parakeets in England]. *Surrey Life* 5: 30.

———. 1980. De gevaren van de halsbandparkiet [Ring-necked Parakeet] in Groot-Britannië. *Vogeljaar* 28: 18–20.

Hawkins, J. E. 1962. Controlling Redpolls in Otago orchards. *New Zealand Orchardist* (May).

Haydock, E. L. 1954. A survey of the birds of St Helena Island. *Ostrich* 25: 62–75.

Heather, B. D. 1982. Cattle Egret (*Bubulcus ibis*) in New Zealand, 1978–80. *Notornis* 29: 241–68.

Heilbrun, L. H. ed. 1976 and 1977. The 76th and 77th annual Christmas bird counts. *American Birds* 30: 155–633; 31: 391–909.

Heilfurth, F. 1931. *Passer domesticus* L. in Mexico. *Journal für Ornithologie* 79: 317–9.

Heim de Balsac, H. 1926. Contribution à l'ornithologie du Sahara central et du Sud-Algérien. *Mémoires de la Société d'Histoire Naturelle de l'Afrique du Nord* 1: 1–141.

Heinzel, H., Fitter, R. S. R. & **Parslow, J. L .F.** 1976. *The Birds of Britain and Europe*. Collins: London.

Heller, D. D. & **Wise, C. D.** 1982. The inevitable: House Finches found nesting in Indiana. *Indiana Audubon Quarterly* 60: 6–13.

Hellmayr, C. E. 1932. Birds of Chile. *Field Museum of Natural History, Chicago, Zoology Series* No. 19.

Helms, R. 1898. Useful and noxious birds: the House Sparrow (*Passer domesticus*), and the Starling (*Sturnus vulgaris*). *Producers' Gazette and Settlers' Record, Western Australia* 5: 178–80, 299–302.

Henry, G. M. 1955. *A Guide to the Birds of Ceylon*. Oxford University Press: London.

Henshaw, H. W. 1900. Introduction of foreign birds into the Hawaiian Islands with notes on some of the introduced species. *Hawaiian Almanack and Annual, 1901,* 132–42.

———. 1902. *Birds of the Hawaiian Islands: Being a Complete List of the Birds of the Hawaiian Possessions with Notes on their Habits*. T. G. Thrum: Honolulu.

———. 1904. Complete list of the birds of the Hawaiian Possessions, with notes on their habits. *Hawaiian Almanack and Annual, 1904,* 113–45.

———. 1911. Report of the committee on the introduction of birds into the Hawaiian Islands. *Hawaiian Forestry and Agriculture* 8: 61–4.

Herklots, A. C. 1961. *The Birds of Trinidad and Tobago*. Collins: London.

Hewitt, J. M. 1960. The Cattle Egret in Australia. *Emu* 60: 99–102.

Hewitt, O. H. ed. 1967. *The Wild Turkey and its Management*. Wildlife Society: Washington DC.

Heyberger, M. 1979. La réintroduction du hibou Grand-Duc (*Bubo bubo*) en Alsace. *Ciconia* 3: 33–41.

Hibbert-Ware, A. 1937–8. Report of the Little Owl food enquiry, 1936–7. *British Birds* 31: 162–87, 205–29, 249–64.

Hicks, L. E. 1933. The first appearance and spread of the breeding range of the European Starling (*Sturnus vulgaris*) in Ohio. *Auk* 50: 317–22.

———. 1936. History of the importation and naturalization of the Ring-necked Pheasant in the United States. *Ohio Division of Conservation Bulletin* No. 106: 1–3.

———. 1940. The role of exotics in the Ohio Valley and the Lower Great Lakes region. Ohio Wildlife Research Station Release No. 133 (4 pp.).

———. 1941. The role of exotics in the Ohio Valley. *Transactions of the 5th North American Wildlife Conference,* 420–4.

Hill, W. R. 1952. The European Starling in Fiji. *Emu* 52: 218.

Hindwood, K. A. 1940. The birds of Lord Howe Island. *Emu* 40: 1–86.

Hindwood, K. A. & **Cunningham, J. M.** 1950. Notes on the birds of Lord Howe Island. *Emu* 50: 23–5.

Hindwood, K. A. & **McGill, A. R.** 1958. *The Birds of Sydney (County of Cumberland)*. Zoological Society of New South Wales: Sydney.

Hines, T. 1971. Tennessee's efforts to introduce Pheasants. *Proceedings of the 24th Conference of the Southeastern Association of Game and Fish Commissioners,* 252–68.

Hirai, L. T. 1975a. The nesting biology of the House Finch in Honolulu, Hawaii. *Western Birds* 6: 33–44.

———. 1975b. The Hawaiian House Finch. *Elepaio* 36: 1–5.

———. 1980. First record of the Warbling Silverbill on Lanai. *Elepaio* 40: 119–20.

Hix, G. E. 1905. A year with the birds in New York City. *Wilson Bulletin* 12: 35.

Hjersman, H. A. 1947. A history of the establishment of the Ring-necked Pheasant in California. *California Fish and Game* 33: 3–11.

———. 1948. The Californian Valley Quail in New Zealand. *California Fish and Game* 34: 33–6.

Hobbs, D. F. 1955. Do newly introduced species present a separate problem. *Proceedings of the New Zealand Ecological Society* 2: 12–14.

Hobbs, J. N. 1961. Birds of south-west New South Wales. *Emu* 61: 54.

Hoffman, E. C. 1930. The spread of the European Starling in America. *Wilson Bulletin* 42: 80.

Hogg, B. 1982. Chaffinch in Tokai Forest. *Promerops* 153: 5.

Holland, C. S. & **Williams, J. M.** 1978. Observations on the birds of Antigua. *American Birds* 32: 1095–105.

Holloway, C. W. & **Jungius, H.** 1975. *Reintroduzione di alcune Specie di Mammiferi e di Uccelli nel Parco Nazionale Gran Paradiso* [Lammergeier and Capercaillie]. Parco Nazionale Gran Paradiso. (See also *Zoologischer Anzeiger* 191: 1–44 (1973) [in English].)

Holman, J. 1846. *A Voyage Round the World.* London.

Holmgren, V. C. 1964. Chinese Pheasants, Oregon pioneers. *Oregon Historical Quarterly* 65: 229–62.

Hollom, P. A. D. 1957. The rarer birds of prey: their present status in the British Isles. Goshawk. *British Birds* 50: 135–6.

Holyoak, D. T. 1974a. Les oiseaux des Îles de la Société. *Oiseau et la Revue Française d'Ornithologie* 44: 1–27, 153–84.

———. 1974b. Undescribed birds from the Cook Islands. *Bulletin of the British Ornithologists' Club* 94: 145–50.

———. 1979. Notes on the birds of Viti Levu and Taveuni, Fiji. *Emu* 79: 7–18.

Holyoak, D. T. & **Thibault, J. C.** 1975. Introduced Tanagers on Tahiti, Society Islands. *Bulletin of the British Ornithologists' Club* 95: 106.

★———. 1984. *Contribution à l'Étude des Oiseaux de Polynésie Orientale.* Mémoires du Muséum National d'Histoire Naturelle, n.s. Série A, Zoologie, Tome 127. Éditions du Muséum: Paris.

Hone, J. 1978. Introduction and spread of the Common Myna in New South Wales. *Emu* 78: 227–30.

Hopwood, C. 1912. A list of birds from Arakan. *Journal of the Bombay Natural History Society* 21: 1196.

Horikawa, Y. 1936. On the animals imported from Formosa. *Formosan Science* 4: 68–70.

Horton, K. J. ed. 1980. Herons to Bermuda. *Michigan Audubon* 28: 1.

Howard, C. W. 1907. Introduction of English Starling. *Journal of the South African Ornithologists' Union* 3: 140–1.

Howard, R. & **Moore, A.** 1980. *A Complete Checklist of the Birds of the World.* Oxford University Press: Oxford (revised edn 1984, Macmillan Papermac: London).

Howard, W. E. 1959. The European Starling in California. *California Department of Agriculture Bulletin* No. 38: 171–8.

———. 1980. Teaching the complex biological problems of wild vertebrate populations. *Environmental Science Research* 18: 205–12.

Howells, G. 1963. The status of Red-legged Partridges in Britain. *Game Research Association 2nd Annual Report*, 46–51.

Huckle, C. H. 1924. Birds of Ascension Island and St Helena. *Ibis*, series 11, 6: 818–21.

Hudson, R. 1965. The spread of the Collared Dove in Britain and Ireland. *British Birds* 58: 105–39.

———. 1972. Collared Doves in Britain and Ireland, 1965–70. *British Birds* 65: 139–55.

———. 1974. Feral Parakeets near London. *British Birds* 67: 33, 174.

———. 1976. Ruddy Ducks in Britain. *British Birds* 69: 132–43.

———. 1978. Stiff-tailed invaders: the Ruddy Duck in Britain. *Country Life* 163: 686–7.

Hüe, F. & **Etchécopar, R. D.** 1970. *Les Oiseaux du Proche et du Moyen Orient.* N. Boubée: Paris.

Huey, L. M. 1932. Some light on the introduction of Gambel Quail on San Clemente Island, California. *Condor* 34: 46.

Hughes, R. A. 1970. Notes on the birds of the Mollendo District, southwest Peru. *Ibis* 112: 229–41.

Hughes, S. W. M. & **Codd, D. W.** 1980. Feral Mandarin in Sussex. *Sussex Bird Report* No. 32 (1979): 72–6.

Hume, A. O. 1873. Additional remarks on the avifauna of the Andamans. *Stray Feathers* 1: 304–10.

———. 1880. The birds of the western half of the Malay Peninsula. *Stray Feathers* 8: 107–32.

Humphrey, P. S., Bridge, D., Reynolds, P. W. & **Peterson, R. T.** 1970. *Birds of the Isla Grande (Tierra del Fuego).* Smithsonian Institution: Washington, DC.

Hunt, C. J. 1926. The English Starling at Chicago, Illinois. *Auk* 43: 239–40.

Hunter, C. 1972. Indian Mynah (*Acridotheres tristis*). *Wits Bird Club News Sheet* 80: 12.

Hurdis, J. L. 1897. Rough notes and memoranda relating to the natural history of Bermuda. Edited by his daughter, H. J. Hurdis. Vol. 8. R. H. Porter: London.

Hutchins, M., Stevens, V. & **Atkins, N.** 1982. Introduced species and the issue of animal welfare. *International Journal for the Study of Animal Problems* 3: 318–36.

Hutchins, R. E. 1938. Invasion of northern Mississippi by the Starlings. *Wilson Bulletin* 45: 140–1.

Hutchinson, F. 1900. Introduced birds of Scinde Island. *East Coast Naturalist* 5: 28.

Hutson, A. M. 1975. Observations on the birds of Diego Garcia, Chagos Archipelago, with notes on other vertebrates. *Atoll Research Bulletin* 75: 1–25.

Hutton, F. W. 1869. The introduction of Pheasants into Auckland Province. *Transactions of the New Zealand Institute* 2: 80.

Hylton, C. G. 1927. Colombo Crows reach Australia. *Emu* 27: 44.

I

Imber, M. J. 1971. The identity of New Zealand's Canada Geese. *Notornis* 18: 253–61.

Imber, M. J. & **Williams, G. R.** 1968. Mortality rates of a Canada Goose population in New Zealand. *Journal of Wildlife Management* 32: 256–66.

Imhof, T. A. 1962. *Alabama Birds.* State Department of Conservation, Game and Fish Division/University of Alabama Press: Alabama.

——. 1978. The spring migration, 1 March to 31 May, 1978: central-southern region. *American Birds* 32: 1017–21.

Immelmann, K. 1960. The spread of introduced birds in northern Queensland. *Australian Journal of Science* 23: 130.

Ingram, C. 1913. Birds of Paradise in the West Indies. *Avicultural Magazine* series 3, 5: 35–41.

——. 1915. A few notes on *Tetrao urogallus* and its allies. *Ibis*, series 10, 3: 128–33.

——. 1943. Birds of the Camargue. *Ibis* 85: 520–1.

——. 1956. Birds of Paradise in the West Indies. *Country Life* 119: 482.

Ingram, W. 1911. Acclimatization of the Greater Bird of Paradise (*Paradisaea apoda*) in the West Indies. *Avicultural Magazine*, series 3, 2: 142–7.

——. 1917. The Greater Bird of Paradise on the island of Little Tobago. *Avicultural Magazine*, series 3, 8: 341–51.

——. 1918. Birds of Paradise in Little Tobago, West Indies. *Avicultural Magazine*, series 3, 9: 279–80.

Inskipp, C. & Inskipp, T. 1985. *A Guide to the Birds of Nepal.* Croom Helm: London.

Irvin, E. W. 1982. A Nanday Conure in coastal North Carolina. *Chat* 46: 43–4.

Isenberg, A. H. 1931–2. Transplantation of foreign birds to the Hawaiian Islands. *Agriculture* 3: 333–4; 4: 70–1.

Ivanauskas, T. & Zubavichus, T. 1955. An attempt to introduce the Grey (-lag) Goose in Latvia. *Byulletin' Moscovskogo Obshchestva Ispȳtatelei Prirodȳ, Otdel Biol.* 60: 97–8 [in Russian].

J

Jack, N. 1952. Goldfinches around Brisbane. *Emu* 52: 222–3.

Jackson, A. S. 1957. Spanish Red-legged and Seesee Partridge introductions in the Texas panhandle. *Proceedings of the 37th Annual Conference of the Western Association of State Game and Fish Commissioners,* 291–4.

——. 1964. A study of the introduction, release and survival of certain European and Asiatic game birds. *Transactions of the 29th North American Wildlife Conference,* 259–69.

Jackson, A. S., De Arment, R. & Bell, J. 1957. Release of the Redlegs. *Texas Game and Fish* 15: 16–17, 26–7.

Jackson, D. F., Stoll, D. & Copper, N. eds. 1978. *Some Endangered and Exotic Species in Florida,* Part 2. Florida International University: Miami.

Jackson, J. A. 1981. The House Finch, a new species for Mississippi. *Mississippi Kite* 11: 7–9.

Jacot-Guillarmod, C. 1960. European Starling, *Sturnus vulgaris,* in Grahamstown [South Africa]. *Ostrich* 31: 173.

Janson, R., Hartkorn, F. & Greene, R. 1971. Ring-necked Pheasant. In T. W. Mussehl & F. W. Howell eds, *Game Management in Montana,* Ch. 18, 153–9. Montana Fish and Game Department: Helena.

Janssen, R. B. 1983. House Sparrows build roost nests. *Loon* 55: 64–5.

Japanese Ornithological Society. 1981. *Nihou San Choryui No Hanshoku Buupu.* [Atlas of Japanese birds.] Kankyocho (Environment Ministry): Tokyo [in Japanese].

Jarman, H. E. A. 1981. Notes on introduced finches [*Lonchura* spp.] occurring in the Heidelberg area, Victoria. *Australian Bird Watcher* 9: 78–9.

Jarvis, P. J. 1979. The ecology of plant and animal introductions. *Progress in Physical Geography* 3: 187–214.

——. 1980. The biogeography and ecology of introduced species. *Department of Geography, University of Birmingham, Working Paper Series* No. 1: 1–40.

Jefferson, K. 1985. How the English Sparrow became a U.S. citizen. *Birds (Magazine of the Royal Society for the Protection of Birds)* 10: 50.

Jenkin, J. F., Johnstone, G. W. & Copson, G. R. 1982. Introduced animal and plant species on Macquarie Island. *Colloque sur les Ecosystèmes Subantarctiques, 1981,* 301–13. Publications du Comité National Français des Recherches Antarctiques, No. 51. Paris.

Jenkins, C. F .H. 1929a. The Starling. *Emu* 29: 49–51.

——. 1929b. Java Sparrows in Western Australia. *Emu* 28: 235.

——. 1959. Introduced birds in Western Australia. *Emu* 59: 201–7.

★——. 1977. *The Noah's Ark Syndrome: One Hundred Years of Acclimatization and Zoo Development in Australia.* Zoological Gardens Board: Perth, Western Australia.

Jennings, M. C. 1981. *Birds of the Arabian Gulf.* Allen and Unwin: London.

Jerdon, T. C. 1863. *Birds of India,* Vol. 2. Military Orphan Press: London.

Jesse, W. 1876. Short notes on several species of birds of Corsica. *Ibis,* series 3, 6: 830.

Jewett, S. G. 1942. The European Starling in California. *Condor* 44: 79.

——. 1946. The Starling in Oregon. *Condor* 48: 245.

Jewett, S. G. & Gabrielson, I. N. 1929. Birds of the Portland area, Oregon. *Pacific Coast Avifauna* 19: 1–54.

Jewett, S. G., Taylor, W. P., Shaw, W. T. & Aldrich, J. W. 1953. *Birds of Washington State.* University of Washington Press: Seattle.

Jobin, L. 1952. The European Starling in central British Columbia. *Condor* 54: 318.

Johnsgard, P. A. 1973. *Grouse and Quails of North America*. University of Nebraska Press: Lincoln, Nebraska.

Johnson, A. W. 1965 and 1967. *The Birds of Chile and Adjacent Regions of Argentina, Bolivia and Peru*, 2 vols. Platt Establecimientos Gráficos: Buenos Aires.

Johnson, A. W., Millie, W. R. & Moffett, G. 1970. Notes on the birds of Easter Island. *Ibis* 112: 532–8.

Johnson, D. A. 1960. Chukars, the exotic partridge. *Naturalist* 11: 29–32.

Johnson, M. 1957. The Hun[garian Partridge] and its limiting factors. *North Dakota Outdoors* 19: 7–9.

Johnston, R. F. & Klitz, W. J. 1977. Variation and evolution in a granivorous bird: the House Sparrow. In J. Pinowski & S. C. Kendeigh eds, *Granivorous Birds in Ecosystems, International Biological Programme* No. 12: 15–51. Cambridge University Press: Cambridge.

Johnston, R. F. & Selander, R. K. 1964. House Sparrows: rapid evolution of races in North America. *Science* 144: 548–50.

———. 1971. Evolution of the House Sparrow: II. Adaptive differentiation in North American populations. *Evolution* 25: 1–28.

———. 1973a. Evolution of the House Sparrow: III. Variation in size and sexual dimorphism in Europe, North America and South America. *American Naturalist* 107: 373–90.

———. 1973b. Variation, adaptation and evolution in the North American House Sparrows. In S. C. Kendeigh & J. Pinowski eds., *Productivity, Population Dynamics and Systematics of Granivorous Birds*, 301–26. Polish Scientific Publishers: Warsaw.

Johnstone, G. W. 1967. Blackgame and Capercaillie in relation to forestry in Britain. *Forestry Supplement* 40: 68–77.

———. 1982. Threats to birds on Subantarctic Islands. Paper read at the International Council for Bird Preservation Conference, Cambridge, England. Mimeograph (49 pp.).

Joiris, Cl. & Tahon, J. 1971. Le problème de l'introduction et de la réintroduction des espèces animales. *Aves* 8: 14–17.

Jones, S. 1942. *Migratory and Permanent Resident Birds in the St Louis Region*. St Louis Bird Club: St Louis, Missouri.

Jones, V. E. 1946. The Starling in Idaho. *Condor* 48: 142–3.

Jouanin, C. 1962. *Zosterops lateralis* (Latham) à Tahiti. *Oiseau et la Revue Française d'Ornithologie* 32: 280–1.

Joubert, H. J. 1945. Starlings and others. *Ostrich* 16: 214–16.

Jourdain, F. C. R. 1912. Extermination of the Sea Eagle in Ireland. *British Birds* 5: 138–9.

Judd, S. D. 1901. The relation of [House] Sparrows to agriculture. *US Department of Agriculture, Division of Biology Survey, Bulletin* No. 15.

Jung, C. S. 1936. The European Goldfinch (*Carduelis carduelis*) in Wisconsin. *Auk* 53: 340–1.

———. 1945. A history of the Starling in the United States. *Passenger Pigeon* 7: 111–16.

K

Kaburaki, T. 1934. Effects of some exotic plants and animals upon the flora and fauna of Japan. *Proceedings of the 5th Pacific Science Congress, Victoria and Vancouver, June 1933* 1: 801–5. University of Toronto Press: Canada.

———. 1940. Effects of some exotic plants and animals upon the flora and fauna of Japan. *Proceedings of the 6th Pacific Science Congress, Berkeley, California, 1939* 4: 229–30. University of California Press: Berkeley.

Kadich, H. M. V. 1899. Quail and Grouse [Prairie-hen]. *Deutsche Jägerz* 33: 517.

Kalmbach, E. R. 1922. A comparison of the food habits of British and American Starlings. *Auk* 39: 189–95.

———. 1928. The European Sparrow in the United States. *US Department of Agriculture Farm Bulletin* No. 1571 (26 pp.).

———. 1930. *English Sparrow Control*. US Department of Agriculture Leaflet No. 61 (8 pp.).

———. 1932. Winter Starling roosts of Washington. *Wilson Bulletin* 39: 65–75.

———. 1940. Economic status of the English Sparrow in the United States. *US Department of Agriculture Technical Bulletin* No. 711.

Kalmbach, E. R. & Gabrielson, I. N. 1921. Economic value of the Starling in the United States. *US Department of Agriculture Bulletin* No. 868 (66 pp.).

Kamstra, J. 1981. Exotics and native fauna. *Trent University Biology Department Ecological Bulletin* No. 5: 13–15.

Katholi, C. 1967. House Finch in eastern United States. *Redstart* 34: 71–4.

Kauffman, H. H. 1962. Pennsylvania wild Turkeys in Germany. *Pennsylvania Game News* 33: 27–9.

Kay, F. C. L. 1904. Capercaillie in Argyll. *Annals of Scottish Natural History*, 189.

Kays, C. E. 1972. Red Junglefowl introductions in Kentucky: a final report. *Kentucky Department of Fish and Wildlife Research, P-R Game Management Technical Series* No. 18 (16 pp.).

Kear, J. 1965. The assessment of goose damage by grazing trials. *Transactions of the 6th International Union of Game Biologists*, 333–9.

———. 1981. The néné success – conservation and captive breeding of large birds. *Countryside* 24: 165–9.

———. 1985. The Hawaiian Goose in the 1980s. *Avicultural Magazine* 91:102–3.

Kear, J. & **Berger, A. J.** 1980. *The Hawaiian Goose: An Experiment in Conservation.* T. & A. D. Poyser: Calton, Staffordshire.

Keefe, J. 1955. Coturnix Quail – a new Missouri game bird? *Missouri Conservationist* 16: 12–13.

Keeler, J. E. 1963. Status of the Red Jungle Fowl in the southeastern states. *Proceedings of the 17th Annual Conference of the South-East Association of Game and Fish Commissioners,* 107.

Keffer, M. O. 1972a. Crested Mynah. In *State of California Department of Food and Agriculture, Division of Plant Industry Detection Manual* No. 7: 6.

——. 1972b. Java Sparrow. In *State of California Department of Food and Agriculture, Division of Plant Industry Detection Manual* No. 7: 11.

——. 1974a. Monk or Quaker Parakeet. In *State of California Department of Food and Agriculture, Division of Plant Industry Detection Manual* No. 7: 15.

——. 1974b. Index of target vertebrate pests for detection. In *State of California Department of Food and Agriculture, Division of Plant Industry Detection Manual* No. 7.

——. 1978. White-eyes. In *State of California Department of Food and Agriculture, Division of Plant Industry Detection Manual* No. 7: 16.

Keffer, M., Davis, L. & **Clark, D.** 1974. *Pest Evaluation: Monk Parakeet, Myiopsitta monachus.* California Department of Food and Agriculture (23 pp.).

Keith, A. R. 1957. Bird observations in Fiji and Samoa. *Elepaio* 18: 25–7.

Keith, K. & **Hinds, M. P.** 1958. New and rare species of birds at Macquarie Island. *Commonwealth Scientific and Industrial Research Organization, Wildlife Research* 3: 50.

Kelham, H. R. 1881. Ornithological notes made in Strait Settlements and in western states of the Malay Peninsula. *Ibis,* series 4, 5: 501–31.

Kellog, F. E., Eleazer, T. H. & **Colvin, T. R.** 1978. Transmission of blackhead [histomoniasis, enterohepatitis] from Junglefowl to Turkey. *Proceedings of the 32nd Annual Conference of the Southeastern Association of Fish and Wildlife Agencies,* 378.

Kelly, W. N. 1927. The Japanese Starling in Vancouver, British Columbia. *Murrelet* 8: 14.

Kendeigh, S. C. 1976. Latitudinal trends in the metabolic adjustment of the House Sparrow. *Ecology* 57: 509–19.

Kendeigh, S. C. & **Pinowski, J.** eds. 1972. *Productivity, Population Dynamics and Systematics of Granivorous Birds (Proceedings of the General Meeting of the Working Group on Granivorous Birds, The Hague, Holland, 6–8 September, 1970).* Polish Scientific Publishers: Warsaw.

Kennedy, J. N. 1914. Notes on birds observed in the Bermuda Islands during the winter of 1912–13. *Ibis,* series 10, 2: 185–91.

Kent, C. C. 1927. The Indian Mynah in Natal. *South African Journal of Natural History* 6: 127–9.

Kenward, R. E. 1981. Goshawk re-establishment in Britain – causes and implications. *The Falconer* 7: 304–10.

——. In press. *The Goshawk.* T. & A. D. Poyser: Calton, Staffordshire.

Kenward, R. E., Marquiss, M. & **Newton, I.** 1981. What happens to Goshawks trained for falconry. *Journal of Wildlife Management* 45: 801–6.

Kermode, F. 1920. Notes on the Chinese Starling. British Columbia Provincial Museum Natural History Report.

Kessel, B. 1953. Distribution and migration of the European Starling in North America. *Condor* 55: 49–67.

——. 1957. Breeding biology of the European Starling (*Sturnus vulgaris*) in North America. *American Midland Naturalist* 58: 257–331.

——. 1979. Starlings become established at Fairbanks, Alaska. *Condor* 81: 437–8.

Keve, A. 1976. Some remarks on the taxonomic position of the Tree Sparrow introduced into Australia. *Emu* 76: 152–3.

Kikkawa, J. & **Boles, W.** 1976. Seabird island No. 15: Heron Island, Queensland. *Australian Bird Bander* 14: 3–6.

Kikkawa, J. & **Yamashina, Y.** 1966. Breeding of introduced Black Swans in Japan. *Emu* 66: 377–81.

Kimball, J. W. 1948. Pheasant population characteristics and trends in the Dakotas. *Transactions of the 13th North American Wildlife Conference,* 291–314.

King, B. 1960. Feral North American Ruddy Ducks in Somerset. *Wildfowl Trust Annual Report 1959,* 167–8.

——. 1976. Association between male North American Ruddy Ducks and stray ducklings. *British Birds* 69: 34.

King, B. F., Dickinson, E. C. & **Woodcock, M. W.** 1975. *A Field Guide to the Birds of South-East Asia.* Collins: London.

★**King, C.** 1984. *Immigrant Killers: Introduced Predators and the Conservation of Birds in New Zealand.* Oxford University Press: Auckland.

King, J. E. 1958. Some observations on the birds of Tahiti and the Marquesas Islands. *Elepaio* 19: 14–17.

King, R. T. 1942. Is it wise policy to introduce exotic game birds? *Audubon Magazine* 44: 136–45, 230–6, 306–10.

King, W. 1968. As a consequence many will die. *Florida Naturalist* 41: 99–103.

King, W. B. ed. 1981. *Endangered Birds of the World: The ICBP Bird Red Data Book.* Smithsonian Institution Press: Washington, DC/International Council for Bird Preservation: Cambridge, England. (Reprint of the *Red Data Book,* Vol. 2: *Aves.* IUCN: Morges, 1978 and 1979.)

Kinghorn, J. R. 1933a. A report of the distribution,

migratory movements and control of the Starling in Australia. *Australian Department of Agriculture Journal* 36: 1154–8.

———. 1933b. The Starling in Australia, its distribution and suggestions for control. *Agricultural Gazette of New South Wales* 44: 512–15.

Kingsmill, W. 1920. Acclimatization. *Journal and Proceedings of the Royal Society of Western Australia* 5: 33–8.

Kinnear, N. B. 1942. The introduction of the Indian House Crow into Port Sudan. *Bulletin of the British Ornithologists' Club* 62: 55–6.

Kinsky, F. C. ed. 1970. *Annotated Checklist to the Birds of New Zealand, including the Birds of the Ross Dependency.* Published for the Ornithological Society of New Zealand by A. H. & A. W. Reed: Wellington.

———. 1973. The subspecific status of the New Zealand population of the Little Owl, *Athene noctua* (Scopoli, 1769). *Notornis* 20: 9–13.

Kiris, I. D. ed. 1973. *Acclimatization of Game and Commercial Animals and Birds in the USSR.* Volgo-Vyatskoe Kn. Izdatelstvo: Kirov.

Kirk, T. W. 1890. Notes on the breeding habits of the European Sparrow (*Passer domesticus*) in New Zealand. *Transactions of the New Zealand Institute* 23: 108–10. (Abstract of, and discussion on, in *New Zealand Journal of Science* 1: 9–12 (1891).)

Kirkpatrick, R. D. 1959. Coturnix investigation; final report. Indiana Department of Conservation, Division of Fish and Game, Indianapolis, P-R Project W-2-R.

———. 1965. Introduction of the Japanese Quail (*Coturnix coturnix japonica*) in Indiana. *Proceedings of the Indiana Academy of Science* 75: 289–92.

Klapste, J. 1982. Xanthochroism in the House Sparrow, *Passer domesticus. Australian Bird Watcher* 9: 172.

Kleinschnitz, F. C. 1957. History of the introduction of the Spanish Red-legged Partridge in Colorado. *Proceedings of the 37th Annual Conference of the Western Association of State Game and Fish Commissioners,* 280–2.

Kloss, C. B. 1903. *In the Andamans and Nicobars.* John Murray: London.

Knock, I., Pringle, S. & **Martin, R.** 1976. Chaffinch. *Cape Bird Club Newsletter* 125: 3.

Koehler, W. 1962. [Introduction of the Pheasant to Poland.] *Chrońmy Przyrodę Ojczystą* 18: 26–30, 54 [in Polish].

Koepcke, M. 1952. El gorrion europeo [House Sparrow] en al Peru. *Mar del Surr* 22: 63–72.

———. 1961. Birds of the western slope of the Andes of Peru. *American Museum Novitates* No. 2028: 1–31.

———. 1970. *The Birds of the Department of Lima, Peru.* Livingston: Philadelphia.

Kolichis, N. 1978. Chestnut-breasted Finch, *Lonchura*

castaneothorax, at Osborne Park. *Western Australian Naturalist* 14: 51.

Korhonen, S. 1972. Tuloksia kanadanhanen istutuskokeilusta inplanterings – forsok med kanadagås (*Branta canadensis*). *Suomen Riista* 24: 52–6 [in Finnish].

Korschgen, L. J. & **Chambers, G. D.** 1970. Propagation, stocking and food habits of Reeves Pheasants in Missouri. *Journal of Wildlife Management* 34: 274–82.

Krabbe, N. 1980. *Checklist of the Birds of Elat.* Copenhagen.

Kragh, W. D. 1982. The Cattle Egret in the Fraser Delta area, British Columbia. *Murrelet* 63: 86–8.

Kricher, J. C. 1983. Correlation between House Finch increase and House Sparrow decline. *American Birds* 37: 358–60.

Kuroda, N. 1913. A flock of Java Sparrows settled down in Haneda village. *Zoological Magazine, Tokyo* 25: 563–6 [in Japanese].

———. 1922. On the birds of Tsushima and Iki Islands, Japan. *Ibis,* series 11, 4: 75–104.

———. 1933–6. *Birds of the Island of Java,* 2 vols. Private Publications: Tokyo.

———. 1937. [Notes on the Java Sparrow.] *Tori* 9: 478–84 [in Japanese].

Kurtz, N. 1980. Nutmeg Mannikin near Mudgee. *Australian Birds* 14: 51.

L

Labisky, R. F. 1961. Reports of attempts to establish Japanese Quail in Illinois. *Journal of Wildlife Management* 25: 290–5.

Lack, D. 1976. *Island Biology, Illustrated by the Land Birds of Jamaica.* Studies in Ecology No. 3. University of California Press: Berkeley.

Lack, D. & **Southern, H. N.** 1949. Birds on Tenerife (Canary Islands). *Ibis* 91: 607.

Lack, D., Lack, E., Lack, P. & **Lack, A.** 1973. Birds of St Vincent (West Indies). *Ibis* 115: 46–52.

Lamm, D. W. & **White, D.** 1950. Changing status of avifauna in the Australian Capital Territory. *Emu* 49: 199–204.

Lancan, F. & **Mougin, J. L.** 1974. Les oiseaux des Îles Gambier et de quelques atolls orientaux de l'archipel des Tuamotu (Ocean Pacifique). *Oiseau et la Revue Française d'Ornithologie* 44: 191–280.

Land, H. C. 1970. *Birds of Guatemala.* Livingston: Wynnewood, Pennsylvania.

Landsborough Thomson, A. 1964. *A New Dictionary of Birds.* Nelson: London.

Lane, S. G. 1964. First arrivals at Lane Cove and North Ryde, New South Wales. *Emu* 64: 47.

———. 1975. The White-winged Widowbird near Windsor, New South Wales. *Australian Bird Bander* 13: 61.

Langseth, R. 1965. Tyrkerduen har nådd Island. *Sterna* 6: 311 [in Norwegian].

Larsen, R. T. F. & **Newlands, W. A.** 1976–7. Reintroduction of the Capercaillie into the Gran Paradiso National Park, Italy. *World Pheasant Association Journal* 11: 62–73.

La Touche, J. D. D. 1925 and 1934. *A Handbook of the Birds of Eastern China*, 2 vols. Taylor & Francis: London.

Lavery, H. J. 1974. Species introduced by man. In *Fauna of Queensland Yearbook*. Government Printer: Brisbane.

Lavery, H. J. & **Hopkins, N.** 1963. Birds of the Townsville district of north Queensland. *Emu* 63: 242–52.

Law, S. C. 1932. Place of the Java Sparrow (*Munia oryzivora* L.) in the Indian avifauna. *Journal of the Bombay Natural History Society* 35: 683–5.

Lawrence, A. M. 1926. Distribution of the Goldfinch [in Australia]. *Emu* 25: 219.

Laycock, G. 1970. *The Alien Animals*. Ballantine Books: New York.

Leach, J. A. 1928. Notes made during a holiday trip to New Caledonia. *Emu* 28: 42.

Leck, C. F. 1973. A House Sparrow roost in Lima, Peru. *Auk* 90: 888.

Leckie, N. 1897. Capercaillie in Linlithgowshire. *Annals of Scottish Natural History*, 44.

Lee, L. 1955. Preliminary observations on the Turkish Chukar in New Mexico. *Proceedings of the 34th Annual Conference of the Western Association of State Game and Fish Commissioners*, 227–30.

Lee, W. H. & **Lewis, J.** 1959. Establishment and spread of the wild Turkey in southwestern Michigan. *Journal of Wildlife Management* 23: 210–15.

Lees, S. G. 1967. The breeding of the House Sparrow, *Passer domesticus*, in Rhodesia [Zimbabwe]. *Ostrich* 38: 3–4.

Leffingwell, D. I. 1928. The Ring-neck Pheasant – its history and habits. *Occasional Papers of the Charles R. Conner Museum, State College, Washington* No. 1 (35 pp.).

Legge, W. V. 1874. On the distribution of birds in southern Ceylon [Sri Lanka]. *Ibis* 4: 7–33.

Le Grand, G. 1977. Apparition des moineaux domestiques aux Açores. *Alauda* 45: 339–40.

———. 1983. Le moineau domestique (*Passer domesticus*) aux Açores. *Arquipelago* 4: 85–116.

Lehmann, F. C. 1959. Observations on the Cattle Egret in Colombia. *Condor* 61: 265–9.

Lehmann, V. W. 1948. Restocking on King Ranch. *Transactions of the 13th North American Wildlife Conference*, 236–42.

Leicester, Earl of. 1921. Date of the introduction into England of the Red-legged Partridge. *The Field* 137: 372.

Lekagul, B. & **Cronin, E. W.** 1974. *Bird Guide of Thailand*. Kuruspa: Bangkok.

Lello, J. 1980. New Maine residents. *Maine Quarterly Audubon Magazine*.

Lemke, C. W. 1957. The Hungarian Partridge. *Wisconsin Conservation Bulletin* No. 22: 19–22.

Lendon, A. H. 1948. A further report on the introduced Grenadier Weaver. *South Australian Ornithologist* 19: 2.

———. 1952. Bulbuls in Melbourne. *Emu* 52: 67–8.

Leopold, A. 1933. *Game Management*. C. Scribner: New York.

———. 1940. Spread of the Hungarian Partridge in Wisconsin. *Transactions of the Wisconsin Academy of Sciences, Arts and Letters* 32: 5–28.

———. 1978. *The California Quail*. University of California Press: Berkeley.

Le Souef, J. C. 1958. The introduction of Sparrows into Victoria. *Emu* 58: 264–6.

———. 1964. Acclimatisation in Victoria. *Victorian Historical Magazine* 36: 8–29.

Le Souef, L. 1912. Acclimatisation. In *Handbook of Western Australia*, 249–52.

Le Souef, W. H. D. 1890. Acclimatisation in Victoria. *Report of the 2nd Meeting of the Australian Association for the Advancement of Science, Melbourne, Victoria, January 1890*, 476–82.

———. 1903. Goldfinch in Australia and Tasmania. *Zoologist*, series 4, 7: 743.

———. 1918. Red-vented Bulbul. *Emu* 17: 236.

Le Sueur, G. 1913. *Cecil Rhodes, the Man and his Work*. John Murray: London.

Lever, C. 1957. The Mandarin Duck in Britain. *Country Life* 122: 829–31.

★———. 1977a. *The Naturalized Animals of the British Isles*. Hutchinson: London. (Paperback edn, Paladin Granada: London, 1979.)

———. 1977b. Britain's naturalized animals. *Illustrated London News* 265: 45–7.

———. 1978. A new place like home. *Bird Life* (July/August): 12–15.

———. 1979a. The invaders. *The Listener* 101: 716.

———. 1979b. A question of survival: introduced animals in Britain. *Country Life* 165: 400–1.

———. 1980a. Naturalized animals of the British Isles. *Animals* 3: 4–7.

———. 1980b. Britain's animal kingdom. *Daily Telegraph*, 21 January.

———. 1980c. Unwanted visitors. In *Wildlife '80*, 76–81. London Editions/World Wildlife Fund: London.

———. 1981. Unwelcome guests. *The Living Countryside* 2 (21).

———. 1982a. Father of wildlife conservation [Charles Waterton and the Little Owl]. *Country Life* 172: 1698–9.

———. 1982b. Avian adoptions [Review of Long 1981]. *The Times Literary Supplement*, 12 March.

————. 1982c. [Review of Long 1981.] *Ibis* 124: 218–19.

————. 1984a. [Review of Love 1983.] *Ibis* 126:267.

————. 1984b. Budgerigar. In I. L. Mason ed., *Evolution of Domesticated Animals*, Ch. 54: 361–4. Longman: London and New York.

————. 1984c. Conservation success for two Bermudan bird species [Cahow and Yellow-crowned Night Heron]. *Oryx* 18: 138–43.

————. 1985a. Goshawk upsets Night Herons [in Bermuda]. *Oryx* 19: 43–4.

★————. 1985b. *Naturalized Mammals of the World*. Longman: London and New York.

————. 1985c. The Little Owl in Britain. *Hawk Trust Annual Report 1984* 14: 12–14.

————. 1985d. Britain's Mandarin. *The Field* 266: 74.

Levi, H. W. 1952. Evaluation of wildlife importations. *Science Monthly* 74: 315–22.

————. 1952–6. Bibliography on the introduction of exotic animals. Wausau Extension Center and Department of Zoology, University of Wisconsin. Mimeograph (20 pp.).

————. 1953. Reports of introductions of animals [to the USA]. Wausau Extension Center, University of Wisconsin. Mimeograph (3 pp.).

Levi, W. M. 1941. *The Pigeon*. R. L. Bryan & Co.: Columbia, South Carolina.

Lewin, V. 1965. The introduction and present status of the California Quail in the Okanagan Valley of British Columbia. *Condor* 67: 61–6.

————. 1971. Exotic game birds of the Puu Waawaa Ranch, Hawaii. *Journal of Wildlife Management* 35: 141–55.

Lewin, V. & Holmes, J. C. 1971. Helminths from the exotic game birds of the Puu Waawaa Ranch, Hawaii. *Pacific Science* 25: 372–81.

Lewin, V. & Lewin, G. 1984. The Kalij Pheasant, a newly established game bird on the island of Hawaii. *Wilson Bulletin* 96: 634–46.

Lewin, V. & Mahrt, J. L. 1983. Parasites of Kalij Pheasants (*Lophura leucomelana*) on the island of Hawaii. *Pacific Science* 37: 81–3.

Lewis, H. E. 1925. The first Labrador record of the Starling (*Sturnus vulgaris*). *Auk* 42: 272–3.

————. 1927. A distributional and economic study of the European Starling in Ontario. *University of Toronto Studies, Biological Series* No. 30 (57 pp.).

————. 1931. Notes on the Starling (*Sturnus vulgaris*) in the northern parts of its North American range. *Auk* 48: 605–6.

————. 1934. Some observations indicating the northeastward extension of the Starling [in North America]. *Auk* 51: 88–9.

————. 1935. Nesting of the Starling (*Sturnus vulgaris vulgaris* L.) in the Labrador Peninsula. *Auk* 52: 313.

Lewis, H. G. 1932. The occurrence of the European Starling (*Sturnus vulgaris*) in the James Bay region. *Auk* 49: 225.

Leys, H. N. 1964. Het Voorkomen van de Turkse Tortel (*Streptopelia decaocto* Friv.) in Nederland. *Limosa* 37: 232–63. (See also *Ibis* 107: 4.)

Lichtenbelt, H. J. 1972. Nijlganzen [Egyptian Goose]. *Vogeljaar* 20: 103.

Liffiton, E. N. 1888. Notes on the decrease of Pheasants on the west coast of the North Island. *Transactions of the New Zealand Institute* 21: 225–6.

Lilford, Lord. 1895. *Notes on the Birds of Northamptonshire and Neighbourhood*. R. H. Porter: London.

————. 1903. *Lord Lilford on Birds*. Hutchinson: London.

Limentani, J. D. 1975. Changes in wintering habits by Canada Geese. *Cambridge Bird Report* No. 48.

Lindemann, W. 1950. Einburgerung der tetraonen. *Columba* 1: 38.

————. 1956. Transplantation of game in Europe and Asia. *Journal of Wildlife Management* 20: 68–70.

Lindley-Cohen, L. 1898. General notes. *Producers' Gazette and Settlers' Record of Western Australia* 5: 28, 162, 223–9.

Lindsay, A. A. 1939. Food of the Starling in central New York State. *Wilson Bulletin* 51: 176–82.

Lindzey, J. S. 1967. Highlights of management. In O. H. Hewitt ed., *The Wild Turkey and its Management*, Ch. 9: 245–59. Wildlife Society: Washington, DC.

★**Linn, I. L.** ed. 1979. *Wildlife Introductions to Great Britain. Report by the Working Group on Introductions of the UK Committee for International Nature Conservation* (32 pp.). Nature Conservancy Council: London.

Lipp, F. 1963. Parakeet [Budgerigar] City – a tourist attraction. *Florida Naturalist* 36(1-B): 1.

Littler, F. M. 1901. European birds in Tasmania. *Emu* 1: 121–4.

Liversidge, R. n.d. Exotic bird species in South Africa. Mimeograph (4 pp.).

★————. 1962. The spread of the European Starling in the Eastern Cape. *Ostrich* 33: 13–16.

————. 1975. Beware the exotic bird. *Bokmakierie* 27: 86–7.

————. 1979. Birds naturalized in South Africa. *Bokmakierie* 31: 43–4.

————. 1980. Exotic birds in South Africa. *Proceedings of the 17th International Ornithological Congress*, 1376.

————. 1985. Alien bird species introduced into southern Africa. In L. J. Bunning ed., *Proceedings of the Symposium on Birds and Man, Johannesburg, 1983*. Witwatersrand Bird Club/Southern African Ornithological Society: Johannesburg.

Lloyd, L. 1867. *The Game Birds and Wild Fowl of Sweden and Norway*. Day & Son: London.

Locey, F. H. 1937. Introduced game birds of Hawaii. *Paradise of the Pacific* 49: 27–30.

Lockerbie, C. W. 1939. Starlings arrive in Utah. *Condor* 41: 170.

Long, J. L. 1964. The Sparrow. *Journal of Agriculture of Western Australia* 5: 357–64.

——. 1965. The Starling. *Journal of Agriculture of Western Australia* 6: 144–7.

——. 1967a. The Indian Crow. *Journal of Agriculture of Western Australia* 8: 170–3.

——. 1967b. The European Goldfinch, *Carduelis carduelis*, in the Metropolitan area of Perth, Western Australia. Unpublished thesis, Institute of Agricultural Technology, Western Australia.

——. 1968. The Spice Finch, the Red-whiskered Bulbul and the Indian Mynah. *Journal of Agriculture of Western Australia* 9: 376–9, 510–11.

——. 1969a. The Java Sparrow. *Journal of Agriculture of Western Australia* 10: 212–13.

——. 1969b. Introduction of the Red-browed Finch to Western Australia. *Journal of Agriculture of Western Australia* 10: 2–3.

——. 1970. The European Goldfinch in Western Australia. *Journal of Agriculture of Western Australia* 11: 152–4.

——. 1971. The Feral Pigeon, *Columba livia* Gmelin, in Western Australia, and control experiments with alpha-chloralose in an urban environment. Unpublished Departmental Report, Agriculture Protection Board of Western Australia, Perth.

——. 1972. *Introduced Birds and Mammals in Western Australia*. Agriculture Protection Board of Western Australia Technical Series No. E1 (30 pp.).

*——. 1981. *Introduced Birds of the World*. A. H. & A. W. Reed: Sydney; David & Charles: Newton Abbot, Devon.

Long, R. C. 1959. The European House Sparrow, *Passer domesticus*, in Swaziland. *Ostrich* 30: 44.

Loustau-Lalanne, P. 1962. The birds of the Chagos Archipelago, Indian Ocean. *Ibis* 104: 67–73.

Love, J. A. 1978. The reintroduction of the Sea Eagle to the Isle of Rhum. *Hawk Trust Annual Report 1977* 8: 16–18.

——. 1980a. White-tailed Eagle reintroduction on the Isle of Rhum. *Scottish Birds* 11: 65–73.

——. 1980b. Return of the Sea Eagle. *British Trust for Ornithology News* 108: 4–5.

——. 1980c. Reintroducing Sea Eagles on Rhum: a progress report. *Hawk Trust Annual Report 1979* 10: 32–3.

——. 1980d. The return of the Sea Eagle to Scotland. *Hebridean Naturalist* 4: 46–8.

*——. 1983a. *The Return of the Sea Eagle*. Cambridge University Press: Cambridge.

——. 1983b. White-tailed Eagle – reintroduction experiment. *Birds (Magazine of the Royal Society for the Protection of Birds)* 9: 27–8.

——. 1983c. A saga of Sea Eagles. *Scottish Wildlife* (September): 12–15.

——. 1983d. First nesting attempts by reintroduced Sea Eagles. *Hawk Trust Annual Report 1982* 13: 21.

——. 1983–4. Nature Conservancy Council White-tailed Sea Eagle reintroduction project reports, 1982 and 1983. Unpublished mimeographs (4 pp. and 5 pp.).

Love, J. A. & **Ball, M. E.** 1979. White-tailed Sea Eagle reintroduction to the Isle of Rhum, Scotland, 1975–77. *Biological Conservation* 16: 23–30.

Lowe, P. R. 1933. The differential characters in the tarso-metatarsi of *Gallus* and *Phasianus* as they bear on the problem of the introduction of the Pheasant into Europe and the British Isles. *Ibis*, series 13, 3: 332–43.

Lueps, P. 1975. The Red-legged Partridge, *Alectoris rufa*, in Switzerland. *Naturhistorisches Museum der Stadt Bern Jahrbuch* 5: 133–51 [in German].

Lund, H. M.-K. 1963. [Canada Geese in Norway.] *Jaktfiske-frilufsliv* 92: 534–6 [in Norwegian].

L'vov, I. A. 1962. [Acclimatization of Pheasants in the Ukraine.] *Ptitsevodstvo* 10: 22–4 [in Russian].

Lyon-Field, B. 1938. Mynah Birds. *Fiji Agricultural Journal* 9: 19–22.

M

Maben, A. F. & **Cruz, R.** 1980. Population size and distribution of Black Francolin on Guam. In *Annual Report of the Guam Aquatic and Wildlife Resources Division, Department of Agriculture*, FY 1980: 169–76.

Mabie, D. W. 1981. Introduction of the Ring-necked Pheasant to the, Texas Gulf coast. *Proceedings of the 35th Annual Conference of the Southeastern Association of Fish and Wildlife Agencies*, 249–55.

McAtee, W. L. 1925. Note on the crested mynah: introduction upon introduction. *Auk* 42: 159–60.

——. 1929. Game birds suitable for naturalization in the United States. *US Department of Agriculture Circular* No. 96 (24 pp.).

——. 1944. The European migratory Quail in North America. *Auk* 61: 652.

——. 1945. *The Ring-necked Pheasant and its Management in North America*. American Wildlife Institute: Washington, DC.

McBride, G., **Parer, I. P.** & **Foenander, F.** 1969. The social organization and behaviour of the feral domestic fowl. *Animal Behaviour Monographs* 2: 127–81.

McCabe, R. A. & **Hawkins, A. S.** 1946. The Hungarian Partridge in Wisconsin. *American Midland Naturalist* 36: 1–75.

McCance, N. 1962. Reckless acclimatization. *Australian Aviculture* (August): 105.

McCaskie, R. G. 1965. The Cattle Egret reaches the west coast of the United States. *Condor* 67: 89.

McCaskill, L. W. 1945. Preliminary report on the

present position of the Australian Magpies (*G. hypoleuca* and *G. tibicen*) in New Zealand. *New Zealand Bird Notes* 1: 86–104.

McCauseland, D. E. 1952. Exotic species at the Cape. *Cape Bird Club News Sheet* 9: 2.

McClure, H. E. 1974. *Migration and Survival of the Birds of Asia*. SEATO Medical Research Laboratory: Bangkok, Thailand.

McCoy, F. S. 1862. Acclimatisation, its nature and applicability to Victoria. Anniversary address to first Annual Meeting of the Acclimatisation Society of Victoria: Melbourne.

McCulloch, D. 1966–70. [Indian Mynah in South Africa.] *Natal Bird Club News Sheet* 140: 3; 146: 4; 162: 2; 173: 4; 185: 1.

MacDonald, D. & **Jantzen, R. A.** 1967. Management of the Merriam's Turkey. In O. H. Hewitt ed., *The Wild Turkey and its Management*, Ch. 16: 493–534. Wildlife Society: Washington, DC.

McGarvie, A. M. & **Templeton, M. T.** 1974. Additions to the birds of King Island, Bass Strait. *Emu* 74: 91–6.

McGill, A. R. 1948. The Asiatic Ring Dove as an escapee. *Emu* 47: 232–3.

———. 1949. Australian status of the Colombo Crow. *Emu* 49: 83–4.

———. 1960. *A Handlist of the Birds of New South Wales*. Fauna Protection Panel: Sydney.

McGregor, R. C. 1902. Notes on a small collection of birds from the island of Maui, Hawaii. *Condor* 4: 59–62.

McIlroy, J. C. 1968. The biology of Magpies (*Gymnorhina* spp.) in New Zealand. Unpublished M.Agric.Sc. thesis, Lincoln College, University of Canterbury, New Zealand.

MacKay, V. M. & **Hughes, W. M.** 1963. Crested Mynah in British Columbia. *Canadian Field-Naturalist* 77: 154–62.

McKean, J. L. & **Hindwood, K. A.** 1965. Additional notes on the birds of Lord Howe Island. *Emu* 64: 79–97.

MacKeith, T. T. 1916. The Capercaillie in Renfrewshire. *Scottish Naturalist*, 270.

McKenzie, H. R. 1953. Virginia Quail in Wairora, Hawke's Bay district. *Notornis* 5: 123.

Mackenzie, S. 1984. Spirit ducks of Asia. *Wildfowl World* 91: 22–3.

Mackenzie, W. D. 1900. Capercaillie in Strathnairn. *Annals of Scottish Natural History*, 51.

McKinley, D. 1960. A chronology and bibliography of wildlife in Missouri. *University of Missouri Bulletin* No. 61.

Mackworth-Praed, C. W. & **Grant, C. H. B.** 1952–73. *African Handbook of Birds*, 6 vols. Series 1 (2 vols): *Birds of Eastern and North-Eastern Africa* (1952 and 1955); series 2 (2 vols): *Birds of the Southern Third of Africa* (1962–3); series 3 (2 vols): *Birds of West Central and Western Africa* (1970 and 1973). Longman: London and New York.

McLachlan, G. R. 1955. European Starling seen in Port Elizabeth [South Africa]. *Ostrich* 26: 157.

McLean, D. D. 1958. *Upland Game of California*. California State Department of Fish and Game: Sacramento, California.

MacLean, G. L. 1962. House Sparrow, *Passer domesticus*, at Van Rhynsdorp [South Africa]. *Ostrich* 33: 76.

———. 1985. *Roberts' Birds of South Africa*. Trustees of John Voelcker Bird Book Fund: Cape Town.

McLennan, J. A. & **MacMillan, B. W. H.** 1983. Predation by the Rook on larvae of the grass grub in Hawke's Bay, New Zealand. *New Zealand Journal of Agricultural Research* 26: 139–45.

McNeel, J. 1973. The Japanese Versicolor Pheasant. *Idaho Wildlife Review* 26: 12–15.

MacPherson, J. 1921 and 1923. Notes on the Red-eyed Bulbul (*Octocompsa jocosa*). *Emu* 21: 145–6; 23: 218–19.

McVicker, R. 1982. Exotic birds in Mombasa. *East Africa Natural History Society Bulletin* (September/October), 74.

Madoc, G. C. 1956. *An Introduction to Malayan Birds*. Caxton Press: Kuala Lumpur, Malaysia.

Mann, C. F. & **Britton, P.** 1972. Naturalized birds on the Kenya coast. *East African Natural History Society Bulletin* (November), 181–2.

Manson-Bahr, P. E. C. 1953. The European Starling in Fiji. *Ibis* 95: 699–700.

Maples, S. 1907. The Little Owl in Hertfordshire. *Zoologist*, 353.

Marchant, S. & **McNab, J. W.** 1962. Iraq bird notes. *Bulletin of the Iraq Natural History Institute* 2: 1–48.

Markus, M. B. 1958. The House Sparrow in Bechuanaland [Botswana]. *Ostrich* 29: 129.

———. 1960. Some records of the House Sparrow, *Passer domesticus*, in the Orange Free State and Cape Province. *Ostrich* 31: 106.

Marler, P. & **Boatman, D. J.** 1951. Observations on the birds of Pico, Azores. *Ibis* 93: 90.

Marples, B. J. 1942. A study of the Little Owl in New Zealand. *Transactions and Proceedings of the Royal Society of New Zealand*, 237–52.

Marples, B. J. & **Gurr, L.** 1953. The Chukor in New Zealand. *Emu* 53: 283–91.

Marquiss, M. 1981. The Goshawk in Britain – its provenance and current status. In R. E. Kenward & I. M. Lindsay eds, *Understanding the Goshawk* (*Proceedings of the Conference of the International Association for Falconry and the Conservation of Birds of Prey*), 43–57.

———. 1983. Goshawk – sporadic success. *Birds* (*Magazine of the Royal Society for the Protection of Birds*) 9: 27.

Marquiss, M. & **Newton, I.** 1982. The Goshawk in Britain. *British Birds* 75: 243–60.

Marshall, H. B. 1907. Capercaillie in Peeblesshire. *Annals of Scottish Natural History*, 224.

Marshall, J. T. 1949. The endemic avifauna of Saipan, Tinian, Guam and Palau. *Condor* 51: 200–1.

Marshall, P. 1934. Effect of the introduction of exotic plant and animal forms into New Zealand. *Proceedings of the 5th Pacific Science Congress, Victoria and Vancouver, June 1933*, 1: 811–16. University of Toronto Press: Toronto.

Mason, I. L. ed. 1984. *Evolution of Domesticated Animals*. Longman: London and New York.

Masson, V. 1959. The Chukar in the southeast region. *Oregon State Game and Fish Commission Bulletin* No. 14: 3, 6–8.

Matheson, C. 1963. The Pheasant in Wales. *British Birds* 44: 452–6.

Mathisen, J. E. & **Mathisen, A.** 1960. History and status of introduced game birds in Nebraska. *Nebraska Bird Review* 28: 19–22.

Maury, M. & **Delvaux, J.** 1974. Réintroduire le Grand Corbeau [Raven] en Belgique? *Zoo, Antwerp*, Suppl. 2: 56–62.

Maxwell, H. 1905. Naturalization of the Golden Pheasant. *Annals of Scottish Natural History*, 53–4.

——. 1907. Capercaillie in the south of Scotland. *Annals of Scottish Natural History*, 116.

Mayr, E. 1945. *Birds of the South West Pacific*. MacMillan: New York.

——. 1965a. Classification, identification and sequence of genera and species. *Oiseau et la Revue Française d'Ornithologie* 35 (Special): 90–95.

——. 1965b. The nature of colonization in birds. In H. G. Baker & G. L. Stebbins eds, *The Genetics of Colonizing Species (Proceedings of the 1st International Union of Biological Sciences Symposium on General Biology)*, 29–47. Academic Press: New York.

——. 1978. *Birds of the Southwest Pacific: A Field Guide to the Area between Samoa, New Caledonia and Micronesia*. MacMillan: New York.

Mead, C. 1986. The Pilgrim feathers? *British Trust for Ornithology Newsletter* No. 145:1.

Meade-Waldo, E. G. B. 1893. List of the birds observed in the Canary Islands. *Ibis*, series 6, 5: 185–207.

Medway, Lord & **Wells, D. R.** eds. 1963–4. Bird reports. *Malayan Nature Journal* 17: 123–44; 18: 133–67.

——. 1976: *The Birds of the Malay Peninsula*, Vol. 5. H. F. & G. Witherby: London; Penerbit University: Kuala Lumpur, Malaya.

Meiklejohn, J., Hodgson, L. K. & **Hodgson, C. J.** 1966. Observations of House Sparrows in Rhodesia. *Honeyguide* 48: 19–20.

Meinertzhagen, R. 1912. On the birds of Mauritius.

Ibis, series, 9, 6: 82–108.

——. 1924. A contribution towards the birds of Aden Protectorate. *Ibis*, series 11, 6: 625–42.

——. 1930. Nicoll's Birds of Egypt, 2 vols. Hugh Rees: London.

——. 1949. Notes on Saudi Arabian birds. *Ibis* 91: 465.

——. 1950. The Goshawk in Great Britain. *Bulletin of the British Ornithologists' Club* 70: 46–9.

——. 1952. An historical note on the Starling at the Cape of Good Hope. *Bulletin of the British Ornithologists' Club* 72: 47.

——. 1954. *Birds of Arabia*. Oliver & Boyd: Edinburgh and London.

——. 1959. *Pirates and Predators: The Piratical and Predatory Habits of Birds*. Oliver & Boyd: Edinburgh and London.

*Meininger, P. L., Mullié, W. C. & **Bruun, B.** 1980. The spread of the house crow *Corvus splendens*, with special reference to the occurrence in Egypt. *Le Gerfaut* 70: 245–50.

Meininger, P. L., Mullié, W. C., Van Der Kamp, J. & **Spaans, B.** 1979. Report of the Netherlands Ornithological Expedition to Egypt in January and February 1979. Middleburg.

Melliss, J. C. 1870. Notes on the birds of St Helena. *Ibis*, series 2, 6: 97–106.

Menzies, W. S. 1907. Capercaillie and Willow Grouse in Moray. *Annals of Scottish Natural History*, 116–17.

Mercer, R. 1966. *A Field Guide to Fiji Birds*. Special Publication No. 1 (39 pp.). Fiji Museum: Suva.

Merikallio, E. 1958. *Finnish Birds: their Distribution and Numbers*. Societas Pro Fauna et Flora Fennica (*Fauna Fennica* 5): Helsingfors, Finland.

Merne, O. J. 1970. The status of the Canada Goose in Ireland. *Irish Bird Report* 17: 12–17.

Merriam, C. H. 1889. The English Sparrow in North America. *US Department of Agriculture Bulletin* No. 1.

Merrill, J. C. 1876. The European Tree Sparrow in the United States. *American Midland Naturalist* 10: 50–1.

Merton, D. V. 1965a. A brief history of the North Island Saddleback. *Notornis* 12: 208–11.

——. 1965b. Transfer of Saddlebacks from Hen Island to Middle Chicken Island, January 1964. *Notornis* 12: 213–22.

——. 1973. Conservation of the Saddleback. *Wildlife – a Review* (New Zealand Wildlife Service) 4: 13–23.

——. 1975a. Success in re-establishing a threatened species: the Saddleback – its status and conservation. *Bulletin of the International Council for Bird Preservation* 12: 150–8.

——. 1975b. The Saddleback – its status and conservation. In R. D. Martin ed., *Breeding Endangered Species in Captivity*, 61–74. Academic Press: London, New York and San Francisco.

Meyer, A. B. 1879. Field notes on the birds of Celebes, Part 2. *Ibis*, series 4, 3: 125–46.

Middleton, A. L. A. 1965. The ecology and reproductive biology of the European Goldfinch, *Carduelis carduelis*, near Melbourne, Victoria. Unpublished PhD thesis, Monash University, Melbourne.

Miller, A. H. 1928. The status of the Cardinal in California. *Condor* 30: 243–5.

Miller, L. 1930. The Asiatic Mynah in Los Angeles, California. *Condor* 32: 302.

Mills, D. H. 1937. European Goldfinch at Hanover, New Hampshire. *Auk* 54: 544–5.

Mills, H. B. 1943. Starlings nesting in Montana. *Condor* 45: 197.

Mills, J. A. & **Williams, G. R.** 1979. The status of endangered New Zealand birds. In M. Tyler ed., *Status of Endangered Australasian Wildlife (Proceedings of the Centennial Symposium of the Royal Zoological Society of South Australia, Adelaide, September 1978)*, 147–68.

Mills, S. 1978. What's wrong with the Néné in Hawaii? *Oryx* 14: 359–61.

Milne-Edwards, A. & **Oustalet, E.** 1888. Études sur les mammifères et les oiseaux des Îles Comores. *Nouvelles Archives du Muséum d'Histoire Naturelle, Paris* 10: 219–97.

Milon, P., Petter, J. J. & **Randrianasolo, G.** 1973. *Faune du Madagascar. Part 35: Birds*. Orstom: Tananarive, Madagascar; CNRS: Paris.

Mitchell, K. D. G. & **Tozer, R. B.** 1974. Feral parakeets and control of introductions. *British Birds* 67: 484–5.

Mitchell, M. H. 1957. *Observations on the Birds of Southeastern Brazil*. University of Toronto Press: Canada.

Moeed, A. 1975. Food of Skylarks and pipits, finches, and Feral Pigeons near Christchurch. *Notornis* 22: 135–42.

Mohler, L. I. 1949. Foods of Pheasants in Nebraska. *Wildlife Management Notes* 1: 27–30.

Moller, A. P. 1980. Is the rook *Corvus frugilegus* in northern Jutland introduced from Great Britain? *Dansk Ornitologisk Tidsskrift* 74: 77.

Monson, G. 1948. The Starling in Arizona. *Condor* 50: 45.

Montagna, W. 1940. European Goldfinch in New York. *Auk* 57: 575–6.·

Montcrieff, P. 1931. Certain introduced birds of New Zealand. *Emu* 30: 219.

Montgomery, S. L., Gagné, W. C. & **Gagné, B. H.** 1980. Notes on birdlife and nature conservation in the Marquesas and Society Islands. *Elepaio* 40: 152–5.

Moon, G. 1979. *The Birds Around Us: New Zealand Birds, their Habits and Habitats*. Heinemann: Auckland.

Moore, H. J. & **Boswell, C.** 1956. *Field Observations on the birds of Iraq*. Publication No. 10. Iraq Natural History Museum: Baghdad.

Moore, J. 1984. European Starling reproduction in central New Mexico. *Journal of Field Ornithology* 55: 254–7.

Moore, R. T. 1935. A new Jay of the genus *Cyanocorax* from Sinaloa, Mexico. *Auk* 52: 274–7.

———. 1938. Discovery of the nest and eggs of the Tufted Jay. *Condor* 40: 233–41.

———. 1939. A review of the House Finches of the subgenus *Burrica*. *Condor* 41: 177–205.

Moors, P. J. 1983. Predation by mustelids and rodents on the eggs and chicks of native and introduced birds in Kowai Bush, New Zealand *Ibis* 125: 137–54.

———. 1984. *Immigrant Killers: Introduced Predators and the Conservation of Birds in New Zealand*. Oxford University Press: Auckland and Oxford (1985).

Moreau, R. E. 1944. Clutch size in introduced birds. *Auk* 61: 583–6.

———. 1960. The Pliocene weavers of the Indian Ocean islands. *Journal für Ornithologie, Leipzig* 101: 29–49.

———. 1966. *The Bird Faunas of Africa and its Islands*. Academic Press: New York and London.

Moreland, R. 1950. Success of Chukar Partridge in the State of Washington. *Transactions of the 15th North American Wildlife Conference*, 399–409.

Morgan, A. M. 1929. [No title.] *South Australian Ornithologist* 10: 132–3.

———. 1933. An addition to the introduced avifauna of South Australia. *South Australian Ornithologist* 12: 31.

Morgan, B. & **Morgan, J.** 1965. Cattle Egrets in Brisbane. *Emu* 64: 230–2.

Morgan, H. K. 1958. House Sparrow (*Passer domesticus*). *Ostrich* 29: 87.

Morony, J. J., Bock, W. J. & **Farrand, J.** 1975. *Reference List of Birds of the World*. American Museum of Natural History: New York.

Morris, A. 1982. Exotic parrots. *Honeyguide* 109: 31.

Morris, J. G. 1969. The control of Feral Pigeons and Sparrows associated with intensive animal production. *Australian Journal of Science* 32: 9–14.

Moulton, M. P. & **Pimm, S. L.** 1983. The introduced Hawaiian avifauna: biogeographic evidence for competition. *American Naturalist* 121: 669–90.

Mousley, H. 1923 and 1925. The Starling (*Sturnus vulgaris*) breeding at Hatley, Quebec. *Auk* 40: 537; 42: 273–5.

———. 1926. Further notes on the Starling in Canada. *Auk* 43: 372–3.

Mowat, C. 1980. Large numbers of House Crows. *Albatross* 260: 4.

Mull, M. E. 1978. Expanding range of Kalij Pheasant on the Big Island [Hawaii]. *Elepaio* 38: 74–5.

Muller, P. 1967. Zur Verbreitung von *Passer domesticus* in Brasilien. *Journal für Ornithologie, Leipzig* 108: 497–9.

★**Munro, G. C.** 1944. *Birds of Hawaii.* Bridgeway Press: Japan. (Revised edn, 1960.)

Munro, J. A. 1921. British Columbia bird notes, 1920–21. *Murrelet* 2: 15–16.

———. 1922. The 'Japanese Starling' in Vancouver, British Columbia. *Canadian Field-Naturalist* 36: 32–3.

———. 1930. The Japanese Starling at Alert Bay, British Columbia. *Canadian Field-Naturalist* 44: 30.

———. 1947. Starling in British Columbia. *Condor* 49: 130.

Munro, J. A. & **Cowan, I. M.** 1947. *A Review of the Bird Fauna of British Columbia.* British Columbia Provincial Museum: Vancouver

Munro, W. T. & **Peter, S.** 1981. *Preliminary Non-Game Bird Management Plan for British Columbia.* Fish & Wildlife Branch, Ministry of Environment, British Columbia.

Murphy, E. C. 1978 Breeding ecology of House Sparrows: spatial variation. *Condor* 80: 180–93.

Murphy, R. C. 1915. Birdlife of Trinidad islet. *Auk* 32: 332–48.

———. 1924. The marine ornithology of the Cape Verde Islands, with a list of all the birds of the archipelago. *Bulletin of the American Museum of Natural History* No. 50: 211–78.

———. 1945. Middle nineteenth century introductions of British birds to Long Island, New York. *Auk* 62: 306.

Murray, J. & **Murray, N.** 1984. Ringnecked Parakeet in Cape Town. *Promerops* 164: 17.

Murray, R. E. 1963. The Black Francolin. *Proceedings of the 17th Annual Conference of the South-Eastern Association of State Game and Fish Commissioners,* 120–1.

Murton, R. K. & **Wright, E. N.** 1968. *The Problem of Birds as Pests.* Academic Press: London.

Murton, R. K., **Thearle, R. J. P.** & **Coombs, C. F. B.** 1974. Ecological studies of the Feral Pigeon *Columba livia. Journal of Applied Ecology* 11: 841–54.

Mussehl, T. W. & **Howell, F. W.** 1971. *Game Management in Montana.* State of Montana Department of Fish and Game: Helena.

Musselman, T. E. 1950. European Tree Sparrows at Hannibal, Missouri. *Auk* 67: 105.

———. 1953. European Tree Sparrow extending its range in the United States. *Wilson Bulletin* 65: 48.

Musson, C. T. 1904–5. The House Sparrow in New South Wales. *Agricultural Gazette of New South Wales* (in *Emu* 9: 159–61).

———. 1907. The House Sparrow in New South Wales. *Agricultural Gazette of New South Wales* 18: 535–8; 19: 914–17.

Myrberget, S. 1976. [Pheasant in Norway.] *Sterna* 15: 174–6 [in Norwegian].

Myres, M. T. 1958. The European Starling in British Columbia, 1947–57. *Occasional Papers of the British Columbia Provincial Museum* No. 11: 1–60.

N

Nagel, W. O. 1939. A preliminary report of Chukar Partridges in Missouri. *Transactions of the 4th North American Wildlife Conference,* 416–21.

———. 1940. The Chukar Partridge and other introduced game birds. *Proceedings of the Minnesota Wildlife Conference: Short Course* No. 2: 12–13.

———. 1945. Adaptability of Chukar Partridges to Missouri conditions. *Journal of Wildlife Management* 9: 207–16.

Nagel, W. O. & **Bennitt, R.** 1945. The Chukar Partridge. *Missouri Conservation* 2: 2, 7.

Nappee, C. 1981–2. Capercaillie and Black Grouse breeding in the Parc National des Cevennes, and first release results. In T.W.I. Lovel ed., *Grouse (Proceedings of the 2nd International Symposium on Grouse at Dalhousie Castle, Edinburgh, Scotland, 16–20 March 1981).* World Pheasant Association: Exning, Newmarket, Suffolk, England.

Narwaz, M. 1982. Re-introduction of wild fauna in Pakistan [*Catreus wallichi*]. *Tigerpaper* 9: 5.

Nature Conservancy Council. 1985. *The Sea Eagle.* Nature Conservancy Council's Interpretative Branch: London (12 pp.).

Navas, J. R. 1981. Los vertebrados exoticos introducidos en Argentina. *Reunión Iberoaméricana Conservacion y Zoologia de Vertebrados 1980,* 128.

Nazarenko, L. F. & **Gurskii, I. G.** 1963. The acclimatization of Pheasants in the area northwest of the Black Sea. *Ornitologiya* 6: 477–8 [in Russian].

Ndao, B. 1980. Le moineau domestique (*Passer domesticus*) espéce nouvelle pour le Sénégal. *Bulletin de l'Institut Fondamental d'Afrique Noire* 40: 422–4.

Neidermyer, W. J. & **Hickey, J. J.** 1977. The Monk Parakeet in the United States, 1970–75. *American Birds* 31: 273–8.

Nelson, L. K. 1963. Introduction of the Blackneck Pheasant group and crosses into the southeastern states. *Proceedings of the 17th Annual Conference of the South Eastern Association of Game and Fish Commissioners,* 111–19.

———. 1964. *A Ten-year Study of Ring-necked Pheasant Introductions in Kentucky: a Final Report.* Kentucky Department of Fish and Wildlife Research, P-R Game Management Technical Service No. 14 (153 pp.).

———. 1972. *A Five-year Study of a Black Francolin Introduction in Kentucky: a Final Report.* Kentucky Department of Fish and Wildlife Research, P-R Game Management Technical Service No. 17 (37 pp.).

Nevill, H. 1971. European Starling in The Transkei. *Natal Bird Club News Sheet* 201:2.

———. 1973. Indian Mynah (*Acridotheres tristis*). *Ostrich* 44: 132.

Newlands, W. A. 1976. Reintroduction of the Capercaillie. In L. Boitani ed., *Reintroductions: Techniques and Ethics*, 197–200. World Wildlife Fund: Rome.

Newman, D. G. 1980. Colonization of Coppermine Island by the North Island Saddleback. *Notornis* 27: 146–7.

Newton, A. & Newton, E. 1859. Observations on the birds of St Croix. *Ibis* 1: 252–64.

———. 1861. [Letters to the Editor.] *Ibis* 3: 114–16.

Newton, E. 1867. On the land birds of the Seychelles archipelago. *Ibis*, series 2, 3: 335–60.

Newton, R. 1959. Notes on two species of Foudia in Mauritius. *Ibis* 101: 240–3.

Newton-Howes, R. 1966. The House Sparrow in Rhodesia. *Honeyguide* 49:19.

New Zealand Acclimatization Societies. *Annual Reports.*

Nicholl, M. J. 1912. *Wild Birds of the Giza Gardens 1898–1911.* Government of Egypt: Cairo.

Nicholls, E. D. B. 1928. The Starling menace. *Emu* 27: 293–4.

Nichols, J. T. 1936. The European Goldfinch near New York City, 1915–35. *Auk* 53: 429–31.

———. 1937. Notes on Starling spread and migration. *Auk* 54: 209–10.

Niethammer, G. 1953 and 1956. Zur Vogelwelt Boliviens. *Bonner Zoologische Beiträge* 4: 195–303; 7: 84–150.

*———. 1963. *Dire Einbürgerung von Säugetieren und Vögeln in Europa.* [Introduced mammals and birds in Europe.] Paul Parey: Hamburg.

———. 1971. Some problems connected with the House Sparrow's colonization of the world. *Proceedings of the 3rd Pan-African Ornithological Congress, 1969; Ostrich Supplement* 8: 445–8.

Nilsson, N. N. 1957 Nevada's experience with exotic game birds. *Proceedings of the 37th Annual Conference of the Western Association of State Game and Fish Commissioners*, 283–5.

Norderhaug, M. 1984. Captive breeding and reintroduction of northern geese *Anser erythropus*. *Norsk Polarinstitut Skrifter* 101: 161–4.

Norman, S. 1975. House Sparrow at Solwezi. *·Zambian Ornithological Society Newsletter* 5: 102.

Norris, R. A. 1956. Introduction of exotic game birds in Georgia. *Oriole* 21: 1–6.

Northwood, J. D'A. 1952. The Myna in Hawaii – asset or liability? *Audubon Magazine* 54: 22–7.

Norton, S. P. W. 1922. Bird notes from Boree (New England Plateau). *Emu* 22: 39–44.

Nowak, E. 1965. *Die Türkentaube (Steptopelia decaocto).* Die Neue Brehm-Bücherei No. 353. A. Ziemsen Verlag: Wittenburg Lutherstadt.

O

Oatley, T. 1973. Indian House Crow: first S. A. sightings. *Bokmakierie* 25: 41–2.

Ogilvie, M. A. 1969. The status of the Canada Goose in Britain, 1967–69. *Wildfowl* 20: 79–85.

———. 1975. *Ducks of Britain and Europe.* T. & A. D. Poyser: Berkhamsted, Hertfordshire.

———. 1977. The numbers of Canada Geese in Britain, 1976. *Wildfowl* 28: 27–34.

———. 1978. *Wild Geese.* T. & A. D. Poyser: Berkhamsted, Hertfordshire.

O'Gorman, F. 1970. The development of game in Ireland. *Proceedings of the 8th International Congress of Game Biologists, Helsinki*, 387–96.

Ohashi, R. J. & Ueoka, M. L. 1977. Nests of the Red-whiskered Bulbul on Oahu. *Elepaio* 38:1.

Ojala, H. & Sjöberg, J. 1968. Turkinkyyhky (*Streptopelia decaocto*) pesinyt Naantalissa. *Ornis Fennica* 45: 139–42 [in Finnish].

O'Keefe, T. M. 1973. Spread of the aliens. *Florida Sportsman*, 44–51.

Oldys, H. 1910. Introduction of the Hungarian Partridge into the United States. *US Department of Agriculture Yearbook, 1909*, 249–58.

Oliveira, R. G. de. 1980. [The Common African Waxbill (*Estrilda astrild*) and its introduction in Rio Grande do Sul.] *Anais da Sociedade Sul-riograndense de Ornitologia* 1: 25–8 [in Portuguese, with English summary].

★**Oliver. W. R. B.** 1930. *Birds of New Zealand.* Fine Arts: Wellington.

★———. 1955. *Birds of New Zealand.* A. H. & A. W. Reed: Wellington.

Olrog, C. C. 1959. *Las Aves Argentinas.* Universidad Nacional de Tucuman (Instituto Miguel Lillo): Argentina.

Ord, W. M. 1963. Black-headed Mannikins and Strawberry Finches. *Elepaio* 23:42.

———. 1964. Fairy terns return to Koko Head, June 7, 1964. *Elepaio* 25: 3–4.

———. 1967. *Hawaii's Birds.* Hawaiian Audubon Society: Honolulu.

———. 1982. Red-eared and Common Waxbills on Oahu. *Elepaio* 42: 89–90.

Ornithological Society of Japan. 1974. *Check List of Japanese Birds*, 3 vols. Gakken Company: Tokyo.

———. 1981. *Nihon San Choryui No Hanshoku Bunpu.* [Atlas of Japanese birds.] Kankyocho (Environment Ministry): Tokyo.

Ortiz-Crespo, F. I. 1977. La presencia del Gorrión Europeo, *Passer domesticus* L., en el Ecuador. *Revista Universidad Católica de Quito* 16: 193–7.

Osborn, T. A. B. 1934. Effect of introduction of exotic plants and animals into Australia. *Proceedings of the 5th Pacific Science Congress, Victoria and Vancouver*

June 1933 1: 809–10. University of Toronto Press: Toronto.

Osmaston, B. B. 1933. Some Andaman birds. *Journal of the Bombay Natural History Society* 35: 891–3.

Osmolovskaya, V. I. 1969. Artificial settlement of game birds as a means of maintaining and increasing their abundance. *Byulleten' Moskovskogo Obshchestva Ispȳtatelei Prirodȳ, Otdel Biologicheskii* 74: 15–24 [in Russian].

O'Sullivan, J. 1981. Introduced birds in the United Kingdom. In N. J. Pinder ed., Conservation and introduced species. *British Association of Nature Conservationists/University College London Discussion Paper in Conservation* No. 30: 24–31.

Ounsted, M. 1985. Fragile eggs to Hungary. *Wildfowl World* 92: 16–18.

Owen, M. 1983. The aliens. *Wildfowl World* 89: 16–19.

Owen, M., Atkinson-Willes, G. L. & **Salmon, D. G.** 1986. *Wildfowl in Great Britain*, revised edn. Cambridge University Press: Cambridge.

Owens, W. S. 1941. The Chukar Partridge. *Wyoming Wildlife* 6: 8, 16–17.

Owre, O. T. 1959. Cattle Egret in Haiti. *Auk* 76: 359.

*★——— 1973. A consideration of the exotic avifauna of southeastern Florida. *Wilson Bulletin* 85: 491–500.

Oxley, T. 1849 The zoology of Singapore. *Journal of the Indian Archipelago and Eastern Asia* 3: 594–7.

P

Packard, G. C. 1967. House Sparrows: evolution of populations from the Great Plains and Colorado Rockies. *Systematic Zoology* 16: 73–89.

Pakenham, R. H. W. 1936, 1939, 1943, 1945 and 1959. Field notes on the birds of Zanzibar and Pemba. *Ibis*, series 13, 6: 249–72; series 14, 3: 522–54; 85: 165–89; 87: 216–23; 101: 245–7.

———. 1979. *The Birds of Zanzibar and Pemba*. British Ornithologists' Union Checklist No. 2. British Ornithologists' Union: London.

Palermo, R. 1968. Louisiana exotic game bird program. *Louisiana Conservationist* 20: 20–2.

Palmer, C. E. 1965. *The Capercailzie*. Forestry Commission Leaflet No. 37. HMSO: London.

Palmer, R. S. ed. 1976. *Handbook of North American Birds*, 3 vols. Yale University Press: New Haven, Connecticut, and London.

Palmer, T. K. 1972. The House Finch and Starling in relation to California's agriculture. In S. C. Kendeigh and J. Pinowski eds, *Productivity, Population Dynamics and Systematics of Granivorous Birds (Proceedings of the General Meeting of the Working Group on Granivorous Birds, The Hague, Holland, 6–8 September 1970)*, 276–90. Polish Scientific Publications: Warsaw.

*★**Palmer, T. S.** 1899. The dangers of introducing noxious animals and birds. *US Department of Agriculture Yearbook, 1898*, 87–110.

Palmer, T. S. & **Oldys, H.** 1904. Importation of game birds and eggs for propagation. *US Department of Agriculture, Biological Survey and Farmers' Bulletin* No. 197 (27 pp.).

Parham, B. E. V. 1954. Birds as pests in Fiji. *Fiji Agricultural Journal* 25: 9–14.

Paker, T. A., Parker, S. A. & **Plenge, M. A.** 1982. *Annotated Checklist of Peruvian Birds*. Buteo Books: Vermillion, South Dakota.

Parker, T. A. & **Rowlett, R. A.** 1984. Some noteworthy records of birds from Bolivia. *Bulletin of the British Ornithologists' Club* 104: 110–13.

Parkes, K. C. 1959. Subspecific identity of the introduced Tree Sparrows, *Passer montanus*, in the Philippine Islands. *Ibis* 101: 243–4.

———. 1962. The Red Jungle Fowl of the Philippines – native or introduced? *Auk* 79: 479–81.

Parr, D. 1972 *Birds in Surrey 1900–1970*. Batsford: London.

Paton, J. B. 1985. The Red-whiskered Bulbul in South Australia. *South Australian Ornithologist* 29: 189–90.

Paton, J. B. & **Barrington, D.** 1985. The Barbary Dove in South Australia. *South Australian Ornithologist* 29: 193–4.

Paton, J. B. & **Pollard, B. M.** 1985. The Peach-faced Lovebird in South Australia. *South Australian Ornithologist* 29: 192.

Paton, P. W. C. 1981a. Yellow-fronted Canary extends range into 'Ohi'a forest on the Big Island. *Elepaio* 42: 11–12.

———. 1981b. Pelagic Kalij Pheasant? *Elepaio* 42: 139–40.

Paton, P. W. C., Ashman, P. R. & **McEldowney, H.** 1982. Chestnut-bellied Sandgrouse in Hawaii. *Elepaio* 43: 9–11.

Paton, P. W. C., Griffin, C. R. & **MacIvor, L. H.** 1982. Rose-ringed Parakeets nesting in Hawaii: a potential agricultural threat. *Elepaio* 43: 37–9.

Patten, G. H. 1982. Project on Ringnecked Parakeets. *Wits Bird Club News* 117: 20.

Paxton, R. O. 1974. The changing seasons. *American Birds* 28: 604–9.

Payn, W. H. 1948. Notes from Tunisia and eastern Algeria, February 1943 to April 1944. *Ibis* 90: 1–21.

Payne, R. B. & **Payne, K.** 1967. House Sparrows reach the Zambezi River in Mozambique. *Ostrich* 38: 283–4.

Pearsall, G. 1946. Notes on some birds of Kauai. *Elepaio* 7: 32–4.

Pearse, I. 1953. European Starling on Vancouver Island, British Columbia. *Canadian Field-Naturalist* 67: 94.

Pearson, A. J. 1962. Field notes on the birds of Ocean

Island and Nauru during 1961. *Ibis* 104: 421–4.

*Pennie, I. D. 1950–1. The history and distribution of the Capercaillie in Scotland. *Scottish Naturalist* 62: 65–87, 157–78; 63: 4–18, 135.

Penny, M. 1974. *The Birds of Seychelles and Outlying Islands*. Collins: London.

Penry, E. H. 1978. The House Sparrow, a successful opportunist? *Bulletin of the Zambian Ornithological Society* 10: 25–7.

Pentzhorn, B. L. & Morris, A. K. 1968. House Sparrow (*Passer domesticus*): new distributional data. *Ostrich* 39: 272.

Perkins, R. C. L. 1913. *Introduction: Fauna Hawaiiensis*, Vol. 1. Cambridge University Press: Cambridge.

Pernetta, J. C. & Handford, P. T. 1970. Mammalian and avian remains from possible Bronze Age deposits on Nornour, Isles of Scilly. *Journal of Zoology, London* 162: 534–40.

Pernetta, J. C. & Watling, D. 1978. The introduced and native terrestrial vertebrates of Fiji. *Pacific Science* 32: 223–44.

Pescott, E. E. 1943. The English Sparrow in Australia. *Victorian Naturalist* 60: 47.

Peters, J. L. and successors 1931–72. *Check-list of the Birds of the World*, 15 vols (8 and 11 in preparation). Harvard University Press and Museum of Comparative Zoology: Cambridge, Massachusetts.

Peterson, R. T. 1954. A new immigrant bird arrives. *National Geographic Magazine* 106: 281–92.

———. 1961. *A Field Guide to Western Birds*. Houghton Mifflin: Boston, Mass.

———. 1984. *A Field Guide to the Birds East of the Rockies*. Houghton Mifflin: Boston, Mass.

Peterson, R. T. & Chalif, E. L. 1973. *A Field Guide to Mexican Birds and Adjacent Central America*. Houghton Mifflin: Boston, Mass.

Peterson, R. T., Mounfort, G. & Hollom, P. A. D. 1954. *A Field Guide to the Birds of Britain and Europe*. Collins: London.

Phelps, W. H. 1944. *Bubulcus ibis* in Venezuela. *Auk* 61: 656.

Philippi, R. A. 1954. Sobre custumbres predatorias del Gorrión comun *Passer d. domesticus* L. *Revista Chilena de Historia Natural* 54: 127–8.

Phillips, J. C. 1915. Notes on American and Old World English Sparrows. *Auk* 32: 51–9.

*———. 1928. Wild birds introduced and transplanted in North America. *US Department of Agriculture Technical Bulletin* No. 61 (63 pp.).

Phillips, W. W. A. 1966. *A Revised Checklist of the Birds of Ceylon* [Sri Lanka]. Natural History Series (Zoology). National Museum of Ceylon: Colombo.

Philpott, A. 1918. Notes on certain introduced birds in Southland. *New Zealand Journal of Science and Technology* 1: 328–30.

Pierce, R. A. 1956. Some thoughts concerning the introduction of exotic game birds. *Wilson Bulletin* 68: 80–2.

Pinchon, R. 1963 and 1976. *Faune des Antilles Françaises. Les Oiseaux*. Fort-de-France.

Pinchon, R. & Benito-Espinal, E. 1980. Installation de nouvelles espèces à la Martinique. *L'Oiseau et la Revue Française d'Ornithologie* 50: 347–8.

Pindar, L.O. 1925. Birds of Fulton County, Kentucky. *Wilson Bulletin* 37: 163–9.

Pinder, N. J. 1979. A policy for faunal reintroductions. *University College London Discussion Paper in Conservation* No. 23 (28 pp.).

———. ed. 1981. Conservation and introduced species. *British Association of Nature Conservationists/University College London Discussion Paper in Conservation* No. 30 (63 pp.).

Pinowski, J. & Kendeigh, S. C. eds. 1977. Introduction. In *Granivorous Birds in Ecosystems: International Biological Programme* No. 12: 1–14. Cambridge University Press: Cambridge.

Pizzey, G. 1980. *A Field Guide to the Birds of Australia*. Collins: Sydney.

Pollard, J. 1967. *Birds of Paradox: Bird Life in Australia and New Zealand*. Lansdowne: Melbourne.

*Popov, B. H. & Low, J. B. 1953. Game, fur animal and fish introductions into Utah. *Utah Department of Fish and Game Miscellaneous Publications* No. 4 (85 pp.).

Poppelwell, D. L. 1929. *Some Ecological Effects of Acclimatisation in New Zealand*. New Zealand Journal of Science and Technology: Wellington.

Porter, R. D. 1955. The Hungarian Partridge in Utah. *Journal of Wildlife Management* 19: 93–109.

Porter, R. E. R. 1979. Food of the Rook in Hawke's Bay, New Zealand. *New Zealand Journal of Zoology* 6: 329–37.

Post, P. W. 1970. First reports of Cattle Egret in Chile and range extensions in Peru. *Auk* 87: 361.

Post, W. & Wiley, J. W. 1976. The Yellow-shouldered Blackbird – present and future. *American Birds* 30: 13–20.

———. 1977a. The Shiny Cowbird in the West Indies. *Condor* 79: 119–21.

———. 1977b. Reproductive interactions of the Shiny Cowbird and Yellow-shouldered Blackbird. *Condor* 79: 176–84.

Potter, E. F. 1964a. First House Finch collected in North Carolina. *Auk* 81: 439–40.

———. 1964b. The House Finch on the Atlantic seaboard: a new species for North Carolina. *Chat* 28: 63–8.

Potter, R. E. 1981. Common Myna and other species in American Samoa. *Elepaio* 42: 137–8.

Potts, T. H. 1884. Some introduced birds in New Zealand. *Zoologist* 8: 448–50.

Powell, J. A. 1967. Management of the Florida Turkey and the Eastern Turkey in Georgia and

Alabama. In O.H. Hewitt ed., *The Wild Turkey and its Management*, Ch. 14: 409–51. Wildlife Society: Washington, DC.

Power, D. M. & **Rising, J. D.** 1975. The Cattle Egret in central Baja California, Mexico. *Condor* 77: 353.

Power, J. H. 1958. House Sparrow in the Northern Cape [South Africa]. *Ostrich* 29: 87.

Powys, Th. 1860. Notes on birds in the Ionian Islands and in Albania [Pheasant]. *Ibis* I: 228.

Pracy, L. T. 1969. Weka liberations in the Palliser Bay region. *Notornis* 16: 212.

Pratt, D. 1977. The Black-headed Munia discovered on Kauai. *Elepaio* 38: 18.

Pratt, T. K. 1976. The Kalij Pheasant on Hawaii. *Elepaio* 36: 66–7.

Prescott, H. E. 1943. The English Sparrow in Australia. *Victorian Naturalist* 60: 47.

Preuss, N. O. 1980. [The Canada Goose as a wintering species in Denmark.] *Feltornithologen* 22: 180–2 [in Danish].

Prévost, J. & **Mougin, J.-L.** 1970. *Guide des Oiseaux et Mammifères des Terres Australes et Antarctiques Françaises*. Guides de Nature. Delachaux et Niestlé Editions: Paris and Neuchâtel.

Price, T. D. 1979. The seasonality and occurrence of birds in the Eastern Ghats of Andhra Pradesh. *Journal of the Bombay Natural History Society* 76: 379–422.

Purchas, T. P. G. 1980. Feeding ecology of Rooks on the Heretaunga Plains, Hawke's Bay, New Zealand. *New Zealand Journal of Zoology* 7: 557–78.

Pushee, G. F. 1948. A survey of Pheasant stocking in the United States. Massachusetts Department of Conservation, Bureau of Wildlife Research Management. Mimeograph (10 pp.).

Pyle, L. 1979. Japanese Bush Warbler and Northern Cardinal on Molokai. *Elepaio* 40: 27.

Pyle, R. L. 1963. House Finch reaches District of Columbia and Virginia. *Atlantic Naturalist* 18: 32–3.

——. 1976. Recent observations of birds on Oahu, July 1975 to April 1976, and May to July, 1976. *Elepaio* 37: 6–9, 45–7.

——. 1976–8. The 1975, 1976 and 1977 Christmas bird counts. *Elepaio* 36: 91–8; 37: 80–7; 38: 85–9.

——. 1977. Preliminary list of the birds of Hawaii. *Elepaio* 37: 110–21.

——. 1979. Japanese Bush-Warbler and Northern Cardinal on Molokai. *Elepaio* 40: 27.

——. 1984. 84th Christmas Bird Count. *American Birds* 38: 396–828.

Pyman, G. A. 1959. The status of the Red-crested Pochard in the British Isles. *British Birds* 52: 42–56.

Q

Quaintance, C. W. 1946. The Starling arrives in Oregon. *Condor* 48: 95.

——. 1949. Further records of the Starling in Oregon. *Condor* 51: 271.

——. 1951. Pioneer Starling nesting in eastern Oregon. *Condor* 53: 50.

Quay, T. L. 1967. House Finch records in the Carolinas, winter of 1966–7. *Chat* 31: 45–9.

Quickelberge, C. D. 1972. Status of the European Starling at its present approximate eastern limits of spread [in South Africa]. *Ostrich* 43: 179–80.

R

Rabor, D. S. & **Rand, A. L.** 1958. Jungle and Domestic Fowl, *Gallus gallus*, in the Philippines. *Condor* 60: 138–9.

Racey, K. 1924. The Japanese Starling in Vancouver. *Murrelet* 5: 12.

——. 1950. Status of the European Starling in British Columbia. *Murrelet* 31: 30–1.

Radcliffe, F. 1910. Starlings in Australia. *The Field* 116: 633.

Raffaele, H. A. 1983. *A Guide to the Birds of Puerto Rico and the Virgin Islands*. Fondo Educativo Inter Americano: San Juan, Mexico, Bogotá, Caracas, Panamá.

Raffaele, H. A. & **Roby, D.** 1977. The Lesser Antillean Bullfinch in the Virgin Islands. *Wilson Bulletin* 89: 338–42.

Raju, K. S. R. & **Price, T. L.** 1973. Tree Sparrow (*Passer montanus*) in the Eastern Ghats. *Journal of the Bombay Natural History Society* 70: 557–8.

Ralph, C. J. 1984. Opportunistic nectarivory in some introduced Hawaiian birds. *Elepaio* 45: 17–18.

Ralph, C. J. & **Pyle, R. L.** 1977. The winter season, December 1 1976 to February 28, 1977: Hawaiian Islands region. *American Birds* 31: 376–7.

Ralph, C. J. & **Sakai, H. F.** 1979. Forest bird and Fruit Bat populations and their conservation in Micronesia. Notes on a survey. *Elepaio* 40: 20–6.

Rand, A. C. 1980. Factors responsible for the successful establishment of exotic avian species in southeastern Florida. *Proceedings of the 9th Vertebrate Pest Conference*, 49–52.

Rand, A. L. 1936. The distribution and habits of Madagascar birds: summary of field notes on the Mission Zoologique Franco-Anglo-Américaine à Madagascar. *Bulletin of the American Museum of Natural History* 72: 143–499.

Randall, P. E. 1940. The ecology and management of the Ring-necked Pheasant in Pennsylvania. Unpublished thesis, Pennsylvania State College (141 pp.).

Raw, W., Sparrow, R. & **Jourdain, F. C. R**. 1921. Field notes on the birds of lower Egypt. *Ibis*, series 11, 3: 238–64.

Recher, H. F. & **Clark, S. S**. 1974. A biological survey of Lord Howe Island with recommendations for the conservation of the island's wildlife. *Biological Conservation* 6: 263–73.

Reed, R. A. 1956. House Sparrows in most parts of the Transvaal. *Wits Bird Club News* 21: 8–9.

Rees, J. P. 1959. The Indian Myna. *Wits Bird Club News Sheet* 31: 5–6.

Reese, J. G. 1975. Productivity and management of feral Mute Swans in Chesapeake Bay. *Journal of Wildlife Management* 39: 280–6.

Reichenow, A. 1980. Vögel von den Inseln Ostafrikas. In A. Voeltzkow, *Reise in Ostafrika 1903–5*. Wissenschaftliche Ergebnisse: Stuttgart.

Reichoff, J. 1976. Some ecological points concerning the introduction of mammals and birds. In L. Boitani ed., *Reintroductions: Techniques and Ethics*, 197–200. World Wildlife Fund: Rome.

Reid, D. N. 1930. Spread of the Capercaillie in Ross-shire. *Scottish Naturalist*, 26.

Reid, S. G. 1884 The Birds of Bermuda. *US National Museum Bulletin* No. 25: 163–279.

Reilly, E. M. 1968. *The Audubon Illustrated Handbook of American Birds*. McGraw-Hill: New York.

Resadny, C. D. 1965. Huns [Hungarian Partridges] on the move. *Wisconsin Conservation Bulletin* 30: 21–3.

Reuther, R. T. 1951. The Chinese Spotted Dove at Bakersfield, California. *Condor* 53: 300–1.

Reuterwall, D. F. 1956. The Collared Turtle-dove (*Streptopelia decaocto*) breeding in Varberg. *Vår Fågelvärld* 15: 262–8.

Reynolds, J. 1982. Variãción y adaptación de poblaciones de *Passer domesticus* en su etapa de colonizatión en Costa Rica. Thesis, Universidad de Costa Rica, Ciudad Universitaria 'Rodrigo Facio' (88 pp.)

Reynolds, J. & **Stiles, F. G**. 1982. Distribución y densidad de poblaciones del gorrión común (*Passer domesticus*) en Costa Rica. *Revista Biologia Tropical* 30: 65–71.

Rhodes, W. 1877. Imported birds for our woods and parks [in Canada]. *Forest and Stream* 8: 165.

Richards, A. 1986. Colourful colonisers. *Bird Watching* (August): 36–7, 42–3.

Richardson, F. & **Bowles, J**. 1964. A survey of the birds of Kauai, Hawaii. *Bulletin of the Bernice P. Bishop Museum* No. 227 (51 pp.).

Richmond, C. W. 1903. Birds collected by Dr W. L. Abbott and Mr C. B. Kloss in the Andaman and Nicobar Islands. *Proceedings of the US National Museum* 25: 287–314.

Ricklefs, R. E. & **Smeraski, C. A**. 1983. Variation in incubation period within a population of the European Starling. *Auk* 100: 926–31.

Ridgely, R. S. 1976. *A Guide to the Birds of Panama*. Princeton University Press: Princeton, New Jersey.

———. 1981. In R. F. Pasquier ed., *Conservation of New World Parrots* (*Proceedings of the International Council for Bird Preservation Parrot Working Group Meeting, St Lucia, 1980*), 293–4. Technical Publication No. 1. Smithsonian Institution Press (Washington) for the ICBP.

Ridgeway, R. 1895. On birds collected by W. L. Abbott on the Seychelles, Amirantes, Glorioso, Assumption, Aldabra and Adjacent islands, with notes on their habits by the collector. *Proceedings of the US National Museum* 18: 509–46.

Ridley, H. N. 1898. Birds of the Botanic Garden, Singapore. *Journal of the Straits Branch of the Royal Asiatic Society* 25: 60–7.

Ridpath, M. G. & **Moreau, R. E**. 1965. The birds of Tasmania: ecology and evolution. *Ibis* 108: 348–93.

Riley, J. H. 1938. Birds of Siam and the Malay Peninsula. *US National Museum, Smithsonian Institution Bulletin* No. 172.

Ringleben, H. 1960. The Pigeon nuisance in cities. *Disinfektion und Gesundheitswesen* 52: 124–8.

———. 1975. Nilgans [Egyptian Geese] und Rostgans als freilebende Brutvögel in Mitteleuropa. *Der Falke* 22: 230–33.

Rinke, D. 1986a. The status of wildlife in Tonga. *Oryx* 20: 146–51.

———. 1986b. Notes on the avifauna of Niuafo'ou island, Kingdom of Tonga. *Emu* 86 (in press).

Ripley, S. D. 1951. Migrants and introduced species in the Palau Archipelago. *Condor* 53: 299–300.

———. 1961. *A Synopsis of the Birds of India and Pakistan: together with those of Nepal, Sikkim, Bhutan and Ceylon*. Bombay Natural History Society: Madras.

———. 1965. Saving the Néné, world's rarest goose. *National Geographic Magazine* 128: 745–54.

⋆**Ritchie, J**. 1920. *The Influence of Man on Animal Life in Scotland*. Cambridge University Press: London.

———. 1929. Northward extension of Capercaillie to Sutherland. *Scottish Naturalist*, 126.

⋆**Robbins, C. S**. 1973. Introduction, spread, and present abundance of the House Sparrow in North America. In S. C. Kendeigh ed., *Symposium on the House Sparrow and European Tree Sparrow in North America*, 3–9. Ornithological Monographs, Vol. 14. American Ornithologists' Union: Lawrence, Kansas.

⋆**Robbins, C. S**. & **Barlow, J. C**. 1973. Status of the North American population of the European Tree Sparrow. In S. C. Kendeigh ed., *Symposium on the House Sparrow and European Tree Sparrow in North America*, 10–23. Ornithological Monographs Vol. 14. American Ornithologists' Union: Lawrence, Kansas.

Roberson, R. C. & **Keffer, M**. 1978. Red-whiskered Bulbul. In *State of California Department of Food and*

Agriculture, Division of Plant Industry, Detection Manual No. 7:4.

Roberts, A. 1940. *The Birds of South Africa*. H. F. & G. Witherby: London.

Robertson, W. B. 1958. Investigations of Ring-necked Pheasants in Illinois. *Illinois Department of Conservation Technical Bulletin* No. 1 (137 pp.).

———. 1962. Observations on the birds of St John, Virgin Islands. *Auk* 79: 44–76.

Robertson, D. B. 1976. Weka liberation in Northland. *Notornis* 23: 213–19.

Robinson, A. H. 1950. Immigration of the Indian Crow to western Australia. *Western Australian Naturalist* 2: 81.

Robinson, C. 1953. Chaffinches. *Cape Bird Club Newsletter* 13: 2.

Robinson, H. C. & **Chasen, F. N**. 1927–39. *Birds of the Malay Peninsula*, 4 vols. H. F. & G. Witherby: London.

Robinson, L. H. 1969. Introduction of exotic game birds in South Carolina. *Proceedings of the 23rd Annual Conference of the Southeastern Association of Game and Fish Commissioners*, 152–9.

Rockafellow, R. R. 1960. Report on Cattle Egrets. *Elepaio* 21: 39–40.

Rockwell, R. B. 1939. The Starling in Colorado. *Wilson Bulletin* 51: 46.

*****Rolls, E. C**. 1969. *They All Ran Wild: the Story of Pests on the Land in Australia*. Angus and Robertson: Sydney.

Roney, K. 1982. Cattle Egret nest record for Saskatchewan. *Blue Jay* 40: 163.

Roots, C. 1976. *Animal Invaders*. David and Charles: Newton Abbot, Devon.

Roscoe, D. R., Zeh, J. B., Stone, W. B., Brown, L.P. & **Renkavinsky, J. L**. 1973. Observations on the Monk Parakeet in New York State. *New York Fish and Game Journal* 20: 170–3.

Rose, C. I. 1978. Introduced species and conservation. Unpublished MSc thesis, University College, London.

———. 1979. Nature conservation and species introductions. *University College London Discussion Paper* No. 26 (47 pp.).

Rosene, W. 1969. *The Bobwhite Quail: its Life and Management*. Rutgers University Press: New Brunswick, New Jersey.

Ross, D. M. 1897. Capercaillie in the mid-Deveron district. *Annals of Scottish Natural History*, 254.

Rostrom, A. 1969. Rosella Parrots: New Zealand's most beautiful pests. *New Zealand Agricultural Journal* 118: 40.

Rountree, F. R. G. 1951. Some aspects of bird life in Mauritius. *Proceedings of the Royal Society of Arts and Sciences of Mauritius* 1: 83–96.

Rountree, F. R. G., Guérin, R., Pelte, S. & **Vinson, J**. 1952. Catalogue of the birds of Mauritius. *Bulletin of the Mauritius Institute* 3: 155–217.

Rowan, M. K. 1952. Chaffinches. *Cape Bird Club Newsletter* 9: 2.

———. 1964. House Sparrow (*Passer domesticus*) reaches the southwestern Cape [South Africa]. *Ostrich* 35: 240.

Rowan, W. 1927. Details of the release of the Hungarian Partridge in central Alberta. *Canadian Field-Naturalist* 41: 98–101.

———. 1936. The Partridge situation in western Canada. *Sportsman* 20: 43, 63.

———. 1938. The Hungarian Partridge on the Canadian Prairies. *Outdoors American* 3: 6–7.

———. 1952. The Hungarian Partridge (*Perdix perdix*) in Canada. *Transactions of the Royal Society of Canada*, section 3, 46: 161–2.

Ruddiman, J. L. 1952. *Corvus splendens* in Western Australia. *Emu* 52: 138.

Ruhl, H. D. 1941. Game introductions in Michigan. *Transactions of the 5th North American Wildlife Conference*, 424–7.

Rutgers, R. & **Norris, K. A**. 1970–7. *Encyclopaedia of Aviculture*, 3 vols. Blandford Press: London.

Rutherford, R. M. 1949. The Chukar makes good. *Outdoors American* 17: 10–11.

*****Ryan, C. S**. 1906. On European and other birds liberated in Victoria (Presidential address to the Australasian Ornithologists' Union). *Emu* 5: 110–19.

Ryan, H. J. 1930. Mynahs and Starlings as potential pests in California. *California State Department of Agriculture Bulletin* 19: 740–6.

Ryan, R. 1972. The problem of exotics. *American Birds* 26: 934–5.

———. 1979. Established exotics in the ABA area. *Birding (Magazine of the American Birding Association)* 11: 164–6, 244–5.

S

Safriel, U. N. 1975. Re-occurrence of the Red Avadavat, *Amandava amandava* (L.) (Aves: Estrildidae), in Egypt. *Israel Journal of Zoology* 24: 79.

Sage, B. L. 1956. Remarks on the racial status, history, and distribution of the Tree Sparrow introduced into Australia. *Emu* 56: 137–40.

———. 1957. Remarks on the taxonomy, history, and distribution of the House Sparrow introduced into Australia. *Emu* 57: 349–52.

———. 1958. Hybrid ducks in New Zealand. *Bulletin of the British Ornithologists' Club* 78: 108–13.

———. 1959. Some recent observations at Aden. *Ibis* 101: 252–3.

Sahagún, B. de [1577] 1963. *Florentine Codex, General History of the Things of New Spain, Book 11: Earthly Things* [Tufted or Painted Jay]. Translated from the Aztec by C. E. Dibble and A. J. O. Anderson.

University of Utah and School of American Research: Santa Fé.

St Amant, J. A. 1977. Some problems with exotic introductions. *Proceedings of the 57th Annual Conference of the Western Association of State Game and Fish Commissioners*, 247–51.

Sakai, H. F. & **Scott, J. M**. 1984. Turkey sighting on Keauhou Ranch, Volcano, Hawaii. *Elepaio* 45: 19.

Sakane, M. 1960. *Bambusicola thoracica sonorivox* increasing in Hyogo. *Tori* 15: 286–9 (in *Auk* 79(1) (1962)).

Salganskii, A. A. & **Salganskaya, L. A**. 1959. [Rheas in the USSR.] *Priroda* 10: 104–5 [in Russian].

Salter, M. T. 1950. Introduction of Starlings. *Victorian Naturalist* 67: 59.

Salter, R. L. 1952. Chukar Partridge introductions in Idaho. *Proceedings of the 32nd Annual Conference of the Western Association of State Game and Fish Commissioners*, 162–4.

Salomonsen, F. 1950. *The Birds of Greenland*, Parts 1–3 [in Danish and English]. Ejnar Munksgaard: Copenhagen.

Salvadori, T. 1905–6. Notes on parrots. *Ibis*, series 8, 5: 401–29; 6: 124–31, 451–65.

Samuel, D. E. 1969. House Sparrow occupancy of Cliff Swallow nests. *Wilson Bulletin* 81: 103–4.

———. 1975. Kiskadee Flycatcher in Bermuda. *Newsletter of the Bermuda Biological Station for Research* 4: 2.

Samuelson, G. A. 1985. Gray Swiftlet sighted in Kahalu'u Valley. *Elepaio* 45: 65.

Sandeman, P. W. 1965. Attempted re-introduction of White-tailed Eagle to Scotland. *Scottish Birds* 3: 411–12.

Sandfort, W. W. 1952. Chukar Partridge. *Colorado Conservation* 1: 15–19.

———. 1955. Evaluation of Chukar Partridge range in Colorado. *Proceedings of the 34th Annual Conference of the Western Association of State Game and Fish Commissioners*, 244–50.

———. 1963. We can have more Pheasants. *Colorado Outdoors* 12: 1–6.

Saunders, H. 1886. Birds of the Island of Diego Garcia, Chagos group. *Proceedings of the Zoological Society of London*, 335–7.

Saunders, W. E 1930–1. Japanese Starlings at Alert Bay, British Columbia. *Canadian Field-Naturalist* 44: 24; 45: 22.

★**Savage, C**. 1952. *The Mandarin Duck*. Adam and Charles Black: London.

Savidge, J. A. 1984. Guam: Paradise lost for wildlife. *Biological Conservation* 30: 305–17.

Scanlon, P. F., Teitt, T. R. & **Cross, G. H**. 1978. An overview of problems of introduced species. *Proceedings of the 30th Annual Conference of the Southeastern Association of Fish and Wildlife Agencies*, 674–9.

Scheffer, P. M. 1967. Exotic non-game bird introductions – pro and con. *Proceedings of the 47th Annual Conference of the Western Association of State Game and Fish Commissioners, Honolulu, Hawaii, 16–20 July*, 113–22.

Scheffer, T. H. 1931. Mynahs at Vancouver. *Murrelet* 12: 84–5.

———. 1935. The English Skylark on Vancouver Island. *Condor* 37: 256–7.

———. 1955. Present status of the introduced English Skylark on Vancouver Island and of the Chinese Mynah on Vancouver mainland. *Murrelet* 36: 28–9.

Scheffer, T. H. & **Cottam, C**. 1935. The Crested Mynah or Chinese Starling in the Pacific northwest. *US Department of Agriculture Technical Bulletin* No. 467 (26 pp.).

Schmidt, R. K., Longrigg, T. D. & **Pringle, S**. 1976. The elusive Chaffinch. *Cape Bird Club Newsletter* 124: 4.

Schneider, C. O. 1938. Notas sobre la aclimatación des algunas aves extrangeras en Chile. *Acta Societatis Scientiarum Chile*, 63–5, 135–8.

Schneider, F. 1957. An introduction of European Gray Partridge of Danish stock into the Willamette Valley, Oregon. *Proceedings of the 37th Annual Conference of the Western Association of State Game and Fish Commissioners*, 271–3.

Schodde, R. 1959. Indigenous and introduced birds recovered from Flinders Range region of South Australia. *South Australian Naturalist* 34: 13–14.

Scholes, K. T. 1954. Notes from Panama and the Canal Zone. *Condor* 56: 166–7.

Schorger, A. W. 1942. The wild Turkey in early Wisconsin. *Wilson Bulletin* 54: 173–82.

———. 1952. Introduction of the Domestic Pigeon. *Auk* 69: 462–3.

Schorger, N. W. 1947. The introduction of the Pheasant into Wisconsin. *Passenger Pigeon* 9: 101–2.

Schrader, T. A. 1944. The Ring-necked Pheasant. *The Conservation Volunteer* 7: 17–22.

Schubert, T. 1973. *Status of Monk Parakeet Program*. New Jersey Division of Fish and Game, Shell Fish Report.

★**Schwartz, C. W**. & **Schwartz, E. R**. 1949. *A Reconnaissance of the Game Birds in Hawaii*. Published for the Territory of Hawaii Board of Commissioners of Agriculture and Forestry (Federal Aid – Wildlife Program, Division of Fish and Game) by The Hawaii News Printshop: Hilo, Hawaii (168 pp.).

———. 1950a. The California Quail in Hawaii. *Auk* 67: 1–38.

———. 1950b. Breeding habits of the Barred Dove in Hawaii, with notes on weight and sex ratio. *Condor* 52: 241–6.

———. 1951a. Food habits of the Barred Dove in Hawaii. *Wilson Bulletin* 63: 149–56.

———. 1951b. An ecological reconnaisance of the Pheasant in Hawaii. *Auk* 68: 281–314.

———. 1951c. A survey of the Lace-necked Dove in Hawaii. *Pacific Science* 5: 90–107.

Scott, J. H. 1882. Macquarie Island. *Transactions of the New Zealand Institute* 15: 484–93.

Scott, K. 1957. A first record of the Cattle Egret in Peru. *Condor* 59: 143.

Scott, P. 1950. Transatlantic voyage of Starlings. *British Birds* 43: 369.

———. 1965. *A Coloured Key to the Wildfowl of the World.* The Wildfowl Trust: Slimbridge, England.

———. 1967. Cause and effect in the introduction of exotic species. *Proceedings of the 10th IUCN Technical Meeting, Lucerne, June 1966,* 120–3. IUCN Publications. n.s. No. 9. Morges.

———. 1972. *The Swans.* Michael Joseph: London.

———. 1985. *Travel Diaries of a Naturalist,* Vol. 2 Collins: London.

Scott, P. & Boyd, H. 1957. *Wildfowl of the British Isles.* Country Life: London.

Scott, S. L. ed. 1984. *Field Guide to the Birds of North America.* National Geographic Society: Washington, DC.

Sealy, S. G. 1969. Starling at Inuvik. *Arctic* 22: 444 (also in *Ibis* 114 (1972)).

Seaman, G. A. 1955 and 1958. Cattle Egret in the Virgin Islands. *Wilson Bulletin* 67: 304–5; 70: 93–4.

Sedgwick, E. H. 1957. Occurrence of the Goldfinch at Albany. *Western Australian Naturalist* 5: 230.

———. 1958. The introduced Turtledoves in Western Australia. *Western Australian Naturalist* 6: 92–110, 112–27.

———. 1976. Supplementary notes on Turtledoves, *Streptopelia*, in Western Australia. *Western Australian Naturalist* 13: 175–6.

Sefton, A. R. & Devitt, J. A. 1962. Additions to the birds from the Illawarra district. *Emu* 62: 186.

Segonzac, J. 1972. Données récentes sur la faune des îles Saint-Paul et Nouvelle Amsterdam. *Oiseaux et la Revue Française d'Ornithologie* 42 (special number): 3–68.

Seibert, H. C. & Donohoe, R. W. 1965. *The History of the Reeves Pheasant Program in Ohio.* Ohio Game Monograph No. 1 (20 pp.).

Selander, R. K. & Johnston, R. F. 1967. Evolution in the House Sparrow.1. Intrapopulation variation in North America. *Condor* 99: 217–58.

Sergeeva, N. A. & Sumina, E. V. 1963. Attempts at acclimatizing *Perdix daurica* and reacclimatizing *Lagopus lagopus* in the central zone. *Ornitologiya* 6: 86–95 [in Russian] (also in *Ibis* 107 (1965)).

Serrano Priego, P. & Cabot Nieves, J. 1983. *Passer domesticus,* nueva especie para Bolivia. *Doñana, Acta Vertebrata* 10: 212–13.

Serventy, D. L. 1935 and 1935 [Acclimatization.] *Western Australian* (4 September and 12 May).

———. 1937. The menace of acclimatisation. *Emu* 36: 189–96.

———. 1948. The birds of the Swan River district, Western Australia. *Emu* 47: 241–86.

Serventy, D. L. & Whittell, H. M. 1951–67. *Handbook of the Birds of Western Australia.* Paterson Brokensha: Perth.

Severin, H. C. 1933. An economic study of the food, of the Ring-necked Pheasant in South Dakota. South Dakota State College and South Dakota Department of Game and Fish. Mimeograph (252 pp.).

Shadle, A. R. 1930. The European Goldfinch at Buffalo, New York. *Auk* 47: 566–7.

Shaffer, C. H. & Gwynn, J. V. 1967. Management of the eastern Turkey in the Oak–Pine forests of Virginia and the southeast. In O. H. Hewitt ed., *The Wild Turkey and its Management,* Ch. 11: 303–42. Wildlife Society: Washington, DC.

Shallenberger, R. J. 1975. African Silverbill. *Elepaio* 35: 55.

*★***Shapiro, A. E.** 1979. Status, habitat utilization and breeding biology of the feral Budgerigar. Unpublished MSc thesis, University of Florida, Gainesville.

———. 1980. Florida's budgies are here to stay. *Florida Naturalist,* 7–9.

Sharland, M. 1944. The Lyrebird in Tasmania. *Emu* 44: 64–71.

———. 1958. *Tasmanian Birds.* Angus and Robertson: Sydney.

Sharpe, R. B. 1889. On the ornithology of northern Borneo. Part 4. *Ibis,* series 6, 1: 409–43.

Sharrock, J. T. R. ed. 1976. *The Atlas of Breeding Birds in Britain and Ireland.* British Trust for Ornithology: Tring, Hertfordshire.

Shaw, W. T. 1908. *The China or Denny Pheasant in Oregon, with Notes on the Native Grouse of the Pacific North West.* J. B. Lippincott: Philadelphia and London.

Shelgren, J. H., Thompson, R. A. & Palmer, T. K. 1975. An evaluation of the pest potential of the Ring-necked Parakeet, Nanday Conure, and the Canary-winged Parakeet in California. California Department of Food and Agriculture, Special Services Unit. Mimeograph (25 pp.).

Shields, T. J. & Neudahl, H. K. 1970. Pheasant release program of the Minnesota Future Farmers of America 1965–69. Minnesota Department of Education. Mimeograph (22 pp.).

Shlapak, G. 1959. [Pheasants on Biryuchiy Island.] *Okhota i Okhotnich'e Khozyaistvo* 3: 13–14 [in Russian].

Shroads, C. V. 1974. Studies on a population of the Canary-winged Parakeet, *Brotogeris versicolurus,* in Dade County, Florida. Unpublished MSc thesis, University of Miami.

Sick, H. 1957. Vom Hausspatzen (*Passer domesticus*) in Brasilien. *Vogelwelt* 78: 1–18.

———. 1959. A invasão da América Latina pelo pardal *Passer domesticus* L., com referência espécial ao Brazil.

Boletín del Museo Nacional de Brazil, Rio de Janeiro: Zoology No. 207 (31 pp.).

———. 1966. Sôbre a espécia existente de *Estrilda* (Ploceidae: Aves) o Chamado Bico-de-Lacre, no Brazil. *Anales de la Academia de Ciencias, Brazil* 38: 169–71.

———. 1967. Introduced species of birds in South America. Paper presented at the International Biological Research Programme Planning Conference, Caracas, Venezuela, 22–24 November, 1967. Section on Animal Species of Expanding Range. Mimeograph.

———. 1968. Über in Südamerika Eingefuhrte Vogelarten. *Bonner Zoologische Beiträge* 19: 298–306.

———. 1971. Notas sôbre o pardal (*Passer domesticus*) no Brazil. *Archivos do Museu, Rio de Janeiro* 54: 113–20.

Siebe, C. C. 1964. Starlings in California. *Proceedings of the 2nd Vertebrate Pest Control Conference, Anaheim, California, 4–5 March, 1964*, 40–2.

Siegfried, W. R. 1962. Introduced vertebrates in the Cape Province [South Africa]. *Report of the Cape Provincial Administration Department of Nature Conservation* No. 19: 80–7.

———. 1970. Wildfowl distribution, conservation and research in southern Africa. *Wildfowl* 21: 89–98.

———. 1971. Chukar Partridge on Robben Island [South Africa]. *Ostrich 42: 156*.

Siegler, H. R. 1949. *The Ring-necked Pheasant in New Hampshire*. New Hampshire Fish and Game Department Survey and Report No. 5 (82 pp.).

Silsby, J. 1980. *Inland Birds of Saudi Arabia*. Immel Publishing: London.

Silverstein, A. & **Silverstein, V.** 1974. *Animal Invaders: the Story of Imported Wildlife*. Atheneum: New York.

Simpson, M. B. 1974. Monk Parakeets breeding in Buncombe County, North Carolina. *Wilson Bulletin* 86: 171–2.

Sims, J. A. 1963 and 1965. Gum Cove Black Francolin release area. *Biennial Report of the Louisiana Wildlife and Fisheries Commission* 10: 87–8; 11: 91–2.

———. 1964. Exotic gamebirds in Louisiana. *Louisiana Conservationist* 16: 22–4.

Sims, J. A., Bateman, H. & **Raiford, J. T.** 1967. Exotic game propagation unit. *Biennial Report of the Louisiana Wildlife and Fisheries Commission* 12: 85–6.

Simwat, G. S. & **Sidhu, A. S.** 1973. Notes on the feeding habits of the Rose-ringed Parakeet, *Psittacula krameri* (Scopoli). *Indian Journal of Agricultural Science* 43: 607–9.

Sinclair, I., Mendelsohn, J. & **Chittenden, H.** 1981. Breeding of the Indian House Crow in South Africa. *Albatross* 262: 8–9.

Sinclair, J. C. 1974a. Arrival of the House Crow in Natal. *Ostrich* 45: 189.

———. 1974b. European Starling (*Sturnus vulgaris*):

new distributional data. *Ostrich* 45: 137.

———. 1980. House Crow in Cape Town. *Promerops* 144: 7–8.

———. 1981. A myriad of parakeets and other birds. *Bokmakierie* 33: 56–8.

Skead, C. J. 1961. Chaffinch, (*Fringilla coelebs*) at Kenton-on-Sea [South Africa]. *Ostrich* 32: 189.

———. 1962 and 1966. The European Starling, *Sturnus vulgaris*, at King William's Town and East London. *Ostrich* 33: 75; 37: 229.

———. 1973 and 1974. House Sparrow (*Passer domesticus*) and European Starling (*Sturnus vulgaris*): new distributional data. *Ostrich* 44: 132; 45: 137.

Skead, D. M. 1966. Birds frequenting the intertidal zone of the Cape Peninsula. *Ostrich* 37: 15.

Skegg, P. D. 1964. Birds of the Hen and Chicken Islands [New Zealand]. *Notornis* 11: 159–76.

Skinner, J. O. 1905. The House Sparrow (*Passer domesticus*). *Smithsonian Institution Report*, 423–8.

Skipworth, J. P. 1983. Aliens in New Zealand. *New Zealand Journal of Ecology* 6: 145–6.

Skottesberg, C. J. F. ed. 1920. *The Natural History of Juan Fernandez and Easter Island*, Vol. I. Almqvist & Wiksell: Uppsala, Sweden.

Skutch, A. F. 1983. *Birds of Tropical America*. University of Texas Press: Austin.

Slater, P. 1970 and 1974. *A Field Guide to Australian Birds*, 2 vols. Rigby: Adelaide.

Slud, P. 1957. Cattle Egret in Costa Rica. *Condor* 59: 400.

Smith, D. S. 1969. An evaluation of Indian Red Jungle Fowl releases in Baldwin. *Proceedings of the 23rd Annual Conference of the Southeastern Association of Game and Fish Commissioners*, 157–71.

Smith J. D. 1950. *The Pheasant Situation in Hawaii, 1950*. Board of Commissioners of Agriculture and Forestry: Honolulu (13 pp.)

———. 1952. The Hawaiian Goose (Nene) restoration program. *Journal of Wildlife Management* 16: 1–9.

Smith, J. D. & **Woolworth, J. R.** 1950. A study of the Pheasant, California Quail, and Lace-necked Dove in Hawaii. *Territory of Hawaii Board of Commissioners of Agriculture and Forestry (Federal Aid – Wildlife Program, Fish and Game Division), Special Bulletin; Progress Report*, Project 5-R-1 (58 pp.).

Smith, K. D. 1956. On the birds of the Aden Protectorate. *Ibis* 98: 303–7.

Smith, L. A. 1978. Rainbow Lorikeets at Safety Bay. *Western Australian Naturalist* 14: 75.

Smith, L. M., Hupp, J. W. & **Ratti, J. T.** 1982. Habitat use and home range of Gray Partridge in eastern South Dakota. *Journal of Wildlife Management* 46: 580–7.

Smith, N. J. H. 1973. House Sparrows (*Passer domesticus*) in the Amazon. *Condor* 75: 242–3.

———. 1980. Further advances of House Sparrows in the Brazilian Amazon. *Condor* 82: 109–11.

Smith, P. W. 1986. Jackdaws reach the New World. *American Birds* 39: 255–8 (see also 272, 294 and 300).

Smith, R. H. 1957. An early attempt to introduce Pheasants to North America. *New York Fish and Game Journal* 4: 119–20.

Smith, T. H. 1967. A sighting of the Colombo Crow (*Corvus splendens*) in Victoria. *Australian Bird Watcher* 3: 49–50

Smith, W. J. 1958. Cattle Egret (*Bubulcus ibis*) nesting in Cuba. *Auk* 75: 89.

Smithers, C. N. & Disney, H. J. de S. 1969. The distribution of terrestrial and fresh-water birds on Norfolk Island. *Australian Zoologist* 15: 127–40.

Smythies, B. E. 1953. *The Birds of Burma*. Oliver & Boyd: London. (reprinted 1981: Sabah and Malayan Natural History Society).

———. 1960. *The Birds of Borneo*. Oliver & Boyd: London.

Snow, D. W. 1950. Birds of São Tomé and Príncipe in the Gulf of Guinea. *Ibis* 92: 579–95.

———. 1958. *A Study of Blackbirds*. Allen & Unwin: London.

Solyom, V. 1940. The Chukar Partridge in Tennessee. *Migrant* 11: 11–12.

Southern, H. N. 1945. The economic importance of the House Sparrow: a review. *Annals of Applied Biology* 32: 57–67.

Sprot, G. D. 1937. Notes on the introduced Skylark in the Victoria district of Vancouver Island. *Condor* 39: 24–31.

Sprunt, A. 1953. Newcomer from the Old World. *Audubon Magazine* 55: 178–81.

———. 1955. The spread of the Cattle Egret. *Smithsonian Institution Annual Report 1954* No. 4198: 259–76.

———. 1956. The Cattle Egret in North America. *Audubon Magazine* 58: 174–7.

Stanford, J. A. 1957. Coturnix or Japanese Quail investigations in the United States: a progress report, October 1957. *Proceedings of the 11th Annual Conference of the Southeastern Association of Game and Fish Commissioners*, 1–8.

Stanford, W. 1973. A note on the birds of Oman and the Trucial States, 1954–1968. *Army Birdwatching Society Publication* No. 1.

Starrett, A. 1985. Warbling Silverbill reported on Kauai. *Elepaio* 45: 117.

Staub, F. 1973. Birds of Rodrigues Island. *Proceedings of the Royal Society of Arts and Sciences of Mauritius* 3: 7–46.

———. 1976. *Birds of the Mascarenes and St Brandon*. Organization Normale des Enterprises Ltée: Port Louis, Mauritius.

———. 1983. [Birds of the Agaléga Islands.] *Proceedings of the Royal Society of Arts and Sciences of Mauritius* 4: 87–110.

Stead, D. G. 1938. Tragedies of Australian acclimatisation, with special reference to recent proposals. *Australian Wild Life (Journal of the Wild Life Preservation Society of Australia)* 2: 33–72.

Stead, E. F. 1927. The native and introduced birds of Canterbury [New Zealand]. In R. Speight, A. Wall & R. M. Laing eds, *Natural History of Canterbury*. Simpson and Williams: Christchurch.

*★**Stebbins, H. G. & Baker, G. L.** eds. 1965. *The Genetics of Colonizing Species*. Academic Press: New York and London.

Steele-Elliot, J. 1907. The Little Owl in Bedfordshire. *Zoologist*, 384.

Steen, M. O. 1949, 1952 and 1955. Introduction of exotic animals. *Proceedings of the 39th, 42nd and 44th Conventions of the International Association of Game, Fish and Conservation Commissioners*, 42–8; 78–81; 89–91.

———.1954. The Pheasant in America. *Missouri Conservationist* 15: 1–3.

Stenhouse, D. 1960. The Redpoll in New Zealand. *Agricultural Bulletin of Wellington, New Zealand* No. 366 (see also *Nature* 186: 488–90).

———.1962. Taxonomic status of the New Zealand Redpoll, *Carduelis flammea*: a reassessment. *Notornis* 10: 61–6.

Stephens, C.H. 1962. Coturnix Quail investigations in Kentucky. *Proceedings of the 16th Annual Conference of the Southeastern Association of Game and Fish Commissioners*, 126–37.

———.1966 and 1967. *Reeves' Pheasant Investigation in Kentucky*. Kentucky Department of Fish and Wildlife Resources, Game Management Technical Services Report No. 15 (32 pp.). And *Proceedings of the 21st Annual Conference of the Southeastern Association of Game and Fish Commissioners*, 222–31.

Stewart, P. A. 1964. Bird notes from southeast Alaska. *Condor* 66: 78–9.

Steyn, P. 1964. House Sparrow. *Honeyguide* 43: 5.

Stidolph, R. H. D. 1933. Destructive civilization in New Zealand. Part 2. *Emu* 33: 93–4.

———.1974. Feral Barbary Doves in Masterton. *Notornis* 21: 383–4.

Stiles, F. G. & Smith, S. M. 1980. Notes on bird distribution in Costa Rica. *Brenesia* 17: 137–56.

Stirling, D. & Edwards, R. Y. 1962. Notes on the Skylark on Vancouver Island. *Canadian Field-Naturalist* 76: 147–52.

Stoddard, H. L. 1941. *The Bobwhite Quail*. Scribner's Sons: New York.

Stokes, A. W. 1948. Status of Pelee Island Pheasants, 1947–8. Paper presented at the 10th Mid-West Wildlife Conference. Mimeograph (3 pp.).

———. 1954. Population studies of the Ring-necked Pheasant on Pelee Island, Ontario. *Technical Bulletin of the Ontario Department of Lands and Forestry, Wildlife Series* No. 4 (154 pp.).

Stokes T., Sheils, W. & Dunn, K. 1984. Birds of the

Cocos (Keeling) Islands, Indian Ocean. *Emu* 84: 23–8.

Stone, C. P. 1983. Hawaiian Goose research and management; where do we go from here? *Elepaio* 44: 11–15.

Stonehouse, B. 1962. Ascension Island: British Ornithologists' Union Centenary Expedition, 1957–59. *Ibis* 103b: 107–22.

Stoner, D. 1923. The Mynah – a study in adaptation. *Auk* 40: 328–30.

———. 1939. Parasitism of the English Sparrow on the Northern Cliff Swallow. *Wilson Bulletin* 51: 221–2.

Stophlet, J. J. 1946. Birds of Guam. *Auk* 63: 534–9.

Storer, T. I. 1931. Known and potential results of bird and animal introductions, with special reference to California. *California Department of Agriculture Monthly Bulletin* No. 20: 267–73.

———. 1934. Economic effects of introducing alien animals into California. *Proceedings of the 5th Pacific Science Congress, Victoria and Vancouver June 1933* 1: 779–84. University of Toronto Press: Toronto.

Storr, G. M. 1965. The avifauna of Rottnest Island, Western Australia. Part 3. Land birds. *Emu* 64: 172–80.

Stott, K. 1957. A first record of the Cattle Egret in Peru. *Condor* 59: 143.

Stresemann, E. 1936. A nominal list of the birds of Celebes. *Ibis*, series 13, 6: 356–68

Stresemann E. & **Nowak, E.** 1958. Die Ausbreitung der Turkentaube [Turtle Dove] in Asien und Europa. *Journal für Ornithologie* 99: 243–96.

Sumina, E. B. 1966. Some results of acclimatization of Chinese Partridge and of re-acclimatization of Willow Grouse, as shown by banding. In Yanushevich, A. ed., *Acclimatization of Animals in the USSR) Proceedings of a Conference at Frunze, May 1963*), 175–7. Israel Program for Scientific Translations: Jerusalem.

Summer, E. L. 1935. A life history study of the California Quail, with recommendations for conservation and management. *California Fish and Game* 21: 167–256, 277–342.

Summers-Smith, J. D. 1956. Movements of House Sparrows. *British Birds* 49: 465–88.

★———. 1963. *The House Sparrow*. New Naturalist Series. Collins: London.

———. 1984. The sparrows of the Cape Verde Islands. *Ostrich* 55: 141–6.

———. In preparation. *The Sparrows: A Study of the Genus Passer.*

Sutton, J. 1935. Acclimatisation in South Australia. *South Australian Ornithologist* 13: 92–103.

Swarth, H. S. 1927. Valley Quail imported from Chile. *Condor* 29: 164.

Swedberg, G. E. 1969. Sightings of wild Koloa on the island of Hawaii, and history of a past release. *Elepaio* 29: 87–8.

Swinhoe, R. 1860. The ornithology of Amoy (China). *Ibis* 2: 45–68.

———. 1861. Notes on the ornithology of Hong Kong, Macao, and Canton, made during the latter end of February, March and April, and the beginning of May, 1860. *Ibis* 3: 23–57.

Swiss Wildlife Information Service. ed. 1981–1985. *Project Bearded Vulture.* Bulletins Nos 1–7. University of Zürich: Zürich.

Syme, R. 1975. *Isles of the Frigate Bird.* Michael Joseph: London.

T

Taapken, J. 1981. [Ring-necked Parakeets in the Netherlands.] *Vogeljaar* 29: 323–4 [in Dutch].

———. 1982. [Black Grouse introduced in the Gooi Heath, Netherlands.] *Vogeljaar* 30: 175 [in Dutch].

Taka-Tsukasa, N. & **Hachisuka, M. U.** 1925. A contribution to Japanese ornithology. *Ibis*, series 12, 1: 898–908.

Tallman, D. A. 1982. House Finches in South Dakota. *South Dakota Bird Notes* 34: 19–20.

Tangen, H. I. L. 1974. Forsok med canadagås [Canada Geese] i Norge. *Fauna, Oslo* 27: 166–76.

Tarr, H. E. 1949. Another introduced bird making headway in Australia. *Emu* 49: 142–3.

★———. 1950. The distribution of foreign birds in Australia. *Emu* 49: 189–95.

———. 1963. Early notes on introduced birds. *Bird Observer* (May): 2.

Tavener, P. A. 1927. Hungarian Partridge v Sharptailed Grouse. *Canadian Field-Naturalist* 41: 147–9.

Taylor, A. L. & **Collins, M. S.** 1979. Rediscovery and identification of the 'mystery' *Garrulax* on Oahu. *Elepaio* 39: 79–81.

Taylor, R. G. 1953. Starlings in Jamaica. *Ibis* 95: 700–1.

Taylor, W. L. 1948. The Capercaillie in Scotland. *Journal of Animal Ecology* 17: 155–7.

Taylor, W. P. 1923. Upland game birds in the state of Washington, with discussion on some principles of game importation. *Murrelet* 4: 3–15.

Teal, J. M. 1965. Cattle Egret in Georgia. *Oriole* 21: 33.

Teixeira, R. M. ed. 1979. *Atlas van de Nederlandse Broedvogels.* De Lange van Leer bv: Deventer.

Temple, S. A. 1981. Applied island biogeography and the conservation of endangered island birds in the Indian Ocean. *Biological Conservation* 20: 147–61.

Terrasse, M. 1980a. Project of re-introduction of the Griffon Vulture in the Cévennes, France. *Vulture News* 4: 7–10.

———. 1980b and 1982. Réintroduction du Vautour Fauvre [Griffon Vulture] dans les Cévennes. *Le Courrier de la Nature* 70: 32–4; 79: 15–24.

————. 1983 and 1984a. Réintroduction du Vautour Fauvre [Griffon Vulture] dans les Cévennes. Rapport d'activités 1983 et chronologie 1984. Fonds d'Intervention pour les Rapaces. Mimeo (5 pp.).

————. 1984b. Reintroduction of Griffon Vultures in the Cévennes, France. In: *Spirit of Enterprise – the 1984 Rolex Awards* (4 pp.). Aurum Press: London.

Terry, M. 1963. Exotic pests? We've got the lot. *People* 14: 12–15.

Thibault, J.-C. 1973. Remarques sur l'appauvrissement de l'avifaune Polynésienne. *Bulletin de la Société d'Études Océaniennes* 15: 262–70.

————. 1974. Les conséquences des variations du niveau de la mer sur l'avifaune terrestre des atolls polynésiens. *Comptes Rendus Académie des Sciences, Paris,* Séries D, 278: 2477–9.

————. 1976. L'avifaune de Tetiaroa (Archipel de la Société, Polynésie Française). *Oiseau et la Revue Française d'Ornithologie* 46: 29–45.

Thibault, J.-C. & Rives, C. L. 1975 *Birds of Tahiti.* Translated by D. T. Holyoak. Les Editions du Pacifique: Papeete, Tahiti.

Thistle, A. 1962. Observations on Cattle Egret, Oahu, July 1962. *Elepaio* 23: 15.

————. 1963. Cattle Egrets. *Elepaio* 24: 14–15.

Thomas, D. G. 1965. Birds of the Royal Australasian Ornithologists' Union 1964 field outing, Bicheno district, Tasmania. *Emu* 64: 172–80.

Thomas, G. 1971. House Sparrow recorded from Northern Province, Zambia. *Zambian Ornithological Society Newsletter* 1: 4.

Thomas, H. F. 1957. The Starling in the Sunraysia district, Victoria. *Emu* 57: 31–48, 131–44, 151–68, 269–84.

★**Thomson, G. M.** 1922. *The Naturalisation of Animals and Plants in New Zealand.* Cambridge University Press: London.

————. 1923. Naturalised animals and plants. *New Zealand Journal of Science and Technology* 6: 223–31.

————. 1926. *Wildlife in New Zealand. Part 2. Introduced Birds and Fishes.* New Zealand Board of Science and Art Booklet No. 5. Government Printer: Wellington.

Thomson, V. & Aspinwall, D. R. 1971. House Sparrow at Chadiza. *Zambian Ornithological Society Newsletter* 1: 3.

Throp, J. 1969. Java Ricebird. *Elepaio* 29: 80.

Thrun, T. G. 1909. Introduction of the English Sparrow. *Hawaiian Annual, 1910, 9.*

Thurber, W. A. 1972. House Sparrows in Guatemala. *Auk* 89: 200.

————. 1986. Range expansion of the House Sparrow through Guatemala and El Salvador. *American Birds* 40: 341–50.

Ticehurst, C. B. 1924. The birds of Sind. *Ibis,* series 11, 6: 459–518.

Todd, W. H. 1925. Two new birds from Porto Rico. *Auk* 42: 282.

Tomich, P. Q. 1962. Notes on the Barn Owl in Hawaii. *Elepaio* 23: 16–17.

Tomlinson, D. 1976. Surrey's Chinese Duck [Mandarin]. *Country Life* 160:1248–9.

————. 1981. Treasures of sea and swamp: a naturalist in Trinidad. Part 2. [Greater Bird of Paradise.] *Country Life* 170: 1227–8.

Toups, J. A. & Hodges, M. F. 1981. House Finch on the Mississippi coast. *Mississippi Kite* 11: 10–11.

Tousey, R. H. & Griscom, L. 1937. Notes on Starling spread and migration. *Auk* 54: 209–10.

Townsend, C. W. 1926. The European Starling in Mississippi and in Florida. *Auk* 43: 371.

Townsend, C. W. & Wetmore, A. 1919. Reports on the scientific results of the expedition to the tropical Pacific in charge of A. Agassiz on the United States Fish Commission steamer *Albatross. Bulletin of the Museum of Comparative Zoology, Harvard* No. 63: 151–225.

Tree, A. J. 1975. House Sparrow (*Passer domesticus*): new distributional data. *Ostrich* 46: 179.

Trenholm, L. 1926. The Starling in Tennessee. *Bird-Lore* 28: 334.

Trimm, W. 1972 and 1973. The Monk . Parrot. *Conservation* 26: 4–5; 27: 32–3.

True, G. H. 1937. The Chukar Partridge of Asia. *California Fish and Game* 23: 299–331.

Trueblood, R. & Weigand, J. 1971. Hungarian Partridge. In T. W. Mussehl and F. W. Howell eds, *Game Management in Montana*, Ch. 18: 153–9. Montana Fish and Game Department: Helena.

Tuck, L. M. 1958. The present distribution and population of the Starling in Newfoundland. *Canadian Field-Naturalist* 72: 139–44.

————. 1968. Recent Newfoundland bird records. *Auk* 85: 304–11.

Tuer, V. 1969. Breeding of the House Sparrow in Bulawayo. *Honeyguide* 59: 34.

Turbet, C. R. 1941. Introduction and acclimatization of animals. *Transactions and Proceedings of the Fiji Society of Science and Industry, 1938–40,* 7–12.

Turbott, E. G. 1956. Bulbuls in Auckland. *Notornis* 6: 185–93.

————. 1957. Native and introduced birds. In *Science in New Zealand*, 97–111. A. H. and A. W. Reed: Wellington.

————. 1961. The interaction of native and introduced birds in New Zealand. *Proceedings of the New Zealand Ecological Society* 8: 62–6.

————. 1977. Rarotongan birds, with notes on land bird status. *Notornis* 24: 149–57.

Turbott, E. G., Braithwaite, D. H. & Wilkin, F. W. 1963. Cattle Egret: a new bird for New Zealand. *Notornis* 10: 316.

Tuttle, H. J. 1959. Virginia's foreign game program: a progress report. *Proceedings of the 13th Annual Conference of the Southeastern Association of Game* and Fish Commissioners, 70–3.

———. 1963. Japanese Green and Kalij Pheasants in Virginia. *Proceedings of the 17th Annual Conference of the Southeastern Association of Game and Fish Commissioners*, 121–3.

Twomey, A. C. 1936. Climatographic studies of certain introduced and migratory bird. *Ecology* 17: 122–32.

U

Udagawa, T. 1949. The eastern Ring-Dove may be extirpated in Japan. *Tori* 12: 267–9.

Udø, O. G. 1979. The Canada Goose in Norway. *Fauna, Oslo* 32: 66–71 [in Norwegian, with English summary].

Udvardy, M. D. F. 1960. The Black-headed Mannikin, *Lonchura malacca atricapilla* – a new breeding bird on the Hawaiian Islands. *Elepaio* 21: 15–17.

———. 1961. The occurrence of the Mocking Bird on the island of Maui. *Elepaio* 21: 72.

———. 1966. [Review of Niethammer 1963.] *Journal of Wildlife Management* 30: 240–1.

Umber, H. 1982. Chukars are back for another try. *North Dakota Outdoors* 45: 2–4.

Urban, E. K. & **Brown, L. H.** 1971. *A Checklist of the Birds of Ethiopia*. Haile Sellassie I University Press: Addis Ababa.

Urner, C. A. 1921. Notes on the Starling. *Auk* 38: 459.

Uys, C. J. 1962. The House Sparrow, *Passer domesticus*, at Grunau [South Africa]. *Ostrich* 33: 39.

V

Van Bruggen, A. C. 1960. Notes on observations on birds in the Transvaal, Southern Rhodesia [Zimbabwe], and Portuguese East Africa [Mozambique]. *Ostrich* 31: 30–1.

Van der Merwe, F. 1984. Europese Spreeus verdring Gryskopspegte. *African Wildlife* 38: 152–7.

Van der Plaat, A. 1952. House Sparrow (*Passer domesticus*). *Ostrich* 23: 64.

Van Nierop, F. 1958. How Indian Mynahs escaped from a pet shop in Durban in 1902. *Wit Bird Club News* 27: 12.

Van Ripper, C. 1973. A comparison of the different nesting locations of the Chinese Thrush in Hawaii. *Elepaio* 33: 91–2.

———. 1976. Aspects of House Finch breeding biology in Hawaii. *Condor* 78: 224–9.

———. 1978. Discovery of the Yellow-fronted Canary on Mauna Kea, Hawaii. *Elepaio* 38: 99–100.

Van Ripper, C., Van Ripper, S. & **Berger, A. J.** 1979. The Red-whiskered Bulbul in Hawaii. *Wilson Bulletin* 91: 323–8.

Van Someren, V. D. 1947. Field notes on some Madagascar birds. *Ibis* 89: 235–67.

Van Tets, G. F. & **Van Tets, P. A.** 1967. A report on the resident birds of the territory of Christmas Island. *Emu* 66: 309–17.

Van Wormer, J. 1968. *The World of the Canada Goose.* Lippincott: Philadelphia.

Vaughan, J. H. 1930 and 1932. The birds of Zanzibar and Pemba. *Ibis* series 12, 6: 1–47; series 13, 2: 351–3.

Vaughan, R. E. & **Jones, K. H.** 1913. The birds of Hong Kong, Macao and the West River or Si Kiang in south east China, with special reference to their nidification and seasonal movements. *Ibis*, series 10, 3: 17–76, 163–201, 351–84.

Vaurie, C. 1961. Systematic notes on Palaearctic birds No. 49. Columbidae: the genus *Streptopelia*. *American Museum Novitates* No. 2058: 1–25.

Vernon, C. J. 1962. Passerinae at Francistown, Bechuanaland Protectorate [Botswana]. *Ostrich* 33: 239–40.

Vicente, R. O. 1969. A new introduced species in Europe: the Red-eared Waxbill. *Ibis* 111: 614.

Vickery, P. 1980. The Cape Elizabeth Monk Parakeets. *Maine Quarterly Audubon Magazine.*

Vierke, J. 1970. Die Besiedlung Südafrikas durch dem Haussperling (*Passer domesticus*). *Journal für Ornithologie* 111: 94–103.

Vincent, J. 1972. A new addition to the list of South African birds [Ring-necked Parakeet]. *Ostrich* 43: 234–5.

Viney, C. A. 1976. *The Hong Kong Bird Report, 1975.* Hong Kong Birdwatching Society: Hong Kong.

Viney, C. A. & **Phillips, K.** 1983. *New Colour Guide to Hong Kong Birds.* Government Information Department: Hong Kong.

Vinicombe, K. E. & **Chandler, R. J.** 1982. Movements of Ruddy Ducks during the hard winter of 1978/79. *British Birds* 75: 1–11.

Vodak, L. 1980. [The Raven in Sumava, Czechoslovakia.] *Ziva* 28: 152 [in Czech].

Von-Essen, L. 1982. An effort to reintroduce the Lesser White-fronted Goose into the Scandinavian mountains. *Aquila* 89: 103–7.

Von Essen, L. & **Fabricius, E.** 1969. Kanadagåsen [Canada Goose] i Sverige. *Svensk Jakt* 107: 13–16.

Von Etzdorf, T. J. R. 1964. European Starling. *Outeniqua Bird Club News* 13: 7.

Von Schwind, H. 1963a. Ausbreitung des Haussperlings [House Sparrows in Namibia]. *Mitteilungen der SWA Wissenschaftliche Gesellschaft* 4: 5.

———. 1963b. Vorkommen des Haussperlings in S. W. A. *Mitteilungen der SWA Wissenschaftliche Gesellschaft* 4: 2.

Voous, K. H. 1960. *Atlas of European Birds.* Nelson: London.

————. 1983. *Birds of the Netherlands Antilles*. De Walburg Pers.

W

Wace, N. M. & **Holdgate, M. W.** 1976. *Man and nature in the Tristan da Cunha Islands*. Monograph No. 6. International Union for Conservation of Nature: Morges.

Wackenernagel, H. & **Walter, W.** 1980. Captive breeding and reintroduction of the lammergeier or bearded vulture *Gypaetus barbatus* – a zoo/nature conservation project. *International Zoo Yearbook* 20: 243–4.

Wagner, H. O. 1959. Die Einwanderung des Haussperlings [House Sparrows] in Mexiko. *Zeitschrift für Tierpsychologie* 16: 584–92.

Wahl, T. R. & **Wilson, H. E.** 1971. Nesting records of European Skylark in Washington state. *Condor* 73: 254.

Wait, W. E 1931. *Manual of the Birds of Ceylon*. Colombo Museum: Colombo.

Walker, A. 1949. The Starling reaches the Pacific. *Condor* 51: 271.

Walker, A. F. G. 1970. The moult migration of Yorkshire Canada Geese. *Wildfowl* 21: 99–104.

Walker, E. A. 1949. The status of the wild Turkey west of the Mississippi River. *Transactions of the 14th North American Wildlife Conference*, 336–54.

Walker, F. J. 1981. Notes on the birds of northern Oman. *Sandgrouse* 2: 33–55.

Walker, H. 1967. Indian Myna. *Natal Bird Club News Sheet* 150: 4.

Walker, R. B. 1952. Indian Mynah on the Darling Downs. *Emu* 52: 64–5.

Walker, R. L. 1967a. Indian Hill Mynah, Cattle Egret, and Red-vented Bulbul. *Elepaio* 28: 23–4.

————. 1967b. A brief history of exotic game bird and mammal introductions into Hawaii, with a look to the future. *Proceedings of the 47th Annual Conference of the Western Association of State Game and Fish Commissioners, Honolulu, Hawaii, 16–20 July, 1967*, 94–112. (Also issued as a mimeograph by the State of Hawaii Department of Land and Natural Resources, Division of Fish and Game (13 pp.).

————. 1970. Nene restoration project report. *Elepaio* 31: 1–7.

————. 1981. List of game birds and mammals of Hawaii. State of Hawaii Department of Land and Natural Resources, Division of Forestry and Wildlife. Mimeograph (2 pp.).

————. 1983. Cattle Egret rookery on Molokai [Hawaii]. *Elepaio* 43: 91–2.

Wall, L. E. & **Wheeler, W. R.** 1966. Lyrebirds in Tasmania. *Emu* 66: 123–31.

Wandell, W. N. 1949. Status of the Ring-necked Pheasant in the United States. *Transactions of the 14th North American Wildlife Conference*, 370–87.

Ward, P. 1968. The origin of the avifauna of urban and suburban Singapore. *Ibis* 110: 239–54.

Ward, P. & **Poh, G. E.** 1968. Seasonal breeding in an equatorial population of the Tree Sparrow (*Passer montanus*). *Ibis* 110: 359–63.

Warner, R. E. 1959. Sighting of the Collared Thrush, *Garrulax albogularis*. *Elepaio* 20: 9–10.

————. 1968. The role of introduced diseases in the extinction of the endemic Hawaiian avifauna. *Condor* 70: 101–20.

————. 1984. Declining survival of Ring-necked Pheasant chicks in Illinois agricultural ecosystems. *Journal of Wildlife Management* 48: 82–8.

Warr, F. E. 1978. *Birds Recorded in the Arabian Gulf States*. Privately printed.

Waterton, C. 1871. *Essays on Natural History*. [Little Owl.] Frederick Warne: London.

Watling, D. 1975. Observations on the ecological separation of two introduced congeneric Mynahs (*Acridotheres*) in Fiji. *Notornis* 22: 37–53.

————. 1977. The ecology of the Red-vented Bulbul in Fiji. Unpublished PhD thesis, University of Cambridge.

————. 1978a. A Myna matter. *Notornis* 25: 117.

————. 1978b. Observations on the naturalised distribution of the Red-vented Bulbul in the Pacific, with special reference to the Fiji Islands. *Notornis* 25: 109–17.

————. 1979. The Bulbul gets a clean bill of health. *New Scientist* 82: 963–5.

★————. 1982. *Birds of Fiji, Tonga and Samoa*. Millwood Press: Wellington, New Zealand.

————. 1984. The breeding biology of the Red-vented Bulbul (*Pycnonotus cafer*) in Fiji. *Emu* 83: 173–80.

————. 1986. Rediscovery of a petrel and new faunal records on Gau Island. *Oryx* 20: 31–4.

Watmough, R. G. 1981. Nutmeg Mannikin in Suburban Adelaide. *South Australian Ornithologist* 28: 167.

Watson, G. E. 1966. The Chukar Partridge (*Alectoris chukar*) of St Helena Island, South Atlantic Ocean (morphology and ecology). *Proceedings of the Biological Society of Washington* 79: 179–82.

————. 1975. *Birds of the Antarctic and Subantarctic*. American Geophysical Union: Washington, DC.

Watson, G. E., **Zusi, R. L.** & **Storer R. E.** 1963. *Preliminary Guide to the Birds of the Indian Ocean*. US National Museum, Smithsonian Institution: Washington, DC.

Wattel, J. 1971. The subspecies of *Fringilla coelebs* L. inhabiting the Cape Peninsula [South Africa]. *Ostrich* 42: 229.

Wayre, P. 1966. The role of aviculture in helping to save threatened species. *Monthly Service Bulletin of the Perth Department of Fish and Fauna* No. 16: 14–17.

————. 1969. *A Guide to the Pheasants of the World.* Country Life: London.

————. 1975a. Reintroduction of the Cheer Pheasant. *Bulletin of the International Council for Bird Preservation* 12: 222–3.

————. 1975b. Pheasants to Formosa. *Wildlife World Conservation Yearbook,* 76–81.

Weaver, R. L. 1939. The northern distribution and status of the English Sparrow in Canada. *Canadian Field-Naturalist* 53: 95–9.

————. 1943. Reproduction in English Sparrows. *Auk* 60: 62–73.

Webb, L. G. 1969. Exotic game bird investigations. *Annual Progress Report of the South Carolina Wildlife Research Department,* Project W–38–5 (81 pp.).

Webb, P. M. 1957. The introduction of the Grey Francolin in Arizona: a progress report. *Proceedings of the 37th Annual Conference of the Western Association of State Game and Fish Commissioners,* 274–6.

Webster, M. A. 1975. *An Annotated Checklist of the Birds of Hong Kong.* Birdwatching Society of Hong Kong: Hong Kong.

Weigand, J. P. 1980. *Ecology of the Hungarian Partridge in North-central Montana.* Wildlife Monograph No. 74 (106 pp.). Montana Department of Fisheries, Wildlife and Parks.

Weisbrod, A. R. & **Stevens, W. F.** 1974. The Skylark in Washington. *Auk* 91: 832–5.

Weissenbacher, B. K. H. & **Allan, D.** 1985. Rose-ringed Parakeet breeding attempts in the Transvaal. *Ostrich* 56: 169.

Welch, G. & **Welch, H.** 1984. Birds seen on an expedition to Djibouti. *Sandgrouse* 6: 1–23.

Welles, M. W. 1969. Potential dangers of exotic waterfowl introductions. *Wildfowl* 20: 55–8.

————. 1980. *The Island Wildfowl.* Iowa State University Press: Ames, Iowa.

Wells, G. R. 1953. Wyoming Chukar Partridge transplant experiences. *Proceedings of the 32nd Annual Conference of the Western Association of State Game and Fish Commissioners,* 168–70.

Wellwood, J. M. 1968. *Hawkes Bay Acclimatisation Society Centenary, 1868–1968.* Cliff Press: Hastings, New Zealand.

★**Wenner, A. S.** & **Hirth, D. H.** 1984. Status of the feral Budgerigar in Florida. *Journal of Field Ornithology* 55: 214–19.

Wessell, C. W. 1939. The Chukar Partridge. *Pennsylvania Game News* 9: 10–11, 31.

Westermann, J. H. 1953. Nature preservation in the Caribbean. *Uitgaven van de Natuurwetschappelijke Studiekring voor Suriname in der Nederlandse Antillen* 9: 1–106.

Westerskov, K. 1949. The recent decline of the Hungarian Partridge *Ohio Conservation Bulletin* No. 13: 20–1.

————. 1953a. Taxonomic status of the Redpoll in New Zealand. *Notornis* 6: 189–91.

————. 1953b. Acclimatization of new game species. *New Zealand Department of Internal Affairs, Wildlife Publication* No. 17 (8 pp.) (Originally published in *New Zealand Fishing & Shooting Gazette* 19(10): 4–8 (July, 1952).)

————. 1954. Spread of the Australian Magpie within the Rotorua acclimatisation district. *Notornis* 5: 243–8.

————. 1955a. The Pheasant in New Zealand. *New Zealand Department of Internal Affairs, Wildlife Publication* No. 40 (35 pp.) (Reprinted 1962.)

————. 1955b. Productivity of New Zealand Pheasant populations: a study of the Pheasant, *Phasianus colchicus,* under New Zealand conditions: its reproductive capacity, taxonomy, distribution, and management. Unpublished PhD thesis, Victoria University College, University of New Zealand.

————. 1956a. History and distribution of the Bobwhite Quail in New Zealand. *New Zealand Department of Internal Affairs, Wildlife Publication* No. 43 (8 pp.) (See also *New Zealand Outdoors* 21: 12–14, 35–6.)

————. 1956b. History and distribution of Hungarian Partridges in Ohio, 1909–48. *Ohio Journal of Science* 56: 65–70.

————. 1957a. Taxonomic status of the Bobwhite Quail in New Zealand. *Notornis* 7: 95–8.

————. 1957b. The Pheasant in Nelson. *New Zealand Department of Internal Affairs, Wildlife Publication* No. 50: 3–12. (Reprinted from the *89th Annual Report of the Nelson Acclimatisation Society,* 15–24.)

————. 1958. The Partridge as a game bird. *New Zealand Department of Internal Affairs, Wildlife Publication* No. 51 (10 pp.).

————. 1960. Danish Partridges in New Zealand: establishing a new breeding stock, 1959. *New Zealand Department of Internal Affairs, Wildlife Publication* No. 70 (11 pp.).

————. 1963. Superior survival of Black-necked over Ring-necked Pheasants in New Zealand. *Journal of Wildlife Management* 27: 239–45.

————. 1964. The recent decline of the Partridge in mid-western United States. *New Zealand Outdoors* 29: 16–19.

————. 1966. Winter food and feeding habits of the Partridge, *Perdix perdix,* in the Canadian prairie. *Canadian Journal of Zoology* 44: 303–22.

————. 1974. Probably the first breeding of the Cattle Egret (*Bubulcus ibis*) in New Zealand. *Notornis* 21: 239–46.

Wetmore, A. 1916. The birds of Vieques Island, Porto Rico. *Auk* 33: 403–19.

————. 1926. Birds of Argentina, Paraguay, Uruguay, and Chile. *Bulletin US National Museum, Smithsonian Institution* No. 133.

————. 1927. Scientific survey of Porto Rico and the

Virgin Islands. *Bulletin of the New York Academy of Sciences* No. 9 (3–4).

———. 1957. An extension in range of the House Sparrow, *Passer domesticus* [in South Africa]. *Ostrich* 28: 239–40.

———. 1963. An early record of the Cattle Egret in Colombia. *Auk* 80: 547.

———. 1964. *Song and Garden Birds of North America*. National Geographic Society: Washington, DC.

———. 1965–84. *The Birds of the Republic of Panama*, 4 vols. Smithsonian Institution Press: Washington, DC.

Wetmore, A. & **Lincoln, F. C.** 1933. Additional notes on the birds of Haiti and the Dominican Republic. *US National Museum, Smithsonian Institution Bulletin* No. 82 (68 pp.).

Wetmore, A. & **Swales, B. H.** 1931. The birds in Haiti and the Dominican Republic. *US National Museum, Smithsonian Institution Bulletin* No. 155 (483 pp.).

Whatmough, R. G. 1981. Nutmeg Mannikin in suburban Adelaide. *South Australian Ornithologist* 28: 167.

Wheatley, J. J. 1970. Status of the Carolina Duck (*Aix sponsa*) in Surrey. *Surrey Bird Club Quarterly Bulletin* No. 55: 15.

———. 1972. Recent Carolina Duck breeding records in Surrey. *Surrey Bird Report* 20: 64–5.

Wheeler, J. R. 1960. Royal Australasian Ornithologists' Union campout on Kangaroo Island, South Australia. *Emu* 60: 265–80.

———. 1962. Observations on the Cattle Egret in eastern Australia. *Emu* 62: 192–3.

Whistler, H. 1923. *Popular Handbook of Indian Birds*. Gurney & Jackson: London.

White, S. A. 1923. Birds observed on and around Mount Remarkable during Royal Australasian Ornithologists' Union visit. *Emu* 22: 216–17.

White, S. R. 1946. Notes on the bird life of Australia's heaviest rainfall region. *Emu* 46: 122.

Whitehead, J. 1899. Field notes on birds collected in the Philippine Islands in 1893–96. Parts 2 and 4. *Ibis*, series 7, 5: 210–46, 485–501.

Whitney, C. 1971. Chukar Partridge. In T. W. Mussehl & F. W. Howell eds, *Game Management in Montana*, Ch. 21: 175–9. Montana Fish and Game Department: Helena.

Whittell, H. M. 1950. The Starling in Western Australia. *Western Australian Naturalist* 2: 137.

Widmann, O. 1889. History of the House Sparrow, *Passer domesticus*, and European Tree Sparrow, *Passer montanus*, at St Louis, Mo. In Barrows, 1889, 191–3.

———. 1907. Preliminary catalogue of the birds of Missouri. *Transactions of the Academy of Science of St Louis* 17: 172.

Wildash, P. 1968. *Birds of South Vietnam*. Tuttle: Vermont and Tokyo.

Wild Bird Society of Japan. 1985. *A Field Guide to the Birds of Japan*. Wild Bird Society of Japan: Tokyo.

Wilhelm, E. 1959. *Birds of the St Louis Area*. St Louis Audubon Society: St Louis, Missouri.

Willett, G. 1930. The Common Mynah breeding in Los Angeles. *Condor* 32: 301–2.

Willey, A., Treacher, W. H., Carey, E. V., Cochrane, C. W. H., Neubronner, A. D. & **Marks, O.** 1903. Acclimatization of Ceylon Crows [*Corvus splendens*] in the Malay Peninsula. *Spolia Zeylanica* 1: 23–35.

Willey, C. H. 1968a. The ecology, distribution, and abundance of the Mute Swan (*Cygnus olor*) in Rhode Island. Unpublished MSc thesis, University of Rhode Island.

———. 1968b. The ecological significance of the Mute Swan in Rhode Island. *Transactions of the Northeastern Section of the Wildlife Society, 25th Northeastern Fish and Wildlife Conference, 14–17 January, 1968*, 121–34.

Williams, G. R. 1950. Chukar in New Zealand. *New Zealand Science Review* 20: 2–6.

———. 1951. Further notes on the Chukar. *Notornis* 4: 151–7.

———. 1952. The Californian Quail in New Zealand. *Journal of Wildlife Management* 16: 460–83.

———. 1953. The dispersal from New Zealand and Australia of some introduced European Passerines. *Ibis* 95: 676–92.

———. 1955. Some aspects of the life history and management of California Quail in New Zealand. *New Zealand Department of Internal Affairs, Wildlife Publication* No. 36 (31 pp.).

———. 1960. The birds of the Pitcairn Islands, central South Pacific Ocean. *Ibis* 102: 58–70.

———. 1962. Story of the New Zealand California Quail populations. *Ammohouse Bulletin* No. 1: 6–8.

———. 1963. A four-year population cycle in Californian Quail, *Lophortyx californicus* (Shaw), in the South Island of New Zealand. *Journal of Animal Ecology* 32: 441–59.

———. 1967. Breeding biology of California Quail in New Zealand. *Proceedings of the New Zealand Ecological Society* 14: 88–99.

———. 1968. The Cape Barren Goose (*Cereopsis novaehollandiae*) Latham in New Zealand. *Notornis* 15: 66–9.

*———. 1969. Introduced birds. In G. A. Knox, ed., *The Natural History of Canterbury*, 435–51. A. H. & A. W. Reed: Canterbury.

———. 1973. Birds. In *The Natural History of New Zealand: An Ecological Survey*. A. H. & A. W. Reed: Wellington.

———. 1976. The New Zealand Wattlebirds. *Proceedings of the 16th International Ornithological Congress, Canberra, 1976*, 161–70.

Williams, J. G. & **Arlott, N.** 1982. *A Field Guide to* *the Birds of East Africa*. Collins: London. (1st Edition, 1963.)

Williams, L. 1968. Med jägarhäläning (om kanadagåas) [Canada Geese]. *Svensk Jakt* 106: 100–1.

Williams, M. 1979. The status and management of Black Swans at Lake Ellesmere. *New Zealand Journal of Ecology* 2: 34–41.

Williams, R. N. 1983a. Bulbul introductions on Oahu. *Elepaio* 43: 89–90.

———. 1983b. The Red-vented Bulbul on the island of Hawaii. *Elepaio* 43: 101–3.

Williams, R. N. & **Giddings, L. V.** 1984. Differential range expansion and population growth of bulbuls in Hawaii. *Wilson Bulletin* 96: 647–55.

Williams, R. N. & **Moulton, M. P.** 1981. Red-vented Bulbul feeding on a gecko. *Elepaio* 42: 30.

Williamson, K. 1945. Some new and scarce breeding species in the Faeroe Islands. *Ibis* 87: 550–8.

———. 1970. *The Atlantic Islands: a Study of the Faeroe Life and Scene*, 2nd edn. Routledge & Kegan Paul: London.

Williamson, M. 1981. *Island Populations*. Oxford University Press: Oxford.

Wilmore, S. B. 1974. *Swans of the World*. David and Charles: Newton Abbot, Devon.

Wilson, A. H. R. 1928. Bird notes from Yarraberb. *Emu* 28: 121–8.

Wilson, C. J. 1924. On the occurrence of a Javanese bird, *Pycnonotus a. aurigaster* (Viell.), in Singapore. *Singapore Naturalist* 4: 86–7.

Wilson, E. 1858. On the introduction of the British songbird. *Transactions of the Philosophical Institute of Victoria* 2: 77–88.

Wilson, H. L. & **Lewis, J.** 1959. Establishment and spread of the wild Turkey in southwestern Michigan. *Journal of Wildlife Management* 23: 210–15.

Wilson, J. E. 1949. A history of the Ring-necked Pheasant in Michigan. *Journal of Forestry* 47: 218.

———. 1959. Status of the Hungarian Partridge in New York. *Kingbird* 9: 54–7.

Wilson, S. B. 1907. Notes on the birds of Tahiti and the Society group. *Ibis*, series 9, 1: 373–7.

★**Wing, L.** 1943a. Spread of the Starling and English Sparrow. *Auk* 60: 74–87.

———. 1943b. The Starlings in eastern Washington. *Condor* 45: 159.

———. 1956. *Natural History of Birds*. Ronald Press: New York.

Wingate, D. B. ed. 1965. Commentarium of J. T. Bartram, Naturalist of 19th Century Bermuda. *Bermuda Historical Quarterly* 22: 1–34.

———. 1973. *A Checklist and Guide to the Birds of Bermuda*. The Island Press: Hamilton, Bermuda.

★———. 1982. Successful reintroduction of the Yellow-crowned Night-Heron as a nesting resident on Bermuda. *Colonial Waterbirds* 5: 104–15.

———. 1985. Exotic cage bird escapes result in the successful breeding and naturalisation of at least one new species on Bermuda. *Department of Agriculture & Fisheries, Bermuda Monthly Bulletin* 56: 27–9.

Winterbottom, J. M. 1951. European Starlings at Heidelberg. *Ostrich* 22: 202.

———. 1952. European Starlings at the Cape. *Ostrich* 23: 220–1.

———. 1953. House Sparrow in eastern Cape. *Ostrich* 24: 130–1.

———. 1955a. Distribution of European Starling. *Ostrich* 26: 46.

———. 1955b. European Starling at Storms River. *Ostrich* 26: 136.

———. 1956a. Red-eyed Dove in the Western Cape. *Ostrich* 27: 184.

———. 1956b. Goldfinches in the Transvaal? *Bokmakierie* 8: 19.

———. 1957a. European Starling, *Sturnus vulgaris* L., at Calitzdorp and Oudtschoorn. *Ostrich* 27: 124.

———. 1957b. European Starling at Matjiesfontein. *Ostrich* 28: 124–5.

———. 1957c. Further records of the European Starling (*Sturnus vulgaris*) in the south west Cape. *Ostrich* 28: 237–8.

———. 1959 and 1961. Expansion of range of the House Sparrow. *Cape Department of Nature Conservation Report* No. 16: 92–4.

———. 1962. The House Sparrow, *Passer domesticus*, at Touws River. *Ostrich* 33: 75.

———. 1965. House Sparrow at Kalkrand. *Ostrich* 36: 91.

———. 1966. Some alien birds in South Africa. *Bokmakierie* 18: 22, 61–2.

———. 1968. Spread of European Sparrow. *Cape Bird Club Newsletter* 87: 3.

———. 1971. *A Preliminary Checklist of the Birds of South West Africa*. South West Africa Scientific Society: Windhoek (268 pp.).

———. 1972. Report on the House Sparrow enquiry. *Bokmakierie* 24: 37–8.

———. 1975. European Starling (*Sturnus vulgaris*). *Ostrich* 46: 178.

———. 1978. Introduced birds. In M. J. A. Werger & A. C. Van Bruggen eds, *Biogeography and Ecology of Southern Africa*, Ch. 30(9): 974–5. W. Junk: The Hague.

★**Winterbottom, J. M.** & **Liversidge, R.** 1954. The European Starling in the South West Cape. *Ostrich* 25: 89–96.

Wise, C. D. & **Cooper, R. H.** 1982. House Finch now breeding in Delaware County. *Indiana Audubon Quarterly* 60: 127–8.

Witherby, H. F. & **Ticehurst, N. F.** 1908. Spread of the Little Owl in Britain. *British Birds* 1: 335–42.

Witherby, H. F. ed., **Jourdain, F. C. R., Ticehurst, N. F.** & **Tucker, B. W.** 1938–41. *The Hand-*

book of British Birds, 5 vols. H. F. & G. Witherby: London.

Wodzicki, K. 1956. Breeding of the House Sparrow away from man in New Zealand. *Emu* 56: 146–7.

★———. 1965. The status of some exotic vertebrates in the ecology of New Zealand. In H. G. Baker & G. L. Stebbins eds, *The Genetics of Colonizing Species* (*Proceedings of the 1st International Union of Biological Sciences Symposium, General Biology*), 425–60. Academic Press: New York and London.

———. 1973. Some problems arising from the invasion and deliberate introduction of exotic plant and animal species in the south-west Pacific. *Proceedings of the Regional Symposium on Conservation of Nature, Reefs & Lagoons* (*Noumea, New Caledonia*), 239–44.

Wolfe, L. R. 1961. Cattle Egret in Mexico. *Auk* 78: 640–1.

Wollard, L. L., Sparrowe, R. D. & **Chambers, G. D.** 1977. Evaluation of a Korean Pheasant introduction in Missouri. *Journal of Wildlife Management* 41: 616–23.

Wood, C. A. 1924. The Starling family at home and abroad. *Condor* 26: 123–36.

Wood, C. A. & **Wetmore, A.** 1926. A collection of birds from the Fiji Islands. Part 3. Field observations. *Ibis*, series 12, 2: 91–136.

Wood-Jones, F. 1909. Fauna of the Cocos-Keeling Atoll. Aves. *Proceedings of the Zoological Society of London* (January/April): 137–42.

Woods, D. L. 1980. House Crow at Zeekoevlei, Retreat. *Promerops* 143: 5.

Woods, R. S. 1968. *Carpodacus mexicanus frontalis* (Say). House Finch. In C. Bent, ed., Life histories of North American cardinals, grosbeaks, buntings, towhees, finches, sparrows, and allies. *US National Museum, Smithsonian Institution Bulletin* No. 237(1): 290–314.

Woods, R. W. 1975. *The Birds of the Falkland Islands.* Anthony Nelson: Oswestry/Lindblad Travel Inc.: New York.

Woodside, D. H. 1970. Edible Nest Swiftlet. *Elepaio* 31: 28.

Wright, C. M. 1925. Goldfinches (*Carduelis carduelis*) at Armidale, New South Wales. *Emu* 25: 43.

Wylde, M. A. 1923. The migrant [Quail]. *Ornithological Notes* 2: 44.

Wyndham, E. 1978. Ecology of the Budgerygah. Unpublished PhD thesis, University of New England, New South Wales.

X

Xavier, A. 1968. Bicos de lacre em Óbidos [*Estrilda troglodytes* in Portugal]. *Cyanopica* 1: 77–81.

Y

Yaldwyn, J. C. 1952. Notes on the present status of Samoan birds. *Notornis* 5: 28–30.

Yamashina, Y. 1961. *Birds in Japan: a Field Guide.* Tokyo News Service: Tokyo.

★**Yanushevich, A.I.** ed. 1966. *Acclimatization of Animals in the U. S. S. R.* (*Proceedings of a conference at Frunze, 10–15 May 1963*). Israel Program for Scientific Translations: Jerusalem.

Yapp, W. B. 1983. Game-birds in medieval England. *Ibis* 125: 218–21.

Yeatman, L. J. 1976. *Atlas des Oiseaux Nicheurs de France.* Ministère de la Qualité de la Vie: Paris.

Yeatter, R. E. 1934. The Hungarian Partridge in the Great Lakes region. *University of Michigan School of Forestry and Conservation Bulletin* No. 5 (92 pp.).

Yerbury, J. W. 1886. On the birds of Aden and neighbourhood. *Ibis*, series 5, 4: 11.

Yocum, C. F. 1943. The Hungarian Partridge, *Perdix perdix* L., in the Palouse region, Washington. *Ecological Monographs* No. 13: 167–201.

———. 1963. Starlings above the Arctic Circle in Alaska, 1962. *Auk* 80: 544.

———. 1970. The Giant Canada Goose in New Zealand. *Auk* 87: 812–14.

Young, H. G. 1984. Night Herons in captivity. *International Zoo News* 190: 9–14.

Young, H. G. & **Duffy, K.** 1984. Night-Herons in Scotland. *Annual Report of the Royal Zoological Society of Scotland*, 40–6.

Young, J. G. 1972a. Distribution, status, and movements of feral Grey-lag Geese in southwest Scotland. *Scottish Birds* 7: 170–82.

———. 1972b. Breeding biology of feral Grey-lag Geese in southwest Scotland. *Wildfowl* 23: 83–7.

Youngworth, W. 1944. The Starling in South Dakota, North Dakota, and Minnesota. *Iowa Bird Life* 14: 76.

Yuen, H. J. 1972. Agonistic behaviour of the Red-crested Cardinal. *Elepaio* 33: 55–61.

Z

Zahl, P. A. 1967. New scarlet bird [Ibis] in Florida skies. *National Geographic Magazine* 132: 874–82.

Zeillemaker, C. F. & **Scott, J. M.** 1976. Checklist of the birds of Hawaii (provisional draft). Mimeograph (7 pp.).

Zeuner, F. E. 1963. *A History of Domesticated Animals.* Hutchinson: London.

Zimmerman, D. A. 1967. *Agapornis fischeri, Lybius guifsobalito* and *Striphrornis erythrothorax* in Kenya. *Auk* 84: 594–5.

Geographical index

Afghanistan

Ring-necked Parakeet (*Psittacula krameri*) 264

Agaléga Islands

Madagascar Turtle Dove (*Streptopelia picturata*) 218
Barred Dove (*Geopelia striata*) 234
Red-crested Cardinal (*Paroaria coronata*) 359
Madagascar Fody (*Foudia madagascariensis*) 473
Common Mynah (*Acridotheres tristis*) 494

Aldabra Island

Madagascar Fody (*Foudia madagascariensis*) 473–4

Algeria

Feral pigeon (*Columba livia*) 211

Ambon (or Amboina)

see under Moluccas

Amirante Islands

Grey Francolin (*Francolinus pondicerianus*) 119
Madagascar Turtle Dove (*Streptopelia picturata*) 218
Common Waxbill (*Estrilda astrild*) 407
House Sparrow (*Passer domesticus*) 444
Madagascar Fody (*Foudia madagascariensis*) 473

Andaman Islands

Chinese Francolin (*Francolinus pintadeanus*) 117
Grey Francolin (*Francolinus pondicerianus*) 119
Common Peafowl (*Pavo cristatus*) 187
Feral Pigeon (*Columba livia*) 210
House Sparrow (*Passer domesticus*) 439
Common Mynah (*Acridotheres tristis*) 492
Jungle Mynah (*Acridotheres fuscus*) 503

Angola

Feral Pigeon (*Columba livia*) 210

Annobón Island

Helmeted Guineafowl (*Numida meleagris*) 192
Yellow-fronted Canary (*Serinus mozambicus*) 381

Antigua

Feral Pigeon (*Columba livia*) 212
Yellow Grass Finch (*Sicalis luteola*) 355
Troupial (*Icterus icterus*) 369
Shiny Cowbird (*Molothrus bonariensis*) 371

Antipodes Island

Mallard (*Anas platyrhynchos*) 45
Dunnock (*Prunella modularis*) 323
Song Thrush (*Turdus philomelos*) 333
Chaffinch (*Fringilla coelebs*) 376
Goldfinch (*Carduelis carduelis*) 392
Redpoll (*Acanthis flammea*) 396
European Starling (*Sturnus vulgaris*) 487, 488

Arabia

(*see also* Bahrain, Oman; Saudi Arabia; United Arab Emirates)

Ring-necked Parakeet (*Psittacula krameri*) 263–4

Argentinia

California Quail (*Lophortyx californicus*) 85
Feral Pigeon (*Columba livia*) 212
Greenfinch (*Carduelis chloris*) 384
House Sparrow (*Passer domesticus*) 450, 454

Ascension

Common Waxbill (*Estrilda astrild*) 408
Common Mynah (*Acridotheres tristis*) 494

Assumption

Madagascar Fody (*Foudia madagascariensis*) 473–4

Auckland Islands

Mallard (*Anas platyrhynchos*) 45
Skylark (*Alauda arvensis*) 308
Dunnock (*Prunella modularis*) 323
Blackbird (*Turdus merula*) 328, 329
Song Thrush (*Turdus philomelos*) 333, 334
Yellowhammer (*Emberiza citrinella*) 351
Chaffinch (*Fringilla coelebs*) 376
Greenfinch (*Carduelis chloris*) 386
Goldfinch (*Carduelis carduelis*) 392
Redpoll (*Acanthis flammea*) 396
House Sparrow (*Passer domesticus*) 457
European Starling (*Sturnus vulgaris*) 488

Austral Islands
see Tubuai Islands

Australia

Ostrich (*Struthio camelus*) 11–13
Mute Swan (*Cygnus olor*) 27
Mallard (*Anas platyrhynchos*) 44
California Quail (*Lophortyx californicus*) 85–6
Chukar Partridge (*Alectoris chukar*) 103
Red Jungle Fowl (*Gallus gallus*) 144
Common Pheasant (*Phasianus colchicus*) 168–9
Common Peafowl (*Pavo cristatus*) 187
Helmeted Guineafowl (*Numida meleagris*) 193
Common Turkey (*Meleagris gallopavo*) 198
Feral Pigeon (*Columba livia*) 213
Spotted Dove (*Streptopelia chinensis*) 226–7
Laughing Dove (*Streptopelia senegalensis*) 230
Skylark (*Alauda arvensis*) 306–7
Red-whiskered Bulbul (*Pycnonotus jocosus*) 313
Red-vented Bulbul (*Pycnonotus cafer*) 315
Blackbird (*Turdus merula*) 326–8
Song Thrush (*Turdus philomelos*) 331–3
Greenfinch (*Carduelis chloris*) 384–5
Goldfinch (*Carduelis carduelis*) 390–2
Nutmeg Mannikin (*Lonchura punctulata*) 423–4
House Sparrow (*Passer domesticus*) 455–6
Tree Sparrow (*Passer montanus*) 465–6
Red Bishop (*Euplectes orix*) 476
European Starling (*Sturnus vulgaris*) 485–7
Common Mynah (*Acridotheres tristis*) 494–6

Austria

Common Pheasant (*Phasianus colchicus*) 152
Common Turkey (*Meleagris gallopavo*) 197

Azores

Red-legged Partridge (*Alectoris rufa*) 108
Canary (*Serinus canaria*) 377
Greenfinch (*Carduelis chloris*) 383–4
Goldfinch (*Carduelis carduelis*) 388–9
House Sparrow (*Passer domesticus*)

Bahamas

Turkey Vulture (*Cathartes aura*) 59
Bobwhite Quail (*Colinus virginianus*) 94
Chukar Partridge (*Alectoris chukar*) 103
Common Pheasant (*Phasianus colchicus*) 168
Feral Pigeon (*Columba livia*) 212
Collared Dove (*Streptopelia decaocto*) 222
House Sparrow (*Passer domesticus*) 451

Bahrain

Ring-necked Parakeet (*Psittacula krameri*) 263
House Crow (*Corvus splendens*) 521

Balearic Islands

Red-legged Partridge (*Alectoris rufa*) 108

Banaba (or Ocean Island)

Red Jungle Fowl (*Gallus gallus*) 147

Barbados

Green-rumped Parrotlet (*Forpus passerinus*) 278
Yellow Grass Finch (*Sicalis luteola*) 354–5
Shiny Cowbird (*Molothrus bonariensis*) 371

Barbuda

Helmeted Guineafowl (*Numida meleagris*) 192, 193

Belau
see Palau Islands

Belgium

Canada Goose (*Branta canadensis*) 35
Red-legged Partridge (*Alectoris rufa*) 108
Common Pheasant (*Phasianus colchicus*) 152
Ring-necked Parakeet (*Psittacula krameri*) 263

Belize

House Sparrow (*Passer domesticus*) 450

Juventud, Isla de la
(*see* Youth, Isle of)

Kenya

Fischer's and Masked Lovebirds (*Agapornis fischeri* and *A. personata*) 259–60
Ring-necked Parakeet (*Psittacula krameri*) 265
House Sparrow (*Passer domesticus*) 442–3
House Crow (*Corvus splendens*) 524

Kermadec Islands

Skylark (*Alauda arvensis*) 308
Dunnock (*Prunella modularis*) 323
Blackbird (*Turdus merula*) 329
Song Thrush (*Turdus philomelos*) 333, 334
Yellowhammer (*Emberiza citrinella*) 351
Greenfinch (*Carduelis chloris*) 386
Goldfinch (*Carduelis carduelis*) 392
Redpoll (*Acanthis flammea*) 396
European Starling (*Sturnus vulgaris*) 487, 488

Korea

Feral Pigeon (*Columba livia*) 210
Collared Dove (*Streptopelia decaocto*) 221

Kuwait

Ring-necked Parakeet (*Psittacula krameri*) 263, 264
House Crow (*Corvus splendens*) 521

Laccadive Islands

Common Mynah (*Acridotheres tristis*) 492
House Crow (*Corvus splendens*) 522

Lebanon

Ring-necked Parakeet (*Psittacula krameri*) 263

Lesser Sunda Islands

Red Jungle Fowl (*Gallus gallus*) 144
Java Sparrow (*Padda oryzivora*) 435
Tree Sparrow (*Passer montanus*) 466

Line Islands

Kuhl's Lory (*Vini kuhlii*) 241–2

Lord Howe Island

Blackbird (*Turdus merula*) 328

Song Thrush (*Turdus philomelos*) 333
European Starling (*Sturnus vulgaris*) 486

Macau

Ring-necked Parakeet (*Psittacula krameri*) 264

Macquarie Island

Mallard (*Anas platyrhynchos*) 45
Weka (*Gallirallus australis*) 202–3
Song Thrush (*Turdus philomelos*) 333
Chaffinch (*Fringilla coelebs*) 376
Goldfinch (*Carduelis carduelis*) 392
Redpoll (*Acanthis flammea*) 396
European Starling (*Sturnus vulgaris*) 487, 488

Madagascar

Chinese Francolin (*Francolinus pintadeanus*) 117
Helmeted Guineafowl (*Numida meleagris*) 191
Barred Dove (*Geopelia striata*) 234
Common Mynah (*Acridotheres tristis*) 493

Madeira

Red-legged Partridge (*Alectoris rufa*) 109

Mafia Island, Tanzania

Laughing Dove (*Streptopelia senegalensis*) 231

Malawi

House Sparrow (*Passer domesticus*) 442

Malaysia

Feral Pigeon (*Columba livia*) 210
Sulphur-crested Cockatoo (*Cacatua galerita*) 243
Java Sparrow (*Padda oryzivora*) 433–4
Jungle and White-vented Mynahs (*Acridotheres fuscus* and *A. javanicus*) 502–3
Crested Mynah (*Acridotheres cristatellus*) 506–7
House Crow (*Corvus splendens*) 522–3

Maldive Islands

House Sparrow (*Passer domesticus*) 439
Common Mynah (*Acridotheres tristis*) 492

Malta

Laughing Dove (*Streptopelia senegalensis*) 230

Qatar

Raoul Island

(*see under* Kermadec Islands)

Rapa Nui

see Easter Island

Réunion

Rodrigues Island

Rumania

Samoa

Sardinia

St Croix, Virgin Islands

St Helena

St John

(*see under* Virgin Islands)

St Lucia

Index of vertebrate species

Main references to introduced and/or naturalized birds are indicated in bold type